REAL WORLD
BRYCE 4

SUSAN A. KITCHENS

VICTOR GAVENDA

PEACHPIT PRESS
BERKELEY, CALIFORNIA

Real World Bryce 4
Susan A. Kitchens and Victor Gavenda

Peachpit Press
1249 Eighth Street
Berkeley, CA 94710
510/524-2178
800/283-9444
510/524-2221 (fax)

Find us on the World Wide Web at:
http://www.peachpit.com

Peachpit Press is a division of Addison Wesley Longman

Editors: Clifford Colby, Becky Morgan
Copy Editors: Becky Morgan, Judy Ziajka
Production Coordinator: Lisa Brazieal
Technical Editors: Steve Lareau, Michael Sigmon
Cover Design: Gee + Chung Design
Cover Illustration: Susan A. Kitchens
Interior Design: Mimi Heft
Compositors: David Van Ness, Owen Wolfson
Indexer: Emily Glossbrenner

ISBN 0-201-35438-1

9 8 7 6 5 4 3 2 1

Printed and bound in the United States of America

DEDICATION

In memory of Rodney L'Ongnion

—Susan

To Linda and Emma, for always being there

—Victor

ACKNOWLEDGEMENTS

ALTHOUGH THE TASK of writing and illustrating various chapters of a book is a solitary activity, in this case undertaken in dual simultaneous solitudes, it could not have been done without the contributions of a host of people.

Of course, this book about Bryce would not have come into being without the software itself. Thanks to all those who've worked on Bryce, now nearly all *formerly* of MetaCreations: Brian Wagner, Aleš Holeček, Ken Musgrave, John Feld, David Palermo, Sam Coroniti, Jackson Ting, Robert Bailey, Josh Bates, Fernando Corrado, and Ian Gilman. They stand on the shoulders of previous Bryce developers: Phil Clevenger, Sree Kotay, Todd Bogdan, Kai Krause and, of course, Eric Wenger. Thanks especially to Brian Wagner and Aleš Holeček who answered many a question and would dip into Bryce's source code to look up all the different keyboard combinations to perform various tasks.

Bryce users are fortunate to be able to participate in an enthusiastic community of helpful fellow-users who are eager to swap tips and share advice. I'm especially grateful to my fellow Bryce Talkers who, when hanging out in the BryceTalk Lobby, would let me barge in to verify some detail that I was working on, to see if it matched with their experience. A special thanks to those who attended my special "Bounce" animation tutorial session; the rough draft generated there (and all the assumptions unmasked) found its way into Chapters 14 and 15.

Book authors' time must be spent making as many details explicit as fast as possible, and therefore we are not gifted with the leisure to make one beautiful scene after another to show off the potential for a given feature. (Besides, all those images by one or two people would get boring!) Thanks to the following people whose excellent work appears in these pages: Janak Alford, Gary Bernard, Sandy Birkholz, Chris Casady, Bill Ellsworth, Chaz Fricke, Ruth "Calyxa" Fry, Clay Hagebusch, Barb Ingersoll, Harald Siewert, Hilary Rhodes, Glenn Riegel, Rodney L'Ongnion, Mark Longo, Sylvia Lutnes, Robert Mann, Carla Moore, Gregory Moore, Martin Murphy, Ken Musgrave, Jan Nickman of Third Planet Productions, David Palermo, Chris Pappathan, Andrew Penick, Mike Pucciarelli, Michael "renato!" Sigmon, Scott Tucker, and Eric Wenger.

For the sections on Bryce animation, I am deeply indebted to Rodney L'Ongnion (oh how I wish you were here to see this result!), Robert Bailey, and Renato Sigmon, all of whom enlarged my understanding.

Portions of this book were technically reviewed by Clay Hagebusch, Steve Lareau, and Renato Sigmon.

The Bryce movie website on the CD-ROM would not have come to be without the the indispensible aid of a few people. Sam DeVore wrote the UserLand Frontier scripts to automatically "render" all those web pages and generate the cross-links. Clay Hagebusch did a tremendous amount of behind-the-scenes production for the animation sample movies. Renato Sigmon contributed substantially with movie production and codec guidance. At the last minute, Richard "Elf" Lo Piccolo also pitched in to re-render some animations.

At Peachpit Press, this book was shepherded along under the editorial guidance of fellow BeanTown alum Cliff Colby, and then by the oh-so-persistent Becky Morgan, whose focused prodding got us all to this finish line. Thanks!!!! The Peachpit design and production crew were ever-superb: Mimi Heft, design queen, Lisa Brazieal, production coordinator, Judy Ziajka, copyeditor, and two masters of page layout, Owen Wolfson and David Van Ness who beautifully laid out text and images. Thanks to Nancy Ruenzel, who oversaw this beast through all its vagaries and twists and turns.

In the category of essential infrastructure, I am grateful for the following: Southern California Edison sold me an unceasing supply of electrons on which my portions of this book took shape. Trader Joe's set up a store within walking distance—yes!! BeanTown supplied coffee beans. At nearby Basil restaurant, I found sustenance in Nina's hospitality and Poky's "food cooked with love."

To Dave Winer and UserLand for making editthispage.com and weblogs.com freely available, thanks. There I found a space where I could blow off steam and experience the immediate gratification of publishing daily ephemera and musings while laboring under the mighty weight of this book and its ever-receding publication date. Thanks also to the friendly community that I found among webloggers, who continued to read and post about my 'blog even when it was filled with whining and rants on technical-writing-hell.

Profuse thanks go to my family and friends who repeatedly listened to those same rants and whines, and offered support and encouragement by way of response. Thanks especially to Cynthia, Julie, Kelly, Liz, and Renato for being there when things got bleak.

Finally, dear reader, thank you for waiting so patiently.

—Susan Aimée Kitchens
September 26, 2000

TO SUSAN'S EXPRESSIONS of gratitude to all who helped to make this book a reality, I add my own loud "Amen!" On a more personal note, I would like to thank my excellent colleagues at Peachpit Press, who provided guidance and comfort while I made my way through my first experience as a book author. Thanks to Publisher Nancy Ruenzel for allowing me to embark on this mad (what *was* I thinking?) but exciting project, and to Executive Editor Marjorie Baer for helping me to balance the demands of my regular workload with the need to Get On With The Book. I could never have made it without the kind words and sage advice of editors Cliff Colby and Becky Morgan, or the technical know-how of Production Coordinators Amy Changar and Lisa Brazieal.

Above all, thanks to my mate, Linda, and our daughter, Emma, for being the most supportive of families. Without their aid in so many forms—moral, emotional, and nutritional—the task would have been much less bearable.

—Victor Gavenda

CONTENTS AT A GLANCE

Preface. xxiii

Chapter 1: In The Beginning...
The History and Background of Bryce 1

Chapter 2: An Introduction to Bryce 21

Chapter 3: Camera and Scene 59

Chapter 4: Brycean Objects 111

Chapter 5: Streamline Your Brycing 157

Chapter 6: Editing and the Internal Bryce Grid 195

Chapter 7: Booleans and Multiple Object Construction 273

Chapter 8: Terrains, Symmetrical Lattices, and the Terrain Editor 331

Chapter 9: Material World I: Materials Lab 407

Chapter 10: Material World II: Picture Textures
and the Deep Texture Editor 483

Chapter 11: Brycean Skies 553

Chapter 12: Brycean EnLightenment 609

Chapter 13: Render Unto Bryce 649

Chapter 14: The Fourth Dimension: Time and Animation 685

Chapter 15: Advanced Animation Techniques 785

Chapter 16: Superlative Nature Imagery 883

Chapter 17: Bryce Eye Candy 919

Index 943

CONTENTS

Table of Contents

Preface . . . . **xxiii**

Chapter 1: In The Beginning…
      The History and Background of Bryce **1**

  Where Did Bryce Come From? 1
  The River Chaos 1
    Fractal Geometry: The River Mandelbrot 2
    The River Chaos: A Newer River 5
    The Musgrave Tributary 6
  The River Bryce 7
    The Musgrave Tributary: Part 2 8
    The Eric Wenger Tributary 9
    Kai Krause and the User Interface Tributary 11
  Continuing Development 13
    Bryce 2 Macintosh 13
    Bryce 2 Windows 13
    Bryce 3D 15
    Bryce 4 16
  Why "Bryce"? 18
  An Emotional Experience 18
  Moving On 20

Chapter 2: An Introduction to Bryce **21**

  A Three-Dimensional World Viewed in Two Dimensions 22
  Walkthrough, Part 1: Bryce at its Most Basic 23
  The Bryce Interface: Tools for Tasks 26
    A Point of View—The Control Palette 26
    Working with Object (Create, Edit, and Selection Palettes) 27
    Environment (Sky & Fog Palette) 28
    Time Palette 28
    Controlling Bryce Itself (Display/Wireframe Palette) 28

Talk 29
Deeper Details 29
Rendering 30
Walkthrough, Part 2: Working With Your Bryce Scene 30
Grayscale Geology 30
Turn the Terrain into an Island 32
Enlarge the Terrain 33
Adjust Your View of the Scene 34
Adjust Haze for Sky and Sun Position 36
Place Rocks in the Scene 40
Adjust the Rocks 42
The Stones' Surface Appearance 44
Animate the Sun and Haze 46
Previewing Your Animation 49
Rendering Your Animation 50
A Bryce World (3 dimensions—X, Y, and Z) 52
World Space 52
Object Space 54
Camera Space 54
Working in Bryce—The Creative Process 56
Drawing or Painting or Photographing a Scenic Landscape... . . 56
...and How Brycing Landscapes is Different and the Same 56
The Bryce User—Artist, Designer, Craftsperson 57
Iterations and Iterations 57

Chapter 3: Camera and Scene **59**
Brycean Kodak Moments 60
"Take a Picture"—How 3D Ray Tracing Works 60
View and Camera Controls 64
Two Perspectives: Camera and Director 65
The View Control 66
View Options Pop-up Menu 68
The Nano Preview 68
Cross Controls 72
Keyboard Navigation 74
The Trackball Control 77

Field of View—A Camera with Different-Sized "Lenses" 80

Pan and Zoom on the Second Dimension 81

Camera Dialog Box 86

How-to: Camera Placement That's Just So 93

The Little Blue Pyramid 93

Targeting an Object in Your Scene 103

Saving Camera Views 105

Think Like a Photographer! 106

Chapter 4: Brycean Objects **111**

Which Objects 112

Infinite Planes Three 112

Terrain/Stone Objects 113

3D Primitives 114

2D Primitives 115

Lights 116

Special Case "Objects" 116

Object Controls 119

Object Attributes 121

The General Tab 121

The Linking Tab 126

The Animation Tab 127

Matrix 127

How Bryce Thinks in Its Own Internal Matrix 127

Practical Matrix Uses 129

Wireframe object 130

Adjustments That Can Be Made to Wireframe Views 130

Wireframe Colors—Object Families 135

Natural Selection 138

The Selection Palette 138

Keyboard Entities 142

Solo Mode 145

Importing Objects 149

How to Import a 3D Object 149

Import Formats 151

Tips for Importing 154

Don't Model It Yourself 154

Moving On 155

Chapter 5: Streamline Your Brycing 157

Optimal Settings 158

    Your Computer 158

    Bryce 160

Setting Up Your Scene 161

    Start Small 161

    Placing Objects in Your Scene: Eric's *Mountain Eroded* Image 163

    Creation and Composition Always Come Before Material Goods 164

    Now Blue Sky It 166

    The Costly Things in BryceLife 166

    What Kind of Time Difference Will Materials Make? 168

Display Controls 170

    Interface Max/Min 170

    Background Pattern 171

    Nano Edit: Dainty (and Fast) Manipulation 171

    Plop-Up Render 173

    Ray Spray 174

    Well-Tempered Wireframes 174

    Wireframe Display Complexity and Animation 176

    Flat Shaded Preview 176

    Make This Scene as Efficient as You Can! 177

Batch Management 178

General Brycean Behavior and Other Technical Considerations 179

    Option-Clicking/Alt+Clicking: Revert and Variations 179

    Naming Scene Files 179

    Preset Libraries 180

    Save Prompts When Closing Files 186

    Preferences 187

    Setting Up Your Own Default Scene 190

    Palette Principles for the Proficient Person 191

    Keyboard Stuff 192

    Palette Placement Tricks and Two-Monitor Brycing 192

Chapter 6: Editing and the Internal Bryce Grid 195

The Underlying Structure of the Brycean Universe 197

XYZ Axes 197

The Grid 200

Other Units of Measurement in Bryceland 203

Changing One Object: Reposition, Resize, Rotate 203

Repositioning Objects in Bryce 204

Resizing 211

Rotation 220

3D Transformations and Other Dialog Boxes 223

The Camera as Object 232

Starting Over: Shades of Undo and the Unity Command 232

Change Object Type 235

Edit Terrain/Object: Focus on Torus 236

Going from One to Many Objects: Duplicating Objects/Replicating Objects 241

Duplicating Objects 241

Replicate Once 245

Multi-Replicate 246

Changing More than One Object 248

Alignment 248

Randomize 258

Group Grope 266

Chapter 7: Booleans and Multiple Object Construction 273

Building Blocks: Using Primitive Objects to Create Conglomerates 274

Build a Little, Duplicate a Lot 274

Complex Composite Objects 275

What is a Boolean? 276

How to Set Up Booleans 278

It's All in the Renderer 279

Booleans in Depth 281

A Few Boolean Examples 289

Object Linking 291

Parent and Child Objects: My Mamma Done Tol' Me 291

Linking and Groups: Who Affects Whom 293

Propagation of the Properties 294

Hierarchical Society 300

Try it Out! A Linked Crane Object 305

Replicating objects 309

Circular Logic: Multi-Replicating into a Circle 309

Macro-Multi-Replication 312

Torus Multi-Replication Variations 314

(Not So) Vicious Circles 315

Terrain Moldings 318

Model Management 319

Merging Scenes 320

Columnar Calamity: A Circumspect Boolean Primer with
Multi-Replication Implications 322

The Main Column 322

Column Base Basics 325

Merging the Two 327

Make It a Relic 329

Moving On 330

**Chapter 8: Terrains, Symmetrical Lattices,
and the Terrain Editor** **331**

Gee Too Aitch 332

The Terrain Editor Controls 333

Overall Structure 333

Resolution in the Grid 334

Preview 335

Elevation Controls 336

Brushes 348

Filtering 352

Pictures 358

Clipping Bracket 360

Preview Color 364

Zoom Area 365

Fave Routines 368

Resolution Fluency 368

Brushing Beauties 370

Raise and Lower 371

Rough Rough Rough 371
Rice Paddies 372
Rivers and Deltas 372
Game Over, Man 374
Waterfall 374
Symmetrical Lattices 383
Working with Other Image Editing Applications 383
Picture Terrain Tricks 387
The Lost Continents of Text-land-is 389
Susan's Text Terrain Recipe 389
Variation—Sloping Letters 392
Altitude Render 394
Recipe: Using Altitude Render to Create a Terrain 395
Digital Elevation Models (DEM) 395
Terrain Export 397
How to Export a Terrain 398
The Terrain Export Lab 399
Moving On 406

Chapter 9: Material World I: Materials Lab **407**
Introduction to the Materials Lab 408
Surface or Volume? 409
The Basic Properties 409
Three Surface Properties.... 410
...Plus One Volume Property 412
Adding 14-Channel Complexity 412
Value: Illumination 415
Optics and Bump 416
Other Value 420
Color 422
Non-Uniform Appearance: Textures 430
The Texture Source: An Introduction 431
Texture-Driven Illumination 435
Texture-Driven Optics 437
Texture-Driven Bump Height 438
Texture-Driven Color 439

Texture-Driven Metallicity 441

Frequency 442

More About Texture Sources 444

But Wait! There's More! 453

Mix and Match 453

A-B Blending 454

A-B-C Blending 456

What About D? 461

Material Options 462

Shading Mode 462

Other Material Options 464

Volume Properties 467

Base Density 468

Edge Softness 469

Fuzzy Factor 469

Quality/Speed 470

Volume Material Options 474

As Painless as Possible: Working with Volume Materials 480

Texture Source Revisited: Practical Tips 481

Moving On 481

**Chapter 10: Material World II: Picture Textures
and the Deep Texture Editor** **483**

2D Picture Textures 483

A Basic How-To 484

The Picture Library 485

Opacity Maps and PICT Textures 494

3D Textures: Deep Texture Editor 496

Overview 497

Quick Tour of the DTE 498

Noise 503

In Your Phase 512

Filtering 514

Output Types 521

Combining Components: Blend Modes 523

Global Output: Combination 527

3D Texture Practicalia 529

Anatomy of a Texture and Material 532

Analyzing Textures 533

Altitude Adjustment: Whole Mountain, Continued... 535

Recipe for the Ringed Planet Material Adjustment 540

Snow Puddles Material 542

Puddlebumps: Bump and Reflections 547

Chapter 11: Brycean Skies **553**

The Sky & Fog Controls 554

Basic Bryce Astronomy 559

Solar and Lunar Direction 559

Sun and Moon Secrets in the Sky Lab 562

When the Moon Hits Your Eye like a Big Pizza Pie 565

Exercise: Solar and Lunar Fluency 567

Clouds, Clouds, Clouds 569

Stratus and Cumulus 569

Cloud Shape 569

Exercise: Adjusting Cloud Shape 569

It's in the Air: Fog, Haze, and Rainbows 575

Fog 575

Haze: On a Hazy Day, You Can't See Forever 582

Rainbows 584

Shadows 585

Shadows and Other Sky & Fog Elements 586

Haze, Fog, and Shadow Walkthrough 587

Color 587

Color and Bryce Atmosphere 588

Color Exercises 589

Sky Mode: Custom Sky Colors 600

Sky Mode: Atmosphere Off 602

Sky Dome Color 603

Random Sky Control 606

Alternative Clouds 606

Infinite Planes and Slabs as Cloud Layers 606

Moving On 608

Chapter 12: Brycean EnLightenment **609**

    Glowing Pseudo-Light Forms 610

    Light Source Primitives 613

    Edit Lights Dialog Box 614

        Preview 615

        Intensity 615

        Softness 618

        Color Controls 619

        Pop-up Menu Items 623

        Falloff 624

        To Infinity…and Beyond! 628

        Visible Lights (Surface and Volume) 628

    Other Light Properties 634

        Express Your Negativity 634

        Caustic Attitude 636

        Increased Render Time 637

        Lights and Solo Mode 639

    Using Bryce Lights: Different Types of Lighting Conditions 639

        What Light Does Aesthetically 640

        Ways to Use Lights 642

        Tips for Setting Up Lights 644

        Gel Cookies 644

        Light Arrays 645

    Example Scenes 646

        Flames Using Light and Pseudo-Light 646

        Shoji Lantern 646

        The Castle Hall Scene 647

        Hall of Kings 647

Chapter 13: Render Unto Bryce **649**

    The Basic Rendering Model 650

        Render Options 651

        "While You Are Working" Rendering 658

        "When You Are Finished" Rendering 662

        Batch Rendering 663

Beyond the Basic Rendering Model 664

   Rendering Large Images 664

   360° Rendering 667

   Render Post-Processing 672

Moving On 684

Chapter 14: The Fourth Dimension: Time and Animation 685

   "…And Then This Happened" 686

  Introducing Time to Bryce 688

   Time, Frames, etc. 688

   Animation Setup 690

  Working with the Time Palette 693

   Time Tools 694

   Animation Preview 703

   Keyframe Tools 706

   AML Doorway 708

  The Things in Bryce that Can Be Animated 709

   States Do Not Animate 710

   Objects (Primitives) 710

   Booleans 711

   Camera 711

   Lights 712

  Animation Controls in the Terrain, Materials, and Sky Labs 712

  The Things that Can Be Animated, Continued 714

   Terrains 714

   Sun 715

   Sky 715

   Materials 719

  Keyframing 721

   Auto-Key On 721

   Auto-Key Off 722

   Advantages and Disadvantages of Each Approach 724

  Trajectories 731

   Bryce's Key Events 732

   Creating Trajectories 732

Moving Trajectory Handles 738

Trajectory Walkthrough 743

Path Object 761

Making and Storing Paths 762

Editing Paths 764

Traveling Along Your Path 767

Paths Walkthrough 771

Tracking 775

How to Track 775

About Face 776

What Moves, What Stays 777

Rendering Animations 778

Test Renders and Stages of Preview 779

Render Animation Dialog Box 781

Moving On 784

Chapter 15: Advanced Animation Techniques **785**

Introduction to the AML 786

Quick Overview 786

Hierarchy List 788

Sequencer 795

3D Preview 802

Time Mapping Editor 803

Bounce Walkthrough (Conclusion) 814

More about Planning Your Animation 819

Building on the History of Cinematography 819

Some Basic Planning and Storyboarding 820

Post-Production 822

Linking and Hierarchies: Camera Cranes 823

Camera Crane and Overall Grooviness: Animation Sequence 824

Camera-Linking Variation 835

Motion Tricks 835

Pendulum 835

Pulsing Light 840

Orbit 842

Spiral Motion 848

Gears 854

QTVR Object Movie 855

Path-ology 862

Multi-Replicating along a Path 863

Several Objects Connected to Path 864

Path Connected to Path 866

Fun with Multi-Replication 867

Linked Hierarchy Multi-Replication Extravaganza 868

Animation Miscellanea 870

Animating Textures (and Materials) 870

Animation and Groups 880

Merging Animated Scenes and Copying/Pasting Animated Objects 880

Whew! 881

Chapter 16: Superlative Nature Imagery **883**

In the Master's Footsteps: Eric's Methods 884

Terrain Placement: Create for Depth 887

Material Frequency Detail 889

Sky Settings for Depth and Realism 889

Eric's Scenery Recap 892

Geology 101: Mountains and Valleys 893

How New Mountains are Created 893

Glaciers 895

Faults 896

Eroded Canyons 896

Volcanoes 900

Multiple Terrains 901

Stones 'n' Water 901

Angled Terrains 902

Undersea Worlds 905

Creating Underwater Plant Life 906

A River Runs Through It 907

Rainy Weather 908

USGS Maps G2H Information 909

The Greening of Bryce 909
Bryce Star Galactica 914
  Recipe for Space Scenes 914
Moving On 918

Chapter 17: Bryce Eye Candy **919**

Still Image Landscapes 920
  David Palermo—*Alien Starburst* 920
  Martin Murphy 920
  Chris Pappathan—*Alaskan Spring* 922
Water, Water, Everywhere 923
  Barb Ingersoll 923
  Mark Longo—*Heavy Seas* 924
  Ruth "Calyxa" Fry—*Rocks, Water, Sand* 925
  Sandy Birkholz 925
Fantastic Visions 927
  Martin Murphy—*Statue* 927
  Chaz Fricke—*Coagulation* 927
  Mike Pucciarelli's Altered States 928
  What's in a Game?—*The Shahnra Project* 929
Painterly Post-Processing 933
  Sylvia Lutnes 934
Martian Water Images 935
Animation 936
  Infinity's Child 936
  Michael "renato!" Sigmon—*Rube Goldberg* 938
  Greg Moore—*Bryce Terrain Flyover* 940

Index **943**

PREFACE

So you went and did it—you bought yourself a copy of Bryce. You saw a beautiful landscape on someone's Web site, or your friend showed you a stunning otherworldly vista she created for a video game, or you saw the program in action on a colleague's computer and were taken with the subtle beauty of the interface. You parted with your hard-earned cash, rushed home with the box and ripped off the shrinkwrap. You put the software through the install-register-serialize routine.

So now what?

You tentatively start clicking things; create a cube, move it around. Click the thing that looks like a mountain at the top of the screen, and BAM—there's a mountain in your picture. Cool! Now you get more adventurous. What happens if you click that tiny little M-thingie next to the mountain? YEOW! What in blazes is that? Don't worry, it's just the Materials Lab, it won't bite…much.

Welcome to Bryce. Throughout the program you'll find over and over again that a deceptively simple surface masks an underlying complexity. You'll also find that Bryce's complexity leads it to trip over its own feet from time to time.

You could grope your way to Bryce-mastery on your own, but you've done a much smarter thing: you've bought this book, which will serve as your guide on your journey of discovery. We'll tell you how to get started in Bryce, how to use the expert tools, where the secret handshakes and decoder rings are hidden, and we won't hesitate to point out the spots where the manual leads you astray or the software is just plain broken.

WHAT THIS BOOK COVERS

This book is a revision of Susan's *Real World Bryce 2*, which in turn was a revision of her earlier *The KPT Bryce Book*. It has been completely rewritten to document software that has undergone extensive modification and enhancements since the last time this tome hit the streets. The book continues on in the tradition of applying a keen observer's eye and answering the questions, "What does it do?" and "What can I do with it?" We observe Bryce's behavior and tell you what it does.

This book covers Bryce 4.0.1 for both the Macintosh and Windows 95/98/Windows NT platforms. At the time of this printing, there are four different shipping versions of Bryce 4 in existence. There's Bryce 4.0 shipped by MetaCreations. There is an updater, 4.0.1, which changes MetaCreations Bryce 4.0 to Bryce 4.0.1. This is the version of the software that we worked with for most of the book. When MetaCreations sold Bryce to Corel, Corel "re-branded" the software with Corel logos on the box, manual and splashscreen, and shipped that as Bryce 4.0; we'll call it Corel Bryce 4.0. Due to a small version error in the Corel 4.0 version, the MetaCreations 4.0.1 updater did not work to update it to 4.0.1. Just as this book went to press, Corel released Bryce 4.1, which includes the 4.0.1 patch. The update works on both the MetaCreations and Corel Bryce 4.0 versions and copies of Bryce updated to 4.0.1. The differences between 4.0.1 and 4.1 are slight—a new starmap with real constellations, some new import and export modes, and some additional volume materials functions.

Note for Bryce 3D users: The feature gap between Bryce 3D and Bryce 4 is much smaller than the gap between Bryce 1 and 2, or between Bryce 2 and 3D. Although this book deals with many specific items in Bryce 4 that won't be found in 3D, much of the coverage, especially the new material on animation and the Materials Lab (including the Deep Texture Editor), is applicable to both Bryce 3D and 4.

In response to readers' requests, we've added a feature for beginners: Chapter 2, "An Introduction to Bryce." If you're new to Bryce, work through the chapter step by step, and in the course of an hour or so you'll touch on most of the program's key features. Although the rest of the chapters provide some background on key concepts, the emphasis of this book is to push you onto the "Bryce Power User" track. Tutorials and guided explorations abound—follow along with the book in one hand, and your computer's mouse in the other.

While we observe Bryce throughout these pages, we are assuming that you know how to use your computer's operating system. If you don't, please refer to the documentation that came with your computer.

Bryce takes you into a complex world—not as complex as our own, but complex nonetheless. In Bryce, everything is related to everything else. When writing about it, there's a risk of oversimplifying while looking at the big picture, or getting mired in the detail while exploring all the possibilities. Our approach cruises between these two risks, providing a look at the big picture while including plenty of detail. Because everything is related to everything else, however, there are numerous cross-references directing you to other chapters.

The Chapters

Here's a basic rundown of what you'll find in each chapter.

The first section unlocks the pieces and parts of the software itself:

• *Chapter 1—In the Beginning…The History and Background of Bryce.* Here, we recount the recent history of chaos theory and fractal geometry and trace their paths into the application Bryce, following it through to Bryce 4.

• *Chapter 2—An Introduction to Bryce.* In this chapter, we introduce you to Bryce and take you on a guided tutorial tour through each major part of the software. If you're just starting out with Bryce, start here!

Now that the basic introduction has been made, the next several chapters take an in-depth look at each section of Bryce.

• *Chapter 3—Camera and Scene.* In this chapter, we go into the concept of camera and scene, introduce ray tracing and explain how to use the Camera controls.

• *Chapter 4—Brycean Objects.* In this chapter we take a look at each of the object types in Bryce and just about all the options for selecting objects and groups of objects in order to work with them. We explore navigating into and out of Solo mode, as well as importing objects.

• *Chapter 5—Streamline Your Brycing.* Here we present a global perspective of the work process in Bryce, all the while sounding the refrain, "Make it efficient." That is, set up your work so as to reduce unnecessary render time. We also discuss general Bryce behavior that's consistent throughout the software.

• *Chapter 6—Editing and the Internal Bryce Grid.* In this chapter, we introduce the unseen grid structure of Bryce and discuss the controls on the Edit Palette, where you can edit single objects, multiple objects, and replicate one object into multiple objects.

• *Chapter 7— Booleans and Multiple Object Construction.* This chapter explores the techniques for working with multiple objects to create models, exploring more of the Bryce multi-replicate options, and taking an in-depth look at boolean functions, merging scene files, linking and object hierarchies.

• *Chapter 8—Terrains, Symmetrical Lattices, and the Terrain Editor.* This chapter explores the Terrain Editor, Bryce's separate "room" for working with grayscale-to-height image processing. The grayscale-to-height image defines the look of Bryce's mountainous forms, used by both terrains and symmetrical lattices. The chapter includes a number of terrain-editing exercises, and also covers exporting terrains.

- *Chapter 9—Material World I: The Materials Lab.* Here we delve into all the intricacies of working with Bryce's Materials Lab to give your objects their surface or volume appearance.

- *Chapter 10—Material World II: Picture Textures and the Deep Texture Editor.* Textures are an important part of materials, and in this chapter we continue our discussion of surface and volume appearance with a thorough examination of picture textures and 3D textures using the Deep Texture Editor.

- *Chapter 11—Brycean Skies.* In this chapter, we discuss all that goes into creating your Bryce environment, exploring in detail the options that make up the shape and color of your Brycean sky, including celestial bodies, haze, fog, shadows, and atmospheric color.

- *Chapter 12—Bryce EnLightenment.* This chapter delves into all things concerning lights, from the pseudo-lights of glowing objects that cast neither light nor shadow to the individual light objects that cast special light into your Bryce world.

- *Chapter 13—Render Unto Bryce.* Here we give some background on how rendering works, tips for rendering, and some ideas for using the alternative render options.

Now that we've examined every aspect of creating still scenes, the next two chapters deal with the process of working with animations in Bryce.

- *Chapter 14—The Fourth Dimension: Time And Animation.* In this chapter, we introduce all of Bryce's basic animation tools and walk you through creating your own simple animations.

- *Chapter 15—Advanced Animation Techniques.* In this chapter, we explore the Advanced Motion Lab, where you can fine-tune your animation, and then delve into advanced topics: creating a camera boom, working with linking and hierarchies and object tracking, paths, multireplication, QuickTime VR and other animation techniques.

The two remaining chapters help you tie it all together; we go beyond the mere recounting of features and tutorial exercises and discuss ways to integrate Bryce's components to achieve certain effects.

- *Chapter 16—Superlative Nature Imagery.* In this chapter, we examine some exemplary scenes drawn from the world around us and analyze the best ways to make scenery that imitates nature.

- *Chapter 17—Bryce Eye Candy.* This chapter features the works of a number of accomplished Bryce artists, discusses their scenes and animations and how they did what they did.

Color Images

There are a lot of illustrations in this book to aid you in your Bryce exploration. The color images have a C preceding their figure numbers, such as C1.4. When you see the C, look in the color section for the figure.

CD-ROM

And finally, the CD. Tucked into the back cover of this tome is a little plastic disc. Take it out and look at what's on it; there's so much more to be seen. Many of the scenes used in this book's illustrations and exercises are included on the CD so that you can go in and poke around yourself. We've set up a folder for each chapter, in which scenes related to that chapter reside; when you see references to files on the CD-ROM, look for them in the folder for the chapter. In addition, there is an on-disk Web site to help you view all the movies for the book, and to keep track of the ones you've already looked at.

When we refer to individual files or folders on the CD-ROM, the name of the file is printed in a special typeface, like so: SCENE FILE. As you may know, any Bryce 4 scene files can be opened on either a Mac or a Windows machine, but the filename must have the extension "*.BR4" in order for the Windows machine to recognize the file as a Bryce scene file. In this book, we've adopted the convention of referring to all scene files using the Mac style, without the extension. We do use the extension "*.MOV" when referring to all QuickTime movies, however, because we often need to talk about a movie created from a scene file, and this helps us to keep them straight, as in: ANIMATION SCENE and ANIMATION SCENE.MOV.

In addition to the tutorials and related scenes for you to work with and explore, there is also a host of goodies on the CD-ROM. You'll find step-by-step slide shows and image samples for different processes, as well as tips, QTVR animations, and animated movies.

Companion Web Site

Don't forget to check out the book's companion Web site for ongoing Bryce developments, stuff that didn't make it into the book, and miscellaneous additional tidbits. It's at: http://www.auntialias.com/rwb4. Go early and often!

A Cross-Platform Book

This book covers both the Macintosh and Windows versions of Bryce 4. When describing key commands and procedures, we will provide first the Mac key command and then the Windows key command. Both platforms use a key called "Control," and each platform uses it differently. In order to avoid confusion between the two, the keys will be described as they appear on the respective keyboards: The Macintosh Control key will be spelled out, and the Windows Ctrl key will be abbreviated, as shown. Where there are simple key combinations, we will use the Macintosh shortcut for the Command key: ⌘, as in ⌘-S. Where there are lengthier keyboard combinations, they will be shown in this fashion: ⌘-Option-E (Macintosh) or Ctrl+Alt+E (Windows). We'll confess to one other Mac-centric bias. Throughout the book we'll call those menus pop-up menus even if they drop down from other spots, although Windows-using folk may think of them as drop-down menus. Bear with us; at least we're consistent about it!

Tutorial Terminology and Your Mouse, or What to Do with Your Mouse

This book contains many step-by-step tutorial walkthroughs, as well as other instructions telling you to "do this then do that." We'd like to spell out exactly what we mean by terms we use for *pointing*, *clicking*, *dragging* and *pressing the mouse*. We will *not* use the term "click-and-drag." (We think that term is a no-no.) So we offer the following explanations of mouse-action directions:

- *Click* is a simple mouse-down-and-up action.

- *Double-click* is a rapid succession of two clicks.

- *Dragging* is the process in which the mouse button goes down and then the mouse is dragged to a new location, where the mouse button is released. But we think that it's simpler to use one word, "drag" to mean all that.

- *Pointing* is the process of rolling your mouse so that the cursor points to a particular item on your screen.

- *Pressing* is the process of the mouse button going down and staying down for a period of time, such as when pressing the mouse at an item to reveal a pop-up menu.

So now that we've gotten this what-where-how business out of the way, settle yourself for this Brycean journey. In the first chapter, we take you through Bryce's history. Then, starting in the second chapter we invite you to roll up your sleeves with this book at your side and Bryce launched on your computer as we dive into working with the software itself, leaving no 3D stone unturned.

CHAPTER ONE

In The Beginning...
The History and Background
of Bryce

WHERE DID BRYCE COME FROM?

Picture yourself, for a moment, hovering over a continent. This is a good place to start—looking over a land mass—since Bryce is about the creation of natural-looking land masses. Spreading its watery fingers over the continent is a large river—you may be thinking of the planet's large rivers: the Nile, the Amazon, the Yangtze, the Mississippi-Missouri. The main river is fed by other rivers, and those rivers are in turn fed by smaller tributaries. Those tributaries are fed by brooks and streams, which are fed by creeks, rivulets, runnels and streamlets. Although the primary channel of the river occupies a single meandering ribbon of land, the larger river system, with all its feeding shoots, reaches over a vast portion of the continent.

THE RIVER CHAOS

This large river is the River Chaos, named for chaos theory, and Bryce River is one of its tributaries, a large stream. The entire aquatic system of the River Chaos covers a vast territory of many scientific disciplines. And these various disciplines, each having reached a stage of maturity where all the obvious questions have been answered, tackle the not-so-easy questions—questions of complexity, irregularity, and widely varying behaviors that at one time seemed to have no recognizable order or pattern. Noise. Weather. Price fluctuations in markets. Fluctuations in population. Turbulence in airflow: the path that a tendril of smoke takes, flowing up, wavering a bit before breaking up into whorls and eddies. Turbulence in fluid flow: clouds in your coffee. Weather storms in the atmosphere; and within a living body, the storms that interrupt life: heartbeat arrhythmia, fibrillation, and cardiac arrest, and the electrochemical storms that drown out all normal brain activity during an epileptic seizure.

In these difficult issues of scientific endeavor, basic linear deterministic thinking— if A happens, then the result is B; if rain falls, then the earth and buildings and people outdoors will get wet—no longer fits the situation. The questions, in fact, are more like this: What conditions lead to the result "it will rain"? Can the rain be predicted? Will it rain today? Next week? Chaos theory discovered and identi- fied deeper patterns to seemingly random events.

Fractal Geometry: The River Mandelbrot

One major portion of the river system Chaos is a river devoted to fractal geome- try, a section that we'll name for Benoit Mandelbrot. The River Mandelbrot lies in an open expanse of the scientific continent, where something like the Tigris and Euphrates of Chaos meet, a fertile crescent of fractal chaos.

Mandelbrot is a mathematician whose pursuits have ranged over a variety of inter- ests and topics: the history of fluctuating cotton prices, noise in telephone lines and resulting errors in transmission, how the distribution of large and small cities have regularities in scaling. He also studied a set of figures and shapes conceived by mathematicians late in the nineteenth century, shapes that had been classified as "monstrosities" and "pathological forms." Mandelbrot's work "defanged" and "harnessed" them. One such shape is the Sierpinski sieve (see Figure 1.1). On each triangular face of the pyramid, an inverse triangle is subtracted, making even smaller triangles (pyramids). The process repeats again, making even smaller tri- angles (pyramids).

A more famous shape, discovered by Mandelbrot himself, is named after him: the Mandelbrot set (see Figure 1.2).

Through Mandelbrot's work and the work of others in the field of chaos theory, complex systems, behaviors—things found all over nature—could suddenly be explained in relatively straightforward mathematics. As Mandelbrot put it in his essay/manifesto *The Fractal Geometry of Nature*, "Scientists will (I am sure) be surprised and delighted to find that not a few shapes they had to call *grainy, hydralike, in between, pimply, pocky, ramified, seaweedy, strange, tangled, tortuous, wiggly, wispy, wrinkled,* and the like, can henceforth be approached in rigorous and vigorous quantitative fashion." Using old mathematics in a new way resulted in a new discipline: fractal geometry.

The term *fractal* was coined from the Latin word meaning "to break," with additional reference to *fragmented* and *irregular*. Geometry is the study of points, lines, angles, surfaces, and solids, so fractal geometry is the study of geometry that has the properties of broken, fragmented irregularity.

In addition to being irregular and fragmented, shapes with fractal geometry have other characteristics in common: The amount of irregularity or fragmentation is the same at different scales of the shape. To generate a fractal shape requires an iterative (repetitive) process of calculation. Finally, the shape has a fractal (fragmented, fractional) dimension.

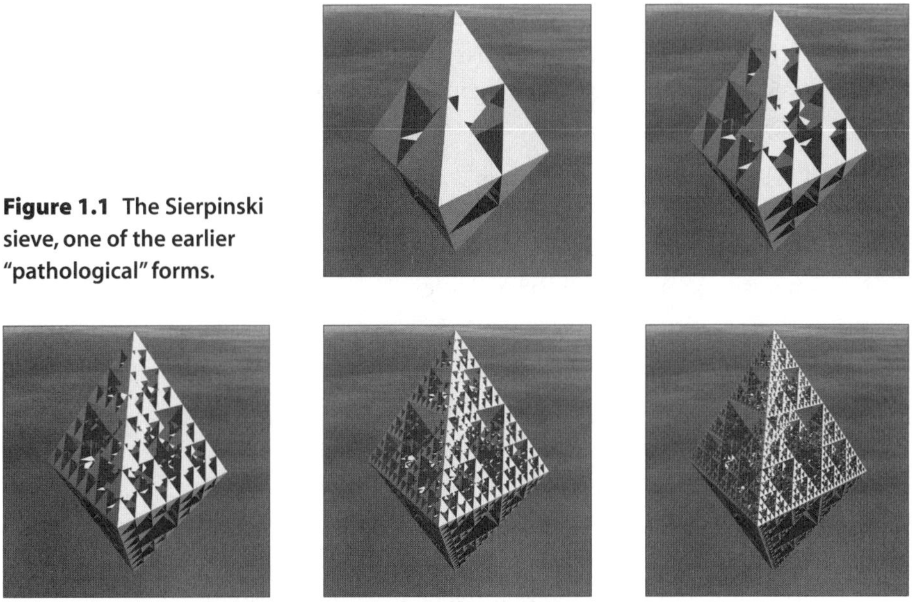

Figure 1.1 The Sierpinski sieve, one of the earlier "pathological" forms.

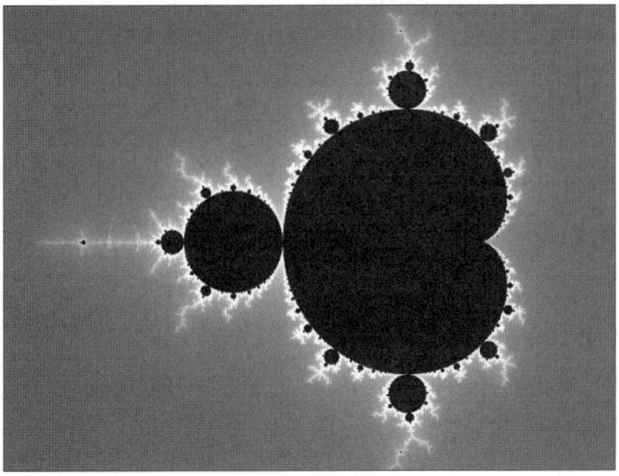

Figure 1.2
The Mandelbrot set, named after Benoit B. Mandelbrot.

Scale and Self-Similarity

The basic phenomenon, or irregular pattern, of a fractal shape repeats itself across different scales; the deeper you go, the same-er it gets. Consider the Sierpinski sieve: The same identifying characteristic is present in all examples. This is true, too, in the complex bug-like geometric shape named after Mandelbrot, with smaller bugs appearing deep in the Mandelbrot set. So, also, the fern leaf is a miniature replica of the fern branch; patterns in craggy rock surfaces are replicated in the boulder and the rocky promontory, in the pebble and the stone. This is why fractals are called self-similar: trees, veins, and rivers branch and continue branching into ever-smaller limbs, twigs, channels, capillaries, and streams.

This chapter's river metaphor was chosen for its self-similarity: The macro scale is the River Chaos, which is fed by other tributaries, one of which, on the micro scale, interests us keenly: the River Bryce.

Iterative Process: A Random Walk

Fractal shapes are generated using an iterative process of calculation. The rigorous quantitative analysis to which Mandelbrot referred is not as simple and straightforward as $3 + 5 = 8$, but something more on the order of quadratic differential equations, which measure change over time. However, the rich fractal irregularities stem from a single equation with a set starting place: Put the initial number into an equation, and the resulting number becomes the origin of the next equation. After a long string of these calculations, the result is a fractal.

Here's a simple example of the iterative process of calculation that does not require mathematical formulæ (thank heavens!). It's an analogy: a random walk. Stand right here (but mark where "here" is). Flip a coin. If it's heads, step forward and right (at about a 45° angle). If it's tails, step forward and left. Flip. Step. Flip. Step. The line that emerges will be jagged, varying this way and that, with the same general characteristics as Figure 1.3.

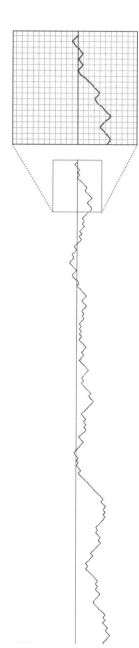

Figure 1.3 A random walk: The path taken by randomly flipping a coin. If it's heads, step right; if it's tails, step left.

Some things, though, are unpredictable. The chances of repeating the exact same coin flips is infinitesimal, so the resulting random walk line will likely never be exactly the same. Yet the path will have the same basic appearance. It will also be nonlinear. And you can approximately measure the length of your stride, but you will not hit that length exactly each time. Yet the iterative process relies on the result of the last calculation as the starting place for the next one.

Fractional Dimensions

Fractal geometric shapes have fractal, or fractional, dimensions. We tend to think of dimensions as being zero, one, two, or three: a point, a line, a plane, a cube (or, if we're mentally adept, we can stretch it to four or five or more). Fractional dimensions, however, lie somewhere between zero and one, or between one and two, or between two and three. Whoa! Really? Fractional? Yes. Mathematicians have rigorous means of precisely determining the dimension of a thing, which we will (mercifully) forego, offering instead a few paltry bread crumbs of analogy. Consider for a moment the path of the random walk. Is it a line? A strictly one-dimensional line is straight, and direction is forward or backward along the line. But the random walk line is not straight. It's not a two-dimensional plane, though. The random walk is a line, but it's more than a line. Like a single-dimension line, the line describing the random walk goes forward and backward, but the path just meanders. It has a fractional dimension that is greater than one, but less than two.

Or suppose for a moment that you were able to look at the Earth's surface from space. At that distance and scale, it appears smooth. If you were to somehow peel it off like a skin and lay it flat, the surface would be flat and two-dimensional. And yet you know, from living in the nooks and crannies of this surface, that the earth is not perfectly flat. It's more than two-dimensional—it is an irregularly shaped plane, with bumps and indentations—yet it retains elements of a two-dimensional surface. The peeled and flattened earth skin has a fractional dimension that is greater than two but less than three. It has more shape than a purely flat plane; otherwise how would you be able to see that continent with the watery fingers of the river system?

The River Chaos: A Newer River

Making a river is slow work. Rain falls, springs burble, and water seeps and furrows over and through the aquifer, seeking and finding paths to run down, down downhill, wandering, rushing, coursing to the sea. Water carves rock and digs channels, scouring away myriad particles of rock, lifting and carrying sediments great distances to drop them on alluvial plains and deltas far away. This is the work of millennia, to carve out riverbeds. Rivers may spring up overnight in dry places, but they follow the paths that have been followed before.

As rivers go, the River Chaos is a newer river, a young 'un sprung and formed in a short period of time—only in the last century. It was formed by a combination of human dredging and computer-aided digging to establish the channels and waterways and rivulets. Once the flood of water began, dried-up dead-ends of scientific inquiry filled with flash floods of inspiration as the discoveries in one discipline led to new springs of discovery in another. Like the awakened (and multiplying!) brooms in *Fantasia's* "The Sorcerer's Apprentice," tirelessly devoted to a tedious task, computers have borne the calculation load that has made the River Chaos possible.

In the last third of the twentieth century, with computing resources ranging from university and laboratory mainframe systems and workstations to the personal desktop computer, chaos theory evolved. Some river channels were laid down in the late 1800s and early 1900s using manual mathematical tools, but slide rules and endless written calculations could only go only so far before a type of calculation white-line-fever set in. Computers get much further in the iterative process than humans. The previous dead ends were renewed and carried forward using computing tools.

Mandelbrot worked at the IBM Research Lab and at Yale University, taking advantage of the computing resources there to explore myriad fractal shapes. He worked with a variation of the random walk to devise a rough, rugged coastline, the initial basis for a landscape. He worked with Richard Voss to generate computer graphic images of a fractal mountain. By writing a computer program to undergo a mathematical process and then displaying the result, Mandelbrot and Voss were able to generate a geometric shape that mimicked the form of our own mountains, islands, and coastlines. The art of fractal computer-generated landscapes was born.

The Musgrave Tributary

In 1987, Mandelbrot, at the Yale University Department of Mathematics, hired a research assistant to create computer graphics to further his work in fractal geometry. The person hired into that position was Ken Musgrave, who was near completion of a master's degree in Computer Science at the University of California at Santa Cruz; his topic: "A Realistic Model of Refraction for Computer Graphics."

Within a couple of weeks of joining Mandelbrot at Yale, Musgrave's own predilection for natural scenic landscapes came to the fore. As he describes it, "A few weeks later,

Benoit was leaving for a trip of several days and I asked if I could make pictures while he was gone. He replied, in true form, 'Render unto Caesar, Caesar's due!' and so I rendered. When he came back, he liked what I had done so much that he never made me do anything else, ever again." Mandelbrot gave Musgrave free reign to create artwork based on fractal mathematics—and a paid assistant artist. What a gig!

The short fellowship turned into a longer one, and Musgrave was invited to pursue his Ph.D. at Yale. He focused on rendering scenic landscapes based on fractal geometry. His dissertation was entitled "Methods for Realistic Landscape Imaging," and his doctorate was awarded in 1993. The series of images in Figure C1.4 are his work, and Figure C1.4a is, as he puts it, "my doctoral dissertation." In addition to devising additional methods to generate mountain terrains, Musgrave focused on atmosphere and environment and the generation of procedural textures to give those landscapes a believable appearance.

The art that Ken Musgrave has created came about through his being a scientist, mathematician, and computer programmer. He is one of a select few who call themselves Algorists. Algorists create original computer art generated by algorithms (mathematical routines) of their own devising. Musgrave takes a pure approach, requiring that his artwork be an exact visual interpretation of his mathematical theorems (in other words, absolutely no post-processing!). Along with this strict and original formal logic is a reverence for nature. As Musgrave says in an artist's statement:

"I do not wish the casual viewer to be confronted with these nasty and alienating technical points of process; those interested can study that in my technical writings. Rather, I wish you to witness my reverence for Nature, and to be drawn in by the quiet beauty I have found there and been able to conjure up in numbers, through a bizarre, improbable, novel and byzantine process. It is all, technically speaking, Magic."

THE RIVER BRYCE

We have followed the River Chaos and traveled up the various tributaries of fractal geometry to the place where mathematical algorithms have been used to imitate the phenomena seen in natural scenery. The form of the River Chaos is a large set of branches, and as we focus on the particular area where fractal geometry begets scenic landscape, we see a smaller set of branching waterways resembling the larger one. That is the history of chaos: a large river with branches and jags and divisions. The history of Bryce is parallel; it is a river fed from some of the same tributaries that feed the River Chaos. The River Bryce, though not as big as the main aquatic artery of the River Chaos, is itself a sizable channel, with brooks and creeks feeding into it. The main spring feeding the river Bryce is the Musgrave tributary, where chaos theory serves the creation of scenic landscapes.

The Musgrave Tributary: Part 2

After his work at Yale, Ken Musgrave went on to become a member of the faculty at George Washington University, where he was Assistant Professor of Engineering and Applied Science. Being in academia, Musgrave did what academics do: he taught and he published.

Academia operates in a paradox: Have you discovered something? Write it up and publish it. Give it away! In exchange for the information, though, the receiver must prove his or her worthiness to freely receive the benefit of another's original work by dint of the hard effort needed to comprehend it. If you really and truly want it, you must diligently apply yourself. Do you want something to work differently? Go write it yourself! If you want to even discuss this topic with me, make sure you've taken the prerequisite courses first.

In keeping with the academic system of meritocracy, Ken's choice of computers—a workstation running UNIX—rewarded those who were diligent enough to master the intricacies of its operating system with an important benefit: stability.. His contempt for constantly crashing desktop operating systems was expressed in a fireball of damning invective at their utter uselessness. He'd rant, "Give me a *real* computer that runs a *real* operating system—UNIX!" A Silicon Graphics workstation running a version of UNIX is stable; it doesn't crash. Musgrave's natural scenery developments were all written in a command-line code, where he recompiled his application—with new numbers each time—to generate a new landscape. His watchword for computer graphics was, "No concessions to the hated user!"

So how did Bryce get from the hands of this algorist artist-mathematician crank with a bemused glint in his eye to software that became user friendly?

The findings, techniques, algorithms, and code devised by Ken Musgrave made their way down Bryce River through the time-honored academic form of dissemination: publishing. Musgrave's work was published in papers, in books, in journals. (Additionally, significant contributions in this field were made by another computer scientist, Ken Perlin, whose work "Perlin Noise" won an Academy Award for Technical Achievement, and who is represented in Bryce 4 by a terrain type called Perlin Hills.)

When it comes to any new advance in computer science and computer graphics, though, the place to publish and present is SIGGRAPH ACM, the Special Interest Group for Graphics of the Association of Computing Machinery. This annual gathering, begun in academia, is *the* place where new breakthroughs are shown. What starts out as a proof-of-concept demonstration this year makes it into a more developed form in the following year or two or three, and probably into a software or hardware product by the year after that.

It was at SIGGRAPH that someone appeared willing to take up the challenge to apply himself and put to work Musgrave's freely offered information about how to generate scenic landscapes. That person was Eric Wenger.

The Eric Wenger Tributary

Eric Wenger, a software engineer, musician, and artist from Paris, France, attended SIGGRAPH every year. The son of a geologist, he grew up with a keen sensitivity to Earth's form and environs. At SIGGRAPH, he was drawn to the lectures by this person who'd use mathematical algorithms to generate natural scenery. He attended, read Mandelbrot's, Musgrave's and Perlin's work, and applied himself to comprehending the material.

Wenger's appreciation of rock forms and natural features was combined with an artist's careful, observing eye. While working on the first edition of this book, Susan saw a landscape triptych of the American southwest desert painted by Wenger; those paintings captured the essence of the area's sweeping basins interspersed with rocky plateaus. To put down all those details on canvas requires that one *see* them. Wenger combined his own exacting scrutiny and creativity and artist's eye with the gist of Musgrave's findings and nurtured it into a Macintosh software application purely for his own enjoyment and self-expression. He called it D3, a playful subversion of 3D, since the output was so different from what was produced by a standard 3D application.

Wenger wrote the landscape software on the side, while working at other tasks. His other software engineering pursuits at the time included a computer graphic and painting application called ArtMixer. (And, after creating Bryce, Wenger founded a company called U&I Software, where he developed MetaSynth, an application that combines imagery and sound, and ArtMatic, an application that combines imagery, sound, and more.)

Creating a landscape application was a personal pursuit, a digital form of grinding his own pigments and mixing them with binder to make paint so that landscape pictures could be painted onscreen. Instead of cadmium, cobalt, and oxide of chromium, Wenger worked with Musgrave's formulations of fractal geometry for generating rugged mountainous terrains. He contributed from his background as artist and musician. Wenger didn't take the pure algorithmic approach that Musgrave had. He added tools from ArtMixer, a digital paintbrush, to manually shape terrain forms, plus the ability to open images generated or worked on in a graphic picture editor. From music, he combined Musgrave's procedural texture work with his own understanding for how sound synthesizers work, generating a set of controls to create and edit visual noise to put realistic surfaces on those rugged terrains. He adapted the atmospheric model and built controls and sliders for adjusting the light source and fog and haze and clouds. He culminated the process by using a ray-tracing renderer as the binder to adhere mathematically derived "pigment" to the computer monitor's "canvas."

Wenger wrote the software for himself—the result of, and for the sake of, his artistic, observing eye. But it was one step further toward placing the software before a wider audience, since it now existed as an application with a minimal user interface that ran on a platform that was in the hands of a wider *user* base—Mac OS.

Wenger showed his software to his friend Pierre Bretagnolle, who, in turn, brought it to the attention of Andreas Pfeiffer, the editor of what was then France's largest Macintosh magazine, *SVM Mac*. Pfeiffer was instrumental in introducing Wenger and his landscape application to John Wilczak and Kai Krause, the co-founders of MetaTools (called, at that time, HSC Software; later MetaTools merged with Fractal Design and became MetaCreations). From that introduction grew the partnership that brought Wenger's personal creation based on the work of Ken Musgrave and Ken Perlin into a form for the general public.

Kai Krause and the User Interface Tributary

Up to this point, the software that existed was either the result of personal mathematical research or was a personal artist's tool based on that mathematical research. The methods for generating landscapes were completely personal and highly idiosyncratic: either a command-line interface and text file, or a personal, rudimentary interface with numbers and sliders. With the next tributary, Kai Krause and the User Interface, the software that Wenger created morphed into a form where it could be used by a larger number of people who had not themselves written the application.

Kai crafted the user interface to take all of the tremendous computing potential, coming as it did from deep mathematics, and put an interface with controls that would let users—lots of users, not just one user—have access to the potential afforded by the mathematics of fractal geometry. He created an interface that put a friendly face on top of powerful features, without bogging down the user in the complex details. Kai had, through his Kai's Power Tools, pioneered precedent-setting new standards for user interfaces that provide tons of functionality while hiding the underlying mathematical complexity. So, continuing in this vein, he worked with Wenger to make Bryce an application that is easy to use. As a result of the shell he created for Bryce, a beginner could get a quick start from the preset combination palettes and, in only a matter of minutes, be on the way to creating a new Brycean world.

Kai made the interface three-dimensional so that a user can instinctively reach for this control or that knob to perform a certain manipulation. Palettes divide the flow of work according to logical sequence. The user can go to different palettes to create objects, to edit them, to design the atmospheric environment, and to render the scene, all the while navigating in the scene using the Camera controls.

Yet the 1.0 version of the software was not the culmination of the dynamic creative process by Wenger and Kai (aided by Phil Clevenger and others at what was then MetaTools). More was yet to come. Even as they shipped version 1.0, they knew that they wanted to add light sources and the ability to import three-dimensional models created by other applications. They wanted to continue working to enhance the interface design to make Bryce even easier to use. But it was time to call a halt to the development process, draw a line in the sand, and say, "This is it. Let's introduce it to the public. Let's put Bryce out there." Thus, the first version of Bryce was released. The interface of Bryce 1 is shown in Figure 1.5.

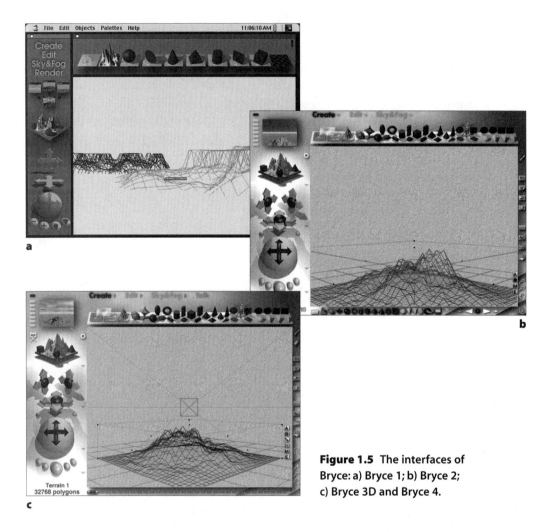

Figure 1.5 The interfaces of Bryce: a) Bryce 1; b) Bryce 2; c) Bryce 3D and Bryce 4.

From a relatively new branch of science and mathematics, to the personal vision of one for whom there was no concession to the hated user, to an artist-musician computer programmer, to a user-interface trendsetter, Bryce evolved from a mathematical idea to software that any person using a Macintosh computer (where the fastest processors were the 68040 Quadra Macs, roughly equivalent to 486-based PCs) could operate. And so Bryce 1.0 was shipped, in July 1994. Rendering took forever. The term *Sleepware* was devised to make the slow render time acceptable: create a scene, set it to render all night, and wake up and see what you wrought. Soon after that, Bryce was ported to operate on the recently shipped Power PC computers, where it and its users enjoyed a substantial power burst.

CONTINUING DEVELOPMENT

Bryce's continued development followed the course of crossing off items from the list of "things we want to do," as well as responding to the demands of an installed user base ("We want more!") and the demands of a technology company eager to grow.

Bryce 2 Macintosh

The developers acted on their wish to improve the software. Bryce 2 saw the addition of a plethora of new features. Wenger worked on the addition of primitive forms, new atmospheric features, separate light sources, the ability to generate random polyhedron rocks, the ability to import 3D models created outside of Bryce, boolean operations, additional terrain processing algorithms, and a far more powerful way to combine textures for more intricate and realistic surface materials. While Wenger pursued the development of new features, Krause and Clevenger set to work on redesigning the user interface, using Bryce itself to create its own interface (see Figure 1.5b). Sree Kotay implemented the interface changes, adding many of his own touches in the antialiased wireframes with depth cueing, more efficient render processes, Solo mode, and Kotay's crowning contribution—the newly revamped Terrain Editor. Todd Bogdan helped to program additional interface implementations. Brian Wagner, who came to the company after working on Pixel 3D (an Amiga/Windows application that generated 3D text and shapes, but which also was used for converting different 3D file formats) wrote the 3D file importers for Bryce 2.1. The Bryce developers stuffed new features into every nook and cranny of Bryce, making the software much more powerful while fulfilling their collective vision to make the application easy and fun to use. They continued the Bryce tradition of software with *soul*.

Bryce 2 Windows

After bringing out version 2.1 on the Macintosh (2.0 shipped in March 1996, and 2.1 shipped in July 1996), the developers took the next step in their Bryce plan. They'd been considering the question of where to go next. Should Bryce become a cross-platform product? Should Bryce animate? The answer to both questions was an enthusiastic "yes!" but the real question to tackle was, "Which one should we do first?" They decided that the next step was to port Bryce to Windows and, in so doing, rewrite it using the company's proprietary graphics libraries, Axiom.

Axiom allowed for further cross-platform development from that point, so that the animation version could be written for both Mac and Windows platforms simultaneously.

The engineering effort to port Bryce 2 to Windows was nothing short of heroic: the task daunting, but doable; the time in which to do it woefully inadequate by at least a good three to six months.

A fair-sized team was assembled for the task. To develop for Windows required, well, Windows developers, so there were a lot of new faces for the Bryce Windows team. From this point, Eric Wenger was no longer directly involved in Bryce development. The effort was headed by a veteran of the Bryce 2 Mac engineering team, Todd "Bogdog" Bogdan. He wrote all the code that tied the underlying features to the controls of the user interface. He was joined by Brian Wagner, who rewrote the ray-tracing renderer from scratch, which involved everything for interpreting Materials—and resulted in the wonderful glass effects. Additionally, Hessan Tchaitchian began work on the Terrain Editor, which was completed by Aleš (pronounced "uh-lesh") Holeček. Ales also contributed the new rendering optimization routines, based on his master's thesis at the Czech Technical University in Prague. John Terrel worked on the code that draws objects on the screen and the internal database that keeps track of all the objects and their whereabouts within Bryce, as well as the part of the software that determines, while rendering, if the ray tracer has "hit" an object (all of these concepts will be discussed in greater detail in other portions of this book). The Deep Texture Editor was ported to Windows by Paul Cattrone and Todd Bogdan. The engineering team toiled long hours, the proverbial 16-hour days, seven days a week, over the course of several long—but short—months.

When Bryce 2 Windows shipped, at the end of September 1996, it was a miracle what had been accomplished in such a short time. But the software was not complete nor stable. It was met with a cry of outrage by the enthusiastic Windows users who, having drooled long enough as they looked over the shoulders of their Macintosh-using brethren and sisteren, gleefully loaded up the software on their own computers running the Windows OS. Instead of being met with magic, they were met by an overabundance of General Page Faults, hangs, and mysterious behaviors. Bryce 2.0 for Windows was shipping, all right, but it simply was not ready for public consumption.

If the history of Bryce is a river, then the events surrounding the development of Bryce for Windows were the rapids—fraught with peril. Here, we follow the self-similarity of the River Chaos with its tributaries to a closer view of the River Bryce and *its* tributaries—one of which is the swiftly moving Technology Software Company Creek. The kinds of tributaries that feed this particular creek—or to put it more accurately, that *flood* this particular creek, can be read about in any Web-based or printed publication that follows the doings of high-technology companies, especially those companies that are newly trading on the public markets. We won't go into those details here, but in the Foreword to the previous edition of this book, Kai Krause summed it up with an eloquent understatement: "Quarterly timing is ruthless."

One of the questions that chaos theory has addressed is the behavior of turbulence, when fluid or air moves at higher speeds, and when two different fluid flows join together. Here the flow of a software application that evolved from personal pursuits met the flow of requirements of a user base, all of which wanted functionality and stability. Those flows, in turn, met the flow of a corporation and its voracious need to continue feeding its own revenue stream (no pun intended). These different tributaries came together in a foamy lather, and Bryce followed a choppy ride through a torrential flow of conflicting forces. Shipping the Bryce 2.1 Windows update in the early part of 1997 made things quieter; the software worked, and it was possible to experience landscape magic.

Bryce 3D

The next major revision of Bryce saw the Windows 2.1 code (which was cross-platform at its base) move forward to satisfy the long-awaited and much-requested ability for a fourth dimension: animation. The goal was the same as the goals for other advances in Bryce: provide features that are easy to use from the get-go, but also provide access to deeper levels of detail for more advanced use. At the same time, whatever the interface was to become, it needed to fit with the look of Bryce 2. Adding time as a fourth dimension required major changes to the underlying function of the application. Whereas before everything worked for still-image creation, now just about every feature of the software had to be made to move over time. Hierarchical links, origin points, and tracking necessitated overhaul of objects and cameras. Then, too, there was the matter of how to represent time in the application: to this end, an animation timeline was added (see Figure 1.5c). This third major version of Bryce was yet another complete overhaul of the application in order to tuck that fourth dimension into every nook and cranny of the three dimensions that were already there.

Who brought the animating version of Bryce into being? On the side of the user interface, there was Robert Bailey and Jackson Ting. On the engineering team,

Todd Bogdan knit together the underlying functionality with the interface, joined by Aleš Holeček and Brian Wagner, two anchor members. Wagner wrote the renderer, materials, and sky, complete with a bevy of new atmospheric and astronomical effects: rainbows, comets, adjustable solar and lunar sizes, interaction between sun and haze color, and a volumetric atmosphere. Holeček continued work with the Terrain Editor and wrote all of the animation code. These were joined by John Terrel, who worked on general editing, and Moe Doucet and Sree Kotay, who wrote the real-time display (Sree3D). Joining Todd Bogdan to hook up the interface was Josh Bates; they implemented the new animation palette, the Advanced Motion Lab, and the redesigned Materials Lab and Deep Texture Editor.

The animated version of Bryce, dubbed "3D," shipped at the end of 1997. This release took place in the still somewhat turbulent waters where all-out software development was combined with corporate pressure to ship *now* rather than later. With such an ambitious number of new features, the software required an update patch to attain full stability. Six months later, the 3.1 update patch was released, with stability (and a few cool new features, naturally!), superceding the original Bryce 3D.

Bryce 4

Bryce 4 is a significant change from the previous two versions in that the engineers had the luxury of building on top of a already built foundation, rather than having to gut the majority of the application and rebuild from scratch. With the basic integrity of the software in shape, the developers turned Bryce outward, so that it could talk and listen to many other applications and their 3D file formats. Bryce 4's Plug-ins folder contains a plethora of import and export modules. In addition to the sheer number of these modules, the fact that there are *export* modules is a major change. Bryce 4, in response to persistent requests, finally exports terrain geometry so that mountains made in Bryce can be brought into other 3D applications. The existence of a more robust set of import and export plug-ins laid a foundation for a possible plug-in development kit for Bryce (though, for reasons we get into later, prospects are doubtful).

In addition to including the Terrain Export lab, Bryce 4 takes skies much further. The Bryce 3D sky features that were crammed into a crowded dialog box were combined with new atmospheric features, precision numerical control, and a new preview to become the Sky Lab in Bryce 4. For better control of animation, a storyboard preview was added, for rendering and playback of the animation frames, as well as navigation to any specific frame of an animation using the thumbnail image. The Terrain Editor sports 26 additional fractal terrain types, and there are new noises in the Deep Texture Editor. Finally, objects can be assigned a Web link, and Bryce will directly export QTVR panorama movies from within Bryce as well as QuickTime movies.

The Bryce 4 development effort was led by Brian Wagner and Aleš Holeček, who respectively worked on Sky Lab and Terrain Export, in addition to cramming lots of little features and adjustments everywhere. Jackson Ting designed the interface for the Sky Lab and the Terrain Export. They were joined by Ken Musgrave working on the algorithm end of Bryce (Yes! He did make one concession to the hated user by working on a landscape application that has more users than just himself!) while Sam Coroniti worked on the import-export plug-in end of the application. Josh Bates did his usual fine job of hooking up the interface, as well as the Animation preview, and Paul Cattrone also implemented interface.

Bryce 4.0 shipped at the end of March 1999 in far more solid and stable a condition than past Bryce *x*.0 releases. An update patch—4.0.1—shipped nearly six months after 4.0 did, but it was not desperately needed in the way that previous update patches had been.

At this point in Bryce's history, the software is more stable and solid and has been filled out in places. By this time in its evolution, it has the fingerprints of quite a few people, as so many different creeks, streams, and tributaries have fed Bryce River.

Toward the end of 1999, the direction of MetaCreations drastically changed: the company divested itself of all its graphics software products, including Bryce. In April 2000, Bryce was bought by Corel, of Ottawa, Canada. What will happen to future development of the software? Since those whose fingerprints are on Bryce 4 have been scattered via resignations, dismissal, or transfer, the future of the software is an open question. We offer no tea-leaf readings here, knowing that prognostication or speculation would quickly be made outdated by real events. This recounting of Bryce's history works well enough in hindsight, but not foresight. Fortunately for Bryce's users, version 4.0.1 *is* stable, and we've much to say about what's contained therein.

WHY "BRYCE"?

So why is the software called Bryce? In the southern part of Utah, there is a national park called Bryce Canyon (see Figure C1.6 in the color section). The park is a place of fantastic geological columnar formations, called hoodoos, that were created by millennia of erosion. The formations look like fanciful images, and many are named for the myths and legends and images that are evoked by their shapes.

Bryce Canyon is not really a canyon; it is a rim, with a drop-off into a deep valley. The high elevation (over 8,000 feet) and high level of precipitation result in snow and freezing temperatures for more than half the year. Because of the daily cycle of freeze and thaw, water works its way into the rock formations and expands as it freezes in the rock crevasses. In the daytime, with each thaw, the water runs off, taking with it a tiny bit of rock. This process produces the crevasses and formations of the hoodoos. The play of light on these formations in the early morning and late afternoon creates dramatic vistas. You can hike down from the rim to walk among the tall hoodoos deep into a wonderland filled with discovery that stirs the imagination.

A natural place of mystery—this is Bryce the place. Bryce the software, which enables you to create your own fantastic creations, is named for that park. It is software that allows you to create your own landscapes—personal visions of mystery and wonder.

AN EMOTIONAL EXPERIENCE

Those visions of mystery and wonder are integral to the experience of working in Bryce. One time early in Bryce's history when I (Susan) had the opportunity to work side by side with Eric Wenger, we talked about the software and its success. He asked me why I thought it is so popular. I answered without hesitation, "It's the emotional experience that comes from working with it." And there is an excitement to working in Bryce. Bryce is addictive. From the first click on the Create Terrain icon on the Create Palette, to watching the erosion process unfold in front of you in the Terrain Editor, to adjusting the clouds and haze to be just so, to the satisfaction at getting the surface appearance just right, to solving a problem or discovering a new way to go about a particular task, to being mesmerized while watching each successive render pass and more and more detail emerge—there is something inherently satisfying about the creative process of working in Bryce.

Upon further reflection, there's more to the emotional experience of Bryce. The *more* part is deeper: it's the fact that, from this thing, this box, this computer, people are given the ability to make creations that mimic our natural environment. It's a primal thing, where we as members of a species living on this planet are able to create environments that echo the places we've been surrounded by from our youth. This is our habitat; this is our world. To be able to switch on a box and double-click an application icon and perform a few clicks and drags and then see the same type of environment emerge on the computer screen strikes us as nothing short of miraculous! Additionally, the process of working with this software makes us, as beings on this planet, more closely attuned to what we see here. If the adage of the artist is that drawing is not a matter of hand skills so much as a way of seeing, then working with Bryce develops in us the eye for our environment. Brycing and observing our surroundings: one informs the other.

And still one other element that makes working in Bryce an emotional experience is that it has been designed to accommodate the creation process. It has been ingeniously adapted to the way artists work, the way the creation process occurs. From the first user interface imprint that Kai Krause (followed by Phil Clevenger and Robert Bailey and Jackson Ting) put on the software, the way that it works *feels* like sculpting, feels like working with art. Some describe it as delightful or as a Zen state. Yes, yes; it is true that, some four versions later and a large population of users later, it's not perfect, and there are some who find the interface a hindrance rather than a help. Plus the ever-moving target of computing power means that the previous designs may turn into hindrances; what was a fantastic innovation two versions ago, in a Terrain Editor fit to a 640 x 480 area, is a hindrance when the baseline monitor size has increased and the canvas display has not (yet) increased with it.

Still, for all of that, Bryce offers you the ability to work with fractal geometry as an artist, not a mathematician, and generate images or animations that have uncanny resemblance to this world, or depart enough from it to be other-worldly while retaining enough elements of perspective and land forms to stay believable. So, swept along in the flow of the Rivers Chaos and Bryce and various other tributaries, here is a software application in which you may work and play.

MOVING ON...

From here on, we turn our attention from introducing how Bryce-the-software came to be to how your Bryce creations will come to be. The next chapter gives you a thorough introduction to the software and elaborates a bit more on the artistic creation process that is a part of working in Bryce.

CHAPTER TWO

An Introduction to Bryce

IN THIS CHAPTER...

- Three dimensions and two dimensions—the software

- A companionable walk through the software, with discussion along the way

- A look at Bryce's 3D space—the x, y and z axes

- A look at the working process

Have you ever attended a party where your host introduced you to all the other guests? At first, your mind numbly grasps their names, along with some relevant tidbit about each person. You forget names and mix up one with another. (Oh, okay...*you* are Shawn—and that person over there is Jamie? Sorry, I was confused.) Later, after talking with Shawn and Jamie and Sandy and others, you recall your initial dazed state when you were first introduced. You find yourself thinking, "Why, of course *that* person is Shawn, and, what's more, Shawn is an artist." How could you have thought otherwise? Still, before you got oriented, everything was new and jumbled. Sometimes you need to hear a thing stated two or three times to get it to stay inside your head.

This book is the party—a Bryce party—and this chapter is the introduction to everyone at the party. (They're all *very cool*, and you'll want to get to know them better!) Don't worry, though, you won't have to make small talk. Just read along, soak it in and follow along with the step-by-step walkthrough in this chapter. You'll become acquainted with the major parts of the application and get a better feel for the three-dimensional environment that is Bryce.

If you find the heft of this book intimidating, this chapter is here to ease your fears. As an introduction and light hands-on walk through the software, it introduces all the topics of the software and is a foreshadowing of the rest of the chapters. (In fact, during the introduction here, each section will point to the chapter where the topic is covered in depth.)

A THREE-DIMENSIONAL WORLD VIEWED IN TWO DIMENSIONS

So what is Bryce? Bryce is software that creates a scenic environment and all the objects contained in the environment. Whereas many other 3D applications devote themselves to modeling objects, Bryce's specialty is scenic landscape—landforms, mountains, bodies of water, skies, fog and the like.

Bryce uses geometry and math to do what it's doing. At first glance, the math is not apparent; it's hidden deep behind an interface where you see your objects in wireframe views (or in very simplistic 3D views) that the computer can quickly draw on the screen. This interface is the main workspace where you do the work, make the adjustments, build some more and tweak tweak tweak. Then, when you are ready to have your computer devote a bit more time to the task, you direct it to render the wireframe into a final, full-color image. If you are working on an animation, you will be rendering a series of images—each one slightly different from the one that precedes it—to create an animated movie.

Bryce, as well as all other applications on desktop computers, works within the limitations of a monitor's two-dimensional image. Bryce uses that flat monitor image to show you a three-dimensional world containing width, height, and depth. While you are working in Bryce, you will be working within the constraints of the monitor and mouse, where your motion is confined to vertical (up-down) and horizontal (left-right) dimensions, but neither mouse nor monitor allow you to work with depth (forward-backward).

In addition to the limitations of a two-dimensional image, displaying three-dimensional objects and environment is a power-intensive and time-consuming task for computers to perform. An enormous number of calculations take place in order to convey the height, width, and depth; to hide the objects that lie behind other objects; and to display the surface details of objects, especially if there are more complex effects such as transparency, refraction, reflection, and volume materials. Bryce, like other 3D applications, has two ways of looking at the objects in your scene—wireframe view, where you can see the basic shape and position of your objects, and rendered view, where you see the completed, rendered image in full color with all indications of three-dimensional depth and surface detail.

WALKTHROUGH, PART 1: BRYCE AT ITS MOST BASIC

We will show you the two ways of looking at the Bryce world by launching the application and seeing what is in an "empty" Bryce world when we render.

1. Double-click the application icon to launch Bryce 4.

   Bryce opens with an interface frame, with controls all around the outside. In the center is a new, untitled document: a gray, paper-textured area displays a wireframe view of a grid, a light blue horizontal line, and a blue pyramid with dotted lines emanating from it. What you see inside this window (on the textured-paper background) is the scene. The viewing area is called the Working Window, or Scene Window. The view that you see in Figure 2.1 is the scene in wireframe view. (Note: Although Bryce's default view, the Scene Window, is a gray paper textured background pattern, we'll be using a white untextured background to make the illustrations in this book clearer).

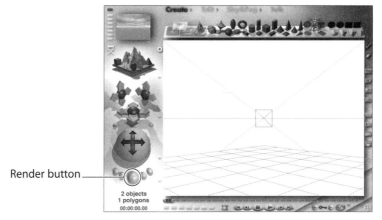

Render button

2 objects
1 polygons
00:00:00.00

Figure 2.1 The Bryce interface, in wireframe mode.

2. Click the render button on the Control Palette, on the left side of the Bryce interface. (Labeled in Figure 2.1)

When you click the render button, the wireframe view is replaced by a plain white background, which quickly fills with colored blocks. The blocks get smaller, showing successively finer detail. The resulting image is a gray ground with a blue sky (see Figure 2.2). There are clouds in the sky and a bit of white haze in the distance, visible on the horizon.

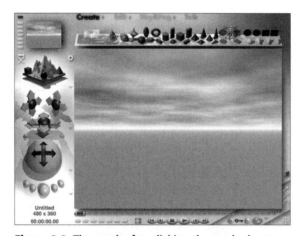

Figure 2.2 The result after clicking the render button.

In Bryce you begin not with a blank page but with an empty world. Well, it's not completely empty—it has a sky, some clouds, a sun, and a bit of haze. There is also an infinite ground plane, a flat gray surface that stretches for as far as you can see. This "empty world" is just waiting for your creative work.

You have a world—a scene. Now put things in that world. You do so by using the Create Palette showing along the top of the Bryce interface. Simply click an object, and it appears in the wireframe view of your scene.

3. Click the Create Terrain icon on the Create Palette (Figure 2.3).

A red terrain wireframe appears in your scene. Whenever a wireframe object is red, it is selected.

4. Click the render button again.

Bryce renders the world, with the terrain. The terrain's surface has a mountainous appearance to it, as shown in Figure 2.4.

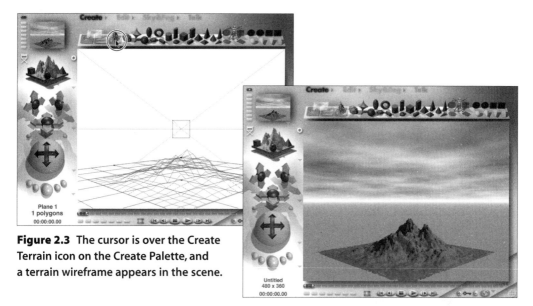

Figure 2.3 The cursor is over the Create Terrain icon on the Create Palette, and a terrain wireframe appears in the scene.

Figure 2.4 The rendered scene with terrain.

You are working with Bryce at its most basic. Start with a world. Put things in the world. Render.

Bryce has two modes—wireframe mode and render mode. Your work in Bryce takes place in wireframe mode. You switch to render mode to render your scene to check the results of your work. The escape (esc) key is the switch that moves you back and forth between them. Check it out.

5. Tap the escape (esc) key a few times.

Each time you tap the escape key, you move from wireframe to render mode and back again.

Bryce makes worlds and then takes rendered pictures of them. Bryce's entire file structure is based on these two processes: working in the three-dimensional world and then taking a two-dimensional snapshot of that world. (When you're animating a scene, the situation is a little more complicated, but as an animation is basically just a series of snapshots, the general principles we expound here are still valid.) In doing these two processes, Bryce creates two documents, one for each mode of operation. The three-dimensional world information—including objects, terrains, materials, sky, and camera settings for the scene—is saved in a scene document. The rendered scene is saved in an image document (PICT for Macintosh, BMP for Windows). Figure 2.5 depicts Finder (Macintosh) or

Explorer (Windows) icons for both documents. On Windows, the file extensions are .BR4 for the scene file, and .BMP for the rendered result; Windows automatically assigns the extensions to your Bryce files. On the Macintosh side, the PICT rendered image file receives a suffix of .PCT, which Bryce automatically assigns when you save a scene.

a
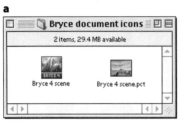

b
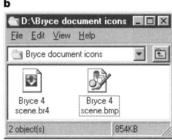

Figure 2.5
The icons for the scene document and image document:
(a) Macintosh;
(b) Windows.

THE BRYCE INTERFACE: TOOLS FOR TASKS

So far, the discussion has been limited mostly to the Bryce scene—the 3D world displayed in the Working Window in wireframe or rendered view. Before we continue with Part 2 of the walkthrough, we'll introduce both the tasks you will do in Bryce—and the portions of the Bryce interface you'll use to accomplish those tasks.

Surrounding the scene window is a frame that contains all the controls you need to get the job done.

In Figure C2.6 (in the color section), the interface frame surrounding the scene window is comprised of different palettes—each devoted to a certain task. Controls on those palettes will lead you to other labs devoted to working on specific tasks. Continue referring to this image throughout this section.

A Point of View—The Control Palette

To work with a three-dimensional world, you need to have a point of view. To borrow an analogy from a real-world three-dimensional artwork—sculpture—you need some kind of device that gives you access to your creation from all sides and all points of view while you are shaping it, such as a turntable or scaffolding. In Bryce, that device is a set of views of your scene, with which you can see your creation from all sides. Some are direct profile views, and others provide a perspective view. The Control Palette, on the left side of the window, provides tools for your point of view. The tools on the Control Palette are an important—and permanent—part of working in Bryce. The palette never goes away.

One point of view is provided by the Nano Preview, a small rendered display of your scene. It's small enough to display quickly and large enough to give a taste for what you're doing. Located below the Nano Preview are the View controls, for choosing different views of your scene. Below that are the Camera controls—the crosses and trackball that you use to move and rotate your perspective cameras. The Control Palette also contains the Render controls. At the bottom of the Controls Palette is the Status Text area, which displays information about your current task.

For further information about the View and Camera controls, see Chapter 3, "Camera and Scene" For more information about rendering, see Chapter 13, "Render Unto Bryce."

Working with Object (Create, Edit, and Selection Palettes)

The top panel of the interface is a set of three interchangeable palettes. Switch to one you want by simply clicking its name. Two of those palettes are devoted to working with objects: the Create Palette and the Edit Palette. The Create Palette is for adding objects to your scene—terrain, cone, light, stone, plane and more.

The Edit Palette contains controls for making adjustments to those objects—the size, rotation and position of each one. How big is it? Which way is it facing? Where is it positioned? Then there is the matter of the object's surface; how does the object respond to light? Is it matte? Shiny? What color is it? Does it have any special optical properties? Is it transparent? Does it reflect light? What is the surface material like? Is it smooth? Bumpy? Is it a surface material or a volume material? All these questions about the object's surface or volume deal with the object's material properties and textures—important building blocks for materials. The Edit Palette not only provides tools for directly adjusting size and position but also acts as a portal to a place for working with the surface appearance.

Below the Working Window is one other palette devoted to objects—the Selection Palette. It enables you to precisely focus on the desired object—handy when you have a scene containing more than a few objects. The Create Palette is covered in more detail in Chapter 4, "Brycean Objects"; the Edit Palette is covered in more detail in Chapter 6, "Editing and the Internal Bryce Grid"; the Selection Palette is covered in Chapter 4, "Brycean Objects."

Environment (Sky & Fog Palette)

Your objects live within an environment. The third palette at the top of the Bryce interface is the Sky & Fog Palette, which contains controls for making your world's environment whatever you want it to be. Bryce's sky contains a light source (sun or moon), clouds, haze, fog, rainbows, halos, stars, and comets. The Sky & Fog Palette provides controls for most of these (more controls live in the Sky Lab).

In addition to the sun (or moon) as a source of illumination for your environment, Bryce generates light objects to shed light on your scene. Lights do not live in the Sky & Fog Palette. However, if you're thinking in terms of "controlling your environment," light objects rightfully belong in the Environment category. For more information on atmosphere, see Chapter 11, "Brycean Skies"; and to learn about the lesser lights see Chapter 12, "Brycean EnLightenment."

Time Palette

The Selection Palette shares space with another—the Time Palette. Almost everything in the scene can change over time—objects, the sun, moon, clouds and environmental characteristics, and the camera. When you are animating your scene, the Time Palette provides you with all the controls for working with the fourth dimension of your scene—time. To switch back and forth between the Time and Selection Palettes, the white wireframe sphere on the right end (lower-right corner of Bryce interface) acts as a toggle switch.

The Time Palette is covered in more detail in Chapter 14, "The Fourth Dimension: Time and Animation."

Controlling Bryce Itself (Display/Wireframe Palette)

The Display/Wireframe Palette (the thin palette on the right) gives you options to control Bryce while working with your scene. The Display controls (top portion of the palette) allow you to customize the appearance of the Bryce interface. The Wireframe controls (bottom portion of the palette) allow you to determine the appearance and behavior of wireframe objects in your scene. For more detail on these controls, see Chapter 4, "Brycean Objects," and Chapter 5, "Streamline Your Brycing."

Talk

Three palettes live at the top of the Bryce interface. Yet a fourth name is there—Talk. Clicking Talk does not bring up another palette, but launches BryceTalk. If your computer is connected to the Internet, you may launch BryceTalk, where you can log in using your unique nickname. Once logged in to BryceTalk, you may talk with other Bryce users.

Deeper Details

Bryce contains additional workspaces dedicated to detail work—terrains, materials, skies, animation. When you go to these workspaces (also referred to as rooms, or labs), you temporarily leave the main Bryce interface. Each room contains many more controls for the fine-tuning of that portion of your scene or animation. The labs are: Terrain Editor, Sky Lab, Materials Lab—with two subsets: the Pictures dialog and the Deep Texture Editor—and Advanced Motion Lab. Most of these include their own version of the timeline; the Advanced Motion Lab is the granddaddy—it controls all aspects of time in your scene. There is also a separate room for exporting terrains.

This book devotes a chapter or a major chapter section to each of these rooms. The Terrain Editor is covered in Chapter 8, "Terrains, Symmetrical Lattices, and the Terrain Editor"; the Materials Lab and the Pictures dialog are covered in Chapter 9, "Material World I: Materials Lab"; the Deep Texture Editor is covered in Chapter 10, "Material World II: Picture Textures and the Deep Texture Editor"; the Sky Lab is covered in Chapter 11, "Brycean Skies"; and the Advanced Motion Lab is covered in both Chapter 14, "The Fourth Dimension: Time and Animation"; and Chapter 15, "Advanced Animation Techniques." The Terrain Exporter is covered in Chapter 18, "Terrains, Symmetrical Lattices and Terrain Editor."

Bryce also contains dialog boxes for working with deeper details of a few other object types—the torus, lights, and meshes (imported objects). These dialog boxes do not take over the entire work area. The Edit Torus dialog box is discussed in Chapter 6, "Editing and the Internal Bryce Grid"; the Light dialog box is discussed in Chapter 12, "Brycean EnLightenment"; and the Edit Mesh dialog box is covered Chapter 14, "Brycean Objects."

Rendering

Many times throughout the creation process—and once when you're done with the scene—you will render. During rendering, Bryce gathers together information about all of the objects and the surrounding environment and then gives them life, taking them from simple wireframe view to their full-color glory.

WALKTHROUGH, PART 2: WORKING WITH YOUR BRYCE SCENE

You started the scene, you created a terrain, you rendered. Now that you've been introduced to the main parts of Bryce's interface and controls, let's get to work and actually do something with each of them.

Grayscale Geology

The next step in the scene is to make some adjustments to the terrain using the Terrain Editor.

Your terrain should still be red—selected. If it is not, click the terrain wireframe to select it. It should turn red and a bounding box should appear, with small square buttons next to it. Those buttons are shortcuts to controls for working with the object. We'll use the E button (for Edit) to access the Terrain Editor.

1. Click the E to edit the object.

   The Terrain Editor appears.

   At the upper right is a view of the grayscale information that gives the terrain its shape—the Terrain Canvas. In the lower left is a 3D preview of the terrain's shape. The three-sided frame around the Terrain Canvas and the buttons on the upper left of the screen contain controls for affecting the terrain's shape.

2. Press the mouse on the Grid name and/or the grid image (see Figure 2.7). From the pop-up menu that appears, select 256—fine. This will add some image detail to the terrain.

3. Click the Eroded button (blue button, upper left). This alters the shape of the terrain to appear eroded.

The Terrain Canvas and the 3D preview change, looking something like Figure 2.8

4. Click the check mark in the lower right to exit the Terrain Editor and return to your scene.

5. Render (see Figure 2.9).

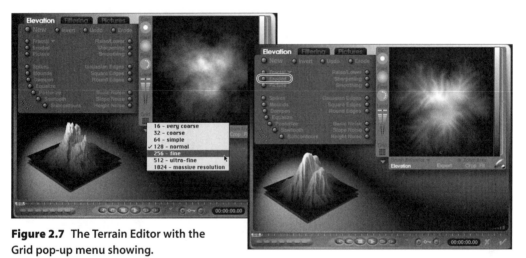

Figure 2.7 The Terrain Editor with the Grid pop-up menu showing.

Figure 2.8 The Terrain Editor after clicking the Eroded button.

Figure 2.9
The rendered scene,
after eroding the terrain.

Turn the Terrain into an Island

That terrain looks awfully funny placed on a flat gray ground. Suppose we make it an island in the midst of water?

We'll grab one of Bryce's preset materials from the Library and apply it to the ground plane.

1. Toggle back to wireframe mode using the escape (esc) key if necessary.

2. Click the ground plane wireframe to select it.

    The ground plane turns red.

3. On the Create Palette, click the triangle just to the right of the word Edit.

    The Materials Library appears with a list of preset categories on the left (see Figure 2.10).

4. Click the Waters & Liquids category.

    New presets of primarily blue watery spheres appear.

5. Click the preset entitled Mercury Surface (see Figure 2.10).

    A red line appears around it, indicating that it is selected.

6. Click the check mark to exit the Materials Preset Library. Render.

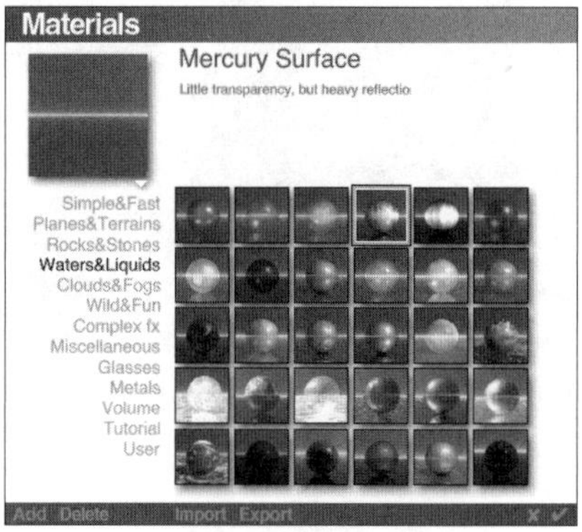

Figure 2.10 The Materials Preset Library, with Waters & Liquids category showing and the Mercury Surface preset selected.

    Speaking of Material Presets, whenever you create a new terrain, Bryce randomly assigns a material preset from the Planes and Terrains category to it. Let's choose a common, unrandom Material Preset for the terrain.

7. Click the terrain to select it. Go to the Materials Library by clicking the triangle next to the word Edit. In the Planes & Terrains category, select the Shaman Cliffs preset, as shown in Figure 2.11. Click the check mark to exit the Materials Library. Render.

    The terrain (which more closely resembles the ones shown here) has a new surface material, and is now surrounded by water. However, it is floating on top of the water's surface. In order to look more natural, it needs to be submerged below the surface a bit.

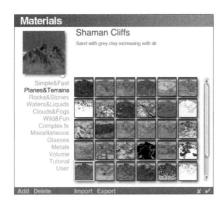

Figure 2.11 The Shaman Cliffs Materials Library preset.

Enlarge the Terrain

The task of enlarging the terrain introduces Bryce's Edit controls, on the Edit Palette. They will conveniently take care of submerging the terrain.

1. Click the word Edit at the top part of the Create Palette. The Edit Palette appears. The Edit Palette contains controls for changing individual and multiple objects.

2. Point your cursor over the center of the resize control, located under the word Edit.

    The cube at the center is displayed at a larger size, and the cursor arrow changes to a proportional resize box.

3. Drag to the right.

    The terrain begins to grow. Continue dragging to the right until the terrain fills the bottom half of the scene window (see Figure 2.12).

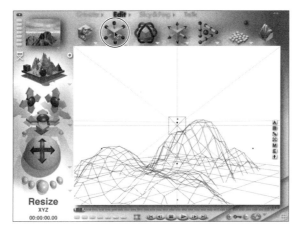

Figure 2.12 After enlarging the terrain using the resize control.

When the terrain increased in size, the base of the terrain was submerged under the ground plane; it is now under water and hidden from view.

You can directly move objects around in the scene by dragging them, however, so we can unsubmerge *some* of the submerged portion of the terrain.

4. Point your cursor over any portion of the red terrain wireframe and drag up a bit, keeping an eye on the terrain's bottom edge. If you see the square edges of the wireframe, you've dragged too high. Drag down again until the terrain is slightly submerged.

Now it fills more of the scene window, as Figure 2.13 shows. You can change your perspective of the scene in order to get a better view.

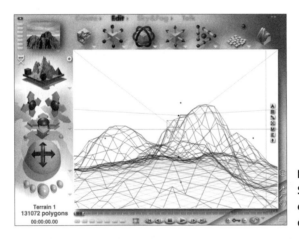

Figure 2.13
Scene Window after enlarging terrain and dragging it up a bit.

Adjust Your View of the Scene

There are many ways to adjust the view of the scene to better position the terrain. For this example, we'll use both the trackball control and one of the cross controls to change the perspective.

1. Point your mouse at the Trackball control on the Control Palette.

The control lightens and the Status Text at the bottom of the palette reads Control Camera Trackball. Drag the trackball up slightly, watching the blue horizon line. Drag up until the horizon line is located about a third of the way up from the bottom of the scene window (see Figure 2.14). (When composing an image it's a good idea to place the horizon line either above or below the exact middle of the picture.)

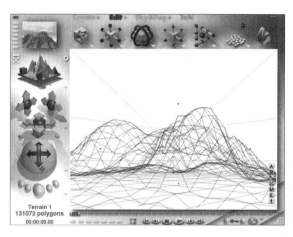

Figure 2.14 After using the Trackball to rotate the camera, thereby lowering the horizon line.

2. Point your mouse cursor over the front edge of the flat cross control, just above the trackball.

    The Status Text reads XZ Camera, and the cursor changes to a Z. When you drag the control from this point, you'll be moving your perspective along the *z* (depth) axis. In other words, you'll move yourself closer to or farther from the objects in your scene.

3. Drag up on the XZ Control. The terrain moves away from you. Continue dragging until your scene looks like Figure 2.15. Most of the terrain appears in the scene, and there is a bit of blank area in the foreground—the water. You look at the island as if from water level, and the island towers above your perspective.

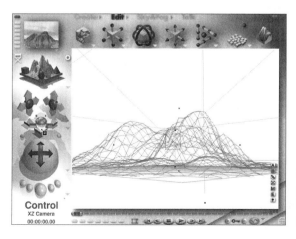

Figure 2.15 After moving your perspective away from the objects in your scene using the XZ Control.

4. Click the render button.

5. Save your scene. From the File menu, choose Save, or type ⌘-S/Ctrl+S. Name your scene "Walkthrough Island."

   Note: Check to see if Bryce saves the rendered image file as well as the scene file. If not, follow the steps in the "Save Image with Scene" sidebar.

SAVE IMAGE WITH SCENE

While you still have Bryce launched and this scene file open, do the following: In your operating system software (Mac OS: Finder; Windows: Explorer) check the location where you just saved the scene file. You should have two files—on a Mac, they will be: Walkthrough Island and Walkthrough Island.pct; on Windows, they will be Walkthrough Island.br4, Walkthrough Island.bmp. If you only have the scene file and not the image file, you need to change the preferences so that Bryce saves the rendered image each time you save a scene file.

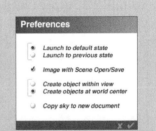

Figure 2.16 Check the Image with Scene Open/Save option in the Preferences dialog box so that the rendered image is saved with the scene.

Under the Edit menu, select Preferences. In the Preferences dialog box, (see Figure 2.16) look for the item called "Image with Scene Open/Save." If that item isn't checked, then you won't find an image file when you save. Click the button to the left of the item to switch it on.

Click the check mark at the bottom of the dialog box to exit. Now resave your scene. The rendered image should be saved with the scene.

Adjust Haze for Sky and Sun Position

Give a new appearance to your sky! For this, you'll assign a sky look from the Sky & Fog Preset Library and then make a minor adjustment or two.

1. Click the word Sky & Fog at the top of the Edit Palette.

   The Sky & Fog Palette appears.

2. Click the triangle to the right of Sky & Fog to open the Sky & Fog Preset Library.

3. Select the preset called Late Afternoon (see Figure 2.17). Click the Render button to see how it looks.

From your perspective, the sun's position is above and left and behind. Not enough of the terrain is in shadow, so it looks flat. Change the sun control to provide more shadow, to add drama to the scene.

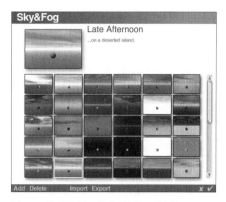

4. Drag the sun control so that the bright point is next to the horizon, at the nine o'clock position (see Figure 2.18). The terrain casts more shadows onto itself.

Figure 2.17 Sky & Fog Preset Library with preset called Late Afternoon.

The Sky & Fog Palette contains six small boxes showing thumbnail images, each of which is a control for changing a different part of Bryce's sky. If you look through all six at once, you see a sample Bryce scene.

SkyLab control

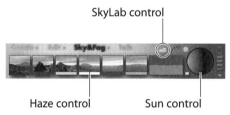

Figure 2.18 Changing the sun to the nine o'clock position.

Haze control   Sun control

5. Point the mouse so it hovers over the thumbnail of the Haze control—just under the words Sky & Fog. The pointer cursor changes to a double arrow, and the Status Text area on the bottom of the Control Palette changes to read both "Haze" and "Haze Color." Drag to the right. As you drag, the Status Display on the bottom of the Control Palette displays numbers that change as you drag. Drag until until the number reads somewhere between 15 and 20 (see Figure 2.19).

Notice that the Haze control thumbnail has changed in appearance: the sky has thickened and the horizon is lighter. Check out the Nano Preview, which shows a miniature render of your scene. Since there is more haze present in the atmosphere, the sky near the horizon is whiter.

We'll go to the Sky Lab to fine tune the haze.

Before

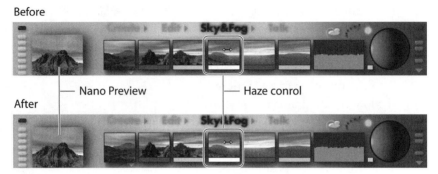

— Nano Preview   — Haze conrol

After

Figure 2.19 Before and after changing the haze setting by dragging the Haze Control.

6. Click the Sky Lab control toward the right end of the Sky & Fog Palette (it looks like a rainbow and cloud) to bring up the Sky Lab. The words at the top label the three main sections.

7. Click Atmosphere to access the section that contains the controls for haze. You should see a panel that resembles that in Figure 2.20. (To see a preview render of your scene, choose the Render in Scene option from the pop-up menu below the preview window.)

Haze controls

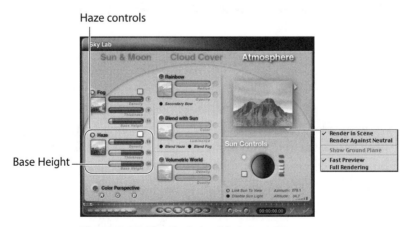

Base Height

Figure 2.20 The Sky Lab, with Atmosphere panel showing.

The Haze controls consist of three sliders. We can thicken the haze in the low foreground by increasing the Base Height. Drag the Base Height slider to 36.

Although the addition of the haze gives the appearance of scale and depth to the scene (this terrain is looking more like a big island now!), it's dulled the patches of blue in the sky. We can add a bit of contrast to the shape of the clouds.

8. Switch to the Cloud Cover section of the Sky Lab (see Figure 2.21a). In the lower center of the section, there is a slider called Amplitude. Drag the slider to the left and the right. As you drag, notice that the slider is orange when dragged to the left and it turns blue as you drag to the right. The orange color corresponds to negative numbers and the blue color corresponds to positive numbers in the numerical readout at the right of the slider. Release the mouse and return the slider to its previous position by typing ⌘-Z/Ctrl+Z.

9. Notice the location of the Frequency slider. Using the Frequency slider's position for comparison, drag the Amplitude slider to the left so that the orange Amplitude slider matches the location of the Frequency slider (see Figure 2.21b.) The cloud has more contrast. (If you want to drag the slider around to get your own result, by all means do so!) Click the check mark in the lower right-hand corner of the Sky Lab to accept your changes.

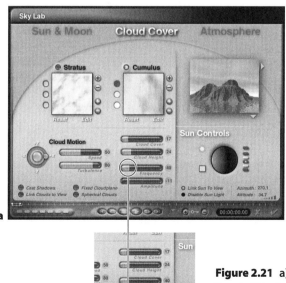

Figure 2.21 a) The Cloud Cover Panel of Sky Lab; b) After dragging Amplitude slider to match slider above it.

Place Rocks in the Scene

Now it's time to place some rocks in the foreground of your scene.

1. Click the word Create to bring the Create Palette to the top.

2. Click the Create Stone icon on the Create Palette. A stone object appears in your scene (see Figure 2.22).

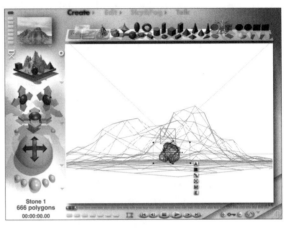

Figure 2.22 After creating a stone object.

The next step involves positioning the stone closer to the viewer. Since we can look at the scene from other angles, top view serves well for this purpose. Once you switch to top view, you need something in the scene that represents the viewer's location. That representative something is the camera object (shown as a blue pyramid in the scene). However, there's a slight catch. Bryce provides two ways to look a the scene from a perspective view. The first is is from the camera object itself; it is called Camera View. The second view is from a location that has no object to represent it, called Director's View, which is the default view upon launching the application. When you are in Director's View, you can see the camera object in your scene (very handy when animating the camera itself). It so happens that you are currently looking at your scene in Director's View. Once you change to one of the other views—top, left, right, front—how can you tell where the Director's View perspective is located? You can move the camera object to the location of the Director's View, so that both Director and Camera views are in the same location. When you look at the scene from top view, you'll have an idea where the camera is, and thus will be able to more intelligently position the stone in relation to the camera. (A comprehensive explanation of the concepts behind Camera and Director's View is in Chapter 3, "Camera and Scene.")

3. From the Camera Options pop-up menu, choose Camera to Director (see Figure 2.23).

   The blue wireframe representation of the camera disappears. It's now in the same position as the Director's View.

Figure 2.23 Moving the camera object to the position of Director's View using the Camera Options pop-up menu.

4. Change to top view either by clicking the View Diorama control twice so that the Diorama changes to a top perspective, or by accessing the View Options menu to the right of the Diorama control and choosing From Top (see Figure 2.24a). The camera is in the lower right hand corner (see Figure 2.24b).

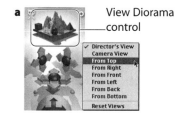

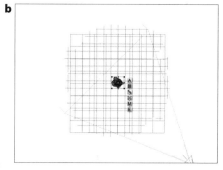

Figure 2.24 Getting to Top view: a) The View Diorama control and the View Options menu; b) Top view of scene.

5. The stone should still be selected (red); if not, you'll have to select it. Directly clicking the stone doesn't work in this case, because the terrain is higher than the stone and "covers" it; when you click, the terrain will be selected instead. Bryce has a clever trick for selecting objects. Hold down the Control or Ctrl key and click where the stone is located. A pop-up menu appears, listing all objects that are located under the mouse (see Figure 2.25). Select Stone 1 from the pop-up menu. When you release the mouse, the stone will be selected.

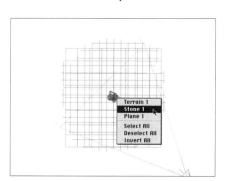

Figure 2.25 The Select Objects pop-up menu, invoked by clicking with Control/Ctrl key pressed.

6. Drag the stone to the lower right, so that it is located near the camera (see Figure 2.26).

7. Create another stone. Each time you click the Create Stone icon, Bryce generates a stone with a random shape. Drag it into position. Repeat this step to create a total of three stones (see Figure 2.27).

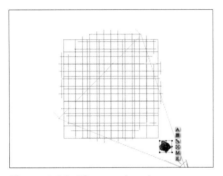

Figure 2.26 After moving the stone closer to the camera.

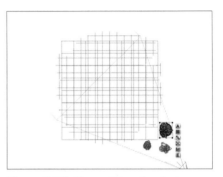

Figure 2.27 Three stones located near the camera.

Adjust the Rocks

Three rocks are in the scene, located in the foreground. However, once you return to Director's View, you'll see that more adjustments are necessary.

1. Return to Director's View via the View Options pop-up menu, the Diorama control, or by tapping the tilde (~) key.

    As you can see in Figure 2.28, the rocks are too far above water and are too big!

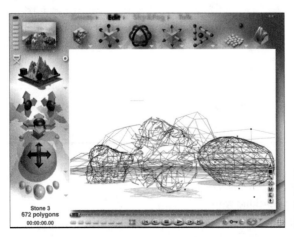

Figure 2.28 Rocks shown from Director's View—they need to be smaller.

You'll need to select all the rocks in order to make changes to them. To do that, you'll use a tool on the Selection Palette.

2. Point your mouse to the white wireframe ball in the lower right hand corner of the interface. The Status Text area says Time/Selection Palette Toggle. Click the wireframe, and the bottom area of the Bryce interface changes to look like Figure 2.29.

The Selection Palette contains options for selecting objects by type.

— Time/Select Pallette Toggle

Figure 2.29 The Selection Palette.

3. Point your mouse to the Select Stones icon (see Figure 2.30). The Status Text readout to the left tells you which object type you are working with. Click the icon.

Figure 2.30 The Select Stones icon on the Selection Palette.

All the stones in your scene are selected. You are now ready to work with them.

4. Drag down to submerge the stones underwater (see Figure 2.31).

They could still stand to be a little smaller in size. Back to the Edit Palette with us!

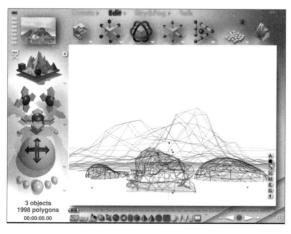

Figure 2.31 After dragging stones down to submerge them.

5. Click the word Edit to make the Edit Palette appear. Locate the Resize tool (below the word Edit). Drag from the center of the tool to the left; the stones shrink in size. Stop when they are an appropriate size (see Figure 2.32).

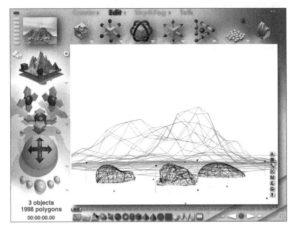

Figure 2.32 After shrinking the stones.

If you need to make additional individual adjustments to the rocks, (changing their position, resizing) do so. You may also go back to top view and change their location so they don't crowd the camera.

The Stones' Surface Appearance

Next, you will give all the stones the same wet rock surface appearance.

1. Once you have made all your size and position adjustments, reselect all the stones by clicking the Select Stones icon on the Selection Palette.

2. On the Edit Palette, click the left icon, the Edit Material icon.

   The main Bryce interface disappears and you go to the Materials Lab (see Figure 2.33), which offers a preview of the surface appearance. The right-pointing triangle to the right of the preview window is another doorway to a place you've already visited—the Materials Library.

To Materials Library

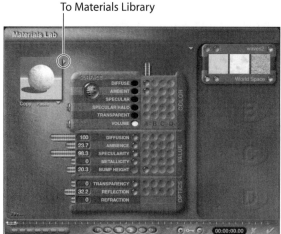

Figure 2.33
The Materials Lab.

3. Click the right-pointing triangle next to the Materials Preview to open the Materials Library. Click the Rocks & Stones category. The preset in the top row, second from the left, should be Wet Rock (see Figure 2.34). Click it and exit the Materials Library by clicking the check mark. You are now back in the Materials Lab.

4. In the Materials Lab, the settings have changed.

    Notice the Ambience setting of 23.7. Ambience determines the overall illumination of the object, especially when it is not in direct sunlight. The Ambience setting for the rocks should match the Ambience setting for the terrain. Why the fuss? You'll want to make

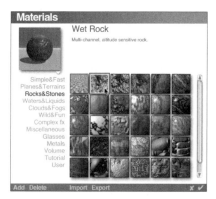

Figure 2.34 Materials Library, with the Wet Rock preset showing.

the Ambience setting for all objects identical, so that they look cohesive, like they belong to the same environment. (More information on this in Chapter 9, "Material World I: Materials Lab" and on the Web site, "What's Wrong With This Picture?") The terrain's Ambience setting is 11.7, so let's make the stones match.

5. Locate the Ambience setting (Figure 2.35). Drag the slider to the right. Alternatively, click the number: a numerical entry box appears, and you may enter the number 11.7. Tap the Return key to accept the number setting.

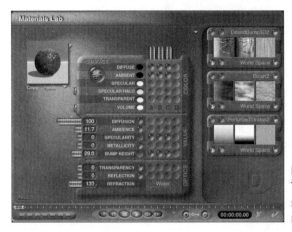

Figure 2.35
The Materials Lab after selecting the Wet Rock material preset.

6. Click the check mark to exit the Materials Lab and return to your scene.

7. Render the scene. It should look something like Figure 2.36.

8. Save the scene.

Figure 2.36 The rendered scene.

Animate the Sun and Haze

To round out this introduction to Bryce, we'll do just a touch of animation, so that you can say that you're acquainted with it. We will animate a couple of things in the sky—the position of the sun and the amount and color of the haze. The first thing we'll need to do is get the Time Palette back.

1. Click the white wireframe sphere in the lower right corner to toggle back to the Time Palette.

2. Ensure that Auto-Key is active (checked) on the Timeline Options pop-up menu (see Figure 2.37).

   If Auto-Key was not active, you'll need to set an initial keyframe. Click the Add Keyframe button.

3. The Time Scrubber is located at the left end of the timeline on the Time Palette (see Figure 2.37). Drag it to the right. As you drag, the Status Text will display the time associated with the Scrubber's present position. Continue dragging to the right until the time reads 00:00:03.00—that's three seconds (the time readout is Hour:Minute:Second.Frame). As you drag, and the Scrubber reaches the right end of the timeline, the white ticker marks on the time timeline will begin scrolling to the left. When the time reads 00:00:03.00, release the mouse. With fifteen frames per second, you have a total of 45 frames in your animation.

You are now in the timeline, three seconds after your initial scene. You may make changes to your scene here, and Bryce will automatically remember the new state and will create a transition from the original state to the new one.

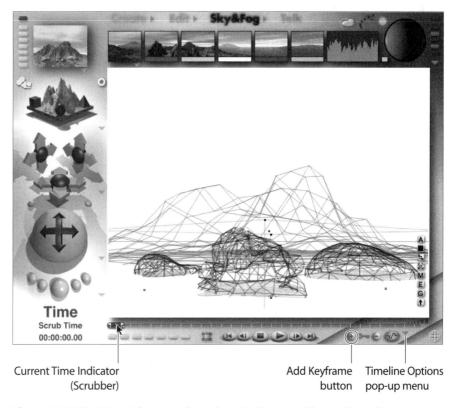

Current Time Indicator
(Scrubber)

Add Keyframe
button

Timeline Options
pop-up menu

Figure 2.37 The Time Palette, ready to drag the Time scrubber to the right.

4. Click the Sky & Fog label to summon the Sky & Fog Palette. Change the sun's position. It's currently low on the horizon, but it could go lower still. Drag the sun control to the left ever so slightly so that the highlight nearly disappears (see Figure 2.38). Do not drag so far that the sun turns into a moon, however (if you do drag too far, undo the last move with a ⌘-Z/Ctrl+Z).

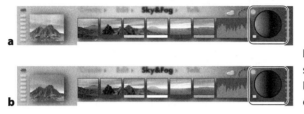

Figure 2.38 Changing the sun's position in the Sky & Fog Palette: a) Before change; b) After change.

5. Since the sun is now closer to the horizon, we can accentuate the moment with reddish haze—the haze is currently white. Locate the Haze Color swatch on the Sky & Fog Palette, underneath the words Sky & Fog. Position your cursor inside the swatch and press and hold. The cursor changes to an eyedropper and a color picker appears. The left side of the color picker is fully saturated, the right side less so (better for nature scenery) Drag to the right where light desaturated pink is located (see Figure 2.39), and let go. You now have a new, pinky color.

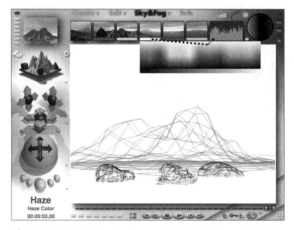

Figure 2.39 Giving the haze a light, desaturated pink color.

6. Now we'll increase the haze amount slightly. Move the mouse into the thumbnail area above the Haze Color swatch. The cursor changes to a double arrow. As you drag to the right a numerical readout appears in the text display area. Drag until the number is between 25 and 35. (The thumbnail appears more murky, reflecting the haze increase; see Figure 2.40.)

Figure 2.40 After increasing the haze amount.

You have now changed your sky in three minor ways. The sun is lower and the haze is pink and a bit thicker. Next you'll preview your animation to see the scene change from the first state to this state you've just created.

Previewing Your Animation

1. Locate the Preview Animation icon on the Time Palette. It looks like a small filmstrip.

2. Click the Preview Animation icon.

The Bryce scene window changes to a storyboard preview. Bryce renders a small thumbnail image for each frame in the scene window (see Figure 2.41). The few frames before the current one are displayed in the Nano Preview, to give you a sense of the action leading up to the current frame. The latest (current) frame in the Storyboard area has a terra-cotta border.

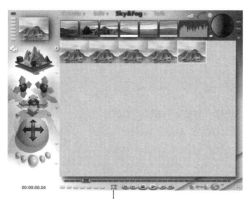

00:00:00.04

Preview Animation icon

Figure 2.41 Bryce's Animation Preview generating a preview of all the frames in the sequence.

When all 45 frames have been rendered, the entire sequence is played back. Three things occur simultaneously during playback: the Time Scrubber marks the current time, the Nano Preview plays the sequence, and the current frame border moves from image to image in the Storyboard area (see Figure 2.42).

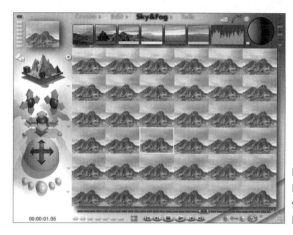

Figure 2.42 The Render Preview when all the thumbnail frames have been generated.

If you didn't like the results of this preview, you could move the Time Scrubber to the end of the sequence, make further changes to the sky, and render a preview again to see the results. Once you are satisfied with the animation, you may render it out to a movie.

Rendering Your Animation

The nice little thumbnail image is all fine and well and good—but small. The image size of the scene is far larger, 480 x 360 pixels. Like the proverbial Goldilocks and the Three Bears, one (the thumbnail) is too small and another other (the scene size) is too big. Your first step will be to get the output size "just right."

1. From the File menu, select Document Setup.

   The Document Setup dialog box appears (see Figure 2.43). In the lower left section, entitled Render Resolution, you may choose to render the scene at the same size as the wireframe, or you can render out a smaller image—half (.50) or a quarter (.25) of the current wireframe scene size.

Figure 2.43 The Document Setup dialog box.

2. Change the Render Resolution to half the current size by clicking the 1:0.50 line. The setting turns dark to indicate that it is currently selected. This new setting will result in a movie that's 240 x 180 pixels. Click the check mark to leave the Document Setup dialog box.

    If your computer is an older, slower model, you may want to select the 1:0.25 Render Resolution in the interest of speed.

    Now that you have the right size, you're ready to get your render going. But first…

3. Click the First Keyframe button (Figure 2.44) to make sure that your Time Scrubber is at the beginning of the sequence (00:00:00.00). If your Time Scrubber was elsewhere, it pops back to the beginning.

Figure 2.44 The Time Palette with the First Keyframe button encircled.

4. Save your scene file.

5. Under the File menu, select Render Animation.

    The Render Animation dialog box appears (Figure 2.45).

6. Make sure that the button labeled "Entire Duration" is active.

    For now, you will accept Bryce's default settings for QuickTime movie and animation. Next, you will choose the location that your movie will be saved.

Figure 2.45 The Render Animation dialog box.

7. Click the Set button and a Save As dialog box appears. Change the location if you so desire. The name "Walkthrough Island.mov" is fine as it is. Click the Save button to get back to the Render Animation dialog box.

8. Click the check mark to exit the dialog box and begin rendering the animation.

Congratulations! You have just created a basic Bryce scene! You have created objects, edited their location and size, assigned them a surface material appearance. You have worked with the Camera and View controls to choose your location and to work in your scene. You've made adjustments to the environment. You added stones, changed their location and assigned them all a common appearance, and tweaked those settings slightly. Finally, you have created an animation and rendered a preview and are currently rendering the movie. When the render is finished, the QuickTime Player will automatically launch and display your rendered movie.

There is much more to go to get you farther and deeper into Bryce. (That's what the rest of this book is for!) But you've made a good start indeed! While the animation is rendering, go ahead and read the rest of this chapter.

A BRYCE WORLD (3 DIMENSIONS—X, Y, AND Z)

Bryce is a three-dimensional world. "Fine," you think. As a three-dimensional being who inhabits a three-dimensional world, you find this an intuitive concept. But how do you refer to each of the three dimensions? Each dimension has a name—the x axis, the y axis, and the z axis—so you can tell them apart and know what's what.

Yet the "what's what" is not so simple and straightforward. The x axis of what? Of the world? The object? Or the x axis of the camera that is viewing the world? The simplicity of the three dimensions is made a bit more complex by the three possible frames of reference in Bryce—World Space, Object Space, and Camera Space. As you continue to work in Bryce, you'll be dealing with all three varieties of xyz space. (Does that make Bryce 9-dimensional? Ouch. Forget we asked…) Here are the main points of each.

World Space

The xyz space that is World Space is the absolute World Space. It's analogous to the compass directions. The x axis is east-west, the z axis is north-south, and the y axis is altitude. You can no more change what the z axis is than you could capriciously shift the direction of north by 28° or so. The xyz axes in World Space are inviolable.

How do you get your bearings in this Bryce World? Which way are the different directions? When towns and cities are laid out on a grid, with streets running north-south, there is what's sometimes referred to as the "zero, zero" block. That's the block where the street numbering begins. The numbers get higher in all directions—100 East Main Street or 100 West Main Street, 100 North Central, 100 South Central. This same quadrant-style numbering system also exists in

Bryce. Rather than have east and west, Bryce has a single axis—*x*. The east side is expressed in positive numbers and the west side in negative numbers. You'll see more of this later in the book, especially in Chapter 6, "Editing and the Internal Bryce Grid." (If you're mathematically inclined, you may recognize the numbering as the Cartesian coordinate style of graph numbering. Ooh la la!)

Bryce's World Center is analogous to that "zero, zero" block. Figure 2.46 compares a downtown street intersection to the Bryce World Space coordinates. When you view your scene from top view, you are looking at the compass points. Up is North, Down is South, Left is West, and Right is East.

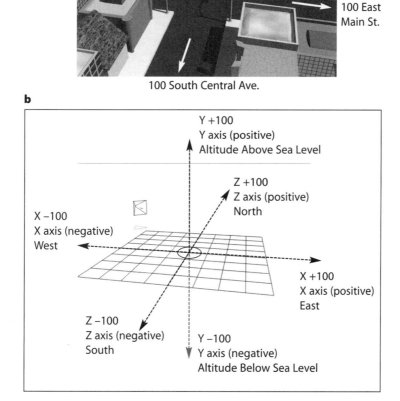

Figure 2.46 Getting your bearings in Bryce: a) A city block, shown with typical street addresses; b) top view of the scene with corresponding Bryce axes.

Object Space

Then there is the *xyz* that is Object Space; this is the object's own width (*x),* height (*y*), and depth (*z*). Working in Object Space means that you can make changes to the object along, say, its own width dimension (*x* axis). Object Space is inconsistently consistent; the *x* axis will always be the object's *x* axis, no matter which Bryce World Space direction the object is facing. After you change the object's orientation, the width part of the object may face Brycean northeast. Figure 2.47 shows a series of objects and identifies their axes in Object Space.

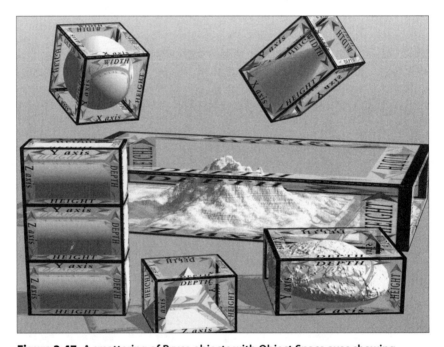

Figure 2.47 A smattering of Bryce objects with Object Space axes showing.

Camera Space

Finally, there is the *xyz* that is Camera Space. The directions of Camera Space are always from the perspective that you view a scene. So the *x* axis is left-right, the *y* axis is up-down, and the *z* axis is forward-backward. Those are the camera's own *x* and *y* and *z* axes, as Figure 2.48a shows. But of course, you're looking *through* the camera, so you can think of those axes in your own point of view—up, down, left, right, forward, back (Figure 2.48b). Those directions refer to the way the camera moves as you look through it. Camera Space is, then, completely subjective. This holds true even when you are looking in views other than "current view." If you were to look at your scene from, say, top view, enlarging an object along the *x* axis will enlarge it left-to-right *as you are currently viewing it* from top view. This is true no matter where the main camera position is. Consider Camera Space the most ephemeral and inconsistent of Bryce Spaces. Once you rotate the camera, the camera's *xyz* space has changed in relation to Bryce World Space.

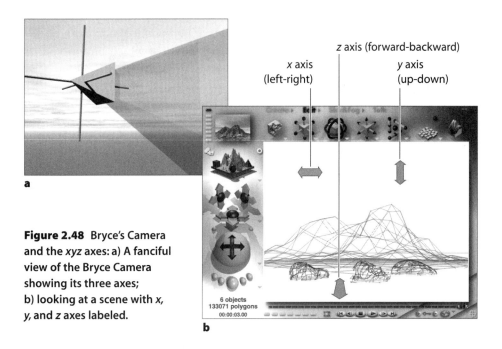

Figure 2.48 Bryce's Camera and the *xyz* axes: a) A fanciful view of the Bryce Camera showing its three axes; b) looking at a scene with *x*, *y*, and *z* axes labeled.

As you work in Bryce, you will encounter the *x*, *y*, and *z* axes again and again, from the perspective of World Space, Object Space, and Camera Space. You'll also see a lot of them in the upcoming chapters on Camera, Objects, and Editing.

WORKING IN BRYCE— THE CREATIVE PROCESS

This last part of the chapter considers yet again the three-dimensional world and the two-dimensional image of that world. However, instead of focusing on what is in the Bryce World or how the software works, or which button you click to get a certain result, we turn our attention to the creative process and what sorts of things happen to *make art* in Bryce. This is a bit of introduction to the *work* you do in Bryce. Most of the book focuses on matters of which button you click to get that results, but as we dish dirt on icons, menus, labs and techniques, the underlying artistic endeavor is never far from our minds.

Drawing or Painting or Photographing a Scenic Landscape...

Suppose for a moment that you were going to some scenic landscape spot with an easel and canvas or a drawing tablet, and pencils or brushes and paint. After trudging to some location carrying your equipment, you reach the spot that you'd like to draw or paint. You set down your easel, place the canvas or tablet against it, examine the landscape, and then begin to place your composition on the page. Drawing, measuring, calculating, line by line, shape by shape, surface by surface, you lay down on that canvas or paper your rendition of what you see there before you. (It's no surprise that the word for drawing, or putting down an impression, is "render," the term borrowed by 3D computer-graphic-ese that describes creating a color image so of your scene.) Or, instead, suppose that you are a photographer in that same landscape. Trudging with your camera, and perhaps, tripod, you arrive at a scenic spot. You compose the image in your view finder. Focus. Adjust exposure. Wait for the birds or the clouds to be just so, or for the light to be just right—and then, trip the shutter to make your picture. You'll have to develop the film and expose and develop a photographic print.

...and How Brycing Landscapes is Different and the Same

How do these processes of drawing, painting or photographing landscapes compare to the process of making scenic landscapes in Bryce?

First, a major difference: when you shoot or paint the Grand Canyon, the place—the Grand Canyon—actually exists. In Bryce, you create the land formations; part of your work is to bring those places into existence. It's as if the Bryce artist is geologist-sculptor, shaping the 3D world.

Second, a similarity: the canvas, the portion of film and the Bryce rendered image are all two-dimensional depictions of a three-dimensional environment.

Third, a similarity: the canvas and the rendered image area do not capture the landscape in its entirety but a certain rectangular portion of it. The Bryce image is actually a small excerpt of a two-dimensional projection of a three dimensional space. Fourth, a difference: in painting or in photography, you basically do not choose your lighting and your sky, or your weather. Those are things which you seek to capture—and do so quickly, before they change. In Bryce you do start with a generic atmosphere, lighting and weather, but the environment controls allow you to determine the time of day and to determine the cloud cover and other atmospheric phenomena.

The Bryce User—Artist, Designer, Craftsperson

The Bryce artist plays several roles: geologist, world creator, architect, sculptor, set designer, builder, photographer, lighting designer, cinematographer, and director. These roles are divided into two main levels. In the first one, creating the world, the creator-sculptor-builder is thinking, "This is my world—this is my dream, my imagination." In the second stage, lighting and setting up the camera and rendering that world, the painter-photographer-cinematographer's work addresses the question, "How can I best show you my world?"

Iterations and Iterations

It's not as though these two main stages of work are separated by a great divide, where first a great flurry of building takes place, followed by a single and final render. Rather, there's constant interaction between the two. Just as each successive render pass results in finer and finer detail, this also describes the process of working in Bryce. First you put things in the world. Render. Adjust and tweak, render, adjust, and tweak. Render again. About this time you get some wild idea and have to go back and build another set of objects to realize it. Render. Tweak. Adjust the way New Idea fits with Older Scene. And then you adjust and tweak some more (and more, and more!) With each step, you add more detail and continue refining as the developing scene draws ideas from you. If you are animating your scene, the process of refinement branches in two directions—perfecting the world, and perfecting the motion until it is time to let your computer take over the work of rendering the sequence.

So…now you've been at this Bryce party for a little while. You've met everyone. We hope that you're feeling a little more familiar with your Bryce companions and are getting ready to dig in. The next chapter takes up the camera in far more detail.

CHAPTER THREE

Camera and Scene

IN THIS CHAPTER...

• How the physical eye sees and how the Bryce cameras see

• The View and Camera controls on Bryce's Control Palette

• How to better work with the Bryce camera

In the previous chapter, we had a sweeping overview of the Bryce application and how it works and how it does what it does. Recall the analogies of artist's easel or photographer's canvas, and the way in which the three-dimensional subject matter finds its way into a two-dimensional image. Similarly, as a sculptor creates a work, the artist looks at the artwork from this perspective and that as the sculpture evolves.

In this chapter, we focus our attention on the point of view in Bryce, both the points of view that you'll use in the scene construction process, and the camera perspective point of view as you create that final rendered image of your scene. These are matters for Bryce's View and Camera controls.

In Bryce, you make scenes and then take pictures of them with your Render "camera." Working in Bryce is analogous to making pictures of our own three-dimensional world. The world itself is three-dimensional, and a still camera captures a two-dimensional representation of one place and time of that world. Similarly, when you're working in Bryce, you are balancing between manipulating the three-dimensional world and moving your camera around to make a two-dimensional snapshot of a particular place and time. By the same token, a movie or video camera captures a series of two-dimensional representations of the world as it moves through the world or as the world changes or both. When you're animating in Bryce, your virtual camera is capturing a sequence of snapshots of the scene you have created. We'll concentrate on using the camera to render still images here, and discuss animating the camera and the world later.

BRYCEAN KODAK MOMENTS

Remember your world in pictures. Bryce creates PICT (Macintosh) or BMP (Windows) images of the wireframe scenes by rendering them. The particular process involved is called 3D ray tracing.

"Take a Picture"—How 3D Ray Tracing Works

To best help you understand how ray tracing works, we'll follow our real world/virtual world model and take a moment to discuss how the eye and the camera register visual information.

How the Eye Sees and How a Camera Sees

In the real world, light emanates from a source (sun, moon, electric lights) and bounces off Earth's surfaces. Depending on the color of those surfaces, different rays of light are absorbed and what is not absorbed bounces. Those bounced light rays that reach the eye are focused through the eye's lens onto the retina. The light information is then transmitted to nerve impulses that travel through the optic nerve to the visual portion of the cerebral cortex of the brain.

The camera "sees" in the same way (see Figure 3.1). Light from the external world passes through the camera's lens and then exposes film. (For this analogy we'll ignore the more up-to-date filmless digital variety.) The film is processed, and prints or slides are created that show the image. The film or transparency and printed photographic paper are all two-dimensional surfaces. (Okay, okay, all have just a touch of thickness, making them three-dimensional. But a millimeter's thickness notwithstanding, they are "flat" surfaces.) The process of seeing with a camera involves a dimension shift from a three-dimensional world to a two-dimensional image.

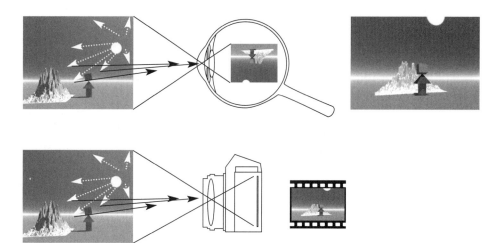

Figure 3.1 The eye and the camera both register visual information. Light emanates from a source, bounces off objects, and registers on the eye's retina or a camera's film.

How Bryce "Sees"

In the real world, there are real objects, real atmosphere, and real light sources. When seeing with your eyes, you are continuously registering moments in time. When making photographs, you capture a particular moment in time.

In a corresponding way, Bryce has a virtual world with virtual objects and virtual illumination. Bryce renders a two-dimensional image to capture a moment in its virtual space and time. How does Bryce do this? By ray tracing. When Bryce renders, it shoots virtual rays into the world to determine the colors of the image. It's not a process of photochemically registering *what is already there,* where the results are seen instantaneously (with the eyes) or with a reasonable delay (film processing). Rather, Bryce's virtual world requires mathematical calculations to follow those rays as they bounce through the world and to record the color of the ray's final destination. Therefore, instead of talking about an entire image, or what can be seen on a piece of film, we'll narrow it down to seeing pixel by pixel.

For each pixel in the scene, Bryce shoots out a virtual ray into the image. Where does it go? For one particular pixel, the ray's path may take it to one side of a terrain. Ah! This particular portion of the terrain has a basic texture color of sienna brown. But the ambient light is a light naples yellow, so the sienna brown is altered based on the ambient light. Further, the surface is very matte, so it doesn't create any direct reflections but rather reflects the light in a diffuse manner. Also, the sun is close to the horizon and is a reddish color. So the color of that portion of terrain is reddened by the sun's color. Now, for a different pixel in the same scene, the ray bounces out into the world to find the ultimate color and light source, so the color may be different where the terrain is in shadow. But the scene also has a few reflective spheres. A ray of light that shoots out toward one of the spheres bounces off the sphere into the world surrounding it. Reflective surfaces increase the ray's journey time. Or, in the case of multiple reflective objects nearby, the ray may bounce from this sphere here to that other sphere, to the terrain way over there. All atmospheric conditions complicate the situation, adding more variables into the calculation that answers the question, "What color will this pixel ultimately become?" If there are transparent objects, then there are further diversions of that ray. And what if the transparent object bends the light as it passes through the object? The ray will go off into a slightly different direction as it seeks out its final color resting place.

As Bryce ray traces, it uses a progressive method. Bryce will go through six passes as it renders. The first pass takes the image in chunks of 256 pixels (16 × 16) and shoots one ray into the scene for each chunk to determine that pixel's color (see Figure 3.2). When it completes that pass, it divides those pixels in half, shooting one ray out for each 64 pixels (8 × 8 pixels). During the second pass, it performs four more calculations than during the previous pass. Each successive pass makes four times the number of calculations as the previous pass, resulting in a more detailed image. Finally, at the fifth pass, each ray shot out into the scene calculates the color for one pixel.

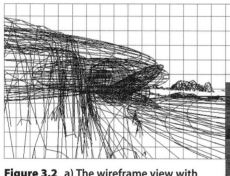

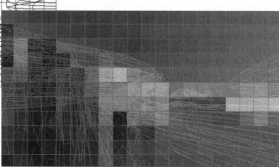

Figure 3.2 a) The wireframe view with a grid composed of 16 × 16 pixels (the first rendering pass) superimposed. For each square, Bryce shoots a ray into the scene to determine the final color.

b) The result after the first rendering pass. (Wireframe view is barely visible for reference.)

Bryce makes that ray-traced calculation for every pixel in the scene. It follows the light to its source to determine what color it is. For a scene that's 640 × 480 pixels, 307,200 rays go out into the world, bouncing here and there to determine the final color for each pixel! (And we haven't even talked about what happens at the antialiasing pass, where several rays are shot out to determine the color of one pixel!) That's a *lot* of calculations! When you first started using Bryce, perhaps you thought all this mumbo jumbo about fast processors for Bryce wasn't really that necessary. Do you think differently now?

A Flexible Approach

So, you have a virtual three-dimensional world that is rendered into a two-dimensional image. This gives you flexibility as you approach world making and rendering.

- *You Can Change Your Mind.* The progressive render process allows you to experiment and then change your mind. After a couple of rendering passes, you can determine if you like what you see so far and then decide whether to let the render progress further. You don't have to wait until the entire image is rendered single pixel by single pixel (whew!). You can stop after a bit and alter the entire scene. Or you can home in on one section by drawing a marquee around the critical section and then letting that render out more fully. Or you can scrap the scene altogether and take a different approach to get your Brycean Kodak moment.

- *You Can Have Multiple Views of One Scene.* All the information for your world is stored in your scene document. You can save several different views of it, and it will all be in one file. (More on this later in the chapter.)

- *You Can Select Different Times of Day.* You can save a series of skies for your scene (times of day, cloud conditions, celestial events, and so on) in the Skies presets or the Skies Memory Dots to keep track of your different times of day for any particular scene. (See the Sky chapter, Chapter 11, for more on this.)

  (However, if you will be rendering your scenes using the drag-and-drop feature, you will need to create individual scene documents for each view of the scene. More on this in Chapter 13, "Render Unto Bryce.")

Obviously, you can spend a good deal of time perfecting one world. Then once it's in satisfactory condition, take rendered pictures of it to your heart's content! Look at it from the south in the morning and then saunter over for an east view in time for Brycean noon. Spend Bryce's late afternoon focused on one detail area, and then at sunset take a panoramic view to the northwest. Don't forget to slip out at night to take it all in once more under Bryce's perpetual full moon. It's all the same world, shown at different times of day focusing on different sections.

VIEW AND CAMERA CONTROLS

Bryce gives you the ability to establish one (or several) points of view on your world through the View and Camera controls. While you're constructing your scene, you can look at the scene in two basic ways. Look at your scene through one of the two perspective views: Camera and Director's View. Or, look at the scene through one of six views along each dimension—orthogonal views. The View and Camera controls on the Control Palette are divided into these two areas. The Camera controls are for positioning Bryce's virtual camera in Bryce's World Space and to adjust the focal length of the lens. The View controls enable you to choose how you view the scene, whether select from the alternate views—the two perspective cameras and the six orthogonal views: top/bottom, left/right, and front/back.

In addition, both ways of viewing your scene have another element in common— the two-dimensional plane onto which the image falls. This flat plane is analogous to film. The Pan and Zoom tools adjust the placement of the image on that plane. Those settings are located on the right interface strip.

Figure 3.3 shows the Control Palette and a cutaway of the narrow palette on the right, with each of the Camera and View controls labeled.

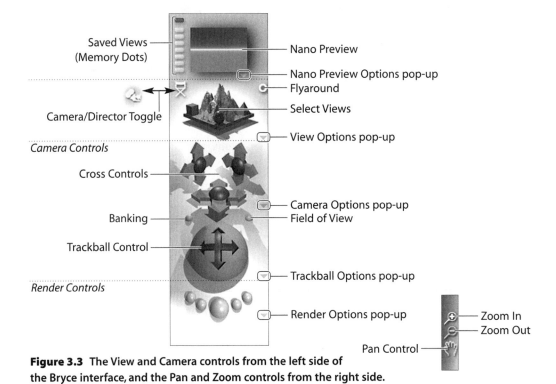

Figure 3.3 The View and Camera controls from the left side of the Bryce interface, and the Pan and Zoom controls from the right side.

Two Perspectives: Camera and Director

The two perspective cameras imitate the performance of a real-world camera. As with any real-world camera, you must consider certain factors when positioning Bryce's camera. Where is the camera in the scene? Is the camera upright? Is it rotated this way or that? Then there's the matter of the kind of lens that's on the camera. How much of the surrounding world enters the lens? A long telephoto lens shows only what's ahead; a wide angle lens shows more of the range.

The original Bryce camera (from Bryce versions 1 and 2) has been split into two different perspective cameras, each with its respective function. For the creation and rendering of a rendered snapshot (a single still-image scene), a basic perspective is all that is needed: the "Director's View" camera. For an animated scene where the camera moves in space and time, there is the camera object: the "Camera View." Since the two cameras evolved from one common perspective camera, the purposes and functions of each may seem confusing—especially for those who've used Bryce since the earliest versions. Plus, when it comes to how you'll actually work with the creation and rendering of your scene, the distinctions we just gave aren't strict. One way to look at the camera functions is to understand how Bryce evolved over its development history. When animation capabilities were added to Bryce 3D, the perspective camera was changed to accommodate the conditions for animation—being able to track a specific object over time, or being able to move around a point of origin that is not in its center (while we're concerned with dicussing history here, we'll get to the specifics of those new functions later in the chapter). Those new abilities went into the Camera View. At the same time, a new viewpoint was added, too: the Director's View. Like the proverbial perspective of a film director, the purpose of the Director's View is to provide you aspiring cinematographers with a neutral vantage point of your scene, allowing you to have an overall view of the spatial relationships among all objects (whether moving or stationary), including the ability to see the Camera View's camera, represented as a blue wireframe object. At the same time, though, all the capabilities of the Bryce 1 and 2 Camera View were retained in the Director's View, (including the old trackball behaviors, to be discussed later). So the newer camera features retain the old name, "Camera View," and the old camera features received a new name, "Director's View."

Though in some ways the Director's View is more limited than Camera View (the Director's View "camera" never appears as an object in Brycean space), it can be manipulated with the same controls as the normal Camera, so most of the following discussion applies to both cameras. When discussing them as a group, we'll call them the "perspective cameras," to distinguish them from the perspectiveless orthogonal views (more about those later).

Property	Director's View	Camera View
Visible in scene	no	yes
Keypad shortcut	~	1
Has origin point	no	yes
Move is undoable	no	yes

The View Control

The View control allows you to look at your Bryce scene from eight different directions. Available views are Director's View, Camera View, top, right, front, left, back, and bottom.

Clicking or dragging the View control changes the preview on the Master Palette. Release the mouse button, and your view of the scene changes to match the control view. If you wanted, say, to put your scene in top view, drag the Select Views control until you see the top view preview and release the mouse—your main scene changes to top view. When the view control is in the three-quarter view showing the scene in perspective, you are using one of the two perspective cameras. To the left of the View control you will see an icon representing either a picture camera or a director's chair to indicate whether the perspective view is Camera or Director's View. A simple click on the icon toggles between the two cameras.

Alternatively you can navigate to other views via the View Options pop-up menu, where you can select—with no possibility of ambiguity—the different views.

> **TIP:** *Here is a speed tip for when you're in another view and you want to go back to Director's View: You can drag all the way to the left to go there directly. Or, Option/Alt-click the View control. This tip is helpful if your machine is slow or if the scene is so complex that Bryce pauses before drawing the wireframe view of the scene.*

TIP: Now, here is a major speed tip. The absolute best way to navigate quickly is to use the number keys to shift between views. Starting with ~ as the Director's View, the numbers correspond to the positions in the Views menu list. Use either the numbers at the top of your keyboard or, on extended keyboards, the numeric keypad. (The latter, of course, lacks a ~ key, so you can't use it to summon Director's view.)

View	Key
Director's View	~
Camera view	1
Top view	2
Right (side) view	3
Front view	4 (Also the = key on the Mac numeric keypad)
First 5 Saved views	5–9

Since this is a holdover from Bryce 1—where there were only front, side, and top views—the keypad numbering has not changed. Therefore, there is no quick way to get to back, other side, and bottom. If this book is biased toward certain orthogonal views, know that it's because the keypad shortcut has made its way into certain working habits, making it harder to get to the orthogonal views that have no numerical equivalents.

Orthogonal Views

When you are looking at your scene in any view other than one of the perspective views, you are looking at the scene in an orthogonal view. What does orthogonal mean? Orthogonal is *not* some fancy term for a hybrid of agony and orthodonture. Orthogonal means that the view is perpendicular; you're looking at the scene from a perfect right angle. When you're in any view other than main view, you won't be looking at your scene in perspective. Should you want to align objects precisely, you'll be able to do so without guesswork.

When you are in an orthogonal view, the Camera controls are grayed out. Should you want to move closer to your object or set the view directly over some other part of the scene, zoom in or out and pan to navigate this way and that. (More on panning and zooming later in the chapter.)

View Options Pop-up Menu

Bryce's View Options pop-up menu, located just off of the View Diorama, has several view options on it. (See Figure 3.4.) Besides the orthogonal views and the camera view, there is another option: Reset Views. This option takes you back to the default Bryce camera position (Director's View) and puts you at the default Zoom setting of 100%.

Figure 3.4 The View control and View Options pop-up menu.

The Nano Preview

The Nano Preview at the top of the Control Palette displays a miniature version of your scene. It displays a preview in three different states: the Sky Only, the Full Scene, or the Wireframe.

When you are looking at the Nano Preview in either the Full Scene or the Wireframe view, you can choose to look at the preview from any of the view options—independent of the main view. Use the pop-up menu to choose a different view or a different mode (see Figure 3.5). You can not only view any of these in the same view as you are seeing in the main work window but also make the preview's view *different* from the one you have in the main window. This is a very powerful feature: When placing the camera, for instance, set the Nano Preview to Camera view. Then you can be in top view in the main window, dragging the camera to different places, and after each incremental adjustment, let the preview render to give you immediate feedback to see if your camera is "there" yet.

Figure 3.5 The Nano Preview and Nano Preview Options pop-up menu.

The same technique works for precise object alignment; you can be in side view in the main window, adjusting the elevation of your object (a body of water, for instance) and pause after each movement to see how it looks as it renders in the preview window.

There are two ways to make the Nano Preview render, one manual and one automatic. The automatic method is simple: The Nano Preview automatically renders after each incremental adjustment is made to your scene. To turn this automatic update off (it is on by default in Bryce), select Auto Update in the pop-up menu, changing the option from being checked (automatic) to unchecked (manual). The manual method to make the Nano Preview render is this: Click directly inside the render window to force the Nano Preview to update.

New to Bryce 4 is the choice of image quality in the Nano Preview. The default setting is equivalent to older versions of Bryce: the preview is complete but a tad grainy, since Bryce is employing a routine that doesn't render each pixel, in the interest of speeding things up. If you have a fast computer and enjoy living on the edge, scroll to the bottom of the pop-up menu and select Full Rendering. Now, each time the preview is updated, you'll be treated to a tiny, finished rendering of your scene, in all its antialiased glory! You will pay for the pleasure, alas, in having to endure more sluggish response from your computer. Indeed, you may find, when working with complex scenes, that you can speed things up significantly by turning Auto Update off.

Why would you want to look at a render in the Nano Preview? First, render time is quicker. You get a literal thumbnail of your scene. Second, it can be more streamlined. You don't have to make a change, switch to render mode, update render, go back to wireframe mode, make another change, switch to render mode, update to see how it went, ad awkwardum. Rather, you can work in the main scene window and see the results of each move or change immediately in the Nano Preview.

Nano Preview Walkthrough

In this sample walkthrough, we'll lead you through some guided steps to work with the Nano Preview. You'll learn how to take advantage of the small rendered image and quick render time while working in the main scene window.

1. Open up the scene NANO PREVIEW SCENE BEGIN from the CD-ROM (see Figure 3.6a).

2. Make sure that your Bryce application settings are as follows: In the Nano pop-up menu, choose the following options: Full Scene, Auto-Update, Camera View, and Fast Preview (see Figure 3.6b). The scene should update in the Nano Preview window. In the Sky & Fog Palette, make sure that Auto-Update is *un*checked (see Figure 3.6c).

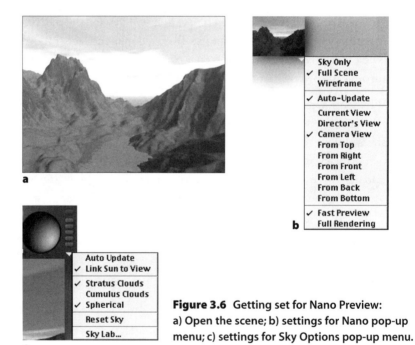

Figure 3.6 Getting set for Nano Preview: a) Open the scene; b) settings for Nano pop-up menu; c) settings for Sky Options pop-up menu.

3. Change the view to top view (see Figure 3.7a). See the set of tori? Position the camera so that you can see into the center of the torus rings by dragging the camera to the left. Figure 3.7b shows the camera after it has moved left, with the corresponding Nano Preview.

4. It's getting there, but it is not completely centered in the rings yet. To do that, the camera needs to be moved vertically. To better see what is going on with vertical camera placement, switch to view from the right (tap the 3 key). Figure 3.7c is the same scene as part b, as seen from side view.

5. Now you can see where the camera is in relation to the tori. Just a lil' move up, and you're there! Figure 3.7d shows the result.

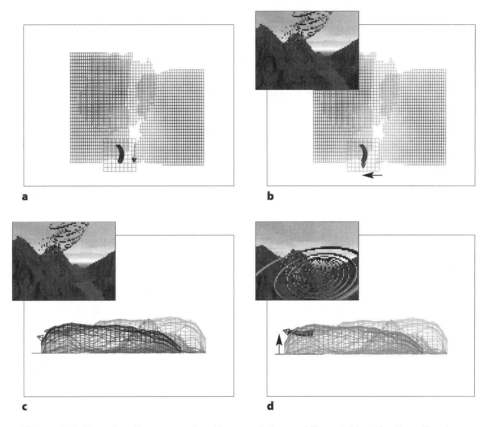

a   b   c   d

Figure 3.7 Changing the camera in orthogonal views while watching the Nano Preview window: a) Begin in top view; b) after moving the camera left; c) same results in side view; d) after moving the camera up.

Since this is the camera chapter, we focused on the Nano Preview for camera movements. But don't be limited by that. This is an excellent way to work in orthogonal views of your scene while editing objects, too.

Cross Controls

The Cross controls move the camera's position from within Bryce. Since the camera is placed in the width, height, and depth of the Bryce environment, the camera position is referred to in *x, y,* and *z* terms. However, these axes are not fixed in Bryce's World Space, where the *x* axis is east-west, the *z* axis is north-south, and the *y* axis is altitude. Rather, the *x, y,* and *z* axes are fixed to the camera's own reference point. Therefore *x* will always be right-left, *y* will be up and down, and *z* will be forward and backward. Those directions will not change, no matter which way you face in the Bryce world. One oddity: the cross controls actually move the camera in the opposite direction from your dragging motion. For instance, if you drag *up* on the *y*-arm of a cross, the camera moves *down*. The scene appears to move *up*, however, which corresponds to the uppishness of your physical motion. Figure 3.8 shows how the camera movements occur independently of the Bryce world orientation. The first panel of the illustration shows the starting place for camera movement. In the second panel, the camera has moved along the *x* axis to its own left (thanks to a rightward drag on one of the *x*-arms); the new camera placement has no bearing on the Bryce World *x* (east-west) axis.

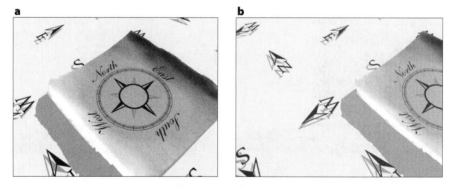

Figure 3.8 a) Starting placement; b) after moving the camera leftward along its *x* axis.

Three crosses make up the Cross controls. Each cross moves the camera along two axes. Each axis is represented twice in the entire set of Cross controls (see Figure 3.9). Each Cross control will move the camera along a plane, whether the movement is limited to the horizontal plane (the X-Z Cross) or to the vertical plane (the Y-Z Cross and the X-Y Cross).

The image in Figure 3.10 shows the camera and the respective planes of motion that are brought about by each of the Cross controls. The two vertical planes represent the range of camera movement using the two upright Cross controls, and the horizontal plane represents the range of motion using the flat Cross controls.

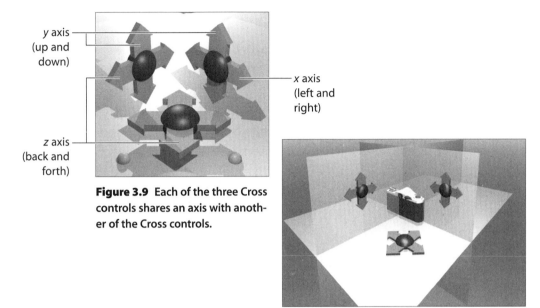

y axis
(up and
down)

x axis
(left and
right)

z axis
(back and
forth)

Figure 3.9 Each of the three Cross controls shares an axis with another of the Cross controls.

Figure 3.10 The virtual camera with three planes emanating from it; the planes match the range of motion provided by each of the Cross controls.

You can constrain all of the camera movements. If you position the cursor above the green dome in the center of one of the crosses, it turns into a little four-arrowed cross, indicating that you are free to move the camera anywhere within that plane. On the other hand, if you move the cursor over one of the terra-cotta arms of a cross, it becomes a single arrow labeled with X, Y, or Z, to show that motion is now constrained to a single axis within that plane. You can also use the keyboard to limit camera motion, according to a rather complicated formula.

Position the cursor over any of the green domes, so that it turns into the four-headed arrow. Now, hold down the Option/Alt key; it turns into a vertical double arrow. Hold down the Control/Ctrl key—now it's a horizontal double-arrow! Here's a table, showing how camera motion is constrained by each modifier key on each cross:

Cross	Control/Ctrl	Option/Alt
Y-Z	z axis	y axis
X-Y	x axis	y axis
X-Z	x axis	z axis

Keyboard Navigation

Tired of dragging from the Cross controls this way and that to move the camera? There are some arrow key combinations that imitate the movement of the Trackball and Cross controls.

The Control (Macintosh) or Ctrl (Windows) key plus the arrow keys moves the camera in trackball fashion. Here are the combinations: The up or down arrow key is the same as dragging up or down on the Trackball control (motion along the *y* axis). The foreground rotates around World Center in the same direction as the arrow; the up arrow moves the foreground up and, consequently, moves your perspective down; the down arrow moves the foreground down, moving your perspective up. The left and right arrow keys, used in conjunction with the Control/Ctrl key, are the same as dragging left and right on the Trackball control (motion along the *x* axis). The foreground rotates to the left with the right arrow, and to the right with the left arrow.

The same arrow keys are used to imitate the Cross control for camera movement, this time using the Control-Option (Macintosh) or Ctrl+Alt (Windows) keys. Control-Option/Ctrl+Alt with the right and left arrow keys moves the camera left and right along the *x* axis. Control-Option or Ctrl+Alt and the up and down arrow keys moves the camera forward and backward along the *z* axis. Sorry to say, the poor *y* axis is left un-keyed.

Note: The Option (Macintosh) or Alt (Windows) key with the arrows moves selected objects within the scene. See Chapter 6, "Editing and the Internal Bryce Grid," for more information.

Camera Controls Pop-up Menu

There are six additional options available in the Camera controls pop-up menu (see Figure 3.11). The Camera control changes the position of the camera in relation to the ground level of the scene or to objects that are in the scene. The Center commands (Center Scene, Center Selection) change the rotation, swinging the camera around so that it points to a particular place. But be warned: If you invoke them while in one of the orthogonal views, they adjust your view of the scene but they do not change the position of the camera!

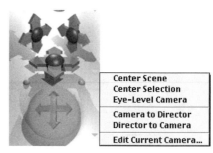

Figure 3.11 Camera controls pop-up menu.

Center Scene. This option points the camera at the center point of your scene. How can you tell what *is* the center point of the scene? If you were to select all your objects so that they had a common bounding box, the camera would be pointing at the center of that bounding box. Although your objects aren't all selected, Bryce knows where that center point is and points the camera there. Figure 3.12 is a series of screen shots, in both main and top view of the default camera perspective (before) and center scene (after). The top view is also shown with all objects selected so that you can see the center point of the bounding box. Note how the "after" camera position points directly to the center of the common bounding box. Use this command to bring your scene back into view if you somehow managed to navigate your camera so that the scene is out of view. (In the sample shown here, the scene is probably a bit more extreme than normal; most scenes are not so widely dispersed.) If you use this command in an orthogonal view, it merely centers the scene in the document window.

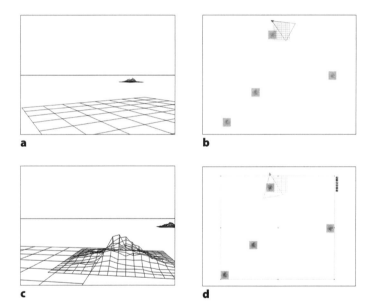

Figure 3.12 Centering the scene: a) Before, in default view;
b) before, shown in top view; c) after centering scene, main view;
d) after centering scene (with all objects selected to show bounding
box's center), top view.

Center Selection. This changes the rotation of the camera, not its position, so that the selected object is smack dab in the middle of your scene window. The same principle as center scene applies; Bryce points to the center of the bounding box. Rather than take the imaginary bounding box for the entire scene, Bryce uses the actual center of the bounding box for the selected object or objects. Use this to point the camera smack dab on a particular object. Once again, in an orthogonal view, this command just causes the view to center on the selected object.

Eye-Level Camera. Unlike the two Center controls, this doesn't operate on camera rotation but on offset. It lowers the camera to about "eye level," which in the camera numerical readout, puts it at 5 Bryce units above the ground, or nearly a grid unit (for more about Bryce units, see the Edit chapter, Chapter 6). Of course, if your camera is placed lower than ground level, it raises the camera to just above ground level. Camera rotation is not changed.

Camera to Director and *Director to Camera*. These commands move one of your perspective cameras to the same position as the other. The wording can be confusing, so think of these commands in this way: "Move the *Camera to* where the *Director* is currently positioned" and "Move *Director's View to* where the *Camera* is currently positioned." So if you are in Director's View, and you want the Camera to jump to the position you are currently looking at in the scene, then select Camera to Director (the bottom option). Conversely, if you are in Director's View and you want to move Director's View to the same position as Camera View, then select Director to Camera (the top option). Depending which view you're in, Bryce changes the order of the two menu items (see Figure 3.13). Before you snarl and gnash your teeth at this inconsistency (it is tempting!), consider the two options in the following way: The result of selecting the top one is that you'll be moving your current perspective away from its position to match the other, different one, in your scene. The result of selecting the bottom one is that you'll be beckoning the other, different camera perspective so that it matches the one you are in right now.

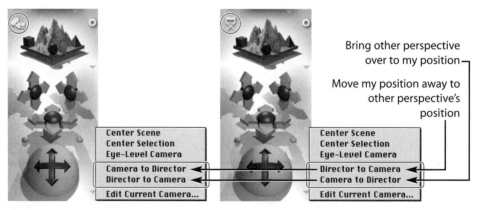

Figure 3.13 Comparing the Camera to Director and Director to Camera menu commands in both Camera and Director's Views.

Edit Current Camera. This takes you to the Camera & 2D Projection dialog box, which can also be accessed by double-clicking the Cross or the Trackball controls. The Camera dialog box allows you to change the numerical values for the camera position. This menu item is the only means to access the Camera dialog box when you are in orthogonal views. In these cases, you won't see the Linking or Animation tabbed panels. That's because these views can't be treated like objects, as the perspective cameras can. We'll discuss the Camera control dialog box a bit later, after going through the rest of the Camera controls.

The Trackball Control

The Trackball control changes the camera position in relation to the entire world. Movement is not restricted to horizontal or vertical but is an integrated rotation around a central point (see Figure 3.14). The Director's View camera has an assortment of modes of rotation, accessible from the Trackball pop-up menu.

Figure 3.14 The Trackball pop-up menu.

Since Bryce 3D, the Camera View camera rotates in Free Camera mode, meaning it rotates around its origin point, wherever it may be (so all the other choices are grayed out). The Camera View Trackball, in Free Camera mode, can be made to imitate any of the modes available to the Director's View Trackball, so we'll describe those first. In its default state, it acts as if it's in Tripod mode.

When you set the Trackball to Trackball mode in Director's View, it works like this: Suppose your Bryce world is inside a globe (see Figure 3.15a). When you rotate the Director's view camera, its distance from the globe's center stays the same, even though it moves up or down or left or right to change position (see Figure 3.15b).

Figure 3.15 The Trackball control, in default mode: a) Before rotation; b) after rotation.

Since the Director's view camera moves relative to Bryce's World Center, then the position of individual objects in Bryce Space will affect apparent camera movements. If you are, for example, trying to rotate the camera around a particular object and you happen to have your object placed way off center, your rotation actions will not be pleasing; the world will seem to rotate on an ellipse.

This is where the second option comes in handy—Center to Selection. In this case, rather than rotating around World Center, the Director's View's rotation is adjusted so that it treats the selected objects as the temporary World Center. So camera adjustments can be made away from World Center without throwing you way off. However, there are a couple of conditions that need to be met for Center to Selection to act as expected. You need to have an object that is selected. If there is no selected object, this mode acts identically to the Trackball mode, rotating around World Center. When you do have an object selected, your camera needs to be pointing directly at it. If not, you'll be rotating around the point halfway between the selected object and where the camera is pointing. The Center Selection menu item under the Camera Crosses menu will rotate your camera so that it points directly at your selected object. Figure 3.16 depicts Bryce's Director rotating around the selected object—the one with the wireframe showing. There will be times when you can easily live with the ambiguity of the not-quite on center in order to make your camera adjustments. But if you were trying to rotate around, say, that cube over there, and it wasn't quite working, your Director's View camera probably wasn't pointing directly at the object.

Figure 3.16 The Trackball in Center to Selection mode.

When you have multiple objects selected, Bryce draws a common bounding box around the objects. When that selection is centered, then you can see the camera rotating around the center control point of the bounding box.

Finally, there is a third option for the Trackball. Selecting Tripod from the Trackball pop-up menu will set the rotation center to be the camera itself, as if it were sitting on a tripod. The entire scene rotates around the camera, while the camera stays stationary (see Figure 3.17).

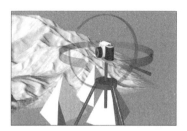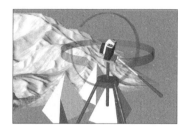

Figure 3.17 The Trackball Tripod rotates the world around the camera location.

In each of these cases, you can use the constrain keys in conjunction with the Trackball for precise movements. To rotate in the *x* direction (around the *y* axis, horizontally), hold down the Control (Macintosh) or Ctrl(Windows) key. This is a very helpful constraining motion to keep the camera from wobbling. To pan up or down from one spot, press the Option (Macintosh) or Alt (Windows) key to constrain movement parallel to the *y* axis (around the *x* axis).

A Point of Origin

A moment ago, we promised to explain how the Camera View's Free Camera mode could be made to imitate the built-in modes available in Director's View. In Camera View, the Trackball rotates about the origin point of the camera. In its default state, this point is at the center of the camera and invisible. If you want to reposition the origin point manually, you first have to make it visible. Open the Camera & 2D Projection dialog box (either double-click one of the camera controls or choose it from the Camera Options pop-up menu). Find the Show Origin Handle item and click it so the box is checked. Close the dialog box, and choose a view other than Camera View. Manuever your viewpoint so you can get an up-close-and-personal look at the camera. You'll see a tiny green dot at its center (look ahead to Figure 3.25). This is the camera's origin point.

Because by default the origin point is at the camera's center, the default Camera View Trackball acts as if it's in Tripod mode. To change the Trackball so that it acts like a—well, Trackball—move the origin point outside to somewhere near the center of your scene. To do this, point your mouse over the green dot and drag from there. Now, manipulating the Trackball will rotate the camera around the origin point. You can also imitate the Director's View Trackball's Center to Selection setting. Choose an object to be the (temporary) center of your scene's universe, and drag the green dot to that object. Adjusting the Trackball will now cause the camera to orbit your favored object. To return the origin point to its default position deep in the belly of the camera, hold down the Shift key and click it.

Banking

There is a functional tilt control for the camera. Adjust it by dragging the Banking control, located to the above left of the trackball. Whatever direction you drag toward, that side of the scene will be raised. So if you drag to the right, the right side of the horizon will get higher than the left (see Figure 3.18). With the addition of this control, you now have full three-dimensional rotation in the Main Palette Camera controls.

Figure 3.18 Banking tilts the world along the horizon line.

Field of View—A Camera with Different-Sized "Lenses"

The Field of View control is analogous to switching lenses on a camera. A wide-angle lens takes in more area than a telephoto lens. For the numerical measurements, though, don't think of Field of View as the equivalent of camera lens focal length. Bryce uses degrees, not millimeters. (The numerical degree measurements are in the Camera dialog box, accessed by double-clicking the Cross or Trackball controls.) The degree number corresponds to the angle that you see. With the largest, 180°, you'll see half the world before you. On the small end, 1° is a tightly focused, narrow view.

Drag to the right to increase the Field of View setting or to widen your perspective. The scene seems to move farther away, but actually, the scene "decreases," since the camera is letting in more image area to the left and right of the scene. Drag left to decrease the Field of View setting. You get "closer" to the image, and the perspective decreases. Move the camera back on the z axis, and you have just created a long-lens telephoto perspective. Figure 3.19 shows a scene at different Field of View settings. As usual, Option/Alt-click the Field of View control to reset to the default setting of 60°.

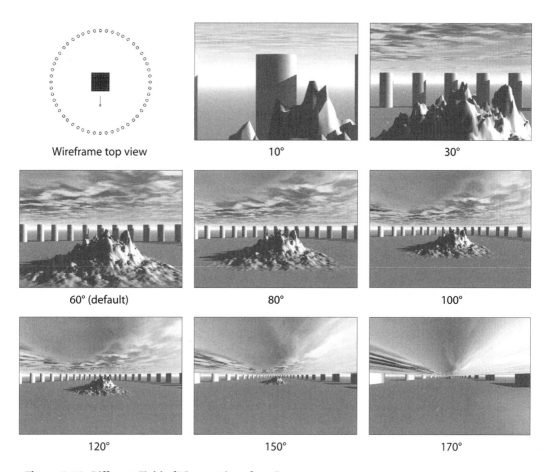

Wireframe top view	10°	30°
60° (default)	80°	100°
120°	150°	170°

Figure 3.19 Different Field of View settings for a Bryce scene.

Pan and Zoom on the Second Dimension

Earlier in the chapter we mentioned that there is an element common to both the View and the Camera controls—the two-dimensional plane. The Pan and Zoom controls allow you to alter the two-dimensional plane on which the Bryce scene is projected. Say what? Weren't we talking about a three-dimensional scene here? Then why all of a sudden are we talking about a two-dimensional plane? If you're asking these questions, keep reading.

Think of the two-dimensional plane as the place where the "film" is, recording the image projected from the scene. Your camera can be oriented in Bryce Space in any position and facing any direction. Wherever the "film" is, the 2D plane extends outward on all sides. The "film" of that camera is measured in pixels. (The size of the "film" is set in the Document Setup dialog box where you choose your scene's resolution.) It is the active "photosensitive" area of the 2D plane that captures light. We refer to this photosensitive area of the plane as the "active image area." The plane can be slid up or down, left or right, to make any portion the active area. You can also zoom into or out from that spot. The Pan and Zoom tools in the lower right-hand corner of the Bryce user interface allow you to do that.

Panning

To scroll along the plane, use the Hand tool. Or press the space bar while dragging the mouse. This infinite plane extends out in all directions (in Figure 3.20, it is represented as finite, if only to indicate its presence). The camera position itself does not change, but the plane may be slid over to determine a new active image area. Think for a moment of the finite infinite plane and ask, "Is the active image area in the upper-left-hand corner? The lower-right-hand corner? How about along the bottom edge in the center?"

Be aware that when you pan while viewing the scene from one of the 3D camera views, you are changing the relationship between the direction the camera is pointing and the portion of your scene it takes in. Figures 3.20c and 3.20d correspond to 3.20a and 3.20b, respectively. Notice that after panning up and to the left, the dotted pyramid (representing the camera's field of view) is no longer lined up with the solid pyramid (representing the camera itself). This can cause all kinds of problems later on, when, for instance, you tell the camera to center on a selected object, and you find yourself staring off into space. The camera may be centered on the selection, but because of your previous panning indiscretion, its view is all cattywumpus. The moral of the story is that it's usually better to save panning for the orthogonal views. If you need to change the view of the perspective camera, move the camera! This is not a hard and fast rule, however. There is one good reason for using the pan control—framing an image.

There are differences between moving a camera up and moving the 2D plane up to "frame" the image just so. In the scene in Figure 3.21a, the horizon line is right smack dab in the middle. There's too much sky and not enough of the foreground terrain. If you drag up on either of the Upright Crosses to move the camera, you'll change the relationship between objects (Figure 3.21b). Instead, scroll up with the Hand tool to maintain the relationship between objects (Figure 3.21c). The camera angle does not change.

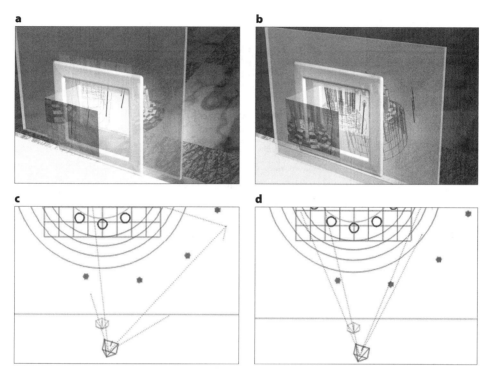

Figure 3.20 a) A virtual Bryce scene on a virtual monitor with a virtual infinite plane (here it is finite so you can tell it is there). b) After scrolling up and to the left, the active image area changes. The figures c) and d) are the wireframe views of a) and b), respectively. Notice that in d) the camera's field of view has pivoted to the left but the camera hasn't moved.

a start   **b** drag up on camera cross   **c** scroll up with hand tool

Figure 3.21 The difference between moving the camera and scrolling the 2D plane: a) Original image; b) dragging up on the Upright Cross; c) scrolling up with the Hand tool.

If you want to reset the Pan back to the default position, press the Option (Macintosh) or Alt (Windows) key and click the hand Pan tool. You'll snap back to the default state.

Zooming

There are several ways to zoom to change the magnification of your image.

- *Magnifier tools.* Clicking the Zoom In magnifier tool—the one with the plus (+)—zooms you into the image. This action is not the same as moving the camera closer to the image. Instead, you are focusing on a smaller area and making that area fill the entire active camera view. Likewise, clicking on the Zoom Out (–) tool expands the view taken in by the camera, rather than moving the camera away from the image. Clicking on the Zoom controls changes your view by set percentages, which we talk about later in the chapter. Here's a neat undocumented trick: press on either Zoom control and drag to the left or the right to zoom in and out smoothly. The two controls work in opposite directions: drag to the right on the (+) control to zoom in, and to the left to zoom out. Drag to the right on the (–) control to zoom out, and left to zoom in.

- *Keyboard modifier clicks.* ⌘-space bar (Macintosh) or Ctrl+space bar (Windows) with a click zooms you in, and Option-⌘-space bar (Macintosh) or Ctrl+Alt+space bar (Windows) zooms you out.

- *Key commands.* On the main keyboard, plus (with the Shift key pressed) zooms you in, minus (Shift key not necessary) zooms you out. A slightly more consistent set of key commands is: ⌘/Ctrl-plus to zoom in, ⌘/Ctrl-minus to zoom out. It's simpler on the keypad for extended keyboards, just tap the plus or the minus key without worrying about the Shift key for plus. This is our zoom of choice. (Beware tapping the equal key alone; equal will change your selection back to unity shape. See Chapter 6 for more on unity.)

To revert the scene back to the default 100% magnification, hold down the Option (Macintosh) or Alt (Windows) key and click either of the Zoom tools.

Zoom to Selection

The Zoom to Selection option is another way to define a view. Suppose there is one area of the image that interests you. "Hey, I'd like to do a close-up on that," you say.

- *Wireframe mode.* Press the ⌘/Ctrl key and space bar. The cursor changes to a Magnifying tool. Drag the tool diagonally across the area you want to focus on. Release the mouse, and that area fills the screen.

- *Render mode.* When you have the rendered image showing, make sure that you have Plop Render switched on (accessed from the Display options to the right). Drag a marquee around the image area you want. Then select Zoom to

Selection from the pop-up menu (see Figure 3.22a). That area then fills the window (see Figure 3.22b). Render again (see Figure 3.22c) and select File > Save As to save your detail image as a separate scene.

You can create several snapshots of the same scene in this way. Consider it your "Postcards from the Bryce Edge."

a   **b**   **c**

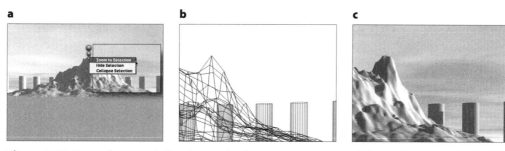

Figure 3.22 Bryce close-ups in Render mode: a) marquee an area and choose Zoom to Selection; b) the marqueed area fills the screen; c) the rendered image.

Zoombiguity

There's a problem with the word "zoom." In camera terms, you can alter the focal length of a zoom lens on the fly. It's a smoother way of changing lenses, say, from 50 mm to 80 mm to 200 mm. You zoom in and out, all the while being positioned in one place. Standing in one place, zoom from 60 mm to 130 mm. This will bring you closer to your subject. This is analogous to the action in the Field of View control.

However, we're talking about using zoom in the computer display sense. In other graphics applications, you change the view of a document by zooming. You can look at something in actual size, you can magnify it, or you can reduce it so that the entire page fits in the document window. This is a two-dimensional zoom process.

When Bryce uses the Zoom In and Zoom Out controls and the Zoom to Selection option in the Plop Render's pop-up menu, it is acting like a zoom-to-magnify feature familiar from graphics applications like Photoshop or QuarkXPress. It is a two-dimensional zoom. The fact that you're in a three-dimensional application that uses something called a camera may make zoom confusing.

When you click the Zoom In or Zoom Out magnifying tools in the lower right hand corner, you are selectively choosing smaller or larger areas of the "scene" to project onto the 2D Projection plane. You're magnifying that particular area when you zoom in and you're reducing it when you zoom out.

Zooming in Orthogonal Views

You can do the same thing in orthogonal views to bring you closer or take you further from your subject. There is a different twist to zooming in orthogonal views. If you have an object selected, the panning will change so that your selected objects are centered in your scene.

In our opinion, zooming works best in orthogonal views. It is a 2D magnification process. Orthogonal views do not have true perspective to them, so zooming works splendidly for enlarging or reducing objects as needed. In the main current view, zooming can result in perspective distortion—this is true especially when you zoom out; you are asking Bryce to put more and more of the entire 2D plane into your little area. The perspective is more extreme the farther away from the center of the image you go.

Camera Dialog Box

To get a little more control over the camera position, select Edit Current Camera from the Camera Crosses pop-up menu. If you're using one of the perspective cameras, you can also double click either the Crosses or the Trackball to open the Camera dialog box (see Figure 3.23). This dialog box allows you to use numerical settings to alter the current camera's angle and position as well as to change where you are on the flat 2D Projection plane from where you view Bryce. We won't go into great detail about it here, because it's a variation on the Object Attributes dialog box, whose discussion comes in Chapter 6. After all, what is the camera but another object in the Brycean universe? We've labeled each item in this dialog box according to its corresponding on-screen controls. Figure 3.23 shows the dialog box in its default state—the position of the Camera in a new document. Figure 3.23b shows this Camera from above. The blue triangle (actually, a pyramid in cross section) is the camera itself; click the Invisible box to make it vanish. When selected, the camera turns red. To render the camera undraggable, check the Locked box (you can still change the coordinates in the dialog box). The Field of View is the large gray triangle (again, a slice through a pyramid) which shows the boundaries of the image the camera takes in. The Origin Handle is invisible by default, because its default position is at the center of the camera. Check this box to make it visible (when the camera is selected) as a green dot, which can be moved anywhere you want.

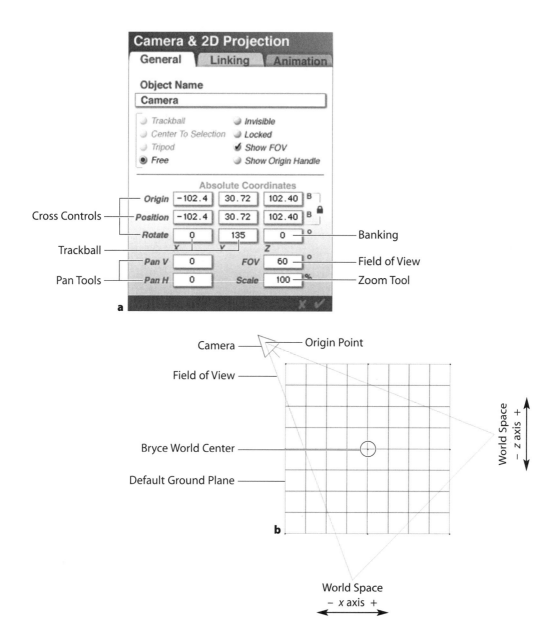

Figure 3.23 The default Camera: a) the Camera and 2D Projection dialog box, labeled to match the items on the Control Palette; b) the default Camera's position and orientation in Bryce Space, as seen from above.

Camera: Position

The Position part of the Camera dialog box is for changing the camera's, well, position, in Bryce Space, in other words, the distance from World Center. World Center is the exact center of the Brycean Universe. Adjusting the Camera with the Cross controls changes these numbers, since you are moving the actual camera location. But beware, don't expect these adjustments to match the numbers in the dialog box exactly—when you drag on the crosses, you are moving the camera in Camera Space but the coordinates in this dialog box represent the camera's location in World Space (see Figure 3.24). The numbers represent distance in Bryce units—hence the "B" to the right of the boxes. Bryce units are the quaint units of linear measurement used by the inhabitants of Bryce space. For example, the grid lines on the Default Ground Plane are 20.48 Bryce units apart. You can use arrow keys to modify the numbers in the dialog box; see "3D Transformations and Other Dialog Boxes," in Chapter 6, where we discuss this in detail.

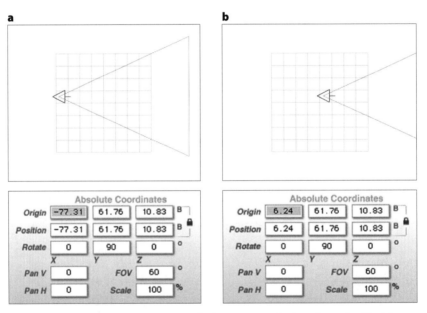

Figure 3.24 a) The Camera's position before moving, facing along the World Space *x* axis; b) after using the *z* axis cross to move the Camera along its own *z* axis. Note that in World Space its *z* coordinate hasn't changed.

Camera: Origin

Here's where you can define the location of the camera's origin point numerically. By default, the numbers will be the same as for the camera's position. If the padlock icon is red and in the locked configuration, any change you make in the Origin's coordinates will be mirrored in the Position coordinates, and vice versa, so the two points will move in lockstep. But suppose you want the camera to move as if in Trackball mode, where the Origin point is somewhere other than the center of the camera. Click the red padlock icon to unlock it (it will turn gray) and type in the coordinates of your desired origin point. Close the dialog box, and *voila!* The origin point is now elsewhere! (See Figure 3.25.) As when moving the camera's position, remember that these coordinates are figured relative to World Space, not to Camera Space. In general, it's probably easiest to move the origin point graphically: Just click the Show Origin Handle button, grab the green dot, and drag it where you will!

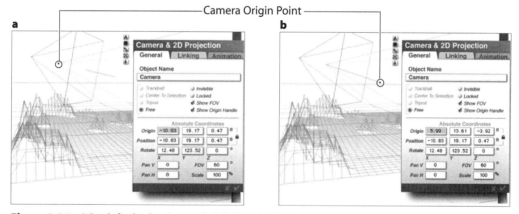

Figure 3.25 a) By default, the Camera's Origin Point is at the Camera's center; b) after typing numbers into the Camera dialog box to move the Origin Point.

Camera: Rotate

The Rotate part of the Camera dialog box describes the camera's orientation in space. The orientation is indicated in degree increments. "Incremented how?" you may ask.

- Rotate *x:* As seen looking along the *x* axis in the negative [–] direction (westward), clockwise rotation is positive. 0° points straight north, 90° points straight down, -90° points straight up.

- Rotate *y:* As seen looking along the *y* axis in the negative [–] direction (down), clockwise motion is positive. 0° points straight north, 90° points east, -90° points west.

- Rotate *z:* Banks the camera. While facing out from the camera along the camera's *z* axis, clockwise motion is positive.

The Trackball changes the settings of the camera angle. However, the Trackball only changes the *x* and *y* value. The *z* value is changed by the Banking control to make the camera do a roll. This is related to the fact that rotation on the *x* and *y* axes is always measured relative to World Space but the *z* rotation is always measured relative to Camera Space.

Field of View

The Field of View part of the dialog box is the number that controls the camera's focal length. The default is 60°. If you need to, you can reset the Field of View here. (You can also Option/Alt-click the Field of View control on the main Control Palette.)

Scale

Scale% refers to the zoom factor. Here are the numbers for the Zoom In (+) or Zoom Out (–) controls. Think of it as the enlargement or reduction of the scene on the active viewing rectangle. The default is 100%. Zoom up or down.

The zoom works in factors of 1.5. So from 100%, it multiplies that figure by 1.5 to get 150. It then multiplies that figure by 1.5 to get 225 and so on up to the maximum. On the Zoom Out side, the zoom takes 100 and divides that by 1.5 to get 66.6, then 44, and so on down to the minimum. Zooming by means of the key commands proceeds by the same ratios.

If you don't like those particular numbers and want to see something in between, say, at 135% or 89%, all you need to do is type your own numbers in the Scale% portion of the dialog box.

When you change scene sizes in the Document Setup dialog box, Bryce adjusts the scale accordingly.

To reset the numbers back to the default of 100%, enter that number for the Scale%. (You can also Option/Alt-click the zoom tools to reset to default.)

Pan V and Pan H

Pan V and Pan H each have a numerical value—*v* is for vertical and *h* is for horizontal. These numbers measure the amount that the 2D projection (film) plane is offset from the center of the 2D projection plane. The default, centered image has *v* and *h* values of 0,0. When you pan to the right, so that you are looking on the left part of the image, the horizontal value will be a positive number. Panning to the left results in a negative number. Likewise, panning up produces a positive value for *v*; and panning down a negative value.

When you change scene sizes, Bryce gives its best guess, putting the old scene in the new active image area. Both the Pan and the Scale% are adjusted. You may need to tweak either setting after changing sizes.

> **TIP:** Remember, you can also use the Camera & 2D Projection dialog box to edit the location and orientation of the orthogonal views. By deftly adjusting the rotation by 90° of, say, the Right view, you could provide yourself with a second Front view, positioned wherever you thought most useful.

Tracking an Object

The advent of animation in Bryce 3D brought a new camera-aiming control which is, of course, present in Bryce 4. It's now possible to have the camera track a particular object, so that the camera stays fixed on that object, no matter where you move the object or the camera.

As usual in Bryce, there are a couple of ways to accomplish this. Simplest is the good ol' point'n'drag method. Make sure you're in a view from which you can see the camera. Click the camera to select it; the Object control icons appear (see Figure 3.26a). Point your mouse at the Tracking icon (the icon looks like a target; Figure 3.26b), press, then drag from the Tracking icon to the object you want the camera to track. While dragging, a blue line extends from the Tracking icon to your pointer's location (Figure 3.26c). Whenever your pointer encounters another object in the scene, the object turns blue while the pointer is over that object. Let go of the mouse when your desired target object has turned blue (Figure 3.26d). There is a gray line extending from the camera to the object, indicating that the camera is tracking that object (Figure 3.26e). If you want to un-target an object, simply click on the Tracking icon. That breaks the tracking connection. The gray line connecting the camera to object disappears.

Figure 3.26 Using the Tracking icon to cause the camera to track an object: a) The camera is selected, displaying the Object Control icons; b) the mouse pointer is poised over the Tracking icon; c) dragging the blue line; d) the pointer is over the intended target; e) the camera swings around, ready to follow the target.

a
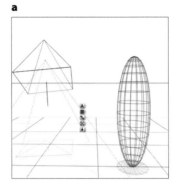

b
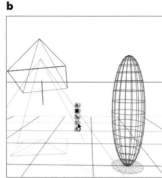

c
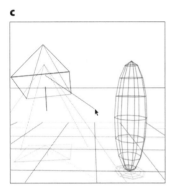

d
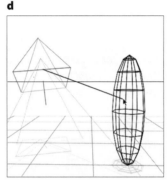

e
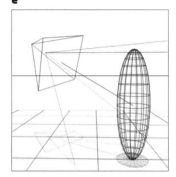

Now, in a crowded scene, it may be hard to snag just the right object, but fear not, Bryce provides another way. With the camera selected, click the Display Object Attributes icon to reveal the Camera and 2D Projection dialog box (or type ⌘-Option-E/Control+Alt+E). Click the Linking tab, and find the Track Object Name pop-up menu (see Figure 3.27). Select your desired object from the menu, and all's well. You'll notice when in camera view that the Trackball control is grayed out. This is because you've locked the camera into a specific orientation with respect to an object, and the Trackball controls the camera's orientation. You can still use the Cross controls to adjust the camera's position, though. Dragging the X or Y (horizontal or vertical) portions of any of the Cross controls will

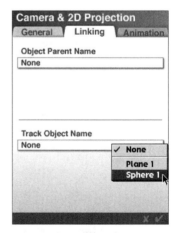

Figure 3.27 The Linking section of the Camera & 2D Projection dialog box, with Track Object pop-up menu set to a particular object.

move the camera in a manner that's similar to the way the Trackball behaves for the Director's View camera set to Trackball mode or Center to Selection mode.

HOW-TO: CAMERA PLACEMENT THAT'S JUST SO

Now that we've talked about the theory of the Camera controls, we offer some additional working information for setting up your camera positions. You don't always need to adjust your camera by using the controls on the Control Palette. You can also directly manipulate it while working in the orthogonal views of your scene or while observing from the comfort of the Director's chair.

The Little Blue Pyramid

When looking at your scene in one of the orthogonal views, or from Director's view, the camera is represented on the screen as a blue pyramid with a line extending from it. The blue pyramid and line is the camera. There is also a larger dotted gray wireframe pyramid hood. The larger gray pyramid indicates the camera's field of view. Like any other wireframe object, both the blue pyramid camera and the gray pyramid hood change to reflect any adjustments made in wireframe depth cueing. (For more information on depth cueing, see the wireframe section of Chapter 4, "Brycean Objects.")

There are two different ways to directly manipulate the camera. The first is to change the camera's position by dragging it to a new location. When you click the camera, it turns red to indicate that it is selected. You can then change the camera's position by dragging the box wherever you want it (see Figure 3.28).

a

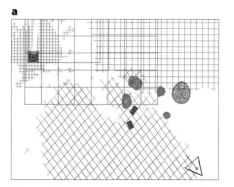

b

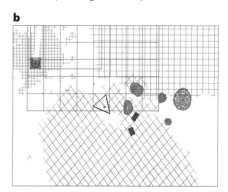

Figure 3.28 Repositioning the camera by dragging the blue pyramid (top view): a) Before (showing where the camera is headed); and b) after.

The second method of direct camera manipulation is aiming the camera. The line, or control handle, can be directly manipulated to change the camera's orientation. You can precisely aim the camera by moving the control handle in the direction you want to point your camera. To aim the camera at a particular object, drag the end of the control handle. When the mouse is close to the control handle's tip, the cursor turns into an arrow-tipped cross. Press the mouse button, and start dragging—a red ball like a clown's nose will appear on the end of the handle. Drag the ball until it touches the object (see Figure 3.29a). When you release the mouse button, the camera retracts to its original size, but is aimed directly at the object (Figure 3.29b). When you go back to main view, the object will be placed in the center of your view (Figure 3.29c). (Since, in this case, the object is tall, changing the track-ball setting to tripod and dragging down on the Trackball control aims the camera up, so that the top part of the lighthouse can be seen. See Figure 3.29d.)

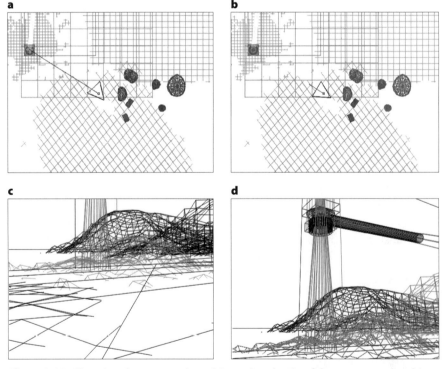

Figure 3.29 Changing the camera view: a) Dragging the tip of the camera to the object (top view) ; b) after releasing the camera (top view); c) the lighthouse in the precise center of the scene (main view); d) after adjusting the camera up using the Trackball.

What, you don't like the result? You can undo any manipulation of the camera by a simple application of the ⌘-Z/Ctrl+Z key combination. Having trouble getting ahold of that slippery camera in the midst of your crowded scene? Press your mouse on the Selection Palette Options pop-up menu and choose Select Camera. Your elusive camera will now be at your beck and call.

Now, say you have a terrain that has deep ravines (see Figure 3.30). You need to get the placement just right or else the camera will be hidden inside the ground. Not a great view. If you use the Cross controls to navigate yourself to that ravine, you will probably put your computer in danger of ruin (or worse!) from your frustrated outburst after many tries to place your camera just so. Don't sweat it. There's an easier way.

Figure 3.30 A scene with ravines that might be difficult to navigate through with the Camera controls.

Precise Camera Placement from Top View

Figure 3.31 shows the terrain from Figure 3.30 in top view. There's quite a bit of dramatic viewing, if only you can get your camera in there. However, placing the camera when you're in the wireframe view of the same terrain is problematical. Depending on the amount of depth cueing and other factors (how close you are zoomed to the entire terrain), you may or may not be able to tell from the wireframe information alone where to put the camera. In this case, depth cueing on the terrain made it fairly obvious (see Figure 3.31a). If that won't work, then render the scene in top view. After a few render passes, the situation will become obvious. You will see where to place the camera. There might be times when seeing the wireframe is also helpful; click twice on the Display Mode button to cycle to the wireframe+rendered mode. Figure 3.31b shows both the top view render and the wireframe as well as the camera. Also helpful are the Flat Shaded Preview modes introduced in Bryce 3D (see Figure 3.31c), which use either OpenGL, Sree 3D, or Direct 3D (Windows only) to generate a basic rendering of your scene on the fly (we'll talk about these more in Chapter 5, "Streamline Your Brycing"). Hold down the mouse button on the Display Mode button to access these modes (Figure 3.32).

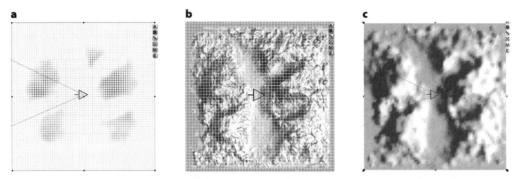

Figure 3.31 Camera placement in top view: a) with wireframe depth cueing; b) showing wireframe and rendering; c) using OpenGL Flat Shaded Preview mode.

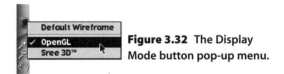

Figure 3.32 The Display Mode button pop-up menu.

Here are a few general Bryce tips to help you while you do this:

- In the Sky & Fog options menu, make sure that Link Sun to View is unchecked. Otherwise you'll get something generally very dark, as overhead sun is actually shining from your horizon.

- Placing the sun not exactly overhead will show the heights and depths of the terrain by casting slight shadows where the canyon is deep.

Flyaround View

For an overall wireframe preview of your scene, and for choosing possible new camera angles, the Flyaround takes you on an aerial tour of your scene. Click the little white donut to the right of the Select Views Control. Alternatively, select Objects > Flyaround or type ⌘-Y/Ctrl+Y. When you adopt the Flyaround view you enter yet another variety of 3D space, which we'll call Flyaround Space. Its center is somewhere in the middle of all the objects in your scene. The scene rotates around this central point, while you are looking on from the distance in a type of God's-eye view. You can see the current camera location; it is indicated by the blue pyramid. If you have set your wireframe preview to have depth cueing, then you'll be able to tell which objects are farther away and which ones are closer while the scene rotates. (For more information on wireframe and depth cueing, see Chapter 4, "Brycean Objects"). Figure 3.33 shows a stuttered "time lapse" of the Flyaround mode as the world rotates before you.

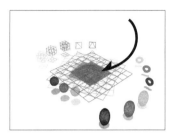

Figure 3.33 The scene in Flyaround mode.

There is more to this Aerial Preview feature than stealing a rare moment to float ethereally above the wireframe as it rotates below, all the while admiring your handiwork (though there are times when that's a fine enough reason to click the doughnut and watch your scene for a bit). The Flyaround provides a fluid way to explore the scene from different vantage points and so to choose a new camera view. There are two steps to the process. In the first stage, explore the view. The second step is to go there and let that become the new camera view. Since the end of the process is much simpler than the beginning, we'll take a moment here and talk about the conclusion before stepping back and discussing the lengthier matters of exploration.

When you get to something that is pleasing enough to declare your new camera view, hit the Return key. The Return key completes the process. If the Flyaround were to be likened to the statement, "Wherever you go, there you are," then the first step of exploration is "wherever you go." The Return key takes you to the new spot, which has now become the current view. The Return key takes you to the conclusion: "there you are."

Of course, you don't have to change your camera view at all; once you click the mouse, you exit Flyaround mode and go back to where you were before. So the click of the mouse key is, "Wherever you went, there you aren't."

That was the conclusion. Now, onto the exploration process. The process always takes longer than the conclusion, and there is always more than one option for getting there. This is yet another case where Bryce Imitates Life. During Flyaround mode, you can use different modifiers along with mouse movements to control the view.

Wherever You Go—Exploration

All the range of movements in the Flyaround mode mirror those of the Trackball (in Trackball mode) and the Z portion of either the YZ or the XZ Camera Crosses. Moving the mouse up and down (not dragging, when the mouse button is pressed, but simply moving the mouse to change the pointer position) will adjust the height of your perspective. The first few times you do this, you're no doubt putting too wide a range of motion, with the result that your aerial Flyaround is bobbing and heaving wildly, threatening to give you motion-sickness. Ouch! Don't pull out the Dramamine, just make sure to keep the mouse movements small and subtle when in Flyaround mode. Is your *mal de Bryce* exacerbated by excessive Flyaround speed? Just hold down the Shift key to slow the spinning to a statelier pace.

There is a method to the movement madness: whatever direction the mouse moves in, it takes the nearer foreground with it. Or, to put it in terms of the x, y, and z axes, the world's rotation on the x axis is controlled by your mouse movement. Flyaround Space acts as if the world has been pierced by a huge skewer that runs parallel to the monitor, and the ground tilts up or down depending on the mouse movement. So when the mouse moves up, the closer ground (between the axis "skewer" and you) moves up closer to you. It will level out, as the ground gets very close to your perspective. Keep moving up and the ground will rotate above your perspective, and you'll be looking up at the ground from below. Conversely, when the mouse moves down, that near ground moves down, placing your perspective high in the air, until you're looking straight down at the ground. Keep moving the mouse down and you'll eventually turn the world upside down as if you're in the air with the ground plane above you, or, to put it another way, you've moved over onto the other side of the world's x axis, suspended upside down. The left column in Figure 3.34 represents the results of moving the mouse up and down while in Flyaround mode.

Mouse Movement (tilt) Command/Ctrl key (near/far) Space bar (rotation)

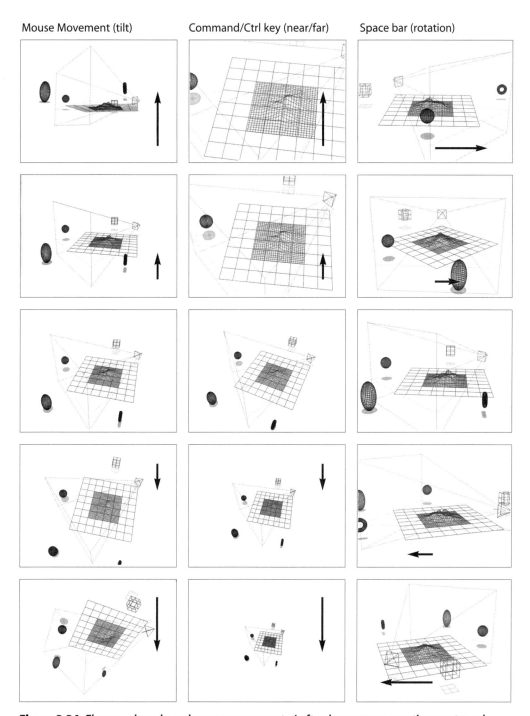

Figure 3.34 Flyaround mode and mouse movements. Left column: mouse motion; center column: mouse motion with Command/Ctrl key pressed; right column: mouse motion with space bar pressed. In each column the central row shows the starting point.

Moving the mouse left to right does nothing (except for random vertical movements, as it's nigh unto impossible to move the mouse horizontally without introducing *some* vertical movement). The range of mouse movement to rotate the entire scene on the *x* axis is limited by the size of your monitor. The larger your monitor, the greater the number of full rotations you can do as you move the mouse up or down.

Now add a modifier key. Press the Command (Macintosh) or Ctrl (Windows) key and move the mouse up and down. This will zoom you into and out of your scene. Command/Ctrl-dragging the mouse down zooms into the scene, and moving the mouse up zooms out again. In Flyaround mode, you don't rotate the world on the *z* axis, you only zoom in the z direction. Once you press the Command or Ctrl key and move the mouse, you'll suspend all of the *x* axis rotation we described earlier. You'll stay at the same angle where you were just prior to pressing the Command or Ctrl key. The middle column in Figure 3.34 shows the results of moving the mouse up and down while the Command or Ctrl key is pressed in Flyaround mode.

Here, too, the limit of motion is determined by the distance between your mouse cursor and the monitor's edge. You may run out of mouse room before you've moved as far into your scene as you want to. (Picking up the mouse and setting it down again does nothing to give you additional room to move. Once you've hit the edge of the monitor, you're stuck there.) To get around this minor edge-of-monitor problem, release the Command or Ctrl key to go back into basic up and down motion, move the mouse up until you do a complete 360° flip of the scene to the same angle, with the mouse's cursor closer to the top of the monitor, then press the Command or Ctrl key and resume moving the mouse down so the scene continues toward you. True Command/Ctrl key gymnastics, that!

Finally, there is one more modifier key—the space bar. Tapping the space bar will pause the aerial rotation around the Brycean *y* axis. Tap again to resume rotation. When it's paused, you can move the mouse left and right to control the rotation of the scene. You'll have none of this autopilot stuff , but you can still move the mouse up and down to adjust the "tilt" of the land and press the Command or Ctrl key as well to move into and out of your scene. The right column in Figure 3.34 represents the change in rotation that occurs when dragging the mouse left to right with the space bar pressed in the Flyaround mode.

And wait, there's more! While you're in this state of suspended animation, you can hold down the Option/Alt key to swivel your viewpoint around. You can't get closer or farther away, or change your altitude, but you can bring a peripheral object closer to the center of your view. Alas, it's only a fleeting glimpse—once you release the Option/Alt key, the view snaps back to where it was.

There You Are—the Conclusion

Finally, remember the Return (or Enter) key. All this mouse movement with the modifier keys amounts to diddly unless you press the Return key at the end to pop your view position into this new place. But which view? Depends on which one you started from. If you were in Camera View when you set out on your Flyaround voyage of exploration, to Camera View you will return when you hit Return/Enter, and your Camera will have moved. If you began in Director's View, then it is Director's View that will move. If you were in one of the orthogonal views, nothing will have changed. (In other words, you can look but don't touch!) Of course, you don't have to have the space bar pressed when you do hit the Return key to end this Flyaround session. Press the Return key while the scene is still rotating. (We knew we had you pegged for the roulette gambler type!)

Before talking about some of the practical ways of working in Flyaround mode, here's a summary review of the process and a table that lists the movements you can make in Flyaround mode:

Flyaround is a combination of x, y, and z movement around "Flyaround Center." It begins with the world rotating on its vertical axis, much as our own Earth rotates (this is the y axis). You can manually control that by pressing the space bar and adjusting the rotation yourself. Then, with the addition of mouse movement up and down, you are adding the x axis, tilting the foreground toward you or away from you. The Command or Ctrl key mouse movement moves you on the z (or distance) axis closer to or farther away from the center of the world. (The z axis extends from Flyaround Center to wherever your camera is located.)

Modifier Key	Mouse Action	Result
	Mouse click	Exits Flyaround view
Shift key		Slows rotation speed
	Move mouse up/down	Changes "tilt"
⌘ or Ctrl key	Move mouse up/down	Zooms in and out
Space bar (tap and release)		Stops Flyaround rotation
(while stopped)	Move left/right	Allows manual rotation
Option/Alt key (while stopped)	Any direction	Pivots viewpoint
Return key		Changes camera view to current Flyaround view

A Bit of Practice

All right. So now you know which is which. Use all three controls! Trade 'em with your friends (ahem, well…)! Once you've gotten the hang of the digital gymnastics (here digital means literal finger-digits), you can use them in combination to navigate your camera to the place you want.

The directions for this little exercise are quite simple; they're intended as merely a guide to show you where to develop fluency and some eye-hand coordination skills. You'll probably have enough going on tangling your Command key (or Ctrl key), space bar, and Return key fingers and mouse up and down movements without having to crane your neck to peer at these pages for the next bit of instructions. What you need to do here is easier *done* than *said!* Think of this as practicing scales on the piano or another instrument; what you're doing right now is not really all that beautiful, but you'll develop skills for beautiful things down the road.

1. Create a scene file with a terrain at its center and various objects surrounding it. Or open up the scene file entitled FLY AROUND ME! in the folder for Chapter 3 on the CD-ROM. Click the doughnut or type ⌘-Y (Macintosh) or Ctrl+Y (Windows). Welcome to the spinning world!

2. Move the mouse up and down. Find an angle that you like.

3. Press the Command key (Macintosh) or Ctrl key (Windows), and move the mouse up and down.

4. Try alternating between pressing and releasing the Command or Ctrl key. When you get up close to the terrain with the ⌘/Ctrl key pressed, let go of the ⌘/Ctrl key and readjust the angle. Press the ⌘/Ctrl key again and move closer or farther. Release the Command or Ctrl key.

    (If you need to move still closer, remember to release the Command or Ctrl key, move the mouse up to completely flip the world back around to place again, then press the Command/Ctrl key again and continue the move-mouse-down to move-Flyaround-Center closer. Snazzy, eh?)

    This next step introduces the space bar:

5. Press the space bar. Move the mouse left and right. Now move the mouse up and down.

6. While the rotation is still stopped, press the Command or Ctrl key and move the mouse up to move closer to Flyaround Center.

7. With the Command (or Ctrl) key pressed, move the mouse left and right. Try moving the mouse in diagonal movements.

8. With the rotation stopped, press the Enter/Return key.

Targeting an object in your scene

Here's a Camera View technique that works well for camera placement in crowded, complex scenes. Create a special object whose existence is devoted solely to camera tracking. Instead of moving your camera using the Cross and Trackball tools, or moving the camera by directly manipulating it in one of the orthogonal or Director's views, this option aims the camera by moving the location of the camera tracking object. So you move the object. Lo, the camera follows it so that the object is always set smack dab in the middle of your scene.

To do this:

1. Create an object, a sphere.

2. In one of the orthogonal views, or in Director's view, select the camera.

3. Point the mouse to the camera tracking icon. Drag from the icon to the sphere until the sphere turns blue (see Figure 3.35).

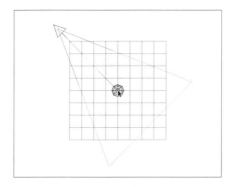

Figure 3.35 (Top view) Dragging from the Tracking icon to the sphere target object.

4. Release the mouse. A gray line should be extended from the camera to the sphere.

5. Select the sphere. Click the Object Attributes icon to access the sphere's Object Attributes dialog box.

6. Check the Hidden option (see Figure 3.36). This will make the object invisible during renders. (Since it is invisible, sometimes this object is referred to as a "null object.")

7. Go to Camera view (see Figure 3.37a). The object is selected, in the center of the working window. Drag the object to some other location (Figure 3.37b). The camera view adjusts accordingly, snapping to position so that the null object sphere is located in the precise center of the Scene window (Figure 3.37c). (If you have offset the 2D Projection plane, the object's placement will be offset accordingly).

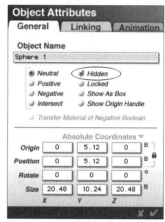

Figure 3.36 The Object Attributes dialog box for the sphere; making the sphere hidden.

This is a technique for using a null object in still scenes. For more information on this technique for animation, see Chapter 15, "Advanced Animation Techniques."

a

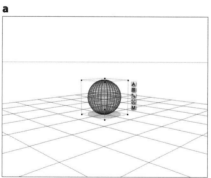

b

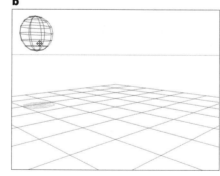

c

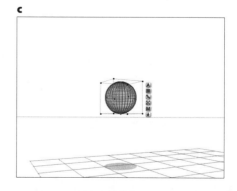

Figure 3.37 How to aim the camera by targeting an object in the scene: a) Looking at selected target sphere from Camera view; b) dragging target sphere to new position; c) the Camera view result after moving target sphere.

Saving Camera Views

The way cool thing about the camera is that you are not limited to one particular view. The freedom to explore a scene from different perspectives leads to the question, "Which one should I pick?" Bryce allows you to store the options so that you can go back and forth between those contenders for *the* perspective on the scene.

Memory Dots

Bryce enables you to save up to seven camera settings simultaneously (besides the default setting) in the Memory Dots section, to the left of the Nano Preview window. The settings are saved with your scene file, so they'll be there when you open up the scene again. When you create a new scene, it inherits the Memory Dots from the previous saved scene. Though you automatically transfer settings to new scene files, you can't transfer them from one saved Bryce scene file to another one that has already been saved. ⌘/Ctrl+N (new scene) transfers settings; ⌘/Ctrl+O (open scene) does not. If you want to transfer a camera setting from one saved scene file to another, select the Camera in the source scene, and use the Copy Matrix command (Edit>Copy Matrix; Option/Alt+C) to copy all the camera's settings, such as the Camera's position and orientation. Open the destination scene, select the Camera, and use the Paste Matrix command (Edit>Paste Matrix; Option/Alt+V) to paste all that data into the Camera. (We'll talk more about Matrices in the Objects and Edit chapters.)

How the Dots Work

The Memory Dots take on three different appearances depending on the state of the dot. When there are no camera views saved, the dot is light gray, matching the background. (Note that we—and the Bryce 4 manual—tend to call these "camera views," but in truth you save any viewpoint, including orthogonal ones). Green means that something is saved. The white spot on green means that "this saved view is currently active;" the camera is using that view dot at the moment. The camera Memory Dots can all be white, all green, or a mix of the two, but you'll never find more than one memory dot that is green with the white spot (see Figure 3.38). This is true even if you click all the dots from the same camera view. Only one will show the green-with-white-spot dot. The top one, set apart slightly from the rest, is hard-wired; it is the default (Director's) view.

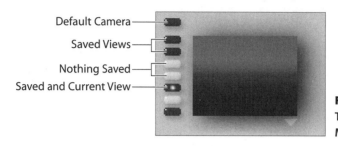

Default Camera
Saved Views
Nothing Saved
Saved and Current View

Figure 3.38
The Saved Views
Memory Dots.

The first click on a gray dot will save that particular camera view. Once clicked, the dot turns green-with-a-white-spot. Suppose you want to alter that particular view? When you move the camera's position (or adjust the 2D plane), the dot loses its white spot. Anytime after the dot is green, a simple click will switch the camera's position to the setting stored there. At that point, the green dot again becomes the green-with-white-spot dot. To clear the camera setting, press the Option (Macintosh) or Alt (Windows) key when clicking the green spot. That turns the dot back to the neutral gray. Remember the Option/Alt-click. After clicking once to create the setting, it's far too easy to do one last little (inevitable) tweak and say, "*Now* it's right," click the green dot again, and—oops!—pop back to the previous position. Don't follow the inevitable tweak with an inevitable sigh or growl, remember to Option/Alt-click to reset the dot. You can then click again to set the new improved tweaked camera view in the camera Memory Dots.

Incidentally, Option/Alt-click-to-reset is a MetaCreations interface standard. Get used to it; you'll be seeing more of it elsewhere, and you won't go wrong to invoke it to clear out a setting back to the default or neutral state.

In a version of Bryce long ago and far away…you could assign descriptive names to saved Camera views to help you remember what they were supposed to represent. Alas, that feature has gone the way of the wookie. The best substitute is good old pencil and paper.

Think Like a Photographer!

A final note. Think like a photographer! You are both creating a world and then making a picture of it, so when you set up your camera position you will be doing the same things that all photographers do when they make pictures: composing the shot.

If you are a photographer, or you've taken any photography classes, you'll recall that the discussion on composition relates to what you're doing in Bryce. Here are a few compositional pointers.

Vary the Horizon Line

Bryce's default position for the horizon line is smack dab in the middle. It cuts your image right in half. It's more interesting and pleasing to place the horizon lower or higher than exact center. Try the upper third or lower third as an alternative. The top row of Figure 3.39 shows different horizon lines. Compare the image divided in half (on the left) with the asymmetrical division of other two. See how boring the half and half is? The others are more pleasing and balanced. In both asymmetrical cases, one side is dominant and the other is secondary. As a result, your eye is led to look at one side or the other.

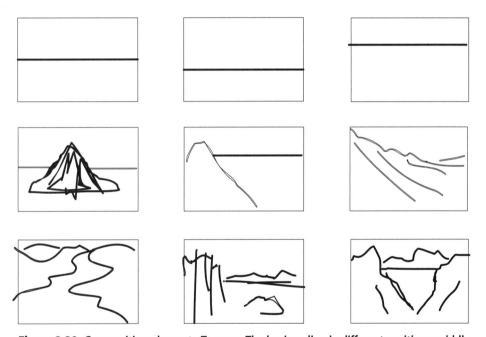

Figure 3.39 Composition elements. Top row: The horizon line in different positions; middle row: dominant element in different positions; bottom row: more complex compositions.

Feature a Dominant Element

Your image will have some elements that are dominant and others that are secondary. If all are dominant or all are secondary, the image will not be as interesting.

Look at your image. Are there lines or elements that lead your eye toward the one dominant element?

The middle row of Figure 3.39 shows various placements of a single terrain in an image. The left image is the standard Bryce default: center terrain on a centered horizon. Boring. The others in that row are more interesting. In the center image, the terrain is not centered. Combine that with a high horizon, and there is a focus on the terrain in the lower left, with a dominant diagonal line, all of which is balanced by the open space to the right. The right image takes things further. A gradual series of diagonals levels out as the terrain becomes more distant.

The images in the bottom row show more complex compositions. The left image has flowing s-shaped lines. Your eye is led from the front to the back. The center image has a contrast between vertical lines on the left and horizontal lines on the right. The right image has foreground elements, which frame the distant terrain.

If all this composition stuff is new to you, try this. On a blank piece of paper, use a pencil to draw a series of rectangular boxes, similar to those shown in the figure. They don't have to be big. Make them about the size of large postage stamps. Then fill them in with different strokes. Round, angular, squiggly, whatever. Make a few strokes in one, then go on to the next. Don't consciously try to make landscape thumbnails. (If you are making landscape thumbnails, fine; don't fight it.) Just play and go for interesting shapes. When you have half a dozen to a dozen, stop and look back over them. Are there any that you prefer? Why? When you can think of why, even if it's not necessarily a left-brain verbalized understanding, you're on your way to developing a sense of what makes a good composition.

Another composition idea: Look at some published material that has landscape or nature photography, such as *National Geographic, Arizona Highways,* and *Audubon* magazines, and coffee table books and Sierra Club calendars. Analyze the images that you find appealing. What is it about this or that one that makes it nice?

If you're interested in more on the composition and design of your world, there is an excellent book on design: *Design Basics*, by David A. Lauer and Stephen Pentak (Harcourt Brace College Publishers). It explains the basics of design, using many examples.

So, as you are composing your picture, keep in mind the following:

- Include some kind of dominant line in the image.

- Sticking with the horizontal format isn't necessary. For a more dynamic, striking image, try vertical.

- Add lines in the image. For example, diagonal and serpentine shapes draw your eye into and through the image.

- Place something close for interest and something far away for scale.

Other things you can do as a "photographer" of your Bryce image:

• Adjust the camera position. What was dull seen from one perspective becomes downright visually engaging when seen from another. Photographers do it all the time.

• Change the focal length of the lens. Use the Field of View control to adjust the angle of the lens. Skies are wonderful when you open the angle of vision way up wide.

• Adjust the time of day. Photographers are notorious for going to places at certain times of day, looking for the most dramatic light. The best time of day is just after sunrise and just before sunset. Midday lighting tends to be harsh. When working in Bryce, though, you don't need to go out at sunrise to capture the delicate light of dawn. All you need to do is adjust the light in your Bryce scene.

All of this thinking about taking photographic concepts into Bryce is reciprocal. The "Photography and Bryce" sidebar by Scott Tucker provides a perspective of an experienced Brycer who finds new depth in his photography after using Bryce for a year and a half.

A PHOTO BONUS SIDEBAR: PHOTOGRAPHY AND BRYCE   *by Scott Tucker*

In photography we are always trying to convey the wonderful landscape we saw and bring it back to the viewer as best we can, just the way we saw it. The challenge comes from representing that 3D world we saw (reality) on a two-dimensional piece of photographic paper or slide. Bryce has made me so aware of the spatial relationships of things and the result is much more depth in my photographs. Technically, I always knew what to do (stop down the lens and use a tripod) but until I gained this heightened spatial awareness (via Bryce), I just wasn't always really thinking about the 3D-ness of what I was shooting. Building 3D worlds in Bryce showed me how objects work together in space—in there I move around objects specifically thinking that my final goal is a two-dimensional representation of these objects in the main view. All this spatial-ness has carried forward to my photography. Now, when I shoot a picture I am automatically aware that I need to convey that sense of depth to the viewer. Now I really see that foreground rock and how it can be used to show that zone in space. Now I really see that middle ground and out to the horizon. Moving objects around in Bryce has taught me how to positively convey a 3D world on a 2D plane.

The best news is this: In Bryce we are always photographing our worlds. I have spent hundreds, probably thousands, of hours in Bryce walking around with that little blue camera and taking photographs. I could never do as much work on my photography as I have in Bryce this past year and a half. Bryce lets me take those field trips at night when the Brycean sun still shines undaunted! Don't get me wrong, Bryce is not a substitute for fresh air, a good hike, and some work on the photographic skills. Bryce is a proving ground, it is a holo-deck for photography—for the art of photography. When I do venture forth into the real world the photos are so much better, because of all the virtual hours I have logged in Bryce.

CHAPTER FOUR
Brycean Objects

IN THIS CHAPTER...

- Bryce objects

- All about the object's Object attributes

- Bryce's internal matrix

- Object wireframes

- Selecting Bryce objects

- Solo mode

- Importing objects

Bryce objects are the building blocks for your scenes. This chapter will take a look at each object type, noting *what* the objects are, and examining the object matrix and object attributes. Since all objects are displayed in wireframe view, this chapter will examine the controls for wireframe display. Finally, this chapter examines the different options available to select an object or set of objects, including the Solo mode. When it comes to the palettes of Bryce, this chapter concerns itself with the Create Palette, the wireframe part of the sometimes hidden Display Palette on the right, and the Selection Palette.

WHICH OBJECTS

With a couple of exceptions, all objects in Bryce are created from the Create Palette (see Figure 4.1). To create an object, click its icon. You have two other ways to bring objects into your scene: One is to import a file created in another program—we'll touch briefly on this method later in "Special Case Objects" and at the end of this chapter—and the other method is to load the object from one of the preset libraries, which we'll discuss in Chapter 5, "Streamline your Brycing." This section will break the objects down into their logical groupings.

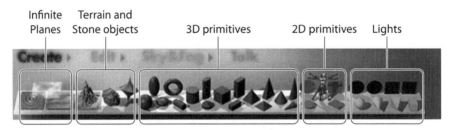

Figure 4.1 Create Palette.

Infinite Planes Three

Bryce has three types of infinite planes: water, ground, and clouds. While in wireframe view they seem to be limited in size, planes actually stretch out infinitely in all four (flat) directions. Figure 4.2 is a scene made from three infinite planes (the ground plane at a tilt). The wireframe for each plane is showing.

Figure 4.2 The three infinite planes create a scene, with wireframes showing.

The original Bryce infinite planes were indeed planes: not only infinite in extent but infinitely thin as well. If you select one and check its attributes, you'll find that its y dimension is 0. Any material applied to it is only skin deep, so the world under a water plane looks pretty much like the world above (save for the reflective surface hanging over your head!). Since Bryce 3D, it's been possible to create infinite planes with depth:

infinite slabs. If your camera is immersed in an infinite slab, the environment will be permeated with the slab's material—great for underwater scenes! Use the same icons to create these slabs—press down the mouse button over the icon rather than clicking, and a pop-up menu will appear, offering you the choice of "Surface" or "Volume." Choose the latter, and you've got a slab. Alternatively, you may hold down the Option or Alt key when clicking any of the three infinite plane icons and Bryce will generate an infinite slab. They all come into your world with a standard thickness, but you can change it to whatever you want. Figure 4.3 shows the default appearance of the two flavors of infinite objects. Note that the wireframe grid of the slab is rotated 45° from that of the plane, helping to distinguish one from the other.

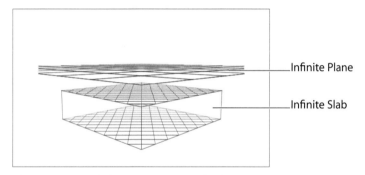

Figure 4.3 The default appearance of infinite planes and infinite slabs.

Terrain/Stone Objects

In the beginning… in Bryce 1… there was but one terrain type—the terrain. There are now two more: the symmetrical lattice, a modified terrain form; and the stone, a freestanding polyhedron mesh (see Figure 4.4).

- *Terrain.* The terrain object is the basis of Bryce's mountains, and other "injection mold" shapes that have nothing whatsoever to do with mountains. When terrains are created, their shape is randomly generated with fractal noise for rugged, rocky shapes.

  This is the old, the familiar, the tried and true staple of Bryce scene making.

- *Symmetrical Lattice.* Cousin to the terrain object, the symmetrical lattice consists of two identical mirror-shaped terrains placed back-to-back. Like the terrain, each symmetrical lattice is created with a unique random shape and is based upon editable grayscale-to-height information that can be changed in the Terrain Editor.

- *Stone.* This is a mesh object, created inside of Bryce. Like the terrain and the symmetrical lattice, each new stone is a randomly generated shape. No two are exactly alike—unless duplicated, of course.

Figure 4.4 The terrain and stone objects: terrain, symmetrical lattice, and stone.

3D Primitives

Bryce primitives are simple geometric shapes—the literal building blocks of Brycean worlds. Most of the 3D Primitives—with the exception of the torus—come with two variations, a stretched and a squashed version. They also may be rotated from their original native position.

- *Sphere.* It's round! It's a geometrical object that is equidistant from one point. It's a sphere. In Figure 4.5a, the bull's eye disk shows how the object's shape radiates from the center.

- *Torus.* This primitive, too, is round, like a tire's inner tube or doughnut. Geometrically, it's a circle with another circle extending from it. The first circle defines how big the object is, and the second defines how fat the tube part is (see Figure 4.5b).

- *Cylinder.* Here's another roundish object. Flat on top and bottom with round sides, the cylinder has a straight vertical spine, and its round barrel side edge is determined by an equidistant measure from that spine (see Figure 4.5c). The cylinder is the variation-hog of the Bryce Create Palette, having the most variations (four). Perhaps it stole one of those spots from the torus, which has but one?

- *Cube.* The basic square building block, the cube is a six-sided square. You can't get more basic than this. See Figure 4.6a.

- *Pyramid.* This is a five-sided polygon, with a square bottom and triangular faces as the object converges to a point at the top (see Figure 4.6b).

- *Cone.* The cone is also a converging shape. It starts out with a circular base, with a smooth, continuous face that focuses at the top (see Figure 4.6c).

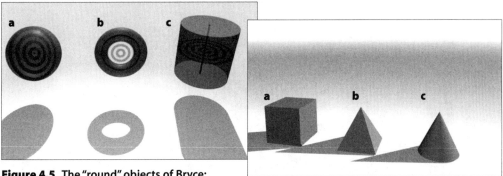

Figure 4.5 The "round" objects of Bryce: a) Sphere, b) Torus and c) Cylinder.

Figure 4.6 Square objects and Cone: a) Cube, or Box; b) Pyramid; c) Cone.

2D Primitives

2D Primitives are flat geometrical shapes; they don't take well to booleanizing. Like Infinite Planes, they come into the world with a thickness of zero. Figure 4.7 shows a sample of each type of object.

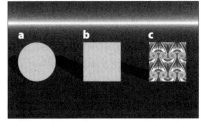

Figure 4.7 2D Primitives: a) Circle; b) Square; c) Pict Object.

- *2D Circle/Disk.* It's round, it's flat, it's a disk (see Figure 4.7a).

- *2D Face.* It's really a square: flat with four sides (see Figure 4.7b).

- *2D Pict Object.* This is a specialized square (see Figure 4.7c). When you click the 2D pict object to create it, the Picture library appears, where you assign the picture for the object, and then the 2D pict object emerges into the scene, scaled to the aspect ratio of the picture.

Lights

Bryce has light sources other than the primary sun. These are shaped like four primitives. Each casts light in a different manner. Figure 4.8 depicts each type of light, casting light alone (default) and creating light patterns using a Pict Gel. We'll discuss more about lights in depth in Chapter 12, "Bryce EnLightenment".

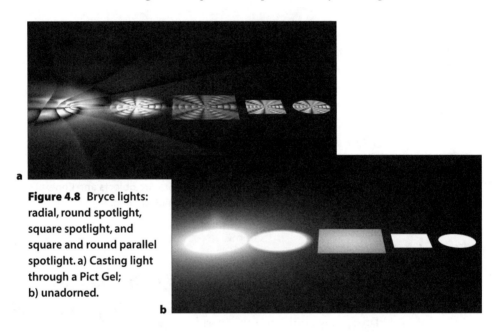

Figure 4.8 Bryce lights: radial, round spotlight, square spotlight, and square and round parallel spotlight. a) Casting light through a Pict Gel; b) unadorned.

- *Radial.* Radial light. A sphere light bulb (or, more accurately, orb).

- *Round Spotlight.* A cone that projects a circle of light in one direction.

- *Square Spotlight.* A pyramid that casts a square-shaped light in one direction.

- *Parallel Spotlight.* A square that projects light without any spread.

- *Round Parallel Spotlight.* A bonus! By pressing the Control/Ctrl key while clicking the parallel spotlight icon, you will create a round parallel spotlight.

Special Case "Objects"

Bryce has several other types of objects. You won't find them in the Create Palette, but Bryce treats them as separate object types in selection controls.

- *File > Import Object.* Import 3D objects created in other modeling applications. Bryce refers to them as "polyhedrons" or "meshes." They don't enter the scene by the Create Palette but by the File menu (see Figure 4.9). The list of import formats available was greatly extended in Bryce 4; we'll discuss them in detail at the end of this chapter.

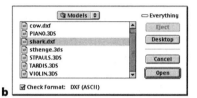

Figure 4.9 Import objects: a) Command from the File menu; b) resulting dialog box for selecting 3D models.

* *Groups.* Here is another not-an-object that is treated like an object. A group is a set of objects that, when grouped, acts like one object (see Chapter 6, "Editing and the Internal Bryce Grid," for more about groups). When it comes to selecting a category of object, though, groups are treated like a distinct object type. Figure 4.10 shows a grouped set of tori along with the other special case objects.

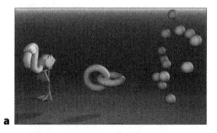
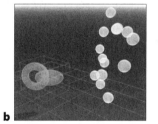
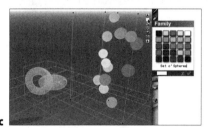
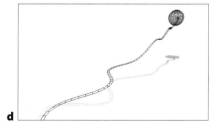

Figure 4.10 Special case objects: a) 3D object import, a grouped set of tori, a family of spheres; b) wireframe view showing family coloring (white) for spheres; c) the Set o' Spheres family selected, showing the Family dialog box (opened by clicking the Families icon). Note that the grouped tori are always enclosed by a bounding box, and the Set o' Spheres family is only enclosed in such a box when the whole family is selected; d) a sphere poised to roll down a roller-coaster path.

- *Object Families.* Though not their own object type, Bryce Object Families are at times treated as an object category all their own. This is a good thing, as you may have different types of objects (say, a sphere, cylinder, and cube) and you want to work with that collection as its own category or family. Object Families will do that. You may have as many as 25 families in a document. Each has its own color and can be assigned its own name, as well. In Figure 4.10b we've assigned all of the spheres to a family and given them the color white.

  When objects are newly created in Bryce they get the charcoal gray "Default Family" designation. Change them to another color using the Family dialog box. The way to the Family dialog box is through the small square color icon that shows when you select a Brycean object (see Figure 4.10c).

- *Paths.* The route, or trajectory, that an animated object follows as it travels through a scene can itself be turned into an object type called a path. One or more objects can then be linked to that path (Figure 4.10d). This simplifies certain aspects of animating your scene, which we'll discuss in more detail in Chapter 14, "The Fourth Dimension: Time and Animation." This also means that paths are exportable objects, so you can collect 'em and trade 'em with your friends (we'll talk about creating and using preset libraries in Chapter 5, "Streamline Your Brycing.")

- *The Camera.* We've already introduced you to the Camera as object in Chapter 3; the Select Options pop-up menu provides the quickest way to select the Camera, especially if it does not appear in your scene window.

- *Web Links.* If you assign one or more object to have a corresponding URL web link, this item in the Select pop-up menu allows you to select all objects that contain web links. (See the section, "The Linking Tab," later in this chapter for more about web links.)

OBJECT CONTROLS

As you've probably figured out by now, a set of controls is associated with any selected object or set of selected objects. They show up in the wireframe view. Bryce has as many as nine quick modifications that can be accessed by the icon controls that are next to the wireframe object. The modification icons show up when the object is selected. Different ones show up at different times, depending on the conditions present (see Figure 4.11). Some of them are doorways to dialog boxes, but some of them are not. Here's a quick listing, with more detailed descriptions to follow later in the chapter.

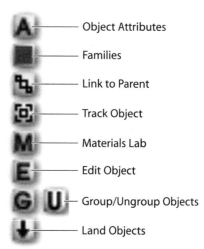

Object Attributes

Families

Link to Parent

Track Object

Materials Lab

Edit Object

Group/Ungroup Objects

Land Objects

Figure 4.11 The Object Control icons.

- *Object Attributes.* The A icon. This opens the Object Attributes dialog box that allows you to define numerically the object's size, position, and orientation in Bryce Space. It is also where you set object properties for Boolean operations, define linking and tracking relationships for animation, and give the object a name.

- *Families.* This color swatch, which matches the object's wireframe color, is the doorway to the Families dialog box. This is where you assign the object to one of the 25 available families and edit the family name or the wireframe color.

The next two icons allow you to define relationships between your current object and other objects. Once a relationship is set up between objects, changing one object may result in a corresponding change in one or more related objects.

- *Link Object.* Use this to define the object as a child of another (parent) object. Whatever you do to the parent object will also affect the child object. If you move the parent, the child obediently follows along (not necessarily like real life!). To link the object, point the mouse at the icon. Drag from the icon—as you do, a gray control handle sprouts from the object. Drag the handle until it overlaps the parent object—the handle and the object turn blue to show you that contact has been made.

- *Track Object*. If you want your object always to face toward another object, click here. Again, your object will grow a handle, which you drag to the desired target object.

- *Edit Object*. For certain objects (terrains, stones, symmetrical lattices, tori, light objects, imported 3D meshes), clicking the E icon will take you into a place where you can perform some edit function that is particular to that object. In the case of terrains and symmetrical lattices, you go to the Terrain Editor; for stones and meshes, you go to the Edit Mesh dialog box; for tori and lights you go to the Edit Torus and Edit Lights dialog boxes, respectively.

- *Edit Materials*. The M icon takes you to the Materials Lab.

The next set of modification options do not take you into a separate room or dialog box.

- *Ground/Land Object*. The up or down arrow will land the object. In other words, the down arrow drops the object onto the next lower object, as long as that object is under the central axis of the current obect. The up arrow brings the object up so that its base rests on the ground plane. If the object's central axis is below another object that itself is beneath the ground plane (see Figure 4.12a), clicking the up arrow brings the object up so its base is at the same level, as shown in Figure 4.12b. (Note that this is not the behavior described on page 300 of the Bryce 4 manual.) A refinement to this feature was added in the Bryce 4.0.1 update: holding down Option/Alt while clicking on the down arrow icon drops the object all the way to ground, no matter what else might be in the way. If the object is below the ground plan, Option/Alt-clicking on the up arrow pops the object into the open air, so it rests on the surface. We talk further about landing and grounding in Chapter 6, "Editing and the Internal Bryce Grid."

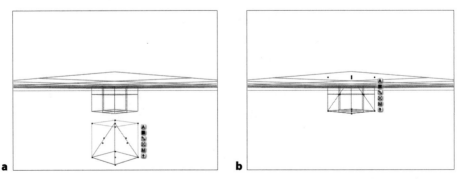

Figure 4.12 Clicking the Land button beneath the Ground plane: a) before; b) after.

- *Group Object.* When more than one object is selected, you can group them together by clicking the G icon.

- *Ungroup Object.* Any grouped object will display the U icon; click to ungroup.

If you have selected several objects, including a group and other objects, you'll see the option both to group all of them and to ungroup the group.

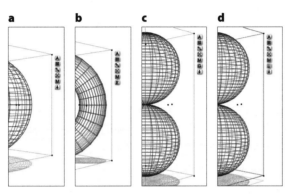

Figure 4.13 Object Control icons for selected Bryce objects: a) single object selected; b) object editable by clicking the E icon; c) two objects selected—G icon allows grouping; d) grouped objects with U icon for ungrouping.

OBJECT ATTRIBUTES

When you access the Object Attributes dialog box (you can also get there by typing ⌘-Option-E/Ctrl+Alt+E), you see three tabs: General, Linking, and Animation (see Figure 4.14). The items on the General tab define some basic properties of the object; the Linking tab defines the object's relationship with other objects; and the Animation tab sets parameters of the object's trajectory as it moves through your scene.

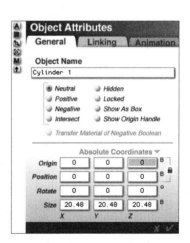

Figure 4.14 Object Attributes dialog box, showing the General tab.

The General Tab

Object Name. When an object is created, it comes into the world with a generic name. When you first open the Object Attributes dialog box, the Object Name field is selected. Just start typing, and you'll give the object a new name. Trust us, naming objects is A Very Good Idea. You'll thank us when you've got a dozen dozen objects in your scene, and you can't remember which round thing is Sphere 46.

Boolean attributes. The left column of attributes has four items that determine how this objects plays with others. When two or more objects overlap, boolean attributes can create an altogether different resuting shape. The default state is Neutral. No substantive change occurs when Neutral objects overlap each other. When Negative is checked, the object's shape will be subtracted from an overlapping Positive object. When Intersect is checked, and your object overlaps a Positive object, all you will see is the area that is common to both objects. The objects must be grouped together to have a boolean effect. (See Chapter 7, "Booleans and Multiple Object Construction," for more about booleans.)

One last boolean parameter: *Transfer Material of Negative Boolean.* This box is checked by default when you check the Negative box. You can use this to create a boolean object whose interior has a diffrerent material from its exterior. In Figure 4.15, we've created a Gouda cheese by covering a squashed sphere with a red waxy material and cutting into it with a soft yellow negative wedge.

Figure 4.15 *Hors d'œuvres,* anyone? The light yellow of the Negative object is transferred to the inner surface of the dark Positive object.

Hidden objects. Check this box, and your object will appear as normal in wireframe view but will vanish from rendered scenes.

Locked objects. When your wireframe appears as locked, the wireframe is gray (actually, a faded version of its Family color). You cannot select it by directly clicking the object, but you can select it by using other select controls (see later in this chapter for more on selecting objects). Even though you can select the object, you cannot edit it by direct manipulation. Figure 4.16 shows a locked object.

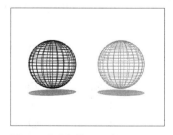

Figure 4.16 Two spheres, one unlocked, the other locked.

You can group a locked object. If you make it negative and then group it with another object, the locked object will be part of a boolean group—but you will be able to move the group. Similarly, any numerical changes that are made in the Object Attributes dialog box will change the object. Consider locking in this way: you won't be able to make accidental changes to the object through an inadvertent drag here or a wayward click there. Doing so in the Object Attributes dialog box will change the object, since, once you've entered there, Bryce assumes that you probably know what you're doing. You can duplicate a locked object, but the newly duplicated object remains locked.

Other things that you can do with a locked object: change its wireframe color, or boolean state. A locked object responds to selecting by family, select all, select by type, tabbing through, and arrow selecting (for more on selecting, see the "Natural Selection" section later in this chapter).

Show as box. This will take the wireframe and display it as a box. The keyboard equivalent for this is ⌘-B/Ctrl+B. To change back to the normal wireframe view, type ⌘-L/Ctrl+L to show as lattice. When you are working with complex scenes where the task of displaying all those wire-frames weighs Bryce down and conse-quently makes it run as fast as molasses, displaying wireframes as boxes will speed things up. See Chapter 5, "Streamline Your Brycing," for a bit more on this. Figure 4.17 displays three objects rendered with wireframes showing; the cube object in the middle is shown in its lattice guise. The lines on the center of each of its six planes distinguish it from the plain-sidedness of the show-as-box object wireframes.

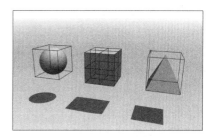

Figure 4.17 Wireframes shown as boxes compared with the normal cube wireframe.

Origin Handle. Each Bryce object has a centerpoint from which all changes to the object—its size, location and rotation—originate. That centerpoint is called the Origin Handle. In certain circumstances you can make that origin handle visible in order to change the object's "centerpoint" to be, well, off center. To do so, check the Origin Handle item in the Object Attributes dialog box.

Check here to display the object's center of rotation. See the "A Point of Origin" section in Chapter 3.

Numerical attributes. Bryce objects have four sets of characteristics, all measured on the *x, y,* and *z* axes. These characteristics can be measured relative to two separate coordinate systems, which you select from a pop-up menu just above the boxes where you enter the numbers (see Figure 4.18). Absolute coordinates are measured relative to World Space, that is, from the fixed center of the Brycean Universe. Definition coordinates are measured in Object Space, the frame of reference that each object carries within itself. We'll tell you more about the use of this pop-up menu in Chapter 6, "Editing and the Internal Bryce Grid."

Figure 4.18
The Absolute/Definition Coordinates pop-up menu.

- *Position*. Each object occupies its own position in the three-dimensional space. Think of this as location. In older versions of Bryce, this attribute was called "Offset," as in, "How far is it offset from World Center (the center of Bryce's world)?" In Bryce 4, "Offset" is used to refer to the distance an object is moved.

- *Origin*. The location of the object's Point of Origin. By default this is at the center of the object.

- *Size*. Each object has its own size, or width, height, and depth dimensions.

- *Rotation*. Each object is oriented in the three-dimensional space. It can be rotated on any of the three axes: *x, y,* and *z*.

The units for both position and size are in Bryce's special binary numbering. The default size of objects is 20.48 Bryce units. Figure 4.19 shows the basic primitives in their freshly created state. Each one fits into a box 20.48 Bryce units on a side. The stretched versions of the basic primitives (Figure 4.19b) are twice as tall (40.96 units) but usually half as thick (10.24 units) in one horizontal dimension. The squashed primitives fall into two groups: the truly squashed and the squashed-and-stretched. The former (squashed sphere, cylinder, and pyramid) cover the same horizontal area as their basic cousins but are one-quarter the height (5.12 units). The squashed-and-stretched primitives (tuboid, brickoid, and squashed cone) don't follow a rule that can be stated succinctly (see Table 4.1).

Squashed-and-stretched primitives	X (Width)	Y (Height)	Z (Depth)
Brickoid	5.12	5.12	20.48
Tuboid	40.96	5.12	5.12
Squashed cone	10.24	10.24	40.96

Table 4.1 The default dimensions for squashed and stretched primitives.

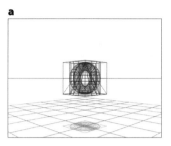
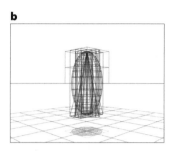
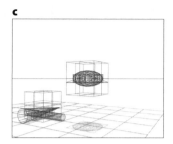

Figure 4.19 Default sizes of different types of primitives, with a basic cube wireframe for comparison: a) Basic standard objects; b) stretched objects; c) squashed objects, with the squashed-and-stretched primitives at the lower left. The squashed-and-stretched primitives were created at World Center; all others were created within view.

The default position depends on a Preferences setting. One choice is to create the object at the center of the current view. Bryce's default is to create the object "at World Center." This is a bit of a misnomer, as the object materializes resting on the ground, so its center is directly above World Center. For an object to be at World Center, it is positioned at 0, 0, 0. The object's position is measured from its own center. So, for an object to be resting on World Center but be grounded on the ground, it will be at 0 x and 0 z, but its y coordinate will be half of its height. For newly created objects that haven't been resized, that amount will be 10.24, since it is half of 20.48, the default dimension for the basic primitives. When objects are created within view, then the position depends on the camera height and orientation—the object pops into existence neatly centered in the Working Window, with no regard for the location of World Center or the ground plane. Figure 4.20a shows an object created at World Center (Bryce's default). When the preferences are set for creating "within view" (Figure 4.20b) the result is as shown in Figure 4.20c. The orientation of the camera is the same in both scenes.

For more particulars on the binary numerical units for Bryce, see Chapter 6, "Editing and the Internal Bryce Grid."

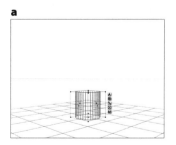
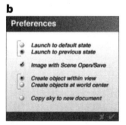
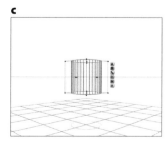

Figure 4.20 a) An object created at World Center (Bryce's default state); b) the Preferences dialog box; c) the object created "within view."

The Linking Tab

Here's where you can set up connections between the selected object and other objects in the scene (see Figure 4.21). We'll just zoom through the settings here, and refer you to Chapter 7, "Booleans and Multiple Object Construction," and Chapter 14, "The Fourth Dimension: Time and Animation," for blow-by-blow accounts.

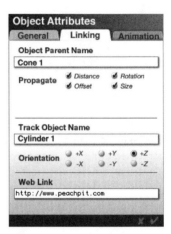

Figure 4.21 The Object Attributes dialog box, showing the Linking Tab.

Linking. This is the dialog box equivalent to the Linking icon referred to earlier. To link your object to another object, click the Object Parent Name pop-up menu and a list of the objects in your scene will appear. Select the one you wish to be the target of your link, and you're done. Now, transformations performed on the target will affect your linked object as well. The check boxes beneath the pop-up menu allow you to choose which transformations will trickle along the link to your object.

Tracking. This is the dialog box equivalent to the object tracking control mentioned earlier. Do you want your selected object always to face another object? Select the desired target object from the Track Object Name pop-up menu. No matter where you move your current object, it will always face the target. Click one of the Orientation radio buttons to choose which side the object will keep pointed at the target.

Web Link. You can export your rendered scene as an HTML image map, with each object a clickable link to another URL. Enter the address you want this object to link to in this box.

The Animation Tab

The Animation Tab (see Figure 4.22) has a set of options which govern the appearance and behavior of a moving object's trajectory. A trajectory is the visible representation of the route an object follows as it moves through a scene. It can also be turned into a path, which itself is another kind of object. We'll discuss these options in Chapter 14, "The Fourth Dimension: Time and Animation."

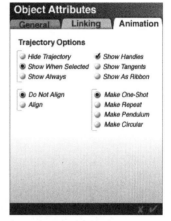

Figure 4.22 The Object Attributes dialog box, showing the Animation Tab.

MATRIX

All the numerical settings in the General portion of the Object Attributes dialog box make up the object's *matrix*. These three sets of attributes are the object's size (height, width, depth); orientation in space (rotation); and location (position). Besides the Object Attributes dialog box, the object matrix can be adjusted in the Edit controls by using the Three Rs controls: Resize, Rotate, and Reposition. The 3D Transformation dialog box, accessed through the Edit Palette, also adjusts the object's attributes. (See Chapter 6, "Editing and the Internal Bryce Grid," for more information on 3D transformations.) You can also copy and paste only the matrix information for an object by using the Copy Matrix and Paste Matrix commands under the Edit menu.

How Bryce Thinks in Its Own Internal Matrix

As you start working in your scene, click the various create object icons and the object wireframes appear. You adjust them and then go on from there. How does Bryce keep track of all objects? It has an internal database of them. As each object is created, it is added to the master list, with all the different attributes following along. The object matrix is a part of the database.

Here's a hypothetical example of a scene. Follow along if you'd like to.

1. Create a new scene (⌘-N on the Macintosh, Ctrl+N on Windows). A ground infinite plane is there already. (Check your Preferences to make sure that "Create object within view" is selected.) Click Create Torus. Press the right arrow key three times to move the torus along the *x* axis.

2. Click Create Stone. Press the down arrow key three times to move the stone forward along the z axis. Click the down arrow to land it on the ground. See Figure 4.23a for the scene at this point.

3. Click Create Pyramid. Press the left arrow key five times.

4. Click Create Terrain. Click the down arrow to land it (see Figure 4.23b).

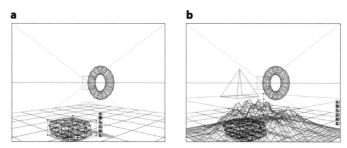

a   b

Figure 4.23 Creating the scene: a) After creating and moving the torus and stone; b) after creating pyramid and terrain.

So how does Bryce refer to the objects? It uses a database with entries for all the attributes. If Bryce were a spreadsheet application, listing the object attributes in different cells, then Figure 4.24 shows what the scene would look like. First, each object type is listed in the order it was created. Then the attributes that make up the object matrix are listed for each object. Finally, additional elements, such as material setting, whether the object is locked or is part of a boolean operation, are included (though not shown in the figure).

		If Bryce Were a Spreadsheet								
Order	Object Type	Position X	Position Y	Position Z	Rotate X	Rotate Y	Rotate Z	Size X	Size Y	Size Z
1	Infinite Plane	20.48	0.01	-20.48	0°	0°	0°	163.84	20.48	163.84
2	Torus	35.84	20.48	-20.48	-90°	0°	0°	20.48	20.48	20.48
3	Stone	20.48	7.78	-35.84	0°	0°	0°	23.8726	15.5934	29.5384
4	Pyramid	-5.12	30.72	-20.48	0°	0°	0°	81.92	20.48	81.92
5	Terrain	20.48	10.24	-20.48	0°	0°	0°	81.92	20.48	81.92
6										
7										
8										
9										
10										

Figure 4.24 Bryce scene seen as a spreadsheet.

How would you like it if *this* were your Bryce scene? Yuck. Yes, we agree. We prefer looking at the wireframe view of the scene to see which is which. Even better, we like looking at the final render. Phooey on all this internal database stuff, right? Well, yes, for the most part. There will be a couple of times when you need to be aware of the database and the *creation order* when you're dealing with sets of Bryce objects. The important thing to note here is that at times the creation order matters.

There will be times when there might be adjustments to more than one object, the "eldest" object will take precedence. This will explain some seeming quirks in editing the materials for several objects. When you select several objects having different surface materials and then you access the Materials Composer, the material you'll edit will be the one belonging to the eldest of the objects. (By clicking the OK check mark to leave the Materials Composer, you'll assign the eldest object's material to all the selected objects.)

Practical Matrix Uses

If you haven't been a matrix copier and paster before now, you will be. Once you've started using the Copy Matrix and Paste Matrix commands, there's no going back. So then, what are some of the practical uses for copying and pasting an object's matrix?

- *Updating different versions of the same scene.* Say you are working on a scene. You have made some adjustments to that scene and saved it with a different name. Your scenes are related, however, and what you've done to the one you want to do to the other. After making one edit to an object, copy the matrix, save the scene, then open up the other scene and select the object and paste the matrix. It pops right into place.

- *Special case alignment.* You have an object that you want to align with another object. You want the new one to take on the exact placement of the older one (or close enough). Instead of using the alignment tools (explained more in Chapter 6, "Editing and the Internal Bryce Grid"), copy and paste the matrix.

- *Generating a new object to take an old object's place.* Say you want to replace a certain object with a newly created object, and you want the newly created object to be sized and positioned right where the old one was. Select the old object. Copy matrix. Delete the object. Create a new object. Paste matrix. *Voilà!!* So easy! So convenient! How did we ever get along without it? (Of course, you may have to copy and paste the old object's material, too…in that case, don't delete the old one just yet.)

A close corollary to copying and pasting the matrix is to use the Object Conversion tool on the Edit Palette, described briefly in the next section, with more elaboration in Chapter 6, "Editing and the Internal Bryce Grid."

WIREFRAME OBJECT

As you work with your Bryce objects, you will be working in Bryce's wireframe view. As part of our consideration of all Brycean objects, this next section examines the workings of wireframes. To the right of the Bryce user interface is the Display Palette (you need to roll your mouse over the palette in order for the controls to appear). The lower grouping of controls affects the appearance of wireframes (see Figure 4.25). These controls aid you in the care and feeding of your Bryce wireframe objects.

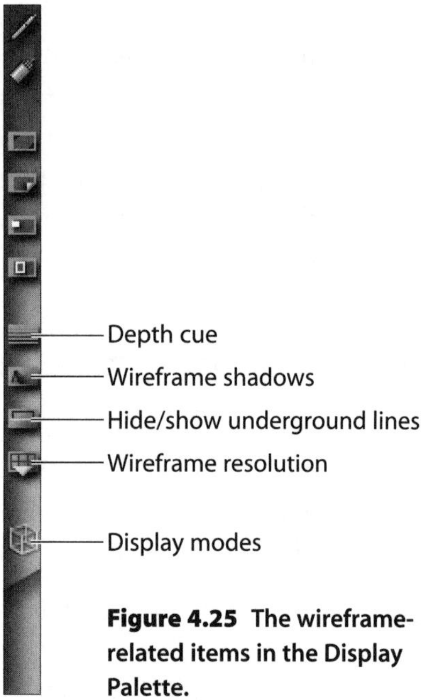

Depth cue
Wireframe shadows
Hide/show underground lines
Wireframe resolution
Display modes

Figure 4.25 The wireframe-related items in the Display Palette.

Adjustments That Can Be Made to Wireframe Views

Bryce's adjustments enable you to change how the wireframe is displayed on your screen. You can determine the level of detail in the wireframe display and how the wireframes of several objects interact with each other.

Wireframe Resolution

Compared to a render, which takes a while to complete, a wireframe view is an instantaneous rendition of the objects in your scene. However, "instantaneous" is a relative term. Depending on the number of objects, the amount of detail to the wireframe, and the speed of your particular computer, Bryce will take *some* amount of time to display the object. The lower the amount of detail, the more "instant" the display. The higher the wireframe detail, the more laggard the display.

You can adjust three distinct states of the wireframe display, which you access from the Wireframe Resolution pop-up menu, near the bottom of the Display Palette. They are Motion, Static, and Selected. In all three cases, the higher the number, the more detail you'll see; hence the longer it takes for Bryce to draw the scene on the screen. This is why the motion wireframe numbers are lower than the static and selected ones; Bryce has to display them while you are dragging the terrain from point A to point B—showing every step in between.

- *Motion*. This is the type of wireframe displayed when you are moving objects, or the camera. It's also used in Flyaround view or when playing an animation.

- *Static*. This is what you see when camera and objects are at rest.

- *Selected*. This is what you see when you have one or more objects selected (while at rest).

The Selected setting lets you look at certain wireframes in higher detail than the rest. After all, it stands to reason that you want to know about the object you've selected. Say, for example, you are moving a terrain. If you set the Static wireframe setting to some obscenely high number (such as 128), it'll take Bryce a while to show your scene. Each time you make a change, you'll have to wait for the wireframe to update in a manner that will be painfully reminiscent of the days of very slow computers. So you can split the difference and make all your wireframes coarser than coarse when they're at rest, and throw all the computing effort into displaying the selected object. That way you can get a feel for more of the object's detail while working with it. Figure 4.26a shows the minimum setting for an object, eight, whereas b shows the maximum, 128.

Figure 4.26 Wireframes at different resolutions: a) Static terrain at 8; b) selected terrain at 128; c) confusing jumble of objects at static setting of 8; d) greater clarity with selected objects at higher setting; e) side view for alignment.

a
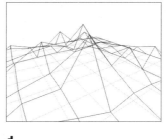

b
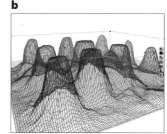

c
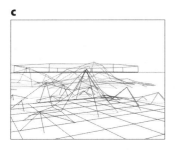

d
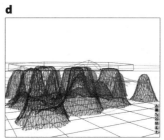

e
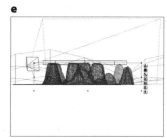

So what setting do you give to each of these three settings? Find a happy medium between the amount of detail you need to see and the amount of speed you can live with. Your happy medium will probably be in the motion numbers; you are given plenty of options for those. Set the numbers lower for general working purposes. If you need higher detail to check something, set the selected object to be higher. You probably won't want to keep to the extremes we chose for Figures 4.26c and d, where the same settings are shown again but with additional objects in the scene. See how jumbled all the wireframes are when they are at low resolution? Even though the selected one is at higher resolution, providing more clarity to the scene as you work, you may find it best to set the Selected setting lower than this one (128). Or you may want to momentarily set it to the maximum for a few brief adjustments and then bring it back down to a lower setting for normal work. You can imagine how this might work in Figure 4.26e, where a side view of the selected terrain makes for ease in precise alignment.

Show/Hide Underground

The next control up the Display Palette is the Hide/Show Underground Lines control. You can show and hide underground lines by clicking the little toggle switch. When you hide underground lines, any wireframe that falls below Bryce's ground level disappears from view. In addition, Bryce displays the blue horizon line. When underground lines are shown, then all wireframe portions are shown and the blue horizon line goes away. When underground lines are hidden, all objects change when they encounter—and drop below—the ground plane level. The horizon line shows, since it is the representation of the ground plane way, way off in the infinite distance. When you show underground lines, it's the same thing as banishing the ground plane and its influence, complete with the horizon line in the distance. Figure 4.27 compares the same scene with wireframes showing (a) and hidden (b).

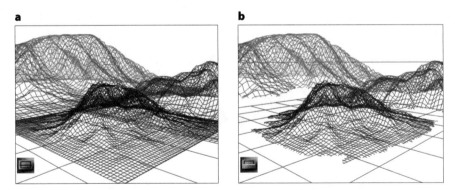

Figure 4.27 Underground lines: a) Wireframes showing and b) hidden. In each case, the current state of the Hide/Show Underground Lines control is shown.

Depending on the kind of scene you're working on, you'll find that either showing underground lines or hiding them is the preferable state. Hide underground lines any time you are positioning objects in relation to the ground. Like wireframe shadows (see the next section), this is a way to see characteristics of your scene in relation to the ground, without resorting to a full-blown render.

When is it good to show them? Show underground lines when you're adjusting terrains or other objects below the surface, especially in the case of an island surrounded by water, or some similar placement where an object is partially "submerged" below ground level. Also, showing underground lines is preferable when you do not have a ground plane in your scene.

Shadows

When the wireframe shadow is invoked, each object casts a small shadow onto the ground plane level of the Bryce Universe. The shadow is cast on the ground plane as if from a light source directly overhead. It's a cue to tell the location of the wireframe. The shadow is cast whether or not you have "hide underground lines" selected or whether or not there is a ground plane present. The object's shadow takes on the muted color of the wireframe itself. Selected objects cast a pale red shadow, default objects cast a pale gray shadow, and objects of other families will cast pale shadows of their family wireframe color.

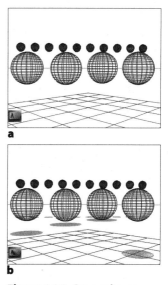

Why use wireframe shadows? They show depth and relative location and, consequently, relative size. The size of the wireframe by itself doesn't necessarily mean anything, as you can see in Figure 4.28a. But when the shadow falls on the ground plane going "up" toward the back, then you know that the wireframe is farther away than some other object (see Figure 4.28b). The horizon line is at eye level in the distance. It represents the ground level. The lower the shadow appears on the ground, the closer it is to the camera. The higher the shadow appears, the farther away it is. The wireframe shadows, then, provide a clue of the object's location and, from that, the relative scale of the object.

Figure 4.28 Four spheres in wireframe: a) Without wireframe shadows; b) with wireframe shadows. We've also shown the current state of the Wireframe Shadows control.

Depth Cue

Depth cue is another means of seeing distance—in fact, it's a purer form than wireframe shadows. Since, as you look at your scene, you see only wireframes, you can't tell right off whether one object is in front of the other. All you see are those little wireframes. Nothing more. Bryce helps you to figure out which object is closer and which is further away by rendering the wireframes in depth cueing. Dragging up on the control will decrease the depth effect, so that all wireframes appear to be bolder with no differentiation between near and far. Dragging down increases the effect of depth, so that you can more easily distinguish whether an object is near or far. Figure 4.29 shows three ranges of wireframe depth cueing states, ranging from no cueing, default, to maximum cueing. As you can see by Figure 4.29c, when maximum cueing is activated, even near objects appear faded. Depth cueing works in all views. Try it out looking at a terrain from top view, as well (see Figure 4.30).

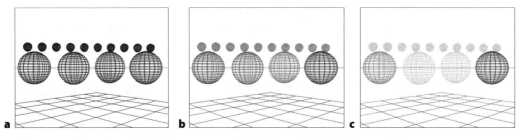

a   b   c

Figure 4.29 Depth cueing in three ranges: a) Minimum; b) default; c) maximum.

Bryce's default state is to have a medium amount of depth cueing. The wireframes are also, by default, displayed with antialiasing applied (this smooths their outlines onscreen). In previous versions of Bryce, Option/Alt-clicking the control caused depth cueing to revert back to its default state. Alas, this feature seems to be broken in Bryce 4. What you can do, on the other hand, is turn off antialiasing and depth cueing simultaneously by Control-clicking/Ctrl+Alt-clicking the Depth cue control.

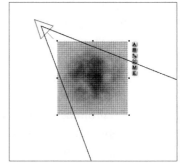

Figure 4.30 Depth cueing of a terrain from top view.

Wireframe Colors—Object Families

Aside from all the wireframe adjustments that can be made using the Wireframe controls on the palette to the right of the scene window, you can also change the wireframe color of an object. This is good for keeping objects in logical grouping types. First we'll talk about the wireframe color and creating different families of objects and then discuss some of the particulars of object groups and wireframe color. Consider this a section that addresses wireframes, paying particular attention to the "special object types" of object families and groups.

Organizing Objects by Family/Wireframe Color

Without using the Group command to make assorted objects into a group, you can roughly categorize different sets of objects by assigning them different colors. There are a couple of good reasons for doing this. First, when you have several objects that all share the same material attribute, make them all the same wireframe color. In this way, if you change the material setting, you can change them all very easily. By selecting by family prior to making the adjustment, none of the objects with that particular material setting will be left out. Second, when you are constructing a very complex conglomerate object with many individual parts, assigning different objects of the conglomerate to be members of different families helps in the construction process. Besides having a number of related objects share a common color, they can also have a name of their own.

Figure 4.31 shows the wireframe view of a lighthouse scene, with the Family pop-up menu showing so that you can see all the names. Notice how the groupings are either logical or are grouped with objects that have the same material setting, for example: lighthouse glass, railings, rocks, chairs (imported objects), near terrains (with textures), and distant terrains (without).

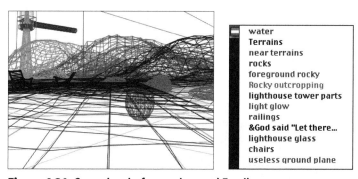

Figure 4.31 Scene in wireframe view and Family pop-up menu.

Color and Grouped Objects

This section is not a discussion of "why to group things that are the same color." It's more a set of warnings about the way object color behaves with grouped objects. It's also a warning that this behavior has changed since Bryce 2.

The default wireframe color is charcoal; when you freshly launch Bryce and create an object, the wireframe color will be charcoal, and the object will belong to the Default family.

Try this:

1. Create a new scene. Create a sphere. Change its family and color to another color, say the lime green of Family 19. Just for fun, let's give this family a name. While the Family dialog box is open, type the word "Lime."

2. Then create a cone. It emerges into Bryce at the default color. Drag it to another location in the scene.

3. Create a cube. Change its color to, say, the navy blue of Family 22.

4. Drag a marquee around all three objects to select them. Notice that the Family icon has turned black to alert you that objects from a variety of families have been selected. Now group the objects by clicking the G icon. The Family icon has now changed to gray, reflecting the fact that the new group has been assigned to the Default family. Click in the background area to deselect the group. See how the group's bounding box has turned gray, but the individual objects have kept their family colors?

    You might be thinking, "Well, Bryce treats groups as objects in and of themselves. Surely I can assign the group to a family without betraying the allegiances of its individual members!" Were you thinking that? Too bad—it ain't true. To continue with our experiments:

5. Select our group again. Click the Family icon and change its color to the vivid orange of number 20. Click in the background to deselect. Uh-oh, all of your objects are now the same color! Never fear, there's a neat trick that lets you select individual members of a group:

6. Hold down the Control/Ctrl key and click the sphere. Up pops a list of all the groups and individual objects under the cursor at that spot (see Figure 4.32). Drag down the list to Sphere 1, and release. *Voilà!* Now, click the Family icon and reassign the sphere from orange to the correct citrus color

(lime). Deselect, and now you have an orange group with one lime member. (Make up your own cliché about comparing apples and oranges...)

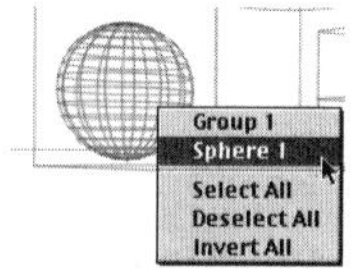

Figure 4.32 The Select Objects pop-up menu.

Let's create some companions for our lone lime.

1. Create a tall cube and drag it off to the side.

2. Create a squashed cone. Add the tall cube to the selection and group. Click the family icon, and assign the group to Family 19 (Lime). Click in the background to deselect.

3. Click the Families button on the Selection Palette, and select Lime from the Families pop-up menu (see Figure 4.33). How about that—you've selected a group of objects, plus an object inside another group.

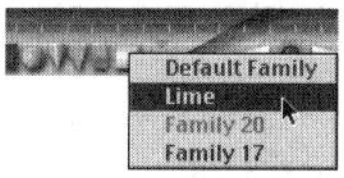

Figure 4.33 The Families pop-up menu, showing the Lime family selected.

But wait—there's more! Your nonconforming lime-in-an-orange-crate possesses dual citizenship.

4. Click once again the Families button and select Family 20. All of the orange group is highlighted, including the renegade lime.

You can use this feature to create powerful cross-group selection parameters, which come in handy when you want to apply the same materials or transformations to many objects scattered across a number of different groups.

(By the way, the Bryce 4 manual would have you believe that you can't select a Family from the Families pop-up menu unless you've formally given the Family a name. Don't you believe it! All the familes you've created will show up in the Families pop-up menu; the ones you haven't given names to will just appear with their default names, for example, Family 20.)

NATURAL SELECTION

Of course, once you have created an object and are viewing it ever-so-nicely in wireframe mode, you may like to do something to it. Move it. Change its size. Give it a surface property. Rotate it. To make any adjustments to an object, you must first select it. There are several ways to select Bryce wireframe objects. You've already seen how to select an object by clicking it or dragging a marquee around it. When you have a scene with several (or dozens!) of objects in it, it's helpful to know all of the ways by which you can select and deselect the objects in your scene. Here are your selection choices:

- Click the object directly. To select more than one object, hold down the Shift key while you click the other objects. Oops, you accidentally selected too many? Hold down the Shift key and click again the offending items. They'll be removed from the selected mob.

- Variation on directly clicking an object—hold down the Control/Ctrl key while clicking on an object or a set of objects. A pop-up menu appears, listing all the objects currently located under the cursor. Then select from the list. This variation is especially handy if you want to select one object in a tangle of overlapping objects. (This option is described in more detail as part of the "Control Key and the Contextual Menu" in the "Keyboard Entities" section a little later in this chapter.)

- Drag the marquee over the centers of one or more objects to select it (or them).

- Use the Tab key to cycle through different objects in a scene.

- The time-honored keyboard shortcut, ⌘-A/Ctrl+A, selects all of the objects in your scene. If you have some objects selected, use ⌘-Shift-A/Ctrl+Shift+A to invert the selection; that is, to select the other objects instead.

The Selection Palette

The bottom of the user interface is the home of the Selection Palette. Figure 4.34 shows the Selection Palette with each option identified. What, you don't see anything that looks like this? Beneath the Working window all you've got is the Time Scrubber and Animation Controls? Well then, you've got the Animation Palette displayed instead. Click the Time/Selection Palette Toggle (in the lower right-hand corner of your screen) to reveal the Selection Palette. Or, just press the S key.

There are four sets of controls:

• Select by object type using object selection icons.

• Select by family (wireframe color).

• Select using the Selection Arrows.

• The Selection pop-up menu, which aids you in selecting miscellaneous items as well as setting some general selection parameters.

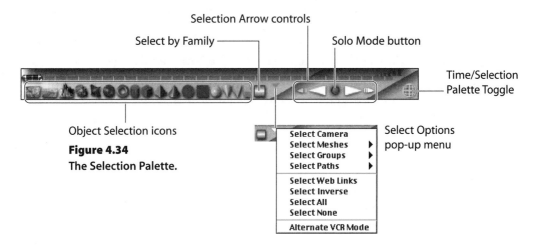

Figure 4.34
The Selection Palette.

Object Selection Icons

The object selection icons are fairly easy to figure out. Click the sphere selection icon and all spheres will be selected. You may also select an individual object of a certain type by name. Instead of clicking, say, the Select Sphere icon, if you press the mouse there, you'll get a pop-up menu. The menu gives you the "Select All of Type" option (equivalent to simply clicking the Select Sphere icon) or you can select any of the individual spheres, which are all listed in the menu. Did we say that naming objects is an advantageous strategy? Here again the naming strategy will come in handy, so that your list of "Sphere 1, Sphere 2, Sphere 3…Sphere 35, Sphere 36" will have more meaningful names.

Selection by Family

Once you have given one or more of your objects different family/wireframe colors (or you have created lights, stones, infinite planes or slabs which all emerge into the scene with a different wireframe color), you can select objects according to the family by choosing from the Family pop-up menu.

The Selection Pop-up Menu

To get at the objects not covered by the Selection Icons or the Family pop-up menu, use the Select Options pop-up menu (illustrated in Figure 4.34).

- *Select Camera.* This allows you to select the Camera (what else?). It's not available when you're in Camera View, though.

- *Select Meshes.* This section of the Selection menu lists any Meshes, or 3D objects, that you've imported into your scene. (Formerly called "Polyhedrons" in Bryce 2 and "Polymeshes" in Bryce 3D. What will they think of next?)

- *Select Groups.* Likewise, this section of the Selection menu lists any groups in your scene. It's a good idea to use the Object Attributes dialog box to give each of your groups a distinctive name. The Select Groups menu isn't much help when all it shows is a long list of items all named "Group X," where X is a number between 1 and umpteen.

- *Select Paths.* Once you've imported or created some paths, they'll show up in this menu.

- *Select Web Links.* This menu item causes all objects with embedded URLs to be selected. Important! All web-linked objects *must* be selecteed *before* rendering, or else your HTML-export will not work.

- *Select Inverse.* This selects all the objects that aren't currently selected.

- *Select All.* Pretty much says it all…

- *Select None.* Ditto.

VCR Mode and Arrows

The other large area on the Selection Palette are the Arrow or VCR controls. They are called "VCR" for their resemblance to the arrows on video cassette recorders (plus, incidentally, a host of other audio-visual equipment). Bryce's Arrow controls have nothing to do with a VCR, however. But you need to be aware of this titling convention because there's an item in the miscellaneous selection pop-up menu that changes the arrows. It's called "Alternate VCR Mode." Aside from that, we shall call them the Arrow controls or Selection Arrows.

There are two sets of arrows for cycling through objects in your scene and two directions to cycle in. They are Previous Object of Type, Previous Object Type, Next Object Type, and Next Object of Type. The larger arrows cycle through object types: infinite plane, terrain, cylinder, and sphere, for example. Once you have hit upon the type of object you want, then the smaller arrows will cycle through all of the objects of that type: first sphere, second sphere, and third sphere, for example.

Those of you who are just joining us from Bryce 2 will remember a peculiarity in the way Bryce advanced through the object types. After proceeding through the list of objects, the Family icon would light up, and all of the objects in one family would be selected. Then if you cycled through all the object types again, another family would be selected, and so on. But no longer—since Bryce 3D, families are ignored in the march from object type to object type.

If you are watching your scene while you click the Arrow controls (and you probably are), you might be confused by the order in which Bryce selects objects, especially if you don't have many objects in your scene, or many object types. As an alternative, to understand what is transpiring as Bryce cycles through object types, click the Next Object Type Button repeatedly while watching the object selection icons on the Selection Palette.

To aid you in this process, open the file located on the CD-ROM's folder for this chapter. The scene document has many object types. When it is open, click the Next Object Type Selection Arrow.

Notice that the scene has several object types in it: a symmetrical lattice, a torus, a pict object (square), a cylinder, a cube, and three radial lights. (See Figure 4.35.) When you open the scene to wireframe view, no object is selected.

Figure 4.35 Wireframe view of the scene entitled *Objects to Select.*

Walkthrough

1. Click the large right arrow on the Selection Palette, and keep clicking it. Watch the Select by Object icons. Notice that as the type is selected, that particular type highlights. Bryce selects objects according to the order of the objects on the bottom panel.

2. When you get to one of the lights, click the smaller arrow to select individual objects from that object type. So Bryce has an agenda here; select this type object, and then, once you're on the particular object, you can cycle through all the other individual objects of that type.

Alternate VCR Mode; Select by Creation Order

Alternate VCR Mode switches the Selection Arrows into a different mode, where the objects are selected in a different order—the order in which the objects were created. The large right arrow cycles you forward from one object to the next, and the large left one cycles you backwards. In the outer set, the arrows cycle you through the different object families. (Incidentally, the Tab key works in the same way as the Alternate VCR Mode Next Object arrow.)

Keyboard Entities

Four types of keyboard keys are used with the selection process. The first type (Tab key) cycles through all objects in a manner similar to the Selection Arrows. The second, the Shift key, acts as a toggle and a way to select or deselect multiple objects. The third, using the key command equivalents to pop-up menu commands, allows you to select all or to select inverse. Finally, holding down the Control/Ctrl key while clicking an object brings up a list of objects under the mouse pointer, with some additional selection commands.

Tab Key

The Tab key cycles through all your objects. If no object has been selected, it starts with the first object created and then cycles through in the order in which objects were created. If an object is selected, it starts with that object and moves through the objects in the order of their creation. If any objects have been selected and then deselected, it continues with the next-youngest nonselected object. The Tab key acts like the Alternate VCR Mode of the Selection Arrows. To reverse the order of selection with the Tab key, hold down the space bar as well.

Shift Key and Selections/Deselections

Get more control of selecting by using the Shift key. Use it to select more than one object or as a toggle to deselect/select an object. This is most intuitive in the direct "click-object-to-select-it" process.

Sometimes when clicking an object, you'll inadvertently select two objects. In the image in Figure 4.36, this happens easily in top view when a portion of the terrain is "hidden underground." You may not be able to see it, but it's still there, and it will be selected when you click it. So if both objects are selected but you want to select only one, hold down the Shift key and click the terrain (or whatever you don't want selected) to deselect it.

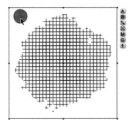

Figure 4.36 Inadvertently selecting two objects when one has underground lines hidden.

Sometimes you will have several objects that are perfectly aligned with the camera. That is, there are several objects, but it looks as if there is only one. In this case, clicking the visible object usually selects the first object and not all the other objects behind. If you want to select all the objects, hold down the Shift key and click. Bryce will select everything under the cursor. Figure 4.37a shows a set of cylinder wireframes that are positioned one behind the other, aligned with the camera's perspective. When holding down the Shift key and clicking, they are all selected (Figure 4.37b).

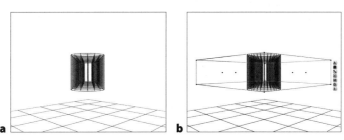

Figure 4.37 Shift-clicking to select all objects located under the mouse's pointer.

You could easily find yourself in a situation where you have several terrains and other objects, all of which overlap one another as you view them from the camera's perspective. With that complex a scene, if you click something directly with the Shift key pressed, you'll select a whole host of objects. It's at that point that you should consider the other options for selecting.

Shift Key and the Select Control Icons

You can use the Shift key in conjunction with the selection icons. Select all spheres by clicking the Sphere Selection icon, and then add to that by pressing the Shift key and selecting the cones as well. You can also use the Shift key and the selection icons to deselect certain objects. Bear in mind, however, that the Shift key works as a toggle, so if you have one of your three spheres selected and hold down the Shift key while clicking the Sphere Selection icon, you'll select the others and deselect the one that was selected.

Say, for example, you have two terrains and a sphere selected and you want to deselect the sphere. Hold down the Shift key and then click the Sphere Selection icon. *Voilà!*

Now, let's say that you have all of those objects selected and you want to add the pyramid to your selection. Hold down the Shift key and click the pyramid. The pyramid will be added to your selection.

In fact, using the Shift key in *all* cases adds to or deletes from a selection, depending on your starting place. This is a good time to point out that the Shift-clicking behavior described on page 30 of the Bryce 4 manual in "To Select Obscured Objects" doesn't work quite as advertised. There it is claimed that Shift-clicking an object that stands between you and other objects will result in all the objects behind the obscuring object will be selected. As we've seen this will actually select all the objects under the mouse pointer. On the other hand, if the frontmost object is already selected, then Shift-clicking it will select all the objects behind it and leave the front object deselected.

Shift Key and the Families Pop-up Menu

If you want to select all of the objects which belong to a single family, say, the Default Family, simply use the Families pop-up menu. Then, if you want to add the objects from another family, hold down the Shift key while selecting that family.

Selecting with the Keyboard

As do most properly-brought-up computer programs, Bryce lets you do a certain amount of selecting without taking your hands off the keyboard. ⌘-A/Ctrl+A selects all of the items in your scene. If you have some items selected, you can instantly select the rest of the items and deselect the currently-selected bunch by typing ⌘-Shift-A/Ctrl+Shift+A (also known as Select Inverse).

Control/Ctrl Key and the Select Objects Menu

Holding down the Control/Ctrl key while clicking one or more objects brings up a handy-dandy contextual menu that helps you pick an object out of a crowd.

Try this trick on a member of a group to select only that item (*à la* Figure 4.32).

In extremely complex scenes, this manuever can be a life-saver: Hold down the Control/Ctrl key and click the desired object (ignore any objects between you and the object). The Select Objects menu will pop up listing all of the objects under your mouse pointer. From the menu choose the object you want to select (see Figure 4.38). As usual, hold down the Shift key to select multiple objects. (The Bryce 4 manual tells you to start by drag-selecting a bunch of objects first, but that's unnecessary.)

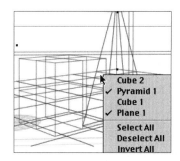

Figure 4.38 Control/Ctrl-clicking the scene causes a list of all the objects under the mouse pointer to pop up. Checked items are selected.

The contextual menu is another argument in favor of naming significant objects; when you look at the list of objects you'll be able to tell that "Sphere in center" is really what you want, rather than "Sphere 37"… or was that "Sphere 38"?

The commands on the menu operate as follows:

• *Select All.* All of the items on the list are selected. Beware! This is not the equivalent of the "Select All" command invoked from the Selection pop-up menu, or by typing ⌘-A/Ctrl+A. It only selects the items under the cursor.

• *Deselect All.* Deselects all of the items on the list (leaving other items in the scene but not in the pop-up menu selected).

• *Invert All.* Nope, it doesn't make all the objects suddenly stand on their heads. All objects under your cursor which were selected are now deselected, and vice versa. Again, not the same thing as ⌘-Shift-A/Ctrl+Shift+A.

Solo Mode

Bryce has an alternative for viewing objects. Select one or a few, and look at those only in Bryce's Solo mode. Activate the Solo mode by clicking the round button between the Selection Arrows on the bottom selection palette (see Figure 4.39). Then only those objects that were selected will appear, and everything else will disappear temporarily—giving you a reprieve from wireframe clutter, and giving your computer a bit of a reprieve; it doesn't have to draw those objects on screen. To get back to regular mode, simply click the red button again. It goes back to its normal green state, and you see everything in your scene again.

Figure 4.39 The Solo mode button on the Selection Palette.

Now that you have a general idea about the way Solo mode works, here is a list of likely reasons you'd want to use it.

Uses for Solo Mode

• Clutter reduction—look at only those objects that you want to see without being distracted by other objects.

• Select individual objects that would otherwise be difficult to select.

• Narrow down selection further.

• Render only certain objects—the same reasons as already given, but instead of selecting and working with only a group, render only the few and the proud and the solo.

Groups and Solo Mode

You'll find that Bryce in Solo mode works just like Bryce in Normal mode, with one exception: if you take an object that's part of a group into Solo mode without its grouped brethren, you won't be able to group it with any other objects. This is a safeguard to prevent you from the unfortunate results you might get if you joined an object to two unconnected groups. Actually, you'll find the same thing is true in Normal mode—if you select one object in a group, Bryce won't allow you to group it with other objects not in the same group. We know, it seems paternalistic of Bryce (watching to make sure our objects don't fall into bad company), but the program does have our best interests at heart. No, really!

Once Inside of Solo Mode

Once you're inside of Solo mode, you'll have your subset of all Bryce objects in your scene. It's almost like declaring those objects that you brought into Solo mode as your temporary universe of fewer objects. Bryce's Selection tools work in Solo mode as well. They'll operate only on those objects that you brought with you. So if you have an overall scene with a dozen spheres and two cylinders, and you brought the cylinders and one sphere into Solo mode, then when you select by object type (sphere), the one sphere will be selected. Bryce temporarily forgets about the objects that aren't in Solo mode. Use the other Selection tools to your heart's content to work with the objects you brought into Solo mode with you. You can select all, you can select by object type, you can select by wireframe family, and you'll select your objects as you see fit.

Selection of the Fittest

Of course, the easiest thing to do is to select something and then go to Solo mode. Work with the objects there, and then go back to normal mode.

But you can also use Solo mode as a temporary state to further narrow down your selection. This technique is based on the original Solo mode cardinal rule: only selected objects will show in Solo mode. If you're already in Solo mode, you can select a subset of objects, pop back out to normal mode, and quickly pop back into Solo mode. You'll only bring the selected objects back with you. Depending on the number of objects in Solo mode, you can directly select everything you want to remain selected or select those objects you want to get rid of, followed by a Select Inverse command.

Figure 4.40 is an example of the Solo mode winnowing process using the Select Inverse command. First the column elements in Figure 4.40a were brought into Solo mode. The objects making up the column base needed to temporarily disappear. So we selected the items and then, from the pop-up menu on the Selection Palette, chose Select Inverse (also ⌘-Shift-A/Ctrl+Shift+A). See Figure 4.40b. A quick click on the Solo button exited Solo mode, then an immediate click reactivated it again, having successfully gotten rid of the unwanted column base (see Figure 4.40c).

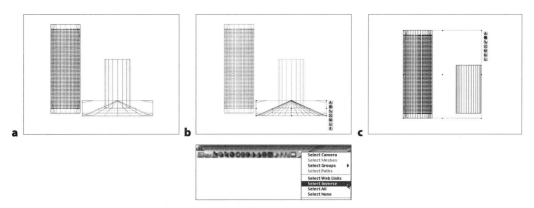

Figure 4.40 Column construction and the solo deselect process: a) Side view of two columns; b) in Solo mode, deselecting the base of column on right; c) after exiting and reentering Solo mode: the pared down wireframes.

Similarly, you can use Solo mode to cut down clutter while you make changes to your selection, exit Solo mode and add another object to the selection, enter Solo mode again and make further changes. To add objects to Solo mode, select all the objects before leaving Solo mode. Leave Solo mode. Shift-click the next object to select it. Go back to Solo mode for further refinements, if necessary.

Here's another example of the way to use Solo mode to successfully deselect some objects. Figure 4.41 shows the top view of a set of tori. From top view, it's a mess. The object here is to place a set of radial lights inside the tunnel created by the booleans. From top view, it's hard to know how to click to select the objects. Selecting by object yields all three of them (see Figure 4.41b). Using Shift-click to deselect will result in a never ending "deselect this while selecting, that, that, and the other one." The smart way to do it is to take those objects to Solo mode (see Figure 4.41c and d) deselect the ones you don't want, and then emerge from Solo mode with the one object selected. Figure 4.41e shows the result of the process.

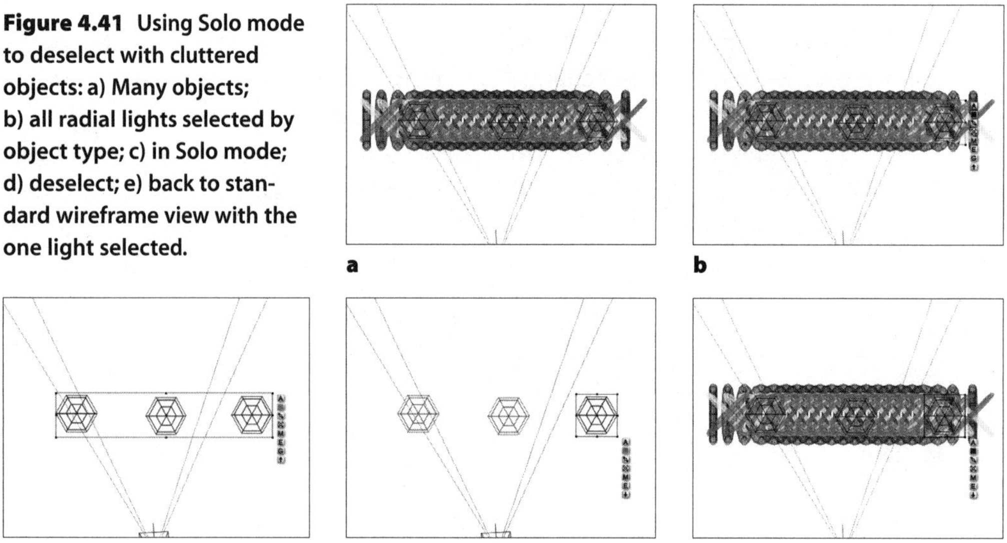

Figure 4.41 Using Solo mode to deselect with cluttered objects: a) Many objects; b) all radial lights selected by object type; c) in Solo mode; d) deselect; e) back to standard wireframe view with the one light selected.

Rendering in Solo Mode

When you render in Solo mode, you will render only those objects that you see in that mode.

IMPORTING OBJECTS

Bryce performs many functions wonderfully, but detailed 3D modeling is not one of its strong points. You'll often discover that the object you need to add just that special something to your scene is impossible to create by clumping together cylinders and cubes, no matter how artfully it is done. Then it's time to leave the confines of Bryce and turn to another 3D program with better modeling capabilities, or perhaps to third-party suppliers of pre-modeled objects. But once you have your finely crafted chair or sword or Ferrari, how do you get it into Bryce? Many of the innovations introduced in Bryce 4 are concerned with helping Bryce to communicate better with the outside, non-Brycean world. Bryce 4 is much happier than its ancestors were to allow you to use objects created in other 3D programs, and will import objects created in a number of different formats.

How to Import a 3D Object

To import a 3D model into Bryce, select Import Object from the File menu. A dialog box will appear, allowing you to navigate to your object. There is a checkbox at the bottom of the dialog box. Checking it makes Bryce scan every item in the current folder to see if it is a legal object type to import into Bryce. This slows down your search considerably, especially if you have to navigate through some crowded folders to get to your target location for the model. We suggest unchecking it and keeping it unchecked until you reach your destination folder.

After you've selected your object, Bryce imports it, complete with the ceremonial progress bar. The larger and more complex the object, the longer it will take, and the more RAM you have to assign to Bryce to successfully import the object.

Once inside Bryce, the object is considered a mesh object. You can perform the same type of edits that you would to any other object. Select it by type using the Meshes option in the Select Options pop-up menu. (The Manual tells you that you can select all meshes by clicking the Stones icon on the Selection Palette. Don't believe it.) Change the object's size, position, or orientation. Duplicate it. Assign it a unique family identity. Give it a material setting. But most importantly, mesh objects (including Bryce's own stones) have an editor all their own for special surface smoothing.

Edit Mesh dialog box

Since meshes are faceted surfaces, your models *could* look quite hackneyed when brought into Bryce. Happily, Bryce supplies a means to get around the faceted look and round out the object. The Edit Mesh dialog box (or Mesh Editor) enables you to smooth the object's surface. When Bryce smoothes, it doesn't add more polygons, but examines what is there and interpolates a smoother surface. The same routine is employed by the Terrain Editor for creating terrain surfaces out of grayscale data.

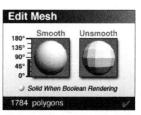

So, when you enter the Mesh Editor (⌘-E for Macs, Ctrl+E for Windows, or click the E icon, or click the Edit Terrain/Object icon on the Edit Palette), there are two buttons and a slider. Although the thumbnail images look like preview windows, they are actually buttons (see Figure 4.42). To smooth the object, click the Smooth button on the left. To unsmooth, click the right button. The slider is for setting the amount

Figure 4.42 The Edit Mesh dialog box.

of smoothness. The numbers correspond to the angle that will be smoothed. The default, at 85°, means that planes at less-than-perpendicular angles will be smoothed into a curve, whereas those at perpendicular angles (90°) and greater will remain sharp angles.

When you click the button, Bryce performs two passes. When it has completed those passes, click the check mark. If you change your mind, you cannot click a Cancel button. To leave the Edit Mesh dialog box, you *must* click the checkmark. To change the mesh back to its former faceted state, you'll have to click the Unsmooth button. Also, once you set the smooth angle to an angle other than the default 85°, it is not automatically set back to the default position the next time you access the

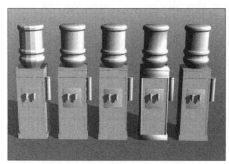

Figure 4.43 The facets of this water cooler were smoothed with several different settings in the Edit Mesh dialog box.

Edit Mesh dialog box. Besides knowing what the setting is and manually dragging the slider to that location, the only other way to reset it is to quit and relaunch Bryce (selecting Edit > Reset To Defaults will not reset it).

If you change the setting to a higher number, you'll get some interesting curvature to the image. In Figure 4.43, the water cooler model has gone through some different smoothing sets. The left model is plain unsmoothed. Next to it is one that is set lower than the default. The center cooler is smoothed with the default settings. The fourth cooler is smoothed at near-maximum settings. The right cooler is smoothed at default settings, clicking the Smooth button twice.

Import Formats

Bryce imports 3D file formats based on the plug-ins in the Bryce applications plug-in folder. If there's a plug-in for a format in the folder, then Bryce can import it. As of Bryce 4.0.1, the list of formats that Bryce will import is impressive (see Table 4.2).

Extension	Format
.3mf/.3dmf	QuickDraw 3D
.3ds	3D Studio [MAX]
.b3d	Bryce 3D
.cob/.scn	Caligari TrueSpace
.ddf	USGS Digital Data File
.dem	USGS or VistaPro DEM
.dxf	AutoCAD
.elev	World Construction Set
.hf	Rayshade Heightfield
.id4	Infini-D
.lws/.lwo	Lightwave
.obj	Wavefront
.pgm	Portable Gray Map
.rds	Ray Dream Studio
.vsa	VideoScape
.wrl	VRML 1.0

Table 4.2 3D graphics formats that can be imported into Bryce 4.

There's not enought room here to describe in detail the ins and outs of importing each of these formats into Bryce; we'll make a few general comments, then briefly discuss the formats you'll encounter most often.

Hopefully, any 3D model that you choose to bring into Bryce will have been intelligently constructed. It should not be a single object, but should be composed of numerous objects corresponding to logical groups within the larger item. For example, a model of a motorcycle might be composed of a body part (or parts), a window, tires, trim, and so on. Once the model is in Bryce, you can select each item individually (using the Select Options pop-up menu or by Control/Ctrl+clicking the object and using the contextual menu) and assign it a characteristic material: bright shiny red for the body group, glass for the window, flat black for the tires, and reflective metal for the trim (see Figure 4.44). While you're at it, give the components descriptive names, if they don't already have them. You can also choose which objects need smoothing in the Edit Mesh dialog box. Come up with your own groupings of objects and assign them to families.

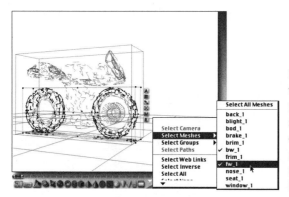

Figure 4.44 A model of a motorcycle in OBJ format, imported into Bryce. The individual parts of the bike already had names; we show the Select Options pop-up menu expanded to display the meshes that comprise the object. The two tires are selected, ready to be assigned to a new family, and to have a suitable tire-like material applied.

TIP: *If there are lots of little bitsy items in the model, increasing the wireframe resolution may help you more easily make out what is what.*

DXF

DXF stands for Digital Exchange Format, a 3D format invented by Autodesk, Inc. It's among the oldest—if not the oldest—interchange file format used by 3D modelers. The file format is in ASCII text, and describes flat surfaces with polygons. There is no such thing as a curved line in a DXF format, just the presence of many polygons joined together in such a way as to appear curved. In a harsh way, a sphere is a multi-polygonal surface, a geodesic dome.

Although this popular format is ubiquitous, it is at the bottom of the 3D-model-format food chain, an unevolved file format creature. The type of information required to represent curved surfaces will require lots and lots of polygons. Lots of polygons calls for a larger file size, and a larger file size means more work for Bryce. But it's there, and it can be used to bring very non-landscapish objects into Bryce.

OBJ

The Wavefront OBJ format is one of the most common formats you'll encounter when downloading 3D objects from various third-party sources; it's also the file used when transferring figures from Poser to Bryce. It's much more compact than DXF—exporting a file as an OBJ instead of a DXF can easily save 50% in file size. OBJ also can include detailed material specifications, so your Poser figure can appear in Bryce wearing the same clothing you gave it in Poser. If there is an accompanying material for the model, it will be in a .MTL file that needs to be located in the same folder as your OBJ file when importing into Bryce. The OBJ format also deals with curved surfaces rather nicely—you probably won't need to smooth imported OBJ meshes once you bring them into Bryce.

3DS

The native file format of the 3D world's 800-pound gorilla, 3D Studio MAX, 3DS turns up just about everywhere. 3DS files are similar to DXF files (not surprising, since 3D Studio was produced by a division of Autodesk). Usually they carry no material information, and they arrive in your scene with their polygons clearly showing. A trip to the Edit Mesh dialog box for a bit of smoothing is definitely called for!

3DMF

3DMF is the file format specific to QuickDraw 3D, a component of Apple's QuickTime. Objects saved in the 3DMF (3D Metafile) format can be imported to Bryce. The 3DMF file format does a very good job of defining (or closely approximating) curves, and imported 3DMF meshes do not improve much with smoothing. Alas, Apple has announced that QuickDraw 3D is history (it's moving its 3D efforts to OpenGL) so 3DMF's importance as a file intechange format will most likely fade in the near future.

Tips for Importing

So, before you import an image, are there any things you can do to make the process easier? More foolproof? Here are a few tips:

- *The Polygon-Memory ratio.* First, know that the greater the number of polygons in your model, the greater the amount of memory that is required to import and work with the model. Also, the more polygons, the slower Bryce will work when handling the model in both wireframe and rendering modes.

- *How you export can make a difference.* Different 3D modeling applications have different options to export a model. The options vary from application to application, but there are options that will result in models that import more successfully. If you find that a model is missing faces or is otherwise strange, then try re-exporting it from your modeling application using a different export option.

- *Selectively reduce model resolution.* While you're working on the model, reduce its resolutions in smart ways to reduce the overall polygon count. A cube needs only six faces, ever. If for some reason you have more detail in that cube, you'll force Bryce to deal with more unnecessary detail than it needs to. Find ways to make your models simpler where you can get away with it.

Don't Model It Yourself

If you want to get your hands on a ready-made model, there are 3D data "clip art" companies that have libraries of models available. In addition to the sets of models that are commercially available, there is an ftp site that has an extensive set of models created and uploaded by 3D artists from all over the world. It's called Avalon, and you can reach it by ftp or via the Web. Usage rights for each model vary and are determined by the artist/owner who uploaded the model. Check it out at http://avalon.viewpoint.com/.

- *Viewpoint Data Laboratories.* Viewpoint has an extensive (and growing!) selection of models of just about anything and everything. They have a four-tiered level of detail: The Titanium Collections are the highest resolution, and are out of Bryce's league (unless, of course, you're that Guinness RAM Book of Records candidate). The Platinum, Gold, and Silver Collections contain models that are progressively lower in resolution, suitable for gaming environments, Websites, or as 3D Clip Art for work using desktop machines. Their

Website usually includes a small assortment of models you can download for free: http://www.viewpoint.com.

• *Zygote.* Specializing in human forms and in characters, Zygote has a growing collection of models, many of which have been used in motion picture and gaming titles. They even sell models specifically in Bryce format: http://www.zygote.com.

• *Acuris.* This firm's collection of 3D models is very strong in architectural items (including furnishings), animals, and vehicles: http://www.acuris.com.

MOVING ON...

You've learned about objects in this chapter, and the camera and the scene in the previous chapter. We will continue our discussion with everything you wanted to know about editing objects, in Chapter 6, "Editing and the Internal Bryce Grid." Bur first, we'll take a bit of time out to familiarize you with all manner of things to help you run Bryce in the smoothest, most efficient way possible in Chapter 5, "Streamline Your Brycing."

CHAPTER FIVE
Streamline Your Brycing

IN THIS CHAPTER...

- Setting up your Mac or PC for efficient Brycing

- The most efficient order to set up scenes

- Effective rendering and batch rendering

- Using Bryce's Display Palette controls for efficiency

- Other general Bryce facts concerning speed and efficiency

- Working with Bryce's Preset Libraries

- Working with Bryce's palettes

- Preferences setup

In this chapter, we tell you how to optimize your Bryce working method and answer the question, "Given the time it takes to render scenes, what is the most efficient way to work in Bryce?" Different activities in Bryce cost more in processing time. It's best when working in Bryce to postpone for as long as possible introducing the effects that cost the most. There are many steps needed to create a scene; ensure that you are getting the most out of the early stages. Then when you perform test renders to ensure that your image is going as planned, you won't have to wait for anything unnecessary to render.

When Bryce 1.0 first came out, it worked on 68K Mac OS machines that were much slower than today's (equivalent to the PC 386 and 486). Render time was at an all-time premium. Renders were time consuming (often overnight!), so it was of utmost importance to keep the most processor-intensive step for last. Happily, over time, computers have gotten faster. From the 68K processor to various generations of the Power PC processor, Mac OS computers have leapt to higher speeds. The same processor speed improvements that have taken place on the Mac have been echoed on the PC side, with ever faster Pentium-class microprocessors. (Bryce 2 entered the PC scene just before the advent of the Pentium II.)

With each speed jump, the old Bryce 1.0 render that took overnight got shortened to a lunch hour, a coffee break, a quick phone call. Bryce has seen speed improvements due to faster machines and render-engine optimization. However, the hardware speed enhancements have allowed room to build additional features into the software. Each new version of Bryce has seen the inclusion of options that weigh down the render process again, from lights and imported objects to animation and volume materials. Thus, whether you have a computer that is simply slower, or you want to take advantage of the power-hungry goodies that are a part of Bryce 4, you'll be better off if you think in terms of efficient working in Bryce.

The basic idea is to work smart, so that the time-consuming stuff—rendering—is not bogged down in all the fine detail until the very end of the process.

OPTIMAL SETTINGS

If you want to work efficiently in Bryce, you'll need all of your computer's processing power available for all those calculations Bryce needs to make. We'll explore some of the settings you can make both to your computer and within the software to make Bryce run at its peak.

Your Computer

Make your computer system run efficiently. To do this, free it from any unnecessary activities that it has to perform. First, make sure that you don't have extensions or programs loading at startup that you don't need. Those blinking eyeballs may be cute, but those and other toys take RAM and CPU cycles away from where you want them dedicated: a bare-bones system, and Bryce.

Macintosh

Now that your system is running lean and mean when it starts up, do the most important thing: For your main Finder windows—the root level for your disk drive(s) and your main folders—set the View Options so that the Calculate folder sizes option is off. Do it *now*! Yes, right now! (You'll thank us later!) Calculate folder sizes is handy when you're trying to find out where the heck all that disk space went when you have to clear off a couple hundred megabytes, but it is not practical for everyday work on the computer, since the system wrests every spare cycle to calculate how much stuff is in each folder. With disk drives ranging from 10 GB and up, that's a lot of calculation that is *not* being devoted to where it should be: Bryce.

This next matter is not as cut and dried as the previous one, but having your computer set for File Sharing slows down the computer. If you have but one computer, go to the Control Panels and turn that damn thing off! If you do have a network, then it's not so simple. You'd be best off doing stealth networking—get by with the minimum amount of shared networking that you can. You can access other computers over a network without enabling File Sharing on your own computer, though when another server goes down, it will take yours with it.

PowerBook

Those PowerBooks are handy things, aren't they? We love 'em. Both Susan's and Victor's primary "Bryce Book" computers are PowerBooks: Portable. Powerful. There's one problem, though. With a PowerBook running Bryce, it seems that by the second or third render pass, the speed of the render slows to a crawl. It's not because all of a sudden Bryce is getting down to the nitty-gritty of the render, either. Rather, the PowerBook is being operated on some assumptions about your behavior with your computer. If you are not tapping the keyboard or moving the mouse, then you're not working, and the computer can lay idle—a smart move for battery consumption, but a bad assumption for Bryce users. Rather that find yourself in the ridiculous position of constantly caressing the PowerBook's trackpad to keep the computer rendering at full speed, you can change your settings in the Energy Saver Control Panel.

The Energy Saver Control Panel has an Advanced Settings section. In the bottom half, there's an option called "Allow processor cycling" (see Figure 5.1). Uncheck it. Make sure it's unchecked for

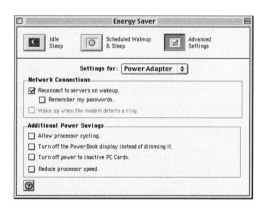

Figure 5.1 **The Energy Saver Control Panel for the Mac OS PowerBook: Disable the Allow processor cycling option to keep renders moving at maximum speed.**

both Power Adapter and Battery (see the pop-up menu toward the top of the Control Panel). That will take care of the insidious processor slowdown.

Windows

If you're using Windows, here are some basic things to make your computer run more efficiently. Don't include anything in the Startup Group unless it's absolutely vital. Once your computer has started up, make sure that you have adequate swap space on your hard drive. Let Windows run the memory management. To keep things running smoothly, run ScanDisk and Defrag periodically to keep your hard disk in healthy shape. Also, anytime you experience a crash (from any Windows software or application) that forces you to restart the computer, run ScanDisk.

Bryce

Now that you've set up the computer for efficiency, turn your attention to making Bryce efficient. Here, your strategy is the same: Make sure that you give as much time to your CPU as you can for Brycing.

What are the things that might take away unnecessary processing time? Most important is the Nano Preview's Auto Update setting. For standard work in scenes, if you've a reasonably speedy computer, you won't notice the time lag. But once you start introducing render-intensive settings to your scene (especially involving Volumetric World or objects with volume materials), you'll notice that having Auto Update switched on causes Bryce to become unreasonably lethargic. If you're used to the brisk pace of Bryce running without it, then when it's on, you'll notice how Bryce gets the blahs. The Auto Update option is a wonderful thing to have on *when you want it on*, but we recommend staying aware of those times when it can slow you down. Also, the Nano Preview does have the option to perform full renders; use that *only* when necessary to get a little more detail in that preview.

Having the Sky & Fog options set to Auto Update is a different thing; it is a matter of personal taste plus the speed of your computer. If you are manipulating objects or camera perspective, you won't encounter any updating. The Sky & Fog Auto Update is not as obtrusive as the Nano Preview. When working with the sky, you may want Auto Update on or off. If you want to see a move-by-move update of what you're doing in the Sky & Fog Palette, but your computer is a slow one, this may be a time to set the Nano Preview to Sky Only and turn Auto Update on. When the Nano Preview and the Sky & Fog Options are *both* set to Auto Update, the priority goes first to the Nano Preview and then to the scene in general. Make your adjustments accordingly.

Auto-Key and File Size

When you first launch Bryce, it automatically generates all new scenes in a state called Auto-Key; you will automatically be working in a state called Auto-Key On. Auto-Key exists to make work in Bryce animation easier. However, Auto-Key is not at all helpful for the simple creation of still images. In the process of setting up each object in the scene, Bryce is creating room in the data file for all that animation information. If you don't intend to animate, you're filling lots of extra room with unneeded fluff that will make your scene files larger and make opening and saving them take a long time, especially if you'll be adding lots of objects to your scene. Turn it off, turn it off, turn that Auto-Key off! To do so, go to the Time Palette at the bottom of Bryce's interface and, on the triangle-indicated popup menu at the lower right, make sure that the Auto-Key item is unchecked. For a detailed discussion of Auto-Key's uses, see Chapter 14, "The Fourth Dimension: Time and Animation."

The procedures described here are a couple of important catch-all time savers. In the next sections, we'll discuss some more strategies for working efficiently in Bryce.

SETTING UP YOUR SCENE

The first step toward efficient working in Bryce is setting up your scene and your working conditions in the program.

Start Small

When setting up your scene, keep in mind that you're working in a three-dimensional world that you will eventually render to a two-dimensional image. When choosing your file resolution, don't think along the lines of, "Well, my final resolution has to be 1500 × 800 pixels," and then create a scene with that render size. You have an entire three-dimensional world there inside your scene, no matter the

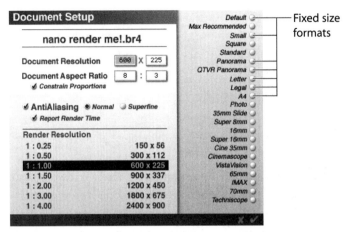

Figure 5.2 The Document Setup dialog box, with fixed sizes indicated.

render size, so take liberties—take *small* liberties. Start small by using Bryce's default setting or one of the settings listed in the Document Setup dialog box or the Render pop-up menu (see Figure 5.2).

When you're first building your scene, it's a good idea to make sure that the scene size is not larger than your monitor size, and that you start with your scene and render at a 1:1 ratio. When your scene is smaller than your monitor, you'll have all your objects on the monitor, present and accounted for (it's a pain to find items that are located off your monitor, and Bryce doesn't allow for a quick zoom out to take a look at the scene in a smaller view, as it does in Render mode). When you are building and rendering at a 1:1 ratio, then there's no guesswork translating to the object location here and where it renders over there. Save those fancy ratios and large scene and render sizes for later, after you've completed the scene building process.

The Document Setup dialog box, with a few exceptions, enables you to accomplish these two efficient-scene setup steps easily. Most of the size ratios that are listed on the right of the dialog box will not go higher than the maximum allowed by your computer. In Figure 5.2, the exceptions are noted as Fixed size formats. No matter what size your monitor is, those options have fixed dimensions. The left side of the dialog box, containing Document Resolution and Render Resolution, allows you to set the scene-to-render sizes at different multiples.

There are actually two different ratios at work here. First is the proportion ratio that you see in the Document Resolution section. The default is 4:3—that is, four horizontal units to three vertical units.

Second, the Render Resolution section has a list of ratios, beginning with 1:0.25 and ending with 1:4.00. These are the ratios between scene size and render size. The default is 1:1. It offers the simplest and most painless way to work. To render at double the size of the scene, select 1:2.00. To render at half-size, select 1:0.50.

If you need to create your scene at half the size that's currently indicated, enter the numbers from that ratio listing in the Document Resolution field above; the numbers below, with all the scene-to-render ratios, will adjust themselves accordingly, and you'll be set at 1:1. (This is especially helpful if you have a small monitor.)

If you know ahead of time that the scene you're working on will eventually become extremely wide or extremely tall, you may not want to go to the Document Setup dialog box just yet. If your scene will have many objects and you need to peer at it a lot from top view, hold off a bit. An extreme aspect ratio will make things more difficult to see when you're looking at top view. A little bit later, when you have most of your objects placed, go ahead and narrow the dimensions.

When you change an image from a basic size ratio to one that is extreme, you may have to change the camera angle somewhat. Bryce gives the newly resized scene its best guess for camera angle and so on, but invariably, you'll have to adjust a little bit to get things just so.

Placing Objects in Your Scene: Eric's *Mountain Eroded* Image

Now that you've optimized your settings for the overall way Bryce works, and you have your scene size established, it's time to focus on ways to optimize the scene creation process. In this section, we'll take a look at a scene created by Eric Wenger, *Mountain Eroded*, using it as an example in discussing what to do during the early part of the creation process, and what to do later.

This scene began with the creation of a distant high mountain range and a foreground range that was shaded by hills. Early on, Eric established the sun's direction.

First, he created the mountains with four terrains. Two terrains are the large mountains in the distance, then there is a lower set of hills, which is eventually to be shaded by a cloud, and then there is a hilly area in the foreground (see Figure 5.3).

Because the cloud shade is a part of the overall composition, creating the shade was the next step. For that, a cylinder was placed above and assigned a cloudy material setting. Here is one case where materials are established early in the

Figure 5.3 *Mountain Eroded* series: a) The terrains in front view; b) part a) shown in top view; c) top view in wireframe for added clouds; d) top view with clouds rendered—cylinder cloud casts shadow on mid-ground terrain; e) after cylinder cloud placement (with and without the rest of the sky and clouds). *Art by Eric Wenger.*

a

b

c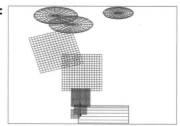

d

e

scene, as the shadow is needed to establish the basic look of the scene. Notice, though, that it was the last element to be established for the composition. Figure 5.3 shows the top view render with and without the clouds in place.

At this point, the other clouds were added to the scene and placed, since they, too, are part of the overall composition of Bryce objects. The final scene before render is fairly complete; a mood is well established long before the terrains have been given custom materials settings.

From this creation-order process, we can draw some conclusions about efficient working in Bryce. We'll discuss them next.

Creation and Composition Always Come Before Material Goods

The single most important thing you can do to save time while working in Bryce is to refrain from assigning any material settings to your objects until the end of your scene creation process. When you first launch Bryce, all primitive objects take on a generic smooth gray surface. Breaking with past tradition, Bryce 4 now creates terrains with automatic material settings, for some ridiculous reason (probably related to increases in processor speed). If you want to live by the "first use gray terrains until you're ready to work on materials" suggestion, you'll either need to hold down the Control/Ctrl key when creating a terrain or change the material back to default gray in the Materials Lab (click the lower bronze button at the side of the grid, near the Volume Color item). For your initial setup, plain gray everywhere is fine. Work first on the overall shape of your world and what goes where before you begin tinkering with the intricacies of materials for each object. And if you have a scene with any complexity at all (more than one object), you *will* have to do a bit of tinkering.

In *Mountain Eroded*, Eric first created the terrain mountain shapes. Fairly early on, he established the camera angle on his scene. (Depending on your working style, you may want to go with this or not. Sometimes it's fun to create a scene and then later discover other ways of looking at it. Take your pick.)

If you need to provide contrast between one object and another while setting up the scene, change one object's color. In the Materials Lab, assign it a different Diffuse Color. You'll be able to distinguish the new object from the others, but you haven't traversed into time-consuming render territory.

There are two different strategies for cutting down on the render time. The first is the one taken here in this *Mountain Eroded* example. Don't assign any material settings, other than perhaps a change in the diffuse color to distinguish one object from another. When you need clouds to be a part of your composition, you'll be able to see them fine.

The second strategy, using the Textures On/Off render button, reduces most materials settings to naught. (The color comes from the Diffuse Color setting and the sun's color.) This will take any materials settings and reduce them to a plain-vanilla plastic, and the object's color will be determined by any colors set in the color swatch controls (exception: if your objects have reflection or transparency, that will show up). The sky will be a flat color, determined by whatever is set as the No Atmosphere color (see Chapter 11, "Brycean Skies," for more informa-tion). This is a good thing to come back to if you find that you need to return to an earlier stage of work in Bryce after assigning materials to your object.

Figure 5.4 *Mountain Eroded* with Textures Off: efficient but unsuccessful.

But there are times when you do *not* want to use this strategy. In the *Mountain Eroded* image, where the spheres were made into clouds for the sake of composition, consider how unsuccessful a Textures Off render would be as all the clouds return to their native spheres, and the opaque cylinder above casts a threatening shadow indeed (see Figure 5.4). Yuck.

Now Blue Sky It

When you are focusing on your sky settings, you'll need to make sure that Textures On/Off is set to On, and it's a good idea to have the Fast Preview mode shut off, since it tends to render the skies inaccurately.

Here are three ways for getting your skies to render quickly. (Your skies will render more quickly than terrains with lots of bump or other details, anyhow.)

• Use the Nano Preview to get a feel for your sky. Set it to either show Sky Only or Full Scene. Set it to Auto Update if you want it to take precedence over everything else when you are working. (When you're done with that portion of work on your scene, switch Auto Update off again!)

• Work inside the Sky Lab and look at the preview window to check out the results of your design decisions for your skies.

• If you are working directly from the Sky & Fog Palette in your main working window, drag a marquee around a partial strip of the image. Set the Sky Options menu to Auto Update (and switch *off* Auto Update in the Nano Preview mode). This is the only place Bryce will render, thereby giving you faster rendered responses to your atmospheric choices.

Now experiment with abandon to get just the right sky setting. Each time you make a change, your preview or strip of image renders again, showing you in a few brief passes what the sky will be like.

Congratulations! You've accomplished much so far in setting up your scene. How much longer would these renders take if you'd included the sluggish parts? Now that you've got everything else out of the way, it's time to bring on that time-consuming stuff!

The Costly Things in BryceLife

What is the time-consuming stuff? The surface attributes of objects, primarily three-dimensional, texture-based materials, cause the rendering process to take longer. Even so, some parts of the materials settings are costlier than others. What are the costly parts of the materials? Reflection, transparency, bump height, and high-contrast detail, and the most extravagant part, volumetric materials. The following list describes these as well as other parts of Bryce that make for expensive render times.

- *Reflection.* As the ray is traced to find the color for that pixel, the material bounces the ray from here to there to some other place to get the final color. Higher physics notwithstanding, the shortest distance between two points is a straight line. By adding reflection, you introduce bouncing rays, and the render time increases.

- *Transparency.* Bryce needs to calculate how much of the ray stays with the object and how much goes through the object to whatever lies beyond. Transparency is a variation on the not-so-short distance between two places, since part of the ray travels beyond the normal stopping place.

- *Bump.* Each individual bump needs to be calculated, and because there's a change in the surface, the new element—height—is added to the width and depth equations. Also, the introduction of indentation in the surface structure results in tiny shadows and light shifts, thereby giving Bryce more to do when it comes time to antialias the image. A bumpy, mottled surface takes longer to render than a smooth surface does.

- *High-Contrast Detail.* When there is a lot of color contrast in a close space, a lot of calculation will take place, especially during the antialiasing pass of the render cycle. Bryce will look to the surrounding eight pixels to determine the final color of the one in the center. If there's high color contrast in those pixels, then Bryce needs to look more carefully to determine the final color.

- *Lighting Costs.* For every light source in your scene, Bryce has to calculate its effect on each object, down to every pixel. The more lights you have in your scene, the more complex is every calculation in the render process, and the lengthier the render time.

- *Volumetric Properties.* Volumetric properties come in three flavors: volumetric materials that are applied to objects, volume visible lights, and Volumetric World, where the entire atmosphere is filled with substance. Choosing to include one of these will significantly increase your render time. Do not—repeat, do *not*—use all three! Be judicious; choose *only* what you need.

- *Imported DXF Objects.* DXF objects, when imported into Bryce, may significantly increase rendering time, depending on their size and complexity and the number of objects in the group.

Figure 5.5 A Bryce scene with volume clouds rendered under different conditions: a) Normal render; b) Texture Off; c) Fast Preview.

What Kind of Time Difference Will Materials Make?

Figures 5.5a through c show a Bryce scene rendered using Bryce's various render options. There are volume clouds there in the lower parts of the scene, amid the fog. Besides the normal render (part a) and the Texture Off render (part b), there is the quick preview for seeing how the scene looks with textures (part c). The quick preview has small blocky-pixel artifacts, but it is great for a peek while work is in progress.

So what kind of time differences does the rendering of materials make? The scene was rendered by different machines under different rendering conditions. In Table 5.1, the results of each of the render reports are listed for comparison. The left column lists different types of computers, to show the relative speed of different types of processors—three Macintosh and two Pentium processors.

	Default Render (Spatial Optimization Low)			
CPU	Txt Off	Fast	Both	Regular
Mac PPC 8100/100	36:10	20:39	17:04	59:23
Mac PPC 8100/100 with G3/333 upgrade card	5:12	3:01	2:18	8:27
Mac G3/400	4:16	2:38	2:00	7:11
Pentium Pro 200 MHz	9:37	6:49	4:30	18:58
Pentium 350 MHz	5:46	4:03	2:40	11:03

Table 5.1 Render Time Comparisons.

The scene has some terrains, each with material settings, an infinite plane set to reflective water, and haze and fog, with low-lying cloud objects. Those low-lying clouds have volumetric textures, making them render-resource hogs.

The results of the Fast Preview are telling. Fast Preview is the fastest option of all, faster even than the No Texture option. Fast Preview, in this case, completed its render in roughly one-third the time of a normal render. Thus, as you begin working with textures in the creation of your scene, use the Fast Preview option! Use it as an intermediate means of checking the overall look of your scene. Once your scene passes muster, then use the regular render method to do the final honing of your scene.

The use of Spatial Optimization does affect render time. We used the default setting, Spatial Optimization Low. In one test, using Spatial Optimization High shaved only 2 seconds off the regular render time. The same scene rendered with Spatial Optimization off had only a difference of 10 seconds from the default. For this scene, at least, Spatial Optimization doesn't yield much—and since it's already switched on for you, there's no sense in our making a big deal about it. For scenes with lots of objects, though, be sure to use Spatial Optimization High. More about this in Chapter 13, "Render Unto Bryce."

Note: The render sample and tests we conducted here compare different rendering conditions for different computer systems. There is a place to go to compare the render times for a single Bryce scene. Run by Fernando Corrado, whose name is on the Bryce splash screen as the Quality Assurance Lead, the Render Times page will show you how different computer systems stack up against one another in rendering the same Bryce scene file. Check out the http://www.gauchito.com/bryce/render_times Web site.

Now that we have discussed the general approach to the working order recommended to maximize efficiency in Bryce, we'll turn to areas of Bryce other than rendering where you can shave your work time.

DISPLAY CONTROLS

The small palette to the right of the scene window holds two sets of controls. They're there to make life easier. The top part controls the displays and the bottom part controls wireframes (see Figure 5.6). For this discussion, we'll talk mostly about the Display controls, since we covered wireframes in Chapter 4, "Brycean Objects." We will briefly discuss how to eke out as much from wireframes as possible though.

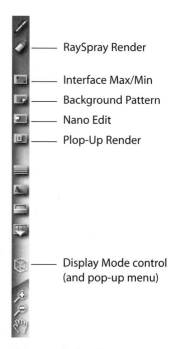

RaySpray Render

Interface Max/Min

Background Pattern

Nano Edit

Plop-Up Render

Display Mode control
(and pop-up menu)

Figure 5.6 The Display Palette, with controls labeled.

Interface Max/Min

The top Display control, Interface Max/Min, determines where the Bryce palettes will be. You have two basic options with Bryce: snuggled next to the scene window or huddled next to the edges of the monitor.

Which one do you choose? It's a personal preference, so choose whatever suits you. If you have a large monitor, you'll find that you're forced to choose between a long mouse journey to the menu bar (Interface Minimum) or a long mouse journey to the controls surrounding the scene (Interface Maximum).

If you are working with animation, more of your timeline will be visible when you use Interface Maximum. Also, if you are working with Bryce on a Mac OS machine, Interface Maximum constantly displays your menu bar, including when you are in Bryce's "rooms" (Terrain Editor, Materials Lab, Deep Texture Editor, Sky Lab, and Advanced Motion Lab). If you need to go back and forth from Bryce to another app (as book authors do), you'll find Interface Maximum your choice for that simple convenience.

Background Pattern

Background patterns are a matter of personal preference. Choose the one you want from the pop-up menu (see Figure 5.7). You can have a textured or a smooth background appearance, or you can choose another color altogether. On the Macintosh, you can also select the options by pressing the Control-Option/Ctrl+Alt keys while typing the numbers: There are nine options on that menu, so numbers 1 through 9 each correspond to a different background pattern.

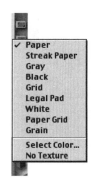

Figure 5.7
Background
Pattern pop-up
menu.

Background patterns are not saved with the scene file. When the application is open, background patterns are defined for the present. When you open or create a new scene file, your background is inherited from whatever the current settings are. The background preferences will stay that way until you change the settings in the pop-up menu during your current working session. If you happen to have your preferences set to Launch to Previous State, then the next time you launch Bryce, your chosen background will appear. If you have your preferences set to Launch to Default State, you will get the default gray paper background each time you launch Bryce.

Nano Edit: Dainty (and Fast) Manipulation

The Nano Editor allows you to make all of your camera adjustments in a smaller view. What does a smaller view mean? It means that instead of having to redraw your full-scene wireframe (at, say, 480 × 360 pixels) each time the camera moves, the Nano Editor displays it at a fraction of that size (160 × 120). And what does a fraction of that size mean? Not as many calculation cycles. And what do fewer cycles mean? Fewer cycles mean speed! The Nano Editor is a way to work faster in Bryce. When you have a complex scene file, with many objects in it, working in the Nano Editor will compensate for the slowdown in the regular-sized window display.

There are two ways to access the Nano Editor. The first, of course, is by switching it on using the control on the Display Palette. Then when you use the camera controls—the Camera Crosses, Banking, Field of View, and Trackball controls—you'll be working with a smaller window while you make your adjustments (see Figure 5.8).

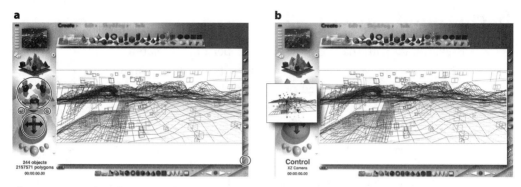

Figure 5.8 a) When the Nano Editor is switched on, the encircled controls will be affected; b) as the Trackball control is activated, a small window appears showing Trackball camera movements.

The second way to access the Nano Editor is on-the-fly. Hold down the space bar and Option key (Macintosh) or space bar and Alt key (Windows) and position your mouse inside the main scene window. The cursor changes to a rotation arrow (see Figure 5.9a). Once you begin dragging the mouse there, a small window appears, showing you live motion of the adjustments you make (Figure 5.9b). You can release the modifier keys once you've begun dragging the mouse. The range of motion is the same as for the Trackball. Dragging left and right rotates the scene; dragging up and down adjusts the tilt up and down. When you press the Command key (Ctrl key for Windows), you can move closer or farther from the center of the scene by dragging up and down (the tilt up and down is suspended while the Command or Ctrl key is pressed).

A simple mouse click on any of the palettes with the space bar and Option key (Macintosh) or space bar and Alt key (Windows) held down will reset the palettes to their default positions, so don't try this procedure indiscriminately.

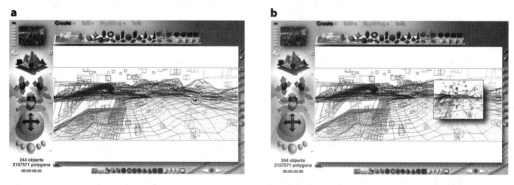

Figure 5.9 On-the-fly Nano Editor: a) Cursor changes to the rotation arrow when both the space bar and Option/Alt key are pressed; b) when the mouse is pressed, the Nano Edit window appears.

Plop-Up Render

The last option on the Display Palette to the right of the scene window is Plop-Up Render. When this option is on (the Display icon is red), your rendered area will plop up from the rest of the scene, separated from all the rest of the scene by a drop shadow. Next to the marquee are three controls. The large sphere is for Clear and Render. The smaller sphere lets you resume rendering inside the marqueed area.

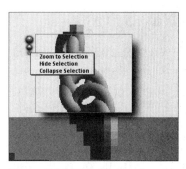

Figure 5.10 Plop-Up Render with its accompanying pop-up menu.

The triangle yields a pop-up menu for three more options: Zoom to Selection, Hide Selection, and Collapse Selection (see Figure 5.10).

If you don't want the Plop-Up Render window showing, you can still render in small areas. Use the Clear and Render button on the main Render Palette or use that ol' ⌘-Option-R (Macintosh) or Ctrl+Alt+R (Windows). The advantage to Plop-Up Render, once you get used to it (it does take a bit of getting used to, in our experience) is that you'll like having the Render button right there.

Zoom to Selection will reset your scene window so that it shows what's inside of the selection marquee. It will zoom in on the 2D Projection plane. If the aspect ratio of the scene window is different from the marqueed area, Bryce will set the new zoom so that the entire selected area is included in the new scene window view; there may be additional portions of the scene showing that weren't inside the selection marquee.

Hide Selection removes the selection marquee from view, without disabling Plop-Up Render altogether. If you select an area and then hide it, you can still render inside that area by using the Clear and Render button or keyboard shortcut. Once an area is hidden, though, the only way that you can see the selection area is to disable and then reenable Plop-Up Render by double-clicking the Plop Render On/Off tool on the Display Palette.

Collapse Selection will get rid of your selection entirely. The marquee goes away, and if you were to test it with a Clear and Render command, your entire scene would be rendered.

The state of the marqueed area is fragile, and it's all too easy to inadvertently drag a new one elsewhere in your scene area when you don't intend to. It's one of those irritating things that won't occur when you want it to and will occur precisely when you don't want it to.

Ray Spray

Speaking of rendering, the Ray Spray Render tool, new to Bryce 4, lives just above all the Display controls. It comes in handy for times when you prefer not to render your entire scene—when you just want to peek at a little corner of it, or when you, perhaps, rendered the whole scene, made a minor tweak in one area, and just want to see the results of that tweak. The Ray Spray Render tool provides a handy way to render bits and pieces of your scene when you're working in either wireframe or render mode. We discuss Ray Spray in some detail in Chapter 13, "Render Unto Bryce," but here are the basics, just for starters: Click the Ray Spray icon, and your cursor becomes a spray can. Drag the spray can across the parts of your scene that you're interested in, and pixel by pixel, the rendered image takes shape where you have sprayed.

Well-Tempered Wireframes

Working in wireframe view is the fastest way to view your scene, right? Well, yes and no. Viewing in wireframe is certainly faster than completely rendering the scene, especially while the scene is still evolving. But there are things you can do to make your computer draw the wireframe onscreen as quickly as possible. You also can reduce the clutter of wireframe objects when you have many of them placed in your scene.

Set up your wireframes so that they don't take more processing than they need. Check out the wireframe section in Chapter 4, "Brycean Objects" for many of the gory details. The basic idea, though, is that the greater the wireframe detail, the more your computer has to think about what it's showing, and the longer time it will take to display things. By lowering the Wireframe resolution you can make this as problem-free as possible, but you'll still run into an updating problem when you use the nudge keys to move objects around (more about nudging in the next chapter). With each move of the object with the nudge keys, the wireframe will snap from still mode to motion mode to still mode to motion mode. Since you're simply wanting to keep your object in motion in very controlled increments, that's a lot of unnecessary processing time. When you have three terrains and a handful of primitives, it won't matter, really. But when you get up there into the dozens, or even the hundreds (or thousands), of objects, Bryce will slow to a moribund crawl. Set all your wireframe resolutions to the lowest level of detail possible.

Another strategy for pepping Bryce out of a torpor is to change your wireframes so that they appear as boxes. Select the object; then from the Objects menu, choose Show as Box or use the shortcut ⌘-B/Ctrl+B. Rather than having to draw all the details of a terrain or torus or other shape, Bryce now has to draw only 12 straight lines to define the edges of the box. (In fact, when Bryce is faced with many objects and wireframe motion, it will momentarily draw all wireframes in Box mode so that it can keep up with your movements.) Figure 5.11 shows a comparison between wireframes when shown as boxes and as lattices in this image by Bill Ellsworth. To create the image, which contains 385 objects, Ellsworth changed all his wireframes to boxes. Even so, it was slow going in Bryce.

The other advantage to displaying some wireframes as boxes is that you can use the highest detail wireframe resolution for those objects you're currently working with, and use the least detailed form—Box mode—for everything else. Along with Static and Selected, you can place the lowest of the low—Box—into your list of wireframe options. Change into boxes the objects that you can ignore for now; you can always change them back later.

a

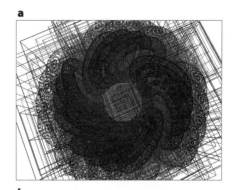

b

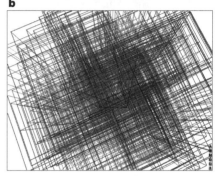

c

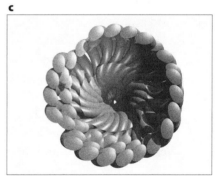

Figure 5.11 Bill Ellsworth wireframe series: a) Wireframe in Lattice mode; b) wireframe in Box mode; c) completed render.

Finally, you can apply the same lattice-to-box action to a set of grouped objects. (More on grouping in Chapter 6.) The group will be changed to a single box.

Wireframe Display Complexity and Animation

The amount of time that Bryce takes to display wireframes will affect the speed of wireframe playback and preview for animation. When Bryce is playing back a wireframe view of an animation sequence, it is not keeping strict time, but rather is playing back as fast as it can. (We've seen it lag slightly behind the actual time in the main window and zoom quickly faster than that time when working in the Advanced Motion Lab.) During playback, Bryce displays the wireframe resolution in Motion mode and will use whatever settings you've established in the Motion menu. You can adjust the Wireframe Preview to change the apparent speed for animation playback. To slow down the preview to nearly the same as actual time in the Advanced Motion Lab, change your Motion wireframe resolution to a high (or maximum) setting. If you have a slower computer and want to speed up the main wireframe view so it is closer to the actual time, then be sure that the motion resolution for wireframes is set to the minimum option, 8.

Flat Shaded Preview

In addition to Wireframe Preview and all of its vagaries and excitements, Bryce provides options that lie between the low-resolution wireframe and the ultra-high resolution ray-traced render. These options are accessed from the pop-up menu that appears when you press your mouse on the Display Modes control, located below the Wireframe controls on the Display/Wireframe Palette. The Flat Shaded Preview comes in two forms on both platforms, Sree3D and OpenGL, and a third for Windows only: Direct3D. Be warned, though, that all of these modes are flaky and are prone to grabbing large quantities of RAM for themselves and causing program crashes when used for long periods of time. When one of these options is chosen, the main scene window is displayed with Flat Shaded Preview. However, the preview is limited to only the main scene window. Other places where the wireframe view of the scene can be displayed (Nano Preview, Nano Editor, other previews in other places in Bryce) will all continue to be displayed as wireframe view.

The Flat Shaded Preview can be very helpful when you're trying to place the camera or another object within the nooks and crannies of a terrain (as we explained in Chapter 3). It has its limitations, however (you've never heard us say that about anything else in Bryce, have you?), especially with regard to the display of boolean objects (we'll talk more about that in Chapter 7). Another annoyance of Flat Shaded Preview is that you can't drag the camera, or even select it by clicking when in top view; you must choose it from the Select Options menu and then use the arrow keys or controls on the Edit Palette to move it around.

Make This Scene as Efficient as You Can!

Here's a scene on which you can practice all your newfound display shortcuts to make work in Bryce as streamlined as possible.

1. Open the scene file NANO RENDER ME! from the CD-ROM. It is quite a scene, with nearly 200 spheres, close to 50 tori, and a handful of the requisite terrains. In addition, just for kicks, it's in a lengthy wide format, just so you can see how the Nano Edit does not display the wireframe in the aspect ratio. (Phooey! Back in the days of Bryce 2, it actually did so.)

Try to make this scene work as smoothly as possible on your computer. There are three areas to make adjustments:

*   *Viewing Efficiency.* Make the wireframes as efficient as possible. Reduce the detail. Change objects to boxes. Group the tori and change the group to a box (see Figure 5.12).

*   *Working Efficiency.* Work in Nano Edit mode. Compare the way the camera tools work in Nano Edit versus the way they work in the normal wireframe scene.

*   *Render Efficiency.* This scene also happens to include a set of render doozies. All those lovely spheres are transparent, reflective, and slightly refractive, making them render hogs. To bypass them (alas, reflective and refractive materials are still rendered when you use Textures Off), try disabling the Nano Preview's Auto Update feature and working in Solo mode with the remainder of the objects if you want to work on placement of the other objects in your scene.

 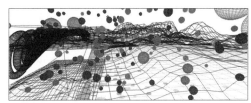

Figure 5.12 Wireframe shown as lattices and as boxes.

BATCH MANAGEMENT

Once you've completed your work on a scene, or a group of scenes, render them all later, when you're asleep or at the gym or watching your favorite soaps. You can do this by batch rendering. Batch rendering is similar on Macintosh and Windows, but there are differences. The basic way to batch render scenes is to drag multiple scene file icons and drop them onto the Bryce application icon. On the Macintosh, you can use an alias in place of either the scene file or the application icon. In Windows, you can use a shortcut in place of the Bryce application icon. (The Explorer's shortcut for a scene file does not work.)

You can begin a batch render whether Bryce is unlaunched or is already running. Once you begin a batch render, Bryce will render the first scene, then save both the scene file and the now-rendered image file, then open the next scene, render and save, and so continue until all the files are rendered, or until you stop the current render. (If you have a power outage, that will also stop a batch render, but we hope that never happens!)

Alas, Bryce does not let you batch render animations. Phooey. Of course, if you're rendering an animation that takes days or weeks to complete, the inability to batch render doesn't matter. But when your set of animations consist of small tests, such as examples that might be part of, say, a chapter or two on Bryce animation for a book on Bryce, then batch render for animations would come in mighty handy.

Suppose you created several scenes and set them all to render overnight. In the morning, you return to your computer...and the renders aren't finished. Assuming that your scenes are together in a single directory or folder on your disk, you can see which ones are finished and which ones aren't by viewing the contents of that directory by date. The scene and render files that are completed will be more recent.

Variation on this theme: (For Macs only) If you are working on several scenes that have documents residing in different folders on your hard drive, create a TO BE RENDERED folder. Make aliases of your scenes in progress and put them in that folder. Drag all the aliases onto the Bryce application icon (or alias) to batch render. The originals stay in their own folders, and you get your batch rendering done.

GENERAL BRYCEAN BEHAVIOR AND OTHER TECHNICAL CONSIDERATIONS

This last section of the chapter turns the focus away from making you a Bryce efficiency expert to making you simply a Bryce expert. Here we discuss some general points about the way Bryce behaves.

Option-Clicking/Alt+Clicking: Revert and Variations

Here is something worth mentioning as a standard all over the Bryce software. After you have manipulated things and you want to reset something to its default state, try Option-clicking (Macintosh) or Alt+clicking (Windows). This works with some camera controls; it removes saved Camera Views and saved skies (both camera and sky Memory Dots), it resets wireframe depth cueing, it resets panning and zooming, it works within the Preset Preview and Terrain Editor to reset the brackets in the Terrain Editor clipping, and perhaps there is another case or so where it restores the default state.

Option-clicking or Alt+clicking is not completely consistent across the board, however, for reverting to the default. In the case of all color swatches, Option-clicking or Alt+clicking brings up a different color picker, and in the Deep Texture Editor, Option-clicking or Alt+clicking a texture component preview brings up a full-screen preview of the texture.

Naming Scene Files

When you name your scene file, Bryce names your rendered image file for you, adding a suffix to the image file name. In Bryce for Macintosh, the rendered PICT file will be assigned a suffix of .PCT. For the file name A GROOOVY OUTTA SPACE SCENE, Bryce will assign the PICT image the name A GROOOVY OUTTA SPACE SCENE.PCT The maximum number of characters in a Mac file name is 31. The example here just happens to hit the upper limit. What happens if you were to go over that limit, say, in assigning a scene name A GROOOVY OUTTA SPACE SCENE2? In cases where your scene file name is 28 or more characters in length, Bryce will truncate the name (at the end) to add the .PCT suffix. The resulting PICT name will become A GROOOVY OUTTA SPACE SCENE.PCT. Ummm, does anybody see a problem with this? When the extra character was lopped off the scene name, the names for both the scene and its image file became exactly the same as the file we previously saved. So the new file and image nuked the first file and image pair, with not so much as a "by your leave"! The moral of the story: When saving a series of files with long names, change characters near the front of the name, not near the back, to distinguish the different versions.

In Windows, Bryce assigns extensions to both the scene file and the image file (.BR4 for scene files, .BMP for rendered image files). When you save the scene file, Bryce automatically writes the rendered image file. Users of Bryce under Windows do not have to be as circumspect as Mac users about the characters at the end of the file name, since Windows 95 and Windows NT allow for file names with up to 256 characters. If you cannot manage to keep your file names under 256 characters (well, 252, actually, but who's quibbling?), then we can offer you no further advice. You can choose whether to show the file name extensions by selecting File > Option, clicking the View tab, and clicking the check box next to the text that says Hide MS-DOS file extensions for file types that are registered. If you do so, the extensions will be automatically added to the files without the possibility of your inadvertently overtyping a part of the extension.

If you are transferring a Macintosh Bryce scene file to Windows, make sure to add the .BR4 extension so that Windows Bryce will recognize it.

Preset Libraries

A Bryce Preset Library exists for each of the three main palettes: Create Palette, Edit Palette, and Sky & Fog Palette. They hold settings for objects, materials, and sky settings, respectively.

To access any of the Preset Libraries, click the triangle next to the name. That palette needn't be active for you to access the library. In Figure 5.13, although the Sky & Fog Palette is currently active, a click on the triangle next to the Edit title will bring up the Edit Preset Library.

Figure 5.13 Accessing the Edit Preset Library when another palette is currently active.

Once inside the Preset Library, you see a list of categories for the objects. The Sky & Fog Library has no categories, though. Figure 5.14 shows an example of each of the three types of Preset Library. To view a type of category, simply click the name

 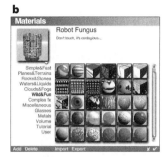 

Figure 5.14   Preset Libraries: a) Object Presets; b) Materials Presets; c) Sky & Fog Presets.

in the left column. The presets from that category will show up. If there are more presets than there are preset image tiles, a scrollbar appears, allowing you to scroll through the entire list.

If you see a preset that you like, how do you apply it? Click the preset tile. The frame surrounding it turns red, and its image shows up in the preview window. If there is a title and a text description for the preset, it shows up to the right of the main preview. Now it is the active one. To apply it, click the OK check mark. Depending on what type of library you were in, you will have a new material surface for the selected object or a new sky setting, or you will have introduced a new object or group into your scene.

When you're inside the Materials Library, you can change your views of the object. From the pop-up menu, you can choose whether the object is viewed close up or at a normal distance (see Figure 5.15). The object can render against a neutral sky or the sky that you currently have established in your scene. (The current sky will affect the appearance of the object or material. Later, under a different sky, you may select that preset and wonder why it doesn't look like the one you saw in the preset tile. The sky made it different.) You can change the object being shown from the current selection to the following primitive types: box, sphere, cone cylinder,

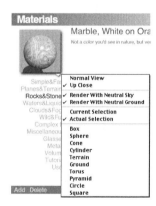

Figure 5.15 Materials Preset Library pop-up menu.

terrain, ground, torus. Besides choosing these options from the pop-up menu that resides under the preview window, you can click directly in the window to momentarily see the corresponding wireframe and drag to customize your view of the object.

Dragging horizontally to the left and right rotates the object in front of you. In fact, you are moving your position around the object. This means that you can check your surface texture in direct sunlight, in shadow, and lit from the side. Dragging down vertically moves you above the object, or even over to its other side. Keep going, and you'll be below it. Pressing the Control key (Macintosh) or Ctrl key (Windows) while dragging vertically moves the object closer or farther away from you. Pressing the space bar while dragging allows you to pan around to change the framing of the object in the preview window. Pressing the Option key (Macintosh) or Alt key (Windows) while clicking the window restores the object to its default position.

Do these settings seem familiar to you? They should—or if they don't, they will soon. These are the same shortcuts for moving your position in relation to the object (or scene, or terrain) that you find elsewhere in Bryce 4. The Nano Edit, Flyaround, and Terrain Editor Previews share most or all of these same manipulations.

The Objects Preset Library has a preview, too, but it's useless for closely examining already stored objects. It displays a canned thumbnail of the object that was created when the object was imported into the library, but if you drag within the window, you don't get to examine the object from various viewpoints. If you had an object selected in your scene, you'll be manipulating that object in the preview, not the preset, as Bryce is assuming that you're getting ready to save a preset for that selected object. Bryce's assumptions fall apart, however, if nothing is selected in your scene: You'll be looking at nothing! Dragging in the preview window does nothing but change your view of the ground plane (if you have one). In any case, as soon as you release the mouse button, the preview reverts to the canned thumbnail.

There's also a preview in the Sky & Fog Preset Library, but it has no options or controls—it's just a larger version of the preset's thumbnail. Each thumbnail and preview includes a sphere object, so you can see the direction and color of sunlight or moonlight, and get a general idea of how objects will react to the sky conditions.

You know the options for manipulating the preview inside the Preset Library. You know how to get a preset from a library into your scene. How about getting something from your scene into the library?

To add a preset, let the preview render. It will take a few passes to completely render (see Figure 5.16a). (If you don't like the appearance, and want to move the object, this is the time to do so. Render again. To force a render from scratch, click in the preview window.) At that point, click the Add button. You'll be presented with a dialog box where you can type a name for your preset. You can also type a pithy description, which allows you to add comments and reminders to yourself about the preset. The description typed in Figure 5.16 and shown in the resulting added texture in part c provides a memory jogger to help you use the preset smartly or do further manipulations later. You can, if you want, add to your description. Make sure that the thumbnail is selected, with the red border surrounding it, and then simply click the text area to make it editable (see Figure 5.16d).

To delete a preset, simply select it and click Delete. You'll be asked if you're sure you want to make the deletion, just in case you accidentally clicked Delete.

What if you want to import or export a set of presets? You can transfer them and trade them with your friends. How do you move them about? First we'll talk about exporting presets, then we'll talk about importing them.

To export presets, you need to select them. The Preset Libraries obey standard conventions for selection in a list of items. Select one item by clicking it. There are two ways to select multiple items: To select everything between two objects, click the first object and Shift-click the last object; everything in between is selected. To select here and there, press the Command key (Macintosh) or Ctrl (Windows) key while clicking each item you want to

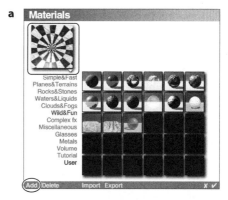

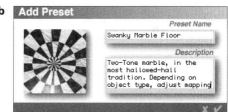

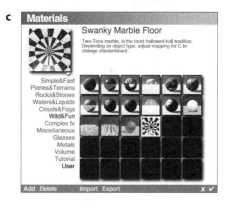

Figure 5.16 Adding a preset: a) Rendering the preset before clicking Add; b) text entry for the preset; c) the result; d) to edit text later, click it.

select. Figures 5.17a through c show the different results of these selection options.

You can select objects from only one category at a time. You cannot select some presets from, say, Rocks & Stones and keep Command-clicking or Ctrl+clicking to add presets from the Waters & Liquids category.

Once you have your preset or presets selected, click Export. You get a standard Save dialog box, and you can name your preset file whatever you like. When you click that Save button, Bryce will write the exported preset file.

To import objects, the process is reversed. Click Import, and you are presented with a dialog box. Select the Preset Library you want to import. There are, however, some things to watch for. You cannot import into more than one category at a time, and you cannot import into a different category than the one you're in at the moment. For example, if you want to import boolean objects, then you'd best select the boolean section of the Objects Preset Library before doing so.

When manipulating large volumes of object presets (either many items or a few complex ones, or both), be aware that patience is called for. The operation may take a long time to complete, and it's not uncommon for Bryce to stop indicating that it's still working; the wristwatch or hourglass (Bryce's

a

b

c

Figure 5.17 Selecting different presets: a) Selecting one preset with a single mouse click; b) clicking again with the Shift key held down selects all presets in between; c) clicking here and there with the Command key or Ctrl key pressed selects non-adjoining presets.

way of saying "I'm thinking! I'm thinking!") may go away, but the program won't respond to your mouse clicks. You may think the program has died and sent your presets to byte heaven—but don't hit the reboot button just yet! Wait a bit longer, and more than likely, Bryce will show signs of life again. Watch out for this situation especially when deleting large numbers of objects from your Preset Library.

There are four preset file types. They are found in the PRESETS folder (imagine that!) inside the Bryce application folder. They have different names:

- NAME.OBP
- NAME.MAT
- NAME.BRT
- NAME.BSK
- ACCEL ENGINE.TME

The first part of the file name, NAME, is a file for the category. You'll see different names that correspond to different categories, such as, METALS.MAT. The second part, .OBP, .MAT, .BRT, and .BSK, identifies which library the file belongs to: Objects, Materials, Textures, or Sky Presets. Each of the library files contain certain data for each preset: the actual information for the objects or materials or sky, the name and description, and a small thumbnail preview image—the one you see in the Preset Library. If you learned to avoid the Preset Libraries because of their flaky behaviors in previous versions of Bryce, you can now unlearn your unlearning: Bryce manages the presets much better than it did in the days of Bryce 2.

That last item in the list, with the .TME suffix, is for Time Mapping Curves that you set in the Advanced Motion Lab. There are two items with that suffix that live in the Bryce PRESETS folder. ACCEL ENGINE.TME is the file in which any user-created Time Mapping Curves are stored; any that you save or delete in the Advanced Motion Lab are stored in or deleted from that file. There's no Add/Delete interface for the Time Mapping Curves as there is for other presets; manipulation is all performed by key clicks with or without modifier keys, which we describe in Chapter 15, "Advanced Animation Techniques." The other file with that prefix, DEF ACCEL ENGINE.TME, is the file that holds the default Time Mapping Curves; don't touch it!

Here's one strategy for transferring library presets. If you want to import presets from one Bryce application to another—say, from Bryce on your home computer to Bryce on your office computer—do a bit of advance planning to make sure you import only the presets you want. Instead of importing *everything* from the other version (where no doubt there is overlap between some presets), open that other version and export only the presets that you want to have. Yes, it requires a bit more painstaking effort, and it's not as graphically intuitive as you were led to believe, but you also won't need to tear the underlying structure of your presets to shreds or risk having to build your presets from scratch, either.

The Objects Library is a nice place to start. The Boolean Objects section of the Objects Library has quite a clever tutorial built into the thumbnails and descriptions. The Objects Library is a good place to get some trees and some animation paths, too—but is this the place where you want to store all your carefully built objects? Maybe and maybe not. There are some who use the Objects Library to keep a collection of objects worked on for a series of scenes. Then when you're through working on the series, you can export and archive all the project's objects. You can do the same thing with a collection of scene files, too. Take your pick.

The Sky & Fog Presets are good places to store various options for skies. In addition to simply collecting them and trading 'em with your friends, you can use Sky & Fog presets when fine-tuning a sky. Save your nearly final candidates as presets while you take one last go-round in the Sky Lab, so you don't have to worry about ruining them.

The Preset Library that we find to be the most helpful is the Materials Preset Library. It is a dual-purpose library, accessed from the Edit Palette as well as from within the Materials Lab. Throughout the rest of the book, we'll refer to the Materials Preset Library the most, followed by the Sky & Fog Preset Library. The Objects Library…well, we mentioned it here, didn't we?

Save Prompts When Closing Files

The standard Macintosh and Windows convention is to present a Save dialog box when you first save a scene document, so you can give it a name. Thereafter, whenever you save, the system merely saves to that same file, without presenting a dialog box, unless you specifically request one by selecting Save As from the File menu. Bryce has a few special instances where the request to save automatically brings up a Save As dialog box. If you merge your scene with another one, when you choose File > Save or type ⌘-S (Macintosh) or Ctrl+S (Windows), Bryce will present you with the Save dialog box so that you may rename the new merged scene. (More about scene merging in Chapter 7, "Booleans and Multiple Object Construction.")

This next instance is a Bryce-prompt-to-save that's worth rejoicing over. When you have completely rendered a scene and close it (by quitting the application, opening another scene, or creating a new scene), Bryce will ask whether you want to save the scene (whew! yes, after all that time rendering, yes, yes, yes!), so click the Save button if you do.

The Revert to Saved function is grayed out (unavailable) in Bryce in the following circumstances: when you have created a new scene and have not yet saved it, when you change from one resolution to another using the Render Options pop-up menu, and when you open a scene with animation and make changes *only* in the Advanced Motion Lab.

Because of Bryce's habit of prompting at various times, you might be confused: Even though you have opened a scene and checked to see that a particular object's material is set to thus-and-so, when you want to close it again and move on to another scene, you will get a prompt asking if you want to save changes. If you select an object or enter any separate dialog boxes to edit objects, terrains, or materials, even though you've made no changes, Bryce will ask you if you want to save. After a while, you get used to these seemingly bogus queries and appreciate the genuine ones (especially at the end of a render!).

Preferences

In the Preferences dialog box (Edit > Preferences), you can choose various states in which to run Bryce. Figure 5.18 shows the Preferences dialog box.

Preferences can be divided into two categories: global preferences that affect the entire application, and "local" preferences for that particular scene file. The global preferences are kept in a small file in your system's Preferences folder, and the local preferences for a scene are kept with the scene file.

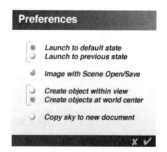

Figure 5.18 The Preferences dialog box.

Then there are the local settings common to both Mac and Windows versions of Bryce: Launch to Previous State and Launch to Default State. These settings primarily affect the way your interface is set up, but they also govern choices you have made regarding Bryce's operation. The following list shows the parameters controlled by the Launch to Default and Launch to Previous State preferences. In each case, the default setting is shown in **boldface**.

Palette Positions

- **Create**-Edit-Sky & Fog Palette showing
- **Time**-Selection Palette showing

Control Palette Options

- Current View (**Director's**/Camera/Top/Left, and so on)
- Camera Trackball Mode (**Trackball**)
- Render Textures **On**/Off
- Fast Preview Render On/**Off**
- AntiAliasing Off/**Normal Quality**/Fine Art(Slow)
- Spatial Optimization Off/**Low**/High
- Gamma Correction **On**/Off
- 48-bit Dithering **On**/Off
- Report Render Time **On**/Off

Display Palette Options

- Interface Max/**Min**
- Background **Paper**
- Nano-Editor On/**Off**
- Plop-Rendering **On**/Off
- Depth-Cue setting
- Wireframe Shadows **On**/Off
- Underground Wireframes On/**Off**
- Wireframe Resolution for Motion (**8**), Static (**16**), and Selected (**32**) modes
- Auto-LOD **On**/Off (when to switch to drawing boxes instead of lattices)
- Display Mode (**Wireframe** or Shaded Preview mode; OpenGL, Sree3D, and so on)

Nano Preview Options

- Nano Preview (Sky Only/**Full Scene**/Wireframe; View [**Current**])
- Nano Preview Auto Update **On**/Off
- Nano Preview Quality (**Fast Preview**/Full Rendering)

Animation items

- Ticker Mark Interval for Timeline (**Every Frame**)
- Movie Preview Options (Storyboard **On**/Off, Frame Borders/**Shadows**, **Line**/Page Scrolling, Play Repeating/**Using Mode**)
- Auto-Key **On**/Off

Miscellaneous Options

- Anchor-Based Aligning On/**Off** (used by the Align tool)
- Sky Auto Update On/**Off**
- Link Sun to View **On**/Off
- Alternate VCR Mode On/**Off**

When Bryce is launched, those things that are remembered as part of the previous state are stored in temporary memory and are applied to each new scene file created during a Bryce session. For those items concerned with the appearance of the Bryce interface, this is irrelevant, but the other options—the Render options, Link Sun to View, and whether Auto-Key is on or off—will actually become a part of the new scene file. Since those scene-specific options are kept with the scene, it is possible, within a given Bryce session, to open a previously saved scene that governs how those items are set and so unconsciously change those previous-state options.

In the case of Auto-Key, where inadvertently having it on during the creation of still-image files adds to your scene file size, it behooves you to be aware of how Bryce treats this. Here's a little scenario for a Bryce working session.

1. You launch Bryce. Since the preferences are set to Launch to Previous State, the Auto-Key setting is the same as in the last scene file you had open during your previous session (if, conversely, you choose Reset to Default, then Auto-Key will be on when you launch Bryce). Let's suppose that the last scene file you had open, which we'll call YESTERDAY, had Auto-Key off. Bryce's setting for Auto-Key will be off.

2. You open that YESTERDAY scene file that you were working with before. Auto-Key is still off. You work for a little while with that scene and finish it.

3. Now you want to refer to another scene, LASTWEEK, that you were working on a little while back. You open it; it is set to Auto-Key on. You check out some little detail that was a part of that scene. Then you're ready to work on something new.

4. You create a new scene file. It inherits settings from the LASTWEEK scene, including Auto-Key on.

The final result, in this scenario, is that in one working session, you've changed from Auto-Key off to Auto-Key on without making a conscious choice or touching the menu where the Auto-Key item resides. The same type of thing will happen for render settings, 48-bit Dithering, Gamma Correction, and Link Sun to View; they will change to reflect the state set in the last open scene. If you have moved any of the palettes to another position by holding the space bar and dragging them, Reset Palettes will straighten them out and send them back to their default positions. Annoyingly, if you had chosen Interface Maximum before, the Reset Palettes command also sends you back to Interface Minimum.

Reset to Defaults doesn't do what you might expect—it does not affect your interface setup, but does reset the sky and the positions of the Camera and Director's Views. It also turns Auto-Key on. On the Sky Options pop-up menu, it enables Link Sun to View and turns on Stratus Clouds and Spherical and turns off Cumulus Clouds. No matter what your settings were on the Nano Preview pop-up menu, they'll be set to the defaults (Full Scene, Auto Update on, Current View, Fast Preview).

So now that we've told you what the Preferences' default or previous state does *not* include, let us tell you what it does include. "Previous" is best thought of as the settings from the previous scene file that you had open.

In general, Bryce launches to a default sky (unless you launch Bryce by double-clicking a scene file, in which case it launches to the sky from that scene). If you have turned on the Copy Sky to New Document setting in the Preferences, the next new scene file you create will inherit the sky from the previous scene file. After you quit and restart Bryce, however, you'll begin with the default sky again.

Here, then is a concluding remark about preferences. You'll probably set them up and forget about them. It's certainly smart; we do the same thing, except for the times when we futz around with them because we have to write about them. Since you can click the Memory Dots to return sky settings to the defaults, and since Bryce launches to a default sky no matter what, we'd recommend keeping your preferences set to Launch to Previous State. It's far easier to make a sky turn back to the default than it is to go back and get a sky from another scene that you just closed.

Setting Up Your Own Default Scene

All this discussion about what's referred to as the previous and default states, and nobody's bothered to ask you whether you'd like to create a Bryce scene that is different from the default Bryce scene. Perhaps you'd prefer to work in a different size or have the Camera or Director's View location in a different spot than what Bryce establishes for you. You can do that by creating your own default scene.

1. Create your scene however you'd like it to be. Give it the dimensions that you prefer. Position the Camera and the Director's View camera where you want them. Make your sky as you prefer.

2. When you have all things as desired, save the scene. Give it the name DEFAULT.BR4 (no matter what platform you're working on, it must have that name). Put that scene file in the folder or directory where the Bryce application is located. There you are!

Bryce launches, and after a moment, it opens your default scene file. Make any changes to it, and when you save it, you'll be presented with a Save As dialog box, with the name DEFAULT.BR4 already in it. Save the scene however you will. If you set up a default scene to make your camera just so (say, for instance, to put it in front as some of our tutorials do, or because you like the camera position from the early days of Bryce 1), then you won't like the next part: Once you save your was-default-scene-but-you-named-it-something-else and then create a new scene, that new scene will inherit the dimensions of your default scene, but *your new scene will not inherit the camera's position you established in the* DEFAULT.BR4 *scene file!* Makes us wonder what it's good for, then! But still, you may find it useful to create your own default scene for the sake of the dimensions. Also, if you want to have a set sky, then it's probably best to check the Preferences item Copy Sky to New Document.

Palette Principles for the Proficient Person

As we mentioned, Bryce has one interface control that lets you decide whether you want the palettes to hug the scene or to hug the edge of the monitor.

There are yet other options. You can drag the palettes around to reposition them; hold down the space bar and drag. This is different from the normal Macintosh or Windows "drag by the title bar" behavior. If you want to reset everything back to normal, then press the Option and space bar (Macintosh) or Alt and space bar (Windows) keys and click a palette—back they go, hugging the edge of your scene. Wait a second. Didn't we talk about that Option (or Alt) and space bar combination earlier? Yes, when you hold down the Option (or Alt) key and space bar and click *inside* the scene area, you get the Nano Edit window. The same key combination applied to a palette brings all the palettes back to their standard home spots. Needless to say, don't click the palettes when you want to elicit the Nano Editor, and vice versa.

Keyboard Stuff

Unless you have concocted your custom setup by dragging palettes this way 'n' that, only one of the Create, Edit, and Sky & Fog Palettes will be showing at a time (and, of course, every time you open or create a new scene file, you'll pop back to the Create Palette). No doubt by now you've discovered that you can make one of the other two palettes active by clicking its title. You can do the same thing using keyboard shortcuts as well. Here are the keyboard equivalents:

Control-1 (Mac) or Ctrl+1 (Windows) = Create Palette

Control-2 (Mac) or Ctrl+2 (Windows) = Edit Palette

Control-3 (Mac) or Ctrl+3 (Windows) = Sky & Fog Palette

Control-4 (Mac) or Ctrl+4 (Windows) = Control Palette

Control-5 (Mac) or Ctrl+5 (Windows) = Select/Animation Controls Palette (whichever happens to be showing at the moment)

Control-6 (Mac) or Ctrl+6 (Windows) = Display/Wireframe Palette

Control-⌘-Tab (Mac) or Ctrl+Tab (Windows) = Toggle Palettes off

The Control-⌘-Tab/Ctrl+Tab toggle is good to use in combination with the others. Suppose you have a small monitor and a large scene, one that's going to take a while to render. You want to watch the render's progress while seeing as much of the scene as you can. Toggle all of the palettes off and then use the key command sequences to bring back only those you absolutely need—most probably Control-4/Ctrl+4, the Control Palette. Then use the space bar drag to move the palette out of the way so that only the render time and render buttons show. Your particular working situation may suggest other alternatives; go to it.

Palette Placement Tricks and Two-Monitor Brycing

When you have a large monitor that displays 800 × 600 pixels or better, you can drag out the other palettes (Edit, Sky & Fog) to other places on your screen so that you can see different palettes simultaneously. If you do that, it's probably better to work in Interface Minimum size, so that the palettes maintain the smaller width, matching the width of the scene. However, if you change the dimensions of your scene the tiniest little bit, the palettes will snap back to their default positions, and you'll have to position your palettes all over again. Thanks for nothing! On the other hand, if you set your display to Interface Maximum and rearrange your palettes, they'll stay put, come hell or high water.

The ability to drag palettes around is a great boon to users of Windows 95 and above, who are blessed (?) with the lovely taskbar. The taskbar, in its default configuration, takes up a good chunk of the bottom of your monitor real estate, and if you like to use the Interface Maximum option, you'll find that the taskbar sits squarely on top of the Selection/Animation Controls Palette. One remedy is to change the taskbar settings. You can turn on the Auto Hide option, so the taskbar stays out of the way until you swoop down to the bottom of the screen to invoke it; but then it's very easy to aim for the Select Spheres button and accidentally cause the taskbar to pop up, blocking your way. You can turn off the taskbar's Always on Top option, but then because the Bryce window is permanently in a maximized state, if you want to get at the taskbar you have to minimize Bryce, which is a hassle. A slicker alternative is to drag the Select/Animation Options Palette a centimeter or so upward, and then it can coexist happily with the taskbar.

A different alternative is to work with palettes in dual-monitor setups (far more prevalent on Macs). Assuming that one monitor is larger than the others, as in the setup shown in Figure 5.19, you cannot see the full length of the Control Palette when it is on the smaller monitor. Its size is determined by the size of the main monitor; though it has been moved to a smaller monitor, the Control Palette still thinks of itself as hugging the edge of the larger monitor. Because of this delusion of grandeur, the bottom text display—the one that tells you what's what—is missing. Likewise, the positioning of certain dialog boxes and the Preset Libraries takes its cue from the position of the main Control Palette and the Nano Preview location, so they must appear.

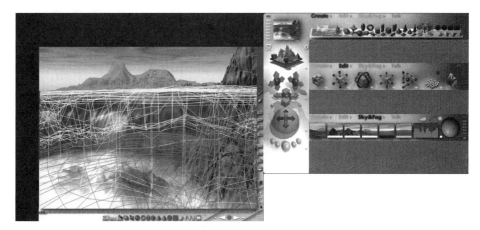

Figure 5.19 A two-monitor working situation, with some palettes arranged on the second, smaller monitor.

Plop-Up Dialog Boxes

Bryce's plop-up dialog boxes have dual-access controls. The plop-up dialog boxes are the Object Attribute dialog box, the Families Attribute dialog box, and the Preset Libraries. They act like both of two standard Macintosh user interface items: pop-up menus and dialog boxes. When they are pop-up menus, you press the mouse on the switch that opens them (either a triangle or an Object control icon) and drag to change the setting, and when you release the mouse, they disappear. To access the same thing as a dialog box, click the switch; the dialog box opens until you send it away by clicking OK or Cancel.

Similar to the plop-up dialog boxes is the plop-render display. It shares the drop shadow with the plop-up dialog box, but none of the other "It behaves like a dialog box! It behaves like a pop-up menu! It's two, two, two functions in one!" attributes.

Monitors: What to Do with Screen Savers, Clocks, and Other Details

You will probably have Bryce render during a time you are away from your computer—for example, when you are asleep or on your lunch hour—so you will inevitably run into the question of what to do with your monitor. Should you keep it on and let your screen saver run?

Some screen savers have been known to interfere with the rendering process because they are continuously asking for the computer's attention. Bryce wants as much of the processor as it can get while rendering; it "concentrates" on the task at hand and does not constantly monitor for keystrokes and mouse clicks. Clocks are continuously updating a portion of your screen. Screen savers are also watching to see how long it has been since the mouse was last moved or a key was pressed.

Who's going to get the upper hand in this situation: Bryce, which wants to ignore all outside stimuli, or the screen saver and/or clock, which prefer to stay aware of the outside stimuli? We'd rather give Bryce the upper hand. Our recommendation here is to disable the screen saver and then shut off the monitor while you're away so that nothing on a system level will interfere with the render process—and if you're the one who pays the utility bills, you'll also save some nickels.

CHAPTER SIX
Editing and the Internal Bryce Grid

IN THIS CHAPTER...

- World Space, Object Space, and Camera Space

- Bryce's internal grid

- Changing a single object: resize, rotate, reposition, flip, align

- Changing object type

- The Torus Editor

- Going from one object to more objects: duplicating and replicating

- Working with a number of objects: aligning, randomizing, and grouping objects

What goes on in the editing process? Editing is the precision adjustment. This is where all your objects get tweaked and otherwise primped, prodded, and poked into the proper position and presentation. To understand what takes place in the editing process, think in terms of several main areas.

- *Awareness of the Bryce Space and units.* What are the units and measures of the Brycean Universe?

- *Adjusting a single object.* Think back on that object matrix and the Three Rs from Chapter 4, "Brycean Objects."

- *Special edits that are unique to an object.* The terrain, symmetrical lattice, mesh, light, and torus all have special Edit controls. The particulars of each will be discussed in other chapters. Terrain and lattices are discussed in Chapter 8, "Terrains, Symmetrical Lattices, and the Terrain Editor," meshes (imported objects) in Chapter 4, "Brycean Objects," lights in Chapter 12, "Bryce EnLightenment." The torus is not significant enough to merit a chapter of its own, so we'll discuss it later in this chapter.

- *Edit materials.* Change the surface appearance of each object. This topic is covered in chapters all its own, Chapter 9, "Material World I: Materials Lab," and Chapter 10, "Material World II: Picture Textures and the Deep Texture Editor."

- *Changing object type.* Transforming from one object type to another.

- *Generating multiple objects from one object.*

- *Adjusting a set of objects.* This includes aligning, randomizing, and grouping a set of objects.

- *Shortcuts.* Nudges and key nudges abound.

We'll discuss these topics in this chapter on editing Bryce objects.

Setting your scene in motion—animation—also involves editing, but we'll save the discussion of that for the Animation chapters (Chapter 14, "The Fourth Dimension: Time and Animation," and Chapter 15, "Advanced Animation Techniques") and for the other chapters where we talk about special kinds of animation (Terrains, Materials, and Skies).

The Edit Palette is where most of the object-oriented activity in Bryce takes place. This palette has eight main controls. Figure 6.1 shows them all. The Edit Materials and Edit Terrain/Object controls are discussed in other chapters. This chapter focuses on the inner controls: Resize, Rotate, Reposition, Align, Randomize, and Object Conversion.

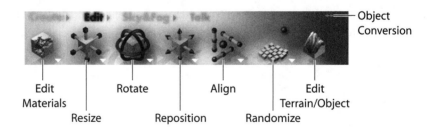

Figure 6.1 The Edit Palette.

THE UNDERLYING STRUCTURE OF THE BRYCEAN UNIVERSE

Once you select an object, you can do something to it. You can change its size, its position, its attributes, or its orientation in the world. This is what the Resize, Rotate, and Reposition controls are for. We'll take a look at each of them in turn, but first we will discuss the Brycean Universe, the *xyz* space, and the underlying grid.

XYZ Axes

Let's do a bit of *xyz* review. Recall from the end of Chapter 2 our discussion of the *xyz* space in Bryce. The three dimensions can be referred to according to World Space, Object Space, and Camera Space. World Space is absolute: *x* is the east-west dimension, *y* is the up-down dimension and *z* is the north-south dimension. Object Space is relative to the object and its dimensions: the object's width (*x*), height (*y*), and depth (*z*). Camera Space is subjective, changing with the perspective from which you view the scene: the *x* axis is left-right, the *y* axis is up-down, and the *z* axis is forward-backward. When thinking editorially about Bryce, you will be dealing with all three varieties of *xyz* space.

World, Object, and Camera Space Edits

When Resizing, Rotating, and Repositioning objects, you can work in any of the three Bryce Spaces. The object will be changed a little differently, depending on which space you're in. How do you know which space you're in? The pop-up menu for each of the Three Rs controls includes options for changing space (see Figure 6.2). When it comes to switching from World to Object to Camera Space, it's "all for one, and one for all." Once you change the state under one menu, say, the Resize menu, the other two menus will also reflect that state.

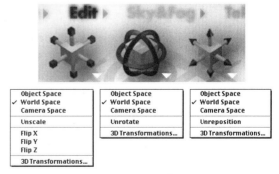

Figure 6.2 The pop-up menus for Resize, Rotate, and Reposition.

World Space

When World Space is selected, an object will be adjusted along the Brycean Universe's x, y, and z axes.

If an object is not lined up along those axes, when you resize along the x axis, there will seem to be an external x force that stretches or squishes the object, no matter what the object's own orientation. The same holds true for rotation. Repositioning will move an object north, east, south, west, or up and down only, regardless of the object's own orientation in space.

The wireframe for World Space is a bounding box with dimensions that are always in alignment with the World Space x, y, and z axes (see Figure 6.3a).

Object Space

When Object Space is selected, the selected object is transformed based on the object's own x, y, and z axes. Working in Object Space is very advantageous, as an object that has already been put into place and rotated one way or another can be made "wider" without losing the integrity of the object's shape (as would happen if the object were "widened" in World Space).

Figure 6.3b shows how the bounding box for Object Space snaps to a snug fit with the boundaries of the object. Like a well-tailored suit, Object Space moves with its wearer.

Camera Space

When Camera Space is selected, object transformations take place relative to the camera's orientation. So no matter how the object is oriented, or where World Space's x axis is, enlarging an object along the x axis when in Camera Space will enlarge it left to right as you are currently viewing it. Notice how, in Figure 6.3c, the wireframe is aligned with the edges of the scene window. When resizing or repositioning the selected object, the x axis is left-right, the y axis is up-down, and the z axis is back-front as you look at the scene. When you rotate objects while in Camera Space, the axes of rotation are parallel to those of the camera. When you pick up an object and drag it elsewhere, you are working in Camera Space (unless, alas, you hold down one of the constrain keys, in which case the object's motion is constrained to movement in World Space). This has been true from Bryce 1.

Figure 6.4 shows the same cube, dragged (using the mouse) to different corners of the scene. The bounding wireframe doesn't keep facing the camera squarely as the center object does; in other words, the z axis doesn't stay pointing at the camera but remains parallel to the z axis that runs through the camera.

Try it yourself: Open the scene file MOVE AND CONSTRAIN from the CD-ROM. Use one of the Three Rs menus to switch to Camera Space. Using the mouse, drag the cube to different corners of your screen. Notice how, in each position, the perspective of the cube's bounding box is different.

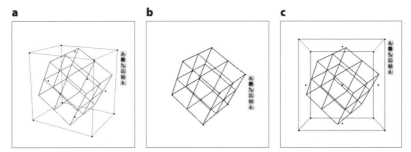

Figure 6.3 Comparison of a) World Space, b) Object Space, and c) Camera Space wireframe bounding boxes.

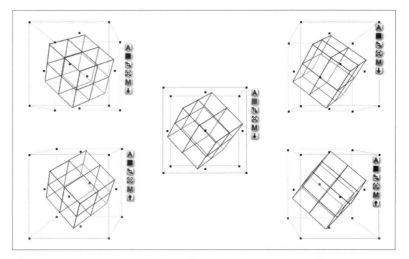

Figure 6.4 At the center, the cube from Figure 6.3c. Surrounding it are depictions of the same cube, dragged to different parts of the scene while in Camera Space.

The Grid

Inside the Brycean Universe is an invisible internal grid. It is referred to in the Snap to Grid command under the Alignment pop-up menu. What is the grid? Bryce has no command for making the grid visible, yet it is the underlying structure of the Brycean Universe, and many of the Edit controls occur in relation to the grid. Figure 6.5 depicts the grid points. You can work more efficiently in Bryce when you are aware of the grid.

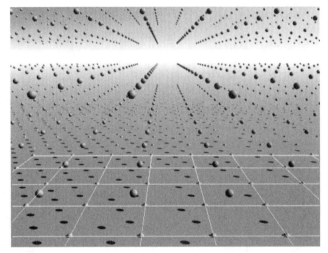

Figure 6.5
Bryce's internal grid.

The grid's unit of measurement is different from those units that correspond to our world. No inches, picas, miles, kilometers, or anything like that. Bryce is a world unto itself, and the Brycean Units and Measurement Council devised this particular set of units based on its own internal logic for our use and pleasure. The grid and units of measurement correspond to the sizes of objects as they come into being in the Brycean Universe. The units are measured in Bryce units, or B for short. You'll see the B symbol in dialog boxes (Object Attributes, 3D Transform, Replicate): B, for Bryce units. Since those measurements are shown for each axis, Bryce units (and our discussion of size in general) describe the linear size of an object on a given dimension. (The real-world counterpart to this is to say something is *n* inches long, not *n* cubic inches.)

When you create a primitive in Bryce, it comes into a certain defined space. We'll call that defined space a unity unit. The unity unit is the size and orientation that objects snap to when you invoke Unity using a key command. (We discuss the concept of Unity later in this chapter.) Figure 6.6 shows the unity unit and the grid points that are part of the unity unit. When you create a terrain, the object comes into Bryce at four times the size of a unity unit. Although terrains pop into the scene covering four times the width and depth of a unity unit, they remain one unity unit high. When you create an infinite plane, its wireframe appears as four times the size of a terrain. However, although their wireframes are sixteen times the size of one unity unit in size, they aren't literally at that scale; infinite planes render on an infinite scale. Figure 6.7 compares the size of the unity unit, a terrain, and the size that an infinite plane wireframe occupies in Bryce Space.

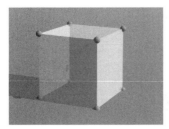

Figure 6.6 The unity unit and the grid points that occupy the space of a unity unit.

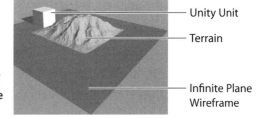

Unity Unit

Terrain

Infinite Plane Wireframe

Figure 6.7 Size comparison of a unity unit, terrain, and infinite plane wireframe.

The unity unit is the foundational unit of measurement, being the basic unit of the Bryce grid. Another important unit of measure is something we call a "nudge unit"—the distance that an object moves when you press one of the arrow keys on your computer's keyboard. There are four of these to a unity unit. (Through Bryce 2, the nudge unit and the grid unit were the same. It was Bryce 3D that enlarged the grid unit to equal the unity unit.) Then, for even further fine-tuning, there is a smaller scale increment—the Option-nudge (Macintosh) or Alt-nudge (Windows) unit. (The unit's name is derived from the action of holding down the Option or Alt key while nudging objects. Hereafter we'll refer to it as the Option/Alt-nudge unit.) There are 64 Option/Alt-nudge units to one nudge unit, and four nudge units to one grid unit. Although we are currently discussing the units of space in Bryce in terms of an action—nudging—we'll discuss the actual process of and strategies for nudging later in this chapter.

Bryce has numeric values for each of these units, and so many of one type equals one of another type of unit. The following chart and Figure 6.8 show you how all of these units fit together.

Bryce unit	=	.01
Nudge unit	=	5.12
Unity/grid unit	=	20.48
8 Bryce units	=	1 Option/Alt-nudge unit
64 Option/Alt-nudge units	=	1 nudge unit
4 nudge units	=	1 unity/grid unit

Figure 6.8 The units of the Bryce grid: four nudge units to one unity/grid unit; four unity units to match the width of a terrain.

Don't blame us for the strange proportions. It's like wondering why there are 12 inches in a foot, 36 inches in a yard, and 5,280 feet in a mile. (And how many inches are in a light-year, anyhow?) Once you live in this world, it makes sense. Or at least you get used to it. Here the same scale is presented again, this time using Bryce unit numbers.

1 Bryce unit	=	0.01 B
1 Option/Alt-nudge unit	=	0.08 B
1 nudge unit	=	5.12 B
1 unity/grid unit	=	20.48 B

Since Bryce is a world that ultimately depends upon ones and zeroes, its numbering units are inherited from them: 1, 2, 4, 8, 16, 32, 64, 128, and so on. By convention, Bryce units put the decimal point in a different place, so that 2048 becomes, instead, 20.48. This is why a single Bryce unit is represented by a Bryce unit number of 0.01B.

We will refer back to these standards of measurement in our discussion of other Edit controls in this chapter.

Other Units of Measurement in Bryceland

In Bryceland, the other unit of measurement is the degree. This is used for measurements of rotation. There are 360 degrees in a complete circle, so the Bryce standard of measurement matches ours for dividing a circle into certain units. Thank God for small mercies.

CHANGING ONE OBJECT: REPOSITION, RESIZE, ROTATE

Now that we've told you about the units of measurement in Bryce Space, we can move on to the Edit controls themselves. The first set of Edit controls we'll examine are those that change the attributes of one object. They're located together on the Edit Palette, roughly occupying its left half (remember, we're ignoring the outside controls on the Edit Palette, since they get their own chapters), as shown in Figure 6.9. The Three R's are Resize, Rotate, and Reposition. They work with single objects. Of course, they can also work with multiple objects, but unlike the two controls to their right, they do not require a multiple object selection to perform their editing magic. These three edit the attributes that are part of an object's matrix (the object matrix was discussed in Chapter 4, "Brycean Objects").

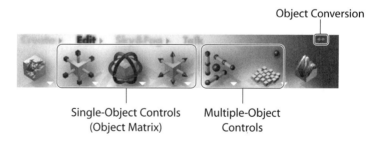

Figure 6.9 column labels:
Object Conversion

Single-Object Controls
(Object Matrix)

Multiple-Object
Controls

Figure 6.9 The Edit Palette's controls broken into their logical control groupings.

You can change an object in Bryce four ways.

- *Edit Palette control.* In the Edit Palette, you can use the Edit Palette control by dragging the appropriate part of the Resize, Rotate, or Reposition control.

- *Direct manipulation.* You can directly change the object in the scene work area by dragging the control handles or dragging the entire object.

- *3D Transformations dialog box.* The pop-up menus for each of the Three Rs controls gives you access to the 3D Transformations dialog box.

- *Object Attributes dialog box.* The Object Attributes dialog box enables you to make changes to the object using absolute coordinates.

Although the Edit Palette presents them in the left-to-right order of Resize, Rotate, and Reposition, we will discuss Reposition first, since there are concepts in repositioning that are more basic to both it and Resize.

Repositioning Objects in Bryce

The first and most basic way you can edit an object is to change its position. Move it from here to there. You can move objects around in your scene in four ways.

With the direct drag method, you select the object and then drag it to some other location in your scene. Drag it from there to here. Simple. Select and drag. Drag in the main view or, for more precision, in top, side, or front view.

You can also use the Reposition control to move an object in a particular direction along an axis. There are times when attempting to drag the object directly will be vexing. The Reposition control will come in handy.

A more precise means of repositioning is to use nudge keys to move the object in one direction by a certain amount.

The fourth method is to change the numerical value for the object's position using one of the dialog boxes that have numerical input. (We'll discuss numerical input later in the chapter in its own section.)

Direct Dragging à la the Constrain Key

Although graphics programs generally use the Shift key to constrain the movement of the cursor, only two directions are involved—horizontal and vertical—as you look at your monitor. Because Bryce works in three dimensions, it departs from the limitations of one constraining key. It has three keys, one for each dimension, as follows:

- The Control key (Macintosh; not Command-Option as the Bryce 4 Manual states) or Ctrl+Alt keys (Windows) constrain along the x axis.

- The Option (Macintosh) or Alt (Windows) key constrains along the y axis.

- The Command (Macintosh) or Ctrl (Windows) key constrains along the z axis.

For the most perfectly aligned movement, make sure you hold down the constrain key before you begin dragging. You can press the constrain key after you begin the drag, but the constraint won't kick in from the point where the object was when you started dragging. It takes effect somewhere in between. For instance, if you were to move an object along the *x* axis and then constrain it a bit later, the object might stray too far up or down from its starting position before the constraint takes place and then be locked into a constrained position along the *x* axis—only higher or lower than where it was before. Bryce seems to pick some arbitrary levels along the grid for constraining in those cases, so make sure that you constrain at the outset.

Unfortunately, you can't follow this precaution when you're using any of the key combinations that involve the Control key on the Mac or the Ctrl key in Windows. Remember: Holding down Control/Ctrl and clicking within the scene brings up a contextual menu with a list of selection choices. Just be sure to hold down the constrain key immediately after clicking the object, to minimize inadvertent object motion.

When you press the constrain key, the cursor changes to a double arrow. Then when you drag, the object will move only on that one axis in World Space.

Reposition Control

The Reposition tool, like direct dragging, gives you the option of moving your object along all three axes. There are no constrain keys for the Reposition control. The movement itself is already constrained. The Reposition control is especially good for moving small objects or moving objects that are positioned in such a way that they're hard to move. The Reposition control, as a member of the Three Rs group, can move an object along, say, the *x* axis of World Space, Object Space, or Camera Space.

To move an object along the *x* axis, drag the Reposition control from either end of the *x* axis point. (The manual is careful to give the two ends of the control arms different names. Why? Who knows—the result is the same no matter which end you drag.) The other two axes behave accordingly. For all three axes, dragging horizontally changes the object's position. Drag right to adjust the object's position in the positive direction, and drag left to adjust in the negative direction.

We said there aren't any constraining keys for the Reposition control, but there is a modifier key (not mentioned in the manual). Hold down the Option/Alt key while dragging the control, and you reduce the rate of the object's motion by a factor of about 10. This degree of fine-tuning comes in handy when you're struggling to position an object so it's just right.

Repositioning and World/Object/Camera Space

So you are repositioning objects. You can work in one of Bryce's three space orientations. Which one? How? For starters, any time you directly drag a selected object, you are working in Camera Space (unless you hold down one of the constrain keys, in which case you shift to World Space). You can drag up, down, left, or right along the camera's orientation.

When you use the nudge keys, you are working in World Space, moving your objects north, east, south, west, or higher or lower in altitude.

When you use the Reposition tool, the objects move according to what type of space is selected in the Three Rs pop-up menus.

Try It Yourself!

Take a look at the differences among the three spaces:

1. Open the scene file MOVE AND CONSTRAIN from the CD-ROM. The object is rotated so that its axes do not match up with the world's axes, nor is the camera aligned on the Bryce World's *xyz* axes.

2. Select World Space from one of the Three Rs pop-up menus. The bounding box around the object changes to align itself with World Space. Drag the arms of the Reposition control and watch the cube move along the gridlines of the ground plane below.

3. Select Object Space. Notice that the bounding box changes to align with the object. (The scene should have been set up this way when you first opened it.) Once again, drag the Reposition control. This time, notice how the cube moves along its own internal axes, without regard to the ground plane grid or the orientation of the camera. Just for fun, try dragging the control while holding down the Option/Alt key. Feels like stirring molasses, doesn't it?

4. Select Camera Space. The bounding box changes again. Its edges are parallel to the frame of your scene, and the box shows perspective. Use the Reposition control to move the cube and notice how dragging the *x*- and *y*-arms of the control move the cube horizontally and vertically. Drag the *z*-arm, and the cube moves in and out, toward you and away from you.

    As long as we're here, let's take note of an unexpected property of Camera Space. First, use File > Revert to Saved to get the cube centered in the window again. Switch to Camera Space. Now drag the Banking control to rotate the camera on its *z* axis. Notice that the cube's bounding box is still parallel to the edges of the screen. Now try dragging the x- and y-arms of the Reposition control. Whoa! The cube doesn't move parallel to the edges of the scene. When you rotate the camera on its z axis, Camera Space doesn't rotate with it. This is a situation you may encounter only rarely, but it's good to know that a gotcha awaits.

Change your camera position with the Trackball and try the exercises again.

When you change from World Space to Object Space to Camera Space, the action of the Reposition tool changes. To return to the original camera position, click the Default View memory dot.

In this next exercise, we'll practice moving the object by dragging it directly, rather than using the Reposition control. You'll find that now the flavor of space you have chosen has no effect on the object's motion.

1.   Make sure you're in Camera Space. Move the cube side to side with the x axis arm of the Reposition control. Now use the mouse to drag the cube from side to side. The motion is exactly the same, right?

2.   Switch to World Space and use the mouse to drag the cube around. See—it's no different from dragging the cube in Camera Space.

3.   Hold down the Control key or Ctrl+Alt keys (to constrain on the x axis) and drag the cube. (Remember, since the Control/Ctrl key will bring up the contextual menu, you need to begin dragging and then immediately press the constrain key.) Notice that the cube moves in the same orientation as the bounding box.

The moral of the story is twofold:

Directly dragging an object with the mouse always moves it within Camera Space—but dragging an object with the mouse while pressing a constrain key always moves the object in World Space.

Moving Things That Are "Hard to Move"

If you're in side or front view and you want to drag something that's flat, such as the ground, a square, a disk, an infinite plane, or an infinite slab, you might have a bit of a problem. Those are difficult objects to select from those angles because Bryce "sees" objects in a ray-traced fashion. In other words, almost all of the rays pass above or below the flat object, so it's hard for Bryce to see at that angle (see Figure 6.10a). But there are times when you must look at your scene from that angle to make your adjustments. There are two options to make your hard-to-move object movable. The first is to use the Reposition control. Once your object is selected, it will go in whatever direction you drag with the Reposition tool. The second option is a sneaky trick for those times when you just gotta get in there and do it directly by dragging about in your Bryce scene. This recipe presents another way to have complete control over that flat object.

Recipe for the Hard of Moving

1. Create a small sphere to use as a "moving buddy" (see Figure 6.10b).

2. Select the flat object (here, a ground plane) and sphere as follows: Select the ground using the Select by Kind pop-up menu on the Selection Palette. Next, hold down the Shift key and select the sphere by directly clicking it.

3. With both objects selected, drag the sphere. The flat object will go along for the ride! (See Figure 6.10c.) Place your flat object wherever it needs to go. When you're done with your sphere moving buddy, delete it.

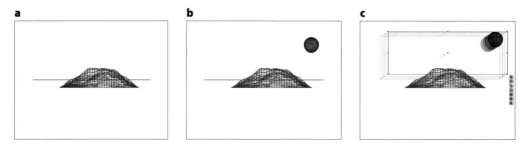

Figure 6.10 Moving using a moving buddy: a) The flat object; b) creating a sphere; c) moving the sphere with the flat object following along.

Never again will you be eluded by an object that doesn't want to move!

Moving Objects by Nudging

You can move your selected object or objects by tapping the arrow keys. You've been introduced to them already in the discussion of the grid: When you press any of the arrow keys to nudge an object, the object will be moved by increments of one-quarter grid unit, which constitutes one nudge unit. That doesn't necessarily mean they will move on the grid, however; they will move over by that grid amount. Of course, if your object is already aligned to the grid, it will stay on the grid as it moves.

You can use the arrow keys and the Page Up and Page Down keys to move objects by one nudge unit, as summarized:

- The *left* and *right* arrow keys move objects horizontally along the *x* axis.

- The *up* and *down* arrow keys move objects horizontally along the *z* axis.

- The *Page Up* and *Page Down* keys move objects vertically along the *y* axis.

Figure 6.11 shows the orientation of the arrow keys in Bryce's World Space. The most intuitive position is from top view, where the keys work to move things front-back-left-right, as the arrow keys themselves are positioned. Since Bryce 4's default camera angle is diagonal to the *x* and *z* axes, sometimes the right-left and up-down arrow combinations are confusing. The arrow keys are tricky when looking at your scene in side view, because the objects move in the opposite direction from what is indicated on the arrow keys. So here, from every view, the arrow keys point in the direction in which things will move in Bryce Space when that particular key is pressed. The arrow keys are locked into Bryce World Space; they do not move things any differently if you have set things to move in Object Space or Camera Space.

Figure 6.11 Bryce Space and arrow key orientations: a) Default Director's View; b) default Camera View; c) top view; d) bottom view; e) right view; f) left view; g) front view; h) back view.

a

Director's view (~ Key)

b
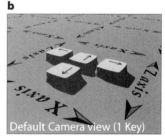
Default Camera view (1 Key)

c
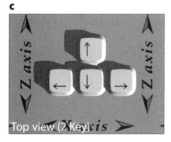
Top view (2 Key)

d
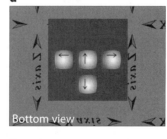
Bottom view

e
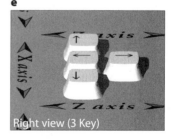
Right view (3 Key)

f
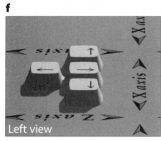
Left view

g
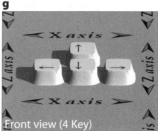
Front view (4 Key)

h
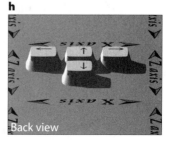
Back view

Now we'll move on to inventory the abundance of alternatives for determining the distance covered in one arrow-key nudge.

Commanding Your Control Shift Options

Bryce is teeming with modifier key combinations to push an object twice or half the distance that a simple nudge will move it, as elaborated in this list:

Shift-nudge	2 nudge units (1/2 grid/unity unit)
Plain ol' nudge	1 nudge unit (1/4 grid/unity unit)
Option-Shift/Alt+Shift-nudge	1/2 nudge unit (1/8 grid/unity unit)
Option/Alt-nudge	1/64 nudge unit (1/256 grid/unity unit)

So, as modifier keys go, Shift makes a move bigger, and Option/Alt makes it smaller. Option/Alt and Shift together make the move larger than the minuscule Option/Alt key move alone. Figure 6.12 shows the relative sizes of the nudge units, with each key combination identified.

We will revisit this list of modifier keys when we discuss numerical entry in the Edit dialog boxes later in this chapter.

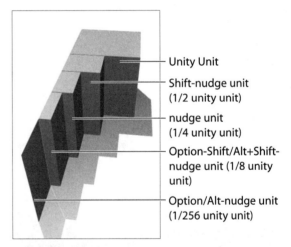

Unity Unit

Shift-nudge unit (1/2 unity unit)

nudge unit (1/4 unity unit)

Option-Shift/Alt+Shift-nudge unit (1/8 unity unit)

Option/Alt-nudge unit (1/256 unity unit)

Figure 6.12 The distances an object will travel when modifier keys are used along with the arrow (nudge) keys.

Nudge Fluency Exercise

If you thought that the "practicing scales" exercise for the Flyaround in Chapter 3 was wacky, then welcome to more scale practice. This will help you gain some fluency with all the Control Shift Option Alt Command keys. Roll up your sleeves and dig right in.

1. Start with the basic nudge arrow keys. If you haven't already played around with moving an object, do so. Create an object and move it this way and that with the arrow keys and the Page Up and Page Down keys.

With a bit of practice, you'll find that knowing which key moves in which direction in which view becomes completely intuitive, although you may still get a bit tangled up in side view.

2. Nudge in larger increments. Press the Shift key, use the nudge keys, and watch the objects move twice as far as they did before.

3. Nudge in smaller increments. Press both the Shift and Option/Alt keys and watch the objects move around in half the space as the nudge units.

4. Nudge in tiny increments. Press only the Option/Alt key while tapping those arrow keys. You'll have to tap a few times before you really see any significant object displacement on your screen.

Resizing

Using the Resize controls, you can take objects that start out symmetrical (a cube or pyramid) and create objects that are far different from their original shape. Bryce's Create Palette, with its "preprocessed" stretched and squashed shapes, is a nod in this direction. Once you change the shape of the original object, the possibilities for modeling objects widen considerably. With resizing, a cube primitive becomes a flat board, a square tile, or a rectangular

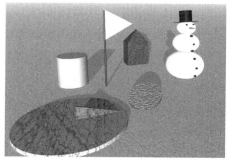

Figure 6.13 A ridiculously simple scene in which all objects were created from primitives.

brick. A cylinder becomes a column, a teeny-tiny tube, almost a piece of string, or a flat coin. A flattened pyramid becomes a flag. This object flexibility is yours with the Resize controls. Figure 6.13 shows several objects created from primitives using the Resize control.

Objects can be uniformly reduced or enlarged, or they can be resized along one axis only. The Resize control and the handles of the selected object work similarly to change the selected object's size.

The Resize control makes the selected object grow or shrink. Point the mouse at the control and then drag. Keep dragging; when you like what you have, let go. Depending on where you first grab the control, you make the object grow or shrink in different ways. As you move the mouse over different parts of the control, you get two sources of feedback to tell you how the object will be resized.

The Object control itself changes, showing you how the object will be changed. The pointer cursor changes, too, to one of four possible cursors. When the mouse is over the object's center, you see the uniform resize cursor. The object also is uniformly enlarged. Roll the cursor over any of the edges of the control, and the cursor changes to tell you which axis you'll be affecting: x, y, or z.

To increase the size of an object, drag to the right. Drag to the left to decrease the size. This procedure holds true no matter which axis you are working with. It does not matter whether you are trying to increase the object's size along the y axis (vertically); you still drag to the right to increase, and to the left to decrease, the size.

You can increase the size of the object in either direction along any axis. In Figure 6.14, a simple cube is resized along the x axis. The cube grows outward in one direction—toward the side where you dragged from in the first place. So if you drag the closer control (on the right), the cube grows out on the right.

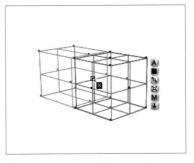

Figure 6.14 An object growing out along the x axis.

The same thing happens when you directly drag the selected object's resize handles. The cursor changes to tell you which axis you'll be affecting. Note that the Resize control has little cubes on each end, to match the shape and position of the handles on the object's bounding box. (The interface design here, with the corresponding look of handles and Resize control handles, is quite handsome!) Here, too, the object will grow or shrink in the direction of the side of the handle you picked—or to put it more simply, the edge that you do not touch stays in the same place.

When you drag from the center of the Resize control, the object grows or shrinks uniformly from its own center. Since there is no control handle at the object's center from which to drag, however, in this case, the direct approach acts a bit differently. The object is resized uniformly when you drag from any of the corners of the object's bounding box. Rather than growing out from the center, though, the object grows toward the corner where you commenced your drag. In Figure 6.15, the cube was grabbed from the upper-left corner and enlarged

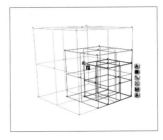

Figure 6.15 Proportional resizing by directly dragging an object: The corner you drag grows in the direction of your drag; the opposite corner stays stationary.

proportionately. The three-step image shows how the opposite corner, on the lower right, stays stationary. The cube grows up and to the left as it increases in size.

A Shift-Clicking Drag

What happens if you want to make an object grow along a certain axis in both directions from the center? For that, you'll need to use a modifier key. This next section will help you familiarize yourself with the dizzying array of modifier options available for resizing your object every which way.

In this section, when we say *grow*, we mean either grow or shrink. While focusing the discussion on the modifier keys, we figured it's best to simplify matters: objects grow. Also, we refer to the *fixed point* and the *grab point*. The fixed point is the part of the object that stays still. The object grows or shrinks from the fixed point. The grab point is the point of the object from which you drag.

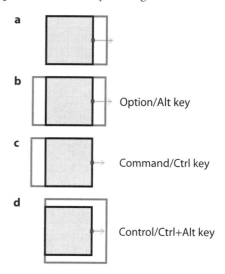

Figure 6.16 How modifier keys change resizing (top view, resizing along the *x* axis): a) No modifier key; b) Option/Alt key; c) Command/Ctrl key; d) Control/Ctrl+Alt key(s).

Option (Macintosh) or Alt (Windows) key. Holding down the Option or Alt key will enlarge or reduce the object from the object's center. This modifier key behavior is consistent with some other applications that change from edge to center when you press the Option/Alt key (for example, Photoshop and Illustrator). See Figure 6.16b. If you use the Resize control, the axis arm under your cursor changes shape when you press the Option/Alt key, to show you that the resizing works in both directions along that axis.

Shift key. Pressing the Shift key constrains an object to 50% increments as it grows. When enlarging, the object snaps to 150%, 200%, 250%, and so on. Reducing, however, happens quite a bit differently, though the manual doesn't let on. When reducing, the object first snaps to 50% of its size and then jumps to 0.1024 Bryce units, or 0.5% of a unity unit. It doesn't matter how huge your object is; the second jump will take you to 0.1024 Bryce units (if you look in the Object Attributes dialog box, you'll see 0.10 because the field shows only the first two digits after the decimal point). In Bryce 2 days, Shift shrinkage progressively halved your object, reducing it to 50%, then 25%, 12.5%, and so on. Now, to accomplish this, you have to perform several distinct Shift-drags: Shift-drag to reduce to 50%, then release the mouse and Shift-drag afresh to reduce to 25%, and so forth. The first step sort of makes sense—Shift-nudge moves an object by a distance of half a unity unit, and Shift-resize reduces a unity-unit–sized object to one half a unity unit in dimension. But going on to 0.1024 on the next step? It's a mystery...

The Shift key can also be used in conjunction with the other key combinations mentioned here. For instance, when the Shift andOption (or Shift+Alt) keys are pressed, the object's size increases or decreases from its center, jumping in the same increments as when the Shift key is used alone.

Command (Macintosh) or Ctrl (Windows) key. When you press the Command/Ctrl key after beginning a drag from a certain point, the opposite side of the object will be resized. The point that you "grabbed" to begin your drag will stay still, and the rest of the object will grow or shrink from that place. See Figure 6.16c.

For kicks, to make your objects do a wireframe dance, begin a drag of an object, and after you begin dragging, press and release the Command/Ctrl key at intervals. If you really get good at it, try it to music! (But please, make the music something other than scales!)

Pressing the Command/Ctrl key before beginning to drag the object will put the object in rotation mode. That is a different kind of dance; we'll discuss it in the "Rotation" section later in this chapter.

Control key (Macintosh) or Ctrl+Alt keys (Windows). Press the Control key or Ctrl+Alt keys after you've started your resize drag. Use this modifier when you want the object to grow or shrink uniformly, but from a certain edge. Drag an axis, and the object will grow from the other side of that axis. See Figure 6.16d, where, looking down at the object from top view, the object is enlarged along the x axis. It is enlarged uniformly, and the fixed point is opposite the grab point.

Pressing the Control key or Ctrl+Alt keys before clicking any control point will snap the object back to unity unit size.

And now, a review: All the modifier keys that are located on the bottom row of the keyboard (Command, Option, Control or Ctrl, Alt, plus the Ctrl+Alt combination) change the resize operation and the fixed point from which the object shrinks or grows. For your reference, the places to remember are the fixed point (the part of the object that is stationary) and the grab point (the point you dragged from).

The standard approach (Look Ma! No keys!) makes the object grow toward the grab point; the fixed point is opposite the grab point.

Option/Alt changes the fixed point to the center. The object grows toward both (or all) sides.

Command/Ctrl changes the fixed point to the opposite end. The grab point becomes the fixed point, staying still while the object grows toward the other side.

Control/Ctrl+Alt enlarges the object uniformly. The object grows toward the grab point; the fixed point is opposite the grab point and stays put.

Shift makes the object grow by leaps and bounds of 50% or shrink to 50% and then to 0.10 Bryce units.

Resize and Nudge Recipe

Follow these steps to create a composite object (see Figure 6.17):

1. Create a cube and a pyramid (see Figure 6.17a).

2. Use the Resize control and Shift-drag left on the z axis to bring the depth of the cube to one-half size (see Figure 6.17b).

3. Select the pyramid. Do the same thing (reduce it to one-half size). See? It's an exact match! No need to eyeball it (see Figure 6.17c).

4. The pyramid should still be selected, so press the Page Up key four times to put the pyramid on top of the cube. Was that easy or was that easy? (See Figure 6.17d.)

5. Extra credit: Flatten the pyramid by Shift-dragging left on the top y axis control. Then group both objects (see Figure 6.17e and f).

Sure, you could've selected both objects and resized them simultaneously. But the point here is that with the internal grid-resize structure, when you get that great idea to add a new object to an already existing object, you should know your resize options.

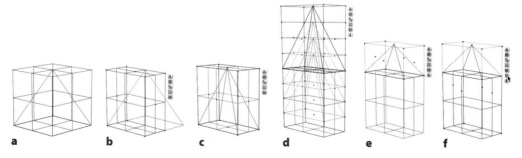

a   b   c   d   e   f

Figure 6.17 Composite object from a cube and pyramid: a) Create cube and pyramid; b) resize cube; c) resize pyramid; d) nudge pyramid up; e) reduce height of pyramid; f) group both objects.

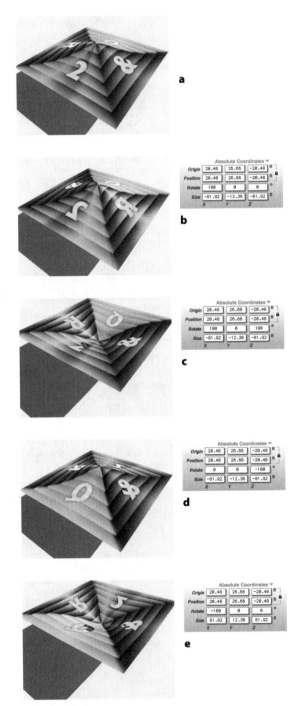

Figure 6.18 Flipping a terrain: a) Before any flipping; b) flip X; c) flip Y; d) flip Z; e) flip Y and Z.

Multiply and Divide

There is a key combination you can use to make proportional enlargements and reductions. In fact, if you want to get to 25% of your object's original size and you are reducing along all three axes, then this is the way to go. To double the size of the object, press the multiply (*) key. To halve the object's size, press the divide (/) key. Pressing the / key twice will, of course, reduce the object to one-fourth its size. You can use the / and * keys located on either the numeric keypad or the regular keyboard. (When you're using the * on the regular keyboard, make sure that you press Shift; otherwise, you'll type 8 and mistakenly change the Camera View. Ow.)

Flip

The Flip controls are found in the pop-up menu under the Resize tool. Flip does just that—flips your object along the axis described. In Figure 6.18, you can see the effect of flipping along each axis—*x*, *y*, and *z*.

Flip X swaps the object's orientation along the east-west axis—what was facing east is now facing west. However, what faced up still faces up and what faced bottom still faces bottom. But the object is inverted. Notice in Figure 6.18b through e that the letters and numbers are wrong-reading because they're flipped.

Flip Z flips the object along the north-south axis. Flip Y flips the object vertically.

Why do the commands for flip live under the Resize menu? A peek in the Object Attributes dialog box provides the clue. The object doesn't really change size per se; rather, it changes orientation or is inverted. Compared to a regular object, the flipped counterpart's size numbers are all negative. Size numbers are either positive or negative; unlike with offset and rotation, there is no mix 'n' match for positive and negative. That is, if all numbers are positive, the object is regular; if they are negative, the object is flipped, an inverted mirror image of itself. Again, there is an exception. As you will see in the numbers for Figure 6.18e, flipping an object twice results in positive size numbers. Remember the old adage: two negatives make a positive.

When to Use Flip

When positioning objects, Flip works well. You don't like your object facing in this direction? Flip it so that it's now facing that direction. That's fairly self-evident. However, when you're creating more complex objects from a series of primitives, Flip is also an excellent tool in your toolbox.

1. Press ⌘-D (Macintosh) or Ctrl+D (Windows) to duplicate the object.

2. Select Flip. The copy will be flipped.

What if you want to flip an object when you are aligning or sizing it carefully? To create the x, y, and z axis arrows in Figure 6.19, we altered a cube primitive object. Then we created a pyramid and positioned it on one end of the rectangle, squashed it, and got it just right. When one arrow was finished, it was time for the other one. Stop. Think about this for a moment. Would you want to go through all that positioning and squashing to get yet another primitive to be just so? No! Neither did we. So we copied the pyramid, pasted it, flipped it, and then moved it to the other end of the flattened cube.

Figure 6.19 Arrows for axes, created with the aid of the Flip command.

Resizing in World Space/Object Space/Camera Space

The significance of resizing in Object Space versus resizing in World Space cannot be underrated. This is one of those features that, when it was added to Bryce, caused an outbreak of riotous thanksgiving and merrymaking. If you haven't joined the celebration already, then try out this resize practice.

Try It Out

Once again, open that same scene file that you used for Resizing: MOVE AND CONSTRAIN. (Or, if it's still open, select File > Revert to Saved.)

1. Change the Space setting to World Space. The bounding box is aligned with World Space, no matter how the object is oriented. This is the first clue that resizing along the world's x axis will warp the cube. Resize along the x axis using the Resize control, by dragging to the right from the Resize x axis. See? It warped the cube. Undo. Try the same thing by directly dragging the x axis control handle. Undo. (Undo after each move.)

2. Change the Space setting to Object Space. The bounding box changes, so it is now hugging the object. Here's your first clue that resizing will behave differently. Again, resize along the x axis using the Resize control. Undo. Now try the direct method on the object's bounding box. Notice how the object, though rotated, is enlarged along its own width. Try the other axes, too. (Undo after each move.)

3. Try out Camera Space. Now the object's wireframe aligns with the edges of the scene window. After changing the setting to Camera Space, try the Resize control and the direct drag-the-control-handle method. Try all three axes. The resizing takes place in relation to your point of view. Try, say, resizing on the x axis, undo, move the camera position, and then resize on the x axis again. Camera Space allows you to be completely subjective when resizing an object.

What Does It All Mean?

The difference between what happens when you resize in World Space and when you resize in Object Space is striking.

In World Space, resizing works from the outside, stretching or pulling on an object along the particular axis. The x force (not to be confused with a popular science-fiction TV show) pays no attention to the object's orientation. In Object Space, the resizing works from within an object, changing the size of the object without destroying the basic integrity of the shape. Figure 6.20 shows the difference between the two. In Figure 6.20a, the World Space *y* force is pushing down on the rotated cone. In Figure 6.20b, the rotated cone is being reduced along its *y* axis.

a

b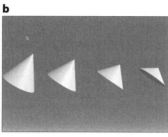

Figure 6.20
Resizing along the *y* axis: a) in World Space; b) in Object Space.

You can work more intuitively, positioning (and rotating) an object, adjusting its size, rotating it a bit more, and resizing again after that. Most of the time, you'll want to work in Object Space for additional resizing if your object has been rotated at all.

However, there may be cases when World Space shape distortion is the desired end. Rotate the object and then make it grow or shrink in any of the three directions to change it into that shape you want. A pyramid can be forced into a right angle, a cone that is off base makes a nice oblique source of light rays, and with judicious use of the Rotate controls, you can coax terrains into having overhanging edges. For more on the thrills of terrain overhangs, see Chapter 16, "Superlative Nature Imagery."

But suppose you subject your object to some fiendish combination of Object and World Space resizings, and the result is a disaster? Not to worry—hidden in the Object Attributes dialog box is a command that will let you come to the aid of your ailing object. Select the offending object and click the A icon (or press ⌘-Option-E/Ctrl+Alt+E) to bring up the dialog box. Click the phrase "Absolute Coordinates" to bring up a pop-up menu. At its bottom is the command Remove Shear. Choose this command and click the check mark to leave the Object Attributes dialog box. Your object will snap out of its funk and look like its old self again.

What did we just do? What's "shear" anyway? Hang on a second and we'll explain. In physics, shear is a force applied to an object obliquely, so that the object's internal axes are deformed. In a sheared object, the axes are no longer orthogonal; that is, they're not at right angles to each other any more. This deformation won't happen if you always transform your object in Object Space, but once you start applying transformations in World and Camera Space, you run the risk of introducing shear (which may be, after all, what you want!).

Figure 6.21a shows one of the sheared cones from Figure 6.20. To return it to its unsheared form (that is, to restore the original orthogonal relationships among its axes), first click the A icon to bring up the Object Attributes dialog box. Figure 6.21b shows you how to get to the Remove Shear command, and the result is shown in Figure 6.21c. If you open the Object Attributes dialog box again, you'll find that all of the numbers are exactly the same. In other words, the object retains its overall dimensions and orientation.

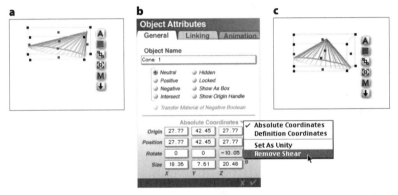

Figure 6.21 Removing shear from an object: a) The sheared object; b) the Object Attributes dialog box, showing the Coordinates pop-up menu and the Remove shear command; c) the unsheared object.

Rotation

The Rotation control is in the center of the Edit Palette. It is the intriguing-looking control with rings around a cube nucleus. When you rotate, you rotate around the axis. The object will always move around its origin point, which by default is at the object's center. Think of the axis as a skewer piercing the object (see Figure 6.22). The object rotates around that skewer, or axis. As we've already mentioned (see Chapter 3, "Camera and Scene," and Chapter 4, "Brycean Objects"), you can move the origin point away from the object's center. This lets

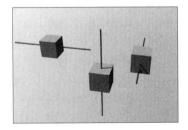

Figure 6.22 Each axis depicted as a skewer.

you move the axis of rotation off center within the object or move it outside of the object altogether. Of all the Edit controls we discuss in this chapter, the Rotation controls are the only ones that have no relation to the grid units.

The beauty of Bryce is that you don't have to complete all your resizing before you do any rotation. Since you can work in Object Space, you can freely move back and forth between resizing and rotation other two Rs, there are no keypad equivalents for rotating an object; there are, however, modifier keys.

Direct Rotation

Place the mouse pointer over a selected object's control handle. When you press the Command (Macintosh) or Ctrl (Windows) key, the cursor changes to a little rotate arc. Now when you drag the handle, you rotate the object. Make sure that you press the Command or Ctrl key before you drag. (Incidentally, this is the counterpart to our earlier admonition—when resizing an object—to press the Command/Ctrl key after you begin the drag.)

Which way will the object rotate? It depends on which control handle you grabbed. Grab one of the face control handles—where the cursor changes to x, y, or z—and you will rotate around that particular axis. Grab one of the corner handles, and you will rotate freely this way and that. If you somehow manage to drag upward in a straight line (the cursor disappears, so you cannot see anything to help with your eye-hand coordination), the object will rotate around one axis. But since hand movement without any visual feedback does not go in straight lines, the object will teeter and reel around freely. Whee!

The Rotation Control

The Rotation control on the Edit Palette works the same way as the direct rotation method, only instead of grabbing a control point for an object's face to rotate, you drag the control for that particular axis. As with the other controls on the Edit Palette that deal with matters of x, y, and z, the cursor will tell you which axis you're going to rotate around, so you know which axis you'll be affecting. The Rotation control has no counterpart to the direct-drag-from-a-corner to rotate every which way.

As with resizing, rotation works by dragging in a left-right direction. Depending on the direction the object is facing, and depending on your camera perspective, the direction of the rotation can be completely counterintuitive. Figure 6.23a shows how, for each axis, there is a clockwise rotation when you drag to the right (yes, we know, it's a right-handed bias; lefties get the upper hand in interface design elsewhere in Bryce). "Clockwise" is determined by the camera's position, however. The z axis rotates clockwise if you look at it from the front, as in the figure. In contrast, Figure 6.23b shows the same configuration from roughly the default Camera View (which is to the rear). From that perspective, the *z* axis rotates counterclockwise. It can be bewildering to those who need to make sense out of object movement in relation to drag movement.

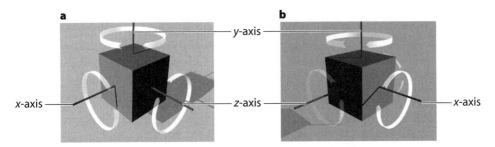

Figure 6.23 a) Rotation occurring in a clockwise direction, as seen from the front; b) the same clockwise rotation seen from the default Camera View.

Constrain Keys

Bryce has a constrain key that enables you to rotate by precise increments. Press the Shift key as you rotate, and the object will pop to 45° positions.

The Option (Macintosh) or Alt (Windows) key, when pressed, provides you with more precise, controlled movement for fine-tuning. In cases where you need to precisely position an object, the Option/Alt key will greatly aid you as you eyeball the object as it rotates. This works for rotating with the Rotation control and is applicable when Command/Ctrl-dragging the object.

> **TIP:** You can better see what is going on for rotation if you set your depth cueing so that the wireframe is fainter on the far sides of your object. Otherwise, you'll be susceptible to those figure-ground optical illusions where you can't tell the near edge from the far edge of the object.

Rotation and World/Object/Camera Space

Rotation, like the other two Rs, operates differently depending on the Space setting. Rotate the object around the world's *x* axis; or around its own *x* axis; or even the camera's *x* axis.

Try It Yourself

For practice, try it out, using that same scene file that you used for Resizing: MOVE AND CONSTRAIN.

1. Change the Space setting to World Space. Rotate along the z axis using the Rotate tool by dragging to the right. Undo. Then find the z axis on the object's bounding box. Press the Command (Macintosh) or Ctrl (Windows) key and drag to the right. Try the other axes, too. (Undo after each move.)

2. Change the Space setting to Object Space. Notice how the bounding box changes, so it now hugs the object. Rotate the object both by using the Rotate control and by directly Command- or Ctrl-dragging the control points.

    Change your camera perspective while you are in Object Space. Rotate on the x axis, and notice how what is clockwise in one direction becomes counterclockwise when viewed from the other side. The object rotates consistently; it's just that your perspective on it changes.

3. Try out Camera Space. After changing the setting to Camera Space, try rotating both by using the Rotate tool and directly Command- or Ctrl-dragging the x axis.

As an alternative, see how rotation on one particular axis changes depending on which space you're in.

P. S.: There is much more to be said about rotation regarding moving the origin point away from its default position at the center of an object. Since this comes up mostly in the context of animation, we'll defer discussion of the subject until Chapter 15, "Advanced Animation Techniques."

3D Transformations and Other Dialog Boxes

Chapter 4, "Brycean Objects," first introduced you to object attributes and the underlying object matrix. The three Edit tools that we have been discussing—Resize, Rotate, and Reposition—work directly with the object matrix, and they are all related. There is one more dialog box for editing your objects, using numerical values instead of clicks, drags, and keyboard constraints. Each of the three Edit tools' pop-up menus contains an option called 3D Transformations. Choose this item to open the 3D Transformations dialog box. In this section, we'll discuss editing your Bryce objects using numerical values in the 3D Transformations dialog box.

But first, here's a quick review of how the tools and dialog boxes are related.

The two dialog boxes—Object Attributes and 3D Transformations—have settings for Position/Offset, Rotation, and Size. These settings correspond to the three Edit controls we've been discussing. Figure 6.24 shows the relationships among the two dialog boxes and the Edit Palette controls. (By the way, for the following discussion, we're assuming that when we're in the Object Attributes dialog box, we're entering numbers in the Absolute Coordinates boxes. Definition Coordinates obey slightly different rules and will be discussed separately.)

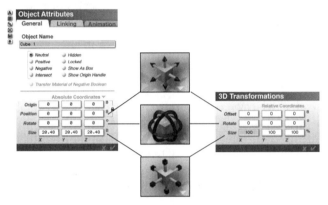

Figure 6.24 The relationships among the Object Attributes dialog box, the Three Rs Edit Palette controls, and the 3D Transformations dialog box.

Offset corresponds to the Reposition tool.

Rotation corresponds to the Rotation tool.

Size corresponds to the Resize tool.

Object Attributes and 3D Transformations each work a little differently. Object Attributes expresses its values using absolute coordinates. When you want to know what the object is, you check Object Attributes. It is thus and such a size and is rotated like so, and is offset from the World Center by such and such Bryce units. Those are specific numbers.

3D Transformations has coordinates in relative values. When you want to change the object, in 3D Transformations, you enter a relative number to determine by what amount you will change it. 3D Transformations starts from where the object is currently located: Move the object over this way by this amount. Rotate it on that axis by that many degrees. Reduce it on two of the three axes by half. Offset is figured in terms of B, that is, Bryce units. Rotate is figured in degrees, and Scale is figured in terms of percent. The 3D Transformations dialog box always opens with the first two rows blank and the third set at 100% size. That is the status quo, and the numbers you put in there will change the object relative to the state it was in.

Choose, then, from the two dialog boxes depending on what you want to do. Do you want the object to be bigger and to be rotated by some amount? Then go to the 3D Transformations dialog box. Do you want the object to be a specific size (say, the same as that other object over there)? Then use the Object Attributes dialog box to enter the precise number.

You can use either dialog box for another handy trick: to resize along two dimensions simultaneously; or very closely related to that, you can use it to reduce in two dimensions while enlarging the third. Figure 6.25 shows three cylinders. The top one is provided for reference, as the basic unity unit size. The middle one has been enlarged on the *y* axis. (In this case, it's handy to get a head start by manually resizing so you know which axis is which.) Its corresponding

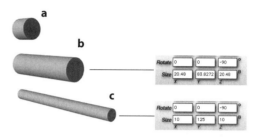

Figure 6.25 Resizing a cylinder on two axes by using the Size fields in the Object Attributes dialog box: a) Cylinder at unity size; b) cylinder enlarged along the *y* axis by entering a number in the dialog box; c) new values entered in the Size fields to reduce the cylinder on two axes and enlarge it on the other.

Object Attributes values are shown. The bottom cylinder has been resized in the Object Attributes dialog box. The two axes that control the width of the cylinder, *x* and *z*, were reduced. The *y* axis that controls the height (or length, since the cylinder is now lying down) was enlarged. These two processes took place simultaneously in this dialog box. You can use either dialog to get the same results; in the 3D Transformations dialog box, you would have entered, say, 75% in both the *x* and *z* numerical entry boxes and perhaps 130% in the *y* numerical entry box.

Object Attributes, 3D Transformation, and World/Object/Camera Space

How are each of the settings in both dialog boxes affected by the different types of space in Bryce?

In the Object Attributes dialog box, the Position value is always calculated in absolute World Space terms. (How else could you measure an object's distance from World Center?) In the 3D Transformations dialog box, the Offset value is relative when it changes the object's position; an object moves over by *n* units from its present position. But does it move based on its own coordinates, that is, in Object Space? No, it does not; the object moves according to World Space orientation.

The following table compares the two dialog boxes, listing which space Bryce is operating in for each of the functions.

Function	Object Attributes	3D Transformation
Offset	World Space	World Space
Rotation	World Space	World Space
Size	Object Space	Object Space

It's worth spelling this out for those of you who may be joining us from Bryce 2, where Offset Transformations behaved differently under Mac and Windows. Yet another platform discrepancy has been deftly eliminated by Bryce's crack team of engineers.

Definition Coordinates

Now it's time to consider the flip side of the Object Attributes dialog box: the Definition Coordinates panel (reached from a pop-up menu on the bottom half of the General Object Attributes tab, or refer back to Figure 4.18). The numbers you type in the Definition Coordinates fields describe the object with relation to its own innate axes, center of rotation, and external boundaries. Work through the following exercise, and you'll see what we mean:

1. Open the file on the CD-ROM named DEFINITION COORDINATES. This is an ordinary cube, created at World Center and still in its default position. Show Origin Handle is turned on, so you should see a little green dot at the cube's center. We've chosen Object Space as our frame of reference (Figure 6.26). Click the Edit button at the top of the screen to switch to the Edit Palette.

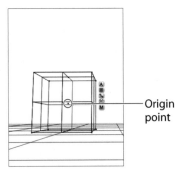

Origin point

Figure 6.26 A freshly created cube, the starting point for our Definition Coordinates exercise.

2. Click the A icon to open the Object Attributes dialog box and hold down the mouse button over the words "Absolute Coordinates." Choose Definition Coordinates from the pop-up menu. Notice that the boxes for Origin are grayed out, and you can type numbers only in the Position boxes. That's because in Definition Coordinates space the origin point of the object is fixed,

and you are defining the position of the center of the object measured in terms of distance and direction from the origin point. Tab to the Position row *y* axis numerical entry box and type 20.48; then close the dialog box. The cube has been moved up, but the origin point remained where it was (Figure 6.27). Use the Rotate control to try out rotation on several axes—the cube swings through space, pivoting about the origin point. Choose Unrotate from the Rotate Options menu to return the cube to its original position.

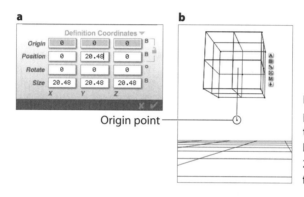

Origin point

Figure 6.27 Adjusting the cube's position: a) Entering numbers in the Definition Coordinates box; b) the result: the cube moves 20.48 units along the *y* axis away from the origin point.

3. Open the Object Attributes dialog box once again and bring up the Definition Coordinates boxes. (You'll notice that each time you enter the Object Attributes dialog box, you have to select Definition Coordinates. That's because Bryce assumes that you usually will want to work with the object rather than redefine its basic coordinates.) Now Tab to the Rotate row *z* axis box and type 45. Close the dialog box. Notice that two major changes have occurred: the cube has rotated around its own center, not around the origin; and the cube has shrunk (Figures 6.28a and b).

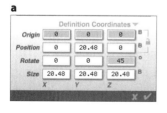

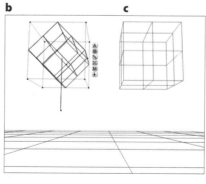

Figure 6.28 Using Definition Coordinates to rotate the cube: a) The Definition Coordinates dialog box; b) the result; c) a new cube, 20.48 Bryce units on a side, for comparison.

So by using Definition Coordinates, you can escape the tyranny of the origin point, and can spin an object about one of its own internal axes, regardless of where the origin is. But what happened to the cube's size? We didn't change any of the size coordinates—compare the Size numbers in Figures 6.27a and 6.28a. For a clue, create another cube and move it next to the first one. Select the first cube and take note of its bounding box: it's the same size as the cube you just created (see Figure 6.28c). When you use Definition Coordinates to rotate an object, the object is confined by the dimensions listed in the Size boxes, so it must shrink to remain within its bounding box. But if you change the size of the bounding box, the rotated object will adjust itself to fit. If you were to rotate by 90° increments, say, to "permanently" orient an object in another direction, you probably won't encounter this situation where the object squooshes to fit inside the bounding box.

4.   Make sure the original cube is selected. Open the Object Attributes dialog box and choose Definition Coordinates. Tab to the Size row x axis box and type 30; then close the dialog box. The cube's bounding box has widened, and the cube inside has stretched to accommodate its new surroundings (see Figure 6.29).

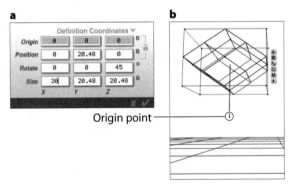

Origin point

Figure 6.29
Growing the rotated cube along the x axis.

Using Definition Coordinates to establish an object's size, rotation, or position redefines the object's basic relationship to Object Space. You are redefining the fundamental parameters of the object—you are saying, in effect, "This is the state of the object as it was created. All further operations use this state as their starting point." This is an important consideration when invoking the Unity command, which we'll discuss a couple of sections from now.

Numbers in the Boxes

Now that we've told you a little about how the dialog boxes work, which space gets affected by which attribute, and how, we'll delve into some specific ways to change numbers in the dialog boxes.

Of course, you can click the numerical entry box you want to change, type the number, and that is that. Slightly higher up on the food chain is the tab technique: tap the Tab key until the particular numerical box you want is selected, so you can then type the number. But wait! There's more! In the survival of the fittest, Bryce power users who master this next technique will evolve into a naturally select group of Bryce Lords and Lordettes. Here is the realm of the up and down arrow keys and all the minion modifier keys. Let Bryce insert the numbers for you.

You can use the up and down arrow keys to increase or decrease the numbers. When you press the arrow keys along with certain modifier keys, the numbers will move up or down in various ways. A dizzying array of options exists for you. We'll break them down as best we can into all the logical groupings.

All of the numerical entry dialog boxes have but three different kinds of numerical units: Bryce units, degrees, and percentages.

First, there are Bryce units. These are used to describe position or offset in both the 3D Transformations and Object Attributes dialog boxes and to describe size in the Object Attributes dialog box.

Then there are degrees. That's a degree (°) sign at the end of row, not a minuscule O! Oh! Degrees are used to describe rotation in all dialog box types.

Finally, there is percentage. This unit is fairly obvious, with the % sign. You'll find it in the 3D Transformations and Multi-Replicate dialog boxes, where change in size is being described.

So, there are three different types of numerical units, and pressing the up arrow or down arrow will increase or decrease the numbers associated with those units. There are also a host of modifiers to make the numbers increase or decrease in different amounts. The amount by which the number will jump depends on both the modifier key and the type of units; that is, the same key combination will affect degrees differently than it will Bryce units; but not even all Bryce units are treated the same, and different dialog boxes accept different combinations. This area is one of the supreme examples of Brycean irrationality—so hang on and follow closely.

Changing Bryce Units

You'll encounter the simplest modifier key combinations most often in Bryce: use the Shift key to raise or lower the number by 10, and the Option/Ctrl+Alt key(s) to change by 0.1. Table 6.1 lists these combinations, which work in the Origin/Position fields within the Object Attributes dialog box. In a moment, we'll show you that they also hold true for other units, and in Chapter 9, you'll find that they also work in the Materials Lab.

Mac modifier	Windows modifier	How numbers change	Numerical result
{Starting point}			20.48
No modifier		Increase/decrease by 1	21.48
Option	Ctrl+Alt	Increase by 0.1	20.58
Shift	Shift	Increase by 10	30.48

Table 6.1 Using the up and down arrow keys with modifier keys to adjust numbers in dialog boxes. These combinations work in the Object Attributes dialog box (Origin/Position fields) and the 3D Transformations and Multi-Replicate dialog boxes (Offset fields).

Recall from earlier in this chapter that Bryce units tend to gather in powers of two: 1, 2, 4, 8, 16, 32, 64, 128, 256, and so forth. Another set of up-and-down-arrow/modifier-key combinations, which now incorporates the Command/Ctrl key, causes numbers to change by those powers of two. Table 6.2 delineates these combinations, which apply in the Size fields of the Object Attributes dialog box, and the Offset fields of the 3D Transformations and Multi-Replicate dialog boxes.

Mac modifier	Windows modifier	How numbers change	Numerical result
{Starting point}			20.48
No modifier		Increase/decrease by 1	21.48
Option	n/a	Increase by .1	20.58
Shift	Shift	Increase by 10	30.48
Command	Ctrl	Increase by 5.12 (nudge)	25.6
Command-Option	Ctrl+Alt	Increase by .08 (Option/Alt-nudge)	20.56
Command-Shift	Ctrl+Shift	Increase by 10.24 (Shift-nudge)	30.72
Command-Option-Shift	Ctrl+Alt+Shift	Increase by 2.56 (Option-Shift/Alt+Shift-nudge)	23.04

Table 6.2 Adjusting numbers in the Object Attributes dialog box (Size fields) and the 3D Transformations and Multi-Replicate dialog boxes (Offset fields). The corresponding nudge unit is shown in parentheses.

How in blazes do you make sense of all of these number units and key commands? Think of it this way: The up and down arrow keys increase and decrease the numerical values (this is true in all the numerical dialog boxes in Bryce). The Option and Shift keys add refinement to the arrow keys. (Sorry, Windows fans;

the Alt key has no effect on its own. That bizarre Ctrl+Alt combo takes its place, and quite neatly destroys the general picture we're so carefully constructing here.) However, since there's an overlap between what the arrow keys do when you're moving selected objects in the Bryce scene window and what the arrow keys do when they're in a numerical dialog box, there is yet another level of modification. By pressing the Command or Ctrl key, you can imitate the moves that happen when you directly nudge—at least so far as the units are concerned. Similarly, pressing the Command key while Option-nudging (or the Ctrl key while Alt-nudging) in the numerical dialog box increases or decreases the amount by Option-nudge (or Alt-nudge) units. The same holds true when adding the Command or Ctrl key to Shift-nudging and Option-Shift (or Alt+Shift) nudging. When you use the Command or Ctrl key with those sequences, the numbers change by the same increments. The Command or Ctrl key causes the numbers to increment by nudge units, rather than tenths, ones and tens (except for that blasted Ctrl+Alt monster).

Changing Degrees and Percentages

Now how about degrees? What modifier do you use to constrain rotation when using the Rotation control or directly manipulating the control handle? The Shift key. Therefore, the Shift key will make the numbers jump up or down by increments of 10°. Likewise, what key do you hold down while rotating an object to refine the object's motion? Why, the Option/Alt key, of course. So the Option key (or Ctrl+Alt key in Windows; the operations are not quite consistent) refines change in the amount of rotation to a tenth of a degree. The resulting set of key combinations is exactly the same as shown in Table 6.1. It just so happens (thank God for small miracles!) that the same system applies to fields measured in percentages, like the Size fields in the 3D Transformations and Multi-Replicate dialog boxes.

Matrix Pasting and Other Variations

Copy Matrix and Paste Matrix are excellent tools for adjusting your object's size, position, and rotation when you want to place something inside another object or in close alignment with it, or when you want to replace an object. We discussed these commands already, in Chapter 4, "Brycean Objects," where we discussed the object matrix, but they bear mentioning here, since you'll use them when you're in your "edit objects" thinking mode.

We will touch on another subset of the 3D Transformations object matrix controls a bit later in this chapter. The Replicate commands are specialized 3D Transformation commands. Since they are part of the process of going from one object to many objects, we'll cover them in the section that discusses that topic. Until then, we'll stick to matters pertaining to editing a single Bryce object.

The Camera as Object

We've mentioned several times that once animation was introduced to Bryce, way back in Bryce 3D, the camera achieved the status of objecthood. It became subject to selection and most of the transformations that apply to objects. Now we'll address the complexities of the camera's "objectness" and look at instances where the camera deviates from ideal objectification.

- *Resize*. None of the Resize commands has any effect on the camera—but then, what purpose would they serve? Fuhgeddaboutit.

- *Rotate*. As you've noticed, the camera, unlike other objects, has no bounding box; it therefore follows, as does the night the day, that it also has no control handles. This makes direct rotation of the camera impossible. Fortunately, the Rotate control on the Edit Palette does work as expected.

- *Reposition*. Rest assured that dragging the camera about the scene works just as with any object, including the effects of dragging with a constraining key held down.

Starting Over: Shades of Undo and the Unity Command

By now you have been resizing and rotating and repositioning your objects. Inevitably, as you hum among the different controls to poke and prod your object into its proud position, you will warp your object in the wrong way. All of a sudden you realize, too late, that you mangled your beautiful object out of alignment. How do you get it back into alignment?

If you warped it just one action ago, there's always Undo (⌘-Z on a Mac, Ctrl+Z under Windows). That's the simplest option—and from the advent of the Macintosh and the Windows adoption of the same, it's been a perennial source of gratefulness!

Most probably, you'll call upon the faithful Undo after a resize or rotate operation, when you realize that you actually wanted to do it in Object Space, but for some reason, you are actually in World Space: Undo. Change Space. Try again.

If you warped your object by more than one action, fixing it gets trickier. You are limited to only one level of undo. However, under each of the pop-up menus for the Three Rs is a command to undo that particular R. Under the Resize control, it's UnResize. Under the Rotate control, it's UnRotate. Under the Reposition control, it's UnReposition. So if you tweaked the rotation, you can undo rotation and start from scratch, without having to change the size of the object. (Undo Reposition is a redundant command; its identical twin, Snap to World Center, can be found one pop-up menu over to the right, under the Alignment pop-up menu. Use whichever one you want.)

If you want to scrap things completely, then there's the Unity command: the Unity command pops your object back into shape. Using Unity is the equivalent of selecting both Undo Resize and Undo Rotate. The Unity button is the "All ye all come free free free!" yell in the hide 'n' seek of Bryce. (Regional yells may vary.) It pops the object back into its original size, shape, and alignment; it aligns it with the grid.

So how do you use the Unity command? There are two ways: First, hold down the Control key (Macintosh; not Command-Option as the Bryce 4 manual says) or the Ctrl+Alt keys (Windows), and then click one of the control points of the object. The cursor should change to a small 1 in a box when the mouse is hovering over a control handle, prior to clicking. The second way is to press the = key. Beware when attempting to go for the + key on the standard keyboard. (The + key, with Shift key held down, acts as Zoom In; without the Shift key, it is the = key, and invokes Unity.) And if you hit the = key accidentally, fortunately Unity is undoable with a ⌘-Z or Ctrl+Z.

Before we go too far into the issue of Unity, a little history lesson is in order. In software, as in society in general, it sometimes happens that there is a discontinuity between the principles by which one claims to live and the realities of day-to-day life. In other words, the Brycean authorities tell us that the Unity command acts one way, when in truth it hasn't acted that way since the first Clinton administration.

Here's what the Bryce 4 manual says about Unity: "Unity is the base size of all primitive objects created in Bryce. Unity is always $2048 \times 2048 \times 2048$" (page 299). Well, it's true that the basic primitives (cube, sphere, pyramid, cylinder, cone, torus) do come into the world at this size (assuming that the manual's authors meant to say "$20.48 \times 20.48 \times 20.48$"). If you had made a nice little brick out of that cube and then activated the Unity control, you would no longer have a brick; it will be a cube again, with the object popped back into the space defined by the unity unit ($20.48 \times 20.48 \times 20.48$).

So where's the inconsistency? It used to be, before Bryce 3D, that invoking the Unity command on the stretched, squashed, and otherwise "-oidal" versions of primitives would zap them back to their truly primitive states—the object that started off as a stretched cube would become a perfect cube, and so on. Other objects (such as the torus, square, and disk) would convert to odd variants of their shapes. Unity-izing a terrain would cause it to squnch up into a cube instead of luxuriating over 16 grid units. But since Bryce 3D, hitting the Unity button causes objects to revert to the shape in which they entered the world, whether stretched, squashed, or otherwise.

The upshot of all this is that Unity still exists as a sort of golden ideal within Bryce; the grid is based on the dimensions of the Unity unit, and the most primitive of primitives are created at this size. But the Unity command no longer resizes all objects to Unity. Moreover, the whole nature of Unity has become relative.

So you don't like the fact that Unity is based on a dimension of 20.48 units? Change it!

Here's what we mean: Create a cube. Enlarge it, stretch it, rotate it—in short, deform the heck out of it. While it's still selected, press the = key. As expected, Bam! It's a perfect cube again. But perfection isn't what we want—we like the deformed version. So, press ⌘-Z/Ctrl+Z to get back to the funky ex-cube. Now (the object is still selected, right?) click the A icon (or press ⌘-Option-E/Ctrl+Alt+E) to bring up the Object Attributes dialog box. Click Absolute Coordinates and a pop-up menu appears (see Figure 6.30) Choose Set as Unity from the menu so a check mark appears by it. From now on, no matter what you do to this weird object, if you click the Unity button, it will return to this perverse shape and size. You have redefined Unity! Likewise, if you change the parameters of the object using Definition Coordinates, you redefine the Unity state for the object.

Figure 6.30 The Set as Unity command, accessed from the Absolute/Definition Coordinates pop-up menu in the Object Attributes dialog box.

This new paradigm of Unity is preserved no matter what you do to the object. Duplicate or multi-replicate it, and the copies inherit the new Unity state. Convert it to another type of object (using the Object Conversion control, described in the next section), and that new object will remember the nonstandard Unity state of the original.

By the way, here's another bit of ancient history: In Bryce 1, the Edit Palette contained a button that invoked Unity, and those among us who have been around

Bryce for a while still find ourselves referring to "hitting the Unity button." This is merely shorthand for "Control-click or Ctrl+Alt+click an object's control point, or press the = key." A more elegant solution, don't you think? Plus, it reminds us of our more youthful days....

The Final Resort

The last option is good to use when you find yourself saying something along the lines of "oh, the hell with it!" The Revert to Saved command lives under the File menu, and you can use it to send everything away that you've done this Bryce session (or since you last saved) and go back to what the scene was like before. If there are things you'd like to bring along with you, select them and copy them. After the reversion, you can paste them into your scene, and they'll pop right back in. Now, that wasn't so hellish, was it?

What? You didn't save your scene, and now it's mangled beyond hope? In that case, the only advice we can tender is that when you express your disappointment, use very colorful language with rich, original metaphors. Fie on thee, Bryce!

Change Object Type

This section offers a genuine reason for appreciation: the Object Conversion control. This is the "quick switch" in Bryce, where you can change one object into another object type. It lives in the upper-right section of the Edit Palette. The double arrows lead to a pop-up palette. If you have a sphere selected, you can change it to a torus. Or a cube. Or a light. Or a terrain. You can change any object to another object type. The only thing that changes is the basic shape. Position, orientation, size—these all are inherited from the object. So you can be working over in this one corner of your Bryce world, get your object all positioned, and then duplicate it (⌘-D/Ctrl+D; we'll talk a bit more about Duplicate below). Change the duplicate to another type. A few taps on one of the arrow keys, and the object is positioned nicely.

Object Conversion is an extremely handy little tool. It is immediately addicting—in the best sense. Once you start using it, you'll wonder what you did without it. The duplication recipe (later in the chapter) incorporates object conversion, so you'll have the opportunity to become addicted, if you aren't already.

One note: If you are looking to convert an object to an Easter Egg object (round parallel spotlight and infinite slabs), Object Conversion won't help you. You can convert each of those objects to another primitive type, but not the other way around. You'll have to use Copy Matrix, create the infinite slab or round parallel spotlight, and then use Paste Matrix to position your object just so. If you want to convert from another light object, you'll have to hand-set all the light settings again for the new round parallel spotlight.

Edit Terrain/Object: Focus on Torus

Before moving on to the process of editing multiple objects, let's discuss the control on the right of the Edit Palette, the Edit Terrain/Object control, specifically as it controls the torus. (The other objects edited using the Edit Terrain/Object control are covered in other chapters.)

What is a torus? It is a circular tube. In what ways can you adjust the size and shape of a torus? Of course, there is the regular Resize control for adjusting its size—its height, width, and depth. But in addition to that, there's that tube. How big is the tube? Is it skinny? Fat? The Torus Editor is the place to control the width of the tube.

You can access the special object editors in several ways. These ways hold true for all object types that have a special editor. When your object is selected, you can click the Edit Terrain/Object control. Or you can click the E next to the object. Or from the Objects menu, choose the Edit Object command, or use the keyboard shortcut ⌘-E (Macintosh) or Ctrl+E (Windows). Use any of these methods with a selected torus, and up pops the Torus Editor.

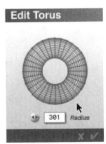

Fine! The Editor looks interesting, but how does it work? To change the tube radius, click anywhere near the torus and drag left or right (see Figure 6.31). Dragging right increases the radius, and dragging left decreases it. To accept changes, press the Return or Enter key, or click the check mark. There are also a couple of modifier-key tricks you can use while examining your torus:

Figure 6.31 The Torus Editor.

- Hold down the Control/Ctrl key to rotate the torus freely about its center point. This key press affects only how the torus looks in the Editor—any changes in orientation are lost once you close the Editor and go back to the Working Window.

- Hold down Control-Option/Ctrl+Alt and drag up and down within the Editor window to move the torus farther away and closer to you, respectively.

- To leave the Torus Editor without accepting changes, press the Escape key. (And, after you've left the Editor, there's always ⌘-Z or Ctrl+Z.)

By the way, the Bryce 4 manual seems to be stuck in an odd time warp with regard to the Torus Editor, describing features and behavior that haven't been present since olden times. When it mentions a "spinning Torus," it's referring to the Bryce 2 Torus Editor, which looked like Figure 6.32, and in which the torus wireframe did indeed rotate just for fun. The manual is also experiencing a flashback when it tells you to "click outside the Torus Editor" to accept changes and to exit the Editor. In Bryce 4, you exit in the normal way, by clicking the check mark or pressing Return/Enter.

Figure 6.32 Bryce 2 Torus Editor with rotating torus.

The text readout area on the Control Palette displays numbers corresponding to the tube's fatness. The numbers range from 0 to 1024, with the default being 256. The higher the number, the fatter the tube. In normal use, you probably won't feel the need to go any higher than 512, which causes the hole in the doughnut to close up completely (see Figure 6.33). You can achieve

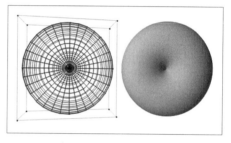

Figure 6.33 A torus of radius 512: a) Wireframe; b) rendered.

interesting effects by using values between 512 and 1024, though. Once you exceed 512, the hole of the doughnut starts to grow inside the tube! (See Figure 6.34.)

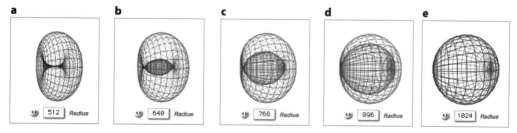

Figure 6.34 Examples of tori with radius 512 or greater.

Come to think of it, this gives you a quick-and-dirty method for creating a hollow globe. The normal method involves nesting a negative sphere inside a slightly larger positive one and then grouping the spheres to create a boolean object (we'll explain that process in more detail in the next chapter). As Figure 6.35 shows, once the torus is rendered (here we've applied a highly refractive glass to both objects), it's practically indistinguishable from the boolean globe. The only fly in the ointment is that you might end up with a tiny speck in the middle of the torus. This is a remnant of the "belly button" at the center of the torus, formed where the sides of the tube overlap each other.

Artifact

Figure 6.35 Two hollow globes: a) A torus of radius 1000 (notice the small speck at the center); b) a boolean object created by nesting a negative sphere inside a slightly larger positive sphere and then grouping the two.

Just as when editing other objects, you can use the arrow-key-plus-modifier combinations to change the number. The up and down arrows increase and decrease the number by 1. Add the Option key (Mac only; no Windows equivalent) to increase or decrease the value by 0.1, or add the Shift key (both Mac and Windows) to change the value up or down by 10.

What do the numbers really mean?

The numbering for the torus tube fatness is set in Bryce units. However, the Bryce units of the Torus Editor are unlike those of the Object Attribute dialog box, in which the numbers have been shifted over by a couple of decimal places. So the 256 you see in the Torus Editor readout is the same as the 2.56 that you see in the Object Attributes dialog box. If 256 torus units = 2.56 Bryce units, does that mean that a setting of 256 in the Torus Editor will be equivalent to the size of, say, a disk that is 2.56 Bryce units? Not exactly. A default torus set at 256 will need a disk that is twice that size, or 5.12, to precisely match up the tube width. The 256 setting in the Torus Editor is not the complete width of the tube; it is the radius, or the distance from the center of the tube to its edge, or one-half of the tube's width.

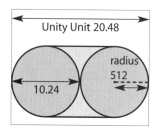

Figure 6.36 shows the relationships among all the numerical units of the torus. This cutaway view represents a torus set to a radius of 512. The overall object's size (unity unit) is 20.48. Each tube is half the width of the object, or 10.24. The radius of the tube is the distance from its center to the edge. That number is 512.

Figure 6.36 Top view "cutaway" of a torus showing its dimensions.

The four tori in Figure 6.37 have different Torus Editor settings, though their external dimensions are those of a freshly created object (Unity). The radius of the top torus is 512 (similar to the one just described), and the radii of the others are reduced by increments of 25%. In the right column are disks of equivalent size, with their dimensions given.

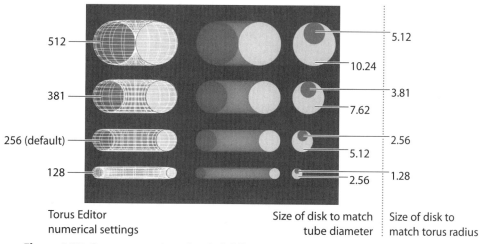

Figure 6.37 Cutaway top view of tori of differing radii but of constant external dimensions. Left column: wireframe view; center column: rendered view with tube cross-section highlighted; right column: disks whose sizes correspond to the tube cross-section and to the tube radius.

So what? Why all of the numerical details? Though math mayn't be your strong suit, it's probably good to know exactly how large to make a torus to fit some other shape.

What if, for instance, you want to create a hollow cylinder that has a rounded edge at the top? You use one cylinder to hollow out another one (for more on booleans, see Chapter 7, "Booleans and Multiple Object Construction"), and a torus atop them will make the rounded edge. Is there a way, other than trial-and-error eye-balling, to determine exactly what the number should be for the torus so that it fits perfectly atop the hollow cylinder?

First, there is the outer size of the cylinder. Both the torus and the cylinder will have the same size: Unity, or 20.48. For this example, you create a torus, which will come into the world with these dimensions: X = 20.48, Y = 20.48, Z = 5.12. Then rotate it 90° on the *x* axis so it lies flat.

The next question—how wide is the lip?—determines both the size of the cylinder that will be subtracted from the outer cylinder and the tube radius for the torus. These are the dimensions:

Outer cylinder	=	[Your choice]
Width of lip	=	[Your choice]
Outer cylinder – 2 × (Width of lip)	=	Size of inner cylinder
1/2 × (Width of lip)	=	Radius of torus

If we choose a lip width of 1.28, and our outer cylinder is Unity-sized:

Outer cylinder	=	20.48
20.48 – 2 × (1.28), or 20.48 – 2.56	=	17.92 (Size of inner cylinder)
1/2 × (1.28), or 0.64, er... 64	=	Radius of torus

Figure 6.38 shows the "cup" made using those dimensions. There is also an arch, where the torus is at default size and radius (256), and each cylinder column is 2 times the torus radius size, or 5.12. The torus was sliced in half by a boolean operation.

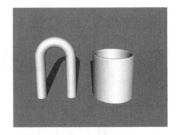

You don't need to keep your dimensions in the strict binary format. But if you do, using the nudge keys for alignment will be much easier, since everything coheres to Bryce's internal grid.

Figure 6.38 Tori at the top of a cup and as part of an arch. In each case, the careful calculation of torus radii ensured a precise fit.

One thing to bear in mind about the 0–1024 scale: it is fixed. If you double the external dimensions of the torus, so that instead of being 20.48 it is 40.96, you will not double the range of the radius to 2048. You have 1024 torus radius units to play with, and that's it. They are calculated for the torus at Unity size, and the entire torus is scaled up or down from that point. The obvious implication, then, is that if you want to perform precise mathematical alignment of the torus with the cylinder or other objects, do it at Unity size. When you're finished with the alignment, group your objects together and resize them as a whole.

GOING FROM ONE TO MANY OBJECTS: DUPLICATING OBJECTS/REPLICATING OBJECTS

Thus far, the discussion has been limited to the Edit controls that work on one object. Of course, you can also resize or rotate more than one selected object; Bryce will perform the edit action on each object individually and simultaneously. If you select several objects and rotate them, you'll have a rotation ballet, with all objects synchronized. (The Windows version of Bryce 2, alas, did not observe this behavior, and the previous edition of this book spilled much ink right here explaining the discrepancy. As of Bryce 3D, on the other hand, the two flavors of the program are synchronized in this regard.) The first step in going from one to many objects is to duplicate or replicate the existing object. Once you have more than one object, you have many edit functions to choose from for working with multiple objects.

Duplicating Objects

Bryce has a command for duplicating objects (⌘-D for Macintosh, Ctrl+D for Windows). It's under the Edit menu, of course. The Duplicate function creates a copy of the selected object right in place, with the newly duplicated object selected. From there, you can nudge the new object into a new place (⌘-D or Ctrl+D, followed by a nudge key).

With a flurry of Duplicate-nudge moves, you can build all sorts of things in Bryce—for instance, build walls by laying a row of bricks: Duplicate-nudge right, Duplicate-nudge right to the end of the row, select all the bricks in that row, and Duplicate-nudge up to create the wall (see Figure 6.39). We'll return again to this Duplicate-nudge method for Brycean mass-production building. But first, we'll focus on the Brycean hand-crafted approach to construction using Duplicate in this tower recipe.

Figure 6.39 Brick wall built by the Duplicate-nudge method of construction.

Duplication Recipe

This tower recipe involves creating only one object from the Create Palette. All other objects are created by duplication and object conversion. While this recipe focuses on duplication and object conversion, it integrates several of the concepts presented so far in this chapter.

1. Create a new scene. Create a cylinder, and then (if your Preferences are set to create objects "within view") ground it by clicking the down arrow (see Figure 6.40a). Make the cylinder taller by enlarging it on the *y* axis. To double the height while dragging directly on the *y* axis, press the Shift key. By the second snap, the cylinder will have doubled in height (see Figure 6.40b).

2. Create a new object from this one. Duplicate the cylinder by selecting Edit > Duplicate or pressing ⌘-D (Macintosh) or Ctrl+D (Windows). Then convert it to a cone, by selecting the cone icon in the Object Conversion control (see Figure 6.41a). The result is shown in Figure 6.41b.

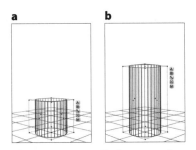

Figure 6.40 a) Cylinder created and b) resized.

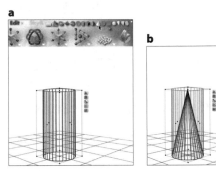

Figure 6.41 The duplicate cylinder is changed to a cone: a) Before and b) after selecting the cone icon using the Object Conversion control.

3. Make the cone go back to Unity size by either pressing the = key or Control-clicking (or Ctrl+Alt-clicking) one of the handles on the bounding box (see Figure 6.42a). Move the cone up by using the Page Up nudge key a few times (see Figure 6.42b).

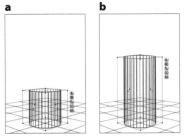

Figure 6.42 a) Cone resized to Unity and b) nudged upward.

4. Flip the cone so that it's upside down. Select Flip Y from the Resize pop-up menu. Figure 6.43b shows the result. Then enlarge the cone uniformly using the Resize tool (see Figure 6.43c). To get more of a squat appearance, reduce the cone along the *y* axis. Grab the *y* axis control handle on the cone's top (here, its flat part) and drag to the left to reduce the cone (see Figure 6.43d).

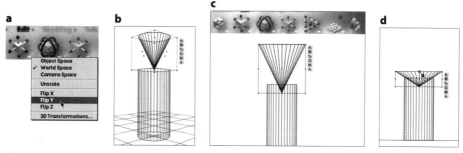

Figure 6.43 a) Selecting the Flip command; b) the result; c) the cone enlarged uniformly; d) the cone reduced on the *y* axis.

5. Duplicate this cone and move the duplicate up using the Page Up key (see Figure 6.44a). Then convert the object to a cylinder using the Object Conversion tool (see Figure 6.44b). It's a squat cylinder. Make the object taller by enlarging it on the *y* axis. Enlarge from the center, using the Option/Alt key (see Figure 6.44c).

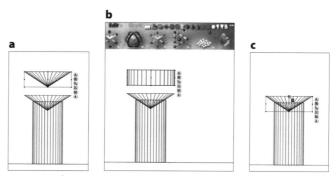

Figure 6.44 a) Duplicated cone is b) converted to a cylinder and then c) enlarged on the *y* axis.

6. Now for a roof. You need another cone. Duplicate the new cylinder and convert to a cone (see Figures 6.45a and b). Remember, we made this cylinder out of a flipped cone, so as far as Bryce is concerned, it's upside down. Select

Flip Y to orient it just so (Figure 6.45c). Move the cone down. To constrain on the *y* axis, press the Option/Alt key before moving the cylinder down.

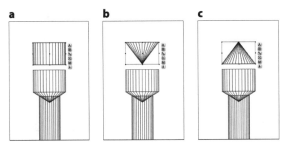

Figure 6.45 a) Cylinder duplicated and nudged up, b) converted to a cone, and then c) flipped.

7. Enlarge the cone slightly so that it has an overhang. Pull the bottom edge of the cone up by resizing along the *y* axis (see Figures 6.46a and b).

8. In the main view, the proportion of the bottom cylinder and the remainder of the tower is a bit extreme. The bottom cylinder needs a bit of thickening. 3D transformation will allow enlargement on two axes. In the case of this object, the vertical axis needs enlarging as well. Figure 6.47a shows the final wireframe result. Then you need to render it. Figure 6.47b shows the finished rendered result.

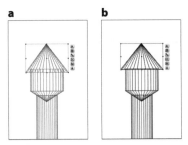

Figure 6.46 a) Cone enlarged and then b) shortened on the *y* axis.

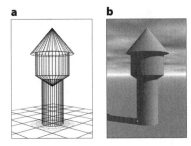

Figure 6.47 a) Final wireframe in the default view; b) final rendered result.

It may not be completely gorgeous (yet), but it's a fine start. More importantly, all the objects are aligned with one another and are automatically centered on the *x* and *z* axes. You only used the Create icon once and built from there, using different Edit controls to duplicate, convert, flip, resize, and otherwise finesse each different object for this tower.

Stop for a moment and consider what you would have had to do if you had created each object from the Create Palette: you would have had to align each object with the others. But the more individual objects you have along one vertical axis, the greater the possibility that you'll misalign one or more with each successive attempt to align the new objects. The method we used here completely sidesteps misalignments.

Replicate Once

Recall the earlier discussion of the brick wall created by Duplicate-nudge. Bryce's Replicate commands automate the process described there. (Henry Ford, take note!) Replicate is a combination of Duplicate and 3D Transform. Bryce remembers the values of the last transformation you made—the last reposition, the last rotation, the last resize. When you select Replicate, Bryce duplicates the object and repeats your previous transformations—repositioning the object, resizing it, rotating it.

So once you've done the first Duplicate-nudge, you can use Replicate to do both actions. Actually, you don't even need to duplicate the object first. Bryce sees what the 3D Transform settings are, and instead of duplicating an object in place, it replicates it—in the new place, position, and size. Continue replicating to build the wall, or to create curlicue spiral natural abstracts.

Try it out!

1. Create an object.

2. Using the direct controls, change the object's location, rotation, and size. Make sure that the size change leans more toward the subtle side, not drastic.

3. Select Edit > Replicate, or press Option-D (Macintosh) or Alt+D (Windows).

4. Continue pressing Option-D or Alt+D and watch a new form emerge.

Now try this again, only this time make the movements infinitesimal. Then try it again and make the movements larger. For extra credit, select all those objects and then use the Object Conversion tool to change them to a different primitive type. Fun!

Multi-Replicate

Multi-Replicate is the same as Replicate, except it adds access to a dialog box (see Figure 6.48). You get to it via Edit > Multi-Replicate or by pressing Shift-Option-D (Mac; not Shift-Command-Option-D, as the manual says—though the Quick Reference Card gets it right) or Shift+Alt+D (Windows). Rather than accepting the last 3D transformations you just performed on your selected object, you can directly enter numbers in the Multi-Replicate dialog box. This

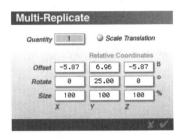

Figure 6.48 Multi-Replicate dialog box.

dialog box is the hands-on executive management response to the laissez-faire come-what-may approach of the simple Replicate command. The dialog box is nearly identical to the 3D Transformations dialog box, with two additions: Quantity and Scale Translation. Quantity is fairly self-explanatory—how many times do you want the object to be replicated? Scale Translation is more complex; we'll discuss it in a bit.

If you've just moved, resized, or rotated the selected object prior to accessing the Multi-Replicate dialog box, you'll see the values of your last move there. If you simply click the check or press Return, your object will be replicated in the same way as if you'd selected Edit > Replicate. Replicate is the eyes-closed version. Multi-Replicate, with the dialog box, allows you to see and to determine what types of changes take place. But both commands perform the duplicate-transform actions described by the numbers in the Multi-Replicate dialog box—with one exception: It doesn't matter what number you type in the Quantity field in the Multi-Replicate dialog box. The Replicate command always acts as if the number is 1. The Bryce 4 manual is, once again, stuck in a time warp. Just ignore it when it says: "The Quantity value entered in this dialog sets the number of duplicates created when you use the Replicate command." That was true way back in Bryce 2 days, but no more.

The numbers in the Multi-Replicate dialog box respond to arrow-key adjustments just like those in the 3D Transformations dialog box, discussed earlier in this chapter. For summaries of the results of using various combinations of arrow keys and modifier keys, see Tables 6.1 and 6.2. Offset can have a value between –99999 and 99999, Rotate can range from –999 to 999, and Size can be any percentage between 0 and 9999. Note: The arrows even work in the Quantity box, where the limit is 999.

The brick wall cited earlier is a fairly simple, highly utilitarian example of the way Replicate works. How many objects do you want? How far over do you want each one to be? Enter those values in the Multi-Replicate dialog box. How much space between objects? 20.48? How many objects do you want in that horizontal row? Twenty? Now that is mass production!

The Scale Translation option is a special-case function for scaling and offset when both take place on the same axis. When Scale Translation is activated, the size scaling also operates on the offset, enabling a cumulative effect. We'll discuss how it works first and then describe the exceptions.

Figure 6.49a shows the difference between a plain-vanilla offset, a plain-vanilla offset with scaling, and a Scale Translation offset with scaling. The original cube was reduced to 90% of unity size. Then, in each case, it was offset using the Multi-Replication command on the x axis by a value of 20.48 (unity units). In the top row, there was no scaling. In the second row, the cube was scaled by 90% on each axis, but Scale Translation was off. The third row was identical to the second, only Scale Translation was on. Notice how the top two rows have identical placement of objects along the x axis. In the bottom row, with each successive cube diminishing in size, the amount of offset is diminished as well.

Then add rotation to the process. The settings in Figure 6.49b are identical to those used in Figure 6.49a, only rotation has been added to each one (X = 5°, Y = 10°, Z = 5°).

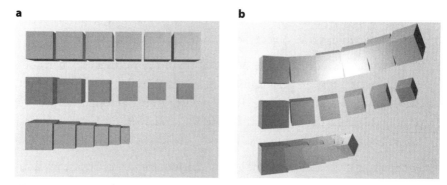

Figure 6.49 Multi-Replicate in action, with and without Scale Translation at work: a) Multi-replication on the *x* axis with no rotation; b) Multi-replication on the *x* axis with rotation added to the mix. (The bottom set of cubes for both examples use Scale Translation.)

As you can see, the rotation numbers are small; the arc-ing effect takes place with the addition of many objects, each with a small amount of rotation. A pattern develops; too much rotation, and the emerging pattern is more hig-gledy-piggledy.

Figure 6.50 shows an abstract image generated by using the same settings and varying negative or positive num-bers in the Offset and Rotate fields. This sends four dif-ferent strands in four different directions. In this chap-ter's folder on the CD-ROM, the Replication folder has all manner of additional examples of images containing replicated objects—plus in the next chapter, we'll go into more detail about multi-replication as we look at multi-ple object construction.

Figure 6.50 Multi-replicated abstract design created using the same basic settings and varying positive and negative values to branch into four directions.

CHANGING MORE THAN ONE OBJECT

Now that there is more than one object in the scene, the Edit Palette has two con-trols for working with sets of objects: Align and Randomize. As their names imply, they are complements to one another: one gathers certain objects into nice, neat, organized places, and the other offers a quick method for distributing a number of objects helter-skelter about your scene. Whether gathering or scattering, you must have two or more objects selected to use these two tools.

To help you conceptualize the organization of the Edit Palette, consider this. Of the Three Rs tools, the Reposition tool is closest to these two gather/scatter tools. Even though we discussed the Reposition tool first among the three, its central position between the other two Rs and the gather/scatter controls is no accident: the Align and Randomize tools are both specialized Reposition tools as well.

Following the discussion of the Align and Randomize controls, we'll discuss the Group command, since group works with more than one object.

Alignment

Alignment precisely lines up two or more objects along a specified axis. The Align control has a rod for each axis—*x*, *y*, and *z*—with three spheres on each rod for the three options for each axis: the center, and either edge. In the center of the control is a sphere that aligns all objects' centers to one place (see Figure 6.51). Like the other iconic controls on the Edit Palette, the Alignment control also has a pop-up menu that provides additional options. These all cause the selected objects to "snap" to certain fixed positions, which we'll discuss later. At the bottom of the menu is an item, new to Bryce 4, that allows the user to determine the behavior of alignment in general.

Figure 6.51
The Alignment control.

What does it mean to align "on" or "along" an axis—for instance, to align on the *x* axis? Aligning on an axis means that all objects will travel on that axis to end up in alignment with one another. Figure 6.52 examines alignment "on" the *x* axis. In each of the three cases, the objects travel along the *x* axis to arrive at a common point along that axis. They share a common Offset X position. (Assuming that the objects are the same size, when aligned on the *x* axis, they'll share the same Offset X setting in the Object Attributes dialog box.) For Align X Left, the objects travel left on the *x* axis to a common point (Figure 6.52a). For Align X Center, they travel in either direction on the *x* axis to reach a common point at the center (Figure 6.52b). For Align X Right, they travel right on the *x* axis to reach a common point (Figure 6.52c).

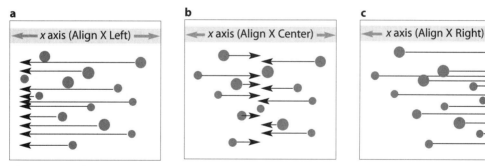

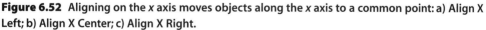

Figure 6.52 Aligning on the *x* axis moves objects along the *x* axis to a common point: a) Align X Left; b) Align X Center; c) Align X Right.

When you are deliberating over which axis to choose, think of it this way: Usually you want everything to align either horizontally or vertically. If you want everything on the same horizontal plane, you'll need to make the objects move vertically—along the *y* axis—until they reach a common point. If you want to stack things up vertically, then you'll need to align on the two horizontal axes, *x* and *z*.

When you align objects, they move along an axis to a common point. How do you determine what that common point is? We're happy to report that Bryce has cleaned up its alignment act since the previous edition of this book was published. Way back then, in Bryce 2 days, the Mac and Windows versions of the program responded to the Alignment commands in dramatically different ways. Not only that, but the Macintosh version was just plain broken. That's all water under the virtual bridge—now the Mac and Windows versions have been brought into alignment in their handling of, uh, Alignment.

How was this discrepancy resolved? Stated briefly, in Bryce 3D, the Bryce 2 Mac version won out. Then in Bryce 4, a variant of the former Windows method of alignment was added as an option. The default method works like so: If you want to align all these objects along an edge, then "the edge"—the common point—is actually the edge of the bounding box of all the selected objects. Align the objects vertically at the top (click Align Y Top), so that they all jump to the top edge of the highest object in the bounding box of all the selected objects. The schematic diagrams in Figure 6.52a through c represent this method. For examples of all of the possible bounding box alignments depicted in Bryce's native habitat, see Figure 6.53.

New to Bryce 4 is anchor-based aligning, which you invoke by choosing Anchor-Based Aligning (duh!) from the Align Options menu, as shown in Figure 6.54. "What if I'm not creating a nautical scene, and there are no anchors lying about?" you ask. No, no; not that kind of anchor! In this context, an anchor is an object to which you want other objects to align. Figure 6.55 illustrates how this works. In each view, the large sphere is designated as the anchor, so when you execute the Align X Left command, the anchor does not move, and the other objects move along the *x* axis so that their left sides align with the left side of the anchor. And how do you designate an object as the anchor? Simple—merely select it first; then add the other candidates for alignment to the selection.

Figure 6.54 Choosing Anchor-Based Aligning from the Align Options menu.

Anchor-based aligning is distantly related to the style of alignment that functioned in the Windows version of Bryce 2. In that long-since-departed software, the common point to which objects aligned was a single object, but it was always the oldest object in the selection—oldest as in first born, earliest created. This caused headaches when you wanted to align a bunch of objects to a younger object, and you were forced to resort to various instant-ageing techniques (sort of like forging a fake ID to buy beer), such as cutting the intended anchor and pasting it back in.

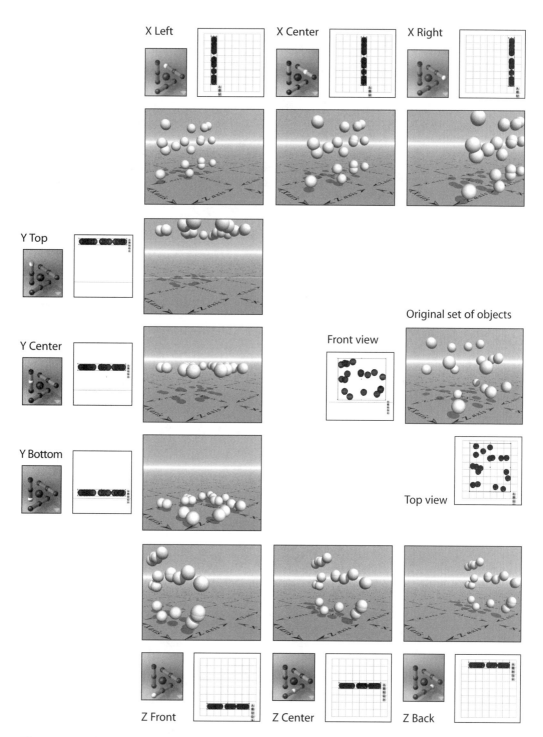

Figure 6.53 Alignment using the default bounding box method.

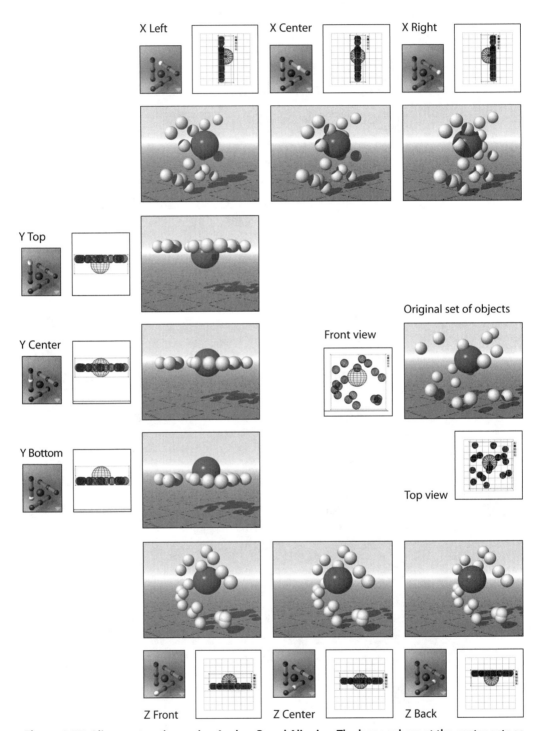

Figure 6.55 Alignment options using Anchor-Based Aligning. The large sphere at the center acts as the anchor.

The new alignment paradigm is indeed an improvement.

Now that the preliminaries are out of the way, let's dust off our hands and get into the real uses for alignment by looking at a couple of examples.

Center Alignment

When would you want to align objects on their centers? When you have round objects and want them to share a common center.

Figure 6.56 features two objects: a cone and a cylinder. When you create them, they pop into the world already in alignment (see Figure 6.56a). Suppose you want to alter their sizes and then align them to create a cylindrical tower with a cone-shaped roof. If you align all (using the spherical button at the center of the Align control), you get the results in Figure 6.56b. That's not the solution, though; the solution is to keep them aligned centered on the *x* and *z* axes (those are the horizontal axes) and place each on a different position on the *y* axis (the vertical axis). (See Figure 6.56c.)

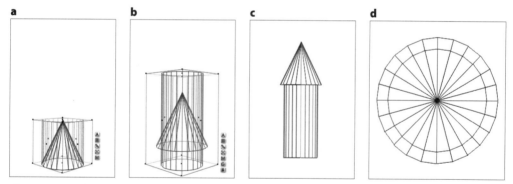

Figure 6.56 Aligning a cone and a cylinder: a) Cylinder and cone as created (main view); b) cylinder and cone after resizing and alignment (main view); c) cylinder and cone positioned (side view); d) cylinder and cone aligned, centered, on both the *x* axis and *z* axis.

> *TIP:* When aligning objects in this type of centered fashion, hop on over to top view to confirm that everything was properly aligned (see Figure 6.56d), or depending on the relative size of your objects in your view, set the Nano preview to top view wireframe.

Edge Alignment

When would you want to align objects flush with one another on their edges? You'll typically use this type of alignment with square-shaped objects: cubes, squares, and pyramids (pyramids have square bases).

Here are the steps for aligning a series of smaller cubes along a larger horizontally stretched cube. The smaller cubes become a set of checkerboard turrets at the top of a castle or fortress wall. Follow these steps (make sure that Anchor-Based Aligning is turned off for this exercise):

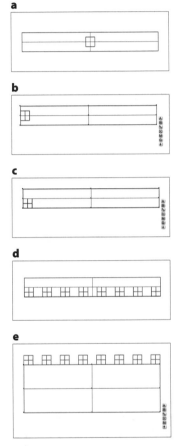

1. Create one cube. Shrink it to one-half size by tapping the divide (/) key. Create another cube and enlarge it on the *x* axis from the center, holding down the Option (Macintosh) or Alt (Windows) key. The top view of the results of the two cubes is shown in Figure 6.57a.

2. Now it's time for alignment. Make sure you're in top view. Select both cube objects. You'll need to perform two align steps to make the cubes flush on two edges. To align them both on the left, click the Align X Left control (see Figure 6.57b).

3. Next, you'll align both objects to the front. Click the Align Z Front control (see Figure 6.57c).

4. Extra Credit: Complete the turret wall. The top cube is flush with the two outside edges of the wall. Now that you've aligned the cube and the wall, you can easily duplicate the top (small) cube along the top of the wall. Select the small cube and then Duplicate-nudge-nudge-nudge-nudge (that's a quadruple-nudge) using the right arrow. Keep doing this to finish the wall (see Figure 6.57d). Of course, to complete the wall, you'll also need to adjust the vertical placement of the turrets in relation to the wall, and heighten the wall accordingly. In front view, the final result should look something like Figure 6.57e.

Figure 6.57 Alignment on the edges: a) Two cubes, top view, after initial resizing; b) top view after Align X Left; c) top view after Align Z Front; d) top view after replicating the smaller cube; e) front view after height and size adjustments for the turret wall.

Make It Snappy

The pop-up menu under the Align control has a series of snappy options. These will work just as well with a single selected object as with multiple selected objects.

Snap to Grid. This option takes your object or set of objects and aligns each one with the internal grid.

Snap Together. This option is a little tricky. Choose an object as your anchor and select it. Now add a bunch of other objects to the selection. Choose Snap Together, and all the objects move to the anchor, so their X, Y, and Z centers are aligned with those of the anchor. Now here's the tricky part: this works only if you have Anchor-Based Aligning turned off! Turn on Anchor-Based Aligning, and nothing happens. Why? Who knows—probably aliens.

Snap to World Center. This command is the same as the UnReposition command under the Reposition Tool. All objects will be snapped together with the centers lined up at World Center. If you select one of these objects post-snap and check its attributes, you'll see that its position is 0, 0, 0.

Snap to Ground. Snap to ground aligns your entire object (or its lowest edge) with Bryce's ground in your scene. (Bryce's ground level is distinct from the ground primitive; a ground primitive is created at ground level but can be moved above or below the ground level.)

Snap to Land. This option is the same as the down-arrow button that appears for selected objects. When you choose Snap to Land, the object will drop to the next-lowest object. Figure 6.58 shows a set of objects before and after landing. This option gives you an excellent way to start having things rest upon others. Why do we say "start"? For one thing, as soon as the object touches the surface of the other object, Bryce considers it done. But for heavy materials like rock, just barely touching is not good enough. Those rocks need to sink into the softer dirt surrounding them, to lend a realistic look to the scene.

a
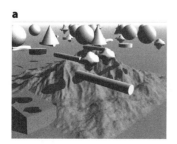

b

Figure 6.58 Many objects: a) In the air; b) after landing on terrains and lower objects.

Snap to Land can act funky at times. The object drops to the next-lowest object—but there are a couple of mitigating (or was that aggravating?) circumstances. First, if the upper object is not completely above the lower object, it will drop below to the next object (or ground). What determines where the landing object stops? Supposedly, the object will stop on the first object directly below its y axis control handle (see Figure 6.59). The top row of Figure 6.59 shows a cube before being snapped to land. In each of the top row images, the cube is in a slightly different position. The bottom row shows the cube after landing. Notice the dotted line directly below the y axis control handle. Whatever is directly below the control handle is what the cube lands on.

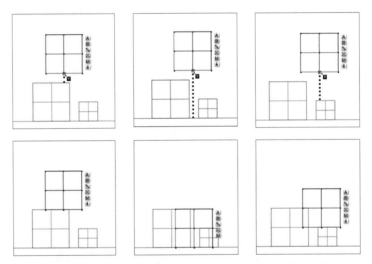

Figure 6.59 Using the Snap to Land command on an object above an uneven surface. Top row: the cube before landing, with a dotted line extending directly below each cube's y axis handle; bottom row: the result of the Snap To Land command.

But what if the dropping object has been rotated, so that the y handle isn't flat on the bottom? Figure 6.60 shows that the reference point for snapping to land is actually the y handle on the object's World Space bounding box. The y handle on the object itself is irrelevant. The same before and after conditions apply as in Figure 6.59. For each cube, the World Space bounding box is shown. The same dotted lines are shown, with an extra dotted line in the first picture to compare the object's own y handle and the World Space bounding box handle.

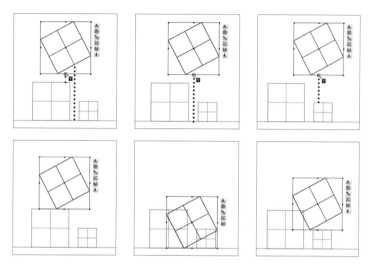

Figure 6.60 Snapping a rotated object to Land. Top row: hovering above the uneven surface; bottom row: after Snapping to Land.

In Bryce 2, several objects that describe a circle on the ground (cone, cylinder, torus) had difficulty supporting objects dropped onto them. In Bryce 3D, and of course, Bryce 4, this is mostly fixed, though a torus, rotated so it's lying flat on the ground, won't support any object dropped onto it, and the cone still has a peculiar problem, as we explain in the following tip.

> **TIP:** To make Snap To Land work most reliably, make sure that the y handles of the two objects involved are aligned. To accomplish this, select both the lander and the landee and click the Align Z Center and Align X Center controls. Inconsistency alert: if the object is landing on the point of a cone, the cone won't support the object if the y handles are aligned. To work around this, just move the landing object along the x or z axis by a tiny amount—an Option/Alt-nudge is enough to do the trick.

Here's one more little gotcha: If the object you are landing is beneath the ground plane, the Snap To Land command will move it upward. All fine and dandy—but things get more complicated if the landing object is beneath another object that is also below the ground plane. Don't believe the story in the Bryce 4 manual (page 316)! There you will read that the lower object will move upward until its top bumps into the object above. The truth is that the lower object keeps moving until its base is aligned with that of the upper object. Figure 6.61 tells the story in pictures.

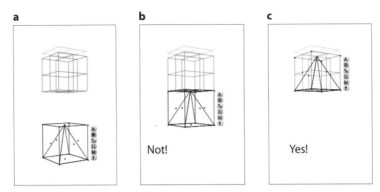

a   b   c

Not!   Yes!

Figure 6.61 Using the Snap To Land command on objects below the ground plane—theory vs. reality: a) A cube and pyramid beneath the ground plane, with the pyramid selected; b) what the Bryce 4 manual says will happen when you snap the pyramid to Land; c) what actually happens.

Randomize

Now that you have all your ducks lined up in a row, we'll talk about the opposite process—randomizing. Randomizing takes your selected objects and scatters them, changing their location, rotation, and size. Lest you think that randomizing is a completely random process (!), Bryce has a set of eight options for chaos control.

The Randomize tool has three parts (see Figure 6.62). The Randomize Mode Selector and the Randomize Options pop-up menu are tied to one another. The menu provides a verbal description of what you may change, and the mode selector supplies a visual representation. They answer the question, "How will you randomize?" Once you've decided how to do it, the Randomize Amount control (the green sphere at the upper right) is the means to activate the randomization. It tells Bryce, "Do it!"

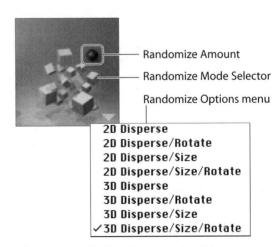

Randomize Amount

Randomize Mode Selector

Randomize Options menu

2D Disperse
2D Disperse/Rotate
2D Disperse/Size
2D Disperse/Size/Rotate
3D Disperse
3D Disperse/Rotate
3D Disperse/Size
✓ 3D Disperse/Size/Rotate

Figure 6.62 The Randomize tool and its components.

Options for Randomizing

The Randomize Options menu lists eight options, but this list disguises the fact that there are actually only five choices you have to make when randomizing. When you add up the combinations of the five choices, you end up with the eight options on the menu.

The one element common to all the options is Disperse. Every option includes it. We suppose you could say that Disperse is not an option; it's mandatory. Disperse takes all those selected objects and moves them every which way. The additional options allow you to make each object change slightly while it's being dispersed. There are two options for changing each object: to change its size or to change its rotation. (Hey! Including Dispersion, which moves objects about in space, there are the Three Rs!)

But the first choice you must make is whether to Disperse your objects in 2D, across a flat, horizontal plane? Or do you want them to spread out in 3D, where objects can be dispersed to different altitudes as well?

Once you've made that choice, next you must decide which of these four basic styles of dispersion you want:

• Disperse alone

• Disperse and Size

• Disperse and Rotate

• Dispersion, Size, and Rotate

These four styles of dispersion are available in 2D and 3D, making for a total of eight possibilities. You can select the eight options from the pop-up menu, or you can cycle through the options by clicking the Randomize Mode Selector. (Dragging works as well for cycling through the options.)

Working the Randomize Control

To start the dispersion process, drag from the Randomize Amount control. The objects move from their original positions into new, random ones. If you drag a little, they move a little. The more you drag, the farther the objects move. Once you let go of the mouse and begin another drag, they move again—in new directions. You can't go back along that dispersion path once you've released the mouse. There is ⌘-Z or Ctrl+Z, of course, to undo. But while you're dragging back and forth in the midst of dispersion, pause for a moment with the mouse still held down to see if this is where you want the objects. More than once we've wanted to move objects back a bit along the paths from whence they came and were not able to do so. In the Macintosh version of Bryce 2, you could simply click the Randomize Amount control to extend the dispersion by a similar amount. Later versions of Bryce, including Bryce 4, adopt the Bryce 2 for Windows behavior, meaning that clicking does nothing—dragging is mandatory.

Additional Notes on the Randomize Options

Randomize Size is now uniform. In Bryce 2, using Randomize Size caused random changes in proportion as well, so a group of spheres, for example, became variously squashed and elongated, and so on. Now they stay nice and round.

Randomize Size now operates in Object Space. In Bryce 2, you ran into problems if you tried to run Randomize Size after a Randomize Rotation operation, because the resizing happened in World Space. Your beautiful cones and cylinders were then stretched into bizarre shapes because they were resized along World Space axes instead of along their own internal ones. This is no longer the case, so you can disperse and resize or disperse and rotate in whichever order you please.

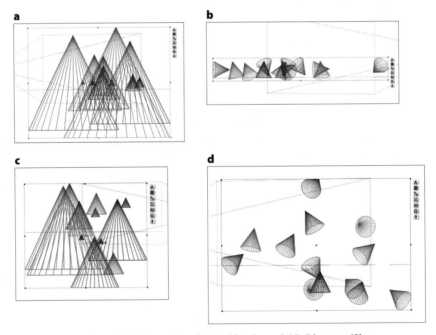

Figure 6.63 2D and 3D dispersions from side view: a) 2D Disperse/Size; b) 2D Disperse/Rotate; c) 3D Disperse/Size; d) 3D Disperse/Rotate.

Use Align along with Randomize. Rotation and Resizing in 2D tend to move objects off the 2D plane. The mechanics of randomizing rotation combined with 2D Dispersion actually do move the objects off a strict horizontal plane. There is a combination of World and Object Space taking place here as the objects move in Object Space, but with rotation thrown in, the 2D horizontal plane along which the object moves is slightly changed in space. The more you drag, the more extreme both the dispersion and rotation are.

Figure 6.63 compares side views of 2D Disperse/Size (a) and 2D Disperse/Rotate (b) and 3D Disperse/Size (c) and 3D Disperse/Rotate (d). Though there is some vertical movement in the 2D processes, it's not as extreme as in the 3D dispersions.

Of course, at any time, if you want to return your objects to a horizontal plane, then a swift click on the Align Y control will return all objects to the same level. In fact, at any point along the way, you can use alignment to help shepherd your objects into certain formations, for controlled chaos.

Suppose you want to create a Lawrence Welk-esque scene filled with bubbles. If you want to make the bubbles float along in a narrow corridor, first disperse them widely into space and then align them on two axes—*y* and one of the others. They'll all be in a row. Then use a subtle 3D dispersion to move them out from that place.

Recipes:

Here are a few related recipes for two different kinds of bubbles, and a variation.

Lawrence Welk Bubble Show

1. Create a new scene file. Select the ground and delete it. Create a sphere. Make many spheres, either by creating more or by duplicating (⌘-D on a Mac, Ctrl+D in Windows). Ten to 12 is a good amount to start (see Figure 6.64a).

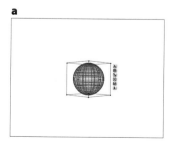 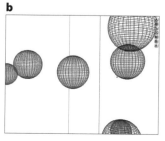

Figure 6.64
a) Create many spheres; b) select all and disperse.

2. Select all the spheres by using the Sphere Select icon on the bottom Select Palette.

3. Randomize: Choose 3D Disperse, and drag to the right on the Randomize Selection control (see Figure 6.64b).

4. Now, to create more spheres that are a different size, duplicate the set that you have (use ⌘-D or Ctrl+D, or Edit > Duplicate). You now have a new set of spheres selected. Make these part of a different family. Change their family color (see Figure 6.65a).

5. Reduce the size of the spheres. Use the Resize control and reduce the size uniformly (see Figure 6.65b). Then drag the Randomize control to change the location of the spheres (see Figure 6.65c). If all the spheres disappear from view when you click the Randomize button, start over by selecting Snap to World Center from the Alignment pop-up menu. Then start your randomizing from there.

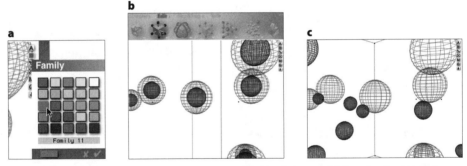

Figure 6.65 Duplicate and uniformly resize a set of spheres: a) Assign the duplicated spheres to a new family; b) resize the new spheres; c) disperse the new spheres.

6. Do you want yet a third size of spheres? Then repeat the process again: use Duplicate, choose a new family or wireframe color (see Figure 6.66a), use Resize, and finally, use Randomize (see Figure 6.66b). At any time, you can select all the spheres of the same size by using the Select by Family pop-up menu. The completed render is shown in Figure 6.66c.

> **TIP:** If you want to add more sets of objects to the mix, here's a quick way to do so: Duplicate, Group the objects, and Rotate the group. This repositions the entire group. Then Ungroup. (More on grouping follows.)

Save this scene file; you'll come back to it in a bit.

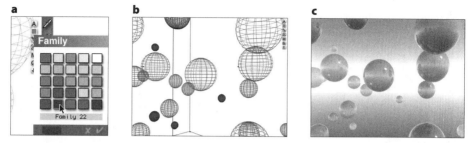

Figure 6.66 Repeat the process a third time: a) Assign the new spheres to a unique family; b) resize and disperse the new spheres; c) complete the render.

Confetti Variation

All this randomizing and we've only used Disperse. How about using Resize and Rotate? Sure, let's do so! The reason that rotation doesn't work with bubbles is that, since they're spherical, it doesn't matter whether they are rotated. If we change to another object type, then rotation will matter.

1. Select all the spheres. Under Object Conversion, select the 2D square object icon (see Figure 6.67a). Now all your spheres are square pieces of confetti. They are all oriented identically, a most unrealistic effect, as you can see in Figure 6.67b.

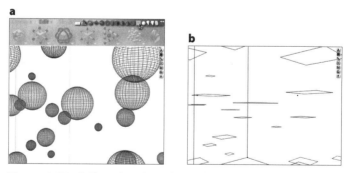

Figure 6.67 a) Changing the spheres to squares; b) the resulting flat squares.

2. Randomize using 3D Disperse/Rotate. *Voilà!* Happy New Year! (See Figure 6.68a.) The confetti may be a bit big, so reduce the size using the Resize tool. Though all the confetti is randomly rotated, the objects may still be flattish. Rotate all the objects on one axis for better visibility. Figures 6.68b and c

show the wireframe and resulting render. (We changed the confetti's material to a less bubbly flat gray and turned off atmospheric effects for clarity.)

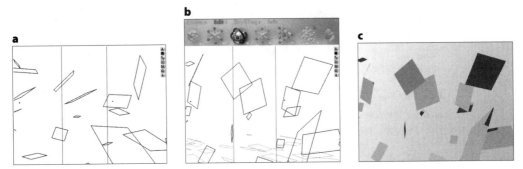

Figure 6.68 a) Randomized squares; b) squares rotating all on one axis; c) rendered result.

3. How about a bit more complexity? Select one of your wireframe families. You can make round "hole-punch" confetti by changing these objects to 2D disks using the Object Conversion control. Do so. See Figure 6.69a. Figure 6.69b shows the rendered result of the conversion (with some additional resizing thrown in for good measure), and Figure 6.69c shows the same scene with the objects all rotated.

4. Now that you've done this, under the File menu, select Save As and name this scene "Confetti."

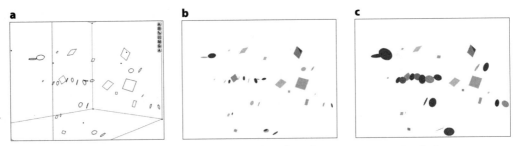

Figure 6.69 More complexity to the confetti: a) After changing some squares to circles; b) rendered result; c) everything rotated and rendered.

Lawrence Welk Bubble Columns

How about a little alignment in the process? Make those bubbles travel in a narrow column.

1. Open up that Lawrence Welk bubble file again.

2.   Select all the spheres. Align them vertically, to set them all on the same horizontal plane. Click one of the Align Y controls. Figure 6.70a shows the scene before alignment, 6.70b shows it after alignment, and 6.70c shows it after a few taps on the down arrow key to center the plane of bubbles.

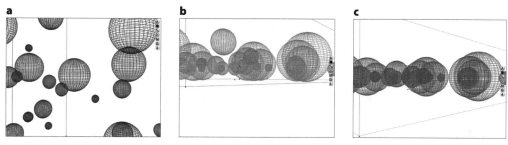

Figure 6.70 Aligning bubbles: a) Select all; b) use Align Y Center; c) move down.

3.   Now align on the horizontal axis. Click either Align X Center or Align Z Center. In Figure 6.71, we chose Align X Center. Then we rotated the camera a bit to get more bubbles into the field of view.

4.   After a bit of assessment, these bubbles seem a bit big, plus there aren't enough of them. First reduce the size by half (Tap the / key or use the Resize control with Shift-constrain). See Figure 6.71b. Then Duplicate and move the bubbles slightly along the z axis (or, if you aligned the other way, then move along that axis). Figure 6.71c shows the result. Now you have a lot of different sized spheres that are aligned in one column.

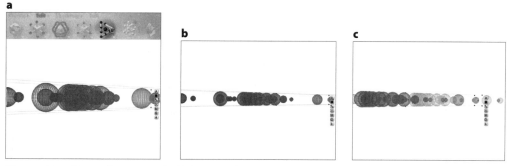

Figure 6.71 More alignment: a) Aligning on the z axis; b) the objects reduced by half; c) the objects duplicated and moved along the z axis.

5. Select all the spheres. Change the Randomize mode to 3D Dispersion. Drag the Randomize control ever so slightly. Easy does it. The spheres are now roughly in a column, but are meandering a bit, as bubbles will do. Figure 6.72 shows the randomizing and the rendered result.

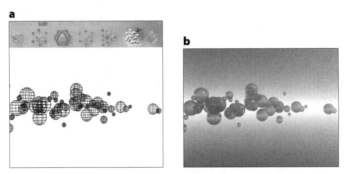

Figure 6.72 Finishing up: a) Dragging slightly with 3D Disperse chosen; b) rendered result.

6. Assign a bubble material setting, and you're ready to polka! (The bubble material setting is on the CD in the Chapter 6 folder.)

Randomize. Align. Randomize again. This is an excellent technique to achieve controlled haphazardness.

Group Grope

Group is a kinda-sorta hybrid between an object type and an edit action. If you think of objects as nouns and edits as verbs, Group is both. Once you select a set of objects and group (edit/verb) them, they become, well, a group (object/noun). As a hybrid, Group lives under the Objects menu and has a listing in the Selection pop-up menu on the Selection Palette. We'll discuss grouping in the edit/verb sense here in this chapter, leaving the object/noun discussion for the next chapter, which is devoted to multiple complex objects and booleans.

First, we'll cover the basic edit/verb actions: how to group. Grouping as an action is very simple. When two or more objects are selected, a G icon is present amid the Edit Objects controls. Click the G to group (or choose Object > Group, or type ⌘-G or Ctrl+G). Ungroup is the counterpart; a U icon is displayed when there's a group. You can click the U, or type ⌘-U (or Ctrl+U) or select Object > Ungroup.

What happens when you group and ungroup a set of objects? When objects are grouped, they no longer act as individual objects; instead, they act as one object. Any Edit function you can perform on one object can be performed on a group. You can change the group's size or orientation. You also can land or ground the group. All Rotation and Resize operations will work on a group of objects as though the group were one object. This means you can go back and forth between Grouped Object Conglomerate and Ungrouped Selected Plethora and perform different actions as you desire.

Uses for Groups

There are three main types of functions for groups in Bryce.

The first function of grouping is an extension of what we've been discussing in the latter part of this chapter: taking a set of objects and making them act as one object for the purpose of an editing process. We will discuss this type of grouping—grouping to perform intermittent edit actions—here in more detail.

The last two functions of groups are for making a set of objects act as one object. First, you can simply keep objects together that belong together, which you will especially want to do when you want to continue editing those objects as a whole. When a number of primitives comprise a conglomerate entity (such as a model of a tower, as in the Edit controls exercise earlier in this chapter), grouping them keeps them together.

Second, you can use grouping with boolean objects. For booleans to work in Bryce, the objects must be grouped. Both of these types of group functions will be discussed in the next chapter, "Booleans and Multiple Object Construction."

Cone Campground Recipe: Grouping

When you are in Edit mode working on adjusting the geometry of your scene and positioning objects, there are times when it will be necessary and prudent to group a set of objects to perform a different kind of resize or rotation operation that will affect the set of objects as a whole. This recipe, to create a cone campground, uses grouping to rotate a set of objects in a certain way. It also reviews many of the other Edit controls explained in this chapter and so gives you an opportunity to try them out together.

1. On the CD-ROM, in the Edit Chapter folder, open the scene file CONE CAMPGROUND START. (Figure 6.73a.)

2. Create multiple cones. We clicked the Create Cone icon 18 times. You can use Multi-Replicate to create 17 additional cones (see Figure 6.73b).

3. Disperse those cones! Select all the cones using the Select Cone icon. From the Randomize pop-up menu, choose 2D Disperse. Then drag the Randomize tool to scatter the cones (see Figure 6.73c).

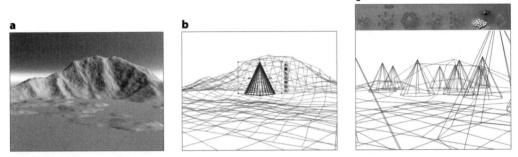

Figure 6.73 Cone campground: a) Beginning scene; b) with multiple cones; c) with the cones dispersed.

4. The cones are a little too big. Reduce them by half. There are at least three ways to change their size: tap the divide key (/); open the 3D Transformations dialog box and enter 50% in all three numerical entry boxes for Size; or use the Resize tool, constraining with the Shift key (see Figure 6.74a).

5. Duplicate and disperse an additional set of cones. Select Edit > Duplicate (⌘-D or Ctrl+D) and then drag the Randomize tool (see Figure 6.74b).

6. Select all the cones by clicking the Select Cones icon. Group the cones by either clicking the G or choosing Objects > Group Objects.

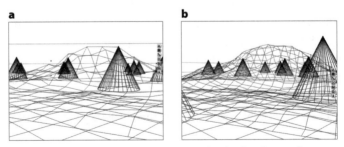

Figure 6.74 a) Reducing the cone size; b) duplicating and dispersing the cones again.

7. Note in the side view (see Figure 6.75a) that the cones are on a horizontal plane. Return to Camera View and change to Camera Space. Rotate the group on the *x* axis so that the close cones are lower and the far cones are higher, descending toward you (see Figure 6.75b).

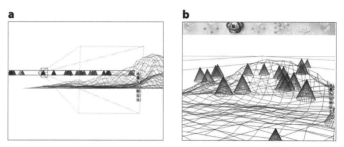

Figure 6.75 Rotating the group: a) Side view of the group for reference; b) the group in Camera Space rotated on the *x* axis.

8. Now it's time to realign the individual cones so that they aren't rotated. First, ungroup the group by clicking the U. All objects are selected, but any Edit actions will operate on each object individually. Then select Unrotate from the Rotation Control pop-up menu. See Figure 6.76a.

Other alternatives: In Object Attributes, for all the still-selected cones, change the rotation to 0° for all three axes. Figure 6.76b shows the Object Attributes dialog box before unrotating. Or in the 3D Transformations dialog box, enter the amount you want to unrotate. (This option is too cumbersome in this case, but it might be just the solution for another time, so we mention it as a possibility here.) The unrotated result is shown in Figure 6.76c.

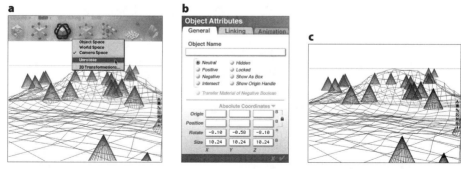

Figure 6.76 Unrotating individual cones: a) Selecting Unrotate; b) entering Object Attribute numbers for still-rotated cones; c) the result.

9. Assign materials to your objects. While the cones are still selected, make them otherworldly by selecting a preset from the Materials Preset Library. Click the triangle to access the presets and select "lit rays" from the complex f/x category (see Figure 6.77a). Click the check mark to get back to your scene. Then select the ground and terrain. (The Edit menu has an inverse selection option. You can also type ⌘-Shift-A on a Mac or Ctrl+Shift+A using Windows.) Go back to the Materials Preset Library. In the Planes & Terrains category, select "Shaman Cliffs" (see Figure 6.77b), or select another preset that tickles your fancy. Click the check to accept the material selection and then render your scene. The final result is shown in Figure 6.78.

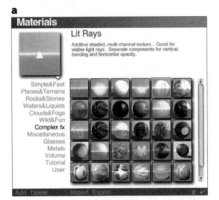 

Figure 6.77 Material presets for objects: a) Cone material; b) ground and terrain material.

Figure 6.78 Final rendered result.

Groups and the Unity Command

So what happens if you use the Unity command on a grouped object? In Bryce 2, the answer was rather sad: each individual object within the group suddenly snapped back to Unity size, turning your delicately constructed composite object into a mess. Since Bryce 3D and, of course, in Bryce 4, there's a happier result. When you group a set of objects, you automatically define a Unity state for the group as a whole. It's as if you used the Set as Unity command right after you clicked the G icon. Now if you reshape or resize the group, just press =, and the group pops back to its initial condition—unless, of course, you perform some transformations on the group and then use the Set as Unity command. Afterward, Unity command will restore the group to its post-transformation state.

Congratulations! You now know how to thoroughly edit your objects. Where this chapter ends up—editing multiple objects and groups—is where the next chapter, "Booleans and Multiple Object Construction," begins.

CHAPTER SEVEN

Booleans and Multiple Object Construction

IN THIS CHAPTER...

- Simple ways to make complex shapes and non-nature objects using multiple primitives and multiple terrains

- All about boolean object construction

- Architectural objects: temples, pillars, and principles

- Circular complex objects, such as spiral staircases and gears

- Merging scenes

- Working with hierarchies and linking

Although the original purpose of Bryce was to be a landscape modeler, it's capable of much more complexity when different objects are constructed together. As Bryce has evolved, the MetaCreations development team has recognized the modeling potential of Bryce and created additional features for more robust modeling. Aside from a variety of primitive types, the ability to combine primitives together using boolean operations gives you, the Brycer, many more options for generating fascinating objects and images. This chapter introduces you to complex objects, booleans, and more in-depth multi-replication in Bryce.

BUILDING BLOCKS: USING PRIMITIVE OBJECTS TO CREATE CONGLOMERATES

First, some term clarifications: When we talk about the creation of an object made from multiple objects, we use the term conglomerate object (or simply conglomerate). we do not use the term group to refer to a conglomerate, since group has a specific meaning in Bryce. A conglomerate object can be grouped or ungrouped. Since boolean objects must be grouped together in order for the special boolean properties to be apparent, we do refer to booleans as groups or boolean groups.

A conglomerate object is a bigger something that is created using many littler somethings. Bryce primitives are the basic building blocks used to create conglomerate objects. Most objects in the real world work this way also; very few objects come prefabricated fresh from a mold. Using this method, you can create all manner of objects—household items, brick walls, gadgets, buildings, whatever your creative eye envisions—using Bryce primitives.

You can also create complex objects in a separate 3D modeling application and then import the object into Bryce (for an introduction to this topic, see Chapter 4, "Brycean Objects"). Modeling in applications other than Bryce goes beyond the scope of this book, however. This chapter focuses on pointers for working within Bryce to model objects.

Build a Little, Duplicate a Lot

When building your conglomerate object, there are a lot of shortcuts you can take. You can duplicate elements to facilitate your construction. To create two sides of a symmetrical conglomerate, build one half first, then group the objects in the first half, duplicate, Flip X (or Z) and put the second half in position. The same thing works for top and bottom—duplicate and Flip Y. "Build a little, duplicate a lot" works at all stages of the process—from the beginning with one or two objects, to later on, duplicating a conglomerate many times over.

This technique is great for architectural objects; put on your Frank Lloyd Bryce hat and build buildings and other fantastic edifices to place into your Bryce world.

As a classic (literally!) example, build a column. Create a cylinder and stretch it up high. Add architectural detailing at the base and at the capitals using other object primitives placed just so. Then, when you have that one pillar, group it, duplicate it and create a row for a portico or arcade. Later in this chapter there is a walkthrough for creating columns that recapitulates the major sections of the chapter—booleans, multi-replication, and merging scenes.

On your duplicitous duplication spree, remember the Brycean universe grid, units of measure, and Object Conversion tool from Chapter 6.

Now that you've built the set of columns, why not build an entire building around them? Figure 7.1 shows the end result of the process of building a complex object—first a column, then a portico, then a roof, a frieze, a bazillion steps, and other things here and there to create an Ode to a Grecian URL (especially if you put an image like this on your Web page; made easier with Bryce 4's ability to export images as HTML image maps. Modeling conglomerate objects using the boolean functions is fun and versatile.

Figure 7.1 Greek Temple.

Complex Composite Objects

The other important use of grouped objects is to control object clutter. In the earlier tower creation exercise, many primitives were used to comprise a complex structure. Grouping allows you to work with all of the objects easily so that they function as a unit.

Figure 7.2 Two towers grouped for convenience.

Another advantage to grouping is that all the grouped objects are selected when you click on any one of them (or anywhere on the group's bounding box). In Figure 7.2, the towers were created with the same basic process used in the earlier exercise. But there are additional objects in there: small, hard-to-select objects, tiny easy-to-overlook objects. The tiny cylinder for the flagpole and pyramid for the pennant could easily be overlooked. Grouping all the objects ensures that all will be selected, so that when you move or resize them, you will move all of them and they will be resized together, not as individual elements.

WHAT IS A BOOLEAN?

What is a boolean? It has nothing to do with a traditional chant sung by loyal throngs devoted to their beloved Ivy League school. "Boolean" refers to a system for describing logical operations algebraically; a system named after its inventor, the nineteenth-century English mathematician George Boole. In Boole's symbolic logic, complex questions can be broken down into combinations of simpler binary propositions: given condition A and condition B, which single condition is the result? The simplest (and most commonly used) Boolean operations are:

- OR (The result is True if either A or B is True)

- NOT (The result is True if A or B is False)

- AND (The result is True only if A and B are both True.)

Boolean logic is the theoretical foundation of the architecture of modern computers, both the hardware and the software. When you do a complex search of a database or a website ("Show me all books about computers and in English but not about Microsoft software") you are using boolean operators. In the case of 3D software, a boolean is the process of combining two or more overlapping objects to result in a new and different shape. (The product of a boolean operation is often referred to as "a boolean," for short.)

There are three possible boolean operations in Bryce, which correspond to the three logical operators listed above:

- Union

- Subtraction

- Intersection

Don't go looking for a "union" command; to create a boolean object in Bryce, you assign boolean properties to the objects you want to combine, then group them. The properties you assign to the individual objects determine which boolean operation takes place.

Every object exists in one of these four states: neutral, positive, negative, and intersect. When you create an object, it comes into the world in the neutral state. Neutral objects do not participate in boolean operations—you must change an object to one of the three other states before the boolean magic can happen (we'll explain how to set those attributes in a minute). Also, one of the objects in a boolean must be positive; you can't combine a negative object with another negative one, or an intersect object with a negative one.

If all the objects in the group are positive, union takes place, and the resulting object is equal to the total volume of all the objects. In terms of boolean logic, any volume that is part of object A OR object B is part of the new object. When a negative object is included, subtraction takes place, and the volume of the negative object is hollowed out of the total. In other words, only the part of the positive object that is NOT shared with the negative object is preserved. Bring an intersect object to the party, and intersection takes place (surprise!). The resulting boolean object consists only of the parts of the original objects that overlap each other: the volumes that object A *and* object B share in common.

Figure 7.3 shows examples of all three boolean operations (from left to right):

- Union: the cone and cylinder are both positive

- Subtraction: the cone is positive, and the cylinder negative

- Subtraction: the cone is negative, and the cylinder is positive

- Intersection: the cone is positive, and the cylinder is set to intersect

a

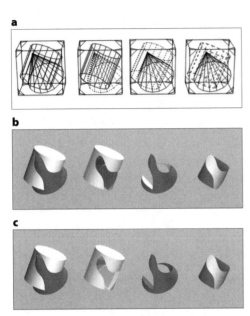

b

c

Figure 7.3 Four boolean constructions:
a) In wireframe view and b) rendered with
default settings; c) rendered with Transfer
Material of Negative Boolean turned off.

Notice the little pyramids in the corners of the bounding boxes. They indicate that the group is a boolean object. If all of the objects in a group are neutral, the group's bounding box has plain corners because it is not boolean.

Bryce has an excellent "online primer" for booleans in the Object Preset Library (find it by clicking the triangle just to the right of the heading "Create" on the Create Palette). Click to select the desired preset tile, and read the description. After perusing the first few rows, you get a good idea of the way booleans work. We will briefly reiterate the basics, then elaborate on implications and techniques. At the end of the chapter there's a sample walkthrough for you to construct your own conglomerate object.

In the previous edition of this book, many paragraphs were devoted to explaining the difference between boolean operations on Macintosh and Windows computers. Fortunately, the Mac and Windows versions of Bryce have put their differences behind them (the system that was introduced in the Windows version of Bryce 2 now reigns supreme), and they have come to an agreement on a common code base. One hesitates to claim categorically that the two versions of the software behave identically, but they're close enough as don't make no never mind.

How to Set Up Booleans

Setting up booleans is simple. Assign the boolean attribute to your object(s), group the set of objects, and render.

To assign the boolean attribute, click the A button next to the object's wireframe or type ⌘-Option-E (Macintosh) or Ctrl+Alt+E (Windows) to open the Object Attributes dialog box. You'll see the four boolean options listed on the left side. Remember, new objects are assigned the neutral attribute by default; they're not booleanable until you assign them one of the other attribute by choosing one of them. If you choose negative or intersect, the wireframe changes from solid lines to dotted (negative) or dashed lines (intersect). Figure 7.4 shows the three different wireframe states for individual objects.

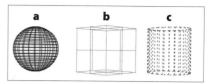

Figure 7.4 The wireframes for each boolean state: a) Solid lines indicate the object is positive (or, confusingly, neutral); b) dotted lines show the object is negative; c) dashed lines show that the object has been assigned the Intersect attribute.

Once you have two or more objects that have a boolean attribute assigned, group them. Select them and click the G icon, or choose Objects > Group Objects, or type ⌘-G (Macintosh) or Ctrl+G (Windows). Then render.

> **TIP:** Use keyboard shortcuts to assign boolean attributes to the selected object without going into the Object Attributes dialog box. Hit the P key to make the object positive, the N key to make the object negative, the I key to assign the Intersect attribute, and the O key (the letter) to turn all attributes off and return to neutral.

It's All in the Renderer

In the more advanced 3D modelers out there, boolean operations are used to permanently change the underlying geometry. When you have a sphere take a bite out of a cube, the result is a new geometric shape that is neither cube nor sphere but something that shares characteristics of both. Bryce's boolean functions differ from those of complex modelers: Brycean booleans do not change the underlying geometry. Sure, you take that sphere and tell it to take a bite out of a cube, but the result is not a new geometrical shape. The resulting render makes it look that way, but what you are seeing is a snazzy rendering sleight of hand. The boolean operation does not change the geometrical shape of the resulting boolean group, but it changes the way the renderer interprets the shapes it encounters when rendering.

The boolean operation takes place during the render, not during the modeling. The ray-tracing renderer sends rays out into the scene to see what's there and what it looks like. The ray tracer sees a group, and asks, "What's in this group? Aah! A sphere and a cube. But wait, the sphere is negative—it's taking a bite out of the cube!" Then the renderer goes to work calculating both the sphere's and the cube's placement. It interprets what portions of those objects will be rendered. "The sphere is not here, but its shape is subtracted from the cube at this location, like so…"

What are the implications of this ray-traced render-based boolean operation?

- *Booleans are Editable.* The individual objects stay what they are—the sphere remains a sphere. After you have assigned boolean properties and grouped the objects, you can still select and manipulate the sphere individually, changing its size, position, and rotation, and so update the look of the entire boolean object. This provides you with editing flexibility throughout the entire scene-making process.

- *All Component Objects are Still Visible in Wireframe Mode.* This next implication may not be so pleasant. Since each shape is maintained through to the end, each shape is visible in wireframe view. If you have an extremely complex object, you will have a far more complex morass of wireframe bits and pieces than if you had said, "Okay, now that my sphere has taken a bite out of the cube, change the shape forever and be done with it!" Unfortunately, you'll have to look at all the wireframe pieces that are non-objects in all their dotted and dashed wireframe glory.

- *All Components are Still Visible in Shaded Preview Mode.* Also potentially unpleasant, this is a corollary to the previous item and is a direct result of the fact that the booleans are created during rendering. Figure 7.5 shows the boolean constructs from Figure 7.3 but displayed with the Sree3D Shaded Preview Mode (the OpenGL preview looks similar). They don't look any different than the equivalent non-boolean groups.

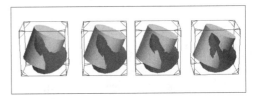

Figure 7.5 The booleans from Figure 7.3, in Sree3D display mode.

- *Surfaces are Based on Individual Attributes.* The surface of the final grouped boolean object is based on the surfaces and boolean attributes of the member objects. The general rule is that each component retains its own material—unless a negative object is involved in the boolean. When you change an object's state to Negative, the Transfer Material of Negative Boolean option is turned on by default (see Figure 7.6). This means that wherever the negative object takes a bite out of the positive one, it will leave its own material behind (the Gouda cheese in Figure 4.15 is an example of this). Back in Figure 7.3, the cones and the cylinders have different surface materials. Figure 7.3b demonstrates the default behavior. The second boolean best displays the result of transferring the material of the negative object—the negative cone cuts out a large chunk of the cylinder and the surface where the two objects are in contact is covered with the cone's darker color. In the third boolean you can just barely see a white strip where the negative cone has subtracted part of the cone and left its lighter material behind. For Figure 7.3c, we turned off the Transfer Material option, so the hollowed-out portions of the cylinder and cone retain the colors of the positive objects. As you can see, when addition or intersection are in force, each component keeps its original material. Planning the surface attributes with these behaviors in mind will make for some boolean objects that are quite fetching.

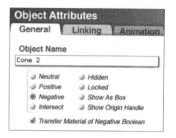

Figure 7.6 The option to Transfer Material of Negative Boolean is turned on by default when an object is made negative.

• *Boolean Objects are not Limited to Certain Types.* We'll include this little note for historical reasons. In Bryce 2, only certain types of objects could participate in the boolean orgy, and the list of acceptable objects was different on Mac and Windows. Now, all objects on both platforms are booleanable, even those that seem extremely unlikely—like meshes and lights, for instance.

Booleans in Depth

With this background in mind, are there any special techniques for using booleans during the construction process? Yes! Use objects as tools for construction—use a sphere to scoop something out. The results of using objects as tools can be widely varied, as various as are the objects in the world. We cannot discuss them all, but we can discuss some principles of construction. You take it from there, being your own architect, contractor, foreperson, and master craftsperson.

Neutral

All objects begin as neutral. There's not much else to say about the neutral state, because it's so…well, neutral. When you group a collection of neutral objects, they just form a group; no boolean operation is taking place. You don't need to group a set of objects in order for the neutral combinations to be visible. For example, refer back to the grand temple image in Figure 7.1. Aside from a small amount of fancy trickery, mostly in the columns most of the objects for the foundations and the steps are neutral objects, positioned just so. They may or may not be grouped.

Union

Union is the most basic of object combinations that actually produces a new object. When you combine positive objects they comprise a more complex shape than either of the two alone. This becomes most readily apparent when you combine objects sharing the same material.

When you are working with transparent objects, the benefit of the union operation becomes clear (pun intended). Since Bryce considers each object to be a distinct element, two overlapping transparent neutral objects will look like two overlapping transparent objects. If you want to combine different objects to make something such as a wine bottle (Figure 7.7), you could run into some problems, as the complex object on the left demonstrates. The complex object on the right, however, doesn't suffer the same fate. All the objects have been assigned the positive attribute and then grouped, producing a nice glass bottle.

Figure 7.7 The grouping of positive objects results in uniting primitives into one shape. The bottle on the left consists of neutral objects; the bottle on the right is assembled from positive objects, which, when grouped, produce a boolean union.

Negative Noodlings and Subtraction Strategies

When you group a negative object with a positive one, you subtract the shape of the former from the latter. Since it's far easier to talk about "subtracting the sphere shape from the cube," we'll speak of negative booleans in those terms rather than the more awkward "make the sphere negative and then group it with the positive cube."

Many consecutive subtractions make for an interesting construction. Figure 7.8 demonstrates a series of boolean operations starting with a simple cube (7.8a1). (The pairs of pictures in the left column show the same object from two different angles.) In Figure 7.8a2 we've used a smaller cuboid (seen in wireframe) to take a chunk out of the original object, resulting in the object shown in 7.8b1. Let's add another cuboid, this time a bigger one, shown in wireframe mode in 7.8b2. Make it positive, and subtract from it the product of our previous booleanizing. Figure 7.8c1 is the result. Lather, rinse, repeat: add a new positive object (the wireframe in 7.8c2), make our previous boolean negative, group, and you get the object in 7.8d1. Finally, add a squashed sphere (7.8d2), subtract 7.8d1 from it, and you've created a lovely, uhhh, paperweight!

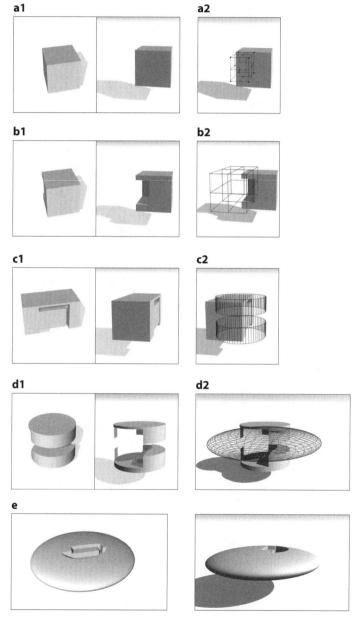

a1 **a2** **b1** **b2** **c1** **c2** **d1** **d2** **e**

Figure 7.8 Cumulative addition and subtraction.

If your negative object isn't big enough to provide the shape you want to achieve, then create a larger subtraction group. Create the several components of your negative group. Ensure that the objects are positive, then select them, group them and make the group negative. Then position the negative group to subtract from your positive object. In Figure 7.9, a pyramid scooping out a shape from a cylinder needs to bore deeper into the cylinder than the height of the pyramid. To do this, group the positive pyramid and a cube , make the group negative, then group this group with the positive cylinder to carve out a shape. This is the technique used with terrains to cut areas out of other objects. We'll elaborate on terrain boolean strategies later in this section.

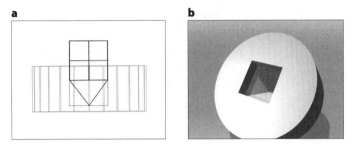

Figure 7.9 **A pyramid and cube combined to make a negative object.**

Of course, for a two (or more) step process, you can use booleans to create your subtracting object. To create the obelisk in Figure 7.10c, in which there are two pyramid shapes, the positive object is the tall, tall pyramid shown in the first figure. But in order to cut it short with another pyramid shape, a double-negative is required. The figure shows the progressive building of the top of the boolean object. First, a negative pyramid is placed in the bottom of a positive cube. Then the two are grouped so the resulting cube has a pyramid-shaped hole in the bottom. After creating and enlarging another pyramid so that it stands very tall, the cube-pyramid boolean is nearly ready to chop off the top of that tall, tall pyramid to finish the obelisk. But first, the cube must grow in height so that it occupies all the area of the top of the tall, tall pyramid (see Figure 7.10b). Once it does that, align it with the positive pyramid (Align X and Align Z; both centered) assign it negative, group it, and render for the result shown.

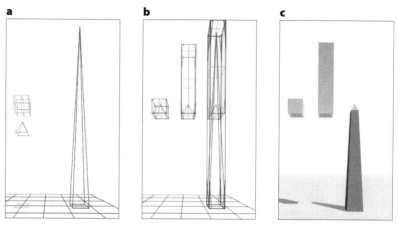

Figure 7.10 Obelisk components and construction: a) The individual objects;
b) creating boolean groups; c) the rendered monument.

Intersection

Intersection takes away everything but the area where the two objects overlap. The surface properties of each object are retained, however, resulting in an object that has two or more different materials. The obelisk in Figure 7.11 is built with intersection, using only two objects, which encompass a much wider area than those in the subtraction example.

When you create an intersection boolean group, you cannot create a group comprised solely of intersecting objects. There must be one object in the group that is positive, no matter how many there are. It also doesn't matter which object is positive and which is intersect, since the result will show only the volume that is common to the two. Multiple intersecting objects can be part of the group. Figure 7.12 shows identical results from

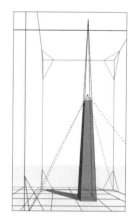

Figure 7.11 Obelisk with intersection wireframes.

two different sets of boolean intersect operations. Each boolean group contains a cone and two pyramids, and the pyramids are offset from each other by 45°. In the set on the left, the cone is assigned to intersect and then grouped with the two positive pyramids. In the group on the right, the two pyramids are made positive, then grouped and the group is assigned to intersect. Then the pyramid group is in turn grouped with the positive cone. The net result of the two processes is the same. You can also group a set of positive objects together and then assign the intersect attribute to the group before joining it with another object. Figure 7.44c, later in this chapter, is the result of that technique.

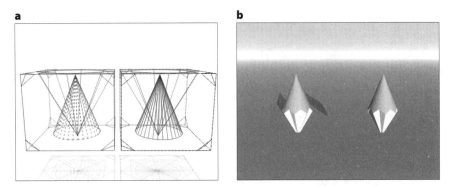

Figure 7.12 Two approaches to intersection: a) Two wireframe boolean object groups; b) the rendered results of the boolean operations.

You can alternate between subtraction and intersection in your boolean groups, but you cannot have both a negative object and intersecting object in the same group. If you are at all mathematically inclined, you'll realize that mathematical equations must first solve one part, and then another. You cannot subtract and divide simultaneously, you have to choose to do one first and then the other. Grouping works in an analogous fashion. If you were to express boolean operations in mathematical terms, the operation might look like this:

(Cube minus sphere) intersected with cone.

The first group consists of the cube and the negative sphere, so the subtraction operation takes place. The first group and the cone (set to intersect) constitute the second group. But remember that groups, just like individual objects, come into the world neutral. You must assign a property to the group before you can continue making boolean constructions with it. In this case, make the first group positive, or nothing will happen when you group it with the intersecting cone.

Booleans and Groups

When you create a group of positive objects and then assign a boolean property to the group, the group's bounding box is changed in wireframe view to reflect the boolean status, not the individual objects themselves. Check out the two wireframe examples in Figure 7.12a. In the example to the right, the boolean property of intersect is assigned to the group, not to the individual pyramids, making the bounding box dashed.

Terrains and Terrains; Terrains and Grounds

Terrains are full-fledged citizens of the Booleanable Objects in Bryce. Since terrains are not simple geometric shapes, as are cubes and cylinders and spheres and the like, there are some special shape considerations to bear in mind when using them in boolean operations. Although a terrain is hollow when you look at it, for boolean purposes, the terrain gets closed off at the bottom to become a solid object. The bottom edge is defined by outside edges of the terrain square. Also, you can set your terrain to be a bona fide solid object in the Terrain Editor (for more information, see Chapter 8, "Terrains, Symmetrical Lattices and the Terrain Editor.") To create a clean terrain-shaped cutout of another object, you need to remember where the edges of your terrain are.

In order for a terrain to cleanly slice out of another object, all its edges have to be clear of the object's edges, otherwise you'll get an overlap. Figure 7.13 shows a terrain (with the Boolean attribute of negative) biting a corner out of a sphere. It has been rotated so that its bottom (where the square edges are) is facing up and out, and its top is subtracted from the object. In Figure 7.13a you can see the terrain wireframe, and Figure 7.13b shows the rendered result. The left half of each image shows the view from the side, and the right half shows front view. Notice that the terrain's bottom edge doesn't completely erase the upper part of the sphere; hence the leftover bit of sphere left floating above the object.

a
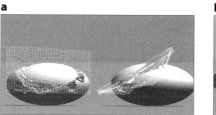
b

Figure 7.13 Terrain being subtracted from sphere: a) Slide view with terrain wrieframe; b) perspective view.

To solve this kind of problem, group the terrain and another object together to make a bigger object. Since the base of a terrain is square, we like to set a cube there. Here's our quick positioning technique:

1. First make sure everything is ungrouped. Duplicate the terrain and change the duplicate into a cube using the Object Conversion tool.

2. In the Edit Palette, change to Object Space and use the Reposition tool (on the *y* axis, most probably) to move the cube so that it extends from the bottom of the terrain.

3.   Make sure both objects are positive, then group the terrain and cube together. Assign negative to the group. The bounding box wireframe changes to dotted lines.

4.   Group the negative terrain-cube group with the positive sphere.

5.   Render.

Simple!

A terrain's height information also plays a role in using it as part of a boolean. Since a terrain changes shape based on the grayscale information (refer to Chapter 8, "Terrains, Symmetrical Lattices, and the Terrain Editor," if this terminology is unfamiliar to you), it's good to know how height information affects the boolean process.

The bottom of the terrain's volume is defined by its lowest points—the darkest parts of its grayscale information. That usually corresponds to the terrain's outside edge. If you want a terrain shape to take a gouge out of another primitive or the ground plane, it seems like there should be two ways to do so. You can position the terrain so that it is upside down, taking that bite out of the object, or conceivably, you could invert the terrain's gray map so that what's high is low and what is low becomes high. But those two actions do not yield the same result. Figure 7.14 shows two terrains positioned with two cubes. Parts a and b show apparently identical wireframes. But the terrain in part a has been flipped on the *y* axis, and the one in part b has had its gray map inverted. In wireframe mode they appear the same, but when they are rendered (Figure 7.14c and d), the differences are striking. The terrain in part c gouges out the volume, whereas the terrain in part d lies inside the cube. Again, it might help to think of a mathematical analogy: the terrain in part c is a positive shape that is turned upside down and given the negative boolean attribute, so it cuts a hole in the ground. The terrain in part d, on the other hand, is already a hole, so assigning it the negative attribute has the same effect as a double negative— it fills the cube rather than digging a hole. (The Terrain Editor preview also gives a nice clue about what is bottom, even for an inverted terrain.)

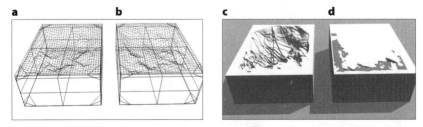

Figure 7.14 Terrains set to negative: a) Wireframe view of a terrain that has been flipped on its *y* axis; b) terrain wireframe with inverted height map; c) rendered view of wireframe from part a; d) part b rendered.

This same type of treatment is effective for taking a gouge out of the ground. The "ground canyon" shown in Figure 7.15 was created by duplicating several terrains that were flipped on the *y* axis, positioning them just above the ground level, then making them negative and grouping them all with the ground. Notice that the highest parts of the terrain approach one level, as if there were a limit to their elevation. That's the effect of the ground plane, from which the terrains were subtracted.

Figure 7.15 Ground Canyon: Many negative terrains grouped with ground.

A Few Boolean Examples

Boolean variety is the spice of Bryce. Here are a few sample images that show Bryce's modeling abilities. In the first, the *Planetary Traveler* probe by Rodney L'Ongnion (see Figure 7.16), a flying ship is created using almost all spheres and cylinders, with a cube thrown in here and there for good measure. Compare the image of the final render with the wireframe view.

a

b

c

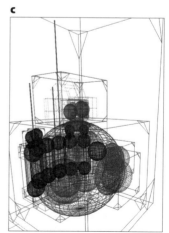

Figure 7.16 *Planetary Traveler* probe: a) Rendered view; b) rendered view of back; c) wireframe view. *Art by Rodney L'Ongnion.*

Hilary Rhodes's *Escher House* (see Figure 7.17) is a Brycean reconstruction of the impossible room that is rightside up and upside down and every which way when viewed from every perspective. Though there is a lot of good old-fashioned addition going on here, judicious subtraction allows the illusion of unreal reality.

a   b

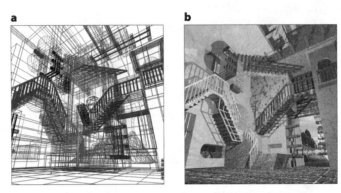

Figure 7.17 *Escher House:* a) Wireframe and b) render. *Art by Hilary Rhodes.*

Harald Seiwert's fairy-tale castle in Figure 7.18 is a study in architectural details. (We must say that European Brycers have a home-turf advantage with the local castles nearby for study!) The double placement of pyramids and cubes (in diamond shape) for the two-sloped roof, the boolean cut-outs for the architectural details on the castle walls, towers, and turrets, and the overall detail in construction make this an exemplary study of the conglomerate Brycean object.

a   b

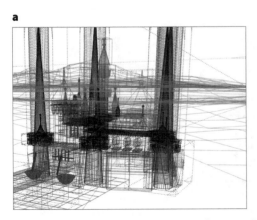 

Figure 7.18 A fairy-tale castle: a) Wireframe and b) render. *Art by Harald Seiwert.*

OBJECT LINKING

When animation was introduced to Bryce 3D, the developers thought it wise to provide a new method of combining multiple objects into larger structures. Grouping is just fine for some purposes, but the rigidity of the group relationship prevents you from creating a conglomerate object whose members have a certain amount of independence. Think about the cars in a train, or the parts of a living organism, or the pieces of a machine: when animating such an entity you want the object as a whole to move together, but you may want its individual components to display a variety of motion behaviors. Object linking was added to Bryce to fill this need.

Parent and Child Objects: My Mamma Done Tol' Me

One can have many objects involved in complex linking relationships, but each link is defined between only two objects at a time. One object is chosen to "lead" the other object; the leader is called the parent, the follower is the child. In real life you cannot choose your parents, but in Bryce, you can. You work with the child object, and from there, choose the parent object. The child follows the parent, but it can also act independently.

Making a Link

The scene file used in the next two examples is included on the CD-ROM. Open it up (it's called LINKING PRACTICE) if you'd like to play along at home. For this exercise, we will be treating the cylinder as the child, and the cone as the parent. There are two methods for linking one object to another. The first method uses one of the Object Control icons: select the child object and drag with the mouse from its Linking icon to the intended parent object (see Figure 7.19). Once you begin to drag, the Object Control icons disappear, and in their place a gray line extends from the child object to your mouse pointer. Continue to drag until the gray line touches the parent object; both line and parent will turn blue to let you know that you've arrived. Release the mouse button, and you're done! To break the link, select the child object and drag from the Linking icon to an "empty" part of the scene, or simply click the Linking icon once.

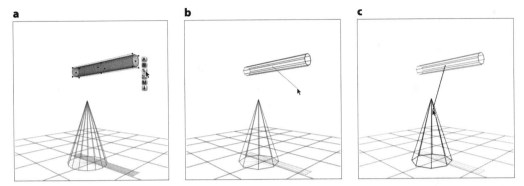

Figure 7.19 Linking a child object to its parent; in this case, the cone is the parent, and the cylinder is the child: a) The child is selected, and the mouse cursor is poised over the Linking icon; b) dragging the link toward the parent; c) the link touches the parent, causing it to turn blue.

The second method involves a visit to the Object Attributes dialog box (as discussed back in Chapter 4, "Brycean Objects"). Let's start over with our cone and cylinder scene. Click the cylinder, our child-to-be, to select it, and then click the A icon. Click the Linking tab in the dialog box, then use the Object Parent Name pop-up menu to choose the object to which you wish to link the cylinder—in this case, the cone (Figure 7.20a). When you release the mouse button, you are confronted with a new set of choices in Propagate (Figure 7.20b). We'll discuss propagation in a bit, but first, some more comparisons between groups and links.

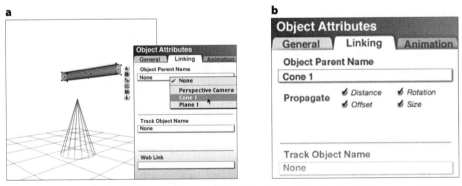

Figure 7.20 Using the Object Attributes dialog box to create a link: a) Choosing a parent for your orphan object from the Object Parent Name pop-up; b) the properties that may be propagated along the link.

Linking and Groups: Who Affects Whom

What's the difference between linking and grouping? Changes made to a group result in a proportionate overall change. When you click a member of a group, you select the entire group. Think of it this way: As you manipulate the group, the transformation energy flows in all directions throughout the group, affecting each of the members equally. (Of course, there are obvious exceptions in the matter of selection; we'll deal with that shortly.)

That's not the case in a linking relationship. With linking, there's a parent-child relationship: changes to the parent affect the child object, but the child may also act independently. Links are always created between two objects at a time, not among multiple objects simultaneously, and the relationship between the two objects is not symmetrical. Transformations performed on the parent travel through the link to the child, but the energy does not flow back in the opposite direction.

Figure 7.21 shows a simple example of this behavior. Our scene consists of two cubes and two spheres. The upper cube/sphere pair is grouped—hence the box around the objects in wireframe view (Figure 7.21a). The lower sphere, on the other hand, is linked to the lower cube: the sphere is the child of the cube. Figure 7.21b shows what happens when we drag both cubes to the left: both spheres move to the left by the same amount. The child obeys the parent. In Figure 7.21c we have dragged both spheres to the right, but this time, only the cube that is grouped with the sphere follows along. The parent, as happens all too often in real life, pays no mind to the wandering child.

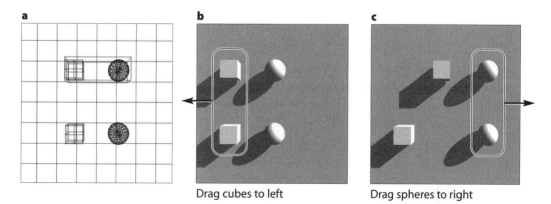

Drag cubes to left   Drag spheres to right

Figure 7.21 Group vs. link behavior: a) The objects at the top are grouped, while those below are linked; b) after dragging both cubes leftward, both spheres follow; c) when both spheres are dragged, only the grouped cube moves.

Although we've just said that a group is completely different from a set of linked objects, there's actually a catch: a group is a very special case of a linked object. When you create a group, you are creating a new object—the group—that is the parent of all the objects in the group. This is the only way you can link multiple objects at once. Figure 7.22 shows the Object Attributes dialog box for a cube that is a member of a group. In the Linking section, notice that the parent is Group 1. The menu item is grayed out, since you cannot change it or disinherit the parent as long as the object is part of the group.

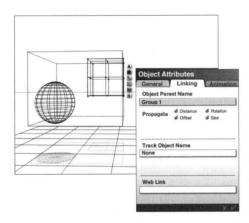

Figure 7.22 The Object Attributes dialog box showing how an object that is a part of a group is actually a child of the object called Group 1.

Propagation of the Properties

We've told you that grouping is a one-for-all, all-for-one arrangement; and linking, with a parent-child relationship, is more selective. A group is totally communal: all members share and share alike. Whatever slings and arrows of outrageous fortune (or 3D transformation) affect one member, affect them all.

In a linked relationship, you can choose which of the parent's properties the child will inherit—a crude sort of genetic engineering, you might say. And you make those choices right on the Object Linking tab (see Figures 7.20b and 7.22). Now, three of these properties should look quite familiar; Offset, Rotation, and Size correlate to the three parameters in the 3D Transformation dialog box, which in turn are derived from the three main controls on the Edit Palette: Resize, Rotate, and Reposition (though not necessarily in that order). The fourth check box, Distance, is a bit cryptic—we'll talk about that one in a moment. For now, we'll assume it's on.

By default, when you create a link, all four of these properties are checked. The resulting link is very sturdy, and the behavior of the linked pair is almost indistinguishable from a group. Toss the parent about in whatever way you will, resize it, distort it, drag it all over creation, and the child is likewise resized, distorted, and shoved around. In only one respect is this linked pair different from a group: a grouped object rotates about the origin point of the group, sort of the center of gravity of the collection of objects. A linked pair rotates about the origin point of the parent.

Things get more interesting when you start turning off those check boxes. Leave only Rotation checked, and you can have objects at opposite ends of your scene, perhaps even moving independently of each other, which rotate exactly in sync. Turn on Offset and turn off everything else, and you can have two objects moving in tandem through your scene, all the while changing shape and rotation individually.

Distance is not a property in its own right, but a modifier of the other properties. If you have Distance on but the other three are off, there is effectively no link. Remember our little metaphor about the transformational energy flowing from the parent to the child? The Distance setting determines what route this energy takes, how it manifests itself.

When Distance is on, there is a powerful, direct conduit of the transformational energy from the parent object to its child. When the parent rotates, the whole parent-child complex rotates about the parent's origin point. When the parent is resized, not only is the child resized but the distance between them is scaled to the same degree. It's as if Distance (combined with Offset) is a rigid stick. It scales, rotates or moves along with the parent object. In Figure 7.23, the Distance (plus Offset) is actually represented as a stick (okay, a cylinder), and you see Distance transformed along with the cube parent object (and, of course, the child cone). When Distance and Offset are off, the transformations are similar but independent—except for reposition, which has no effect on the child at all. Offset is a bit more complicated: when it's on, if the parent moves, the child moves with it, but if the parent also turns, as when tracking another object, the child moves so that it is always "connected" to the same point on the parent's surface.

If Rotation is on and Distance is off, the parent and child spin along parallel axes and at the same speed, but each one rotates around its own origin point. Resizing the parent causes the child to resize proportionally, but the distance between them does not change. If the parent is Offset, the child follows but does not try to stay pointed to the same face on the parent object.

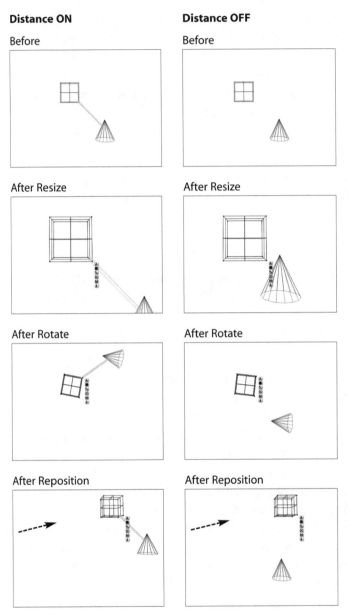

Figure 7.23 Distance represented as a stick, where cube is parent and cone is child object: Left column: Distance on; Right column: Distance (and Offset) off. Top row: Original state before any transformations; the lower three rows show the results of performing a transformation on the parent. Second row: Resizing; Third Row: Rotating; Fourth row: Repositioning.

To tease out all the differences, take a look at Figure 7.24. It shows six sets of parent-child links, side by side; in each case, the pyramid is the parent. Each child inherits the parent's properties in a slightly different way. The propagation particulars are shown at the top of the image. On the left half (the first three images of each row), the sphere inherits size, and on the right half, it does not. With the exception of size, the settings mirror one another, from left to right: A-B-C C-B-A. Figure 7.24a is the before state, Figure 7.24b is after resizing the pyramids. In Figure 7.24c, the before and after states are superimposed so you can see precisely what happened during the transformation. The origin handles for each object are shown so that you may compare their locations and the relationship between objects. In the process of growing in size, the pyramid's origin changes position slightly. (This is a result of resizing proportionately by dragging on the corner control handle so that the pyramid grows up and to the left.)

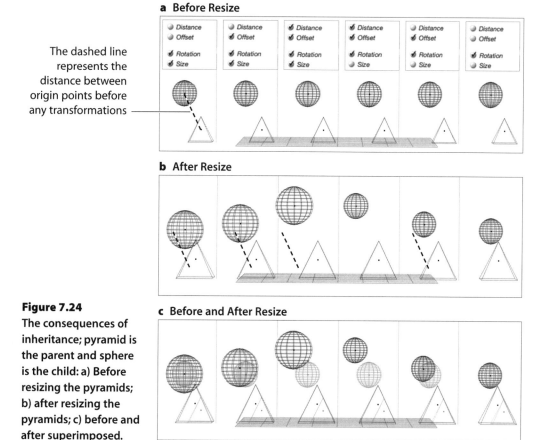

The dashed line represents the distance between origin points before any transformations

a **Before Resize**

b **After Resize**

Figure 7.24
The consequences of inheritance; pyramid is the parent and sphere is the child: a) Before resizing the pyramids; b) after resizing the pyramids; c) before and after superimposed.

c **Before and After Resize**

Notice that in the first set, where neither Distance nor Offset is propagated, the sphere inherits the parent's change in size. But the sphere's location does not change at all; the origin points for the sphere are in the exact same place. In the second example, where the sphere inherits the pyramid's Offset, the sphere grows and changes position to match the change in position of the pyramid's origin point. The relationship between parent's and child's origin points stays constant. The third case includes Distance in the mix. When Distance is inherited, it is as though there was an invisible stick connecting the parent with the child. When the parent is enlarged, the Distance—or invisible stick—between them is also enlarged, and, of course, the child is also enlarged. The fourth option is identical to the third, only the sphere does not change size. The Distance "stick" grows along with the pyramid parent's growth, moving the sphere farther away, but the sphere does not change in size. The fifth option is similar to the second one, except that the sphere does not change in size. The Offset is inherited, so that the relationship between both objects' origin points remains constant. The sixth option is similar to the first—though without size—neither distance nor offset is inherited. In this case, the sphere remains the same in position and size. The same pyramid-sphere linked sets are shown, this time inheriting Rotation, in Figure 7.25. The left three spheres all inherit the Rotation of the parent. In the first two examples, the sphere rotates in place without moving. In the third, both Distance and Offset are inherited and the sphere rotates around the parent pyramid's origin point. In the fourth example, Distance and Offset move the position of the sphere, but, since it does not inherit the parent's Rotation, it stays in the same orientation. The fifth and sixth see no change in the child sphere in response to the parent's rotation. If you are counting your lists and checking them twice, you may have noticed that there is no condition where Distance is on and Offset is off. Astute observation! The result of that condition is identical to the second one. Don't take our word for it, though, feel free to try it out yourself; look for the scene file in the Chapter 7 folder on the CD-ROM. It's called Distance Offset Sixsome.

a **Before Rotate**

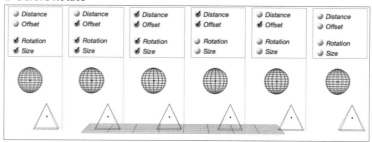

b **After Rotate**

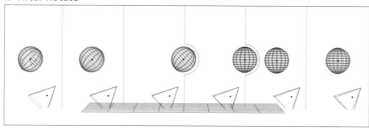

c **Before and After Rotate**

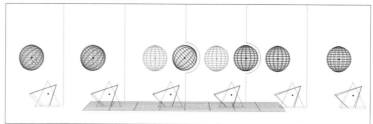

Figure 7.25 The child (sphere) inherits the parent's (pyramid's) Rotation with or without Distance and Offset (pyramid parent; sphere child): a) Before rotation; b) after rotation; c) before and after superimposed.

But wait—there's more! What happens if you change both the Size and Rotation? In doing so, you'll also affect position. Figure 7.26 shows the conditions before and after the transformation, with the superimposed before and after together so you may carefully analyze what took place.

a Before Rotate and Resize

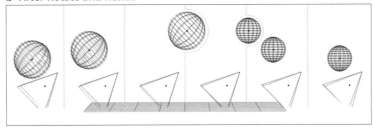

b After Rotate and Resize

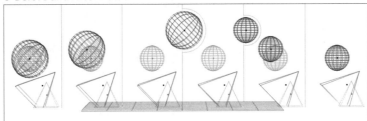

c Before and After Rotate and Resize

Figure 7.26 Inheriting the parent's Rotation and Size with or without Distance and Offset (parent: pyramid; child: sphere): a) Before rotation and resizing; b) after rotation and resizing; c) before and after superimposed.

Hierarchical Society

The existence of links between parents and children has some hierarchical implications. The "chain of command" can move down across generations, extending the "parent directs the child but the child can act independently" into more complex variations. There are also some surprises when you try to work with parent and child(ren) the same way that you work with a set of unrelated objects. Being able to tell what is part of the hierarchy will help in the construction and process of working with your scene.

Multi-generational Inheritance

Just as you can have grouped groups, you can also have linked links. In the scene file DOUBLE-HIERARCHY (in the Chapter 15 folder on the CD-ROM), shown in Figure 7.27, you see a torus that has four pyramids linked to it. Linked to each of those pyramids is a smaller torus, which, in turn has four pyramids linked to it. The most-parental torus rotates and all follow along. (If this is the top object in the hierarchy, does that make it a matriarch or patriarch object?!) But each of the smaller tori also rotate in the opposite direction, creating an effect similar to that scrambler carnival ride that made us woozy in our youth! See this effect on the movie file, DOUBLE-HIERARCHY.MOV in the Chapter 15 folder on the CD-ROM.

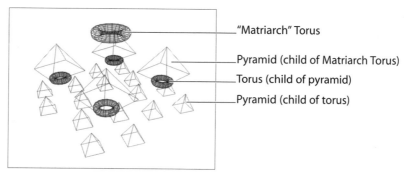

"Matriarch" Torus

Pyramid (child of Matriarch Torus)

Torus (child of pyramid)

Pyramid (child of torus)

Figure 7.27 Linked links: The top torus is the "matriarch" with four pyramid children, each of which have a torus child that has, in turn, four pyramid children.

Dual Transformations

One thing to watch out for with both groups and links is transforming both parent and child objects. (For this purpose, the group is the parent and the individual members of the group are the children.) In the case where you select both the parent and the child and then make some transformation—move, resize or rotate them—you will be performing a double transformation on the child object. The child is transformed in an exaggerated fashion, since the same transformation occurs twice: transformation inherited from the parent, and transformation to itself. This is true for groups as well, since a group is a parent object to all the (child) group objects. Figure 7.28 compares four sets of objects. The top two sets of objects are grouped, and the bottom two are linked together. The contextual selection menus for each set show precisely which objects are selected. Notice the difference in the before and after: When the group and a member of the group (the top pair) are both selected, the cube in the group moves farther than the group does; the relationship between the members of the group is changed.

Likewise, the third pair (the top linked pair) has both the parent sphere and the child cube selected. The result is identical, with the child object moving much farther out than the parent. What's happening here? The child object is moving twice as far, since it's both inheriting the parent's move and moving of its own accord.

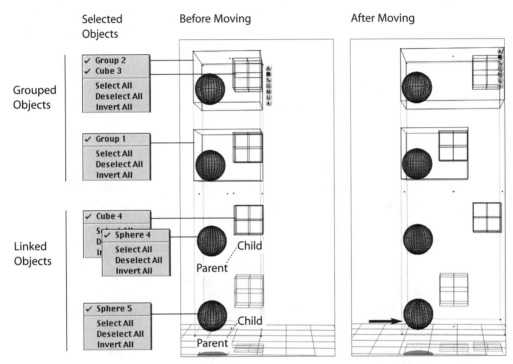

Figure 7.28 Results of selecting and transforming both parent and child, as compared to performing same action on a group and its contents: Left column: selected objects; Center column: Before moving objects; Right Column: After moving objects. Double selections move the child object twice as far as the parent object.

The practical implication of this is extremely important! When you are making changes to linked objects, be sure to change only the parent!

Making the Hierarchy Explicit

Right about now you may be thinking, "Gee, it would be nice if there was some way to keep track of all of these complex inter-object relationships." It would certainly help to see who's linked to whom to avoid the situation just described, right? Alas, Bryce doesn't give you any visual clues as to tell you what objects are linked to each other as you look at your scene. (With groups, at least there's a big box around their wireframes.) However, there is help, of a sort, in a place you might not expect it.

Let's go back to the scene we used in Figure 7.21, one sphere and cube grouped, and another sphere and cube linked. For an overview of all of the objects in the scene and their structural relationships, we need to pay a visit to the Advanced Motion Lab (AML). To get there, either click the Advanced Motion Lab icon on the Time Palette (Figure 7.29), or type ⌘-T/Ctrl+T.

Figure 7.29 Click this icon to enter the Advanced Motion Lab (AML).

Ta-daa! (See Figure 7.30a.) An impressive piece of (faux) hardware, *n'est-ce pas*? We'll save a thorough discussion of its workings for Chapter 15, "Advanced Animation Techniques," because we're only interested in one feature right now. Unfortunately, that feature isn't displayed when you first open the Lab; to remedy that, press your mouse on the little triangle on the right edge of the Lab (circled) and drag to the second item on the pop-up menu, Show Animated (which means Show only Animated), turning it off (Figure 7.30b). (If any of the objects are selected, you need to turn off Show Selected—which actually means Show only Selected—to see the whole list of objects). Make sure that the third item, Display Hierarchy, is checked.

The bottom half of the AML will now be filled with a multi-layered timeline; the part we're looking for is at the left end (Figure 7.30c). At first glance, it seems to be a list of the objects in your scene, but on closer inspection it proves to be missing a few items. How does it decide which objects to show and which to hide?

You'll notice that two items have little triangles next to their names. These items are both representatives of conglomerate objects: Group 1 (the Top Cube and Top Sphere) and Bottom Cube (parent of Bottom Sphere). Click the triangles and the object list expands to show all of the components of the conglomerate objects in a sort of outline format (Figure 7.30d).

This "outlined" list of objects has a hierarchical look to it, doesn't it? That's because this is a representation of the object hierarchies within your scene. Remember back in Chapter 4, we mentioned that Bryce maintains an internal spreadsheet with data about all the objects in a scene. Within that spreadsheet, Bryce uses each object's place in the object hierarchy to keep track of its relationships with other objects, especially those with which it is grouped or linked. Look once again at Figure 7.30d; the leftmost items in the cascading list are at the top of the hierarchy (they're also the only items that show up when the hierarchy is collapsed, as in Figure 7.30c). The objects farther to the right are deeper in the hierarchy. In a scene with many complex linkages and groupings, you quickly overflow the small space allotted to the list (Figure 7.31). Bryce's object hierarchy list is limited compared to similar features in other 3D programs, but it's better than no list at all, as in Bryce 2 (which, of course, also had no hierarchies).

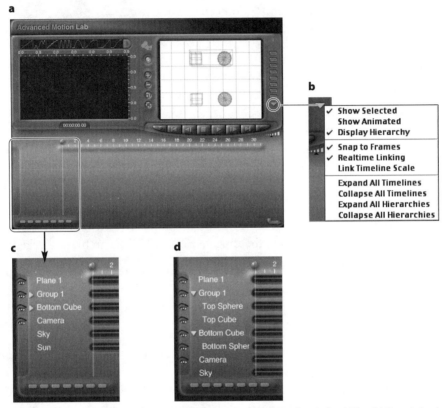

Figure 7.30 Displaying hierarchies in the Advanced Motion Lab: a) The AML as it looks upon opening; b) the AML Options menu, with Show Animated turned off; c) the Object Hierarchies display area, with hierarchies collapsed; d) Object Hierarchies expanded.

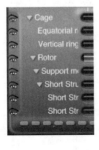

Figure 7.31 Part of the Object Hierarchy list for a gyroscope, a complex structure of many groups within groups.

Try it Out! A Linked Crane Object

To conclude this section on linking, we'll construct an elbow crane. Why an elbow crane? This is a camera crane that we'll discuss in greater detail in Chapter 15, "Advanced Animation Techniques." Here, you'll use linking and hierarchies (and the changing of origin points) to create an object that will support a camera for some natural-looking animated camera movements. We won't discuss the use of the crane in this chapter, but we'll use the linking techniques to make the crane for later.

1. Create a new Bryce scene and create a cube in it.

2. Rotate the Director's View perspective camera to view your scene from the front. It should look something like Figure 7.32a.

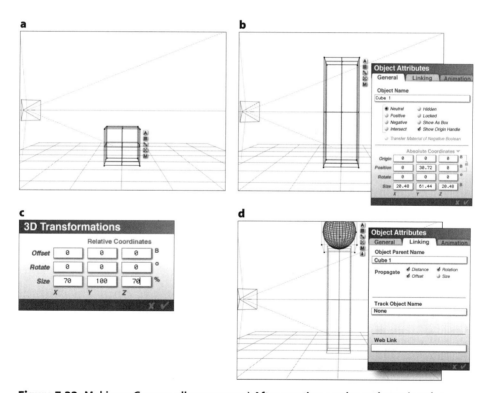

Figure 7.32 Making a Camera elbow crane: a) After creating a cube and rotating the Director's View to "front;" b) changing the cube's origin point in the Object Attributes dialog box; c) the 3D Transformations settings for narrowing the cube; d) linking settings for the sphere.

3. Drag from the top control handle to enlarge the cube vertically on the *y* axis.

   If you want to be precise about it, press the Shift key and drag up until the cube snaps to the fourth place. The top of the cube will be a little bit below the top of your scene window (assuming, of course, that it's the default scene size).

4. Now you'll need to change the origin point of the cube so that it's at the bottom center of the object. Click the A icon to access the Object Attributes dialog box (see Figure 7.32b). Click the Show Origin Handle option to activate it.

   You can place the origin handle manually by exiting the Object Attributes dialog box and dragging the green origin handle point. Or, you can place the origin handle numerically here in the Object Attributes dialog box. This is the approach we'll take.

   Click the little lock icon in the Absolute Coordinates section so that the lock is open. This will allow you to make the origin point a different place than the object's position. For origin Y, type 0. Your numbers should look like the Object Attributes dialog box in Figure 7.32b. Click the check mark to leave the dialog box.

5. Next, reduce the width and depth of the cube. Click the word Edit at the top of the screen to make sure that the Edit Palette is showing. Under either the Resize, Rotate, or Reposition pop-up menus, select 3D Transformations. In the dialog box, enter 70% for the Size settings on both the *x* and *z* axes (see Figure 7.32c). Click the check mark to exit the 3D Transformations dialog box.

6. Create a sphere. Tap the Page Up key until the sphere rests on top of the elongated cube (12 taps). Look at the object from side view (hit the 3 key) or front view (the 4 key) to double-check that the bottom of the sphere just touches the top of the cube.

   The sphere will be the elbow part of the elbow crane. The next step will be to link the sphere to the cube.

7. Go back to Director's View (~ [tilde] key). The sphere should be selected. Drag a connection from the sphere's Link icon to the stretched cube underneath it. As you drag, a line should extend from the sphere to your mouse pointer. When your pointer passes over the cube, the line and the cube should turn blue; let go of the mouse. The sphere is now the child of the cube.

   Now you have to change the sphere's attributes so that it does not inherit all of the propagation properties of the cube.

8. Click the A to open the Object Attributes dialog box for the sphere. Click the Linking tab. Click the Size check mark to deactivate it (see Figure 7.32d). Click the check mark at the bottom to accept your changes.

9. Save your scene. Call it "Camera Elbow Crane.br4."

10. Try out your crane—select the cube, then rotate the cube using the rotation tool on the Edit Palette. That was just a little try-it-out test. Undo the rotation.

Now it's time to create the top part of the crane.

11. Make sure the cube is still selected, and from the Edit menu, choose Duplicate (⌘-D/Ctrl+D). Notice that when a parent object is duplicated, the child is duplicated along with it! We're duplicating the cube because it already has its origin point set at the object bottom. (Note: if you have changed any of the propagation properties, those won't be duplicated. All properties will be active in the newly duplicated linked set.)

12. Look at your scene from side view (tap the 3 key); you'll see plenty of area above the cube and sphere. The newly duplicated cube should still be selected. Tap the Page Up key until the entire duplicated assembly rests on top of the first sphere, as shown in Figure 7.33a.

a

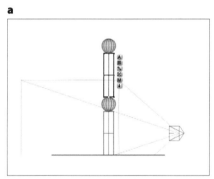

Figure 7.33 Completing the Camera elbow crane: a) The duplicated cube-sphere assembly placed on top of original one; b) converting the top cube to a pyramid; c) Object Attributes settings for the pyramid; d) testing the assembly by rotating the bottom cube.

b

c

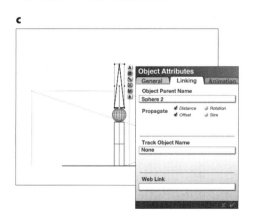

d

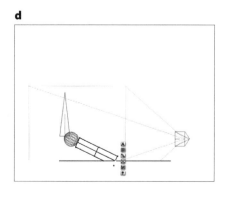

13. Select the top sphere and delete it (you can delete a linked child without any harm coming to the rest of the objects).

14. Make sure that the Edit Palette is showing, and select the top cube. Using the Object Conversion tools, convert the cube to a pyramid (see Figure 7.33b).

15. Link the pyramid to the sphere. Drag from the Linking icon to the sphere until both the sphere and the line extending from the pyramid turn blue. Open the pyramid's Object Attributes dialog box and click the Linking tab. On the linking panel, uncheck both rotation and size (see Figure 7.33c). Click the check mark to accept your changes, and save your scene file again.

Now check out the result!

16. Select the bottom part of the crane, the cube, and rotate it. Notice that the cube and the sphere maintain a common rotation angle, and although the pyramid stays attached to the assembly, it does not bend the same way as the rest of the elbow assembly (see Figure 7.33d).

In time, you will be able to rotate the top pyramid part of the crane assembly to work independently of the bottom one for a camera assembly. We'll work more with this object in Chapter 15, so hold on to this scene file!

> **TIP:** When you want to get the object back to the normal rotation, select the cube, and under the Rotation pop-up menu on the Edit palette, choose Unrotate. The same goes for the pyramid object.

Note: if you simply can't wait until Chapter 15, and want to know the "camera crane punch line," move the camera object to the tip of the pyramid, link it to the pyramid, and assign only Distance and Offset. If you set your camera to track an object, you can get very smooth camera operation by rotating the crane. And that's all you're going to get about the camera part of the camera crane in this chapter! Go to Chapter 15 for the rest of the goodies. Be sure to stop by Chapter 14, "The Fourth Dimension: Time and Animation" first.

REPLICATING OBJECTS

When you are creating a conglomerate object or using many identical objects to create something bigger, be sure to use the Multi-Replicate command. It's an excellent tool for creating objects in circles, for example.

Circular Logic: Multi-Replicating into a Circle

With all the opportunities to use numbers in Bryce, it's helpful to know how to use them and under what circumstances. Here, we'll examine the formula for creating a number of objects in a circle. How do we know which numbers to enter into the Multi-Replicate dialog box? First of all, you have to decide on the number of objects you want to end up with—let's say 12 objects. Because a circle has 360 degrees, in order to get a complete circle of objects, you need to divide 360 by the number of objects. Since 360 divided by 12 equals 30, enter 30° (or -30°) as the value for rotation. As for the number of objects, type into the Quantity box the number you want minus one—if you want 12 objects total and you already have one (you have to have one to multi-replicate!), then you want to make 11 new objects. How big do you want the circle to be? The amount you enter into the offset box determines the circle's size. Figure 7.34 shows three different circles created using different amounts of offset. The offset value for the cones is 10.24 (half unity unit size); the offset value for the cylinders is 20.48 (unity unit size, same as the object's size); the offset value for the pyramids is 30.72 (one-and-a-half unity unit size). Whatever axis (or axes) you offset the object along, do not also rotate on the same axis. (If you do, you won't get a circle.)

Figure 7.34 Offset value affects the overall size of the circle: three circles created using the same rotation amount but different offset amounts.

Which axis do you want your circle to rotate around? If you want a circle of objects flat on the ground, then choose the *y* axis for rotation. In Figure 7.35a and b, the rotation takes place on the *y* axis, but the offset is on different axes. For all these images the opaque objects are rotated at 30° and the transparent ones are rotated at –30°. The encircled pyramid is the original starting place.

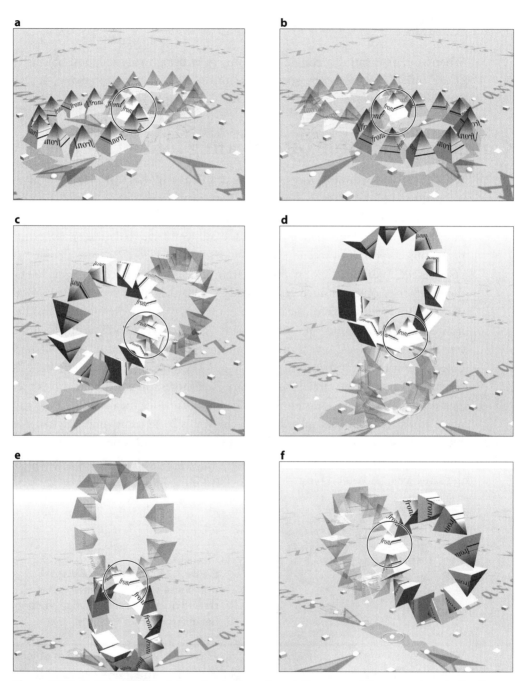

Figure 7.35 Multi-Replication into a circular form, by rotating around the *x*, *y* and *z* axes. Top Row: Horizontal rotation around the *y* axis; a) offsetting *x*, and b) offsetting *z*. Middle Row: Rotating around the *x* axis; c) offsetting *y*, and d) offsetting *z*. Bottom Row: Rotating around the *z* axis; e) offsetting *x*, and f) offsetting *y*.

Remember, in the Multi-Replicate dialog box, the offset is relative; it offsets from the previous position. This is most apparent when seeing the "front" of the object in relation to the previous one. Notice the difference in the rotation style for each axis. As each object is rotated, what is "front" differs from the X rotation (where all the fronts face inward) to the Z offset, where the fronts line up one behind the other.

Figures 7.35c through f show the same type of rotation variations for the x and z axes, where the circle shape is vertical, like a Ferris wheel. Again, the opaque objects are rotating 30° and the transparent ones are rotating –30° from the same original pyramid.

To summarize multi-replication for circles:

1. Quantity: Enter the total number of objects you want, minus 1.

2. Rotate: For the degree of rotation, divide 360 by the total number of objects.

3. Offset: Enter a number that's larger than the object size. Do not use the same axis as rotation. You can enter numbers into one or both of the other axes.

The multi-replication feature of Bryce allows for immense diversity. For another circular variation, take an object and rotate successive copies with no offset whatsoever. That's how the extraterrestrial flower in Figure 7.36 was made: first, a single petal was constructed out of two spheres (one hollowing out the other) and two cubes (grouped, made negative, and subtracted from the hollow sphere). Then we multi-replicated the petal, rotating the copies in place.

a
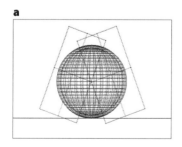

b

c
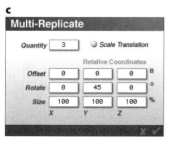

d

Figure 7.36 Using Multi-Replicate to create an alien flower: a) The boolean underpinnings of the original petal; b) the petal, seen in perspective view and rendered; c) creating three rotated copies of the petal with the Multi-Replicate command; d) the final flower, rendered.

Macro-Multi-Replication

Sometimes, when you open the Multi-Replication dialog box you'll see numbers already present. Where did they come from? You put them there! OK, you didn't necessarily type them in, but these figures are a record of the last operation you performed on the object. Bryce keeps track of this data for each object in your scene, and when you select an object and execute the Multi-Replicate command, the numbers are automatically plugged into the dialog box, just in case your intent was to perform the same editing operation again. It's almost like having a little macro program running in the background, recording your most recent actions so you can repeat them with a click of the mouse.

This comes in very handy when you want to multi-replicate an object, but you'd prefer to set the relationships among the objects by eye, rather than by calculation. Create the first object, duplicate it and transform (Move, Rotate, Resize) the duplicate to set up the pattern that will be followed. Bring up the Multi-Replicate dialog box, enter the quantity of objects you want to create (the other parameters will already be entered) and click the check mark.

Here's how to use this method to build a spiral staircase. Figure 7.37a shows the first tread: a cylinder squashed on the y axis and stretched on the z axis. In the Object Attributes dialog box, make sure that Show Origin Handle is checked. Drag the origin handle to the point you want the stairs to spiral around. Duplicate this tread, then rotate the copy around the y axis and raise it upward along the y axis until you're happy with the relationship between the steps (Figure 7.37b). Now comes the magic: summon the Multi-Replicate dialog box (Option-Shift-D/Alt+Shift+D) and see that the transformations you just applied to the second tread have been recorded. Hmmm…we rotated the tread about 20°, which means that if we want to end up with a full circle of treads, we'll need a total of 18 of 'em. We've already got two, so we'll enter 16 into the Quantity box (Figure 7.37c), hit Return/Enter, and bingo! One elegant spiral staircase, ready for use! To finish the job, we duplicated the whole flight of stairs and stacked the copy on top of the original, giving us a two-story staircase; then we provided a central pole for support. Some simple materials and a few lights complete the scene.

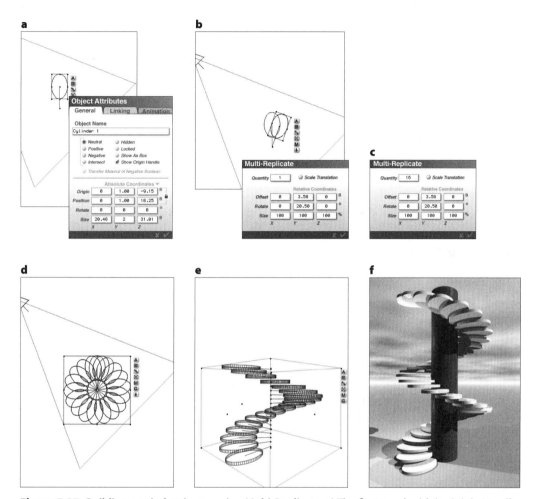

Figure 7.37 Building a spiral staircase using Multi-Replicate: a) The first tread, with its Origin Handle moved to the axis of the spiral; b) after duplicating the first tread and rotating and elevating the copy along the *y* axis, the transformations are automatically entered into the Multi-Replicate dialog box; c) change the quantity to 16 so we end up with 18 treads; d) completed stairs from top view; e) seen in perspective; f) the finished product.

Torus Multi-Replication Variations

Using Multi-Replicate to rotate only (without offset) works nicely with the torus. The torus, with its hollow center, can be used to create a delicate interwoven form resembling a basket or ball of twine. As with the circular rotation discussed above, the torus conglomerate follows the formula of number-of-objects × rotation amount = 360. Figure 7.38 shows several examples. Part a shows the torus rotated on the x axis by a constant amount, 15°, with 23 replications. This holds true for all of the examples, though the others add more than the x axis rotation. Parts b through d add rotation on the z axis, with uniform, lower and higher amounts respectively (the final object in Figure 7.38d is rotated slightly so that the side detail is visible). The last two, parts e and f, add rotation on the y axis as well. Generally, the size of the opening corresponds to the amount of the rotation on the secondary and tertiary axes; the smaller the amount of rotation, the smaller the opening. The larger the amount, the larger the opening. You can have a lot of fun with this one.

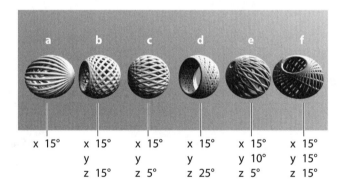

Figure 7.38 Different sets of tori duplicated and rotated, but not offset.

How about one more twist before we're through? What happens if you offset each replication slightly? Figure 7.39 experiments with an offset on the x axis with scale translation turned off and on. The initial torus is given a radius of 96, then doubled in overall size. The four examples show different settings for the replications. The first is offset on the x axis by 10, while the size stays the same. In the next three replications the size is reduced to 90%, so each newly replicated torus is 10% smaller than the previous one. The second and third set have identical settings, except that scale translation is off on the second and it's on with the third. The offset amount is also determined by the scale of the object. The fourth example has scale translation on for all axes, with an offset of 10 on all three axes.

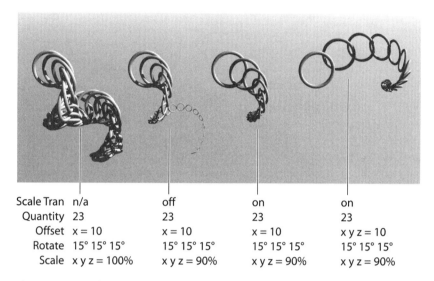

Scale Tran	n/a	off	on	on
Quantity	23	23	23	23
Offset	x = 10	x = 10	x = 10	x y z = 10
Rotate	15° 15° 15°	15° 15° 15°	15° 15° 15°	15° 15° 15°
Scale	x y z = 100%	x y z = 90%	x y z = 90%	x y z = 90%

Figure 7.39 Scale translation and offset for tori conglomerates.

(Not So) Vicious Circles

There's an older way to create a circular set of objects in Bryce that doesn't require numbers and calculations and the Multi-Replicate dialog box, but it does the trick. Sometimes it's preferable to use this method to create something in a circular form.

To create a circular form without using the Multi-Replicate dialog box, duplicate the first object, move the duplicate object elsewhere and then group two objects together. Now these objects, being grouped, will move around a common center when you rotate them. Duplicate, then rotate (see Figure 7.40a), holding down the Shift key to make the rotation snap to increments of 45°. Select both groups, duplicate the both of them, and then Shift-rotate again. (Be sure to select the groups, not the cylinders themselves; or else the cylinders will just spin in place). Keep duplicating and rotating until you have filled up the circle. Of course, if you want a circle with 12 evenly spaced objects in it (or any number that's not a power of 2), you can't use the Shift-rotation trick once you've got four objects. Figure 7.40d shows the final step for this 32-object circle.

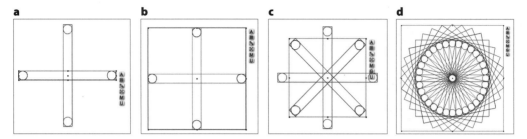

Figure 7.40 Creating circles by duplicating then rotating: a) After the first duplicate-then-rotate; b) the two groups grouped; c) the second group duplicated and rotated; d) completed circle after more duplicate-then-rotate steps.

Gear Variation

Another variation is gears. Cubes are good for this—instead of flat stair objects, make these upright. Use either method, the "duplicate and rotate" on-the-fly method or the Multi-Replicate dialog box and calculator method (see Figure 7.41). Once you have your set of gears, you can use rotation to make them perform all sorts of fascinating or sick and twisted maneuvers. Choose between Object Space and World Space to get a variety of effects.

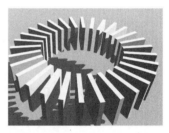

Figure 7.41 Freshly created gear.

While the objects (the gear's teeth) are still selected, rotate them. The top row of Figure 7.42 shows a set of gears whose teeth are rotated on each axis in Object Space. The bottom row is a set of gears whose teeth have been rotated on each axis in World Space. The ones for the x and z axes are bizarre in a fascinating way. After rotating the teeth on only a single axis, have some more fun! Figure 7.43 shows gears whose components have been rotated on all three axes.

Finally, for more abstract fun, create a set of gear teeth, duplicate them, then change the duplicates to another object type using the Object Conversion tool. (Variations: change size or rotation only and not object type.) Set the new objects to negative, group the whole thing and check out a new intriguing abstract. Use all of the Three Rs tools in Object Space to set each of the new objects in a uniform relation to each of the old ones, even though they are rotated and facing in every direction to begin with. Figure 7.44 shows some samples. Part a has negative tori; part b gets more complex, with an additional set of boolean objects (created by the duplicate and convert method); part c has the tori intersect. The tori were grouped together as positive objects, then the group was changed to intersect in order to get this effect.

x axis   y axis   z axis

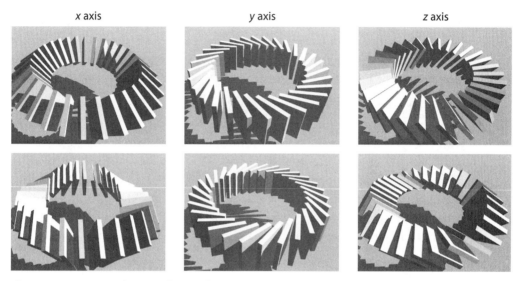

Figure 7.42 Gear teeth rotated on each axis. Top Row: Object Space; Bottom Row: World Space.

a   b   c

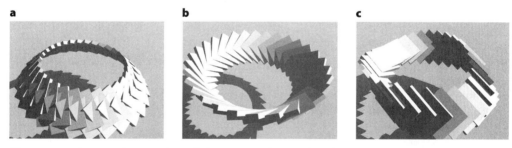

Figure 7.43 Gear teeth rotated on all three axes: a,b) Rotated in Object Space; c) rotated in World Space.

a   b   c

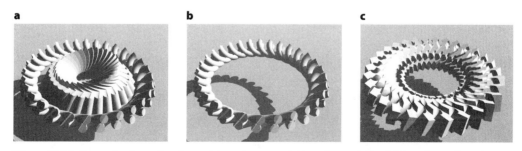

Figure 7.44 Some duplicate boolean object changes: a) Negative tori; b) additional set of booleans; c) intersect with tori.

TERRAIN MOLDINGS

If you want to get fancier with the construction of your model, include terrains and symmetrical lattices (we'll discuss them in detail in the next chapter) as a part of your conglomerate object. The terrain objects do not function as a mountainous surface but as a component for a conglomerate object. A grayscale-to-height map, combined with terrain clipping, gives you two powerful features for creating unusually shaped objects.

Figure 7.45 shows the famous *Bryce Big Rig*, by Jackson Ting and Robert Bailey. Though created in Bryce 1, it stands as a classic example of the versatility of grayscale-to-height maps. The figure includes several wireframe views of the scene, if only to convince you that this was indeed generated using terrains. Notice the enormous amount of detail in this model. There are a mere 174 objects and a paltry 94 terrains. (It's safe to say that this was not created on a computer with 8 MB RAM!) Many of the different elements were created in Adobe Illustrator and imported into Bryce via Photoshop.

 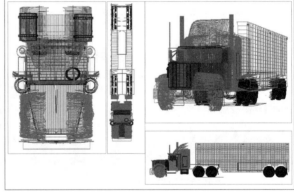

Figure 7.45 *Bryce Big Rig:* Tractor-trailer truck constructed in Bryce from terrains and primitives—174 objects total and 94 terrains. *Art by Jackson Ting and Robert Bailey.*

This next example uses Bryce's symmetrical lattices to create architectural details. *The Tower*, by Chris Casady, has a number of different elements that use grayscale information to define the shape. In Figure 7.46 the construction is broken down, complete with a wireframe view of all the symmetrical lattices in the scene and a couple samples of their grayscale information.

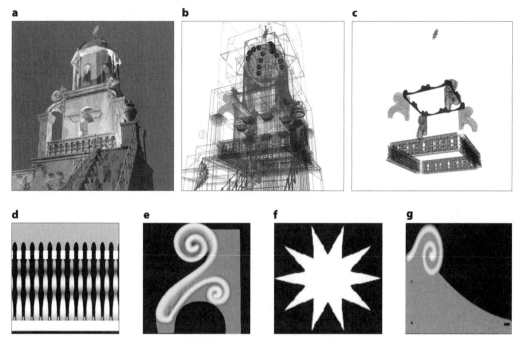

Figure 7.46 Tower and symmetrical lattices: a) Rendered image; b) wireframe; c) wireframes for symmetrical lattices. Bottom row: Graymaps for d) balustrade; e) curlicue cornice; f) star; g) decoration. *Scene by Chris Casady.*

MODEL MANAGEMENT

When creating a conglomerate object scene, embrace a strategy for isolating each task into a manageable portion. Although you could work in one scene file and keep adding to it and saving as you go along, it's a good idea to create a separate scene file for each element of your colossal conglomerate object scene. Save the pillar over here, save the initial temple over there, then put them together in a third scene file. If there are additional buildings, keep them in a separate scene file and merge them later.

One advantage to keeping the different elements in different files is that you don't have to juggle all of your objects while you are still working on construction. As you continue adding here and there—and Bryce has a tantalizing way of leading you on to "create just one more thing to get that bit of detail"—you will be placing more and more objects in your scene. The greater the number of objects, the slower Bryce will run. Also, with a greater number of objects, Bryce's occasional tendency toward forgetfulness during resizing and swapping the y and z axes may well become a frequent tendency. By working on elements separately, you prolong the state of manageability and the fleetness of Bryce's response until you can no longer delay the inevitable convergence of all your glorious creations into one triumphant but lethargic scene file. The temple scene file shown in Figure 7.1 is a handful shy of 1000 objects. With each exciting improvement—the temple, the pillars, the base, the steps—Bryce responded to the building tasks with a growing fatigue. (Of course, if your idea of a conglomerate scene is a mere hundred objects to the temple's thousand, then you'll be spared the anguish of waiting after each move.)

Merging Scenes

So, you've created this splendid conglomerate object; it's in this document over here. And over there, in another document, is another exquisite conglomerate. You want to put them together. For extremely simple objects, you can copy an object (or several objects) from one scene and paste them into another. They'll be placed in the new scene file in the exact place they occupied when they were copied from the previous one. But Bryce gives you another option—merge scenes.

Merging in Theory

What happens when you merge scenes? Here's the theory behind merging. You already have a scene open, called the host scene, as it will invite another scene (the guest) within. The invitation is extended via the Merge command. All objects from the guest scene are brought into the host scene in the same position they previously occupied—a terrain at World Center in the guest scene comes into the host scene at World Center. However, sky, camera, family, and render settings of the guest scene stay behind; those of the host scene prevail.

Merging in Practice

What happens when you merge scenes in practice? We do not mean to imply that practice deviates from theory, as in "do as I say, not as I do." Rather, here is the sequence of events you'll go through when merging:

1. To bring two or more scenes together, use the Merge command in the File menu. If you didn't save your current (host) scene after manipulating objects, Bryce asks you if you want to save your scene. Click OK to save the scene, if you want to.

2. The Open dialog box appears. Select the guest scene and click OK.

3. Bryce merges the scenes. All objects from the guest scene come in selected (red wireframes). You may want to group objects, deselect or move them, or you may want to change all items to one color. But host and guest are now together in one scene.

> **TIP:** *If you want to make any adjustments to the newly merged scene, activate Solo mode immediately after merging. The guest scene will be displayed in its entirety; you can select objects, delete superfluous objects (the ground plane?), rename families, and make other adjustments without mixing the guest and host scene components.*

One slightly annoying "feature" of the merge process is that Bryce will switch you to Director's View, no matter which view you were using before. If you had assigned custom family and wireframe color settings for the guest scene, the family names and custom colors will take on the names and colors of the host scene. So in your guest scene you might have a family called "foothills." (Formerly it was, say, Family 12, and had a different wireframe color.) When it comes into the host scene, it takes on the host scene's name and color for Family 12. Also be aware that your guest scene loses any animation when merged into the host. The moral here is that if you're assembling an epic motion picture, save all your animation efforts for the host scene.

Here's a handy subset of the Merge command: hold down the Option/Alt key when you choose Merge from the File menu, and only the guest scene's sky will be imported.

If you plan to use Merge to join different conglomerate object scenes into one master scene that will contain all the objects, don't build any extra objects into the individual scene documents. When you merge scenes, all guest objects (including grounds) will be imported into the host scene. You don't need multiple grounds or other extraneous objects in your final scene, do you?

COLUMNAR CALAMITY: A CIRCUMSPECT BOOLEAN PRIMER WITH MULTI-REPLICATION IMPLICATIONS

This exercise gives you an opportunity to create an object using the techniques discussed in this chapter. In creating the column, you'll work with both negative and intersecting booleans, multi-replication, merging scenes, and the fine art of making a terrain boolean work properly. Starting from a basic cylinder primitive, you'll carve out flutes, create a base, and merge scenes to put it all together.

The Main Column

In the beginning there was the Cylinder. And it was tall. It had a base and it had a capital. It was very good.

1. Start by creating a cylinder. Enlarge it along the y axis so that it is somewhat tall (see Figure 7.47a). This is the main cylinder.

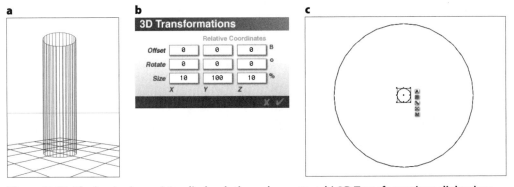

Figure 7.47 The beginnings: a) A cylinder doth a column start; b) 3D Transformations dialog box settings for duplicated flute-cylinder; c) result of resize, top view.

To make this column fancy with fluted cutouts, a series of narrower cylinders will be used to scoop out column portions. You need to create the first flute-cylinder, change its size, and then replicate it to create a set of flute-cylinders that are evenly spaced in a circle.

2. Duplicate the main cylinder (⌘-D/Ctrl+D). Now you are ready to resize this new cylinder to flute-cylinder size.

3. In the Edit Palette, under any of the Three Rs controls pop-up menus, choose 3D Transformation. Here you'll maintain the height (y axis) but enter 10% for the x and z axes (see Figure 7.47b) to narrow the cylinder. Click OK. From top view, your wireframe should resemble Figure 7.47c.

4. Now it's time to multi-replicate that narrow column. Choose Edit > Multi-Replicate or type Shift-Option-D/Shift+Alt+D. How many flutes should there be? In this example, we used 24, so 23 is the quantity, with 15° rotation for Y (15 × 24 = 360). For offset X, use a value of 2. The Multi-Replicate dialog box is in Figure 7.48a, and the results (from top view) are shown in Figure 7.48b.

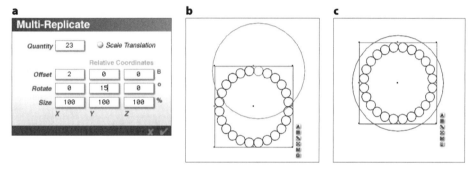

Figure 7.48 Making many flutes: a) Multi-Replication dialog box and values; b) results shown in top view; c) main column cylinder aligned with the group of flute cylinders.

5. Well, shoot—the circle of flute-cylinders isn't aligned with the main column. To align them, first Shift-click the original flute-cylinder to add it to the selection (the freshly created flute-cylinders should still be selected), then group. While you're at it, assign the flutes a unique family color and name. After grouping the flute-cylinders, add the main cylinder to the selection. Looking at the scene from top view, align by clicking the Align X and Align Z tools at the center points (see Figure 7.48c). Once they're aligned, deselect the main cylinder.

6. The circle of flute-cylinders is not quite big enough. While the fluted cylinders are still grouped, enlarge them uniformly using the Resize tool (see Figure 7.49a), then ungroup and reduce all cylinders uniformly. Each individual cylinder will be reduced simultaneously, though each centerpoint will remain the same. Stop when they're just nicking in the main cylinder (see Figure 7.49b). This is the home stretch for flutedness! In the Object Attributes dialog box, assign negative (or type N while the flutes are selected).

Also, assign the main cylinder to positive (select it and type P). Group the flute-cylinders with the main cylinder and render. Figure 7.50 shows the side view wireframe and the rendered result. Note: With the enlargement and reduction, the flutes stop a bit shy of the overall height of the column. Since the ends will have fancy-schmancy base and capital treatments, this is just fine for now.

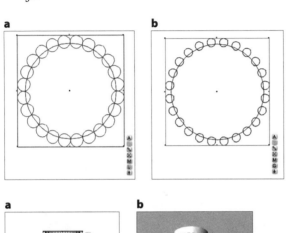

Figure 7.49 Adjusting the size of the flute-cylinders: a) After enlarging the grouped cylinders (top view); b) after ungrouping and reducing the cylinders (top view).

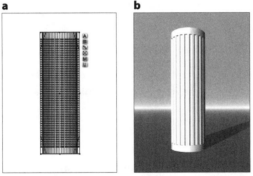

Figure 7.50 The end of the first phase: a) Side view of wireframe; b) rendered result of flute-cylinders, with ugly abrupt endings at top and bottom.

At this point, you may look at the top and bottom edges of the flutes and say, "But they cut off abruptly rather than gently scooping in!" (See Figure 7.50b.) Yep, we said that, too. Working in Bryce is filled with "Do something cool, render, hmmmm… finesse" procedures. Here's how to make a nice gentle scoop.

7.   Ungroup the column-and-flutes group. Select the flute-cylinders and duplicate. Change the duplicated cylinders to spheres using the Object Conversion tool. Now the spheres are perfectly aligned with the flutes, however elongated they are.

8.   Reduce the spheres along the *y* axis using either the direct manipulation handle or the Resize tool. Make the spheres slightly oblong, then align them at

the top of the flute-cylinders so that the center equator of the spheres matches up perfectly with the top edge of the flute-cylinders (see Figure 7.51a).

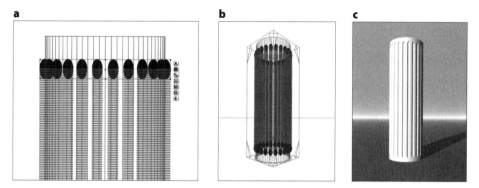

Figure 7.51 Fluted spheres: a) Spheres reduced and aligned with cylinders; b) main view
of column with sphere sets at top and bottom; c) rendered result.

9. Duplicate those spheres and move the new set to the bottom, as shown in
    Figure 7.51b. (Hint: If you are directly dragging the objects, remember to
    press the Option or Alt key to constrain movement along the *y* axis)

10. Once you have the spheres placed top and bottom, select the flute-cylinders
    and the spheres and group, then group the group with the main cylinder,
    then render. As you can see in Figure 7.51c, there are pretty smooth
    scoops on those flutes! (Note: Since you duplicated an object assigned a
    negative attribute, the duplicates, the spheres, were also negative. Once
    they were grouped with the main positive cylinder the spheres began their
    scooping action!)

There, you've successfully made it through step one. We trust you are none the
worse for wear with all this circuitous advice and negativity! Save this scene file
and set it aside for the moment.

Column Base Basics

Now that you have a basic column, how about a fancy base for it? The options
here are numerous; we'll show you a few different directions you could go, and
then pursue one in particular.

If you weren't using any boolean operations, you could make a base using a cube
or a cylinder, depending on whether you want your base to be round or square.

Figure 7.52 shows a half-dozen non-booleaned simple bases in rendered and wire-frame form, so that you can tell what was used to create them. (The scene file is also on the CD-ROM.)

a

b

Figure 7.52 Examples of non-booleaned bases: a) Rendered and b) wireframe.

Once you get into booleans, though, you can get a bit more tricky. Intersection is good for taking other shapes and combining them with cylinders. Cones and spheres come to mind here (see Figure 7.53).

a

b
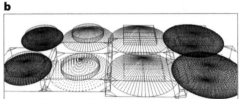

Figure 7.53 Column bases created using boolean combinations of objects: a) Rendered and b) wireframe.

Flattened cylinders and flattened cubes make the basic form, and cones and spheres make up the secondary shape. Choose whichever one tickles your fancy.

1. In a new scene file, create the basic shape (cylinder or cube). Hold down the Shift key and drag leftward on the cube's y control handle, halving the cube's height. Release the mouse button, and Shift-drag again. Do it a third time, so the cube is flattened to one-eighth of its original height.

2. Create your secondary shape. Make it wider than the first by enlarging on both the *x* and *z* axes. If it's a sphere, its top point shouldn't be higher than the top of the cube or cylinder (see Figure 7.54).

3. Assign one of the shapes to intersect and then group them. This is the beginning of your base. Topping the group with a cone helps to smooth the transition into the column. Now you can add some decorative elaboration—the torus is excellent for this purpose. In Figure 7.54c, the thicknesses of the tori have been reduced in in the Torus Editor.

a

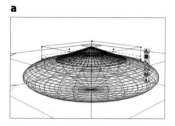

b

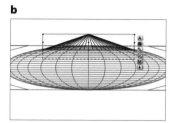

c

Figure 7.54 Making a column base: a) The primary shape (here, a cube) intersected with a sphere, topped with a non-boolean cone; b) side view of the same; c) the rendered result, with the addition of tori.

4. Create your own elaboration using the torus. When placing it, match the center of the tube of the torus to the point where the column and the cone intersect. If a torus is being used as a decorative edge for a vertical and horizontal object, only a quarter of the tube should show. This is also true when the torus is negative, as in Figure 7.55. This figure is a variation on the theme, and not a direct result of the steps described here. But then again, we told you that this portion of the walkthrough has more "dealer's choice" options in it.

Figure 7.55 Tori used to subtract portions from the base.

5. Once you have completed a base, save the scene file.

Merging the Two

Now it's time to put the column and the base together. For this, you'll use Bryce's Merge command.

1. Open your base scene file, if necessary. Under the File menu, choose Merge. Select your fluted column scene file in the dialog box that appears, and click OK (Open).

2. Your fluted column scene comes into your base scene file with all the elements selected. Go straight to Solo mode to edit any object in the newly imported scene. You probably brought in a ground plane, too—you'll need to delete it, since only one ground plane is necessary. Select the ground and delete it, then exit Solo mode.

3. Match the position of the fluted column with the column base. For this procedure, you'll need to go into orthogonal views. Unless you moved either

one during the making, they probably match up horizontally. However, the fluted column probably needs to be moved up along the y axis so that you can see the bottom fluted edges. (If you need to align them horizontally, make sure that the base is grouped together. The fluted column should already be grouped. Select both and click the Center options of the Align tool on the x and z axes.)

4. You may need to make some adjustments to your base in light of the position of the fluted column. A torus may need a bit of tweaking, which you can do from side or front view. See Figure 7.56 for some non-verbal pointers on fine-tuning.

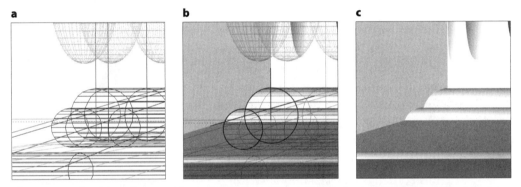

Figure 7.56 Precision alignment for tori at column base (all side view): a) Wireframe view; b) wireframe superimposed on rendered view, with tori, cone and cylinder position emphasized; c) rendered side view.

5. Group the objects together. Render (see Figure 7.57a).

Once you have created a base, you can duplicate it and position it on the top. After duplicating, select Flip Y from the Resize pop-up menu. Depending on the shape of your base, you may need to reduce the top one for better proportions' sake (see Figure 7.57b).

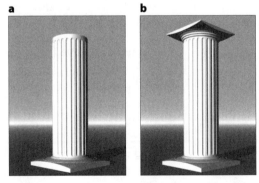

Figure 7.57 Column and base rendered together: a) Base only; b) base duplicated, resized slightly, and positioned at top of column.

Make It a Relic

If you want to forego the capital altogether, use boolean combinations with a terrain to antique the column. The terrain will carve out bits of broken column fragments. In order to bite off a nice chunk of column, you'll have to group the terrain with a cube and then make the group negative.

1. Start with your column and base. Create a terrain and move it to the side so that it does not overlap the column. Reduce it to half size by pressing the / key.

2. Duplicate the terrain (⌘-D/Ctrl+D) move it up by tapping the Page Up key twice. Select the bottom terrain and change it to a cube using the Object Conversion tool (see Figure 7.58a).

3. Make any adjustments to your terrain's shape in the Terrain Editor. When working in the Terrain Canvas, make sure that the edges of the terrain grayscale map stay black, so they stay in contact with the cube object below.

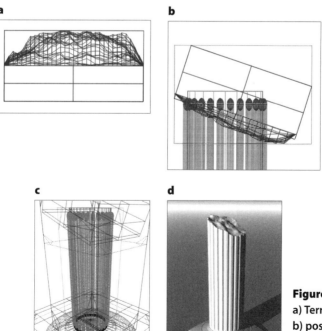

Figure 7.58 Antiqued column: a) Terrain atop cube, grouped; b) positioning group at top of column; c) wireframe from main view; d) completed render.

4. Group the two together and move them to the top of your column. Rotate the terrain so that it's more or less upside down. Position the group so that it takes a bite out of the column, similar to the position shown in Figure 7.58b. You may need to make adjustments to each of the objects in the group at this point; the cube may need to be elongated or the terrain squashed flatter. Change to Object Space and use the Control/Ctrl key contextual menu to select the individual member of the group you need to adjust. Enlarge or reduce along the *y* axis as needed.

5. Select the column group and assign it positive. Group the terrain and cube again and change the group to negative. Then add the column to your selection, group, and render.

6. You may need to do some finessing; the cube and the terrain may need to overlap a bit more, or you may need to enlarge the entire terrain-cube group or reposition it.

7. When you're finished making your tweaks, render. Figures 7.58c and d show the completed wireframe and render.

MOVING ON…

The incredible thing about multiple object construction and boolean operations is that you get an infinite variety of objects. This is a place to let your imagination go wild! The few samples presented in this chapter barely scratch the surface of multiple object construction. Check out the conglomerate object studies in the Chapter 7 folder on the CD-ROM.

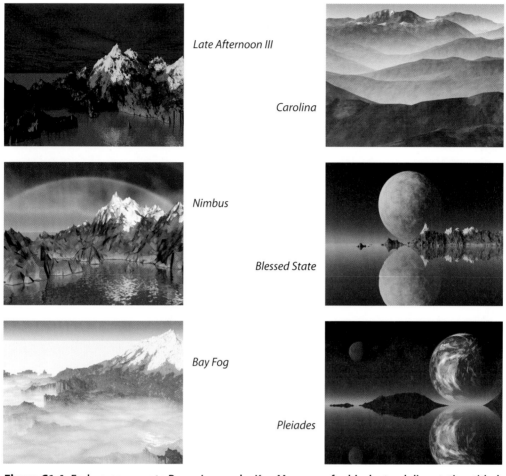

Late Afternoon III

Carolina

Nimbus

Blessed State

Bay Fog

Pleiades

Figure C1.4 Early precursors to Bryce. Images by Ken Musgrave, for his doctoral dissertation, titled "Methods for Realistic Landscape Imaging."

Figure C1.6 Bryce Canyon National Park at sunrise. *Photograph by Susan A. Kitchens.*

C2

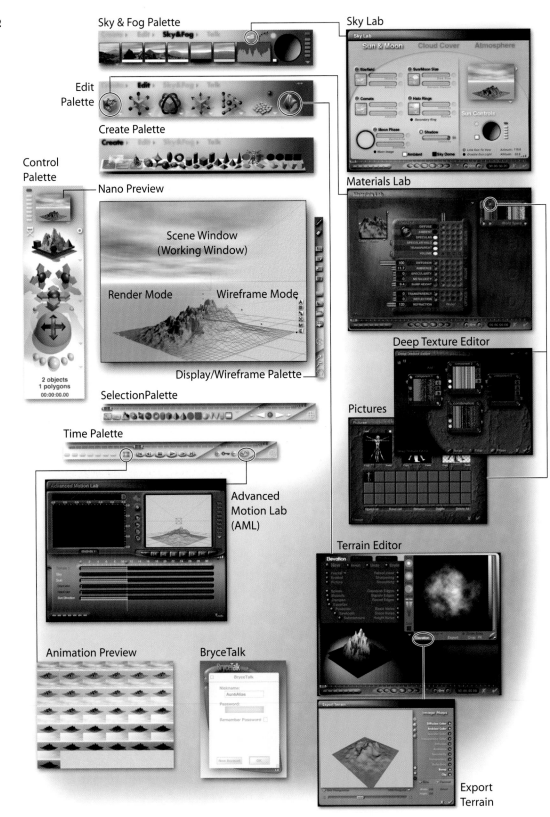

Sky & Fog Palette

Sky Lab

Edit Palette

Create Palette

Control Palette

Nano Preview

Scene Window (Working Window)

Render Mode

Wireframe Mode

Display/Wireframe Palette

2 objects
1 polygons
00:00:00.00

SelectionPalette

Materials Lab

Deep Texture Editor

Pictures

Time Palette

Advanced Motion Lab (AML)

Terrain Editor

Animation Preview

BryceTalk

Export Terrain

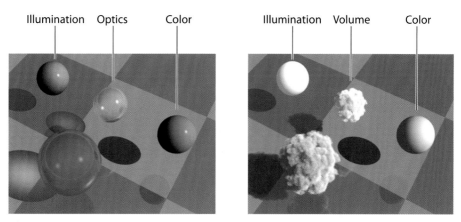

Figure C9.2 The three surface and volume properties of an object.

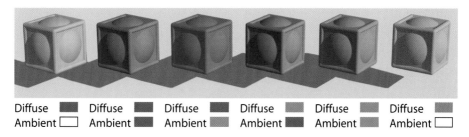

Figure C9.12 Diffuse and Ambient Color working together: The Diffuse and Ambient Color settings for each object are below that object.

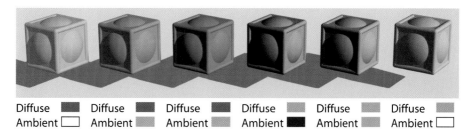

Figure C9.13 The Ambient Colors for these objects range from white to dark gray.

Opposite:
Figure C2.6 The Bryce Interface: The main palettes in Bryce and the controls that lead to the special task areas, also known as Labs or Editors.

C4

Diffusion = 0

Diffuse Color

Diffusion = 50

Metallicity = 0   20   40   60   80   100

Figure C9.14 Metallicity settings. Top row: No Diffusion (diffuse illumination); Bottom Row: Diffusion set to 50.

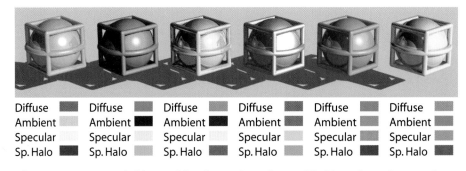

Diffuse	Diffuse	Diffuse	Diffuse	Diffuse	Diffuse
Ambient	Ambient	Ambient	Ambient	Ambient	Ambient
Specular	Specular	Specular	Specular	Specular	Specular
Sp. Halo	Sp. Halo	Sp. Halo	Sp. Halo	Sp. Halo	Sp. Halo

Figure C9.17 A set of objects with color settings shown. All objects have these settings: Diffusion: 89.4; Ambience: 31.3; Specularity: 100; Reflection: 19.6.

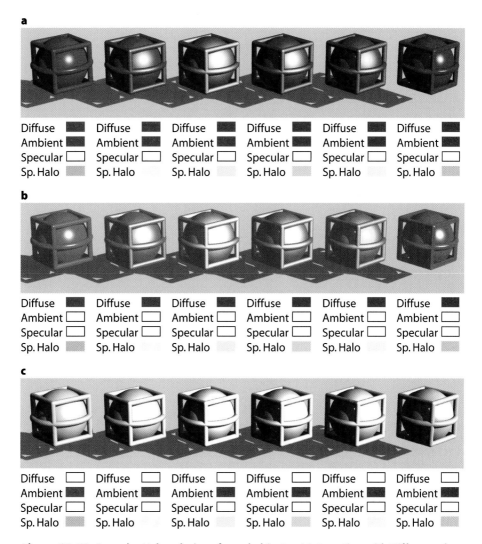

Figure C9.18 Specular Halo colorings for red objects: a) Interacting with Diffuse and Ambient Color; b) white Ambient color; c) white Diffuse Color.

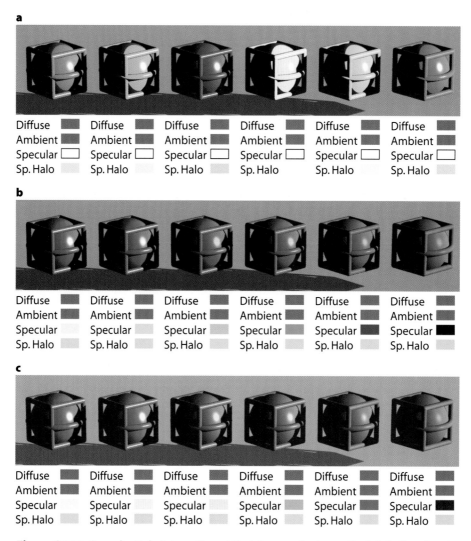

Figure C9.19 Specular Halo interaction: a) Each hue pushed over the bright line threshold; b) detail of blue Specular Halo with neighboring hue cyan Specular Color; c) detail of blue Specular Halo with complement, yellow, for Specular Color.

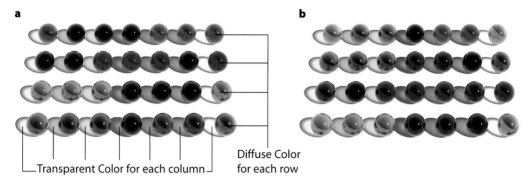

Diffuse Color
for each row

Transparent Color for each column

Figure C9.20 Transparent Color interacts with Diffuse Color: a) Diffuse Colors are mostly the primary colors—red, blue, green; b) Diffuse Colors are mostly secondary colors— orange (containing yellow), aqua (containing cyan), and purple (containing magenta).

Diffuse Color
Transparent Color

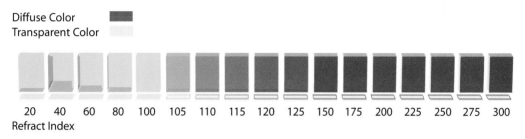

20 40 60 80 100 105 110 115 120 125 150 175 200 225 250 275 300
Refract Index

Figure C9.21 The interaction of Transparent and Diffuse Color at different Refract Index settings.

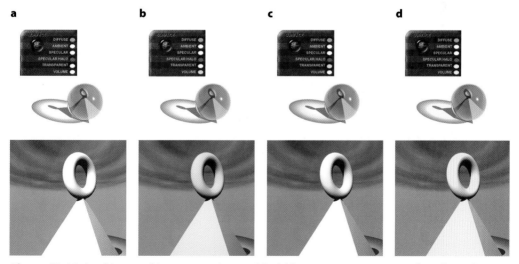

Figure C9.22 Looking at white torus and pyramid within a transparent green sphere from the inside and the outside: a) Sphere's Transparent and Volume Colors are both white; b) Transparent and Volume Colors are both yellow; c) Transparent is white and Volume is blue; d) The combination from (c) was switched, with Transparent blue and Volume white.

C8

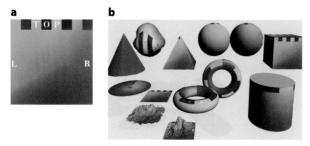

Figure C9.29 Parametric mapping places a) the image b) onto the objects in proportion to each object's shape.

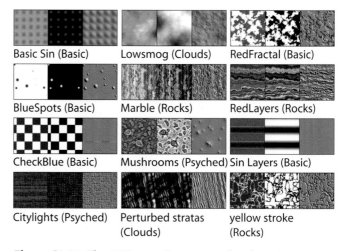

Basic Sin (Basic) Lowsmog (Clouds) RedFractal (Basic)

BlueSpots (Basic) Marble (Rocks) RedLayers (Rocks)

CheckBlue (Basic) Mushrooms (Psyched) Sin Layers (Basic)

Citylights (Psyched) Perturbed stratas (Clouds) yellow stroke (Rocks)

Figure C9.30 The 12 Texture Sources used as the primary examples for this chapter (Category names are in parentheses; we abbreviated "Psychedelic" to "Psyched").

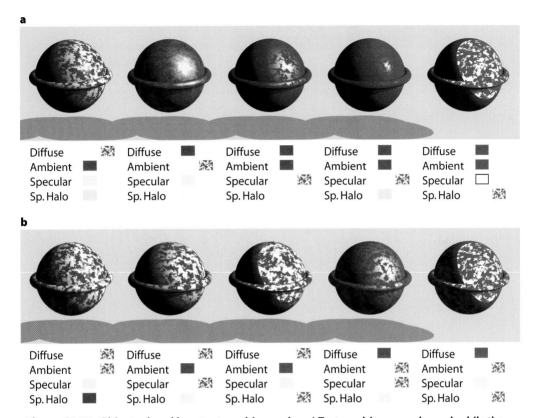

Diffuse	▓	Diffuse	■	Diffuse	■	Diffuse	■	Diffuse	■
Ambient	■	Ambient	▓	Ambient	■	Ambient	■	Ambient	■
Specular		Specular		Specular	▓	Specular	▓	Specular	☐
Sp. Halo		Sp. Halo		Sp. Halo		Sp. Halo		Sp. Halo	▓

Diffuse	▓	Diffuse	▓	Diffuse	▓	Diffuse	■	Diffuse	■
Ambient	▓	Ambient	■	Ambient	■	Ambient	▓	Ambient	▓
Specular		Specular	▓	Specular		Specular	▓	Specular	
Sp. Halo	■	Sp. Halo		Sp. Halo	▓	Sp. Halo	▓	Sp. Halo	▓

Figure C9.36 Object colored by a texture-driven color: a) Texture drives one channel, while the rest of the channels have uniform coloring; b) texture drives two of the three channels.

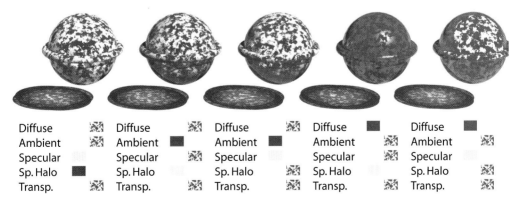

Diffuse	▓	Diffuse	▓	Diffuse	▓	Diffuse	■	Diffuse	■
Ambient	▓	Ambient	■	Ambient	■	Ambient	▓	Ambient	▓
Specular		Specular	▓	Specular		Specular	▓	Specular	
Sp. Halo	■	Sp. Halo		Sp. Halo	▓	Sp. Halo	▓	Sp. Halo	▓
Transp.	▓	Transp.	▓	Transp.	▓	Transp.	▓	Transp.	▓

Figure C9.37 Texture-driven color for Transparent Color and two other channels (adapted from Figure C9.36b).

Figure C9.38 Texture-driven Transparent Color interacting with Diffuse Color.

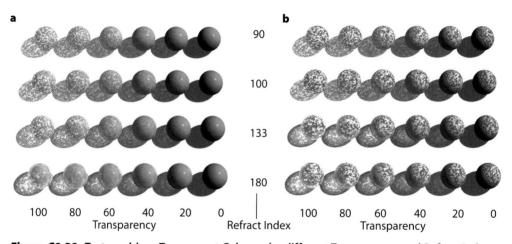

Figure C9.39 Texture-driven Transparent Color under different Transparency and Refract Index settings: a) Transparent Color is the only texture-driven color; b) Transparent and Diffuse Colors are both driven by a texture source.

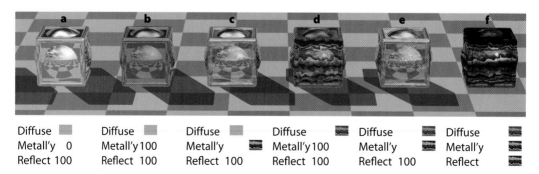

Figure C9.40 Texture-driven Metallicity, using the RedLayers texture: a) Reflection only; b) uniform Metallicity; c) texture-driven Metallicity; d) uniform Metallicity with texture-driven Diffuse Color; e) texture-driven Metallicity and Diffuse Color; f) texture-driven Reflection, Metallicity and Diffuse Color.

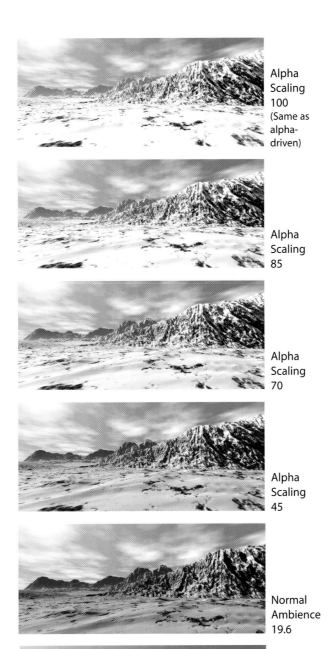

Texture Source for
Snow Material

Alpha
Scaling
100
(Same as
alpha-
driven)

Alpha
Scaling
85

Alpha
Scaling
70

Alpha
Scaling
45

Normal
Ambience
19.6

Alpha Map
(Ambience)

Figure C9.43 Texture-driven Ambience using Alpha Scaling: Different settings using the slider affects the brilliance of the snow.

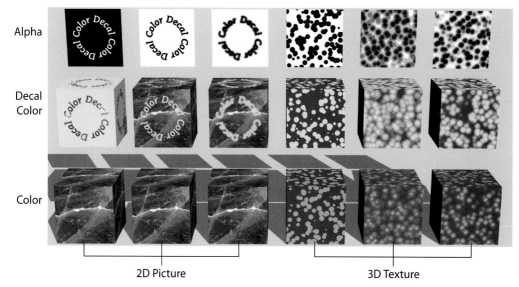

Figure C9.46 Decal Colors. Top row: alpha channel information for each object; middle row: Decal Colors; where alpha channel is black, the texture color is replaced by the swatch color; bottom row: the standard material, with coloring supplied by the Texture Source.

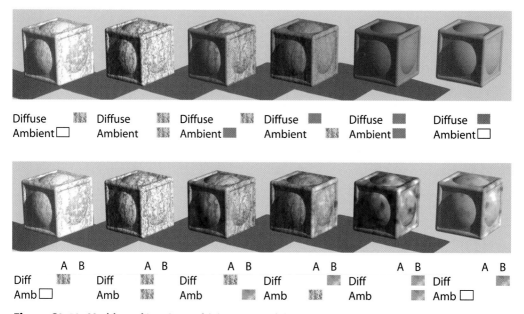

Figure C9.48 Marble and LowSmog driving some of the color channels.

Figure C9.54 Changing the Source C texture changes the way that textures A and B are blended together.

a   b   c

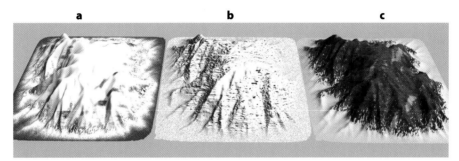

Figure C9.55 Whole Mountain material broken down into the three surface properties: a) Illumination; b) bump; c) color.

a

b

Figure C9.56 Whole Mountain color breakdown, from left to right: a) Hills texture driving Diffuse Color only, Diffuse Color and Diffusion, combined colors and Diffusion using all three Texture Sources; b) pebbly Diffuse Color only; Diffuse Color and Diffusion, combined colors and Diffusion.

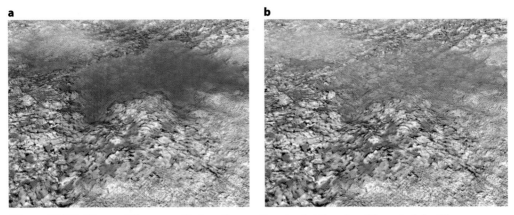

Figure C9.58 What a difference a Texture Source D makes! a) Terrain with material settings as shown in Figure 9.57, including a Texture Source D to drive the Diffusion channel and provide the appearance of moisture; b) the same scene without any Texture Source D.

Volume Blend Altitude

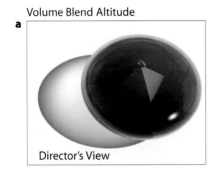

Director's View

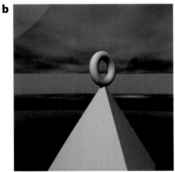

Camera View

Figure C9.65 Volume Blend Altitude, as seen from the inside and the outside of an object: a) Volume Blend Altitude outside the object; b) Volume Blend Altitude inside the object.

Volume Blend Distance

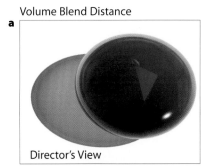

Director's View

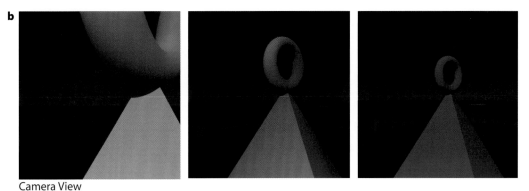

Camera View

Figure C9.66 Volume Blend Distance, as seen from the inside and the outside of an object: a) Volume Blend Distance outside the object; b) Volume Blend Distance inside the object, at different distances from pyramid and torus.

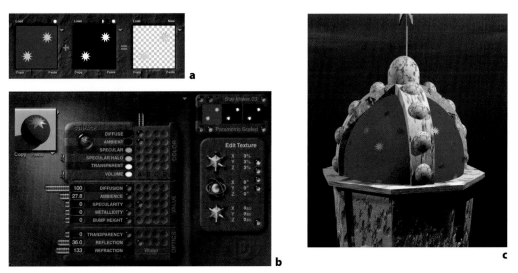

Figure C10.7 *Tower Blues*, by Chris Casady, made from a picture Texture Source: a) The Texture Source and its alpha channel; b) the Materials Lab settings for the material; c) the rendered result.

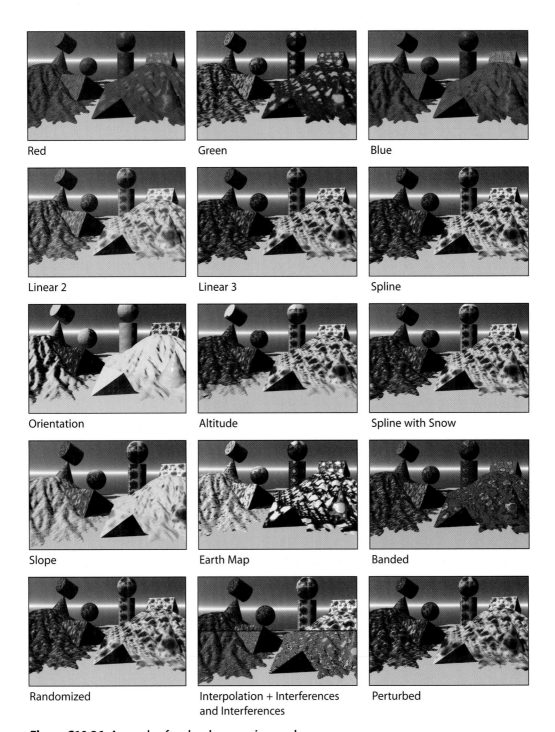

Figure C10.26 A sample of each color mapping mode.

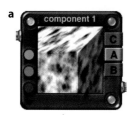

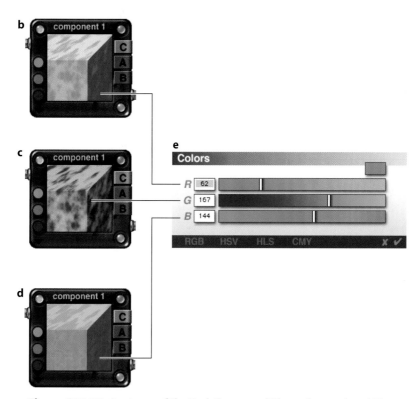

Figure C10.27 Anatomy of the Red, Green, and Blue color modes: a) The texture displayed to output as alpha; b) the same texture using the Red color mode to output Color; c) the same texture using the Green mode; d) the same again outputting Blue; e) the RGB Color Picker for the top color swatch.

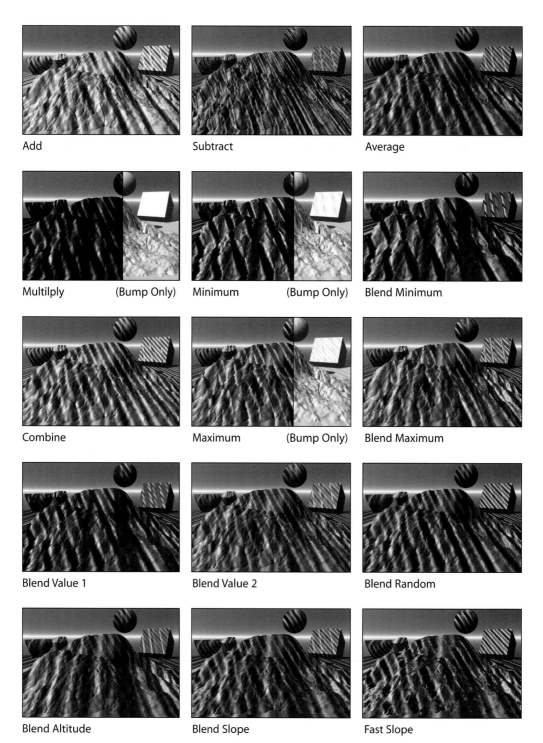

Add

Subtract

Average

Multilply   (Bump Only)

Minimum   (Bump Only)

Blend Minimum

Combine

Maximum   (Bump Only)

Blend Maximum

Blend Value 1

Blend Value 2

Blend Random

Blend Altitude

Blend Slope

Fast Slope

Figure C10.28 Blend options in the Deep Texture Editor for combining texture components.

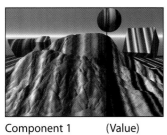 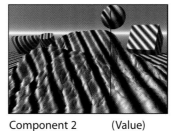 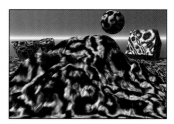

Component 1　　(Value)　　Component 2　　(Value)　　Component 3 (for Parallel)

Parallel

Procedural Blend

Difference

Blend Orientaton

Figure C10.28 *continued*

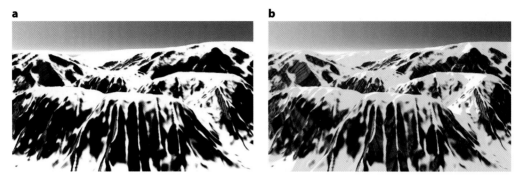

Figure C10.35 The snow rendered: a) The Snow Preset; b) with the Ambient Color modified.

Figure C10.36 *Puddlebumps*, final result of a Deep Texture Editor recipe.

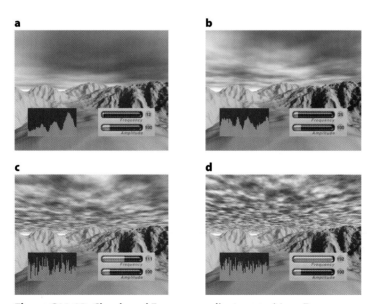

Figure C11.12 Clouds and Frequency adjustment: a) Low Frequency; b) default Frequency; c) higher Frequency; d) near maximum Frequency.

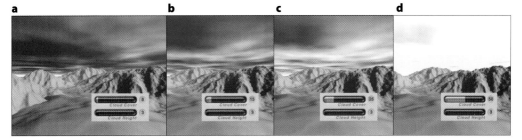

Figure C11.13 Adjusting cloud coverage with the Cloud thumbnail changes cloud amounts so they range from daintily decorating the sky (left) to dominating it (right). The Cloud Cover sliders from the Sky Lab are also shown.

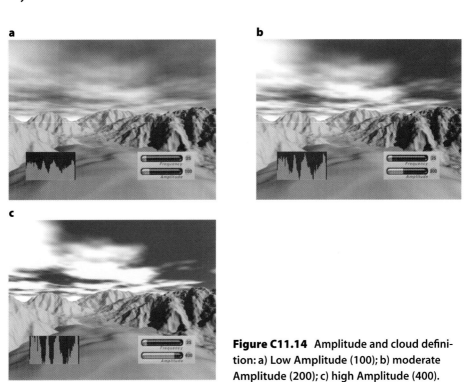

Figure C11.14 Amplitude and cloud definition: a) Low Amplitude (100); b) moderate Amplitude (200); c) high Amplitude (400).

Figure C11.15 Cumulus clouds with a) positive and b) negative Amplitude.

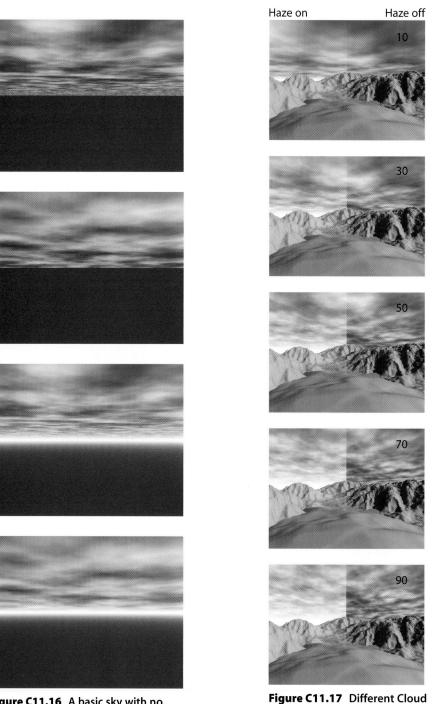

a

b

c

d

Haze on   Haze off

10

30

50

70

90

Figure C11.16 A basic sky with no ground plane: a) Spherical Clouds turned off, no haze; b) Spherical Clouds on, no haze; c) Spherical Clouds off, a small amount of haze; d) Spherical Clouds on, a small amount of haze.

Figure C11.17 Different Cloud Height settings change how many cloud forms can be seen, as well as modulating the haze height. The Cloud Height setting is shown for each example.

a

b

c

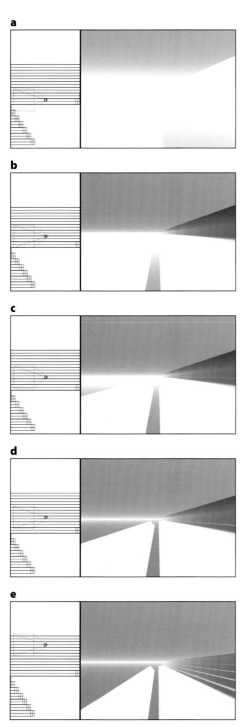

d

e

Figure C11.26 Localized fog created by means of a uniformly transparent sphere.

Figure C11.25 The appearance of fog changes depending on the camera position: a) Lowest position; b) low position; c) higher position; d) still higher position; e) highest position.

Haze Density: 7   Haze Density: 35

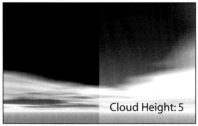

Cloud Height: 5

Cloud Height: 20

Cloud Height: 40

Cloud Height: 80

Cloud Height: 100

Figure C11.27 In each image, the cloud cover, frequency, and amplitude are the same, but the Cloud Height increases from top to bottom. In the left column, the Haze Density is 7; on the right, it is 35.

Figure C11.28 Three terrains of different sizes seen through Brycean haze of varying densities (shown for each image). Thickness and Base Height are left at their default settings, namely 50 and 0.

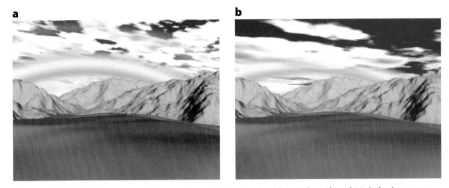

Figure C11.29 Brycean rainbows in relation to clouds: a) the Cloud Height is set to 72 and the clouds float serenely above the rainbow; b) at a Cloud Height setting of 18, the rainbow's head is lost in the clouds.

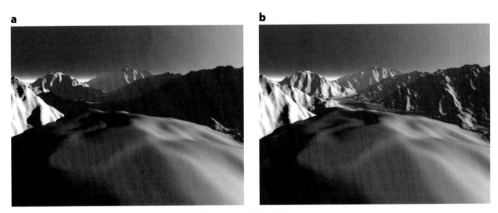

Figure C11.30 Shadow set to a) maximum and b) minimum.

C26

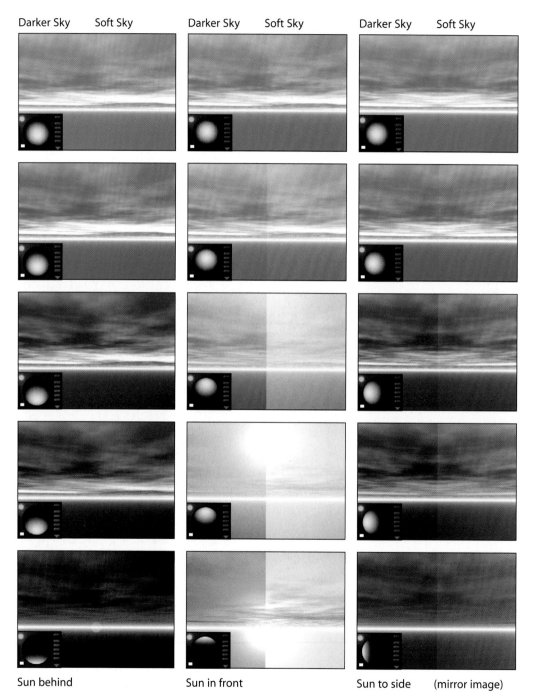

Figure C11.32 Different sun positions and the effect on the Brycean sky dome.

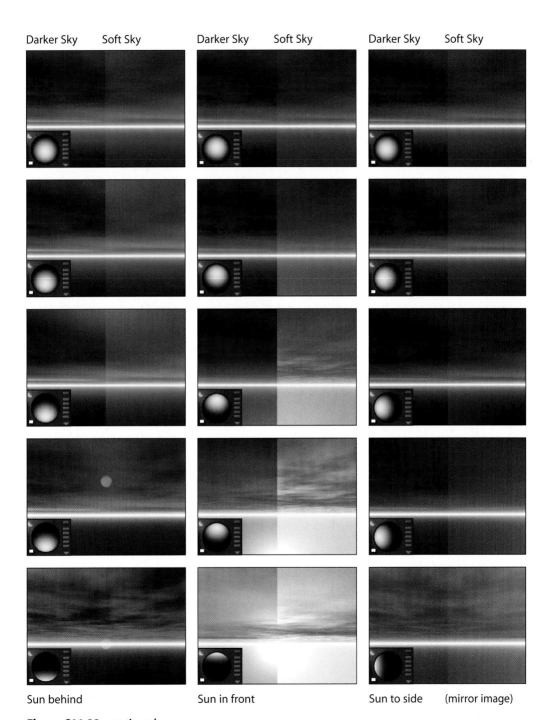

Figure C11.32 *continued*

C28

Sun in high position

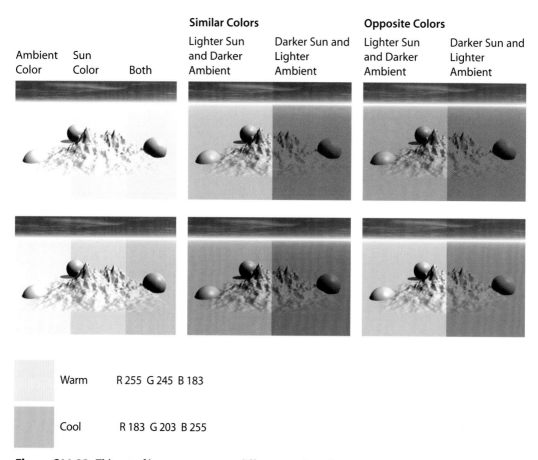

Figure C11.33 This set of images compares different settings for Sun Color and Ambient Color. Sun is in high position.

Sun in low position

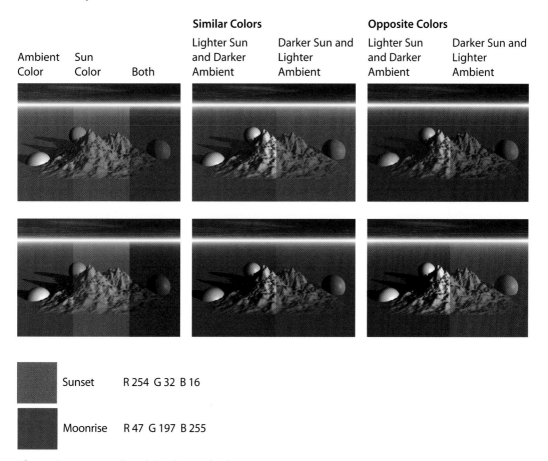

Similar Colors

Opposite Colors

Ambient Color · Sun Color · Both · Lighter Sun and Darker Ambient · Darker Sun and Lighter Ambient · Lighter Sun and Darker Ambient · Darker Sun and Lighter Ambient

Sunset   R 254 G 32 B 16

Moonrise   R 47 G 197 B 255

Figure C11.33 *continued.* Sun is near horizon.

C30

Cloud Height 3   Cloud Height 20   Cloud Height 40

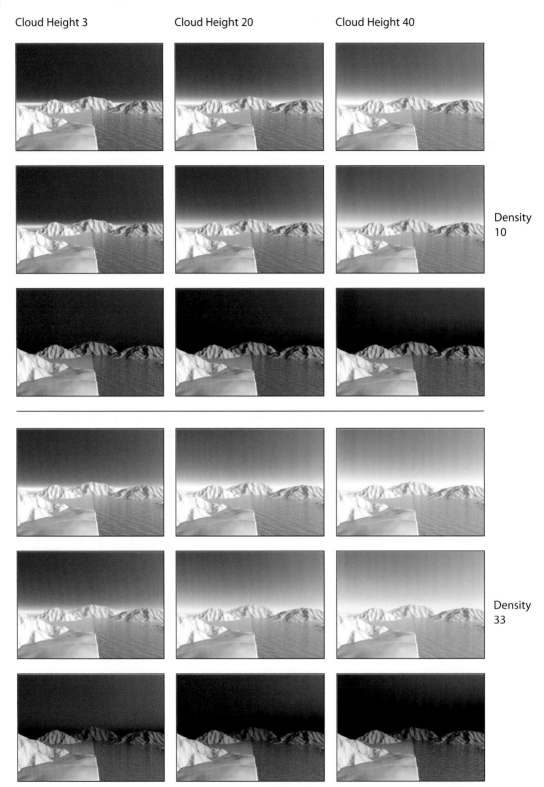

Density
10

Density
33

Cloud Height 3   Cloud Height 20   Cloud Height 40

Density
65

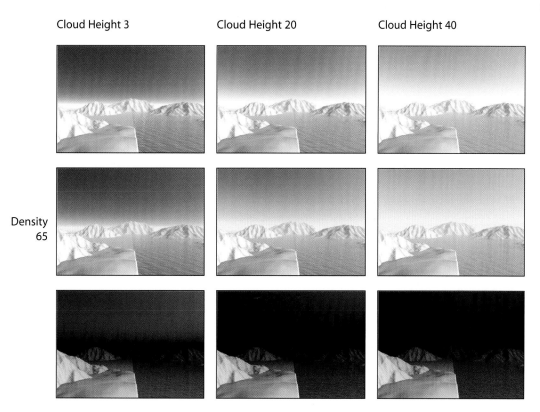

Figure C11.34 Variations in haze. Changes of color (white, ivory, and black), Density (10, 33, and 65) and Cloud Height (3, 20, and 40) affect the appearance of near and distant objects in this scene.

C32

15/15
higher
camera
position

15/15
lower
camera
position

15/75
higher
camera
position

15/75
lower
camera
position

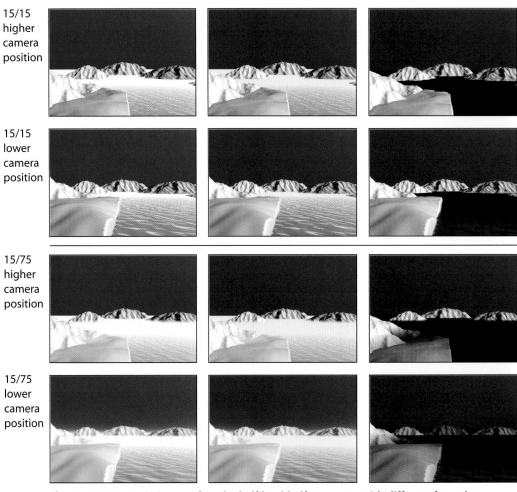

Figure C11.35 Variations on fog. The half-land/half-sea scene with different fog colors, heights, and amounts; and varying camera perspectives.

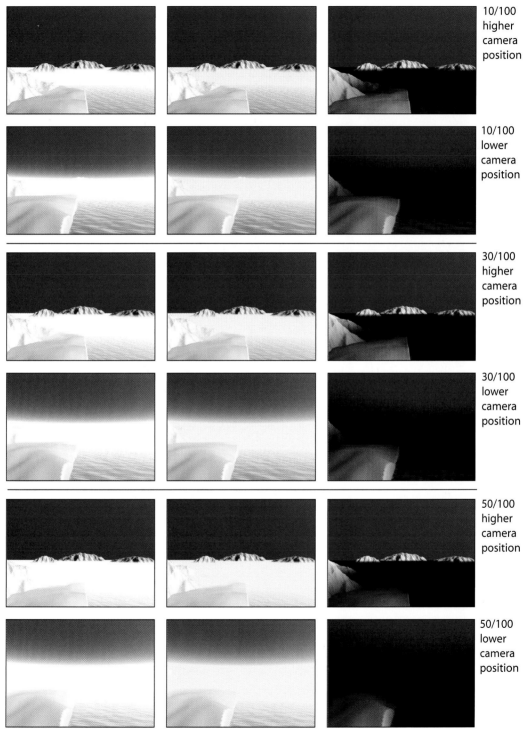

10/100 higher camera position

10/100 lower camera position

30/100 higher camera position

30/100 lower camera position

50/100 higher camera position

50/100 lower camera position

Figure C11.35 *continued*

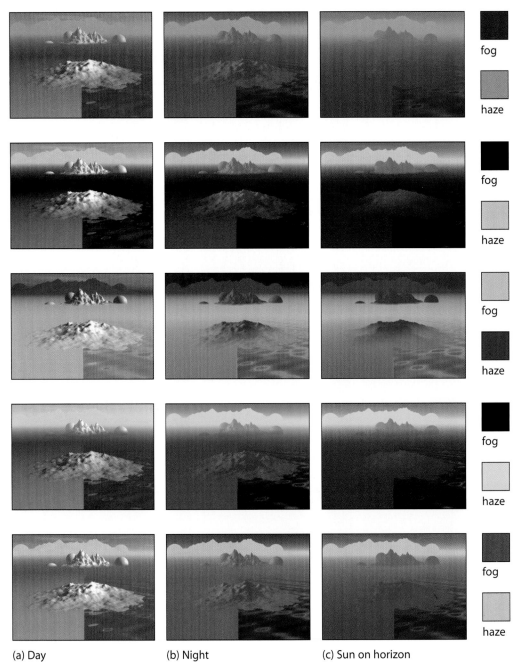

(a) Day (b) Night (c) Sun on horizon

Figure C11.36 The combination of different fog and haze Colors; each combination is shown at three different times of day.

Blend Haze with Sun
OFF

Blend Haze with Sun
Color 50
Luminance 50

Blend Haze with Sun
Color 100
Luminance 100

Sun Altitude 60°

Blend Haze with Sun
OFF

Blend Haze with Sun
Color 100
Luminance 50

Blend Haze with Sun
Color 100
Luminance 100

 Sun Color   Haze Color

Figure C11.37 Using the Blend with Sun feature with Haze.

Sun Altitude 9°

Blend Fog with Sun
OFF

Blend Fog with Sun
Color 50
Luminance 50

Blend Fog with Sun
Color 100
Luminance 100

Sun Altitude 60°

Blend Fog with Sun
OFF

Blend Fog with Sun
Color 100
Luminance 50

Blend Fog with Sun
Color 100
Luminance 100

Sun Color   Fog Color

Figure C11.38 Using the Blend with Sun feature with Fog.

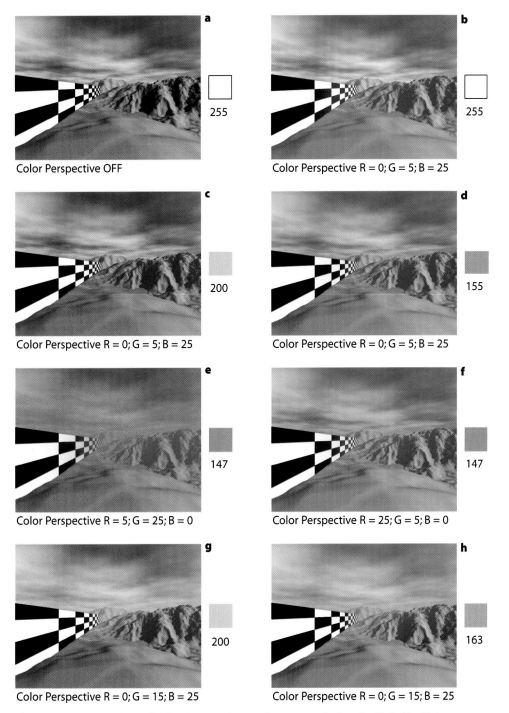

Figure C11.40 A variety of Color Perspective settings as applied to the Plain Vanilla! scene. For each image, the Color Perspective control settings are given. To the right of each image is a color swatch showing the haze color—the number beneath it is the Lightness value of the color (as measured in the HLS color model).

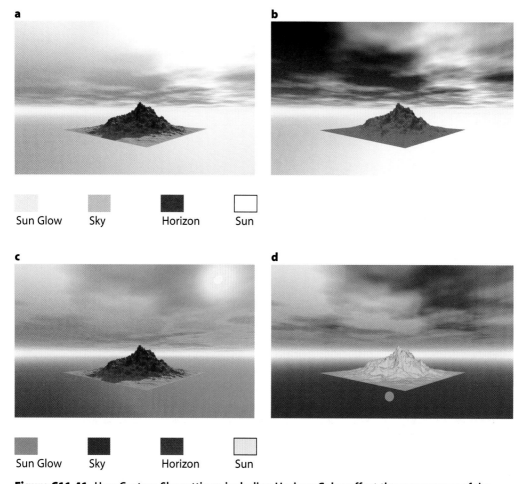

a

Sun Glow   Sky   Horizon   Sun

b

c

Sun Glow   Sky   Horizon   Sun

d

Figure C11.41 How Custom Sky settings, including Horizon Color, affect the appearance of the sky: a) moderate colors, sun above horizon; b) same colors, sun below horizon; c) wild colors, sun above horizon; d) wild colors again, sun now behind camera (but above horizon).

Figure 11.42 Custom Skies in Panorama View with the custom colors as insets. Left column: Horizon Color is white; Right column: Horizon Color is not white, and is picked up by the stratus clouds.

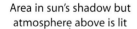

Area in sun's shadow but atmosphere above is lit

Figure C11.43 A side view of a planet shows how an area can be in the sun's shadow while the atmosphere is lit by the sun and thus can be illuminated by the Sky Dome Color.

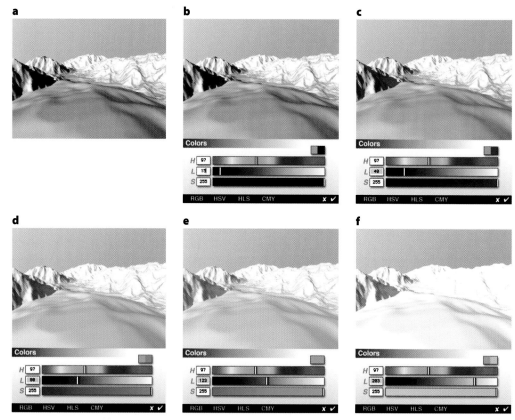

Figure C11.44 Sky Dome illumination in a Custom Sky, showing the effect of progressively higher Sky Dome Color Lightness levels (shown by the color pickers beneath each image).

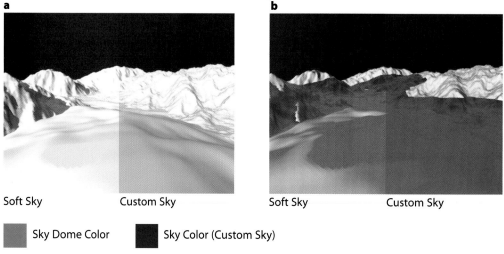

Figure C11.45 Comparing how Sky Dome illumination works with a Soft Sky and a Custom Sky: a) Sun well above the horizon; b) the same sky settings but with sun positioned exactly on the horizon (Altitude = 0).

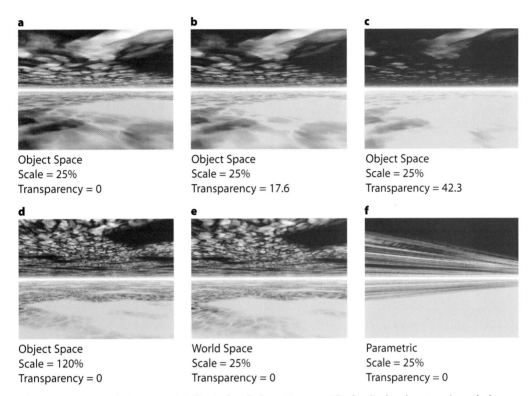

a

Object Space
Scale = 25%
Transparency = 0

b

Object Space
Scale = 25%
Transparency = 17.6

c

Object Space
Scale = 25%
Transparency = 42.3

d

Object Space
Scale = 120%
Transparency = 0

e

World Space
Scale = 25%
Transparency = 0

f

Parametric
Scale = 25%
Transparency = 0

Figure C11.46 Variations on an infinite cloud plane. Top row: The basic cloud texture is scaled 25%, uses Object Space mapping, and the material's transparency is texture-driven with various slider settings; bottom row: the same texture, with transparency = 0, is applied using different scales and mapping modes.

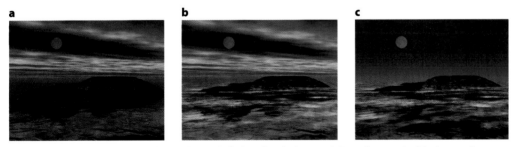

a

b

c

Figure C11.47 A nighttime sky with two infinite cloud planes: a) Top plane only; b) planes above and below; c) bottom plane only.

Figure C11.48 Examples of infinite cloud slabs: a) An infinite slab with the same material as Figure C11.39a; b) the view inside the cloud slab, with rocky peaks piercing the cloud layer; c) the same, now with a volume material applied to the slab.

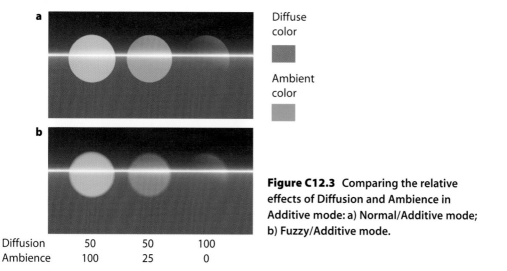

Diffuse color

Ambient color

Figure C12.3 Comparing the relative effects of Diffusion and Ambience in Additive mode: a) Normal/Additive mode; b) Fuzzy/Additive mode.

| Diffusion | 50 | 50 | 100 |
| Ambience | 100 | 25 | 0 |

Figure C12.9 A square spotlight and a 2D Pict Gel make Bryce very good for projecting slides.

Parametric   Object Space   Spherical

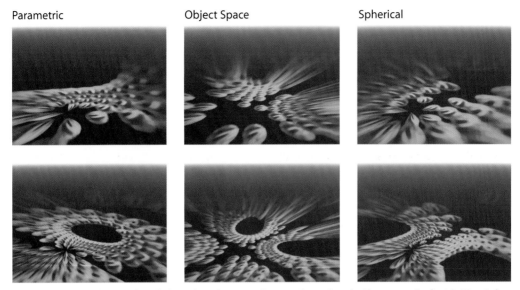

Figure C12.10 The results of changing the mapping mode and scale (frequency) of a 2D Pict Gel applied to a radial light. Top row: Texture scale = 0%; bottom row: Texture scale = 5%.

a   b

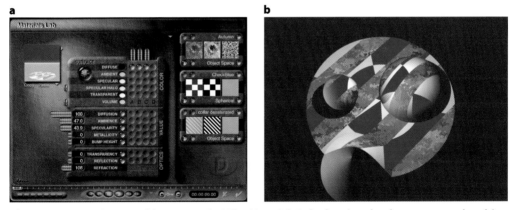

Figure C12.11 Using a multitexture gel: a) The Materials Lab, showing the three textures that drive the material's Diffuse Color; b) the rendered scene.

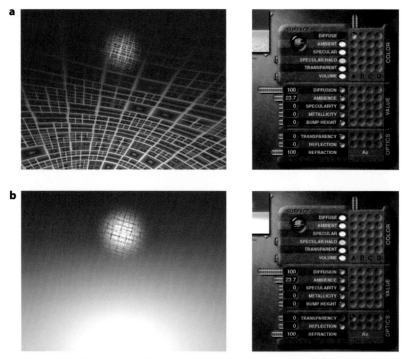

Figure C12.12 A gel applied to a visible light: a) A visible light with a gel applied in the normal way (the gel drives the Diffuse Color of the light); b) the same light, with a Diffuse Color of pure white and Transparency driven by the gel's texture.

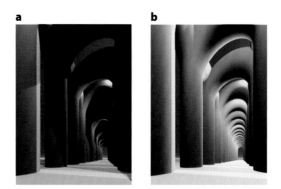

Figure C12.13 A row of arches interspersed with radial lights: a) The lights cast shadows; b) the lights have Disable Cast Shadows turned on.

Figure C12.14 "Boolean Potato Skins": a) No lights; b) a white radial light at the center casting a shadow; c) a white radial light with Disable Cast Shadows turned on; d) yellow visible radial lights added to each bowl, casting shadows; and e) not casting shadows.

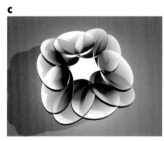

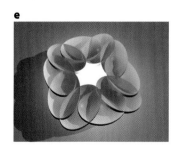

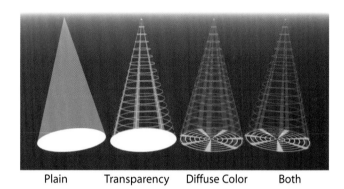

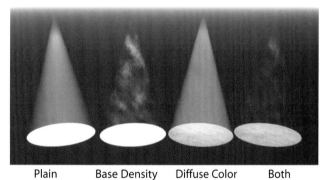

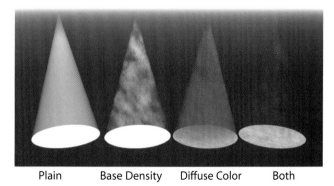

Figure C12.25 Visible Lights and Material settings. Top row: Surface lights; middle row: volume lights, additive; bottom row: volume lights, not additive.

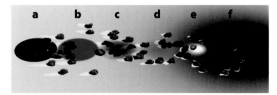

Figure C12.29 Negative Lights: a) White spotlight, intensity −25; b) orange spotlight, intensity −100; c) white spotlight, intensity −13, softness 20; d) magenta spotlight, intensity −25, softness 40; e) white spotlight, intensity 25, softness 70; f) white radial light, intensity −45.

a

b
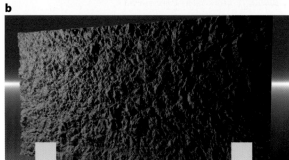

c

Figure C12.30 How adding a negative light adds drama: a) A terrain wall lit by orangish light from the upper left; b) the same terrain wall with an identically colored negative light on the right side of the terrain; c) the negative light's color has been changed to an aqua green to provide reddish shadows for the terrain wall. (Color swatches indicate the lights' colors.)

Figure C12.32 Lights with a caustic texture illuminate this aquatic scene. *Image by Susan A. Kitchens and Scott Tucker.*

Figure C12.35 *Wine Cellar. Image by Gary Bernard.*

C48

Figure C12.38 *Hammersmith Odeon. Image by Robert Mann.*

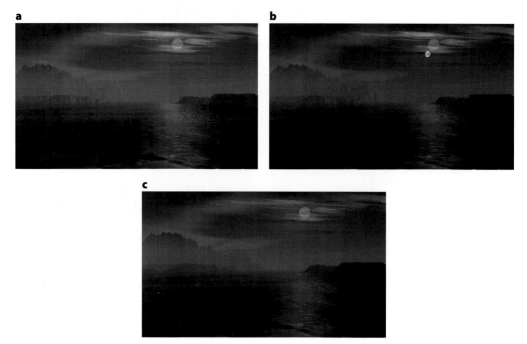

Figure C12.39 *Moon Water*: a) Rendered scene; b) scene showing radial light wireframe; c) scene rendered without the supplemental light. *Image by Eric Wenger.*

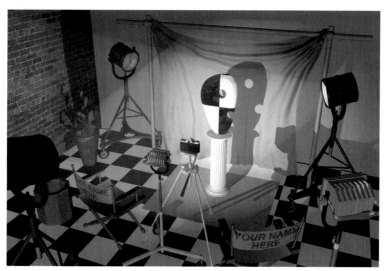

Figure C12.40 A studio with the different kinds of studio lights.
Image by Chris Casady and Susan A. Kitchens.

Figure C12.41 *Cappuccino on the Rocks:* a) Lit from the right only; b) the stealth approach—lit from both sides, but only the light from the right casts shadows; c) lit from both sides, but only the light from the left casts shadows; d) lit from the left only. *Image by Susan A. Kitchens.*

C50

Figure C12.42 *Cappuccino on the Rocks* setup: Give one light a different color to test its effect on the scene.

a

b
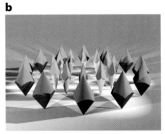

Figure C12.43 Scene with lights rendered with a) Textures On, and b) Textures Off.

Figure C12.44 Two spotlights using a hand-painted foliage gel cookie, cast shadows onto the wall and ground, suggesting the presence of trees and the moon above.

Figure C12.46 *Chandelier* and *Water Temple at Night. Images by Susan A. Kitchens.*

Figure C12.47 *Shoji Lantern. Image by Carla Moore.*

Figure C12.48 *Castle View. Image by Glenn Riegel.*

Figure C12.49 *Hall of Kings. Image by Janak Alford.*

a

b

c

Figure C16.3 a) *Fjord Mud*; b) *Abisko Pine Trees*; c) *Valley*, all by Eric Wenger.

Figure C16.4 Abisko Trees with volume clouds. This variation of Eric Wenger's scene was adapted by Susan Kitchens to use volume clouds.

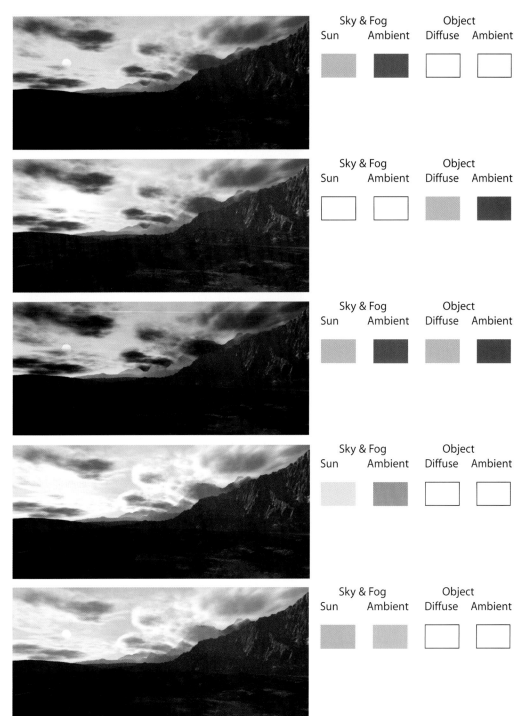

Figure C16.5 The subtle colors of volume clouds: a) White clouds, orange sun, blue ambience;
b) the reverse, with orange and blue clouds and white sun and ambience; c) orange and blue
clouds with orange sun, blue ambience; d) white clouds, yellow sun, pale blue gray ambience;
e) white clouds, yellow sun, pale gray ambience.

	Bkdrp	Amb	Fog	Haze	Sun
R	103	255	172	105	255
G	198	161	85	132	201
B	171	39	64	170	103

	Fog	Haze	Shadow	Cl Height
Amt	72	93	10	6
Ht	47.9			

	Bkdrp	Amb	Fog	Haze	Sun
R	103	255	14	140	121
G	198	161	0	173	119
B	171	39	102	176	255

	Fog	Haze	Shadow	Cl Height
Amt	28	96	10	13
Ht	92.9			

	Bkdrp	Amb	Fog	Haze	Sun
R	103	129	223	69	223
G	198	177	233	162	233
B	171	33	197	181	197

	Fog	Haze	Shadow	Cl Height
Amt	12	91	10	13
Ht	35.9			

	Bkdrp	Amb	Fog	Haze	Sun
R	103	144	198	149	121
G	198	122	154	153	119
B	171	25	0	57	255

	Fog	Haze	Shadow	Cl Height
Amt	36	81	10	11
Ht	55.9			

Figure C16.21 Four sea scenes with different colors set in the Sky & Fog Palette.

Figure C16.24 Waterfall created by using clipped terrain to make the water cascade. *Scene by Susan A. Kitchens.*

Figure C16.29 *Gorge Greek. Scene by Sandy Birkholz,* ©2000.

Figure C16.34 *Bushes,* created by using lots and lots of small terains and a picture texture. *Scene by Andrew Penick.*

Figure C17.1 *Alien Starburst.*
Image by David Palermo.
©2000.

Figure C17.2 *Old Shore.*
Image by Martin Murphy,
©1999.

Figure C17.5
Alaskan Spring. Art by Chris
Pappathan, ©2000.

Figure C17.7 *Brave Boat Harbor, Art by Barb Ingersoll,* ©2000.

Figure C17.8 *Shore. Art by Barb Ingersoll,* ©2000.

Figure C17.9 *Water Under Water. Art by Barb Ingersoll,* ©2000.

a **b**

Figure C17.10 a) *Heavy Seas* and b) *Tsunami Buoy* detail. *Art by Mark Longo, Highmark Design,* ©2000.

Figure C17.11 *Rocks, Water, Sand. Scene by Ruth "Calyxa" Fry—Calyxa's Cartography,* ©2000.

Figure C17.12 *Tides. Scene by Sandy Birkholz,* ©2000.

Figure C17.13 *Woodlights. Scene by Sandy Birkholz,* ©2000.

Figure C17.14 *Statue. Scene by Martin Murphy,* ©2000.

Figure C17.15 *Coagulation. Scene by Chaz Fricke,* ©2000.

a

b

c

d

Figure C17.16 a) *Lotus;* b) *Organikscape;* c) *Techscape;* d) *Ernst. Images by Mike Pucciarelli,* ©2000.

Figure C17.17 *Alien Borealis. Art by Clay M. Hagebusch,* ©2000.

Figure C17.18 *She Plays With Magic. Image by Clay M. Hagebusch,* ©2000.

Figure C17.19 *Galahfana's Amulet. Art by Clay M. Hagebusch,* ©2000.

Figure C17.20 *Tollerè Submersible. Image by Clay M. Hagebusch,* ©2000.

Figure C17.21 *Timerip. Image by Clay M. Hagebusch,* ©2000.

Figure C17.24 *Mikkahl Desert Region. Image by Clay M. Hagebusch,* ©2000.

Figure C17.25 *Mystic's Rock. Image by Clay M. Hagebusch,* ©2000.

Figure C17.26 *Rocky Beach. Scene by Clay M. Hagebusch,* ©2000.

Figure C17.27 *Ned's Dock* images. Top left is original Bryce render; other three are the results of post-processing in Photo-Paint. *Art by Sylvia Lutnes*, ©2000.

Figure C17.28 *Rocky Shore. Art by Sylvia Lutnes,* ©2000.

Figure C17.29 *Eagle. Scene by Sylvia Lutnes*, ©2000.

Figure C17.30 Ancient, water-covered Mars and Mars today. *Images by Susan A. Kitchens for Scientific American,* ©1996.

Figure C17.31 *Infinity's Child* images, courtesy Third Planet Productions. ©1999.

CHAPTER EIGHT

Terrains, Symmetrical Lattices, and the Terrain Editor

IN THIS CHAPTER...

- How to work with the Terrain Editor controls to create terrains and symmetrical lattices

- How to create clipped terrains for waterfalls and special effects

- How to create unusual terrain forms from words and images

- How to create terrains using United States Geological Survey (USGS) Digital Elevation Models (DEMs)

- How to export terrains

Each time you click the Create Terrain icon on the Create Palette, a terrain is randomly generated from a Fractal Noise map. As of Bryce 4, a randomly selected texture is applied to your new terrain—but holding the Control/Ctrl key while clicking the Create Terrain icon disables this feature so that the terrain comes into the world with the good ol' Flat Gray texture. No two Bryce terrains are alike. (Unless you duplicate the actual wireframe, of course!) The same is true for symmetrical lattices in Bryce; the same random generation process happens when you click the Symmetrical Lattice icon (with texture randomly applied), and each one is unique unless the object itself is duplicated.

You control the terrain information in the Terrain Editor by clicking the E edit icon next to the wireframe, typing ⌘-E/Ctrl+E, or clicking the Edit Terrain/Object icon on the Edit Palette. Bryce's Terrain Editor is rich with features and controls for making mountains, molehills, or other monuments (see Figure 8.1). Though the Terrain Editor is the place to edit both terrains and symmetrical lattices, we'll primarily talk about terrains in the editing process. When we discuss some editing procedures that focus more on symmetrical lattices, we will refer to the object as the symmetrical lattice.

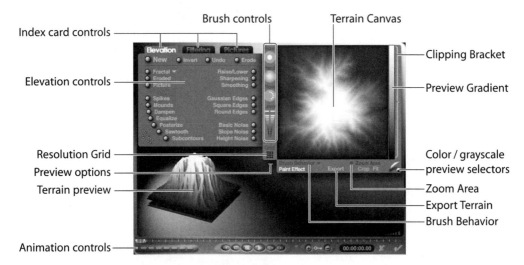

Figure 8.1 The Terrain Editor.

GEE TOO AITCH

The Terrain Editor is the master source of Bryce's land formations. How does Bryce control the shapes of a terrain? It generates them from grayscale image information. Different levels of gray correspond to different heights. The lowest elevation is represented by black and the highest elevation by white. This is called a grayscale-to-height map (or G2H map for short).

The G2H map is a top-view, two-dimensional grayscale representation of a three-dimensional entity. As you look at the G2H terrain image in the Terrain Editor, you need to make a mental shift away from looking at a two-dimensional image as a picture in which light and dark are shadow and highlight. Think of light and dark as different heights: if it's darker, it's at a lower altitude; if it's lighter, it's higher.

THE TERRAIN EDITOR CONTROLS

The grayscale *image* determines the shape of the terrain, so the Terrain Editor is actually a specialized *image editor.* It offers numerous controls for adjusting and shaping the grayscale image to create your terrain.

Overall Structure

The Terrain Editor is divided into several major areas. The main area, the Terrain Canvas, shows you the G2H information for your current terrain. To the left of the Terrain Canvas are three sets of controls, organized by index tabs. They are the Elevation controls, the Filtering controls, and the Picture controls. Click the word on the tab to make that set of controls active (see Figure 8.2). Also, you can step through the different sets of controls by tapping the Tab key (tapping Control-I accomplishes the same thing on the Mac, though less intuitively). Immediately surrounding the Terrain Canvas are the Brush controls, the Zoom and Crop controls, and the Clipping and Color Mapping controls. In the lower-left hand corner are a couple of pop-up menus, including the Grid pop-up menu, where the terrain resolution is set, and some other general controls that affect the preview (see Figure 8.3).

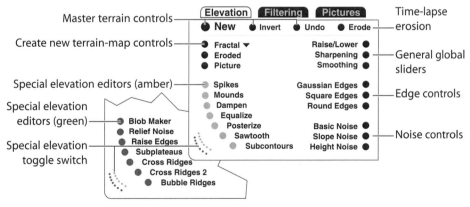

Figure 8.2 The Terrain Editor file card controls:
Elevation, Filtering, and Pictures.

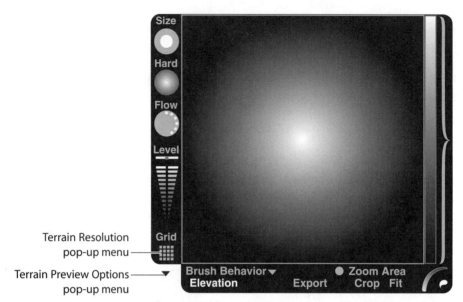

Terrain Resolution
pop-up menu

Terrain Preview Options
pop-up menu

Figure 8.3 The controls surrounding the Terrain Canvas.

Resolution in the Grid

Terrains come in different resolutions. The Grid control at the lower left of the Terrain Canvas panel (see Figure 8.3), has a pop-up menu for editing the terrain's resolution. (This Grid, with its pop-up menu, does not have any relation to the internal grid discussed in Chapter 6, "Editing and the Internal Bryce Grid.") Like any other image editor, you determine how much image information you want by choosing the resolution. The numbers in the pop-up menu refer to the number of pixels along one side of the terrain G2H map. Each pixel represents a datum, or point of information. The higher the number for resolution, the more detail you have for transitions from one point to the next. The default size, 128, stands for 128 × 128 pixels. Under most circumstances, 256 is the minimum terrain size we use. However, we don't always start with 256; we may do some manipulations at one resolution and then enlarge or reduce the resolution a bit later. There are times when a 16 × 16–pixel terrain is adequate. (Andrew Penick, who used customized terrains to build leaves for a plant, used terrains set to 16 to create the mesh shape. See Figure 16.33 in "The Greening of Bryce" section in Chapter 16.)

The largest terrain resolution is 1024 (1024 × 1024 pixels). Bryce 2 could handle such high resolutions internally, but could not copy and paste them. If you copied a 1024 × 1024 resolution and pasted it into Photoshop, the image would be resampled to 512 × 512. Since Bryce 3D, this is no longer true—you can export via the Clipboard even the largest grayscale maps. Pasting grayscale maps *into* the Terrain Editor is another matter, though. The resolution you have chosen in the Grid menu will override the resolution of the incoming image. If your grid is set to 64, and you paste a 1024 × 1024 pict image into the Editor, it will be sampled down to 64 × 64.

> **TIP:** *(Windows only) If you are copying from an image-editing application and pasting to Bryce, your image must be in RGB mode (even though the pixels are shades of gray) for the paste to work correctly.*

You'll find more discussion of when to use high or low terrain resolution in Chapter 16, "Superlative Nature Imagery," and you'll learn more about changing resolution as part of the terrain shaping process later in this chapter. For now, suffice it to say that higher resolutions require more RAM, increase your file size, and jack up the rendering time for your scene—but used judiciously, higher resolutions are worth it.

Preview

The preview in the lower-left part of the Terrain Editor shows you what your grayscale map looks like as a real honest-to-goodness elevation. Like the other previews in Bryce (in the Preset Library windows, in the Materials Composer preview window, and in the Flyaround view), you can manipulate the preview to change your perspective. Here's a brief recap of the controls:

- Drag right and left to rotate the terrain.

- Drag up and down to move your perspective down and up.

- Hold down the Shift key and hold down the mouse button to start the preview rotating. While it's spinning, drag left and right to change the rotation direction. On the Mac, you can drag up and down to change the orientation of the preview (the axis of rotation remains the *y* axis of the terrain, no matter what). You can combine the Shift key with the next two key commands to add rotation to the geographical gymnastics.

- Option/Alt-drag up and down to zoom into or out of the preview. This isn't a linear zoom—the horizontal dimension changes more than the vertical dimension, so when you're zoomed way out, the terrain looks tall and skinny, but if you zoom in close, it looks squashed. (This has no effect on the actual terrain itself.) To return the view to normal, click the preview while holding down Option-Control/Alt+Ctrl.

- Control/Ctrl+drag to exaggerate the vertical scale of the preview. Again, this doesn't change the terrain itself, and to return to a normally scaled preview, execute the ol' Option-Control/Alt+Ctrl and click.

You can also select from the preview pop-up menu to make your preview respond in real-time to your edits on the Terrain Canvas, spin around, or fill your screen with a bigger preview.

Elevation Controls

There are many different options available to you in the Elevation controls window, what with all the different buttons you can click and drag from. Since the preview gives you immediate feedback on your actions, and since the particulars of each are well documented in the Bryce 4 manual, it's not necessary for us to go through the list and provide individual descriptions of each Elevation editor. Rather, we shall categorize the controls and describe the ways to work with them.

The Different Types of Elevation Editors

The Elevation index card, shown in Figure 8.2, provides a series of buttons for the various types of elevation edits.

At the top, above a dividing line, are the master terrain buttons: New, Invert, and Undo. These operate with a single click. They also have key command equivalents. New is ⌘-N (Macintosh) or Ctrl+N (Windows). On the other hand, Control-click (Mac) or Ctrl+click (Windows) the New button if you're thoroughly disgusted with your terrain editing; the terrain will revert to the way it was when you entered the Editor. The keyboard equivalent (which was changed, by the way, in the 4.0.1 update) for this is ⌘-Shift-N (Mac) or Ctrl+Shift+N (Windows). Invert is ⌘-I (Macintosh) or Ctrl+I (Windows). Undo (which undoes only your most recent edit) is ⌘-Z (Macintosh) or Ctrl+Z (Windows). The key commands work for all sections of the Terrain Editor. Two of the buttons also support dragging: drag to the right on the New button to fade the terrain to black; drag to the right over the Invert button to gradually turn all the white parts of the image black, and vice versa.

The last button on the top row is the time-lapse Erode. This control erodes for as long as you have the button pressed. (If your terrain is of the high-resolution variety, you may not be able to see the results without using the Zoom Area function.) Think of the eons of geological change you can make just by holding that button down for a few seconds!

Two master terrain buttons that could be on the Elevation index card but are not are Copy (⌘-C for Macintosh or Ctrl+C for Windows) and Paste (⌘-V for Macintosh or Ctrl+V for Windows). The standard key commands work for copy and paste at all times in the Terrain Editor.

Underneath the dividing line are the remainder of the elevation editors. They are grouped into different categories which we'll describe momentarily, but they all have one thing in common: they are applied both by clicking and by dragging. Each button works as a slider. A drag to the right gradually applies the effect one way, and a drag to the left applies it another way. A click on the button is equivalent to dragging the slider all the way to the right.

The first set of controls creates new terrain shapes. There are three main sources: Fractal, Eroded, and Picture. Clicking Fractal or Eroded creates new terrain maps based roughly on the existing image information (in contrast to the way that the other Elevation controls make slight alterations to the existing image.) You can click to fully apply the effect or slide to partially apply it. But wait—there's more! Bryce 4 has many new options for the Fractal control (reached by way of a pop-up menu to the right of the button's label). We'll describe those in the next section. There is a key command shortcut to apply Eroded: ⌘-Shift-E/Ctrl+Shift+E. The Picture create tool is the one exception to the each-button-is-also-a-slider rule (there always has to be *one* exception, right?). The Picture button brings up an Open dialog box (indeed, ⌘-O/Ctrl+O accomplishes the same thing) for you to select any picture file. The list of importable formats was vastly expanded in Bryce 4 (see Table 8.1); you can make any image the basis of your terrain elevation data. And never fear, slider fans! There is a provision within the Terrain Editor for incorporating pictures via slider control. It's on the Pictures tab of the interface, and we'll discuss it later in the chapter.

> **TIP:** *Option/Alt-clicking the Picture button will display the image's color information in the terrain preview. Tra la la.*

The Elevation controls on the right side are more basic editors. At the top of the right side are a set of global editors: Raise/Lower, Smooth, and Sharpen. To remember which way to drag for the desired raise or lower effect, let the placement of the words be your guide. Drag to the right (the word *lower* is on the right) to lower and to the left to raise. Or use the handy-dandy key command equivalents: lower the terrain by typing ⌘-X/Ctrl+X; raise the terrain by typing ⌘-Shift-X/Ctrl+Shift+X. The amount the terrain will be raised or lowered is determined by the placement of the red dot in the Levels control. When the control is high (light end), the terrain will move in smaller increments; when the control is low (dark end), the terrain will move in larger increments. For more on the Levels control, see the "Brushes" section later in this chapter.

Extension	Format
.psd	Photoshop
.tif	TIFF
.pct/.pict/.pic	PICT (Mac only, or Win with QuickTime 3 or later installed)
.bmp	Windows bitmap (Win only)
.sgi,	Silicon Graphics bitmap
.iff	Amiga
.rle	Compressed BMP
.dib	BMP & RLE
.emf	Enhanced Metafile (a flavor of BMP)
.flm	Filmstrip
.fpx	Flash Pix
.gif	GIF
.jpg	JPEG
.mac	MacPaint file (Macintosh)
.pcx	PCX
.pxr	Pixar
.png	PNG
.pnt	MacPaint (Macintosh)
.icb	Targa
.tga	Targa
.vda	Targa
.vst	Targa

Table 8.1 2D graphics formats that can be imported into Bryce 4.

Below the edges are the noise editors: Basic, Slope, and Height. Basic applies noise all over, Slope applies noise only on the transitions from high to low (it makes for great cliff faces!), and Height applies only at higher altitude.

The last set of editors, the special editors, located in the lower-left corner, is the largest and most exotic group. Within the two sets of special editors are two main types of effects. The first type takes the existing image information and transforms it in some way. the amber button editors and a couple of the green button editors transform existing information. When your mouse is positioned over the buttons for these editors, the cursor changes to a double arrow for dragging left and right. The second effect type adds completely new grayscale information to the terrain map. Most of the green button editors, the ones with *blob* and *ridges* in their names, add new information. When your mouse is over those buttons, you see a four-way crosshair for positioning. As soon as you begin dragging, you're determining where the effect will be placed in the grayscale map.

Switch from one set to the other using the smaller rows of buttons in the corner (or by pressing Shift+Tab). One set of editors has amber buttons; the other set has green. The special editors use a variety of image processing algorithms that'll put some fun (and convincing!) geological phenomena on your terrain maps.

Dragging the Elevation Editors

The default drag direction is to the right. Dragging right has the same effect as simply clicking the button, but to a different magnitude. In most cases, dragging right increases elevation by lightening the grayscale map. Similarly, dragging to the left darkens the map. For example, dragging to the right on the Spikes or Mounds control creates spikes or mounds that rise from the ground. Dragging to the left on the same controls produces spike- or mound-shaped pits. Figures 8.4a and b show the results when dragging to the right and left on the Subcontours control (Figure 8.4c is the basic erosion map). Figures 8.4d and e show the same thing using a different special editor: Sawtooth.

There is at least one notable exception to the drag-right-to-lighten rule: when you use the Raise/Lower editors. The Smoothing and Sharpening controls also apply a lightening effect when you drag to the left. Also, the noises tend to apply the same type of noise regardless of the direction you drag. The same is true of the Posterize control. For the most part, though, the right/left lighten/darken rule applies to the special editors.

When you drag to make changes, try out small distance drags. If you are trying to make ever-so-subtle alterations, you will probably pass the subtle "mark" before you can really see the changes in the Terrain Canvas. Once you are able to see the changes, they've gone beyond subtle toward exaggerated. This is a spot where the Zoom Area feature comes in handy (as will be discussed in detail later).

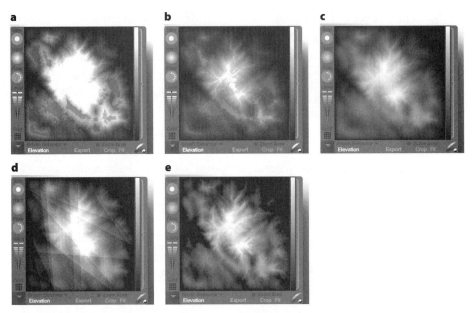

Figure 8.4 Dragging to the left and right applies different lighten and darken effects: a) Subcontour dragging left; b) Subcontour dragging right; c) the terrain before the effect. Different applications of the Sawtooth control: d) Sawtooth dragging left; e) Sawtooth dragging right.

Fractal Terrains

The Fractal button is considered a source generator. When clicked, a new terrain map is created using a fractal number generator (see Chapter 1 for a description of fractal geometry and its significance in the history of Bryce). Before Bryce 4, Bryce employed only one fractal algorithm, so all the terrains you could create by this method looked pretty much alike. Now, more than two dozen types of terrains are available (this feature was added to Bryce 4 very shortly before it shipped, so you won't find it mentioned in the manual, but it is described in the README file).

To get at this cornucopia of landscapely delights, use the pop-up menu to the right of the Fractal button (see Figure 8.5). As pop-ups go, it's a big one: the first 27 items are the different terrain models you can generate. Bryce Classic is equivalent to the lone model available in previous versions of the program; the others are all new. Next on the list are

Figure 8.5
The Fractal Terrains pop-up menu.

parameters that let you select the degree by which various terrains created with the same model differ from each other (not available with Bryce Classic, and so grayed-out in this image). These are followed by options for creating terrains that will match up smoothly when you place them side by side.

Figure 8.6 shows what the different fractal terrain models produce, with six examples provided for each, using different "randomness" settings. Notice that the ancient and venerable Bryce Classic model is the least flexible of the bunch, allowing little variation among generated terrains.

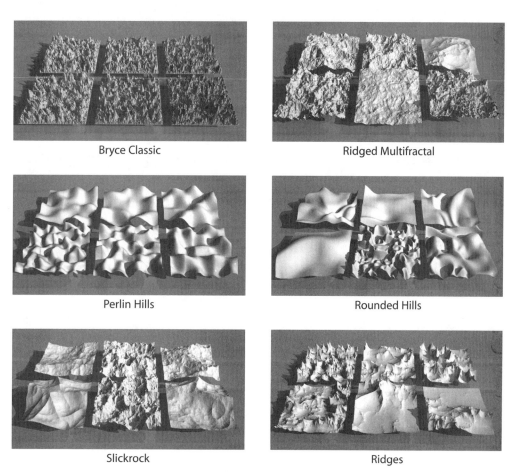

Bryce Classic

Ridged Multifractal

Perlin Hills

Rounded Hills

Slickrock

Ridges

Figure 8.6 Examples of each of the fractal terrain types.

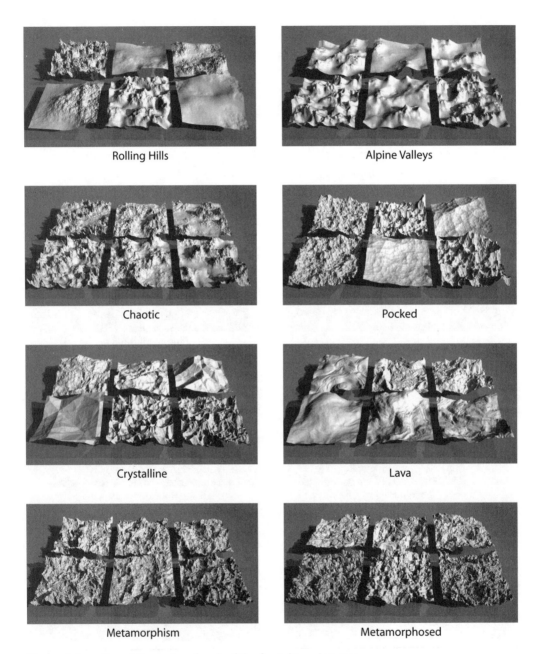

Figure 8.6 *continued* Examples of each of the fractal terrain types.

Fractured

Weathered Dikes

Warped Slickrock

Warped Ridges

Zorch

Warped Zorch

Mordor

Shattered Hills

Figure 8.6 *continued* Examples of each of the fractal terrain types.

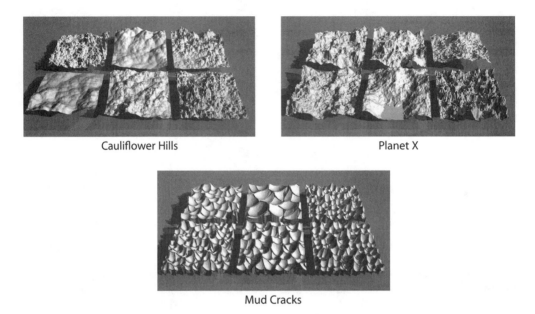

Cauliflower Hills

Planet X

Mud Cracks

Figure 8.6 *continued* **Examples of each of the fractal terrain types.**

How do the randomness settings work? Think for a moment about the nature of the fractal terrain models. The manual says they are based on "fractal patterns," which is close to the truth but not right on. The models don't obviously form patterns, at least not in the sense we think of patterns, because they don't repeat in a regular way—which makes sense, because if they were too regular, our eyes wouldn't accept them as natural landscapes, right? The mathematical models on which they're based do have a certain degree of periodicity, though, which means that elements recur over and over again, but just not in easily discernible patterns. It's this degree of recurrence that is adjusted by the randomization settings. When Random Extent is on, the overall size of the units of the terrain varies randomly. When Random Position is on, the position of the grid bearing the units of the terrain will change at random. Random Character allows other parameters that govern the overall look of the terrain to change at random.

The Fractal button can apply these models in several ways: first, if you already have a terrain map showing in the Editor window and you are working with the Bryce Classic fractal type (the default terrain), a click on the Fractal button generates a new terrain and merges it with the existing terrain. As with the other buttons on the Elevation index card, you can use the button as a slider to vary the amount of the effect: The more you drag to the right, the stronger the influence of the new terrain on the map; the more you drag to the left, the more the inverse fractal is blended into your terrain grayscale map (what was light when you dragged right is now dark, and what was dark is now light). Dragging to the center of the range makes your map retains its original appearance.

You can also use the Fractal button to create an entirely new terrain from scratch. Click the New button to nuke the current terrain completely and start with a blank slate. Now click the Fractal button and choose a mode from the pop-up menu, and a fresh landscape pops into view. Also see the "Game Over, Man" recipe later in this chapter for more on starting from scratch.

The new fractal models that the Bryce programmers have so thoughtfully provided produce landscapes that are much more interesting, and often more realistic, than the old Bryce Classic version. A click of the Fractal button when one of the new fractal types is active produces an entirely new terrain. Period.

The mathematical processing invoked during the creation of one of the new fractal types hogs up your computer's processor and consumes time. It will take more time with a higher resolution, but you can cut out unnecessary waiting by doing your terrain shopping at a lower resolution.

There's a trick to "shopping" for a fractal terrain and saving time as you do so.

1. Set your terrain grid to 128.

2. Select the fractal style in the Fractal pop-up menu.

3. Click the Fractal button to generate a new fractal. Keep clicking until you find the one you want.

4. Once you find that, shut off all the random generators—deselect Random Extent, Random Position, and Random Character so that there are no check marks beside any of them. (Alas, this process takes you down the long menu three times, but the eventual results are worth it.) While you're there, make sure that there is no check mark by any of the Tile options (Tile North and so on) below the Random options.

5. Change your terrain grid to make it larger: 256, 512, 1024—whichever you prefer.

6. Click the Fractal button one more time. Without any of the random generators, Bryce will generate the exact same terrain and will add in extra-juicy detail for your chosen grid resolution.

    The next time you go fractal shopping, you'll need to switch on the Random generators again.

Another approach is to blend the fractal with the existing terrain. You may do so by sliding the Fractal button rather than clicking it. However, you'll have to accept the first fractal generated by Bryce (then again, there's always Undo, so you're not limited solely to that fractal). You'll have to keep the mouse pressed on the button until the wristwatch/hourglass cursor goes away. One option is to blend the two together using the Pictures function of the Terrain Editor rather than risk giving yourself carpal-tunnel syndrome pressing and waiting for as long as it takes to generate the fractal. We discuss the Pictures tab of the Terrain Editor later in this chapter.

Tiling

The tiling options let you create a linear series of terrains that fit together seamlessly. Here's how:

1. Create a new terrain and open the Terrain Editor.

2. Browse the fractal terrains until you find one that you like, such as the one in Figure 8.7. Close the Editor.

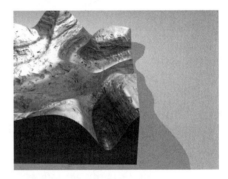

3. Duplicate the terrain and position the duplicate immediately adjacent to the original terrain in the direction you want the tiling to proceed (in this example, shown In Figure 8.8, we're tiling to the North, or in Brycean terms, in the positive direction along the z axis). If you haven't

Figure 8.7 The starting terrain, created using the Rounded Dunes model.

resized the terrain, you can use key combinations to move the new terrain by a distance equivalent to its own dimensions—holding down Shift and pressing the up arrow key eight times should do it.

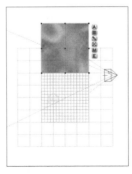

Figure 8.8 The duplicate terrain is moved to abut the original terrain on its northern side.

TIP: Keep your terrains at their default size while tiling. That will make it easy to place them precisely using the nudge arrow keys. When you are through generating the tiles, resize them as a block: select them, group them, and enlarge them to the desired size.

4. Open the Terrain Editor again. Access the Fractal pop-up menu, make sure that all randomization options are unchecked, and choose Tile North. Click the Fractal button, wait for the new terrain to be created, and then close the Editor.

5. Render your scene. You should find that the new terrain matches the original almost perfectly (see Figure 8.9a). If the terrains don't quite touch, scoot the new terrain back toward the original, using Option/Alt-arrow key. It will probably need only a few nudges to cover the gap (see Figure 8.9b).

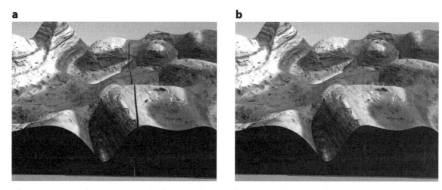

a   b

Figure 8.9 a)The new terrain in position and rendered, but still showing a small gap between the terrains; b) after Option/Alt-nudging the new terrain back toward the original—the gap has vanished!

Even though this technique only creates matching tiles in a line, if you're careful and follow a back-and-forth plowing pattern, you can fill a large space (see Figure 8.10). What—you're amazed that Bryce can remember what the edge of square 1 was like when it gets to square 6? Here's a little secret: the terrains match up not because Bryce contrives each new terrain to fit with the adjoining one, but because Bryce is progressively revealing pieces of a larger terrain whose parameters were established when you created the first terrain. (Incidentally, this is also why some terrains you generate with the new fractal style are in tones of middle-gray: the entire range of black-to-white spans an area that is larger than a single tile of that terrain, and your currently gray terrain happens to lie in the middle-gray segment of the larger terrain pattern.)

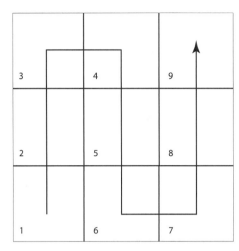

Figure 8.10 Follow this zigzag pattern when creating tiling terrains to fill a large space seamlessly.

Brushes

On the left and bottom edges of the Terrain Canvas display area are controls for the brush. The controls on the left side determine the brush's behavior. The effects of two of them, Size and Flow, are increased by dragging to the right and decreased by dragging to the left. To increase the brush's hardness, on the other hand, you drag to the left; to feather its effect around the edges and soften it, you drag to the right.

When you move the cursor over the Terrain Canvas, the crosshair cursor changes to a circle, indicating the brush's size. Size is fixed; a given brush size represents the same number of pixels. Thus, a brush that is very large on a 128 terrain will be much smaller on a 1024 terrain. Figure 8.11 shows the same brush size applied to

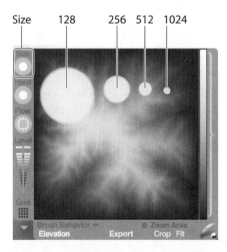

Figure 8.11 The same brush size when applied to a terrain that is 128, 256, 512, and 1024.

a terrain that has been set to different resolutions: 128, 256, 512, and 1024. The size control is not particularly smooth; the brush size tends to jump from one increment to the next without all the in-between sizes. If you need to brush a certain size and can't seem to do so, try changing the resolution and using a different-sized brush.

Hardness determines whether the brush has a soft or hard edge. A soft brush allows you to create subtle effects without betraying your moves with brush tracks.

The Flow control governs the rate at which the digital paint comes out of the brush. Flow can also be thought of as opacity. (Although the interface indicates different flow amounts by placing dots along the control's circle, a circular motion of the mouse will not change anything; the control works by dragging right and left.)

You can constrain the motion of the brush by holding down the Shift key when you start to paint. Press the Shift key, and you will only be able to drag the brush horizontally or vertically or at a 45° angle. Here's another handy key modifier trick: if your computer is too slow to allow you to keep Realtime Linking permanently turned on (in the terrain preview Options menu), hold down Control/Ctrl while brushing and the results of your painting will instantly appear in the terrain preview.

The default Brush Behavior setting is for Elevation (the Brush Behavior pop-up menu is located on the left side of the panel below the Terrain Canvas). The Level control, located on the left panel underneath the Size, Hardness, and Flow controls, sets the elevation—or gray level—for the brush. Drag the little red indicator up or down to the desired level. To move the red indicator, press anywhere in the Level control; you don't need to aim right for the couple of pixels of the indicator itself. As a shortcut, you can also paint the inverse level (black instead of white, dark gray instead of light gray) by pressing the Option (Macintosh) or Alt (Windows) key before or while dragging the mouse to make a brush stroke. You can also use key commands to set the indicator to the highest and lowest levels. ⌘-L/Ctrl+L sets the red indicator to the highest (white) level. ⌘-Shift-L/Ctrl+Shift+L sets the red indicator to the lowest (black) level.

There is another handy method for choosing a brush color. Pressing the space bar temporarily turns the brush cursor into an eyedropper. Point the cursor over an area of the Terrain Canvas whose elevation you want to copy to another spot and press the space bar. The brush picks up the color from the spot where you sampled.

(The Level control adjusts accordingly, as Figure 8.12 shows.) Be careful not to click the mouse when you sample! If you do click, you will then be *painting* that grayscale level into your Terrain Canvas.

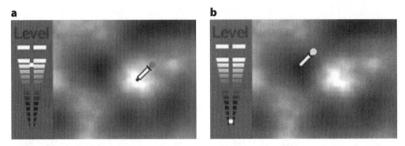

Figure 8.12 The eyedropper in action: a) sampling in a light area causes the Level control to rise; b) sampling in a dark area leads to the opposite result.

Brush Behaviors

Not only does the brush paint in certain elevations, but the Brush Behavior pop-up menu has other options: Paint Effect/Unpaint Effect, Minimum/Maximum, and Erosion.

The most powerful of these by far is the Paint/Unpaint Effect set. Rather than painting a certain gray level, you can paint a portion of an effect you previously applied. After applying and then undoing, say, mounds, you can now paint the mounds effect only in the places you want, rather than applying the effect to the entire terrain. Paint the mounds in the darker, lower places. The east-facing slopes. The heights. You choose. Then you paint.

Brush Behavior Walkthrough

Try it out.

1. Create a new Bryce scene document. Create a terrain. Go to the Terrain Editor. Click Eroded to create an eroded terrain (see Figure 8.13a).

2. Press the Option key (Macintosh) or Alt key (Windows) and drag slightly to the right on the Posterize special editor until the terrain pattern looks slightly pixelated. (Note: This is a variation on the usual Posterize, the Mosaic tool; see Figure 8.13b.)

3. Click Undo or type ⌘-Z (Macintosh) or Ctrl+Z (Windows).

4. Switch the Brush Behavior pop-up menu to Paint Effect. Now you can paint the pixelated terrain in places on your eroded terrain (see Figure 8.13c).

5. If you painted too much, switch to Unpaint Effect and "erase" the pixelated effect so that the eroded terrain shows.

> **TIP:** *You can switch between Paint and Unpaint on the fly by pressing the Option key (Macintosh) or Alt key (Windows) while you paint.*

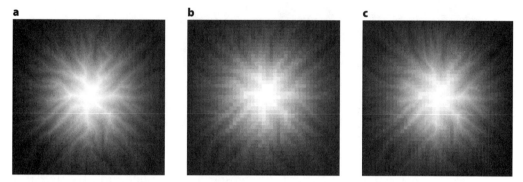

Figure 8.13 Do-undo-Paint Effect: a) Original eroded terrain; b) after applying Option/Alt-Posterize; c) after undoing and then painting using Paint Effect.

This do-undo-paint-only-where-you-want-to technique is extremely handy in Bryce. We use it all the time. Keep in mind that you can combine it with a light application of the brush, with a very soft edge. Between the gradually adjustable elevation tools and the do-undo-paint-only-where-you-want-to technique, you can add layer upon layer of subtlety. This technique also works with the other two types of terrain edits, from the Filtering and Pictures sections of the Terrain Editor (explained later in the chapter). Look at some of our fave terrain routines later in the chapter for some additional techniques.

> **TIP:** *There is an additional shortcut method for Paint Effect. Press the space bar while clicking an Elevation Effect button. The Brush Behavior mode is automatically switched to Paint Effect, and you may begin painting that effect. Of course, if you want to use the slider to determine how much of an effect to apply, use the normal do-undo–Paint Effect method.*

The Brush Behavior also has another pair of options: Minimum and Maximum. These are analogous to the lighten-only apply mode and darken-only apply mode in Photoshop. With Maximum (lighten only), once you choose an elevation level, you can paint the elevation; the result will be whichever is lighter: the brush color or the existing terrain (see Figure 8.14a). With Minimum (darken only), the result will be whichever is darker: the brush color or the existing terrain (see Figure 8.14b).

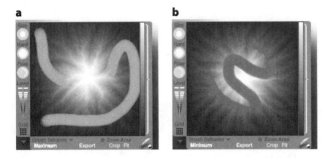

Figure 8.14 a) Maximum and b) Minimum Brush Behavior modes.

The final Brush Behavior option is Erosion. Paint erosion wherever you'd like it. This is a splendid idea—don't erode everything uniformly, but erode it here and there, as you see fit. Unfortunately, Brush Erosion is not sensitive to the Flow amount, so you cannot brush subtle applications of erosion. Although the terrain resolution does affect the outcome (the erosion is more subtle on a 1024-sized terrain than on a 128), we prefer to paint our erosion using the do-undo–Paint Effect method using an application of the Erode button. You can control the softness, the size of the brush, and the all-important flow, too.

Filtering

The second of the index card tabs in the Terrain Editor contains the Filtering controls. The title of the control is Filtering. To avoid confusion between the *action* of *filtering* and a *thing* called a *Filtering control,* we'll use the word *Filter* when referring to the control. The Filter allows you to change the shape of your terrain.

Like the old computer-ese saying GIGO (garbage in, garbage out), referring to a special event (or, in GIGO's case, a lack of it) that occurs between incoming and outgoing information, a Filter places you between the incoming gray values and the outgoing gray values. It allows you to tweak the gray values to your heart's content. If you've worked with the pencil tool in Photoshop's Curve control/Arbitrary Map, the Terrain Editor's Filter control will be familiar to you.

The Filter control has several parts. The Filter control itself is at the left of the Filtering index card, bisected by a diagonal line. To its right is a small preview of your terrain, showing how it looks based on the Filter setting. Across the top of the Filtering index card are nine presets. Below the Filter control are the Reset and Smooth buttons. The Apply button is located at the bottom of the index card. There are also two pop-up menus: one under the Filter control, and the other under the preview. The first allows you to choose options for combining the filter effect with a grayscale ramp; the other allows you to process your terrain map with Photoshop-compatible plug-ins (we'll discuss the latter later, in the section "Working with Other Image Editing Applications") (see Figure 8.15).

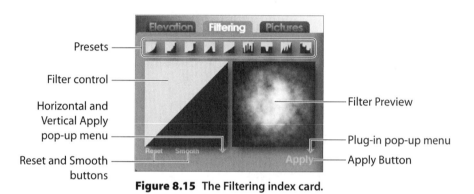

Presets —

Filter control —

Horizontal and Vertical Apply pop-up menu —

Reset and Smooth buttons —

— Filter Preview

— Plug-in pop-up menu

— Apply Button

Figure 8.15 The Filtering index card.

Filter as a "Side View"

Think of the Filter section as a cutaway of your mountain terrain. The terrain's shape will be determined by the shape of the diagonal. In its default (reset) state, the straight diagonal line represents a smooth gradation from black to white. Change the Filter to other shapes by dragging in the area (see Figure 8.16). When your cursor moves over the Filter, it changes to a pen. The cutaway follows as you draw.

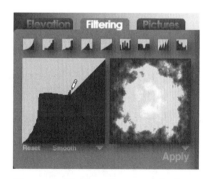

Figure 8.16 Drag the cursor in the filter to change the Filter's "shape."

When you look at a G2H map, you may be fooled into trying to read a three-dimensional illusion in that two-dimensional depiction. The image in Figure 8.17a appears to be a sphere. It's not a sphere, however; it's a cone (see Figure 8.17b)—the gray values move evenly from black to white. Your eyes need to undergo a bit of retraining if you are going to work a lot with the grayscale terrain maps (and, if you like this thing called Bryce, you probably will!). The Filter portion of the Terrain Editor may help take the edge off of this visual illusion.

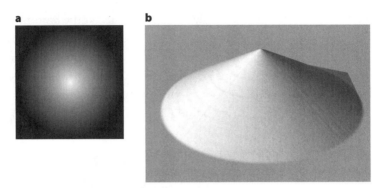

Figure 8.17 Cone or sphere? a) G2H map appears to be a sphere; b) when rendered, it is a cone.

Let's look at a series of terrains and their Filter adjustments. Figure 8.18 has three rows: the top row shows G2H terrain maps, the middle row shows the filters for the G2H maps, and the bottom row shows the rendered terrains. The left G2H map has a black-to-white-to-black gradation. To help shift you away from seeing this as an illusion of a three-dimensional tube, notice how the Filter and the rendered terrain correspond to the G2H map's linear transition from black to white. This is no tube; it's a straight diagonal wedge. This wedge terrain map is the starting place for every other G2H map in this figure. To create the other maps in the series, the Filter shapes in the middle row were created first. They were then applied to the wedge-shaped G2H map to result in the other G2H terrain maps in the top row. The rendered terrains in the bottom row show the final result. Each filter in the middle row is a cutaway view of the corresponding rendered terrain below it.

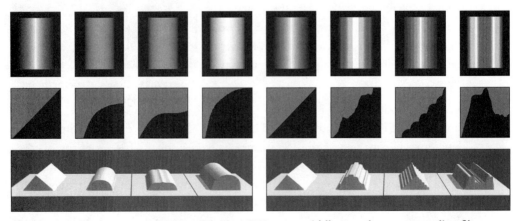

Figure 8.18 Filters as cutaway views. Top row: G2H maps; middle row: the corresponding filters that shaped them; bottom row: rendered results.

Of course, a terrain won't precisely follow the Filter's shape, since terrains aren't conical. Terrains go down in some places and up in others. (That's all a part of their charm!) The terrain will roughly follow the Filter's shape, complete with all those charming irregularities. But once you apply the Filter, the terrain itself changes. After any change, the new terrain shape acts as the straight diagonal wedge once again. If you continue to apply the same Filter over and over again to a terrain, you will get widely differing results (depending on the original image, the Filter, and the subsequent images).

Smoothly Reset the Apply

After you have changed the Filter, you have three options: use Reset to get back to the default, Smooth to soften harsh transitions, or Apply to use the current settings to change your terrain. When you apply the Filter, you can undo the action and paint effect or unpaint effect, if you desire.

> **TIP:** You have the option to try before you apply—to apply the Filter effect temporarily in the terrain preview. To do so, click in the Filter preview. The terrain preview will display the Filter effect for as long as the mouse is pressed. But wait—there's more! While you are holding down the mouse button, the cursor will change to a four-headed arrow. This is a visual clue that you can manipulate the terrain preview. Drag the mouse around, and sure enough, the terrain preview rotates, just as if you were dragging the preview itself.

Reset pops the Filter back to its normal diagonal state. One click on the Smooth control flattens out the bumps in your Filter pattern—but for a little mindless entertainment try holding down the mouse button on the control. The smoothing action is continuous for as long as you press, and what's more, you get to see the effect of the filter changing in real time in the Filter preview. If you hold down the button long enough, eventually the Filter pattern returns to its default diagonal shape—just as if you had clicked the Reset button.

Filter Presets

The Presets are at the top of the Filtering area. Clicking any of them will apply them to the Filter ramp. Once you change your filter, you can't undo it; you will lose what was there before. You can, however, undo any change made to the terrain map itself.

Also, you cannot place your own custom Filter in the Filtering area. (This would be handy for production-type work, where you apply the same Filter action to a series of terrains.) If you want to do that, you'll need to copy and paste terrains from Bryce to Photoshop and save an arbitrary map/curve there and apply the curve to a series of images. With one or two possible exceptions, we find that most of the presets are fairly worthless for normal Filter use.

Horizontal and Vertical Options

The pop-up menu below the Filter control has options to take the Filtering information and apply it differently to your Terrain Canvas. The additional options are Apply Vertical, Apply Horizontal, Apply Vertical Add, and Apply Horizontal Add.

At this point the Filter control changes. In the GIGO analogy, the horizontal and vertical options are GO (garbage out). These options do not process any input information; they apply the Filter map as output information only, so the Filter becomes a directional height generator. When using the Apply options, the filter no longer processes the pixels of the Terrain Canvas, it merely overlays the grayscale map suggested by the filter onto the Terrain.

When the filter is applied horizontally, it results in vertical bands of some sort. That's because the filter was applied across the horizon of the terrain. The same holds true for the vertical application, which creates horizontal bands. It's worth noting that in this context *vertical* and *horizontal* don't have the usual geographic meanings of "toward or away from the center of the Earth" and "parallel to the surface of the Earth," referring to the height or breadth of your terrain. They merely refer to the plane of the Terrain Canvas on your computer screen. If this is confusing to you, remember the key combination for Undo; it applies here. Note that the Add algorithms are not the classic Add calculation mode, but a special means of intensifying what is already present: darks get darker and lights get lighter.

So what are these options good for?

To generate a basic ramp, create a new grayscale map. Then click Reset to make sure that the Filter is a straight diagonal line. Then select Apply Horizontal or Apply Vertical (one, not both). You get a basic ramp. Repeated applications (especially using the Add option) will make the ramp climb from black to white. This is good for creating terrain shapes where you need a one-sided ramp. As a variation, try using the same filtering curve, first horizontal and then vertical. The symmetrical plaid effect in Figure 8.19 was obtained by using one application of Horizontal Add and one of Vertical Add.

Figure 8.19 A strange symmetrical plaid effect created by applications of Add Horizontal and Add Vertical.

The Vertical and Horizontal applications are seemingly meaningless when you are working on a normal terrain that rests upon the ground. Sure, you can make your trippy Madras plaid and all, but that's not what this control is good for. The Horizontal and Vertical applications are better put to use on terrains that stand up vertically, such as sheer cliff faces, or for symmetrical lattices. For the vertically placed objects that take advantage of this type of construction, some of the previously meaningless presets now have become slightly useful.

The hoodoos in Figure 8.20 were created using a symmetrical lattice that stands upright. Starting with a new (black) terrain, some bumps were drawn across the middle of the Filter control. The basic G2H shape was created by repeated Apply Horizontal and Apply Vertical filtering. Repeated applications accentuated the shape; the Add mode exaggerated the lights and the darks to make the top thinner and the bottom fatter. Figures 8.21a through c show the first few steps used to create the shape of the individual hoodoos (the entire sequence is on the CD-ROM in the HOODOO HOWDUNNIT folder).

Figure 8.20 Scene with hoodoos created using the Vertical and Horizontal applications for the Filtering control.

The last step is shown in Figure 8.21d. The entire grayscale map was created in the Terrain Editor, in one editing session. No other imaging applications were used, and brushing was limited only to do-undo-paint-where-want-to applications of the algorithmic elevation effects.

There's one last little pop-up menu to discuss. It's almost hidden, tucked away under the Filter preview area. Indeed, you won't even find it mentioned in the Bryce 4 manual, because it was added at the very last minute, just before the release of Bryce 4 (it is mentioned in the README file, however). It lets you run Photoshop-compatible filters on your grayscale terrain map without leaving Bryce. We talk about this menu later, in the section "Working with other Image Editing Applications."

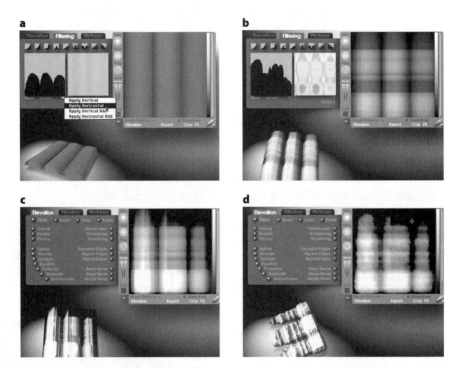

Figure 8.21 Some of the Terrain Editor steps used to create the hoodoo symmetrical lattice: a) After applying Horizontal; b) after applying Vertical repeatedly; c) after adjusting contrast; d) final terrain map.

Pictures

The third index card is for adjusting pictures. You can take any two images and blend them together in some way to create a resulting image from your Terrain Canvas and, ultimately, your terrain.

There are three preview windows in the Pictures portion of the Terrain Editor. When you first click the Pictures tab, your existing terrain (from the Terrain Canvas) is displayed in the left window (see Figure 8.22) and the middle window is filled with white. The right window shows the results of blending the two. You can replace the contents of either the left or the middle window with an image. There are two ways to accomplish this: you can paste the image from the clipboard, or you can load a graphic file from elsewhere on your computer. The roster of image formats you can import is quite lengthy in Bryce 4; refer to Table 8.1 for a complete listing. To load an image, click the Load button above the window in which you want your picture to appear. A standard Open dialog box allows you to navigate to wherever your file is stored.

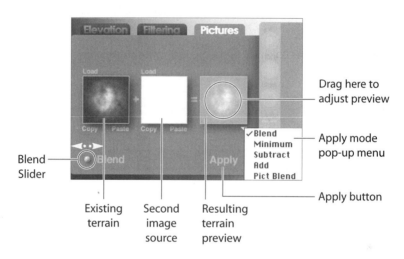

Figure 8.22 The Pictures index card with the Apply mode pop-up menu showing.

The Load buttons also act as pop-up menus (see Figure 8.23). Hold down the mouse button on either one to activate the menus. Choosing the first item, Load Image, is equivalent to clicking the button—an Open dialog box appears. Current Terrain loads the terrain displayed in the Terrain Canvas in its present state (merely clicking the window performs the same function), and Original Terrain loads the terrain as it was when you opened the Terrain Editor. You can

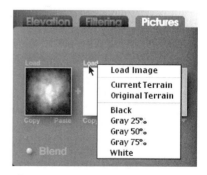

Figure 8.23 The Load Image pop-up menu.

also fill the window with black or white or one of several intermediate shades of gray. A blend of the contents of the two windows appears in the rightmost window.

To adjust the weight of the blend, adjust the slider button at the bottom of the Pictures index card. Drag in the third window to display the blend results in the 3D preview window, where you can rotate the preview to better see those results. Once you get a result that you like, click the Apply button.

You can adjust the mix of images in five different ways using the Blend modes in the pop-up menu: Blend, Minimum, Subtract, Add, and Pict Blend. To adjust the mix between the two images, drag the slider below them. There's immediate feedback, so you can see the results of each method. As you move the slider, the weight shifts between the two images.

- *Blend.* Performs a simple average combining of the two images.

- *Minimum.* Compares the two images and accepts the darker regions.

- *Subtract.* Performs a calculation between the two images, where the value of one pixel is subtracted from the other. In grayscale, 0 equals black and 255 equals white. Subtract tends to result in lower (or even negative) numbers, so the image will get darker and move toward black. You end up with terrains that have more area that is "flat on the ground."

- *Add.* Takes the values of individual pixels and finds their sum. The larger the number, the lighter the images. At 255 or more, the result is white. Add is a fine way to create high plateaus.

- *Pict Blend.* This option is an alternative algorithm. When you drag to the left, it multiplies the two sources together, and when you drag to the right, it performs a weighted subtract of the two (the second source becomes inverted and then some). When you're in the middle, between the multiply and the weighted subtract, it's pretty ugly.

Clipping Bracket

The Clipping Bracket, on the right of the Terrain Canvas, cuts an adjustable portion off the top or bottom of the terrain so that it won't render (see Figures 8.24a through f). In the preview (Figure 8.24e), the top is shown flat when clipped, although because the terrain is actually hollow, no flat surface will appear in the rendered scene (Figure 8.24f). (You can remedy the hollowness by choosing Solid from the pop-up menu in the lower-left corner of the Terrain Canvas.) This enables you to create grayscale-to-height forms that aren't necessarily square. For symmetrical lattices, the bottom clipping point defines the place where the two back-to-back terrains join.

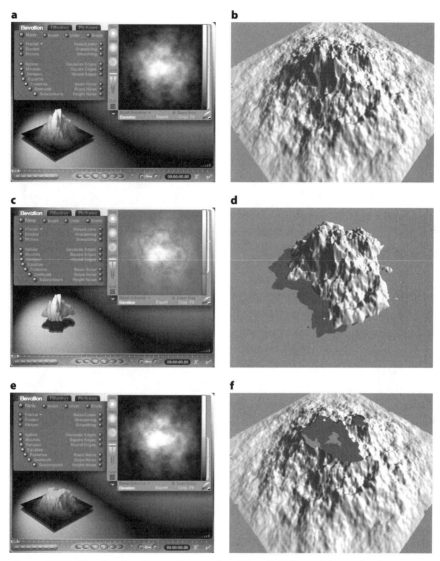

Figure 8.24 Clipping Bracket and a terrain: a) Terrain Editor with no clipping; b) rendered result; c) Terrain Editor with bottom clipping; d) rendered result; e) Terrain Editor with top clipping; f) rendered result.

These are all the ways you can adjust the Clipping Bracket:

• Drag either end to adjust that end.

• Drag from the center to reposition the entire bracket.

• ⌘-A (Macintosh) or Ctrl+A (Windows) selects all (resets the bracket).

- Option-clicking (Macintosh) or Alt-clicking (Windows) anywhere on the bracket also resets it.

A second function served by the Clipping Bracket is to restrict the part of the Terrain Canvas subject to editing. Clipping creates a selected area; whatever elevation edits you make will not be applied to the area that lies outside the Clipping Bracket. In the terrain map shown in Figure 8.25, the higher elevations were clipped and then an Erode effect was applied. Afterward, the bracket was returned to the default position. Notice how the highest areas are smooth and erosion begins below.

Figure 8.25 Terrain edited using the Clipping Bracket to apply an effect to a portion of the terrain.

The good news is that you can use the Clipping Bracket to isolate certain elevation special effects to particular elevations. Make the top half eroded and the bottom half sawtooth—all you have to do is isolate one portion before applying the effect. If your effect lowers or raises the terrain so that it fits into the clipped elevation, the clipping preview will change accordingly. But although you can add to the clipped area, it's extremely rare that you would take away from it (exceptions to the clip rule: Posterize,

Figure 8.26 A terrain form created by clipping the top and bottom, applying an effect, and then unclipping.

Equalize, and the Bubbles and Ridges in the special editors). You can create a whole set of terrain edits by taking advantage of this feature. Figure 8.26 is a terrain made from clipping top and bottom, dampening the center (by dragging left), unclipping all, and then finishing up with touches of Slope Noise, Erosion, and Smoothing (not necessarily in that order).

The bad news is that you may have a clipping effect in place already and when you go to apply something new, whoa! it isn't applied as expected. We've often discovered this when we have a terrain clipped at the bottom and add an effect—say, Dampen. The new effect changes what was in the center, but the outer information is caught between being changed by the dampening and being clipped and is therefore unaffected by the change. Figure 8.27 shows the same symmetrical lattice before and after dampening. Note the tiny fringe of terrain on the dampened version. To drive that fringe away, you would have to retouch your terrain map by painting black or by enlarging the clip area to include everything, making your adjustments and then resetting the clip to what it was before. The first process is time-consuming, and it's too easy to forget to do the second one.

Oftentimes the little leftover bits on the outside stay there, and a pile of rubble accumulates at the outer edges of the object. See for yourself. Create a symmetrical lattice and then open the Terrain Editor. Flip the grayscale map so you can see light at the lower end (⌘-F on Macintosh or Ctrl+F for Windows). Click the Dampen button repeatedly and watch how the detritus gathers.

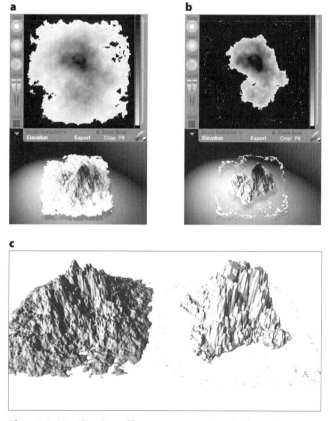

Figure 8.27 Clipping affects area near the clip boundary:
a) Terrain Editor for symmetrical lattice before and b) after
applying Dampen; c) rendered results of the before and
after states.

Preview Color

Related to terrain clipping is the color of the terrain preview. The default is black when terrain is low, and white when high. By holding down the mouse on the rainbow icon, you can make a set of colors appear. Choose any of the color sets to show different color schemes for the terrain. Different colors are good for working on elements at certain elevations. The default dark gray tends to obscure the details at

low elevations, so you're not completely sure what is happening at that level. A different color scheme brings out the detail. Or you can flip any gradient by typing ⌘-F/Ctrl+F. There is a third option as well for changing the gradient. Dragging up or down directly in the Gradient area cycles the gradient around so that a different color corresponds to a certain elevation.

This third option is good for marking certain areas. For instance, if you have clipping set to a certain level, you can cycle the gradient around so that the sharp transition matches that level. Change the clipping to perform certain edits and then change the gradient back again (Option-click or Alt+click resets the position).

When the Terrain Canvas is displayed in color, you can also adjust the Filter using colors. There are times when this is very helpful to isolate a certain level for making adjustments. The sharp transition between

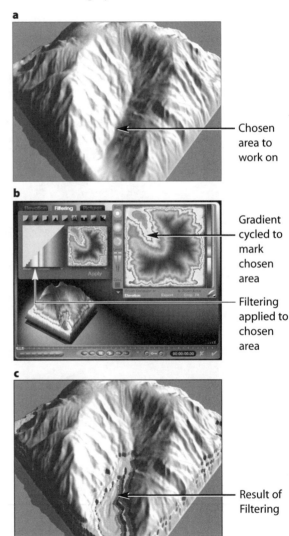

a

Chosen area to work on

b

Gradient cycled to mark chosen area

Filtering applied to chosen area

c

Result of Filtering

Figure 8.28 A cycled gradient marks the exact position of a certain part of the terrain, making adjustment using the Filter much more precise.

the top and bottom of the gradient makes an excellent marker; position the gradient so that the transition is right where you want it. In Figure 8.28, note how the color gradient has been repositioned to mark a valley in the foreground. In the Filtering area, the gradient matches, so it's easier to make adjustments to the terrain.

> **TIP:** You can have your terrain preview drawn in the terrain's current texture by typing ⌘-T/Ctrl+T. You're in for a longish wait after issuing the command, but the effect is lovely. Unfortunately, it only works if your terrain is set to a resolution of 128—no more, no less.

Zoom Area

Zoom Area has three buttons: an On/Off toggle, Crop, and Fit. The default is Off, and the preview represents the entire Terrain Canvas. When you click the Zoom Area button, a square marquee appears on the Terrain Canvas. When your pointer is over the marquee, the cursor appers as a grabbing hand or an arrow (see Figure 8.29a). The preview changes to show only what is within the bounds of the marquee. To change the position of the marquee, drag it by its sides (see Figure 8.29b). To change the area, drag from any corner to enlarge or reduce the size (see Figure 8.29c).

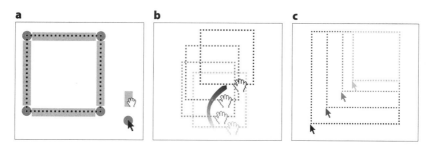

Figure 8.29 Working with Zoom Area: a) Active areas of marquee; b) repositioning marquee; c) resizing marquee.

Why would you crop a terrain? If your perspective calls for a high-detail terrain but a very limited camera perspective, you can cut away the parts that are off-camera and devote all the terrain's size to the portion that faces the camera. Or use it as a step in the whole terrain shaping enterprise. You don't want a basic Gaussianized version, but one shaped differently—use the Cropper to change the overall basic shape of your terrain and then go back and finesse from there.

The Fit function is more interesting. Take all your existing terrain data and fit it into the area described by the marquee. In other words, put your existing terrain into a smaller area surround by more black lowlands. Why would you want to do this? Say you're working on a terrain and the combination of a few edits (Stones, Dampen, and other lightening special editors) makes your terrain perilously high, perilously close to the edge of the terrain. You can't have any dramatic drop-offs to nothing; the terrain has to go from way up high down to ground level without falling off the edge of the terrain square. Use Fit to fit the entire terrain into a smaller space. Figure 8.30 depicts the basic problem and solution, with sufficient space surrounding the terrain to add transitional terrain detail.

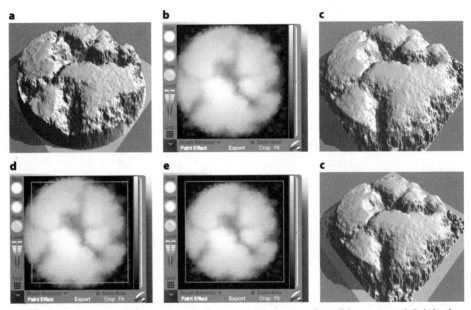

Figure 8.30 Fiddle as a Fit—using Fit to give a terrain some breathing room: a) Original terrain, in danger of "falling off the edge;" b) an application of mounds raises the terrain's edge off the ground; c) rendered view of too-high terrain; d) positioning the zoom Area; e) after fitting; f) the new terrain, with room all around.

Cool Zoom Tricks

One advantage of the new fractals (discussed in the section "Fractal Terrains" earlier in this chapter) is that their edges are such that you can tile 'em together. The disadvantage is that, if you want to make a single terrain out of a collection of them, the edges of the aggregate terrain won't be low. There's a lovely Zoom feature that will help you get low edges on your beautifully exotic fractal.

When Zoom is turned on, the marquee bounding box defines the area to which the fractal is applied. Figure 8.31 shows how this works. In Figure 8.31a, the terrain canvas displays the "before" state, with a terrain map in place. Then we switched on Zoom, and we adjusted the bounding box so it is inside the borders of the terrain (see Figure 8.31b). Figure 8.31c shows what happens when a new fractal is applied. It is applied only within the bounding box. The edges are blended together so there is no harsh transition to the area outside and inside the marquee.

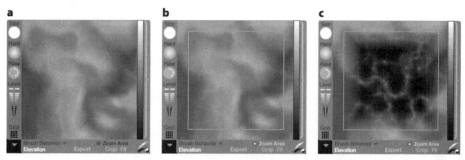

Figure 8.31 Using Zoom to apply a fractal to a smaller area in the terrain canvas: a) Terrain Canvas in the "before" state; b) after activating Zoom and adjusting the marquee position; c) after applying a new Fractal, which applies only within the zoom marquee.

(This is similar to what would happen if you were, say, to first apply the fractal and then apply Square Edges with an extreme drag to the left. The result is that the edges are squared off.)

This handy trick of using the zoom marquee to selectively apply a fractal has practical applications: Start with a new, dark canvas, set the zoom marquee to the edge of the terrain canvas, and then apply your fractal. Rather than having light edges, the terrain will be dark (low) at its edges. Figure 8.32a shows a terrain created by filling the Terrain Canvas with a fractal all the way to its edges. Compare Figure 8.32b, which uses the same fractal terrain, but applies it within the zoom marquee, which in turn hugs the outside edge of the Terrain Canvas. Of course, in the latter, the edges slope uniformly, and when the grayscale map is translated into a 3D object, the lower parts of its sides will resemble the bottom of a pyramid. You will probably need to retouch the edges with a bit of judicious painting or lightening or darkening.

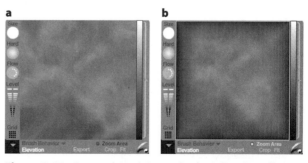

Figure 8.32 Comparing: a) A standard application of a fractal with b) the same fractal applied to a new, blank terrain canvas with the zoom marquee set to the edge of the Terrain Canvas.

Another use for the Zoom tool is to apply one fractal (remember: all Random settings off!) terrain-wide, and then to apply the same fractal again (and again) inside a number of smaller zoomed areas. The entire fractal pattern is scaled down to fit within the marquee each time. Figure 8.33 shows the result of this technique with the Mud Cracks fractal. We used the Equalize command on the first terrain-wide application to get full tonal contrast (and height), and then the subsequent smaller patterns were applied without retouching afterwards, giving them less height. Cool, eh? We're sure that you'll come up with some other great variations!

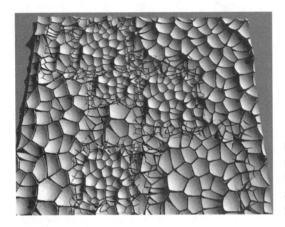

Figure 8.33 The result of reapplying the same fractal inside the zoom marquee around different parts of the Terrain Canvas.

FAVE ROUTINES

Now that we've introduced the Terrain Editor, it's time to discuss a few of the fun things you can do while you are in it. We will briefly describe the few steps to get each type of terrain, with the idea that in 1-2-3-4 steps or so, you can have a respectable shape that is not the normal humdrum terrain. Step one begins after creating terrain and opening the Terrain Editor. By the time you get through this, you'll also get a feel for some of the Zen of working in the Terrain Editor. For these (and more!) steps to create terrains, look for the STEP-BY-STEP folder in this chapter's folder on the CD-ROM.

Resolution Fluency

When you are working in the Terrain Editor, your fluency in changing resolutions—depending on the task you are doing—will help you obtain certain types of terrain effects.

The lower the resolution, the more powerful the erosive prowess of the Eroded (time lapse) button. Conversely, when it comes to using the Eroded button in creating a terrain, the higher the resolution, the more refined and detailed the original erode. Figure 8.34a shows a set of terrains from the same starting place. A click of the Eroded button was applied at each of the four higher resolution settings: 128, 256, 512, and 1024. Using a slightly different approach, Figure 8.34b represents four steps in a terrain creation process. First, the Eroded button is clicked for the 128-sized terrain. Then that terrain is changed to 256 resolution, where it becomes the basis for the next eroded terrain. The result of that is the basis for another Create Eroded at 512, and the result of that is used to create eroded terrain at 1024. It's not necessary to end up with a high-resolution result, though. Figure 8.34c shows the 1024 terrain beside the exact same terrain reduced to 256.

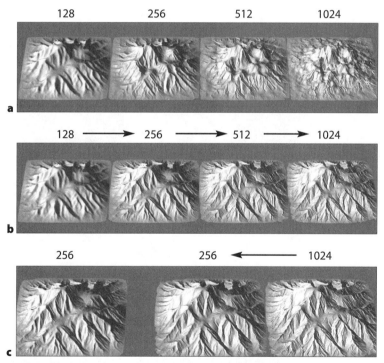

Figure 8.34 Terrain resolution and visible detail: a) Clicking the Eroded button to create a new terrain form at different sizes; b) starting at 128 and clicking Eroded, each terrain is the basis of the eroded terrain to its right; c) eroding at 256 versus eroding at 1024 and then resizing down to 256.

So what does this mean? You can increase the resolution to perform some specific action in the Terrain Editor and then reduce the resolution afterward, or you pack as much detail as you can into a 256 terrain.

For each of the next set of quick terrain tips, we're assuming that you're in the Terrain Editor and that your terrain resolution is 256.

Brushing Beauties

For subtle terrain effects, or for effects only-where-you-want-them, follow these steps:

1. Click the Eroded button to create an eroded terrain.

2. Click the Mounds button.

3. Undo.

4. Change Brush Behavior to Paint Effect and paint mounds only in the lowlands (see Figure 8.35).

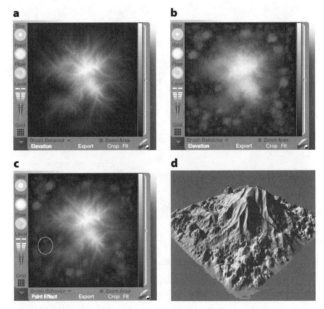

Figure 8.35 Brushing Beauties: a) Eroded terrain; b) after clicking Mounds; c) brushing the Mounds effect in the lowlands; d) rendered terrain.

Raise and Lower

The "Brushing Beauties" technique is excellent for selectively lightening (raising) or darkening (lowering) a terrain. Use it when you need to darken a terrain portion. Here's how to use it for raising a terrain:

1. Decide which portion of a terrain you want to lighten.

2. Drag the Raise/Lower slider at the left (lighten), keeping your eyes on the part you want to lighten. Don't worry if other parts become solid white.

3. Undo.

4. Using Paint Effect, brush in the lightened, raised terrain.

Rough Rough Rough

1. Apply Sawtooth with a subtle drag to the right (see Figure 8.36a).

2. Apply Sawtooth again, this time with a drag to the left (see Figure 8.36b).

3. Drag to the right again (see Figure 8.36c).

4. Drag again to the left (see Figure 8.36d).

5. For better definition of the blocks, apply Subcontours very gently, until you just see darker contours between gray levels (see Figure 8.36e).

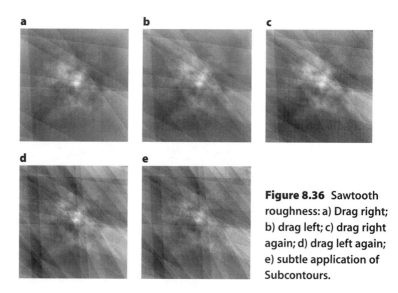

Figure 8.36 Sawtooth roughness: a) Drag right; b) drag left; c) drag right again; d) drag left again; e) subtle application of Subcontours.

Rice Paddies

1. Click Eroded to create an eroded terrain form.

2. Apply Posterize to get a terrace effect; drag until there are about a dozen levels.

3. Click OK to exit the Terrain Editor. In the scene, duplicate the terrain.

4. Go back to the Terrain Editor with one terrain selected. Change the resolution to 512. Apply Subcontours with very slight drag to the left, so the edges are barely higher (see Figure 8.37a). Click OK to go back to the scene.

5. Select the other terrain. Give the second one a water appearance, adjust the height positioning, and plant some rice. Add mist and brush calligraphy for a terraced rice paddy (see Figure 8.37b).

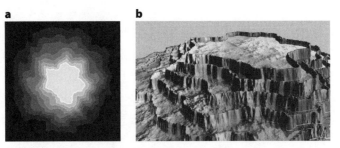

Figure 8.37 Rice Paddies: a) After using Subcontours to slightly lighten the edge; b) the rendered rice paddy.

Rivers and Deltas

1. Click New and then Invert to get a white terrain.

2. Brush a basic path into the terrain (see Figure 8.38a).

3. Increase the resolution to 512. Clip off the bottom and drag the Eroded slider to erode the top part (see Figure 8.38b).

4. Copy the terrain.

5. Clip off both the top and bottom and apply Dampen on the left (see Figure 8.38c).

6. Option-click or Alt+click the Clipping Bracket to reset it, to turn off clipping. Switch to Pictures.

7. Click within the first window to force it to display the image on the Terrain Canvas. Paste the previously copied terrain into the center (second) source.

8. Switch the Blend mode to Subtract. Move the slider all the way left and then to the right slightly until the river area darkens (see Figure 8.38d).

9. Apply Slope Noise and Erode (time lapse).

10. Reduce the terrain's (wireframe) height slightly and render (see Figure 8.38e).

a
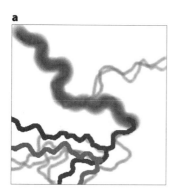

b
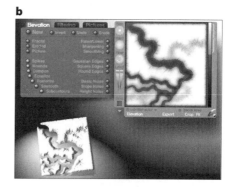

c
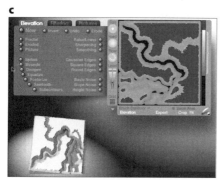

d

e
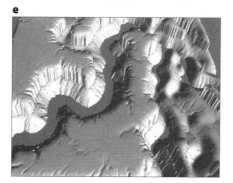

Figure 8.38 Rivers and deltas: a) After brushstrokes; b) clipping the bottom and eroding the top; c) clipping the top and bottom and dampening the left; d) merging the eroded river and dampened river using Subtract; e) the rendered terrain.

Game Over, Man

After trying something in the Terrain Editor, do you ever just want to start with a new terrain form without creating a new terrain? To start over from within the Terrain Editor:

1. Click New

2. Invert.

3. Click Gaussian Edges. Do so again.

4. Click Fractal.

Or…

1. Click New

2. Click Blob Maker (once or twice).

3. Click Fractal.

All of these steps are illustrated on the CD-ROM. In addition, there are more step-by-step procedures to create original terrain forms. Let these be an inspiration to guide you into new areas of exploration.

Waterfall

A waterfall is a multilevel entity. When water's at rest, it is flat; then it falls to a lower level, where it is flat again. To make a waterfall in Bryce, use a terrain. But the water also must fit inside a container of some kind—there is a bank or a shore of land on all sides. The land-container is also a terrain. So a waterfall, then, is a water terrain tucked within a land terrain. Making an exact fit of the water within the land requires some intricate work, since the two terrains are very closely related.

To be convincing, the land terrain needs the following characteristics:

• Suitably shaped pockets to hold water

• The bank is higher in elevation than the flat water level.

• Dual-level rock; there must be a precipice over which the water falls to another level below.

• The bank below must contain (or partially contain) the lower water level.

The water terrain needs to have the following characteristics:

- The water terrain is two basic gray levels—one for high water, another for low water—and all else is black (clipped).

- The flat areas of the water need to be wide enough to completely fit within the rocky area; otherwise it's not convincing, as shown in the one-level lake terrain in Figure 8.39b.

- The flat areas need to be the proper shade of gray to match the rock elevation and fit within the rock terrain.

- The transition between the two levels is sudden.

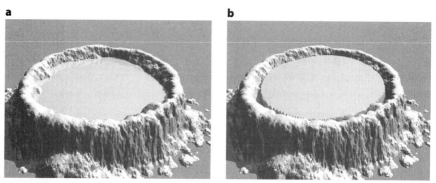

Figure 8.39 Making a water terrain wide enough to fit within a rock terrain: a) Water terrain that is wide enough; b) water terrain that is not wide enough.

Terrain Process Overview

Here's an overview of the process for creating the two terrains.

1. First, the land terrain is created and edited. It determines the *shapes* and *heights* that will hold the water.

2. Second, the terrain is duplicated to form the basis of the water terrain.

3. Next, the water terrain is edited based on the information from the land terrain. The area of the water terrain needs to match the *shape* of the rocky river bed. The grays used to define the flat water levels need to make the water at the right *height* so that it will be above the ground.

4. After the basic gray levels of the water are created, the river bed on the rock terrain is lowered a bit.

5. Finally, add fine tunings and tweaks and application of materials, and there's your waterfall! Add additional stones and other river-type objects to complete the scene.

Because of the close relationship between the two terrains, we find that the Terrain Editor's brushes are inadequate for the job. Even though the current version of the Terrain Editor allows you to copy (using the Space bar method) specific shades of gray to match elevations in various parts of the terrain, it is still not powerful or flexible enough for scenes like our waterfall, which consists of several similar tightly nested terrains. This type of job requires the heavyweight features of an image processor like Photoshop.

Step-by-Step Waterfall

1. First, create your land terrain. In the example shown here (see Figure 8.40), the upper and lower pools aren't completely enclosed. There's a higher side and a lower side, and the rocky enclosure forms a bank. (Note: The illustrations here were created in Photoshop 4, but the same procedure works equally well in later versions.)

    Start by opening up the scene file WATERFALL START on the CD-ROM.

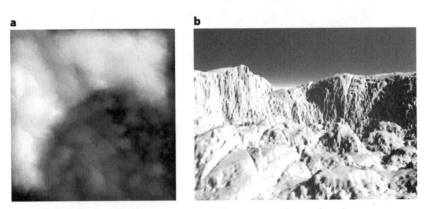

Figure 8.40 First terrain image: a) Grayscale map; and b) rendered.

2. Open the Terrain Editor. Copy the terrain. Click OK. Then open Photoshop. Select File > New. Photoshop automatically assigns a size for a new document based on the contents of the Clipboard. Accept the size suggestions Photoshop offers to create a grayscale document. Paste into your new document window. Your terrain map should now be in the window.

3. In Photoshop, duplicate the terrain by creating a duplicate layer. (Drag the layer name to the New Layer button at the bottom of the Layers Palette.) Name your two layers. Name the new layer "Water Terrain" and the background layer "Original Terrain." The first thing you will do to the Water Terrain layer is create a separate selection that defines the area, or *shape*, of the water. You can do this in at least a couple of ways. You can select a certain gray level by using the Magic Wand, or you can switch to Quick Mask mode and paint a selection area.

4. The Magic Wand method requires a bit of painstaking care, but yields better results, since you're getting exact elevation levels. For the Magic Wand Options, set Tolerance to 10 and make sure that the Anti-aliased box is unchecked (see Figure 8.41a).

   Concentrate on one major puddle area at a time. Select the lower area. Click in the dark areas. Shift-click to add to the selection (see Figure 8.41b). When you have determined the perimeters of the selection, switch to Quick Mask mode (see Figure 8.41c). From there, you can do some of the last bits of cleanup by painting out the little islands to leave a clear selection area. When you have finished cleaning up the little islands, switch from Quick Mask back to selection.

5. Take your selection and create a separate channel for it. Choose Select > Save Selection and make the destination a new channel. Name the channel "Lower Level Selection."

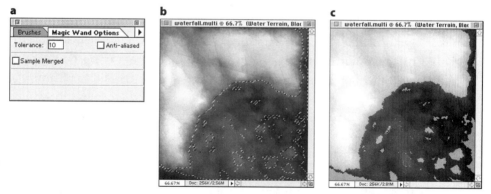

Figure 8.41 Using Photoshop's Magic Wand to select the water area: a) Magic Wand settings; b) Magic Wand selection marquee in progress; c) Quick Mask mode ready to clean up the last little bits of the selection area.

6. When you are finished with the lower selection area, deselect it. Now go back and repeat the same process for the upper water area. Select with the Magic Wand and clean up the edges with the Paint tool in Quick Mask mode. Save the selection and name it "Upper Level Selection."

7. Join the two areas into one selection to create the water area mask. Create a new channel (which should have a black background). Load the selection channel for the lower pool and fill with white. Then load the upper pool selection and fill with white. Using white, paint in the transitional area between the two pools, indicated by the encircled area in Figure 8.42. Name the channel "Water Selection Area."

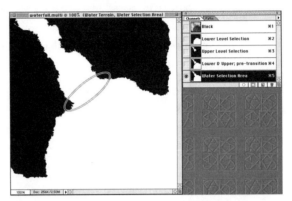

Figure 8.42 Water Selection Area channel and Channel Palette.

You'll use this mask for several things. You will use it as the basis for creating the flat area in the water terrain. You will also use it to select the area in the rock terrain that will be lowered (darkened) slightly later on.

If you haven't done so before now, save your Photoshop file. Make sure you save it using the Photoshop format (.PSD) to keep the layers intact.

8. Now that the Water Selection Area channel has been created and saved, make the Water Terrain layer active and load the Water Selection Area channel. Since you must ensure that the water is wide enough to fit snugly into the rock, the selection needs to be expanded. From the Select menu, choose Modify > Expand and enter three pixels as the expansion amount. The selection size will increase ever so slightly. (For all of these selection areas, make sure that you select with antialiasing switched off.) Save this selection for reference, by choosing Select > Save Selection. Save it in the same document as the new channel and name it "Larger Water Selection."

9. This expanded selection is what you'll use to paint the flat areas of your water terrain. Now that you know the area you'll be painting into, it's time to decide what level of gray to paint. Look at the rocky area within the confines of the selection. Sample a gray level from the lighter values there—say, near

the shore, where the selection area meets the rocky part above ground. Select the gray and then paint in the lower water area with solid, normal brush strokes (see Figure 8.43a). Paint the lower level just over the water spill.

10. Repeat the process for the upper area. Select a gray level from the lightest parts of the area enclosed by the upper pool. Using that gray, paint the entire water terrain upper pool area (see Figure 8.43b). When you are done, you should have something like what is shown in Figure 8.43c. Outside the selected area is the same old terrain data, and inside the selected area are two levels of gray, with a place of transition.

a
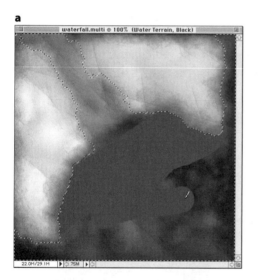

b
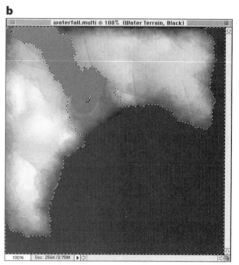

c
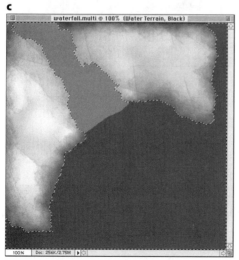

Figure 8.43 Painting the water terrain:
a) The lower gray area with a flat water surface gray; b) painting the upper water area; c) after painting all water levels.

11. There are two remaining details to fix here. The first is the transition. The water should spill out *over* the rocks, not cut under the edge to go *through* the rocks. Therefore, the lighter area should project out ever so slightly into the darker pool area. Set the layer blending mode to Lighten to help you judge how far to project the water. If you see rocky area peeking through at the waterfall transition, then the water will be cutting under the rocks. It's okay if there is rock peeking out elsewhere from the water, but not at the waterfall's edge. The transition should be sudden. Use the Smudge tool to create the transition (see Figure 8.44a). A couple of judicious smudges here and there make for a wall of water that's not perfectly uniform.

12. You'll also need to fix the rest of the terrain area. Whatever isn't water (what is still rock) should be at the darkest level. Select Inverse, so that all the extra nonwater area is selected. Fill it with black. You'll clip the black part so that the water does not even show in those areas (see Figure 8.44b).

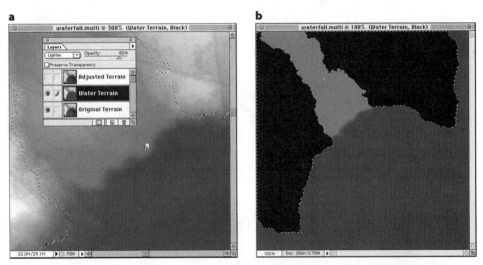

Figure 8.44 Finishing touches: a) Using the Smudge tool to make the waterfall transition between the two levels; b) filling all nonwater areas with black to finish the water terrain grayscale map.

13. In the Layers Palette pop-up menu, select Duplicate Layer, and where Photoshop asks you to specify the destination, select a new document. Save that new document as a PICT file (Macintosh) or TIF file (Windows). To do so, you may need to delete the extra channels. Name the new file "Water Terrain" and close it. Hang onto your master Photoshop file with the layers and selection masks. (In fact, save it again.)

14. Now you have one terrain map completed. Hooray! The second terrain map you'll make is a variation on your original one, the rocky terrain. Make your original terrain layer active. (Make sure no other layers are visible.) Load the Water Selection Area channel. This smaller selection is the exact area the water will fit into.

Since you sampled an elevation from here for your water, the water is now too shallow. Deepen it by darkening this selected area where the water will be. Access the Levels dialog box (Image > Adjust > Levels or ⌘-L on a Mac/Ctrl+L in Windows) and move the middle gray (gamma) triangle slider ever so slightly toward the white end. The numeric readout should change from 1.0 to something in the 0.90s. This darkens your selection a bit. Remember, it doesn't take much to make the elevation fall off. Even if it's subtle to your eyes, the change will be significant in elevation (see Figure 8.45).

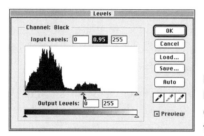

Figure 8.45 Using Photoshop's Levels dialog box to lower the rocky pool area.

15. Duplicate this layer in a new document and save it as a separate PICT or TIF file. Call it "Adjusted Terrain." Save your multilayer multichannel scene file and head on back to Bryce. Quit Photoshop.

16. Select your terrain (actually, it should still be selected). Open the Terrain Editor. Click the Picture button. Select the image file ADJUSTED TERRAIN. (When it loads, it shouldn't change much, just darken the current one in places.) Click OK to exit the Terrain Editor.

17. Duplicate the terrain. Open the Terrain Editor and click the Picture button again. This time, select the image file WATER TERRAIN. Once it loads into the Terrain Editor, slide the Clipping Bracket up from the bottom so that the low black terrain disappears (see Figure 8.46). Your body of water should be trimmed to the dimensions of the water. All those sixteen steps led up to this single drag of the Clipping Bracket for this waterfall! Click OK.

18. For the sake of clarity when the terrains render, change the surface of this waterfall to the basic blue option in the Materials Preset Library. Now when you render, you'll know what is water and what is not (see Figure 8.47a).

19. Render and see if all works according to design. Make any necessary adjustments.

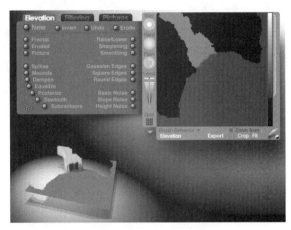

Figure 8.46 Clipping off the bottom of the water terrain.

Do not adjust the placement of the terrains, since they fit snugly together. If you need to make adjustments to ensure that the water is higher than the land or some other tweak, do so in Photoshop and adjust the grayscale map. If you need to move or resize the terrains overall, group them together before committing yourself to any move.

Assign surface materials and tweak. Be sure to check out the special waterfall material file in the WATERFALL folder on the CD-ROM. Congratulations! You've just made a waterfall in Bryce! Figure 8.47b shows a completed render, with all the material settings. (The color image for this scene is Figure C16.24, in the color section for Chapter 16, "Superlative Nature Imagery.")

a

b

Figure 8.47 Rendered waterfall: a) With water changed to flat dark color; b) complete with materials.

SYMMETRICAL LATTICES

The symmetrical lattice is a fine way to create "injection mold" objects. The symmetrical lattice is the equivalent of placing two terrain halves back to back. In nature scenes, you can create freestanding rocks, arches, and rocky-slab forms. The hoodoos shown earlier (see Figure 8.20) in the discussion of the Filtering controls were created using symmetrical lattices. For modeling, you can create pretty much anything you can imagine! The tower architecture image by Chris Casady at the end of the previous chapter (see Figure 7.46) uses symmetrical lattices to construct architectural elements.

When making objects with the symmetrical lattice, the most critical point is to create the grayscale map so as to minimize the seam where the two halves join. The Filter is excellent for creating a curve to minimize this seam; see the example in Figure 8.48. The trick is to make a very sudden transition from black to a lighter color.

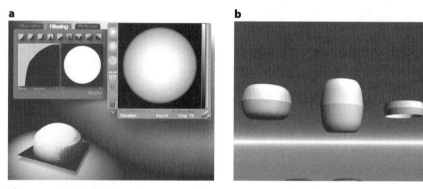

Figure 8.48 Minimizing the seam: a) The settings on the Filtering control; b) rendered result with different object height settings and with clipping at the top, too.

WORKING WITH OTHER IMAGE EDITING APPLICATIONS

Of course, since the Terrain Editor is a special-case image editor, you can also use other image editors (such as Photoshop) to create or alter images to use as terrains. The Picture Import option and the Pictures index cards are admissions of the fact that images created elsewhere make good terrains. Of course, you can start from scratch in the other image-editing application (as was done for the sun-baked mud cracks shown in Figure 8.49, which were created using a technique developed by Chris Casady), or you can import terrain image information and further manipulate it using additional options available elsewhere. Trivia note: If you've explored all the new fractal options, you've probably gathered that this particular Photoshop terrain-making method has been superceded by the Mud Cracks fractal style (in fact, we used an example of this fractal earlier in this chapter). But Chris Casady's mud cracks technique was the inspiration for that very fractal method!

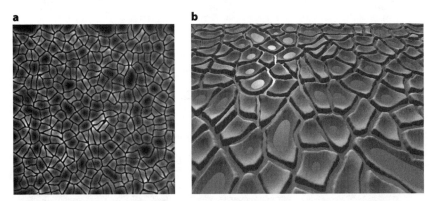

Figure 8.49 Mud-baked tiles à la Chris Casady, with the terrain created in Photoshop.

Figure 8.50 shows a series of images created by manipulating a single terrain using various Photoshop filters. More samples are also available on the CD-ROM. In previous versions of Bryce, this required going through a tedious process: copy your terrain map, paste into a new image in Photoshop, run that through a filter, paste it back into the Terrain Editor to see the results, lather, rinse, repeat. As mentioned earlier, a brand-new feature of Bryce 4 is the ability to use Photoshop filters directly within the Terrain Editor. Figure 8.51a shows the new pop-up menu through which you access these filters. Choose the item Select Plug-ins Folder to bring up an Open dialog box to tell Bryce where you keep your plug-ins, whether installed with Photoshop or another program that supports Photoshop-compatible plug-ins, like Corel Painter or Photo-Paint. Not all Photoshop-compatible plug-ins will work, however; Bryce has a "filter filtering" mechanism that allows only Bryce-friendly plug-ins to appear in the pop-up menu.

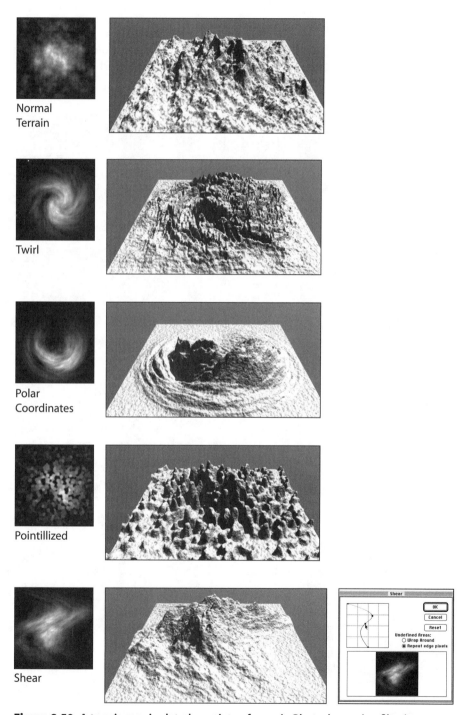

Normal
Terrain

Twirl

Polar
Coordinates

Pointillized

Shear

Figure 8.50 A terrain manipulated a variety of ways in Photoshop using filtering
techniques.

Figure 8.51 The pop-up menu on the Filtering index card that lets you use Photoshop filters directly within Bryce.

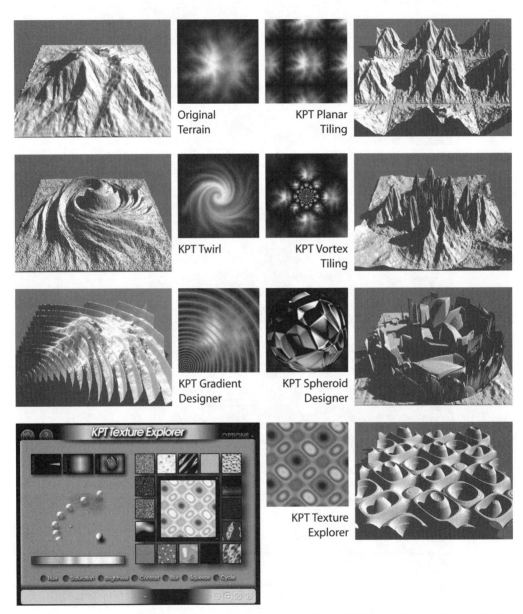

Figure 8.52 Examples of terrain effects you can achieve with the KPT filters that are included with Bryce 4.

In case you don't have one of these applications, Bryce 4 comes with a sampling of filters from Kai's Power Tools, version 3. Figure 8.52 shows examples of each of the filters, as applied to an ordinary terrain. The Gradient Designer example uses the preset Complex Gradients > Emanating ling waves, the Spheroid Designer example uses the Gold Aspheroid preset, and the Texture Explorer example uses a randomly generated texture (from the Texture Explorer dialog box).

Another idea in Photoshop is to create your own custom brushes to paint your terrains, whether they are footprints, geological phenomena, or some other wonderful invention.

Picture Terrain Tricks

Any image is game to become a terrain. Some of the more interesting (and, at times, horrifying) terrains are those created from an image source. Save the image as a PICT (Macintosh only) or as a BMP, PSD, or TIF (TIFF) file and then import it into the Terrain Editor using the Picture option. Bryce will create the terrain based on the values of the image. This works well when the image is also mapped onto the terrain as the 2D Picture texture.

When you want to make the image-as-terrain recognizable, lower the terrain's overall wireframe height in the Edit Palette. In the Terrain Editor, the Smooth button comes in handy, as sharp transitions from light to dark take on a more mellow, melted appearance.

Two sets of images in Figure 8.53 show examples of this process. The clock parts image is the basis for a terrain shape in Susan's *GlockenFondue*. It illustrates the pleasing way that images create abstract forms. And Phil Clevenger's *Necrofelinia* sets the standard for using Bryce's Terrain Editor to make sinister Mr. Hyde transformations from sweet, furry, adorable Dr. Jekyll images.

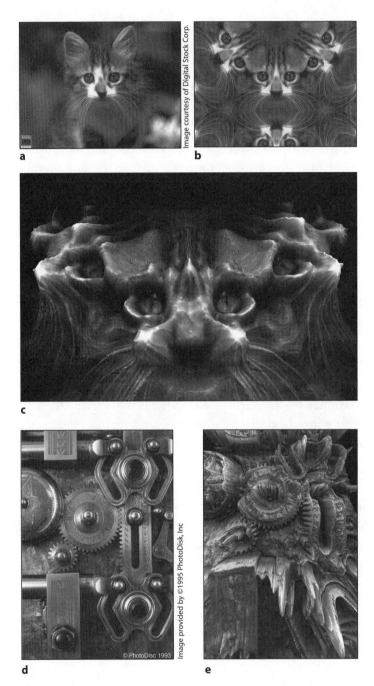

Figure 8.53 Using a picture to create a G2H map: a) Original kitty image for *Necrofelinia*; b) G2H map; c) rendered *Necrofelinia*. *Art by Phil Clevenger*. d) clock parts images for *GlockenFondue*; e) rendered *GlockenFondue*. *Art by Susan Kitchens*.

THE LOST CONTINENTS OF TEXT-LAND-IS

By now, the implications of using the Terrain Editor as a special image editor to create different heights might be working its way into your brain. Besides allowing you to exercise your mad geological creativity to make mountains, there are other things you can do—for example, create terrains out of words. Here are the basic steps and issues for creating literate land from text terrains. Use this technique with hand-lettering (Susan's personal favorite), typography, and logos. If your logo is in a PostScript format, rasterize it directly into Photoshop and take it to Bryce from there.

Susan's Text Terrain Recipe

1. Create the text itself as line art. In this case, I wrote out the words by hand with brush, ruling pen, and ink on paper and then vectorized this in Adobe Illustrator. From there I rasterized the art in Photoshop and saved it as a PICT file, but TIFF or the native Photoshop format would work as well. (In Windows, the rasterized image would be saved as a BMP file.) You can start with a scan, type created in Photoshop, or type rasterized from Illustrator. I prefer an original image that has a resolution of 512; 1024 is even better. If the resolution is 256 or smaller, you risk losing some detail in the actual letter forms.

    The terrain will be square. If your words do not fit into a square format (the likely case), pad your word/image document with empty white space to make the format square.

2. For a little flexibility in manipulating your image, create two more variations. Besides your original, create a slightly blurred and an extremely blurred version of your word or logo. Figure 8.54a shows three variations used for this text terrain.

3. Once you have all of your variations created as image files in the proper format, create a new scene file with a new terrain. In the Terrain Editor, change the resolution to 512 or 1024 and then click Picture to import your text image. (If you do not change the resolution before importing the picture, the imported image information will be interpolated down to the default resolution of 128. Ick.)

4. Now make the word more terrain-like. Notice in Figure 8.54a that as a black-on-white image, it will be initially translated to an inverted "valley" position in the Terrain Editor. For this technique, you may be doing a lot of work-then-invert, since the terrain needs to be merged with fresh source copies in order to maintain legibility.

    Invert the image so that the text is white (higher) (see Figure 8.54b). Click the Eroded button to make an eroded land mass based on the text-based information already there (see Figure 8.54c). At this point, you can continue working with the terrain for a while or try another merge in the Pictures index card area. Use any and all of your favorite tricks with the Terrain Editor.

5. When you are ready to merge the image again, you can invert it or not as you see fit. The keyboard combination, ⌘-I (Macintosh) or Ctrl+I (Windows) works the entire time you're in the Terrain Editor. Load the original image again and blend the two images together.

    The Pict Blend option actually works quite well in this situation. Choose whichever method you want to use: normal terrain (white letters on black lowlands) and Pict Blend (drag all the way to the right; see Figure 8.54d), inverted terrain and Pict Blend (drag all the way to the left; see Figure 8.54e), or inverted terrain and Minimum blend (drag to the middle to evenly weight the two).

    For this merge variation, use one of the blurred versions of the original image. The merge will beef up the terrain heights just around the edges of the word. Make your adjustments so that the text form is the most extreme value—the whitest of the whites or the blackest of the blacks, depending which of the three blend mode methods you chose.

6. Go back to the Elevation controls and continue working with the terrain. Add whatever effects you want. Beware the Mounds, Relief Noise, and Subplateaus controls, which all tend to shift the terrain's bulk to the left. If you shift too much, the land mass will be out of alignment with the text form. Figure 8.54f shows the terrain after erosion is added.

7. When you have completed the exploration process (please feel welcome to apply intermediate merges, too!), perform one last blend merge to make the text stand out from the rest of the terrain ever so slightly (see Figure 8.54g).

Why this last blend merge? It makes the word itself easily visible. Even when you have the word blurred or mostly light, any irregularities in tone will create elevation differences in the terrain that will make the word more difficult to read.

Remember—for the umpteenth time—that you're translating grayscale information to height. You may be able to read it fine in the Terrain Editor preview window, but it will be harder to read once you've rendered the terrain. After you've made the word the final flat top plateau surface, you can, of course, add a last touch of erosion for a more "natural"-looking word. The rendered result of this process is shown in Figure 8.54h.

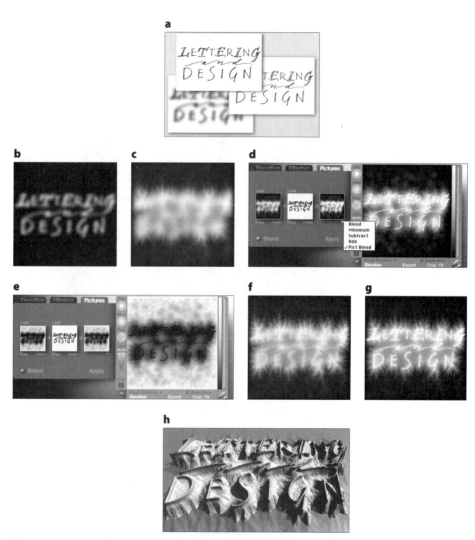

Figure 8.54 Creating text terrains: a) Three original source images; b) after importing to the Terrain Editor and inverting; c) after clicking Eroded; d) remerging with the original using Pict Blend and sliding to the right; e) and to the left; f) additional erosion; g) after merging one last time; h) completed render.

Variation—Sloping Letters

Another variation doesn't use the image processing power of the Terrain Editor beyond assigning text and gradations to a terrain. Figure 8.55 shows three different gradations on words, where the lights to darks flow in different directions, with differing results in the rendered terrain.

In Photoshop, create a document and fill it entirely with black. Create a text selection. Fill the text with a gradation. Try using gradations that run from left to right or front to back, or a radial depression. The three text gradients (with their respective G2H maps) show both. Save your terrain as a PICT (Macintosh) or BMP (Windows), TIF, or PSD file to import using the Picture control button.

Figure 8.55 Three different text-gradient graymaps and the resulting three terrains.

Beefing Up Serifs

When working with text terrains, you must take pains with serif fonts. The font shown in Figure 8.56a (Bodoni Poster) has thick portions joined together by very delicate branches. Normally, when a font like this is rasterized in Photoshop, the delicate joins show up as gray aliased transitions. This presents no problem when the text is a flat two-dimensional image; the grays help convey the shape of the letter.

However, you aren't thinking two-dimensional here when you're looking at the G2H map. (At the risk of bordering on the repetitive, "Howmanytimesdoihaftatellya?" wheeze, you'll often encounter the ingrained manner in which you rely on two-dimensional image information to perform three-dimensional optical illusions. Only after a few nasty surprises, when the terrain doesn't behave properly, do you start to see G2H maps for what they are.) In a G2H map, those delicate, slightly blurred branches between letter portions will end up at a different height. The joins *will* be there, but far below the level of the rest of the letter surface (see Figure 8.56b). Compound this by the fact that you're going to make the letter surface a variable gradient, and you've got a tricky situation. You can't simply work exclusively in the world of sans-serif type, with its more uniform widths. (We can just see that client looking over your shoulder, saying, "But I want you to use that other typeface!") So how do you navigate through *this* one?

First, adjust the word so that it will live on the same level. In Photoshop, beef up the joins and serifs. We prefer using the Burn tool (set to shadows) or the Levels command to darken the serifs, to get results similar to what is shown in Figure 8.56c. Invert the image (white text on black background). You'll need to perform both of these steps prior to adding any gradients.

To complete the process for this circular serifed type extravaganza, two circular gradients were applied using the KPT Gradient Designer. The first gradient was set lower in the image to bend the letters so that the open ends of the horseshoe were lower than the top of the circle. A second gradient was applied to make the tops of the letters higher than at the baseline (see Figure 8.56d). The text face is slightly curved as a result, and all the serifs are there (see Figure 8.56e).

Figure 8.56 Beefing up serif text: a) Original text in Illustrator; b) terrain with collapsed serifs; c) beefed up text; d) additional gradients sculpt text levels; e) final render.

ALTITUDE RENDER

Bryce's Altitude Render is a good way to create a terrain from a render of top-view objects, to create a new terrain based on objects that are already in your scene. This approach is especially good if you are trying to align several terrains in a mountain-valley formation. Alignment of the valley terrains with the mountain terrains can be tricky. This technique allows you to get the alignment close and then take a slightly different tack to get it right. Altitude Render creates a grayscale image in which grades go from black at the bottom to white at the top; so an Altitude Render from top view creates, in essence, a new G2H map of all the objects within view.

Recipe: Using Altitude Render to Create a Terrain

1. Set up a scene with multiple terrains. Make one terrain the rolling valley floor if you like.

2. From the Master Palette's Views pop-up menu, select top view.

3. In the Render Palette, select Altitude Render.

4. Render the scene.

5. From the File menu, select Save As and give this file a different name. You will open this file in Photoshop or another image-editing application to set the proper size of the file.

6. In Photoshop, open the file. Crop it into a square format. Crop out all the unnecessary image area.

7. Invert the image in Photoshop (⌘-I/Ctrl+I), if necessary. You now have your terrain map. Save the file or else copy it, making it ready to paste into Bryce's Terrain Editor.

DIGITAL ELEVATION MODELS (DEM)

To create terrains based on existing land forms, use what is called a Digital Elevation Model (DEM). DEM data files were devised by the USGS as a means of storing topographical information electronically. In the last couple of years, the USGS has introduced a new format for DEM data, which bears the less-pronounceable acronym SDTS (Spatial Data Transfer Standard). SDTS files end up being much more compact than the older-style DEM files, which is a blessing. Bryce 4 can work with both.

The DEM file is a text file describing the elevation for each point on a mesh for a map. Imagine a grid laid over an area of land. The question "What's the elevation here?" is asked at each point where a grid intersection occurs. This is called a sample.

Samples are taken for each point on the grid, resulting in a text description of the actual terrain. If you convert this DEM information to a grayscale image, where each point on the grid is represented by a pixel, you have a G2H map. The pixel color indicates the elevation, so you can build a terrain based on real data from the real world.

DEM measurements are discussed in two ways: the amount of area covered and the amount of detail for an area. For the amount of land area covered, the measurements are conveyed in terms of Earth's basic measurements: latitude and longitude. Units of latitude and longitude are expressed in degrees, then minutes, then seconds. If you see reference to a two-degree map and a 15-minute map, the 15-minute map takes in a smaller area than does a two-degree map.

The other way of discussing DEM measurement, amount of detail, is referred to as meter samples. How many meters do you travel between one elevation sample and the next? A 100-meter sample is not as detailed as a 30-meter sample, since the 30-meter sample obtained about 10 times the amount of data as the 100-meter sample did. There is a relationship between the amount of area in a DEM and the amount of detail in a DEM. For any number of data points in a DEM, questions of scale and resolution are asked: "Is this a highly detailed map of my four little acres?" "Is this a moderately detailed map that spans four big counties?" The larger the area, the less detail; the smaller the area, the more detail.

So how do you get from DEM/SDTS to Bryce? In previous versions of Bryce, you had to process the DEM file through a third-party program, which converted the numerical data into a grayscale graphic, which you could then use like any other image in the Terrain Editor. Saints (and engineers) be praised, this is no longer necessary in Bryce 4. Just use the Import Object command (under the File menu) to bring in DEMs and SDTSs directly. Because each DEM is a single (often humungous) file, loading it is relatively simple. Importing an SDTS file is a slightly more complex matter, though, because it is actually a folder full of files.

Figure 8.57a shows the Import Object dialog box in Windows. We've chosen USGS DEM/SDTS (*.DDF) as the file type we're looking for, but within this whole folder (which represents a single map) are a slew of files. Always open the file that ends with …CATD.DDF. This is the core file, which tells Bryce what other

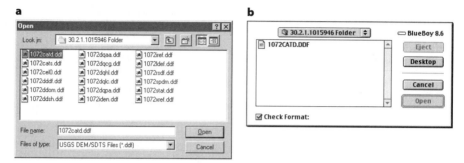

Figure 8.57 The Import Object dialog box: a) In Windows, showing all the files in an SDTS folder; b) in Mac version, with the Check Format box checked.

files to look for and what data will be found in each file. The Mac version of this dialog box is a little more user-friendly (Figure 8.57b); if you keep the Check Format box checked, it will automatically sort through the forest of files and show you the crucial one.

The SDTS file comes into your scene as a terrain object and can be edited like any other terrain object. On the CD-ROM, in the DEM INFO folder, you'll find a small sampling of DEM/SDTS data as well as information about where you can go to download more by Web surfing or Anonymous FTP from Internet sites.

The ability to take real-world topographic data into Bryce has its scientific uses for visualizing planetary surfaces at times or in places where humans cannot visit. Bryce has been used to generate models of past geology as well as models using elevation samples taken from spacecraft orbiting neighboring planets to enable earthlings to place themselves on Martian and Venusian soil and take a look around. Not only can you create any land forms you have imagined or seen in Bryce, but also you can boldly Bryce where no one has gone before.

TERRAIN EXPORT

New in Bryce 4 is the ability to export your terrains (and symmetrical lattices), complete with materials, as files that can be imported into other 3D applications. Bryce can export files in a wide variety of formats, including the native file formats of many popular 3D programs. Here's the complete list:

Extension	Format	Extension	Format
.3ds	3D Studio Max	.mts	MetaStream
.cob	TrueSpace	.obj	Wavefront OBJ
.dem	USGS (US Geological Survey)*	.pgm	Portable Gray Map*
.dxf	AutoCAD	.rds	Ray Dream Studio
.hf	RayShade Heightfield*	.vsa	VideoScape
.id4	Infini-D	.wrl	VRML 1.0
.lws/.lwo	Lightwave		

Table 8.2 3D graphics formats that can be exported from Bryce 4. The asterisk (*) indicates formats for which Bryce does not generate image maps.

For most of these formats, Bryce performs what it calls *MetaTerrain Export*—it exports the terrain as a collection of files: the physical shape of the terrain object is exported as a mesh (with no material information), and the terrain's material is exported as a set of graphics files or image maps. For some graphics file formats (those shown by an asterisk (*) in Table 8.2), Bryce performs a simpler type of export: it exports a single file containing the height information in the terrain.

How to Export a Terrain

Select a terrain. Choose Export Object from the File menu; or, if you've already got the Terrain Editor open, click the Export button; a Save dialog box appears (see Figure 8.58). Choose a file format for your exported terrain. By default, Bryce automatically inserts the name of your terrain object (from the Object Attributes dialog box) and appends the relevant suffix to your filename. If the file format you've chosen does not have "MetaTerrain Export" after its name, that's all there is to it! If it does, then after you click the Save button, the Terrain Export Lab will appear. (A MetaStream file can be exported with a material applied, but the material is not exported as a separate file, so it doesn't count as a MetaTerrain.) Choose mesh and image map options for your terrain, and click the check mark. The next sections will take you through that last step in more detail.

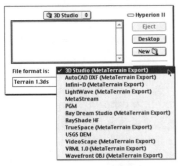

Figure 8.58 Choosing a file format for an exported terrain.

Mesh Controls

Image Map
Controls

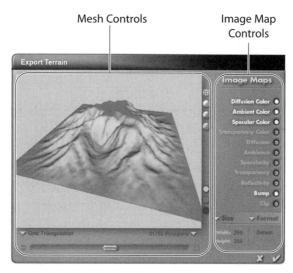

Figure 8.59 The Terrain Export Lab, showing the two
main parts of the interface.

The Terrain Export Lab

The Terrain Export lab is where you customize the file parameters for your exported terrain object (see Figure 8.59). Its interface is divided into two parts: on the left
is the terrain preview and controls for adjusting the degree of detail in the mesh in
the exported object; on the right are the controls for the image maps that are
exported along with the mesh.

The Mesh Controls

The polygonal mesh portion of the Terrain Export Lab is dominated by the
Polygonal Mesh Preview window (see Figure 8.60). The buttons that run down
the right side of the window allow you to customize the preview to your own
taste. Below the window are controls for adjusting the size and complexity of the
polygonal mesh itself. You can drag within the window to rotate the mesh preview
this way'n'that, just as in the Terrain Editor Preview. Confusingly, the key commands for modifying the dragging are not the same as those in the Terrain Editor:

• Simple drag. Rotates the terrain in place.

• Space bar-drag. Moves the terrain within the window.

• ⌘-drag/Ctrl+drag. Zooms in and out.

- ⌘-Option-drag/Ctrl+Alt+drag left and right. Adjusts the contrast of the preview.

- ⌘-Shift-drag/Ctrl+Shift+drag left and right. Adjusts the brightness of the lighting in the preview.

You have a choice of four display modes for the mesh preview, which you choose by clicking one of the buttons at the upper right edge of the window. The default display mode is Shaded (shown in Figure 8.60), which shows a rendered view of the terrain, without textures. Also available is a view of the terrain with an approximation of the material applied in the scene (Figure 8.61b). The third, Wireframe mode shows the actual polygons that will comprise the exported mesh (Figure 8.61a). Finally, the fourth button overlays the wireframe (using a different color from the simple wireframe preview) onto the textured preview (Figure 8.61c). Note: you must click the Textured mode button to produce the materials preview before clicking the Textured with Wireframe Overlay button to get the full effect. If you don't, you'll just get the wireframe overlaid on the ordinary shaded preview.

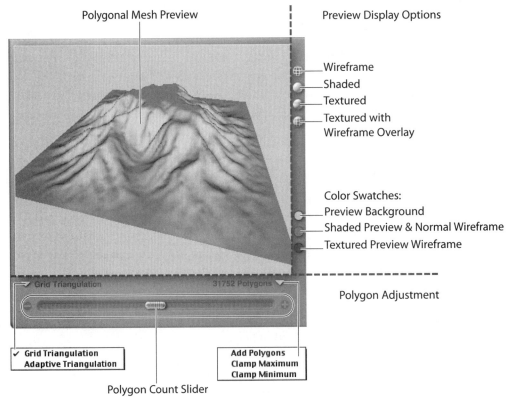

Figure 8.60 The Polygonal Mesh portion of the Terrain Export Lab.

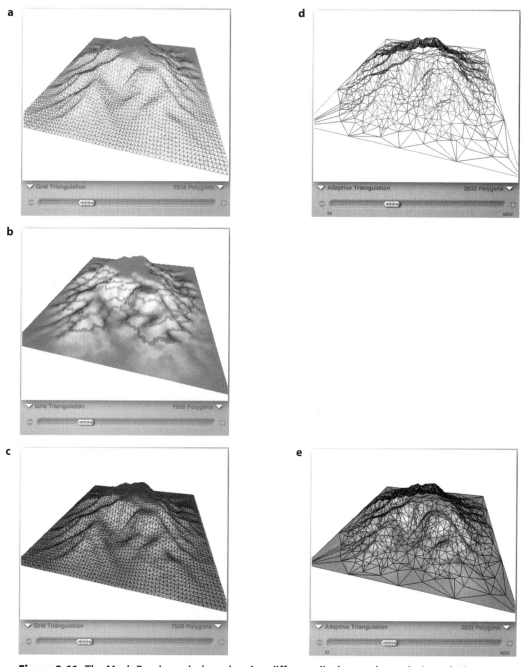

Figure 8.61 The Mesh Preview window, showing different display modes and triangulation options: The left column shows Grid Triangulation: a) Wireframe mode; b) Shaded Preview mode; c) Textured Preview mode with Wireframe Overlay. The right column shows Adaptive Triangulation: d) Wireframe mode; e) Textured Preview mode with Wireframe Overlay.

Below the display mode buttons are three color pickers. The top one chooses the background color for the preview window. The second button chooses a color that will be used for the Shaded Preview mode and for the wireframe in the simple Wireframe mode. At the bottom is the picker for the alternate Wireframe mode, used when overlaid on a Textured Preview. These pickers work like other color pickers in Bryce: drag on one and a spectrum of color choices pops up. Alas and alack, the good ol' Option/Alt+click trick doesn't work—there's no way to get to the precise (RGB, HLS, etc.) color pickers from these controls.

So much for the mesh preview. What control do we have over the mesh itself? In order to better see what's happening, we recommend switching to Wireframe view mode. You'll notice that the entire terrain is covered with equal-sized triangles (see Figure 8.61a). Bryce calls this technique of constructing a mesh *Grid Triangulation*. Beneath the lower right corner of the preview window you'll see the number of triangles Bryce has used to define the terrain. In Grid Triangulation, this number is more or less a function of the resolution of your terrain, as Table 8.3 shows:

Terrain Resolution	Number of Polygons in Mesh
16	50
32	242
64	1154
128	5000
256 and above	7938

Table 8.3 The number of polygons Bryce uses by default to describe terrains of different resolutions.

These numbers are just Bryce's defaults; you can change 'em if you need to by moving the Polygon Count Slider left or right. (The minus and plus signs at each end of the slider look like buttons, but they're just there to tell you which direction to slide for greater or smaller numbers—as if we couldn't figure that out for ourselves.) Why do we need to be concerned about the number of triangles in the mesh at all? More triangles means smaller triangles, and the smaller the triangles, the more closely the mesh can follow the details of the landform's contours. At the same time, the more triangles, the bigger your exported file will be. If your terrain is particularly convoluted and you move the slider way over to the right in hopes of capturing all of the detail, you run the risk that Bryce will bump its head on your RAM ceiling. Bryce will yell "Ouch!" (that is, give you an error message) and stop the export process.

So, finding the right balance between mesh detail and file size is a tricky business. The problem with Grid Triangulation is that as you increase the polygon count to create smaller triangles to fit the smallest details in your terrain, you generate tons of triangles in the flat and/or smooth areas where you don't need them. Fortunately, Bryce provides a way to get around this problem: use the pop-up menu at the lower left corner of the preview window to switch from Grid Triangulation to Adaptive Triangulation (the menu is illustrated in Figure 8.60). Figure 8.61d shows the results of employing Adaptive Triangulation: Bryce surveys the terrain and assigns more triangles to surfaces with lots of fine detail (like the slopes on the sides of the mesa), and fewer triangles to relatively uniform surfaces (like the flat top of the mesa and the gentle slopes at the edge of the terrain). The numbers under the lower right corner of the preview window tell the Tale of the Triangles: When Grid Triangulation was used for this terrain, Bryce generated a mesh of 7938 polygons; switching to Adaptive Triangulation slashed that number by a large percentage. Again, you can adjust the amount of detail in the mesh by means of the Polygon Count Slider. Or, you can approximately double the polygon count in one fell swoop by choosing Add Polygons from the pop-up menu at the lower right corner of the preview window (this item is only available when using Adaptive Triangulation).

There's one more set of options in the same pop-up menu: Clamp Minimum and Clamp Maximum. These are specific to one export format, MetaStream (they're grayed out for all other formats). Before we can tell you what these options do, we first have to explain a bit about the MetaStream format. MetaStream is a proprietary format, developed by MetaCreations, for interactive display of fully textured 3D content in Web browsers. "Interactive" means that the user can manipulate the model in real time, rotating it, zooming in and out, changing the display of textures and lighting, and so on. Obviously, for some detailed models, or for slow Internet connections, the user might experience sluggish performance, so the MetaStream viewer allows the user to adjust the number of polygons displayed in the model. Lowering the number helps the model to respond to the user's commands, and raising the number lets the user examine the model in greater detail. So what does all this have to do with those Clamp items? When you export the MetaStream model from Bryce you can use these options to set the range of detail in the mesh. Use the Polygon Count Slider to choose the smallest polygon count (the least amount of detail) you want the user to select, then choose the Clamp Minimum option. Move the slider to the largest polygon count (the largest file size) you want the model to contain, and choose Clamp Maximum.

Image Maps

So much for the 3-dimensional outlines of your exported object. What about its appearance? When exporting in any of the formats marked as MetaTerrains in the Save dialog box described earlier, Bryce will export information from the individual channels of the terrain's material as separate image maps, which can then be loaded into your target 3D application and applied to the terrain mesh. You choose which channels to export and set other image parameters using the right side of the Terrain Export Lab (see Figure 8.62).

We'll pause here for a moment and warn you that the next few paragraphs will sound like gibberish if

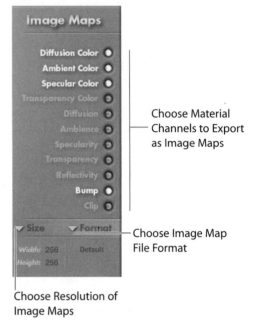

Choose Material Channels to Export as Image Maps

Choose Image Map File Format

Choose Resolution of Image Maps

Figure 8.62 The Image Maps portion of the Export Terrain Lab.

you haven't skipped ahead and read the next chapter, Chapter 9, "Material World I: Materials Lab." We just figured that if you were already at the point where you had a finished terrain ready for export, complete with materials, then you must be up to speed on that...uh...material.

The first ten items in the Image Maps portion of the Terrain Export Lab correspond to ten channels in the Materials Lab (Specular Halo, Volume Color, Metallicity, and Refraction are not included). If the material of the terrain you're exporting uses a texture to drive any of these channels (in other words, if there's a marker in column A, B, C, or D), the name of that channel will be highlighted, and the orange dot next to the channel's name will light up. By default, Bryce will export an image map for every highlighted channel, based on that channel. If you wish to export only certain channels, click the other channels' orange dots to turn them off. Their names remain highlighted to show you that they're still available for export. Figure 8.63 shows the products of the export of a terrain whose material used the same texture to drive every possible channel. We've grouped the file icons according to whether they're derived from a Color channel, a Value channel, or an Optics channel.

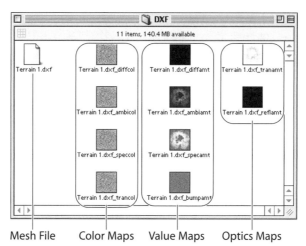

Mesh File   Color Maps   Value Maps   Optics Maps

Figure 8.63 The collection of files that results when a terrain is exported in DXF format.

The pop-up menus below the materials channel buttons allow you to set the parameters of the image map files themselves. Choose a file resolution between 64 × 64 and 4096 × 4096 from the Size menu—the default is 256 × 256, no matter what the resolution of your terrain is. If your terrain will be viewed up close and personal when it's imported into another program, you'll be happier if you choose a large resolution for the image maps. Choose a graphics file format from the Format menu. If you are exporting the terrain in a specific 3D format for import into a specific 3D application, it's best to leave this menu set to Default. Bryce will export the image maps in the format that the target 3D application expects to find. But if you're mainly interested in the image maps themselves, you can export them in almost any of the 2D graphics file formats that Bryce supports; in other words, everything listed in Table 8.1 except for .SGI, .DIB, .EMF, and .FLM.

What are these image maps? They're simply bitmapped image files, each one containing the color, or value, or bump information contributed by one channel to the material as applied to the terrain. You can open 'em up and look at 'em in an image editor like Photoshop. The Diffuse Color image map, for example, can be described this way: Imagine driving the Diffuse Color with a texture, moving the Diffusion slider to maximum (100), and setting all the other sliders to 0, then rendering the terrain. If you were somehow to shine a light from beneath the terrain so the image of the terrain was projected onto a flat surface, the result would be equivalent to the exported Diffuse Color image map.

If you are using only one texture to drive your Color channels, you can see that all the Color channels driven by that texture will produce identical image maps. The image map that is exported for Diffuse Color (to take one example) contains only the color information that was calculated for that channel—it contains none of the information that comes from the Diffusion channel, which modulates how the Diffuse Color is applied to the material. The setting of the Diffusion slider is ignored.

The maps produced for the Value and Optics channels are purely grayscale. They are the result of "mapping" the grayscale information from the Value and Bump components of the texture driving them onto the terrain.

Putting these maps together in your target 3D application to reconstruct the material your terrain had in Bryce can be challenging, and is different for every application—limitations of time and space prevent us from giving more than general outlines here. Some applications expect to find textures in a specific folder, so you must be sure to transfer the exported image maps to that folder. Other programs prefer to have all the image maps together in one place with the mesh that you're importing. After you import the terrain mesh into your 3D program, you will probably have to build a new material using the image maps. Usually you will tell the program "use *this* file for the Diffuse Color (the map whose filename ends with diffcol) and map it onto the object using *this* texture file (the map whose name ends with diffamt)," and so on for each image map you export.

Here's another limitation to keep in mind when using exported terrains and image maps: One of the wonderful things about Bryce's 3D textures is that they're procedural—that is, they're recalculated afresh every time you move the object they're applied to, or move the camera, and so on. They never get pixelated when you look at them up close, like picture textures do. Alas, you lose that feature when you export the material's components as image maps. They're fixed at a single resolution, so if your terrain will be imported into a scene where it will be part of the foreground, it would be best to set your image map resolution to a high number.

MOVING ON...

Congratulations! So far, you've learned to set up a Brycean scene, position your camera just so, and populate your scene with objects of every description. But up til now, those objects have all been dull dull dull gray. Ready for a little color in your Bryce-made world? In the next chapter, we'll show you how to clothe your objects in splendid materials.

CHAPTER NINE

Material World I: Materials Lab

IN THIS CHAPTER...

- What object surfaces are made of: illumination, optics and bump, and color
- Bryce's 14 channels for controlling surface appearance
- The Materials Lab interface and overall organization
- Texture Sources and how they drive the material channels
- Texture mapping and additional Texture Source options
- Volume materials
- Different methods for combining multiple sources into one material channel
- A deeper explanation of each part of the Materials Lab
- Discussion of some practical approaches to working in the Materials Lab

Bryce allows you to make pictures of a virtual world. To give that world a sense of reality, you have to make the objects' appearances convincing. Since you cannot leave the chair in front of your computer and jump inside your monitor to wander around that world, all of your cues and clues about what makes up that world are visual, represented on that rendered two-dimensional image. How can you tell what the objects are? What are they made of? Are they metal? Granite? Glass? Steam? Wood? Sand? Crystal? Cloud vapor? The appearance of the object provides substantial clues to the nature of the matter. The Materials Lab is where you compose the matter of your objects. (The relationship of the two words *material* and *matter* is no coincidence.) Here you blend your artistic vision with a type of mad-scientist (or is that "mat" scientist?) observation, bringing as much from the disciplines of geology, chemistry, and physics as you can muster into your crafting of the surface appearance of the Brycean objects in your world.

This chapter will unfold the concepts that comprise an object's surface material and the Materials Lab user interface controls, starting with the simple and introducing additional levels of complexity as we go along.

Instead of the exercises that we have been offering in other chapters, this chapter has lots of illustrations that show all of the Materials Lab settings. You can follow along and re-create the combinations that you see in these pages, or open the example scene files on the CD-ROM in the folder for this chapter and use them as a starting place for your own material explorations.

INTRODUCTION TO THE MATERIALS LAB

Before we discuss what the Materials Lab does, we'll review our setup. There is an object in the scene. The renderer will shoot a ray (actually, many rays) into the scene that will intersect the object. What happens at that point? What information about the object is discovered? Where does the ray go after that? It will bounce off and go somewhere—to a light source or to other objects, eventually deriving a color for that pixel.

The Materials Lab is where you determine the appearance of the object—whether surface or volume. You set properties for each object so that it has its own particular appearance. Settings in the Materials Lab determine the answers to these questions: How will the ray bounce? Will rays of certain colors be absorbed and others be reflected? Will the ray bounce directly, creating a specular highlight, or will it bounce from all directions, an indication of diffuse light? Is the object a volume, with lots of texture permutations within the object, or does the object have a hard surface? Is the object transparent, with some of the rays passing through the object to what is on the other side, or is the object reflective, bouncing the ray to that other object over there, which is reflected on the surface of the primary object? Is the object matte or shiny? What color is it? Are there patterns of colors? What are the shapes of those color patterns? Is the actual surface smooth or are there indentations?

The Materials Lab controls the sum total of the object's surface or volume properties—the way it absorbs, reflects, or transmits light, surface texture, color, small surface indentations (bumps), and volume density. More than a uniform means of coloring the object, the surface appearance may change depending on altitude, orientation, or slope (how level or upright the surface is). The Materials Lab is the place to define *every aspect* of the object's surface or volume.

When discussing how an object appears, it might be tempting to use the words *materials* and *texture* interchangeably. Don't. Each has a specific meaning; materials and texture aren't identical. Material is the *overall* appearance of the surface of an object. Texture is *a part of* the object's surface appearance. Our discussion in this chapter concerns how textures fit into the big material appearance puzzle; we reserve next chapter for the in-depth examination of the creations and editing of the textures themselves.

Surface or Volume?

Bryce's material properties are not limited to the surface only. The Materials Lab also provides access to controls for the object's volume appearance, where the object's details are not limited to its surface, but can be seen inside the body of the object. (The volume option has been available in Bryce since Bryce 3D.) The distinction between surface and volume is pretty much fixed: You cannot decide that a single object is a volume here and a surface there; it's one or the other. We'll look at surface first, since that is the more common (and more swiftly rendered) option available to you.

THE BASIC PROPERTIES

Surface. Volume. Texture as a part of a material. Color. Transparency. Reflection. There are so many things that go into the makeup of a material that it's downright overwhelming. The controls in the Materials Lab, too, are plentiful and daunting, as Figure 9.1 shows. (We've labeled only the most basic parts for now; we'll add more as we go.) Where's a person to start? We'll begin with the broadest categories of material properties and build from there with an analysis of the different elements that comprise the appearance of an object. We begin by discussing the basic properties of the surface of an object.

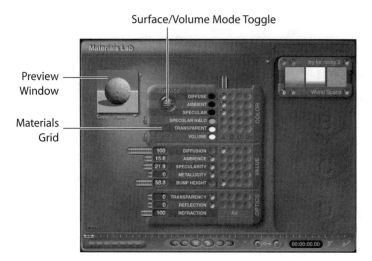

Figure 9.1 The Materials Lab.

Three Surface Properties...

So what are the most basic material properties anyhow? All the surface properties can be broken down into three categories: illumination, color, and optics (plus bump) (see Figure C9.2 in the color section). For volume objects, the basic properties are illumination, color, and volume.

In the previous version of this book (which covered Bryce 2), Susan divided the properties into three categories: illumination, optics (plus bump), and color. Since Bryce 2, the Materials Lab has been revised and the properties have been divvied up a little differently. A category called Value includes illumination and bump and metallicity (which is closely related to optics). We'll ultimately use both sets of terms here. We feel that the previous book's terms (illumination, optics plus bump, color) are still useful for understanding which does what and why, and of course, you're confronted with Bryce's divisions (color, value, optics) each time you're in the Materials Lab.

Illumination refers to the channels that determine the way that an object's surface responds to atmospheric light. Ranging from a glossy shine with bright highlights to a duller, matte surface, to self-illuminating glow, the object surface's response to lighting gives you information about what material comprises the object. The term *illumination* does not appear in the Materials Lab interface; it was coined back in Bryce 2 days, when all the object-lighting channels were placed together in a single group. Illumination is now part of the Value category in the Materials Lab.

Color is what reaches your eyes when light rays bounce off objects. In the real world, a green object absorbs all but the green rays in the light spectrum. The green light rays reach your eyes, causing you to see green.

Optics are special-case situations where the renderer's ray is divided as it hits the object's surface. If the object is reflective, then you'll be able to see the likeness of the surrounding objects and environs in the object's surface. If the object is transparent, then light rays pass through the object, and you'll see what lies behind it. Depending on the nature of the substance, the light may refract as it passes through the object. Figure 9.3 compares the most basic rendering conditions for an object's material: normal surface (no optic conditions), reflective, transparent, and volume. The hash marks along the gray ray-trace path indicate a point where a rendering sample is taken. For a surface object, there is only one such point: where the ray encounters the surface of the object. For reflective objects, there are

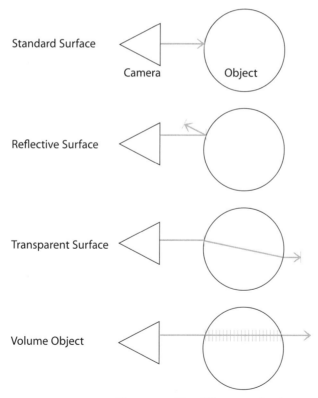

Figure 9.3 The different paths that the ray takes with standard surface, reflective surface, transparent surface, and volume objects.

two: the surface of the object and the surrounding area that is reflected by the object. For transparent objects, the renderer samples the object's surface as well as a point beyond the object (the illustration shows a bent ray, indicating that light is refracted as it travels through the object). We discuss the volume object in a bit.

There is another surface "special event" that we previously lumped together with optics: bump. (The Materials Lab now places bump in the Value category.) No matter where it lived or lives, bump works in this way: The ray encounters bump information and creates surface indentations that tell your eyes about the tactile qualities of the object's surface. The object may be nubbly or smooth, pitted, or wavy.

To recap: Surface materials have illumination, color, and optics plus bump. Bryce arranges these in the Color, Value, and Optics categories in the Materials Lab interface.

...Plus One Volume Property

When you switch from surface to volume materials by clicking the Surface/Volume toggle, the Optics and Bump items go away. They are replaced by another property. That one property, unique to volume materials, is—are you ready for this?—Volume. The Volume property is concerned with the density of an object in its interior. Is there substance in the interior of the object? Are there places where there is nothing? Or as Gertrude Stein put it, is there any *there* there? By working with the density of the object, you can essentially change the object's shape, and carve away portions of the object. Volume renders are much more time consuming. Figure 9.3, which shows the path that the rendering ray takes, shows how a volume render has multiple samplings of the object's material within the object's interior. Each little hash mark represents a sample taken. Compared to a surface object's single render sample and a surface reflective or transparent double sample, the volume multiple sample requires a far greater number of computations to come up with a color for that one pixel.

Adding 14-Channel Complexity

There is obviously more to each of the three material properties—illumination, optics plus bump, and color. Figure 9.4 shows all the different channels and the broader property categories to which they belong. Volume and Surface share much between them. Notice that non–illumination value channels disappear when Surface is changed to Volume. (This is an argument in favor of our Color,

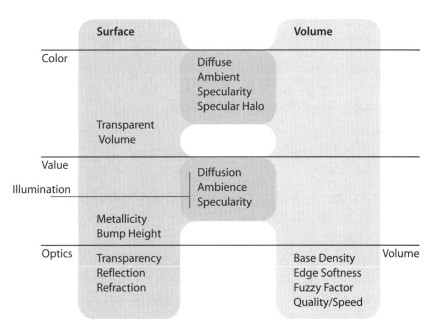

Figure 9.4 Surface and Volume materials and the material channels used by one, the other, or both.

Illumination, Optics plus Bump categories. But we won't insist on it and will use both our and Bryce's labels.)

We will first concentrate on surface materials and introduce the surface properties. Later (toward the end of this chapter), we'll introduce the volume properties.

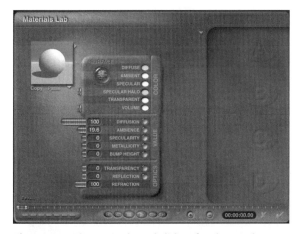

Figure 9.5 The controls and sliders for the 14 channels in the Materials Lab grid.

All the material properties are displayed in the central part—the grid—of the Materials Lab. For this discussion of the channels used by the three surface properties, Figure 9.5 shows the user interface collapsed so that only certain elements are showing. (This and other figures where the user interface is collapsed are reconstructions for illustrative purposes; don't even try to find the secret key ingredient to collapse the Materials Lab into the form you see pictured here! If you want to see the Materials Lab labeled in its entirety, see Figure 9.47.) There is a preview window, the Surface/Volume toggle, and a set of sliders and color pickers.

The top group of channels provide six different kinds of color: Diffuse, Ambient, Specular, Specular Halo, Transparent, and Volume Color. These all belong to the Color category. Each item has a color swatch.

The second group is Value. It includes the Illumination group: Diffusion, Ambience, and Specularity. Metallicity and Bump Height are also part of the Value group.

The third group is Optics. It consists of Transparency, Reflection, and Refract Index. The last two groups have sliders that extend to the left from 0 to 100.

The Bryce interface displays Color at the top based on the assumption that the first thing you want to do with an object is change its color. However, the color channels also depend on the illumination and optics. We're left with a chicken-egg problem here: Describe the color first and let you flail around trying to understand the illumination or optic property upon which the color is based, or take things slightly out of order (the method we've chosen), first introducing illumination and optics and saving color for last.

If these 14 basic channels seem confusing to you, just refer back to Figure 9.4, where you can see them grouped in their main categories: Illumination, Optics plus Bump, and Color.

About Those Sliders…

When you make adjustments with the sliders, be careful to limit your mouse movements to the horizontal level where the particular slider lives. If your mouse strays above or below, you'll end up adjusting those other sliders, too. The usual user interface standard is that once you have pressed the mouse button and started adjusting the one control, all other controls are off-limits while your mouse remains pressed. This standard is upheld throughout the rest of the application, but not here with the sliders; they're all live. One vertical drag of the mouse will leave a trail of ravaged settings in its path as you inadvertently readjust the sliders for all six channels. Happily, ⌘-Z or Ctrl+Z undoes the last move you made, so the destruction needn't be permanent.

If you prefer the direct approach, you can use the Tab key to cycle through the fields to type in your own numbers. You can even use the up and down arrow keys in combination with modifier keys (see Table 6.1) to adjust the numbers.

Value: Illumination

The value channels are mostly concerned with the illumination of your object and allow you to control the way light interacts with it. (We'll get to the other value properties later—hang tight!) Light bounces off the object and hits your eye. Or, in the ray-tracing analogy, once the ray hits the object, it bounces from the object to the light source. The three illumination channels determine how that ray will bounce and thus how the object is lit.

Diffusion

When light strikes a rough surface, it doesn't bounce in a particular direction—it scatters, bouncing away in all directions. Consequently, the surface appears matte (flat). The object is in direct light, or it is in shadow, but there is no hot highlight. Figure 9.6a shows a sphere with the maximum Diffusion setting, and Figure 9.6d shows Diffusion mixed with Ambience and Specularity.

For many of the objects created in Bryce, especially ground and terrain surfaces, a high Diffusion setting is the norm. Much of the natural world has rough surfaces, and light bounces away from a matte surface in all directions.

Figure 9.6 These spheres are in partial shadow, showing illumination in direct light and shadow: a) Maximum Diffusion; b) maximum Ambience; c) maximum Specularity; d) Diffusion mixed with Ambience and Specularity; e) Ambience mixed with Diffusion and Specularity; and f) Specularity mixed with Diffusion and Ambience illumination channels.

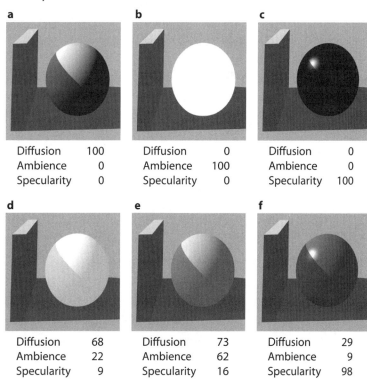

a			b			c		
Diffusion	100		Diffusion	0		Diffusion	0	
Ambience	0		Ambience	100		Ambience	0	
Specularity	0		Specularity	0		Specularity	100	

d			e			f		
Diffusion	68		Diffusion	73		Diffusion	29	
Ambience	22		Ambience	62		Ambience	9	
Specularity	9		Specularity	16		Specularity	98	

Ambience

When an object has ambience, it is self-illuminating: It resists shadows, and at the extreme end, it glows in the dark. Figure 9.6b shows a sphere with a maximum Ambience setting. Although the path from the light source is obstructed by another object, the sphere is not in shadow. When Ambience is mixed with diffuse illumination, the shadows falling on the object are not as dark and pronounced (see Figure 9.6e). Most natural objects (terrains and such) produce little to no ambient light. A low setting (Bryce's default is 50) allows you to see some surface detail for portions of the object that are in shadow.

Important note: It's crucial that the Ambience setting be consistent for most of the objects in your scene (stay tuned for exceptions). If you place one object that has a low Ambience setting next to an object that has a high Ambience setting, they will not appear natural. The edge between the two objects will seem artificial, especially when the edge is in shadow.

In cases where you want an object to be especially bright, such as snow (atop a darker, rocky surface) or a glowing object, the Ambience setting should be different. Also, when an object has a 2D Picture for its surface and you want the details of that image to be readily apparent, give the object a higher Ambience setting.

Specularity and Specular Halo

When light hits a hard, polished surface and bounces directly off it, the result is a *hot spot*, or specular highlight. Figure 9.6c shows a sphere with maximum Specularity, and Figure 9.6f shows a sphere with some Diffusion and a tad of Ambience added to the high Specularity setting. An object with a high Specularity setting appears very shiny, glossy, or wet. In its most basic form, the size of the specular hot spot is set using the Specular Halo control. Specular Halo happens to be a color control, so we'll get back to Specular Halo when we discuss color.

Optics and Bump

The optics channels control special case situations when the object's surface is something other than basic opaque. The optics channels allow you to determine whether light passes through or reflects off the object. Reflection, in this case, is mirroring, not diffuse illumination's scattering reaction to direct light sources. Reflection and Transparency each determine the manner and amount in which the renderer's ray is split—the ray is traced to the object itself, and the ray is traced *through* to the other side or *mirrored* to the surrounding area for additional information to calculate the image of the object in the scene. Naturally, adding more complexity by splitting light rays means a longer render time, since more calculations must be made to chase down those rays to their sources.

We consider the Optic properties a little out of order from the way they're listed on the Materials Lab interface, since Reflection stands alone, and Transparency and Refract Index go together.

Reflection

In the case of Reflection, the ray will bounce off the object to other surrounding objects—and the light source—in the scene. The Reflection slider determines to what extent the object reflects light. The slider is weighted: Low Reflection results in little reflected surroundings in the object's surface, and high Reflection results in more reflected surrounding area than object surface. Those rays of light bounce off that reflective surface and go elsewhere, to another surface. Of course if that other reflected surface is an object that also has a lot of complexity, then the renderer will take its sweet time calculating all that detail. If that object is also reflective, then the "bounce rays into surrounding areas" process begins all over again. The maximum number of reflective bounces is six; after, that the reflection is black.

Unlike in a real world, where light rays can travel infinitely down a "hall of mirrors," Bryce would be brought to its knees by infinite recursion. You'd never see any render progress! Figure 9.7 is set up as an infinite hall of mirrors, as two reflective surfaces face one another. At the sixth reflection, the object turns black. Water, mirrors, and metals are reflective. Adjust to taste.

Figure 9.7 Bryce's six-reflection limit.

Transparency

With Transparency, one part of the ray will be traced through the object to what lies on the other side (and, further, if there is refraction, the ray will be bent as it bounces). The other part will bounce off the object until it reaches the light source. How much light passes through the object? The Transparency slider determines that amount, balancing the strength of "the surface" information with the "on the other side" information. A low Transparency setting casts the weight toward the information about the surface, while a high Transparency setting will swing the weight to the other side, with more of the objects beyond showing through.

Of course, once the light passes through the object, the question arises: "Do the light rays bend as they pass through?" That's where the Refract Index comes in.

Refract Index

The Refract Index determines how much light bends as it passes through an object. By adjusting the number scale, you can suggest what the transparent object is composed of. In the real world, different types of physical matter refract light differently depending on their molecular structure and other physical and chemical properties. In this virtual 3D world that you're creating, you get to play molecular physicist by tweaking the numbers. Want air? Set the Refract Index to 100. Want water? Set it to 133. How about glass? Take it on up to 152. The higher the number, the more light bends. You'll reach a point where the world turns upside down through your refracted object. (This is especially true of spheres.) If you want to play virtual mineralogist, check out a paper written by Linda Ewing (a geologist, of course!) about the refraction index for different gem and mineral substances. It's on the CD-ROM in the Tips folder.

Changes in refraction can be quite dramatic taken in the small increments. The Refract Index is a control to use with subtlety. Also, despite the Refract Index given for certain materials, there may be times when you want to cheat a little and have a lower refraction rate in the interest of allowing the viewer to see more easily through the object.

Figure 9.8 shows a sphere at different Refract Index settings. The Refract Index for these spheres changes by a factor of 5. The neutral Refract Index is 100; it's the same as for air. As the Refract Index moves up, the world turns upside down. When the Refract Index goes below 100, light bends and behaves as it does when passing through a concave lens (think of glasses for nearsightedness).

Figure 9.8 Refract Index settings.

With judicious use of refraction, a couple of intrepid Bryce users have set up telescopes to take advantage of the laws of physics inside their ray-traced worlds! Whatever you do, don't create a magnifying glass through which to focus the sun, so that you burn holes in your Brycean ground. No screen saver will help in that case!

Additionally, if the only optic property you have in your material is transparency and your object does refract slightly, then you'll see a slight reflection at the edges, where light rays bounce off of the object at an oh-so-slight angle. This is one of the qualities that makes Bryce so prettily glassy eyed.

Bryce handles transparency in two different ways, each dealing with the way Bryce behaves when the Refract Index is set to 100. The control to switch between the two lives in the Material Options pop-up menu; we'll go into the details when we get to this menu.

Combining Reflection and Transparency

You can, of course, make your object have both transparency and reflection. If your object has both, you'll need to watch out that the object does not get too bright. Combining both Transparency and Reflection settings will make the object appear brighter, since more light will reach the camera from the object (see Figure 9.9). When the object reflects, the surrounding light bounces toward the camera. When it's transparent, light passes through, so you see light from the other side and also light from everywhere else. If your object is a primitive with an enclosed shape, such as a sphere, there may be additional reflection as light bounces around inside.

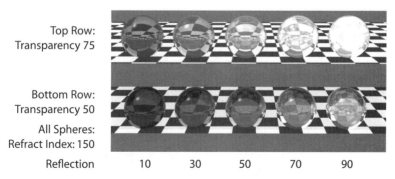

Top Row:
Transparency 75

Bottom Row:
Transparency 50

All Spheres:
Refract Index: 150

Reflection   10   30   50   70   90

Figure 9.9 Combining reflectivity and transparency makes the object brighter—more light comes from the object to the camera.

For an object with high Transparency and Reflection settings, make sure Diffusion is set to 0. If you don't want the object to be too bright, make sure that the sum of Transparency plus Reflection does not exceed 125. (Technically, to emulate the real world, the threshold cutoff is a sum of 100, but the level of brightness can still be acceptable until the sum reaches 125 or so.) Figure 9.10 shows sets of spheres with sums of Transparency and Reflection ranging from 88 to 142. Each row of images uses a different approach to reach the sum: for example, using 50:50, 60:40, and 70:30 ratios of Reflection and Transparency.

Other Value

We return again to the Value category to cover two more of the material channels.

Metallicity

Metallicity is a modifier of optics and color. It modifies Reflection by mixing in color. Bryce places Metallicity in the Value category, though since it modifies an

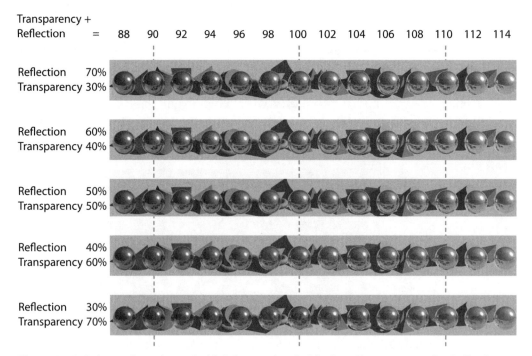

Figure 9.10 Spheres along the optical brightness threshold, where Transparency plus Reflection ranges from 88 to 142.

optic category, we place it with optics. When your object is reflective, Metallicity will make the object reflect some color as well. Copper, gold, bronze, and brass not only reflect the environs, but take on the object's particular color. Since Metallicity works with Diffuse Color, we discuss it in more depth as part of our exploration of Diffuse Color.

Bump Height

Bump Height is another hard-to-classify material channel because it, too, is not a normal-basic-opaque surface. To convey the impression that the surface has tactile texture, the Bump Height channel tells the renderer to create an optical illusion. But Bump Height doesn't split the ray during rendering so much as add a depth dimension to the object's surface. Mostly, Bump Height is in the Value category because it doesn't easily fit anywhere else.

Also, although Bryce places Bump Height in the Value category, the information governing Bump Height does not come from the value (alpha) portion of a texture. It comes from the bump portion.

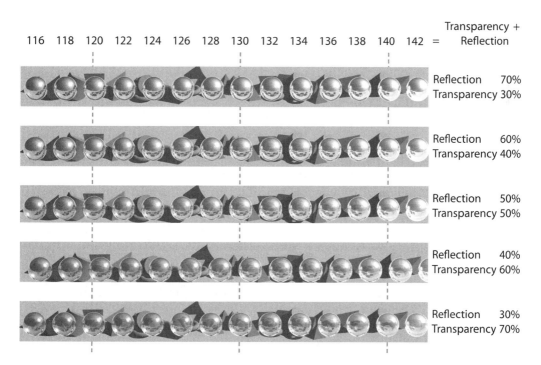

Like the optics, Bump Height can be render intensive. Since Bump Height *requires* texture information to wield its effect, and since we've not yet talked about Texture Sources, that's all we'll say of Bump Height for the moment.

Color

The color channels determine how an object's surface will be colored. What color bounces off the object and to your eyes? The color channels echo the illumination channels, with some additions: Diffuse Color is tied to Diffusion (diffuse illumination). Ambient Color is tied to Ambience. Specular Color and Specular Halo are tied to Specularity. Transparent Color is tied to Transparency.

First, you activate or adjust the type of illumination, and then you determine the color for that illumination channel. The colors you set for your object in the color channels depend on the amount of illumination for that corresponding channel. If you wanted to have, say, shocking pink ambient color but the Ambience slider is set to 0, then you won't see any shocking pink, since the object is not responding to ambient lighting at all.

Before discussing the different individual color channels, let's discuss the Bryce color picker.

The Bryce Color Pickers

There are three types of color picker in Bryce. The first is the pop-up color picker. Press the mouse on any of the color swatch areas in the Materials Lab (as well as in the Deep Texture Editor, on the Sky & Fog Palette, in the Sky Lab, and in the Edit Lights dialog box, all introduced in subsequent chapters), and up it pops. Drag to your desired color and release. The left half is a fully saturated spectrum, and the right half is a desaturated spectrum, very handy for more subdued coloring in nature scenery. Beneath both color spectrums is a strip of gray tones, ranging from black to nearly white.

To access the second color picker, hold down the Option key (Macintosh) or Alt key (Windows) and click again on the color swatch. This one adjusts with sliders and gives you a choice of four different color models: Red Green Blue (RGB), Hue Luminance (Lightness) Saturation (HLS), Hue Saturation Value (HSV), and Cyan Magenta Yellow (CMY). For Brycean color subtlety, we like the HLS and HSV pickers, and of those, we prefer the HLS (see Figure 9.11a).

Figure 9.11 Desaturating light colors: a) Original saturated color; b) pulling back saturation; c) increasing lightness.

Drag the Saturation (S) slider to pull the saturation back so that the color is more gray (see Figure 9.11b). With dark colors, that's probably all that is needed. With lighter colors, desaturating the color will make it darker, and you may need to bring up the Lightness (L) value to get back in the same general range (see Figure 9.11c).

You may continue to go color shopping at this point if you like. Once you find an acceptable level of saturation and lightness, drag the Hue (H) slider to find a different hue in the same general range.

For those who are CMYK oriented, the CMY color picker is not a CMYK picker with a missing K. It is the complementary side of the RGB picker. Red's complement is cyan, green's is magenta, and blue's is yellow. Select a color and look at it with the RGB slider and then the CMY slider. They're opposite. The sliders are flipped end to end. If there's a color that will be outside of the CMYK gamut by RGB standards, it will also be outside the CMYK gamut in the CMY color picker.

The third color picker, should the first two be insufficient for your needs, is the color picker that is supplied with your computer's operating system. The key combinations for it are Control-Option (Macintosh) or Ctrl+Alt (Windows).

Color Picker Gripe

When using the pop-up color picker, you can also select a color from anywhere on your screen, assuming that you can get out of the Materials Lab to do so (this is easier if you have a two-monitor setup, or when selecting colors from swatches available elsewhere in Bryce). The Materials Lab is a separate room, so you're cut off from anything else on the Mac. Although the color picker—in theory—allows you to select a color from anywhere, you cannot select from anything other than the Materials Lab interface. Alas, the only way you can get pure white is by using one of the other white swatches (if you have the default settings) or by Option-clicking/Alt+clicking the color swatch and entering numbers for white. Amazingly enough, the pop-up color picker does not have absolute white (255); the nearest it gets is 253 or 254.

Diffuse and Ambient Color

Diffuse Color is the color of an object when it is lit by diffuse light. This is the color of the object when it is directly lit. Ambient Color is the overall color, but primarily the color that you see when the object is in shadow. These two colors, as a rule, are the same when you want your object to be uniformly colored. However, you needn't limit yourself to making Diffuse and Ambient Color identical. Setting different colors makes an interesting color shift, much like In a fabric weave that shifts between two colors. Figure C9.12 shows a set of objects with illumination settings of Diffuse 100 and Ambient 31.3, but different settings for Diffuse and Ambient Color. The colors are mixes and matches of blue, pink, and white. The most brilliant pure colors are the objects with identical Diffuse and Ambient Color settings. The outside objects are Diffuse Color, and Ambient is white. The center two objects are a mix of Diffuse and Ambient.

When you use two different colors, a darker Ambient Color setting will give the object more contrast. When the Ambient Color setting is lighter, the object looks washed out and flatter—as opposed to strikingly dimensional. (You'll revisit the advantages of a darker Ambient Color when you adorn your entire environment in the Sky & Fog Palette settings, in Chapter 11.) Figure C9.13 shows sets of objects whose Ambient Color settings range in the grayscale, for objects with a blue Diffuse Color and objects with the default gray Diffuse Color. The outside set of objects has an Ambient Color setting of white. The Ambient Color gets darker for the objects located closer to the center.

Diffuse Color and Metallicity

Recall our earlier discussion about Metallicity. Metallicity is the control that enables you to give reflective objects a color cast that conveys what the metallic substance is—gold, brass, bronze, copper. Metallicity works in conjunction with two other controls in the Materials Lab: Reflection and Diffuse Color. Metallicity acts as a filter controlling how much of the Diffuse Color is included in the reflection. At zero, no Diffuse Color is cast through the reflection, so the reflection is like a mirror. A maximum setting provides the strongest color cast by the Diffuse Color. When Metallicity is active, it doesn't matter whether there is any setting for the Diffusion illumination channel; Diffuse Color will still be seen through the reflection. (This is similar to the way that Diffuse Color is seen in an object with Transparency when the Refract Index causes the two colors to interact.) Figure C9.14 demonstrates the range of Metallicity. There are two rows; the bottom row has some diffuse illumination in addition to maximum Reflection; the top row has no diffuse illumination. The range of Metallicity settings is shown. The objects on the left have no Metallicity, so the reflections are mirrorlike. The objects on the right have maximum Metallicity, and so the reflection takes on a gold cast.

Specular Color (and Specular Halo)

The Specular hot spot's color is not the object's color so much as the color of the light that strikes the object. Specular Color is the color of the light, and the Specular Halo color acts to control both the size and the color of the specular highlight. We'll first consider Specular Halo as the item that determines the size of the hot spot.

Specular Halo and Hot Spot Size

A black or dark Specular Halo color will make a small, pinpointed highlight, and a very light color gray-to-white will make a very large highlight. It's probably most helpful to understand Specular Halo color from the color's numerical settings. Getting into the numeric nitty-gritty of RGB color, the numbers for red, green, and blue range from 0 to 255. When all three numbers are identical, the result is a shade of gray. We'll use a shortcut and provide only one number (although in reality, all three are used and are set the same): 0 is black and 255 is brilliant white. For these precision settings of Specular Halo, we use the Option-click/Alt+click method to use the alternate color picker (the one with numbers).

Figure 9.15 shows three spheres with three different Specular Halo settings for otherwise identically illuminated objects. The small highlight has a Specular Halo setting of 0; the large highlight has a Specular Halo setting of 250, just shy of the maximum. The size of the highlight changes (note how 205 is seemingly closer to zero than 250). In Figure 9.16, the nuances of the maximum are shown with every setting from 255 down to 246. Obviously, a Specular Halo setting of 255 is brilliant, with maximum illumination on the entire

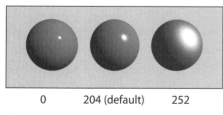

| 0 | 204 (default) | 252 |

Figure 9.15 The setting for Specular Halo changes the size of the specular hot spot.

| 246 | 247 | 248 | 249 | 250 | 251 | 252 | 253 | 254 | 255 |

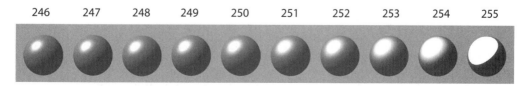

Figure 9.16 A detailed examination of the high end of the Specular Halo. The sharp border is visible above 249 or 250 or so.

hemisphere of the object that faces the sun and/or light sources. Just below maximum is a level we call "pretty dang bright," where the crisp edge of light is distinguished from shadow. As the setting moves down into the high 240s, the crisp edge disappears. The high 240s and low 250s are acceptable for bright highlights if you want to avoid that crisp line. If you've ever wondered why the bright line is on some of your objects, now you know. Crank down the Specular Halo a tad.

Having divulged how Specular Halo alters the size of the hot spot, we'll move on to Specular Color itself. We'll come back in a bit to discuss Specular Halo for colors other than shades of gray.

Specular Color Interactions

Specular Color conveys the color of the light source bouncing off the object. Of course, depending on the nature of the surface you are trying to create, Specular Color adds a nuance of surface texture, polish, or sheen. In Figure C9.17, the brightly polished objects have high specular sheens or gloss that suggests either wetness or shellac. Adding a touch of Reflection heightens the effect.

In addition, Specular Color and Specular Halo interact to determine the size and color of the hot spot. The colors are combined, and, depending on the specific colors, one may augment, complement, or counteract the other. Diffuse and Ambient Color settings also play parts in the interaction.

To understand the color interaction dynamics of the Specular Halo and the object, it helps to understand additive (RGB) color theory. (Yes, not only do we insist that you become familiar with the 0 to 255 numbering, but now we urge you to understand what it all *means*. The nerve!) The sum of all colors is white. Earlier you saw that if Specular Halo is set too high, you get a bright white highlight with a crisp border between "lit" and "unlit" areas. So how can you get a nice strong white without that harsh border? Use the complementary color. In Figure C9.18, top row, Diffuse and Ambient Color are set to red. There are different Specular Halo settings for the objects. The left two are gray shades. The center two are cyan shades. The right two are the other RGB complements: yellow and magenta. But those center two don't show any cyan at all; they appear to be a nice, bright white. Why? Red plus cyan equals white! This is a way to tiptoe around the "if it's too bright, you'll get a harsh border" situation. Notice that the halo around the two objects on the right contains a more intense red. That is because yellow is red plus green, and magenta is red plus blue. The red resulting from the Diffuse and Ambient Color settings is intensified by the red in the yellow and magenta.

The middle and bottom rows of Figure C9.18 are variations on the top row. The Specular settings (both Specular Color and Specular Halo) are identical, but the middle row's Ambient Color is white, and the bottom row's Diffuse Color is white. When the Specular Halo is not the exact complement of the Diffuse Color and Ambient Color, you can see a bit of the Specular Halo color. Notice the center two objects in the bottom two rows. Because white is either the Diffuse Color or Ambient Color, you can notice an ever-so-slight tint of cyan.

The same extreme highlight as the white is generated when one or two of the RGB values exceeds the 254 threshold (see Figure C9.19a).

In the same way that the Specular Halo interacts with Diffuse Color and Ambient Color, the Specular Halo color and the Specular Color also interact. In Figure C9.19b, an object with a blue Specular Halo interacts with a "neighbor" Specular Color, cyan (cyan is the combination of blue and green). The entire intensity range of that cyan hue is shown. Conversely, Figure C9.19c demonstrates the interaction of the blue Specular Halo with its complement, yellow. As the intensity of the yellow Specular hue decreases, the combination of both colors sucks any hue out of the Specular Halo.

Transparent Color

Transparent Color is the color of light that passes through an object. Transparent Color is applied to an object when the Transparency channel is active. The higher the Transparency setting, the more you will see the Transparent Color. Not only does the Transparent Color affect the color of the transparent object, but the shadow that is cast by the transparent object will be the Transparent Color. (The Sky & Fog Palette setting for Global Shadows determines the strength of the transparent shadow.)

Transparent Color does not operate on its own. As already mentioned, it is tied to the Transparency setting. In addition, Transparent Color is also tied to the Refract Index setting. The Diffuse Color is also incorporated into the object's color, *even if there is no Diffusion setting!* The manner in which Diffuse Color is applied to the object depends both on the Refract Index setting and whether or not you also have a distinct Volume color.

Transparent Color will always have an effect on the object's color, as long as the Transparency setting is something other than 0. The mix of Transparent Color to Diffuse Color changes depending on the Refract Index.

When the Refract Index setting is above 100, the Transparent Color and Diffuse Color combine to form a new color. Figures C9.20a and b shows several sets of transparent spheres. You can always tell what the Transparent Color is, since that is the color of the shadow cast by the object. The same Diffuse Color is used for the entire row of objects. The object at the right end of the row is the Diffuse Color only—the Transparent Color is white—so use the sphere at the right to evaluate all the other color interactions for that row.

For Diffuse and Transparent Color, complementary colors combine to make the object darker. In Figure C9.20a, where there is a row each of red, blue, and green, three of the color variations are extremely dark. The dark spheres combine two primary colors (red and blue, for example) or a primary with a secondary color that is itself the combination of the other two primaries (for example, green with magenta, which is produced by combining red and blue). Check out the top row of Figure C9.20. The Diffuse Color of each of these spheres is red. The dark spheres in that row combine the red with Transparent Colors of green and blue (second and fourth from the left, respectively) and the secondary color, cyan (third from the left). Cyan is composed of green and blue and is also the complement to red. Notice that the front row's Diffuse Color is a pleasant mocha brown, a color that liberally mixes each of the primaries. There is no complementary cancellation, so all six Transparent Colors interact with the Diffuse Color in a pleasing way. Figure C9.20b is a similar set of spheres, only the Diffuse Colors are more of the secondary range—orange, aqua, and purple (which are, respectively, composed of lots of yellow, cyan, and magenta).

Bryce modulates the Transparent Color and the Diffuse Color depending on the Refract Index setting. Figure C9.21 shows a series of objects with the Refract Index settings indicated. The Transparent Color (yellow) is present when the Refract Index is set to 0. As the Refract Index increases, the two colors are mixed together as the Diffuse Color (magenta) gains in strength. The Refract Index is related to the density of the substance—the higher the Refract Index number, the greater the density. A substance with a high density slows down light passing through the object, and the high Refract Index means that when that light reaches the object's surface, much of it is reflected back into the object. The result is a greater visibility of the Diffuse Color.

Volume Color

Bryce's surface objects are hollow in the sense that once you place yourself inside an object, you are located within the contained space that is bordered by the outer surface skin of the object's geometry. What's it like within the object's interior? Volume Color is the material channel by which you determine the interior color of an object.

Volume Color is important under two conditions: when you're inside an object, and when an object is placed inside another transparent object. Object transparency is optional: When you're inside an object and there's a light source, you have a self-contained world. Think of Volume Color as a special-case Ambient Color that exists only inside of that object.

We set up an example to illustrate how Volume Color works. Figure C9.22 shows an object, a transparent sphere, with a pyramid and torus inside. For each state, there are two views: one from within the object, and the other looking at the object from the outside. (We also included the color settings for the sphere's material.) The sphere's green color is set by Diffuse Color. The objects within the sphere, the pyramid and torus, are white. Looking from the outside, you can see at the bottom that a teeny part of the pyramid pokes out of the sphere. That part is white, no matter what color the objects appear to be when you look at them from inside the sphere.

Since a transparent object is also affected by Transparent Color, how can you know how much of an effect Transparent and Volume Color have? We'll look at both colors. In the first example, the Transparent Color and Volume Color of the sphere are both white. The shadow cast by the sphere is white, too. In the second example, both the Volume Color and Transparent Color are yellow. Notice how the sphere's shadow is yellow—this comes mostly from the Transparent Color setting, as we'll see momentarily—and from inside the sphere, the pyramid and torus are a bright, saturated yellow.

On the bottom row, we tease out the difference between the Transparent Color and Volume Color. In the left example, the Volume Color is blue, and the Transparent Color is white. The sphere's shadow is a pale blue, but the interior color is a vivid blue. Volume Color strongly affects the color of objects within the object, but only minimally affects the shadow cast by the object. The example on the right is the opposite situation: a white Volume Color and a blue Transparent Color. The shadow cast is much stronger than the color of the objects within, which is affected only slightly by the transparent color.

The Volume or Transparent Color also slightly affects the green of the sphere. Compare the background green colors of all four examples, especially with the upper left (white Volume or Transparent Color). The green is slightly warmer with the yellow and slightly cooler with the blues. Both of the mixing colors are fairly light in value. When colors are deeper or move toward the complement of the diffuse color, the mixed color gets stronger and perhaps stranger. If you want a smoky-colored sphere rather than going for one that is a straight gray, add interest to it by working with complementary colors.

> **TIP:** Create underwater effects by using a Volume slab, assigning an appropriately aquatic Volume Color, and placing your camera within the slab.

NON-UNIFORM APPEARANCE: TEXTURES

So far, everything we've said has concerned an object with a uniform surface appearance. How do you get from uniform to non-uniform, where much of the power of the Materials Lab lies? You use the grid in a slightly more unfolded form (see Figure 9.23). This expanded grid includes an A column. To the right, the area marked A is now filled with a box. The box with three windows is the Texture Source. To make the Texture Source box appear, click anywhere in the A column of the Materials Lab grid. (Our favorite place to click in the A column is in the Diffuse Color row.) A marker appears where you clicked, and a Texture Source appears at the top right, with a randomly assigned texture. No doubt you've noticed that there's room for a total of four Texture Sources, but in this unfolding explanation of the Materials Lab, we'll focus on the first one.

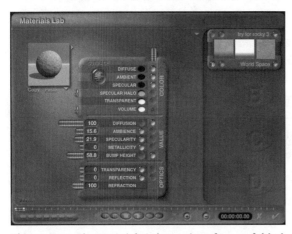

Figure 9.23 The Materials Lab user interface, unfolded a step to show the grid for column A as well as Texture Source A.

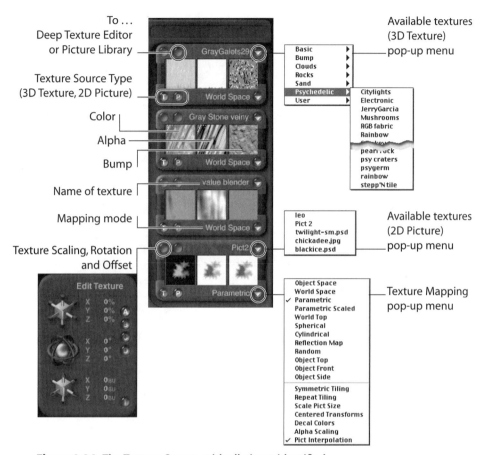

Figure 9.24 The Texture Source, with all pieces identified.

The Texture Source: An Introduction

The Texture Source allows you to select a texture to drive some or all channels of your surface material. Figure 9.24 shows four different Texture Sources occupying the Texture Source area; we'll describe the features common to all of them. Each Texture Source contains several parts. There are buttons, pop-up menus, and three windows. The buttons on the lower left of each Texture Source, marked T and P, are for choosing the texture type: T for 3D Texture and P for 2D Picture. The 2D Picture source uses images from the Picture Library, and the 3D Texture Source uses textures created by Bryce's powerful Deep Texture Editor. We'll get to the other buttons after we discuss the three windows.

The three windows show the three properties of the texture. The left is color, the center is alpha (or value), and the right is bump. These three texture properties are used in the different material channels to drive the amounts or colors using the non-uniform aspects of the texture. Figure 9.25 shows which Texture Source properties provide the information for which channel. The illumination and optics channels are driven by the texture's alpha information, Bump Height is driven by the texture's bump, and the color channel is driven by the texture's color.

Textures created in Bryce's 3D Deep Texture Editor have three possible output types, which correspond to the three texture properties: color, alpha, and bump. (Alpha is sometimes referred to as value.) The 2D Picture textures have both color and an alpha channel; alpha is used for both alpha and bump information. (You may want, then, to duplicate your picture source if you require different alpha and bump information for a given texture.)

In the top section of the window, the name of the current texture is displayed. The button to the right of the name has a triangle on it; pressing the mouse on the button elicits a pop-up menu from which you can choose all the available textures. If 3D Texture is selected, then the pop-up menu will list all of the possible 3D Texture Sources. If 2D Picture is selected, then the pop-up menu will list all the available pictures from the Picture Library.

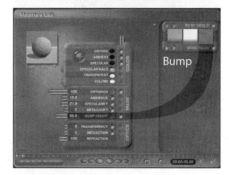

Figure 9.25 Three texture properties—color, alpha, and bump—supply the information to the color, illumination and optics, and Bump Height channels of the texture.

There is another way to select from the available textures if you're working with a 3D Texture. This second method allows you to choose from visual previews. (Undocumented feature alert!) Point your mouse at the texture name. Hold down

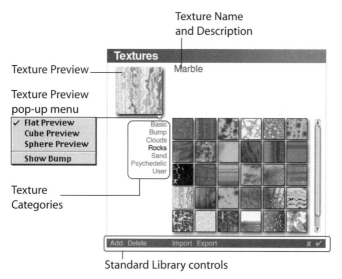

Figure 9.26 The Texture Library, accessed by pressing the Shift key while clicking the texture name in one of the Texture Sources or while clicking the combination in the Deep Texture Editor.

the Shift key and press the mouse. The Texture Library appears (see Figure 9.26). You can search for a texture by picture, or you can save the current texture that is displayed in the Texture Source. (You can access this same Texture Library in the Deep Texture Editor as well. See the next chapter, "Material World II: Picture Textures and the Deep Texture Editor," for more about the Deep Texture Editor.)

Texture Mapping

In the bottom frame of the Texture Source, the current mapping mode is displayed. To the right of the mapping mode is another triangle-clad button. It, too, connects to a pop-up menu. From the top portion of the menu, you can select from the available mapping options. Mapping answers the question, "How will this texture be applied to my object?"

For 3D Solid Textures, the default answer is in World Space.

In World Space, the texture has an orientation in the world. Any object that uses the texture—no matter what its position, rotation, or elevation—will take on the texture for that coordinate in the world. Move the object, and the object's texture will change to reflect what the texture is like in that other part of the world. This explains why Bryce provides seamless textural transitions between the ground plane and the terrain that rests on the ground. They both use the same texture in

a

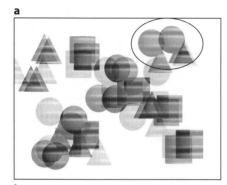

b

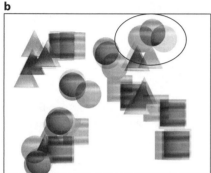

Figure 9.27 Mapping spaces: a) The surfaces of objects mapped to World Space change when the objects are moved; b) the surfaces of objects mapped to Object Space do not change when the objects are moved.

World Space. (It also explains why your objects change when they move when you are attempting to animate in Bryce.) The objects in Figure 9.27a are all mapped with World Space using the Sine Layers texture. Notice how the stripe changes as the objects are higher or lower in elevation. There are ghost images of the objects as they are moved around in the World Space. The texture belongs to the world, and the object's surface changes as its position in the world changes. Also check out the movie called WORLD-OBJECT SPACE.MOV on the CD-ROM in this chapter's folder.

In contrast, the same set of objects mapped in Object Space will display the texture the same way no matter what the position, as Figure 9.27b shows (with the same ghosted moved images, for comparison).

A corollary to World Space is World Space Top. This reorients the direction of the overall space. It comes in handy in cases where a perfectly decent texture is oriented toward the "front" in World Space, so that a flat surface, like a ground plane, has only variegated stripes. In Figure 9.28a, a set of objects facing in all directions has had the Mushrooms texture applied to it in the standard World Space mapping. Notice how the "front" has the full benefit of the texture, but on flat horizontal surfaces, all you see are stripes. Figure 9.28b shows the same texture mapped to World Space Top, which reorients World Space from Front to Top, making the texture visible on horizontal flat surfaces. Make World Space Top your first recourse when you find a great texture for your ground plane, but the texture turns out to look like an incomprehensible set of lines.

The answer to the "How will this texture be applied to my object?" question for 2D Picture textures is using *parametric mapping*. Parametric mapping is proportional to the object. Figure C9.29 shows a set of Bryce objects with a Picture texture mapped to them. The picture is different at the top, bottom, left, and right, so that the mapping approach is clear for all the different objects. If the object gets larger, the picture is enlarged as well.

a b

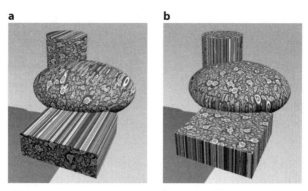

Figure 9.28 A texture mapped in a) World Space and b) World Space Top.

In the list of options in the Mapping pop-up menu, no doubt you notice some old friends: World Space and Object Space. (No, there is no such thing as mapping a texture onto an object based on Camera Space!) Are these identical to the World and Object Spaces of the Edit Palette? Well, no and yes. They are similar in that World Space is oriented according to the Bryce world, and Object Space is oriented to the object. They are not, however, sensitive to the option selected in the Edit Palette pop-up menus.

Also located below the divider line in the bottom half of the Mapping menu are a hodgepodge of useful texture options. We'll revisit them two more times in this chapter, in the context of our unfolding discussion. The Alpha Scaling option comes at the conclusion of this Non-Uniform Texture section. The options that manipulate 2D Pictures comes toward the end of the chapter, when we discuss 2D Picture textures further.

In the meantime, we'll continue discussing how Texture Sources are used to drive material channels. For our explanation and demonstration, we will draw primarily from a set of twelve 3D Texture Sources. Each one is quite distinct in color and value. Figure C9.30 shows them with their three properties and provides the names so that you may follow along and match the examples you see in these images.

Texture-Driven Illumination

You've met the various material channels. You've met the Texture Source, with color, alpha, and bump. It's now time to combine them. Yippee! This is where the Materials Lab starts to get fun.

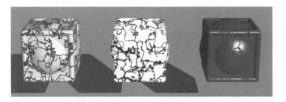

Texture Source Alpha

Figure 9.31 Texture-driven illumination using the Yellow Stroke texture: Diffusion, Ambience, and Specularity.

The alpha portion of the texture may be used to drive the object's illumination. How does the texture's alpha property correspond to the texture? If the marker is in the left column of the Materials Lab grid (no texture), then the slider for that attribute will uniformly control the amount. When you click in the A column to place the marker there, your slider no longer determines the amount for that channel. You may have a uniform (slider) setting for, say Diffusion, or your object's response to diffuse light may be driven by a texture. It's an either/or relationship; the lighting is determined *either* by the slider for uniform illumination *or* by the texture for non-uniform illumination, but never by both. (Well, we had to get complicated on you: There is an exception to this "never both" rule, but we'll save that for later.)

When a marker is placed in the A column (or one of the other columns), then the alpha portion of the texture(s) will control where and how much of that lighting property affects the object. Where the texture's alpha is white, the object's response to the lighting effect is at the maximum; it's the same as pulling out the slider all the way to the maximum. Where the texture's alpha is black, the object's response to light is at the minimum, the same as if the slider were close to 0 (see Figure 9.31).

For the majority of Bryce objects, illumination channels are set to uniform slider amounts. When would you want to use textures for illumination?

- *Terrains That Are "Wet."* Driving Diffusion with a 2D Picture texture that matches the terrain's form will make terrain darker at lower elevations, giving the appearance of wetness near a body of water, as if water has seeped into the ground. The mud in Figure 8.49 and the water pond in Figures 9.57 and C9.58 both have their wet edges created by a Diffusion texture.

- *Dirty or Scuffed Surfaces.* Driving Diffusion with a lower-contrast texture (such as Low Smog) will result in surfaces with a mottled, dirty appearance. The objects in Figure 9.49 use texture-driven diffuse illumination for a dirty, industrial look.

- *Blinding Snow.* Driving Ambience with the alpha information of certain textures will make brilliant snow. The ground (non-snow) is generally dark, with low Ambience. But snow is brilliantly white. To make the white snow bright, assign a high ambient lighting property to only the area that has the snow. Having the snow texture's alpha information drive the amount of Ambience will result in snow that is blindingly light, while the rocky places that peek through the snow will stay darker and dimmer. The snow in the top image in Figure C9.43 uses a snow with texture-driven Ambience.

- *Textured Sheen.* Driving Specularity with the alpha information of certain textures provides additional detail. For a brushed metal surface, without the render cost of Bump Height (or in addition to Bump Height), a textured specular highlight provides clues to the nature of the object's matter; it can be dewy and wet, or textured, or something else. Figure 9.32 shows a sphere and a torus, each with a different Specularity texture. The sphere uses the value component of BlueSpots, and the torus that of Uranus (in the Clouds set). See how

Figure 9.32 Texture-driven Specularity provides additional clues about what the object is made of.

much information is conveyed in the different patterns of shiny highlights?

Texture-Driven Optics

The optics channels likewise use the texture's alpha properties as the basis for non-uniform Transparency or Reflection in an object's surface. The optics channels do not have an either/or relationship between the slider and the texture when it comes to what drives the intensity of the effect; the relationship is "both/and," where information about the optics channel is derived by *both* the slider *and* the Texture Source. Figure 9.33 shows an example of each type of texture-driven optic material.

With Transparency, the object is transparent when the texture's alpha is black. When the alpha is white, the object is opaque. No matter where the slider is set, a black value equals a transparent object. The slider affects the Transparency of the *remainder* of

Figure 9.33 Texture-driven optics, again using Yellow Stroke: Reflection, Transparency, and Bump Height.

Figure 9.34 How Reflection looks under different circumstances. The two objects on the left are for reference; the center two objects have standard high Diffusion with maximum (top) and minimum (bottom) Reflection; the right two objects have Reflection settings identical to those of the center objects, but have low Diffusion settings. The RedFractal texture is used in all cases.

the object, where the alpha is white or some other nonblack shade of gray—or to state it differently, the slider affects the uniform Transparency of the object, but since part of the object is already transparent and can't become extratransparent, that part can't be affected. In the case of Reflection, when the texture's value is black, the object is immune to the actions of the Reflection slider. When the texture's value is white, the object is sensitive to the amount of Reflection determined by the slider. In addition, the white areas are no longer responsive to diffuse illumination. To see the reflection, however, you must use the slider. The slider setting determines the degree to which the reflect areas (white alpha) reflect. For 2D Picture Texture Sources, the situation is reversed.

The objects in Figure 9.34 show the range of possibilities for the Reflection slider. The left column of objects is for reference. The top object shows the alpha information for that Texture Source. The bottom object shows a plain-jane object with Diffusion. The center column of objects places the texture in the Reflection channel. The bottom object in that row has the Reflection amount set to zero, and the top object has the Reflection amount set to the maximum (100). The right row is identical to the middle row, except that no Diffusion is set. The bottom object is uniformly dark. Notice how the gray shade matches the dark areas of the bottom object in the center row. The reflection area has no Diffusion, and the normal area has no Diffusion. Of course, the top right object has Reflection set to the maximum.

Texture-Driven Bump Height

Bump Height determines the degree to which your surface will have perturbances. Of all the 10 channels, Bump Height stands alone when it comes to the texture–slider relationship. Bump Height is the only channel driven by the third texture property: bump. (In the case of picture-based textures, it is driven by the image's alpha channel.) In addition, this channel *requires* a Texture Source that affects the object's surface. There is no such thing as a uniform bump in the same way that there is uniform Diffusion or uniform Reflection. It doesn't matter if the slider is pulled all the way out to 100, the maximum; if there is no texture driving

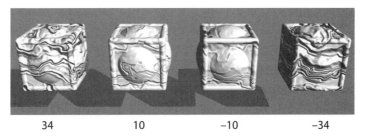

34   10   −10   −34

Figure 9.35 Object employing the RedLayers texture with four different Bump Height settings.

bump, the net result will be nothing: flat; smooth; plain. Your tactile illusions require that the marker move from the left "home" position to one of the texture columns. In addition to providing a Texture Source, you must also set the slider to something other than zero to see the bump effect. You can set the bump to a positive value (drag to the left for the olive green slider) or a negative one (drag to the right; the slider frankly turns scarlet, and what was poked out is now poked in). Figure 9.35 shows an object bumped both positively and negatively.

The actual surface geometry of the object is not changed in bumping. Bryce takes the bump information and very smartly "embosses" the surface appearance to create the illusion of all those perturbances. Bump Height makes rendering costly, since bump information is used to tell Bryce to move a texture on the y axis, as well as on the x and z axes. Additional calculations occur to create the appearance of displacement on the object's surface. When working with the nonterrain primitives, you won't see little perturbances if you look closely at the edges of objects. (This is also an excellent argument for using a terrain, no matter how flat, for extreme foreground ground when you have anything more than a mild bump.)

Texture-Driven Color

In the color channels, texture-driven color allows you to color your object using different Texture Sources. You can pick and choose which color will show for which type of illumination. Where the object is lit by diffuse light, there is one type of coloring. Where the object is illuminated by Ambience, there is another (or the same) type of coloring. Where the object is lit by Specularity, there can be a third type of coloring. If the object is transparent and the Refract Index is set to anything other than 100, then the color of light that passes through the object can be set using the Transparent Color. (There is no such thing as a texture-driven Volume Color, however.)

The color of the object for any color channel is an either/or choice: Either you have a uniform color set by the color swatch, or you have a color driven by one or more of the Texture Sources. Ah well, to every rule there are exceptions; we'll get to those toward the end of the chapter when we delve into Texture Sources and Picture textures. (When you render your scene with Textures off, any texture colors "go away," and the object is rendered using the uniform color set in the color swatch.)

Of course, texture-driven color behaves the same way as uniform color: The amount of illumination for a channel also determines the strength of the color for that channel.

Figure C9.36 is a series of studies for placing a single Texture Source into the different channels. In C9.36a, the RedFractal Texture Source is first placed in each channel: Diffuse Color, Ambient Color, Specular, and Specular Halo. There are two samples of texture-driven Specular, with different Specular Halo settings: very bright and medium bright.

To see which is doing what, you need to know where ambient, specular, and diffuse illumination fall on the object. You see the Ambient Color where the object is in shadow. You see the Diffuse Color where the object is lit by the sun (or light source). The specular highlight is the hot spot, though the hot spot can grow or shrink depending on the Specular Halo.

Use a bright Specular Halo and texture-driven Specular Color to get effects that you wouldn't first think of as "shiny" or "glossy." As you can see by the right example, where the texture drives Specular Halo, the result is a high-contrast between what is lit and what is in shadow. (In this case, the white in the texture produces the equivalent effect of a white uniform Specular Halo color.) This strategy was used to get the high contrast between sunlight and shadow in the image of the globe in Figure C11.43 (in the Sky chapter's color section). Specular Color is driven by the texture, with a white Specular Halo used to create the nice, crisp boundary between sunlight and shadow.

Figure C9.36b shows texture-driven color for two of the channels. The remaining two channels use uniform colors. For most typical Bryce objects, the same Texture Source drives both the Diffuse and Ambient Color channels, with uniform colors for Specular and Specular Halo.

What's happens when we add Transparent Color to the texture-driven color mix? Figure C9.37 shows a series of objects whose Transparency is set to 50 (and that have a Refract Index of 130). With the presence of Transparency, the application of

Transparent Color takes effect. The materials use texture-driven Transparent Color in addition to two other texture-driven color channels as an adaptation of Figure C9.36b.

Like uniform Transparent Color, texture-driven Transparent Color interacts with Diffuse Color to create a new hybrid color. Figure C9.38, a texture-driven remake of Figure C9.20, shows the interaction of colors. A different texture-driven Transparent Color is used in each column. The samples demonstrate how the Transparent Color can be the only texture-driven color channel, with others uniformly colored.

The appearance of the texture-driven Transparent Color changes with changes in Transparency and Refract Index settings. Figure C9.39a shows a set of spheres with Transparent Color texture-driven, and Diffuse and Ambient Color uniform. The left column is completely transparent, and the right column completely opaque. The rows are have different Refract Index settings. Compare the different Refract Index settings for a single transparency setting. Figure C9.39b has the same Transparency and Refract Index settings as C9.39a, but Diffuse Color, as well as Transparent Color, is texture-driven.

Texture-Driven Metallicity

Metallicity tints the reflection with Diffuse Color. Since Metallicity works with Diffuse Color and Reflection, each of which can also be texture driven, there are many possible ways to have texture-driven Metallicity. Figure C9.40 shows the various combinations. The first object is set to maximum reflection, without any Metallicity; the object mirrors its surrounding environment. The second object has maximum Metallicity as well, so that the surrounding environment is mirrored through a coppery Diffuse Color. The third object has texture-driven Metallicity; the Diffuse Color is still the uniform copper color, but it is reflected based on the texture's alpha. In the fourth object, Metallicity is *not* texture driven, but the Diffuse Color is; Metallicity is set to the maximum, and the texture's color is reflected through the object. In the fifth object, both Metallicity and the Diffuse Color are texture driven. In the sixth object, Reflection is also texture driven, resulting in portions that aren't reflective. The set of objects do not have any diffuse illumination, so the areas that aren't reflective in the sixth object are dark. You could, of course, add Diffusion, and that would change the appearance, allowing the coppery Diffuse Color to show—oh, the possibilities are just endless!

Frequency

At the top of each Texture Source column in the grid is a Frequency slider. Frequency determines the texture's size in an inverse relationship: the greater the frequency, the smaller the texture size. Drag up on the slider to increase the frequency, which shrinks the texture so more of it fits into a given space. Dragging down on the slider has the opposite effect. The slider does not have numbers, since it is possible for you to adjust frequency along each dimension. These Frequency sliders atop the A, B, C, and D columns in the Materials Lab grid are tied to the Frequency controls in the Edit Texture Palette, which we'll discuss next.

> **TIP:** Frequency usually needs to be set higher for objects that are closer to the camera than for those that are far away. For any textures that are altitude-based, increasing the frequency will lower the altitude.

Edit Texture Palette

The top-left button of the Texture Source takes you to the Edit Texture Palette, where you can adjust the texture's frequency, rotation, and position. The Edit Texture Palette lets you go beyond the uniform frequency available in earlier versions of Bryce (1 and 2). When your mouse hovers over the top-left slightly greenish button of the Texture Source, the Status readout says "Editor." Then, when you've opened the Edit Texture Palette, the status readout says "Transformation Tools," although the text at the top of the palette itself says "Edit Texture." Of the three terms used, we chose Edit Texture, since that text appears constantly on the Edit Texture Palette itself. The Edit Texture Palette is shown in Figure 9.41.

Figure 9.41 The Edit Texture Palette, accessed from any one of the four Texture Sources in the Materials Lab.

The three controls should look familiar to you; they're nearly the same as the Resize, Rotate, and Reposition controls on the Edit Palette. They are called Scale, Rotate, and Offset. Instead of working with objects, these tools work with textures. (Trivia note: The golden metallic appearance is the one surviving remnant of what at one time might have been a complete metallic overhaul of the entire Bryce user interface. Some have taken to calling the tools on the Edit Textures Palette the "golden tools.") You can move the Edit Texture Palette to any place on your monitor, even (and especially) off the main area of the Materials Lab to the black background area.

Next to each control is a numerical readout. Scale is expressed as a percentage, Rotate as degrees, and Offset as Bryce units. The numbers, incidentally, are editable. Click a number and a numerical entry box appears. When the Edit Texture Palette is open, tapping the Tab key cycles through numerical entries for all the materials channels and then cycles through the numbers on the Edit Texture Palette. Alas, there is no way to cycle backward. By the way, you can use the Up and Down Arrow keys, together with modifier keys, to adjust the quantities (see Table 6.1 for the relevant key combinations).

The Edit Texture Palette has five buttons, four of which are labeled by the letters A, B, C, and D. These four correspond to each of the four Texture Sources. The button for the active texture is highlighted, and the numeric settings reflect the state of that particular Texture Source. If your material calls for multiple Texture Sources, you can make adjustments to, say A, and then click the B button and make adjustments to Texture Source B. (The highlight color may be purple or bronze; unhighlighted, the button is gray. Don't ask what the logic is behind the purple-bronze color shifts; the logic, *if any*, is extremely obscure.)

The bottom button, a downward-pointing arrow, dismisses the Edit Texture Palette. It isn't mandatory for you to click the bottom button to send the Edit Texture Palette away, however. You can just leave it there, and then leave the Materials Lab. When you come back, the Edit Texture Palette will have snuck away on its own. That auto-sneak may be A Bad Thing if your work is at a stage of tweak, leave Materials Lab, test render, return to Materials Lab (hey! where'd that Edit Texture Palette go?), tweak.

The settings in the Edit Texture Palette stay with that Texture Source. Most of the time, you will leave Rotation and Offset at zero, but very often you will need to change Scale. Should you decide to rearrange your textures as part of a mix-and-match, or to arrange textures into an A-B blend or an A-B-alpha-C blend (to be covered later in the chapter), then you need to double-check the Edit Texture Palette settings.

Suppose you select a texture for A and then select the same texture for B—with a minor alteration (B can be a slight variation on A in order to drive a slightly different variation, say, Ambient Color). For whatever reasons you use the same or nearly the same texture for two different sources, you need to make sure that they are in sync with each other, so make sure that the Edit Texture Palette settings for each are identical.

If you've ever looked at your object in World Space and thought, "Yes, well, but I want everything in that texture to take one giant step backward along the *z* axis," you can use the Reposition tool to make this happen. (Of course, you're not limited to World Space; these tools work no matter what the mapping or whether the texture is a 3D (Procedural) Texture or a 2D Picture texture.)

More about Texture Sources

When we introduced the Texture Source, we told you enough to help you understand how the texture is used with the Materials Lab grid. This aspect of the texture is used by that material channel to get a certain result. Now that we've been through that, we take you back to discuss some other options available in the Texture Source. The options we describe are located in the bottom half of the Texture Mapping Mode pop-up menu, at the lower right of the Texture Source.

Alpha Scaling

You've already seen how the alpha portion of the texture may drive certain material channels, such as, say, Diffusion. Where the alpha is white, the effect is fully applied (maximum Diffusion, for example), and where the alpha is black, the effect is not applied at all (no Diffusion). Is there any way to tone down the alpha channel's effect while still keeping all the information contained in the alpha channel? The Alpha Scaling option allows this to happen. For Value—Illumination, Metallicity, Optics, and Volume—the material properties driven by the texture's alpha component, Alpha Scaling allows you to change the degree to which the alpha is applied when driving a particular property. It so happens that all the channels that are alpha driven also have a numerical slider. When Alpha Scaling is on, a channel's slider controls the strength of the alpha to drive that particular material channel. Although bump lives in the Value category, it is not affected by Alpha Scaling, since the texture that drives bump is not the alpha, but bump. Figure 9.42 compares the alpha scaling and non–alpha scaling for all the surface material alpha-driven options.

Previously, we described two different behaviors related to sliders: either/or and both-and. With the either/or behavior, you either use the slider to determine the uniform quality, or you use the Texture Source to drive the quality. The alpha-driven channels in the Value category (Diffusion, Ambience, Specularity, and Metallicity) all respond in this either/or manner. With the both-and behavior, in the Optics category, you can use only the slider to affect optics uniformly, or you can use both the Texture Source and the slider to affect the outcome for that channel.

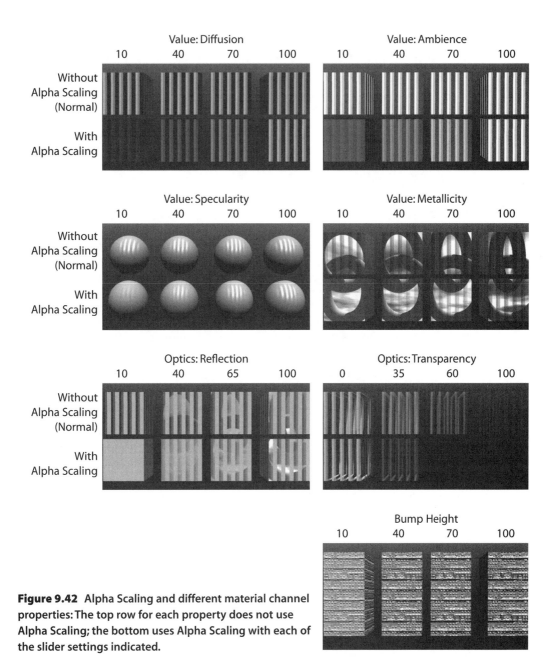

Figure 9.42 Alpha Scaling and different material channel properties: The top row for each property does not use Alpha Scaling; the bottom uses Alpha Scaling with each of the slider settings indicated.

In Figure 9.42, the top row does not use Alpha Scaling. Notice that for Diffusion, Ambience, Specularity, and Metallicity, although the sliders are set to different positions (respectively, 10, 40, 70, and 100), the results in the top row are identical. In the bottom row, however, the effect is weighted, with the lightest application at the left, with a setting of 10. The middle two increase in strength, and the one on the right, with a setting of 100, is identical to the top row examples. For the either/or behaving properties (Value), the texture-driven effect is weighted, ranging from full strength to no strength whatsoever. With Alpha Scaling, you can apply the effect so that it is less than full strength. Alpha Scaling will take alpha's white (full strength) and tone it down to gray, or even to black. But you cannot take black and strengthen it to white.

For the Optics and Value examples shown in Figure 9.42, the top row shows different slider settings without Alpha Scaling applied. Reflection is applied only to those areas that the texture allows.

For texture-driven Reflection, a setting of 0 marks a portion of the object as having the potential to reflect; this setting is identical to no Diffusion and lots of Specularity, as we pointed out earlier. As the Reflection setting gets higher, the surroundings are visible in those places where the texture's alpha is at the maximum—that is, where the texture's alpha is white. Where it's black, the object never reflects. In the bottom row, where Alpha Scaling is on, the maximum setting (100) is identical to the maximum setting in the row above. But see the difference at a setting of 0! There's none of that dark no-Diffuse, maximum Specularity, potential-for-reflection. The object is uniformly lit, with only Diffusion and Ambience. As more Reflection is applied, the reflection does get stronger. There's no extra darkness where the object is darker and the reflection weaker, though. Alpha Scaling is very handy to get a totally different (and better) reflection behavior.

Transparency works differently. For texture-driven Transparency, where the alpha is at maximum (white), the object is transparent. The slider affects the uniform transparency of the remaining (opaque) part of the object. The Alpha Scaling and non–Alpha Scaling results are identical when the slider is set to 0. Alpha Scaling only amplifies the tendency to make everything transparent. You probably don't need to use Alpha Scaling with Transparency; working in the standard way is good enough.

Now that you've been introduced to the behaviors of Alpha Scaling, we offer some gratuitous practical advice. No doubt, the reason you'll use Alpha Scaling is to scale back the alpha-driven properties of a single alpha channel (our guess is Ambience, but we'll gladly allow you to prove us wrong). In Figure C9.43, we show an example of alpha-scaled Ambience. All objects in the scene use a snow material. The material uses a single Procedural Texture to drive Diffuse Color and Ambient Color, Ambience, and Bump Height. The only alpha-driven material channel is Ambience. The alpha information that corresponds to the snow is white. The remainder, corresponding to the location of the underlying foliage, is a shade of gray roughly equivalent to the default Ambience setting. (The bottom image is a full-context render of the scene showing only the material's alpha information.) The top four images were all rendered with Alpha Scaling active. The Ambience setting is shown next to each image. A setting of 100 is equivalent to not applying Alpha Scaling at all. Below the four Alpha Scaling examples is an example of the material with no texture-driven Ambience; instead, uniform Ambience is given the default setting of 19.6.

Chances are, you may be using the same Texture Source in other material channels. Since Alpha Scaling applies to all channels that use that Texture Source, you'll need to ensure that you don't apply Alpha Scaling in the other channels (unless you actually want to). If the other material channel is a color channel, then don't worry. Alpha Scaling applies only to channels that use the alpha portion of the texture. That excludes color and bump. If one of your other channels does use alpha, you have two options: First, you can make sure that any other channels that use the Texture Source have the slider set to the position where Alpha Scaling is not applied. Second, if you are not using all your Texture Sources, you can use the same texture in another channel, using the mix-and-match method. You'll need to make sure that you save the texture in the Texture Library. If you make any adjustments to either one, you'll need to save it again and then reload it to the second Texture Source. You'll also need to make sure that the settings in the Edit Texture Palette are identical for both textures. The second one does not have Alpha Scaling set.

Picture Mapping Options

The bottom part of the Texture Mapping Mode menu provides a number of options devoted specifically to pictures as the source of textures. Click the P button at the lower left of the Texture Source to change to a Picture texture. Although we've use a picture of ice skates as our sample picture, the Leo picture will work as well for this exploration of the Texture Mapping Mode pop-up menu. (For more about selecting and managing pictures, see the next chapter, "Material World II: Picture Textures and the Deep Texture Editor.") Of the options listed in the bottom half of the Texture Mapping Mode pop-up menu, we've covered Alpha Scaling already, which is ambidextrous and works with both 3D and 2D Picture textures. Although the menu contains a number of items, each of which can be set to active (checked) or inactive (unchecked), working with the items is not a simple matter of choosing only one of the menu items. You can combine different menu options to produce widely varying results. The picture mapping options work closely with

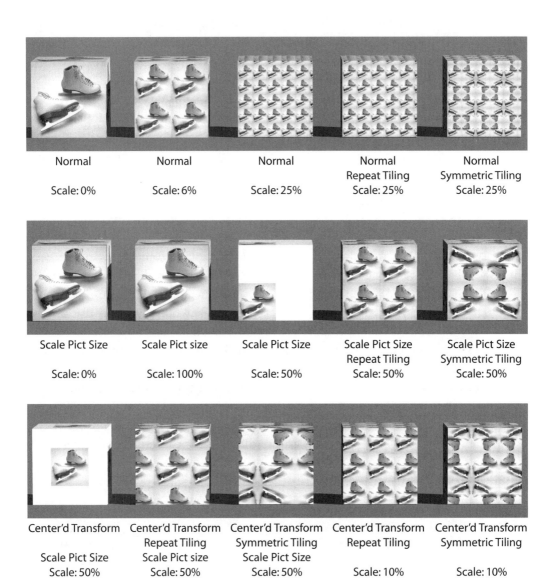

Figure 9.44 The Picture mapping options combined. Top row: tiling options; center row: Scale Pict Size combined with tiling options; bottom row: Centered Transform used with or without Scale Pict Size and tiling options.

scaling. Mind you, "scaling" is the frequency scaling that is controlled with the Edit Texture Palette Scale Transformation tool; it has nothing whatsoever to do with the Alpha Scaling option we just described. Figure 9.44 shows the results of different scales and different menu items. We'll explain as we go.

There are two tiling options that govern what the picture will do when the scale determines that more than one image can fit on the face of a surface:

- *Symmetric Tiling.* Symmetric tiling mirrors the images as they're tiled, making for smooth transitions between edges.

- *Repeat Tiling.* This default mode butts bottom against top, left against right.

Notice that in the top row of Figure 9.44 the first three options are unlabeled where tiling is concerned, yet they still appear to be tiled. What's up with that? The labels for each example indicate what menu option is active. Even though the first three lack a tiling option from the Texture Mapping Mode pop-up menu, the net effect when scaling is set to a value other than 0% or 100% is that the image repeats, or tiles. (Scale settings of 0% and 100% produce identical results; more on this in a moment.) The second and third options are two different scale options. The third option, Normal/Scale = 25% is identical to the fourth, where Repeat Tiling is used. The fifth option uses Symmetrical Tiling; there the images mirror one another as they are repeated. If neither tiling option is active, the result is the same as when Repeat Tiling is active. Why have the Repeat Tiling option at all, then? The next item in the menu requires Repeat Tiling. Read on!

- *Scale Pict Size.* This option, when chosen, changes the way scale is interpreted in mapping a picture to an object. The net effect is that you can apply a picture to the object and then adjust the size of that picture by adjusting the scale. Normally, when Scale Pict Size is off, the scale is interpreted the same as the scaling of Procedural Textures. An increase in the percentage number increases the frequency of the scale; more copies of the picture appear in the same space. However, 100% is the same as 0%. When Scale Pict Size is on, the scale applies to the size of the picture. Again, 0% and 100% produce identical results (go figure): this time, a perfect 1:1 ratio of picture size to object size; 50% yields half of the object size, 25% yields a quarter of the object size, and so forth. (A negative percentage, say, –50%, flips the image upside down.)

The second row of Figure 9.44 shows different Scale Pict Size options. The first three are displayed without any tiling. Notice the third image, where the scale is 50%. The picture occupies an area that is smaller than the surface of the object. The remaining area is colored by the uniform swatch color, which, for this object, is white. The last two images in the second row are tiling options combined with Scale Pict size. When Scale Pict Size is active, there's quite a difference between Scale Pict Size and a 50% scale when no option is selected and when Repeat Tiling is selected! Compare the third and fourth sample in this row to the third and fourth in the row above; in both cases, the difference between the third sample and the fourth is that the fourth sample uses Repeat Tiling.

Further, compare the fourth Scale Pict size sample (second row) with the second sample in the top row. The net result is identical, but the scaling applied is very different. The scale is 6% in the top row option.

> **TIP:** When adjusting the frequency of pictures mapped to an object, and when Scale Pict Size is off (default state), use multiples of 6 to evenly map the image without any leftover portions of image: 6%, 12%, 18%, 24%, and so on. When Scale Pict Size is on, divide 100 by the number of times you want the image to map: 100%, 50%, 33.3%, 25%, 20%, 16.6%, and so on.

- *Centered Transform.* This option places the image at the center of the object. Changes in scaling occur from the center and move out. Center Transform can work in combination with Scale Pict Size and the tiling options.

The bottom row of Figure 9.44 shows different Centered Transform options. In all cases, the picture is applied from the center. The first sample shows the result when Scale Pict Size is on and no tiling option is applied. The second and third samples show Scale Pict Size with the two different tiling options. The last two options show Centered Transform with tiling and without any Scale Pict Size (notice the difference in scales with and without Scale Pict Size.)

The last option in the menu exists to enhance the quality of the render of the image.

- *Pict Interpolation.* Suppose that you had a picture whose resolution was 128×128 pixels, and you were applying that to, say, a cube object in your scene. Suppose the render resolution for that scene is the standard 480×360 pixels, and your cube is so large that it occupies most of the scene. If the number of pixels required to render a face of the cube is greater than the 128×128 pixels of the original image, how will Bryce treat the task of enlarging the picture image to fit the size of the cube? Pict Interpolation is the process whereby Bryce smoothly enlarges the image as it renders. When this option is active (it's on by default), Bryce requires an additional bit of processing power to produce a higher quality result. If the picture weren't reinterpolated when enlarged, you'd simply see larger blocks of pixels rendered. We compare an enlarged view of the brrrryce-skate with and without pict interpolation in Figure 9.45. One portion is shown without anti-aliasing; the other is shown with it. Antialiasing does get rid of some of the jaggies, but it doesn't fix them entirely. Bryce sets this option to on by default; do keep it that way!

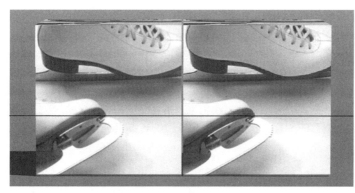

Without antialiasing

With antialiasing

Pict Interpolation ON   Pict Interpolation OFF

Figure 9.45 Pict Interpolation smoothes out a picture: Pict Interpolation shown on and off with and without antialiasing.

In a couple of the picture mapping options we mentioned, if the picture is smaller than the surface area and is not tiled, the object's color will be a combination of the picture (a texture-driven color) and the swatch color. This is one case where the color is not *either* swatch or texture, but *both* swatch and texture. The last option we explore, Decal Color, is another case of both swatch and texture color.

Decal Colors

The term *decal* evokes childhood days of building model airplanes, where certain identifying numbers need to applied to the constructed aircraft. Those numbers are either on a peel 'n' stick sticker or attached to paper and removed by soaking in water. Once freed of their backing, the decal numbers are carefully applied to the appropriate place on the airplane.

The decal, providing a local surface appearance, has three characteristics: The decal usually has different coloring than the remaining surface area, it covers only a portion of the object, and it has an irregular shape. Bryce has a decal function: the Decal Colors menu item. When active, it allows you to apply *both* the texture-driven color and the generic swatch color to the object. What is used to mix the two together? The alpha channel. The information in the alpha channel provides the irregular outline of the decal and makes the decal occupy only a portion of the object.

Decal Colors can be used with both 2D Picture and 3D Texture Sources. Although both types of Texture Sources have the requisite alpha channel information, 2D Pictures work better. A picture easily lends itself to having an alpha channel that appears significantly different than the RGB color information. Text or numbers can be placed in the alpha channel of an image in an image editing application (such as Photoshop), and the resulting image can be imported to Bryce through the Picture Library (more on that in the next chapter). You can also use the Picture Library to copy and paste color and alpha channel information from one or another image. That, too, is covered in depth in Chapter 10, "Material World II: Picture Textures and the Deep Texture Editor." For now, we'll look at how Decal Colors work with precreated images.

Figure C9.46, shows six samples of Decal Colors—three using 2D Picture textures and three using 3D Textures. The top row shows only the alpha channel information for each object. The bottom row shows the texture-driven color for each object. The center row shows the result of applying the Decal Colors menu item for each object.

The left three objects have 2D Picture textures. The right three have 3D Texture–based textures. Where the alpha channel is white, the texture color is applied. Where the alpha channel is black, the swatch color (yellow) is applied. We've included samples where the alpha channel contains gray tones, resulting in a mixture between the the texture and swatch color.

Notice that the picture examples take advantage of the inherent ability of an image to contain different color and alpha information. The color is from a photograph of blue-gray cracked ice. The alpha channel is text. Depending on whether the alpha channel is dominated by black or by white, the swatch color dominates or the Picture texture dominates.

> **TIP:** To increase or decrease the size of a picture-based decal, set the Scale Pict Size menu option to on and then use the Edit Texture Palette's Scale control to adjust the size. Move the decal to other locations on the object by using the Offset controls.

What if you wanted to, say, combine a picture-based decal with a 3D Texture background? Combining two different texture types is not possible using Decal Color; Decal Color works only for combining a texture with a single swatch color. To combine textures, you'll have to work with multiple Texture Sources—which happens to be our next topic. (The ABC Texture described in this next section is the solution to the question we just posed.)

BUT WAIT! THERE'S MORE!

There's more to the grid than what we've described thus far. We've described only one column, the A column—but there are four Texture Sources in the grid. (See Figure 9.47, an image of the Materials Lab interface that actually matches what *you* see when *you* access it.) When it comes to those four Texture Sources and the placement of markers to make textures drive certain channels of the surface material, you can invent all sorts of interesting ways to mix and match. There are three strategies for combining your Texture Sources: mix and match, A-B blend, and A-B-C blend.

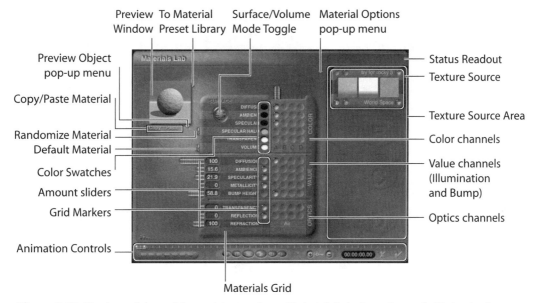

Preview Window / To Material Preset Library / Surface/Volume Mode Toggle / Material Options pop-up menu

Preview Object pop-up menu
Copy/Paste Material
Randomize Material
Default Material
Color Swatches
Amount sliders
Grid Markers
Animation Controls

Status Readout
Texture Source
Texture Source Area
Color channels
Value channels (Illumination and Bump)
Optics channels

Materials Grid

Figure 9.47 The bona fide, real, honest-to-goodness Materials Lab. Accept no substitutes (unless they are interpretive illustrations that help you understand how the whole thing works!).

Mix and Match

You can combine different Texture Sources to drive different channels. For instance, you can choose one Texture Source to drive the Transparency of the object, and choose another one to drive Bump Height, Diffuse Color, and Ambient Color. Combine that with, say, a 2D Picture-based alpha to drive the Diffusion channel, and you've got yourself one interesting, complex surface material. This is the mix-and-match method.

Taking up the texture color refrain from the earlier section, the Ambient and Diffuse Color channels needn't necessarily both be driven by the same texture. Figure C9.48 shows some different mix-and-match possibilities using two Texture Sources: Marble and LowSmog.

Figure 9.49 shows a possible set of options for a material. For this, we have taken liberties with the user interface in the hope of reinforcing the idea that different sources are called upon to do different things when they are selected.

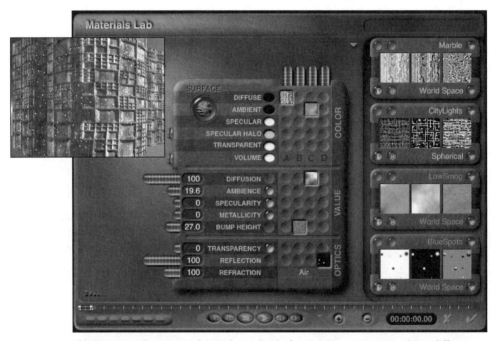

Figure 9.49 The mix-and-match method of assigning textures to drive different material channels.

A-B Blending

The second and third methods of combining your Texture Sources get a bit craftier. No doubt you look at the grid and say, "But is there any way to combine more than one source in the same channel?" There certainly is! There are two possible combinations: A and B; and A, B, and C. Press the Control key (Macintosh) or Ctrl key (Windows) and click in the B column. Markers are placed in both the A and B columns. Or press the Control key or Ctrl key and click in the C column to place markers in A, B, and C. Why are there only these two combinations—why not B, C, and D, for example? Read on!

When two Texture Sources are combined in one material channel, the sources are blended together. The two possible combinations correspond to the two blending types. But don't think that a mere two blending types constrict you unnecessarily. The possibilities are vast. For the first A-B combination, the two Texture Sources are blended together via altitude. Source A is in full effect at ground level. Moving up in altitude, A begins blending into B. At the highest altitude, B is in full effect. In Figure 9.50, the Texture Source A (Mushrooms) and Texture Source B (City Lights) are combined.

What constitutes the lowest point? The highest point? It is not the height of the object. The lowest and highest points are calculated based on the total altitude of objects in your scene. In Figure 9.50b, the only thing that changed from Figure 9.50a was the addition of a pyramid that was higher, forcing the total altitude to be higher and a remapping of the blend between the two Texture Sources. Figure 9.50c adds a cube that is as tall as the pyramid; its material is the same as that of the first cube. You can see where the Texture Source B material went with the addition of taller objects in the scene. Depending on your scene composition, you may run the risk of ruining your altitude-blend-mapping by adding just that last

Figure 9.50 Combining two textures in an A-B blend: a) The A-B blend applied to one existing object; b) the presence of another object skews the blend between textures A and B; c) the tall cube shows where the higher altitude part of the blend has been skewed.

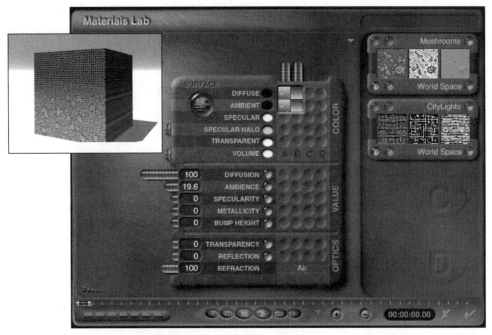

Figure 9.51 The A-B blend in the Materials Lab, with the blend directions indicated in the Diffuse and Ambient Color channels.

one object. Figure 9.51 shows the grid with the textures and the Blend mode interpreted for you.

A-B-C Blending

The second multiple–Texture Source blend option (and the third grid strategy overall) is the A-B-C blend (also known as A-B-alphaC). Like the A-B blend, it is a blend between two Texture Sources. Instead of a straight altitude blend between them, however, the A-B-C blend uses the alpha information from the C source to blend the two A and B sources. In Figure 9.52, the placement of textures in the grid for the Diffuse Color and Ambient Color channels reflects which goes where. The A and B source textures are color, and the C texture is alpha information. This means that where Texture Source C's alpha is black, the color from Texture Source A is applied; where Texture Source C's alpha is white, the color from Texture Source B is applied.

The A-B-C blend is extremely powerful. Consider that your 3D Texture Sources can also pay attention to altitude, slope, and orientation. (We'll go into altitude,

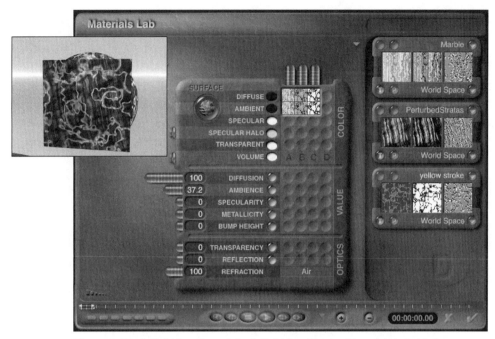

Figure 9.52 A-B-C blending: a) An A-B-C blend in the Materials Lab; b) the rendered object.

slope, and orientation in detail in Chapter 10, "Material World II: Picture Textures and the Deep Texture Editor.") Combine these with the basic textured noise, and you have random patches of two different textures on your object.

When creating A-B-C textures, you needn't limit yourself to the same mapping for all three Texture Sources. The marble tile steps in the *Water Temple at Night* image (shown in Chapter 3, "Camera and Scene," and in Chapter 12, "Brycean EnLightenment") use an A-B-C texture blend. The two marbles in A and B are set to map in World Space, but the CheckBlue texture in Texture Source C is set to Spherical Mapping.

Analysis of the Mountain Material Preset

Eternal Lake, by Eric Wenger, made in the era of Bryce 2, uses a by-now famous A-B-C Texture Source material. Indeed, this material preset has been used a lot in Bryce imagery; it's a beautiful surface material. Knowing how it was created will give you the courage to alter it and to come up with your own texture creations. Each of the scene files for analysis of this material are in the WHOLE MOUNTAIN folder in this chapter's folder on the CD-ROM.

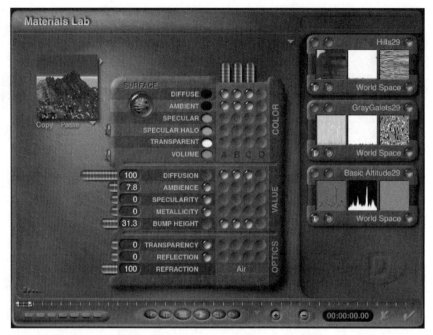

Figure 9.53 The Materials Lab settings for the Whole Mountain material preset.

Create a terrain. Open the Materials Lab. In the Preset Library, select Planes & Terrains > Whole Mountain. Click the check mark to leave the library and go back to the Materials Lab.

Take a look at what you have here. There are three Texture Sources. Source A is a greenish, brushy texture. Source B is a pebbly, light sandy texture. Source C has some spiky things and is colored wildly (see Figure 9.53). By now you know that when there are A-B-C blend textures, the color of C matters not a whit; the C source is there for the alpha information.

Just so you get a feel for what Texture Source C is doing, try changing it momentarily. Select another texture. Try CheckBlue and Sin Layers. You may need to lower the frequency for Texture Source C in the Materials Lab grid.

For Figure C9.54, we have created two additional terrains using the same material, and for each, we have replaced the source C texture with a new texture. The material for the terrain on the left uses CheckBlue, and that for the one in the middle uses Sin Layers (the terrain on the right still has the original Whole Mountain material). The new source C texture determines the manner of variation between the sandy pebble texture and the green hill texture. Although the new variations are bizarre, they're instructive. The C Texture Source is the switch for the two other textures. In the case of the original Whole Mountain preset, the C Texture Source determines where it's pebbly and where there's vegetation. Mostly, the pebbly part is lower and the vegetation is higher, but there are higher pockets where the pebbly part peeks through.

The Texture Source C switch works for all three of the basic surface properties for this Whole Mountain material. (Reminder: The basic three properties are illumination, optics and bump, and color.) In Figures C9.55a through c, the three surface properties are isolated. The left terrain shows only the illumination, the center terrain shows bump, and the right terrain shows only color. Since C is the Texture Source that does the mixing, the Value illumination, bump, and color information for Texture Sources A and B is consistent. If Texture Source C determines that "A shows here," then A's Diffusion, Bump Height, Diffuse Color, and Ambient Color will all be there together.

The illumination example in Figure C9.55a shows the variations in light and dark within the material as it is applied to the terrain. (We produced this image by setting the Diffuse and Ambient Colors to white and turning off the bump channel.) The combined alpha channels of the A-B-C textures determine where the object responds completely to light (where it's white), and where it resists diffuse light (dark). At the bottom of the terrain, near ground level, the alpha is dark (when the Basic altitude texture was created in the Deep Texture Editor, its alpha channel was designed to react to altitude—but we'll explain how that works in the next chapter). The darkness corresponds with the bottoms of the green vegetation and the pebbly areas. The pebbles, when they reach ground level, are dark, or wet. This surface material was designed to be used with water.

The terrain in Figure C9.55b has only the bump information applied to it (for this image, we set the color to white and turned off the illumination channel, Diffusion). Notice that bump, too, changes according to the placement, as determined by Texture Source C, of Texture Source A or Texture Source B. The Bump Height information varies from one texture to the other.

The terrain on the right (see Figure C9.55c) shows the color information (we turned off the illumination and bump channels in the material). The lower part is sandy (from the GrayGalets texture), and the higher part is green with streaks of brown (the Hills texture). (Also, in places where the terrain is vertical, there is a brown rocky cliff color.) Again, the alpha channel of the Basic altitude texture, which is derived from the altitude and to some extent the slope of the underlying terrain, determines the placement of these colors. See how the entire bottom portion is a consistent sandy color? Compare the diffuse illumination and color examples at corresponding locations on each of the two terrains. (Since these textures are mapped to the object in World Space, you won't see an exact correspondence of streaks to dark places from one terrain to the next.)

Figures C9.56a and b focus on the coloring and diffuse illumination for each texture. Part a shows the hilly texture, and part b shows the pebbly texture. For each of the two images, the left terrain shows the texture color with uniformly bright diffuse lighting. The center terrain shows the texture color and also includes the texture-driven diffuse lighting, with lights and darks. The right terrain shows the final result, combining both Texture Source A (hills) and Texture Source B (pebbles) with illumination and color.

> **TIP:** If you want to isolate one part of the surface properties to analyze which is doing what, then place all the other markers in the default "home" column in the Materials Lab grid. If you want to look at a texture for alpha only (to see what is driving illumination and optics for the object), then set Diffuse Color and Ambient Color to white (no textures), and have the textures drive the Diffusion and/or Ambience information. All other channel markers are in the home position. Include or omit texture-driven Ambience depending on whether you also want to see shadow portions of the object. To show shadows in Figure C9.56, we didn't include texture-driven Ambience. You can do the same thing to isolate the Bump Height information or the color information.

We've already said that some portions are such-and-such close to sea level. But why are they so? Why is the area closest to sea level dark? Why does the Gray Galets (pebbly) texture fall mostly at the areas close to sea level? The alpha information for each texture is paying attention to altitude. Herein lies the genius of Bryce's 3D Texture Generator: Your texture information is intelligent and knows how high or how flat or in which direction that part of the object's surface is, and the texture is adjusted accordingly. This altitude sensitivity is integral to the final look of the texture. We won't go into the particulars of creating a texture with altitude sensitivity here; the next chapter, "Material World II: Picture Textures and the Deep Texture Editor," discusses that. We will be examining Whole Mountain's underlying textures in depth in the next chapter when we discuss the Deep Texture Editor.

You can adjust the different frequencies independently. This will become important when you use the Whole Mountain material. Depending on the scale of your terrain, the pebbles may be too big or too small. Since they're from Texture Source B, you can adjust the frequency for Texture Source B, and the texture's scale will change.

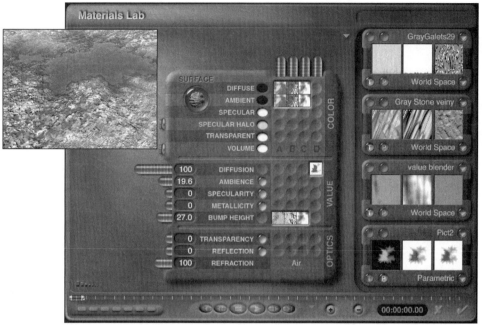

Figure 9.57 Using Texture Source D for diffuse illumination: Materials Lab that includes A-B-C texture combination with a D source to darken the ground near the water puddle, along with the rendered result. (Color image of rendered result is shown in Figure C9.58.)

What about D?

In all this discussion, poor Texture Source D has been neglected. Isn't there any special blend combination for D? No. D is the maverick. D stands alone. The advantage to having one last Texture Source available is that you can tie up three textures for certain purposes and then tie up a fourth for a different purpose. A-B-C together can drive the color and bump information for a texture, while D drives, say, Diffusion. If you want a complex set of textures on a terrain to show wetness near a water source, then you have one remaining Texture Source card to play: Texture Source D. Figure 9.57 shows the Materials Lab for a material where Texture Source D is used to drive Diffusion. (Again, we have taken liberties with the user interface to show which Texture Source is being applied where.) Texture Source D is a picture (a dampened variation of the terrain map) that is driving the Diffusion channel to convey moisture. The result of the A-B-C and D combination is shown here in grayscale. In Figure C9.58a and b (in the color section), the result is shown in color, along with the identical scene *without* Texture Source D. Figure C9.58b lacks the extra Diffusion information, and there is nothing to give the impression of moisture seeping through the ground near the mud hole. What a difference a D makes!

MATERIAL OPTIONS

There is one last major part to the Materials Lab that needs describing. At the top of the Materials Lab, just to the left of the Texture Sources, is a pop-up menu where you can choose the material options for your object's surface (see Figure 9.59). Four options are listed above the divider line, and then seven options below the divider line.

The four options above the dividing line are the material shading modes.

Figure 9.59 The Material Options pop-up menu for surface materials.

Shading Mode

The shading modes allow you to select different effects. To understand a bit about how these work, consider again the render process. As the renderer encounters objects in the Brycean world, it doesn't necessarily stop when it reaches the one sphere. With a rendering X-ray vision, the renderer, if directed, will also find out about the objects beyond the object, calculating what lies behind the sphere. What is the advantage to that? There are different ways to combine the object and what lies behind.

Normal

Nomal is the plain, basic shading mode. For transparent objects, even when there is no refraction (a setting of 100), there is a noticeable brightening of the object as light passes through it. Of course, at a setting other than 100, Bryce uses a different, more complex ray-tracing routine to bend the rays and create refraction. The Normal state will add lighting highlights to the object rather than create a straight blend between the object and the background (Blend Transparency).

Blend Transparency

Blend Transparency is similar to Normal in every way except for the treatment of transparency. Blend Transparency provides a way to use the texture alpha channel to

Global Transparency   Alpha-driven Transparency

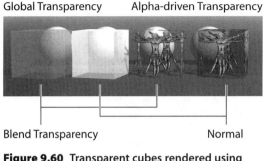

Blend Transparency   Normal

Figure 9.60 Transparent cubes rendered using Blend Transparency and Normal shading, for cubes with uniform Transparency and cubes with alpha-driven Transparency.

determine what sections of the object are actually rendered. When Blend Transparency is selected, the renderer calculates the appearance of both the object and whatever lies behind it. The final result will be a mix of the two, as determined by the setting for the Transparency slider. It's a two-step process: First, the renderer performs computations for both objects, and second, the renderer creates the final result by weighing the two in a blend. This is why a Transparency setting of 1 is just as costly as a setting of 99; both require that double render of the object and whatever lies behind it. Figure 9.60 shows a scene with two sets of cubes so you may compare the effects of Normal and Blend Transparency.

Blend Transparency struts its stuff when alpha information is used to make a portion of the object transparent. When there is a 2D Picture texture or a 3D Texture including some type of alpha-driven transparency, the Blend Transparency shading mode works beautifully. There are portions where the object shows, and other portions where the background shows. The alpha information determines which part will show, as a comparison of the right two objects in Figure 9.60 shows.

(Back in the days of Bryce 2, Blend Transparency was the default Macintosh transparency mode, and the Windows version used Normal shading, but offered the Blend Transparency option. If you open a Bryce 2 Mac scene in Bryce 4, transparent objects will automatically be set to Blend Transparency. Some of the scene files on this CD-ROM date back to that time, so you may see some Blend Transparency shading modes if you look hard enough.)

Fuzzy

The Fuzzy option gives your object a diffuse edge for a soft look. To create a fuzzy edge, the renderer calculates the surface of the object and then blends in the calculated result of the area beyond the edge of the object. Figure 9.61 compares Normal, Fuzzy, and Light shading modes. Use the Fuzzy options on any primitive object aside from flat objects, mesh-based objects, lights, and terrains. Fuzzy is excellent to use on fake glowing pseudo-light sources, planetary atmosphere, or spheres that will be free-standing clouds (assuming that you don't want to go with a volume material, that is). Fuzzy is a very cheap form of volume density; an object with Transparency set to Fuzzy will not refract the light that passes through it.

Light

The Light shading mode is auto-matically selected when you create light object primitives. Bryce's renderer calculates the object in a semi-glowing fashion. When an object is set to Light, it does not respond to any of the illumination

Figure 9.61 A cylinder rendered with (left to right): Normal, Fuzzy, and Light.

controls. Figure 9.61 shows a light object. Notice that unlike the other options, this one does not cast a shadow. The only channels that affect the appearance of a Light object are Transparency (or Base Density) and Diffuse Color. Both uniform and texture-driven variations can be used to good effect. You probably won't be surprised to learn that more discussion of this particular shading mode appears in Chapter 12, "Brycean EnLightenment."

Other Material Options

In addition to the shading modes, some other options are available to you.

Additive

When the Additive option is selected, Bryce uses a special process when rendering the object. The ray finds the object and determines its surface appearance. It then finds whatever is *behind* the object, whether an additional object or atmosphere. When it determines the final pixel color for each, it adds the two together—the object and what is behind the object. For pixel values, 255 is the lightest, and 0 is the darkest. Adding numbers together results in a number of greater magnitude and, therefore, makes the object brighter. You have probably seen this if you've worked with Add in other image processing situations, or if you've used the Add option in the Pictures portion of the Terrain Editor. This brightening effect gives the object the appearance of glowing. Figure 9.62 shows Additive when

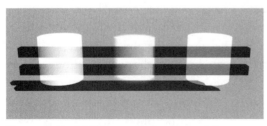

Figure 9.62 Additive applied to Normal, Fuzzy, and Light shading modes.

applied to Normal, Fuzzy, and Light objects. Notice how none of the objects casts any shadow. (See Chapter 12, "Brycean EnLightenment," for more on creating glowing objects.) When Additive is combined with fuzziness, you can create glowing atmospheres and light bulbs. When it is not combined with fuzziness, you can create moons. Make sure Diffuse is your only illumination.

Shadow Options

"The Shadow knows," or so the saying goes. Actually, for 3D realism, the shadow *tells*: It tells you information about the object and its relationship to the ground and to other objects. Unlike in the real world, where you either have shadows or you don't, you can choose whether to have shadows on Bryce objects. In fact, you can choose the extent of shadowing to a degree unheard of in the real world! Figure 9.63 shows all the options.

Cast Shadow. The object casts shadows onto other objects. This is probably the quickest option of the bunch to calculate. Among surface material objects, the differences in render time for shadow options are negligible. We'll revisit the question of shadow options and render time when we discuss volume materials toward the end of the chapter.

Receive Shadow. The object receives shadows cast onto it by other objects. It will receive the shadow of any other object that casts shadows.

Self Shadow. The object casts shadows onto itself. Since this option involves both casting and receiving shadows, it should be used in addition to the other two. You can see the effects of this option much more clearly with surface objects, as Figure 9.63, the example of the surface torus, shows. The distinction is subtle: For the object labeled Cast + Receive or Self + Receive (in other words, only two out of the three shadow conditions), portions of the torus are darker because they cannot respond to diffuse light—but it's as though the top part of the torus doesn't exist, and the light is shining straight through to the bottom. When all three conditions are present—Cast, Receive, and Self Shadow—a pronounced shadow falls from the top part of the torus to the bottom.

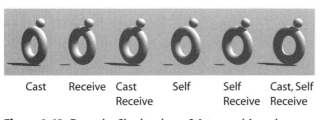

| Cast | Receive | Cast Receive | Self | Self Receive | Cast, Self Receive |

Figure 9.63 Does the Shadow know? A torus object shown with different combinations of shadow options: Cast Shadow, Receive Shadow, and Self Shadow.

The default state for objects is to have all three shadow options in effect. All the objects shown in the shading mode section (Normal, Blend Transparency Fuzzy, Light, plus Additive) were rendered with all shadow options enabled. Shadows cannot be cast by objects that are additive or are in the Light shading mode. In addition to those conditions where you *can't* have an object cast or receive shadows, there may be times when you want an object that resists shadows (February 2 is one of them!). This is different from the resistance to shadows that takes place with a high Ambience setting.

When would you shut off the shadow? When you want to reduce the shadow clutter. The objects in Figure 2.47 have the Shadowable setting switched off, since there's sufficient visual detail in the frames already; we don't need the shadows to get in the way, too.

Distance Blur

Distance Blur is a special-case option you can use when you use Bump Height in your surface appearance. Distance Blur tells the renderer to ignore Bump Height the farther in the distance the object (or portion thereof) is located. This reduces excessive noise (and render time) in the distance. The tests we set up for this, however, revealed scant difference between Distance Blur on and off. Render times were identical, too, so this option may not be as handy as we first thought it was. Figure 9.64 shows a ground plane without bump, with bump (but without Distance Blur), and with bump and Distance Blur.

Volume Color Blend

When Volume Color is applied to an object (we'll call it the main object), the resulting color of both the inside surface of the main object and an object inside the main object is a mix of the object's Diffuse Color and the Volume Color. The volume blend options allow you to determine how those colors are mixed together.

a   b   c

Figure 9.64 What's the big idea? Distance Blur and bump under different conditions: a) No Bump Height setting; b) Bump Height, normal; c) Bump Height, with Distance filter on—no apparent difference from b). Humph.

Volume Blend Altitude

When Volume Blend Altitude is active, the Volume Color is rendered at lower altitudes, and the Diffuse Color at higher altitudes. Figure C9.65 shows the blend. The green color in the background is actually the Diffuse Color of the main object, and the Diffuse Color of the torus and pyramid are white. At lower altitudes, the blue Volume Color shows; at higher altitudes, the objects' own Diffuse Colors show. You can also play the movie VOLUME COLOR ALTITUDE.MOV, in the folder for this chapter on the CD-ROM, to see how the objects inside the main object are colored as you travel around inside the cube.

Volume Blend Distance

When Volume Blend Distance is active, the Volume Color and Diffuse color are mixed based on distance from the camera. When you are close to the objects, they take on their own Diffuse Color, but when you are far away from them, they take on the main object's Volume Color. Figure C9.66 shows an exterior and three interior views of a green transparent sphere with white objects inside. Inside the cube, the closer parts of the torus and pyramid are whiter, and where they are farther away, they take on the blue Volume Color. The main object, the sphere, is green. When viewed from the outside, the Volume Blend Distance setting mixes Diffuse Color near the objet's surface, with the Volume Color appearing deeper in the center of the object. It's as if the cube had a green (Diffuse Color) transparent skin, and the guts are dark blue (the Volume Color). There is a movie for this example, too: VOLUME COLOR DISTANCE.MOV. Moving around within the object is instructive. The Volume Color acts like a thick haze: Up close to the objects, you see the object's color; farther away, all you see is the haze color.

VOLUME PROPERTIES

A hard-edged surface is not the only type of object appearance that you can create in Bryce. The Materials Lab in Bryce 4 (and indeed, since Bryce 3D) offers controls for affecting the volume appearance of an object.

The volume channels work primarily with density. Density is the thickness, or degree of impenetrability, of a substance. Put in quantitative terms, density is the amount of something per unit measure (such as unit length, area, or as we examine here, volume.)

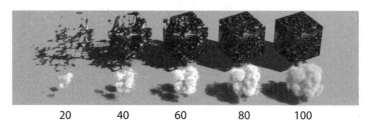

Figure 9.67 Two different volume objects shown at different Base Density settings.

To change your material to a volume material, click the Surface/Volume toggle. The list of properties changes. The Optics settings, which focus on optical properties of the surface of an object, go away, as do Metallicity and Bump. The volume properties take their place.

Base Density

Base Density in Bryce is the channel that determines the amount of the object's interior thickness. Think of Base Density as the property that carves out the shape of the volume, determining what is solid and what is not. Usually the Base Density is driven by a texture, and indeed, of the Volume controls, it's the only one that can be driven by Texture Sources. The Texture Source's alpha is what's used to drive Base Density. This is where the volume texture starts; the other attributes are modifiers of Base Density. That is why this attribute is driven by textures, and the other volume attributes aren't; they don't add anything new, but rather, modify the Base Density setting. The Base Density slider determines the strength of the texture, with 100 indicating the maximum strength, and 0 indicating no strength whatsoever; that is, a texture with a Base Density setting of 100 is more dense, or more opaque, and one with a 0 setting is of no density, or fully transparent. Figure 9.67 shows a series of objects at different Base Density settings, so you get an idea of what takes place when you move the Base Density slider.

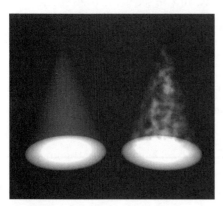

Figure 9.68 Two volume visible lights, without (left) and with (right) a texture to drive Base Density.

One exception to the driven-by-an-alpha texture tendency is the volume visible light, which doesn't necessarily have to be driven by a texture. If there is no texture, the Base Density determines how thick the volume space is, resulting in a hazy-lit-atmosphere appearance. Figure 9.68 shows two volume visible lights: one (on the right) with a texture for Base Density, and one (on the left) without a texture.

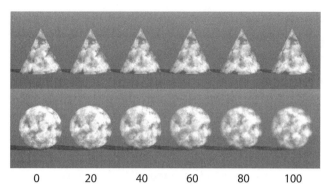

Figure 9.69 Edge Softness and object type: Edge Softness applied to spheres obscures the sphere's edge, whereas identical settings with cones have scant effect.

Edge Softness

Edge Softness removes the appearance of the primitive's shape. It's a location-specific density changer; the location in question is the object's surface. This control works best for obscuring the surface edges of sphere objects, for clouds. Figure 9.69 shows a set of cones and a set of spheres with a volume material. Each of the spheres has a different Edge Softness setting. All other settings are identical. Compare the edges of the objects. Edge Softness makes a noticeable difference in the spheres, whereas the cones seem untouched by it. Use the Edge Softness control when you want to disguise the primitive shape of your volume object—especially clouds.

Fuzzy Factor

Fuzzy Factor is a secondary control of Base Density. For any given level of texture density, you can exaggerate that setting to create either a harder edge or a fuzzier edge. The default setting, 100, makes no change from what is determined by the Base Density setting. Between 100 and 0, the density increases, resulting in harder edges; between 100 and 300, the edges become fuzzier. We'll discuss some practical tips

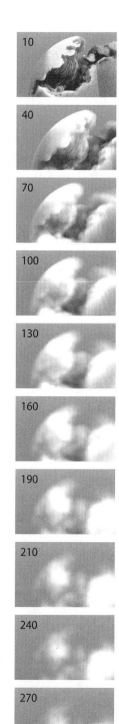

Figure 9.70 Different Fuzzy Factor settings applied to a volume texture.

for using Fuzzy Factor when we introduce the volume material options in the next section. Figure 9.70 shows a series of objects with a single Base Density setting, but a range of Fuzzy Factor settings

The Materials Lab has a lovely preview window to show you the results of the current settings. This is highly advantageous if you want to dink around with one or more of the material channel sliders and see the results. You can use this method to figure out how material channels interact. But the advantage is limited mostly to surface materials. Once you start working with volume materials, the preview render pace creeps along at glacial speed. Oh the temptation to move on and make the next adjustment when the previous adjustment has only rendered a small portion of the preview! (We speak from experience, having succumbed to that temptation more often than we care to admit.) And since each render time takes so long, by the time one finishes, you've forgotten what you saw before. If it takes nearly an epoch to render one lot of volume materials settings, how's a dedicated Brycer ever going to be able to work with the volume channels in any satisfying way? We've taken care of this for you. The CD-ROM in this chapter's folder contains a set of QTVR movies with the fully rendered results of the slider positions shown.

Quality/Speed

The Quality/Speed slider is not a material property so much as it is a control to govern the amount of detail that Bryce goes into when it renders the volume material. Recall our earlier discussion of the manner in which the ray "marches" through the object, taking a sample, then another sample, then another one, cre-

ating a calculation for each spot, until the entire object has been marched through by the ray-tracing renderer, or the result is something wholly opaque. The higher the quality, the greater the number of samples that Bryce will use to calculate the material inside the object.

Figure 9.71 Two sets of objects rendered at different quality settings. The top row uses a distance origin texture; the bottom row uses a cloudy texture.

Figure 9.71 compares the output of a render at different quality settings using a distance origin and cloudy textures (a distance origin produces a noise at the World Center or Object Center). See Figure 9.72 to compare the render times for different quality settings.

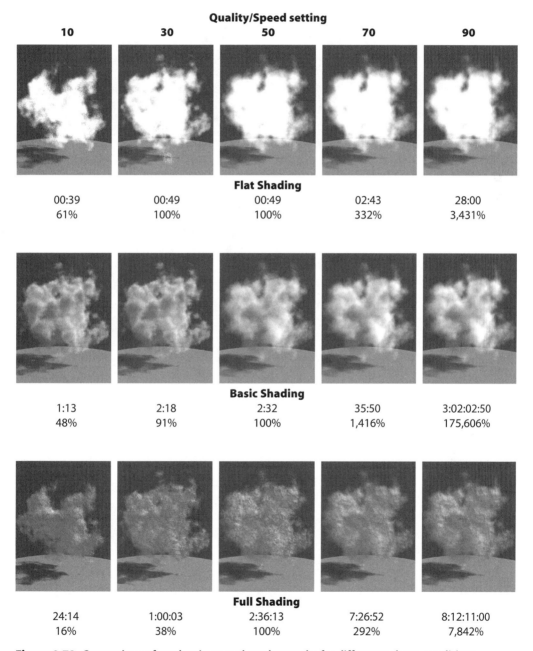

Quality/Speed setting

10	30	50	70	90

Flat Shading

00:39	00:49	00:49	02:43	28:00
61%	100%	100%	332%	3,431%

Basic Shading

1:13	2:18	2:32	35:50	3:02:02:50
48%	91%	100%	1,416%	175,606%

Full Shading

24:14	1:00:03	2:36:13	7:26:52	8:12:11:00
16%	38%	100%	292%	7,842%

Figure 9.72 Comparison of render times and render results for different volume conditions.

Flat Shading, Quality/Speed = 50

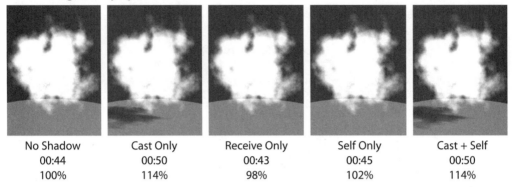

No Shadow	Cast Only	Receive Only	Self Only	Cast + Self
00:44	00:50	00:43	00:45	00:50
100%	114%	98%	102%	114%

Basic Shading, Quality/Speed = 50

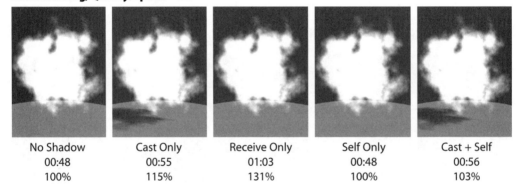

No Shadow	Cast Only	Receive Only	Self Only	Cast + Self
00:48	00:55	01:03	00:48	00:56
100%	115%	131%	100%	103%

FullShading, Quality/Speed = 50

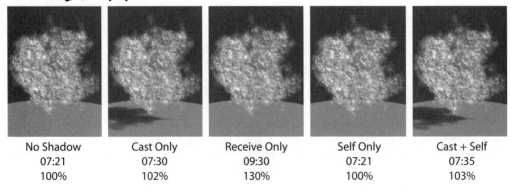

No Shadow	Cast Only	Receive Only	Self Only	Cast + Self
07:21	07:30	09:30	07:21	07:35
100%	102%	130%	100%	103%

Figure 9.72 *continued* Comparison of render times and render results for different volume conditions.

Flat Shading, Quality/Speed = 50

Receive + Self	Cast + Receive	Cast+Receive+Self
00:45	00:50	00:49
102%	114%	111%

```
FlatShading; Quality/Speed =50
          No Shadow . . . . 0:44
          Cast Only . . . . 0:50
       Receive Only . . . . 0:43
          Self Only . . . . 0:45
         Cast + Self . . . . 0:50
      Receive + Self . . . . 0:45
      Cast + Receive . . . . 0:50
Cast + Receive + Self . . . . 0:49
```

Basic Shading, Quality/Speed = 50

Receive + Self	Cast +Receive	Cast+Receive+Self
01:05	02:37	02:32
129%	327%	317%

```
BasicShading; Quality/Speed =50
          No Shadow . . . . 0:48
          Cast Only . . . . 0:55
       Receive Only . . . . 1:03
          Self Only . . . . 0:48
         Cast + Self . . . . 0:56
      Receive + Self . . . . 1:05
      Cast + Receive . . . . 2:37
Cast + Receive + Self . . . . 2:32
```

FullShading, Quality/Speed = 50

Receive + Self	Cast +Receive	Cast+Receive+Self
9:29	2:36:09	2:36:13
129%	2,129%	2,130%

```
Full Shading; Quality/Speed =50
          No Shadow . . . . 7:21
          Cast Only . . . . 7:30
       Receive Only . . . . 9:30
          Self Only . . . . 7:21
         Cast + Self . . . . 7:35
      Receive + Self . . . . 9:29
      Cast + Receive . . 2:36:09
Cast + Receive + Self . . 2:36:13
```

Figure 9.72 *continued*

Although the slider goes all the way up to 100, we urge you never to use that setting. The difference in appearance between 60 or 70 and 100 is negligible when compared to the overwhelming increase in render time for a setting of 100. Figure 9.72 charts the render time for different quality settings of the same material. Of course, the times are relative to one another and depend on other factors, such as the type of texture used to drive the Base Density, the speed of your CPU, and so on. (In case you were curious, the computer we used is a Power Macintosh 8100 with a 333 MHz G3 Sonnet upgrade board.) Still, it serves as a guide to help you judge how to get the best render bang for the time buck.

Volume Material Options

Figure 9.73 The Material Options pop-up menu for volume materials (the bottom options, which do not function for volume materials, are crossed out).

Earlier in this chapter, we went through the material options for surface materials. When the Surface/Volume toggle is set to Volume, the items on the Material Options pop-up menu change to specific items for volume materials. The options are grouped in two categories: shading style, and shadow and other options. Figure 9.73 shows the Material Options pop-up menu for volume mode.

Shading Style

The shading style options determine the extent to which Bryce's shaders interact with the volume. As the ray-tracing ray marches through the volume and encounters texture, does it merely note it, or fully give it all the nuances of shading, or something in between?

Flat Shading

Flat Shading is the simplest option (see Figure 9.74). Bryce notes that the volume texture is there and distinguishes present from absent. But when the volume texture is visible, it has a basic, flat appearance. Diffusion and Ambience and Diffuse and Ambient Color are calculated, but that is all. Objects with Flat Shading can cast shadows but cannot receive shadows cast upon them.

Figure 9.74 Three volume shading styles: Flat Shading (left), Basic Shading (center), and Full Shading (right).

Table 9.1 compares the available options for each of the three volume shading options. The significant difference between Basic and Flat is that Basic allows the object to receive shadows. The significant difference between Basic and Full is that Full also allows the use of Specularity and Specular Colors.

	Flat	Basic	Full
Color			
Diffuse Color	√	√	√
Ambient Color	√	√	√
Specular Color			√
Specular Halo Color			√
Value (Illumination)			
Diffusion	√	√	√
Ambience	√	√	√
Specularity			√
Shadows			
Cast	√	√	√
Receive		√	√
Self		√	√

Table 9.1 Comparison of Material Controls Available in Each Volume Shading Mode.

Basic Shading

Basic Shading is a step up from Flat Shading. Designed with clouds and gaseous forms in mind, Basic Shading improves the interaction of light within the volume material, and the volume can receive shadows cast onto it and can cast shadows on itself. Basic Shading's illumination consists of Diffusion and Ambience. Basic Shading's color consists of Diffuse and Ambient Color.

Full Shading

Full Shading is the high-end version—All shading is calculated for each part of the volume. The result tends to be darker than in other cases.

Full Shading adds specular illumination and specular coloring to the object. Since, within the volume, the ray will encounter an abundance of tiny surfaces as it

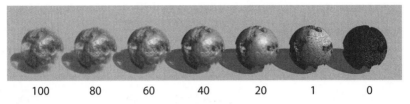

| 100 | 80 | 60 | 40 | 20 | 1 | 0 |

Figure 9.75 A volume object with Full Shading, at different Fuzzy Factor settings

marches through the object, calculating specular highlights for each one encountered significantly increases the render time. Full Shading works better with hard-surfaced objects. Use it with a Fuzzy Factor at a setting under 100. That way you can have an object with a complex surface, but you don't need to calculate surface after surface after surface within the object. Since you don't have to take as many samples within the object, your Quality/Speed setting can be lower, much more toward the speed end.

Figure 9.75 compares a single Full Shading volume texture. The only thing that differs from sphere to sphere is the Fuzzy Factor setting. The most dramatic difference from one setting to the next is the one between a setting of 1 and a setting of 0. If you want your volume to be completely hard, use 1!

> **TIP:** *If you are making soft, wispy volumes such as clouds, set the Fuzzy Factor to a higher number. If you are making hard-edged rocky items, set the Fuzzy Factor to a lower number.*

Light Sensitive

Light Sensitive is different from the other options; it is the option Bryce uses when you set a light to be volume visible light. (See Chapter 12, "Brycean EnLightenment," for more about lights in general.) When light strikes a light-sensitive volume, the light will make the texture glow. There are no shadows or opacity of textures. The texture glows uniformly; it doesn't matter which direction the light is coming from. (As a result, this option renders more swiftly.) The Light Sensitive option was designed to simulate tiny particles floating in the air. Light Sensitive is also one of the volume options that works without any texture whatsoever. If there's no texture for density, then what you're left with is light that picks up the fine particles floating in the air. It's haze that is located only in the light beam itself.

We compare Light Sensitive applied in different conditions in Figure 9.76. The left object, a, is a volume visible light with no texture. (Note: Bryce's default Base Density setting for volume visible light is too low; we cranked ours up to over 80

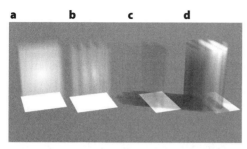

Figure 9.76 Light Sensitive option applied to different objects: a) Volume visible light; b) volume visible light with texture-driven Base Density; c) cylinder object set to Light Sensitive; d) cylinder that is not Light Sensitive, but set to Basic Shading. Both c and d are partially lit by parallel spotlights to show the material's behavior in the presence (and absence) of light.

to make the density more visible.) The second object, b, is identical to the first, except that this one has texture-driven Base Density. The third object, c, is a cylinder set to Light Sensitive. The cylinder has the texture, and one half of it is under a parallel spotlight. The lit part is thicker than the unlit part, but it is hardly as bright as the light, the second object. The fourth object, d, is the same textured cylinder, but set to Basic Shading and not set to Light Sensitive. This set of objects demonstrates that using the Light Sensitive option with actual light objects is better than using the option with standard objects that are being lit by a different light source.

Additive

The Additive option, shared with the surface materials options, makes the object significantly lighter. For eerie glowing ghost effects, using Additive with Basic Shading may be a better option than using Light Sensitive.

Shadows

The three shadow options are identical to those of the surface material options. An object can cast shadows onto other objects, an object can have a shadow cast onto itself by another object, or an object can cast a shadow onto itself. Figure 9.77 shows examples of different combinations of the shadow options

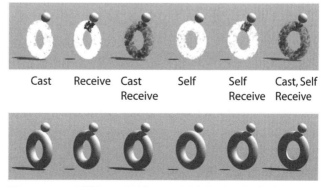

Cast Receive Cast Self Self Cast, Self
Receive Receive Receive

Figure 9.77 Different shadow options for basic volume, with surface object shown beneath for comparison.

- *Cast Shadows.* The object casts shadows onto other objects. This option is available with all three volume shading options (Flat, Basic, and Full Shading). When used alone, that is, the object only casts shadows, it is the least render-intensive option.

- *Receive Shadows.* The object receives shadows cast onto it. This option is available only with Basic and Full Shading; objects with Flat Shading will not receive shadows. For volume objects, Receive Shadows and Cast Shadows can be combined so the object casts shadows onto itself. This significantly increases render time.

- *Self Shadows.* This third option, which provides a specific and notable effect for surface materials, is nearly redundant for volume materials. The difference between objects with Cast + Receive + Self Shadows and those with only Cast + Receive Shadows is hardly noticeable. We conducted an experiment and found that the render times differed oh-so-slightly, and that there was a tiny difference between images (when analyzed using Photoshop's Difference mode to locate where they differed). When the images are looked at side by side, however, the difference is negligible.

Sampling Blur

In volume textures, as the rendering ray marches through the object, it strikes the object at distinct intervals. This may result in ugly banding artifacts. Sampling Blur is an antidote. Sampling Blur staggers the distinct intervals, making banding artifacts less likely to occur. Think of Sampling Blur as a form of antialiasing for volumes. No; it's not an oversampling process, but one of fudging the sample intervals, resulting in a smoother appearance. Always keep this option on!

Volume Blend Options

Although Volume Blend Altitude and Volume Blend Distance appear in the Materials Options pop-up menu when the Materials Lab is in Volume mode, these are meaningless options for volume materials. They modify Volume Color, which, oddly enough, doesn't work in volume materials. These two items shouldn't be on the menu. Unfortunately, they are, resulting in more confusion for you, and more work for us, since we now have to tell you to ignore them and why. Not that we're complaining; we're just suffering along with you. If you simply must know why these two menu items are bogus, we'll spell it out. Although both options have *volume* in their names, they work with the modification of the interiors of solid objects. Volume Color works in the hollow interior of an object.

Volume materials determine whether density is present or not throughout the object. There is either density or nothing; "hollow" does not exist for volume materials. So although the word *volume* will trip you up with the empty promise of significance, ignore it; the two options do nothing for volume materials.

Alpha Scaling and Volumes

Since Base Density is driven by the alpha portion of the Texture Source, you can set it so that Alpha Scaling works with Base Density. Recall our earlier discussion of Alpha Scaling. We mentioned all the surface material options, but postponed the Volume option until now. Base Density is the one volume material attribute that is driven by a Texture Source. Since it is driven by the texture's alpha, Base Density can be set to work with Alpha Scaling. Base Density is similar to Transparency in the following ways: Alpha determines what is "there," and what is "not." When alpha decrees that density is there, a setting of 100 makes density the maximum. Applying Alpha Scaling to Base Density changes the weight of Base Density at the lower end of the scale so that the texture density disappears entirely. Figure 9.78 shows what happens to Alpha Scaling and Base Density. Compare it with Figure 9.42, which shows Alpha Scaling and surface material attributes. When would you want to use Alpha Scaling with Base Density? You'd use it when you want to uniformly tone back all densities. In that case, start with a higher setting. With the presence of the Fuzzy Factor, though, you'll probably not have to use Alpha Scaling much with volume textures—but since it's an available option, we felt compelled to mention it.

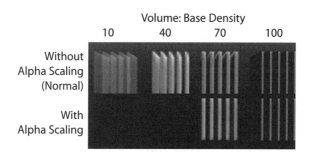

Figure 9.78 Alpha Scaling with Base Density. The top row shows different settings with Alpha Scaling off; the bottom row shows the same settings with Alpha Scaling on. Compare this figure to the other Alpha Scaling examples in Figure 9.42.

As Painless as Possible: Working with Volume Materials

Volumes are often frustrating to explore, because the consequences of each move of the slider are so time consuming. It's a wonder that you work with volumes at all, since doing so requires a dose of patience. You need a strategy to reduce the render pain to a bare minimum.

Here are the factors that affect render time:

- *Shading Method.* Your choice of Flat, Basic, or Full Shading affects the render time. Flat requires the smallest calculation resources, Basic requires more, and Full requires the most.

- *Quality/Speed Setting.* Properly setting this control determines whether you stay sane or altogether give up working on volume materials. Though the slider goes up to 100, do not even think of using it at 100! Refer to our master grand info-graphic figure (Figure 9.72) to compare the results of quality settings with the render times incurred.

- *Shadow Mode.* The final render time increases significantly if the volume object both casts and receives shadows.

- *Type of Texture Driving the Volume Material.* Some textures are based on noises that take longer to calculate. Sometimes you can do something about this, and other times you can't. Of the factors listed here, this one is the least important. See the next chapter, on textures, for more information.

In addition, if you have the Nano Preview set to update automatically, working in your scene in the main Bryce scene window will be a tremendously sluggish experience.

Here are our suggestions to make working with volumes tolerable:

- Turn Auto-Update off in the Nano Preview.

- For a volume material, set the Quality/Speed slider toward the speed end. Make it lower than 50—say between 10 and 35 when you're just starting out.

- Work in Flat Shading mode to begin with, or in Basic Shading without receiving any shadows.

- Once you've worked with your volume and texture to get your object to appear the way you want it to appear, add a bit more quality by increasing the numeric setting on the Quality/Speed slider, or set the object to receive shadows, or do both. Your volume material's particular requirements will dictate which of the two to do first.

Elsewhere in your scene, don't make the volume material do any more than it absolutely has to. If you have created some volume clouds for the purpose of casting shadows on objects in the scene, while those clouds are off camera, set them to Flat Shading mode.

Texture Source Revisited: Practical Tips

Once you place any of the channel markers in any of the columns to drive that channel, Bryce randomly assigns a 3D Texture to the source. So if, say, you place the Diffusion marker in column D, then Bryce will assign a 3D Texture to Texture Source D.

If you exit the Materials Lab, you'll lose any Texture Source that isn't actively placed in one of the channels. At times, Susan has momentarily gotten rid of a texture to see how the material—minus that one Texture Source—renders in the scene. But she doesn't want to lose the texture entirely, so she places the marker in an unused channel, which serves as a holding spot. Assuming that there are no other Texture Sources in these two channels, two favorite places are the Bump Height (with the slider set to 0) and Transparent Color (with slider set to 0) channels. The Texture Source will still "stay" there, so you can use it later, but won't affect the render.

When you open the Materials Lab, there is a priority order in the rendering of previews. First, the preview window renders. When that is finished, each Texture Source preview will render.

MOVING ON...

Congratulations on coming this far through material-dom! We continue the quest for the perfect surface or volume in the next chapter, where we examine textures in minute detail.

CHAPTER TEN

Material World II: Picture Textures and the Deep Texture Editor

IN THIS CHAPTER...

- 2D Picture textures: descriptions, how-to's, and pointers
- 3D Textures and the "shallow" Texture Editor
- The Deep Texture Editor: a dissection of each part
- How to analyze any material
- Building a couple of material settings from the ground up

In the previous chapter, we examined materials. This chapter focuses on the textures that are used to make certain materials. There are two types: 2D Pictures and 3D Textures. We refer to them as pictures and textures, to match the P and the T buttons of the Texture Source in the Materials Lab.

If you're reading this chapter to get to the goods without having familiarized yourself with the Materials Lab, we wish you luck. This chapter builds on the foundation laid in the previous chapter.

2D PICTURE TEXTURES

The Picture Library holds images with their alpha masks: an RGB-color image for your Texture Source, and a grayscale image for alpha, which will be the alpha and bump information of the Texture Source.

Bryce's 2D Picture options allow you to wrap images onto any object. The most common formats are these: PICT (native to the Macintosh but available to Windows users if they have installed QuickTime 3.0 or greater), BMP (native to Windows but also available to Mac users with QuickTime installed) , PSD, TIF, GIF, JPG, TGA (targa), RLE, IFF, PCX, and PNG. See Table 8.1 in Chapter 8, "Terrains, Symmetrical Lattices, and the Terrain Editor" for a full list. You can have a texture that repeats again and again, or you can place a single photographic image into your scene as a separate object.

A Basic How-To

To put a photograph into your scene as a cutout, you need two image files: the object itself and a mask. The mask trims away any extraneous image area so that your image retains its own shape inside the Bryce scene. The mask or alpha channel can be viewed in the Bryce Picture Library; it can drive any of the illumination or optics and bump channels in the Materials Lab. There are other uses that Opacity Maps can be put to with the aid of the Materials Lab, but we'll first focus on the basic transparency model.

How to Create a Photographic Two-Dimensional Image with an Alpha Channel

Making an object using photographic image with an alpha channel is pretty straightforward:

1. Click the Create Picture Object icon (the gold Leonardo-man) in the Create Palette.

2. Bryce opens the Picture Library. Select an available picture or click the Load button above the top-right window to import an image from your hard disk to the Picture Library (see Figures 10.1a and b).

Figure 10.1 Loading pictures into the Picture Library: a) Clicking the Load button; b) navigating in the dialog box for the desired image; c) the selected image in the Picture Library preview windows.

3. The selected picture should appear in the previews at the top of the Picture Library. If the image has an alpha channel, it will appear in the second window. Click the black-and-white circle above the center preview window to invert the alpha channel, if need be. The window on the right shows what is clipped and what is not (see Figure 10.1c).

4. Click the check mark. Your image is applied to the object. Bryce takes care of the Materials settings automatically.

5. Render.

Figure 10.2 is a series of many picture images brought into a Bryce scene using this method.

Images courtesy MetaPhotos

Figure 10.2 "Occupational Hazard," a series of picture objects. (Images courtesy MetaPhotos.)

The Picture Library

Bryce keeps all of the images in a Picture Library. The previous little walkthrough indicated one way to access it. There are several others. In the Materials Lab, click the Texture Source Editor button of the Texture Source. (The texture needs to be a picture texture; otherwise, that Edit Texture button will take you to the Deep Texture Editor.) On the Edit Palette, select Edit 2D Pict Textures from the pop-up menu underneath the Edit Materials icon. From the Objects menu, choose Edit 2D Pictures (or ⌘-Option-M on the Macintosh or Ctrl+Alt+M using Windows).

Figure 10.3 The Picture Library.

The Picture Library (see Figure 10.3) has two main parts. The top part, with the larger windows, is the place for working with the active picture. Below are holding places and thumbnails for your collection of pictures.

Image Thumbnail Area

The Image Thumbnail Area displays small previews of whatever images are currently present in the Picture Library. When your mouse pointer hovers over an image thumbnail, the name of that image appears in the status text display at the lower left of the Picture Library. To select any of the pictures, click the thumbnail. The thumbnail is outlined in red, and that image appears in the top three windows.

Clicking an empty, gray thumbnail is the equivalent of clicking the Load button (as previously mentioned in the "A Basic How-To" tutorial). Click an empty thumbnail to get an Open dialog box, where you can navigate to your desired image and bring it into the Picture Library.

Below the image thumbnail area, five commands are displayed. Two of them affect the currently selected image. Rename brings up a dialog box where you can rename the image, and Delete allows you to rid the library of the image. (After, of course, Bryce displays the obligatory dialog box that asks you if you're sure you want to delete—are you ever really sure?) We'll get back to the other three commands in a bit.

The observant (or bored) person may note that there are a total of 30 spaces for image thumbnails. The total capacity, however, is greater than 30 images. When there are 31 or more images, a scrollbar appears to the right, so that you may see them all. (Once you add more than 30, however, the order in which they're displayed may change.) What is the upper limit to the number of images displayed in the Picture Library? We tried to find out and concluded that the limit is constrained by the system memory assigned to Bryce, or to one's sanity. If you keep adding images, you'll hit the ceiling of one or the other.

The Top Three Windows

The top part of the Picture Library, composed of three windows, provides a preview of the selected picture. The left two windows correspond to the first two Texture Source properties: color and alpha. The third window is a combined view showing the way the alpha information will affect the object. (The alpha information also determines the bump information; there is no third information source that drives Bump Height.) The little gray equation tells how it all works: Color (left) plus Alpha (center) equals the Combination (right).

Load Image

At the top left of each window is a Load button. Clicking it evokes an Open dialog box to load an image from your disk into the Picture Library. For the first two windows, the Load button loads the image *into that particular channel*—either color or alpha. Whatever image was displayed before loading is replaced by the new one. The third window's Load button imports a new image. It doesn't matter which thumbnail is selected below; the result of clicking the right Load button always brings a new image into the Picture Library.

New Image

The Combination (right) window also sports a New button. Clicking that brings up a dialog box where you can specify the settings for a new, blank image (see Figure 10.4). You can name the image, specify its size, and select a color for it (good if you need a plain-colored image for whatever reason).

Figure 10.4 a) New Image dialog box, for generating a new, blank image in the Picture Library; **b)** Image Size pop-up menu for the new image.

Why would you want to generate a new image within Bryce's Picture Library? Here are some possible reasons we could think of; you may come up with some more:

• A plain-colored texture where you need to use a picture-based alpha channel

• A Decal texture where you have an image for the alpha channel (that is the shape of the decal), but you need to generate the color that will be either the decal or the background

• A plain image that you will later embellish using one of the available filter tools that Bryce 4 provides for you (there's more on filters at the end of this section)

Once you decide to create a new image, the dialog box offers you these choices: Name, Image Size, and Background Color.

Naming is straightforward: Type a name in the text box. If you don't want to do so, Bryce supplies a name for you.

For the image size, you can enter numbers (for pixels) in the numerical entry boxes or select from the options on the pop-up menu (see Figure 10.4b). That triangle next to the Image Size label would, of course, lead you to believe that there's a pop-up menu displaying a number of standard image size options—and if you're using Bryce on Windows, there is. But if you're using Bryce on a Mac, you must use Windows-like mouse actions to get a menu: Click and release; the menu will then appear. If you engage in normal Mac menu-eliciting behavior, just pressing the mouse button, you will not see the menu. (It took Susan forever to discover that a menu was even there, poor Mac-using slob that she is. Once she discovered the existence of the menu, she regretted having to delete what she'd written about the lack thereof.)

To select a background color for your image, press your mouse in the color swatch to access the pop-up color picker. If you want to be more precise by using the alternate color pickers, beware of this consequence: When you Option-click/Alt+click or Control-Option-click/Ctrl+Alt+click the swatch to access the alternate color pickers, you are given access to the other color pickers. However, when you leave the color picker dialog boxes and go back to the New Image dialog box, the swatch will not be updated. Lest you think all is lost, Bryce is ultimately obedient to your color whims; it at least applies the color to the image when you click the check mark to create the New Image.

Black and White Circles

Above the Color and Alpha windows are small, circular buttons: black, white, and for alpha, half and half. The solid black or solid white button, when clicked, will delete the contents of whatever is displayed, making the window solid black or white (depending which button you clicked). Although you may be thinking to yourself, "I want to put a solid white alpha channel in this image," Bryce treats the whole process as deletion, and it offers you that "Are you sure you want to delete?" dialog box to confirm. Humor the silly application; it is concerned with deleting what is there in order to replace that with solid white or solid black, while all you're thinking of is filling that channel with solid white or black.

The alpha channel's additional circular control—half-black, half-white—inverts the alpha channel, to crop the other part of the image (see Figure 10.5).

Figure 10.5 Inverting the alpha channel: The half-black/half-white circle inverts the alpha channel, making different portions of the color show.

Copy and Paste

Underneath each window are Copy and Paste buttons to copy that particular channel and to paste to that particular channel.

- *Color.* Copies or pastes only the color information. Paste overwrites previous color information for that image.

- *Alpha.* Copies or pastes only the alpha information. Paste overwrites previous alpha information for that image.

- *Combination.* Copies both color and alpha information. Paste generates a completely new image. (Using Paste Combination is the fastest way to fill up the Picture Library.)

Copy 'em all! Paste 'em with your friends! Or rather, copy and paste and trade—trade color and alpha information among the color and alpha parts of an image! You can click the Copy button under the Color window (Bryce's Display Status calls the Copy button the Pict Image) and then click the Paste button under the Alpha window to create an alpha channel that is a desaturated, grayscale version of the picture. That's a quick 'n' dirty way to create an alpha channel for an image that doesn't have one. It may not be perfect, but it has its uses.

Filtering Images

You have the option of using Photoshop-compatible filters on your images right there in the Picture Library. The triangle to the right of each window accesses a pop-up menu with all your filters. The bottom item lets you select your plug-ins folder. (You can do the same thing in the Filter menu in the Terrain Editor; whatever is chosen here will affect what filters appear in the Terrain Editor's menu, and vice versa.)

There are advantages and disadvantages to working directly in the Picture Library with Photoshop-compatible filters:

Advantage: It's quick and dirty. You can quickly apply an effect to an image.

Disadvantage: There's no Undo option available. If you don't like the effect, you'll have to delete and reload the image.

Advantage: You can copy and paste the combination image to work on a duplicate. If you don't like the effect, simply delete and paste again to try another time.

Disadvantage: Unlike Photoshop or Painter, this Filter menu does not give you an item for "last-used filter." If you possess a fair number of filters, you'll need to navigate through the menu hierarchy again to get to any particular one. After a while, the quick and dirty advantage is not so quick and is downright filthy; test your own threshold to find the point where you'd rather adjourn directly to Photoshop for more control.

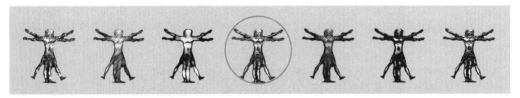

Figure 10.6 Leo picture after different Photoshop filters were applied (ringed Leo in the center has no filter applied).

Figure 10.6 shows a series of Leonardo images that were copied, pasted, and then filtered. Different filters were applied to each image (the center image, with a ring around it, is the normal Leonardo image.)

Global Picture Behaviors and Commands

Now that you know about most of the items in the Picture Library, let's talk about the library itself and what to do with it.

The Picture Library is the place to hold a given picture. You can work with it while thinking, "I want to apply *this* picture to *this* object," and the Picture Library is the place where *this* picture lives. But the Picture Library can also be a place where a collection of pictures live, which may or may not be applied to objects in your scene. The Picture Library has a separate little existence from your scene. And indeed, some of the pictures have a separate existence from anything. Our discussion of global behaviors for the entire Picture Library will help you navigate this in-between area, so that if you create something here, you may actually keep it, rather than inadvertently losing it when you quit Bryce. Your actions in the Picture Library cannot be undone with ⌘-Z or Ctrl+Z. While you are in the Picture Library, you're living on the edge. Everything you do matters. So what good is the Cancel button when you leave the Picture Library? When you cancel out of the Picture Library, you are not changing the library itself, but are choosing not to apply the selected contents of the library to the object. If you got to the Picture Library by creating an object, then canceling from the Picture Library prohibits the object from coming into being. If you got to the Picture Library via the Materials Lab, then canceling from the library means that no changes are made to the object. But any changes you made to the library itself, or to the pictures, will be permanent.

Suppose, for instance, that you earlier applied an image to an object. We'll call that image, say, "Face," and let's suppose that it has both color and alpha, and that the alpha is used as a transparency mask. You could select the object, go to the Materials Lab, and go from there to the Picture Library. While in the Picture Library, you could load another image into the color channel of Face. You have just permanently altered the contents of an image in the Picture Library. If you then cancel out of the Picture Library, the appearance of the Texture Source in the Materials Lab does not change. Bryce thinks, "All right, the user canceled, no changes were made; there's no need to update the image preview in the Texture Source." However, when it comes to rendering the object, Bryce refers to that image, the one called Face. And that image, as you know, just changed. So the rendered image changes, even though you canceled out of the Picture Library. It's tricky that way, but there is an obtuse underlying logic.

Since the Picture Library is a separate entity, how do you manage the image data that's in there? This question is especially pertinent if you happened to, say, copy and paste a bunch of images within the library and apply different Photoshop filters to them and then apply some—but not all—to objects in your scene. You have created new art, some of which exists *only* in your Picture Library. How do you keep it from unintentionally going to File Heaven?

One of the three global commands is the Save List command. Use this to save the contents of your Picture Library to disk. When you save the list, Bryce will suggest the name 2DTEXTURES.LST in the Save dialog box. Keep the .LST suffix and name the file whatever is meaningful to you. Of course, there's the counterpart to saving the list, Open List, which allows you to open a saved list library (Bonus: Older libraries, such as those in the Bryce 2 format, can be opened by Bryce 4). When you open a list, the contents of that list are added to what was already in the Picture Library.

The last of the global commands, Delete All, clears all the contents of the library, leaving you with Leo, the sole survivor.

Saving and opening lists and deleting all are not the only ways to change the contents of your Picture Library. Opening scenes that contain pictures will also change the Picture Library, replacing what was in the library with the picture contents contained in the scene. If you have images in the library that exist only there (such as those filtered copies of an image mentioned earlier), be sure to save the list first, before you open a Bryce scene file. It's okay if, during a single session in Bryce, you create new scene file after new scene file after new scene file. The Picture Library contents will not change from new scene to new scene. But once you open a previously saved scene, the Picture Library will change to whatever was in that scene, *even if the scene you open contains no pictures!* In that case, you'll just get Leo, the default picture.

You can save the list, open the scene file, and then open the list again, and it will be added to what was in the Picture Library.

A Sample Work Session in the Picture Library: How It Changes and Why

Here is a scenario illustrating the change in the Picture Library in the course of a working session.

Launch Bryce. The default picture image, Leo, is in the library. You create a picture object and load an image, Face, and apply that to the object. Then you create another picture object, Arch.

Contents of the Picture Library: Leo, Face, Arch.

You save the scene file and create a new scene file. The contents of the Picture Library are still the same. You apply any of the pictures to objects in the new scene file and save that. The contents of the Picture Library are *still* the same.

Next, you open up a scene file you saved previously. The scene file contains an object whose picture texture is called Ice. Once you open a previously created scene file, the contents of the Picture Library are changed...

Contents of the Picture Library: Ice.

In the Picture Library, you copy Ice and paste it into the Combination window, resulting in Image 2. Next, you apply a filter to Image 2. But this wasn't exactly what you wanted for this scene. After a moment, you remember another scene for which the filtered Image 2 would be perfect, so you cancel out of the Picture Library...

Contents of the Picture Library: Ice, Image 2.

...and open that other scene file. The one you just opened has no pictures in it. Once you open the Picture Library to apply that cool, filtered ice to an object, you discover that—it's gone...

Contents of the Picture Library: Leo

Hey! Where did Image 2 go? It wasn't saved to disk, so it went to file heaven when you opened a previously saved scene file. Gotcha! And...ouch! Fortunately (sort of), you can probably paste the Ice image again and filter it again, if you haven't done any copying or pasting in the meantime. Do you remember what filter you applied? Do you remember the settings?

Image Names, Library Lists, and Disaster Avoidance

When you import an image into the Picture Library, Bryce will remember the name of the image. The name will show up in the list of available 2D Picture textures in the Texture Source pop-up menu. That name information is saved in the scene file. This is not a publish and subscribe situation, though. You've brought the image into the scene, and there it stays, no matter what changes you might make to the original image. The presence of the name will help if you want to reimport an altered image.

Image Resolution

Older versions of Bryce were persnickety about the image resolution; a resolution of 72 ppi would work better than, say, 300 ppi. In Bryce 4, the image density no longer matters.

However, it's a good idea to pay attention to the overall size of the image, that is, the total number of pixels. Is it 128 × 128 pixels? 256 × 256? 512 × 512? Bigger than that? In the earliest days of Bryce (Bryce 1), you couldn't possibly have an image larger than 512 × 512 pixels. The image needs to be held in memory while you're working. (An image of 1024 × 1024 that has RGB + alpha channel is 4 megabytes in size.) The rule of thumb is to keep the image the smallest size possible without sacrificing quality. Before you make the image larger, make sure that it's at 72 ppi. The final render size will also determine the resolution of the image for the picture texture; if your final render is going to be 640 × 480, then there's no sense in having a source image that's 1024 × 1024. Not only will you have to keep that huge image in memory, but during the render, Bryce will have to interpolate the image to a smaller size. With Pict Interpolation turned on (the default state), it's not a problem, whether you have to render the image larger or smaller than its original size. (Note: This discussion concerns the total number of pixels to use in a picture texture. Render resolution and changing the final render to be something other than 72 ppi is a different subject entirely. See Chapter 13, "Render Unto Bryce," and "Printing Bryce Images" (a chapter on the Website), for more about image resolution that is other than 72 ppi.)

Opacity Maps and PICT Textures

Now that you have the basic idea of how to wrangle picture textures inside the Picture Library, what sort of cool tricks can you try with images? Remember from

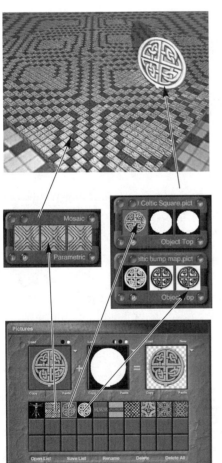

the previous chapter on the Materials Lab that the Texture Sources can drive color, alpha, and bump. For picture textures, the alpha channel drives both alpha and bump.

Here is a classic case of using an alpha channel to create some optics and illumination. The dome of the tower by Chris Casady (see Figure C10.7) features a cobalt-blue flat surface with gold stars. The Texture Source is a picture and alpha channel. The color information in the picture is the blue field with gold stars. The alpha channel isolates the gold stars and drives both Reflection and Specularity. Putting Reflection and Specularity only where the gold stars are gives the impression that the stars are gold foil applied to a matte cobalt-blue surface. The scene file for this image is in this chapter's folder on the CD-ROM.

To create picture-driven bump information, place bump information in the alpha channel for the picture. You can also create a different image for bump information only. Figure 10.8 uses two

Figure 10.8 Tiles and Medallion scene and the Picture Library show different methods for creating bump information from picture sources. (Images from "The Grammar of Ornament" by Direct Imagination.)

different methods to create bump information for the objects. For the tile floor, the color image was pasted into the alpha channel to provide luminosity-driven bump information. For the Celtic scroll medallion, a second picture was created from the color of the first, after blurring and adjusting the contrast. The original alpha information was necessary to outline the shape. (The source for the images is "The Grammar of Ornament," by Direct Imagination—a CD-ROM with a wealth of historical ornament and decoration.)

Similarly, you can apply filters to the alpha channel that will be used to drive bump. Here's a variation on our filtered Leo series from Figure 10.6. Two different pictures were used to get the results for each Leo shown in Figure 10.9. The color information was not filtered, but it was copied and pasted into the alpha channel of a second picture texture, where a filter was applied. In the Materials Lab, two picture texture sources were used: first, the plain Leo to drive color and transparency information, and second, the filtered-alpha Leo to drive bump information. The bottom row of Figure 10.9 shows the bump information only.

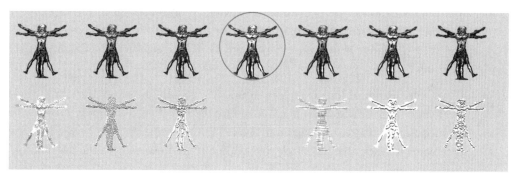

Figure 10.9 A second Leo Texture Source, with a filtered alpha channel, drives Bump Height for each of these Leo examples: The first Texture Source is the standard Leo. (The ringed Leo is plain.) The bottom row shows bump information only.

TIP: Here's a way to do some quick picture editing without leaving Bryce. Copy your picture and then select (or create) a terrain. Open the Terrain Editor, paste the image, and then alter it using the tools available in the Terrain Editor. When you are through, copy the completed image, cancel out of the Terrain Editor (to leave the terrain unchanged), open the Picture Library, and paste the image back into the target spot, or into the Combination window to create a new terrain-based picture.

3D TEXTURES: DEEP TEXTURE EDITOR

3D Textures are what underlie all those natural-looking terrains and Brycean landscapes. These are what you use to set textures that respond to altitude, slope, and orientation, so that your Brycean landscape will differ depending on whether there's a sheer cliff face, a flat lowlands or highlands, or north-facing rocks that have lichen growth.

The 3D Textures are based on mathematical procedures; hence, they are sometimes referred to as Procedural Textures. By the time you are through with this portion of the chapter, we trust that your eyes will be glazed over in response to the depth of detail and the myriad ways that you can forge all those mathematical procedures into believable life-like textures for your Bryce scenes.

Access the Deep Texture Editor (the DTE) from the Materials Lab by clicking the Edit Source Texture button of a Texture Source. This access method assumes, of course, that you have an object selected and are editing its materials. There are two other ways to access the DTE without having an object selected: You can choose Edit 3D Textures from the Objects menu, or from the Edit Palette, you can access the Edit Options menu (underneath the Edit Materials icon) and choose 3D Textures.

The Deep Texture Editor is the procedural Mecca—the heart of Bryce. It evolved over years of Bryce's development while Eric Wenger shaped the application. As he needed a new texture, he added it to the DTE. Over time, it grew. It was, for him, a personal solution that he could work with, but not meant for public distribution.

When Eric Wenger's application was being transformed into version 1.0 of Bryce, the developers weighed the question of whether to include the DTE. The Procedural Textures from the DTE were vital to the software, and yet the DTE was complex and arcane. There certainly wasn't available time to make the Deep Texture Editor accessible in the same way that the main parts of Bryce were made accessible. The developers opted to include the Deep Texture Editor, but not to document or support it. If the bold user wanted to explore, then hail and welcome—but no tour guide was offered. It was only after the Deep Texture Editor was given a new face in Bryce's third major version (Bryce 3D) that MetaCreations documented it. In fact, the official documentation is based on the discussion of the Deep Texture Editor in the previous edition of this book.

Overview

The Deep Texture Editor is analogous to a musical synthesizer. A synthesizer sends a tone through one or more filters to produce a new variation with unique qualities. Bryce's Deep Texture Editor does the same thing, only instead of synthesizing sound, it synthesizes visual noise. The result is visual texture.

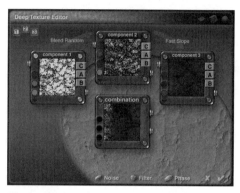

Figure 10.10 The Deep Texture Editor.

Figure 10.10 shows the Deep Texture Editor itself. There are four framed windows. The top three are for texture components, and the fourth is the combination window. The schematics in Figure 10.11 show the logical order of the Deep Texture editing process.

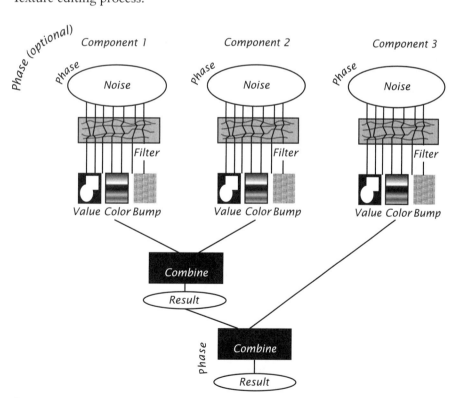

Figure 10.11 The logical sequence used by the Deep Texture Editor to create textures.

Here in the Deep Texture Editor you can start with one, two, or three components. For each component, assign a noise. Then put the noise through a filter. At that point, you need to choose among three output options: Will the component be output as Color, Alpha (which has also been known as Value; hence, the Value area of the Materials Lab), or Bump? Or will the output be some combination of the three? If there is more than one component, how will they be combined? The first two components are combined to form a new hybrid. If there are three components, the hybrid of the first two will be combined with the third component.

Finally, you can apply some global settings to the combined result of the component process. Overall frequency, a final color scheme, a final filtering of the combined alpha, a final apply of global phase completes the texture. The result of the combined components in the Deep Texture Editor will become a *single* Texture Source in the Materials Lab.

This has been a quick take on the process; now we'll tie the process together with the controls in the Deep Texture Editor. As we continue through the chapter, we'll stop and explore the eddies and pools of complexity at each step along the way.

Quick Tour of the DTE

The DTE has three component windows and a combination window at the lower center. Around the edges of the Deep Texture Editor are general controls. The upper left corner houses the control for setting the number of texture components. Click the 1, 2, or 3 to set that number of components. The numbers act as toggles to shut off a component as well. In the upper right corner is the Preview control, for looking at your textures as flat 2D squares, cubes, or spheres. In the lower left corner is the status display, which describes the item that the mouse cursor is pointing to, and if the item is a control, what that control will do. At the bottom of the DTE are buttons labeled Noise, Filter, and Phase. Each button is a toggle to make its control appear or disappear (more on these in a bit). Figure 10.12 shows the results of clicking these buttons. There are two similar-looking palettes for Noise and Phase, and a squarish palette for Filter. The Noise, Phase, and Filter Palettes all have a component indicator, for selecting the active component—or combination. The Noise, Phase, and Filter Palettes can be dragged to other locations on your monitor, should you care to place them elsewhere (the component and combination window frames aren't moveable).

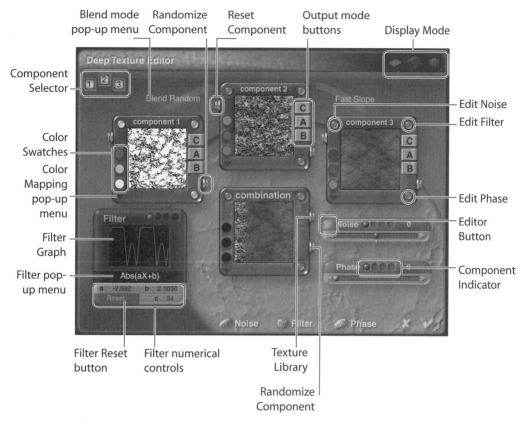

Figure 10.12 The Deep Texture Editor, with the Noise Palette, Phase Palette, and Filter Palette showing.

Component Windows

The component windows and combination window display a texture preview. The window frame has controls for that particular component texture. Each frame contains three buttons, in the corners: one for Noise, one for Filter, and one for Phase. Clicking a button invokes that particular palette. If that palette is already present, then clicking the button will select the component.

Selecting Components

1. Launch Bryce, create an object, go to the Materials Lab, and click the A column for Diffuse and Ambient Color.

   This randomly assigns a Procedural Texture for Texture Source A.

2. Click the pale pink button labeled Texture Source Editor to go to the Deep Texture Editor.

   You should now be in the Deep Texture Editor. The texture that is displayed may or may not have three components to it. It doesn't matter if it doesn't, since you can wake up textures in all components by clicking the 3 in the upper left corner.

3. If all three texture components aren't present, click the 3 in the upper left corner. Three Texture Sources should appear.

4. Click each of the buttons at the bottom for Noise, Filter, and Phase. The respective palettes appear, and the DTE should look like Figure 10.12, though in all likelihood, the textures in the window will be different; don't worry about that.

   Now that all three components contain textures and the three palettes are present, experiment to see how to make each component active.

5. Click in each space in the Noise Palette's component indicator.

   With each click, the component indicators for Phase and Filter match the Noise Palette's component indicator. The buttons around the component windows and the combination window light up to indicate the active component.

6. Now click the buttons on each of the component windows.

   The component indicator button appears in the space for the component you just clicked.

   The controls for Noise, Filter, and Phase change to the active component. There are four buttons, one for each of the three components and one for combination. (The Noise combination button is misleading, as there is no such thing as a combination noise.)

Component Output

Each texture component is assigned one or more of these output types: color, alpha channel, or bump map. The component window's right frame contains three buttons, labeled C, A, and B. Click a button to activate it; it turns a lighter shade of gray (an inactive button is a darker gray and slightly recessed). Bryce automatically applies alpha and bump to the texture, but offers you many choices for color. The lower left side of the frame contains three color swatches for color, and a triangle below those accesses a pop-up menu where you can choose different color mapping modes.

Each component has two switches: one to randomize the component and another to reset the component. Clicking Randomize will shuffle all possible settings, but only for that single component. Clicking Reset will revert the texture to its original state. The original state may be the state of the texture when you first came to the Deep Texture Editor, or if you loaded a new texture from the Texture Library, then clicking Reset will revert back to the state of that newly loaded texture component.

Combination

The combination control, at the bottom, displays the result of the other controls. It does not have any C, A, or B output controls, since those are determined by each individual component. However, color *can* be displayed and selected. There are color swatches and a pop-up menu of color mapping choices. (Often the combination's color mode is set to None.)

Combining Components

When there is more than one component, they are combined using one of several blend modes. The current blend mode is displayed at the curved arrow that arcs between components. Components 1 and 2 are combined, and the result of that is combined with component 3. Pressing the mouse on the term brings up a pop-up menu, where you can select a different blend mode (see Figure 10.13). Later in the chapter, we'll get into the nitty-gritty of how each blend mode works. For now, you just need to know where to find 'em.

Figure 10.13 The Blend Mode pop-up menu.

Combination Window

The combination window displays the final texture. There are no C, A, or B buttons, as the color, alpha, and bump information was already chosen for the individual components. However, you can add a final color cast using the Color Mode pop-up menu and the color swatches.

The combination frame has two buttons, on the side. One randomizes the entire material; the other provides access to the Texture Library. Instant access to the Texture Library is handy when you have a texture you're proud of and want to save it as a preset. Beware of clicking another preset once you're in the library—you'll pop back to the DTE, and all your work will be erased. Fortunately, Undo (⌘-Z/ Ctrl+Z) returns you to the previous state.

Clicking the Randomize Combination button generates entire new textures from any possible combination. Just in case you were curious about the total number of possible combinations of 3D Textures back in the days of Bryce 1, we calculated the number:

1,097,135,300,000,000,000,000,000,000,000,000,000,000,000,000,000,000, 000,000,000,000,000,000

(The calculator stopped filling in specific numbers after the first eight decimal places.) This is a 1 followed by 72 zeroes. Some additional options have been added since Bryce 1, providing more combinations than those originally calculated here—but when you have a number of that magnitude, what's a few zeroes among friends?

Be careful when you want to save your texture; one button (Randomize) will destroy it, and the other button will allow you to save it. Unfortunately, there's precious little to help you distinguish between the two buttons. (Yeah, a little bronze color—so what?) Go slowly here, point your mouse at the button, and look at the status display in the lower right corner. If the unforeseen happens, fortunately ⌘-Z/Ctrl+Z saves you from permanently throwing away the texture you so painstakingly created. But there's another way to avoid the button confusion altogether. Hold down the Shift key and click the word "Combination" at the top of that frame to access the Texture Library. The Shift-click here in the Deep Texture Editor is equivalent to the Materials Lab's means of accessing the same Texture Library by Shift-clicking the top of any of the Texture Sources. If you're already in the Shift-click habit, you can avoid button mixup altogether. It does require two hands, though.

Now that we've taken a whirlwind tour of the DTE, we'll settle down and dig deeper, beginning with the texture's beginnings: noise.

Noise

Noise is the source for textures in Bryce. There are two controls directly associated with noise: the Noise Palette and the Edit Noise dialog box (which we'll also refer to as the Noise Editor).

Noise Palette

The Noise Palette appears when you click the Noise button on one of the components, or when you click the Noise button at the bottom of the Deep Texture Editor. What you see is a slider with the component indicator and a glowing green corner. You may be asking, "Is this *all* there is?" No. The Noise Palette can be continuously present, and it is the doorway to the far more powerful Edit Noise dialog box.

The left corner of the Noise Palette is both a status display and a button. If noise is present for the selected component, the corner will glow green. If there is no noise present, then when your mouse hovers over the button, it will turn green, indicating "I'm a button! Press me!" Of course, if there is noise present, the corner is continuously green, and it glows a bit brighter to taunt you to click it. When you do click the button, the Edit Noise dialog box appears. This is where the real meat of noise editing transpires.

Edit Noise

The Edit Noise dialog box is the place to edit this noise; it is the beginning place for your work with textures (see Figure 10.14).

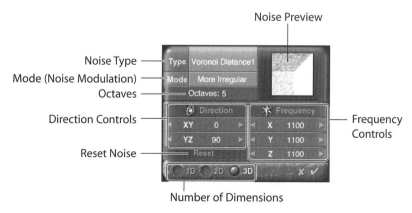

Figure 10.14 The Edit Noise dialog box.

As with the Noise and Phase and Filter palettes, you can drag the Noise Editor around to any place on your screen. By now, though, you've probably noticed that there is no traditional title bar from which to drag. Any part of the Noise Editor (and of the other palettes, too) that does not operate a control or access a pop-up menu can be dragged. Sometimes you may think you're dragging the control only to find out that you're actually changing a setting. Dragging by the outside edges or the image preview area is your best bet with the Noise Editor. (By the way, the new positions of the Noise Editor and the palettes aren't remembered from one Bryce session to the next.)

Edit Noise is a modal dialog box. You can move its position elsewhere, but once it's there on the screen, you cannot work with any of the controls on the component frame while the dialog box is still open. However, you can change the filter settings (stay tuned; more on filters to come!). You can also work with the Noise and Phase Palettes when the Edit Noise dialog box is open. (We'll leave the phase discussion for later.) It's possible to edit the noise for more that one component in a single trip to the Edit Noise dialog box. You could, say, open the Noise Editor while component 1 is active, edit that noise, then click the component indicator for component 2 on the Noise Palette, edit *that* noise, and repeat the process for component 3, all without leaving the Edit Noise dialog box. Although it is possible, we don't recommend it. What if you like the changes you made to component 1 and don't like the changes to component 2? You can undo your changes with ⌘-Z/Ctrl+Z, but you'll end up undoing all the work you did while in the Edit Noise dialog box.

Now that we've dispensed with all the mechanics and vagaries of the Edit Noise dialog box itself, let's discuss its purpose for existing: editing noise.

The Edit Noise dialog box contains controls for the following:

- Type of noise
- Number of dimensions
- Mode (noise modulation)
- Octaves
- Direction (spatial orientation)
- Frequency
- Resetting the noise

Noise Type

First, select the type of noise to generate. The pop-up menu has a whopping 50 noise types. (Bryce 4 includes a whole new series called Voronoi noises; many are slight variations on each other.)

The Noise Editor quickly previews the noise, and then the component window is updated for the noise setting, and after that, the composite window is updated as well. The component and composite renders take place in two steps: first rough, and then detailed. The length of time it takes to render the previews gives you an indication of how computationally expensive the particular noise is. However, there is a very annoying bug in the Noise Editor. The preview is the inverse of the way the texture appears in the component preview. To see what your texture *really* looks like, look at the component preview with only the alpha (A) setting activated (see Figure 10.15).

Figure 10.15 Noise Editor display bug: The preview in the Noise Editor is the inverse of what's shown in the main component window (alpha output). Believe the main component window!

Different noises take different amounts of time to compute. RND Continuous does not take a long time to compute. Among the most expensive noises are Vortex Noise, Voronoi noises, Leopard, Waves, Fractal Stone, and Spots. If you're working with a fast computer, however, you'll hardly notice the time hit. Don't avoid the costly noises altogether—after all, they're there for a purpose—but if you're just experimenting and you're using a slower computer, don't use them cavalierly, unless you have all day, and then some. As we continue, we'll point out the other factors that may make a texture expensive to use.

Number of Dimensions

Set the number of dimensions for your noise with the buttons at the bottom of the dialog box. Noise that is 1D is one-dimensional, 2D is two-dimensional, and 3D is three-dimensional. The number of dimensions for the noise is integral to the two controls described next: Frequency and Orientation.

Frequency

There are two ways to adjust the frequency of your noise to shape the look of your texture. Under the noise preview, the control next to the Frequency label will proportionately adjust the scale of the texture; drag to increase or decrease the frequency on all axes (you can drag the control or the word itself). You may also adjust frequency independently on each dimension using any of the three sliders below the Frequency label. Click the arrows to change the frequency by one number at a time, or keep the mouse pressed to keep the number moving. You can also drag the numbers to quickly adjust them. Alas, woe and alas! You can no longer type numbers directly. (We loved this feature in Bryce 1 and 2 for the Macintosh. Really. Truly.) Although all three frequency settings are constantly available for adjustment, you won't always need them. To determine which ones you'll need, check to see how many dimensions your noise has. One-dimensional texture is on the x axis, two-dimensional texture adds the y axis, and three-dimensional texture adds the z axis. Don't try to fiddle with the z adjustment if you have a 2D texture. If you do, the Noise Editor will take the time to recompute the noise, but nothing will change. When changing frequency on an individual axis basis, drag the numbers or type them directly.

There are a couple of exceptions to the strict correspondence between one dimension and x axis, two dimensions and $x + y$ axes: The Leopard, Stone Cliff, Liquid, and Turbulence noise types, when set to one-dimensional, also receive input from the y and z frequency amounts. (Liquid and Turbulence receive input from the y axis when they are one-dimensional noises.) It's as if, for this noise, 1D defines the direction of the grain, and the noise itself will vary when you change the frequency adjustments on all three axes. Check out the Leopard noise slide show on the CD-ROM (10 MATERIALS II > DTE > LEOPARD NOISE SLIDE SHOW).

In addition to adjusting the noise proportionately using the Global Frequency control in the Edit Texture dialog box, you can also use the slider on the Noise Palette to proportionately adjust the frequency. The slider has only comparative numeric settings, with 0 as its starting place. You can even use that slider while the Edit Noise dialog box is open. The proportional slider is similar to the Materials Lab's vertical sliders above the A, B, C, and D columns on the materials grid. They are not tied to any persistent, meaningful numbers, since the frequency setting can be different on each dimension.

When you preview the noise from within the Noise Editor, the part of the cube that faces the front is the same as in the two-dimensional preview in both the Deep Texture Editor and the Texture Source preview. (You can switch this view by 90° in the Materials Lab by selecting World Top for mapping; what is facing front here in the Noise Editor will face up in Bryce.)

When you set the frequency of the noise, the *x*, *y*, and *z* axes are established first. After that, you can rotate the noise in any general direction using the Direction controls, which are discussed next.

> **TIP:** To make a noise that's generally consistent across two dimensions but without the rigid uniformity of a two-dimensional noise, use three-dimensional noise and vary the frequency along one dimension. For noise that has a vertical grain, reduce the frequency on the y axis. For noise that has a horizontal grain, reduce the frequency along both the x and z axes or increase it along the y axis. Figure 10.16 compares a two- and a three-dimensional noise.

2D Noise with uniform texture along the *y* axis

3D Noise with reduced frequency on one dimension.

Figure 10.16 Three-dimensional noise with a two-dimensional look to it.

Direction

Noise, whether it comes in one, two, or three dimensions, has a grain, or a fixed spatial orientation. In your scene, the direction in which that noise "points" will stay consistent no matter what the objects are or how they are oriented in space. The default mapping for 3D Textures' World Space is based on this orientation.

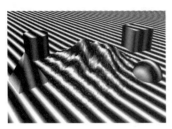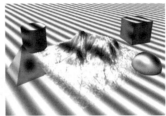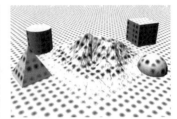

Figure 10.17 One-, two-, and three-dimensional noise oriented in space.

Here in the Noise Editor, you can change the orientation of the noise by rotating it. (You can also change its orientation using the Edit Texture controls in the Materials Lab.) To rotate, use the Direction control on the left side of the Edit Noise dialog box. Drag to change direction. While the mouse is down, you'll see a very rough preview of the grain of the texture. The rough preview looks like cross-hatching, to show you the general orientation. When you release the mouse, the actual texture appears. For precision (or to start over), use the numerical controls at the left. Click the arrows to increase or decrease by single increments, or drag up and down for very quick adjustments. We repeat our lament over the lack of direct text entry capability for number settings in the Deep Texture Editor.

Figure 10.17 shows one-, two-, and three-dimensional noise at Noise Editor settings 0 and 0. Settings at 0 and 0 favor the front of the preview cube in the Noise Editor, which corresponds to the place closest to front view in Bryce World Space. If you want to change the orientation to the top of your object, then you need to rotate so that the cross-hatches appear on the top of the small preview cube in the Noise Editor.

Octaves

Octaves in Bryce's Noise Editor are similar to musical scale octaves. The C that is an octave below middle C is the same note, but lower. (Mathematically, the frequency is half.) Adding an octave in Bryce is analogous to playing both middle C and the C below it at the same time. The result is more complex than if you played only one note. (In fact, for cloud textures in the Sky Lab, when you add complexity by clicking the blue Plus buttons next to the cloud texture previews, you are increasing the Octave setting for the noise.)

You change the Octave setting by dragging horizontally to increase or decrease the number. The lowest value is 0 and the highest value is 8. Each time you set Octave to a higher number, you are adding more processing time, as the noise has to be run through more frequencies for each octave that is computed.

When you add octaves to your noise, you can modulate the noise using one of the several options available on the Mode pop-up menu.

> **TIP**: *Adding octaves tends to make the overall appearance of the texture larger. You can compensate for the change in texture feature size by increasing the global frequency.*

Noise Modulations

When you add an octave, the noise is also generated at a lower frequency with longer wavelengths. Figure 10.18 shows a wave and its lower-octave relative. The original noise is represented by the thick line, and the added lower octave is represented by a thin line. So what happens when there are additional octaves? The Mode menu allows you to tweak these in different ways. For instance, Maximum and Minimum take the combined noises and select only the top and bottom values for the scale. This is analogous to using Photoshop's Lighten and Darken modes.

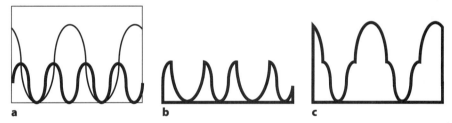

a   b   c

Figure 10.18 Octave and modulation: a) A noise wave (thick line) and its lower-octave cousin (thinner line); b) Minimum modulation; c) Maximum modulation.

Here are brief descriptions of each of the noise modulations. Figure 10.19 shows examples of octaves and modulations. Two different noise types, RND Continuous and Sine, are shown at four Octave settings. RND Continuous noise is shown in each modulation option. To make modulations work, make sure you set Octave higher than 0. Remember: The higher the Octave setting, the longer the processing time, so set Octave judiciously. In addition to the examples shown here, there are more samples (using Voronoi noises) of noise variations, octaves, and modes on the CD-ROM, in this chapter's folder.

- *Standard.* This default modulation adds the new octave at half the frequency and twice the amplitude (see Figure 10.18a).

- *Irregular.* The same as Standard, but more weight is given to the higher frequency noise, resulting in a noise with more detail.

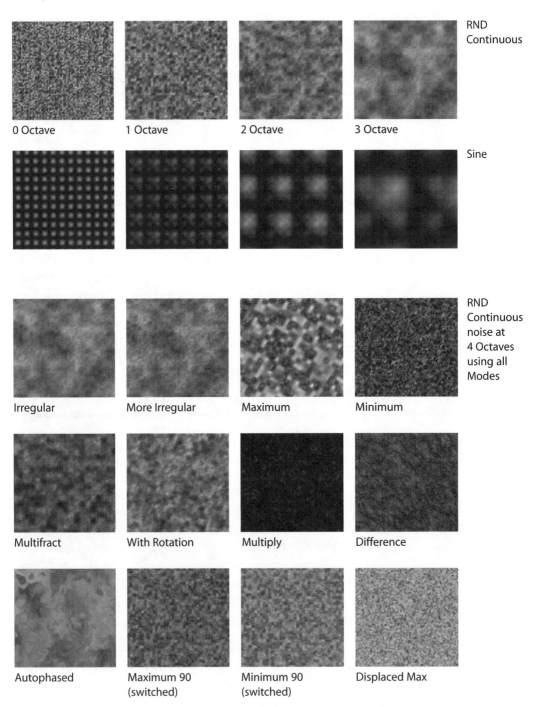

RND
Continuous

0 Octave | 1 Octave | 2 Octave | 3 Octave

Sine

RND
Continuous
noise at
4 Octaves
using all
Modes

Irregular | More Irregular | Maximum | Minimum

Multifract | With Rotation | Multiply | Difference

Autophased | Maximum 90 (switched) | Minimum 90 (switched) | Displaced Max

Figure 10.19 Two different noise types—RND Continuous and Sine—at four Octave settings; RND Continuous noise is shown for all modulation options.

- *More Irregular.* Same as Irregular, but intensified. Compare More Irregular to Irregular when you have a noise modulated at several octaves; More Irregular adds many small details that simply aren't apparent with Irregular.

- *Maximum.* Analogous to Lighten Only, takes the highest (lightest) values to produce the resulting noise (see Figure 10.18c).

- *MultiFractal.* Lighter values mean more high-contrast noise.

- *With Rotation.* Puts a spin on the noise so that each additional octave is rotated in space. This is most easily seen in linear noises, such as a one-dimensional Sine, or RND Linear.

- *Minimum.* Analogous to Darken Only (see Figure 10.18b). Selects the lowest (darkest) values of the combined noises.

- *Multiply.* Also gives a darker result. The different values are multiplied together.

- *Difference.* Difference subtracts the value of one octave's noise from that of the other and displays the result as an absolute value. Absolute values pay no attention to whether a number is positive or negative, representing all results as positive numbers. Think of white as 1 and black as 0. Where the values are identical, the result is black. For instance, white (1) minus white (1) equals 0. Values that are different produce shades of gray; the greater the difference, the lighter the shade. Values that are diametrically opposed, that is, black and white, produce white. Black (0) minus white (1) equals –1, but since the answer is expressed as an absolute value (that is, positive), then the result is white (1). For some strange reason, Difference works even at 0 octaves (we don't know exactly how; we're just reporting the facts, ma'am). The higher the number of octaves, the darker the resulting noise.

- *Minimum 90.* Repeats the noise at a 90° angle from its original orientation and combines the two, finding the *maximum*. Say what? How come it's the maximum combination when the option name is *Minimum*? Because the Minimum 90 and Maximum 90 options are switched. A leftover bug—from Bryce 2, for goodness sake!—lives on even in Bryce 4, and what with that inverse-display bug in the Edit Noise dialog box preview, it looks correct in the Noise Editor, though it is, in fact, incorrect in the actual texture component. This mode is good for woven patterns, where woof and warp are used.

- *Maximum 90.* Repeats the noise at a 90° angle and combines the two, finding the *minimum*. Its name is switched with Minimum 90.

- *Auto-Phased.* Automatically introduces phase to the noise modulation itself, rather than requiring the use of the separate Phase control (see "In Your Phase" for more about phase). Like Difference, Auto-Phase also works when the Octave setting is 0.

- *Displaced Max.* Displaces, or offsets, the noise by a small amount and shows the lightest of the two places where they overlap. This is good for pebbles and stones.

Reset Noise

The Reset Noise control is a button that lets you switch your noise back to its original state. You can revert to the noise you began with without having to leave the Edit Noise dialog box.

In Your Phase

Earlier in our overview of the Deep Texture Editor, we briefly mentioned phase. Phase is an added level of turbulence. (In the Sky Lab, you are adjusting phase when you click the white plus or minus buttons next to the cloud texture previews.) When working with textures, you can apply phase to any one of your individual components or to the combined texture (or both!). When you are working with the Deep Texture Editor, you usually work for a while and then decide later that a bit of phase would do the trick. However, as Bryce's Deep Texture Editor processes things, it looks at phase first to see how the turbulence displaces everything else. So first Bryce will look at the global phase, then phase settings for individual components, and then individual noises, and so on through the loop.

To work with phase, click the Phase Dialog button at the lower right corner of any of the component or combination windows. The Phase Palette will appear. (You can also click the Phase button to get the Phase Palette) The Phase Palette looks similar to the Noise Palette. There is a slider and a button at the left. Click the button and *surprise!* You find yourself in what gives every appearance of being the Edit Noise dialog box. But if you got there by clicking the Edit Phase button, you are in the Edit Phase dialog box. Editing phase is just like editing noise. All the particulars for editing noise apply to creating and editing phase as well, with two important distinctions:

- The only place where you can set the phase frequency is in the Edit Phase (Edit Noise) dialog box. The little slider on the Phase Palette allows you to adjust amplitude. This slider determines how much phase will interfere with the component's noise. (More on this in a moment.)

- There is no such thing as filtering a phase. The filter applies to the noise. Once you have introduced phase into the equation, the combined phase-noise will be percolated together through the filtering process.

Since our entire discussion of filtering follows this section, we'll let the filter matter rest here and take up again with this amplitude business.

The amplitude of the phase refers to the degree of the phase's effect. The higher the amplitude, the more "offset" the original noise is. Figure 10.20 shows a sample of this. On the left is the noise all by itself. Next to that is the phase that's all by itself (although phase can't be seen "by itself," for illustration purposes we substituted a noise here with the exact settings for the phase to show you what the phase looks like, so you can understand how noise is changed by phase). On the right, the phase is applied to the noise at different amplitude settings. As amplitude is increased, you see more interference with the original noise. You don't need to set amplitude very high for phase to have a marked effect. In fact, restrain yourself to the lower parts of the amplitude scale until you have a good grasp of what is happening.

Of course, by now you're starting to get a feel for the costliness of the process. When you introduce another element to offset all other elements, you're asking Bryce to process more, and so your rendering time will increase. Phase in your cost! Have a care when using phase. By all means, use it when the situation calls for it, but don't use it willy-nilly because you think it will be cool to run into the Deep Texture Editor and tweak a few dials.

> **TIP:** Here is a phase housekeeping tip. Check each component to see that phase isn't called upon unnecessarily. The button in the left corner will glow green if there is phase. To turn phase off, click that button to go to the Edit Phase dialog box and set the noise type to Nothing. If you have a noise type selected, even if there's no amplitude, you will still force Bryce to think about that noise type before it gets the all-clear signal from the zeroed amplitude slider. When Bryce is forced to think about things needlessly, your render time increases.

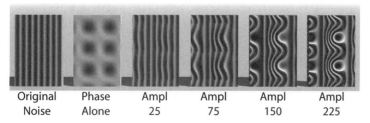

| Original Noise | Phase Alone | Ampl 25 | Ampl 75 | Ampl 150 | Ampl 225 |

Figure 10.20 Phase amplitude adjustment: The original noise is at left, and phase (pictured as if it were alone) is next to it; phase is applied with increasing amplitude settings.

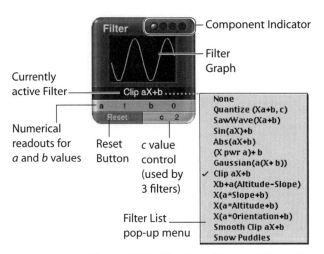

Figure 10.21 The Deep Texture Editor's Filter.

Filtering

Filtering is an extremely powerful feature of the Deep Texture Editor. When you refine a noise through a filter, you alter it in some fashion—by increasing the noise's contrast, posterizing the noise, pulling out additional details, or making the noise occur only at certain altitudes or other spatial orientations.

Filter Area: The ABCs

The Filter Palette is the place to alter the noise. You first select a filter type and then make adjustments to that particular filter. Click the upper right button on the component or combination window frame, or click the Filter button at the bottom of the DTE. The Filter Palette (see Figure 10.21) contains a graph and some numbers for a, b, and c. Choose which of the filter functions you want to apply from the Filter pop-up menu, accessed by pressing the mouse at the name of the filter (which is None if no filter is selected). The filter has a Reset button; click Reset to change the values and graph to make no alteration to the noise; this is equivalent to selecting None for that particular filter. When exploring what these filters do, use Reset as a starting point.

Drag the graph to change the filter. Dragging horizontally changes the a number, and dragging vertically changes the b number. You can also drag the numbers themselves to change the graph's shape. There is also a c variable, which plays an active part in the filter equation for a couple of the filters. It can only be changed by dragging the number setting; there is no graph-drag counterpart. The inability to directly type numbers or to click to change the setting for c (as you could do in Bryce 2) may put you at risk for repetitive strain injury if you make a lot of adjustments to the filter setting. While you're aiming to get the precise setting for c, keep your mousing hand as relaxed as possible. Generally, the a control adjusts the intensity of whatever effect you're applying, and b adjusts the overall height of the graph. In some filters, a and b may stand for other things.

Visualize the top part of the range as being white and the bottom part as black. Figure 10.22 shows the filter graph next to a gray ramp. Or think of the graph's range as a side-view cutaway of a bump map; the deepest dents are at the bottom, and the heights are at the top.

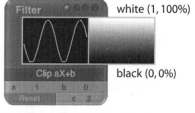

Figure 10.22 The filter graph, with a grayscale gradient next to it for comparison.

The filters use two sets of number schemes. In the graph, which you should visualize as a continuum from black to white, the bottom (black) is 0, and the top (white) is 1. If you think of 0 and 1 in terms of percentage of brightness, then the bottom is 0% bright (or black), and the top is 100% bright (or white). The *graph* will not go lower than 0 or higher than 1 (what's blacker than black or brighter than white?). The other set of numbers are those that drive the graph: *a, b,* and *c*. Those numbers range all over the place.

To get the best feedback from your work with the graph, set the output of your texture component so its only output is alpha; make sure that the A button is the only one that is light gray. You should then be able to see your texture in grayscale.

The Reset button sets the filter back to the neutral position for that filter. In all cases, the numerical settings are changed to $a = 1$, $b = 0$, and $c = 2$.

Now let's get down to specifics. The following descriptions show the relationship among the filter formula, the graph appearance, and the final noise result. The discussion will take the filters in a logical sequence, not necessarily the order they're listed in the pop-up menu. We begin with Clip aX + b because it is the most basic of the filters.

Clip aX + b

The most often-used, ubiquitous contrast filter, Clip gets its name from portions of the noise being clipped at the upper and lower ends, for higher contrast. When you adjust the sliders, *a* controls the contrast, and *b* controls the overall brightness.

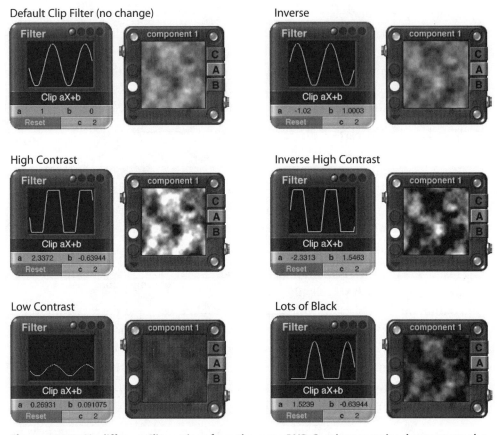

Figure 10.23 Six different Clip settings from the same RND Continuous noise demonstrate the range of possibilities.

For a low-contrast effect, make the wave smaller. Decrease *a* to reduce the size of the wave, and increase *b* to move the entire wave up. All the noise information will be output as expressions of middle grays for low-contrast noise (see Figure 10.23).

For a high-contrast effect, make adjustments so that the wave hits the top and bottom edges. When the wave hits the top, it clips at white; when it hits the bottom, it clips at black. The wave actually ascends above and descends below the limits, but the top represents white, and you can't get any whiter than white by going "beyond" white. Give *a* a large number for a higher range of wave motion; give *b* a negative number to move the entire curve down, and then center it so that portions clip at top and bottom.

When interpreting the graph it may be helpful to read the slope of the line as indicative of the amount of contrast. A steep line means quick transitions between

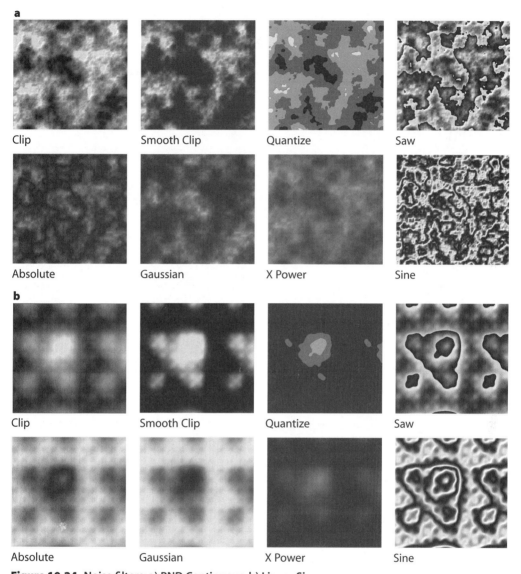

Figure 10.24 Noise filters: a) RND Continuous; b) Linear Sine.

light and dark (high contrast), whereas a gentle slope means gradual shifts from light to dark (low contrast).

To invert the noise (white changes to black), make a negative and adjust b to the corresponding level. (To invert the default filter, set $a = -1$ and $b = 1$.)

For the following filter descriptions, Figure 10.24 shows examples of all filter types as they are applied to two types of noise: Random (RND) Continuous and Linear Sine. Here are the starting settings for each noise before the filter is applied.

- Random Continuous: 3D noise, 3 Octaves Standard Mode, Direction is 0,0 and Frequency is $X=171$, $Y=171$, $Z=170$.

- Sine is identical to the Random Continuous example, except the noise type is set to Sine.

See this chapter's folder on the CD-ROM for the actual textures used in Figure 10.24.

Smooth Clip aX + b

Smooth Clip is the same as Clip aX + b except that it smoothes out the hard transitions near black and white.

Quantize

Quantize, analogous to the Terrain Editor's (and Photoshop's) Posterize, creates discontinuities as gray values stair-step from one level to the next. The setting for c determines the number of levels between black and white, and the settings for a and b determine overall contrast and height.

SawWave

SawWave starts as a contrast filter (when there's a small curve in it). When the curve reaches the limits, instead of the top and bottom being clipped, the curve is bounced back in the other direction. The result is high-contrast discontinuity, like a saw. Use this with color output to get portions of high-contrast alternating color. When you set a high, so that there are many waves bouncing top to bottom, you'll get areas that have a lot of noise. Use care in setting a, the height, when using SawWave to filter noise for bump output.

Sin(aX) + b: Sine Wave

The Sine Wave filter gives you a high number of lines that follow the same path. Use it for creating things such as wood textures or perhaps rippling desert sand. The number of lines is determined by a. This filter is continuous. As a increases, the curve maintains its curved shape as it bounces back down from the top. Higher numbers, say, 10 or 20, are best. The value for b, as usual, adjusts the entire curve and determines the clipping at the top or bottom.

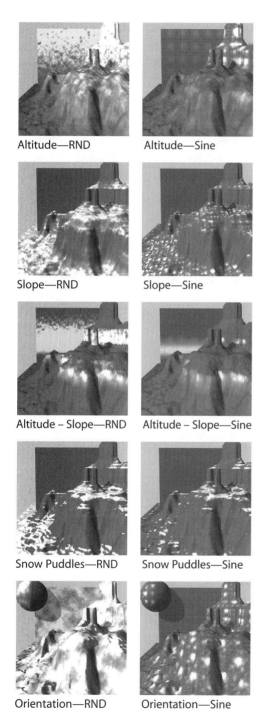

Altitude—RND Altitude—Sine

Slope—RND Slope—Sine

Altitude – Slope—RND Altitude – Slope—Sine

Snow Puddles—RND Snow Puddles—Sine

Orientation—RND Orientation—Sine

Figure 10.25 3D Noises (RND Continuous and Sine) applied to a vertical face and a terrain.

Abs(aX + b): Absolute

The Absolute filter, analogous to the Difference calculation (recall our explanation of the Difference noise modulation earlier in this chapter; we mentioned absolute value there, and lo! this filter's name is Absolute), takes the absolute value of the noise sine wave. Thus, where the curve would otherwise clip at black because the filter sine wave is below 0 and so has a negative number, it instead pops back up. This results in more light areas and additional complexity for bump maps, especially in those places where the bump would be flat (or 0). Absolute will clip at white if given the opportunity. To get twice the bump information as you would with no filtering whatsoever, make $a = 2$ and $b = -1$.

Gaussian(a(X + b))

Gaussian creates a bell curve and clips at 0. The variable for a determines how spiky or pinched the curve is; b determines the upness and downness of it (whether toward white or toward black). You get smooth areas near 0, and bump when the value is higher, toward white. When the value is up at white, Gaussian bounces it down, resulting in noisier areas in the light range.

(X pwr a) + b: X Power

X Power is similar to Gaussian. Both smooth out the darkest areas as they get to the bottom. However, X Power clips at white, whereas Gaussian bounces the curve back down. X Power's curve is offset halfway from Gaussian's, so what Gaussian clips is what X Power actually shows.

The next five filters adjust the noise and apply it according to the object's orientation in the three-dimensional World Space. Their curves move in a diagonal direction. Figure 10.25 shows each filter applied to Sine and RND Continuous noise. All the examples use the same settings in the Noise dialog box:

• Modulation: Standard; Octaves: 3; Direction: 0,0; Frequency: 171.

The textures are in a folder for this chapter on the CD-ROM.

X(a★Altitude + b): Altitude

The Altitude filter modulates the noise according to altitude. The setting for *a* determines how rapidly the noise is scaled by altitude. A lower number will result in a gradual transition, whereas a higher number will result in a sharper transition. To apply noise at a high altitude, make *a* a positive number. The *b* setting determines the onset of the transition; the lower the number, the higher the onset of transition to noise. To apply noise at a high altitude, usually you will have to make *b* negative. To apply noise at a low altitude, reverse the settings so that *a* is negative and *b* is positive.

X(a★Slope + b): Slope

Slope works the same way as the Altitude filter, except that it uses slope. It applies the noise according to the object's orientation, ranging from flat and horizontal (no slope, or the graph at 0) to sheer and upright (high slope, or the graph at 1). This is the filter to use to restrict textures to vertical cliff surfaces or flat surfaces.

In the 2D Preview of the texture, the left side represents no slope (or flat areas), and the right represents high slope (or upright areas). The best preview to look at, however, is the Spherical Preview, since you can see all of the transitions from flat to vertical.

The value for *a* determines the steepness of the noise; –4 is completely flat, while 4 is sheer upright. The value for *b* adjusts the starting point of the transition and controls clipping at the sheer vertical or flat horizontal extremes. When the slope is 0 (as determined by the graph), only the setting for *b* acts on your noise, so if you want a little noise where there are flat places, set *b* slightly above 0 (to 0.1 or 0.075).

• Noise on upright surface: *a* = 4 (or high 3's); *b* = –2 (or –2.5).

• Noise on flat surface: *a* = –4 (or high –3's); *b* = 1.5 (or 2 or more).

X(a★Orientation + b): Orientation

Orientation operates similarly to Altitude and Slope, only instead of change being oriented to degrees of height, it is oriented to degrees of east and west.

Xb+a (Altitude–Slope): Altitude Minus Slope

Altitude Minus Slope puts the noise only at certain combinations of slope and altitude. When *a* is positive and *b* is negative, the result will be noise at high altitudes and flat surfaces. When *a* is negative and *b* is positive, the result will be noise at low altitudes on upright surfaces.

Snow Puddles

The Snow Puddles filter turns noise into snow patches. The value of *a* determines the degree to which snow is affected by the noise. When *a* = 0, the noise doesn't apply at all, so the snow is uniform. When *a* is higher, the snow takes on the look of the noise. The value of *b* shifts the altitude, or the snow level. The Snow Puddles filter has a *c* value, too, which determines the slope; the higher the number, the flatter the surface needs to be for snow to stick to it.

Output Types

Now that the noise has been generated and filtered, it's time to determine the output type. The three options are Color, Alpha, and Bump, and they correspond to the color, alpha, and bump in the Materials Lab's Texture Sources. You can also combine them so that a component can have any one, two, or three output types.

Alpha and Bump both take their information from the gray values of the noise. But if the output will be Color, then how will the colors be chosen? It should come as no surprise that Bryce provides plenty of options!

Color and Color Mode

There are three color swatches, which behave like all other color swatches. Pressing the mouse pointer inside a swatch invokes the pop-up color picker. Using the Option/Alt key in combination with a mouse click inside a swatch brings up the alternate numerical picker. Pressing Control-Option/Ctrl+Alt while clicking the color swatch brings up the operating system color pickers. Once you have assigned the colors for the texture, how will the color be mapped to the noise? You can select from over a dozen options on the Color Mode pop-up menu. Here is a description of each color mode option. Figure C10.26 (see color section) shows a sample of the results of each. For all but the top row, the same set of colors was used. Also, there are two sets of textures for each image comparison: The objects on the left use a texture generated with Random Continuous noise; the objects on the right use a texture from Sine noise.

- *RGB/HLS.* The first two items on the Color Mode pop-up menu aren't modes in themselves. They allow you to choose which color model will be used in the color blending process. RGB applies colors to the noise according to the Red-Green-Blue model; HLS applies colors according to the Hue-Saturation-Lightness model.

- *None.* No color blending occurs. The component's color output consists merely of the top swatch's color.

- *Red or Hue, Green or Lightness, Blue or Saturation.* Take Red, for example. Red or Hue outputs only red values if the color model is RGB, or Hue values if the model is HLS. But try making the top color swatch white and choosing Red or Hue with the RGB model. You might naturally expect that the red part of the white light would dominate, but all you see is cyan (red's complement) and white. Now try changing the top swatch to black; you'll see red!

  Figure C10.27 shows what's going on. At the top, Figure C10.27a shows a texture set to Alpha output; the grayscale values will be the basis of three texture components (see Figures C10.27b, c, and d) that will be output using the Red, Green, and Blue color modes, respectively (see Figures C10.27b, c, and d). We're using the RGB model for this example. On the right is the RGB color picker for the color in the top swatch. On the color picker, notice the R spectrum. If the texture component is set to Red color mode (Figure C10.27b), the range of colors in that spectrum will be mapped to the grayscale values in the component's alpha channel, with the color at the left end of the spectrum taking the place of black, and that at the right end of the spectrum taking the place of white. Likewise, for the Green and Blue color modes, the G and B spectra, respectively, are mapped to the grayscale values of the texture's alpha information.

- *Linear Interpolation 2.* Creates a straight two-color blend. The colors in the top two swatches will be used, with the top color being assigned to areas with the darkest values.

- *Linear Interpolation 3.* Creates a linear blend between the three selected colors. The top color swatch is assigned to the darkest values, the center swatch to the middle values, and the bottom swatch to the lightest values.

- *Spline.* One of the more common color mapping options, it is similar to Linear Interpolation 3.

- *Spline with Snow.* Same as Spline, except it adds snow on top according to the altitude of the object.

- *Altitude.* Puts white snow level on your colors. Vary the snow level using the Material Lab's Frequency control. Anything below ground level is automatically colored ochre.

- *Randomized.* Applies color using standard interpolation and randomizes it afterward in RGB space by means of a noise that Bryce generates internally.

- *Earth Map.* Generates color according to the bump map. Besides the colors you've selected, which are applied in the middle of the bump range, blue is applied at the lowest values. There are also white polar ice caps. Use this with Color-Bump on spheres in outer space for planets.

- *Perturbed Map.* This mode applies colors with additional irregularities.

- *Banded.* This version applies the colors in bands. Rather than the normal trek through the lowest-midpoint-highest color associations, this mode cycles back through the color again, in a sequence that looks like low-middle-high-middle-low.

- *Interferences.* The individual red, green, and blue values for the *first* color create a repeating pattern around the contours of the noise. It's wild 'n' crazy.

- *Interpol+Interferences.* A combination of Linear Interpolation and Interferences.

- *Slope.* Gives an object a different color depending on its slope.

- *Orient.* Assigns the colors to the object according to east–west orientation.

Combining Components: Blend Modes

By now you have generated noise, filtered it, assigned an output type of Alpha, Bump, or Color (or a combination of those), and assigned color maps for your color components. Assuming you have more than one component, now is the time for you to choose the parameters for the combined output and the way that the individual components interact with one another. The parameters can be set in the pop-up menus between the previews for each of the three components. Figure C10.28 shows the result of each of the blend modes.

Bryce compares the two components to be combined and, based on whatever method you choose, produces a result. Since a component can be output as color, alpha, and/or bump information, what is Bryce using to compare? In most cases, Bryce uses the alpha information—that is, the basic grayscale noise information plus whatever filtering you've applied to that noise. Since it's possible to have, say, a light color applied to the area of the noise that's represented by dark values of the alpha, it's important to understand that Bryce considers lights and darks according to the alpha information and not the color information. If you're outputting Color and the results aren't what you expect, temporarily change the output type to Alpha to check.

Maximum/Blend Maximum

With Maximum, Bryce compares the two components, and whichever is lighter is the final result. If you are familiar with channel operations or Apply modes in Photoshop, you will recognize that this is the same as Lighten Only.

Blend Maximum is the same as Maximum, except it creates blurring at points of harsh transition. When you use Blend Maximum for basic bump mapping, the resulting bump map will generally have more high points and dip into low points only occasionally.

Minimum/Blend Minimum

Minimum is the complement of Maximum. Instead of the lighter portions of noise prevailing, the darker ones do. It is analogous to Darken Only in two-dimensional imaging blends or channel calculations. Blend Minimum smoothes out any abrupt transitions between the two components.

When creating bump maps, use Minimum when you want areas that are generally lower but with some higher points. The same situation about so-called darker and lighter colors holds true for Minimum as for Maximum. These combination modes work best for components that use Bump as an output type.

Parallel

Parallel is a nonblend mode. Use it when you're using the Bump output type for one component, Color for another, and Alpha for another. If you have one output type that is shared by components, such as *Color*-Bump and *Color*-Alpha, you won't get your desired result for Color. The color will be taken from the first component only.

Combine

Combine is a blend mode for color only. For each component, you can assign three colors. Combine uses component 2's top swatch color as an alpha channel. Wherever that color is located in component 2, you'll see component 1 in the combined result. (This is similar to the behavior of Decal Color, described in the previous chapter on the Materials Lab.) Note: Combine is an exception to the rule that Bryce always uses alpha for the blend mode. Here, Bryce uses color, so your final combined result will look different if component 2's color mode is Linear Interpol 2 or 3 or Spline or Banded. In fact, all Combine does is combine color. The final alpha and bump information come straight from component 1.

Average

Average is a normal blend between the two components, where all elements are mixed with equal weight. If one is black and the other is white, the result will be gray. This is a good, all-purpose output type for Bryce textures, and another bump combination workhorse.

Multiply

Multiply combines both components in such a way that they get darker. In the case of Alpha or Bump, when one component is black, the result is black. When one is white, the result is whatever the other one is. Where both are shades in between, they are proportionately darkened.

When using Multiply with the Bump output type, the result is a completely flattened bump map, even though it would seem that the result would be darker shades of gray produced from multiplying two light or medium gray tones together, resulting in a subtle bump pattern). Multiply has worked successfully under very strict conditions: The first component must be set to Bump, and the second, high-contrast component must be set to Alpha. The second component also affects the bump of the first, without its being set to Bump. The Puddlebumps recipe at the end of this chapter is set up this way. For all that, two Bump components do not successfully combine using Multiply.)

Add

Add combines colors so that they are lighter.

Sub (Subtract)

Subtract is a blend mode that, in grayscale, tends to go toward black. In Color output mode, Subtract results in brilliant and bizarre combinations that lean toward the complement of the original color. Be adventurous with color here.

Blend v1, Blend v2

Since you are never blending more than two components, you always choose between the first and the second. These modes blend the two components according to the alpha (er, that's value, actually—the v1 and v2 are leftovers from the day when alpha was called value) of the first one (v1) or the second one (v2). Essentially, these modes allow you to use one or another of your noises as an alpha channel for blending.

Blend Slope/Fast Slope

These modes blend two different components according to slope. The first component is applied to areas that are flat; the second is applied to areas that are upright (or have high slope). Fast Slope is a variation that blends in a more abrupt manner.

Blend Altitude

Blend Altitude blends the two different components: the first one at a lower altitude and the second one at a higher altitude.

Blend Orientation

This blend mode faces one component in all directions and blends the other component on one direction only (used for such things as moss that grows only on the north side of trees and rocks).

Blend Random

Blend Random is another alpha channel type of blend. A low-frequency random noise becomes the alpha channel. It chooses one component here and the other component there for the final version. Of course, since you're adding another layer of noise, you get that much more noise for your two or three components. But this mode is costlier, too.

Difference

Difference finds the difference between the noises of the two components. It operates only on the output types common to both components. If the first component is Color-Alpha and the second is Alpha, then the first component's color will be passed on straight while the alpha will be "differenced."

Difference is too complex to go into here, but it does some pretty wild things to your colors. A light color combined with another color will invert the other color, so you'll find a lot of complementary-color relationships using Difference.

Procedural Blend

Procedural Blend combines the two textures so that the color and value of the first is applied to the second, based on the gray values of the second. Where the second's is light, the first is not applied. Where the second one is dark, the first one's is made darker. Where the second is a straight medium gray, the first is applied without change. Blending using this method usually results in colors that are more saturated. You may need to adjust your original colors to get the right combination.

Global Output: Combination

What happens to the textures when they are combined? That is determined in the Blend Mode pop-up menus, which are between the components.

Saving the Texture

At this point, you can do several things with your combined output. The options should be familiar to you, since you can also use them while working on the individual texture components. Set the component indicator to the fourth position, so that the combination texture is active. Then choose an option.

- *Preview Combined Components.* When you look at a preview, you'll see the combined texture. Click inside the window to see a full-screen preview. The Deep Texture Editor disappears for the moment and is replaced by a rendering view of your texture. When you've seen enough, click the texture to get back to the Deep Texture Editor.

- *Adjust Frequency.* Using the Noise Palette set to the fourth spot on the component indicator, you can adjust the global frequency of the entire texture by dragging the little red Frequency control.

- *Filter Combined Output.* Choose a filter and settings for the combined texture by editing the filter for the fourth (combination) spot. The filter will affect the combined alpha for the texture.

- *Add Global Phase to the Combined Texture.* You can add phase that will affect the entire texture. This is similar to adding phase to any of the individual components.

For the final output combination, Bryce draws on the output types of the individual components. Usually, you will have set Color, Alpha, and Bump in your individual components. Occasionally you will not. What happens then? Here is a collection of consequences for combination output.

- If you do not set Alpha as the output type, Bryce compensates for it without any trouble or weirdness.

- If you set the Color output type only, Bryce handles color and alpha just fine.

- If the only output mode is Bump, you won't see anything alarming in the Deep Texture Editor, but once you return to the Materials Lab, the color preview of the Texture Source will be psychotic. Further, the color behavior will be even more psychotic; once you make the texture drive color, the object's surface won't match what you see in the color preview for the Texture Source, until, of course, you activate Bump Height. Don't say we didn't warn you.

- If the only place you want to set the Color output type is in the combination texture and not in any individual component, you must ensure that the Alpha output type is active in at least one of your texture components, or else combination color will not work.

3D Texture Practicalia

At last it's time for the real housekeeping hints! Here's an assortment of important things to know that don't fit into the overall conceptual information we presented previously.

> **TIP:** When working in the Deep Texture Editor, choose bright saturated colors (at first) so that you can clearly see what each color is doing. When all is balanced to your liking, then you can go back and make fine-tuning adjustments to your color.

Adding and Copying Textures

There are two ways that you can manipulate texture combinations and components: Add a combination Texture to your collection of textures, and copy a texture component from one component window to another.

To add a texture to your permanent collection, click the Texture Library button in the combination window to go to the Texture Library, where you can add the texture. You can also Shift-click the word "Combination" to go to the Texture Library.

In days of old, you used to be able to copy—and paste— textures from one component window to another. That function has been replaced by the ability to drag a texture from one component window to another. Of course, the texture being replaced goes away and does not come back (unless you immediately undo the texture-drag).

Texture Library

A note about the permanence or ephemerality of textures: The Texture Library is the permanent repository of textures. You can pull a texture up from that collection, but once loaded into a Texture Source, it takes on a new existence. In days of old, if you were to go to the Deep Texture Editor and change the texture, you'd change every instance of that texture used in a scene. But when animation was introduced to Bryce with Bryce 3D, that edit-once, affect-all behavior changed, so that you can now animate the texture data over time. All in all, this is A Good Thing. However, if you don't want to lose the changes you made to *this* texture, you must save the texture in the Texture Library. If you have edited the texture at all and need to change the order of textures, by all means, save it in the Texture Library. Otherwise, in the Materials Lab, when you load the texture by name, say, My Stunning Texture, you will discover that the texture you loaded is the old, saved one, which has just replaced all your texture work. Stunning indeed! Quick; undo that action and then save the texture you just worked on. Whew! That was a stunning rescue!

In the Materials Lab, you cannot drag and drop a texture from one source to another, so you need to go to a single place from which to load the texture. If you changed that texture from what it was when last saved, you risk losing all your texture work. (If your first encounter with Bryce is version 3D or 4, then you can dismiss the aha-surprise of this statement as the incoherent ramblings of a Bryce old-timer. But if you're one of the Bryce old-timers, well then, you *know!*)

Frequency

There are several places where you can adjust texture frequency. They are all related to one another, from the individual noise frequency in the Edit Noise dialog box, to the Frequency slider for that component, to the Global Frequency control, to the Materials Lab's Frequency control for that Texture Source and for all the textures combined.

Randomize Component/Randomize Combination

If you find all of this Deep Texture Editor detail too much to deal with, you can submit yourself to the Random Muse and shuffle all the combinations together by clicking the Randomize Component button in any of the three component windows or clicking the Randomize Combination button on the combination window. 'Round and 'round and 'round it goes, and where it stops, nobody knows. Whee!

Component Order

The order in which the components are created sometimes makes a difference. How? In the way things are blended together. Depending on the output type, you may need to change them around. We cover this further in the "Snow Puddles Material" exercise at the end of this chapter.

Names in the List

The textures are listed in a hierarchical menu. On each menu, the textures are listed in a peculiarly computerish alphabetical order. Capital letters come before lowercase letters, so "Zebra stripe" (capital *Z*) will come before "aardvark skin" (lowercase *a*). Makes sense to you, eh? Nope? It doesn't? We agree; it's lame computer-think. Also, in the Texture Library, there's no limit to the number of characters you can assign to your texture name. However, when it comes to what shows up in the pop-up menu, you're limited to about 30 characters (32 for Macintosh, 30 for Windows).

Shortcut to the DTE

To jump straight to the DTE from the working window, choose Edit 3D Solid Textures from the Edit Options menu on the Edit Palette, or choose Edit 3D Textures from the Objects menu, or press Option-M/Alt+M.

In Bryce days of yore, this shortcut to the DTE was designed as a timesaver, so that you wouldn't have to travel through the Materials Lab to get to the DTE. By the time you get to the stage where making your scene just so involves careful work fine-tuning a texture, you'll be going back and forth from test renders in the scene window to the DTE, where you'll tweak, tweak, tweak. When working like that, the trip through the Materials Lab to the DTE is simply an unneeded extra step. Hence, the shortcut. But now the shortcut is not as handy as it once was, as going to the DTE changes the settings in the Materials Lab. If you are working in the main scene window with a selected object and take the shortcut to the DTE, where you edit and accept some texture for that object, Bryce will automatically choose these material settings for that object: Texture-Driven Diffuse Color, White Ambient Color, Diffusion setting of 100, and Ambience setting of 19.6. Everything else is in the state of default color. If you have made any custom material settings, *do not* take the shortcut to the DTE, or you will throw away all your previous work in the Materials Lab! However, if you are just beginning to work on an object, the changes in the Materials Lab will hardly affect you. Also, if your purpose in Bryce is simply to work on the creation of textures that you'll be saving in the Texture Library, then use the shortcut with impunity. But for the original purpose of working back and forth in the scene and in the DTE to perfect a texture's appearance, the shortcut is hosed.

Going to the DTE from the Terrain Editor

There is yet another shortcut to the DTE from the Terrain Editor. This is a fantastic little side tunnel that allows you to work in the DTE to create texture information that will then be used to create your terrain canvas for your terrain or symmetrical lattice. In the Terrain Editor, press ⌘-Option/Ctrl+Alt while clicking the Picture button. (Remember to increase your terrain resolution to 256, 512, or

1024 before applying anything to it!) Rather than getting a dialog box that allows you to select an image file on your disk drive, you are whisked to the DTE. Work in the Deep Texture Editor to your heart's content, and when you leave, what you've created will be applied to your terrain. (It takes a little while to apply your work to the terrain; please be patient!) To get the best results, you need to watch out for these conditions:

- *Alpha Output.* In the DTE, make sure that your output for all components is set to Alpha only. Bryce takes whatever the combination output is and converts that to grayscale. If you have color there, Bryce will use that. (If you simply must use color output to get a special effect, say by applying the Banded or Perturbed color mode, then use black, white, and gray for your colors, so you can better predict your results.)

- *Flat Preview.* In the DTE, set your Render Preview to Flat. If you don't believe us, try it with Square or Sphere Preview and see what results you get in the Terrain Editor.

- *Frequency Is Your Friend.* Use Frequency in the DTE to squash the texture in the same direction that you want to stretch the terrain. For instance, if you are constructing a wall with a terrain, you may wish to rotate it on its side and then widen it. If you were, say, to make it three times as wide as it is tall, then you can accordingly increase the noise frequency three times on the same axis, so that the terrain doesn't look squashed or stretched. We've provided a scene, TERRAIN FROM DTE, located in the folder for this chapter on the CD-ROM, so you can see how we did it. Hidden behind the terrain wall is a cube with the material applied. Select the cube and then go to the DTE via the Materials Lab to see how we adjusted the noise frequency. This is an incredibly slick trick to get detail upon detail for your terrains.

ANATOMY OF A TEXTURE AND MATERIAL

By now, we have poked into every nook and cranny of the Deep Texture Editor. But what does it all mean? How do you use it? This Journey-to-the-Center-of-the-Earth has shown what everything is, but so far it hasn't provided a look at a real-live texture and how it was put together. That time has now arrived! We'll take a look at some specific textures and examine them in the Deep Texture Editor to discuss how they work, paying attention to how they'll be used in the Materials Lab.

We'll bite off and chew six separate Deep Textures:

- The three textures in the Whole Mountain preset examined earlier

- Planet Rings: Variations on an existing Materials preset

- Snowed Under: Snow atop a rock

- Bump and Reflections: Bumps with reflective puddles

Analyzing Textures

"Okay," you say, "All of those mathematical equations were simply fabulous. Do you have any more like them? Any more that will help me get just that right look for my terrain?" Look, just admit it. Your eyes were glazed over during that section. It's perfectly understandable. Susan's were rather glassy the first time she heard Eric Wenger's explanation for how the equations work. The explanations provided here are a resource for you to turn to when the right time comes. Once you get to working with the textures a bit, you'll turn back to refer to them. "But how do I *start* working with the textures?" you reasonably reply. The first thing you do is analyze the textures that you like. We'll do a bit of that here. There is enough depth and complexity to the Deep Texture Editor to merit a book all its own, and so even as a thick part of a very thick chapter in a rather thick book, we cannot go into all the lurid details for every one of those options. The next best thing is to break down a few textures and analyze how they work. Before doing so, however, we'll provide a few clues about how you can do your own exploration, just in case the texture that has caught your eye doesn't happen to be one discussed here.

- *Orient Yourself to Orientation.* Look for the overall orientation. Is the texture doing something in Bryce's World Space that relies on altitude or slope or orientation? You can see the orientation effects in the filtering (for the individual component or in the global), in the blend mode between components, and in the color mapping.

- *Simplify Multicomponent Textures.* When a texture has two or three components, switch down to a lower number and look at the combination preview or exit the Deep Texture Editor and go back to the scene and see how it renders. You'll be able to see how—by its absence—that second or third component interacts with the first (or the combination of the first and second), and how the blend mode does what it does. You needn't worry about the texture component going away and getting lost somewhere. After you're through poking at the simpler texture, click the proper button to bring all the components back again.

- *Look at the Various Preview Views.* Check out the various preview modes by clicking the 2D square, the cube, and the sphere in the upper-right corner of the DTE. The default preview is the 2D Preview (though once you select another preview option, Bryce remembers it until you change it to something else for the duration of your current work session). All the previews will display spatial-specific aspects of the texture—texture that's dependent on altitude, slope (flatness/uprightness) orientation (east/west), and so on. However, spatial orientation is easier to interpret when the texture is displayed in the Cube and Sphere Preview modes, so remember that there are two options besides the default preview. Although the Cube Preview will show some slope qualities—the flat part will show on the flat part, and the upright parts will show on the uprights—you will not see the subtle shifts at differing slopes. The 3D Sphere Preview will show you that. In other cases, what occurs at low altitude will show up best in the 2D Preview. Altitude runs from bottom to top, slope runs at an angle, and orientation runs from left to right. Knowing how each spatial filter is expressed in 2D preview is helpful when scrolling through textures in the Texture Library, where the preview is most often the flat 2D version. You'll be able to better predict the spatial changes to the texture from simply looking at the flat preview.

- *Explore the Noise.* It's fairly easy to see what's going on with noise without necessarily changing the numerical settings (for frequency and direction). You can change the noise, you can change the number of octaves, and you can change the modulation. If you don't want to keep your exploratory changes, click Cancel when you leave the Noise Editor.

- *Switch Off the Filter Momentarily.* When looking at the filter graph, with numbers out to the fifth decimal place, it's easy to be intimidated. You may find yourself fearing, "If I touch it, I'll ruin it!" and thereby talk yourself out of exploring the filter. There are at least two ways to explore safely without budging a thing. First, you can switch the filter from its present form to None. The numbers won't change; you'll just momentarily deactivate the filter. Then you can see how the noise operates alone. When you're done looking at that, select the filter again. All the numbers are still there, down to the last decimal place. Whew!

- *Remember Undo.* You always have ⌘-Z/Ctrl+Z available to revert the filter (or noise, or any single action you take in the DTE) to its previous state. If your texture has only one or two components, you can preserve a component by dragging it to the unused third component (this will "wake up" the third component, but you can easily put it back to sleep again).

We mourn the loss of the ability to copy components, which was available in Bryce 1 and 2. Dragging from one component to another is handy, yes, but it is very difficult to do from one texture to another, and the old copy-and-paste did that well.

• *Use the Ultimate Undo.* Of course, you can always cancel out of the Deep Texture Editor after you're through, and none of the changes you have made will affect the texture.

This set of options should make your explorations easier.

Altitude Adjustment: Whole Mountain, Continued…

In the previous chapter, we performed a thorough exegesis of the Whole Mountain material in the Materials Lab. Let's take up the Whole Mountain discussion once again to understand the underlying textures. There are three of them: Hills 29, Gray Galets 29, and Basic Altitude 29. (The number 29 is the heritage of an older version of Bryce, which added a number to the texture when renaming it. The names of the first two textures are also relics of a past version of Bryce; you'll find these textures in the Bryce 4 Preset Library as good hill! and leopard. They're both in the Bump category.) Hills is Texture Source A; Gray Galets (pebbly) is Texture Source B; and Basic Altitude is Texture Source C, which switches between A and B.

Hills 29 Texture

The Hills 29 texture is a three-component texture (see Figure 10.29). Each component is set to Color-Alpha-Bump. There are a couple of World Space orientations. The color mapping mode for component 1 is set to Altitude. The filter for the global texture is set to Altitude as well. The high numbers and extreme waves on the filtering graph also indicate that there's *something* going on with that altitude as well; it's pretty extreme. There is also another World Space orientation operating; the blend mode between components 1 and 2 and component 3 is Slope, so component 3 texture is applied only under certain slope circumstances.

How about the individual noises? Component 1's noise is modulated to Displaced Max. This means that there is lots of detail, and it's lighter detail. Noise that is darker has been obliterated by the Maximum setting. Component 2's noise swoops in wide, circular streaks. The blend mode between the two, Minimum, makes sense

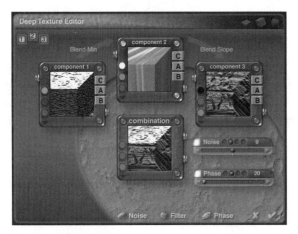

Figure 10.29 Deep Texture Editor settings for Hills 29.

Component 1 Noise

Component 2 Noise

Component 3 Noise

Component 1 Filter

Component 2 Filter

Component 3 Filter

Combination Filter

1 and 2 filtered to take advantage of a Blend Minimum combination.

Combined components (shown as Alpha) with and without composite filtering

1 and 2; no composite filtering

1 and 2; yes composite filtering

1, 2, and 3; no composite filtering

1, 2, and 3; yes composite filtering

when you see the filtering for each. The higher, lighter noise in component 1 is filtered to stay in the mid-to-high range. The sweeping paths are filtered for smooth, high contrast in the entire range. This filtering is for bump. Visualize the two filter paths superimposed, and you'll understand how those dirt scars (or clearings) show up here and there in the hilly texture. Wherever component 2's noise is lower, the result is a scar in the vegetation. Therefore, it's important that the second component is higher everyplace else. Setting a mid-to-high range for the first noise ensures that it will be lower than the second dirt noise's high (non-dirt scar) area. The dirt scars shouldn't show up all over the place, so the frequency for the second noise is much lower.

Component 3 is a departure from the foliage-and-dirt-scar combination. The third component is blended according to slope, so it provides the appearance for any vertical faces of the terrain. The noise modulation, Maximum 90 (remember, they're switched; it really is Minimum 90) applies the same noise to itself at 90°, with the lower portions taking a bite out of themselves. This accounts for the horizontal gashes.

Finally, the global filtering settings will determine the final alpha information that will drive the diffuse illumination for the texture. Look at only the alpha information for all components. To so do, switch all other Color and Bump buttons off. Compare the global filter with a preview of what the alpha looks like when there is no filtering. There are gray tones all over the place. The consequences of all that gray is that the diffuse illumination will be darker in those areas, making the Hills texture significantly darker. To have full diffuse illumination, the alpha needs to be made primarily white. However, there are spots for it to be dark, at low altitudes. Therefore, the altitude filter is used, and the numbers are set to make the vast majority of the altitude range white, with only little rough dark patches at the bottom, as well as the most extreme of the horizontal gashes in the vertical cliff face.

Gray Galets 29

The second Texture Source, the pebbly one, has two components (see Figure 10.30). The first one uses the Leopard noise to create the pebble shapes. For the shapes, Color-Bump is the output mode. The second noise is for determining color and alpha. Altitude comes into play here. For the noise itself, the pebbles at lower altitudes are a darker, richer beige than they are at higher altitudes. More than that, though, this second noise is the basis for the final alpha, which will determine the diffuse lighting conditions for the overall texture. The global filter alters the texture's alpha based on an extremely high-contrast altitude filter. This removes any traces of darkness at higher altitudes. In other words, the beach will be darkened only at the very lowest altitudes, although the color of those pebbles will be darker at higher altitudes. Refer back to the color images of the textures in Figures C9.54 and C9.56. Then notice how the higher the number is for *a* in the

Gray Galets Cube Preview

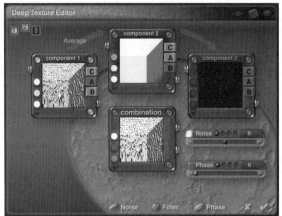

2D Preview

Combination
Alpha Only
no Combination
Filter

Combination
Alpha Only
yes Combination
Filter

Component 1 Noise

Component 2 Noise

Component 1 Filter

Component 2 Filter

Combination Filter

Figure 10.30 Deep Texture Editor settings for Gray Galets 29.

altitude filter equation, the more extreme the altitude contrast and the more white area when the noise is viewed as values only.

Basic Altitude 29

The Texture Source C noise, Basic Altitude 29, is the texture that determines what's going to show at any point on the object: Texture Source A (Hills) or B (Galets, er, pebbles). (See Figure 10.31.) Since the pebbly beach material is lower than the hilly vegetation, it's no surprise that the texture is based on altitude. Both noises are altitude noises. The first noise establishes a high-contrast, low-altitude barrier between light and dark values. This is for the boundary between the two textures. The second noise has lower-contrast altitude filtering, allowing the lower texture to creep up into the higher regions at little spots here and there. When the

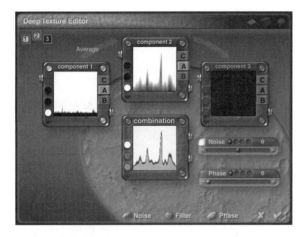

Component 1 Noise

Component 2 Noise

Component 1 Filter

Component 2 Filter

Combination Filter

Figure 10.31 Deep Texture Editor settings for Basic Altitude 29.

texture components are combined for the final output, the filter used is Clip, which creates an extremely high contrast between the two. A lower contrast would have fuzzy edges that are partially stony and partially hilly; and a diffuse boundary between the two areas would not be as dramatic—nor realistic—as two crisp edges. Hence, the high-contrast Clip. The negative number inverts the value so that black is above and white is below. In the usual altitude order in the Materials Lab, Texture Source A is used for the lower-altitude texture, and Texture Source B is used for the higher-altitude texture. Though this altitude texture adds noise, the white-above, black-below of the component noises follows suit. Only because the higher-altitude texture was placed in Texture Source A was it necessary to invert the final value. Since this material was created by Eric Wenger, for whom adjusting the clipping for a value is as simple as switching Texture Sources, it's a trivial matter to change the filtering to accommodate the established Texture Source order.

Color was assigned from the combination color. The yellow-blue-red coloring is meaningless for what the texture is intended for: a texture-based alpha channel to switch between the hilly vegetation and pebbles.

Recipe for the Ringed Planet Material Adjustment

This recipe is an example of how you might use an existing preset as a starting point to create some other effect. In the realm of space, a sphere is a planet, and a squashed sphere (or squashed cylinder) is a planet ring object. To create the rings, alter one of the existing presets in Bryce's Materials Presets. Start a new scene and delete the ground plane. Create a sphere (for the planet) and then duplicate it (for the rings). Enlarge the duplicate and flatten it on the *y* axis from the sphere's center. Switch to the Sky & Fog Palette and set up your scene so that there's no haze (drag to the left on the fourth thumbnail from the left until the numerical readout at the bottom of the screen says 0). Use the pop-up menu under the leftmost thumbnail to turn Atmosphere off, and use the color swatch at the bottom of the same thumbnail to set the background hue to black.

1. Begin with the Materials preset Dali Bee Stripes in the Wild & Fun category (see Figure 10.32a). You'll try some successive attempts to get these to look like planet rings. The rings themselves are too even and too regular. How would you make them irregular? By changing the underlying noise!

2. Next, change the noise. Go to the Materials Lab and then to the Deep Texture Editor. This is a one-component texture. Click the Edit Noise button on the Noise Palette to access the Noise Editor. You will see that the noise is square and one-dimensional (see Figure 10.32b). Are there other noises that would do as well? Let's try Random (RND) Linear. Just by changing the noise, you get many different shades of gray, rather than simple black and white. Click OK to get back up to the main level of the Deep Texture Editor. Check out the preview.

3. Look at the preview windows to see how the color works. (Incidentally, with the color settings here, the gray is in the locations where the transparent areas are going to be. That gray color corresponds to black when the texture is viewed without color settings. Bear that in mind as you make adjustments.) Change the coloring of the other two swatches if you'd like. Two different yellows are, well, rather yellow. Click OK to exit the Materials Lab and do a little test render of your scene (see Figure 10.32c).

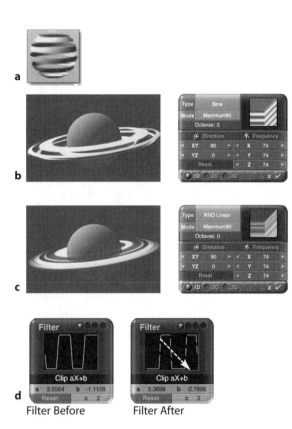

Filter Before   Filter After

Figure 10.32 Adjusting an existing Materials preset to create planet rings: a) The starting preset; b) Sine noise results in too-regular ring stripes; c) changing noise to RND Linear for irregular rings; d) Filter control settings before and after adjustment; e) rendered image after adjusting the Clip filter.

4. Go back and adjust the noise a little bit. We mentioned that the black in the noise is the part of the texture that is transparent. You'll need more gray, somehow, to create the in-between areas of your ring stripes, so go get back in the Deep Texture Editor. Proceed directly to component 1 and play with the filtering (see Figure 10.32d). The filter is the ubiquitous Clip. Where the

curve reaches the top, it clips at white, and where it reaches the bottom, it clips at black. Fine. But you want more black, so get the curve to be more "bottom-y." (No relation to a lobotomy!) Drag the graph down. Drag far enough so you can see the tops of the curves and then drag to the right to increase the overall contrast range. (The arrow in the figure indicates the overall direction of the adjustment drag for the filter.) The dark areas are larger now; that's good. Click OK to exit the Deep Texture Editor and also the Materials Lab and do a test render (see Figure 10.32e).

Now you're getting somewhere! The stripes are fainter and there is more in-between area.

5. Adjust the Mappings setting. Notice that the stripes are strange as they come around from behind the planet to the front. Perhaps the way the texture is mapped to the object could change a bit. Look at the Mappings control. Up to now, this texture has been applied in Object Space. Other potential Mappings settings are Parametric, Spherical, and Cylindrical. Try Cylindrical.

6. As a final noodle, try adjusting the frequency in the Materials Lab. Then try again with those different mapping options. The one we finally settled on was Spherical. Finally, experiment in the Material Options menu with both Blend Transparency and Fuzzy. Our final choice was Fuzzy. A fuzzy object has a bit of something in its interior; the color of the interior is determined by the component's top color swatch. We changed the top color to black back in step 3, and you can see the result in the center part of the ring. You may or may not want to change the color to something that matches the background or other environs; that is a matter of personal taste.

Snow Puddles Material

This next material description is not a walkthrough so much as an analysis of a material setting that already exists. In examining all of what goes into this material, you'll get a feel for how the controls in the Deep Texture Editor work together.

Here's a material that uses two components to create a snowy terrain. It is found on the CD, in the Bryce file entitled SNOWED UNDER. It is also the basis of the Material preset called Mid Winter, in the Plains & Terrains category (see Figure 10.33). (Trivia note: This texture first came into existence during the time that Eric Wenger was teaching Susan about the DTE for the very first edition of this book. Through Eric, it subsequently made it into Bryce's Preset Library.)

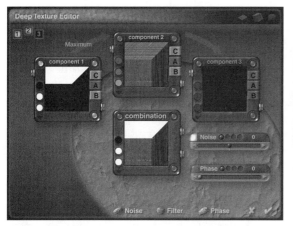
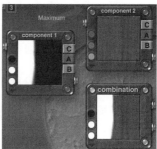

Component 2 noise, filtered, shown as Alpha

Component 1 Noise

Component 2 Noise

Component 1 Filter

Component 2 Filter

Combination Filter

Figure 10.33 Snowed Under Deep Texture Editor settings.

We'll begin by taking a look at the Deep Texture Editor to see what is there.

The Snow Component

The first component, snow, has its noise oriented in such a way that the noise detail is visible on the top as well as in front. The significance of this will be apparent shortly.

Now take a look at the filter. It's Snow Puddles, the three-variable filter that makes snow occur at certain altitudes and slopes.

Remember that *a* determines how much the snow patches are influenced by the noise. The higher the number, the greater the noise's influence on the snow. Here, the number is 3.99221. The *b* value shifts the altitude. The number is fairly close to 0, meaning the snow patches occur at pretty much any altitude.

The c value determines the extent to which slope influences whether the snow appears. When c is 0, it does not matter whether the terrain is flat or upright; snow will stick to the terrain. The higher the number, the flatter the surface needs to be for snow to appear. Here, c is 2, thereby requiring that the terrain be somewhat flat for the snow to stick to the ground. Snow won't stick to the upright surfaces, and the rocky portion of the texture will show through.

Now look at the output type. This component will be output as Color-Bump. Bump is for the bump. Where the noise is white, the surface bump will be highest. This ensures that the snow sits atop the terrain. Where there is no snow, the noise is black. The color mode is set to Linear Interpol2. This means that the color is linearly interpolated between two colors: black and white. The reason for the black will become apparent shortly when we discuss the interaction of the components. But first, take a look at the other component.

The Rocky Mountain Component

The second component is created from a three-dimensional noise, Random (RND) Lines. Notice that the frequency for y is much less than that for x and z. This is a real-life example of how to make a three-dimensional noise with a vertical grain. This creates a two-dimensional effect without the complete uniformity of a two-dimensional grain. Notice that there's no rotation to the noise, and it's one octave with a More Irregular mode. Thus, there's a bit of complexity to the noise and some random strains that aren't completely vertical or horizontal.

The noise has the same output type as the first component—that is, Color-Bump. Bump is the bump map, and Color, of course, provides the color for the object. Now take a look at the filter for this component. The filter is set to make the bumpiness of the rock a certain height. The standard contrast filter, Clip aX+b, is used. The b value (which controls the height of the graph) is negative, thereby making the range of output about half height. Think about this for a moment. If the graph went from the bottom to the top, you would have a bump that goes the full range, from lowest to highest. But this rocky texture will be combined with snow, and the rocky surface had better jolly well be located *underneath* the snow. So the filtering curve that determines the rocky surface bump keeps it in the bottom-to-mid range of the bump. The lightest (highest) values of the combined output are reserved for the snow. (See, it all makes sense, doesn't it?) The actual shape of the curve is not changed much. It goes to about 60 percent of its height (a = .57746), and the bottom edge just dips below the bottom black part, thereby creating more pronounced bottom edges.

Look at the result of this filtering. (In Figure 10.33, we show it using alpha for the moment, a handy little trick for seeing the component solely in terms of the gray values.) The values shown are all middle to dark gray.

Component 2's output is Color-Bump. The color map is Linear-Interpol 3. The three colors are generally closer to one another, not widely divergent.

Combining the Components

Now that we've looked at each individual component, we'll examine how the two components are combined. Each individual component has its output type set to Color-Bump. Look for a moment only at the bump. The snow needs to be higher than other elements. Maximum (analogous to Photoshop's Lighten Only) compares the two components and takes the lightest one as the result. Where it's white, there will be snow with a higher bump. Everything else will be the underlying rocky matter.

There is a combination filter, Quantize, that adds a bit of high contrast in a posterized fashion. This filter operates only on the alpha portions of the noise—the part that will drive Ambience, resulting in an alpha channel that is either black or white. (We'll further explore filtering at the combination stage in the next material exercise.)

Render the snow. Notice that there are little indentations in the snow, as if there were animal tracks or tufts of grass peeking out through the layers. This effect is a result of the two-dimensional noise rotation that included the top as well as the front orientation.

Suppose you wanted to add a third component to the texture. The rocky substance is rather uniform and might be nice with something else to break it up, perhaps some horizontal coloring of some sort. Think about this. If you add a third component, you'll want to change the order of the components, since you want the snow to come out on top. The snowy portions need to be highest, so Maximum is the blend setting. Any combination blend other than Maximum (Multiply, Add, Average) will result in funky snow.

If you don't believe us, try it out yourself. (You will anyway!) Switch the number of components to 3. For component 3, select some noise, give it some color, make the second blend Average, and see what kind of madness ensues. Recall from the overview diagram in Figure 10.11 how the results of the first two textures are combined with the third texture. For the snow-on-top-blended-using-Maximum to work, it must be a sole operator in the combination process, either as one of two, or as the third component to blend with the results of the first two components. It cannot successfully work as one of the first two components to blend with a third component. To rectify the situation, drag your snow component to component 3. Then create your rocky matter inconsistencies in the component where the snow used to be (in this case, component 1). Remember to filter the new noise so that it stays below the top. Your snow must be the highest thing in this texture. Set the first blend to Average and the second to Maximum so that the snow in combination with the result of the first two components will have a "come-out-on-top" result.

Snowed Under in the Materials Lab

Now how is this snow texture worked in the Materials Lab? (See Figure 10.34.) As a Texture Source, this texture is driving Diffuse Color, Ambient Color, Ambience, and Bump Height. To create the full illusion of height for the snow, Bump Height is set to a strong level (54.9). The texture's frequency depends more on the amount of detail you want to see in the object and is adjusted interactively while you are working on the particular object in the scene. (For objects closer to the camera, the frequency will need to be set higher than for those far away.)

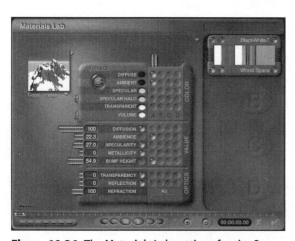

Figure 10.34 The Materials Lab settings for the Snow preset.

There is a problem with the existing Mid Winter preset. With Ambience being driven by this texture, there is either full ambient light (where the snow is), or there is little to no ambient light (where the rocky part is). This means that where there are shadow areas, the rock will be black. If the Ambient Color in the Sky & Fog Palette is white, then no matter where the sunlight or shadow is, the snow will be uniformly blindingly white. To change this so that you can tell that there is shadow on the snow, you need to make the Ambient Color darker. You can do this in the Sky & Fog Palette. You may also want to scale Ambience back just a tad by applying Alpha Scaling to the texture. (See the previous chapter for the nitty-gritty on Alpha Scaling.) Another possibility is to change the Snowed Under material's Ambient Color to a uniform color and select a light blue or lavender. When snow is in shadow, you'll be able to see the shadow. Other solutions to this extreme Ambience problem are in the SNOW CONES folder on the CD-ROM. Figure C10.35 compares the normal preset version of the snow with our Ambient Color modification.

Puddlebumps: Bump and Reflections

The final 3D Texture that we will work with here uses the filtering in the combination output to get its result. It has a bump and also (you guessed it!) reflection. (See Figure C10.36 in the color section.) If you belong to the rare society of Bryce 1 veterans, you might recognize an old preset that uses this technique, where rocky mass is interspersed with flat reflective puddles.

Do the Bump

1. For component 1, start by generating a noise. Open the Deep Texture Editor for any texture and change the first noise to Random (RND) Continuous. In the Noise Editor, make adjustments to component 1 so that the noise is three-dimensional, with three octaves, and is set to the Irregular mode (see Figure 10.37a). Set Frequency to about 450 for all three axes and then leave the Noise Editor. Set the filter to Clip and adjust it to high contrast. Set the output mode to Bump for a gray bumpy surface.

a
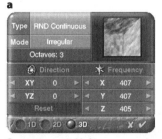
Component 1 Noise

b
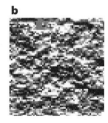

c

Component 1 Filter

Figure 10.37 Component 1's: a) Noise setting; b) filter setting; c) 2D preview.

2. For component 2, begin with the same type of noise as in step 1 (drag component 1 to component 2) and then tweak. Adjust component 2's noise to a lower frequency setting. Bring the Octave setting down to 2 (see Figure 10.38a). Now filter this with Clip. Adjust it to match the filter shown in Figure 10.38b. The filter graph is fairly steep, which creates significant areas of black. Set component 2's output type to Alpha. Why Alpha? The alpha

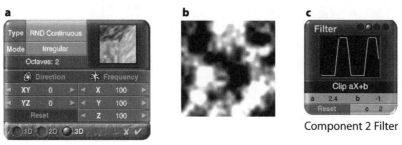

Component 2 Noise

Figure 10.38 Component 2's a) Noise setting; b) filter setting; c) 2D preview.

information will be used in the Materials Lab—in this case, it will drive Reflection. There, a Reflective setting will provide areas that will be reflective for the puddle surface.

3. Now it's time to set up the blend between the two texture components. The first and second noises will be multiplied together, so choose Multiply. The black portions of component 2's noise, when multiplied with component 1's bump map, will result in flat areas (no bump) in the combined final texture. This combination works on the bump map, even though it's an alpha component that's doing the work. Now that you see where the large flat areas come from, you can see why the second noise was set to a smaller frequency than the first. Figure 10.39a compares a portion of the two components side by side with their multiplied result. You can see where the second noise is used to create flat areas. (Bryce is very peculiar when it comes to multiplying a bump with an alpha. Component 1 must be bump only, and component 2 must be alpha only. If you set things up any other way, this operation will not work.)

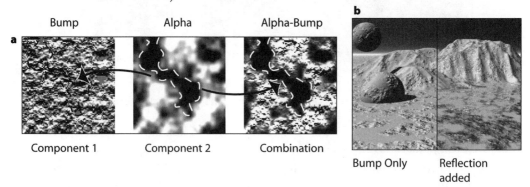

Figure 10.39 a) Multiplying the two components to get flattened areas; b) the result so far has flat areas interspersed with bump.

4. In the Materials Lab, make the Texture Source drive both the Reflection and Bump Height channels. Be sure to set the Reflection amount, too! Make it at least 50. Set the Bump Height to something moderate. Render. Take a quick peek at what's been created so far as it applies to the object's surface (see Figure 10.39b). The resulting image has areas that are flat and areas of Bump Height. However, the alpha-driven reflections occur in the high portions, not the low portions.

   Why is the reflective area in the bumpy area? Component 2 is set to Alpha output mode. Where alpha is white, you'll get reflective areas from using the alpha-driven Reflection. But where there's black, you're combining it with the bump information in noise 1 to flatten out the bump. You want portions that are flat and portions that are bumpy. You need the black to flatten the bump, but you also need to somehow swap the alpha information so that the flat part is reflective.

   You can't change anything in components 1 or 2. You *can,* however, change the final output. If you can somehow reverse the final combination's alpha and invert it there, then you will end up reversing the alpha information without touching the interaction of the two components to create bumpy and flat areas.

5. Adjust the combination filter to invert the alpha setting. When component 2 is set to Alpha output mode, then it becomes the alpha of the combined texture, so component 2's filter settings can be the basis for the combination filter. All you need to do is invert the combination. (To clearly see what you are doing, temporarily disable all output settings other than component 2's Alpha.) Component 2's filter is Clip aX+b, where a is 2.4 and b is –1.

   Now, before you invert the combination, a bit of background on Clip aX+b: The default values (no clipping) for this filter are $a = 1$ and $b = 0$. A straight inversion is $a = -1$ and $b = 1$. To invert *any* setting, change the value for a from positive to negative (or vice versa), and for b, change the number from negative to positive (or vice versa) and then add 1 to the number. For this example, a straight inversion ($a = -1$, $b = 1$) would not provide sufficient contrast for the reflection. It's a start, though, and it gives the flat areas a white alpha. After initially setting the combination filter to Clip aX+b and getting close to the straight inversion formula, continue increasing the contrast. Increase the contrast after the initial inversion to more clearly define the area that will be reflective. We set our combination filter to Clip aX+b and adjusted the values to (roughly) $a = -4$ and $b = 1.5$.

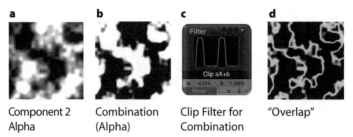

a	b	c	d
Component 2 Alpha	Combination (Alpha)	Clip Filter for Combination	"Overlap"

Figure 10.40 Changing the alpha to make the reflective area flat:
a) Component 2; b) combination after inverting; c) filter settings
for inversion; d) overlap to create wet edges.

If you decide not to follow the straight mathematical route, you'll need to tweak and preview. (Actually, no matter what, you'll have to tweak and preview; the entire process is fraught with tweaking.) Make sure that component 2 and the global output previews are the inverse of one another. You'll need to play with this one a bit to make sure the white areas (reflection) are showing in the right places. If you make your combination white area grow a bit so that it overlaps into component 2's white area, areas of reflectivity will move up into the bump, thereby creating an illusion of wet land right where the two meet. (Figure 10.40 shows component 2 and the combination, along with the filter setting.) Although Figure 10.40d shows something called overlap, you won't

ever generate any little outline by playing with the filter settings. The overlap is a doctored image created from the component 2 and combination images to show you where the overlap happens to be. Figure 10.41 shows the result of the combination filter inversion.

Now that you've inverted the alpha for your global output, take stock of this texture.

Figure 10.41 Swapping the alpha in the global filter creates flat reflective surfaces.

6.   The color for this texture, which is something of a land mass, goes to component 2. Until now, the output type has been Alpha. Change the output type to Color-Alpha and set your colors for component 2. In this example, the color map is Spline Interpolation. For the final combination, choose None from the Color Mode pop-up menu (since you already set it in component 2). Now you're set.

Finally, adjust the contrast for the combination filter to fine-tune the partially reflective wet edge around the puddle. Semi-reflective areas are gray in the final value, and they overlap very closely on the "shores" of the other bumpy areas.

7. Click the Texture Library button on the Combination Palette (or Shift-click the word "Combination") to get to the Texture Library; then click Add to create and name this texture of yours. Call it Puddlebumps (or whatever you'd like).

Congratulations! You've made your way through four different forays into the Deep Texture Editor as well as many explorations of the Materials Lab. With this as a foundation, and knowing how to analyze existing textures, you've more than scratched the surface of the techniques for creating realistic surface materials in Bryce.

CHAPTER ELEVEN

Brycean Skies

IN THIS CHAPTER...

- The multitudinous controls on the Sky & Fog Palette and in the Sky Lab
- Positioning the sun and moon in your Brycean sky using the Sun control
- Changing cloud shape and color
- Fog and haze—controlling atmospheric moisture in Bryce
- All about color—how each color setting for Sky & Fog affects your Bryce scene
- Advanced sky tricks
- Infinite cloud planes and slabs

In Bryceland, you can create an atmosphere to mimic the best day you ever had in your life—or any other kind of day. Working with the Sky & Fog Palette and the Sky Lab to make that atmosphere is a mixture of incredible ease and daunting complexity. The Palette's controls are easy to work with: Drag one of the controls to make an adjustment. Controls in the Sky Lab, besides governing even more parameters, allow greater precision in that you can enter numerical values directly. Since there are so many interconnecting variables in the Sky & Fog controls, the complexity comes in figuring out which control to drag at what time to get that specific result you want.

If you aimlessly drag here or there and watch the preview to see what happens, you may get something you like—or you may not. The hit-or-miss approach may work fine at the beginning, but it gets old quickly. It's better if you know how to go straight to a particular control to change some aspect of your Brycean sky.

In this chapter, we'll look at each Sky & Fog control in turn, isolating each to see how it influences all the others. As we go, we'll point out those features of the sky that can be animated by giving you the special names under which they're known in the animation interface (keyframe menu, Advanced Motion Lab Hierarchy List) in italic text, within square brackets [*like this*]. (The practical worth of this information will become more obvious after you've read Chapter 14, "The Fourth Dimension: Time and Animation.") We'll do the same in the figures—if the illustration shows an interface element that controls a sky property that can be animated, we'll add the animation name in an italic typeface.

THE SKY & FOG CONTROLS

The Sky & Fog Palette has been a feature of Bryce since the beginning. It has many controls, each with additional options. Figure 11.1 shows the palette with all its controls labeled. It offers a number of variables that you can manipulate to create your Brycean sky: six swatches for choosing color, three sets of cloud controls to manipulate Bryce's cumulus or stratus clouds, and controls for fog and haze and

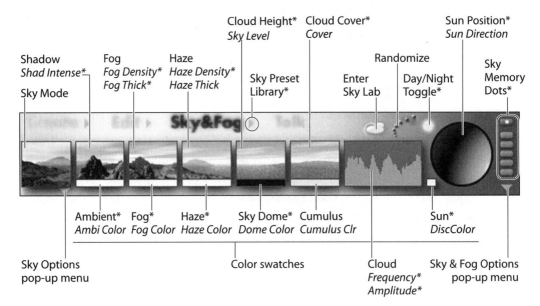

Figure 11.1 The Sky & Fog Palette. Labels in italic type indicate properties subject to keyframing. An asterisk (*) indicates that the item can also be adjusted in the Sky Lab.

shadow. You'll find light source directions—both day and night—that influence the rest of the scene. Four different sky modes, including Atmosphere Off with a color swatch and the Custom Sky option with yet another three color swatches, bring the color swatch total to 10. Any one setting will influence the outcome of any other setting.

The design of the Sky & Fog Palette echoes that of the Edit Palette: Move the mouse pointer over one of the controls, and the control's name appears at the lower left of the screen, at the bottom of the Control Palette. (Option/Alt+click any control to deactivate the feature it affects—the control will lose its color and turn gray.) Drag with the mouse on the control, and a numerical readout replaces the control's name. This arrangement is somewhat cumbersome, because the numbers are a long way from the control you're adjusting; what's more, if you want to see how your changes have affected your scene, you have to render the entire image. As more and more sky editing capabilities were added to successive versions of Bryce, the program sprouted new dialog boxes rather than trying to squeeze the new features onto the Sky & Fog Palette. Bryce 4 introduced a new solution to the problem of where to put the proliferating sky controls: the splendid Sky Lab. This is a large-scale editing "room," like the Materials Lab or the Advanced Motion Lab; you get there by clicking the cloud-and-rainbow icon on the Sky & Fog Palette (see Figure 11.1) or by typing ⌘-K/Ctrl+K. The Sky Lab duplicates most (but not all) of the controls on the Sky & Fog Palette (and adds a few more for good measure), allows you to adjust meteorological parameters by directly typing in numbers, and even provides a real-time preview of your work. Figure 11.2 shows the complete Sky Lab. Controls that lack names on the interface are labeled in normal type; controls that can be animated are labeled with the term used in the keyframe menus and Advanced Motion Lab.

The Sky Lab is more or less a tabbed interface. We say "more or less" because clicking the headings "Sun & Moon," "Cloud Cover," and "Atmosphere" bring different layers of the interface forward, but the headings don't sit on visible tabs. In Figure 11.2, each tabbed layer in turn is brought to the fore. You'll notice that the right third of the Sky Lab never changes; this permanent panel holds the Sun Controls and the preview window.

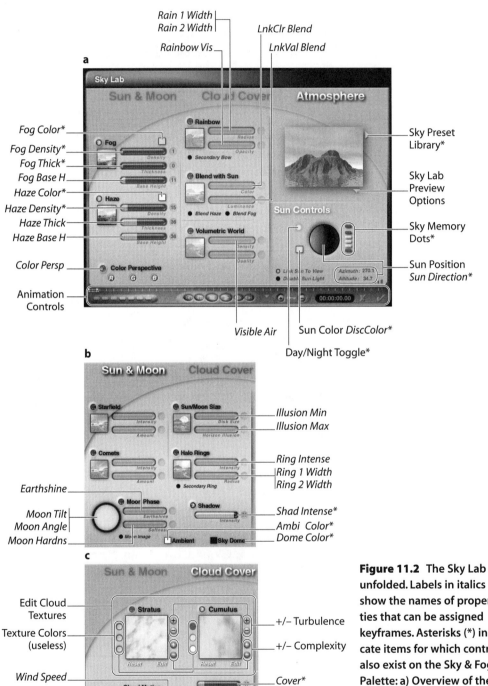

Figure 11.2 The Sky Lab unfolded. Labels in italics show the names of properties that can be assigned keyframes. Asterisks (*) indicate items for which controls also exist on the Sky & Fog Palette: a) Overview of the Sky Lab, with the Atmosphere tab showing; b) the Sun & Moon tab; c) the Cloud Cover tab.

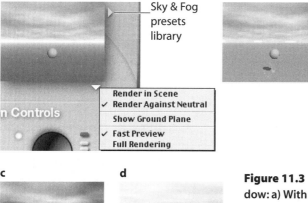

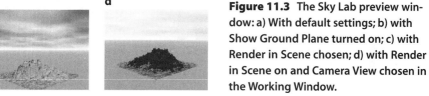

Figure 11.3 The Sky Lab preview window: a) With default settings; b) with Show Ground Plane turned on; c) with Render in Scene chosen; d) with Render in Scene on and Camera View chosen in the Working Window.

The Sky Lab preview is very much like the other Nano Previews scattered throughout Bryce, only bigger. Figure 11.3 shows the preview in all its many moods, as it depicts a scene with default sky settings (but with Link Sun to View turned off). Figure 11.3a shows the default preview, in which a solitary sphere floats free in the Brycean sky. For increasing degrees of realism, you can add a ground plane (Figure 11.3b) or look at a rendering of the sky in the actual scene (Figures 11.3c and d). When you open the Sky Lab, the preview generally starts by showing you the sky from Director's View, with these exceptions: If you were looking at the scene from Camera View before you invoked the Sky Lab, then Camera View is what you get in the preview; and if Render Against Neutral is checked, the window shows the view from the default Director's View (that is, from the southeast).

As in the other Nano Previews, you aren't stuck with the beginning viewing angle; you can change your point of view. Drag (not Option-drag/Alt+drag as the manual says) within the preview window to make the view swivel around its center in trackball fashion. If Render Against Neutral is checked, Option-click/Alt+click to return to the default Director's View; if you've chosen Render in Scene, Option-click/Alt+click switches the viewpoint to the general direction of the default Director's View, but lower and closer in. Hold down Control/Ctrl to constrain the motion: Dragging left and right rotates the scene within the horizontal plane, and dragging up and down zooms out and in. Dragging with the space bar held down pans the scene in any direction.

Next to the Nano Preview is a triangular button; pressing it opens the Sky & Fog Preset Library. This works just like the other preset libraries in Bryce: Click a preset's thumbnail to apply the preset to your scene; click the Add button to add the current sky to the library; click Delete to remove a preset; click Export to save selected presets to a file that can be shared with other Bryce users; click Import to bring in presets from an exported file.

There's another familiar feature just below the preview window: a set of Memory Dots. Again, they behave like their brethren elsewhere in Bryce. Click an empty dot to save a sky configuration; click a green dot to load a saved sky; Option-click/Alt+click a green dot to clear it. And, contrary to the manual, the saved skies will still be there after you quit and restart Bryce. The top dot returns you to the default sky, equivalent to choosing Reset Sky from the Sky & Fog Options pop-up menu (more about that in a moment). One detail to keep in mind: If you change any of the cloud textures in your sky (we'll talk about how to do that in "Exercise: Adjusting Cloud Shape"), the Memory Dots will forget the previous textures, and the new textures will be stored as part of the default sky for your scene.

Another way to reuse a particularly memorable sky in a new document is to turn on the "Copy sky to new document" option in the Preferences dialog box. This option does pretty much what it says: The next new document you create will inherit the sky properties of the document you're currently working on.

Of course, the Memory Dots and the Sun control are present not only in the Sky Lab—they're reproduced on the Sky & Fog Palette as well. There's one more place where you can get at several of the sky controls: the Sky & Fog Options pop-up menu (see Figure 11.4). None of the items on this menu is unique. They're all available somewhere else, but it's handy to have these commonly used controls here, rather than buried in the Sky Lab.

Auto Update forces the scene to rerender each time you make a change to the sky parameters. This can be useful if you're in experimentation mode, allowing you to tweak the sky and see the results of your tweaking immediately. We'll discuss Link Sun to View in detail in the section "Solar and Lunar Direction," but for now, suffice it to say that this control keeps the sun at a constant angle to your camera's perspective. Stratus Clouds and Cumulus Clouds are switches that turn these cloud varieties on and off, and Spherical Clouds keeps your clouds looking natural as they recede into the distance (more about those in the section "Clouds, Clouds, Clouds"). We've already mentioned Reset Sky, and the final item takes you to the Sky Lab (though there are easier ways to get there!).

Because there are so many interconnected elements, a lot of this chapter's step-by-step directions will simply be exploratory exercises to help you become fluent with all of the Sky & Fog parameters. Once you see what each one does to the sky and the scene as a whole, you can go on to create more complex sky effects.

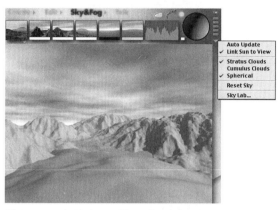

Figure 11.4 *Plain Vanilla!* scene, showing the Sky & Fog Options pop-up menu.

All of the exercises in this chapter use the scene called PLAIN VANILLA! from the Chapter 11 folder of the CD-ROM (see Figure 11.4). The scene has the Bryce default sky set among several terrains with default flat gray surfaces. The mountain forms will let you see how changes to the sky affect the entire scene. If your experimentation takes you too far afield, you can get back to this original state by choosing Reset Sky from the Sky & Fog Options menu or by clicking the topmost Memory Dot.

This chapter's game plan for sky exploration consists of two major sections. The first section covers all the elements that give "shape" to the sky, starting with the solar and lunar direction and then continuing with all the forms of atmospheric moisture: clouds, haze, and fog. The second section explores all the different ways to put color in your sky, including Sky modes.

BASIC BRYCE ASTRONOMY

At the outer limits of the Brycean world is a sphere. This virtual edge is Bryce's sky dome. On the surface of that sky dome are Bryce's principal light sources. The sun illuminates the world during Bryce's daytime, and the moon comes out during Brycean night.

Solar and Lunar Direction

How do you set the time of day? Use the Sun control [*Sun Direction*]. Think of the Sun control's different locations as different times of day. There is a sunrise position, a high-noon position, late morning and early afternoon positions, and so on.

A different way to think of the Sun control is as the top view representation of the Brycean sky dome. You place the light where the sun shines in the sky. At the edges of the circle are different points along the horizon, and at the center is light from the top of the sky. In that case, the top edge is the northern horizon, bottom is south, and east and west are at the left and right sides, respectively (see Figure 11.5). No, this is not a strict "the sun rises in the east and sets in the west"

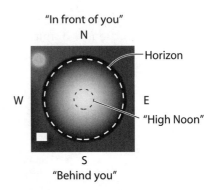

Figure 11.5 The Sun control with Bryce sky dome positions superimposed.

situation. Remember that Bryce is another world entirely. You can make your sun rise and set wherever you want.

Of course, the north-east-south-west orientation can be relative or absolute depending on the status of Link Sun to View. By default, Link Sun to View is on. (Use the Sky & Fog Options pop-up menu if you need to change it; see Figure 11.4.) No matter from which direction you look at your scene, the Sun control position will match your view as seen from directly beneath High Noon; thus, the north horizon will always be directly in front of you when Link Sun to View is on. In other words, it's most helpful to keep two separate frames of reference in mind: When Link Sun to View is on, the different quadrants of the control represent "in front of you," "behind you," and so on; but when Link Sun to View is off, you can think of the control as a compass, showing north, south, east, and west.

Recall from Chapter 6, "Editing and the Internal Bryce Grid," that you can edit your objects from World Space or Camera Space (or Object Space). Using Link Sun to View is analogous to selecting World Space or Camera Space to orient your skies. When Link Sun to View is unchecked, the sun's position (and the entire sky) is oriented in World Space, regardless of your camera perspective on the scene. When Link Sun to View is checked, the sky is oriented in Camera Space as the sun's position follows the camera position.

When you create a new scene, the camera is in the default view, rotated 135° around the y axis, and Link Sun to View is on. If you uncheck Link Sun to View while looking at your scene from the default view, then the sun position will move by 135°.

Figure 11.6 shows just such a scene, start- **a**
ing with the camera and sun in their
default positions. Figures 11.6a and 11.6b
show the scene with Link Sun to View on
and off, respectively. The inset in the
upper right corner of each image shows
the Sun control. Figure 11.6c shows the
scene in Wireframe mode from top view,
with the camera in its default position to
the northwest. Notice that at first, with
everything in the default position, the **b**
sun is about 45° to your right, casting a
nice glancing light across your landscape.
But in Figure 11.6b, with Link Sun to
View turned off, the sun, together with
the whole dome of the sky, has spun
around 135°, so it's shining practically in
your face. The Sun control doesn't show
any sign of this change, so we've rotated
the inset to show the effective sun angle. **c**
To sum up: With Link Sun to View on,
the Sun control reads as "off to the right";
and with Link Sun to View off, it reads as
"shining from the southeast." If you are
creating a Bryce scene as a static illustration, then it doesn't matter if you have
Link Sun to View selected. But if you are
creating an animation, you'll need to
make sure that the sun's position is oriented to World Space. That way, when
your camera moves through the scene,
the sun (or moon) will stay in one place,
as it would in the real world.

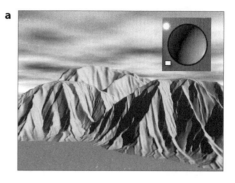

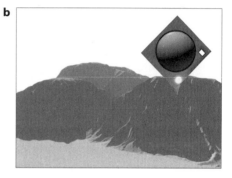

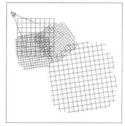

Figure 11.6 Link Sun to View changes
the sky, depending on the camera's
position. Scene from the default Camera
View (including inset picture of the
Sun control) with Link Sun to View
a) checked and b) unchecked; c) wireframe view from top.

When working on a scene, you may want to render from top view and turn off Link
Sun to View. Otherwise, the areas of sun and shadow will be bizarre, since they are,
of course, linked to your view!

On the top left part of the Sun control is the Day and Night button. To change from day to night, simply click the sun. It changes to a moon, and it's now nighttime in Bryceland (where a certain King has been heard to croon, "Love Me Render"). You'll notice that the big glowing blob that represents the sun's position on the Sun control has been replaced by a delicate little smudge, which shows the moon's location. Click again to change back to day.

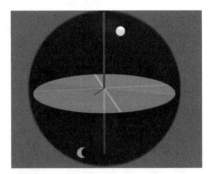

Figure 11.7 Bryce sky dome with the sun opposite the moon.

You may have noticed in your explorations that the sun and moon are on the same continuum—they're at the opposite ends of the sky. If you create a scene that has no ground in it, change the day to night, set the sun in the direct center, turn off view linking, and then point your camera down into the depths…peek-a-boo! There's the sun! (You can also do the opposite, where you look into the depths to see the moon when the sun is out above your head.) In fact, anywhere you place the sun, the moon will ride along opposite it. Figure 11.7 shows a miniature Bryce sky dome sphere, with the sun above and the moon below halfway around the Brycean world.

Sun and Moon Secrets in the Sky Lab

The Sun control on the Sky & Fog Palette was designed for pure intuitive play with your light sources. Drag the sun to the position you want, and there you are. You don't need to deal with numbers to get the sun's position just so. In the Sky Lab, however, you can alter the numbers for the Sun controls. This is good for precise incremental changes for animations or other sequential events.

Here's what happens numerically when you drag the Sun control. (This changed drastically in Bryce 4, so listen up, folks.) Previous versions of Bryce identified the sun's position relative to the *x*, *y*, and *z* axes, but Bryce 4 uses only two parameters: Azimuth and Altitude. Azimuth refers to the point on the horizon directly beneath the sun and is measured in degrees from due north, which is 0°—so due east is 90°, south is 180°, and so on. If you look at a good compass, you'll see the same numbers there. Altitude is the sun's height above the horizon. The maximum is 90°, straight overhead, 45° is halfway up, and at the moment of sunrise or sunset, the sun's altitude is—you guessed it—0°. Negative values are fair game, putting the sun below the horizon and bringing the moon out of hiding to illuminate the scene. (The manual hiccups on this point, saying that the range of Altitude values is from –99 to +99. That was the range for various parameters in the old three-axis system, but no more.)

One of the advantages of this system is that it's also used by astronomers to pinpoint heavenly bodies in the real (non-Brycean) sky. For example, let's say you construct a model of Stonehenge, and you want to capture the effect of the sun rising over the Heelstone at dawn on the Summer Solstice (a matter of great concern to the Druids among you). Just look up the celestial coordinates of the sun for that date and location in a good almanac, plug the values into the Sky Lab, and you're ready for some human sacrifice!

Figure 11.8a is a schematic representation of the Sun control, with the Azimuth scale made visible. The glowing spot shows the sun's default position. Figure 11.8b shows both the Azimuth and Altitude scales from a vantage point low and to the south-southeast. The white globe represents the sun at its default position

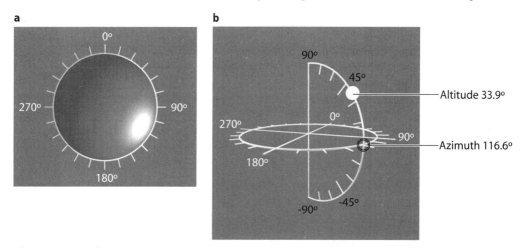

Figure 11.8 Default sun position: a) Top view showing the sun's azimuth; b) side view showing Azimuth and Altitude. The white numbers are on the Azimuth scale, and the black numbers are on the Altitude scale.

at Azimuth 116.6°, just a little bit south of east, and Altitude 33.9°, a little more than a third of the way up the dome of the sky. Refer back to Figure 11.2 to see the Sun Position control in the Sky Lab (by the way, there's a quick way to get there: double-click the Sun control on the Sky & Fog Palette).

You can change the Azimuth and Altitude numbers by selecting them and typing new numbers in the data fields, or you can use the up and down arrow keys (with modifiers) to adjust the values. The keyboard modifiers available are a subset of those used in Edit dialog boxes, as listed in Table 6.1. The only ones applicable here are Shift (+/– 10) and Option/Alt (+/– 0.1). Notice that the numbers always refer to the sun's position, no matter whether it's day or night. Figure 11.9a shows the Sun Position control in a daytime setting. If you click the Day/Night control, Figure 11.9b is the result. The moon and sun swap places, and the small white dot shows the moon's position. Azimuth and Altitude have changed, too: Since the sun has moved to the opposite side of the Azimuth scale, add 180° to (or subtract 180° from) the Azimuth quantity, and since the sun is now below the horizon the same distance it was above the horizon, the Altitude value goes from +57.4° to –57.4°.

Figure 11.9 The effect on the Sun controls of clicking the Day/Night button: a) The sun's position during the day; b) the result of switching the control to night.

Wait, what's that you say? You don't conceptualize the sun's position in the sky numerically? And the God's-eye view provided by the Sun Position control doesn't work for you either? You'd rather just be able to point to a spot in the sky and say "Sun here!"? Well, thanks to a secret key combination (almost as good as a secret handshake, right?), Bryce will allow you to do just that. Double-click the Sun control while holding down Control-Option (Macintosh) or Ctrl+Alt (Windows). You won't get any feedback to speak of—that's just how Brycean Easter Eggs are. Then, holding down the same keys, single-click your scene on the spot where you want the sun to be. A little gold star appears. (See Figure 11.10. Yes, it really is gold—but it's made up of lines that are only one pixel wide, so the

color doesn't show up well.) Render the
scene, and there's the sun, right where you
put it. Not quite what you wanted? Switch
back to Wireframe mode, Control-Option-
click/Ctrl+Alt+click somewhere else, and
the sun takes the new position. Designing a
night scene? Click the Day/Night toggle on
the Sky & Fog Palette, and the star turns
dark blue—it now marks the moon's position. Alas, this trick isn't perfect (remember,
that's just how Brycean Easter Eggs are). If
you change to night and then click the scene
as if to move the moon, Bryce rather rudely
dumps you back into daytime and puts the sun where you just clicked—so to set
the moon's position, put the sun where you are sure you want the moon to be and
then switch to nighttime. Also, when you open a new scene or restart Bryce, you
have to go through the double-click rigmarole again.

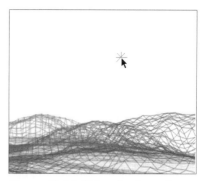

Figure 11.10 Using the Control-
Option-click/Ctrl+Alt+click Easter
Egg to position the sun in the sky.

When the Moon Hits Your Eye like a Big Pizza Pie

Bryce, in its infinite wisdom, lets you adjust not only the position of the sun and
moon, but their sizes and other parameters as well. Open the Sky Lab and click
the Sun & Moon tab to bring forward the options for those celestial bodies. Before
we plunge into descriptions of the individual controls, we'll tell you how they
work in general. Typically, they have an on/off switch, a square thumbnail illustrating the property they affect, and two sliders with a numerical entry field next
to each. The sliders work like their counterparts in the Materials Lab: Drag the
end of the slider to adjust, or click the spot where you want the slider to stop. To
enter a quantity directly, click the number, and it turns into an editable field.
There's another choice: Move the mouse over the thumbnail itself, and the
pointer changes to a four-headed arrow, showing you that you can drag to change
quantities. The general rule: Dragging left and right adjusts the upper slider; dragging up and down adjusts the lower slider.

• *Sun/Moon Disk Size.* This control sets the diameter of the sun or moon,
  whichever is showing. When you first turn this control on, it's preset to 10,
  the default [*Illusion Min*]. Have you ever watched the sun set on a lazy summer's eve and noticed that it seems to get bigger as it sinks out of sight? In
  Bryce, this effect is controlled by the Horizon Illusion slider. The higher the

number, the larger the sun (or moon) at the horizon, and the higher above the horizon the effect kicks in [*Illusion Max*]. (Minor buglet: When you drag the thumbnail, the mouse pointer becomes a two-headed arrow, rather than a proper four-headed one.)

- *Halo Rings.* A high layer of cold air infused with ice crystals will cause the sun or moon to be surrounded with a gossamer halo. Turn on Halo Rings to get this effect in your Bryce scene; click Secondary Ring to add a faint outer ring. The Intensity [*Ring Intense*] and Radius sliders affect both rings simultaneously, but you can animate the radii of the two rings separately [*Ring 1 Width, Ring 2 Width*]. "Radius" is a misnomer—this slider actually adjusts the breadth of the rings, not their radii.

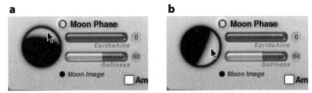

Figure 11.11 The Moon Phase controls: a) After dragging up on the moon's phase; b) after dragging down and to the right.

- *Moon Phase.* Want more than a flat disk in your night sky? Turn on this option to add a romantic crescent moon to your scene. Drag in any direction on the Moon control to choose the moon's phase [*Moon Angle*] and its position on the face of the moon [*Moon Tilt*] (see Figure 11.11). Earthshine [*Earthshine*] adds some illumination reflected from the Earth to the shadowed part of the moon. Softness [*Moon Hardns*] adjusts the sharpness (or lack thereof) of the boundary between light and shadow on the moon's surface. Want your moon to look more like The Moon? Turn on Moon Image. Want to see a truly frightening effect? Here's the secret: ⌘-click/Ctrl+click the Moon Image button, and a pop-up menu appears with a list of names. These folks are the Bryce 3D development team (many of whom were also involved in work on Bryce 4, but some of the crew changed, and the list o' names doesn't reflect the new crew); pick one from the list and render your scene. Whoa! You've heard of The Man in the Moon, but this is ridiculous! If this gives you nightmares, bring up the secret menu again and choose Normal to make the scary face go away.

- *Starfield and Comets.* Use these to populate your nighttime sky. The Amount sliders govern the quantity of objects spangling the heavens, and the Intensity sliders adjust their brightness relative to the background. Alas, these features cannot be animated, so you can't create the effect of stars winking out one by one or a meteor shower building in intensity.

Exercise: Solar and Lunar Fluency

To limber up your "work with the Brycean sky" muscles, open up the PLAIN VANILLA! scene file on the CD-ROM. Shut off Auto-Key from the pop-up menu on the Time Palette; since the aim of this exercise is to make multiple variations on the scene, you want to ensure that the scene file size will be as small as possible. Limit yourself to using the Sun control for changing the sun's position and changing from day to night and vice versa. For this exercise and the others, the aim is to create as many quick sketches as possible. If you've ever taken drawing classes or tried drawing exercises, you've probably done quick gesture drawings, where you try to capture the basic pose or attitude with just a few quick strokes. When you've made those few marks on paper, you move on to the next exercise. The aim is not to complete a detailed drawing, but to work quickly with fluidity, going from one sketch to another to another in rapid succession.

This exercise works in the same way. (If you're already familiar with Bryce animation, we present a slightly different strategy for this exercise in the Tip after step 5. Read the steps to familiarize yourself with the routine and then follow the alternative advice in the Tip.)

Make sure that you have between 20 and 50 megabytes of disk space free on your hard drive for this exercise (and the exercises that follow in this chapter). Each copy of the scene file and image file takes up about a megabyte and a half. (The CD also contains a lower-resolution version that should be in the neighborhood of 600K, if your disk space is tight.) Later, when the exercise is over, you can trash the scene files.

Give yourself about 10 to 15 minutes for this exercise. Create between 10 and 15 (or more, even!) different versions of the scene, each with a unique sun or moon position. The idea is to create as many *different* versions of lighting as you can.

1. Make a move with the Sun control. Render a couple of passes. You don't need to finish the scene.

2. Select Save As and give your new version of the Plain Vanilla! scene a unique name. The easiest way to do this is to add a number to the end of the name (PLAIN VANILLA!-1). Each time you save a variation using Save As, Bryce will increase that number by one.

3. Start again. Make another move with the Sun control. Render a few passes. Select File > Save As and give this version a unique name and number. Continue on with your sky gesture drawings.

4. Put the sun in your scene so you can see it. Put the moon in your scene. When you're working on the moon, pay particular attention to the lunar opposition to the sun and decide beforehand to make a lunar shadow from *some* direction. Then place the Sun control to make it so.

5. When you are finished, or when the time is up, prepare your files for a later batch render. In the Macintosh Finder or in Windows Explorer, display the folder in list view by type so all of the scene file icons are together. That way, it will be easy to do a batch render later. To batch-render, drag the scene file icons to your Bryce application icon, alias, or shortcut.

Note: As you work on your Plain Vanilla! scenes, please refrain from making any changes to the terrains that are already in the scene (unless you want to adjust the terrain resolution to create a smaller scene size). There are other chapters in this book for working on other parts of Bryce. Right now, you are concentrating on skies, and the scene is provided so you can see how various changes in the Sky & Fog Palette and the Sky Lab affect your scene. At the end of this chapter, you will have amassed a collection of sky variations, and it's valuable to have a common reference to the same set of terrains.

> **TIP:** *If you are already familiar with animation (to be introduced in Chapter 14, "The Fourth Dimension: Time and Animation"), you can set up the fluency exercises in a different way. Start with Auto-Key on, and set an initial keyframe for the scene. Set ticker marks to be displayed every five frames. Instead of saving a new scene file for each variation, advance the Time Scrubber by five frames (tap the period [.] key to move to the next ticker mark), and then set up a new sky variation. Not only will you see the results of each of your explorations, but you'll see the states in between as well. Since you are adding so many extra renders for each change you make, set your render resolution to 1:0.50 or use the supplied PLAIN VANILLA ANIM! scene file for the exercise.*

CLOUDS, CLOUDS, CLOUDS

In this section, we'll examine all the different ways to adjust and manipulate clouds in Bryceland. There are many different factors to manipulate. This section explores them individually so that you can be aware of which control influences which behavior.

Stratus and Cumulus

Brycean clouds come in two flavors: stratus and cumulus. You can set up either or both types of clouds in your scenes. You do so by selecting one or both from the Sky & Fog Options pop-up menu.

Here are the main differences between the two types of clouds:

Stratus	Cumulus
Higher, wispier cloud	Lower, more substantive cloud
Color comes from Sun Color	Color comes from Cumulus/Ambient Color
High amplitude, high definition	High amplitude, high definition
Low amplitude, wisps dissolve	Low amplitude, low definition into high-altitude haze

Cloud Shape

You can adjust your clouds in several ways. In the Sky & Fog Palette, the four means of adjusting clouds are Altitude, Cover, Frequency, and Amplitude. (You can also adjust Cumulus Color in the Sky & Fog Palette as well, though we're not focusing on color at the moment.) The Sky Lab has numerical settings for each of those controls. Refer back to Figures 11.1 and 11.2c.

This next exercise explores all that goes into the creation of cloud shape. Both stratus and cumulus clouds are included in this study of Brycean cloud shapes.

Exercise: Adjusting Cloud Shape

Set aside another 20 minutes or so for this exercise. First you'll learn to adjust specific controls in response to questions about which way to change the clouds. Later, after you've gone through each of the questions, spend some time freely playing with the different controls. Each time you create a unique look for your sky, select File > Save As and give your scene a unique name.

The scene file PLAIN VANILLA! starts with the basic default sky that ships with Bryce (refer back to Figure 11.4). Notice that in Bryce 4, the default sky is not a blank slate, but includes stratus clouds. This provides your initial cloud setting for this exercise.

Answer these questions:

1. Do you want more clouds?

    More clouds in the sky, that is, more individual cloud shapes, can be obtained via the Frequency control. Drag the graph to the right to increase frequency and to the left to decrease frequency [*Frequency*]. Figure C11.12 (in the color section) shows a series of clouds with different frequency adjustments. Part b uses the default frequency; part a uses lower value, and parts c and d use higher values. The frequency graph for each rendered image is inset on the image, as is the frequency Slider from the Sky Lab (the range of permissible values is 0 to 200).

2. Do you want more cloud cover?

    Drag the Cloud Coverage thumbnail. Dragging to the right increases cloud coverage, and dragging to the left reduces it [*Cover*]. Coverage determines the amount of cloud cover in your sky. You can have the same number of cloud puffs (frequency), but you can change how much of the sky they cover (coverage). By adjusting the Cloud Coverage thumbnail, you can make the same number of cloud puffs grow in proportion until they dominate the sky or shrink back to daintily decorate it. Figure C11.13 shows a series that progresses from lower (left) to higher coverage (right).

3. Do you want the clouds wispier or more defined?

    Adjust Amplitude to control how wispy or well-defined the clouds are [*Amplitude*]. When you drag down so that the graph gets spikier, your clouds become more defined (see Figure C11.14). When you drag up, the graph becomes flatter, and the clouds become more diffuse at their edges.

    The Sky Lab includes a section for numerical entry of the amplitude. The numerical range is normally 0 to 500 (–500 to 0 values are also possible; we'll discuss negative amplitude in a moment). The higher the number, the spikier your graph; the lower the number, the smoother your graph. With an Amplitude setting of 0, you won't be able to see your clouds at all.

Note: With stratus clouds, a lower Amplitude setting—or wispier clouds—results in a high-altitude haze. The less defined the stratus clouds are, the greater the high-altitude mist, since the clouds are dispersed. Figure C11.14 shows the default stratus clouds at three ranges of amplitude: low, default, and higher. So if you want a hazy sky when you don't have haze elsewhere, use a lower Amplitude setting and stratus clouds.

4. Do you want the clouds placed differently in the sky?

   Would you rather your clouds changed places with the sky? You can swap your cloud and sky areas by setting Amplitude to be positive (see Figure C11.15a) or negative (see Figure C11.15b). The default is usually positive. Compare the images in the figure. The basic cloud shape is the same, but a positive Amplitude setting puts the cloud here and sky there, whereas a negative setting swaps the sky and cloud.

   Note: In the Sky Lab, achieving a negative value by dragging the Amplitude slider is a slightly mysterious process: Drag the slider to the left all the way to 0 and then keep dragging. A new gold slider will begin to sprout in place of the blue one. Drag the gold slider to adjust negative values.

5. Do you want your clouds to be at a different altitude?

   Changing the altitude will change the way your clouds look in the sky. Change the altitude setting by dragging the Cloud Height thumbnail [*Sky Level*]. The default setting, 8, is pretty low considering that the range is from 0 to 100. In some ways, adjusting the altitude will have the same effect as adjusting the frequency of the clouds—the higher the clouds, the higher the frequency. Your eye is able to see more area farther away, so the clouds farther away (higher) seem to have a higher frequency. When the altitude is lower, you can see fewer clouds. And while we're on the subject of the distant edges of clouds, this is a good time to mention the Spherical Clouds option. Contrary to what its name might imply, it doesn't make individual clouds spherical. Rather, it maps the entire cloudplane onto the surface of a sphere so that as the clouds recede into the distance, they dip below the horizon. If Spherical Clouds is turned off, the cloudplane is an infinite flat plane. Distant clouds become smaller and smaller along the line of sight, until the horizon is lined with little tiny cloud granules, as you can see in Figure C11.16a. With Spherical Clouds turned on, the clouds keep a more natural shape along the full distance to the horizon (see Figure C11.16b).

For this example, we turned off haze completely to make the effect clearer—though to be fair, we should mention that even a little bit of haze tends to mask the effect, as shown by C11.16c and d.

However, lest you think that Cloud Height is merely another means of adjusting frequency, Cloud Height also affects the way that you see haze in your sky. (We weren't kidding when we said that everything is tied to everything else!) We'll talk more about this when we discuss haze later in the chapter. Figure C11.17 illustrates how different altitude levels affect the haze modulation. For each altitude level, the left half of the image has the default amount of haze (Density = 8; Thickness = 50); and the right half has no haze. The higher the altitude, the more clouds that can be seen. Likewise, the height of the haze layer increases with the cloud height—you can see this most plainly in the bright band along the horizon, which gets thicker as the cloud height goes up. If you raise the cloud level, you may have to reduce the frequency afterward to compensate for the apparent increase in the number of clouds.

6. Do you want different clouds?

Change from stratus to cumulus clouds via the Sky & Fog Options pop-up menu. (Or, as a variation, select both. Try both on your own; continue this exercise by working with cumulus clouds only.) Figure 11.18 shows the result of using the Sky & Fog Options pop-up menu to switch Cumulus Clouds on.

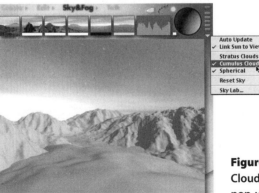

Figure 11.18 Choosing Cumulus Clouds from the Sky & Fog Options pop-up menu.

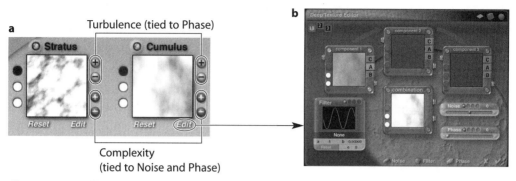

Figure 11.19 Editing cloud textures: a) Using the Sky Lab to perform small-scale editing; b) the Deep Texture Editor showing the cumulus cloud texture

7. Do you want the clouds to look different?

You can tweak the clouds' appearance directly in the Sky Lab by clicking the + and – buttons to the right of each cloud panel (see Figure 11.19a). The upper pair of buttons for each cloud type controls the turbulence of the pattern— how convoluted it is. The lower pair controls the complexity of the texture— how much fine detail is incorporated. Contrary to the manual, there's no Randomize button here. Disregard also the manual's comment about the color controls to the left of each cloud panel: They are completely useless. Bryce takes information about value (levels of light and dark) only from the texture and ignores the color information. If you're not satisfied with your new pattern, click Reset to return to the default cloud shapes—or...

To make your clouds depart completely from their current shape, click the Edit button below the Stratus or the Cumulus panel (see Figure 11.19a). Doing this will take you to the Deep Texture Editor (see Figure 11.19b). The Deep Texture Editor was discussed in lurid detail in the previous chapter; go there if you need a brush-up. In the Deep Texture Editor you have access to the full range of Bryce's texture-editing capabilities, minus, of course, the color features, but including the Randomize button. (For truly bizarre and nightmarish sky effects, try some of the geometric texture presets!). Note that any editing you did in the Sky Lab shows up here as well; adjustments to the Turbulence and Complexity buttons are reflected here in the Noise and Phase settings. The default cloud textures use only a single component, but you can add more components in the DTE. If you use a multicomponent texture, changes you make with the Turbulence and Complexity buttons are applied equally to each component.

Clicking the Turbulence buttons adjusts the global Phase setting of each component and of their combination: Click + to increase global Phase by 20; click – to decrease by the same amount. Adjustments made with the Complexity buttons affect Noise and Phase. Clicking the + button doubles the frequency of, and adds an octave to, the Noise of individual components; it also doubles the frequency of, and adds an octave to, the Combination Phase (clicking the – button halves the frequency and removes an octave for both individual component Noise and Combination Phase). For example:

Starting with:	Frequency = 375	Octaves = 4
After clicking Complexity +:	Frequency = 750	Octaves = 5
After another click:	Frequency = 1500	Octaves = 6

In other words, because of the way that the Octaves setting works in the Deep Texture Editor, the frequency is adjusted to compensate for the new level. With the addition of each lower octave, you need to increase the frequency to see the same shape, but that shape, with the additional octave, has greater richness and complexity of detail.

Here's something to keep in mind: If you change either of the cloud textures, the new texture becomes part of the Default Sky settings for this document; any further use of the Reset Sky command or clicking of the Default Sky Memory Dot will conjure up clouds containing your new textures.

8. Do you want to create even more variations?

Continue creating variations on your Plain Vanilla! scene. Work with all of the cloud controls: Altitude, Coverage, Frequency, Amplitude, switching between Stratus and Cumulus and using both. Add the Sun control to the mix. Tempting though it may be, do not use the other Sky & Fog controls just yet. In the space of another 15 to 20 minutes, create as many different scene files as you can. Aim to create 15 in a 20-minute time span. (If you don't create that many, don't worry; the time and quantity are guidelines to help get you going at a quick-quick-quick pace.)

Clouds and Sunlight

Whatever their size and shape, Bryce clouds won't obscure the sun's light, unless you go to the Sky Lab and turn on the Cast Shadows switch to allow the clouds to block the sun's light. Doing so dapples your landscapes with subtle patterns of shadow that follow the clouds lazily across the sky. To adjust the appearance of your cloud's shadows in your scene, you may need to tweak Amplitude, Cloud Height, and/or Frequency. If, for whatever reason, you choose to forego cloud shadows in a sky with lots of cloud cover, be sure to pull back your Shadow setting (described in a few pages) to make the direct sunlight less apparent.

Finishing Touches

The last few cloud-related options in the Sky Lab are mostly of concern in animated scenes. True, we're jumping the gun a bit, since animation is introduced in Chapter 14, but file these bits of info away for future reference. By default, your clouds will drift slowly across the sky during an animated sequence, governed by the Cloud Motion settings. The round gizmo at the left sets the direction from which the clouds flow [*Wind Dir*]—just drag the shiny blue ball to the desired point of the compass, which represents the axis of World Space. The sliders at the right adjust the speed [*Wind Speed*] and turbulence [*Wind Turbu*] of the cloud motion. To stop cloud motion altogether, click the large button at the center of the round gizmo; the sliders for both Speed and Turbulence will be set to zero.

Link Clouds to View freezes the clouds to the camera's point of view—in other words, they move in Camera Space. Otherwise, the clouds move in sync with the landscape, in World Space. Compare the two movies on the CD-ROM, CLOUDS LINKED TO VIEW.MOV and CLOUDS NOT LINKED TO VIEW.MOV.

IT'S IN THE AIR: FOG, HAZE, AND RAINBOWS

Fog, haze, and rainbows are all manifestations of moisture in the air. Fog is localized moisture clinging to the ground; haze is overall moisture. When moisture conditions are right and the viewer looks at the right part of the sky with the sun at a certain angle, a rainbow is visible.

Fog

Fog, in real life, is a cloud layer that clings close to the ground. Bryce's Fog control allows you to create a ground-hugging mist of any color. Aside from its color, three parameters determine the fog's appearance: The overall amount of fog is set by Fog Density, and the height of the fog layer is set by Fog Thickness (in previous versions, this setting was called Height). The thumbnail control on the Sky & Fog Palette gives you two directions to drag to change either setting. Dragging right and left changes the density of the fog [*Fog Density*]; dragging up and down changes its thickness [*Fog Thick*]. Two corresponding sets of number readouts tell you what you have. The Sky & Fog dialog box allows for precise numerical entry of these parameters, plus a third: Fog Base Height [*Fog Base H*]. This latter setting provides nuance for the first two, so we'll discuss it later, after we've introduced you to the more basic parameters.

Fog is at maximum in the infinite distance of the horizon. This is true even with the slightest Fog Density setting: 1. But what determines the volume of the fog at places other than infinity, at points closer to you? The three Fog controls do.

Density determines the amount of water per cubic volume of air in the fog layer. Density is defined by a single number, but the density will vary vertically within the fog layer, diminishing with altitude. You observe the fog's density most dramatically as you look down the camera's depth (z axis) from the foreground to the infinite horizon (presuming the camera is near the ground). Figure 11.20 shows three representations of fog density. (Here, maximum fog is considered black.) All three scenes are completely "socked in" at the horizon. The fog in each dissipates differently as it moves from the distant horizon to the near foreground. The fog in the left image dissipates in the distance, with very thin fog in the foreground. The fog in the center image still has some density in the mid- to foreground. The fog in the right scene is quite thick, with some thinning in the foreground. In these simple illustrations, which scene do you suppose has the lowest Fog Density setting, and which one has the highest? (Tick tick tick tick tick—beep! Time's up!) The left one has the lowest Fog Density setting, and the right one has the highest.

Figure 11.20 A schematic representation of various amounts of fog density, increasing from left to right.

The second part of the fog volume equation is fog thickness. Thickness determines the vertical dimension of the fog layer. It answers the question: How much room is there for the transition from solid "socked in" fog (at the bottom of the fog bank) to no fog (at the top of the fog bank)? Figure 11.21 shows yet more simplistic representations of three different Fog Thickness settings. Which one do you think is maximum? How about minimum? (Insert the theme song from "Jeopardy" here!) If you matched up minimum with the left and maximum with the right, then you're right! ("Now tell our contestants what they've won, Jay!")

Figure 11.21 More schematic representations of fog, this time showing fog thickness. The lowest setting, at the left, not only provides a thin layer of fog, but the opacity of the fog itself must change rapidly from opaque at the bottom to ethereal at the top. When the layer is thicker, as at the right, the opacity changes at a more leisurely rate (with default Base Height settings).

Now that we've established what the two main parts of the fog volume equation are, it's time for some observations about the relationship between the two. Fog at low thickness is different above ground level than below ground level. In the first image in row a of Figure 11.22, settings of Density = 5 and Thickness = 5 with a bowl-shaped crater below ground level shows the fog below ground level solidly socked in, whereas above ground, it's not. (Note: All objects that are at ground level are just a teensy smidgen *above* ground level.) Why is this? The Fog Thickness setting tells how much vertical room there is to make the transition between solid fog (where fog covers everything) and no fog (where fog obscures nothing). With a low Fog Thickness setting, there's scant room for any transition between everything and nothing, giving the impression of a very thin layer of solid fog. Above ground level, you get mostly nothing, and below ground level, you see everything. The remainder of the images in row a of Figure 11.22 have more vertical room to modulate from solid fog to no fog. The scenes all have the same density, but thickness increases from left to right. Compare the images in row b, where the Thickness setting is kept constant, but the Density value increases from left to right (in both these sets of images, Base Height is left at the default setting).

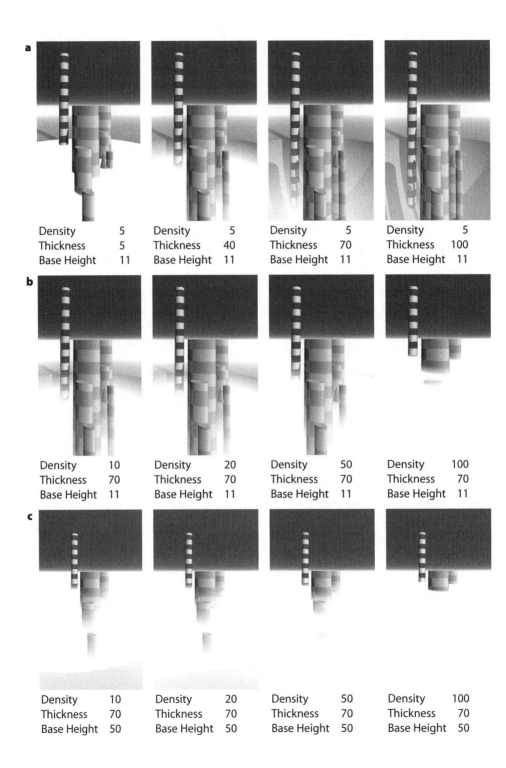

a

Density	5	Density	5	Density	5	Density	5
Thickness	5	Thickness	40	Thickness	70	Thickness	100
Base Height	11	Base Height	11	Base Height	11	Base Height	11

b

Density	10	Density	20	Density	50	Density	100
Thickness	70	Thickness	70	Thickness	70	Thickness	70
Base Height	11	Base Height	11	Base Height	11	Base Height	11

c

Density	10	Density	20	Density	50	Density	100
Thickness	70	Thickness	70	Thickness	70	Thickness	70
Base Height	50	Base Height	50	Base Height	50	Base Height	50

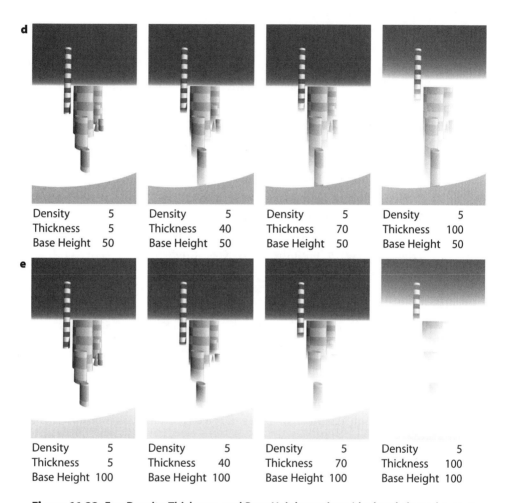

Density	5	Density	5	Density	5	Density	5
Thickness	5	Thickness	40	Thickness	70	Thickness	100
Base Height	50	Base Height	50	Base Height	50	Base Height	50

Density	5	Density	5	Density	5	Density	5
Thickness	5	Thickness	40	Thickness	70	Thickness	100
Base Height	100	Base Height	100	Base Height	100	Base Height	100

Figure 11.22 Fog Density, Thickness, and Base Height settings (the bowl-shaped cutout is below Bryce's ground level): a) Low Density setting, with Thickness increasing from left to right; b) moderate Thickness setting, with Density increasing from left to right; c) same Density and Thickness settings as for b, but Base Height of 50; d) same Density and Thickness settings as for a, but Base Height of 50; e) same as d, but Base Height of 100. The default amount of haze is also present.

> **TIP:** As a general rule, avoid low Thickness settings unless you want to struggle with sudden socked-in layers of fog. As an emphatic rule, if you have anything in your scene that is below ground level, avoid low Thickness settings like the plague.

So what about this Base Height thing? Remember that you can assign a Density quantity to fog, but for any given Density setting, the fog will have a range of density, thinning with altitude. The Base Height setting allows you to adjust this variation in density to taste. Figure 11.23 shows schematically how changing Base Density alters the vertical distribution of density within a fog layer. The gradient in each square shows the lessening of density with altitude, and the dashed white line marks the height at which the density has dropped to half its value at ground level. The leftmost graph shows the default Base Height—the fog is mostly concentrated near the ground (the manual errs in saying that the default Base Height value is 0; if your Base Height setting is 0, you are fogless!). As you increase Base Height, the 50% mark moves higher, redistributing the moisture throughout the fog layer. This comes in handy if you need to place your fog in a valley so it's just so. Adjust Base Height up and down until the fog is densest right where you need it.

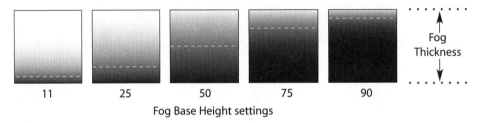

Fog Base Height settings

Figure 11.23 How adjusting the Fog Base Height setting redistributes density within the fog layer. The squares represent fog layers of a certain thickness with different Base Height settings.

The fog layer has an absolute upper limit, defined by the Thickness setting. (There's an absolute maximum height for fog in Bryce, too, above which the fog never intrudes; it's at about 50 Bryce Units above the default ground plane.) *In* Figure 11.24, we've added a huge mountain to the scene used in Figure 11.22 (it's about 550 Bryce units tall). Figure 11.24a shows a low-Density layer of fog at 100% Thickness and default Base Height. Notice how far the fog extends up the mountain. In Figure 11.24b, we've increased Base Height to 50. The fog layer is more opaque (because we've moved the moisture higher within the fog), but the layer itself extends no farther up the slope. Along the fog's "shoreline," the layer is still slightly translucent, because there is still some relatively thin fog at the top of it, but in Figure 11.24c (where Base Height is 100), the layer is solid.

Fog is calculated in the render as part of the shading process. There's a relationship between the Fog settings, the camera position, and the other objects in the scene. The appearance of fog in a scene changes radically depending on the presence or absence of objects—especially a ground plane. At the same time, though,

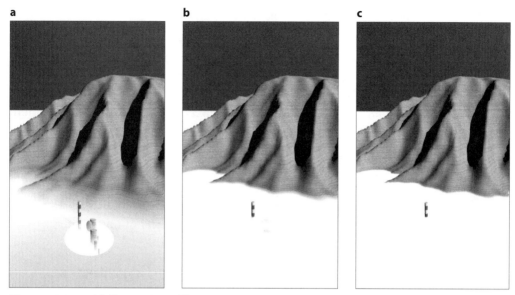

Figure 11.24 A bird's-eye view of fog. In each example, Density = 5, Thickness = 100: a) Base Height = 11; b) Base Height = 50, c) Base Height = 100. Haze was turned off for this example.

the position of the camera in relation to the objects—or to the horizon in general—also affects the appearance of fog. In Brycean terms, the whole purpose of fog is to obscure objects in the scene. When there are no objects, there's nothing to obstruct. In most scenes, you'll have a ground plane. As it extends into horizontal infinity, the ground plane is obscured by the fog. But if you delete the ground plane, then fog acts differently, in what seems like a bizarre fashion. Figure C11.25 (in the color section) shows a series of scenes. There is a pseudo-ground plane on the right (it's just a square occupying the right side of the scene, and it stretches way, way back). There are steps on the left that descend into the infinite sky abyss, and steps on the right that ascend toward the sky. All of the scenes have identical Fog settings: Density is 37, Thickness is 100, and Base Height is 11, the default. What is different about each one is the camera placement; the cameras are at five different heights. (For reference, there is a side view of the wireframe next to each rendered image.) What the camera sees differs depending on the camera's height and, consequently, its viewing angle for each object. The camera's Rotate settings (as set in the Camera controls dialog box) do not change. But as the camera's position is raised, its perspective of the foreground changes. The higher the camera position, the more directly the camera looks down into an infinite sky. Since it's hard to measure precisely how to obstruct "nothing" stretching way off into infinity, Bryce does not do so. What you see instead is the wild blue yonder—literally.

Freestanding Fog

If you want to create freestanding fog that is local to one particular area in your scene, you can use a sphere or cube primitive and give it foggy material attributes. Figure C11.26 shows a localized fog bank made from a basic sphere. In the Materials Lab, the Shading mode is set to Fuzzy. Diffusion is set to maximum (100) and Ambience to medium (51.7), and there is some transparency as well (8.2). The Diffuse and Ambient Colors are white. To adjust the visibility of the edges, increase the Transparency setting or change the size of the sphere. Make the localized fog sensitive to shadow by ensuring that there is some diffuse illumination. You can do the same sort of thing with freestanding clouds to get localized fog effects. We'll talk about freestanding clouds at the end of this chapter.

Haze: On a Hazy Day, You Can't See Forever

Haze indicates distance. As you walk to and fro upon the Earth, haze is one visual cue that something is far away. The farther away an object is, the more its details and color intensity are obscured by the water moisture in the air—or to put it differently, the more haze you have to look through, the farther away the object will appear. The Haze control on the Sky & Fog Palette works very simply: Drag left or right in the Haze thumbnail control to change the haze amount. Assign the haze a color from the Haze Color swatch. In the Sky Lab, you'll find a bit more complexity: three sliders, for Density (the parameter set by the control on the Sky & Fog Palette) [*Haze Density*], Thickness [*Haze Thick*], and Base Height [*Haze Base H*]. At first glance, it would seem that these are analogous to the controls for Fog, but the relationship isn't so simple, as we shall see.

A little haze goes a long way. With the lowest possible Haze setting, you will see the haze line on your horizon. Indeed, even if you check the Disable Sun Light option, as long as there is the tiniest bit of haze in your sky, that glowing band along the horizon will be there. If your scene is just a plain blue sky, the presence of the minimum amount of haze (set Density to 1 out of 100 in the Sky Lab) will make all the difference as you look off in the infinite distance.

Once you start adding objects to your scene, however, a higher Haze setting will give the appearance of distance. Take a look at the scenes by Eric Wenger on the Bryce CD (and on the book's CD, too). The Haze setting is often above 11 for a sense of distance and scale. (It can go much higher, especially when you're set to lower altitudes.) What was just a dinky-looking terrain swells to massive grandeur once all the haze is there to tell you that the mountain is really quite large.

Of course, if Earth-bound realism isn't your thing, you can turn off Haze completely for that extraterrestrial look. Nothin' says "vacuum" like a hard-edged, crystal-clear sky!

Getting back to those pesky controls—Density works very much like its foggy cousin. It sets the overall quantity of moisture in the air, thickest near the ground and thinning with altitude (and the default is 8, not 4 as the manual claims). When adjusting haze, you'll probably get the best results by working with the Density control; after all, there's a reason it's the one Haze parameter you can adjust on the Sky & Fog Palette. You can do most of the work without ever cracking the Sky Lab at all. When you're ready to do your final tweaking, call up the Sky Lab, where reside the Thickness and Base Height controls.

These last two don't work quite the same way as their fog-bound cousins. What does "thickness" mean when speaking of haze, anyway? With fog, it's pretty clear-cut: Fog is a distinct layer, and Thickness tells you, well, how thick (high) the layer is. But haze is different—it pervades the atmosphere and often doesn't form itself into a neat layer—so the Thickness control governs not the vertical dimension of the haze layer, but how much haze affects the visibility of far-off objects. The higher the Thickness setting, the faster the increase in moisture with distance from the camera. You can see the effect of changing Thickness most clearly by watching the bright line on the horizon. Even with a high Density setting, you can make that line razor thin by turning down Thickness. Likewise, using a high Thickness setting with a low Density setting will produce a thick line.

Haze, like fog, also has a Base Height setting, which should, in theory, shift the entire pattern of density up or down. It doesn't quite work this way in actual practice. In general, Base Height adjusts the overall intensity of haze. Increasing Base Height fills in the foreground areas, even if Density is at a moderate level.

Not only can you change the amount of haze by dragging the thumbnail to a different setting, or by typing numerical entries into the Haze portion of the Sky Lab, you can also modulate the height of haze by making adjustments in the Cloud Height control. Haze is the moisture in the atmosphere between ground level and cloud level. If the cloud level is higher, then haze exists in those higher areas.

Figure C11.27 shows some samples of the same cloud settings, where only Cloud Height is changed. The left half of each image has a Haze Density setting of 7, and the right half has a Haze Density setting of 35, so that you can see how altitude affects lesser and greater amounts of haze.

How much distance and size cueing you get from your haze also depends on the size of your terrains. This is something that's rather self-evident: The larger the terrain, the more space it occupies. The more space, the more distant portions the terrain has, the more exaggerated the depth effect. In Figure C11.28, each image has three terrains at different sizes. The left part of each image shows the terrain at the default size (when it enters the Bryce scene). In the center of each image, the terrain has doubled in size. On the right side of each image, the terrain has doubled in size again. The four images have different Haze settings. The larger the terrain, the more pronounced the distance effect. (This is really our under-handed way of urging you not to be shy; make your terrains bigger to get better haze effects!)

Rainbows

A rainbow is one of the most beautiful of meteorological phenomena, made all the more precious by its rarity. A rainbow appears only when special conditions have been met: The air must contain billions of tiny droplets of water of just right size, which act as tiny prisms. Each one refracts a beam of light from the sun, splitting its white light into its multicolored components. For the refractions from all the drops to create a coherent pattern, the sun must be directly behind the viewer.

The colors fan out in this order (from longest to shortest wavelength), starting at the outer edge: red, orange, yellow, green, blue, indigo, violet. Under certain con-ditions, as the beam of sunlight passes out of the water droplet, part of the light bounces back into the drop for another round of refraction. This reflected beam produces a secondary bow above the curve of the main bow. The secondary rain-bow is fainter than the main one, and its colors are reversed.

Bryce allows you to add a lovely rainbow to your scene: On the Atmosphere tab of the Sky Lab, click the Rainbow button. If the sun is above the horizon (but not higher than 45° or so) and at your back, a rainbow will appear. By default, the sec-ondary bow is switched on when you activate the main bow. The two controls at your disposal for tweakage of the same are Opacity and Radius. Opacity [*Rainbow Vis*] adjusts the intensity of the color—how well the rainbow stands out against the sky. As with the Sun Halo Rings control, the Radius slider is somewhat mis-leadingly named. The control doesn't adjust the radius of the rainbow, but rather the width of the bow (if you want to get picky, it's the difference between the radii of the outer and inner edges of the bow). An animation note: The Radius slider adjusts both the main and the secondary rainbows in tandem (ignore what the manual says about the "Intensity" field), but the two bows are separately keyframeable ([*Rain 1 Width*] and [*Rain 2 Width*], respectively), so through the magic of animation you can change their sizes independently.

A couple more notes about rainbows: They're influenced by the sun's color and intensity. As long as the sun is a normal whitish sort of hue, they will display all the colors for which they are renowned. Give the sun a distinct color, and the rainbow will take on the same tinge; dim the sun's light, and the rainbow will turn grayish as well. Finally, the manual tells us that rainbows are "infinitely distant," but in Bryce, some things are more infinite than others. A glance at Figure C11.29 shows that rainbows can be closer than clouds, depending on the Cloud Height setting. As Cloud Height descends, portions of the rainbow will disappear. (See also the movie on the CD-ROM, RAINBOW & CUMULUS HEIGHT.MOV.) What is true is that rainbows will always remain distant from your vantage point—no matter how far you move the camera in their direction, they will recede just as far. Just as on Earth, you'll never find that pot of gold....

SHADOWS

Bryce allows you to control the harshness of the shadows with the Shadow control. Shadow is a universal setting for your entire scene. It determines to what extent objects will block light from reaching other objects that are exposed to the sun. A setting of 0 results in no shadow, and a setting of 100 results in maximum shadow [*Shad Intense*]. Even if you have your Shadow setting at minimum, the part of the object that is not facing the sun will be darker, depending on its setting for diffuse and ambient illumination in the Materials Lab. In Figure C11.30, you can compare the maximum and minimum Shadow settings. With maximum shadow, the terrain on the scene's right blocks light from reaching other surfaces that lie "behind" the terrain relative to the sun. When shadows are set to minimum, the sun shines "through" the terrain to illuminate what lies behind it. However, in both cases the parts of the objects that do not face the sun are in shadow regardless of the Shadow setting.

Since this is not the real world, but a virtual ray-traced world, you can make separate determinations about any object's acceptance of or resistance to shadows. Related to the Sky & Fog Palette's Shadow control are a couple of settings in the Materials Lab for the surfaces of objects. An object lit by diffuse light will display light and shadow, even on its shady side, when the Shadow setting is at a minimum. Besides the basic diffuse light setting to enable light and shadow on an object, the Materials Lab has a special control to determine whether any one object will accept shadows independent of the diffuse light setting (the Receive Shadows item on the Material Options pop-up menu). See Chapter 9, "Material World I," for more on this Shadow setting. Also, if you are using any of Bryce's light sources, you can decide whether any or all of them will cast shadows. See Chapter 12, "Brycean EnLightenment," for more information about enabling or disabling cast shadows.

Shadows and Other Sky & Fog Elements

Bryce sky elements don't have object surface properties that are sensitive to diffuse, ambient, or specular light. Therefore, their response to direct sunlight and shadow is different from what you'd expect of their real-world counterparts.

You can choose whether your Bryce clouds cast shadows; the switch is on the Cloud Cover panel of the Sky Lab. By default, cloud shadows are turned off, so it is easily possible to set your cloud coverage to 100% and have the sun still shine on your scene, bright as can be. This is advantageous for creating those days that have a front of dark storm clouds off in the distance while the sun is shining overhead, or if you want to have an overcast sky, tone down the harsh light by reducing the shadows. Adjust the degree of shadow in the Sky & Fog Palette.

In the same vein, Bryce's fog pays no attention to shadows. You can have a dark area completely shaded, and the white fog glows merrily in shadow as much as it lurks brightly in the sunshine. This resistance to shadow enables you to make some clever eerie fogs in dark Brycean places. When you're aiming for dead-on realism in sunlight and shadow, you'll have to augment Bryce's fog with additional effects.

Bryce's haze also has no sensitivity to light and shadow. Try though you might (and we have) to duplicate high moisture atmospheres to see rays of light passing through hazy air, you cannot achieve that effect using Bryce sky parameters alone.

To get atmospheric effects that are sensitive to light and shadow, you have to use actual objects that are editable in the Materials Lab. Fortunately, the diligent Brycer's efforts will be rewarded. The last section of this chapter covers clouds as infinite plane or slab objects, and the sample images demonstrate solutions for each of the nonshadowed situations described here.

HAZE, FOG, AND SHADOW WALKTHROUGH

Continue your walkthrough exercise with the Plain Vanilla! scene. No doubt by now you have the routine down.

1. Work in the Sky Lab with the three sets of controls—Shadows, Fog, and Haze—and create as many different scene files as you can with as much variety as you can.

2. Make sure to use the other controls as well—the Sun control and the four Cloud controls. Make sure to create some scenes with stratus clouds, some with cumulus, and some with both. When it comes to haze, make sure that you work with the Altitude control! Steer clear of the color swatches for now.

3. Save each scene variation as a separate scene file. Do so after a couple of render passes. Remember that the idea is to create as large an assortment of images as you can, with as much variety as you can. Try for a 20-minute session working with the Fog, Haze, and Shadow controls.

COLOR

Until now, we've discussed the Sky controls without introducing color. We've examined the shape of the sky— the type of clouds, the sun and moon, fog and haze, and the extra options in the Sky Lab. Now is the time to focus on color. Bryce's atmospheric controls provide a rich and varied capacity for color to create the subtlety that is inherent in natural landscapes. There are over a dozen different colors to mix and match: Sun Color, Ambient Color, Fog Color, Haze Color, Sky Dome, and Cumulus Color. When it comes to the color of the sky itself, you can select among two "normal" types of skies (Soft Sky and Dark Sky) or set your own sky color in the Custom Sky (with its three color swatches), or if you don't want to have a sky with clouds, sun, or moon, you can select Atmosphere Off and determine a backdrop hue. In each of the three normal sky modes, the color of the sky dome (and optionally, haze or fog) also changes by the position of the sun (or moon). All of these colors interact with one another, resulting in sophisticated color combinations. We'll explore them here, one by one.

Of course, the best way to learn how these colors interact is to play with them and see what happens. This discussion will be a guided play time interspersed with discussion about the significance of each color.

If you need a review of methods for using the color picker, check in Chapter 9, "Material World I," where we discuss it in depth.

DOUBLE TIP: Here's a color picker tip. When you're choosing white, don't drag at the far end of the grayscale part of the gray ramp in the pop-up color picker. To get white, you'll be aiming for a tiny area. If you're set to Interface Maximum, there's an ocean of pure white on the Control Palette, just below the Render controls. Otherwise, in Interface Minimum, aim for the area near the View controls on the Control Palette; there's quite an area of white available there. Figure 11.31 shows the area of pure white, with nonwhite areas darkened.

Figure 11.31
Color picking tips for Sky & Fog: The pure white area surrounding the View control, a fertile source for white color-picking.

Since you can select colors from elsewhere on your monitor, select colors from your partially rendered scenes or the Nano Preview. Render a bit and then choose your color from that rendered area. If you need to desaturate the color, mix it with some white haze or fog, render a portion again, and then send your eyedropper in search of a toned-down color.

Color and Bryce Atmosphere

The controls for adjusting color are the following:

- *Sun/Moon Position.* Not a direct color control, but sky dome, cloud, and haze color are affected by it nonetheless.

- *Sun.* The color of the actual sun (when it's visibly positioned in your sky) and the color of diffuse light as it falls on objects in your scene.

- *Ambient.* The color of indirect light everywhere in your scene, especially in shadow.

- *Cumulus Color.* The color of your cumulus clouds.

- *Fog.* The color of the localized moisture that clings to the ground level in your scene.

- *Haze.* The color of the general water moisture, dust particles, and all other airborne matter that's suspended in your Brycean sky.

- *Sky Dome Illumination.* A general overall light source from the atmosphere illuminates your scene, if you so desire.

- *Sky Mode.* Bryce offers four sky types. The "normal" ones, Soft Sky and Dark Sky, use the controls just mentioned to modulate the sky color, more or less according to natural earthly models. Custom Sky allows you to set your own sky colors for a fully functioning sky that obeys its own rules. Atmosphere Off allows you to set a color for the sky, but without clouds, and without the sun or moon visible. The first part of the following exploration will assume that you have Soft Sky or Dark Sky selected; we'll discuss the other modes later in the chapter.

- *Blend Haze/Fog with Sun.* When this control is on, the color and illumination of haze and/or fog is influenced by the sun's light.

- *Color Perspective.* New to Bryce 4, this feature shifts the color of objects depending on their distance from the camera.

Color Exercises

In these exercises, we'll alternate explanation and exploration. These exercises are not intended to help you make that killer sky in three easy steps; rather, their goal is to help you become fluent at navigating through all the complexities. This will be a guided exploration of colors while you work in your Plain Vanilla! scene. All the controls you need are on the Sky & Fog Palette, so you can let the Sky Lab lie dormant for a while. If you see anything you like, save it under a unique name and then keep going in your explorations. At the end of this chapter, you will have quite a body of work, showing you the variety of looks you can give your scenes simply by changing the sky.

To create your initial sky setting, open the scene file PLAIN VANILLA! from the CD-ROM, then follow these steps:

1. Start again with Bryce's default clouds (Stratus).

2. Drag up on the graph to increase the Amplitude slightly for better cloud definition (you'll get a spikier graph).

Time of Day

The first color manipulation is time of day. You set time of day with the Sun control. This control affects the color of Bryce's sky dome, which changes color according to the Sun control position. It also affects cloud color.

Recall the Sun control conventions mentioned previously. Bryce's high noon is the Sun control at the center. Place the sun at the top horizon (northwest) for sunset.

1. Let's explore stratus clouds and Sun control position. Drag the Sun control preview to the bottom (south). The stratus clouds turn red. Drag up in increments toward the center, letting Bryce render between each little movement. The clouds change from red to yellow to white. Drag the Sun control up toward the top (to north, sunset, twelve o'clock). The clouds turn reddish again, although the glare of the sun may make it hard to see this. Compare Soft Sky and Darker Sky modes when the sun is visible. Drag along the horizon's edge off to either side. Change to Night View and look at the different colors again depending on the Sun control's position.

    Make sure you save a few interesting variations in your PLAIN VANILLA! file.

2. Before continuing, save the stratus cloud setting in one of the Sky Memory Dots to the right of the Sky & Fog Palette (you'll come back to it later). Add cumulus clouds. To get decent and recognizable clouds, you'll probably have to increase the frequency and perhaps amplitude. (An increase in altitude helps, too.) Drag the sun position all around the sky, repeating the movements from the previous step. Does sun position act the same with cumulus clouds as it does with stratus clouds? How about when the sun is shining from behind the clouds when you drag the Sun control toward sunset?

    Keep those Plain Vanilla! variations coming! Save interesting scenes as you see them!

Figure C11.32 explores different sun positions as they affect sky dome color and cloud color. Each image is divided, comparing Darker Sky (left half) and Soft Sky (right half). The sun is shown at five different basic heights, from three perspectives: behind, in front, and to the side. Side and behind are almost identical. Although the Soft Sky on the right of each image is flipped, it shows the portion of the sky closest to the sun. When the sun is on the horizon, the haze and clouds are red. When the sun is near the horizon, the sky is violet, and the haze and clouds are orange-beige. When the sun is at mid-sky, the sky is a vivid blue, and the clouds and haze are white. When the sun is directly overhead, all colors are washed out to a lighter blue. When the sun is facing you, the same is generally true, except the sky color is lighter and is reddened by the sun's presence. (Changing to Darker Sky in the Sky Mode pop-up menu deepens the sky dome color, especially for the half of the sky, where you face into the sun.)

When the sun is closer to the horizon, all sky colors take on a reddish cast. This is similar to the way light works in real life, since the sun's rays have to travel through more atmosphere to reach your eyes. Longer distance draws out the longer red-light wavelengths. Conversely, when the sun is positioned directly overhead, the sky is blue because the shorter light waves bounce about. The strongest red is when the light is "behind" you (bottom position).

Go inside the Sky Lab to numerically manipulate the Sun control. Sky color is determined by the Altitude setting. The reddish horizon corresponds to an Altitude of 0; the sun is on the horizon, and the overall color is red.

3.   Change from day to night and move the Sun control to different places. The right-hand spread of Figure C11.32 shows the same set of variations, but with the Sun control set to night. The sky dome is noticeably darker, and the cloud color stays in the same general range as it was during the day. Notice the continuity when the sun is close to the horizon. Whereas the biggest change in day is when the sun is in front, night's biggest change is when the sun is behind and the moon is in front.

The Sun's Color

Now that you've played with the bare-bones sky and light source position, it's time to give some color to that light. Sun Color affects the scene overall, primarily where light falls directly on objects. However, Sun Color also has an effect on cloud color.

1.   Change the cloud type back to Stratus Clouds only. (Before doing so, save your cumulus cloud in a Memory Dot; then go back and click your Stratus Memory Dot.) Now assign a Sun Color. Switch the Sun control back to Sun (day). Sun Color is transferred to the clouds. Stratus clouds take on the Sun Color.

2.   Drag the Sun control around. Notice that when the sun gets down toward the horizon, the cloud color mixes oranges and reds into whatever the Sun Color is.

3.   Have an Amplitude adjustment hour. Place the sun closer to the center (close to noon) than to the horizon. Drag down the Amplitude graph to even out the spikes somewhat (that is, lower the amplitude) and notice that stratus clouds become hazier. The overall high haze takes on the Sun Color.

4.   Change the Sun control to night and drag it around. Sun Color has no effect during Bryce's deep midnight. Only when the sun nears the horizon does Sun Color creep into the clouds. Change back to daytime.

5.   Alter Sun Color and cumulus clouds. Change the clouds to cumulus alone and select a different color for the sun. Compared to the stratus clouds, with cumulus clouds, there's only a subtle change in cloud color. Drag the sun all around to see how the color affects things at different times of day. Try the same thing for night. Set the sun to white again.

The stratus clouds easily pick up the color of the sun, so to change the color of the stratus clouds, change the Sun Color. To a limited extent, choosing a different Sun Color influences the cumulus cloud color, but it's more of a little color lacing the edges than it is a pure color.

So far, this exploration has shown that a change in Sun Color affects the color of other objects in the scene, but it hasn't yet addressed the question of *which* color. Cast an overall tone in your scene by your selection of Sun Color. Warm up your scene with a warmer Sun Color. Likewise, cool it down with a wintry chilly color. At this point, you may want to change the Diffuse Color of your Plain Vanilla! terrains from the default gray to a lighter gray, or white, so that they'll respond to the all the colors to be used in these exercises. Figure C11.33 shows two sets each of images showing warm Sun Colors and cool Sun Colors. The leftmost image in each column is split into three parts: In the left third, the Sun Color is white, and the color comes from the Ambient Color; in the middle third, the Sun has the color, and the Ambient Color is white; in the right third, the same color serves as both Ambient and Sun Color. The rows emphasize the warm, cool, sunset, and moonrise colors, respectively.

When the sun is high in the sky, it's realistic to make the colors subtle. For that glowing sunset and the red rays just before dusk, change the Sun Color to a more intense red-orange and place the sun low on the horizon. (Of course, if you want to make a fiery red-orange sun at high noon, go right ahead. It's your world.) A deep blue sun casts a strong "moonlight." This is an effective color alternative, as long as you don't want to have much sky showing, or—heaven forbid!—the moon itself.

In the images for the figure, the ground, terrain, and sphere all have Bryce's basic white material setting, there is a bit of white haze, and the Cumulus and Ambient Colors are white, so you can see how much influence the Sun Color has on the entire scene. Portions of the images have an Ambient Color setting as well. We'll discuss Ambient Color momentarily.

The Sun Color is apparent by the color of the sun's light. When you position the sun so that you can see it directly, it is, well, the Sun Color! Think about making your sun ultramarine or black or Day-Glo green for skies that do not resemble our home world. You're not limited to the yellows, oranges, and reds that are associated with Earth's sun! The sun, when seen directly, is affected by the amount of haze and fog. With the presence of haze, it might lose its strength, so be gentle with it.

Incidentally, there is no corresponding control for the moon's color. It never changes.

Ambient Color

In the same way that Sun Color affects the overall scene, so also does ambient light [*Ambi Color*]. Ambient light is the sum total of all light in your scene. The color of ambient light affects the color of objects both in direct sunlight and in shadow, but it is far more pronounced in shadow. For the general color of light in your scene, think of the Sun Color as the color of direct light, and the Ambient Color as the color of shadow. There are more subtleties to it than that, but that's the gist of the situation.

Figure C11.33, previously discussed as a part of Sun Color, uses the same set of warm and cool colors for Ambient Color. The left portion of the images in the left column has only Ambient Color and a white Sun Color. The presence of *any* Ambient Color is better than white, since white tends to make the shadows look washed out. When both the Sun and Ambient settings have color, the result is a richer-looking scene. Bear in mind, of course, that these samples are using the white matte material setting. Your mileage may vary with material settings that have different colors. You may not require Sun and Ambient Colors of this intensity to get a rich effect.

The RGB values for the four different colors are provided so that you can try out your own Ambient and Sun Color combinations. In the top two rows, the sun is in a high position, and in the bottom two rows, the sun is in a lower position. Compare the different images, especially in the shadow and highlight areas. The middle column compares warm with warm colors and cool with cool colors, whereas the right column compares mixtures of dissimilar colors.

For images with good lighting contrast, use a darker color for ambient light than for your Sun Color.

Bearing these points in mind, try a bit of Ambient Color choosing yourself:

1. Try different Ambient Colors in your scene. Change your cloud type back to Cumulus. Select a lighter Ambient Color and see how it influences the clouds and your objects. Move the sun into a high position and then to a low position.

2. Select a darker Ambient Color and look for the same things. (Of course, check out these colorings at night, too!) Then change the Ambient Color back to white. Make sure you save any variations that are interesting to you.

Cumulus Color

Cumulus Color is the first of the moisture-atmospheric color conditions. The following is self-evident: Setting the Cumulus Color swatch will affect the color of the cloud [*Cumulus Clr*]. But lest you think this is *too* simple, read on.

1. Change your cloud type to Stratus. For comparison's sake, select a deep color for the Cumulus Color swatch control. No change. *Stratus clouds are not affected by Cumulus Color, only by Sun Color.*

2. Now change to cumulus clouds. Change the Cumulus Color. This time you will see a far more dramatic color influence on the clouds.

Haze Color

Haze Color tends to give an overall color cast to a sky (and all objects in it) [*Haze Color*].

When the haze density is high enough, Haze Color will interact with Ambient Color. Your Haze Color will provide a secondary Ambient Color. In some cases, that little bit can be too much.

In most standard day-sky scenes (Soft or Darker sky, sun roughly overhead), a white haze gives the scene a bluish cast. When the sun is close to the horizon or in Bryce nighttime, the haze takes on a reddish cast.

Figure C11.34 shows different Haze settings in a scene that is half sea, half land. Notice the distance of terrains from the camera and how their details are obscured by haze.

All that we said earlier about the sun's position and sky color also applies to haze. Moving the Sun control will change the color of haze. In fact, there are two color changes occurring simultaneously: While the sky dome changes from light blue to deep blue to violet, haze changes from white to light orange to red.

Now try this exercise:

1. First, modify Haze Color and stratus clouds. Then change the color (and amount) of haze. Increase the Haze Amount to somewhere in the 30 to 40 range and assign a color to the haze.

2. Try these settings for a night sky, too.

3. Adjust the altitude of clouds to see how this affects the overall color of the haze.

Fog Color

Here's another simple, self-evident statement for you: Set your fog's color with the Fog thumbnail color swatch [*Fog Color*]. (Yawn.) Figure C11.35 shows some examples of different fog densities and fog thicknesses. The same three color variations are used as in the haze example in Figure C11.34—white, ivory, and black. For each of the Fog Thickness and Density settings, the scene is rendered from two different camera angles. The scenes with the lower camera position show less fog in the foreground than those with the higher camera position and the same Fog Thickness and Density settings. Compare how the appearance of the other objects in the scene changes with Fog Color.

Fog will also add a tint to the sky, assuming that your camera position is low and your fog height is high. (See especially the examples in Figure C11.35, where the fog thickness is 100 and the camera is lower.) Try this exercise. Give your scene some fog and give the fog a color. Drag the Sun control around and add colors for both Sun and Ambient. Notice that Fog Color is not affected by the lighting colors. For that matter, fog is not affected by sunlight or shadow either (unless you turn on the Sky Lab's Blend with Sun option, which we'll discuss in a moment).

Combining Haze and Fog Color

Combining Fog Color and Haze Color takes you to an interesting place. You can select a color to be distinct by itself or select one to mix with your Haze Color. Fog Color can be intriguing, yea, exciting, when combined with the color of haze. Though fog maintains its color when mixed with lighting controls, the combination of haze and fog creates some very subtle and pleasing effects. If your fog is dark and the haze is light, then the resulting combination can be downright fetching. Try a light yellow haze with any dark color fog. Black fog provides a delightful surprise, as does dark green.

Figure C11.36 shows the same scene with different combinations of Haze and Fog Colors. For each color combination, the light source is shown in three different positions—daytime, nighttime, and dusk, with the sun on the horizon. The double combination of haze with sun position and Fog and Haze Colors results in a surprising new color. The result is not a straightforward mix of the Fog and Haze Colors, as other factors are at work. Sun position, sky color, and Ambient Color all enter into this delightfully complex area of atmospheric color.

Would You Like That Blended or Straight Up?

Even though the haze shifts color a bit according to the sun's position, it ignores (by default) the color and intensity of the light coming from the sun. If you would like to link the illumination of your haze and/or fog to that produced by the sun, use the Blend with Sun control. This control has two components: Color [*LnkClr Blend*] and Luminance [*LnkVal Blend*]. The Color slider governs the degree to which Haze or Fog Color is influenced by the sun's hue, and the Luminance slider determines how the haze or fog responds to the brightness of the sun's light.

If you try this control with the default colors for haze or fog and sunlight, you won't see any change in hue or luminance because the haze or fog and the sun are already the same color—white! You'll see no effect from using the Blend with Sun control unless either fog or haze or the sun is a color other than white. For greatest realism, keep the controls at 100%; the Blend with Sun effect is so subtle that moving the controls down below about 50% is equivalent to turning them off.

Figures C11.37 and C11.38 show the results of using the Blend with Sun control with haze and fog, respectively. The scene is our old friend, Plain Vanilla!, but rendered using the 360° Panorama option, so we see the sky in all directions. The sun is at the far right, nearly at the edge of the picture, so the middle of the picture is the part of the sky directly opposite the sun. For the first three images in each figure, the sun was placed low in the sky, and for the bottom three images, it was moved up to 60° altitude. Keep in mind that all of the objects in this scene have the default gray material, so any color you see comes from the sun (to which we've assigned a pale goldenrod) or the haze or fog (slightly bluish-gray in our case).

The first and fourth image of each figure show Blend with Sun turned off, the default for Bryce skies. You'll notice that both haze and fog are uniform in color, all the way 'round the horizon. Skip down to the third and sixth images in each figure—here Blend with Sun is turned on full blast. Both fog and haze are tinted yellow where they are closest to the sun, and they revert to their normal gray hue at a distance. Follow the horizon along to the center of the picture, where the sky is farthest from the sun—notice how the haze or fog darkens with distance from the sun, responding to the weakening sunlight.

Get Some Perspective!

If you stand on a height and a take in the sweeping vista, you observe that the farther an object is from you, the more indistinct its appearance. Not only that, but distant objects all tend to look the same color, almost neutral but with a bluish cast. What you're observing is *aerial perspective* (as opposed to *linear perspective,* which causes more distant objects to appear smaller than closer ones). Aerial perspective has two components: *atmospheric perspective,* which is the loss of contrast with distance, and *color perspective,* the perceived shift in hue of distant objects.

Bryce has given you control over atmospheric perspective since the beginning— that's the role haze plays in your scene. But controls for color perspective are new in Bryce 4, and you'll find them tucked away on the bottom of the Atmosphere tab in the Sky Lab. This book is not the place for a complete explanation of the theory and practice of color perspective—for that, we're happy to send you to the Website of Ken Musgrave, the guiding genius behind much of the algorithmic substance of Bryce (see Chapter 1, "In the Beginning…The History and Background of Bryce") at http://www.wizardnet.com/musgrave/4_persp.html. From that page, you can download a technical document that even gives you the mathematical formulas for atmospheric and color perspective—if you're into that sort of thing.

Here's the story, in brief: Light traveling through the atmosphere is subject to scattering and absorption according to its wavelength, so light reaching your eye from a distant object will shift in hue. In general, dark colors move toward blue, and lighter colors move toward yellow and then red. The principle has been known for a long time; color perspective was first put into practice by Flemish painters in the early fifteenth century, and its use in landscape painting is one of the hallmarks of the Renaissance style. A well-known example is the rocky background of the *Mona Lisa*, by Leonardo da Vinci (http://www.louvre.fr/img/photos/collec/peint/grande/inv0779.jpg), in which the nearer terrain is earth-toned, and more distant pinnacles become progressively bluer. Meanwhile, the somewhat brighter sky starts out as a pale greenish-brown, but turns yellowish near the horizon.

So much for theory. Truth be told, you have to set up your Brycean sky carefully to have color perspective work like that. First of all, color perspective takes effect only if you have haze in your sky—and what's more, you must have nonzero values for both the Density and Thickness parameters. The Color Perspective control resides on the Atmosphere tab of the Sky Lab (refer back to Figure 11.2, the top image). Figure 11.39 shows the control up close and personal,

Figure 11.39 The Color Perspective control.

though we've taken a couple of liberties with the image to show different ways of adjusting it simultaneously. The controls work similarly to other numeric controls in Bryce; you can drag to make changes or click the numbers to get data entry boxes where you can directly type the values. But there are no sliders, so where do you drag? Place the mouse cursor over one of the individual color controls (R, G, or B), and it turns into a double-headed arrow, as we've illustrated for the green control. Drag left and right to decrease or increase the value for that color. Or click one of the numbers, and a data entry box appears (as we've shown for blue) into which you can type a value. If the box is active, you can also adjust the numbers by pressing the up and down arrow keys (the modifiers listed in Table 6.1 apply here). Take note that these are not your usual RGB values, but percentages—they don't range up to 255, only to 100.

For our examples, we're using a variant of our Plain Vanilla! scene, into which a crazed Bulgarian artist has plopped a long wall that stretches far into the distance. The black-and-white pattern helps us track the changes in hue wrought by Color Perspective. Figure C11.40a shows our scene with default sky values and no Color Perspective. In Figure C11.40b, we've turned on the Color Perspective switch, with its default setting of red = 0, green = 5, and blue = 25. If you look carefully at the black panels in the fence, you'll see that the more distant ones are distinctly bluer, as are the shadows in the distant hills. Now here's something really useful: Check out the boundary between two terrains about a third of the way up from the bottom (indicated by arrows). In Figure C11.40a, the two gray terrains seem to be adjacent, but with Color Perspective, it's obvious that the second terrain is much farther away, because its color has shifted toward the blue. That shows you how important color perspective is in providing clues to the location of objects in space.

Now, what about the white panels in our fence? They should be shifted toward yellow, right? Nope—if you check them with the eyedropper tool in Photoshop, you'll see that they're all pure white, right back to the horizon. This is because color perspective works properly only when haze is a neutral (gray) color, and we're still using the default haze, which is white. In Figure C11.40c, the haze is gray, with a lightness value of 200 (using the HLS color model), and in C11.40d it is a gray with a lightness value of 155. Now the white panels of the fence take on a yellowish hue as they recede into the distance. In the second example, even the stratus clouds are affected.

To sum up: If haze is a neutral gray, dark areas of the scene will be tinted by the hue defined in the Color Perspective control, depending on their distance from the camera. Conversely, the same color will be sucked out of lighter areas, causing them to move toward the hue's complement. Of course, nothing says you have to make your scene resemble the ordinary state of things on Earth; Figure C11.40e shows the result when Color Perspective is set to R = 5, G = 25, and B = 0 (haze is made even grayer, at 147). The shadows and other dark regions take on an eerie green color, and the white panels of the fence and the clouds shift toward green's complement, magenta. The result of another unnatural experiment is shown in Figure C11.40f, where Color Perspective is set to R = 25, G = 5, and B = 0, turning the dark areas red and the light areas toward cyan.

Speaking of naturalism, we feel that the default Color Perspective setting is weighted too heavily toward the blue component to create a truly realistic effect. For some alternatives, we suggest a little less blue or perhaps a little more green, as shown in Figure C11.40g. The setting R = 0, G = 15, and B = 25 allows for more of a layered look, with nearby hills showing just a touch of color, the next-most-distant range turning blue, and the most distant terrain tinged with cyan. (The other parameters for haze in this scene are Density = 54 and Thickness = 20, and the color is gray with a Lightness setting of 200.) If you need to depict an extra-smoggy or smoky day, just darken the haze color a bit, and the most distant parts of the sky will be tinted with red, as one might expect (Figure C11.40h; Haze Lightness = 163).

Time Out!

Try this exercise free-for-all: Lay down this book, put *all* the Sky & Fog controls to work with all their colors, and simply play.

But by now, this will not be hit-or-miss playing. When you tweak here and adjust there, your playing will have more direction to it. If you find yourself gravitating toward this or that control to move further in a particular direction, then congratulate yourself! You've started building an internal sense for all of Bryce's atmospheric controls. (If not, don't fret. Keep working and exploring; it will come.)

Sky Mode: Custom Sky Colors

For those situations where the typical Bryce sky just won't work right, try the Custom Sky. In the Custom Sky, you set your own colors for the sky. After you choose Custom Sky from the Sky Options pop-up menu (under the left thumbnail on the Sky & Fog Palette), you will find three color swatches to control the sky.

- *Sky Color.* The center swatch is the Sky Color [*Base Color*]. This is the overall color of the sky. Here's where you can create a soft faint blue, or an angry burnt orange, or a surrealistic aquamarine sky.

- *Sun Glow Color* (not *Solar Halo Color*, as the manual says). This is the color swatch at the left [*Halo Color*]. This color is assigned to the area of the sky that surrounds the sun. Make it closer to a shade of the Sun Color, or warmer or cooler than the rest of the sky. Even when the sun is not in the sky, this color can become the partial Sky Color.

- *Horizon Color* (formerly *Haze Shift Color*). This is the color swatch at the right [*Horiz Color*]. Its function has changed since Bryce 2, where it added a tint to the haze in places away from the sun's location. and had a minor effect on the color of stratus clouds, too. Now it primarily colors stratus clouds near the horizon and adds a bit of tint to haze, especially haze below the horizon.

Figure C11.41 shows one scene (a lone terrain floating majestically in space) with two different Custom Sky color settings, with two sun positions for each one. The top row shows a relatively conservative set of colors: pale peach for Sun Glow, a light blue-gray for Sky Color, and a bright red Horizon Color. In the left image, the sun (whose color is just plain white) is in the upper right corner. Its white disk merges into the peach halo, which then fades into the Sky Color, except near the horizon, where the stratus clouds pick up the red. The sky below the horizon is a mixture of Sky Color and Horizon Color. Note that the terrain (which has the default gray material) is affected only by the white sunlight. The image at the right is the same, but the sun is an equal distance below the horizon.

For the second row of images, we chose slightly more extreme colors, the better to show you which parts of the sky are affected by which parameters. Figure C11.41c is the same scene as C11.41a, but with a new color scheme: The Sun Color is a vivid yellow, the Sun Glow Color is a deep green, the Sky Color is deep blue, and the Horizon Color is the same red. Notice that the cloudless parts of the sky near the sun take on the Sun Glow Color, while the nearby clouds get their color from the sun itself. Again, as the clouds near the horizon, they take on the Horizon Color. In Figure C11.41d, we've moved the sun behind us, but at the same altitude as the previous scene. Now the sky is unaffected by the Sun Glow Color, and the clouds show more influence of the Sun Color and less of the Horizon Color.

If you want to see the below-horizon effects with your Plain Vanilla! scene, simply select faraway terrains (but not the closest one), or no terrains at all, and enter Solo mode. When you render, you'll be able to see down into the sky abyss below.

The images in Figure C11.42 are 360° panoramas of custom skies, with different colors and positions of the sun. Since you can see the entire panorama, it's easy to note the color closest to the sun, farthest from the sun, and everywhere in between. The custom color swatches are included in the lower left corner of each scene. Only the scenes in the right column have nonwhite Horizon Colors; these scenes have a pinch of stratus cloud added to show them off.

Exercises for a Custom Sky

Try the Custom Sky yourself!

1. Open that ol' PLAIN VANILLA! scene. For the first part of the exercise, turn off all clouds and choose Custom Sky from the Sky Mode pop-up menu.

2. Change the Sky Color and move the sun around to different positions.

3. Assign a Sun Glow Color and continue moving the sun to different positions.

4. Add a Horizon Color and move the sun to different positions. Add stratus clouds and see how the presence of the Horizon Color affects the cloud color. Move the sun to different positions.

5. Increase haze, fog, and altitude as you see fit. Add cumulus clouds.

6. Assign colors for the sun, ambient, fog, haze, and clouds.

7. Change to night—the color shift is not so dramatic as with Bryce's Soft and Darker Skies.

8. Save lots of variations of your work. There are so many options here, from the beatific to the hellacious.

Sky Mode: Atmosphere Off

When you select Atmosphere Off, the sky's color is set by the Background Hue swatch on the Sky Mode control [*Def Color*]. The clouds, sun, and moon will no longer be visible in your scene. Haze, fog, rainbows—all are gone (don't believe the manual when it tells you to turn Haze down to 0 to prevent a horizon line from showing). However, you can still see sunlight or moonlight reflections off a reflective surface. The sky will be one flat, featureless color, but that color won't affect anything in your scene—unless it happens to be a highly reflective surface, of course, and mirrors the sky. Some of the normal color sources work, but don't affect the sky: Ambient, Sun, and Sky Dome Colors will color the objects in your scene. Atmosphere Off is especially useful when rendering individual objects against a plain background. Set the Background Hue to black and arrange some lights around your object, and it will be displayed like jewelry on a velvet pillow.

Atmosphere Off Exercises

Try this series of exercises to develop your "Atmosphere Off" fluency:

1. Open the your PLAIN VANILLA! scene file from the CD-ROM. From the Sky Mode pop-up menu, select Atmosphere Off.

2. In the Sky & Fog Palette, set Sun and Ambient Colors to white. Sky Dome Color should be black (off).

3. In the Backdrop Hue color swatch, select a color. (Make it a deep, dark color.) Change the sun's position a few times, just to see how it affects the objects but not the sky.

4. Add color to sun and ambient and compare day and night effects. See how the Sun and Ambient Colors affect objects in your scene? The degree of effect differs depending on whether it's night or day.

Sky Dome Color

Sky Dome Color is an extremely diffuse light source [*Dome Color*]. Light falls from above, reflected through the atmosphere. By changing the color—and the value—of the Sky Dome Color, you determine the color and strength of the subtle illumination that descends through the atmosphere.

What's all this about light reflected from the atmosphere, anyhow? If you've been outside before sunrise or after sunset, when the sun is below the horizon and there is no direct sunlight shining on anything, you've probably noticed that a very faint diffuse light comes from above. Though you are in the shadow of the Earth, the atmosphere above is not. Light strikes the atmosphere above, descending to where you are after being thoroughly scattered in the atmosphere. The result is a soft illumination that comes from directly above.

Figure C11.43 depicts the Earth, the atmosphere, and the shadow of the Earth to show what portions are in sunlight and shadow. If you are in the shadowed portion of the earth near direct sunlight, the atmosphere above is lit. Of course, you don't *have* to be at a dusky spot to take advantage of Sky Dome illumination. You can use it whenever you want. But you'll use it most for an overall light fill when you have your sun close to the horizon.

So how does it work? There are two dynamics taking place; both are controlled by the color you select. The value of the color (or brightness) determines *how much* light falls onto your scene from above. The hue of the color determines the color of the light. (Saturation will determine how muddy or pure the hue is.) When you use the color picker, look at it for the two color dynamics. Move left to right to choose the color, and up and down to choose the amount of light. Dark, dark colors will still make a noticeable difference in your scene! Figure C11.36 shows five variations of green in the Sky Dome illumination, with a neutral reference scene (we're using a Custom Sky with Sun Glow and Horizon Colors set to white, and Sky Color set to a very light gray). For each Sky Dome-illuminated scene, the color picker values are shown. In the first variation, even though you cannot tell what color the Sky Dome is, you see the result in a subtle green. A look at the numerical values show that the green is nearly black—yet see how much green has entered the scene from this Sky Dome Color! Each of the other variations is made by sliding the L (Lightness) slider toward white.

When the sun is overhead, you won't need very much Sky Dome illumination. In fact, as you can see by the last sample in Figure C11.44, too much will blow out the highlight areas of your scene. When the sun is overhead, use dark colors to provide color shift subtlety. When the sun is not overhead, a stronger Sky Dome illumination is more effective; anything from dark to light color is appropriate here.

Now YOU try it!

Spend a little time playing with the Sky Dome Color.

1.   Whip out that PLAIN VANILLA! scene file.

2.   To make the ground more sensitive to the changes in the diffuse light, alter the Diffuse setting a bit. Select all terrains (or simply select all objects).

3.   In the Materials Lab, change the Diffuse setting from 100 to something lower. Then change the Diffuse Color to white or very nearly white.

4.   Try different colors. Experiment with all the lightness variations of any hue by using the HLS Color Picker. (Remember: To get there, Option-click/Alt+click the color swatch.)

5.   Try the same set of lightness variations with the sun in different positions.

6.   Change the Sun control to night and see what kind of Sky Dome illumination you get.

7.   You *are* saving interesting variations, aren't you?

Sky Dome Color and Different Sky Modes

It just so happens that the Sky Dome Color works differently when you use Custom Sky and Atmosphere Off than when you are in either of Bryce's "normal" skies, Soft Sky and Darker Sky. In either of the latter modes, Sky Dome Color has a different effect on your landscape. Figure C11.45a shows our Plain Vanilla! scene using a deep green Sky Dome Color in both Soft Sky and Custom Sky modes (Soft Sky is the left half of the image; Custom Sky is the right half; the Custom Sky color is a blue that nearly matches the Soft sky color). The scene is strongly influenced by the value (lightness) portion of the Sky Dome Color, but only slightly by the hue. Figure C11.45b shows the same two scenes, now with the sun on the horizon (at 0 altitude)—notice how the Sky Dome Color is expressed in the shadowed part of both the Soft Sky and Custom Sky halves of the scene. The shadows in the Soft Sky scene are illuminated from above, but the color is completely desaturated, whereas the Custom Sky scene is illuminated from above with saturated green.

Plain Vanilla! Conclusions

At this point, you have amassed quite a collection of Plain Vanilla! scenes that are by now neither plain nor vanilla. What will you do with them all?

1. First, finish rendering them. Select the scene file icons and drag them onto the Bryce 4 application icon. Then go outside and take a look at the sky or visit people in the real world while your Bryce skies finish their rendering, or if it's late at night, go to bed and have a restful well-earned sleep.

2. Put your files all in a folder together with a copy of QuickShow, or use another slide show application to view your rendered images. (QuickShow is on the Bryce application CD-ROM for both Mac and Windows versions, as well as this book's CD-ROM in the Software folder.)

3. Let the slide show run while you look at all the scenes. Notice the incredible variety in the appearance of all your scenes. All the scenes have identical objects. You haven't changed their appearance (well, maybe you lightened the gray of the terrains for some of the Sky Dome Color scenes)—the only thing you have changed is the sky. See how much mood and feeling in a scene comes from your atmospheric settings?

   No doubt, there are some skies that you think are real "keepers." These are the ones you'll open again and add to the Sky Presets (we discussed Preset Libraries in Chapter 5, "Streamline Your Brycing"). Since the file names are displayed on the screen with each image, you can make a note of which scenes you want to keep.

4. Once you have opened all your "keeper" scene files and saved the presets, you can trash the scene files if you need the rest of your hard disk back! Keep the rendered images to look at for inspiration or to help get you out of a rut.

By this time, you will probably have an internal gut sense about skies. Perhaps as you go through the slide show, you might see a scene and find yourself with an intuitive sense of how to fix it or tweak it or do something else to it. If you do have that sense, congratulations! You have managed to wrap your brain and your senses around a very complex set of interweaving controls, with 10 shape parameters and 11 color parameters. This was no simple task!

Random Sky Control

"Now wait a minute!" you may be saying, "There's one sky control that this chapter hasn't covered yet." Yes, that funky doo-hickey little set of spheres is located just to the left of the Sun control. If you've worked with Kai's Power Tools, you know that it's a tiny version of the Mutation Marbles. Unlike the full-scale Mutation Marbles, these do not require you to click a specific marble for a weaker or stronger mutation—they're too small for that! Simply click the marbles-in-general to randomize the Sky & Fog settings. After a few clicks, you'll see a range of Sky & Fog fog, haze, cloud, sun, and color settings as Bryce zigs and zags through some seemingly improbable options.

You've probably already visited this bastion of random skyness before you cracked open this chapter, right? We saved the discussion of the Random Sky control until last, since you now know how you can use it. When you get a random sky, you may or may not have something useful. If you don't know what to change to make something weird and ho-hum into something that's Wow! Original! Spectacular! you may end up clicking many times until you get something moderately useful— or you might have been tempted to abandon use of it altogether. If, after all the plain vanilla-ing, you've got the gut sense that tells you, "Tweak *this* (but not *that*; that is okay for now)," you can use the Randomize control to launch into new directions.

ALTERNATIVE CLOUDS

Brycean clouds are wonderful inventions of a mathematical nature. However, there are some limitations. They don't cast shadows by default, and when you do set them to cast shadows, the shadows themselves are rather diffuse, and perhaps don't quite create the "sun-dappled hillside" effect that you're looking for. In this section, we explore real shadow-casting Brycean clouds in their various forms— infinite planes and slabs and freestanding spheres.

Infinite Planes and Slabs as Cloud Layers

You are not restricted to the pervasive, environmental clouds that are the default in Bryce, and which are controlled by the Sky & Fog settings. You have the option of creating layers of clouds that behave more like normal objects: the infinite cloud plane (of 0 thickness) and the infinite cloud slab (with substantial thickness). When either is created, Bryce automatically assigns a material setting from the Clouds&Fogs section of the Material Presets. Note also that the infinite cloud plane object enters the Bryce world with a different family wireframe color than the default charcoal gray.

When tweaking the clouds in the Materials Lab, make sure to play with the Frequency and Transparency sliders. Also take a look at the mapping options for the infinite plane/slab materials that are in the other presets. Object Mapping is frequently used. What happens if you change to Parametric? World Space Top? Figure C11.46 shows a basic cloud infinite plane with transparency adjustments (top row) and mapping and frequency adjustments (bottom row).

When you use a cloud infinite plane, you're not limited to one. Figure C11.47 shows a rocky island at night with two cloud planes, above and below the camera level, and no atmospheric clouds. Only in the center image are both layers shown at once.

The infinite cloud slab is much like the infinite plane, only thicker. Figure C11.48 shows some examples. The first image shows the same material from the infinite cloud plane in C11.46a applied to a slab. The overall appearance is much the same, but the clouds seem to have more heft, more depth, and the shadows they cast are more distinct. One of the uses of infinite slabs is to provide an immersive environment—you can put the camera inside the slab, and it will be surrounded by cloud.

In practice, the results aren't totally satisfactory; check out C11.48b, which shows the view from the midst of the slab in the previous image, with a couple of rocky tors poking through for dramatic effect. We don't really get the feeling of being engulfed in the cloud—we're just floating between two parallel identical cloud planes above and below. That's because the cloud planes come into the world with surface materials applied. The view improves immensely if you switch them to a volume material, as you can see in Figure C11.48c. Accomplishing this is a long and complex process; Richard vander Lippe has posted an exhaustive online tutorial at http://www.vanlippe.com/volume/volume1.html, along with some sample volumetric materials preset files. Here's the short version: You need to start from scratch with the Deep Texture Editor, because none of the built-in cloud presets works very well as a volume material. Build a single-component texture (alpha output only) with a basic noise (RND Continuous is a good choice) set to 4 Octaves, irregular modulation, Frequency around 200, no phase, no filter. In the Materials Lab, set all the color swatches to white, put the Texture A marker in the Base Density channel, and move the Base Density slider to about 50%. Adjust Fuzzy Factor to 300 and set the Quality/Speed slider to 0. That's enough to get you started; naturally, you can make things more interesting by adding phase, experimenting with the frequency of the noise, and so on. Check this chapter's folder on the CD-ROM for some sample files. For more advice on working with volume materials, see the "Volume Properties" section of Chapter 9, "Material World I."

Some things to be aware of when using infinite cloud planes and slabs: They are objects, not atmospheric phenomena, so they don't automatically interact with other components of the atmosphere like the "normal" clouds do. For example, their color doesn't vary with the sun's position—they don't automatically turn pink and red as the sun dips toward the horizon. If you've applied a volume material to your infinite cloud object, you can get around this limitation. The material will by default be set to Flat Shading, so it responds to light passing through it in the simplest possible way. Change the Shading mode to Basic, and the material will interact with the colors emanating from the sky. If you use these cloud objects in a sunset scene, you'll have to adjust the Sun Color, the Ambient Color, and the colors of the clouds themselves by hand to get the proper range of hues.

For some more about freestanding volume clouds, see Chapter 16, "Superlative Nature Imagery," and Martin Murphy's Ansel Tribute in Chapter 17, "Bryce Eye Candy."

MOVING ON…

You've now made your way through Bryce's atmosphere and its "natural" light sources. In the next chapter, we'll explore Bryce's "artificial" light sources: light objects.

CHAPTER TWELVE

Brycean EnLightenment

IN THIS CHAPTER...

- Creating pseudo-light forms from glowing primitives

- Bryce's light primitives and how they work

- Practical tips for using light objects

- Different types of light objects and how to create them

- Sample lighting scenes

Bryce allows you to play the role of lighting director. Dramatic lighting is what separates the ho-hum scenes from those eliciting an exclamation of "Wow! Incredible!"

There are pseudo-lights in Bryce, where special Shading modes give the appearance that self-illuminating glowing objects throw off light, even though they do not. And there are light sources that actually throw light elsewhere in the Bryce scene as well as cast shadows. The chapter begins with a discussion of the glowing forms and then continues with discussion of the light objects and how to use them. The chapter concludes with several examples of lights as used in completed scenes.

A word to the wise before we start: The behavior of Brycean lights changed drastically between the Mac and Windows versions of Bryce 2, and the previous edition of this book took great pains to elucidate the differences. Later versions (on both platforms) of Bryce have continued to follow the Bryce 2/Windows way of handling lights, which makes writing about it easier for us (hooray!), but this also means that if you open in Bryce 4 a scene created with the Mac version of Bryce 2, your lights may act in bizarre ways. We'll point out things to watch for as we go along.

GLOWING PSEUDO-LIGHT FORMS

The pseudo-light approach makes any Bryce primitive object glow. This is not the specialized light object, where light is projected and shadows cast. With a glowing object, you can make suns and moons, lightbulbs, tubes, and cones of light.

How do you make any Bryce primitive glow? Use the Materials Lab. Three options contribute to an object's glow: Shading mode, Ambience, and one or both of Ambient and Diffuse Color. First, choose one of these Shading modes: Normal, Fuzzy (these two with or without the Additive option), or Light. Second, in the Materials Lab grid, hone in on Ambience and Transparency (the Ambience setting has no effect on the Light Shading mode). Third, select your color. If you've chosen the Additive shading modifier, Ambient Color will play the greatest part in determining the color of your object. If you've chosen the Light Shading mode, Diffuse Color will determine the color of your glowing object. Keep in mind that the different Shading modes exact different costs in rendering time.

Figure 12.1 shows the results of the different Shading modes. The objects in the top row have some transparency, and those in the bottom row have no transparency. The objects in Figure 12.1a are set to Normal Shading, but have Ambience set to 100%. This is the quick-and-dirty method of creating glowing objects and is the cheapest in terms of rendering time. It's not ideal—the objects have no three-dimensional character and are just flat, bright shapes—but if you want a lot of bright spots in the background and depth isn't important, this is the way to go. Notice also that you need to turn off all the shadowing options (as we've done with the lower torus), or you will get the unrealistic effect of a light casting a shadow (as with the upper torus). Figure 12.1b shows objects set to Normal Shading with the Additive option turned on. The objects have hard edges. We changed the Ambient color of the objects' material to gray and turned down the Ambience; otherwise, the objects would already be so bright that adding the brightness of the pixels behind them wouldn't make any visible difference. This Shading mode can be a little costly, because (as we explained in Chapter 9) the program has to render the scene behind the object as well as the object itself and add them together. In Figure 12.1c we changed the Shading mode to Fuzzy, with

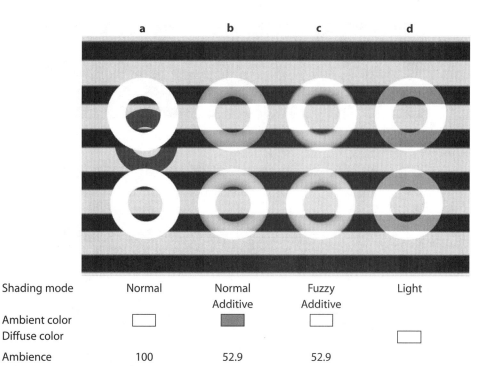

Shading mode	Normal	Normal Additive	Fuzzy Additive	Light
Ambient color	□	▦	□	
Diffuse color				□
Ambience	100	52.9	52.9	
Diffusion				100

Figure 12.1 A torus made to glow using various Shading modes: a) Normal; b) Normal with the Additive option turned on; c) Fuzzy/Additive; and d) Light.

the Additive option turned on. Not only are the edges of the object fuzzy, but the objects behind it are fuzzed, too. This added complication makes for the most expensive glowing lights. Finally, Figure 12.1d shows you objects using the Light Shading mode. The tori have a hard edge, are translucent, and appear as glowing, flat silhouettes.

Figure 12.2 shows a series of glowing objects created using the Fuzzy Additive mode. In all of them, the horizon intersects the object so that you can see the additive effect at work.

There are three sets of glowing objects. The top row shows different values for Transparency (all of the spheres have an Ambience of 50). Higher Transparency settings result in a fuzzier object. In the case of the spherical objects shown here, the Transparency setting causes the spheres to maintain their round shapes. The second row has different Ambience settings (but Transparency is set to 0). As the Ambience setting is decreased, the object loses its glow, but the lesser glows appear

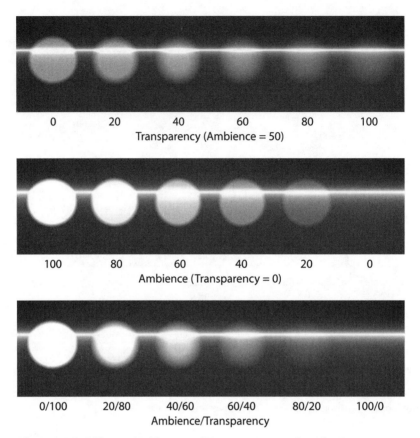

Figure 12.2 Different Ambience and Transparency settings for Fuzzy Additive glowing objects.

flat, and a 0 setting is still barely visible! The bottom row adjusts both Ambience and Transparency in proportion to one another. As the glow decreases with Ambience, fuzziness increases with Transparency, resulting in definite spherical shapes. The sphere on the right has now completely disappeared.

Another word about the Additive option: The Bryce manual tells you that for best results, you should set Ambient Color to zero. But if you do that, you get a faint, ghostly apparition (which may be just the effect you want). To create a vivid glowing object, crank up the Ambience setting. Figure C12.3a shows three spheres, set to Normal/Additive mode, with a Diffuse Color of orange and an Ambient Color of green. The first sphere, set to Diffusion=50 and Ambience=100, glows bright green. The second sphere, with much reduced Ambience but still Diffusion=50, glows more faintly, but is still green. Only the third sphere, with Diffusion cranked up to the maximum and Ambience turned off, shows any trace of the orange color. Figure C12.3b shows the same spheres set to Fuzzy/Additive mode.

Since you can get different levels of glow, you can put one object inside another for a lightbulb-and-halo effect—that is, a lightbulb in a frosted globe.

You can also use the Light Shading mode for some light-related effects. In the image of the slide projector shown later, in Figure C12.9, the dusty light beam from the projector uses a pyramid set to the Light Shading mode with the Transparency information coming from a 3D texture.

LIGHT SOURCE PRIMITIVES

Bryce has five types of light source primitives (see Figure 12.4). They are based on geometric primitives that already exist, but they project light. They are the radial light (sphere), the spotlight (cone), the square spotlight (pyramid), the parallel light (cube), and the cylindrical parallel light (cylinder). To distinguish them from the solid primitives upon which they are based, the lights entering your scene are assigned to Family 4, which gives their wireframes a bright yellow color. The wireframes are also drawn at a lower resolution than the equivalent geometric primitives. All of these light sources can be made visible or invisible (more on that in a moment), and you can adjust the softness of the edges of all the lights except for the radial light.

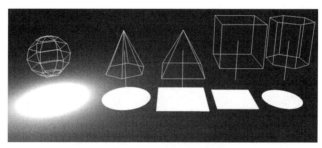

Figure 12.4 Bryce's light objects, showing for each its wireframe and the pattern of light it projects, from left to right: radial light, spotlight, square spotlight, parallel light, cylindrical parallel light.

- *Radial Light.* A sphere lightbulb (or more accurately, orb). It radiates light in every direction from the center of the radial light object.

- *Spotlight.* A cone that projects a circle of light resembling the classic spotlight: the farther the light travels before hitting another surface, the larger the spread of the light. This is a directional light; the needle pointing away from the cone indicates the direction the light will travel. The light emanates from the pointy end of the cone (though the light's exact origin is the center of the wireframe, at the position of the default origin point).

- *Square Spotlight.* A pyramid that casts a square-shaped light; The light is projected from the square side of the pyramid. This is good to use as a "slide projector" for projecting images or patterns onto other objects in the scene.

- *Parallel Light.* A square that projects light without any spread. The final size of the area of light thrown matches the surface area of the light object, no matter how far the light travels. So if your *x* and *z* size dimensions are 20.48 units apiece, it's impossible for the size of the light thrown from that parallel light object to be any bigger than 20.48 × 20.48.

- *Cylindrical Parallel Light.* This object is a little harder to get to—to create one, you have to Control-click/Ctrl+click the parallel light icon on the Create palette. Other than being round, it acts just like the square parallel light. (Hint: Think "Laser Beam"!)

EDIT LIGHTS DIALOG BOX

All of the lights can be adjusted in the Edit Lights dialog box (reached by typing ⌘-E/Ctrl+E, clicking the Edit Terrain/Object icon on the Edit Palette, clicking the small E icon next to the selected object, or selecting Objects > Edit Object from the menu). (See Figure 12.5.)

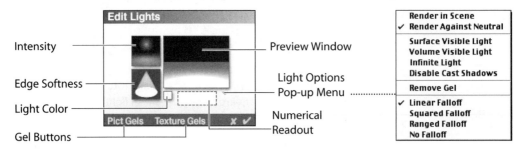

Figure 12.5 The Edit Lights dialog box, where lighting features are controlled.

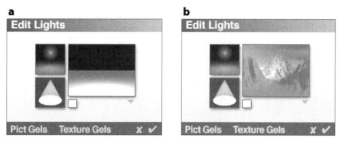

Figure 12.6 Two different types of preview: a) Render Against Neutral; b) Render in Scene.

Preview

The Edit Lights preview can be viewed in two forms: Render Against Neutral and Render in Scene. Choose between the two in the pop-up menu. You can show the illumination effect against a neutral background (default), or you can show the light in the scene (see Figure 12.6). Depending on the complexity of your scene, the Render in Scene option provides the better preview. However, if you have a costly scene or so many objects that you spend more time waiting for the preview to update than you do making the changes to the light settings, Render Against Neutral is the better option.

> **TIP:** Preview while you work! When you're working directly in your scene and placing lights hither and yon, get immediate feedback on the light's placement. Make sure that the Auto Update option is activated in the Nano Preview pop-up menu. Then press the F10 key while dragging your light around and watch the Nano Preview window update in real time. Pretty snazzy, eh?

Intensity

How brightly does the light shine? Dragging in the Intensity control adjusts the amount of light. The numbers range from –999 to 999 (we'll discuss the negative part of the range in a moment), but to see those numbers, you need to click the control.

When it comes to measuring intensity, there are two different factors to consider. Of course, the first factor is the numerical setting for intensity. The second factor is the size of the light object—a given numerical setting will have a different brightness depending on the size. When any light is at the default unity size, the lower numbers are adequate for adjusting the light strength. Beyond a certain point, the

Radial Lights

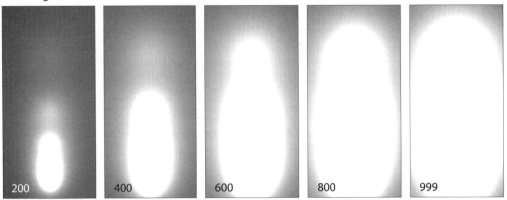

Round Spotlights

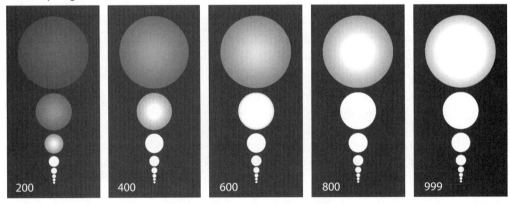

Square Spotlights

Figure 12.7 Top view renders of light forms of different sizes. All lights in an image share the same intensity setting. Within an image, each light is twice the diameter of the one below it.

Parallel Lights

Cylindrical Parallel Lights

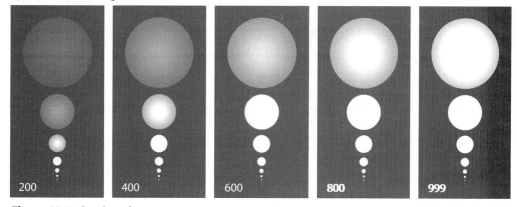

Figure 12.7 Continued.

light just doesn't get any brighter. But when the size of the light is doubled, tripled, quadrupled, or and-them-some-pled, the higher numbers become useful.

The series of images in Figure 12.7 show how a range of light intensity settings affect lights of different sizes. All the images are top view renders of each of the Brycean light forms. In all of these images, each light is twice the size of the one below it, and the intensity setting is identical for all lights in that image. The intensity value is indicated for each image. Notice that the larger lights are still dim when the smallest ones are at a maximum brightness.

Also, intensity has different results with different light forms. In the case of the square lights, when the light is still dim, the light has a round hot spot in the center and the square edges are slightly less intense.

What are the implications of all of these size and intensity studies? If you enlarge the lights, you may be able to get a more subtle range of illumination intensities. If you find that your current light settings have too many jumps from one level of light to the next, then enlarge the light.

> **TIP:** *To enlarge everything in your scene, select all and group. Then enlarge using the Resize tool. All your objects will retain the same relationship, though they all will be bigger. You'll have to readjust the camera's position. You can anticipate this by creating a small cube and aligning it exactly with the camera before you group and enlarge the entire scene. Afterward, align the camera to the new box position; it will precisely match the old one. Delete the box when you're through.*

Warning for veteran Brycers: Bryce's handling of lights changed rather drastically between Bryce 2 and Bryce 3D/4. For one thing, in Bryce 2, the range of possible intensities is 0 to 100, but in later versions it extends from 0 to 999. Say, for example, you have an old Bryce 2 scene with a light whose intensity is 90—that's almost as bright as you can get. But open that same file in Bryce 4, and the light's intensity will still be 90, or only about 10% of maximum. Of course, the relationship between the old and new values is not linear, so you'll have to do some experimenting to figure out how to reconstruct the previous light levels.

Here's something that'll knock your socks even farther off: Say you have an old scene created in the Mac version of Bryce 2 that contains parallel lights of either the square or the cylindrical variety. Get ready for a surprise when you open the file in Bryce 3D or 4: The intensity of the lights is reset to 0! And what's more, the color of such lights is set to pure black! Not only that, but the lights remain essentially dead no matter how high you adjust the intensity. What were they thinking?

Softness

The softness control determines how sharp or smooth the transition is from "all light" to "no light" at the edges of the light. You might infer from the Bryce 4 manual that the control applies to all the lights, but you would be wrong—it has no effect on the radial lights. Figure 12.8 shows the result of varying softness settings for each of the applicable light types. The settings range between 0 at the left (completely hard-edged, the default) to 100 (the softest) at the right. Intensity is left at 25, the default.

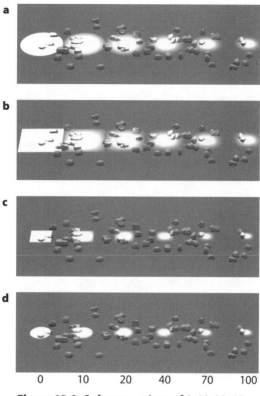

Figure 12.8 Softness settings of 0, 10, 20, 40, 70, and 100 for: a) Round spotlight; b) square spotlight; c) square parallel light; and d) cylindrical parallel light.

Color Controls

Three controls in the Edit Lights dialog box govern the color of the light projected by your light object. The Light Color swatch lets you choose a single uniform color for the light (pure white is the default, naturally). The Pict Gels and Texture Gels buttons at the bottom of the Edit Lights dialog box allow you to apply more complex colors to your light. With the former, you can choose a picture for your light to shine through, rather like a slide projector. The latter allows you to assign a preset from the Materials Library to the light.

Uniform Color

What color is the light? If you want to project a uniform color, choose the color by clicking the color swatch. Like all other color swatches in Bryce, this one accesses the pop-up color picker and brings up the Color Editor (with numerical values) when you press the Option (Macintosh) or Alt (Windows) key as you click the color swatch.

Setting the uniform color of the light is similar to setting the Sun color in the Sky & Fog Palette. The color is the color of diffuse light that emanates from that light source, and, if the light object is visible, it is also the color of the object itself.

There's Always Room for a Gel

If you do not want to have a uniform color but rather a variety of colors or a stencil effect, then use one of the gels. In real-world lighting, a gel is a piece of film (the earliest ones were made of gelatin, hence the name *gel*) placed in front of the light to give a light color. When you want multicolored light, Bryce allows you to select from its two types of gels: Pict Gels and Texture Gels. When you select either of those, you'll go to libraries to select a texture from the appropriate type. Pict Gels takes you to the 2D Picture Library, and Texture Gels takes you to the Materials Preset Library. The two gel types—3D Textures and 2D Pictures—are components of the Materials Lab. Even though this discussion revolves around the Edit Lights dialog box, when you work with gels, you will possibly need to go outside that dialog box to the Materials Lab. To complete the discussion of gels, we will definitely take you to the Materials Lab.

Pict Gels

A Pict Gel is any picture image that is loaded into the Bryce Picture Library. Here is the source for "slides" to project slide images. Load any pict image into the library and so into the light. The light will project in the pattern of the image. The square spotlight is a good one for the slide projector type of image. A very literal application is shown in Figure C12.9 (see the color section). When your good friend's old college buddy gets you onto the White House lawn for Fourth of July fireworks, you simply *must* take a picture to remember the moment and you're obligated to show it off at every opportunity. Bryce's slide projection ability gives you yet another means to bore your friends with your vacation snapshots. There are, incidentally, more lights in this scene besides the one square spotlight projecting the slide show image. For the terminally curious, the scene file for an earlier version of this image (the final scene file is too large) is on the CD, in this chapter's folder, along with that entire boring slide show (in the Portfolio folder). Although square spotlights take to the Pict Gel the best, any light of type can be used.

> **TIP:** When creating square spotlights that are true image slide projectors, it's best to give the square spotlight the exact aspect ratio of the image (Otherwise, the picture will be squashed to fit the square shape of the spotlight). To do so, try this handy trick: Make sure that you have your picture image all ready saved on disk as a picture file. Then create a picture object by clicking the Leonardo tool. The first thing that happens is that you go to the Picture Library and select the picture. When you complete that step, Bryce creates a picture object that exactly matches the aspect ratio of the picture. Now change the picture object to a square spotlight using the Object Conversion tool on the Edit Palette. One problem happens at this stage: Your light object is squashed to match the dimensions of the picture axis, which has barely any discernable size on the z axis. The fix is simple, however: In the Object Attributes dialog box, just copy the y axis size into the box for the z axis size. If the picture's aspect ratio creates an image that is wider than it is high, then the y dimension will be the default 20.48, whereas the x dimension will be something larger than that; you needn't do anything to change the y axis size. If the image is taller than it is wide, then x will be 20.48, and the number for y will be larger. After you copy the number for size y to size z, then it's probably a good idea to change y back to the default of 20.48. This resizing in the Object Attributes dialog box is a slight pain, but knowing that your projected light will exactly match the aspect ratio of the picture it is projecting will make it worth the trouble.

> **ALERT!** If you open an old Mac-created Bryce 2 scene in any other version of Bryce, you'll find to your dismay that any slides projected by square spotlights will have disappeared. Take heart—they're not lost; they're just disoriented. In Bryce 2/Mac, when you create a square spotlight, it enters the scene facing downward like any other spotlight, but internally its x axis rotation is set to 90°. If you change the light's rotation, the spotlight is still measured relative to the initial 90°. Thus, when you open the scene in another version of Bryce, the program reads the numerical value of the rotation parameter and merrily points the light in a direction you did not intend. A common example of this problem is a square spotlight that you've rotated 90° so that it projects a slide onto a vertical surface, as in Figure C12.9. If you open the file in Bryce 4, you'll find the light pointing in exactly the wrong direction. Open the Object Attributes dialog box for the light and change the x axis rotation by 180°.

The color of the light projected through the gel is determined by the Light Color swatch in the Edit Lights dialog box, and the gel image or texture will be strongly tinged with this color. It's not true, though, that choosing a nonwhite color will cause that color to override the colors in the gel, as the manual claims. After assigning a Pict Gel, if you go to the Materials Lab, you may notice that the light object uses a picture texture source. Bryce has assigned the default picture configuration in the Materials Lab for the light object: Parametric is the mapping style, the material's Transparency will be driven by the picture's alpha channel, and the picture texture drives the color for the Diffuse Color channel. Even though there's texture-driven Transparency, that alpha channel information will not limit the pattern of light cast from the light object in the same way that it would limit your ability to see portions of a normal picture object. The only thing in the Pict Gel that determines where light is cast is the Diffuse Color (possibly influenced by the light's uniform color setting). Wherever there is black in the Diffuse Color, no light will be projected. (We'll happily contradict ourselves later in this chapter when we discuss visible lights.)

The options in the Materials Lab that you can adjust are texture frequency and mapping. (Incidentally, these options are the same for Texture Gels, which we'll discuss next.) Figure C12.10 in the color section shows some light variations using the same picture source with different mapping and frequency options.

Texture Gels

The Texture Gel is similar to the Pict Gel, except it uses the information from a 3D texture in Bryce to create the gel's color. Again, the diffusion color is all-important for determining the color emitted from the object. For the 3D texture to work with a light, there needs to be enough color information in the texture itself to drive Diffuse Color. In other words, if you go to the Materials Preset library and choose a solid color or a reflective optic effect, the net result from a light gel standpoint is nil. The texture takes its information from the 3D texture's color information only.

As with the Pict Gel, you can make some adjustments in the Materials Lab to the Texture Gel for effects. You can adjust the frequency and mapping, and if you have a visible light, the Transparency information will affect the appearance of the light.

What about more complex multichannel textures? If your mind works in wicked "what if" ways, then the thought has (or will) occur to you. You can apply a multisource texture gel to a light, but the results may not be what you expect. In Figure C12.11, we applied a three-texture material to a round spotlight. Figure C12.11a shows the Materials Lab settings for the preset; C12.11b shows the rendered result. As you'll recall from our discussion of A-B-C materials in Chapter 9, the material draws color information from the A and B textures only; the alpha information in the C texture determines how the other two textures are blended: Where the C texture's alpha is black, the color comes from the A texture; where the alpha is white, the color comes from the B texture. The alpha/Transparency information is also meaningful when the light itself is visible. (See the discussion of visible light a bit later in this chapter.) In normal (non-gel) lights, the entire light is visible. When the alpha channel drives the texture, then you see the portions of the light that the alpha channel allows you to see. You can mix and match the Diffuse Color so that the light object looks like the light it projects, or like it has alpha channel holes cut into it while projecting. Figures C12.12a and b show two variations on visible light with a Texture Gel applied. Part a shows the basic visible light. Part b shows what happens when you have a solid Diffuse Color (white, in this instance) with no gel driving the projected light, but a gel that drives the transparency of the visible light object. The Materials Lab settings for each version are shown as well.

Pop-up Menu Items

The Edit Lights dialog box has a pop-up menu for certain options. Use this menu to choose the preview mode, the visibility, the falloff, whether the light casts shadows, and to clear your gels.

Remove Gel

Although Remove Gel is not the first option listed on the pop-up menu, we mention it first since this discussion of the pop-up menu immediately follows the discussion of the gels. If you have 'em, this one will get rid of 'em and get you on the straight and narrow again. (In the Materials Lab, you can do the same thing by clicking back into the default column for Diffuse Color.)

Render Window Preview

At the top of the menu, choose which kind of preview you want to see in the preview window.

Disable Cast Shadows

The Disable Cast Shadows switch will disable the light from casting a shadow.

Brycean lights differ from real-world lights in that you can control whether or not they cast shadows. Since the Bryce world is visualized by means of ray tracing, the creation of shadows is a separate, additional routine. Therefore, you can decide whether or not you want the renderer to go through that routine to have shadows cast from lights. (If you want to explore all of Bryce's shadow side, check out these chapters: Chapter 9, "Material World I," Chapter 11, "Brycean Skies," and Chapter 13, "Render Unto Bryce.") Figure C12.13 shows a scene where the lights (a row of radial lights tucked up amongst the arches) cast shadows and the same scene where those lights do not. When you do not use shadows, other objects in the scene do not block light. This can have a wide variety of effects, from subtle (the additional light sources do not betray their presence with a shadow) to eerie (where is the light coming from?) to the bizarre.

The ability to disable shadows opens up a whole realm of possibility for lighting and coloring effects. Figures C12.14a through e shows a series of images we call "Boolean Potato Skins." This series explores a whole range of light possibilities. It starts with no special light source (part a) and then adds a white radial light in the center that casts shadows (part b) and does not cast shadows (part c). Then visible yellow lights are placed in the bowls of each of the half-sphere objects, both casting shadows (part d) and not casting shadows (part e), resulting in an ethereal glow.

Falloff

In Bryce, you can control the degree to which light weakens as it travels away from its source, or you can turn off the weakening entirely, through the use of the falloff options on the Edit Lights pop-up menu. The default setting is Linear Falloff (the only choice for Bryce 2 lights), which establishes an inverse relationship between the brightness of the light on the object or surface and the amount of space projected. The farther away the light is from the object, the dimmer the light is as it falls on that object. At the same time, the area that's illuminated increases in size as the light is moved away. Linear Falloff is an especially good choice for spotlights and parallel lights; the slow lessening of the light's energy nicely reinforces the effect of a focused beam. It's also useful for radial lights in outdoor scenes. Figure 12.15 shows a series of sample scenes illustrating the results of using Linear Falloff with different light positions.

Figure 12.16 compares the nondefault falloff settings to Linear Falloff. If you want the intensity of your light to die away more quickly, use the Squared Falloff setting. The name refers to the inverse square law, which governs the dissipation of

Close   Distant   More Distant

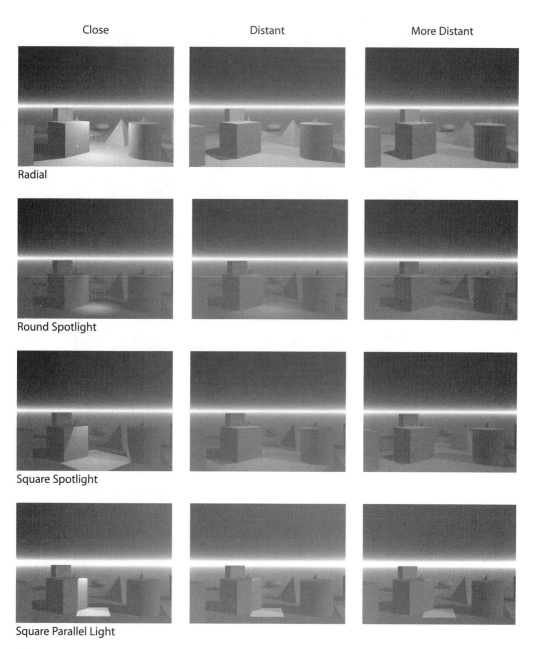

Radial

Round Spotlight

Square Spotlight

Square Parallel Light

Figure 12.15 The relationship among distance, brightness, and the illuminated area with Linear Falloff.

light from a point source, like a lightbulb or a candle: The intensity of the light decreases proportionally to the square of the distance from the source. In other words, at a distance of two units away from the light, the intensity will be one-

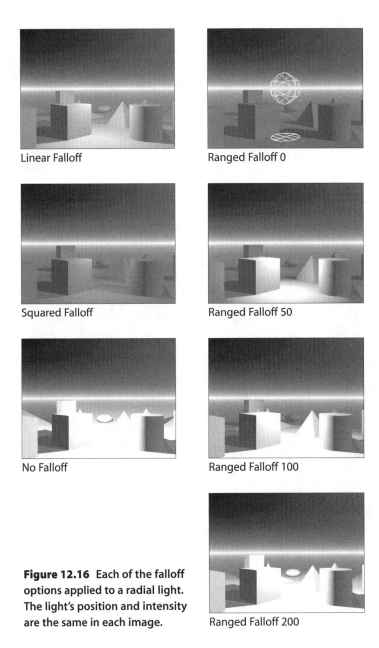

Linear Falloff

Ranged Falloff 0

Squared Falloff

Ranged Falloff 50

No Falloff

Ranged Falloff 100

Figure 12.16 Each of the falloff options applied to a radial light. The light's position and intensity are the same in each image.

Ranged Falloff 200

fourth of what it was at a distance of one unit. Use Squared Falloff for radial interior lights, where you just want a modest glow around a light source, or for those instances where you want to use real-world light behavior. The No Falloff option gives you exactly what the name implies: The light never dims, even at an infinite distance from the source. Parallel lights benefit most from this option; it allows you to make laser beams that travel long distances without any change in brightness. It's also useful for projecting gels onto a surface a long distance away.

The final option, Ranged Falloff, is new in Bryce 4. It's somewhat similar to No Falloff in that there's no gradual dimming of the light: The light just stops at a set distance from the source. You can see the effect of different Ranged Falloff settings in the right column of Figure 12.16; the white wireframe in the first image shows the location of the light. Alas, the manual lets us down once again, referring to a dialog box where you can enter the light's range. Seek, if you must, the Lost Dialog Box, but we'll let you in on an undocumented secret (you knew you bought this book for a reason!): To adjust the range of Ranged Falloff, first make sure that Ranged Falloff is checked on the Edit Lights pop-up menu; then hold down the Option/Alt key and drag within the preview window. A zero will magically appear in the Numerical Readout part of the dialog box, and as you drag to the right, the number will increase. Be prepared to keep dragging for a long time—the maximum value is 9999! Obviously, it's designed to work with lights in large-scale exterior scenes. Figure 12.17 shows our old friend, the Plain Vanilla

Ranged Falloff = 100

Ranged Falloff = 500

Ranged Falloff = 1000

Ranged Falloff = 1500

Figure 12.17 The results of applying various falloff ranges to a distant radial light.

scene, with a radial light hovering over the distant mountain peak. We've turned it into a visible light so you can see it, and we've set its intensity to 50. The sample scenes show that you can fine-tune how far the light spreads over your scene by adjusting the Ranged Falloff setting.

To Infinity…and Beyond!

The Edit Lights pop-up menu has an option that may seem confusing at first blush: Infinite Light. "What's the difference," you may well ask, "between a light with No Falloff and an Infinite Light?" And the answer is: the Infinite Light setting does not apply to the light cast by your light object, but to the light object itself. The option works only for lights that have been made visible (see the next section). Without the Infinite Light setting, a visible light shows up as the size of its wireframe when rendered, but if you make the light infinite, the light itself extends as far as you can see, making for a much more realistic effect. Figure 12.18 shows ordinary visible lights compared to infinite lights; the wireframes of all the objects are the same size.

Figure 12.18 Infinite lights side by side with ordinary visible lights. From left to right: Round spotlight, square spotlight, round parallel light, square parallel light.

Visible Lights (Surface and Volume)

Your lights can have visible light sources. Not only will the object cast light, but you can see the light source itself when one of the visible light options is checked. The available flavors are surface visible lights and volume visible lights. What's the difference? Here's the short answer: Surface visible lights come into the world with a surface material; volume visible lights have a—wait for it—volume material. We cheerfully refer you back to Chapter 9, "Material World I," where there is a wealth of information about surface and volume materials. We'll go a little deeper into the distinction as it applies to lights in a moment, after a little more in the way of introduction. Figure 12.19 shows a sample of each kind of visible light. Because one of the principal uses for visible lights is to create beams of light, it's usually a good idea to turn on the Infinite Light option, as Figure 12.20 shows (radial lights, however, are unaffected).

For surface visible lights, visibility is separate from light intensity. In fact, a surface visible light can be set to 0 intensity and still be a visible object. (Setting the

a

b

Figure 12.19 Visible lights: a) Surface; b) volume. Front row, left to right: Radial light, round spotlight, square spotlight. Back row: Parallel lights, square and cylindrical.

a

b

Figure 12.20 Infinite visible lights: a) Surface; b) volume. Front row, left to right: Radial light, round spotlight, square spotlight. Back row: Parallel lights, square and cylindrical.

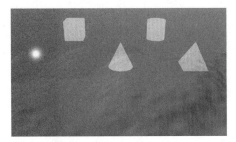

Figure 12.21 Surface visible light sources with intensity set to 0.

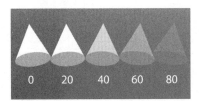

Figure 12.22 Surface visible spotlights (intensity = 0) at a range of Transparency settings.

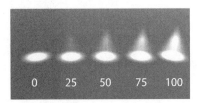

Figure 12.23 A volume visible spotlight at different Base Density settings.

intensity of a volume visible light to 0 renders it, well, invisible!) Figure 12.21 shows a sample of each of the surface visible light sources with intensity settings at 0. What governs the visibility of the light, then? For surface visible lights, it's the Transparency setting in the Materials Lab. In Figure 12.22, the lights have different Transparency settings. The one on the left is 0 (most opaque). Each light to the right has a setting incremented by 20, and the last one has a setting of 80 (higher values render the light essentially invisible). The quality to use for adjusting the visibility of volume visible lights is the Base Density. By default, volume visible lights are created with a Base Density of 15.3—rather a low figure, which accounts for the faint appearance of most of the lights in Figures 12.19b and 12.20b. Figure 12.23 shows a set of volume visible spotlights with various Base Density settings.

How to characterize qualitatively the distinction between surface and volume visible lights? The difference shows up most clearly when the light beam interacts with something else. We'll refer to Figure 12.24 to illustrate. The image shows two infinite parallel lights, both with the same wood grain material applied, the one on the left set to surface visible, the one on the right to volume visible. A horizontal cylinder cuts through both lights. Notice how the surface texture on the left light acts like a skin wrapped around the light—almost like a soap-bubble film. One doesn't have the sense that the texture exists inside the beam. The cylinder passing through the light interrupts the beam enough to cast a shadow, but then the light reforms into its original shape and continues on its merry way.

Compare the volume visible light on the right. Every cubic inch of the beam seems to emit light, and we have the sense that the texture fills the beam. It's almost as if the light and its texture have physical substance. Notice what happens when the light beam is interrupted by the cylinder: Not only does the cylinder cast a shadow, but it shuts off some of the flow of the light. The light beam itself is

Figure 12.24 Two visible lights, surface on the left, volume on the right, with the same texture applied.

reshaped, as a stream of water is diverted around obstacles in its path. The surface visible light doesn't quite obey real-world lighting conditions, especially where the light encounters the lower side of the cylinder. Assuming that the cylinder is opaque (which we can safely do here), it should "stop" all light from passing through it.

Visible Lights and Materials/Gels

Earlier we mentioned that when a gel is assigned to a light, a connection is forged to the Materials Lab, and that the only possible thing you can manipulate within the Materials Lab is the Diffuse Color. Well, we lied. Sort of. As we already said, once you make a light visible, it has two distinct properties: its visibility and the intensity of its illumination, or the light it casts on other objects. Remember that a light can be visible even though its intensity is set to 0, so it illuminates nothing. Our earlier statement about Diffuse Color was no lie with regard to illumination: Diffuse Color is the only Materials Lab property that affects the quality of light shining upon another object. However, visibility is a whole 'nother thing. Once you make a light visible, you can use other parts of the Materials Lab to affect the appearance of the visible part of the light object. For a surface visible light, you can use Transparency. For a volume visible light, you can use Base Density, and its modifiers: Fuzzy Factor and Quality. Table 12.1 compares the different material properties that operate in the different kinds of lights.

Property	Surface Light	Volume Light
Shading mode	Light	Light Sensitive
		Additive
Color (gel)	Diffuse Color	Diffuse Color
Appearance (visible lights only)	Transparency	Base Density (plus modifiers)

Table 12.1 Material Properties That Can Be Applied to Lights.

Figure C12.25 is an overview of the various visible light options. The top row shows surface visible lights, and the bottom two rows show volume visible lights. In each case, the leftmost light is plain white, with no gel. The other three lights use a texture to drive at least one property of the light's material. In the surface visible light examples, the texture drives (from left to right) Transparency only, Diffuse Color only, and both Transparency and Diffuse Color. How can you tell which is which? Whatever is in the Diffuse Color channel governs the illumination shed by the light, whereas the texture in the Transparency channel affects what portions of the visible light object are, in fact, visible. The center row, volume visible lights with the Additive option turned on, is presented in a similar pattern: Plain, texture-driven Base Density, texture-driven Diffuse Color, and both Base Density and Diffuse Color driven by a texture. The bottom row is exactly identical to the middle row except that the Additive option has been disabled. What a difference Additive makes!

Smoky Spotlight Walkthrough

A classic use of volume visible lights is to create a spotlight whose beam is given substance by traversing a smoke-filled room. We'll show you how:

1. Create a new scene. Type ⌘-K/Ctrl+K to open the Sky Lab. Click the sun icon to switch to night time, and then click the dot next to Disable Sun Light so the option is turned on (that is, so Sun Light is disabled). Close the Sky Lab. (Optional: To heighten the effect, we also chose the Atmosphere Off option from the Sky Options menu on the Sky & Fog Palette.)

2. Click the round spotlight icon on the Create Palette. Move the newly formed object higher in the scene, to get a better view of the light.

3. Click the E icon, or type ⌘-E/Ctrl+E to open the Edit Lights dialog box. Choose Volume Visible Light and Infinite Light from the Options pop-up menu.

4. Now we need an appropriately smoky texture for our spot. Click the M icon next to the light (or type ⌘-M/Ctrl+M) to open the Materials Lab. Before we go texture shopping, first open the Material Options pop-up menu at the upper-right of the Lab to see what Shading mode was applied to our light when we made it volume visible. It came into the world with the Light Shading mode; now it's been switched to Light Sensitive mode with the Additive option turned on.

5. Diffuse Color is one of only two channels we can do anything to that will affect our volume visible spotlight, so click the materials grid in the Texture A column for Diffuse Color. A random texture preset appears in the Texture A source. Whatever texture the program has conjured up for you probably isn't anything like smoke, so let's find a texture that is. Click the Texture Library pop-up menu and navigate to the Psychedelic category; find the Smokey preset (see Figure 12.26a). Close the Materials Lab.

a
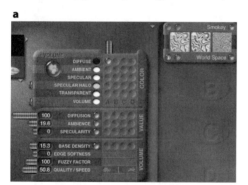
b
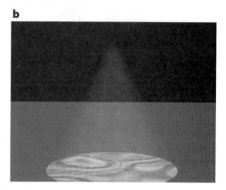

Figure 12.26 Our first attempt at a smoky spotlight: a) The Materials Lab, showing the application of the texture preset Smokey to the Diffuse Color channel of the volume visible light. Base Density is set to its default value, 15.3; b) the rendered result.

6. Let's see what we've got—render the scene (see Figure 12.26b). You'll probably find that the smoke is a little too diaphanous for the effect you're trying to achieve, so head back to the Materials Lab. Boost the Base Density by a goodly amount, and your smoke will have more body to it (see Figure 12.27).

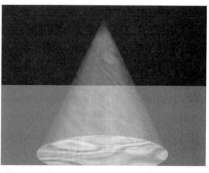

Figure 12.27 Our smoky spotlight after boosting Base Density to 32.2, about double its default value.

7. We'll add a further refinement: Our light looks fairly smoky, but it still has a sort of general glow, an evenness that doesn't look quite right. Remember that we can use our texture to drive one other channel of our volume visible light's material: Base Density. Click the Texture A column next to Base Density and move the slider to a yet higher value. *Voilà!* You're on your way to a perfect nightclub atmosphere (see Figure 12.28). Say, isn't that Piaf I hear?

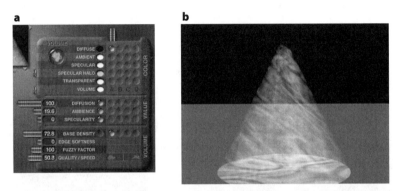

Figure 12.28 Our finished smoky spot: a) The Materials Lab, showing the texture driving Base Density, and the Base Density slider adjusted to 72.8; b) the rendered light.

OTHER LIGHT PROPERTIES

Now that you've been introduced to the basics of the light objects and the means of manipulating them in the Edit Light dialog box, we'll discuss light in the real world, light in the Brycean world, and a few practicalities in terms of scene complexity and render time.

Express Your Negativity

Here's an item from the Odd But True department: You can have lights of negative intensity in Bryce, something that you can't do in the physical world. What the heck does that mean? Think of it this way: With a conventional light, turning up the intensity causes more and more light energy to pour into the scene. A negative light sucks light energy out of a scene, and the more negative the intensity, the more it, uhhhh…sucks. What's more, if you apply a color to a negative light, that color is removed from the scene wherever the light strikes, leaving the color's complement behind. To illustrate, we created Figure C12.29, which is based on Figure 12.8a. We changed the intensity of the leftmost light (C12.29a) to –25, and now it casts a hard-edged cone of blackness. The second light, C12.29b, has an intensity of –100, and we gave it a deep orange color, resulting in a circle of vivid blue, the complement of orange. C12.29c, in the middle, has a small negative intensity (–13) and a softness of 20, so it just creates a smudge of darkness. The fourth light, C12.29d, is magenta, with an intensity of –25 and a softness of 40, creating a soft-edged puddle of green (magenta's complement). We left C12.29e unchanged for comparison (intensity 25, softness 70). We saved the most dramatic change for C12.29f, which we transformed into a radial light, and to which we gave an intensity of –45; it not only creates a great inky spot beneath itself, but its light streams in all directions, affecting the rest of the scene. Notice the funny flame-shaped halos around the pebbles? Those are shadows: When an object obstructs a negative white light, which for all practical purposes casts black light, it throws a white shadow! Because negative lights are contrary to nature, use them for unnatural effects or to set an eerie mood. Want a mysterious shadow where none should exist? Use a negative light.

For normal scene making, use negative-intensity lights in the same way that photographers use black screens to absorb light. You can create darker shadowy places that way. For those kinds of effects, you don't need to crank the intensity far into the nether negative regions; just a slight bit of negativity may do the trick. Likewise, if you don't want to deal with positive (that is, white) shadows, then choose the Disable Cast Shadows option in the Edit Lights pop-up menu. For the three scenes shown in Figure C12.30, we created a rock wall using the DTE-terrain-making trick described at the end of Chapter 10. What better thing to do than to use lights to emphasize all those nice rocky shapes in our terrain wall? Figure C12.30a shows the scene with a single, positive light shining from the upper left. (The color swatch at the lower left shows you the light's color.) Figure C12.30b has a negative light in the lower-right of the terrain. It's the exact same color as the pale orange light, and it sucks out all the pale orange from the scene, resulting in a dark blue. Figure C12.30c has the same negative light, colored green this time. When it sucks the green from the scene, the result is a dark reddish shadow. Whichever color option you choose, the negative light adds so much depth and drama to the wall as a whole, doesn't it?

Caustic Attitude

There are a couple of real-world light conditions that are not captured in the ray-trace process. They both concern secondary illumination effects as light passes through objects or bounces off other objects. The first one, highlights from water, is the effect where the bending in the water's surface act as a lens to focus light. When that light passes through water to a solid surface below, wavy lines shine on the solid surface. In the same way, reflections off the water's surface onto other areas also reflect those wavy lines. The wavy line refractions and reflections are called *caustics*. Though caustics exist in the real world, they are not created by ray tracing.

The second type of light condition is the reflection of light from an object. If light bounces off a brightly colored object onto another object—especially one that's a light color—a bit of the bright color will be reflected onto the object. The rendering method that treats every object as a potential light source is called *radiosity*. With all the added rendering calculations, radiosity is an extremely time-consuming method. (Radiosity is not used in Bryce.) The light bouncing off brightly lit objects is the subtle version. The more obvious version uses a reflective object—say, a mirror. If a light is shining toward a mirror, when you look into the mirror, not only do you see the light, but the light shines into your eyes. (A car rear-view mirror is a real-world example. The little switch that adjusts the tilt so that the glass is not as reflective as the mirror is an eye-saving invention that compensates for this light reflecting tendency.) But if you set up a rear-view mirror in Bryce, it will not work that way. For an excellent brief introduction to these phenomena, with illustrations, produced in a program that does render caustics, see the article "A Look at Caustics" by Jeremy Birn, at www.3drender.com/light/caustics.html.

For any of these kinds of phenomena to appear in your scene, you'll have to find a way to create them.

Figure 12.31a shows Susan's version of a caustic light. There are two ways to generate the light: by using a picture or by using Bryce's Texture Generator. The latter is preferable, though Susan continues to search for that "just right" caustic wave pattern. (The aquatic image in Figure C12.32 and the temple image in Figure C12.46 also use a caustic texture for watery illumination.) Depending on the situation, the type of light you select to illuminate the caustic will vary. If the light is shining down onto a surface below, such as a swimming pool, fountain, or other shallow water, then use a parallel light. In the case of the rocks lit by the caustics reflecting off of water, we use a spotlight. Experiment for the best results. Look on

a

b

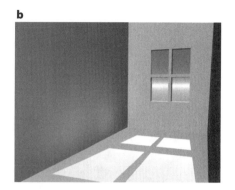

Figure 12.31 Emulating real-world lighting conditions using Bryce lighting tricks:
a) A parallel light with caustic texture throws fake caustics on the bottom of this pool
of water; b) round spotlights cause the illusion of light bouncing off a brightly lit area
and reflecting on a nearby wall.

the CD-ROM in the folder for this chapter to find a scene file that has several
lights with different caustic textures.

To get a radiosity type of reflection from a light or brightly colored object, use a very
weak radial light or spotlight. The spotlight can project on the surroundings, and
since it has a narrow beam, it won't shed additional light on the object that's reflecting onto other objects. Figure 12.31b uses two round spotlights to create the illusion
of light bouncing off the brightly lit floor onto the wall. For best results, give the
light the color of the object that's "reflecting." Creating the bouncing light reflection
is a painstaking extra step, but if you're going for drop-dead realism, the difference
will be convincing, and you'll no doubt be extremely satisfied with the results.

Increased Render Time

As with every other part of Bryce, when you employ lighting effects, there's a constant obsession with rendering time: Is this costly? Is it efficient? Each light source
in the scene increases your render time. Why? Unlike in the real world, where the
addition of lights does not add to the time required to perceive objects in your
environment, the addition of light increases the number of calculations required
to render the scene. Each time a ray intersects an object, it then bounces toward
the light source to determine its effect on the object and hence the object's color.
Bryce always does this type of calculation for the primary light source: the sun (or
moon). When there are multiple light sources, however, there are multiple calculations. When the renderer finds an object in the scene, it asks, "What influence
does the radial light have on this object?" If there are several additional lights, it

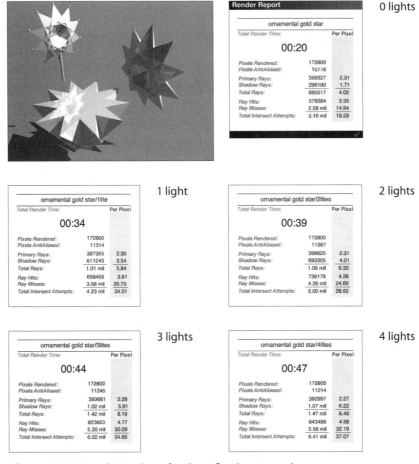

Figure 12.33 Rendering times for the reflective star series.

asks the question for each one. Figure 12.33 shows a scene with some reflective primitives in it, plus the render time and calculations when lights are added to the scene one at a time. For this sample, where the longest render time is just under a minute (on a 350 MHz Power Macintosh G3; your mileage may vary), the times don't seem all that long. But consider that the addition of the first light nearly doubled the rendering time, then succeeding lights each added about 10%. When you have a whole host of lights (see the "Light Arrays" section later in this chapter), the scene becomes very expensive. The real-world analogy that fits, it seems, is electricity: When you have a whole wad of lights, someone has to foot the electric bill.

Of course, there will be times where you need each and every light source to create just that perfect look for your well-lit Brycean masterpiece. That's what they're there for! But if you've added a bunch of lights willy-nilly and wonder why your render has slowed to a crawl, consider the impeding effect of the addition of all those light sources.

Lights and Solo Mode

When you go to Solo mode, you will see the influence of lights, even when the lights aren't there. If you have set your light objects to be visible (spotlight, radial light, and parallel light), the light objects must be in Solo mode for the visible part to render.

Lights are hybrid objects. They can be created, selected, and edited like objects, but once they're in the scene, the renderer treats them like skies and environment; their influence is global.

USING BRYCE LIGHTS: DIFFERENT TYPES OF LIGHTING CONDITIONS

This next section addresses the question, "But what do I use lights *for* in Bryce?"

There are lots of technical considerations for lighting, most of which we've discussed so far, and then there is the aesthetic decision-making process. Betty Edwards, in her book *Drawing on the Right Side of the Brain*, makes the case that learning to draw is not so much a matter of developing eye-hand coordination; rather, it is a matter of learning how to see. Using Bryce is an extension of this process, and indeed, if you have found yourself more aware of the environment and atmosphere and lighting conditions outdoors, Bryce has been guiding you to look at the world a little differently.

If you've had studio photography experience where you need to light objects, you're at an advantage. If you haven't, there is a body of reference material about lighting from experts in that profession. John Alton's *Painting with Light* is a discussion of lighting for cinematography and is considered a canonical reference on light in motion pictures. Though not all of this book applies to Bryce, the discussion of the different lights and their uses in combination with each other will increase your awareness of ways to set up lights for your scenes.

In a different vein, Burne Hogarth's *Dynamic Light and Shade* discusses light and shade in drawing. Though nearly all of his examples are hand-drawn—and what beautiful images!—his discussion of different lighting considerations throughout the book will help you to analyze the world around you. In short, this book will help you learn how to see light. There are plenty of landscape samples—all in grayscale, so you can see how much is conveyed in a reduced palette. Besides landscapes, Hogarth's book is filled with drawings of the human figure and other objects and environs.

These are not the only reference works available, but they are two from among of the best practitioners in their fields, and one emphasizes technical aspects of lighting, while the other concentrates on aesthetic judgments about light.

What Light Does Aesthetically

What else does light do in a scene? If you've gone through all the Plain Vanilla series of Sky & Fog variations in the previous chapter, you know how much light and atmosphere affect the appearance and overall tone of a scene. Lighting is a continuation of the atmosphere process. Here are some of its important functions:

- Lighting helps to define the full dimensions of form. This is a three-dimensional world, rendered in a two-dimensional image. Lighting helps to establish a sense of depth. Light and shadow push objects out toward you and pull them away into the distance. Notice in Figure 12.34 how the flat overhead gray light makes the objects dull and flat. In the other examples with additional lighting, a sense of depth is added to the scenes.

- Lighting establishes mood. Is the scene hot or cool? Is it happy or sad? Is it bright or drab? Is it commonplace or mysterious? Lighting helps establish the feel of a scene. Look at the scenes in Figure 12.34 again. Notice the difference between the lighter and darker versions. Do you get a different feeling from them? A different emotional tone? How about the difference between left and right lighting and front and back? The backlight adds drama and intrigue.

  This *Wine Cellar* scene by Gary Bernard (see Figure C12.35 in the color section) uses lights to help establish the environment and create a mood. The warm yellow lights—are they actual flame torches or lights made to resemble torches?—bespeak an indoor environment, and together with the rest of the scene, they invitingly beckon the viewer to share a glass of the finest.

- Lighting defines textures. In the samples from Figure 12.34, the objects are primarily smooth. But when there is a tactile sense of the object, light is the means of conveying it to your eyes, which in turn tell your fingers what it

Figure 12.34 Three-dimensional forms and lights.

Figure 12.36 Lighting shows the texture of an object.

would feel like to touch the object. Figure 12.36 shows a version of the scene in Figure 12.34 using surface textures on all the objects.

• Lighting emphasizes a focal point, or points of interest. In Figure 12.37 the pyramid—which was almost lost in the other images—is shown highlighted. Once the single bright light is on it, your eye goes to it first. The emphasis on one object poses a question: Why is the pyramid singled out for special notice? Lighting, then, can be used to help tell a story.

Figure 12.37 Lighting serves to focus your attention on a particular part of the scene.

Ways to Use Lights

The previous section discussed ways to use light to enhance your composition and tell a story. This section discusses ways to use light in a more logical, "what kind of light do you want?" sense. This is a counterpart to the cinematographic guide to which light does what and under what circumstances do you use each. Although it's entirely probable that your fertile imagination will find uses beyond those mentioned here, we'll get you started with a basic list of uses.

• *Artificial Light.* This is probably the most common form of light you'll create in your scenes. It is the light form that is not the sun. Besides the primary light source, there is the additional light source, whether it's electric or flame or something else. This is also the type of lighting you have in indoor environments, such as the *Wine Cellar* image. In the scene *Triad: Live at the Hammersmith Odeon,* by Robert Mann, spotlights create the feeling of a live amphitheater (see Figure C12.38 in the color section). The variations on artificial lights are legion, from flame to lamp to incandescent light to spotlight. Go for it!

• *Augmenting Light.* Augmenting light is a subtle addition to what is already present in the scene. Add to the light source that is already there, or use lights to make up for what is lacking in the ray-tracing procedure. In the moonscape over the water in Figure C12.39, a radial light adds strength to the light reflection on the water. The scene by Eric Wenger has a radial light placed between the camera and the moon. It adds some subtle lighting to the shores as well as to the watery surface. In Figure C12.39, note the superimposed wireframe for the radial light and compare the finished render with a version of the scene rendered without the light. Though the highlight still is there on the water, the subtle added moonlight created by the radial light is missing.

Caustic lights and subtle reflection lights, discussed earlier, fall into the augmenting light category.

• *Studio Light.* Use studio lighting for your still-life Bryce image; fill in shadows or add drama with additional lighting. Here is where you set up a scene with the key light, or principal light (usually your sun, though not always), a fill light to fill in harsh shadows and a back light or kicker light to shine on the object from behind for added drama, or to shine onto the background area to illuminate it adequately and separate it from the foreground object. Figure C12.40 shows a Brycean studio complete with studio lighting.

• *Stealth Light.* Stealth lighting is any lighting for added effect that does not have shadows. The advantage of this type is that it lets you carefully light a scene and highlight certain portions with lights without giving away the light source by shadows. In artificial environments, multiple light sources might be perfectly acceptable. In nature scenes, the presence of artificial lights is, well, artificial. In *Cappuccino on the Rocks*, two radial lights illuminate a cappuccino machine nestled in a rocky enclosure. The light to the right is the main one (shown as the only one in Figure C12.41a); a second, weaker light, which serves to fill in the shadow, is on the left (see Figure C12.41b). When the secondary light casts a shadow, there are a few places (note the top of the cappuccino machine, the area behind the carafe, and the right part of the rock wall "behind" the unit) where the presence of a second shadow contradicts the impression that all light comes from the above right, cast by the primary light (see Figure C12.41c). For reference, there's an image (Figure C12.41d) where light comes only from the left. Stealth lighting is not limited to positive lights; try negative lights (without casting shadows, of course!) to judiciously suck light out of portions of your scene, too.

Tips for Setting Up Lights

If you are mixing different lights and want to see which one is doing what, try giving each a different light color. That way you can judge which one is lighting up what space. In a variation on the *Cappuccino on the Rocks* scene, Figure C12.42 shows a view of the forward light tried as a spotlight. The light is red. It's easy to tell where the light is falling and whether it's aimed correctly.

The time to place lights in your scene varies. If your wild inspiration springs fresh from the Muse with an integral lighting plan, or if a light is the main part of the scene, you may set up your lights early in your scene-making process. On the other hand, lighting may be one of the final steps after completing many other steps in your scene construction. At either stage, you'll encounter the clashing of two expensive processes: rendering multiple light sources and rendering those beautiful material surfaces. When you're placing your lights, use the Textures On/Off switch on the Render controls (it's the control on the left) to turn off your textures. Lights will show up when the Texture Off Render mode is active. Figure C12.43 compares a scene with several spotlights when textures are turned on and off. Though the ground texture and presence of haze changes, the presence of the spotlights does not change, and Textures Off mode can be significantly faster. Of course, the beauty of the final process is seeing how the presence of additional lights enhances the look of those beautiful, expensive textures. But that's what sleep is for.

Gel Cookies

When designing your lights, make sure to consider Pict Gel cookies. What is this: some new, weird combination of chocolate chips and Jell-O? (Eeeew.) No. *Cookie* is the time-honored term used by cinematographers for an opaque stencil that blocks light in some shape and casts shadows onto a surface. The presence of black in the pattern of a Brycean gel will accomplish the same purpose. Use a specific picture (or texture) to make a certain type of shadow. Make a foliage shadow (see Figure C12.44 in the color section) or smoky, eerie lighting effects. When it comes to shadow casting, Bryce creates hard-edged shadows. If you try to use actual objects to block the light, you won't get soft shadows. Look again at the foliage cookie image. The shadows are soft because you can create a nice, fat, blurry pattern by painting in Photoshop.

Another use of Pict Gel cookies is for a bit of judicious touch-up to the lighting to shape the pool of light just so. In the highlighted pyramid back in Figure 12.37, a Pict Gel cookie would have handily cut away the light that spilled beyond the pyramid itself. This type of situation calls for back and forth work in Photoshop and Bryce (or try it in the Terrain Editor with a throw-away terrain and copy and paste) and a lot of top view renders, assuming that the light is being cast from above.

Light Arrays

In Bryce, all shadows are hard-edged. If you want a soft-edge shadow, you'll have to go to additional lengths to get it. One way is by using an array of lights. Figure 12.45 shows a series of images by Robert Mann that compares a light array to a single light source. Mann adapted a technique described in *3-D Artist* magazine (issue 25, "Shadow of Doubt: Mechanics of Realism," by Timothy Wilson). A spiral light array (rendered as spheres for the purpose of illustration in Figure 12.45e)

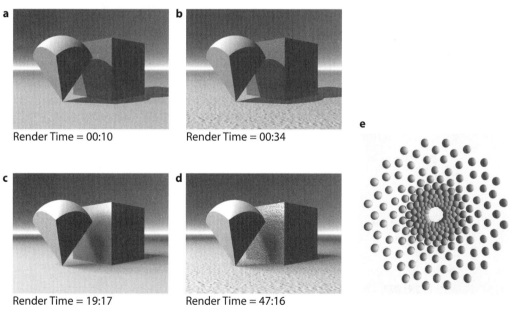

Figure 12.45 Using a light array to create a soft shadow. Top row: Single light source; object surfaces are a) smooth and b) bumped. Second row: Light array; object surfaces are c) smooth and d) bumped. At the right: e) Light array pattern rendered as spheres. Render times are based on a 266-MHz Macintosh PowerBook G3.

casts light onto the scene. The figure shows two versions of objects: with smooth edges and with bumped edges. The array technique is more convincing with the bump, since the shadow pattern is obscured. Because of the number of additional lights in the scene, render time is tortuously prolonged.

EXAMPLE SCENES

This last section examines a few scenes containing lights. It analyzes different techniques, goals, and effects for lighting.

Flames Using Light and Pseudo-Light

The two scenes, *Chandelier* and *Water Temple at Night*, in Figure C12.46, both employ the same type of flame and light effect. In addition, *Water Temple at Night* has two other types of light sources. Each of the flames in both scenes actually uses two spherical objects to create the light effect. The flame itself is not a light source; the flame is a sphere whose material uses a fire texture and whose Shading mode has the Additive option turned on. This is the Bryce pseudo-light technique. The actual light illuminating the scene comes from the radial light that occupies the same space. In *Chandelier*, the lights are larger and visible. The visible part acts as the glow very close to the light "source," the flame. The texture source for the lights' materials drives both Diffuse Color and Transparency. (The scene file is supplied on the CD for this chapter; be sure to check out the construction of the candles—both for their construction as objects and for their use of texture-driven materials.) The glow is not as apparent in the *Water Temple at Night* scene. The light with pseudo-light is a tricky hack: The flame is not the light source; the glow is the light source while acting as the glow from the flame pseudo-light source.

Besides the flame lights in *Water Temple at Night*, there are spotlights to highlight the objects in the temple's center and the pillar area. In addition, a parallel light projects the water caustics onto the marble floor.

Shoji Lantern

Carla Moore created a strikingly beautiful scene through the use of a simple lighting scheme, in keeping with the timeless elegance of her subject (see Figure C12.47). Carla originally set up the lantern to be the source for an animated GIF, with candlelight flickering gently behind rice paper screens. To focus attention on the light produced by the lantern itself, sunlight is turned off. A single pale beige spotlight provides the only external illumination for the lantern object. Five radial lights, all set to Squared Falloff, create the candle radiance from within the lamp. The central radial light, a volume visible light colored pure white, provides general illumination and serves as the visible source of the illumination. Nestled within it are four small radial lights, arranged in a tight diamond formation. These lights are somewhat brighter than the larger white one and are colored various shades of yellow and orange. A flickering flame does not throw a uniform shadow—hence, the multiple light sources. For her animation, Carla rendered a series of variations on this scene, each time moving two or three of the colored flames by a tiny amount (less than 0.10 Bryce units on any axis). Each rendering served as one frame of her animation. (The scene file and the animated GIFs are provided on the CD-ROM for your delectation.)

The Castle Hall Scene

The extremely complex scene in Figure C12.48, by Glenn Riegel, created for the Sanctuary Web-game project, uses lighting superbly. The light sources are radial lights, and there are *many* of them in the scene. In some places, two are doubled up at the same location to create extremely bright light. Notice how lighting establishes focal points and dimension in this hall. Although the camera is placed in the middle of the room, you don't really notice the ground you're standing on, since it's dark. The points of emphasis are elsewhere. Stairs lead up to a second level. A banner hangs from the wall in the center back. Lights located upstairs and downstairs against the wall not only define the building's dimensions, but they suggest places that you could walk to. There is light off to the right side. Don't you want to just turn to the right and see what's there? Lighting in this scene does three things: It establishes the full dimension of the place, it establishes mood with warm flame lamps with yellowish glows, and it suggests possibilities for further game play. The main focal points are the stairs, the flag, an undefined area to the right, and places along the perimeter of the scene. Look at the scene again and notice how your eye moves from one to another area in the scene. When designing your own images, use light to establish priorities for the viewer and tell your story.

Hall of Kings

Janak Alford's monumental architectural study uses Volumetric World to create great streaming floods of light (see Figure C12.49). The Volumetric World Density setting (the controls are on the Atmosphere tab of the Sky Lab) is cranked up to 90%, almost the maximum, giving the light a rich texture. The Quality setting has been reduced a bit from the default level, to 39%, to improve render time. Sun light has been disabled; the principal light source is one huge, intense, yellow-orange parallel light positioned above and to the right of the structure (the building has no roof). This light has been expanded enormously along its z axis, so that it is longer than the building. It is angled down and to the left, parallel to the beams of light that fill the center aisle. There's only one other light in the scene: a very faint radial light (also yellow-orange) that extends the length of the main hallway, just above and to the right of the camera. It provides a touch of ambient light, filling in areas not reached by the parallel light and bringing out the bump mapping on the columns on the right. Because this scene lives in Volumetric World, both lights act like volume lights, though the weak radial light doesn't really show it. As the illumination from the parallel light streams through the architectural elements, its flow is interrupted by the objects it encounters. The light that gets through appears as distinct beams, falling from above. The light takes on a tangible quality, in splendid counterpoint to the massive stone structures it illuminates. (Make sure to inspect the scene file, on the CD-ROM in the folder for this chapter.)

CHAPTER THIRTEEN

Render Unto Bryce

IN THIS CHAPTER...

- How ray tracing works
- Spatial optimization
- Tips and tricks for rendering while you are working on your scene and when you're done
- The Render Report
- Batch rendering
- Large-format rendering
- 360° rendering
- Distance rendering
- Mask rendering
- Semi-antialiasing tricks

Everything we've talked about in earlier chapters—objects, terrains, materials, and sky and fog—culminates in rendering, which is the creation of a two-dimensional PICT or BMP image of the scene. The main concern in the scene creation process is the creation of a great image. Very closely tied to this is the creation of an efficient scene. This chapter begins with a deeper look into the mysteries of ray tracing, complete with some time-saver tips so you can make your scenes render more quickly. Then it continues with discussions of rendering during the working process and rendering when the scene is complete. From there, the chapter treats batch renders and then beyond-the-basic renders, including renders of large images to 360° renders and the use of other render modes for post-processing of your scenes.

"But what about rendering animations?" you might ask. Quite a reasonable question to ask of any book on Bryce 4—but for now, we'll defer the answer to the next chapter, "The Fourth Dimension: Time and Animation."

We'll start things off by saying that the first Windows version of Bryce introduced many significant changes in the rendering procedure; so much so that the previous edition of this book expended many photons in explicating the differences between the Mac and Windows versions. Since then, the innovations in Bryce 2 for Windows have become standard equipment on both platforms.

THE BASIC RENDERING MODEL

What takes place during ray tracing? When rendering an image, Bryce's normal procedure is to shoot a ray into the scene for each pixel. What is rendered depends on what is or isn't struck by the ray. When the ray doesn't intersect an object, it renders sky. When it does intersect an object, it bounces off of the object. Then, depending on the surface features of the object, it bounces elsewhere until it finds the light sources that contribute to that object's color. From that, the ray determines one final color for the pixel. Of course, the area that Bryce considers a pixel changes with each progressive rendering pass. Recall that in the first pass, Bryce determines a color for an area that is actually 16 × 16 pixels. The second pass covers an 8 × 8 area, the third pass 4 × 4, and so on until every single pixel has been rendered. The final antialiasing pass shoots nine rays to determine a color for each pixel (in those areas of high contrast), averaging all the information to come up with a color for that one pixel.

If there are 16 objects in a scene, then Bryce must test for 16 objects for each ray that goes out in your Bryce world. Each ray "knows" how many objects are out there. It will ask: "Did I hit one object? Did I hit two objects? Did I hit three? Did I hit four?" and so on. The greater the number of objects in your scene, the greater the number of queries to see if the ray struck any of them; the more queries, the slower the render. This process occurs for each ray that is shot out. The same 16 questions are asked each time. There are no shortcuts.

Render Options

Fortunately, Bryce allows you to adjust certain parameters, which gives you some control over the speed of rendering. You can set Bryce's render options using the Render pop-up menu and a cluster of buttons, all on the Control Palette (see Figure 13.1). The buttons have two modes of operation: Apply a simple click to one of the three on the right to get a rendering process going, but the two on the left are switches that toggle back and forth between two states; click once to change the button's state, and click again to return to the default state. It's easy to tell when one of these buttons is in the nondefault state: It gets a dimple in the side, making it look like a collapsed ping-pong ball.

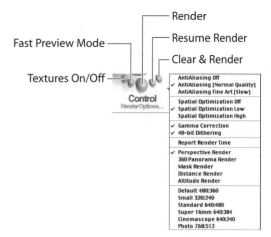

Figure 13.1 Render controls on the Control Palette and Render pop-up menu.

Spatial Optimization Off/Low/High

Remember our rays that are shot into the scene, asking, "Did I hit anything?" Suppose there was a way to tell the ray ahead of time, "Don't even bother to look in these parts of the scene, because there aren't any objects there." Well, there is! It's called *Spatial Optimization*. The goal is to divvy up the objects in the scene to cut down on the unnecessary part of rendering. We described the process as the renderer asking if something was there. If you're geeky enough to actually write the code for a ray tracer, you'd call the process *testing*; the ray tests to see if something is there. To accelerate the process, arrange the scene so that the rays perform only the necessary tests.

The Spatial Optimization Off option performs the most infinitesimal bit of optimization. Bryce assigns everything in the scene to a bounding box. If the area of the bounding box is limited, then the ray must ask the additional questions only a few times, in comparison to all the times it would ask about one object, two objects, three, four, and so on, for the rest of the rays shot into the scene. Although you may lose a bit of speed when the ray must ask about the specifics of the group, you gain speed because it doesn't have to ask about the specifics of that group everywhere else. When rendering things outside of that bounding box (sky), Bryce won't even test for objects; all it cares about is sky. For all practical purposes, however, when the Spatial Optimization Off option is active, you get very little speed-up. It works fine when you have fewer than five objects in your scene. Above that, you'll need to move up to real optimization.

If you invoke Low or High Spatial Optimization, Bryce subdivides the scene's bounding box into smaller bounding boxes, each containing a certain number of items. It doesn't perform any tests for objects in *this* part of the world when it's over there rendering *that* part of the world. The only difference between Spatial Optimization Low and High is that the bounding box of all objects is divvied up into different quadrants.

Each of the subdivided quadrants for Low contains a lower number of items, and each of the quadrants for High contains a higher number of items. This may seem backward—for the same scene, there are fewer total quadrants for Spatial Optimization High than there are for Spatial Optimization Low. Consider it from the perspective of the number of questions each ray must ask, however. In a scene with 300 objects, it's better to require each ray to ask six questions about sets of 50 than it is to require each ray to ask 60 questions about sets of five objects.

This explains the rule of thumb for which option to use: When you have fewer than five objects, Spatial Optimization Off is fine. When you have more than five objects, but the numbers don't run up into the hundreds, Spatial Optimization Low is fine. In fact, Low is the default render method in Bryce 4. If you've come this far in this book, the majority of your scenes probably contain over five objects. When you create scenes with objects numbering in the hundreds, use Spatial Optimization High. By now it should be obvious that for medium-sized scenes, dividing the bounding box into fewer quadrants containing many more objects may be more trouble than it's worth.

Antialiasing Options

You have three flavors of antialiasing to choose from, and your choice will affect rendering time significantly. Quickest, naturally, is turning antialiasing off altogether. The default Normal Quality antialiasing adds a moderate amount of time to your render, but the Fine Art variety will give you a serious lesson in the virtues of patience. In addition to letting you select from those options on the Render Options pop-up menu, Bryce also allows you to make your antialiasing choice in the Document Setup dialog box. (The Render Options pop-up menu's Fine Art setting is equivalent to choosing Superfine AntiAliasing in the Document Setup dialog box.)

The standard process of antialiasing takes place after the five render passes. At the conclusion of those passes, Bryce conducts a special render pass. First it decides whether to antialias the pixel or not. To do so, it examines each pixel and the pixels below and to the right (see Figures 13.2a and b). If there is a high contrast between the target pixel and the ones below and to the right, it then conducts a supersample. It shoots extra rays around the rest of the eight pixels surrounding the one pixel (see

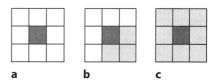

Figure 13.2 Antialiasing strategy: To determine if a) the center pixel will be antialiased, b) additional rays sample the area below and to the right of the center pixel; if there's high contrast, then c) the remainder of the eight surrounding pixels is sampled.

Figure 13.2c). The result of the supersampling is weighed together with the center pixel to arrive at the final color for that pixel. The image is smoothed as a result. The basic process is to perform a regular render for five passes and then conduct a post-processing supersample pass at the end to smooth out the areas that need it. The areas that will be antialiased are areas of high contrast, and high-frequency textures.

The AntiAliasing Fine Art [Slow] option approaches antialiasing in a different manner. Rather than conducting five normal render passes and saving the super-sampling for the end, the Fine Art method conducts the supersampling during all five render passes. If you wondered why this method is slower than the others, this is the reason! Further, for each supersample, instead of shooting out a set of rays in a 3×3 formation, for a nine-times oversample, the Fine Art method shoots out sets of rays in a 4×4 formation, for a total of 16 rays per pixel. After five passes, the render is complete. After supersampling throughout the process, there is no need for an antialiasing pass to cap it off.

But wait! There's more! Each time those 16 rays are shot into the scene, they are randomly jittered. (In Normal Quality antialiasing, the ray is shot out to sample the upper-left corner of the pixel.) Figure 13.3 shows how the arrangement varies

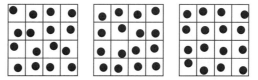

Figure 13.3 Fine Art AntiAliasing pass randomly jitters the placement of each of the 16 rays that are shot into the scene in order to determine one pixel's color.

from one sample to the next. The result of this random jitter is a better-looking final image. Additional detail that might otherwise be lost in the standard ray tracing is picked up by those jittered rays. The kinds of artifacts that create aliasing tend to occur from repeated patterns, rather than randomness. For those familiar with offset printing technology, the difference between the basic line screen halftone and the stochastic screen halftone is analogous to the difference between the regular render method and the jittered sampling method. The line art screen has artifacts (moiré); stochastic screening lacks moiré and has crisper detail.

Color Adjustments

Bryce's internal rendering engine calculates colors to a high degree of precision, but when the results of these calculations are displayed on physical computer monitors, a good bit is lost in translation. Bryce 4 introduced the Gamma Correction and 48-bit Dithering options in an attempt to compensate for the deficiencies of computer display mechanisms, with mixed results.

48-Bit Dithering

When Bryce calculates the value for the color of a pixel, it produces a real number—a number that might have an infinite number of digits after the decimal point. A computer monitor can, at its 24-bit best, only display colors whose red, green, and blue components are each an integer between 0 and 255. If Bryce rounded off the real numbers directly to these integers, your image might end up with awkward jumps between neighboring colors, leading to the heartbreak of unsightly bands of color. When 48-bit Dithering is turned on, Bryce first converts the real numbers to 48-bit color; then it dithers the color to 24-bit color, which your monitor can display. The result is smoother gradients, especially in skies and atmospheric phenomena such as moon halos. There's no performance penalty when you use 48-bit Dithering, so we recommend keeping it on all the time (some people report seeing minor artifacts in the ground plane when it's on, but this is rare; if it happens to you, just turn 48-bit Dithering off).

Gamma Correction

The Gamma Correction option was added to Bryce in a noble attempt to solve a two-fold problem: The gamut, or range, of colors produced by Bryce's rendering engine is much greater than can be displayed on a computer monitor, and the same color calculated by Bryce on two different computers won't necessarily look the same on the monitors of those machines. The latter problem primarily manifests itself when comparing images on Macintoshes and Windows machines, because the two operating systems display colors differently onscreen. When Gamma Correction is turned on, Bryce attempts to tweak the colors it sends to the screen to account for this difference, so that the same scene rendered on a Mac and a Wintel box will produce similar output.

Unfortunately, Gamma Correction, as implemented in Bryce 4, is not quite ready for prime time. Part of the problem is that it doesn't know how your particular monitor and video hardware display color; it can only make guesses, treating all Macs and all PCs alike—so if you're really concerned about precise color control, keep Gamma Correction turned off, and do all your color correction with specialized hardware and software: Use a calibrated monitor, make sure your ColorSync settings (Mac only) are up-to-date, and process your images through Photoshop or some other editing program with sophisticated color-matching tools.

Report Render Time

Initially installed as a testing device when the developers were working on the rendering part of the software, the Render Report has remained in the software to indicate render time and recount what's transpired during the render process for still images. We'll discuss the significance of items listed in the report after focusing on the practical uses of selecting the Render Report (or not). You can activate the Render Report either through the Render Options pop-up menu or through the Document Setup dialog box.

Besides telling you how long Bryce took to render the image, this feature provides another significant function. It provides a system alert when the image has completed rendering. Any time you're in a production environment where you need to actively attend a set of renders (on one or multiple machines), the system alert is your friend, telling you to come back after working on the other computer (or paying your bills or practicing your juggling) to save this image and go on to the next.

What is the significance of the report itself? Aside from the total render time, what additional meaning can be abstracted from the report and all those numbers? (See Figure 13.4.)

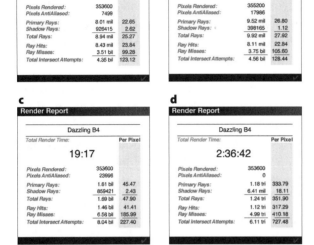

Figure 13.4 Render Reports for: a) Scene with Textures off; b) scene in Fast Preview mode; c) scene rendered normally with Normal Quality AntiAliasing; d) scene rendered with Fine Art AntiAliasing.

As you look at the rows of items in the report, you see three main categories. The first has to do with the number of pixels in the scene. The second concerns the number of rays that are "shot out" into the scene to render the image. The third tells how many of those rays hit objects and how many missed.

The first category concerns the number of pixels in the image. The first item, Pixels Rendered, is simply a count of the pixels in your scene. That number is fixed at the time you set the document and render resolution in the Document Setup dialog box. The second item, Pixels AntiAliased, depends on the contents of the scene. If you have a completely smooth image where no antialiasing occurs (for instance, rendering a cloudless sky with no haze), then the number would be 0. An image with more complex surface detail would have a higher number. If you render using the Fine Art AntiAliasing method, the result will also be 0 pixels antialiased (see Figure 13.4d).

The next section concerns rays that are shot into the image. For each pixel, rays shot into the scene calculate that pixel's color. How many rays are shot out? Primary rays include the first set of rays and the antialiasing rays. Shadow rays shoot out from "found" objects to determine if a shadow is cast onto it. If you have the Shadow control in the Sky & Fog Palette set to anything other than 0, then Bryce will shoot out shadow rays as appropriate while it is rendering the scene.

The final set of items concerns whether the ray hits an object or not. For a sky scene with no objects, all you'll have is misses. Recall from the initial render discussion that when a ray is shot into a scene, it either finds something (a hit) or it doesn't (a miss). In a scene where the camera looks down from above onto a ground plane, every one will be a hit. Between those two extremes of all sky or all object are all the hit-or-miss possibilities in Bryce.

By the way, if you're applying your mathematical due diligence to the report, adding up the numbers here and there to see if they reconcile (Ah! But you're reading this because you're an artist, not because you're an accountant, right?), you may have noticed that the total number of rays does not always equal the total number of intersect attempts. That's because there are other rays in the render process, but they aren't listed in the Render Report. What are they? Why, secondary, tertiary, and additional rays that are shot out under special optical conditions (reflection, refraction, transparency). Those additional rays are factored into the Total Intersect Attempt number. They result in many more misses, since they may bounce off an object and into the sky.

The Render Report is a good diagnostic tool for reducing the expense of a scene and making it render more efficiently. How do you conduct a diagnosis of a scene?

First, look at the number of Pixels AntiAliased. The number can be no higher than the Pixels Rendered number. The higher the number is, the longer the rendering takes.

Next take a look at the total number of rays shot into the scene. In a scene created at Bryce's default size, the resulting numbers are in the hundreds of thousands and low millions. It's hard for numbers of that magnitude to be meaningful, but when they are divided by the total number of pixels, a baseline ratio emerges. It becomes meaningful when you consider the number of rays per pixel or the number of intersections per pixel. One ray per one pixel is extremely efficient. (The lowest number we've seen is 1, when the camera points straight down at a plain ground plane that's had all shadow options disabled in the Materials Lab's Material Options menu. It was very efficient, but visually boring!) The higher the number, the more complex and costly the scene is. We've seen scenes using the normal render method that hover near and even exceed 10 rays per pixel. (Of course, the Fine Art method *starts* at 16 and goes up from there, as Figure 13.4d shows.) Needless to say, those have longer render times.

Finally, take a look at the relationship between the Total Rays Per Pixel and the Total Intersect Attempts Per Pixel. The Total Intersect Attempts will be equal to or higher than the total number of rays shot. It can very easily be two, three, four, or five times as many. When you add lights and other optic conditions to your scene, then you're making that ratio higher.

We're not saying to try to keep the numbers equivalent. Pretty scenes in Bryce will require expensive components. It's just that it's best if you *choose* to use the expensive ones rather than have a pricey render foisted upon you by a lack of familiarity with the software. If you need some measure of your scene's efficiency, you'll find it here in the Render Report.

Before leaving this topic, we'd like to briefly mention what types of Bryce settings affect the outcome of the Render Report.

- *Antialiasing.* The factors that determine antialiasing are the joining of one contour to another, the presence of a bump map, the presence of high-contrast color, and the presence of high-frequency detail.

- *Primary Rays.* These are determined by the total number of pixels, the total number of antialiased pixels, and a third category that's harder to quantify: the specialized optic conditions. Additionally, if you happen to be rendering any objects with volume, your primary ray count will be affected. Strangely enough, there appears to be an inverse relationship between the quality setting and the primary ray and secondary ray counts. At lower quality settings, the primary ray count is higher, and the shadow ray setting is low. At higher quality setting, the shadow ray count shoots way high, and the primary ray count is lower.

- *Shadow Rays.* These are determined by the shadow settings in the Materials Lab's Material Options pop-up menu, the shadow setting in the Sky & Fog Palette, as well as the presence and number of additional light sources in a scene. The shadow ray count shoots way up for objects with volume materials that use Basic Shading or Full Shading mode.

- *Ray Hits and Ray Misses.* These counts will be significantly larger due to optical material surfaces and additional light sources. Also, hits and misses are determined by the overall structure of objects: how many there are and whether or not they occupy the greater part of the scene.

So reduce those numbers if you dare—or can. For a better understanding, look at several scene files and read their render reports. Check the Render folder of the CD-ROM for a set of examples to study.

"While You Are Working" Rendering

Of course, in Bryce you don't simply build a scene, place objects hither and thither, and assign materials and sky settings without also performing many intermediate, "Am I on the right track?" renders along the way. Bryce has a couple of render modes just for working on in-progress renders: Textures Off and Fast Preview modes. Bryce 4 added a new mechanism for rendering small portions of your scene on the fly: the Ray Spray tool.

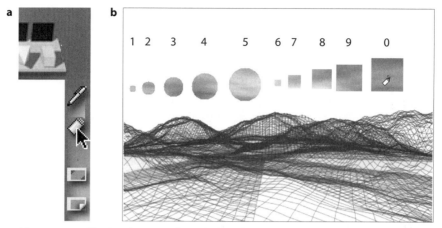

Figure 13.5 The Ray Spray tool: a) Finding the control on the Advanced Display Palette; b) the available nozzle sizes and the corresponding key commands.

Ray Spray

The Ray Spray tool changes your cursor into a little spray can—drag your mouse across an area of your scene and it will "spray" pixels of the rendered image as it passes (no antialiasing is performed, however). The longer you scrub that area with the Ray Spray tool, the more image detail fills in. Normally out of sight, the control that turns on the Ray Spray tool lives on the hidden Display/Wireframe Palette. Move your mouse over the strip of gray along the right side of the Bryce working window to make the icons appear (see Figure 13.5a); click the spray can icon to enable Ray Spray. You have a choice of 10 nozzles for your faux spray can, five round and five square, in a range of sizes. Pick a size by typing a number from 1 to 0 on your keyboard; Figure 13.5b shows each size with its assigned number.

Ray Spray works slightly differently depending on whether you're in Wireframe mode or Render mode.

Wireframe Mode

In Wireframe mode, the Ray Spray product is a temporary preview; as soon as you click the mouse to dismiss the Ray Spray tool, your rendered pixels disappear.

Render Mode

The portion of your image that you Ray Spray while in Render mode becomes part of the rendered image of your scene. If you choose Resume Render after using Ray Spray, the sprayed area is incorporated into the image.

Textures Off Render

When the Textures Off render option is selected, most of the surface attributes of the objects in your scene will not be rendered. Likewise for the sky—clouds, haze, and fog will be absent. This setting is good for determining the basic shape of your image and for setting up the geometry and composition. The colors of objects can vary widely, however. That's because they take their color information from the diffuse color in the Materials Composer. Even if the object's surface color is determined by a 3D texture source, whatever color is in the color swatch for Diffuse Color will be the color of the object—ignore what the manual says about a color being taken from the Ambient Color channel. To double-check, move the marker out of the Texture Source columns back into the Color Swatch column and see what the Diffuse Color value is. If you need to distinguish objects from one another, you can quickly sneak in a global Diffuse Color "under" the texture color.

Notice that we said most of your objects' surface attributes won't be rendered. In spite of what the Bryce manual says, if you have assigned reflection or transparency to any objects, they will render as such even when you select Textures Off. By now, you should understand that reflection and transparency are two of the more expensive items contributing to your render time—too bad they never fixed that No Texture Render bug, which has existed since Bryce 2 Windows.

Fast Preview Render

Fast Preview is a two-pass version of a basic render. It renders surface textures and fog, haze, and clouds, trading off speed for some imperfections in the rendered results. Use it while you are working on in-progress renders, when you've moved from the basic composition to decisions about material settings. With its speed and imperfections, Fast Render's not the option of choice at the stage where you are checking minute details of your sky or objects. It won't provide meaningful feedback on, say, the detail pattern of the surface's bump map. But if you want to test whether the snow is falling where you want it, this quick render will do the job admirably.

Rendering in Progress: Earlier Stages

To get a better sense of overall image detail, zoom out while in Render mode (click the Zoom tool or tap the minus key on the keypad) and then begin rendering your scene. Those first few passes will give you a general sense of the image. Reducing the image's size onscreen increases the apparent resolution, so you can get a better idea after one or two passes of how the image is developing.

Rendering in Progress: Later Stages

This render technique is good for the later stages of scene building, when you're doing some serious fine-tuning—when you have performed at least one initial render and you come back to the scene the next day or after your lunch hour or…

Suppose you have a scene and a PICT or BMP saved from a previous working session. You open the image and decide it needs further tinkering. After tweaking it here and there and doing little test renders for each tweak, what do you have? Many subtle changes displayed in a fine mess of coarse pixels. What if you want to get a quick look at the changes—against a completely rendered background—before you leave your computer to complete its rendering work in peace?

Select File > Open Pict (Macintosh) or Open Image (Windows) to go back to your original rendered image. Think of this move as a partial revert to saved. With it, you revert to the saved image but retain all the intermediate changes you made to your scene document when you were having that fruitful dialog with the Bryce Muse. (Bryce will ask you if you want to save changes when you open the image. You don't. Of course, if you've saved your scene document along the way, the newly opened image might not be as dramatic when you go to rerender over the image from when you saved the scene yesterday.) After you open your original image, simply drag a marquee around the area you want to render and then select Clear and Render. The rest of the image stays. You can clearly see the changes you made. Your scene document underneath keeps the changes.

You can render on top of *any* image, even if it's not an image created with Bryce. If you're looking for a new experimental medium for creating rendered abstractions, open any image file, drag a marquee around an area, and render. The Abstract Muse will tell you what to do next.

When you save the scene (and your Preferences are set to Open and Save Image with Scene), Bryce will write the new image over the old image. Say you have opened a scene document called ORIGINAL SCENE (Windows: ORIGINAL SCENE.BRC). The accompanying image document is called ORIGINAL SCENE.PCT (Windows: ORIGINAL SCENE.BMP). Then you open an image from a variation on this scene that is named SECOND SCENE.PCT (Windows: SECOND SCENE.BMP). Opening a subsequent image closes the first one. You render over portions of the new image to see changes made since you worked in SECOND SCENE and SECOND SCENE.PCT (Windows: SECOND SCENE.BRC and SECOND SCENE.BMP). When you save the scene (⌘-S or Ctrl+S), then this new rendered image will be renamed ORIGINAL SCENE.PCT (Windows: ORIGINAL SCENE.BMP). The scene document that is open takes precedence in the writing and naming of the accompanying image document.

This technique of opening older images is good for seeing changes in a scene's object placement, size, materials, position, and sky. It is not as successful for seeing changes in camera position, since everything in your scene will have changed.

"When You Are Finished" Rendering

You have finished working with your scene. Now it's time for the final render.

For your final render, make sure that you start from scratch. On the Control Palette, click Render Scene, or when you are in Render mode, select all and then select Clear & Render. You can select Clear and Render from the Edit menu by clicking the Clear and Render button on the Control Palette or by using the keyboard shortcut, ⌘-Option-R (Macintosh) or Ctrl+Alt+R (Windows).

Why do either of these things? In all likelihood, you made minor changes since the first tentative pixels were rendered at the beginning of your session. Perhaps you moved the camera slightly or changed the orientation of the 2D Projection plane. If you just click Resume Render (or type ⌘-R or Ctrl+R), you will not completely overwrite the older rendered portion. In fact, the finished render will have ghosts of the old render. This is especially true in the Macintosh version, where the fourth channel of the PICT image keeps track of the render's progress. The fourth channel has different patterns for each stage of the render. During the render, Bryce looks at the fourth channel and says, "Yes, well, but that's been done already" and so overlooks the area for the next couple of passes. However, that portion that's been "done already" may not be the most recent revision of the scene; the PICT's fourth channel remembers where the render left off, but it doesn't check to make sure that what it calls "rendered already" is, in fact, the *latest* version of the scene. That's for *you* to do, and it's easy enough: Just click that big Render Scene button on the Control Palette.

The Windows version does not have an alpha channel to track the render's progress, and the bitmap file format does not even contain a fourth channel, so it cannot keep track of the render's progress on a pixel-by-pixel basis. So where does the information about the render's progress reside? Bryce Windows keeps track of it and stores it in the scene file itself, noting the line number and general location of the render progress.

Batch Rendering

One of the joys of Bryce is its ability to do batch rendering. It works through the computer system's drag-and-drop feature. Drag the scene icons (*not* the PICT or BMP icons) and drop them onto the Bryce Application icon (or alias or shortcut). We keep an alias to the Bryce application on each of our desktops and drag all of our scene icons onto them. When batch rendering, Bryce opens a scene, renders it, saves the image and the corresponding scene file, and then moves on to the next one on the list.

Of course, batch rendering, like other complete renders, should be started over again from a fresh new render to ensure that there are no weird in-progress render anomalies left from previous work on the scene. Before you save a scene to be batch rendered, click the Render Scene button and let the render go for a single pass (or even less if you're fast enough!). Click again to stop the render and then save the scene file, which is now ready for batch rendering. When it batch renders that scene, Bryce will pick up the render from the point you just left off.

As with so many other things in Bryce, batch rendering sets a trap for the unwary. Make sure not to include any scenes that have been completely rendered among the group you batch render. If you do, Bryce will render on its merry way through the various scenes until it reaches a scene file that's completely rendered. Upon encountering that file, it comes to a halt, thinking, "Well, obviously my work is done," and renders no more. Unless that scene was the last in the batch queue, Bryce has prematurely stopped the batch render. Oops!

Of the selected scenes that are dropped onto the Bryce application icon, how do you know which one will render first? On the Macintosh, that depends on how you selected the scene files. If you Shift-click to select a number of files, the scenes are rendered in the order in which you selected them. If you drag a marquee around a group of files, whether in List or Icon View, Bryce renders the scenes in the order of the files' creation dates, from newest to oldest. What about the order for Windows? In Windows, scenes are rendered according to their creation dates, from oldest to youngest.

BEYOND THE BASIC RENDERING MODEL

Everything we've discussed so far fits into the category of basic rendering—how Bryce operates during rendering and how you can make your trips to RenderLand more pleasant. In this section, we depart from the basic. First, we discuss the rendering of large images and the option of rendering really large images to disk. Then we consider each of the other render options available on the Render pop-up menu: 360° Panorama and rendering for post-processing using Distance Render, Altitude Render, and Mask Render.

Rendering Large Images

How large can you make your Bryce images? Bryce gives you an array of options in the Document Setup dialog box. It's very easy to proportionately enlarge an existing size to one of the available ratios: 1:1.5, 1:2, 1:3, or 1:4. To create render resolutions that are even larger, say 1:6, you can see what the resolution is at 1:3. Enter those numbers in the Document Resolution section and then select 1:2.

If you don't have enough memory to render at a large resolution, then you can always use the Render to Disk option (see the next section). (If you run into any memory ceilings, you will be told along the way that Bryce won't participate to your liking.)

Here are some image resolution and memory considerations to keep in mind. Bryce will limit your maximum image size according to the amount of memory available. If you have chosen a size larger than what Bryce will be able to accommodate, you will get the alert "An unexpected error has occurred (out of memory)." Not to worry—your image just returns to its previous resolution.

The maximum size of a rendered PICT image (on the Macintosh) is 4096. Bryce—for both platforms—goes up to only 4000; that is the maximum size that Bryce will render or save an image. When you're in the Document Setup dialog box, you won't be able to enter anything higher than 4000 for sizes. You can, however, render larger than that to disk. The TIFF file format and the Photoshop 3.0 file format are not limited by a maximum size, so you can create sizes larger and actually save them. Although the Render to Disk dialog box for naming your file gives you the options of choosing among the three file formats, if you're using a Mac and have selected, say, a 6000 × 6000 image, you can still select PICT and

Bryce will begin rendering away. We didn't hang out long enough through a render of that size to see what Bryce does at the end, but if you want to try it for kicks, go ahead. It won't be pretty.

a

b
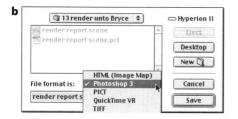

c
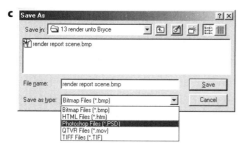

d
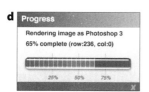

Figure 13.6 Render to disk: a) The Bryce Render to Disk dialog box; b) the File Save dialog box with the File Format pop-up menu and the same file name as a scene file (Macintosh); c) the Save As dialog box in Windows; d) the Render to Disk progress bar.

When you're rendering large format scenes (ones that take 12 to 24 or more hours to render), saving the scene from time to time is a good precaution. Then if a thunderstorm winks your electricity off and sends that big, beautiful render to file heaven, you'll at least have the rendered image data from the last time you saved the render.

Also, any time you increase the render resolution, you may need to increase your terrain resolutions accordingly. Although a terrain with a resolution of 256 may serve admirably in the foreground of a scene that's at Bryce's default size, once you double or triple the render resolution, you may get triangle-shaped pock marks in a terrain of that size. Increase the resolution of your terrains if you need to.

Render to Disk

To render to disk, select Render to Disk from the File menu. You'll be presented with a dialog box that enables you to select your final size (see Figure 13.6a). Unlike normal rendering, which requires enough RAM to keep the Bryce application, the scene file, and the number of pixels for the rendered image all in dynamic memory, the Render to Disk option enables you to render an image larger than your RAM would allow. So if you have, say, 64 MB of RAM on your computer and a scene file that would render fine at, say a 1:1.5 ratio but chokes when you try to render it at a ratio of 1:2, 1:3, or 1:4, you can render the scene to disk and sneak around the memory limitation.

You can select the final size and determine the image resolution, that is, the number of pixels that are displayed in an inch (if you're a centimeter person, well, sorry!). Bryce calculates the total number of inches for the scene.

You can an also choose the QTVR option. We'll discuss that in a separate section on rendering 360° panorama views.

When you have set up your dimensions and click OK, you'll be presented with a dialog box for naming your image (see Figures 13.6b and c). The current file name is there for you Macintosh Brycers already (see Figure 13.6b). It is the name of your scene file.

Urgent Warning! Make sure that you change the name slightly. Otherwise, you'll overwrite your scene file and cause untold hours of frustration and misery as you wonder where in tarnation it went. (It was replaced by a rendered image.) If you realize you just overwrote the scene file while the scene is yet rendering to disk, you still have an escape hatch: Resave the scene file under a different name. At the end of a completed render, Bryce will usually ask you if you want to save the scene (and image). Do so. Give it another name, just in case. Windows users need not worry about accidental overwrites since Windows automatically appends the file extension to the file name and does not place the current file name in the Save As dialog box.

Once you've sent the render on its merry way, you'll see a modal window with a progress bar (see Figure 13.6c). At that point, you can put Bryce in the background so that you can do other tasks on your computer. Just pray that the second software that you're using is not buggy or allergic to Bryce or vice versa, because if something should go wrong, all your rendering is down the drain. In fact, you cannot save a partially rendered render-to-disk image; it's all or nothing. Nor can you start a render and resume it. Once you commit yourself, you're committed (this is why you pray that all your software is very stable).

At the end of the process, you will be presented with the beloved Render Report (if you have chosen this option). This is helpful for, among other things, conducting tests of rendering capabilities. Seriously, though, the information is helpful if, say, you use this procedure to render an image that's a rough; then you know approximately how long it took so when the client asks you to make some changes and then deliver it in *n* minutes/hours/days, you'll know exactly what you're up against.

360° Rendering

To render the entire panorama encircled by the camera position, select 360 Panorama Render. First we'll talk about the general procedures for setting up Bryce to render panorama images. Then we'll give you a short introduction to creating a special kind of panorama: a QuickTime VR movie.

Whatever your current image size is, the 360° panorama will be squished into that space—and squished is an accurate word, especially if your image format is nearly square (see Figure 13.7). A 360° panorama is best for very wide images.

a

b

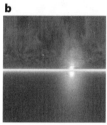

Figure 13.7 a) Wide and b) squished panoramas.

Bryce's Document Setup dialog box gives you a couple of options for panoramas. There's the simple Panorama aspect ratio, which is good for nice wide scenes. Then there's the QTVR Panorama aspect ratio, useful for—you guessed it—creating QuickTime VR movies.

Bryce's 360 Panorama Render is like projecting the entire scene onto the round vertical wall of a cylinder. The image comes to a stop at top and bottom; this is not a spherical render.

It is critical to ensure that your camera is level. An unlevel camera causes your horizon to undulate like a sine wave, as shown in Figure 13.8. Ensure that your horizon is level by double-clicking the Camera controls on the Main Palette to access the Camera dialog box. There, the Camera Angle values of x and z should be 0. For a 360° panorama that takes in what's below and above as well as both horizons, enter 90 for either the x or the z axis.

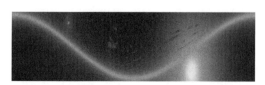

Figure 13.8 A wavy horizon resulting from an unlevel camera.

To have convincing image detail close to the camera and larger terrains far off (see Figure 13.9a), set up a whole series of small terrains very close to the camera. In fact, make sure that a terrain is placed *under* the camera. It needs, of course, to be a higher-resolution terrain. Figure 13.9b shows the top view of the scene with terrains on all sides of the camera.

a

b

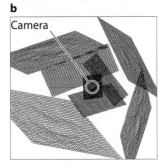

Figure 13.9 A 360° render where land surrounds the camera: a) 360° render; b) top view of wireframe.

Because you are creating a panorama that goes in a complete circle, you need to look at your scene from different perspectives as you set it up. Use the Camera Memory Dots to add different perspective views so that you can move back and forth between them, or go to the top view and move the camera position and then switch back to Camera View and add that view.

Or enter the numbers in the Camera dialog box. Note that if you want to position your camera at World Center, then set the offsets for *x* and *z* to 0. Offset *y* refers to how far off the ground the camera is. The camera angle *y* points your camera to the four directions: 90, 180, 270, and 0 (or 360). Enter those numbers and save a view for each. You can work with developing your scene that way. In the end, your panorama will incorporate those views.

Here's another way to preview the placement of objects in a panorama: Use the Perspective Trackball. Press the Control (Macintosh) or Alt (Windows) key and then drag the Trackball. The camera will be constrained along the *x* axis and rotate in a circle. You can check for object positioning in wireframe view.

The Zoom and Field of View controls have no bearing on 360° rendered scenes. Your placement of the camera in the 2D Projection plane, however, does affect the way the final render appears. In fact, if your image is rendering very strangely and you're hard pressed to know how to fix it, pan up or down to change the placement of the 2D Projection plane. Often the wireframe view and the rendered view do not match. Make sure that the rendered view takes precedence.

QTVR

QuickTime Virtual Reality (QTVR) is a movie format available for both Macintosh and Windows. In a QTVR movie, you can navigate through areas at will. There are two different QTVR movie formats. The panorama movie places you in the center of a virtual cylinder (just like the cylindrical images created by Bryce's 360 Panorama Render). You can turn in any direction to look at any area of the cylinder. Zoom in or zoom out. Look up or look down. The second type of movie is an object movie. In an object movie, you can "pick up" an object and examine it on all sides by dragging vertically and horizontally. We'll tell you how to use Bryce to create an object movie in Chapter 15, "Advanced Animation Techniques."

When Apple first introduced QTVR, the technology was intended only for photography, and Apple offered specialized photographic equipment to create a perfect panorama and software that required stitching several image portions together. Some quick-thinking Brycers realized that the 360° Panorama Render would work beautifully to create a QTVR movie, merrily skipping the process of the careful photographic and stitch process. The Bryce QTVR process has been on the virtual-reality creation scene ever since. (Trivia note about those quick-thinking Brycers: One was David Palermo, who in pre-QTVR 1.0 days worked for Apple Computer, Inc. He went on to become the QuickTime VR Product Manager at Apple, and then later became the last Bryce Product Manager at MetaCreations, before the company decided to divest itself of its professional graphics product line. Since Palermo had—and has—such a passion for both technologies, we can't help but wonder what QTVR goodies would have lain in store in the MetaCreations' version of Bryce 5.)

Creating and tweaking QuickTime VR movies is a rich and complex process, and we can only give you the basics here. For a deeper understanding of the subject, we happily refer you to another book by Susan, *The QuickTime VR Book*, also published by Peachpit Press:

http://www.peachpit.com/ books/catalog/69684.html

There are two basic procedures for making a QuickTime VR panorama with Bryce: the quick and dirty version, which is open to both Mac and Windows users, and the slightly more involved, sophisticated version, which requires a Macintosh (though the original image can be created on a Windows machine). We'll start with the latter.

Create a scene in Bryce. In the document Setup dialog box, choose the QTVR Panorama option. You can choose the dimensions yourself, as long as the aspect ratio is 13:4, the width is divisible by 96, and the height is divisible by 4. Render the scene in 360 Panorama mode. You can then render the panorama and perform some manual tweaks to it, or render automatically. (We'll describe both approaches so that you understand what the automatic version is doing.)

The manual method: When you have completed and saved the render, open it in Photoshop (or some other graphics editing application) and rotate it 90° (for this, rotate it counterclockwise). This puts it in the vertical orientation that QTVR needs to create a panorama movie. If you're creating the image in Windows, convert it from a *.BMP to a *.PCT file at some point along the way.

The automatic method: Bryce will both render and rotate for you if you select File > Render to Disk and check the Rotate 90° option in the Render to Disk dialog box that Bryce displays.

The Macintosh freeware applet QTVR Make Panorama 2 allows you to make a panorama movie. You can download it from Apple's QTVR Web site:

http://developer.apple.com/quicktime/quicktimeintro/tools/

If you have other QTVR panorama-creation software, by all means, use it! If you're using Windows, you may be interested in the offerings of VR Toolbox (www.vrtoolbox.com), which has Windows-based applications as well as MacOS ones.

1. Launch QTVR Make Panorama 2. The applet gives you an Open dialog box for loading your PICT image. Load your image.

2. You do not see the image, but you get a dialog box for choosing options to create your movie. (See Figure 13.10a for the QTVR Make Panorama dialog box.) There are a set of options for Compression, Size, Horizontal Pan, Vertical Pan, and Zoom, along with options to name and choose the locations for the files that the panorama maker will create for you.

3. Determine the Compression setting. The default option, Cinepak, will create QTVR movies that are compatible with the widest variety of platforms and older versions of QuickTime. If you are reasonably sure that

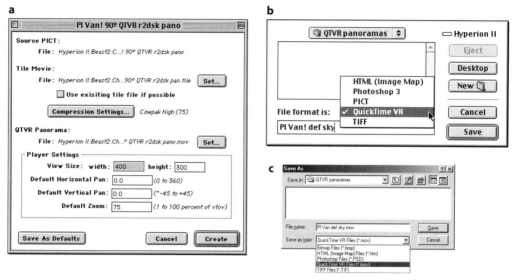

Figure 13.10 Making QuickTime VR panorama movies: a) The dialog box for Apple's freeware Make QuickTime Panorama 2 application; b) selecting the QTVR option to have Bryce automatically render and then save a QTVR panorama movie for you in the Mac OS; c) rendering a QTVR panorama to disk in Windows.

your audience will have access to recent versions of QuickTime (3 and above), you might want to try other types of compression, like JPEG or Sorenson Video, which produce higher-quality output. For more information on various compression schemes (or codecs, from "coder-decoder,") consult Terran Interactive's Web site, Codec Central:

http://www.terran.com/CodecCentral/index.html

4. Set the View Size. This option determines the size of your QTVR window when you open the movie. Make sure to choose dimensions that are no higher than the actual Bryce render image size. When your QTVR window size is significantly smaller (such as half or a quarter of the height of the scene render image size), then you'll be able to use the QTVR viewer's zoom tools to zoom in on the scene for more detail.

5. Set the Horizontal and Vertical Pan. These options allow you to choose where the virtual camera focuses when you first open the QTVR movie. The horizontal rotation starts by focusing on the left edge (well, the right edge, too, since they end up being set next to one another). If the object you want to focus on is in the middle of your image (probably a more natural way to work when in Bryce, since Bryce's camera aim puts the part of the image that the camera sees in the center of the rendered strip), then you'll

need to enter 180° to place the focal part of the render into the center part of your panorama movie.

Vertical Pan has a range of positive or negative 45° for looking up or down. Depending on your subject matter, you may find yourself wanting to adjust up or down.

6. Determine the Zoom. Since a QTVR panorama movie allows zooming in and out, you can set the default zoom: 1000 is zoomed all the way in (very blocky pixels, yuck!), and 0 is zoomed all the way out. For a nice, pleasing look, start with something in the 0 to 50 range.

7. Once you have all those settings in place, click the Create button. After a bit of Bryce cogitation, you'll have a completed movie! Open it in the QuickTime Player, and there you go!

Now for the quick and dirty version: One of the new features in Bryce 4 is the capability to export a QuickTime VR movie directly, without going through another program like QTVR Make Panorama. Be forewarned, though, that you get none of the nice bells and whistles that Apple's free utility provides. Bryce picks a default size, camera orientation, zoom, angle, and compression scheme (Cinepak), and that's it.

Set up your file as described for the QTVR Make Panorama procedure and choose 360 Panorama Render. Use the Render to Disk command, and check the 90° rotation option. When you are presented with the Save dialog box, choose QTVR movie from the pop-up menu (see Figure 13.10b). Let Bryce do its stuff, and a lovely QTVR movie is the result.

Render Post-processing

Besides Perspective and 360 Panorama, the Render pop-up menu offers three other options: Mask Render, Distance Render, and Altitude Render. These are useful for creating post-processing effects after the initial render, as well as for other kinds of scene-building techniques. With them, you're not choosing either one or the other; you can do both. First, perform the basic Perspective Render; then go back and render an additional image: a mask to use for special post-processing. You can do the same with Distance Render. Since Mask and Distance Renders are both much faster than a basic Perspective render, you can render live and export the image. We'll discuss Distance and Altitude Renders first, since they have aspects in common, and then discuss Mask Render afterward.

Distance Render

Distance Render creates a grayscale image based on the distance of the object from the camera. The closer the object is, the darker the value that is rendered; the further away the object is, the lighter the value. Sky far away is white.

The range of gray values is determined by the overall placement of objects in your scene. If your camera is located outside of the bounds of all objects, then you will see a full range of black to white. (This includes the placement of the ground plane, even though it renders infinitely. Its placement in the scene will affect the overall tonal range.) Often your camera is placed within the scene, so the range of grays are more limited.

Distance Render is handy for creating selection masks that vary depending on distance for such things as motion blurs, depth-of-field focus, and so on. In the raytracing render model, all objects are rendered "in focus." To create a realistic unfocus, use Distance Render.

For those objects whose materials are other-than-plain-ol'-normal (alternative Shading modes of Fuzzy, Fuzzy Additive, Light, or Additive; Alpha-driven Transparency, Volume material, with or without texture-driven Base Density), Bryce will not take any of the peculiarities of the shading mode into account during its Altitude Render. The object will be rendered the same as if it had that default plastic gray material.

Creating Blur Effects with Distance Render

Although in some cases you'll do a partial render without saving the resulting image, using Distance Render to create a selection mask requires that the entire scene be rendered and the image saved. (Use Save Image As or Export Image from the File menu; if you use the Save command, the Distance Rendered image will overwrite your color *.PCT or *.BMP file.) As a naming convention, we add -DX (hyphen DX) to the file name; resource documents on the CD-ROM with that suffix are Distance Renders.

In a Distance Render, the gray levels provide you with the means to create a blur based on distance from the camera. Although you see a grayscale image, the Distance Render is still an RGB image with four channels. In Photoshop, load one channel as a selection for the basic Perspective image (see Figure 13.11a). If you invert the selection, the blur will take place in the foreground (see Figure 13.11b). If you leave the selection as is, the blurring will occur in the distance.

Figure 13.11 Distance Render blurring: a) Distance Render mask; b) foreground blur; c) Distance Render using Blur More; d) distance blur using Gaussian Blur; 3) detail comparison of Blur More and Gaussian Blur.

We find that several applications of the Blur More filter (see Figure 13.11c) are better than a single application of Gaussian Blur (see Figure 13.11d). In Gaussian Blur, the edges of the mask will prohibit the blur from being applied to the masked-off area. However, it will not prohibit the blur from picking up information from behind that mask to mix with the neighboring pixels. The result is a strange, unnatural glow. See the close-up of the two types of blurs in Figure 13.11e. Blur More is on the left, and Gaussian Blur is on the right.

Another approach to blurring is to change the selection mask to create a depth-of-field blur. The blur is applied to the foreground and background, with the area in the middle ground staying in focus. To do this, you need to use Photoshop's Curves. The grayscale information in the selection mask is based on distance, so if you change the gray values to make portions lighter or darker, you will enable something that affects only that one area.

Figure 13.12a shows a grayscale image. In the middle ground is a cabin and water-wheel. Those objects need to be changed to black (or very dark gray), so that the image will be in focus and any blurring applied won't affect them. Change it using the Curves dialog box in Photoshop (see Figure 13.12b). Adjust the curves so that the darkest colors, up close, are lighter. Darken the tones where depth-of-field sharpness is important. The resulting blur is applied to the foreground and in the distance (see Figure 13.12c).

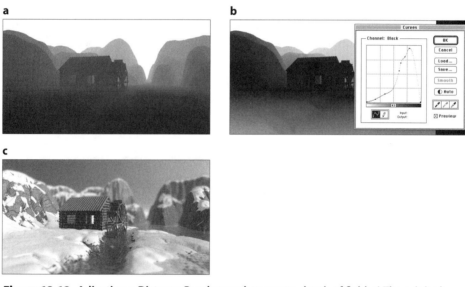

Figure 13.12 Adjusting a Distance Render mask to create depth of field: a) The original mask; b) masking adjusted with Photoshop's Curves; c) resulting blur.

Altitude Render

A cousin to Distance Render, Altitude Render takes all points at the same elevation and gives them the same gray or color value. Like in the Terrain Editor's grayscale-to-height map, the highest points are white and the lowest points are black. Unlike Distance Render, where the camera angle has everything to do with the final render, Altitude Render's camera perspective doesn't have any affect on the ultimate values rendered. Everything located at the "light gray" elevation will be that light gray, no matter which way you look at it.

Like Distance Render, Altitude Render determines the full range of gray from the highest point of the highest object in the scene to the lowest point. If you add an object that's higher than all the rest and rerender, Bryce will have adjusted for this new highest height and reset the range of grays. Altitude Render provides an excellent method for the impromptu creation of terrain or other grayscale data from top view.

Using Altitude Renders to Work with Terrains

When rendering from top view, Altitude Render is good for working with the scene as a whole. Use Altitude Render while your work on a scene is in progress. Suppose you need to take a look at a terrain's shape in the context of the scene. Your terrain is in place, resized, and rotated, and you don't want to touch its orientation. You do, however, want to shave off or augment a ridge for aesthetic balance. To know which part of the terrain to darken, you need to understand how the terrain is oriented. An Altitude Render from top view (see Figure 13.13a) will give you a grayscale image, and you'll be able to recognize the landmarks so that you can alter the terrain as need be in the Terrain Editor (see Figure 13.13b).

a   b

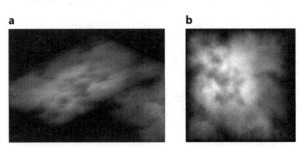

Figure 13.13 Altitude Render for terrain context:
a) A top view Altitude Render of the terrain in position;
b) grayscale-to-height map of that same terrain

To create the Altitude Render, go to top view. Locate the terrain and then tap the Escape (esc) key to switch to Render mode. Draw a marquee around the area to be rendered. In the Render pop-up menu, change to Altitude Render and then click Clear and Render. After a few passes, you will see the orientation of your terrain.

You can also use Altitude Render to create a larger terrain comprised of smaller ones, or a sandy build-up at the base of other objects, whether terrains or other

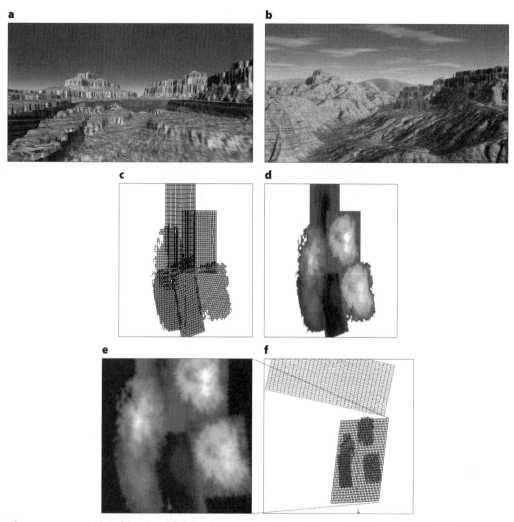

Figure 13.14 a) The old scene; b) the new scene; c) top view wireframe of old scene; d) the Altitude Render; e) the new terrain grayscale map based on the Altitude Render; f) wireframe for the new scene.

objects. When creating mountains and valleys, do an Altitude Render from top view. The render will become the image used to create the larger terrain that incorporates transitions between smaller terrains (see Figure 13.14).

In this scene, Distance Render was used to solve the problem of creating a smooth transition from mountain to valley (see "Superlative Nature Imagery," Chapter 16). Rather than the scene's having four separate terrains (three as mountains and one as valley; see Figures 13.14a and 13.14c), the entire area was rendered from the top as an Altitude Render in order to incorporate both mountain and valley.

1. To create a new terrain map, the scene was rendered from top view using Altitude Render (see Figure 13.14d).

2. Then the rendered image was exported as a ⋆.PCT or ⋆.BMP file, using the Save Image As command. (If you want to work on-the-fly, you can do the same thing with a screen capture utility that allows you to draw a marquee around the specific area you wish to capture.).

3. The old terrain that had been the valley was selected and then the Terrain Editor was accessed. Using the Pictures tab, the Distance Rendered image was brought into the Terrain Editor (see Figure 13.14e).

4. Finally, the terrain was spread out over the area covered by the Altitude Render (see Figure 13.14f).

Mask Render

Mask Rendering takes a selected object or objects and renders a mask. The selected objects (see Figure 13.15a) will be white, and all else will be black (see Figure 13.15b). If the object is behind another object, then only the portion that is visible to the camera will render. If everything is selected (see Figure 13.15c), then all objects in the scene will be rendered as a mask; the sky will be black, and every-

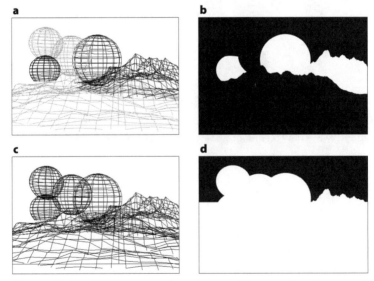

Figure 13.15 a) Objects are selected and so b) are rendered as a mask; c) all objects are selected and so d) all are rendered as a mask.

thing else will be white (see Figure 13.15d). If nothing is selected, then nothing will render as a mask.

Mask Rendering for Work in Progress

Use a Mask Render while you work to determine if a particular object is showing and, if so, how much of it is showing from a particular camera angle or from the object's placement. Mask Render helps you fine-tune the positions of the object and the camera. Like Distance Render, Mask Render requires much simpler computation by Bryce's renderer. Figure 13.16a shows Mask Render used to verify that the waterfall can be seen from the indicated camera position (see Figure 13.16b).

Figure 13.16 Mask Render used in progress: a) Mask Render; b) final render.

Mask Render is good to use when one terrain (such as rocks) is poking out of another terrain. When the scene is viewed as a wireframe, you can see what part of an object is above ground level. But when both objects are above ground level, you can't easily see whether one object pokes out beyond another object. Select the one underneath and use Mask Render.

Because Mask Render allows you to specify which object or objects will render, you can test certain things by selecting the objects and rendering. Suppose a scene with many objects appears on screen as a confusing jumble. You want to know whether object A has the same wireframe color as the others (you want to assign the same material setting to the whole set, and you want to ensure that all are included). Select by family and then render as a mask. If you can see object A in silhouette, you'll have your answer. If the jumble of objects is sufficiently confusing, using this method may be faster than tabbing through the lot until the desired object is selected.

Mask Render and Transparent Objects

Rendering selected objects doesn't work in all cases as you'd like it to—at least, if you have a picture object (like that Leonardo guy or the glasses shown in Figure 13.17a) and want to render a mask of the object in position in your scene, you won't be able to. The object is the square, and individual points of transparency as introduced by the image mask won't affect the rendering of the object's shape. (The same holds true for partially transparent objects in 3D Solid textures, which is why you'll never be able to make an accurate mask of freestanding clouds.)

There are workarounds for this, however painstaking they may be. To render a mask of a picture object, you need to fake the mask part. You don't need to create a whole new scene for this; Solo mode will do admirably when combined with another trick or two.

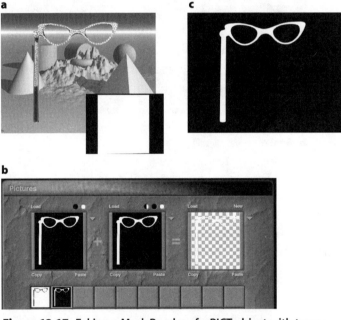

Figure 13.17 Faking a Mask Render of a PICT object with transparency: a) The scene before Mask Render with a standard Mask Render inset; b) the mask image pasted in both the image and mask areas; c) the final faked mask rendered in Solo mode.

1. Save your scene before you try any of the next steps. You won't save anything that you'll do to the scene file, and you can simply use Revert to Saved to get back to where you were.

2. Save your current sky with a Memory Dot. Then change the sky mode to No Atmosphere and select black for Background Hue.

3. Select your picture object. In the Materials Lab, select source B (or C or D) and assign it to 2D Picture. Click the Texture Source Editor button to access the Picture Library. When you're there, copy the mask from the source image. Select a new item in the library and paste the mask in both the first and the second areas (see Figure 13.17b).

4. In the Materials Lab, assign Ambient and Diffuse Colors to column B where your mask picture is. (The reason for not assigning the transparency as well is that you'll keep the old source. Later it's a matter of clicking column A to revert your object to its former state.)

5. Go to Solo mode and render the white mask against a black sky. Export the image to a new mask file (see Figure 13.17c). Was that easy or was that…well, at least a way to get your desired result?

Also, if you need to create a mask of a partially transparent object, such as a cloud, create a separate scene file with different settings. Get rid of other objects in the background and make the sky a flat color (black or white). Change your object's color to white with high ambience so that even shadowed areas render. A normal render will create an alpha channel mask that you can use for compositing transparent, wispy, cottony, or otherwise semi-visible objects.

Mask Render for Finished Rendering

Of course, Mask Render also creates a mask for selections to use in post-processing. Select all elements in your scene to render a mask that will have only your sky showing. If you need to do any post-processing of only the sky, then you can easily select just that one part of the scene with the mask.

Mask Render, Antialiasing, and Compositing

What if you want antialiasing only on the edges of objects? Making this happen involves a bit of extra work, but for the right scene, it's worth it. The scene in Figure 13.18, *Deep Undulating Canyon*, has a lovely texture when seen in the last

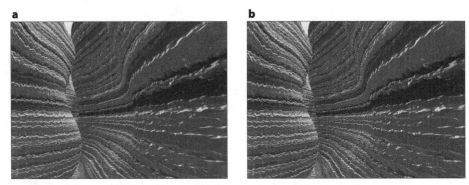

Figure 13.18 Scene shown rendered: a) With and b) without antialiasing

render pass. It's rough, and you can just sense the sandpapery texture of the rock face by the way the render looks. Once it's antialiased, the rock will be metamorphosed into some other thing that, well, might be plastic (see Figure 13.18a). Needless to say, the un–antialiased version is better (see Figure 13.18b). However, the edges of objects are a bit too rough; those are the areas that need to be antialiased. How to do it? Combine Mask Render in Bryce with some Photoshop manipulation to create masks for the edges and then happily marry the two render versions: antialiased and rough.

Case Study: Antialiased Edges in a Rough Rendered World

To create a Bryce scene that mixes antialiasing and non-antialiasing, follow these steps:

1. Use Mask Render to create masks of each individual object (see Figure 13.19a). This render generally happens pretty quickly, so you can use the one scene document and export the rendered mask images, giving each one a different name.

2. Change the Render option to Perspective. Then save the scene with a suffix that includes something meaningful, such as -NO AA. In the Render pop-up menu, uncheck the AntiAliasing option so that this first render will not have antialiasing. When the scene is finished rendering, save it again.

3. Immediately save the scene document with a different name, changing the suffix to -YES AA. Change the Render option so that antialiasing is *on* and then click Resume Render or type ⌘-R or Ctrl+R. (Don't start from scratch; you've already done the first five passes!) When the antialiasing pass is completed, save the scene and image combination again.

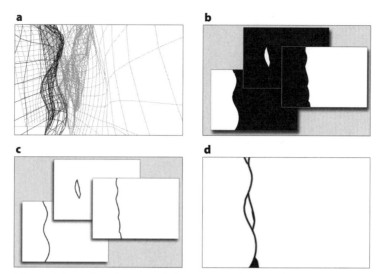

Figure 13.19 Creating a mask for compositing: a) Selecting one wireframe;
b) mask for each object; c) blurred and Find Edges; d) combined edges mask.

Continue in Photoshop or some other image editing application with these steps:

4. Open each of the mask images and change them to grayscale. Blur each one slightly and then apply the Find Edges filter (see Fig. 13.19c).

5. Create a combined edges mask. Make each mask a layer in a composite image document and set all but the bottom layer to the Darken mode to combine them (see Figure 13.19d). (In this case, the area at the bottom where the water is located was added to the mask using a painting tool.)

6. Open both of the rendered color images of the scene. Invert and load the combined mask as a selection into the non-antialiased version. The edges should be selected. In QuickView, check that the mask area has taken in sufficient border area and, if necessary, adjust using Levels.

7. Change back to the selection. Copy all of the antialiased version and paste it inside the selection. Adjust the opacity; this sample (see Figure 13.20) had the anti-aliased edges at 70% strength.

Figure 13.20 Antialiased edges and non–antialiased everywhere else.

There you go! You have your beautiful, rough, rocky surfaces and smooth transitions from edge to edge.

> **TIP:** *There's a secret way to keep individual objects from being antialiased, but the setting affects the entire object, not just the edges: Select the object and open the Object Attributes dialog box (⌘-Option-E/Ctrl+Alt+E). Don't change anything, but hold down the key combination Control-Shift/Ctrl+Shift while you click the check mark to close the box. To turn on normal antialiasing again, open the Object Attributes dialog box, and this time hold down Option-Shift/Alt+Shift. Your object will return to its regular smooth self.*

MOVING ON...

We offer you the sincerest congratulations for having reached this point; you've completed all the chapters that focus on the different aspects of working in Bryce to create still images. Animation awaits you in the next two chapters. If you are solely concerned with still images, then we invite you to Chapter 16, "Superlative Nature Imagery," where we address some overall concepts about nature-scene making.

CHAPTER FOURTEEN

The Fourth Dimension:
Time and Animation

IN THIS CHAPTER...

- Time and Bryce

- The Animation controls

- Previewing animations

- Generating animations

- What can be animated in Bryce

- Keyframes and key events

- Object trajectories and paths

Bryce provides you with the ability to make motion in your scene. For the purposes of keeping things straight, let's call a Bryce scene a scene. If it contains animation, the item that Hollywood calls a scene we'll refer to as a sequence, just so you know what's what.

Don your director's hat, get out your director's chair, grab your megaphone (even if it's only a virtual one), and get ready to roll!

This chapter will acquaint you with everything there is to know of Bryce's Animation controls. This is the part where we explain How It All Works. Once you know how it all works, though, there's the finer art of the approach to creating motion, and advanced tricks and other fine things for making good animated motion in Bryce. We'll leave these topics for the next chapter, "Advanced Animation Techniques."

". . .And Then *This* Happened"

At its most basic, an animation strings together a series of images, each one very similar to, but not exactly like, the next one. When they are shown in succession, the human eye and brain are tricked into thinking that there's a continuous moving image. This grand perceptual twist is called *persistence of vision*. (How many other perceptual tricks have led to mega-industries like the film industry? Gives pause for consideration!)

In any time narrative, things are strung together with events. Events are occurrences, the points where one says, "and then this happened." To bring it to a mundane level: "The alarm clock went off (then this happened). I batted at it until it stopped (and then this happened). I guess I was awake then, so I got out of bed (and then this happened)." Each of those points of description can be thought of as a *key event*. In Bryce, animating the camera or objects is done by stringing together key events. Your work in Bryce animation is to create the "this happened" and then move to the next event. What constitutes an event may be mundane: It may involve the laws of physics, it may involve mystery and chance. Your job as Bryce animator is to weave all those things together to tell your story.

The story that we'll be using for most of this chapter is the story of a ball. It rolls off the top of a cylinder, falls, and bounces on the ground; then it flies up into the air again and falls to the ground again (see Figure 14.1). Like so many layers laminated together, a variety of key events are taking place. The ball rolls. It follows a certain path in space. When it bounces, it flattens (the force of momentum, gravity). It continues to spin as it falls and bounces. (You can find the scene file and the movie file in a folder called BOUNCE contained in this chapter's folder on the CD-ROM.)

Figure 14.1 The bouncing ball animation that will be our companion for a lot of this chapter. The route the ball takes is lightly superimposed in this set of images.

The overall workflow of creating an animation is depicted in Figure 14.2 and discussed here.

- *Pre-production: Storyboarding and Planning.* Plan what the animation is going to be and do at the very beginning of your scene creation process. Planning, storyboarding, previsualization are all terms for the initial process. We will mostly just mention it here so that you know it comes at the beginning. Our intention for this chapter is to ensure that you're familiar with all of Bryce's Animation controls, so merely mentioning storyboarding will do for the moment.

- *Constructing the Scene.* Once you know what story you're going to tell and have planned it out, you should then construct the scene. Creating a scene for animation is much the same as creating any other scene in Bryce, except, perhaps, for the fact that you know you're not going to look at it from a single perspective if your camera will be moving.

- *Animating the Scene.* Once your scene is constructed (or mostly constructed), then begin animating it. At this point, you'll be working with time in Bryce and using the Time Palette and all the controls.

- *Preview and Tweak.* Preview your work and then go back and tweak it some more. There are a number of Animation Preview tools at your disposal that you can use to check the progress of your animated sequence as you work on it. Fine-tuning can be done in a number of ways. The Advanced Motion Lab comes into play here for working with the mapping of time to animation events.

The spark, inspiration, or challenge for an animated sequence

Pre-production
　　　Planning the movie
　　　(storyboard)

Constructing the scene
　　　Creating and editing
　　　Test render
　　　Tweak and adjust
　　　Test render
　　　...ad infinitum

Animating the scene
　　　Plotting out motion
　　　Fine-tune motion

Preview and Tweak
　　　Playback preview
　　　Additional animation
　　　Tweak and adjust
　　　Playback preview
　　　Adjust some more
　　　And some more
　　　...ad tedium

Render Animation Sequence

Post-Production
　　　Movie compression
　　　Editing with other sequences
　　　Convert for delivery

Figure 14.2 Overview of the workflow to create an animation in Bryce.

- *Render.* Finally, render your animation, either to a movie or to a series of still images.

- *Post-production.* After rendering, work with your output to edit it together with other sequences, compress it for your final output, composite with other graphics, and deliver your final animation product.

We'll talk more in depth about all the steps of production, omitting the pre- and post-production. Our main focus for this chapter is working with the Animation controls of Bryce.

INTRODUCING TIME TO BRYCE

Once you begin to animate in Bryce, you are ushering in the fourth dimension: time. The first thing you need to learn is how to tell time in Bryce. Thankfully, there's no need to figure out what time it is when the big hand is on one thing and the small hand is on another. Bryce tells you the time in a numerical readout. Still, it's good to know what refers to what.

The status display also lists the current time in Bryce. Obviously, if you have not set up anything in your scene to animate, then the time readout is a series of zeroes.

Time, Frames, etc.

Bryce measures where you are in time in two ways: by counting frames, and by simultaneously noting time and frames, referred to as SMPTE. (We'll discuss SMPTE in a bit.)

No matter which method of keeping track of time you use, you'll have to contend with one of the (so-called) joys of computers. Computers, and the software that runs thereon, tend to be enamored of the snazzy mathematical concept introduced by the ancient Arab civilization— the zero. Bryce, too, is entranced by the zero. The first frame is numbered zero—but it's not an empty place holder; you'll actually have a rendered frame at frame 0, which will be numbered 0. By the time your sequence gets to the one-second mark (assuming, for a moment, that you're rendering at 15 frames per second), you'll actually have created 16 frames of animation, with the first one numbered 0. And you thought Y2K was bad! If this strange fact of Bryce Life is going to make you crazy, then you can start rendering your animations from Frame 1; check out the section, "Render Animation Dialog Box" later in this chapter for juicy tidbits on how to do that. (In the next chapter, we set up the QTVR Object movie example to sidestep Frame 0.)

SMPTE

This arduous acronym (pronounced "simptee") stands for the Society of Motion Picture and Television Engineers. The Society sets standards for the various equipment involved in creation of film, TV, and video. The standard that is referred to in Bryce is the standard for digital time and control code for use in film, video, and TV (any of which may include audio) operating at 24 frames per second (film) and 25 or 30 frames per second (video and TV).

Trivia hint: it's numbered SMPTE 12M-1995. (Cure your curiosity—or your insomnia—with a little surf to www.smpte.org and read about all their standards!) So what is the time display standard for? It divides the time into hours, minutes, seconds, and frames, like so: HH:MM:SS.FF (see Figure 14.3).

Figure 14.3 The SMPTE code and what it means.

What this standard means is that the time displayed is divided into hours, minutes, seconds, and frames. The time is calibrated to your setting for the number of frames per second (or fps). Note: the standard frame settings are: 24 fps for motion picture film, 25 fps for European-standard video (including the former Soviet Republic and Middle East), and 30 fps for United States-standard video. Why the difference in frame rates? Video needs to be synched up with the electricity that is supplying it, so that all those electrons dancing across the screen do so in harmony with the overall flow of electrons in electricity. Europe and the U.S. have different electric currents, so the frame rate for video differs. The film rate, 24 fps, is simply tied to the number of frames that can be flashed in succession to provide the illusion of persistence of vision.

The setting for frames per second determines the length of time your animation plays. In theory, it should work this way: You could set an animation of 26 frames' duration. To convert that to SMPTE, you would need to supply a setting for frames per second (fps) to obtain the actual playback time for your animation.

So suppose that you had a grand total of 26 frames; what would that look like in SMPTE time? It depends on the frames per second.

Total Frames	24 Frames per Second	15 Frames per Second
26	00:00:01.02	00:00:01.11

The total number of frames is divided by the frame rate to arrive at the time portion of SMPTE (HH:MM:SS), with the remainder being the number of frames (.FF). Thus, 26 divided by 24 is 1 second, with a remainder of 2 frames; and 26 divided by 15 is 1 second with a remainder of 11 frames. So 26 frames may play for a longer or a shorter time, depending on the frame rate.

We mentioned that this is how it should work "in theory." Alas, "in practice" is different. Since Bryce counts frame 0 as an actual frame, there will *always* be one additional frame beyond the final frame number. If you set an animation to what, for all appearances, is 26 frames duration, you will actually end up with a total of 27 frames, since Bryce appends frame 0 at the beginning of the 26 frames. Bryce won't ever let on that there are 27 frames. It will begin its count at frame 0, and continue counting up to the final 26th frame (or display the equivalent SMPTE time code, as shown above). But if you were to render that "26 frame" animation so that each frame is a separate image file (we'll tell you how to do that at the end of this chapter), the result will be 27 rendered images. The total number of frames will always be whatever number Bryce states plus one. Throughout this chapter, when we discuss SMPTE time code as provided by Bryce, we will follow Bryce's deluded SMPTE numbering, because that is what Bryce's time display reads.

Unless your animations call for precise timing, you can ignore the initial Frame 0 and just live with an extra frame in your animation. When precision is critical, toss out that first "Frame 0" frame.

Whither Frames or SMPTE?

When should you work with your animation using SMPTE, and when should you use a basic frame count? If you are creating a short animation, say, for the purpose of creating an animating GIF or for a QTVR object movie (as Susan is wont to do), then a simple frame count will suffice. You may find yourself saying, "I need 20 frames for this animation—that is all." At that point, messing with seconds, minutes, and hours is just extra hassle. When you're planning a sequence to fit into a specific amount of time, say, 24 seconds, then the SMPTE method of tracking time will work better.

Animation Setup

The Animation Setup dialog box is the place for you to set up the time settings for your animated sequence. Here, you have precise control over all matters of time for your sequence (in the next section, we'll introduce you to the Time Palette, where you can interactively work with the same settings we discuss here.)

The Animation Setup dialog box is accessed in two ways from the main Bryce interface: by choosing from the File menu (with the keyboard shortcut ⌘-Shift-N/Ctrl+Shift+N), or by double-clicking the Time Scrubber. The Animation Setup dialog box is shown in Figure 14.4. The dialog box is divided into three parts. The top part tells you where you are right now—the current time in the animation. At the right, it tells you the number of the frame you are on, and, based on the frames per second, supplies numbers according to SMPTE code accordingly. The current time corresponds to the location of the Time Scrubber, located on the Time Palette. The middle part, labeled Duration, is where you define the length of the animation. Between the top and middle areas is a small box labeled FPS, for Frames per Second; this is where you set the frame rate for the animation. The bottom part has controls for you to control playback (you can play once, repeat playback, or play back as a pendulum) and for you to specify how you want the time readout displayed. Those last two options are also controlled from the Animation Options pop-up menu on the Time Palette.

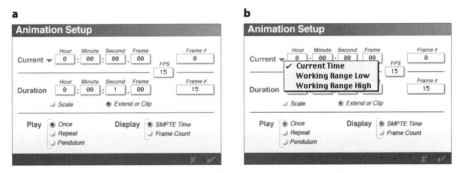

Figure 14.4 a) The Animation Setup dialog box, b) shown with the pop-up menu choices for what the top time can refer to.

When you make adjustments in the Animation Setup dialog box, you can enter a frame number and the SMPTE time will be calculated automatically. The reverse is also true: Enter the SMPTE time and the frame number will be calculated for you. For a shorter sequence, enter the frame number and let Bryce deal with the SMPTE time code.

The Animation Setup dialog box is a master area for controlling aspects of time in your scene. Many of the controls there can also be accessed from other parts of the Bryce interface, but the dialog box is a central place to control them.

Animation Setup Dialog Box Walkthrough

1. Open the scene file called BOUNCE, located in this chapter's folder on the CD-ROM.

2. Tap the Escape (Esc) key to switch to wireframe view, then click the Play button.

3. From the File menu, select Animation Setup. A dialog box appears.

4. Right now the setting is probably on Extend or Clip. Click the button for the Scale option. Then increase the time. Enter the number 50 in the box that is encircled in Figure 14.5.

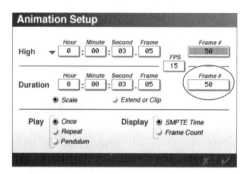

Figure 14.5 Scaling the animation to a longer time: The Scale button is active, the duration is set to 50 frames (encircled), and the Working Range High (boxed) value is also set to 50 frames (also boxed).

5. Next, you'll need to change the Working Range High value to match the new time. (We'll explain the Working Range in a bit; for now, just humor us!) Click the word "Current." A pop-up menu appears (see Figure 14.4). Select Working Range High. The result is shown with a box around it in Figure 14.5. Enter the number 50 in the Frame# box at the right of the Working Range High row (it's also highlighted in Figure 14.5). Click the check mark to accept those changes and go back to your scene.

6. Play the animation sequence by clicking the Play button. Notice the difference in how it plays this time and how it played before. It should now take longer to play.

7. Open the Animation Setup dialog box again. This time, clip the time. Click the Clip or Extend button and enter 2 seconds, 2 frames into the numerical entries, as shown in Figure 14.6. Click the check mark to go back to your scene and play the animation. This time it stops just before the ball gets to the top of the arc.

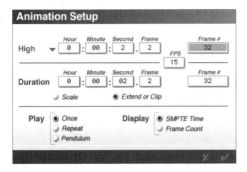

Figure 14.6 The Animation Setup dialog box set to clip the sequence at 2 seconds, 2 frames.

8. Revert to the saved version: Choose File > Revert to Saved to throw away all these changes and go back to the way the scene was.

Now that you've experimented a bit with changing the time in your animation, let's discuss the Time Palette itself.

WORKING WITH THE TIME PALETTE

Bryce's Time Palette holds the Animation controls, all the controls you need to work with time. The Animation controls are repeated in three other places in Bryce: in the Terrain Editor, the Materials Lab, and the Sky Lab.

The Time Palette controls, shown and labeled in Figure 14.7, can be roughly divided into four categories. First, the time and playback tools are for working with time in your scene. Next, the keyframe tools are for displaying the status of the key events in your sequence and for adding and deleting key events. Third, the Animation Preview is for generating and working with a thumbnail preview of your animation sequence. Finally, the Advanced Motion Lab doorway takes you to a special room where you can work very specifically with time and each key event for each item that is being animated in your sequence.

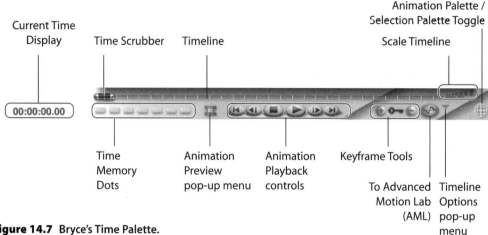

Figure 14.7 Bryce's Time Palette.

Time Tools

You use the time tools to set up the entire range of time, find out where you are in time right now, and navigate to any point in your time sequence.

Timeline

The timeline is the primary control for showing you where you are in the sequence and for navigating to any other spot. The timeline shows the beginning, end, current time, and working range high and low of your scene. The timeline is infinite. It begins at 0 and can move up to, say, 99 hours. (You won't ever want to set it to that!) The BOUNCE sequence that we'll be using to demonstrate the Time Palette and controls is a little over one-and-a-half seconds.

Time Scrubber

The Time Scrubber (also referred to as the Current Time Indicator in the Bryce documentation, though we'll stick with Time Scrubber) is the green control that you can slide along the timeline. It performs two main functions. It shows you what the current time is and where it lies on the visible portion of the timeline. It also lets you navigate to any particular time of your choice. Also, during playback or preview, it moves to indicate the current time. Double-clicking the Time Scrubber brings up the Animation Setup dialog box. If you hold down the Option or Alt key while moving the Time Scrubber, the time changes without the live wireframe preview. Use this feature when you want to navigate to a new place without waiting for the wireframe preview to redraw.

Time Scrubber Walkthrough

1. Open the Scene file BOUNCE, contained in this chapter's folder on the CD-ROM.

2. Drag back and forth on the Time Scrubber. Watch the animation play as you do so.

3. Press the Option/Alt key and then move the Time Scrubber again. Notice how it moves but the wireframe view of your scene does not change. Now let go of the Time Scrubber. The scene updates to that position in the timeline.

4. Double-click the Time Scrubber. You see your old friend from the previous exercise, the Animation Setup dialog box. Click the X to leave the dialog box.

Playback/Navigation Controls

In addition to the Time Scrubber, which tells you where you are in time, there are the Playback controls, for playing your animation and navigating to other points in time in the sequence (see Figure 14.8).

Assuming that you've used a tape player or an audio CD player, you are familiar with the Play (and Pause) and Stop controls. The controls at the ends take you to the beginning or end of the sequence. The controls in between are for navigating to the next and previous keyframes. (We'll talk more about keyframes in a bit.)

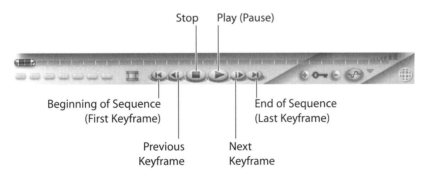

Figure 14.8 The Playback controls on the Time Palette.

When a scene contains animation, clicking the Play button will bring about two different consequences, depending on what mode you're in:

-   *Wireframe Mode.* Clicking the Play button will cause your wirerframe preview to animate. The animation plays while the scene is in wireframe mode, playing in time with the time track.

- *Render Mode.* Clicking the Play button will start the process of rendering the animation. It brings up the Render Animation dialog box, where you establish settings for your animation.

Table 14.1 has the keyboard shortcuts for the Playback/Navigation controls. This table includes key commands for ticker marks, the small white markings on the timeline that often represent each frame. We fully describe ticker marks later in this chapter, in the "Ticker Marks" section.

	Shortcut
Previous Ticker Mark	, (comma)
Next Ticker Mark	. (period)
Previous Keyframe	<
Next Keyframe	>
Sequence Beginning	[
Sequence End	]
Play/pause	\

Table 14.1 Keyboard shortcuts for the Playback controls.

Note to Macintosh users: The "next ticker mark" key equivalent is a period. This is true even if you have the Command key depressed. You know what this means: Your habitual ⌘-period behavior is not going to be accepted by Bryce in the same old way. Bryce will interpret your "No! Wait! Stop! Interrupt!" behavior as a request to move the Time Scrubber to the next ticker mark. If you haven't already, make a conscious decision to use the Escape key. To stop, use Escape; to interrupt, use Escape; to cancel, use Escape. If you feel really inclined, repeat this as a mantra. One exception is render: anything you type during a render, including ⌘-period (except for Shift-T, which launches or activates BryceTalk), will interrupt the render's progress.

Time Playback/Navigation Controls Walkthrough

1. Make sure that you are in wireframe mode.

2. Click the Play button. The sequence plays through to the end.

3. Click the Play button again, and, while the animation is still playing, click the Pause button. Click the Play button again. The sequence plays, stops at pause, and then resumes to play to the end.

4. Click the Beginning button and End button. Watch the time jump to the beginning and end of the sequence.

5. Switch to render view. Click the Play button. The Render Animation dialog box appears. Click the X to cancel rendering of the animation. (It is sufficient to simply see the different consequences while clicking the Play button in different modes.)

Working Range

The Working Range is a subset of the total sequence or Recorded Area. In many cases, the two will be identical, but you can shorten the time that you're actively working with if you want to concentrate on one particular area. The part that is active is green; the remainder of the Recorded Area is dark gray.

Working Range Walkthrough

1. Drag the Time Scrubber back and forth to watch the action of the bouncing ball. Notice that the ball just starts falling off the edge of the cylinder at around Frame 2.

2. Click the timeline area just inside the left edge and drag to the right. The green Working Area timeline moves to the right to follow your mouse pointer, leaving behind a dark gray area at the left.

   You can follow the same procedure on the other end to adjust the working area. Be careful, though, not to drag from the actual green Set Duration dot, but drag from just inside it, as Figure 14.9 shows.

Click inside Sequence duration ┘ └ Sequence duration

Figure 14.9 Making the working range shorter than the duration of the animation: Click just inside the green area to change the working range.

Another way to set the working range involves the Animation Setup dialog box.

3. Scrub the time to the upswing of the bounce, before the ball reaches the top (Frame 12 to 14 or thereabouts). Double-click the Time Scrubber to access the Animation Setup dialog box. Notice the frame number (Frame 13 in Figure 14.10a.)

4. Click the word Current to access a pop-up menu and choose the Working Range High option. In the frame number box, type 13 (from the current one) (see Figure 14.10b).

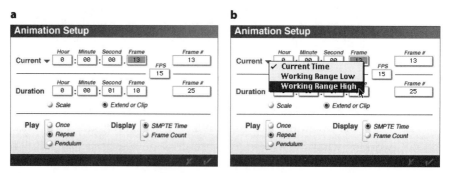

Figure 14.10 Setting the working range using the Animation Setup dialog box: a) Noting the number of the current frame; b) after changing the option to Working Range High and entering that same number in the Animation Setup dialog box.

5. Click the check mark to leave the dialog box. Your working range is now smaller than it was before, letting you focus on the bounce (see Figure 14.11).

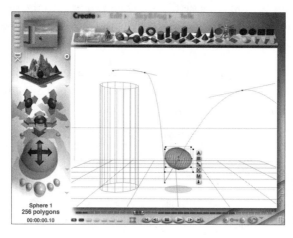

Figure 14.11 After setting the working range to isolate the bounce.

Recorded Range

The Recorded Area is the range between Time 0 and the time when your animation sequence ends. Although the Status Display refers to it as the Recorded Area, we'll use the term sequence or duration or sequence duration. Usually the sequence duration is displayed on the green part of the timeline, unless you've set your working range to be different than the recorded range (more on that in a moment).

Caveats and warnings: Time can extend beyond the recorded range, and keyframes can exist beyond it, too, but this is the upper limit of the animation sequence that your scene file is currently set to. Also, remember that Bryce adds that extra frame at the beginning, so although Bryce may display a certain time duration in the Animation Setup dialog box, the true time will be that time plus one frame.

There are three ways to establish your sequence range:

• Use the Animation Setup dialog box. Enter either a time in the SMPTE portion or a number of frames in the Frame Number portion. Click the check mark to accept this value as your new duration.

• If you have turned on the Auto-Key option and have no green in your timeline, you can drag the Time Scrubber out to some time mark. Perform some action in the scene. You can create an object, edit an object, edit the sky, or edit the camera in your scene. (If you're looking at your scene from Director's View, and you use one of the camera controls to change it, the change won't be recorded as part of the animation sequence. However, if you make camera adjustments from Camera View, they will be recorded, and the timeline will fill in green up to the position of the Time Scrubber.)

• Drag the Time Scrubber out of the way of Time 0 at the left end of the timeline. You'll see a green dot. Drag that green dot to set the duration of your sequence. Similarly, to change the duration after it's been set, find the green dot and drag it to a new position (see Figure 14.12).

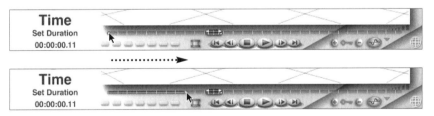

Figure 14.12 Setting the animation's duration by dragging the green dot to the desired time.

There are also ways to change existing sequence ranges to lengthen or shorten them. You can, of course, manually extend the sequence by dragging that green Set Duration dot either to the right to extend the sequence time, or to the left to shorten the duration of the sequence.

You can also use the Animation Setup dialog box to lengthen or shorten the sequence. Two options are available for you: To simply add more time onto the end or curtail the existing time by some amount, select the Extend or Clip option. Suppose, though, that you want the animation, along with all the events or actions that take place, to be proportionately lengthened or shortened along with the overall sequence duration. For that, choose the Scale option.

Scale Timeline

Time is infinite, but the area for displaying the timeline on the Animation Palette is not. It is limited by the scene size and your monitor size. Assuming, for a moment, that you have your Bryce interface set to hug the scene (Interface Minimum), and that your scene size is the Bryce default, you can see about 30 frames worth of time on your timeline. Suppose your animation is longer than that, and the green working area extends off to the right; you can scroll with the Time Scrubber to move to that later point in time. If you want the entire green working area of the timeline to appear at once, though, use the Scale tool to squeeze all of your sequence onto the visible portion of your timeline. Dragging to the right compresses more time into the visible area, and dragging to the left expands the currently visible time, making less time visible.

> **TIP:** In addition to using the Scale Timeline tool, there is another way you can make more time visible on your timeline. When you set your interface to Interface Maximum (hugging the edge of the monitor), the timeline will expand to show as much time as your monitor width will allow. (Move the Animation Palette closer to your scene by pressing the space bar while dragging the Animation Palette to where you want it.)

Scale Timeline Walkthrough

1. Point your mouse at the timeline Scale control (see Figure 14.13). Drag right. Notice that more ticker marks appear as more time is compressed into the visible area. Drag left. Notice that the timeline expands, with less time visible.

2. If your interface is hugging the Bryce scene, click the UI Min/Max button on the Wireframe/Display Palette. When the interface expands to hug the monitor's edge, notice how much more of the timeline is visible (see Figure 14.13). Click the UI Min/Max control again to make the palette hug the edge of your scene window.

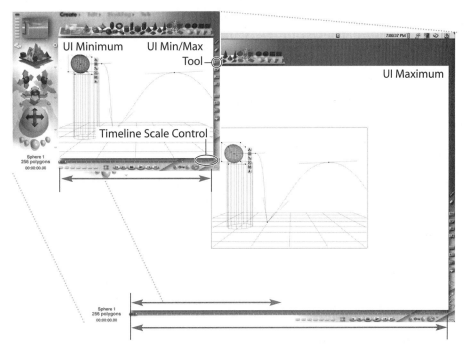

Figure 14.13 How to show more time. Use the timeline Scale tool (circled) to display more time, or maximize the Bryce interface to display more time. The timeline measurement arrow for UI Minimum is set next to UI Maximum for a 1152 x 870 monitor size.

Ticker Marks

On the timeline, there is a series of white ticker marks, to mark time. They can be set to different scales, ranging from every frame to every 5 seconds. Change the settings from the Timeline Options pop-up menu. Generally, Every Frame is good for shorter animations; for longer animations, setting to Every Second generates one ticker mark for 15 frames (assuming a frame rate of 15 fps).

Ticker Marks Walkthrough

1. Remember that exercise from the Animation Setup dialog box where we scaled the time to 50 frames? Do that again. In the Animation Setup dialog box, click the button for the Scale option, and then enter the number 50 into the Duration: Frames box. Set the Working Range High numbers to match (see Figure 14.5). We're scaling to 50 frames to give ourselves lots more ticker marks.

2. Scale the timeline so that all the time shows. Drag to the right on the Scale control. The ticker marks should squeeze together.

3. From the Animation Options pop-up menu, change the display of the ticker marks to other options besides every frame. Try 'em all!

Memory Dots

The Animation Palette has a set of Memory Dots that you can use to mark certain time spots in your sequence. There may be spots in your animation sequence that you want to be able to come back to immediately, without having to resort to dragging this way and that or (horrors!) setting an arbitrary keyframe. For this purpose, Memory Dots are a tremendous convenience; they can get you back to the spot where you want to be.

To use the Memory Dots, click to create a Memory Dot. This marks the current time. To remove a Memory Dot, Option-click/Alt+click. Memory Dot information is saved with the scene file. The set of Memory Dots also appears in all the other places where there are timelines: the Terrain Editor, Materials Lab, Sky Lab, and Advanced Motion Lab.

Memory Dots Walkthrough

1. Move the Time Scrubber to the beginning of the working range.

2   Click a Memory Dot to save that time.

3. Move the Time Scrubber to the end of the working range.

4. Click a Memory Dot to save that time.

5. Move the Time Scrubber to another time; then click one of the green Memory Dots. Notice that the time scrubber snaps to the place where it was when that dot was set.

6. Option-click/Alt+click one of the Memory Dots to reset it to blank.

Animation Options Pop-Up Menu

The Animation Options pop-up menu, shown with all the options in Figure 14.14, has controls for four different items or sets of items.

• *Auto-Key.* This option determines whether Bryce automatically watches for each move made over time and generates a keyframe whenever anything changes, or whether you will manually set all keyframes. Auto-Key is discussed at length in the "Keyframing" section of this chapter.

- *Ticker Marks.* The Ticker Mark section allows you to choose the number of frames (or seconds) between ticker marks.

- *Play Mode.* Then there is the playback option for how the Animation Preview should be displayed: play once through (abc), repeat the sequence (abc abc abc, ad infinitum), or play the sequence as a pendulum going back and forth (abcbabcba, ad infinitum).

- *Time Display.* You can choose the way the time is displayed: as SMPTE time code or a simple frame count.

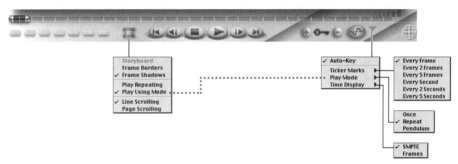

Figure 14.14 The Time Palette and its pop-up menus: Animation Preview (left) and the Animation Options menu (right).

Time Display Walkthrough

1. Change the Time Display from SMPTE to Frames and back.

Thrilling, wasn't it?

Animation Preview

The still-image process of working in Bryce is "create, tweak, render; tweak and render; tweak and render." The animation process is no different. It's true that you're dealing with still-image features, but you're adding time and changes over time to the whole mix.

You need to preview your work in the most efficient way for the stage of the animation you're working on. The progression goes from quicker to slower, from lesser to greater detail, before you're ready to commit the computer to a full render.

The most preliminary feedback comes from quick previews. We already introduced you to the simplest preview option, the wireframe preview. Taking things up a notch, the Time Palette has the Animation Preview control, for generating a quick, thumbnail render of your sequence.

Once you create a sequence, you can render a series of rough thumbnail images for each frame and watch a miniature version of your animation. The Animation Preview control is the tool that allows you to do that. For a single little control, it offers several options, depending on whether you select options from its pop-up menu or simply click the control to generate a preview.

Press for Pop-Up Menu Options

Pressing the Animation Preview control brings up a pop-up menu listing options for working with your preview (see Figure 14.14). If you want to see only the Nano Preview, deselect Storyboard before you click the Animation Preview control to generate a storyboard; the playback will take place only in Nano Preview once the preview render is completed. But the storyboard area is there to look at, so why not keep the Storyboard option active so you can better keep track of the context of the current frame of the Animation Preview?

There are three options for the appearance of the storyboard preview:

• *Off.* Thumbnails have neither a shadow nor a border.

• *Shadow.* Each thumbnail has a drop shadow.

• *Border.* Each thumbnail has a border.

The latter two options allow you to see each individual frame better, but you can't get as many frames into a row. Depending on the length of your sequence, it may be better to have more frames visible at once; use the Off option for that. The pop-up menu also contains two playback options: Play Repeating or Play Using Mode. When you select Play Repeating, the sequence plays over and over again. If you want to play once or play pendulum, then choose Play Mode > Pendulum from the Timeline Options pop-up menu and then set the Animation Preview pop-up menu to Play Mode. (You could, of course, set the Timeline Options pop-up menu to Repeat, accomplishing the same result as if you'd set the Animation Options pop-up menu to Play Repeating. Whee.)

The Animation Preview will preview only your working area, so if you don't want to preview the entire sequence, (oh, yes, that five-minute sequence takes *so* long to preview, yikes!) you can simply set the working area to the particular spot you're interested in and then render the preview for only that area; it's automatic. You don't have to do anything other than to set the proper limits of your working area; Bryce automatically takes care of limiting the Animation Preview to the working area.

When your Animation Preview has a larger number of frames than can be displayed in the Animation Preview at one time, the current frames scroll into position while the old ones scroll up and away. The last menu item lets you choose whether they scroll up a line at a time or a page at a time. It's a matter of Dealer's Choice here, a purely personal preference.

Click to Play

Clicking the Animation Preview control produces slightly different results depending on where you are:

- *Wireframe or Render mode.* Clicking generates and plays a preview.

- *While the preview is being generated.* Clicking stops generating the preview.

- *After the preview has been completely generated.* Clicking returns you to wireframe mode. If viewing the preview without the storyboard, the wireframe view remains visible throughout the preview; clicking the Animation Preview control will cause the preview to play again.

- *Wireframe or Render mode after a preview was generated and no changes occurred to scene.* Clicking pulls the preview from a temporary cache—that is, the preview is generated quickly! The already rendered frames are cached for as long as you have the scene in its current condition; Bryce does not have to re-render them when you click the Preview Animation button a second time. Once you make any change to your scene (including simply switching to wireframe mode or moving the Time Scrubber), Bryce will have to regenerate the next Animation Preview.

Animation Preview Walkthrough

Continue working with the BOUNCE scene for this walkthrough.

1. Click the little filmstrip. The sequence renders in small bits 'n' pieces.

2. Give the preview a border by selecting Frame Border from the Animation Preview pop-up menu.

3. Change the preview to no border or shadow by unchecking Frame Border on the Animation Options pop-up menu. Click the Play button. Change the preview to include a drop shadow again.

4. Change the preview to Play Using Mode (from the pop-up menu).

5. Change the mode on the Time Options pop-up menu to Once. Click the Play button again.

6. Change the mode on the Time Options pop-up menu to Repeat. Click the Play button again (this is the same as the Animation Preview Options pop-up menu's default mode of Play Repeating).

7   Change the mode in the Time Options pop-up menu to Pendulum.

8. On the Animation Preview Options pop-up menu, change to Page Scrolling. Click the Play button. Change back to Line Scrolling and click Play again.

    You'll have your own preferences about which options to use; now that you've seen them all.

9. One last thing. Make the working range smaller, to include only the bounce part. Then click the Preview button again.

10. When Storyboard is showing, click the preview once to go back to wire-frame view. Now press the menu. You see that the Storyboard option isn't grayed out. Choose Storyboard to turn off this option. Now click the animation preview control again. See how the animation preview plays in the Nano Preview window, but it does not show the storyboard in the main window? You also don't get to see the animation in wireframe, either.

Keyframe Tools

In your animation sequence, you are working with the key events (recall the "and then this happened" discussion from the beginning of the chapter). Bryce works with key events, also referred to as keyframes, in its animation system. There's the first condition at the first event, and then another condition at the final event. Bryce interpolates a set of steps between those two events to make the scene change over time. The marker events are called keyframes, since, at a particular frame, a key event occurs.

We will discuss how to set up keyframes and use Auto-Key in more detail in the "Keyframing" section of this chapter. For now, though, we'll introduce you to the controls on the Time Palette and let you see how to work with them in an already created animation sequence.

Keyframe Navigation

The Playback/Navigation controls allow you to navigate to various keyframes in your scene. To navigate by keyframes, use the buttons between the center Play and Stop buttons and the Begin and End sequence buttons on the ends.

You may have many more key events in a scene than you are able to get to by clicking the Previous Keyframe and Next Keyframe buttons. The stops that occur are for the selected objects only, so if you have nothing selected, and if all of your animation takes place with one or more objects in your scene (no sky animation), then clicking the Next Keyframe control will take you from the beginning to the end of your sequence. Select the object and then see what kind of stops you get along the way!

If you have no objects selected, Bryce will stop at any keyframes that exist for the sky, assuming that you've animated your sky. Any keyframes for object materials will not cause Bryce to stop, even when that object is selected. The only place to navigate among materials key events is in the animation controls in the Materials Lab and the Advanced Motion Lab (more on the Advanced Motion Lab in the next chapter).

Keyframe Status

During playback, and when navigating using the Next and Previous Keyframe controls, Bryce indicates to you that a keyframe exists by displaying a darkened keyframe icon. It is otherwise half transparent (see Figure 14.15).

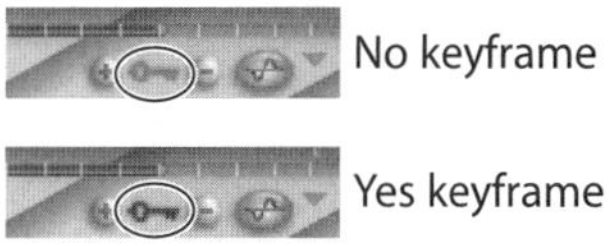

No keyframe

Yes keyframe

Figure 14.15 The Keyframe control is grayed out in its normal state and turns a dark green when a keyframe is present for the selected object or for the sky or the camera.

Adding or Removing a Keyframe

A simple click on the Add Keyframe control will record the state of each and every selected object, the sky, and the sun in a new keyframe. If you are viewing your scene from Camera View, all camera information will be recorded as part of that new keyframe as well. If no object is selected when you click the Add Keyframe control, then only the sky, sun, and camera (if the scene is being viewed from Camera View) will be recorded in a new keyframe. Clicking the Remove Keyframe control (as you might expect) consigns existing keyframes for that particular time to oblivion. The controls also house pop-up menus (see Figure 14.16) that allow you to selectively remove or add only certain attributes to the key event. Press the mouse until the menu appears, and you have a list for all options for the selected objects, camera, and sky. The Add/Remove Keyframe controls are available not only when you're editing keyframes manually, but also when Auto-Key is on.

Figure 14.16
The pop-up menu accessed from the Add/Remove Keyframe controls provides precision keyframe addition and removal.

Keyframe Control Walkthrough

1. Click the Next Keyframe button. Keep clicking. Notice that there are points where the sphere stops even though there aren't those blue marker points. Those other stopping places correspond to keyframes that are set for something other than the sphere's position. (We'll be exploring all the possible options later in the chapter.)

2. Deselect the sphere and click the Next or Previous Keyframe control.

AML Doorway

The Enter Advanced Motion Lab control leads to the working area in Bryce where you can fine-tune key events and time behaviors as well as clean up after wayward keyframes that might have slipped into your scene. The Advanced Motion Lab is discussed in detail in the next chapter, "Advanced Animation Techniques."

AML Doorway Walkthrough

1. Select the sphere. Click the AML Doorway tool to go to the Advanced Motion Lab.

2. Click the name Sphere 1. The line expands to display a number of options for Sphere 1, as shown in Figure 14.17.

   In the green rows that appear, notice the little white ticker marks; they represent key events for each of the attributes of Sphere 1 that are being animated in this scene.

3. Click the arrow at the bottom to leave. (We'll come back and visit the AML in depth in the next chapter.)

You've just gotten the barest taste for the attributes of an object that can be animated. In the next section, you can gorge yourself with detailed knowledge about each and every attribute in Bryce that can be animated. *Bon appetit!*

Figure 14.17 The Advanced Motion Lab, with the animated attributes for Sphere 1 displayed, the result of clicking the name Sphere 1.

THE THINGS IN BRYCE THAT CAN BE ANIMATED

So now that you've looked at all the choices in the Time Palette, what in Bryce can be animated?

This section exhaustively lists all the things in Bryce that can be animated. The definitive list is derived from the items on the pop-up menu for adding and deleting keyframes. We list items first by the name on the pop-up menu and then provide the alternative name used in the rest of Bryce's user interface. More often than not, the menu name (which is also used in the Advanced Motion Lab) is different from the label for the attribute as it appears on the user interface. The Bryce creators think that you users are genius enough to figure out the differences between the menu item label and the user interface label all by yourself; we realize that you might find them confusing and take pity on you by listing both here. Also, with each item that we list, we provide a brief description to remind you of its function.

We discuss the animation attributes in the order in which you encounter them. A basic set appears on the Add and Delete Keyframe pop-up menus in the Time Palette. The controls on the Time Palette, though, are repeated in three other places in Bryce: the Terrain Editor, the Sky Lab, and the Materials Lab. Depending on what you are animating, you may need to go to one of those places to add or delete keyframes. This makes sense, actually; you can make materials adjustments only in the Materials Lab, so you can delete material-based keyframes only in the Materials Lab on the timeline that is there, or, of course, in the Advanced Motion Lab.

This chapter's folder on the CD-ROM contains animation samples for each of the items listed here. The samples are movies on a Web site, presented with links, so that you can tell what you've seen already and what you have not. The scene files are also supplied, so that you can examine the scene files used in making the sample movies.

States Do Not Animate

Bryce will animate anything that is not a state. This is not to imply something about California versus Illinois versus Rhode Island. Rather, a state is a condition that cannot be changed during the sequence. You can establish (and edit) the condition, but you can't change it mid-course. It's more of an either-or situation. For instance, an object is either hidden or normal; or an object is either a pyramid or a cube—there's no morphing transition between them. Animation takes place within a state, but does not change from one state to another; a cube remains a cube but can change position and size and so forth.

So there are some things that will animate, and there are other things that will not.

Objects (Primitives)

Recall from Chapter 6, "Editing and the Internal Bryce Grid," the ways that you can edit an object. The changes to an object are attributes that can be animated over time.

Pop-up Menu Name	Regular Name	Description
Position	Object Position	Location of the object in space
Rotation	Rotate, Rotation	Object orientation; which way it faces
Origin	Origin	Location of object's origin point
Scale	Size, Resize	The object's size
Shear	Shear distortion	Combination of size and rotation; Works together with Rotation

Booleans

When you have two objects that are in a boolean relationship (one object is positive, the other object is set to be positive, negative or intersect, and both objects are grouped), they can move relative to each other over time, and so the boolean object can change its shape over time. The boolean relationship stays constant, and interesting things can take place within it; you can make things disappear by flying them into a "negative" shape (a portal, for instance).

See the examples on the CD-ROM in the folder for this chapter.

Camera

All editable attributes of the camera object can be animated to change over time.

Pop-up Menu Name	Regular Name	Description
Position	Camera Position (coordinates)	Location of the camera in space
Origin	Origin	Location of camera's origin point
Rotation	Rotation	Orientation; camera's rotation on *x* and *y* axes
Banking	Banking	The camera's rotation around its own *z*-axis
FOV	FOV (Field of View)	The amount of area "seen" by the camera
Pan X	Pan H	Horizontal panning on the 2D projection plane
Pan Y	Pan V	Vertical panning on the 2D projection plane
Zoom X	Scale (Zoom)	Horizontal scaling of 2D projection plane
Zoom Y	Scale (Zoom)	Vertical scaling of 2D projection plane

Lights

Light objects can have most of their light-casting attributes change over time.

Pop-up Menu Name	Regular Name	Description
Position, Rotation, Origin, Scale, Shear		All Standard Object Options.
Color	Color Swatch Color	The color that is cast by the light.
Intensity	Brightness	Numerical setting for casting or absorbing light.
Range	Ranged Falloff	How far the light is projected from source.
Falloff	Softness (Spotlights)	The softness of the edge of the light beam; for square lights, Falloff is expressed in terms of Falloff X and Falloff Y.
Light Gel (Materials)	Pict or Texture Gels	When assigned, this is a material setting. Use the Materials Lab to animate the light's gel.

Use the Materials Lab to animate the light's gel. If you attempt to animate the gel from the Edit Lights dialog box, you will wipe out any other light gel settings you may have keyframed.

We interrupt this presentation of the list of things that can be animated in Bryce to introduce you to the animation controls that live in portions of Bryce devoted to specific tasks; we'll continue with the animation lists from there.

ANIMATION CONTROLS IN THE TERRAIN, MATERIALS, AND SKY LABS

There are time controls in the other parts of Bryce: the Terrain Editor, the Materials Lab, and the Sky Lab. Each of the labs has, of course, a set of Animation controls that match the Time Palette's controls. The Animation Options pop-up menu thoughtfully provides access to the Animation Setup dialog box. (After all, you don't have access to that item under the File menu when you're inside one of the labs!) The menu also matches the Time Palette's menu options for the Ticker Marks, Play Mode, and Time Display controls.

The Playback controls are inside the labs, too. Do not overlook the Play button. The Play button will preview the animations for terrains, materials, and skies. If the Sky Lab preview is set to Render in Scene (accessed from the pop-up menu below the Sky Lab preview window), then not only will you see a preview of the sky, but a preview of the entire scene. The sky will animate, but the remainder of the scene does not; it stays in whatever state it was in when you entered the Sky Lab.

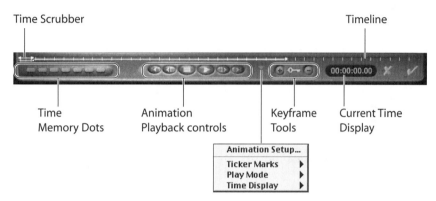

Figure 14.18 Lab Animation controls in the Terrain Editor, Materials Lab, and Sky Lab

Next Keyframe and Previous Keyframe will track the keyframe progress for the attributes of that particular lab. Suppose you are in the Materials Lab animating the material for an object. Although your selected object might, say, change location, rotation, and so forth, the Materials Lab's Next/Previous Keyframe button will stop only at keyframes for changes in the object's material; it blithely ignores any other type of key event. The Add/Delete Keyframe menus, accessed by pressing the Add/Keyframe button until the pop-up menu appears, will display only those attributes that can be edited inside whatever lab you happen to be in. Here's a description of what can be edited where in the Bryce main area and the various labs.

- *Terrain Editor.* Key events for attributes unique to terrains can be added or deleted in the Terrain Editor, Advanced Motion Lab, and main Time Palette.

- *Materials Lab.* Materials attribute key events can be added or deleted in the Materials Lab and Advanced Motion Lab; they cannot be worked with in the main Time Palette.

- *Sky Lab.* Sky and Sun attribute key events can be added or deleted in the Sky Lab, Advanced Motion Lab, and main Time Palette.

We have provided a crude but effective scene file that you can look at to see animation in the different labs. The file is called TERRAIN-MATERIAL-SKY. The terrain geometry changes, the material changes, and fog rolls in. None of these things take place at precisely the same time, though. You can see this by opening the scene file, going to the various labs, and clicking the Next and Previous Keyframe buttons to see where the key events fall. (The Advanced Motion Lab also will give you an at-a-glance look at the timing for the various animated changes.)

THE THINGS THAT CAN BE ANIMATED, CONTINUED

Now that we've introduced you to the animation controls in the labs, our tour of the things which can be animated continues with animatable attributes for terrains, skies, and materials.

Terrains

Terrains, as objects, have attributes that can be animated just like any other Bryce object. In addition, there are several animatable terrain attributes that can be animated by changing settings in the Terrain Editor. All animated transitions that are generated inside the Terrain Editor are straight blends from one keyframed condition to the next.

Pop-up Menu Name	Regular Name	Description
Position, Rotation, Origin, Scale, Shear		All Standard Object Options.
Geometry	Terrain Canvas	Grayscale information for terrain, symmetrical lattice.
Gradient	Preview Gradient Color	Change from one grayscale or color gradient ramp to another. Apply preview gradient as a material.
Grad Shift	Preview Gradient Shift	Change in appearance of a single gradient ramp; drag gradient color up or down to animate. Apply preview gradient as a material.
Low Clip	Clipping Bracket	Adjust to make low parts of terrain disappear.
High Clip	Clipping Bracket	Adjust to make high parts of terrain disappear.

In order to apply the preview gradient as a material, and therefore see the results of the two gradient options in the main scene, you must follow these three steps: First, in the Materials Lab, set the material to default. Then you must activate the Keep Gradient menu option. Finally, apply the gradient as a material by pressing the Control/Ctrl key when exiting the Terrain Editor *each time* you leave the Terrain Editor after editing the terrain.

Sun

The animation items for the sun include those for lights and objects. Internally, Bryce considers the sun to be an object and a light. You can't make changes to the sun as an object, nor to establish its intensity or range settings. Those are inside Bryce's sky model, so far out into the Brycean distance that you can't reach them!

For Sun options, we add a new category to our chart: Where the item is accessed. Possibilities are Sky & Fog Palette, Sky Lab, both, or n/a for those attributes that, although listed, do not have user-defined controls.

Sun states that do not animate are these: Link Sun to View, Disable Sun Light.

Pop-up Menu Name	Regular Name	Where Accessed	Description
Standard Object Options		n/a	Position, Rotation, Origin, Scale, Shear. (Warning! These options don't work!)
Standard Light Options		n/a	Color, Intensity, Range. (Same warning as above)
Disc Color	Sun Color	both	Color of visible sun disk and color cast by the sun.
Halo Color	Sun Glow Color	Sky & Fog	Sky Mode Control: Custom Color Swatch; Color of sky surrounding sun.
Sun Direction	Sun Control	both	Position of Sun; set by Sun Control or Azimuth/Altitude settings.

Sky

There are many things that can be animated in the sky. The first time you look at the list of pop-up menu items with the short, abbreviated list of names, you may wonder which does what and what corresponds with what else. Some of these controls are accessed from the Sky & Fog Palette, and others from inside the Sky Lab, and some are accessed from both. This list tells you where to access control for each particular item.

Although all of these items are listed in the Animation Keyframe pop-up menu, not all of them may be active. In addition, some are red herrings; although they are in the list, you'll never be able to make any changes for that attribute. For any sky move, they'll show up at the first and final keyframe of your scene, although they will not necessarily all be active. This is a supreme bummer. If you are working on an animation sequence where it's very important to know precisely what is being changed over time, your only recourse is to go to the AML and "clean up" your sky keyframes. We'll discuss this cleanup process in the next chapter, under the heading "If You Don't Read Any Other Section in This Chapter, Read This One!"

Pop-up Menu Name	Regular Name	Where Accessed	Description
Sky Level	Cloud Height	both	How high cloud plane is.
Cumulus Clr	Cumulus Cloud Color	Sky & Fog	Color of cumulus clouds.
Stratus Clr	Stratus Cloud Color		A pseudo-setting; controlled by Sun Color, which affects the stratus color.
Cover	Cloud Cover	both	How large each cloud puff is.
Amplitude	Amplitude	both	Contrast between cloud and sky.
Frequency	Frequency	both	Cloud pattern frequency.
Base color	Sky Color	Sky & Fog	Sky Mode Control: Custom Sky; Sky Color swatch; color of background sky.
Horiz Color	Horizon Color	Sky & Fog	Sky Mode Control: Custom Sky; Horizon Color swatch.
Dome Color	Sky Dome Color	both	The color and intensity of general light that falls down from above.
Def Color	Background Hue	Sky & Fog	Sky Mode Control: Atmosphere Off; Background Hue color swatch.
Shad Intense	Shadow Intensity	both	The strength of shadows cast by all objects.
Ambi Color	Ambient Color	both	Color of ambient light.
Ambi Intense	Pseudo-setting	n/a	Part of internal sky model; no controls.

Pop-up Menu Name	Regular Name	Where Accessed	Description
	Note: The Sky portion of the Keyframe pop-up menu contains two sections for haze and fog: this one, toward the top, and another one, toward the bottom. The top set is primarily for the fog and haze controls located both on the "outside" Sky & Fog Palette and in the Sky Lab, whereas the lower ones are mostly for additional fog and haze controls located in the Sky Lab.		
Haze Color	Haze Color	both	The color of haze.
Haze Density	Haze Density	both	How dense the haze is.
Fog Color	Fog Color	both	The color of fog.
Fog Thick	Fog Thickness	both	Thickness of fog. (In Sky & Fog Palette, set by horizontally dragging Fog control.)
Fog Density	Fog Density	both	Density of fog, filling in from horizon toward camera's position. (In the Sky & Fog Palette, set by vertically dragging the Fog Control.)
Moon Angle	Moon Control	Sky Lab	Moon Phase must be activated; how much of moon's surface is visible. Auto-Keyed together with Moon Tilt. When Moon Control is used, it generates information for both Moon Angle and Moon Tilt.
Moon Tilt	Moon Control	Sky Lab	Moon Phase must be activated; which way the lit surface of the moon "faces."
Earthshine	Earthshine	Sky Lab	Moon Phase must be activated; amount of "reflected" light appearing in shadowed portion of moon.
Moon Hardness	Softness	Sky Lab	Moon Phase must be activated; the fuzziness or sharpness of the border between light and shadow on the moon.
Illusion Min	Disk Size	Sky Lab	Sun/Moon Size; Disk Size slider. The size of sun or moon's disk when it is located high in the sky, away from the horizon.
Illusion Max	Horizon Illusion	Sky Lab	Sun/Moon Size; Horizon Illusion slider. The maximum possible size of the sun or moon when the sun or moon is located on the horizon.
LnkClr Blend	Color	Sky Lab	Blend With Sun; Color slider. The degree to which fog and/or haze color takes on the sun's color.
LnkVal Blend	Luminance	Sky Lab	Blend With Sun; Luminance. The degree that fog and/or haze color's luminosity takes sun color's luminosity.

Pop-up Menu Name	Regular Name	Where Accessed	Description
Ring Intense	Halo Rings: Intensity	Sky Lab	The intensity of ring or rings (when Secondary ring is active).
Ring 1 Width	Halo Rings: Radius	Sky Lab	Width of first halo ring.
Ring 2 Width	Halo Rings: Radius	Sky Lab	Width of second halo ring.
Rainbow Vis	Rainbow Opacity	Sky Lab	How opaque the rainbow appears.
Rain 1 Width	Rainbow Radius	Sky Lab	Width of rainbow.
Rain 2 Width	Rainbow Radius	Sky Lab	Secondary Rainbow option must be active; width of second rainbow.
			Note: When Auto-Key is active and you change the Rainbow Radius in the Sky Lab, Bryce will set a keyframe for both Rain 1 Width and Rain 2 Width.
Visible Air	Volumetric World: Density	Sky Lab	Density of visible atmosphere.
Wind Dir	Cloud Motion control	Sky Lab	The ring slider location matches the location of the wind source—that is, where the wind is blowing from.
			Note: Shut this off completely by clicking the Cloud Direction control's center button.
Wind Speed	Cloud Motion: Speed	Sky Lab	The speed of the wind carrying clouds.
Wind Turbu	Cloud Motion: Turbulence	Sky Lab	The degree of change of the clouds as they are blown by the wind.
Color Persp	Color Perspective	Sky Lab	How haze changes color over distance. RGB numerical settings.
Haze Base H	Haze Base Height	Sky Lab	This controls the onset of haze, how high it is.
			Note: Recall that there are two sets of fog and haze attributes in the list; this is the second set.
Haze Dist	Pseudo-setting	n/a	Some part of internal sky model that never received actual user controls. *Presence in menu and AML is meant to confuse you and test your character.*
Haze Thick	Haze Thickness	both	How much or how little haze exists.
Fog Base H	Fog Base Height	Sky Lab	The onset of fog as a function of height (altitude).
Fog Dist	Pseudo-setting	n/a	Another part of internal sky model that that lives deep in Bryce but has no user controls. *You will be a stronger person for having to navigate around this item in menu and AML lists.*

There are no animation settings for stars or comets. Obviously, phenomena like that, being way out in space, move at such relatively glacial speeds that the sky is unchanging. Even though the planetary rotation in a night's time causes the stars to move around Polaris, Bryce is a different world in that way.

Materials

Materials, when animated, contain two or more sets of timelines. There is the timeline for the material settings themselves, and, if one or more textures are used in a material, there is a separate timeline for each one.

Materials Timelines

The following chart lists all material properties that can be animated. The items listed live in the Materials Lab's grid.

Pop-up Menu Name	Regular Name	Description
Diff Color	Diffuse Color	The color of the object when it is struck by diffuse light.
Ambi Color	Ambient Color	The color of the object in ambient light.
Spec Color	Specular Color	The color of the object when it is struck by specular light.
Spec Halo	Specular Halo	The color of the specular halo (also thought of as how large or small the specular highlight is and whether or not it has a color cast).
Trans Color	Transparency Color	The color of the object when it is transparent, or the color of the shadow it casts when light shines through the object.
Diffusion	Diffusion	This is the amount that the object is illuminated by soft, diffuse light.
Ambience	Ambience	The amount that the object is lighted everywhere by ambient light (also can be thought of as how light the object is when it is in shadow).
Specularity	Specularity	The amount that the object is lighted with a bright hotspot.

Pop-up Menu Name	Regular Name	Description
Transparency	Transparency	The amount of light that is able to pass through an object.
Reflectivity	Reflection	The amount of surrounding light that is reflected off the surface of the object.
Bumpiness	Bump Height	The amount of texture-driven surface bumps.
Metallicity	Metallicity	Where Diffuse Color is shown in reflection.
Vol Density	Base Density	The amount of density for a volume object.
Vol Color	Volume Color	The color of the interior of a solid object.
Refraction	Refraction	The measure of light bending as it passes through a transparent object.
Vol Softness	Edge Softness	The amount of softness of the edge of a sphere volume object.
Vol FuzFact	Fuzzy Factor	The amount of extra hardening or softening of the base density volume texture.
Vol Quality	Quality/Speed	The setting for the number of rendering calculations of the volume object's interior. (high quality is slow; low quality is faster)

Texture Timeline

When a texture is applied to the object, the texture's name (such as, say, "RedFractal") becomes a separate item on the Keyframe pop-up menu. For texture components, you have these timelines:

Pop-up Menu Name	Regular Name	Description
Mapping	Texture Mapping Mode	Changes from one Texture Mapping Mode menu item to another.
Scaling	Scale Control	Changes in the Scale control settings of the Edit Texture Transformation Tools.
Offset	Offset Control	Changes in the Offset control settings of the Edit Texture Transformation Tools.
Rotation	Rotate Control	Changes in the Rotate control settings of the Edit Texture Transformation Tools.
Texture Data	Deep Texture Editor	Any change made in the DTE to the texture's noise, phase, filter, and the like.

To properly animate textures, you'll need to pay attention to the dependencies between texture attributes and material attributes. A texture, although a separate entity, is a subset of a material. Therefore, when setting keyframes for a texture, you must also set a keyframe for the material as well. No texture will successfully be animated on its own unless there is at least one keyframe set for the material property that is driven by the texture. If the texture drives more than one material property, it is necessary to set a keyframe for only one material property. So, for instance, if a single texture drives both Diffuse and Ambient Color, it will be necessary to set an initial keyframe for only one of those, say, Diff Color.

KEYFRAMING

Key events, or keyframes, are the structural anchor points that hold together the animated sequence. Key events are the "and then this happened" points of the animation story. They are like telephone poles, between which are suspended the wires of animated transitions as something changes from one condition to another. You will use key events to set up your animation and tell the story.

When it comes to setting up keyframes, the intent is this: Set a starting time and condition. Generate a key event for that time and condition. Move to a later time and change the condition; then generate a key event for that second time and condition. Move to a yet later time, change the condition, and generate a key event for that third time and condition. Keep doing this until all the key events are generated for all the different conditions that exist in the sequence.

Bryce has two strategies for generating key events. Auto-Key is the automatic strategy, where Bryce "watches" for all the changes in the objects over the duration of the sequence and generates key events for every change that takes place. In the manual option (Auto-Key off), you manually set the key events for different changes in objects over time. We'll discuss these both in depth.

Auto-Key On

When Auto-Key is on, Bryce watches for each and every change that is made to an object over time. Bryce remembers the changes and automatically records key events for each change. When you play back the sequence, all the changes that were made will be played back.

The rough order of work flow with Auto-Key on is this: Start. Drag the Time Scrubber to another time. Change something in the scene. Drag the Time Scrubber to another time (the time can be forward or backward). Make another change to the scene—or to put it more succinctly: Start. Change the time and then change the scene. Change the time again and then change scene again. Repeat until all changes are made. Stop.

The left column of Figure 14.19 shows the process of creating a three-event trajectory with Auto-Key on.

Auto-Key On Walkthrough

1. In a new scene, create a cylinder. Reposition it at the lower-left corner of the working window.

2. Drag the Time Scrubber to some arbitrary point on the timeline.

3. Drag the cylinder to a new position at the upper-right corner of the window. As you drag, a blue line is drawn. It marks the route of the cylinder.

4. Release the mouse button. The timeline segment between the starting point and the scrubber fills in with dark green. At the same moment, the little key icon between the Add and Remove Keyframe controls darkens to indicate that a keyframe was added.

5. Drag the scrubber back to the left, so it's somewhere around the midpoint of the dark green segment of the timeline. As you drag the scrubber, the cylinder retraces its steps backward along the blue line.

6. Drag the cylinder upward. The blue line is reshaped as you drag, and when you release the mouse button, the key icon once again darkens. Each time you move to a new point on the timeline and change the condition of the selected object, a new keyframe is automatically added.

Auto-Key Off

When Auto-Key is off, you're on your own; the process of adding keyframes is completely manual. The rough order of work flow with Auto-Key off is like so: Set up the initial condition at the beginning time (00:00:00.0). Click Add Keyframe to record that initial condition. Move forward to a new time and change the condition. Add a keyframe to record that change. Move to yet another point in time. Change the condition again and add a keyframe. Continue in this fashion until all changes are made. Stop.

Auto-Key On   Auto-Key Off

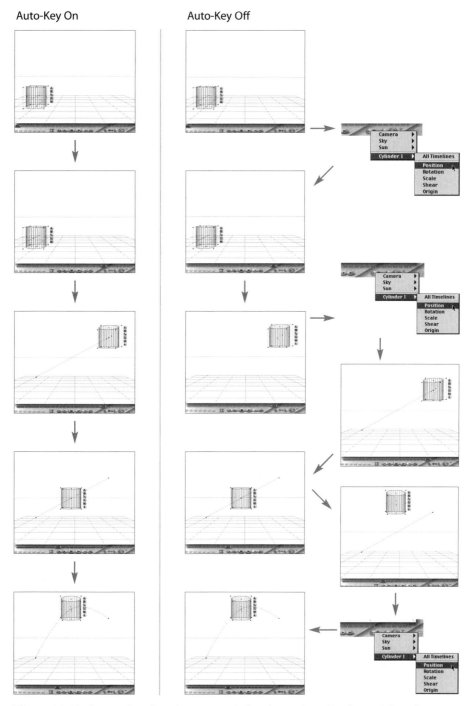

Figure 14.19 Generating three key events. Left column: Auto-Key is on; right column: Auto-Key is off.

Figure 14.19 (right column) shows the process of creating a three-event motion trajectory with Auto-Key off. The results are identical to those with Auto-Key on, so you can compare the two approaches.

Auto-Key Off Walkthrough

1. Create a new scene. From the Timeline Options pop-up menu, choose Auto-Key to turn it off.

2. Create a cylinder and position it as in the example with Auto-Key on. From the Add Keyframe pop-up menu, choose Cylinder 1 > Position. A keyframe is created representing the starting point of the sequence, and the key icon turns black.

3. Drag the Time Scrubber some distance to the right.

4. Drag the cylinder to the upper-right corner of the window. Notice this time that no blue line is added to the scene. Pay a visit to the Add Keyframe pop-up menu, choose Cylinder 1 > Position, and *voilà!* A keyframe is added, and the blue line appears.

5. Drag the scrubber back to the left, and the cylinder follows along.

6. Drag the cylinder upward, away from the blue line.

7. Visit the Add Keyframe pop-up menu one more time, to add a keyframe for the cylinder's new position, and the blue line is redrawn to follow suit.

Advantages and Disadvantages of Each Approach

Each of these strategies is totally viable for animating in Bryce. Each approach has its advantages and disadvantages.

With Auto-Key on, you always need to know when you are. With Auto-Key off, you need to know what exactly you're affecting and to be sure to record each change as you make it.

Auto-Key On

When Auto-Key is active, the good news is that any change that you make to an object over time will be recorded. The bad news is that any change that you make to an object over time will be recorded.

Of course, it all depends on whether the change that you made is one you intended for a certain portion of the time (the good-news scenario), or whether you intended to make a global change to an item for the entire sequence and actually made a local change for a portion of the sequence (the bad-news scenario). It's good when you want it to happen, and it's bad when you don't want it to happen.

The advantage to using Auto-Key is that your work is reduced to moving to a new time and then editing objects, the camera, or the environment. You are freed from the added thought process and actions needed to generate keyframes for each move your objects make. Auto-Key is quite a boon, especially when you're just starting out with animation in Bryce, because you can concentrate on questions such as "What does this thing do for animation?" and not have to worry about remembering to add the keyframe at each of the appropriate times.

The main trick to working with Auto-Key is to know when you are in relation to the attribute you are modifying.

Auto-Key and Scene File Size

At the same time, though, entrusting Bryce with the task of adding all those keyframes results in something we call "Auto-Key droppings," where initial keyframes exist for all items in your scene. The larger the scene, the larger the Auto-Key droppings pile—and those droppings can create quite a pile of Auto-Key guano for scenes with lots and lots of objects.

A scene file filled with Auto-Key droppings is a larger scene file. Once Bryce considers an object to be animating, it allows scads more room to the file to accommodate all those real or mythical changes the object undergoes during the course of animation.

Our most flagrant example of conspicuous Auto-Key waste is the scene file for the Sierpinski object shown in Chapter 1. The scene file was constructed with Auto-Key on and has a total of 3,125 pyramids. Big mistake. The file size weighed in at over 27 MB and took forever to open and save (26 minutes to save the scene file!). When keyframes were removed from the scene, the scene took less than a minute to save, and the final file size was just over 7 MB. Auto-Key can get ugly. Very ugly.

Auto-Key Off

When Auto-Key is off, the good news is that you can exercise precise control when adding each keyframe to the sequence. The bad news is that you must exercise precise control when adding each keyframe to the sequence.

When Auto-Key is off, you need to be extremely conscious of each change that you are making to your objects or environment in your sequence. Not only do you need to know when you are, but you also need to know precisely what you are changing. For those attributes whose keyframes are set in tandem (Zoom X and Zoom Y, Moon Angle and Moon Tilt, sometimes Scale and Shear) you need to save keyframes for both.

You have to be master of each and every setting there is, including knowing which of the items on the Add Keyframe pop-up menu are worthless dead ends. Since we just provided you with the exhaustive list of what does what, it is possible to follow each and every animated attribute. If in doubt, you can always add a keyframe for All Timelines for a particular object.

The advantage of an Auto-Key off sequence is that you won't have any Auto-Key droppings that you need to manage. Turning Auto-Key off is essential for large scene files containing lots and lots of objects.

The drawback to turning Auto-Key off is that you may go to a new time, make a change, and then forget to record or add it. Once you have introduced time into your scene and are animating with Auto-Key off, you must record the result of each and every change. If you don't, once you press the Play button, Bryce will display whatever has been keyframed and will disregard anything not keyframed. Your oh-so-carefully applied edit will be completely lost if you inadvertently failed to record it. (Here's a hankie!)

Not Either/Or, but Both/And

So far, we've been describing how each keyframe generation strategy works. We're not implying that you must work only one way or the other way. You can combine both methods. In fact, it may be more efficient at times to go back and forth between Auto-Key off and Auto-Key on. Before launching into possible mix-and-match methods, we'll lay out scenarios for the way that key events can exist for a given option over the duration of a sequence. This will help you understand how to work with Auto-Key on and off and to move between the two approaches.

Keyframes and Animation Scenarios

Figure 14.20 shows an un-animated state plus four possible scenarios for object animations that take place over time. (Although the same scenarios can exist for skies or object attributes, we use objects for ease of reference.) The little vertical bars mark the key events. You may recognize the general appearance of these options when you visit the Advanced Motion Lab (more on the AML in the next chapter).

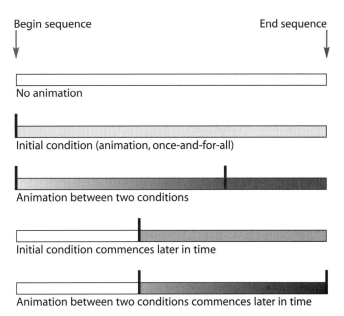

Figure 14.20 An object's attribute being animated. Top: No animation (no keyframes, no nothing). Second row: Animation exists as an initial state, but does not change for the duration of the sequence. Third row: Animation from one condition to another. Fourth row: Initial condition is established at a later time. Bottom row: Animation between two conditions begins later in the sequence.

Here are the four scenarios:

- *Not Animated.* There are no keyframes for the object; it is not animated. This is the normal scenario with Auto-Key off. If you have Auto-Key on, you need to make a change to the object's keyframe(s) to put it in this state (we'll tell you how later). If an object is not animated, you can change it no matter what the current time is set to. That's because there is no initial state for Auto-Key to compare against, so there's no possible way to record a change as a new key event.

- *Animated Initial Condition.* This is the normal scenario for all objects created when Auto-Key is on. The initial condition persists for the duration of the sequence. Therefore, if you need to change something for the entire sequence, tap the left bracket key ([) to move the time to the beginning, make your change, and then go back to whatever point in time you were at before doing the once-for-all change. (Otherwise, the change you make will look like the next option, Animated Object.)

- *Animated Object.* Two or more animated conditions exist, and there is a transition from condition A to B, and so on. For animation in Bryce, this is the most common scenario.

- *Delayed Initial Condition.* The initial keyframe is set not at the beginning of the time, but at a later point in time. With no additional changes after the initial keyframe, the object exists in a single-condition. When Auto-Key is off, this might happen if you record the first keyframe at that later point. You can also change the second scenario (Animated Initial Condition) into this one by moving the key ticker mark's position in the Advanced Motion Lab (more on that later).

- *Delayed Animation.* A delayed initial keyframe is followed by another keyframe later in the sequence, resulting in an animated transition from one condition to another. This scenario is identical to Animated Object except that the animation commences later in the sequence. Like the previous scenario (Delayed Initial Condition), this scenario is more apt to occur when working with Auto-Key off and setting the initial keyframe later in the sequence.

When to Work with Auto-Key On

When you're just starting out with animation, turn Auto-Key on; you need only worry about the current time and editing your object.

If you're creating a scene that doesn't have a lot of items in it, use Auto-Key.

If you're animating many objects at once, as with, say multiple objects, hierarchies, and the like, use Auto-Key to record the changes for all the objects as you go. Otherwise, you'll have to click the Add Keyframe button to add keyframes for all the objects, and possibly add keyframes for other things besides what you want to.

When to Work with Auto-Key Off

If you positively abhor the notion of Auto-Key droppings (and there are some Brycers who are adamant!), then don't use Auto-Key!

If you are working with a scene that contains lots and lots of objects, then don't use Auto-Key. Chances are pretty good that, of all those objects in your scene, not all of them will be animating. (If they are all animating, then we welcome you to the loony bin with open arms!)

When Auto-Key is off, you will need to manually create a keyframe for each animated change you wish to occur in your sequence. Although we walked you through a specific example earlier in this Keyframing section, we outline the most basic steps to adding keyframes with Auto-Key off:

1. Set your Time Scrubber to the desired time.

2. Make the change to the object or the environment.

3. Click the Add Keyframe icon until the pop-up menu appears (see Figure 14.16). Select the option from the pop-up menu for the object and attribute you just changed. Either choose the option, say, Scale, or else choose All Timelines for that object.

   Simply clicking the control will add keyframes for all selected objects in your scene, plus keyframes for the sky and sun, as well as a keyframe for the camera if you are in Camera View. This may add too many key events and may result in weird playback behavior. Then again, it may not. But you never know.

Going from Auto-Key Off to Auto-Key On

You can combine things, though. You can build a scene with Auto-Key off. Then, when you are ready to animate, turn Auto-Key on. You still need to create initial conditions for the animating objects to make Auto-Key work. Starting with Auto-Key off, look at your scene from Camera View and select only those objects you will be animating. Record an initial keyframe by clicking the Add Keyframe control. You will now have an initial keyframe for your objects, the camera, and the sky and sun (if you don't want to animate the sky or sun, you'll have to remove those). Then switch to Auto-Key on to record the moves for your chosen objects over time. You will not have the burden of file size dragging you down, and you get the advantages of Bryce's remembering the changes that you made to those objects.

The problem with going back and forth between Auto-Key off and on is that there's no way to tell at a glance which mode you're in. You have to look at the Animation Options pop-up menu to see. You can tell pretty quickly by behavior, however. But until you are absolutely confident that you can tell, you may do something you regret. As one aphorism puts it, "Experience is a great teacher, but she sends terrific bills."

Removing Keyframes

Working with keyframes involves more than simply adding them to your scene. Inevitably, after putting them into your sequence, you'll want to take them out.

Well, not all of them. Just some of them. Or one of them. Or that problem one over there. You need to know what to do to backtrack and clean up after yourself, because, as sure as the sun rises in the east, you'll end up doing something that you'll need to undo later.

Removing keyframes is a simple reversal of the process that you used in the first place to add a keyframe (select the object, go to the time, change the object, add the keyframe).

1. Select the object whose keyframe you want to remove.

2. Use the Next/Previous Keyframe buttons to navigate to the particular keyframe you want to remove.

3. Press the Delete Keyframe (–) button to make the pop-up menu appear. From the listing under the object, select the attribute you want to remove.

   If you want to remove more than one attribute for that object, you can either select All Timelines rather than an individual attribute or continue deleting the attributes for that keyframe until all the ones you want to get rid of are removed.

   If you want to remove all keyframes for an object and it has only an initial state recorded (a single keyframe), then navigate to that keyframe where the initial state was recorded and delete All Timelines for the object. (You can also easily do this in the Advanced Motion Lab; we'll describe this in the next chapter.)

The result of removing a keyframe for an object containing multiple keyframes is that the removed keyframed condition goes away. Conditions that had surrounded the removed keyframe are now blended together. Suppose that the color of your object starts out with three keyframes: blue, then green, then white. If you remove the center (green) keyframe, the result will be a two-keyframe transposition from blue to white. If, instead, you removed the last (white) keyframe, the result is a two-keyframe transition from blue to green. If you start with two keyframes and remove one of them, the object will change to the remaining keyframe's condition. For example, if you have two keyframes, blue and green, removing the first (blue) one will result in a green obect that doesn't change. The converse is true: removing the second (green) keyframe results in a single, continuous blue condition. When there is only a single (initial state) keyframe, the object doesn't change to any other condition; it simply ceases to have any animated state. For an object with a single blue keyframe, removing that keyframe does not cause the object to cease being blue, it causes the object to cease being animated. Sometimes to see the effect of keyframe removal, you may need to move to a new frame and back, just to coerce Bryce to update its display with the new keyframe-less condition of the object.

On a slightly different approach to removing keyframes, suppose you are working with Auto-Key on, creating or working with motion trajectories. You create a keyframe, look at it, exclaim, "My God, what have I done? How did I get here?!" and immediately repent doing the deed, invoking the Undo command. Your object moves back to its previous position, but the key event stays. Your trajectory is marred; it's not the same as it ever was. You'll have to manually remove the keyframe by navigating to that spot in time and then using the Remove Keyframe control as we just described. And the days go on.

At the beginning of this section, we said you don't want to take out all the keyframes, just some of them. But there are times when you really do want to remove each and every keyframe in a sequence. What do you do then? The ultra mega remove every single last keyframe from your scene key command is this: Press ⌘-Option-Shift/Ctrl+Alt+Shift and click the Remove Keyframe button. Bryce presents you with two highly cryptic alerts, composed, no doubt, in the wee hours. The first is, "What're you up to?" and the second one is "Done!" Warning! Once you've committed yourself to this option, there is no going back. Those cryptic alerts have no Cancel buttons, only OK buttons. If you're not sure about removing all keyframes, save the scene beforehand. You can then revert to the saved version as a last resort.

TRAJECTORIES

Bryce objects and the camera (which, for the purpose of this discussion, we'll treat as an object) move along a trajectory—a motion path through Bryce space. Since we'll later refer to a related item called an object path, we'll stick to the term *trajectory* for the editable path that travels through Bryce space.

Trajectories represent two simultaneous concepts: movement in space and movement in time. The key events for a trajectory are marked with the blue handle points. Each trajectory handle represents the location of the object at a particular moment in time. Depending on the type of trajectory an object may have, the location itself may be fairly complex in its own right. Ultimately, you'll get more control over your scene if you can separate the location trajectory from the moments-in-time trajectory. We'll discuss strategies for doing exactly that as we continue.

Bryce's Key Events

In the creation of motion trajectories, you are dealing with two elements of object motion: the location and the timing of that motion. There are a few ways to approach the generation of motion trajectories:

1. Pay no attention to timing; think location-location-location. Work only on the shape of the trajectory; worry about the timing later (we'll get more into this with motion trajectories and with object paths).

2. Work with both location and timing from the outset.

3. Using a hybrid approach, you can roughly block out the timing, but pay more attention to location. Afterward, tweak the timing to match.

The latter two options require some forethought about time. Of course, the first option requires afterthought about time. Taking the action in the BOUNCE sequence as an example, consider how long a bounce will take. To establish the time for your clip, get a stopwatch or a watch with a sweep second hand (in a pinch, your computer's clock will do if you can get the seconds to show). Mark the beginning of the time and then picture the event in your imagination: "Mark! Roll, fall, bounce! Up arc, down, bounce. Mark!" How long did that take? Set that time as the length of your sequence. For this example, we set it to be 1 second, 10 frames (00:00:01.10).

Creating Trajectories

To set up a trajectory, you use both time and position. First, set a time with the Time Scrubber. Then position with the object. One way to do this, if you've a sense for how long the entire duration is going to be, is to set your last point on the trajectory and then go back and set the in-between spots. Set the trajectory's start (at time 00:00:00.0) and its end (at Time End). Then move the scrubber back to in-between spots and set in-between places. We'll use this method in the tutorial exercise at the end of this section to re-create the BOUNCE scene that you've been working with so far.

When Auto-Key is on, simply move the scrubber and then move the object. When Auto-Key is off, you move the time, then move the object, and then set a keyframe—it's best to press the mouse on the Add Keyframe button and let the pop-up menu appear and then choose Object > Position.

Moving Key Points/Position

Bryce calls them handles, the little things on
a trajectory. Figure 14.21 shows a trajectory in
wireframe view with the parts labeled.

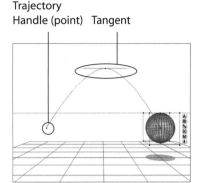

Trajectory
Handle (point)   Tangent

Figure 14.21 An object and its
trajectory.

- *Trajectory.* This is the line of the trajectory.
  The line will be a different color, depending on the family color of the object. The
  camera, being blue by default, will have a
  blue trajectory, lights will be yellow, most
  other objects will be gray, and so on.

- *Trajectory Handle Points.* This is a tricky one;
  although the manual refers to these as
  handles, which does accurately imply something by which you can grab and
  manipulate something else, our years of experience working with Bézier handles shows us there can be confusion. Therefore, we'll be sure to use the word
  points to be wholly unambiguous and, on whim, will call them either trajectory
  points or handle points.

- *Trajectory Tangents.* These will be introduced in the next section; they are made
  visible or not by settings in the Object Attributes dialog box. (*Tangent* is the term
  for the item that, in 2D vector drawing applications such as Adobe Illustrator or
  Macromedia FreeHand, may be called *handle*; hence our pointed attempt to
  avoid confusing the terms *tangent* and *handle*. If you are unfamiliar with those
  vector drawing applications, then please excuse this extra explanation.)

Object Attributes Dialog Box: Animation Tab

For each object in Bryce, the Object Attributes dialog box has an Animation panel
for setting preferences for the object's motion trajectory. Figure 14.22 shows the
Animation tab of the Object Attributes dialog box.

Trajectory Visibility

Depending on the task you are working on, you may want your trajectory showing,
not showing, or showing only when selected. Here are some possible reasons for
each choice:

- *Show When Selected.* This is the default state and is good for most occasions.
  When the object is selected, the trajectory line appears. When the object is
  deselected, the trajectory disappears.

- *Show Always.* When you are analyzing an object's motion and want to see its entire path, even when another object is selected, use this approach.

- *Don't Show.* Suppose that you are setting an object's rotation. The object's control handle may be in the exact same location as the trajectory keyframe handle. When the trajectory is showing, Bryce favors the trajectory over the rotation. To rotate the object, press the Command/Ctrl key, and the cursor changes to the rotation arrow. But when you are moving a blue trajectory handle, pressing the Command/Ctrl causes the handle to move on the *z* axis. To ensure that you are, in fact, rotating the object, make the trajectory disappear and rotate to your heart's content. (You'll have an opportunity to do just that in the tutorial!)

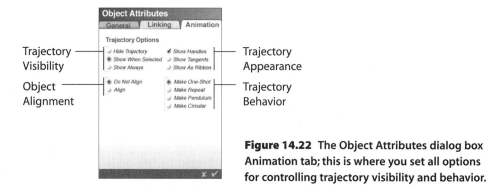

Figure 14.22 The Object Attributes dialog box Animation tab; this is where you set all options for controlling trajectory visibility and behavior.

Trajectory Appearance

The three options at the top right of the dialog box are for choosing the appearance of the trajectory and the parts of it that appear when it is visible. Figure 14.23 shows each of these options.

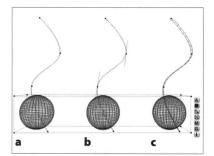

Figure 14.23 Trajectory appearance: a) Show Handles; b) Show Tangents; c) Show as Ribbon.

- *Show Handles.* Set the visibility of the blue trajectory handle points with this option. The default setting is on. When trajectory handles are showing, you can edit and move them. When they're not showing, they cannot be edited. Also, showing the entire path without the blue trajectory points allows you to focus your attention on the shape of the entire trajectory pathway without being distracted by individual points.

- *Show Tangents*. A tangent is a line that touches but doesn't intersect another line. In trajectories, the tangent displays information about the curves of the trajectory surrounding the particular handle point. The tangents are a visual representation of what Bryce is using to interpolate from one point to the next as it draws the best, smoothest route from one point to the next. (If you've worked with Bézier handles, you'll probably recognize these.) Tangents are for display only, to provide information about the shape. They have no direct editing function; you cannot drag a tangent to change the trajectory's shape. We will discuss how to edit trajectory handle points and change the appearance of tangents a little later.

- *Show as Ribbon*. Sometimes a single small line is simply too narrow. Show as Ribbon widens the trajectory, making it easier to see and easier to select. A ribbon is similar in appearance to a path, but the two, in fact, are different. (A path is an independent object, whereas a ribbon trajectory will appear and disappear depending on your visibility setting.)

Object Alignment

The Align to Trajectory option in the Object Attributes dialog box lets you align an object to the trajectory. The idea is to change the object's orientation so that it follows the trajectory path. The purpose is to make the object continually face in the direction of the trajectory line. It's a shortcut that's easier than, say, continually rotating the object so that it faces in the direction of its motion. However, there's a sticky problem with alignment in how it actually plays out. The trajectory information that says "you are here" can pull some funny loop-the-loops going around curves and arcs and the like. Changing the path or the trajectory ever so slightly when the object is aligned may bring on this problem. Look at Figure 14.24, which shows two nearly identical pyramid trajectories. Notice that in the first stages of travel along the motion path, the top pyramid does a funky flip. Lowering the second anchor point just a tad takes the extra arc out of the path that causes the flip. At this point, there is no known cure for this problem, so if you do align an object to a path, beware the flip.

> **TIP:** For object alignment, you may have to change the object's Definition Coordinates to make it face along the path. For the pyramids in Figure 14.24, the Definition Coordinates were changed to rotate the pyramids 90° on the x axis so that the pyramid "pointed" toward the path. The same is true of cone objects as well, since they "point" in a manner similar to pyramids.

When you choose Align to Trajectory, the object follows the direction of the trajectory, "pointing" in whatever direction the trajectory is facing. Of course, each object has a default way that it faces, based on the Definition Coordinates of the object. When you set up cones and pyramids to align to the trajectory, they don't move around facing point first, but they lumber along side first. You need to redefine the Definition Coordinates to make them point down the trajectory. It's a pretty simple thing to do, and you're already in the Object Attributes dialog box anyhow. Click the General tab, and, from the pop-up menu triangle next to the Absolute Coordinates, select Definition Coordinates. For Rotate, enter 90° on the x axis. The object will now point forward down the path.

Whether lumbering sideways or pointing, your object may still have some overall orientation troubles when it is aligned to the trajectory. Depending on the shape of the trajectory and the arcs and curves in it, the object may roll around this way and that. Figure 14.24a shows two nearly identical object trajectories. Notice that the second trajectory handle point is positioned slightly differently. Figure 14.24b is a series of rendered frames (with wireframes superimposed) of the point where the top trajectory directs the object to flip around. Compare the materials for both objects, and for the first three images for the top object; something is afoot, Watson! That teeny extra arc in the trajectory is all it takes to make the object oriented another, weird, way. It's apparently a function of the mathematics involved to calculate and mark the trajectory, and there is no fix for it in Bryce 4 (4.0 or 4.01). In this case, it seems that a workaround involves being a little more straight.

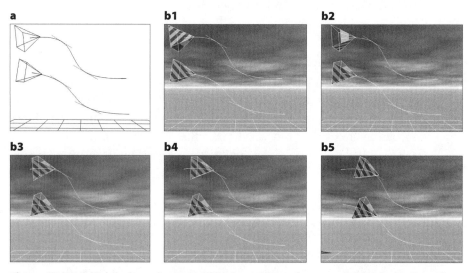

Figure 14.24 A kink in the trajectory: a) Wireframe view of two nearly identical trajectories; b) the material settings and superimposed wireframes on these rendered images from the sequence demonstrate the twist that occurs at the very beginning of the sequence.

If, as you work with your own trajectory, you get the seemingly random flip around, move your Time Scrubber to the time when the object flips. Then adjust the trajectory points following the object to see if you can get things straightened out.

Trajectory Behavior

Trajectory behavior addresses the question: "How does the object travel along the trajectory over time?" All of the trajectory behavior options address the issue of what takes place when the available time extends beyond the final trajectory handle point.

The scene file, TRAJECTORY BEHAVIOR, located in this chapter's folder on the CD-ROM, contains four pyramids, all with identical trajectories and each set to one of the four behavior settings. The final key event takes place at Frame 24 (or time 00:00:01.09), even though the time extends to Frame 91 (or 00:00:06.01). Figure 14.25 shows the wireframe view of the scene, though it must be seen on your computer screen for full effect.

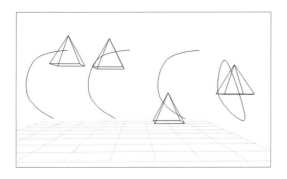

Figure 14.25 Trajectory behavior: Wireframe view of a scene that shows the different trajectory behavior options.

- *Make One-Shot.* The default behavior, Make One-Shot, is a simple one-to-one correlation between time and location. The object goes from the beginning to the end of the trajectory and then stops, even if the available time continues after the end point.

- *Make Repeat.* With this option, the motion along the trajectory repeats again and again for as long as the time exists. If the trajectory is keyed to time period from A to B, but the duration extends beyond B, the trajectory motion will repeat again and again to the limit of the duration.

- *Make Pendulum.* This option, like the Make Repeat option, extends the same trajectory motion beyond the time limit to fill the duration of the time. However, instead of repeating the motion each time, the pendulum goes back and forth.

- *Make Circular.* This option differs from the others; it actually changes the geometry as well as the behavior. The last trajectory handle point is changed to occupy the same point as the first handle point. To define a circular trajectory, you need a minimum of three points. (You actually need an extra, fourth, point, since the last one will move to the same location as the first when you choose the Make Circular option.) Figure 14.26 shows a trajectory with five points before and after it has been made into a circular trajectory. You can, of course, add additional points to the trajectory once you've closed the circle. If the duration extends beyond the time associated with the last point, the object will continue to move along the circular path again and again for as long as the time duration will allow.

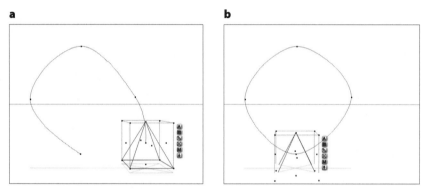

a   **b**

Figure 14.26 When a trajectory with five points is made into a circular trajectory, the first and the last point occupy the same space, giving the circle the appearance of having only four points.

Moving Trajectory Handles

With Auto-Key on:

- Moving the object at a new time (no keyframe existing) creates a keyframe for that new position.

- Moving the object at an already-existing keyframe changes the position of the object for that keyframe.

- Moving one of the trajectory control handles changes the position of the object for the particular keyframe associated with the control handle (as in the previous example, except instead of moving the object and having the trajectory move with it, moving the point on the trajectory).

• Moving the trajectory at a point other than any of the keyframe control points moves the entire trajectory. No new keyframes are added.

You may encounter a little "gotcha!" when moving trajectory handles when Auto-Key is on. (You'll never catch us declaring that Bryce 4 is bug free, oh no! Bryce 4 has bugs, and this is one of 'em.) When you are moving an object at an existing keyframe (the second example listed above), sometimes Bryce will not move the object and existing trajectory handle, but will instead add a new keyframe and trajectory handle. Yes, that's right: two keyframes at one time. Ouch! You'll recognize this by the kink in the trajectory. The fix for this problem involves moving keyframes in the Advanced Motion Lab, discussed in the "Key Event Ticker Marks" section of the next chapter.

Entire Trajectory

You can move the entire trajectory by dragging it. Select the object; the trajectory should be showing. Then move your mouse so that your pointer is located on any part of the trajectory that is not the object and is not any of the trajectory handle points. Drag the trajectory. The entire trajectory moves as one. Note that since the trajectory line is very thin, you'll have to make sure that the tip of the pointer arrow is actually over the trajectory line. Don't be surprised if this procedure doesn't work on the first attempt. If you have the trajectory showing all the time, you can also select the object by clicking the trajectory. The handle points appear, and the object is selected.

> **TIP:** You can move the entire trajectory using the Reposition tools or the Reposition shortcuts (arrow keys). Select the object and then click the trajectory itself. Once you have clicked the trajectory, you can use the Reposition tools or arrow keys to move the entire trajectory!

Trajectory Handle Points

For the trajectory, Bryce draws the best, smoothest path from one point to the next. However, it's highly likely that you don't want the trajectory to follow the best, smoothest path. That bounce scene, for instance, has a trajectory that comes to a sharp point. When you want to alter the shape of the trajectory and change the curves from the default curves, work with the trajectory handle points. There are three ways to change the shape of the curves when working with the trajectory points; they use the special modifier keys T, C, and B.

Tension

Tension adjusts the amount of tension in the curve surrounding the point, creating a fuller curve or a not-so-full curve. To adjust tension, press the T key. When the T key is down, point the mouse at the trajectory handle you want to adjust. The handle is outlined, and the pointer changes from an arrow to a double-cross arrow. Drag the mouse either left or right. (Once you begin dragging the mouse, it's no longer necessary to keep the T key pressed down.) You'll see the tangent handles extend or contract and the trajectory change accordingly. In addition, in the status display, you'll see a numerical readout. Note that 0.00 is the standard, default position of tension. If you want to get back to this normal tension, then you'll need to drag the handle again with the T key held down (see Figure 14.27). Also, once you begin changing tangents, you have ventured beyond the realm where you can undo the last move; ⌘-Z/Ctrl+Z does not work with changes to tangents.

Continuity

Continuity, activated by pressing the C key before dragging the trajectory handle, controls whether the curve is continuous or broken. Continuity is the key to making the path go to peaks (such as, for instance, the point of a bounce).

Bias

Bias, adjusted by pressing the B key before dragging the trajectory handle, controls whether the curve favors one or the other side of the trajectory handle (see Figure 14.27).

Twist

There is another option: twist—but although you can attempt to use twist on a trajectory, it doesn't work. Twist really comes into its own when used with an object path, discussed in the next section.

Straight Lines

In addition to making the adjustments we've just mentioned, you can completely remove the smooth curve (called a spline) from the trajectory by a little trick in the Advanced Motion Lab. (The Advanced Motion Lab is discussed in depth in the next chapter; you may need to turn there to completely understand these instructions.) For the selected object, look at the Position Attributes timeline in the Sequencer. Click the ticker mark and tap the I key (I stands for interpolation);

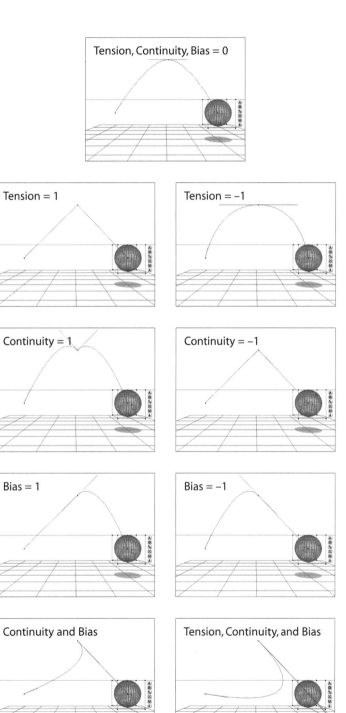

Figure 14.27 Tension, continuity, and bias.

the segment of the trajectory from the selected ticker mark to the next trajectory point is straightened out to a line. Tapping I again will change the trajectory segment back to a smooth spline shape (see Figure 14.28).

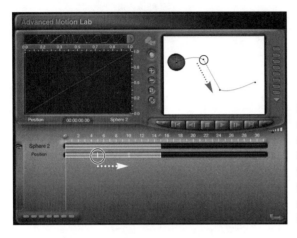

Figure 14.28 Straightening segments of a trajectory in the Advanced Motion Lab: The encircled ticker mark corresponds to the encircled control point on the trajectory. A tap of the I key straightened the segment that falls after the control point.

Constrained Adjustment of Points

You can drag a trajectory point around to move it. That's the simple way. Surprise, surprise, surprise: Bryce also has an option to move trajectory points with precision, to constrain movement along one axis. (Who woulda thunk it? Bryce? Provide more detailed precision? But of course!)

- X *axis*. To move only on the *x* axis, press the X key and then drag the point. You can also use the Control key on the Macintosh or the Ctrl+Alt keys in Windows.

  However, using the Windows key combination of Ctrl+Alt, you need to time the pressing of the keys oh so carefully, or else! If you press the modifier keys before you press the mouse, you will not move the *x* axis; you will instead twist the point. Oops! So the mouse button must go down (and stay down) before the modifier keys are pressed. However, once the mouse button is down, also be careful to press Ctrl+Alt *before you begin moving* the mouse. Otherwise, with the mouse down and moving prior to activating the constrain keys, the motion will not be constrained, and that trajectory control point will move willy-nilly. Did your eyes glaze over? We don't blame you. Skip over this tortured "do this before that but not before the other" froo-frah and just press the X key to constrain on the *x* axis.

- Y *axis*. To move only on the *y* axis (adjust its vertical position), press the Y key, and drag to change position. (You can also press the Option/Alt key, but the same tortured warnings apply to the use of the Option/Alt key as for the Windows key combination above. Save yourself the hassle and just use the Y key.)

- Z *axis*. To move the trajectory handle only on the *z* axis, press the Z key or press the Command key (Macintosh) or Ctrl key (Windows).

Trajectory Walkthrough

We've used the BOUNCE scene to demonstrate various animation features. Now we're going to work step by step to re-create and animate that scene. We'll take things in roughly this order: Create the objects in the scene, then create a trajectory for the ball's location, and finally add rotation and the bounce-impact squash. In the next chapter, after we've introduced the Advanced Motion Lab, we'll make speed adjustments to the animation.

Create a Scene and Set Up the Camera and Initial State

1. Create a new scene at Bryce's default size. Make sure that your preferences (Edit > Preferences) are set to Create Objects at World Center. For this tutorial, we're

Figure 14.29 Making sure Auto-Key is on at the beginning of the work session.

going to be using Bryce's Auto-Key feature. Auto-Key is on the Animation Options pop-up menu, to the right of that AML entryway button. Make sure it's checked, as shown in Figure 14.29.

2. Create a cylinder.

3. Move your camera perspective so that the camera is roughly in front. Right now, you're in Director's View. The Trackball is useful for rotation of this sort. To constrain the Trackball on the horizontal axis, hold down the Control (Mac) or the Ctrl (Win) key. Then drag to the right (you will appear to be traveling left) until you are sitting in front of the cylinder and the grid, and the center wireframe line of the cylinder aligns with the center grid line of the ground plane's grid. You've roughly eyeballed yourself to a position right out in front (see Figure 14.30).

4. Next, let's place the camera in exactly your position. From the Camera pop-up menu, select Camera to Director (see Figure 14.31).

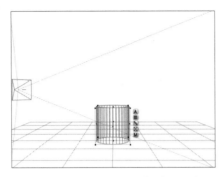

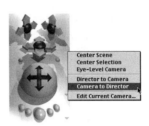

Figure 14.30 Using the cylinder and the ground plane to help align the Director's View out in front on the z axis.

Figure 14.31 Camera to Director menu command on the Controls Palette

> **TIP:** Reminder! The bottom option on the menu is always the one that moves the other perspective camera to your current location.

The result is that now, if you look at your scene from the top view, your camera will be in the position of Director's View. Making Director's View and Camera View one and the same will make the Director's camera visible when you are looking at your scene from other views. If you checked it from top view, go back to Director's View.

5. Move the cylinder to the left. About 8 taps on the left arrow key moves you to the left side of the frame as you look at it, as in Figure 14.32.

6. Now let's make the cylinder grow taller. Point your mouse over the top center, so the pointer changes to the Y cursor. Press the Shift key so that your resizing will be incremental and will stay snapped to the grid, which will make it a cinch for us to

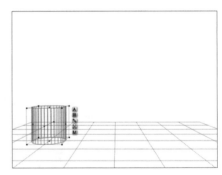

Figure 14.32 Move the cylinder to the left.

plop a sphere on top of the cylinder. Drag up until the cylinder snaps three times. The top will fill two-thirds of the scene window. The final height on ours was 51.20 (see Figure 14.33).

7. Create a sphere. With ten taps on the Page Up key, its bottom should be even with the top of the cylinder; eight taps to the left should place it right on top of the cylinder, as Figure 14.33 shows.

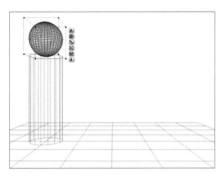

Figure 14.33 The cylinder is increased in height, and the sphere now rests on top of it.

Compared to the cylinder, that ball is a little too big. It needs to be small enough to convincingly roll on the surface of the cylinder. You can reduce it by eye (see Figure 14.34), but if you want to check with our measurements, the sphere ended up measuring 14.67 on all three axes.

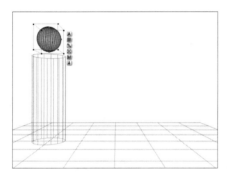

Figure 14.34
After reducing the sphere.

Now the sphere is slightly smaller. It also happens to float slightly above the cylinder. If it isn't one thing, it's another. (This is just How Bryce Is.)

8. Click the down arrow (the Land Objects Down icon) to land the sphere on the cylinder below.

9. Next, set the sphere's position a little to the left on the cylinder. It does need room to roll, after all! To precisely see its position, switch to front view (Tap the 4 key). You can see exactly where the sphere is located in relation to the cylinder without any confusing perspective. Option-Shift/Alt+Shift and a tap on the left arrow key moves the cylinder in half-nudge increments. We tapped ours twice, which is the same as a single tap on the left arrow (sometimes it's nice to have finer control). See Figure 14.35.

We now have the sphere in the starting position. Let's assign it a material setting. We'll be grabbing a material preset and altering it slightly.

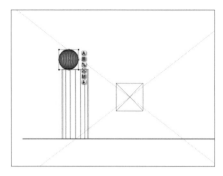

Figure 14.35 The sphere is nudged left on the cylinder, so that it has room to roll (scene in front view).

10. Click the M to go to the Materials Lab. A click on the right-pointing triangle next to the preview window (circled in Figure 14.36a) takes you to the Materials Library. Once you are there, go to the category Wild&Fun and grab the preset "Clown Collar" (see Figure 14.36b).

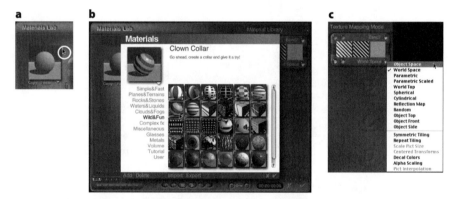

Figure 14.36 Assigning a material to the sphere in the Materials Lab: a) Accessing the Materials Library from the Material Preview; b) selecting Clown Collar from the category Wild&Fun; c) changing the mapping to Object Space.

Our Clown Collar material is currently set to World Space. Once this ball starts flying in the air, that will look really weird; it won't tell the story we want to tell. (Why? Because as the object changes position, the material doesn't "stay" with the object. It's as if the ball is flying through a great big invisible amount of this material; wherever the ball is, it shows the material for that quadrant of the world—interesting, but ultimately uncredible.) Therefore, we'll change the mapping to Object Space.

11. Press the triangle next to the text "World Space." A pop-up menu appears, as Figure 14.36c shows. Select Object Space.

12. Click the check mark to leave the Materials Lab; save your scene! If you want to admire your hard work thus far, go to the main view (either Camera or Director's; they'll be the same) and render.

Adding Time to the Scene

1. Go back to wireframe view, and switch back to front view. Front view will provide the best way to view the scene as you add time and motion trajectories to it.

2. Generate your initial time settings. Go to the Animation Setup dialog box and make sure that your settings are for 15 frames per second and that the time display is SMPTE (they're the default settings, but it's possible that you've changed them to something else). See Figure 14.37.

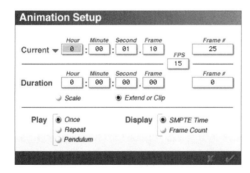

Figure 14.37 Ensuring that the frame rate is 15 frames per second in the Animation Setup dialog box.

3. Drag the Time Scrubber out so that it reads 00:00:01.10 (1 second, 10 frames), as Figure 14.38 shows.

Figure 14.38 The Time Scrubber set to the end of the sequence: 00:00:01.10.

Since we have the ball in the first, initial position and the Scrubber set to the end point of the sequence, the next move will be to place the ball in the final position. You have Auto-Key on, so the next move will be automatically recorded by Bryce.

4. Move the ball to the final position, as shown in Figure 14.39. When you drag the sphere elsewhere, the timeline will fill in green.

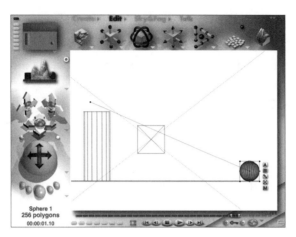

Figure 14.39 The result of dragging the sphere to a new position: The timeline has filled in between the beginning and the current time, and the straight line trajectory goes from the initial position to the current position.

5. Play what you have thus far. Click the Play button on the Time Palette or press the \ (backslash) key. Right now, you have a sphere *seilbahn* (that's German for aerial tram), without the bounce we're after. Still, it's motion.

Make the Trajectory into a Bounce

1. That straight line trajectory doesn't look like a bounce, so we'll go back in time and add a bounce to the trajectory. The comma (,) and period (.) keys will take you to the previous and next ticker mark. (A ticker mark, by default, is one frame.) Tap forward or backward until your time reads 00:00:00.07. Lo! Your sphere moves back along the trajectory (see Figure 14.40a)!

2. Once you are at Frame 7, move the sphere down and slightly left to the bounce position, at ground, nearer to the cylinder (see Figure 14.40b). You simply drag the sphere to move it.

    Looking at the sequence so far, it's pretty obvious that we need to add some more key positions to get our trajectory looking less tragic and more bounce-like. The next one we'll create is just outside the top-right edge of the cylinder. This point will make the ball miss the cylinder's edge as it rolls and falls.

3. Move the Time Scrubber close to the beginning of the sequence: to Frame 00:00:00.02. Figure 14.41a shows the position of the ball at Frame 00:00:00.02, before we do anything to move it.

4. Drag the ball up and right, so that it clears the edge of the cylinder, as shown in Figure 14.41b.

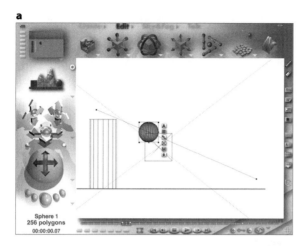

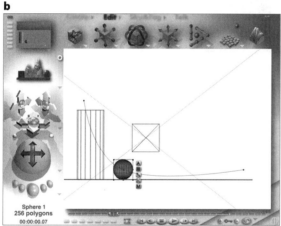

Figure 14.40 Working at time 00:00:00.07: a) The sphere moves backward along its trajectory; b) dragging down to position the sphere where it bounces.

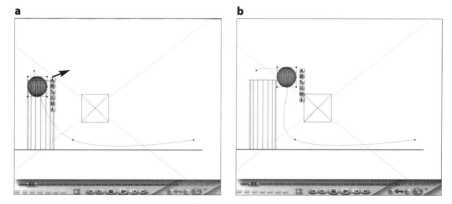

Figure 14.41 Working at time 00:00:00.02: a) The Time Scrubber and sphere in position for changing the sphere's location; b) after moving the sphere.

Yes, the trajectory shape is funky still. We will fix that in a bit, but first we'll create one more point in the trajectory: the bounce up!

5. Move the Time Scrubber to 00:00:01.02, so that the sphere is roughly halfway between the bounce down position and the final position (see Figure 14.42a).

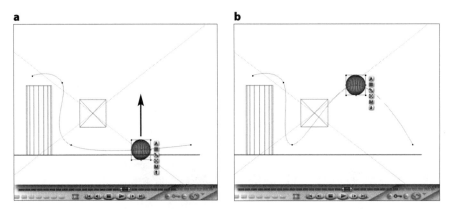

Figure 14.42 Making the arc of the bounce: a) After positioning the Time Scrubber; b) after changing the sphere's position.

6. Drag the sphere up to make a bounce arc (see Figure 14.42b). Don't drag as high as the ball's beginning spot on top of the cylinder, since we need to take gravity into account. Generally, things don't bounce as high as their starting places, unless you happen to be on a trampoline (which we're not).

7. Check out the animation; click the Play button or tap the backslash (\) key. Save your scene.

Adjusting the Trajectory

We have the basic positions set in the trajectory. But they need to be adjusted so they become a lovely bounce.

1. To adjust the trajectory's shape, we need to see the tangent handles. (Well, strictly speaking, we don't have to, but it certainly is helpful.) Click the A button to get to the sphere's Object Attributes dialog box. Click the Animation tab and click the option for Show Tangents. Figure 14.43a shows the Object Attributes dialog box, and the resulting view of your Bryce scene is shown in Figure 14.43b.

    Those tangent handles help us see more of what's going on with the trajectory. We need to get that smooth arc out of the bounce bottom and make it a nice! sharp! point! In other words, we need to alter its continuity. Now, continuity begins with a C, and that's the key we'll use (right here in River City!).

a
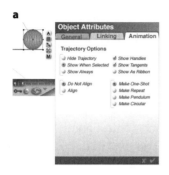

b
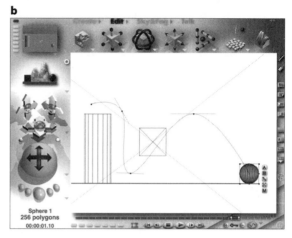

Figure 14.43 Working with tangents: a) Choosing the option to make them visible in the Object Attributes dialog box; b) the result.

2. Point your mouse over the bounce bottom control point. The cursor changes to a double-cross. Hold down the C key and then drag to the left. Watch the status display on the Controls Palette as you do. The numbers change along with the shape of the curve. Let go of the mouse when the Continuity status display is at about –1. The result is shown in Figure 14.44.

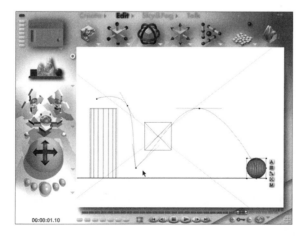

Figure 14.44 Breaking the continuity of the trajectory by pressing the C key and dragging until the status display reads –1.

Next, let's work with the curve of the trajectory where the sphere tumbles over the edge of the cylinder. Currently, it rises up to go out. It needs to travel straight instead. That means we have to change the way the curve bulges, and that's the same as bias. Both bulge and bias start with B, so that's the key that we'll use, right as the ball falls! (Can't you just hear the *Music Man* chant in the background: "bias! bias! bias! bias!"? Then again, maybe not.)

In the next steps, we'll be adjusting trajectory handle points only to make adjustments to the trajectory curve itself, without moving the sphere to that position.

3.   Point your mouse over the trajectory's second control point. The cursor changes to crossed arrows. Press the B key and drag to the right, until the numeric readout on the Controls Palette reads 1 (that means that the bias is completely in one direction; a setting of –1 would send the bias in the other direction). See Figure 14.45.

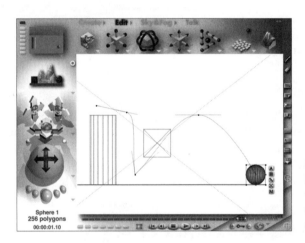

Sphere 1
256 polygons
00:00:01.10

Figure 14.45 Changing the bias of the control point at the top right of the cylinder flattens the trajectory leading to the point.

Now that the trajectory has been flattened out, we'll have to move the point up a little bit to make a straight line between the first and the second trajectory point.

4.   Set the Time Scrubber to frame 00:00:00.01 (Frame 1). You can see the unwished-for consequence of the current placement (see Figure 14.46). The sphere scoops down and into the top of the cylinder!

5.   Zoom comes in handy to help fix the problem. Tap the plus key (+) on the keypad. Your view will center on the selected object (the sphere). It's plenty big so that you can adjust its position and see clearly what you're doing. Drag the trajectory's key position up; do not drag the sphere (see Figure 14.47a). The result of dragging up at the point fixes the problem that's most apparent when the sphere is at frame 00:00:00.01 (Frame 1).

Now that we've changed the bias of that curve, the point is too far out, as Figure 14.47b shows (the ball's position is at Frame 00:00:00.02). The ball shouldn't roll out sideways into the air before it falls. (This is not a Saturday morning cartoon!) This next part is a little tricky. You need to position the point on the trajectory so that the sphere does not gouge into the cylinder at any point while it tumbles over the edge. Although you could add a point on the trajectory for each critical point in the ball's motion, we'll move our existing point left and then adjust the shape of the curve to do the rest.

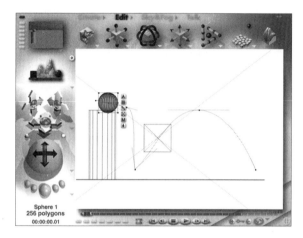

Figure 14.46 The need for further adjustment is demonstrated by the way that the sphere scoops down into the cylinder.

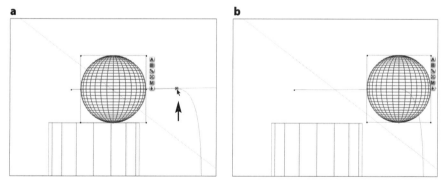

Figure 14.47 Adjusting the key point where the sphere spills over the cylinder's edge: a) Dragging up on the key point; b) after moving .

6. Move the Time Scrubber to 00:00:00.02 (Frame 2). The sphere is located on the keyframe point. You can see where the ball rolls *beyond* the cylinder's edge. Move the point left, so that the ball just touches the edge of the cylinder (see Figure 14.48a).

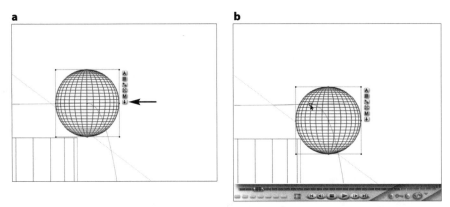

Figure 14.48 More adjustments to the point where the sphere spills over the edge of the cylinder: a) Moving left; b) increasing the fullness of the curve by adjusting the tension.

Now we come to yet another control point modifier. We've used C that stands for continuity! And we've used B that stands for bias! Now we'll use T that stands for tension, to change the fullness of our trajectory! So that we can complete this tutorial! Right here in River City! First, though, we'll change the time to position the sphere at the most critical spot on the trajectory.

7. Change the time to the next frame by tapping the period (.) key once. The Time Scrubber moves to 00:00:00.03 (Frame 3). The sphere moves down into the spill and gouges the side of the cylinder.

8. Point your mouse at the blue trajectory point (not the sphere's center point) until the cursor turns into a crossed arrow. Press the T key and drag to the left. Watch the edge of the sphere and the cylinder. Stop when the sphere is just touching the edge of the cylinder (Figure 14.48b). The numerical setting here is not as important as eyeballing it to make sure that it's right.

Next, we'll double-check to make sure that all is working well by playing the animation. To do this, you'll create a custom range to see only the part you're interested in, and you'll make the Play mode repeating so you can concentrate on just that one part.

9. Change the working area of your sequence so that only the beginning part is active. Point your mouse to the ticker mark on the timeline that is one ticker mark shy of the final point. Drag left from there. The green part retracts to the location of your mouse pointer and leaves behind a dark gray line. Keep dragging until the green extends a frame or two beyond the current Time Scrubber's position, as Figure 14.49 shows.

Figure 14.49 Setting the Play mode to Repeat, with the working area shortened to include only the first few frames.

10. Now, from the Animation Options pop-up menu, select Play Mode > Repeat. This will make your sequence repeat over and over (see Figure 14.49). Then click the Play button and double-check your animation.

11. Zoom out to look at the entire trajectory by clicking the minus (–) key on the keypad.

When you take a look at the entire trajectory, you can see that more tweaking is in order. It's pretty clear at this point (see Figure 14.50a) that the position of the ball bounce (where it impacts the ground) needs to be closer to the cylinder. After all, a ball falls down and not out.

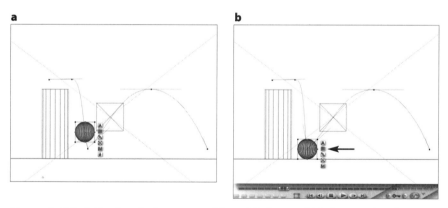

Figure 14.50 Adjusting the bounce position: a) Before and b) after moving the sphere left slightly.

12. Go to 00:00:00.07 (Frame 7) and then move the sphere to the left slightly. You can use keyboard combinations to move the ball; we used the Option-Shift-Left Arrow/Alt+Shift+Left Arrow combination to move the ball to where it is in Figure 14.50b.

13. Let's make one last preview of the trajectory as an animation. Click the timeline just inside its final point. The green Working Range line expands to fill the entire sequence duration. Click the Play button on the Time Palette.

Rolling Along

We have the bounce and have finalized the path position for the ball's position. Now it's time to get the ball rolling (ahem!). We'll be adding rotation to the sequence. The animation begins with the ball rolling along the top of the cylinder. As it falls, that rotation continues to the point of impact. The second arc of the ball will also have rotation, but not as extreme as in the first segment.

Bryce records rotation in terms of overall, cumulative gyration. Therefore, it's not something you can work with using numerical entry in either the Object Attributes or 3D Transformation dialog box. The numbers don't tell you in which direction you have rotated to reach that place. Additionally, when rotating, Bryce records the change from the first state to the next. Therefore, if you rotate by precisely 360° or multiples thereof (720, 1,080, and so on), then the animated result will be no motion whatsoever, since the end is no different than the beginning.

1. Navigate to the keyframe that's at the bottom of the bounce. (If you were at the beginning, click the Next Keyframe button twice or tap > (Shift-period on U.S. keyboards) twice, until you're at 00:00:00.07 (Frame 7), or the point where the sphere touches the ground.

Here we encounter an interesting fact about trajectories and their control points. Normally, with any object, if you press the Command/Ctrl key when the mouse pointer is over the object's control point, you'll get the rotate arrow cursor, and the object will rotate as you drag the mouse from that position. However, when a trajectory is showing, that won't be the case, since Bryce favors the trajectory handle point over the object's own control point. You could, of course, bypass this circumstance by using the Rotate tool on the Edit Palette, but, in our "Brycing builds your character" school of thought, we'll learn how to deal with this pointed conflict. To directly rotate a selected object that has a trajectory, you'll need to hide the trajectory.

2. Click the A icon to get to the Object Attributes dialog box; then click the Animation tab. Click the Hide Trajectory option (see Figure 14.51). Now you can directly rotate the sphere using ⌘-drag or Ctrl+drag.

3. Point your mouse at the object's control point (in the sphere's center). The z axis cursor appears. Then, when you hold down the Command or Ctrl key, the cursor changes to the rotate arrow cursor. Drag to the right so that the sphere rotates end over end and then a little bit beyond that. Watch the status display on the Controls Palette. We stopped our sphere at around −225.0°. (You can get exact 45° increments by holding down the Shift key.)

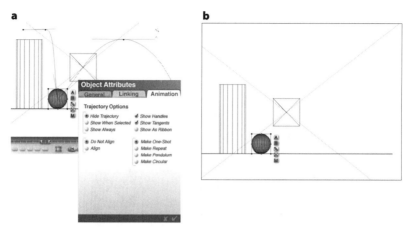

Figure 14.51 Hiding the trajectory: a) The Object Attributes dialog box; b) the result.

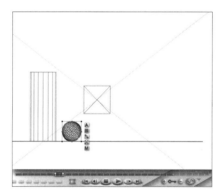

Figure 14.52 After rotating the sphere.

(What happens if you don't hide the trajectory and do this same move? Using ⌘-drag or Ctrl+drag on a trajectory's control point will move the point in a constrained manner along the z axis.)

4. Play the animation to see the result of the first rotation. Click the Play button.

5. Move the Time Scrubber to the end of the sequence, to 1.10. The sphere moves to the final position. For the final keyframe, after the bounce in the air, we'll rotate some more, continuing further in the same direction.

6. Repeat the rotation process for this keyframe. With the sphere selected, the Command or Ctrl key held down, and the mouse positioned over the z axis control point, drag to the right. This time, put less spin on it. Our numeric settings for this step are around −143 or −143.5.

7. Click the Play button to play the animation in wireframe mode.

8. Save the scene file. Create an Animation Preview so you see a teeny thumbnail of your sequence. Click the Animation Preview button on the Time Palette and play your animation (see Figure 14.53).

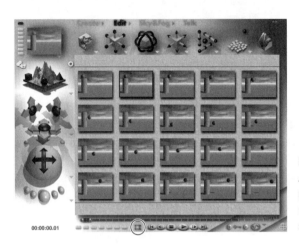

Figure 14.53 A click on the Animation Preview button produces a thumbnail-sized rendered preview of your sequence.

The Ball Goes Squash

To convey the idea of the ball's substance (rubber or plastic and filled with air), it will need to squash when it hits the ground, so we'll make changes to its size at the bounce point (Frame 00:00:00.07). However, if we were to just resize it at that bounce point, then there'd be a nice, smooth transition from roll start to roll end where the object would gradually get compressed. Instead, the compression should be quick, taking place just as the ball contacts the surface, and not throughout its entire trajectory toward the ground. To make that happen, we'll set keyframes right before and after the bounce. The new keyframes will be the commencement and conclusion of the squash.

1. Get ready for the work to do for the squash; switch back to wireframe mode. Let's switch the trajectory back on so it's showing again. In the Object Attributes dialog box, on the Animation tab, click the Show When Selected option and then click the check mark to leave the dialog box.

2. If you managed to get out of front view, go back to front view (press the 4 key) so you can see the entire trajectory. Set the Time Scrubber to the frame just prior to the bounce, 00:00:00.06 (Frame 6), as shown in Figure 14.54a.

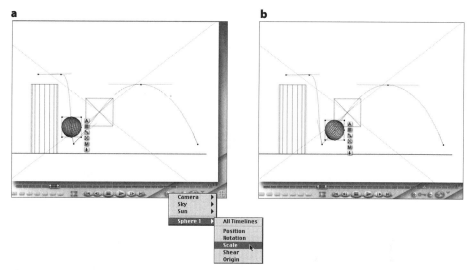

Figure 14.54 Setting keyframes before and after the squash at the bounce: a) At time 00:00:00.06, add keyframes for scale (and shear); b) the sphere at time 00:00:00.09, ready for the same keyframes to be added again.

Now you're ready to set up the "commence" key event. You'll add two different keyframes for scale and shear using the pop-up menu for the Add Keyframe button. Why do this? When an object changes in size and rotation, the object's shear is changed as well. We already rotated the object, so we'll need to set keyframes for both the scale and shear parameters.

3. From the Add Keyframe pop-up menu, select Sphere 1 > Scale. Then go back and add another keyframe: Sphere 1 > Shear (see Figure 14.54a).

4. Next, create the key events for the end of the squash-on-bounce. Move the Time Scrubber to 00:00:00.09 (Frame 9). That time is two frames after the bounce bottom, as shown in Figure 14.54b.

5. At that time (00:00:00.09, Frame 9), press your mouse at the Add Keyframe button to display the pop-up menu. Do the same thing as before. For Sphere 1, add a keyframe for scale. Then add a keyframe for shear.

6. Now we're ready to squash the ball. Move to 00:00:00.07 (Frame 7). Double-check that you're in World Space, by checking the pop-up menu under the Resize, Rotate, or Reposition tool on the Edit Palette.

The resize will have two parts: On the y axis, the sphere will be reduced. But it will be expanded on the horizontal (x and z) axes, since the ball is a volume, and that squashed portion has to go somewhere (it goes out). We will uniformly enlarge the sphere and then reduce it on the vertical axis.

7. Enlarge the sphere proportionately using the Resize tool on the Edit Palette. Figure 14.55a shows the sphere before and Figure 14.55b shows the sphere after enlarging.

8. Next, reduce the sphere on the vertical axis. Hold down the Option or Alt key and drag from the top (y axis) control handle to resize from both the top and bottom, until the bottom of the sphere is resting on the ground, as shown in Figure 14.55c. Release the mouse.

9. Without using the Option or Alt key this time, drag down again from the y axis control point to continue reducing the sphere, until it looks about like the one shown in Figure 14.55d.

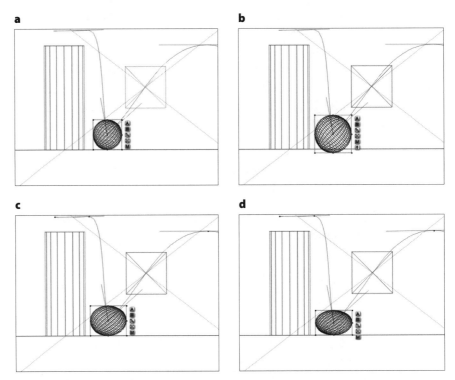

Figure 14.55 Squashing the sphere: a) Before squashing; b) uniformly enlarged; c) symmetrically reduced on the y axis until the bottom of the sphere rests on the ground; d) further reduction on the y axis.

10. (Optional) If you want to double-check that you've set all the keyframes you need, you can check them in the Advanced Motion Lab. Click the AML button or press ⌘-T/Ctrl+T to go directly there. When you expand the listing for Sphere 1, so that you can see all of Sphere 1's attributes, it should look like Figure 14.56. At Frames 6, 7, and 9, there are ticker marks for Scale and Shear.

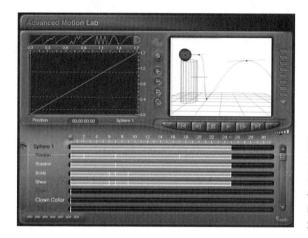

Figure 14.56
Double-checking the keyframes for the squash action: Keyframe ticker marks exist for Scale and Shear at Frames 6, 7, and 9.

(If for any reason, you made those beginning and end keyframes at another spot, say at Frame 5, 8, or 10, you can simply select the ticker marks and move them over so that they occur at the right time.)

Leave the AML and go back to the main scene.

11. Click the Play button to play your animation. The ball falls. It rolls. It smooshes. It bounces back again. It's getting there! It now needs a bit of acceleration on the downward path. Save your scene file.

Since acceleration falls under the realm of the Advanced Motion Lab, and since we haven't discussed that yet, we will leave off with this tutorial for now and complete it at the end of the AML discussion in the next chapter.

PATH OBJECT

A Path object, or an object path, is a specific object type that is, in many ways, similar to a trajectory. But one significant way in which it differs is that, once you turn a trajectory into a path, you sever the tie between location and time, so that each can operate separately. Ultimately, that results in smoother object movement.

The magic trick to paths is that objects can be linked to paths, and their positions along the path can be changed over time. The number of objects linked to a path may be one, or it may be many; there is no limit. (There may be an arbitrary upper limit; we didn't try a brute-force experiment to see just how many objects can possibly be linked to a single path. If you want to try this how-many-angels-on-the-head-of-a-pin experiment, we welcome you to do so!)

Once a trajectory is changed to a path, those old trajectory handle points now determine the path's geometry points. They can be edited in the same way that trajectory points can be edited, with a couple of differences, which we'll discuss. However, the path as a whole is one unit, so an object can travel from one end to another in a very smooth way using two key events: beginning and end. Also, a path can itself be animated: Its position can change (and have its own trajectory); it can be scaled, rotated, and sheared; and its geometry can change over time.

Making and Storing Paths

With these benefits to paths, do you want to rush out and create and work with them? Sure! It's good to weigh your reasons for using them, though; there are times when it's best not to change a trajectory into a path. Once you do decide to make a path, though, it's pretty easy, and paths have the advantage of being portable, since they're objects.

When Not to Use Paths

The BOUNCE tutorial we just went through is a good example of when not to use a path. There, the time and location keyframes are joined together nicely for the bottom-of-the-bounce event; splitting them apart by creating a path and then rejoining them for the bounce moments and squoosh and all would be more trouble than it's worth. But for meandering motion and fly-bys, paths are great. In the path tutorial, we'll be working with a fly-by trajectory and change it to a path, so you can appreciate the difference between the two animation approaches.

Creating Paths

Create a Path object using the Objects menu: Objects > Create Path. The keyboard shortcut is Option-P/Alt+P. A path is created based on the trajectory of the selected object. If nothing is selected, then Bryce supplies a basic sine-shaped path.

If you are creating an animation magnum opus, it's a good idea to save a copy of your scene with the object trajectory, since, by the time you've completed the process of working with the path, you'll have sent the trajectory to bit heaven. The previously saved version of the scene is nice to fall back on.

Figure 14.57 shows the process of creating a path from a trajectory. 14.57a is the before state, a camera trajectory. Then the path is generated, and in Figure 14.57b you can see the camera's trajectory is still present along with the newly created (and selected) path. Once the camera is linked to the path, in Figure 14.57c, its own trajectory disappears, vanishing for all time.

a
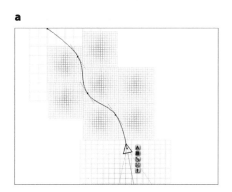

b
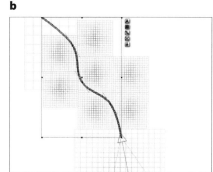

c
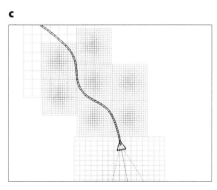

Figure 14.57 Making a path from a trajectory: a) Before: the camera trajectory; b) after a path is created, where both the trajectory and path exist; c) after the camera is linked to the path (its trajectory has disappeared).

Storing Paths

Paths, as objects, can be stored in the Objects Library and thus imported and exported. (Make 'em! Trade 'em with your friends!) Select the path, click the triangle just to the right of the Create icon, click the Paths category, and add your path. However, you cannot store a path that has a camera linked to it.

Editing Paths

Once you have created a path, there are some ways that you can edit it. Of course, you can perform the same object transformations to a path that you can to any object, changing its position, its size, or its orientation in space, as well as its shear. In our discussion of editing paths, we focus on the object path's unique feature—its geometry.

Creating New Geometry Points

You can add new geometry points to a path by Option-clicking/Alt+clicking the path. A new blue point appears on the path. (Warning! You cannot undo the addition of a new geometry point. Take precautions: Save your scene file so you can revert to the previous state, or copy the path first, or save the path in the Objects Library.) Creating a new geometry point is not the equivalent of creating a new point on a trajectory. (Scrub to the appropriate time to position the object there and add a keyframe. Hmmm. Then again, trajectories don't accept new points without a little squiggle of change either.) The new point may not appear exactly in that position, though. Paths seem to have their own internal logic that determines where the new points appear. Unfortunately, that logic is rather opaque. It probably stems from the underlying geometry of the point's continuity, tension, and bias. Chances are, you'll have to adjust the point's position or its continuity, tension, and bias to get the new point to fit in smoothly. Still, you can decide later whether you need to add more points to the path, and you'll be able to do so.

Selecting Geometry Points

You can select one—or more—geometry points and alter it (or them). Working with a single point is no different than working with a trajectory. When your mouse is over a point, a small black box appears around it, and your pointer changes to the crossed-arrow cursor.

If you want to select more than one geometry point, hold down the Shift key and click the point. It changes from blue to cyan. You can continue Shift-clicking points to select additional ones. Any change made to one will affect all of them—moving location as well as changing tension, continuity, and bias.

Bryce has a wrinkle in the multi-geometry point selection process. Suppose that you have two geometry points selected. You could go and work with still another (unselected) geometry point. Once your cursor hovers over that point, the black line will appear around it, and the cursor will change. You can move or otherwise alter that other point, and the first two cyan points stay selected and just go along for the ride. Afterward, you can go back to one of those selected points and move or change it—thereby moving and changing all the cyan selected points—and Bryce merrily does so. Here, Bryce has a funky way of communicating with you about what it's doing, ambiguously telling you that it is working with two different selected states, but at least the behavior and results turn out okay.

Altering Geometry Points

You can change path geometry points in pretty much the same way that you changed trajectory points. Path geometry points differ from trajectory points in two ways: First, changes to tangents (adjusting tension, continuity, bias, and twist) are undoable. Second, with paths, you cannot get any tangent lines to appear. The only way that any tangent lines appear is with a trajectory. The reason for this is somewhat simple (or awkward, or understandable), once you finally "get it." A path is an object that can itself be moved over time. When it is moved over time, the path will have a trajectory. The trajectory options in the Object Attributes dialog box will apply to the path's trajectory. You can, of course, assign the tangents to appear. Figure 14.58 shows an example of the default sine wave path, which has moved along a trajectory whose tangent handles are showing (the origin handle is showing as well, just to make it easier to see how the path is connected to the trajectory). If you wanted the path's geometry points to have tangent lines appear, you'd need to click some other option—one that simply doesn't exist in Bryce.

Path point adjustments are pretty much the same as for trajectories; we note the major difference here. Tension, continuity, and bias work the same way as with trajectories. Twist, however, works differently with paths. In fact, compared to trajectories (where twist is useless), twist just plain works!

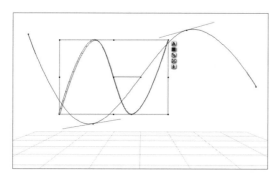

Figure 14.58 A Path object, though it has geometry points that have adjustable tangents, does not display the tangent lines, since the path can also move on a trajectory that may have visible tangent lines.

Twist

Twist works on a path that has at least three points. Don't waste your time trying to do anything with a two-point path. And by the way, don't bother checking any of this in the manual 'cause it ain't there! Twist is a totally undocumented feature.

Imagine a strip of crêpe paper attached to a flat surface by several pieces of tape along its length. The strip of paper is analogous to a path, and the pieces of tape correspond to control points. Applying twist to a control point is like picking up one of the pieces of tape so the paper is free to move, twisting the paper, and then sticking the paper in place with the tape again. The portion of the path on both sides of the control point twists with the point, but the twisting diminishes along the path as it gets closer to another point, which acts like one of the pieces of tape still holding the paper down.

Figure 14.59 shows several groups of three paths systematically twisted in various ways. A light-gray background line marks the locations of the points. The set of paths labeled 3.0 is shown again at the right, with specific twist settings indicated for each point. The left path in the group has a single point twisted at a setting of 3.0. Notice how the path segments above and below that point twist in opposite directions. They appear symmetrical.

The middle path of the group has subsequent points twisted the same amount, so that the second, third, and final points are all given a twist setting of 3.0. The result is a twist in the first (top) segment, and then the remaining segments continue straight at the angle where the twist ended. To put it another way, the bottom segment's opposite twist was removed by continuing the twist setting to the other points in the path.

The right path has cumulative twisting, where the sum of the previous twists is added to the current twist, to perpetuate the twist in a single direction. The second point is twisted to 3.0, the third point to 6.0, and the final point to 9.0.

For the other sets of twists shown in the main (left) image in Figure 14.59, the same methods were applied, respectively, to the left, middle, and right paths in the group. Rather than using 3.0 as the twist setting, the paths were twisted by settings of 1.0, 2.0, and 4.0. Each whole number twists the path by 60°, so for a complete revolution, you'd need a twist setting of 6.0.

To twist the path, point your mouse at the geometry point you wish to twist. Press the Option/Alt key and then drag the mouse. The direction of the twist changes depending on the direction in which you drag.

It's important to press the Option/Alt key before you depress the mouse button to begin dragging. If you press it afterward, you will instead be moving the point while constraining on the y axis. One can only wish that this "one key does two completely different things" matter would be resolved by giving the twist, say, the W key. Oh well. (But then, where would we be with our River City song, anyway?) This potential problem is further exacerbated by a pernicious little detail. Suppose that you inadvertently move the point and instead of twisting it, something easily done by not pressing the Option/Alt key at the right time. Invoking the Undo command will not only undo the move, but it will untwist the portion of the path governed by that point.

Also, twistedness is a state. You cannot animate it or have a gradual onset of twistedness. (All right, all right; keep your snickers to yourself. Yes, we know how much this statement imitates real life!)

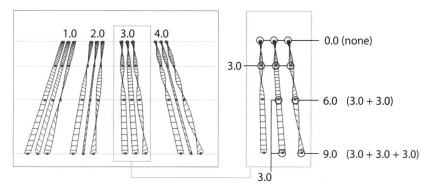

Figure 14.59 Twist and Shout! Variations on twisted paths. Each group has been twisted by a particular number: 1, 2, 3, or 4. For each group, the setup is similar, as the labeled guide at the right shows. For each group, the first (top) point has been twisted by the same amount. In the middle option, all subsequent points are twisted to the same number. The right option is the cumulative twist, where the sum of the previous twists is added to the current point.

Traveling Along Your Path

Now that you have your path shaped the way you want it, attach objects to it! The way to do so is to link your object to the path. Then, to make it move along the path, you change the constraints of the object over time, and the object travels along.

Linking and Constraining

Linking an object to a path is the same as linking an object to anything else. Select the object. Point your mouse at the Link Object icon. Drag from that icon to the path. As you drag, a blue line extends from the object. When the path turns blue, let go of the mouse; the object is linked to the path. In fact, the object's position changes so that it's now located on the path at the spot where you dragged the blue link line. It is both linked and constrained to the path.

The other way to link is to use the Linking section of the object's Object Attributes dialog box and to make the path the object's parent (see Figure 14.60). Once an object has a path for a parent, the Object Attributes dialog box displays the option to constrain to a path. Click that. At this point, having both linked and constrained the object, you've completed the equivalent of dragging from the Link Object icon (which links and constrains simultaneously). When the object is constrained, there is a numerical entry box and a slider.

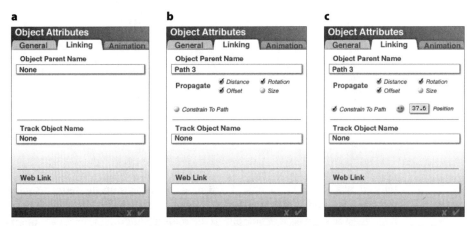

Figure 14.60 Linking the object to a path in the Object Attributes dialog box: a) Before selecting the path; b) once the path is selected, the Constrain option appears; c) when Constrain is checked, a numerical entry box and slider appear.

What does constraining mean? Is this something that has to do with constraining the object so that it doesn't stray from the path by some numerical setting—a margin of error of sorts? No. Constrain assumes that the object is located where the path is. The numbers determine how far down along the path the object travels.

The range of numbers is expressed as a percentage, with 0 to start and 100 to end, on an open-ended path. Circular paths, created from circular trajectories, have numbers that go far higher than 100, since the object can go around and around and around and around and... well, you get the idea.

That Constrain number can change over time. Thus, with two key events, you can position the object at 0 and 100 to make it travel along the entire path. Navigate to the beginning of your sequence, set Constrain to 0, and if you have Auto-Key off, add a keyframe. Go to the end of your sequence, set Constrain to 100, and if need be, add a keyframe.

You can also do the same thing by directly dragging the object in the Working Window, without having to go to the Object Attributes dialog box. Once the object is linked and constrained to the path, it will move only along the path as you drag it. Drag right and left, and the object will change position along the path. (Do not try to drag so that your movements follow the path position; Bryce responds only to right and left dragging in this case.) The dragging motion is limited by the monitor's edge, so depending on the length of the path and the size of your monitor, you may have to drag in two or more stages to get the object to the other end of the path.

The way that Bryce measures the numbers for constraint is a little strange. If an object constraint is set to 50%, the object is actually positioned halfway through the number of geometry points, not halfway through the entire path. If you have several points clustered around one end of the path, then 50% is weighted severely toward that end. In a case such as that, the direct drag method is good for visually positioning objects along the path.

Alignment

In addition to linking an object to a path, you can align it so that it changes direction to follow the path's orientation. In the Object Attributes dialog box, in the Animation section, just click Align. In this circumstance, the title in the Animation section, Trajectory Options, is a misleading misnomer. You can align the object to a path, which is not a trajectory. The other options apply to the object's trajectory. In the case of an object linked to a path, that means that they aren't available.

Path alignment shares that unfortunate tendency of trajectory alignment: Your object is subject to flipping around at curved spots.

What about alignment and twist? We just spent all sorts of time discussing how to twist the path. When you align an object to a path, it will follow the outrageous twists of fortune that you impose on the path—well, most objects will do so. The camera will not, so those nice little banking movements will have to be accomplished using one of two workarounds:

- *Let the banking be your guide.* Twist the path, align the camera to it, and then use that as a guide to manually bank your camera. Figure 14.61 compares two states of banking for a camera attached to the path. Figure 14.61a shows the camera perspective, where the path is banked. Notice by the level horizon line that the camera, however, is not banked. In Figure 14.61b, the twisted path was used as a guide to bank the camera, so that the path lines are level, but the horizon line is not.

a   b

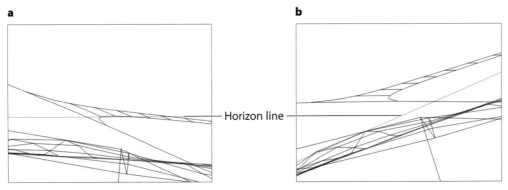

— Horizon line —

Figure 14.61 Manually aligning a camera to a path: a) The level horizon line demonstrates that a linked, aligned camera doesn't bank with the twisted path; b) after manually banking the camera to match the path's twist.

- *Link the camera to an object that is linked (and aligned) with the path.* This convoluted workaround is reminiscent of that song about "dem bones, dem bones, dem dry bones." The camera is connected to the object. And the object is connected to the path. Of course, at this point, you're still subject to that aggravating flip-around that happens when the path curves in a way that reorients the object in some undesirable manner. Figure 14.62 demonstrates this. The camera is linked to a cylinder that is linked and aligned to a path. The path, of course, is twisted, and it bends around in that flip-susceptible way. We captured the before and after flip frames in wireframe and show the thumbnail sequence so you can see the sky and ground swap positions at the flip point.

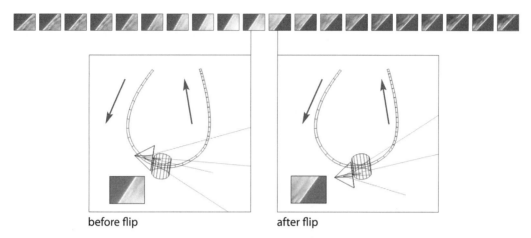

before flip   after flip

Figure 14.62 The perils of aligning and constraining to a path: The camera is linked to a cylinder that is linked and aligned to the path.

Paths Walkthrough

In this walkthrough, we'll work with a scene file called TRAJ-TO-PATH-BEFORE. The scene contains a large terrain for land mass, with a few similar ones in the distance, and another terrain for the lake—all in all, a pretty simple and straightforward scene. The camera is on a large, sweeping, C-shaped trajectory. The camera is tracking a sphere in the center. (Actually, the camera is tracking the water terrain, more or less near the center of the lake. We'll cover the hows and whys of tracking in the section that follows. For now, just trust us!)

There are a couple of problems with the trajectory. The trajectory point locations are not evenly spread out over the duration of the sequence, so the camera speeds up in some places and slows down in others.

In this tutorial exercise, we will convert the trajectory to a path and then cause the camera to follow the path over the sequence duration for a much smoother camera motion.

1. Open the scene file TRAJ-TO-PATH-BEFORE, located in the folder for this chapter on the CD-ROM.

2. On the Controls Palette, click both the Render Textures On/Off and Fast Preview Mode controls so that they are both depressed and the render in Nano Preview appears tan and blue.

3.   Click the Play control to play the animation through in wireframe mode. Notice the spots where the camera seems to whip around a bit more swiftly? Let's take a closer look.

4.   Click the Animation Preview control to generate an Animation Preview (see Figure 14.63). The sequence is seven seconds long, so it will take a bit to render (on a Power Macintosh G3/400, it took just under 50 seconds). Keep reading here while it renders!

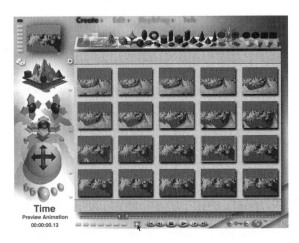

Figure 14.63
The Animation Preview for the scene, rendered with textures off and in Quick mode.

5.   Play the preview. Now you have some more visual information in the form of rendered surfaces. Notice how the camera swoops around the beginning part as it draws close to the lake.

Convinced that a change would do this good? Good! (If not, please humor us and go along with it anyhow!)

6.   Switch to top view (keypad: 2) so that you can see everything in the scene. Click the Time/Selection Palette toggle to switch to the Selection Palette. From the Selection Options pop-up menu, choose Select Camera. The camera is selected, and its trajectory appears, as shown in Figure 14.64.

7.   Go to the Object menu and choose Create Path. A path appears in the same position as the camera's trajectory (see Figure 14.65).

Right now the camera's motion is still governed by the trajectory. If you were to click the Play button, the camera would animate, but it's the old trajectory that's working here. To get the camera to follow the path, it needs to be linked to it.

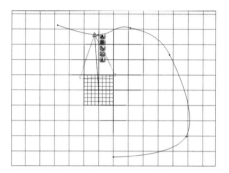

Figure 14.64 The camera and trajectory, seen from top view.

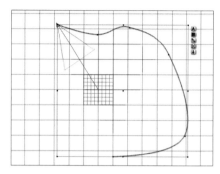

Figure 14.65 After creating a path.

8. Make sure that the camera is selected and that the Time Scrubber is at the beginning of the sequence. Point your mouse at the camera's object linking control (among the object options controls). Drag from the linking control to the newly created path, until the path turns blue. When it turns blue, release the mouse (see Figure 14.66). (If you accidentally linked to the wrong object, a simple click on the camera's link control will unlink the camera.)

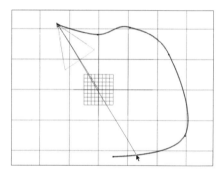

Figure 14.66 Linking the camera to the path.

Sometimes the object path will not turn blue because there is another object that lies between it and the current camera's line of sight, or the wireframe of the Path object is too difficult to "hit" with the mouse pointer. Here is the sure-fire way to link the camera to a path:

Click the A icon to get to the Object Attributes dialog box. Click the Linking tab. From the Object Parent Name pop-up menu, select Path 1. Once you select the path, the Constrain to Path button appears; click it. Click the check mark to accept these changes and return to your scene.

9. Just for grins, click the Play control. No camera movement. That's because you need to set new keyframes. When you linked to another object, your camera tossed away its trajectory and all its keyframe settings for position; now you need to create new key events for its position. All righty then, let's get to it!

10. Set the Time Scrubber to the beginning of the sequence. Open the Object Attributes dialog box again and go to the Linking tab. In the Object Parent Name section, there is a numerical entry box for Constrain. Since you're at the beginning of your sequence, enter 0 (see Figure 14.67). Click the check mark to leave. The camera may or may not have jumped to a new spot (it depends on whether you dragged from the Linking tool, and where along the path you linked; the camera's position was there).

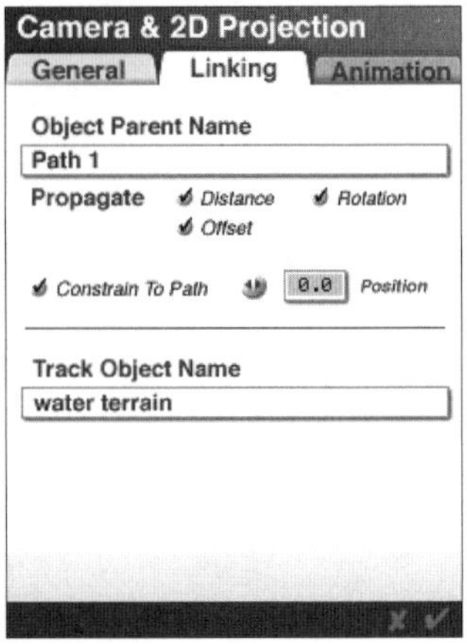

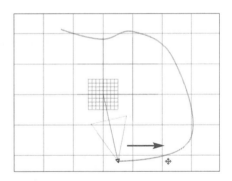

Figure 14.67 The Object Attributes dialog box Constrain setting for the beginning of the sequence (first keyframe).

You've now placed the camera in position for the beginning of the sequence. The scene that you opened up was saved with Auto-Key on, so that should simply do it for you. If, however, you were working with Auto-Key off, you would need to add a keyframe at this point for the path position.

11. Leave the Object Attributes dialog box and set the time to the end of the sequence. To get the camera to the end of the path, we'll use the other method for moving an object along a path. Your camera should still be selected. Adjust your top view of the scene so that you can see the entire path and camera. Point your mouse so that the pointer arrow is aimed right at the camera. Drag right from that position. As you drag, the camera scoots along the path. Keep dragging right until the camera reaches the end of the path, as Figure 14.68 shows. This is your second key event, for the end. (If you had Auto-Key off, this is where you'd add another keyframe for the path position.)

Figure 14.68 Dragging the camera to position it along the path at the end of the sequence.

12. Click the Play button. It works, it works! Now go to Camera View and click the Play button again. Does the smoothness feel better this time around?

13. Extra Credit: If you want to continue altering the geometry of the path to make it smoother, you may do so. Set the Time Scrubber to the beginning of the sequence. Select the path. (If you're in top view, you may want to first select then lock the terrain so that it doesn't get in the way; Lock is an option in the Object Attributes dialog box.) Then drag the blue points to new positions. The reason we told you to make sure the Time Scrubber is at 0 is that path geometry is an animation property. You want to change the path for the whole thing rather than a little here, a little there.

TRACKING

Tracking in animation is useful for so many things. Tracking is a way to create and smooth object rotation and, in the case where the camera is the tracker, smooth camera movement. When an object tracks another object, one object is set to "face" another object. We'll call them, for the sake of clarity, the tracker (the object that's tracking another object) and the trackee (the object being tracked). Tracking is an object rotation shortcut; rather than describing an object's orientation, tracking establishes a relationship between two objects, where one object lives by the rule "Face that other thing, and keep facing it, no matter what happens!" It is an alternative to manually making changes in the orientation of the tracker object. The position of the trackee determines the rotation of the tracker.

How to Track

To make an object track another object, select the tracker-to-be. Point your mouse on the Tracking icon. Drag from there to the trackee object. As you drag, a blue line extends from the tracker. When your target trackee turns blue, let go of the mouse. Figure 14.69 shows the sequence of actions and the consequences using a round spotlight to track the sphere for a variation on the bounce scene we've been working with.

You can also set up a tracking relationship by using the Object Attributes dialog box, on the Linking tab, where the bottom half is devoted to tracking. Select from the pop-up menu of objects to choose the one you want to track (see Figure 14.70).

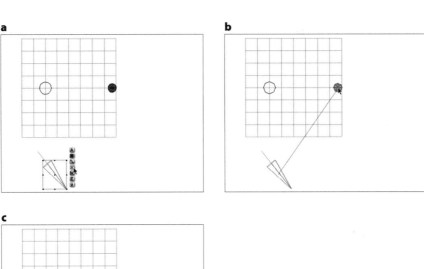

Figure 14.69 Establishing a tracking relationship between two objects:
a) Dragging from the tracking icon;
b) contacting the trackee; c) the tracker facing the trackee.

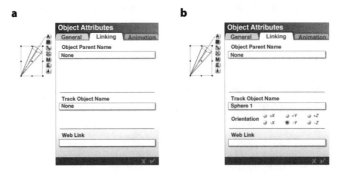

Figure 14.70 Setting up object tracking using the Object Attributes dialog box.

About Face

The tracker faces the trackee. But how do you determine what side of the tracker object will be the face that always looks toward the trackee? There are six possible options, two for each of Bryce's three dimensions; they are listed in the Tracking section of the Object Attributes dialog box. Figure 14.71 shows a still image from a movie, XYZ TRACKING PATHMOV, created to show every possible angle of tracking for every object in Bryce. For cones, pyramids, and terrains, tracking along the *y* axis points the tip of the object toward or away from the trackee. For the cylinder and the torus, the the *y* axis points along rounded part of the ring. (Note: The scene file is on the CD-ROM in the folder for this chapter.)

Figure 14.71 Different object types, in each of the six possible "face" orientations, tracking a glass sphere.

What Moves, What Stays

In the relationship between tracker and trackee, which is moving and which is staying still? There are four possible options:

- *The tracker and trackee are both still.* What good is it for both objects to be still? Tracking is good for scenes where a light shines on an object and the tracking relationship is set up merely to ease the process of aiming the light. Track the object and then adjust the light's position until you're satisfied. A similar procedure works with positioning the camera in a complex scene populated with many objects: Create an object whose only purpose is to be the trackee. In the Object Attributes dialog box, make the object hidden; it will be visible in wireframe, but not during the final render. Look through the camera at the object, and move the object to adjust the camera's position.

- *The tracker is still while the trackee is moving.* This is probably the most common relationship. It was used in the XYZ TRACKING movie we just mentioned. It also works well for, say, a camera or for lights that follow a moving object. When the tracker is still, following a moving trackee, the tracker is *not* considered to be animated, even though it does appear to be moving. You won't find it in the list of animated objects; it won't appear in the Advanced Motion Lab with a colored bar in the Sequencer and key event ticker marks (unless, of course, you created the object while Auto-Key was active, in which case, it will have a single, initial keyframe ticker mark but no colored bar to indicate animation over time). The only moving object is the trackee. What does exist is a tracking relationship. Tracking is a state; either an object is tracking another object or it is not, and in the case of the tracker, provided that it is motionless, it is not animated.

- *The tracker is moving while the trackee is still.* This option is the one used for orienting the camera in the trajectory-to-path animation earlier in this chapter. The camera moved along the path, all the while facing the lake terrain as it circled around. The moving camera faces the same object. As the camera changes location, its rotation changes to keep it facing that trackee object.

- *The tracker and trackee are both moving.* The trackee moves. The tracker faces it, and it moves too. The trajectory-to-path animation could easily be changed to this type by adding a hidden object that moves over the terrain and setting the camera to track that hidden object. This is an alternative to aligning the camera to an object's path. Have the camera track an object that is moving just ahead of it on the path, or that is moving along a slightly different trajectory or path.

Tracking provides for a whole number of sophisticated camera and object movements. By exploring these alternatives here, we're just straddling the line that divides an introduction to animation from more advanced techniques. We will take up some more of these in the next chapter, "Advanced Animation Techniques."

But first, it's (finally!) time to render animations!

RENDERING ANIMATIONS

At last, at last! The moment we've all been waiting for, when we can render the animation! You're almost done! Or wait…are you? Before you complete your ultimate and final render, you'll probably render your animation several times as a preview. Earlier in the chapter, we mentioned preview methods—playback in wireframe mode and the Animation Preview, where Bryce swiftly renders a small thumbnail of each frame. The first renders you will do of your animation are test renders, so that you can see what you've been working with and see what else needs to be done.

Test Renders and Stages of Preview

Of course, when you're working, there are test renders. The first and easiest level of test is the Wireframe Preview. The second level of test is the Render Preview (the Storyboard Preview).

Once you've gone through those preliminary stages, the next one commits you a bit more. The third test level involves actually letting Bryce render an animation for you and saving it to disk, so that you can get an idea that what you're doing is on the mark. Since it is saved to disk, you will have it there in perpetuity, or until you decide you don't need it anymore and throw it out, or until your hard drive crashes and takes all your data with it. (Um, you do back up your data, don't you? Don't you?! Hope so!)

There are some things that a moving wireframe will never show you that the render will. In the process of first creating the bounce sequence used in this chapter, the question of whether to move the camera to follow the ball arose. Since this is a beginner scene, the idea was to keep it as simple as possible. We thought, "Oh well, there's a bit where the ball is out of the frame of view." However, after rendering, the fact that the ball's shadow was still visible added a nice touch. The stationary camera turns out to be not only a good idea for an introductory sequence, but an excellent means of concluding the sequence with the ball's shadow. That discovery wasn't made until the scene was previewed as a rendered movie.

Test Render

Your next step will be to render an animation and generate an actual movie file with it. That way you can see what is going on. "But," you may be wondering, "won't that take too long to do?" Well, yes and no. Rendering animations is a more time-consuming process than rendering still images. If you want your animation work process to be, "Think up a movie and then, presto! it's done," however, you might as well pursue some other quest than animating with Bryce. (On the other hand, of course, the speed increases in processors is bringing the cost-of-entry threshold down to the level where mere Bryce mortals can do something interesting using a desktop computer.) Further, there are some tricks you can employ to get the biggest preview bang for the smallest render-time buck. Don't stop reading!

The test render, like any other "real" render, can be a movie or a set of still images. And as with any other render, you can choose the render settings for the sake of efficiency. Do you want a normal render or Fast Preview? Are textures on or off? Is the render resolution the same size, smaller, or larger than the wireframe size (smaller is good for test renders)? Is your render antialiased or not? You can choose settings that shorten your render time while still getting meaningful information from the rendered result.

For your first animation test, be sure to visit these places in Bryce for a test render procedure check.

- *Document Setup dialog box.* The document setup dialog box gives you the option to render at a smaller size. Use it! Set Render Resolution to 1:0.5 or 1:0.25. The render doesn't need to be full size for you to see if you're on the right track.

- *Deactivate antialiasing.* You can do this in either the Document Setup dialog box or on the Render Options pop-up menu (on the Controls Palette).

- *Render Options buttons on the Controls Palette.* Choose Fast Preview Mode, Textures Off, or both. (If you are animating sky effects, Fast Preview Mode will give you, at best, blurry effects. Try it and see.)

Table 14.2 lists a number of options for previewing your animations, including the Wireframe and Storyboard Previews, and rendered movies. The further you get in the construction of your sequence, the further down the list you'll go.

	Wireframe	Storyboard	Render
Full/Partial Sequence	✔	✔	✔
Fast/Full Nano		✔	
Fast Preview Mode		✔	✔
Textures On/Off		✔	✔
Antialiasing On/Off			✔
Render Size	✔		✔

Table 14.2 Preview and Render options for animation sequences; choose from these to reduce render time for test animation renders.

At first, just to make sure that you're getting where you want to go, you'll use the quick, early-in-the-process ways to check your work.

> **TIP:** *(advanced tip) If you are rendering volumetric materials during a test render, move the Quality slider to Low Quality/Fast Speed. The material will be grainier, but because so much time is involved in a full-out render, you want to make sure that you devote your computing resources to the final version, not another razzum-frazzum-this-razzum-thing-is-taking-forever draft. Don't put in the final rendering time until you absolutely need to.*

Render Animation Dialog Box

The Render Animation dialog box (see Figure 14.72) has three main sections. In the top section, choose how much of the sequence you want to render: the entire sequence, or the working range, or a specific range that you can enter there in the Time entry boxes. (Note: If you discounted that first Frame 0, you'd set the beginning of your range to Frame 1.)

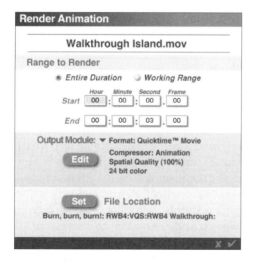

Figure 14.72 The Render Animation dialog box.

In the center section, choose the type of output: a sequence of still images, QuickTime movies, or AVI (Windows only). If you are creating roughs or very simple animations, choose the movie option and accept the default compression settings (QuickTime: Animation; AVI: Full Frames). For more complex or final-draft renders, choose still images. Why? If Bryce can produce output as a movie, then rendering to still images seems to be a step backward. Perhaps, and perhaps not. Suppose that your final render, at final resolution, will take four days. Suppose that, with all but five frames to go, your electricity cuts out for a minute, or some other emergency occurs that stops Bryce in its tracks. With a movie file, you've lost nearly four days' worth of work, whereas with a sequence of still images, you've only lost whatever render time was committed to the current frame. A movie file is not completely written and saved until the last frame is rendered. Also, if you have more than one machine to devote to rendering, you can have them all work on separate portions of the sequence.

Note: Once you create a movie that is made from a set of pict or bitmap images, you'll need, at minimum, the QuickTime Pro upgrade from Apple to generate a continuous movie from all the images. Also, the QuickTime Player does not like there to be any numbers in the file name other than the frame numbers themselves. Beware!

(Lest you think that four-day renders are excessive, the computer that is Susan's back-up renderer for this book—and the main computer on which *Real World Bryce 2* came into being—began its work history as a part of the *Planetary Traveler* renderfarm. Four-day renders were quick on that project; there were some renders that took weeks to complete!)

Finally, at the bottom, choose the location where your movie or image frames will be saved to disk. Then click the check mark.

> **TIP:** *Pressing the Shift key while clicking the check mark to exit the Render Animation dialog box will result in Bryce's creating a movie of the wireframe. Cool, eh? The CD-ROM contains many examples of wireframe-based animations shown concurrent with the rendered results to give you a sense of what's going on. Of course, whatever your settings are for wireframe view will be recorded in the movie: background texture; visibility of horizon line and underground lines; amount of detail of the wireframe; and whether the wireframe is visible in wireframe, OpenGL, Sree 3D, or (Windows only) Direct3D mode. Also, despite whatever render resolution you choose, your wireframe will be made into a movie at 1:1 size. When you render a wireframe movie, you are accepting the settings for your wireframe, not for your render.*

Bryce renders the movie, providing you with the status of its progress on the Time Palette. At the conclusion of the render, Bryce launches the application to display the image format or the movie format. The application launched will be whatever is the default image editor for pict or bitmaps (probably Photoshop, but your mileage may vary). For animations, Bryce will launch the QuickTime Player for .MOV files, and the Windows Media Player for .AVI files.

We will walk you through rendering a movie when we finish the Bounce tutorial in the next chapter. In the meantime, if you want to try creating test or real renders, work with the TRAJ-TO-PATH scene file and compare your render results to ours. For this, we used a Power Macintosh G3/400 Powerbook.

	1:0.25 Render Resolution	1:0.5 Render Resolution
Textures off	2 minutes	7.5 minutes
Textures off/Antialiasing on	8 minutes	26 minutes
Quick Preview	4 minutes	14 minutes
Quick Preview/Antialiasing on	23.5 minutes	82 minutes
Full Render	5 minutes	21 minutes
Full Render/Antialiasing on	29 minutes	108 minutes

Table 14.3 Results of render tests using different settings on a PowerMac G3/400 Powerbook.

As you can see here, for test renders, the single most time-saving action you can take is to turn off antialiasing—the difference is dramatic!

Render Animation Gotcha

Bryce has a very cryptic and unfriendly alert that may show up just at the point where you click the check box to begin rendering your animation. This unfriendly alert says the following, "A file error has occurred (i/o, bad media)" (see Figure 14.73). Relax! You don't have bad media! The alert is really just a sheep in wolf's clothing.

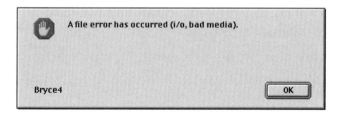

Figure 14.73
The cryptic i/o error alert, a sheep in wolf's clothing.

There are two possible reasons why this alert appears, neither of which really has anything to do with bad media. Suppose you render a movie; it will automatically be opened in your movie viewing application. After looking at what takes place in it, you inevitably decide to tweak something in the sequence. Hmmm…tweak… hmmm, tweak. When you're through making your adjustments, you go to render the movie again. Bryce offers you the name of the previous movie in the movie

Save As dialog box. Should you save the movie while the first version of it is still open, you'll get that alert because the file can't be overwritten while it is open.

If that's not the case, then chances are your movie file name is one or two characters too long. (This situation is more likely to occur on Macs.) And, no, that's not "bad" either, seeing as how that silly dialog box allowed you to enter up to 31 characters in the first place. The situation is simple to remedy. But first you have to click OK, and then Bryce dumps you straight back into your scene, so you'll have to start the whole process over again in the Render Animation dialog box to retry.

But what is this about two characters too long? If the name fit into the Save dialog box, why is it too long? The reason is that when Bryce renders a movie, it generates a temporary file that it writes to while the render is ongoing. Suppose that you have a movie named MOVIEFILENAME.MOV. Bryce writes the temporary file as MOVIEFILENAME.MTEMP. The temporary file's name is two characters longer than the original name. This is not a problem if you're using Windows, where you're given over 200 characters for file names, nearly sufficient for writing a sonnet. (Well okay, maybe a limerick or a haiku, if not a full sonnet!) But for the Macintosh file system, with a 31-character name limit, the two extra characters may force extra brevity on you.

MOVING ON...

If you've made it through this whole chapter, including all the walkthroughs, we salute you! This is a lot of animation knowledge to get under your belt! We shall move on in the next chapter to the Advanced Motion Lab (and take care of the finishing touches of that bounce tutorial!) and get into fine-tuning animations, camera moves, and more good motion fun.

CHAPTER FIFTEEN

Advanced Animation Techniques

IN THIS CHAPTER...

- Introduction to the Advanced Motion Lab
- Working with a camera boom
- Animation case studies
- Leveraging animation
- Linking, hierarchies, and groups
- Working with paths

This chapter takes up more advanced animation techniques. We begin by introducing you to the one part of Bryce that has the word *advanced* in its name: the Advanced Motion Lab. Once you've been through the Advanced Motion Lab, you'll be familiar with all of Bryce's animation controls. At that point, it will make sense to talk about how to plan your animations, since you'll then have an idea of what you're getting into. From there, we delve into advanced camera techniques, the camera boom, and additional motion tricks and things to do with paths.

INTRODUCTION TO THE AML

The Advanced Motion Lab (AML) is where you do the work to make your motions seem more natural and to make little fixes to your animations and keyframes. At the beginning of the previous chapter, we mentioned that key events may involve forces of physics (such as the flattening of a ball when it hits the ground). Another force of physics is gravity. Objects do not travel with a uniform motion. When they start moving, they take a little time to get going, and once they're in motion, they take a little time to decelerate before completely stopping. Much like the atmospheric effects that make your Bryce world believable as a snapshot of another place, the motion subtleties are what will make your animation believable. The place you do the fine-tuning is the Advanced Motion Lab.

You can edit objects and their key events, move those events around, get rid of them entirely (nice for cleanup), make adjustments to the way events occur over time, and change time itself for any given object or for any object property.

Quick Overview

Recall from the last chapter that animated key events take place in both space and time. Here, in the Advanced Motion Lab, you wedge yourself between the two and adjust the relation of time to space.

To get to the AML, click the Advanced Motion Lab button on the Time Palette or type ⌘-T/Ctrl+T. The Advanced Motion Lab reflects the separation of time and space in the way it's organized, as Figure 15.1 shows. The AML is divided into a few main areas. (The following list details five areas, but when it comes to actually working in the AML, there are actually only four—or maybe even just three.)

- *Time Mapping Area.* At the upper left of the AML, the Time Mapping area allows you to edit the time part of the key event. You can adjust the velocity of objects and otherwise tweak time to make your object behaviors as believable as possible.

- *Preview Area.* The 3D Preview, at the top right, is devoted to space, so that you can see your objects move in space. The preview area is at the upper right. There you see your scene in wireframe view. You can switch back and forth between Director's View and Camera View and adjust your perspective.

- *Time/Playback Controls.* Running across the center part of the Advanced Motion Lab, like a belt at the waist, are the controls for time: the time readout, the Playback controls, and the Time Ruler—the AML's equivalent to the Time Scrubber and working area.

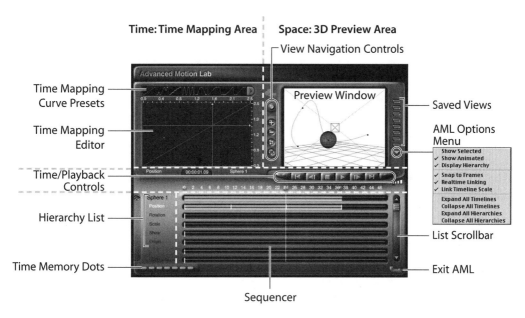

Time: Time Mapping Area   Space: 3D Preview Area

View Navigation Controls

Time Mapping Curve Presets

Time Mapping Editor

Preview Window

Saved Views

AML Options Menu

Show Selected
✓ Show Animated
✓ Display Hierarchy
✓ Snap to Frames
✓ Realtime Linking
✓ Link Timeline Scale
Expand All Timelines
Collapse All Timelines
Expand All Hierarchies
Collapse All Hierarchies

Time/Playback Controls

Hierarchy List

List Scrollbar

Time Memory Dots

Exit AML

Sequencer

Figure 15.1 The Advanced Motion Lab, with each major section labeled.

In the bottom half, below the waistline of the AML, are the Hierarchy List and the Sequencer. This is the place where you can see at a glance what is being animated and can home in on objects, their attributes, and specific key events.

- *Hierarchy List.* Each animatable object, and each object attribute that is being animated, can be listed here. We say "can be" because you can choose exactly what appears and how it appears—more on that in the section devoted to the Hierarchy List.

- *Sequencer.* To the right of the Hierarchy List is the Sequencer, where you can carefully select and manipulate any key event for any point in time. For each item in the Hierarchy List (which can be an object or attribute of an object), there is a horizontal timeline, where you can see whether animation is taking place at all for that object (a summary that includes all attributes) or for that attribute. Each key event is marked with a little vertical ticker mark, which we'll call the key event ticker mark.

Now that you've got an overall feel for each area, we'll delve into each in greater detail. However, we'll proceed in reverse order, starting with the objects and attributes in the Hierarchy List. But first, a word of caution.

Oh, and When You Leave…

When you navigate to the AML, you come to one of Bryce's special "rooms." Unlike every other room in Bryce, this one has an arrow to return you to Bryce. There is no option to either cancel or accept changes; this is a place where there's no Undo. Well, that's not exactly true. You can undo a move you just made in the AML; you just can't decide, at the end of all your workings and tweakings, to say, "Hmmm…I think I'd like to throw the whole thing out and start over, so I'll click the Cancel button." You can undo one move at a time, but that is all. Whatever you do here in the Advanced Motion Lab you do for all time in Bryce.

Hierarchy List

At the bottom half of the Advanced Motion Lab are the Hierarchy List and Sequencer. The Hierarchy List is a good place to start our AML tour, since the list names the items that are in the scene and shows what is animated. For each object whose name appears in the list, there is a sublist containing each property or attribute that is animated. A simple click on the object name will expand or collapse the list of properties. Properties? Attributes? What are those? Recall the previous chapter's long list of what can be animated; those are animatable attributes. Each object in the scene can be expanded to display those attributes. Each attribute can have its own individual settings.

The text labels in the Hierarchy List can be one of four colors. Each color indicates the status of that particular item or attribute.

- *Red*. Red indicates that the object is selected. The red name corresponds to the selected red wireframe. The red color is limited to the name of the object; none of the object's attributes can ever be displayed in red.

- *White*. White indicates one of two things. It may indicate that there's more contained in that object: A container item is a timeline that contains additional timelines. The most obvious example is the name of an unselected object, which is displayed in white; it can be expanded to show the attributes for that object. White text also indicates that the attribute is animated using a minimum of two keyframes. (There are many objects and object attributes that contain only one keyframe—typical when working with Auto-Key on.) Usually when a timeline is a container, it cannot itself be animated, so the item displayed in white text will either be a container or an animated attribute.

- *Yellow*. Yellow indicates that the particular animated attribute is selected. When the attribute is selected, you can work with it in the AML (we discuss specifics later in this chapter).

- *Gray*. Gray indicates the end of the line. The attribute is not actively animated—that is, it contains only an initial single keyframe (this is often the case when Auto-Key is on). Also, an item that is gray cannot be expanded to contain additional timelines. (There is one confusing exception to this no-expand rule, which we discuss in the "Animating Textures (and Materials)" section at the end of this chapter.)

Besides displaying the attributes in one of those four colors, Bryce offers you some options for which items are displayed in the Hierarchy List and how those items are displayed. The AML normally displays only your selected objects in the Hierarchy List. This assumes, of course, that you were working with an object in the main scene window, and that, with the object selected, you decide to go to the Advanced Motion Lab and tweak the object a bit. When you come into the AML, the object name appears in the Hierarchy List; and it is red, to indicate that the object is selected. But there are additional options besides that default state.

What Exactly Do You Want to See?

There are three main options for determining what gets displayed in the Hierarchy List. You can access them from the AML Options menu at the right edge of the Advanced Motion Lab window. Our descriptions for each of the items assumes that only that option is active.

Show Selected displays only selected objects in the Hierarchy List. Note: since the sun and the sky cannot be selected or deselected; they are always visible in the Hierarchy List.

Show Animated displays only those objects that are animated. It does not matter whether or not they are selected.

Display Hierarchy shows parent-child relationships as a series of collapsible lists.

Show Selected and Show Animated both act as filters to determine what is displayed, and Display Hierarchy determines how the displayed objects appear in the AML if they are part of an object hierarchy.

Show Selected

There are things you can do to affect the preview. You can, in the AML, select or deselect objects. Selected objects are shown in red in the list. To select or deselect the object, ⌘-click/Ctrl+click the object name. The Wireframe Preview should change to or from red, depending on whether it was selected in the first place. Once you select additional objects, those objects stay selected in your scene after you leave the AML.

If you want to, say, increase the number of items appearing in your Hierarchy List from what was in the list when you first entered the Advanced Motion Lab, you can do so by a little bit of selection trickery. Try this: In the Display Options pop-up menu, deselect Show Selected to see everything in your scene. Then ⌘-click/Ctrl+click the names of the items you're interested in seeing. Then go back and select Show Selected to make all the other items go away.

Suppose you want to go the other way and make fewer items appear by using Show Selected and deselecting objects. When you have a selected object and you use ⌘-click/Ctrl+click to deselect it, it does not automatically disappear from the list when you deselect it; you need to deactivate and reactivate Show Selected from the pop-up menu or leave and return to the AML. In addition, at least one object must be selected for the others to go away using this method.

Show Animated

We mentioned that Show Animated displays all animated objects whether or not they are selected. This is true when Show Animated is checked and Show Selected is unchecked. If both are checked, however, then only those objects that are both animated and selected will be displayed.

Display Hierarchy

Here's a guided walkthrough to show you how hierarchies are displayed in the Advanced Motion Lab.

1. Open the scene DOUBLE HIERARCHY and go to the Advanced Motion Lab.

2. If these settings are not already in effect, select Show Animated and Display Hierarchy on the menu and disable Show Selected (see Figure 15.2a). There is a blue triangle next to Torus 2, indicating that it is the parent of a child or children (see Figure 15.2b).

3. Click the triangle, and the top level of the hierarchy unfolds. Notice that Torus 2 has four children: the four pyramids. (see Figure 15.2c.)

4. Click the blue triangle for the first pyramid. There is one child, Torus 4 (see Figure 15.2d).

5. Click the triangle for that object. The hierarchy expands to show Torus 4's child objects: an additional four pyramids (see Figure 15.2e).

Of course, for each of the other four objects, you can show or hide the children as well. And of course, you can show the attributes for them.

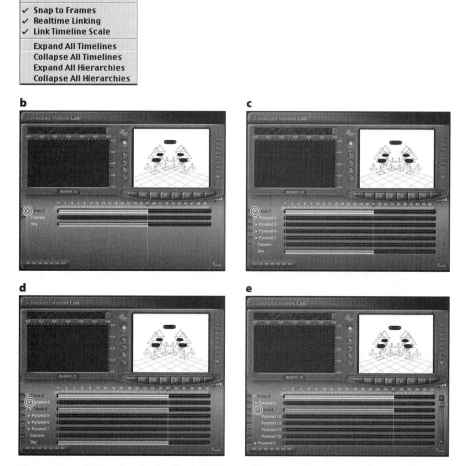

Figure 15.2 Hierarchy display in the Advanced Motion Lab: a) Initial AML Options Menu setting; b) the AML with the objects listed; c) expanding the hierarchy for Torus 2; d) expanding the hierarchy for the first pyramid; e) expanding the hierarchy to display Torus 4's children.

For now, we'll skip the items in the middle section of the AML Options menu, but we'll return to them in a moment when we discuss the Time Ruler and its controls. The bottom part of the menu contains commands that help you speed through the Hierarchy List:

Expand All Timelines

This option expands all the timelines so that the properties for all projects are expanded and visible. Well, they'll be visible when you scroll through the list.

Collapse All Timelines

This is the cleanup command; it closes all the expanded object timelines so that the Hierarchy List displays only the list of objects.

Expand All Hierarchies

When you are looking at your Hierarchy List as a hierarchy, this option expands all the hierarchies, so you can see who belongs to whom. (In the awkward case where there are so many nested children that the list is indented out of the Hierarchy List area and into the Sequencer area, this command provides the only way to see all of the objects when the list is displayed as a hierarchy.)

Collapse All Hierarchies

This option is the cleanup option for hierarchies, collapsing them into their top-most parent objects.

The thing to note about navigating in the Hierarchy List is that you can show or hide whatever you want. It would be easier, of course, if the AML were to magically expand to take up more of your desktop real estate. One can only hope that Bryce will borrow that aspect of Poser; it sure would make things simpler in the Advanced Motion Lab. In the meantime, there are myriad little ways to display your objects, their attributes, and their children—or not.

Eyes Wide Shut

Notice that to the left of each object there is an eye. That means that the object is displayed. If you click the eye to shut it, the object disappears from the 3D Preview window. Suppose you are animating an object that is located behind another object for a portion of the animation. To fine-tune that object's motion, you need to temporarily hide the one in front of it. Shut the front object's eye, and you have an unoccluded view of the object you're interested in. Making objects invisible in the AML 3D Preview has no effect on the visibility of objects in your main scene window. Clicking the eye hides or shows the object in the preview window; it will remain displayed in the Hierarchy List and Sequencer.

If you are looking at the list in Hierarchy View, with the collapsible arrow, then Option-clicking/Alt+clicking the eye of a parent object affects the visibility of both it and all its children. Even after you've made a multiplicity of items invisible with one stroke, you can still go back and show or hide individual items by clicking their respective eyes.

If You Don't Read Any Other Section in This Chapter, Read This One!

When you move the pointer arrow over one of the objects or the object properties in the Hierarchy List, hold down the Shift key, and then press the mouse button, a pop-up menu appears (see Figure 15.3). This menu accomplishes exceedingly useful tasks for you. Notable is the item at the bottom: Delete All Keyframes. "What's so great about that?" you may ask. "We already learned about the magical Remove All Keyframes key combination back in the last chapter, for which, by the way, we are exceedingly grateful." Here's the difference: That com-

Figure 15.3 The pop-up menu for the objects or attributes listed in the Hierarchy List.

mand removes every blessed keyframe from your entire scene; this menu command removes keyframes from only the animation property on which your mouse is poised. This one item is one of the primary purposes for visiting the AML. If you decide that, so far as Bryce is concerned, the AML is non-territory for you, this one item should be the reason for an exception to the "I won't go there!" rule. Use this command; you'll thank us for it. (Of course, we hope that you'll use other parts of the AML anyway.) The Delete All Keyframes command is splendid for scene cleanup. Bryce has a habit of throwing nasty Hierarchy List property detritus all over, listing useless attributes left and right (well, to be technically accurate, which we strive to be, even under duress, the useless properties are listed up and down). They're no damn good. You don't need 'em, so get rid of them.

It often happens that many items in the Hierarchy List will acquire keyframes at the start of a sequence. This normally happens when you have Auto-Key on, and you go to the beginning of the sequence to edit an object. Going to the beginning ensures that there is no change to the object over the duration of the sequence, but by recording a keyframe, you increase the file size, and you provide more junk to wade through in the AML. You can delete all keyframes for an object, or for individual properties of an object.

Aside from the all-important Delete All Keyframes command, the menu has other options, which will cause other interesting animation effects to occur. They are: Pendulum Movement, Circular Movement, Repeat, and the "tag home base" option: One Shot. These fascinating options are discussed in more detail later in this chapter.

Keyboard Shortcuts

Here are the keyboard shortcuts that apply to the Hierarchy List in the Advanced Motion Lab.

Basic Keyboard Shortcuts

⌘-Z/Ctrl+Z	Undo last action.
Return/Enter/Esc	Leave AML. (Esc is not cancel! There is no cancel in AML!)

AML Options Menu Shortcuts

⌘-S/Ctrl+S	Show Selected (toggle on or off).
⌘-A/Ctrl+A	Show Animated (toggle on or off).
⌘-H/Ctrl+H	Display Hierarchy (toggle on or off).
⌘-Q/Ctrl+Q	Expand/collapse the sequencer/timeline information for all the objects.
⌘-E/Ctrl+E	Expand/collapse the hierarchy information for the objects. (This option works when Display Hierarchy is on unless Show Selected is on as well.)

Hierarchy Key Shortcuts

⌘/Ctrl+Click Object Name	Select/deselect the object (in the AML preview and also in the scene itself).
⌘/Alt+Click Object Name	Expand/collapse timelines of the object and all object properties.
Shift+Click Object/Attribute Name	Displays pop-up menu with animation options for object or animation attribute.
Option/Alt+Click Eye	Show/hide the object and its children (if applicable).
Option/Alt+Click Hierarchy triangle	Expand/collapse the hierarchy of object's children.

Sequencer

The Sequencer is the other part of the lower section of the Advanced Motion Lab. It's where the stuff of time is adjusted. For each item in the Hierarchy List, there is a horizontal bar that indicates where key events are (vertical ticker marks) and when in time the object or property is being animated (the colored bar). When each object is collapsed, the main Sequencer bar for the object provides a summary, indicating that change is taking place in one or more of the object's attributes. The Sequencer bar for that object is not editable. By clicking the object name, so that all the properties are displayed, you can edit the actual animation properties.

Generally, different objects have different-colored "temperature bars." The camera is red, the sky is blue, and objects are green. If there is an object hierarchy, the parent object is purple. It doesn't have to be like this all the time, though. Now, through the use of a very spiffy Easter Egg key, you can cycle though all manner of colors in the Advanced Motion Lab. That's right; with one tap of the C key, you can change the color. When you tap seven times, you're cycled back home to the colors you began with. It's an aesthetic treat for your Advanced Motion Lab working pleasure.

No, Not Quite a Time Lord

At the top of the Sequencer area is the Time Ruler. The Scale control is to the right; it operates the same way as the Scale control on the main Bryce Time Palette or in the Terrain Editor, the Sky Lab, and the Materials Lab. As promised, now we'll tell you what those items in the midsection of the AML Options menu are for (refer back to Figure 15.2a).

Snap to Frames

When active, this option forces all movement of the Current Time indicator and the keyframe ticker marks to snap to frames. It is on by default. It probably should stay that way.

Realtime Linking

When active (it's on by default), this option displays the 3D Preview in real time when the Current Time indicator is moved. Otherwise, you first move the Current Time indicator, and then when you stop, the 3D Preview changes to reflect the new current time.

Link Timeline Scale

This option synchronizes the scale of the Time Ruler in the Advanced Motion Lab with the timeline on the Time Palette. Scale it down here in the AML so that you see only the first several frames, and when you leave the AML and go back to the main Bryce work area, the timeline there will be scaled accordingly. To synch or not to synch: that is the question; whether 'tis nobler to check this item on the pop-up menu. Doing so produces different results depending on how you have the Bryce interface set up. With the default (Interface Min) setting, whereby the program's controls stick tight by the edges of the working window, the length of the AML's timeline will be the same as the one on the main Time Palette. On the other hand, if you've chosen Interface Max from the Display Palette, so that the interface hugs the edges of your screen, the Time Palette's timeline will be longer than the one in the AML. But if Link Timeline Scale is on, the two timelines will rescale proportionally.

Figure 15.4 shows the bottom half of the AML, with everything labeled. In addition to the Sequencer, the other Time controls are labeled.

There's one other element in the Sequencer area that is not strictly part of the Sequencer. It's the time display, located at the bottom of the Time Curve Mapping area.

The Sequencer area includes three controls for indicating where you are currently and for setting limits to the range of animation.

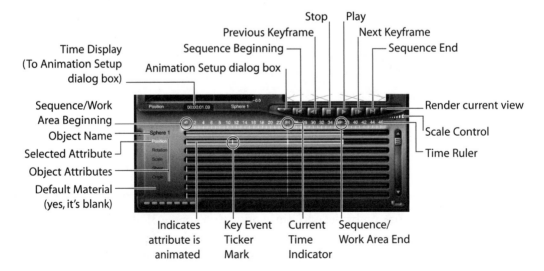

Figure 15.4 The Sequencer with all the parts labeled.

Time Controls

The Current Time indicator is a vertical line that indicates where "now" is. The lavender knob at the top both marks the current time on the Time Ruler and is a control knob for dragging the current time to another spot. It is translucent at all times, except when your pointer rests over it or when you are dragging the control around. Similar to the lavender knob are two tan knobs that mark the beginning and ending points of your sequence. Normally they mark the beginning and end of the entire sequence duration, but they also mark the limits of the working range. They, too, are translucent except when the mouse pointer is over them or when you are moving them around. Changes made to the working range in either the AML or the Time Palette will be updated in the corresponding Time Ruler.

Suppose your Time Ruler is scaled so that only part of the sequence shows—say, the second half of it. How do you get to a point in the first half? The obvious method is to drag the current time marker to the left end of the ruler and beyond, which will cause the whole shebang to scroll to the right. The other, less obvious method is to drag the ruler itself. Go ahead and try it—put the mouse pointer anywhere on the Time Ruler (make sure you're not on top of one of the control knobs) and drag left and right. How's that for a feeling of power?

The other control for time is at the middle right: the Playback controls. These have the same functions as the ones on the main Time Palette, with the inevitable couple of exceptions. First, the AML's Play controls are inconsistent with the Play controls elsewhere in Bryce (in the Time Palette, Terrain Editor, Materials Lab, and Sky Lab). In the Advanced Motion Lab, the Play button does not act as a toggle with Pause. You click one button, Play, to go, and you click another button, Stop, to either pause or stop. The other exception concerns the two unlabeled buttons to either side of the begin and end keys. The one on the right is a render preview; it will render a still frame of the preview currently displayed in the window. The one on the left will invoke the Animation Setup dialog box. By the way, clicking the current time readout will do the same.

AML Animation Setup Dialog Box Warning

Warning! Danger, Will Robinson! If you go to the Animation Setup dialog box, do not under any circumstances scale the scene to increase or decrease the time. (Well, okay; if you want to experiment to see if we're telling the truth, then go right ahead. Verification is A Good Thing!) For some reason, your doing so here inside the AML will cause the timeline here and the timeline "out there" on the Time Palette to no longer coincide. Further, the current time readout will show funny numbers when you begin dragging things around. Basically, it's a nice attempt at continuity, but, in this case, we say to you, as parent to young toddler, "Oh, honey, hot! hot! No, don't touch! It'll burn you! Ow!"

The Animation Setup dialog box in the AML is accessed in two different ways. One is by clicking the time counter. The other is by clicking the unlabeled button to the left of the Playback controls.

Sequencer Keyboard Shortcuts

Here are the keyboard shortcuts that apply to navigating the Time Ruler and the Sequencer in the Advanced Motion Lab.

Time Navigation Keyboard Shortcuts

, . (comma, period)	Go to previous frame/next frame. In AML, movement is strictly by frame and not by ticker marks.
< >	Go to the previous/next keyframe. (Use the Shift key with the comma/period on U.S. keyboards.)
[ ]	Go to the beginning of the work area/end of sequence (oops! a bug).
\ or P	Play the animation; pause if playing. (P does not work in the main Bryce interface.)

Sequencer Navigation Keyboard Shortcuts

Home	Go to the very top of the timeline list.
End	Go to the very last timeline.
Up/Down Arrow	Scroll timeline list up/down one line at a time.
PgUp/PgDn	Scroll timeline list up/down one page at a time.

Click 'n' Drag with Sequencer

Click keyframe	Select keyframe.
Delete (Macintosh) Backspace (Windows)	Delete selected keyframes.
Shift+Click keyframe	Multiple keyframe selection and Toggle keyframe selection.
I (with keyframe[s] selected)	Toggle between spline (curved) and linear interpolation of keyframe.
⌘/Ctrl+drag keyframe	Make copy of selected keyframes.
Option/Alt+drag keyframes	Proportionally scale the time between keyframes (three or more have to be selected for you to see the effect).

Sequencer Item List

To edit an animated property, click the name of the property or its colored bar on the timeline in the Sequencer to select it. Remember that you can't select the timeline of an object; you must display its individual timelines and select one of those. When you select a timeline, that property becomes active in the Time Mapping area.

Key Event Ticker Marks

You can also select one key event ticker mark, or multiple ticker marks for a single timeline, or multiple ticker marks across multiple object property timelines.

Click a key event ticker mark to select it. (It is white when selected.) Hold down the Shift key to select additional ticker marks. You can also drag a marquee around multiple ticker marks to select them (this works horizontally or vertically). (See Figure 15.5.)

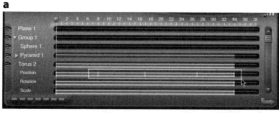

Figure 15.5 Dragging a marquee around Sequencer ticker marks selects multiple ticker marks; this works a) Horizontally or b) vertically.

Once a ticker mark is selected, you can move it to another place on the line. The best, easiest, and most satisfying thing to do with one selected key event ticker mark is to adjust its position in time. If you're editing a trajectory position, here is a place in the AML where you can separate *where* the key event occurs from *when* it occurs—make it happen later, or earlier. If you've created a whole bunch of position points, then this is where you can even out the timing of the object as it moves through all those positions. Adjust the spacing of the times so that the key events occur uniformly. (Of course, using the Path option is another way to ensure uniform motion, but sometimes a trajectory with four keypoints is all you need.)

Caution—dragging keyframes in the AML can be precarious, since they'll slide around really fast. It's as though you're trying to run down greased steps. Precision control is sometimes hard to achieve, especially if you want to move over a great distance. Changing the scale to enlarge the space between the frames may help.

If you drag the key event ticker marks beyond other ticker marks, you'll change the shape of your trajectory or the order in which things take place. This is handy when it's what you intend, and baffling when it isn't.

The second-most satisfying thing to do with key event ticker marks is to get rid of them. If there is but one ticker mark for a given property (a common artifact of Auto-Keyed animation) and you delete it, the whole property goes away from the AML. O blissful AML housecleaning! So, if you are animating a couple of items in the sky and want to clean up the remaining nonanimated attributes, drag a vertical marquee around as many of those leftover key event ticker marks as you can and, with them selected, tap the Delete or Backspace key to send them away.

a

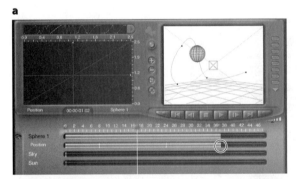

b

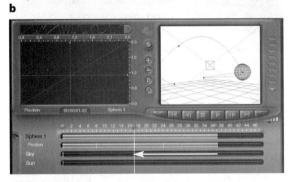

Figure 15.6 Duplicating a key event in the AML by ⌘/Ctrl+dragging the key event ticker mark to a new position: a) Before; and b) after.

There are more things to do with key event ticker marks than moving and removing them. You can create a copy of a selected keyframe by dragging it with the ⌘/Ctrl key held down (don't believe the manual when it tells you to use the Option/Alt key). If you are creating a sequence where an object moves back to a single place and then goes elsewhere and returns again and again in a bouncy fashion, this is a good way to get the return part. Create the trajectory with the first return in it, and then duplicate the returns in the AML. Figure 15.6 shows before and after states for key events duplicated in the AML. The final keyframe is duplicated and brought to the position where the Current Time indicator is. Compare the 3D Preview for both situations.

We just told you how to duplicate a key event ticker mark; what if you want to get rid of an unwanted duplicate key event ticker mark? In the previous chapter, in the section "Moving Trajectory Handles," we mentioned a bug where Bryce sometimes adds a duplicate keyframe and trajectory handle on top of an existing one. Now that we've explained key event ticker marks, we can tell you how to fix the problem. Navigate to the time in question. Select and move the key event ticker mark. Moving it will reveal the presence of another one "underneath" it; that is the duplicate. Determine which of those two key events you don't want; then select the unwanted one and delete it.

In addition to moving multiple selected key event ticker marks, you can scale multiple ticker marks to expand them or squeeze them. You need to have three or more selected for this operation to work. To scale the key event marks, hold down the Option/Alt key while dragging. Figure 15.7 shows the before (Figure 15.7a) and after (Figure 15.7b) state of three selected key event ticker marks. The final ticker mark was dragged to the left; this caused them all to be scaled smaller. Had it been dragged to the right, they would have been scaled larger. The relationships among the ticker marks are preserved as they scale (in this example, the space between them is mostly uniform, so the preservation of scale is not as readily apparent). We have two warnings for you, though: First, if you are scaling multiple ticker marks to the left, toward 0, and you continue the drag left *past* 0, you'll lose the relative relationships among them. Carried to extremes, they'll pile up one by one at the zero spot; but even if you drag slightly past 0, the relationships will warp slightly. Undo and try again, if necessary. Second, if you are going to scale multiple ticker marks, selecting key event marks across different timelines will deliver some strange results. Let's hope you don't have to adjust tons and tons of key event ticker marks.

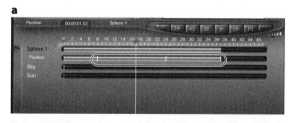

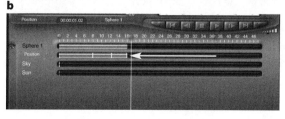

Figure 15.7 Scaling multiple key events: a) Before scaling, with three ticker marks selected; b) after dragging the rightmost ticker mark to the left with the Option or Alt key pressed.

3D Preview

The preview area in the AML lets you see the result of your work. You can see the objects in motion while you adjust the timing. The preview window is a miniature wireframe display of the scene. You can navigate around in it to adjust your view, and you can determine whether an object is visible or not (see "Eyes Wide Shut" earlier in this chapter).

However, when you click the Play button in the AML to preview your animation, you are not following strict SMPTE time. Bryce plays your animation as fast as it can, taking less time than the amount allotted for your sequence. (In fact, Bryce doesn't follow strict SMPTE time in the main preview, either; the wireframe playback takes longer than the time allotted.) The faster playback pace in the AML could be a good thing, if you want to rush through a long time sequence. However, there may be times when you're fine-tuning, and the rushedness of the AML preview makes it difficult to judge the subtleties of motion differences. In that case, you'll have to see the motion in the main Bryce Working Window. You can slow down the AMC preview by selecting a more detailed wireframe setting. From the Wireframe Resolution pop-up menu on the Display/Wireframe Palette, choose the highest setting for Motion: 64.

Camera and Director's Views

To the left of the window are the Animation Preview controls (see Figure 15.8). The top control toggles you back and forth between Camera View and Director's View. When you are looking through the camera, the little green status light is on. (Michael "renato!" Sigmon gave this the nickname "belly button;" it's an "innie" or an "outie" depending on whether it's on or not.) (The Camera icon also changes shades of gray depending on whether the camera is active or inactive. But it's much easier to just look at the green light and see whether it's on or off.) When you're looking at the preview from Camera View, the other controls are disabled.

When the light is off, the camera is dimmed to darker gray, and the Director's View controls are usable. From top to bottom, they are: zoom in, zoom out, reset to the default Director's View (the corner arrangement), and pan in any direction.

You can also change the Director's View by using direct mouse manipulations inside the 3D Preview. Drag left, right, up, or down to change the rotation. (It's similar to using a trackball, no?) To move forward or backward, press the Control/Ctrl key and drag up to move forward or drag down to move backward. Dragging left and right with Control/Ctrl held down moves your view left and right.

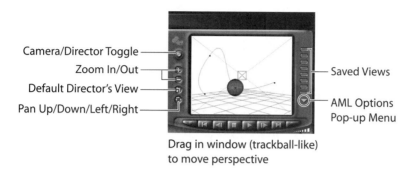

Camera/Director Toggle
Zoom In/Out
Default Director's View
Pan Up/Down/Left/Right

Saved Views

AML Options
Pop-up Menu

Drag in window (trackball-like)
to move perspective

Figure 15.8 AML 3D Preview, labeled.

You can save your Director's View animation previews by setting the purple memory dots (in a vertical row, to the right of the 3D Preview window). Those memory dots are saved for the duration of the time that Bryce is open during the current session. If you want to preserve your views, then don't shut down Bryce! If you do, say bye-bye to anything saved with the purple memory dots. Likewise, each time you start Bryce afresh and enter the AML, the Animation Preview Director's View camera will be reset to its default position, regardless of its position in the scene itself.

Here is a summary of the shortcuts you can use in the 3D Preview:

Keyboard Shortcuts

Drag up/down/left/right	Rotate trackball perspective around world center.
Control/Ctrl+Drag up/down	Move in/out in Preview window.
Control/Ctrl+Drag left/right	Move left/right in Preview window.

Time Mapping Editor

The Time Mapping Editor is where you get to work with time and its relation to the events in your animated sequence. Slow down or speed up the time between events. Or vary it so that you start off slow, get moving, and then, just before the end, slow down again. You can even make time go forward while the event order goes backward!

Before you begin doing all these wonderful things to time and events, let's talk about all the pieces and parts of the Time Mapping Editor. Figure 15.9 shows the Time Mapping Editor, with its components labeled.

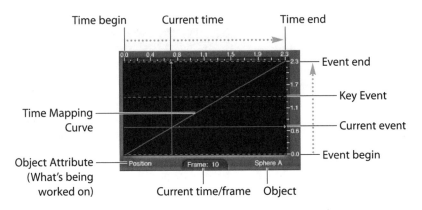

Figure 15.9 The Time Mapping Editor, with all its parts labeled.

Horizontal Axis: Time

Along the top of the Time Mapping Editor is a timeline that represents true and actual time (well, from a simple, common-sense Brycean perspective). The vertical crosshairs mark the position of the current time, which is also displayed numerically at the bottom of the window. The readout takes the form you've chosen in the Animation Setup dialog box (which you can get to by clicking the readout): either SMPTE time or frame count. (By the way, don't try to use the Animation Setup dialog box for anything other than changing from frame to SMPTE format or the other way around.)

The left-to-right movement of time matches the movement of time for the AML in the Sequencer and the forward progression of time for timelines and Time Scrubbers in each place where you work with animation: the Time Palette, Sky Lab, Terrain Editor, Materials Lab, and of course, here in the Advanced Motion Lab. Time marches on; it moves from left to right.

Vertical Axis: Events

Along the right side is the timeline that represents the series of events taking place in the sequence. From the initial state at the bottom to the final state at the top, each key event is represented as a horizontal dotted line. As the events occur, the horizontal crosshairs mark the current event.

The Time Mapping Curve

Trace a line through all the points of intersection for time and events, and the result is the Time Mapping Curve. Here's the real significance of the curve: The slope of the curve at each point where the timeline and the event line intersect gives you the rate of change of time at that point. In the default state of a Bryce animation, the map is a straight diagonal line. The slope of a diagonal line is the same at every point, which means that time proceeds at the same, uniform rate throughout the sequence.

But fortunately, the shape of that Time Mapping Curve can be changed to vary the way that events occur over time. Here's why that's a good thing: In a default, garden-variety Bryce sequence, time marches on in a nice, forward, orderly fashion. Time begins at the beginning, with the first event, in the lower-left corner. When half the time has transpired, you're halfway through the event sequence. When you reach the end of time, you have just concluded the final event. That is a nice, orderly, linear, time-event progression. It also happens to be boring! It's a total giveaway that the animation is being accomplished by computer! Yuck! It's a lie, a big, big lie! Well, at least if you're trying to imitate the action of the real world, it's a lie.

The number of things in this world that move and change at a completely uniform pace are a scant few. The Time Mapping Editor is the place to accelerate and decelerate your objects as they move. That's why the Time Mapping Curves are sometimes referred to as the velocity curves; you're adjusting the velocity of movement over time.

Now that you've taken a look at what is in the Time Mapping Editor, let's take a look at five different objects, all traveling the exact same path, with the same number of keyframes. Figure 15.10 shows five objects that follow an identical trajectory (except, of course, for vertical position). The Time Mapping Curve for each one is different, however. All of them use preset curves. Each object has a different time map and, consequently, is located in a different position for that point in time. (You can play the QuickTime movie that corresponds with this illustration; it is called TIMEMAPPINGCOMPARED.MOV and is located on the CD-ROM in the folder for this chapter.)

There are three columns. Each column represents a point in time. The top row, Sphere A, has the straight, default Time Mapping Curve. Notice how, at Key Event 1 and Key Event 2, the sphere is centered right at the trajectory control point. However, the other objects are either ahead of or behind the trajectory control point.

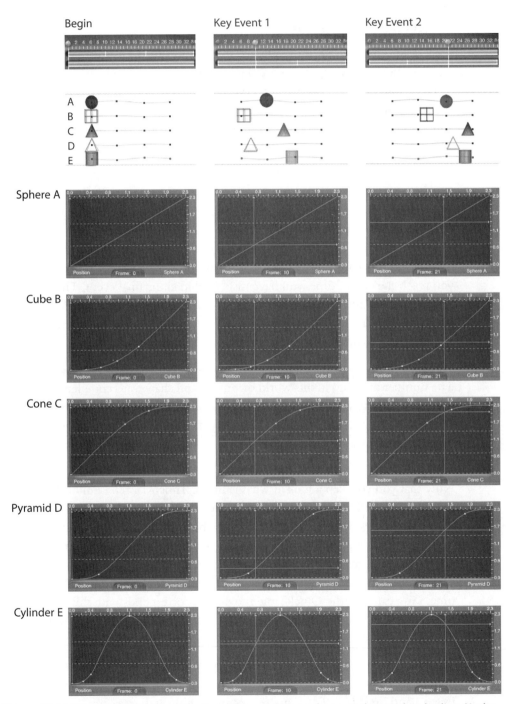

Figure 15.10 Time Mapping Curves for five different objects, shown at three points in time. Notice the difference in the location of the crosshairs showing the relationship of the current time and the current event. Compare the position of each object along its trajectory with the time-to-event curve.

Cube B is on an acceleration curve; the cube begins slowly and then moves at a uniform rate once it gets going. At Key Event 1, Cube B lags behind Sphere A, since the cube is taking time to build up its acceleration. At Key Event 2, it still lags behind Sphere A. Most of the Time Mapping Curve for Cube B is flatter, with a shallower slope than Sphere A's standard diagonal Time Mapping Curve.

Cone C starts off at a uniform rate and then decelerates as it reaches the end. At Key Event 1, Cone C is ahead of Sphere A, and it continues to be ahead of Sphere A at Key Event 2. The first two-thirds of Cone C's Time Mapping Curve slope is steeper than the default diagonal of Sphere A.

Pyramid D combines the previous two Time Mapping Curves to accelerate and decelerate. The S-shaped Time Mapping Curve is also called the ease-in and ease-out curve. At Key Event 1, Pyramid D lags behind Sphere A. At Key Event 2, it is slightly ahead of Sphere A. Although Pyramid D's Time Mapping Curve is flatter at its beginning and end, the slope in the middle is slightly steeper than that of the default diagonal line (Sphere A).

Cylinder E behaves quite differently from all the other objects. At Key Event 1, Cylinder E is about two-thirds of the way to the end of the trajectory. By Key Event 2, it has reached the end and is beginning to make its way back on the return trip. The Time Mapping Curve ascends to the top more sharply than any of the other curves and then changes direction to slope downward again. The top position of the curve represents the end of the trajectory. As time continues going forward (to the right), the event sequence moves down, regressing backward through the events to move the object backward along its trajectory.

Notice how, with all the Time Mapping Curves for each column, the vertical crosshairs representing the current time are all lined up. The horizontal crosshairs, however, are above or below the dotted key event line, matching the Time Mapping Curve location for the vertical point in time. When the horizontal crosshairs are below the dotted line (representing the key event), motion is slower than normal (that's why the cube is behind the sphere), and when the crosshairs are above the dotted line, motion is faster than normal—well, at least "normal" as defined by a perfectly straight diagonal line (as in the case of the sphere at the first key event).

When the Time Mapping Curve does not match the normal, standard one, the point where the key event "normally" would take place is either before or behind the point in time. When you click the Playback controls, you'll find seemingly extra keyframes that you can't account for. The extra pauses in the Next Keyframe button sequence are really the places where the keyframe would have been if it had stayed normal and linear. You can see this by opening the scene file TIMEMAPPINGCOMPARED and working in the AML. If you set the time to the beginning and then click the Next Keyframe button, you'll see many stops along the way where no white key event ticker marks exist. That's because Bryce stops at each horizontal event line wherever it happens to be, whether advanced or retarded in time due to the Time Mapping Curve. Every extra stopping point corresponds to a horizontal broken line in the Time Mapping Editor.

When the curve is steeper than the normal diagonal line, events happen faster. Time is faster (like Internet time, yuk yuk!). When the line is straight up and down, events jump from one to the next in no time at all! When the curve is flatter than the normal diagonal line, events are s-l-o-w-e-d down. When the line is completely flat, time passes, but no events transpire. If the line slopes down in the other direction, then time goes backward, backtracking through events.

Time Mapping Editor: Numerical Readout

The edges of the Time Mapping Editor contain numbers to help you know where you are in time. The numbers adjust to the active animated time for a particular object attribute. When no object attribute is selected, they simply read 0.0 for all points on the scale.

The area is divided, rather arbitrarily, into sixths of the duration for time (across the top) and quarters of the duration for events (along the right edge). What's common to both is the beginning, midpoint, and end. There are additional points for each, but they belong to different scales.

The boundaries of the Time Mapping Editor are the only places where time is normally displayed using a scale other than SMPTE or basic frames. Here, a decimal scale is used, with time divided into minutes, seconds, and tenths of seconds. How do you get this time scale to match the time scale that Bryce uses the rest of the time? Just about now you've gotten used to looking at SMPTE and interpreting everything to the right of the decimal place as the frame count. Elementary, my dear Watson; there's an Easter Egg that will make the time display work in decimal format. It expands the display to three decimal places, showing you time in thousandths-of-a-second increments. And how, pray tell, do you invoke this Easter Egg? Press the D key (for decimal—get it?) and then click the Time Scrubber or tap the period (.) or comma (,) key to move the time forward or backward by a frame, and lo, the display changes to thousandths of a second (see Figure 15.11). Doing this will make the time markings of the Time Mapping Editor far less mysterious. Incidentally, once you leave the AML and go back to the main Bryce interface, the time display there will also be in decimal form. The same goes for the other places in Bryce where a timeline is displayed: the Sky Lab, Materials Lab, and Terrain Editor. To change the time display back to frame or SMPTE format, simply select either option from the Animation Options pop-up menu, or double-click the Time Scrubber or otherwise invoke the Animation Options dialog box where you can change it back to one or the other.

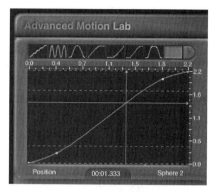

Figure 15.11 Time displayed as decimals, invoked by tapping the D key in the Advanced Motion Lab.

Those numbers along the side tend, as a rule, to be uncooperative as you work with your scene. The numbers will scale properly if you follow certain rules.

If you try to change the total animation time in the Animation Setup dialog box, you may get different results depending on whether you clip or extend the time or scale the time. (Remember not to access the Animation Setup dialog box from within the Advanced Motion Lab to make any changes other than to the time display; leave the AML and go to the main Bryce interface to make changes in the Animation Setup dialog box.) Clipping or extending the time makes no difference to the appearance and behavior of the numerical scale, since what is being displayed in the Time Mapping Curve is the timeline for that particular attribute; you are changing the overall time, and not the time for the attribute. However, changing the duration by scaling the time will break the numerical readout for that attribute. Scaling the time scales all timelines contained in it, and the Time Mapping Curve just doesn't have the capacity to follow the new timeline and accurately display it. You will forever be stuck with the old time, no matter if you save, save as, or copy and paste the object to another scene file. (Well, actually, if you copy and paste the object to a new scene file, it comes in set to the old, prescaled time; at that point, you could select all key event points in the timeline and hold down the Option/Alt key to scale them to whatever time you like.)

There is one other persnickety way in which the numerical scales do not behave politely as you work in the Time Mapping Editor. We'll save it for the discussion of zooming later in this section of this chapter.

Preset Curves

So it's not necessary that your Time Mapping Curve be the default diagonal line. How do you get your curve to be something different? First, there are the preset curves (shown in Figure 15.1), which supply you with the most useful, basic time-event alterations, or a starting point for your own alterations. To use one of them, simply click the desired Time Mapping Curve preset. That preset appears in the Time Mapping Editor area.

If you create something and want to save it as a preset for later access, you can do so. Scroll through the list (click the Scroll Presets button at the right). There is always one blank spot at the end of the list of presets. Click the blank spot, and your Time Mapping Curve will be saved in that spot. There will be a new blank spot for the next preset you want to save. To delete one of your custom presets, Option-click/Alt+click it.

Bryce's default Time Mapping Curves are blue lines with white dots. Any curve that you save will be displayed as a blue line with little yellow dots.

Where the Presets Are Stored

The presets are stored in two different files in the presets folder. The default set of presets is stored in a file called DEF ACCEL ENGINE.TME. Any Time Mapping Curve presets that you create will be written to a file called ACCEL ENGINE.TME. There is one key combination that will wipe out your presets; there will be no way to recover them (short of opening up whatever scene files contain the curve that is saved for various objects and their attributes and saving new presets again). If you press the Option/Alt key while clicking the Time Mapping Curve Scroll Presets button, you'll send all your presets away—permanently. So use care.

Adding and Removing Points

Of course, you don't have to accept the curves as given, but can make your own. That's the best part!

When your mouse pointer is positioned over the curve, the arrow changes to a pen cursor, for drawing the curve. Click the blue line to create a yellow control point. If your mouse pointer is positioned over an existing control point (such as the one just created in the last sentence), the cursor changes to double arrows, indicating that you can move the point's position. These are the ways to affect the Time Mapping Curve points (and you won't find most of them in the manual):

- *Add Point.* Point the mouse at the area of the curve where you want to add a point. If no point exists there and the mouse pointer changes to a pen, click. *Voila*: a new point, bright and yellow!

- *Move Point.* Point your mouse at an existing point. The pointer changes to crossed arrows. Drag the point's position to wherever you desire.

- *Remove Point.* Point your mouse at an existing point. Then press the Control/Ctrl key and click the point. It goes away.

- *View Curve Tangents.* Point your mouse anywhere in the Time Mapping Curve area. Hold down the Option/Alt key and click. In addition to the curve, the tangents that create the curve are also displayed (see Figure 15.12).

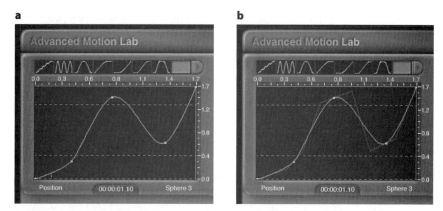

Figure 15.12 Time Mapping Curve: a) Without and b) with tangents appearing; Option/Alt clicking in the Time Mapping Editor toggles between these two states.

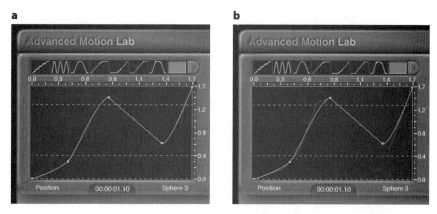

Figure 15.13 Making one segment of the Time Mapping Curve a straight line by Shift-clicking the control point: a) Without and b) with the tangents showing.

• *Make a segment of the curve a straight line.* Press the Shift key and click a control point. The next segment after the point will change to a straight line, with no curve whatsoever. Shift-clicking the point will make the segment curved again. See Figure 15.13, where the straight segment is shown with and without tangents for comparison.

Zooming

Once you start working with Time Mapping Curves, you'll be tempted to work in finer detail in the Time Mapping Editor. If your sequence is longer, this temptation will be nearly irresistible. The window size is fixed; you cannot change the window shape to accommodate a longer sequence, with a larger number of events. Give in to temptation by zooming in. Rather than making the Time Mapping Editor larger, zooming in makes the curve itself larger. No doubt you've noticed that when your mouse is in the Time Mapping Editor and it isn't a pen or four-headed arrow, it is a zoom magnifying glass. However, it doesn't work simply by clicking. Place the magnifying glass in the center of the area you want to zoom in on. Drag the mouse. As you do so, a white border is drawn, representing the area that will be included in the Time Mapping Editor window when you release the mouse (see Figure 15.14).

a
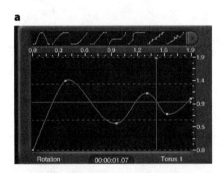

b
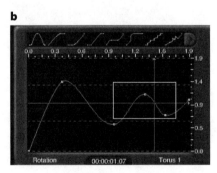

c
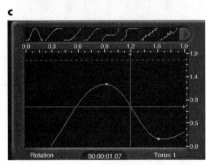

Figure 15.14 Zooming in with the Time Mapping Editor: a) Time Mapping Editor before zooming; b) the dragged marquee; c) the resulting close-up look at the Time Mapping Editor.

Once you're zoomed in, you may want to look at another part of the Time mapping curve. Panning makes it so. To pan, hold down the space bar; the cursor turns into a hand, and you can drag whichever way you want.

To zoom out, hold down the Shift key and click. (The Shift key?!? Not the Alt or Option key, as in most other applications, including Bryce's main Working Window?! Yes, the Shift key.)

We promised you more persnickety details about the numerical scale that's along the outside of the Time Mapping Editor; we shall not disappoint! Once you're zoomed in, the numerical scale does not follow your position. A reasonable person would expect that, like Buckaroo Banzai, wherever you zoom, there you are, with the numerical scale reflecting the new zoomed-in reality. But no! It turns out that the scale stays fixed at the fully zoomed-out position. Notice in Figure 15.14c the discrepancy between the vertical crosshairs location (along the timeline) and the time readout below.

Miscellany

We've supplied you with some additional types of Time Mapping Curves for you to explore. These are variations on a theme of sudden starts and stops, with the lines alternating between flat and upright (good for those sudden one-frame jumps). There is also an object that gets bumped and rotates back and forth on its way to a stable state again. Look for them on the CD-ROM in the folder for this chapter, in the AML SAMPLES folder.

Time Mapping Curve Keyboard Shortcuts

Click on Time Mapping Curve	Create new control point (not undoable).
⌘-click/Ctrl+click control point	Delete control point (not undoable!).
Option/Alt+Click in Editor	Toggle display of curve tangents.
Option-Shift-click/Alt+Shift+click in Editor	Reset curve to default straight line (not undoable!).
Drag in Editor Area	Zoom in.
Space bar+drag in Editor/ Shift+click in Editor	Pan view of Time Mapping Curve.
Shift+click control point	Toggle next segment as straight line / curve.
Click empty preset tray	Saves current Time Mapping Curve as Preset.
Click preset curve icon	Places that curve in Time Mapping Curve.
Option-click/Alt+click Preset icon	Delete that preset (must have yellow control points).
Option-click/Alt+click Preset Scroll button	Reset to default curve presets (not undoable).

Bounce Walkthrough (Conclusion)

Now that we've discussed the AML, we can return to the bounce tutorial and adjust the acceleration of the bouncing ball.

We left off in the previous chapter with the bounce animation set up. But we need to make some adjustments to account for gravity and to make the whole animation more realistic. We'll use the Advanced Motion Lab for these tasks.

If you are joining us here without having completed the tutorial in the previous chapter, you'll find it hard going. We won't provide additional explanation or context, so you're starting three-quarters of the way through. It's really better if you work through the first part. We have, however, provided a scene file that you can work with; it's called BOUNCEAMLSTART.

Acceleration and Other Time Mapping Adjustments

We need to add some acceleration on the downward fall—so back to the Advanced Motion Lab we go!

1. Under Sphere 1, in the Hierarchy List, click the word Position. The word turns yellow, and a blue diagonal line appears in the Time Mapping Editor (see Figure 15.15).

Figure 15.15 The Advanced Motion Lab with Sphere 1's Position attribute selected so that its time mapping curve appears (here, a straight line) in the Time Mapping Editor.

2. Click the Play button to play the animation here in the AML. Notice that as time moves forward (from left to right), the events proceed from bottom to top. For each spot on the Position timeline in the Sequencer, there is a horizontal dotted line in the Time Mapping Editor.

    Notice the two lines that correspond to Frames 2 and 7. The first, at Frame 2, represents the ball as it begins to fall, and the second, at Frame 7, represents the ball's point of impact on the ground. This is a section we want to speed up.

3. Make sure that the current time is at frame 2. Click the Next or Previous Keyframe button to get it there (see Figure 15.15).

4. Point your mouse right where the crosshairs are. Whenever the mouse is over the Time Mapping Curve line, the cursor changes to a pen. Click the mouse at the intersection. A yellow point appears on the curve. Point your mouse at the place where the diagonal line intersects the next dotted line. Click again, and another yellow point appears (see Figure 15.16a).

a

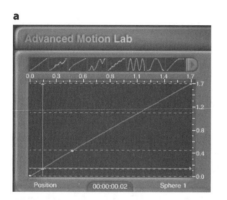

b

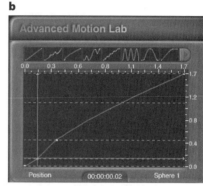

Figure 15.16 Adjusting the Time Mapping Curve for Sphere 1's position: a) After generating two new control points; b) after accelerating the segment by dragging the second control point up a bit.

We'll accelerate the next step by steepening the line between these two points.

5. Drag the second (higher) point left slightly, so that it stays intersected with the dotted line, but does so earlier in time. The line segment between the two points is steeper than the rest of the Time Mapping Curve (see Figure 15.16b).

6. Check out the change by clicking the Play button in the AML. Pretty fast going, isn't it?

   One bad thing about the AML is that it plays each frame as fast as it can, which will be much faster than the number of seconds allotted for the sequence. The faster your computer's processor, the faster the renderer—a good thing. But here, the faster the processor, the faster the animated preview—groan. Alas, the Advanced Motion Lab, where you work with time, is itself not a good judge of time. To see what's really going on, in real time, you need to leave the AML for a moment and go to the main scene window.

7. Click the arrow to leave the AML and go to the main scene. Click the Play button on the Time Palette.

Don't worry about the funky position of the squash. It no longer coincides with the bounce. We'll fix that in a moment. Just look at the scene for acceleration as the ball falls.

8. Go back to the AML. If you need to, click Position in the Sequencer to make its curve appear in the Time Mapping Editor.

    Now it's time to slow things down just a bit as the ball moves up after the bounce. Point the mouse at the intersection of the Time Mapping Curve and the next horizontal dotted line, corresponding to Frame 16 (or 01.02), or the top of the ball's arc. A yellow point appears on the line. Drag slightly to the right to flatten the line a tiny bit (see Figure 15.17a).

    Now the ball will slow down a bit as it travels up, and it will speed up ever so slightly as it falls again.

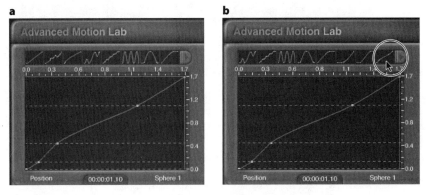

Figure 15.17 Making another adjustment to the Time Mapping Curve to slow down the ball as it moves uphill: a) After creating a control point and dragging it down slightly; b) saving the curve as a preset by clicking the blank spot in the Curve Preset tray.

9. Save this Time Mapping Curve as a preset. Click the arrow on the Time Mapping Curve presets until you see the blank preset. Then click that blank. Your current Time Mapping Curve is now a preset (see Figure 15.17b).

    We will use this curve to apply the other Sphere 1 attributes, Scale and Shear, so that they'll obey the same mapping as Position.

10. In the Hierarchy List, click the word Scale so the word turns yellow. Then click the preset you just loaded into the Time Mapping Curve presets. *Voila!* The curve appears in the window. Click the word Shear so that it turns

yellow and do the same thing to assign the curve to it, too. Leave the AML and go to the main scene to see how things are shaping up.

The rotation is still a little funky. The same curve needs to be applied to the rotation, but it also needs some further adjustment. Back to the AML we go!

11. Go back to the AML and click the word Rotation so it turns yellow. Assign it the same preset curve as the other attributes. Set the current time to the impact of the bounce and continue making adjustments to the curve position while watching the sphere in the 3D Preview window. By adjusting this curve, you ensure that the ball's flattening occurs on a dimension parallel to the ground. Figure 15.18a shows the AML with the point being adjusted.

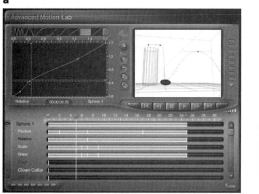 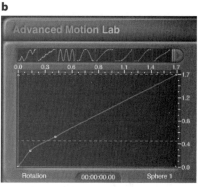

Figure 15.18 Adjusting the Time Mapping Curve for Sphere 1's rotation: a) Adjusting the rotation for the bounce bottom so that the flattened sphere is actually flat on the ground; b) after removing the point for the bounce top and adjusting the first point to speed up the rotation for the ball roll.

12. Remove the yellow point that corresponds to the top of the arc. There's no change in the rotation energy. ⌘-click/Ctrl+click that yellow point to remove it.

13. Adjust the first point upward a bit, to speed up the rotation as the ball rolls along the top of the cylinder (see Figure 15.18b).

14. Leave the AML and go to the main scene. Click Play to preview the animation in Wireframe mode. Click the Preview Animation control to create a thumbnail preview of it, if you'd like (see Figure 15.19). Save the scene.

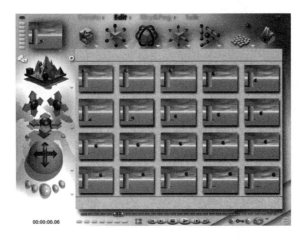

Figure 15.19 Previewing the animation one final time before rendering.

15. Render your animation. Go to the Document Setup dialog box to set your output size to half the current size (see Figure 15.20). Render a still frame by clicking the Render button.

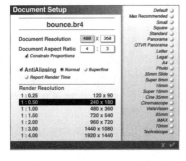

Figure 15.20 The Document Setup dialog box for the bounce scene, with the render resolution set to half size (0.50).

16. Begin rendering the animation. Since the scene is in Render mode, you can click the animation Play button, or tap the backslash key (\) to display the Render Animation dialog box. (This is in addition to the Render Animation command in the File menu.) Select Bryce's default settings for a QuickTime movie (Animation codec, millions of colors) and the location to which your rendered movie will be saved, click the check mark, and let 'er rip!

Congratulations! You've created a bouncing ball and have used many of Bryce's animation tools to do so!

MORE ABOUT PLANNING YOUR ANIMATION

Although we mentioned planning your animation at the beginning of the previous chapter, if you didn't know much at all about animation, the details of making plans about a bunch of processes as yet unknown to you is only so much wasted breath on our part. Better to know what you're in for first, before you get an idea for how to plan. So, we revisit the topic again here.

Now that you've got an idea about what Bryce does to animate your sequence, think again about how to plan it. Of course, as with any new endeavor, the first forays often involve getting in over your head, and later, you will draw on all sorts of wisdom along the lines of "I should have planned it better, and now that I've been through it once, I can really see how planning this, that, and the other thing would have helped."

Building on the History of Cinematography

For close to a century, the art of cinematography has trained us how to see motion. Follow those guides from the giants of movie making; consult all the resources available to you, watch movies, read books about film appreciation, take film appreciation classes. Watch movies and be aware of "how they did what they did to tell the story."

One excellent resource is a book called *Film Directing Shot by Shot: Visualizing from Concept to Screen*, by Steven D. Katz (Focal Press, 1991). It covers preproduction, production design, and storyboarding and discusses how to go from creating storyboards to actually planning camera shots. Of course, the book is written with the assumption that the movie will involve actual actors and sets and physical cameras, but the decisions discussed are the same as the ones you'll have to consider when working with Bryce. And the storyboards reproduced on the book's pages are a treat in themselves: from *Citizen Kane*, *The Birds*, *The Graduate*, *Blade Runner*.

As you start getting into traditional movie-making terminology, here's a new word to add to your vocabulary: shot. A shot refers to one camera point of view, such as a long shot, a close-up shot, an establishing shot. Given that Bryce has but one camera for a scene, shot and sequence may be synonymous. But then, what if you have the same 10 seconds of activity shot from two different angles? If it's the same 10 seconds, is it the same sequence? A shot, then, might be the same as a sequence, but if a sequence is broken into smaller portions, those portions are shots.

Some Basic Planning and Storyboarding

Preplanning your animation is not necessarily a matter of focusing your mind on Bryce and its animation capabilities. Rather, your focus should be on the story as you ask and answer the question, "What do I want to convey?" The second part of storyboarding and planning takes the answer to that question and applies it to Bryce and its capabilities. There are some simple techniques for figuring out what you're going to say.

Get Your Story Straight

First, you need to decide on your narrative. As an example, we'll take a sequence constructed by Michael "renato!" Sigmon. In Sigmon's animation of a Rube Goldberg device, a metal ball travels a course and does several things to several objects as it rolls on its merry way. First it goes down a spiral, picking up speed. Then on the straightaway, it triggers some additional balls that spill onto paths perpendicular to the first path. Hoisting checkered flags as they go, the balls pour into a cup that weighs down one end of a balance, while the original ball spills off the straightaway and lands on a seesaw and a figure flies through the air, where it lands on the other side of the balance, which swings upward. That balance hand is attached to the balance arm, and it sets the dippy bird in motion, so that it smacks the dippy bird's head down onto a, well…we won't give that away, but will let you see how it ends yourself. The movie RUBE.MOV is on the CD-ROM in the folder for this chapter.

With this basic narrative, the planning involves defining the cast of characters: the surrounding environment, the ball, the track, the flags, the teeter-totter, the man, and the dippy bird, and their respective actions—plus the surprise ending. Then the question is, what camera shots will best tell the story?

You Don't Need a Single, Continuous Shot

It's common for the first-time animator to think that one, single, gargantuan scene has to be created, with one single, long camera shot. "Create the big scene. Animate the big scene with one long, continuous camera shot. Render. Okay, then: done!" Well, not exactly. It's also customary in motion pictures to tell the story using a series of shots, which are then edited together.

A scene can start with an establishing shot, to provide the overall context for the action taking place. Then a close-up on thing A, to establish thing A's role in the location. Then a shot of thing B. Or follow thing A as it goes through some action. Or thing C. These variations depend on the story and what the animator is trying to convey.

The alternative is to not have an establishing shot, but to start with a close-up of the object. If you want to deliberately mislead viewers into thinking that they are watching one thing when really it's something else, save the establishing shot as a sight gag punch line—ha! fooled you! The choice to do one or the other depends on the story you want to tell and how you want to tell it.

The Rube Goldberg sequence starts with an establishing shot to provide the context, which is followed by a series of shots that follow the first ball—or the set of additional balls—as the Rube Goldberg device goes through its paces. Each successive shot tells what happens next.

When it comes to planning your different shots, do check out the *Film Directing Shot by Shot* book; it says it all about how to plan shots.

Create Storyboards

It's a good idea to generate storyboards: Sketch out each shot with its camera angle. You can create picture sketches, or if your scene is already constructed, still image sequences. The sketches convey the action taking place and the general framing of the camera, as well as camera motion.

Get a Stopwatch

Once you have a set of shots and you're ready to plan the action in each one, get out that trusty stopwatch for estimating the timing. Let the scene play in your mind with the stopwatch running, and you'll get a good idea for how long each sequence is supposed to last. Start the watch, let the sequence play in your mind's eye, and when it's done, stop the watch. Did it take 12 seconds to play? Plan that sequence to be 12 seconds, then.

Perhaps Create Some Proof-of-Concept Animations

Depending on what's taking place in your animations, you may need to do some proof-of-concept work. After all, some concepts don't spring forth as fully developed complete realizations from the mind, but rather are borne from a dialog between an appealing but hazy idea and some work to flesh out that idea.

Or it may be that your initial animation work in Bryce is simply the result of working with the software to figure out how something works in Bryce. First you're figuring out how to solve some motion problem, and then flash! there in your brain pops a Grand Animation Idea. Then you figure out how to tell a story with it. Sometimes the work is suggested from the exploratory proof-of-concept work. (Many of the examples used in this book were initially suggested by the process of simply working with the software.) Other times, the idea for a story demands proof-of-concept work to test whether it is really possible to bring it to fruition in Bryce.

The former, exploratory type of proof-of-concept work certainly was what was used in the case of Sigmon's Rube Goldberg series. The Mousetrap board game was the initial idea. The first step was to develop each of the elements of the cast of animated characters. The development turned into motion tests, just to see if the idea would work. Some of the problems solved during this stage: getting the ball to roll on tracks, tripping the gates to hoist the flags, the teeter-totter with the Poser figure, the dippy bird. The story was honed by the process of generating motion tests to work out the concept of the Rube Goldberg device. For instance, the flags changed. After all the tests, the various elements then were put together.

In some ways, the planning, production and motion tests, and revision are the animation process's equivalent of the still scene's process of construct, render, tweak. In the case of animation, the process takes place on two fronts. First, you work with all the elements of a still-image scene (create objects, position and edit them, give them material appearance, add sky and lighting, and so forth). Then, on top of that, to animate the sequence, you have all the considerations of time and motion.

Whether creating a still image or an animated sequence, you will probably engage in a dialog between the idea in your head and the realized one in the scene until you make things work to your satisfaction. (Or as Susan crudely puts it, when you first construct a scene, it sucks. Then you work on it and it sucks less. You keep working on a scene until it stops sucking. Sometime after it stops sucking, it gets to the point where it actually looks good and is exciting or compelling. It's somewhere around that point that you can call the work finished.)

Post-Production

No matter how you started work on your sequence, eventually your task changes from planning to full immersion in the work of producing your animation sequence. You gratefully emerge from this process with a result: one or more rendered animation sequences. If you have more than one sequence, you'll need to edit them together.

Editing Sequences Together

When you move to the task of editing your sequences, you're no longer talking about working in Bryce; you'll need to work with an application for video editing. Bryce produces either a series of still frames or a QuickTime or AVI movie format.

Think of this as the raw stuff that you composite with dissolves, cuts, fades, and the like. If you are adding a sound track, then you'll use the movie editing software to put that in as well. The postproduction editing process is way beyond the scope of this book. (Besides, isn't this tome thick enough as it is? We certainly think so!) However, here are some applications to consider if you want to pursue editing further:

• *QuickTime Pro.* The MoviePlayer application that comes with QuickTime Pro has basic editing functions, and it's cheap; Mac and Windows.

• *Adobe Premiere.* For entry-level video compositing; Mac and Windows.

• *Adobe After Effects.* A professional-level video and film compositing tool; Mac and Windows.

• *Final Cut Pro.* Apple's professional video-editing tool; Mac only.

Now that we've discussed all the matters of planning with a deeper look at the preproduction stages, you're ready to be introduced to some production techniques for generating good camera motion.

LINKING AND HIERARCHIES: CAMERA CRANES

Back in Chapter 7, "Booleans and Multiple Object Construction," we introduced linking and hierarchies. These really come into their own for animation, since child objects can be related to their parent objects and yet have independence as well.

Here is a series of animation ideas, mostly for cameras or for trajectory motion. The first set, Camera Crane, is a progressive build on the idea of linking and animation and tracking and animation. Each step builds on the previous one. Be sure to look at the scene files and the movie files on the CD-ROM. To get the most out of these examples, play not only the rendered movies, but click the Play button while looking at the scene files themselves. Don't forget that you can also play the sequences while looking at the scene from any view: not only Camera View, but Director's View, front view, top view, and so on. Using different views is especially valuable for those examples where the camera is attached to the crane—the only way to watch the dynamics of the scene is to step back a bit and take it all in from a distant vantage point.

Camera Crane and Overall Grooviness: Animation Sequence

This animation series is based on a pyramid that moves from point A to point B, traveling between a row of cylinders and a row of cubes. In each of the animation scenarios described, the pyramid movement and the cylinders and cubes are identical. The pyramid does travel based on the ease-in, ease-out curve in the Advanced Motion Lab. To find the specific files on the CD that match the descriptions here, look for PYRAMID ## or PYRAMID ##.MOV, where ## is the number at the start of each topic heading.

1. Pyramid Moves from A to B

This is the starting place, the baseline. The camera is stationary, looking at the pyramid as it travels. The pyramid's motion is governed by the simple ease-in, ease-out curve applied in the AML (see Figure 15.21).

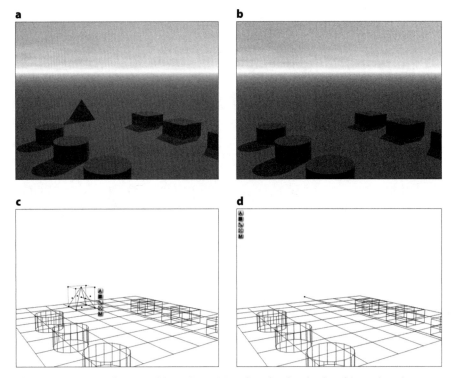

Figure 15.21 Simple pyramid motion: a) Rendered at beginning; b) rendered at end; c) wireframe at beginning; d) wireframe at end.

2. Light Follows Pyramid

In the second variation, one change is added. A light is linked to the pyramid. The pyramid is the parent of the light. It travels along with the pyramid, making the pyramid easier to see (see Figure 15.22).

a b

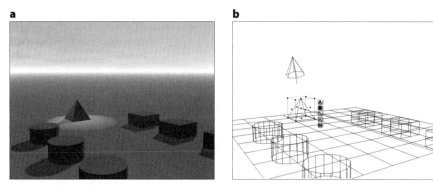

Figure 15.22 A spotlight illuminates the pyramid, shown in a) Rendered and b) wireframe views.

3. Camera Linked to Pyramid (Dolly)

In this variation, the camera is linked to the pyramid, so when the pyramid moves, the camera moves, too. The pyramid is the parent of the camera. This is a simple dolly move, where the camera moves in a straight line, as governed by the pyramid's movement in a straight line. The camera and pyramid are in perfect sync with one another (see Figure 15.23).

4. Camera Tracks Pyramid.

In the fourth variation, the camera was unlinked so that its position is stationary. Instead of being linked, the camera tracks the pyramid, as the Object Attributes dialog box, Linking tab, shows in Figure 15.24c. Since the camera is tracking the pyramid, the pyramid stays in the absolute center of the frame.

a

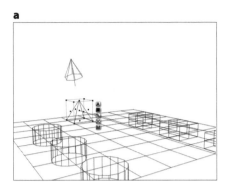

b

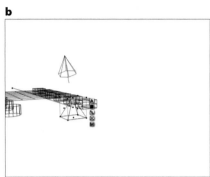

c

Figure 15.23 Camera linked to pyramid: a) Sequence beginning; b) sequence end; c) Object Attributes dialog box for the camera.

a

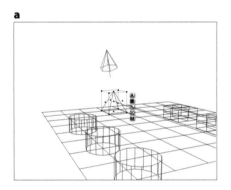

b

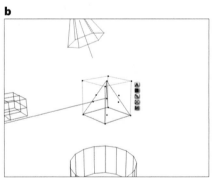

c

Figure 15.24 Camera tracking the pyramid: a) Sequence beginning; b) sequence end; c) Object Attributes dialog box for the camera.

5. Light Linked to Camera

In this variation, we added another light to the scene. The new light is positioned just to the left of the camera (from the camera's perspective), facing the direction of the pyramid. The light was linked to the camera (so that the camera is the parent and the spotlight is the child). Now when the camera's position and rotation change, the light's position and rotation change as well. The result is that the light generally fills the scene from near the camera (see Figure 15.25).

a

b
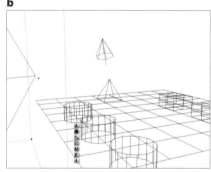

Figure 15.25 A fill light is positioned to the left of the camera (and linked to it), shown in a) Rendered and b) wireframe views.

6. Light Changed to Track Pyramid.

In the sixth variation, a small change was made to the light. In addition to being linked to the camera, it is set to track the pyramid. The result is a better, more even (and predictable) lighting of the pyramid object (see Figure 15.26).

7. Tracking a Null Object

Variation 7 introduces a significant change. In variation 4 and following, the tracking of the pyramid meant that the pyramid was always in the center. That's far too close of a correlation between object movement and camera movement. No human camera operator can position a camera in perfect synchronization with the movement of the object that is being tracked. There's usually a bit of reaction

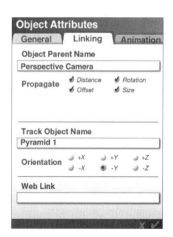

Figure 15.26 Object Attributes dialog box for the light, showing its parent (the camera) and the object it tracks (the pyramid).

time, during which the camera either slightly lags behind or anticipates the motion of the object. Also, the object doesn't necessarily have to be framed precisely in the center of the image frame.

To address this problem, we created a special null object: a sphere. We used the Object Attributes dialog box to hide the sphere and then animated the sphere so it travels a path nearly identical to, but slightly shorter than, the pyramid's, as Figure 15.27a shows. Then we set the camera to track the null object, resulting in a view of the pyramid that is not in the exact center. With this, we avoided that icky Hey-ma!-it-looks-like-a-computer-animated-this-camera! appearance.

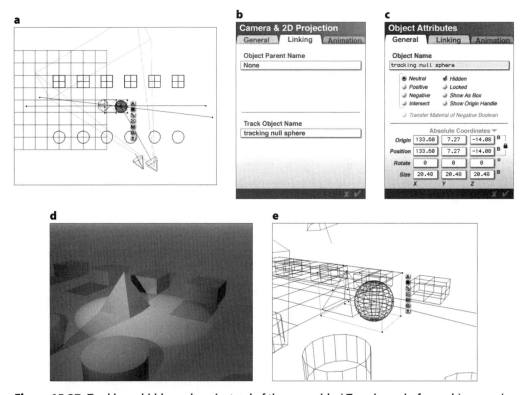

Figure 15.27   Tracking a hidden sphere instead of the pyramid: a) Top view, wireframe; b) camera's Object Attributes dialog box showing that the camera is tracking the sphere; c) sphere's Object Attributes dialog box showing that the sphere is hidden; d) rendered and e) wireframe views of the scene from Camera View.

8. But Wait! There's More! Da Crane! Da Crane!

Professional moviemakers use moveable cameras mounted on cranes, dollies, and the like. We as movie viewers are used to seeing motion pictures that were filmed by cameras using all of those devices to govern their motion. To create similar animation in Bryce, imitate the pros in da biz! Create cranes and attach cameras to them. The motion that results appears wholly natural, and it looks just like it does at the movies.

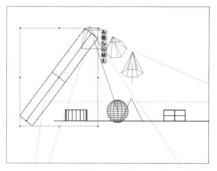

Figure 15.28 Side wireframe view of scene, showing the camera crane.

For variation 8, we introduce a simple crane into the scene (see Figure 15.28). It's the same one that you built in the object-linking tutorial in Chapter 7, "Booleans and Multiple Object Construction." You can also see the scene file, called CAMERA ELBOW CRANE, located in Chapter 7's folder on the CD-ROM. The crane is a cube whose origin point is at the bottom. The camera is positioned at the top and linked to the pyramid. Rather than moving the camera, move the boom of the camera arm. In this case, the boom was rotated on its *x* axis to generate the movement. The *x* axis rotation determines the height of the camera as the boom stretches out low or is upright.

9. This Is Gettin' Pretty: Two Axes of Rotation

In this variation, the camera boom rotates on two axes, so that it can determine the height of the camera (*x* axis) and the position of the camera boom as it (thinking from top view) swings to the left or to the right of the pivot point (*y* axis). See Figure 15.29.

a

b

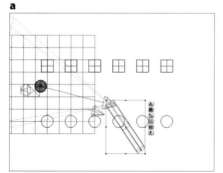
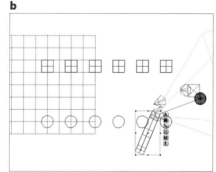

Figure 15.29 From top view, it's easy to see the camera crane pivoting around the *y* axis from a) Left to b) right. Less obvious is the crane's rotation around its *x* axis, which is apparent only in the foreshortening of the crane as it tilts up toward the viewer.

10. Three Axes of Rotation

The tenth variation adds movement on the third, z axis. Considering the range of motion available to us in the first two axes, the addition of a third axis takes away from the others. You can check out the substandard results of this move in 10 CRANE (X&Y&Z AXIS).MOV on the CD-ROM. It was the result of logically expanding the number of ranges of motion. We'll take that idea in another direction in subsequent steps.

11. Dollying Crane

There are other ways to get a third range of motion. One way is to actually move the camera boom while it is rotating on two axes.

Variation 11 involves moving the entire camera boom assembly. Since the assembly acts as though it's set on a dolly, this is called a dollying move. In this case, the dollying movement travels in the direction opposite to the pyramid. At the place where the camera whips around, the Time Mapping Curve is set to slow down the motion of the dolly so that the viewer doesn't get visual whiplash. Open the scene and see what it was like without the Time Mapping Curve adjustment, to see the type of accelerated whip-around that we avoided. In the AML, click the Crane Base item in the Hierarchy List to display the animated parameters for that object; then click Path Position to see the dolly's Time Mapping Curve (see Figure 15.30).

a
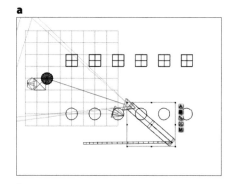

b
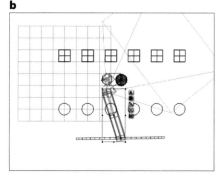

c
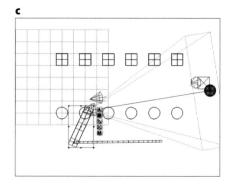

Figure 15.30 A dollying crane: a) At beginning; b) middle; and c) end of the sequence.

12. Following Halfway

Variation 12 is another crane-and-dolly move. In this case, the crane starts even with the pyramid, follows halfway, and then comes to rest partway along the dolly track, at the place where the camera was positioned for most of the early camera variations (see Figure 15.31).

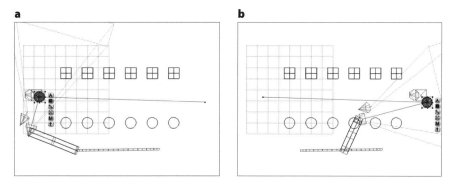

Figure 15.31 Another crane-and-dolly move, where the crane a) starts out at roughly the same place as the pyramid and travels only b) halfway down the line by the end of the sequence.

13. Dolly Moves and Rotates

Well, we had to get tricky on you. The dolly track itself moves and rotates. (This is one scene file where it's really crucial to watch the action from above.) This is one of those moves that can be done more easily in a 3D application than in a real studio. It might be worthwhile to build another joint for the crane, providing an elbow to give another degree of motion (see Figure 15.32).

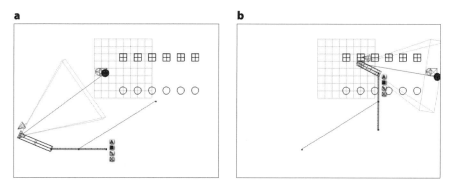

Figure 15.32 Yet another crane-and-dolly move, where the dolly both moves and rotates: a) Sequence beginning; b) sequence end.

14. Elbow Crane

This variation adds that extra motion, using an elbow crane. The first joint is identical to what we've been working with so far. The second joint is a sphere, an elbow bearing. A second limb, a pyramid, is attached to the sphere, with its origin point at the base, right next to the elbow sphere. The advantages of an elbow crane are added height, so that the camera can smoothly move from way high to level with the object, and an additional range of motion.

When moving an elbow crane, take it in this order: first, establish the base joint rotation. Second, rotate the elbow sphere. Do not rotate the pyramid; it is linked to the sphere. It's there simply as the arm that is connected to the elbow.

After rotating the base joint and then the elbow sphere, you may need to go back and adjust the base joint again to put the camera in a better position. Unlike your own elbows, you cannot adjust both elbows in Bryce simultaneously. This version has some nice motion, but the ending is lacking—it's too short or something. To fix that, we'll add a dolly track and move the whole shebang a bit away from the pyramid (see Figure 15.33).

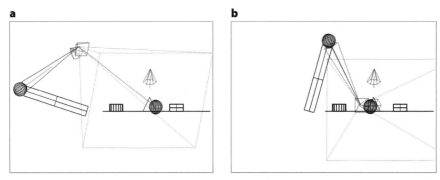

Figure 15.33 Camera on an elbow crane: a) Beginning of sequence; b) end of sequence.

15. Elbow Crane on a Dolly

In this variation, the elbow crane travels along a dolly as the elbow crane swings around (see Figure 15.34).

16. Elbow Crane on a Dolly: In Front of the Pyramid

In this variation, the dolly and elbow crane allow the camera to get out and stay out in front of the pyramid (see Figure 15.35).

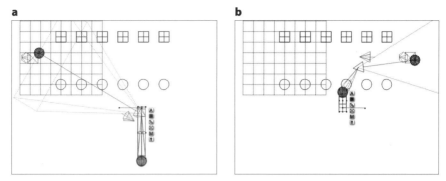

Figure 15.34 The elbow crane on a dolly: a) Beginning; b) end of sequence.

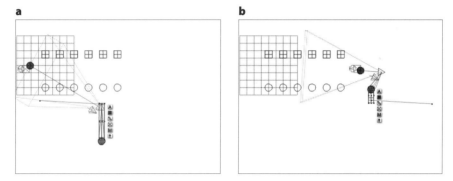

Figure 15.35 The elbow crane on a dolly moves the camera out in front of the pyramid: a) Beginning; b) end of sequence

17. Elbow Crane Travels with Pyramid

The elbow crane is linked to the pyramid, so that it moves in perfect synchronization with it, while the crane action goes from high above the pyramid to down in front of it. The elbow crane rotation is identical to that in the previous version (see Figure 15.36).

18. Crane Swings around Behind Cylinders

In this last variation, the camera starts behind the pyramid, swings around behind the cylinders, travels along, and then comes out in front of the pyramid to watch it come to a rest (see Figure 15.37).

The variations can be endless. But you can see how, starting from a stationary camera watching a pyramid move, we gradually added components to light the scene and made the camera and the lights track objects. Then we gave sophisticated movement to the camera that is more consistent with the way we've been taught to view movies by the mechanics of cameras, dollies, and cranes from the motion picture industry. Please experiment on your own with variations on these moves, using the supplied scenes as a starting place!

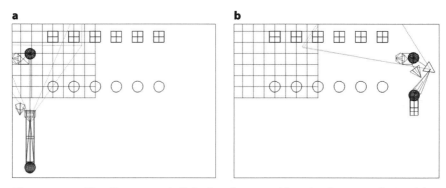

Figure 15.36 The elbow crane is linked to the pyramid so that it moves along with the pyramid: a) Beginning; b) end of sequence.

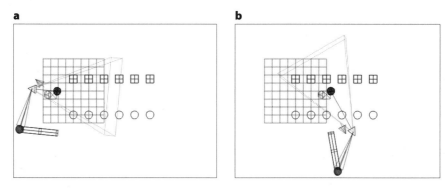

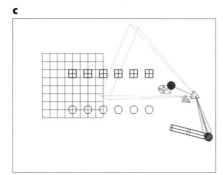

Figure 15.37 The elbow crane on a dolly enables camera to a) start behind the pyramid at the beginning; b) move behind the row of cylinders as the crane moves forward with the pyramid; and c) end out in front of the pyramid by the end of the sequence.

Camera-Linking Variation

The previous examples of linking all involved linking the camera to a boom. Here is a variation on the concept that was brought to our attention by Michael Fenimore (BryceTalk: M'Kell). It's a variation on the "moving buddy" concept that we discussed in Chapter 6, "Editing and the Internal Bryce Grid." Fenimore links his camera to a sphere. Then, rather than moving the camera about in the scene, he moves the sphere. The advantage is that he avoids changing the angle or focus of the camera, something that is possible to do if one doesn't click or drag in the exact right place. He uses this technique for both still images and animated scenes.

We took this technique and applied it in a new way, to generate a camera path that follows the contours of a number of tiled terrains. For successive points in time, the sphere was moved over a different part of the terrain mass and then landed there. The result is a trajectory that follows the contours of the terrain. That trajectory was tweaked and then made into a path. The path's horizontal altitude was adjusted and the camera linked to it. You can see the resulting movie as TERRAIN TILING CAMERA.MOV on the CD-ROM in this chapter's folder.

We'll present additional techniques for linking as we continue through this chapter.

MOTION TRICKS

In various places in this book, we've mentioned the Advanced Motion Lab and the tendency of objects to have origin points at some place other than their own centers. You've seen already, for instance, how an origin point at the base of an object enables the camera boom crane to work.

Pendulum

A pendulum is something allowed to swing free so that it is moves only by gravitational force. A popular interpretation is that the something moves back and forth. That certainly is the basis for Bryce's use of the term *pendulum* for describing action. There are two—well, actually three—places in Bryce where you can apply pendulum actions or behaviors to your objects as they animate. We use two of them here in a scene that is a literal pendulum, making this a thrice self-referential pendulum exercise. We'll explain what each of the pendulums are so that you can follow along.

The Pendulum Scene

The working part of the pendulum consists of three objects. The weight, at the bottom, is a sphere. It is connected to a cylinder, which, in turn, connects the weight to the actual rotating part. The rotating part here, the pivot, is a small cylinder. In the linking hierarchy, the rotating cylinder is the parent. Its child is the long extension cylinder, which is parent to the weight sphere (see Figure 15.38).

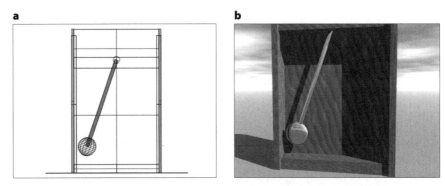

Figure 15.38 The pendulum scene: a) Front view of the wireframe; b) rendered from the camera perspective.

(As an alternative, you could make a simpler pendulum out of only two objects. Omit the small pivot cylinder and then move the extension cylinder's origin point to its upper end, so the whole rotates about that point.)

Animating a Single Swing

We've provided you with two pendulum scene files on the CD-ROM in this chapter's folder. PENDULUM is the complete, animated scene, for reference. PENDULUM-NOANIM is the built scene, with no animation. Work along with that latter scene. For this scene, we'll work with Auto-Key off for a change.

1. Go to front view (tap the 4 key). The small cylinder should be selected. Its name is Cylinder Pendulum Parent.

2. The Time Scrubber should be at 00:00:00.00. Press the mouse on the Add Keyframe menu and choose Cylinder Pendulum Parent > Rotation. The keyframe indicator darkens (see Figure 15.39a).

3. Drag the Time Scrubber out to 2 seconds (00:00:02.00).

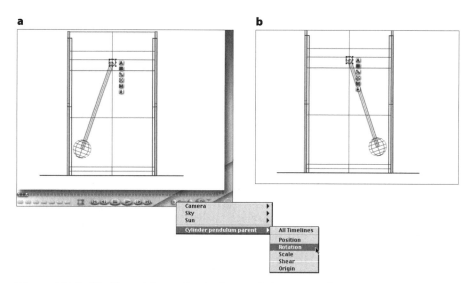

Figure 15.39 Working with rotation in the pendulum scene (front view): a) Adding the first keyframe; b) after rotating the pendulum assembly to the right.

4. Next you will rotate the cylinder so that the pendulum assembly swings to the other end. Take a moment to note the current position of the pendulum assembly so you can judge where your rotation should end.

   Point your mouse at the center control point of the cylinder. The cursor changes to the *z* axis cursor. Press the ⌘/Ctrl key and drag to the left until the pendulum assembly swings to the other end (see Figure 15.39b).

5. Add this keyframe: From the Add Keyframe pop-up menu, select Cylinder Pendulum Parent > Rotation (the same as in step 2).

You have now animated the pendulum movement with a single swing from left to right. The only object in the scene that is animated is Cylinder Pendulum Parent. Its motion is governed by all of two keyframes: the stopping point of the leftward swing of the pendulum, and the stopping point of the rightward swing. Stay tuned; you'll do more to get the pendulum swinging properly in both directions.

The Time Mapping Curve Creates Pendulum Movement

We'll continue working with our pendulum scene in the Advanced Motion Lab.

1. Go to the Advanced Motion Lab, and click Cylinder Pendulum Parent in the Hierarchy List to display its animated properties. Rotation is the only property animated. (Ah, the advantages to working with Auto-Key off!)

2. Click the word *Rotation* so that it turns yellow and the diagonal default Time Mapping Curve appears in the Time Mapping Editor.

3. Now assign this a new preset Time Mapping Curve. Look for the bell-shaped curve in the preset list. Click it. That curve now appears in the Time Mapping Editor (see Figure 15.40a).

4. Click the Play button. The pendulum assembly swings from left to right and back again.

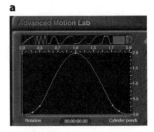

a

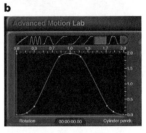

b

There are two things taking place with that Time Mapping Curve you just set for the cylinder's rotation. First, time is mapped forward and backward using a bell-shaped curve. Halfway between your starting time (00:00:00.00) and your ending time of 2 seconds (00:00:02.00), the time-event crosshairs meet at the top of the curve, at the point where the pendulum assembly has swung to the right. The time is at 1 second (00:00:01.00). As time continues from 1 to 2 seconds, the crosshairs follow the downward slope of the Time Mapping Curve, making the event move backward. The cylinder rotates in the

Figure 15.40 The Time Mapping Curve pendulum: a) The preset curve that turns a forward event into a pendulum event; b) after making adjustments so there is slowdown at the right end of the swing.

opposite direction: the pendulum assembly swings back to the left. The shape of the curve is the basis for the pendulum movement. It is what causes the pendulum assembly to swing forth and back, whereas you animated the pendulum assembly to swing only forth. The 2 seconds you originally planned for the swing from left to right were cut in half so that the swing takes only 1 second.

> **TIP:** *When you plan on animating using a pendulum-producing curve, set your initial keyframe to twice the time involved; the Time Mapping Curve will cut the time in half.*

The second thing that the Time Mapping Curve does is adjust the speed of the pendulum's motion over time, so that the pendulum starts its swing slowly, picks up steam at the middle of its rightward swing, slows a bit at the right edge, speeds up on the return voyage, and then gradually slows as it reaches the left extreme. Unfortunately, the preset bell-shaped curve doesn't provide for equal decelerations at each end of the swing—the slowdown is greater at the left end of the swing than at the right.

5. Modify the Time Mapping Curve to flatten out the top of the curve (which corresponds to the right end of the swing) so it more closely matches the contour of the curve at its two ends (see Figure 15.40b).

    Hint: After placing each of the two new points in the curve, use the cross-hairs to double-check alignment of the points on the curve so that they're symmetrical.

Repeating the Action over Time

Up until now, we've been talking about a single event that takes place: The pendulum assembly swings to one end and returns to the beginning. But we want the pendulum assembly to swing back and forth and back and forth for as long as we can endure it. To fix this, you'll need to extend the time in your scene past 2 seconds.

1. In Bryce's main window, double-click the Time Scrubber to display the Animation Setup dialog box. Locate the numerical entry boxes for Duration and enter a number in the Seconds box that is an even multiple of 2 seconds (such as, say, 12 seconds, or 14 seconds, or 30 seconds). Make sure that the Extend or Clip option is active; then leave the dialog box.

    If you do not set the time to an even multiple of 2 seconds, then the animation will end somewhere in the middle of a pendulum swing.

    Now that we've got the time in which the pendulum swing can occur, we need to tell the cylinder to rotate in perpetuity. As long as there is any animation time, the pendulum assembly will swing. How do we tell the cylinder to rotate past the 2-second mark? Tell it to repeat.

2. Go to the Advanced Motion Lab and make sure that the Cylinder Pendulum Parent's Rotation attribute is visible in the Hierarchy List. Hold down the Shift key and press your mouse on the Rotation name. A pop-up menu appears, as Figure 15.41 shows. Choose the Make Repeat option. Click Play. The pendulum assembly should swing and continue swinging for the duration of your animation.

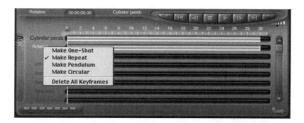

Figure 15.41 The pop-up menu to change animation behaviors of any attribute in the Hierarchy List.

Since, in our example, the action is the same forward as it is backward, we had the option of setting the action to either Make Repeat or Make Pendulum. Faced with a choice, we went with Make Repeat. Supposing that all things weren't equal; what's the big difference between Make Pendulum and Make Repeat? Figure 15.42 shows the standard ease-in, ease-out Time Mapping Curve set up as Make Pendulum and Make Repeat. When the Time Mapping Curve isn't symmetrical, there's a vast difference between these two options!

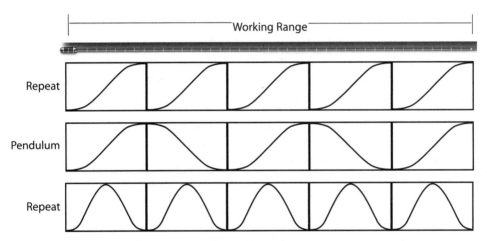

Figure 15.42 The Time Mapping Curves for various repetition modes: in the top row, the ease-in, ease-out curve is set to Make Repeat; in the second row the same curve is set to Make Pendulum. For comparison, the third row shows the pendulum Time Mapping Curve preset in Repeat mode. The overall shape of the curve is similar to the ease-in, ease-out curve in Pendulum mode, but it cycles faster.

We worked with a Time Mapping Curve that creates pendulum behavior. We considered the use of the Make Pendulum option from the pop-up menu. Have we exhausted all of Bryce's pendulum offerings? Well, no and yes. Yes, there is another pendulum offering, located on the Animation tab of the Object Attributes dialog box. However, the options listed there are for the object trajectory position only. So if you want to have any pendulum (or repeat, for that matter) action for rotation or size or other animation attributes that don't follow a trajectory, you must use the menu option we just described in the AML.

Pulsing Light

Pulsing light is another animation example that uses the repeat animation command in the AML and makes judicious use of Time Mapping Curves. No objects move, but the lights change in intensity and visibility. The lights start out bright and then go dim. The animation takes place over the first few frames, but is set to repeat, so that the pulsing takes place for as long as the animation sequence is set to occur. See Figure 15.43 and, on the CD, look for PULSINGLIGHT.MOV and PULSINGLIGHT in the PULSING-LIGHT folder on the CD-ROM in this chapter's folder.

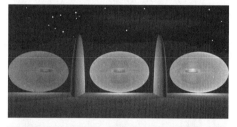

Here's how we animated the lights. Although each of the three lights has a slightly different setup in the Time Mapping Editor, the underlying animation is identical. Select all three lights and go to the Advanced Motion Lab. You'll have to unfold the Hierarchy List a bit to see the animated properties for the lights. To simplify the list, make sure that Show Animated is checked in the AML Options pop-up menu. Then click the name of any of the lights to display its animated properties.

There are two animated properties: Intensity and Material. For Intensity, there are two keyframes, one at high intensity and the second at low intensity. For each light's material, we animated its Base Density and Fuzzy Factor properties. (According to the AML, the property of Volume Softness is included with the other animated properties, although there's no discernable change in the actual Materials

Figure 15.43 Pulsing light animation, where lights pulse brightly and then fade in intensity.

Lab.) How'd we know what to animate for the material? Since we set the lights to Volume Visible in the Edit Light dialog box, and since the visibility of that volume is controlled in the Materials Lab, we animated the volume properties to make the volume less visible, matching the lower intensity of the second keyframe. The Material settings' two keyframes, for higher density and lower density, correspond with the keyframes for the light's high intensity and low intensity.

The animation for each light begins and ends at the same time, but the subtleties of timing are tweaked. The secret to the pulsing is the Time Mapping Curve. Each of the different pulse arrangements has its own Time Mapping Curve. The curve for the green light, on the right, is just a straight linear change from the bright to dim. The yellow color gets a standard ease-in, ease-out pattern. The curve for the red light is flattened at the left end (where the light is bright), which means it fades slowly at first, and then the rate of fade accelerates.

Other possible examples are: mostly dark with a brief pulsing to bright, and gradual brightening and gradual fade. Suppose that instead of the repeat we used a pendulum; what would happen then? In the second example, PULSE-PENDULUM.MOV, we've changed the animation from Make Repeat to Make Pendulum, so that there's a fade-on, fade-off action. In that case, at each repetition, the Time Mapping Curve flips back and forth, as shown Figure 15.42, second row.

Orbit

For the sun and planet orbit scene (ORBIT-ORIGIN, in the Orbit folder in this chapter's folder on the CD-ROM), we moved the origin point of one object outside of itself to create an orbit. The planet's origin point was placed at the center of the sun, so when the planet rotates around the sun, it actually orbits the sun.

Setting Up an Origin-Based Orbit

There are three main players in this scene: the sun, the planet, and the moon. Once constructed, the main action in the scene is the rotation of the objects.

- *Sun.* A sphere in the middle is set to Additive material so that it will glow. A radial light set "inside" the sun casts the light. The sun stays stationary.

  Sun Position Note: To make it easy to set the planet's origin point, the sun's position coordinates are 0 for both the x and z axes.

- *Planet.* The planet's origin is set to match the center of the sun sphere.

  Planet Position Origin Note: Once the sphere for the planet is in place and the origin point made visible, using the constrain key—Control/Ctrl—to move the origin along the x axis is helpful in getting the origin point over to the sun sphere. For fine-tuning, unlocking the origin and position coordinates in the Object Attributes dialog box lets you enter 0 for origins x and z without affecting the current position of the actual planet sphere.

See Figure 15.44 for a top wireframe view of the planet and its Object Attributes settings.

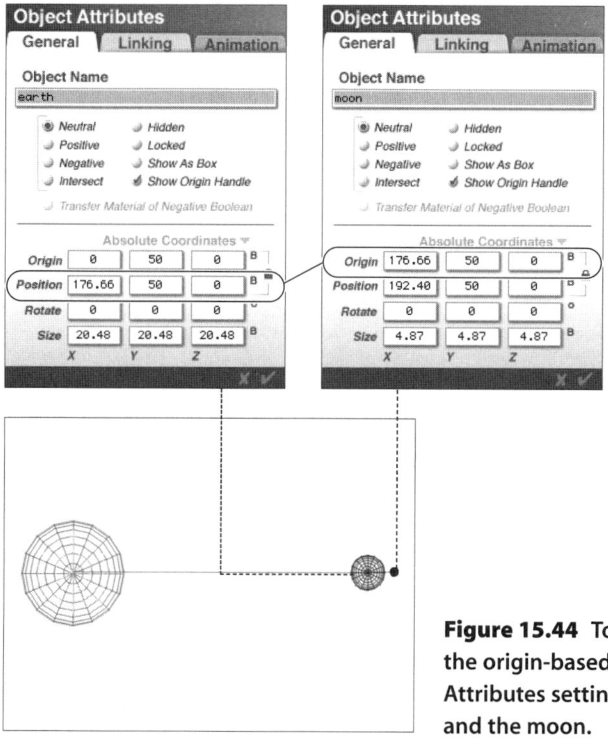

Figure 15.44 Top wireframe view of the origin-based orbit with the Object Attributes settings for both the planet and the moon.

- *Moon.* The moon's origin point is located at the center of the Earth. In addition, the moon is linked to the Earth, with the distance, offset, and rotation propagated.

  Moon Position Origin Note: The moon's origin point matches the position of the planet's offset—that is, the default position of the planet's origin point (see Figure 15.44).

- *Rotation Calculation.* Both the moon and the planet are rotated and animated. The moon's rotation around the Earth takes place over eight frames. Since one of these rotations is equivalent to a month, and the Earth takes 12 months to go around the sun, our total animation will be $12 \times 8 = 96$ frames.

Figure 15.45 shows three successive frames of the orbit in the top wireframe view.

There is a problem with this setup, however. In the real (non-Brycean) universe, the moon shows the same face to the planet all the time, but the Earth does not keep the same face to the sun, as our model does. It rotates on its own axis as well as revolving around the sun. To implement all the different rotations and revolutions, we'll have to take a different approach and create a separate object for the orbit: a circular path.

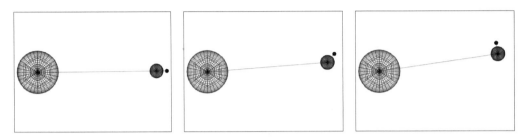

Figure 15.45 The origin orbit, seen as three frames in wireframe from top view.

Creating a Circular Path (Trajectory)

As the first step in creating an orbit along a path, we created a perfectly circular trajectory. Then we moved the planet along the trajectory and rotated it along its own axis while the moon operated the same as before.

A Perfectly Circular Trajectory

To create our circular trajectory, we started with a new scene file. The creation of a path object is an intermediate stage; we work with a duplicate of our orbit scene file after the circular path is complete.

First, we created a cylinder. We then enlarged it so that its circumference matched the wireframe size of the ground plane. The cylinder will serve as a template, to indicate the shape of a perfect circle. As a template, its height doesn't matter. Just to keep it out of the way, we reduced the cylinder's height until it was quite flat.

Next, with Auto-Key on, we created a sphere. Working in top view, we positioned the sphere so that it was at the top edge of the cylinder, in the twelve o'clock position (see Figure 15.46a). Then we repeated this basic process to set up the next positions: We advanced 10 frames by tapping the period (.) key 10 times. (Why 10? It's easy to remember the number!) Then we moved the sphere to the next position—three o'clock (16 arrow taps in one direction and 16 in the other). After that, we moved the Time Scrubber out another 10 frames and moved the sphere to 6. Then we advanced 10 frames, and then moved the sphere to 9 (see Figure 15.46b).

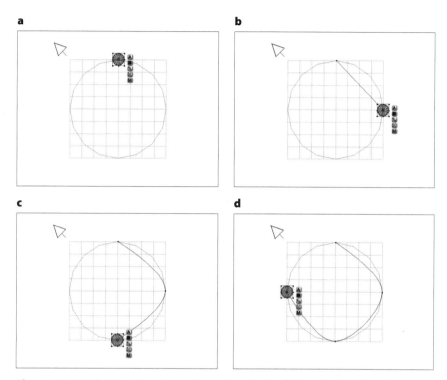

Figure 15.46 Plotting the points of a perfect circle: a) After the initial point;
b) after the second point was created; c) after the third point was created;
d) after the fourth point was created.

For the final loop-closing move, we advanced the Time Scrubber another 10 frames and moved the sphere anywhere. (You'll see why in a second.) Then, in the Object Attributes dialog box, on the Animation tab, we clicked Make Circular to close the loop. The trajectory didn't look like a circle, but a curved diamond shape (see Figure 15.47a). The T key, for tension adjustment, was handy here. For each point, we set the tension to –0.4. Once we did, our trajectory matched the outline of that cylinder: round, perfectly round (see Figure 15.47b). We created a path from that trajectory and went from there!

Now that we've made our circular path, we can copy and paste it into another scene file or save it as a path object in our Preset Library for use in other scene files.

a

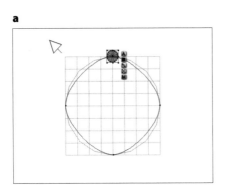

b

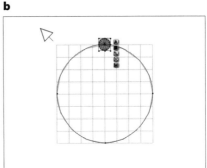

Figure 15.47 Closing and tweaking the circle: a) After the trajectory has been made circular; b) after the tension on all the points was adjusted to –0.4.

Rebuilding the Scene

Working with a duplicate copy of our origin orbit file, we first worked with the planet sphere. We retracted the origin point of the sphere into the object's own center. (Hint: There are two ways to accomplish this: by Shift-clicking the origin point, or by entering the Object Attributes dialog box, unlocking the relationship between the two objects, and making the origin coordinates match the position coordinates.) Once this is done, the moon will fly away from the Earth, because its relationship to the Earth is defined as an offset from the Earth's origin point— which has just moved from the center of the sun to the center of the Earth (press the 2 key to switch to top view and you'll see).

Since the moon object is a child of the Earth object, retracting the planet's origin point caused the moon to move to a new position, to keep the same relationship between it and the Earth's origin point. We set the moon's origin point to be the same as the planet's. We noted the origin attributes in the planet's Object Attributes dialog box and entered those same numbers as the moon's origin settings in the Object Attributes dialog box. (We didn't touch the moon's position settings since we wanted to keep the same origin-to-position relationship with the moon.) When we changed the moon's origin point, two things happened to its animation attributes, as seen in the Advanced Motion Lab. First, a keyframe was added to the very end of the animation, to match the planet's final rotation keyframe. Second, the moon's rotation lost the Repeat attribute, reverting to the default Make One Shot. So in the Advanced Motion Lab, we selected and deleted the final keyframe on the Rotation timeline and then Shift-clicked the label Rotation and chose Repeat from the pop-up menu.

With those changes in the AML, the moon still follows the same rotation pattern as it did in the first scene. The planet rotates in place; it does not move around the sun. Before, in the origin example, the planet's rotation essentially determined its position. This time around, position and rotation are taken care of separately, and the planet rotates freely.

In the next step, we took care of the planet's position.

Remember the circular path we created before we began working on this scene? (See previous section.) Having saved a copy of it in the Object Library, we now loaded the path from there into this scene and then doubled its size by tapping

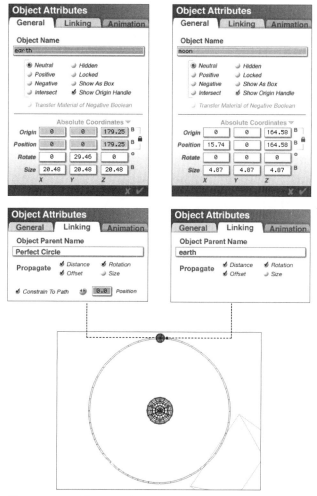

Figure 15.48 The sun-planet-moon orbit and Object Attributes settings for the planet and the moon.

the ∗ (multiply) key. Then the planet sphere was linked to the circular path, and constrained to position 0.

To get the right approximate relationship among the various rotations, since this version adds the planet's own rotation in addition to the orbit around the sun and the moon's orbit around the planet, the entire animation's duration (time) was scaled to about four times the size (384 frames); when we did so, we had to expand the Working Area to match the new overall sequence duration. Then we rotated the planet on its own *y* axis in about five frames. Note that in this case, all the rotations proceed to –359.5°, since rotating to –360° (or +360°) would not work right. (We discuss a way to create a perfect 360° rotation in the "QTVR Object Movie" section later in this chapter.) We then moved the Time Scrubber to the final frame and constrained the planet's position to the 100.0 position on the circular path.

Once all the keyframes were set, we did a little cleanup in the Advanced Motion Lab. We deleted the final keyframe for the Earth's rotation from the very end of the sequence (similar to what we did with the moon earlier) and then set Rotation to Repeat.

Figure 15.48 shows the top wireframe view of the scene at the beginning of the sequence, with the object attributes for both the planet and the moon.

Spiral Motion

Spiral motion is a variation on the theme of origin points and rotation. You can give an object spiral motion by changing its distance from its origin point over time and then rotating it around the origin.

Helix

In the scene HELIX (and the movie HELIX.MOV), three pyramids change position, from high to low. We moved the pyramids' origin points away from the center of the object. For the object on the left in the scene (see Figure 15.49), the origin's position stays a constant distance from the object. Each of the other two pyramids (at the center and right) begins with its origin at the object center. As the object moves down, the origin point moves farther and farther from the original center point. These two pyramids spiral wider as they descend, whereas the one on the left simply spirals straight down the side of an imaginary cylinder.

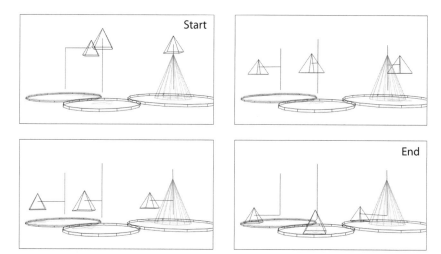

Figure 15.49 Helix animation using rotation and position and a different origin point location. The left object has its origin displaced by a constant distance; center and right objects change from centered origin points at the start to maximum origin displacement at the end.

To generate the corkscrew animation that has consistent displacement (similar to the left pyramid), follow these steps (with Auto-Key on):

1. Create an object, make its origin point visible, and then change the origin point so that it is offset from the object's center.

2. Position the object at the beginning of its spiral. (In the case of descending spirals, place the object higher.) (See Figure 15.50a.)

3. Drag the Time Scrubber to a new time and position the object at the end of the spiral—that is, lower. At this point, you will have a simple position change from high to low (see Figure 15.50b).

4. Staying at the new time, rotate the object on its y axis. (Hint: To keep your rotation in 45° increments, hold down the Shift key to constrain the object as you rotate it.) Be sure not to end the rotation at 360° or a multiple of 360° (720, 1080, and so on). (See Figure 15.50c.)

5. Check your spiral animation! (See the Bryce scene file HOW HELIX 1-2-3.)

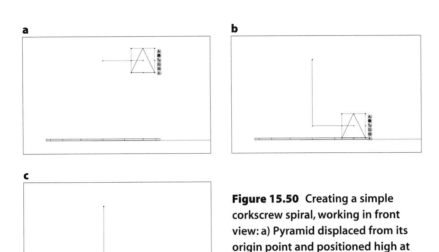

Figure 15.50 Creating a simple corkscrew spiral, working in front view: a) Pyramid displaced from its origin point and positioned high at starting time; b) pyramid positioned lower at end time; c) pyramid rotated at end time to create a spiral.

Spiral

To generate the spiral whose radius changes over time, follow these steps:

1. Create an object, make its origin point visible, and position it at the spiral's beginning (in this case, at the high point). See Figure 15.51a, which shows the scene from front view.

2. Drag the Time Scrubber to a new time and position the object at the spiral end—that is, lower (see Figure 15.51b).

3. In the Object Attributes dialog box, in the Animation options, check Hide Trajectory. Then, using the Control/Ctrl key to constrain motion on the *x* axis, move the object's origin point to the left to change the origin point. Figure 15.51c shows the result of this step.

   (The reason for hiding the trajectory is that trajectory control points take precedence over the origin point; by hiding the trajectory, you give the origin point precedence again.)

4. In the Object Attributes dialog box, in Animation options, set the trajectory back to Show When Selected. The result should look like Figure 15.51d.

   The next step is to shift the ending origin point back to the same position as at the beginning.

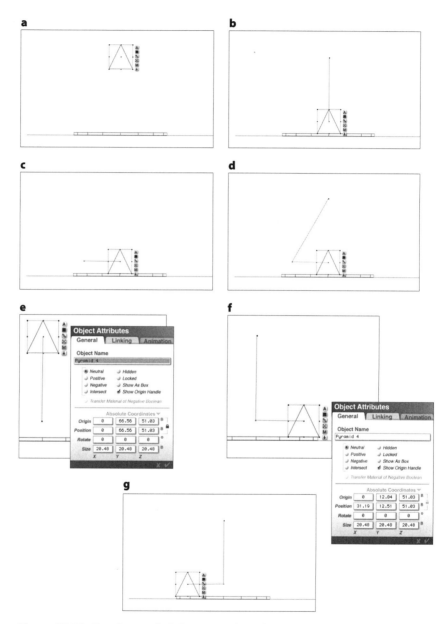

Figure 15.51 Creating a spiral that expands as the object descends: a) The object at start time with the origin point showing; b) at the end time, the object is moved to final position; c) after hiding the trajectory and moving the origin point d) and then showing the trajectory again; e) object attributes for the start time; f) object attributes for the end time, with the origin point's *x* axis matching the start time's origin point; g) after rotating object.

5. Move the time back to the beginning. Check the object attributes for the object's origin, noting its placement on the x axis (see Figure 15.51e). Move the time to the end and open the Object Attributes dialog box. Enter that previously noted number (in this case, zero) for the origin's x axis. (The y axis will have changed, naturally, since the object's vertical position has changed. The z axis should be identical, since you constrained the origin point to the x axis in step 3.) (See Figure 15.51f.)

An alternative approach is to constrain again on the x axis and move the origin point so that it is positioned below the first one. Since you have the trajectory showing, you won't be moving just the origin point but the entire object. To get it exact, however, you'll have to go to the Object Attributes dialog box.

6. Continuing at the end time, the final step is to rotate the object on its y axis. Be sure to keep clear of 360° or multiples thereof (see Figure 15.51g).

7. Check out your animation!

Spirals Using Paths

The other way to create a spiral involves creating an actual spiral path. It's a variation on the circular trajectory technique described earlier. At each quarter of a circle, tap the Page Up (or Page Down) key to make the trajectory ascent (or descend) by an even increment. (Note: The final points on the trajectory get different settings than those in the middle of the trajectory: Continuity is 1.00, Tension is 0.3—that's right, positive!) Naturally, since the object's travels along the helix do not begin and end in the same place, we didn't use the Make Circular option in the Object Attributes dialog box. The wireframe view of the scene file HELIX TRAJECTORY is shown in Figure 15.52.

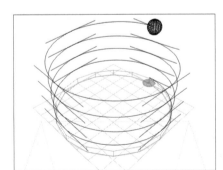

Figure 15.52 A helix trajectory was created by animating an object using the circular-path method, where the vertical position is changed at each quarter of the circle.

The trajectory, of course, is the basis for generating a path. The advantage of a path is that it can be resized as a whole. Figure 15.53 shows the path based on the trajectory from Figure 15.52 lengthened vertically and shortened on both horizontal axes.

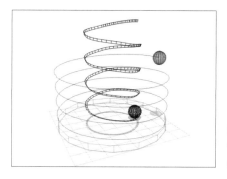

Figure 15.53 The helix path generated from the trajectory is lengthened on the vertical axis and shortened on the horizontal axes.

For the movie generated from the helix path (HELIX PATH.MOV), we constrained a sphere to the path. We didn't generate a rolling rotation, but we did get the right feel for the sphere's picking up speed on the descent by using the default accelerate Time Mapping Curve (it starts out flat and grows steeper as it moves to the right).

Getting fancier, in the RINGS N THINGS variation, shown in Figure 15.54, a number of torii are constrained to the path. The torii do not animate. To get them all to face in the proper direction, we set them all to track the center cylindrical object on the *x* axis. If they had been set to align to the path, the twists and curves of the path would have made the whole setup utterly hopeless.

a
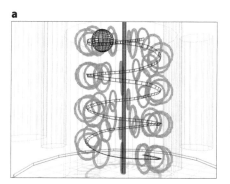

b

Figure 15.54 Rings and Things variation on a path helix shown in a) Wireframe and b) rendered views.

Yet another trajectory-turned-path variation is changing both the altitude of the object (to descend or ascend) and the size of the circle so that the spiral winds in closer. We've gone to the trouble to do so, and made the path shown in Figure 15.55.

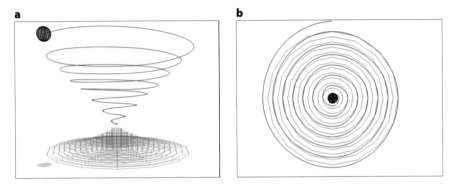

Figure 15.55 The spiral trajectory: a) Camera perspective; b) top view. Changes in elevation and in the size of the circle (using cylinders and guides) generate the spiral shape.

Gears

Moving far, far away from the natural landscape scene and deep into mechanical matters, we lugged out our copy of David Macaulay's *The Way Things Work* and researched gears. The scene shown in Figure 15.56 is the result. The number of teeth that fit around a gear is directly proportional to the gear's circumference, so the larger gear, with twice the circumference of the smaller gear, has two times the number of teeth. (Circumference is the length of the x or z axis times π.) The gears turn in opposite directions, and the smaller one rotates twice for each rotation of the larger one.

Twice as big
24 teeth (double)
Rotates opposite
Rotates 270° (half)

Half as big
12 teeth (half)
Rotates opposite
Rotates –540° (double)

Figure 15.56 The relationship between two gears in construction and animation: The smaller gear is half the size of the larger one, has half the number of teeth, and rotates at twice the rate.

QTVR Object Movie

A QuickTime VR object movie is an interactive movie that allows you to view an object from all sides. Breaking down the interactive movie into the individual still images of the object results in a two-axis array of views of an object. That series of views is what you need to generate to create your own QTVR object movie. Shoot your object from every perspective, as Figure 15.57a shows. Each intersection of the white tubes represents a place from which to grab a view of the object. You can create a movie that will display an object from every perspective, as shown in Figure 15.57a, or you can create a partial perspective, where the total number of views is limited (as in Figure 15.57b). There are even variations that work from a single view of an object that may have two different degrees of movement (you'll see them on the CD-ROM). Here, we'll show you how to work with Bryce to make the traditional view-from-all-sides QTVR object movie.

Note: To learn all about QTVR movies, please see Susan's book, *The QuickTime VR Book*, published by Peachpit Press. There you'll find lots more detail about the entire process of generating QTVR, whereas here we're just discussing how to work with Bryce to get the right kind of camera movements to generate a QTVR object movie.

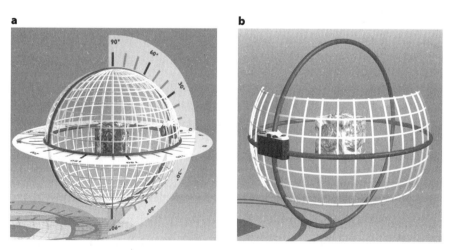

a   b

Figure 15.57 Taking pictures from all (or many) sides of an object: a) From all possible views, with degrees of rotation indicated; b) a partial set of views of the object.

Object Movie Strategy

You saw all those precisely located white-tube intersections. To create a movie with the views from those exact locations, you need to exercise exact mathematical precision when rotating the camera around the object. For our movie to come out right, we must have a certain number of frames, spaced at regular intervals, and the spacing is determined by the amount of rotation between shots.

Single-Row Movie

For a simple, horizontal QTVR object movie, you want to have regular intervals. The idea is this: The movement looks smoothest when there is a difference of 10° between views. For a single-row movie, that comes out to 36 frames. Because in Bryce the first frame is Frame 0, alas, the last frame is numbered 35. However, since this technique can be expanded for use in creating multi-row movies, and since the "what frame number corresponds with what view at what rotation?" problem increases with additional rows, we've addressed this issue from the start. We've created our sequence so that the first frame is a throwaway frame, to begin the count at 1. We did this by generating a starting condition at Frame 0 and then advancing the Time Scrubber to Frame 1 and saving a keyframe there. By rendering to individual images, we simply throw out the frame numbered 0000—a slight waste of rendering time, to be sure, but not as confusing as doing all the mathematical calculations and staying off by 1.

How do you get exact rotation increments then? Let's say that we want 36 images altogether, in one row around the object, spaced at 10° intervals. You might think that it would be simplest to set up a 36-frame sequence and then define a keyframe at rotation 0° and another at 360°—but you would be wrong. There are two arguments against this course of action. First, of course, is that Bryce sees no difference between 0° and 360°, and it will not animate the camera between the keyframes. The second reason is that starting at 0° and going to 360° will actually give you 37 frames, so to get 36 images, you will start at rotation 0° and end at 350°.

Here's the method we used: We moved the camera's origin to the center of the object being photographed; then we rotated the camera. Another possible method for moving the camera is to constrain it to a circular path; however, you cannot get the kind of precision that a QTVR object movie requires.

We tried both approaches and show you side-by-side (and top view) comparisons. See Figure 15.58, a single frame from the QuickTime VR movie, COMPOSITE OBJECT.MOV. The movie compares two QTVR movies of the same object. In one, the camera moves on a path (the left half), and in the other, the camera rotates around its origin point, located at the object's center (the right half). In the top view, you can see the two circles, each with 36 cones, corresponding to the 10° position changes for each view of the object. We merged the two movies into a single movie, in which the two play in parallel, frame for frame. Open the movie and drag left and right to create the animation. Notice that the alignment cones, in the bottom of the image frame,

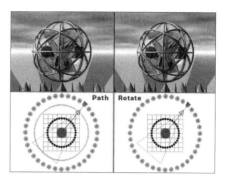

Figure 15.58 A still image from a QTVR movie comparing path position and rotation methods (rotation wins!).

drift left and right in the path-based version, whereas in the rotation version, they stay completely still. Although the path version's key events are set at 90° rotation, 180° rotation, 270° rotation, and 350° rotation, the in-between spots are not dead-on as they are with the rotation method. That's why the drift is there.

Multi-Row Movie

A multi-row QTVR object movie is more complex than a single-row one. It uses two sets of rotations. In addition to the camera's horizontal rotation around the object, as seen in the single-row example (the camera's y axis rotation), there is vertical rotation as well. If the horizontal rotation around the y axis could be compared to longitude, then vertical rotation, on the camera's x axis, is the camera's latitude position. Vertical rotation determines the camera's position above, level with, or below the object. For the most convincing movies, you need to have even increments of rotation all the way around. For the example discussed and shown in this section, we spaced the camera's locations 20° apart on both the vertical and horizontal axes.

We mentioned previously that 10° of rotation between views provides the smoothest playback of the QTVR object movie. We'd like to note, however, that the total number of frames skyrockets from 180 to over 600 when a movie with 20° increments changes to a movie with 10° increments. Figure 15.59 shows the number of camera positions for both 20° and 10° increments on circles that represent cutaway views of the vertical and horizontal axes of rotation (see Figure 15.57a for the vertical and horizontal axes.) The reason for the jump in views is that the total number of vertical spokes is multiplied by the total number of horizontal spokes. Table 15.1 compares the number of rows and columns and total number of views for movies where the rotation increments are at 10, 15, 20, and 30 degrees for both axes, using full vertical rotation.

Degrees between Views	10°	15°	20°	30°
Vertical (180°)	19	13	10	7
Horizontal (360°)	36	24	18	12
Total Views (v x h)	684	312	180	84

Table 15.1 Total Number of Frames/Views for a QTVR Object Movie in Relation to the Number of Degrees between Views

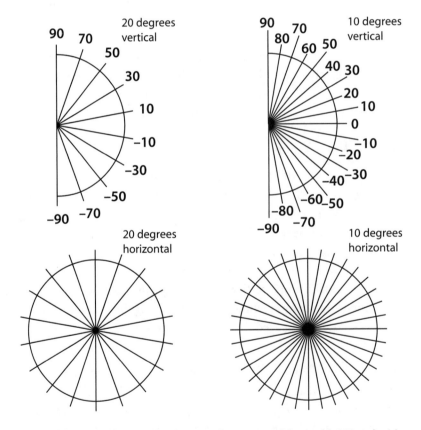

Figure 15.59 Comparing the density of camera positions with 20° and with 10° spacing. The top row shows the view from the side, looking along the *x* axis, and the bottom row shows the view from the top, looking down along the *y* axis.

We've provided you with a template scene for the 20° option shown in Table 15.1, QTVR MULTIROW OBJECT MOVIE. The camera and its animation are already set. If your movie will show the object from all sides, use one of these scenes, turn Auto-Key off while you build your scene or object, and adjust the camera's position. You can change the relationship between the camera and its origin point, but only on the camera's z axis, extending the camera further out from the object.

Here's how we calculated the total frame count for a QTVR object movie. First, we decided how many degrees of rotation we wanted to have between views. That number needs to divide evenly into 180. We then added one row to that result, to come up with the total number of rows. So, to take 20° increments as an example, $180 \div 20 = 9$. Another row gave us 10 rows. Second, to calculate the number of horizontal views (columns), we divided 360 by our degree increment: $360 \div 20 = 18$. Multiplying the number of rows by the number of columns gave us the total number of frames: $10 \times 18 = 180$. If you're going to create a QTVR object movie that examines a land formation, then you'd probably render all the camera locations with positive rotation on the x axis, but not the ones with negative x axis rotation, because those are below the ground level. Because each of these sequences begins at the top, you can stop the below-ground action by limiting the duration of the object movie.

If you want to create a partial object movie, then you'll have to generate one of your own. On each row, the camera will move in the regular direction, and the place for the next row goes back to the beginning, so that the camera always moves in the same direction for each row. (Zigzagging back and forth down the rows will not work when it comes to putting your object movie together.)

Animating Your QTVR Sequence

Suppose you didn't want to work with the QTVR object movie scene we supplied, but wanted to make your own: How would you do that? The following is not a step-by-step so much as a discussion of the order in which you proceed.

1. Determine the total number of frames you need to generate for your scene.

2. Set Time Display to Frames. Then make the first frame disposable by creating two key events for the beginning state: one at Frame 0 and another at Frame 1. You'll be able to count and keep track of your calculations more easily that way.

3. Place the camera in the highest position looking at the object (see Figure 15.60). Set a keyframe. Advance the time to the frame corresponding to the last view of that row. Then rotate the camera to that position. If your views

are spaced 20° apart, as in our 180-frame sample, then frame 18 will be at 340°. Set another keyframe. To use a clock analogy (as shown here), start at six o'clock and rotate around the clock to five o'clock.

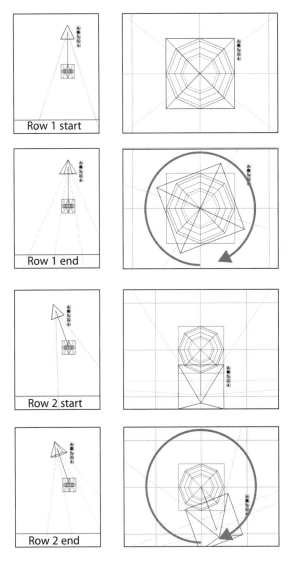

Figure 15.60 Setting keyframes for the QTVR object movie, side and top view.

4.   Advance one frame. Rotate the camera 20° on the *y* axis (to bring it back to the starting place). Then Rotate Camera 20° on the *x* axis (to move it down to the next row) Set a keyframe. Then rotate the camera around for that row (340°) and set a keyframe. Continue rotating and setting key events for each row.

TIP: The camera is the one object in Bryce whose rotation you can animate numerically. As you go, notice that the numbers keep getting higher and higher and higher to display the cumulative rotation on that particular axis at that particular point in time. You won't ever see that kind of cumulative rotation numbering with any other Bryce object.

Figure 15.61 shows the whole strategy for setting up keyframes for object movies. The places where keyframes are set are indicated by the downward-pointing arrows. Actual frame numbers are shown for 10-, 15-, 20-, and 30-degree rotation increments for the first five rows of the movie. You should be able to take it from there with a bit of paper, pencil, and methodical figuring.

	Frame 0 ▼	Row 1 Start ... End ▼ ▼	Row 2 Start ... End ▼ ▼	Row 3 Start ... End ▼ ▼	Row 4 Start ... End ▼ ▼	Row 5 Start ... End ▼ ▼	Total: Rows Frames
10°	0	1 35	36 71	72 107	108 143	144 179	19 rows 684 frms
15°	0	1 23	24 47	48 53	54 77	78 101	13 rows 312 frms
20°	0	1 17	18 35	36 53	54 71	72 89	10 rows 180 frms
30°	0	1 11	12 23	24 35	36 47	48 63	7 rows 84 frms

Figure 15.61 Setting up keyframes in Bryce for a QTVR object movie for 10-, 15-, 20-, and 30-degree rotation increments.

Making Your Render into an Actual QTVR Object Movie

Once you have all your keyframes set, double-check them in the AML to see that you've set them at the right time and place. If there's an even, consistent pattern to the row of ticker marks there, then you're okay. If not, then you need to do some investigating to see what's wrong. If you need to make corrections, just slide the position of the ticker mark to the proper location.

At that point, you're ready to render your movie. Render as an image sequence; that will make it easy to throw out the first frame.

Some QTVR object-creation software (such as the free-for-the-download Macintosh utility called Edit QTVR Object) requires that you begin with a QuickTime movie file. If you render to a movie, there are two things you need to do. First, make sure that you set up your movie to have no keyframes, as the dialog box in Figure 15.62 shows. Some compression codecs use temporal compression, where one frame records only what has changed from the previous one, and keyframes mark the real and whole frames that are the bases of change. Temporal compression and keyframes won't work with an object movie, where the movie can go up, down, left, and right, and where the idea of a strict sequence of frames is irrelevant. The second precaution to take when rendering to a QuickTime movie is to set the working range so it is from Frame 1 to the last frame, because you don't have an easy way to get rid of Frame 0.

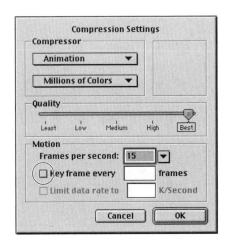

Figure 15.62 Ensure that a QTVR object movie render has no keyframes by unchecking the Key frames option in the Compression Settings dialog box, reached from the Animation Setup dialog box.

There are various applications for converting your set of rendered images or QuickTime movie to a QuickTime VR object movie. Apple's QuickTime VR Authoring Studio (Mac OS only) and VR Toolbox's Object Worx or full-featured VR Worx (Mac OS and Windows) are commercial applications. If you use the Mac OS (or have a friend who does), Apple offers a very basic way to generate an object movie with its free utility application, QTVR Edit Object, which you can download from Apple's QuickTime Web site: http://www.apple.com/quicktime/developers/tools.html.

PATH-OLOGY

We begin our little path-ology discussion with a review of what you know so far about paths.

- Paths are objects.

- Their geometry can be adjusted over time.

- Objects can be constrained to them; the position of that constraint may or may not change with time.

- You can constrain more than one object to a path.

Once you combine these path characteristics in an animation, you have the power to create remarkable effects. You will be able to generate complex motion for multiple objects without having to individually animate each object.

"So," you may be wondering, "What types of powerful things can I do with paths?" Here are some ways you can work with paths; we'll explore them in depth.

- *Paths Connected to Paths.* A path (let's call it A) can be connected to another path (Path B). Path A is animated to travel down Path B. Objects that are constrained to Path A can then travel along Path B.

- *Objects Constrained to a Changing Path.* You can constrain several objects to a path; the path geometry changes and takes the objects wherever the path goes.

- *Objects Moving along a Changing Path.* A variation on the previous item; the objects also move along the changing path.

Multi-Replicating along a Path

By the time you get into the placement of multiple objects along a single path, it's time to get the wish list out again and add "multi-replicate along a path" to it. An object that is constrained to a path can be duplicated, and the new object will also be constrained to the path. However, there's a bit of cognitive dissonance: The new object appears in the same position as the old, but when you look at the numerical entry for Constrain in the Object Attributes dialog box, the newly duplicated object reads 0.0. This dissonance is easily overcome, however, by dragging the object to the desired location along the path. An attempt to duplicate multiple objects along a path will result in many objects in new positions. Once you begin to move them, all duplicates jump to a common position underneath your mouse. So much for any attempts at efficiency.

If you duplicate a path that has objects constrained to it, the objects will all jump to a common position (the exception seems to be any object that is constrained to 0; since that's where it is and that's where the numbers say it is, then all goes well.)

After wracking our brains trying to find a better way, it seems that the best option for multi-replicating along a path is to simply duplicate the object (⌘-D/Ctrl+D) and drag it to another location along the path. (You can also use keyboard shortcuts to move it along; they're similar to the nudge key command shortcuts.)

Several Objects Connected to Path

Constraining several objects to a path makes for some interesting animation opportunities. For example, in a still-image category, you can string pearls or stones along a path to create a necklace, chain, or some other thing like that. We made a very simple turquoise necklace using stone objects constrained to a path. Interspersed among the stones are little silver beads (see Figure 15.63). Other Brycers have used this technique to create a linked chain that doesn't obey a simple straight-line configuration.

Figure 15.63 A turquoise and silver necklace created using objects constrained to a path.

All right then. That's a still image. But this is a chapter on animation. So we'll take the next step and get those paths moving and see what can be done. What happens when you animate the geometry of the path and keep all the objects in their same positions relative to the path? Here are a couple of examples: an inchworm and some wacky underwater plants.

Caterpillar

The caterpillar in Figure 15.64 is a path with many spheres linked and constrained to it. Using the Object Attributes dialog box's Percentage field to position objects along the path provides unpredictable results. (Depending on the number and placement of points in the path, objects may not be spaced correctly.) Therefore, we eyeballed the spheres' placement and manually dragged them to their positions. We animated the path over time to imitate the action of an inchworm. The path changes in geometry and location.

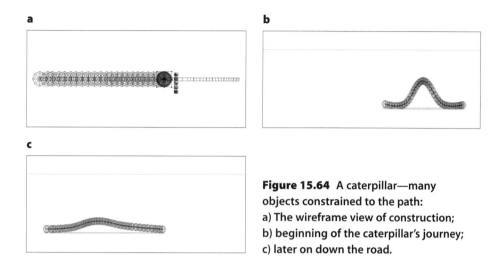

Figure 15.64 A caterpillar—many objects constrained to the path:
a) The wireframe view of construction;
b) beginning of the caterpillar's journey;
c) later on down the road.

Wacky Plants

Here is a another example of objects linked to an animating path: wacky plants. This technique that doesn't strive for realism so much as caricature. (Whoever heard of seaweed made of pyramids?) The plant fronds stay anchored at the base and then float and sway and bob at the other end. Movement of the object provides important clues about what the object is made of and what kind of environment it is in, as these wacky underwater plants attest (see Figure 15.65).

Figure 15.65 A plant dancing in the water's current—many objects constrained to several paths: a) The wireframe view of construction; b) one frame in the animation; c) another frame.

Path Connected to Path

Nothing provides control over the motion of several objects in a complex scene quite so well as connecting one path to another. The Jet Race scene (JET RACE and its associated movie, JET RACE.MOV), shown in Figure 15.66, has three jets attached to a path. (Yes, yes, it's true; we used a very low-tech version of a jet: a lengthy cone. In this case, the animation principles were more important than the construction of an elaborate jet.) We'll call the paths the jet path and the motion path.

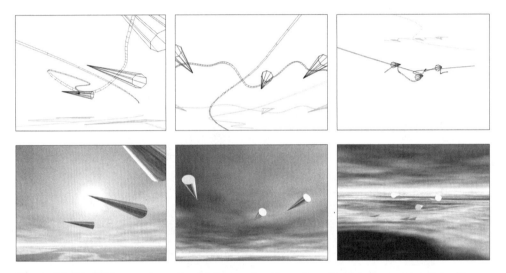

Figure 15.66 Still images from the Jet Race animation, where the jets (cones) are linked to one path that travels along another path.

There are five elements of movement in this scene:

• The jets move back and forth slightly along the jet path.

• The geometry of the jet path changes over time; this causes the jets to move about relative to each other as they travel.

• The jet path moves along another path. This is how the jets cover real distance.

• The motion path's geometry changes over time, too. As time goes forward, the motion path increases in size, providing an acceleration burst. The jet path is set to move from one point of the motion path to another in a given amount of time. If the space between those points increases, as it would with an increase in motion path size, then the jet path will need to travel faster to cover more territory.

- The camera tracks the jet path, and the camera moves along its own trajectory as it follows the jets.

All of these changes are isolated and illustrated in the movie JET RACE HOW.MOV on the CD-ROM in this chapter's folder. The movie is a series of wireframe movies showing each of the animations just described individually before the different parts were put together into the final animation.

A similar effect was achieved with a set of little yellow balls that spiral downhill into the blue upside-down-cone abyss. In this case, the balls are linked to a path that itself moves along the spiral path. To get the objects to face the right way, the yellow ball path tracks a hidden object in the center of the spiral. See Figure 15.67 and see DOWNHILL SPIRAL.MOV AND DOWNHILL SPIRAL on the CD-ROM.

a   b

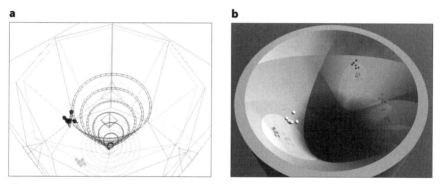

Figure 15.67 The a) Wireframe and b) Rendered views of the downhill spiral, where one path moves along another path.

FUN WITH MULTI-REPLICATION

We've been exploring linking in many ways, with objects linked to objects, objects linked to paths, and paths linked to paths. This next example examines objects cumulatively linked to objects linked to objects linked to…well, you get the idea. Get ready for some fun and fascinating results in this ode to a Bryce multi-replication Easter Egg.

Linked Hierarchy Multi-Replication Extravaganza

Here's something that's simply fun: linked hierarchies up the yin-yang.

1. Create a new scene. Open the Preferences dialog box (under the Edit menu) and make sure that Create Objects at World Center is checked. Drag the Trackball to the right while holding down the Control/Ctrl key to constrain movement horizontally. Stop when the center line of the ground plane grid runs up and down (see Figure 15.68).

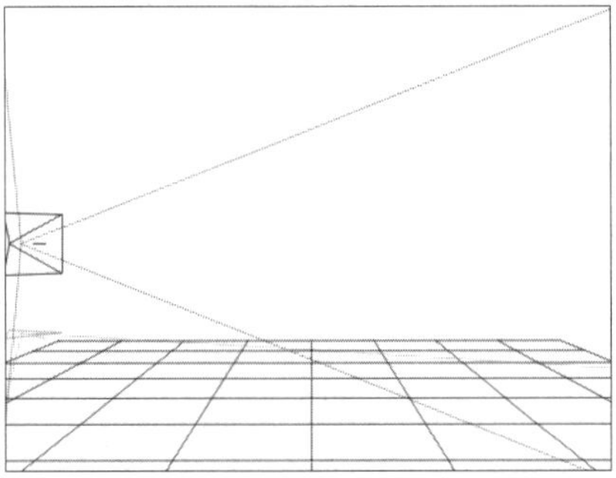

   Figure 15.68 After rotating the Director's View so that you are facing the ground grid squarely.

2. From the Camera pop-up menu (on the Controls Palette), choose Camera to Director. The blue outline of the camera disappears. (The camera is in the same place that you are!) Click the Director/Camera icon on the Controls Palette so that the Camera icon appears. You're looking at your scene through Camera View.

3. From the Animation Options pop-up menu, make sure that Auto-Key is on. (You'll be creating many animating objects, and you do not want to manually set keyframes for them all!) Create a cone.

   Next, you will multi-replicate this cone into a circle of cones on the ground.

4. From the menu, choose Edit > Multi-Replicate. Enter these numbers into the Multi-Replicate dialog box (see Figure 15.69): For quantity, enter 30. To keep the cones on the ground, they need to be replicated around the y axis only. A circle is 360°, and we'll have 30 items (well, actually 31, counting the first, original object; for this exercise the extra object doesn't matter). Divide these to get the number of degrees separating the copies: 360 ÷ 30 = 12. Enter 12 into the Rotate Y box. Finally, set an amount for Offset. Since the cones are all going to sit in the same plane, the offset should be on either the x or z axis. Enter 5 for Offset X. Don't leave the dialog box yet!

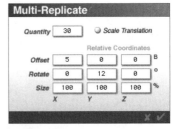

Figure 15.69 The Multi-Replicate settings for the cone.

5. Now comes the fun part! There's a magic trick that will link each successive replicated cone to the previous one: Hold down the Control-Option/Ctrl+Alt keys as you click the dialog box's check mark to leave. Your results should look like Figure 15.70.

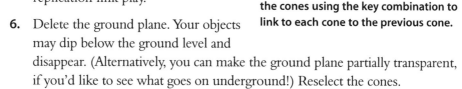

The next few steps will get you all set for the remainder of your multi-replication link play.

Figure 15.70 After multi-replicating the cones using the key combination to link to each cone to the previous cone.

6. Delete the ground plane. Your objects may dip below the ground level and disappear. (Alternatively, you can make the ground plane partially transparent, if you'd like to see what goes on underground!) Reselect the cones.

7. Drag the Time Scrubber out to some time marker. It may be a function of having a large monitor and making the interface hug the monitor's edge, but we've been setting up scenes with about 64 frames, or a little over 4 seconds long (at 15 frames per second).

8. Save your scene. (You want this state to come back to, or if you get carried away on a jag because this is so much fun, you can continue to create additional scene files by selecting Save As and giving the new scene a new name.)

All set now? Let the games begin!

9. Use the Rotate, Reposition, and Resize tools to make your set of objects move.

They are already rotating on the y axis; they'll wind up or unwind with additional rotation on the y axis. What happens when you rotate on the x or z axis?

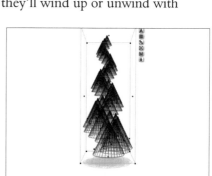

Try resizing to make the objects smaller or larger. What happens?

Try repositioning the objects on one or more axes.

Figure 15.71 shows one sample result of working with Resize, Reposition, and Rotation.

Figure 15.71 One result of using Resize, Reposition, and Rotate with multi-linked multi-replicated objects.

10. When you have a result that you like, hit the backslash (\) key to play the movie. If you like it, save it with another name. (We figure you'll want to try this more than once! Keep the original scene file for that.)

11. Render your animation. Giggle!

> **TIP:** *It makes a difference whether you're in World Space or Object Space when you make these subsequent multi-replicate monster manipulations! Try it out in both spaces!*

ANIMATION MISCELLANEA

Before we abandon the topic of advanced animation, we have a couple more tidbits of miscellaneous animation wisdom to offer you.

Animating Textures (and Materials)

Animation of textures (and materials) shouldn't be an undertaking only for "advanced" work in Bryce; it should be simple and straightforward. But it's not. There are several debilitating bugs in Bryce that make the task of animating materials far more difficult than it needs to be. Alas, this is one of those insidious user-unfriendly things that requires mastery of all the concepts involved before you can begin to comprehend and work around the buggy behavior. So now that you're familiar with all the concepts involved, we can divulge secrets. We lay it all out for you here, with the promise that, once you get past the landmines, you will be able to reliably work with animated textures (and materials).

Materials in the Advanced Motion Lab

First, let's understand how materials appear in the AML Hierarchy List. A material, belonging to an object, is listed as one of the attributes in an object's timeline. (Alas, if you create a path object with Auto-Key on, Bryce will automatically assign material attributes to that path in the Advanced Motion Lab—a wholly unnecessary complication!) The object's timelines are slightly different depending on whether you are working with Auto-Key on or off.

- *Auto-Key On.* When creating an object, all timelines for that object are created, including the materials timeline.

- *Auto-Key Off.* When creating an object and then setting an initial keyframe in the Time Palette's Add Keyframe pop-up menu (Object Name > All Timelines), only keyframes for the object attributes (position, rotation, scale, shear, origin) are created. No materials timelines are created until and unless they are added in the Materials Lab.

When a materials keyframe is created, it will be displayed in the AML in one of three conditions. First (this occurs only with Auto-Key on), for objects with Bryce's default gray material, the material is a big, fat nothing (see Figure 15.72a). Yes, that's right; where the title for the material should be, there is a blank. Perhaps

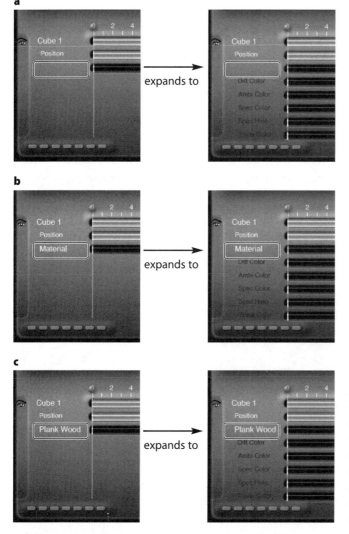

Figure 15.72 Three ways that Bryce displays the object's material in the Advanced Motion Lab's Hierarchy List: a) The default material, displayed as a blank (Auto-Key On only); b) generic material; c) material with a specific name (material comes from the Materials Preset Library). Each option is shown collapsed and expanded.

the assumption that Bryce makes here is that no animation takes place with the default material, so there's no sense in displaying it. But still, to display it as *a blank*?!? What were those Bryce creators thinking? Once you *do* make any change to the default material (change color, change one of the sliders, assign a texture to drive one of the materials attributes), the material will be displayed in the second condition: The material is labeled "Material"—pretty much what you'd expect (see Figure 15.72b). The third condition is a specific name (see Figure 15.72c). Any material stowed in the Materials Preset Library has a name. If that material is applied to an animated object, then that material's name will be what you see in the Hierarchy List for that object.

Textures as a Subset of Materials

In the Materials Lab, textures drive one or more of the material attributes. In your normal work in the Materials Lab, if you don't assign a texture source to drive one of the material properties, then that texture source will disappear once you leave the Materials Lab. The texture *depends* on that material attribute. That same dependence is reflected in the way the Advanced Motion Lab displays textures.

There are three places in Bryce where the relationship between texture and material are displayed. First, there's the Materials Lab grid, where markers are placed on the grid to show which texture source is driving which material property.

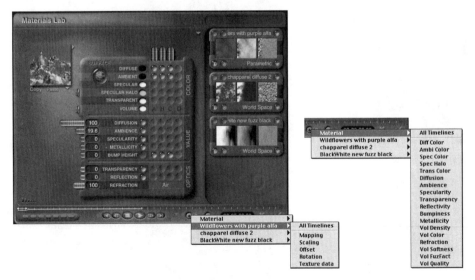

Figure 15.73 Textures among material properties in the Materials Lab: Texture sources are assigned to material properties in the grid and also appear in the Add (and Remove) Keyframes pop-up menus.

Second, in the Materials Lab, the Add and Remove Keyframes pop-up menu displays separate hierarchical menus for the material and for any one of the textures. Third, the Hierarchy List in the Advanced Motion Lab displays the textures as a subset of the material properties to which the texture is assigned. Figure 15.73 shows examples of the two places where textures appear in the Materials Lab (we'll get to the Advanced Motion Lab in a bit).

The Materials Lab's pop-up menu, with its separate listing for materials and texture, might lead you to believe that in the AML's Hierarchy List, somewhere at the bottom of the list of material attributes, you will find the texture name containing the texture's attributes. Not so! The texture and its attributes are contained within the appropriate materials attributes. Figure 15.74 shows the Hierarchy List for a material where a texture is contained both in the Diffuse Color and Ambient Color properties. Display of textures is not limited to a single texture, however. Since you can have up to three textures

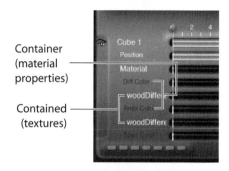

Container (material properties)

Contained (textures)

Figure 15.74 Misleading appearance of material properties: Hierarchy List of materials, showing the material property container items and the contained textures. The material properties do not have white text that tells you "this is a container item."

simultaneously driving a material property (two properties in an A-B blend; three properties in an A-B-alpha C blend), the Hierarchy List for a material property can contain up to three textures, as Figure 15.75 shows.

Let's get back to this matter of the material property as a container of a texture. In the game of animated attribute hide 'n' seek, Bryce plays a dirty trick on you by not correctly displaying the status of that attribute. The first thing you may notice is that the Diffuse Color (Diff Clr) attribute is not displayed in white—that is, as a container timeline. If you are unsure whether texture timelines are hidden among your material properties, use the Option-click/Alt+click method to expand or collapse timelines. Use Option-click/Alt+click on the material item to expand its contents. Doing so will also expand any texture-containing material properties so you can see them all.

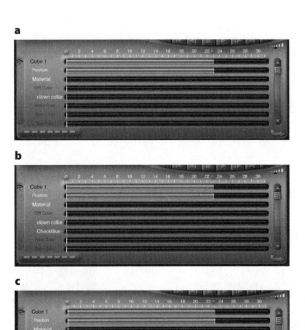

Figure 15.75
A material property timeline may contain as many as three textures: a) A single texture; b) two textures, an A-B blend; c) three textures, an A-B-alpha C blend.

The reason why Bryce plays such a mean game of hide 'n' seek here may be due to the inherent ambiguity of the material property. Consider, for example, Diff Clr (Diffuse Color): Is it a container item or an animated item? It could be one, the other, or even both!

- *Container Item.* When a material property is a container item, its name will be gray. If a contained texture is animated, then the colored bar in the timeline will have only a single white key event ticker mark, at the beginning. (A minimum of one keyframe must be saved for the material property to display the subordinate texture.) (See Figure 15.76a.)

- *Animated Item.* When a material property is animated with a minimum of two keyframes, its name will be white, and when selected, will turn yellow. The timeline will have a colored bar that contains white key event ticker marks (see Figure 15.76b).

Note: The color of the material property's timeline is the same, whether it is animated or whether it is a container. Search very carefully for those key event ticker marks, as those are the only indication of which is which. Well, that is, except for...

• *Both Container and Animated Item*. The material property can simultaneously be animated and be a container item for one or more textures. The item's name will be white, and the colored bar will be the same color as for either a container or animated item. Key event ticker marks will appear where there are keyframes. What happens if the times for the material property's animation and the contained texture's animation do not coincide? The material property's timeline will contain both key event ticker marks and will extend beyond those, as Figure 15.76c shows. Isn't the ambiguity the most charming thing you ever did see? We didn't think so either.

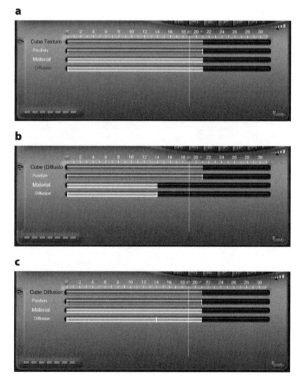

Figure 15.76
Material property as:
a) A container for textures;
b) an animated property;
and c) a container that is
also animated.

Our three-steps-forward, two-steps-back tour of texture animation continues with a peek at the texture timeline. The texture timeline is a container for the texture attributes. As a container, its name does appear white in the Hierarchy List. Whew! But not so fast there. By looking at the texture's timeline, can you tell that it contains actual animation data with a minimum of two keyframes? Look at Figure 15.77, where the texture timeline is shown closed and open. There are three texture sources used here. (In fact, you're looking at the texture in the AML that you saw in the Materials Lab back in Figure 15.73.) Only one of the textures is animated. Can you tell by looking at Figure 15.77a which texture is animated? (We can't.) Notice, in both cases, that the material property container (Diff Color) is not animated (it has no ticker marks), and it does have a colored bar, which indicates that it contains an item that is animated. Yet the texture container timeline does not display a similar bar. However, when the timeline is expanded, showing its contents, one of the texture attributes is, in fact, animated! So the texture container timeline does not report the true status of its contents. Grrr! Grrrrr! (All right, take a deep breath. Do not shoot the messenger! We are only here to report to you the condition and behavior of Bryce 4.0.1 as we found it! Complain to MetaCreations. Oops. Complain to Corel. Um. Just complain! Take that breath first, though.)

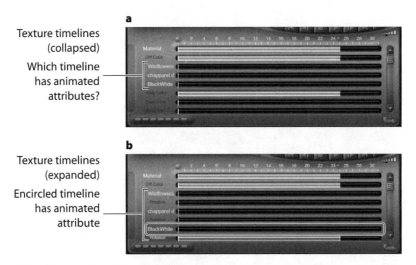

Figure 15.77 How the texture timeline lies to you, and how to force it to tell the truth: Timelines for Diffuse Color, and texture with the texture timeline a) Collapsed and b) expanded.

Would you believe that you can force the texture timeline to display a colored bar? Indeed! It's true; you *can* force the software to behave. Here's what you need to do. You must have the texture container timeline visible. Then alter the scaling of the timeline using the timeline Scale tool. *Voila!* The texture item's timeline will all of a sudden display a colored bar to indicate that animation is taking place (see

Figure 15.78). If you change the scaling of the timeline without the texture container item displayed, it will not work. The "transformation" will not be saved with the scene file. Saving the scene in the changed state and then closing and opening it again will result in a start-all-over texture item keyframe that will not be displayed. Now who'd have thought that, merely to see the current status of your animation in the Advanced Motion Lab, you'd have to futz around with the timeline Scale tool to force Bryce to properly display what it should have been displaying all along?

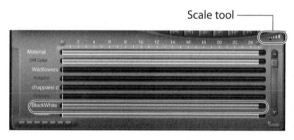

Scale tool

Figure 15.78 Forcing an update: The expanded texture properly displays the timeline after all timelines are adjusted using the timeline Scale tool (circled).

Animating Textures

Now that you are familiar with the ins and outs of how material and texture timelines are (or aren't) displayed in the Hierarchy List and Sequencer of the Advanced Motion Lab, let's turn our attention to what you need to do to animate textures.

Because the texture depends on at least one of the material properties, you must set a single, initial keyframe for one of the material properties that is being driven by the texture.

When you create an object with Auto-Key on, initial keyframes for materials are automatically created; you do not need to create additional keyframes. When you work with Auto-Key off, you need to set an initial keyframe for one of the material properties using the Add Keyframe pop-up menu. You do not need to actually animate that property over time; simply create a single keyframe at the beginning of the sequence. Now that a material property keyframe is in place, you can animate the texture, and the animation will "stick." (We've heard complaints of texture animation not working; it turns out that those who've done the complaining are those who work with Auto-Key off. This step in creating a material property keyframe is not explained in the documentation, nor is there anything in the way that Bryce behaves that guides you toward this task.)

Now that you have a keyframe for the material property, it's time to animate the texture. If you are working with Auto-Key off, you will, of course, need to set an initial keyframe for your beginning condition, and one or more subsequent keyframes for animation that takes place over time. If you are working with Auto-Key on, you can advance the Time Scrubber to your desired time and then make a change to the texture. However, if you're working with a material (and, consequently, a texture) from the Materials Preset Library, then you will need to manually set an initial keyframe as well. When you load a material preset, the initial state of the texture is not automatically recorded by Bryce.

Removing Material Property Keyframes in the AML (Don't!)

There is one last little bit of buggy behavior that we feel compelled to describe to you. Normally, you'd think that you can remove keyframes for an object or one of its attributes in the Advanced Motion Lab by holding down the Shift key while pressing the mouse on the item name in the Hierarchy List and then selecting Delete All Keyframes from the resulting pop-up menu. However, under very specific circumstances, that procedure won't work. If you have an object with a material that has several texture-driven material properties, and one of those textures is animated (even if it contains a single, initial keyframe), do not try to delete all keyframes for *any* of the material properties that are texture driven. You only need to have one of the material properties animated with an initial keyframe, so you'd think you could get rid of the others, right? (You probably won't find yourself in this situation unless you are working with Auto-Key on.) If you try to delete any texture-driven material property in the Advanced Motion Lab, the unfortunate result is that far more timelines will disappear—at minimum, all material keyframes, and at maximum, all keyframes for that object, will just go away—poof! That's a shocker! Since removing keyframes in the Advanced Motion Lab is not undoable, it's definitely a good idea to save your scene file first before you take a trip to the Advanced Motion Lab for keyframe cleanup. You will have no problem, however, if you delete keyframes for individual material properties in the Materials Lab using the pop-up menu accessed from the Remove Keyframe control.

Textures and Materials Animation Recap

Congratulations! You've just successfully made your way through a bug-riddled section of Bryce. Navigating through this part of Bryce is apt to turn you into a parody of 2001's Dave Bowman: You say, "My God! It's full of bugs!" Then, as you enter the depths of Bryce animation, snapshots flash different views of your face contorting in response to the cruel extremities of the Advanced Motion Lab, and flashes of timeline Sequencer color bars reflect off of your face visor. If you survive without becoming a wizened old person or a fetus orbiting the planet, then good for you!

Here's a quick summary of the things you need to look out for while animating textures:

- You must have a keyframe for at least one of the material properties that are driven by the texture that you want to animate.

- No matter whether you are working with Auto-Key on or off, you must manually set the initial keyframe for whatever texture property you are animating if you are working with a preset material. Otherwise, with materials that you build in the Materials Lab, work as you normally would (Auto-Key off: manually set keyframes; Auto-Key on: set the Time Scrubber and then make adjustments to textures).

- In the AML, the timeline for the texture will be hidden beneath the timelines for any or all of the materials properties that are driven by that texture. The material property item in the Hierarchy List breaks the rule that says that items are displayed in white if "more is here." Instead, the material property appears gray.

- The material property will, however, display the colored bar to indicate that animation takes place in this timeline. However, the color is the same as if the material property itself were animated. The only difference is the lack of a ticker mark at the later end of the bar.

- The texture timeline also expands to display the properties contained therein. The texture timeline is properly displayed in white. However, when one of the properties is animated over time, the texture name does not reflect that same time by displaying a colored bar. Once you use the Scale tool in the AML to change the display of the timeline, however, the colored bar will appear in the texture name's timeline.

- Attempting to remove all keyframes for a texture-driven material property in the AML will result in removal of all keyframes for the entire material (or even the object!). If you want any material keyframes to remain, use the Materials Lab's Remove Keyframe pop-up menu to remove keyframes for individual texture-driven material properties.

Animation and Groups

If you animate a group so that its position changes, resulting in a trajectory, and then later ungroup the group, all of the group members inherit the group's trajectory, with the result that each object will have its own trajectory. The same thing occurs with linked objects. (After all, a group is a parent to all the group's members.) A child object, when unlinked from the animated parent object, will retain the parent's trajectory path.

Knowing this, if you ungroup a group after animating it with a motion trajectory, you'll have several trajectories whereas before there was one. You can make one object the parent of the others, or keep the group, or live with your several and varied trajectories.

Merging Animated Scenes and Copying/Pasting Animated Objects

Naturally, if you are creating an animation extravaganza, you'll be tempted to increase your efficiency by building different elements in different scenes and combining them later by merging. This is an excellent strategy. Merged and copied and pasted objects retain all their animation information.

Suppose, for instance, that you set out to create a scene with several animating widgets in it. The entire duration of the animation is 10 seconds. Widget A moves from second 1 to second 4, Widget B moves from 3 seconds to 7 seconds, and Widget C moves from 6 to 10 seconds. If each widget is built in a separate scene, then setting up each scene for 10 seconds and animating within that time will allow the animation to beautifully coalesce when the different scenes are merged together. You can set the working time to surround the animation in question, so that the scene for Widget A starts at either time 0 or time 1, and the end of the working time is at 4 seconds.

Here are a couple of interesting points on retaining animation information. If you generate an animation and then later scale the timeline, a copied animated object will paste into a new scene with its original timeline scale. The AML's ability to scale multiple key event ticker marks will help you scale it out again, and here's hoping that you don't have tons of properties animated in that one object. The second item is a much sadder point. For paths containing objects constrained to it, such as those earthworms, seaweeds, and pearl necklaces, copying and pasting and merging will cause all the objects constrained to the path to jump to a common position.

Whew!

Congratulations, Bryce animator! You've made it through this chapter. It, and the previous one, are only the beginning of animation adventures. We wish you swift renders! For some real-life stories of Bryce animation, do check out Chapter 17, "Bryce Eye Candy," for examples of who did what, and why and how.

CHAPTER SIXTEEN

Superlative Nature Imagery

IN THIS CHAPTER...

- At the feet of the Master—dissecting some scenes by Bryce creator Eric Wenger

- Tips for specific nature effects

- Geology 101—how Earth formations occur and how to create them in Bryce

- Undersea worlds

- Rainy weather conditions

- Outer space

In this chapter, we'll jump back and forth between the natural world "out there" and the virtual world of Bryce "in here." There is an interactive process between using Bryce and being outdoors. The best way to make natural-looking Bryce landscapes is to spend some time outdoors observing the lay of the land. After you've worked in Bryce, you'll start noticing things about the environment— you'll observe geological structures, habitats, and atmospheric conditions. After inspecting the way things look in the natural world, you will apply your observations to your Brycean scenery. You'll set up your skies with haze and fog that's just so. Your Bryce terrains will benefit from all that careful scrutiny of the local land, and working in Bryce will give you a keener eye when you're out-of-doors.

To give you a head start on the reciprocal observation process, this chapter discusses some of the common solutions for making convincing nature scenery. Not all natural possibilities can be explored in detail in this (or any!) book. We will, however, cover some common tricks. With basic understanding of nature scenery and a few tricks as a foundation, you'll be able to continue on and more readily translate the outdoors to the inner workings of Bryce.

IN THE MASTER'S FOOTSTEPS: ERIC'S METHODS

The absolute master of creating nature scenes is Eric Wenger, creator of Bryce. After all, he wrote the software to tickle his own funny bone long before Kai, Phil, and Sree became involved with putting together a version for public consumption. Eric knows it best. The best school of instruction for getting natural-looking images is to study the methods of his Brycean madness. This section will do just that, exploring a few of his images and examining the characteristics common to superlative scenery. After reading this section, take a look at Eric's scenes on this book's CD-ROM.

Here is a brief list of the principles that can be deduced from Eric's images. We'll discuss each one in turn. You can always turn back here for a master reference list of masterful techniques.

• Create multiple terrains.

• Create a sense of relative distance from the camera with terrain size and resolution.

• Put all the detail right in front of the camera.

• Enlarge the terrains that go way off in the background (usually).

• Create a sense of scale with Atmosphere and Materials settings.

• Pay attention to those Sky settings!

We'll explore these concepts by examining three scenes (see Figures 16.1 and 16.2). They are shown in both final rendered state and in wireframe from top view. The final renders are also shown in Figure C16.3 in the color section. Figure 16.1 is *Fjord Mud*; Figure 16.2 has two images, *Abisko Pine Trees* and *Valley*. You can find the scene document for both figures on the CD-ROM in this chapter's folder.

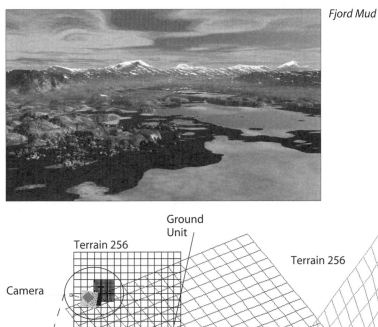

Fjord Mud

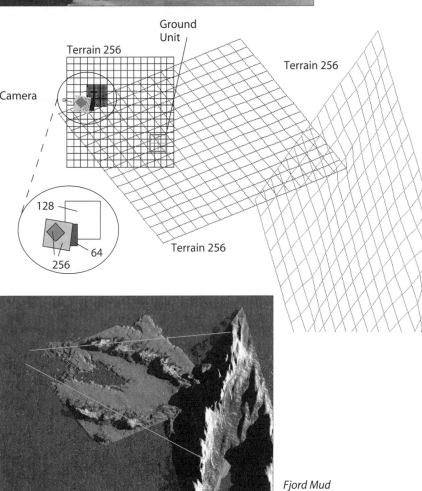

Fjord Mud
top view rendered

Figure 16.1 *Fjord Mud. Art by Eric Wenger*

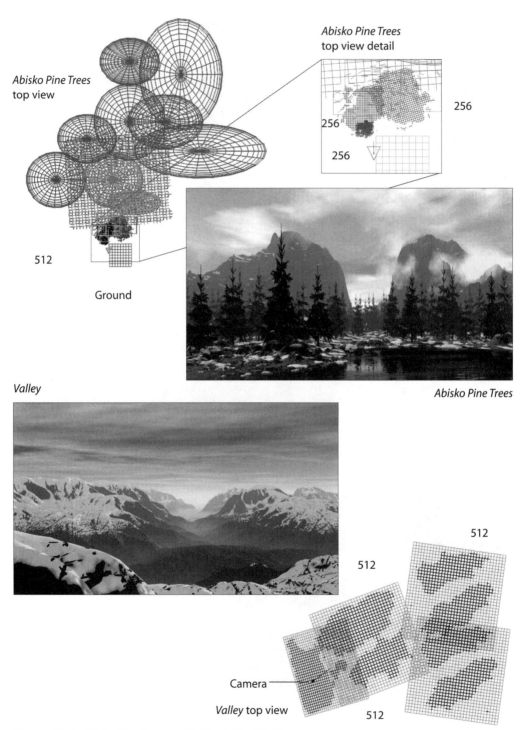

Abisko Pine Trees
top view

Abisko Pine Trees
top view detail

256

256

256

512

Ground

Abisko Pine Trees

Valley

512

512

512

Camera

Valley top view

512

Figure 16.2 *Abisko Pine Trees* and *Valley*. *Art by Eric Wenger*

Terrain Placement: Create for Depth

Eric's placement of terrains—their position and size—provides a sense of scale in his nature scenery. Multiple terrains are placed in the scene, and their resolutions and wireframe sizes vary depending on the distance from the camera.

Wireframe Analysis from the Top Down

Figures 16.1 and 16.2 show wireframe top views for each of the three scenes. In each of the figures, the ground is highlighted so that you can compare the relative sizes of the terrains. Notice that the camera is at one end and the small terrain sizes are closest to the camera in *Fjord Mud* and *Abisko Pine Trees*. Farther away, the terrain sizes become gargantuan in comparison. Nearly all of the terrains have been enlarged from their original sizes. The farther away from the camera the terrains are, the larger they are. This establishes a sense of scale.

Now that we've told you one thing, we're going to contradict ourselves right here! You don't *always* have to have larger terrains in the distance. *Valley* (in Figure 16.2) successfully uses several terrains of the same size. Here, the mountains are all high detail and large size. With the proper camera perspective, the result is a nice sense of overall distance and grandeur from the height of a snowy mountain top.

The figures have numbers indicating the terrain resolution (set via the Grid pop-up menu in the Terrain Editor). Close to the camera, they are generally 256 or 512. But far away, the amount of resolution detail does not increase in proportion to the increase in wireframe size. The larger the terrain's resolution, the more RAM is required to process your scene. Terrain far away from the camera doesn't require the same detail.

Fjord Mud has high detail right in front of the camera. The four terrains in the foreground (shown in an enlargement) are mostly medium- to high-resolution. Their wireframe sizes have been *reduced,* creating even higher detail (see Figure 16.1).

Open up the FJORD MUD, VALLEY and ABISKO PINE TREES scene documents on the CD-ROM. Notice that the terrain maps for many of the terrains in each scene are the same. You can also see this trend toward sameness in the top-view render of *Fjord Mud* as well as the scene file for *Valley*. You don't need to create and painstakingly perfect a separate G2H map for every terrain. You can reuse the same one and change the terrain's orientation (rotate it on the y axis). Or make it a bit different with a slight tweak, if you must.

Having analyzed the scenes from top view, you may think that the general order of business is to create and place terrains from that view. A potential top-view formula would go like this:

Start in top view. Create a terrain. Duplicate it and move it away from the camera. Enlarge it some. Stretch it out on one dimension. Duplicate the terrain again. Move it over and back a bit. Enlarge it. Rotate it around. Now create a ground. Give the terrains and ground a material setting. Add haze to taste. Go back to Camera View. Sashay the camera back and forth to get the right perspective. Render. *Voilá!* Instant natural scenery!

This process will work, since it bows respectfully to the Major and Minor Deities of depth and scale. But the scenes shown here weren't created that way. Eric created them while in main view, with forays into top view to make adjustments. In the next section, we discuss camera perspective as part of the scene-building process.

Camera Perspective

Each of these scenes was created for a one-camera perspective. They also were created in the days before Director's View, when Camera View was the only perspective view available. They were not meant to sustain the perspective of a complete circular panorama. In all of these, the camera's active image area determines the location of the terrains in the three-dimensional world. In the *Fjord Mud* example, shown rendered in top view, the lines roughly indicate the edge of the camera's field of view (see Figure 16.1). Like a movie set where not all of the beams and frames can be seen by the camera, Bryce terrains end abruptly off-camera. This is a natural outcome of the process of working in Camera View; as long as the object looks fine through the camera, it doesn't matter how it appears elsewhere.

If you are going to create a scene for a 360° render or for animation, you'll have to work a bit differently. Smaller, detailed terrains are close to the camera, with larger terrains spread out along the perimeter. (More on 360° renders can be found in Chapter 13, "Render Unto Bryce.")

In *Fjord Mud* and *Abisko Pine Trees*, the camera is located close to the ground. If you were to somehow take a Fantastic Voyage and actually enter Bryce Space, your eyes would be located—you guessed it—close to the ground. The mountains would be huge—hundreds of times taller than you are. To put you in your humble place, select the Eye-Level Camera item from the Camera Options pop-up menu. As a result, those massive terrains will appear to be just that—massive. In *Valley*, the camera is on higher ground, atop a terrain. The same "be close to the ground" rule applies; it's just that you're close to higher-elevation ground. The Eye-Level Camera item does not work for higher elevations.

Material Frequency Detail

The terrain placement and camera position are adjusted to give an overall sense of scale. Continue the illusion of realism in the Materials Lab. In these scenes, the amount of surface detail is adjusted to ensure authenticity. The adjustments are most critical for objects right in front of the camera. When an object in the foreground looks blurry, increase the frequency to add more detail. There are a couple of ways to do so. In the Materials Lab, adjust the Frequency using the Edit Texture control. In the Deep Texture Editor, adjust the Noise Palette's frequency slider for each component. These detail-increasing controls are covered in detail in Chapter 9, "Material World I: Materials Lab."

Material Setting: Ambient

To give the all the scenes' elements a sense of cohesion, the objects' Illumination settings contain an identical amount of Ambience in the Materials Lab. If each of your objects' ambient settings differs, the scene won't look natural. The discrepancy between objects will be most apparent in their shaded areas. On occasion you can beautifully exploit different ambient settings. If you have one terrain object with dark rock and another terrain with snow, for example, the ambient settings will differ. However, in most cases, giving all your objects a consistent ambient setting will help them live together harmoniously in your Brycean habitat.

Sky Settings for Depth and Realism

The sky settings contribute to the natural look. How did Eric set up his skies in these scenes? For our analysis of the three scenes, we'll focus on haze, sky colors, freestanding clouds, and the choice of atmosphere.

Haze and Sky Settings

The Haze setting provides a feel of true depth and perspective. All the strategic placement and sizing of terrains does nothing without adequate haze to infuse distance into the scene. The objects close to the camera are clear; the distant mountains *are* far away. The presence of haze—in generous proportions—is common to these and most of Eric's landscape scenes.

What differs from scene to scene is the Haze Color setting. The haze in *Fjord Mud* is a pale bluish-gray, and *Abisko Pine Trees* has a pale azure haze. In *Valley* the haze is lavender. In these instances, the Haze Color generally matches the overall color tone of the image. Don't take this as a strict rule, however.

If you *do* want to take a color observation as a rule of thumb for realism, we offer you this: The color of ambient light should be in medium values on the cool side of the spectrum. Not only does it influence areas in shadow, but it influences the color of other areas in the scene. In *Abisko Pine Trees*, the Ambient Color is a medium blue. In *Fjord Mud*, it is a pale aqua—most noticeable in the cloud layer above. *Valley* has a mauve-gray Ambient Color, which is most noticeable in the color of the snow when in shadow.

Shadow color depends on three things: the Shadow setting in the Sky & Fog Palette, the Ambient Color, and the Haze Color. In *Fjord Mud*, gray ambient and blue haze mix to create the overall shadow color; the Shadow setting is maximum. Of course, you can have one color or the other dominate, depending on the amount of haze in your scene. An increase in haze will always make that color dominate the shadow area.

Clouds Are Huge

Freestanding clouds can add to a scene's sense of realism. Look at the top view of the *Abisko Pine Trees* image. The spheres are the clouds. Because this is an ancient Classic Bryce scene, these clouds aren't volume clouds, but spheres set to Fuzzy Shading mode. They are huge, especially when compared to the terrains in the scene's foreground. This is not merely a matter of creating a sphere, flattening it somewhat, and then applying a cloud material setting to it. No, these puppies are grandiose. Remember, this is a *world* you're creating, and clouds are large-scale objects. Creating and seeding clouds is not something you've had day-to-day practice in—until now. So think big!

Volume Clouds

Freestanding clouds that use volume materials ("volume clouds," for short) present some requirements and challenges. If your scene uses volume clouds, be sure to review the "As Painless As Possible" section at the end of Chapter 9 to bone up on practical tips for working with volume materials. The clouds in Eric's Abisko scene, revisited in Figure C16.4, were converted into volume clouds; the result is a different appearance.

Volume clouds, when you're using the basic shading mode, will show diffuse color highlights and have darker, thicker spots of Ambient Color. In direct light, an object's color is the combination of Sun Color (or light color) plus the object's own Diffuse Color. In shadow, the object's color is the combination of the sky's Ambient Color with the object's Ambient Color. The most satisfying volume clouds are the result of a judicious blend of coloring in the Materials Lab and the Sky & Fog Palette. Since there are so many small texture particles that are rendered, the interaction of the cloud's Ambient Color with the Sky Ambient Color is quite sensitive.

If you're aiming for realism, then keep the actual cloud colors subtle. After experimenting with the volume clouds provided in the Materials Library, we found that cloud colors set very close to white worked well when we used the Sky & Fog Palette to provide overall color to the scene. Figure C16.5 compares different colorings in same scene. Figures C16.5a and b use the same colors but apply them differently. C16.5a applied white to the clouds' Diffuse and Ambient Colors, whereas the sun is orange and the Ambient Color is a muted blue. C16.5b reversed the situation, with the clouds being given the orange Diffuse Color and blue Ambient Color, and the Sun Color and Ambient Color both white. The appearance of the sun, clouds and the light on the mountains does not blend together as well as when the scene is colored in the Sky & Fog Palette, as was done in C16.5a. Figure C16.5c uses both cloud and sky colors. C16.5e and f show the same scene with white clouds, with slight variations on the Sun Color and Ambient Color. Unless you are going for highly stylized dramatic coloring, apply color to either the sun and ambience or to the clouds, but not both.

The ability to create volume clouds is both a blessing and a curse. It's a blessing, of course, because, after having been desired by so many Brycers for so long, there is finally a means to make clouds look great! Laying aside the obvious curse in render time (you knew that nice clouds came with a price, did you not?), the real curse of volume clouds is that a certain render shortcut prevents them from looking as good as they could. As the ray marches through that volume object, calculating sample after sample of the material, it completely ignores the haze atmosphere setting. When your volume clouds are floating far away among those distant terrains, the terrains will be affected by the haze in your scene, but the

Figure 16.6 The distant clouds of this volume cloud infinite slab are not affected by haze in the same way that the distant terrains are.

clouds will not. Figure 16.6 shows a scene in which an infinite slab was used to generate clouds. As they recede into the distance, the clouds do not match the haziness of the distant hills.

Eric's Scenery Recap

Here's a summary of all of the tips we covered during our examination of Eric Wenger's scenes:

- *Number of Terrains.* There is more than one terrain in these scenes, ranging in number from four to seven.

- *Terrain Proportions.* Close to the camera, terrains are relatively small; farther away, they are spread out and larger.

- *Terrain Size.* Terrains both close up and far away use a size of 256×256. Terrains closer to the camera need a higher level of detail. Far away, the same terrain resolution suffices even when the terrain wireframe is greatly enlarged.

- *Detail Right in Front of the Camera.* The greatest amount of detail is right in front of the camera.

- *Low Camera Position.* All of the camera views are close to the ground, whether at ground-level elevation, or close to terrain level at a higher elevation. Because the terrains far away are large, the low camera position tells you that you are in a big, big world.

- *Carefully Calculated Material Detail Frequency.* The material setting frequency is finessed to give the proper sense of scale. If repeating patterns or bump maps are too large, it makes the object seem too small.

- *Haze to Create Distance.* Haze provides a visual cue that an object is located far away.

- *Cool Ambient Colors.* Make your Ambient Color cool and medium-valued for realistic outdoor coloring.

- *Huge Clouds.* Spheres used for freestanding clouds are not small. Make 'em big!

- *Volume Clouds.* Pay attention to the sane methods of working with volume objects and let white clouds be colored by the Sky & Fog Palette's Sun and Ambient Colors.

GEOLOGY 101: MOUNTAINS AND VALLEYS

Making landscapes in Bryce is not about creating things that you think up in your head. (Well, then again, yes it is!) Even a fantasy landscape looks more impressive when it's based on some sort of reality, or at least a perception of reality. To aid your reality perception process, this section examines some basic matters of geology, or how Earth was formed. We're not talking about the big plate tectonics stuff all the world over but rather what happens on a local level.

While enjoying the vista at a scenic spot, you may have wondered how Earth got to be the way it is. How were the canyons formed? Why do the mountains there look different than the mountains you're used to seeing at home?

How New Mountains are Created

New mountains are created in four basic ways:

Volcanic Activity

Magma from inside the Earth forces its way to the surface. Lava spills onto the surface, thereby creating successive layers that build a mountain. Volcanoes are known for their central hole or crater, from which lava emerges. The eruption of Mount St. Helens in Washington is one notorious example of volcanic activity.

Volcanoes in Bryce

Use the Filtering control in the Terrain Editor to draw a downward line to make the top portion of the terrain descend (see Figure 16.7a). Figure 16.7b shows two Bryce volcanic cones. One is has a level top; the other is jagged after applying Noise in the Terrain Editor.

a b c

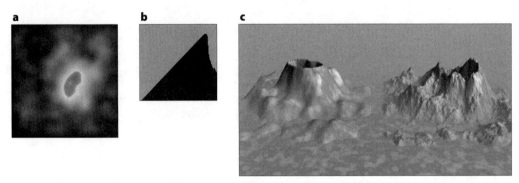

Figure 16.7 Volcano terrain map: a) The grayscale map; b) filter settings to create volcanic dent; c) two rendered volcano terrains.

Compression

Land masses are forced together. Where they collide, Earth's crust shortens and becomes thicker. What Earth's crust calls "thick," we call mountains. This process gives us folding and faulting and earth-shattering experiences. The Alps in Europe are mountains created by the compression of Earth's crust.

Compressed Land Masses in Bryce

There is no characteristic look to this mountain-making method. Just click the Terrain icon on the Create Palette and you'll be okay. However, bear this in mind: If land masses come together quickly, there will be a rapid rise with high relief faces where mountain-building vastly outpaces erosion. If the two land masses are compressed together more slowly, slopes won't be as steep and there will be more erosion.

Extension

Earth's crust is stretched apart. As it is stretched and thinned, cracks form, creating new faults. Some of the crustal blocks sag into the thinner crust along these faults (see Figure 16.8). Those crustal blocks that don't sag become mountains by default (pun intended!). The Basin and Range Province of Arizona and Nevada was created by extension.

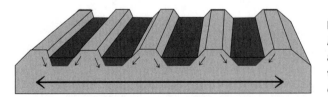

Figure 16.8 Extension: As Earth's crust is stretched apart, faults form and matter sags into the thinner crust along the faults.

Extension Mountains in Bryce

Extension mountains create an alternating sequence of parallel mountain ranges and basins. Set up a ground terrain with multiple terrains for a basin-and-range effect.

Broad Upwarping

A large mass of crust bulges upward, creating broad mountains. The Black Hills of South Dakota were created by broad crustal upwarping.

Broad Upwarping in Bryce

Enlarge your terrain with the Proportional Resize tool and then reduce it on the *y* axis (height) for extremely broad rolling hills.

Then, on the other hand, there's the matter of valleys. Once you have the mountains, how are the valleys created?

Glaciers

Some landscapes have been formed by glacial erosion. During the Ice Age, massive ice sheets, drawn by gravity, crept downhill ever so slowly. In the battle between ice and land, these enormous glaciers won. They carved a path for themselves, leaving behind huge sweeping U-shaped valleys as they retreated.

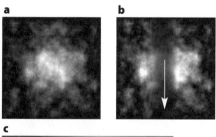

Figure 16.9 Brycean glacier-making: a) A normal terrain; b) after brushing with a fat brush; c) the rendered terrain.

The *Abisko Pine Trees* scene in Figure 16.2 has a broad U-shaped valley. Although a peek at the terrain from top view shows that the valley does not extend over a long distance (proper glacier-formed valleys do), it has the right shape.

Create a Brycean glacier using brush tools. In the Terrain Editor, use a brush tool with the elevation set to low (dark). Make the brush wide, soft, and set the Flow (opacity) to low-moderate. Or, use the brush tool in Photoshop and set the apply mode to Multiply. Either way, wield that brush and cut a wide swath in your terrain. Your brush is now the glacier. (How's that for being a virtual ice mass?) Figure 16.9a shows a normal terrain that was taken into Photoshop. The terrain was then brushed with a large (150 pixel) brush in

Photoshop using the Multiply mode (see Figure 16.9b). The final rendered terrain has the characteristic U shape (see Figure 16.9c).

Faults

All the world over, Earth's crust has cracks, or faults. Check out the guide for terrain fractal styles in Figure 8.6 to see which of the styles is apt to produce cracks or add faults and diagonal roughness to your terrains by using the Sawtooth control in the Terrain Editor. (Hey! You can even add sawtooth to one of the special fractal generated terrains!) When you run diagonal lines through your terrains, the land masses break up as though different layers of rock had shifted. It may be San Andreas running through your terrain or it may be a little localized action.

Eroded Canyons

How are canyons created?

The Colorado Plateau, in the southwestern United States, has over 30 wilderness areas set aside—either as national parks, national monuments, or national recreation areas—because of their scenic beauty. The Plateau is home to such wonders as Zion National Park, Bryce Canyon National Park, the Grand Canyon, and Canyonlands National Park. When it comes to erosion, this region's geology beckons a closer look.

In your library or bookstore, peruse any publications showing pictures of the American Southwest (*Arizona Highways Magazine, Islands in the Sky, Tony Hillerman Country,* John Blaustein's *The Hidden Canyon*, Time-Life books, and so on). Many places in this region boast fascinating land formations that are worth studying.

How did this type of land come into being? Once, the entire area was under water, which deposited layer upon layer of sedimentary rock. Eventually, the water receded. That was the beginning—layers of rocks.

Then along came some source of erosion—more water. Combine that with vast amounts of time, some wind, and Earth's gravity, and *voilà!* Layer cake geology!

How are canyons formed? At the base of the canyon is usually a river (or wash or arroyo). Depending on the hardness of the rock that the water cuts through, different types of canyons are formed. Figure 16.10 shows different types of valleys formed by erosion, depending on the hardness of rock. The darker substance is hard rock; the lighter substance is soft rock. Hard-rock valleys are narrow and

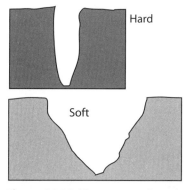

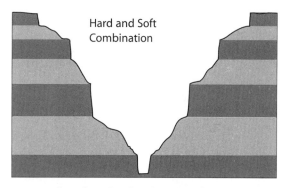

Figure 16.10 Three types of eroded valleys: narrow valleys from hard rock; wide valleys from soft rock; stair-step canyons from alternating layers of rock.

V-shaped; soft-rock valleys are wide and V-shaped. Valleys with alternating layers of hard and soft rock are called stair-step canyons.

Soft Rock

Water cutting through soft rock will make canyons shaped like a wide V. As the water washes away portions of the ground, higher rock breaks off and follows gravity's inexorable pull down to the water source, where it is washed away. The process continues, deepening and widening the V-shaped valley.

Making Soft-Rock Valleys in Bryce

To make Bryce create soft-rock canyons, you don't have to do much to change the default terrains. Use the Terrain Editor's Filtering tool to make the canyon walls the shape that you want them. That little diagonal line in the Filtering tool is like a cutaway side view of the shape of the mountain or valley (see Chapter 8, "Terrains, Symmetrical Lattices, and the Terrain Editor " for more details on this). Since it's already V-shaped (well, half of a V-shape), you don't have to do much else to shape it that way. To make the valley broader, stretch out the terrain using the Resize controls on the Edit Palette. In Figure 16.11, a terrain was widened via the Edit controls to make a wider valley.

Figure 16.11 Soft-rock V-valley.

Hard Rock

Over time, water acts like a saw, digging a deep gulch into the rock. Canyons formed in hard rock will be deep, narrow, and V-shaped. Water cuts through just the one section of rock, but the newly exposed rock is more resistant to erosion. See Figure 16.10 for a side view diagram of this type of hard-rock valley.

Making Hard-Rock Valleys in Bryce

Set up your Bryce scene in one of two ways. You can try to get the hard rocky valley effect using only one terrain. But there will probably not be enough terrain detail once you put your camera in there. So try the second alternative; set up multiple terrains, where each terrain is a portion of the deep gorge walls. Four terrains, two on each side, is a good start. You may want to use more if your scene calls for it.

The scene in Figure 16.12 was created to resemble that kind of canyon. The terrains are all set up sideways to represent the canyon walls. From the camera angle, you're not even able to see the canyon's rims, so no terrains are placed there.

Figure 16.12 Hard-rock canyon with vertical walls was created by standing a set of terrains sideways.

Vertical Cliffs

Vertical cliffs are formed in rock that is generally hard but which has softer areas. As water cuts through an area where the softer rock is under some hard rock, the softer rock is worn away, undercutting the harder layer of rock above. The weight of the rock causes the overhanging area to break off, thereby forming a sheer vertical surface.

Making Vertical Cliffs in Bryce

Form vertical cliffs using the Filtering tool. You can also create cliffs by putting in a vertical drop-off using the Filter tool. Drag the cursor so that there's a vertical drop off.

You can also exaggerate vertical cliff faces by enlarging the terrain on the y axis.

Stair-Step Canyons: Mix-and-Match Rocks

In the formation of sedimentary rock, multiple layers of different types of rock were deposited at different times under different conditions. When water cuts through more than one layer of rock, each layer erodes in its own way. Where hard rock alternates with soft rock, the manner of erosion alternates as well. Hard rock erodes to form vertical cliff formations; soft rock erodes in gentle sloping formations. The resulting series of straight cliffs interspersed with gentler slopes forms a stair-step canyon. See Figure 16.10 for a side view diagram. The most famous example of a stair-step canyon is the Grand Canyon.

Making Stair-Stepped Terrain in Bryce

Figure 16.13 shows the process of creating a stair-stepped canyon. The canyon begins with a meandering river (see Figure 16.13a). The Terrain Editor coaxed it into a broader terrain with a click on the Erode button (see Figure 16.13b). After the basic shape was created, the terrain was inverted. Then the terrain was

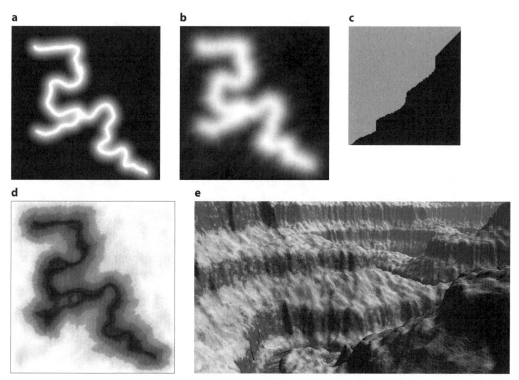

Figure 16.13 Creating a stair-step canyon: a) Beginning with a meandering river; b) using Erode to broaden the terrain in the Terrain Editor; c) stair-step filtering on the inverted terrain; d) resulting terrain map; e) final rendered canyon.

stair-stepped by an application of the Filtering control (see Figure 16.13c) to result in the terrain map shown in Figure 16.13d. With materials and haze, Figure 16.13e is the rendered result.

Volcanoes

Earlier, we discussed volcanoes as one way new mountains are born. A volcano can be the beginning of the mountain's life. Later, after time and erosion have worn down the volcanic combination of hard and soft rock, a different type of volcanic terrain develops. The hard and soft rock are a result of the volcanic birth. The volcano erupts, spewing material everywhere. The channel through which lava passes is called a root, or throat. Molten magma that subsided back into the throat, never erupting, is harder than the surrounding pile of volcanic debris. Over time the surrounding apron of debris from the outer volcano erodes away, leaving the now-solid core of harder rock that remained in the neck. That becomes a cylindrical high plateau or spire.

Shiprock in New Mexico and other dramatic vertical rocks of the American Southwest are ancient volcano plugs. Make your own by using the Subcontours control and the Filtering tool in the Terrain Editor. Figure 16.14a shows a volcanic plug scene and 16.14b, the subcontoured terrain that created it.

a
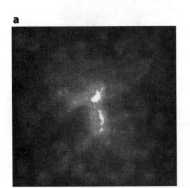

b

Figure 16.14 Volcanic plugs: a) Terrain map with Subcontours applied; b) the rendered scene.

MULTIPLE TERRAINS

The earlier discussion of multiple terrains focused on the use of several different-sized terrains placed in different locations in order to create a sense of depth and scale in the scene. But there is also a way to use multiple terrains in close proximity with one another for a different natural effect. Portions of one terrain protrude from another to create realistic image detail: stones scattered over a landscape; high-relief cliff faces emerging from a gradually sloping valley; rock formations that jut at an angle—all can be created by popping one terrain out of another. The element common to all is one terrain emerging from another. There are peculiarities with each, the lurid details of which we will divulge in these pages.

Stones 'n' Water

This first technique allows you to scatter stones across a landscape or plop them in shallow water. The foreground of *Fjord Mud* was created this way. Various rock elements protrude from the water. The stones are in a separate terrain positioned under the main water plane, or the main terrain. (Spain has nothing to do with it, 'enry 'iggins!) The stone terrain varies in height. It is lower in most places, except, of course, where the stones pop through the top. Figure 16.15 is a side view diagram of two terrains. The stone terrain pokes through the main one.

Figure 16.15 Side view of one terrain poking out of another.

Terrain Stone Shaping

There are two things necessary for creating nice boulder-like stones: The stones should have a pleasing rounded shape, and they should be distinct from one another. To create the rounded shape, your terrain map should have diffused blotches of gray. If your G2H map has points of light, you will create pointy rocks, which won't be as convincing. So, to make stones that *are* convincing, use a few specific Terrain Editor tricks.

1. Create a terrain. In the Terrain Editor, enlarge it to at least 256.

2. To get your diffused patches of gray, try applying Mounds or Subplateaus (or both). Subplateaus has a definite left-creep effect on the terrain. To put the

terrain back in the center again, activate the Zoom area, position the marquee so it occupies most of the Terrain Canvas area—but is on the right—and then click the Fit button. Deactivate the Zoom area.

3. Follow with an application of Subcontours to make the stones distinct.

The areas in between stones are darker, making each one "freestanding." The rendered result of this process is shown in Figure 16.16.

Of course, another way to create stones is to take that ol' paintbrush and put a dollop of light gray or white pixels on each place that you desire a rock to be. For the squarish boulder-like effect, pass your rocks through that Subplateau control, or use a Photoshop-compatible filter to diffuse and lighten the terrain. (Working in Photoshop, use a Diffuse filter with a Lighten mode.)

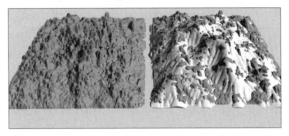

Figure 16.16 A stony terrain ready to poke above water or another terrain.

Obviously, there is more than one way to create stone boulders. Consider this a starting point and don't ignore the little leanings that strike you along the way.

Angled Terrains

Not all rock formations are conveniently vertically oriented; some rocks jut from the ground at an angle. If you rotate the terrain to put it at an angle, you'll get the very unrealistic result of the higher edge poking out from the ground. Not cute. Here's a method to get around that high edge: Create the elusive angled terrain *with overhangs*. The secret to making terrains with angled orientations is in the Edit Palette.

Recipe for a Terrain Overhang

1. Create a terrain (see Figure 16.17a).

2. In the Edit Palette, check to see that you're working in World Space. Rotate the terrain along the z axis so that the terrain is tilted diagonally as you look at it from the front (see Figure 16.17b).

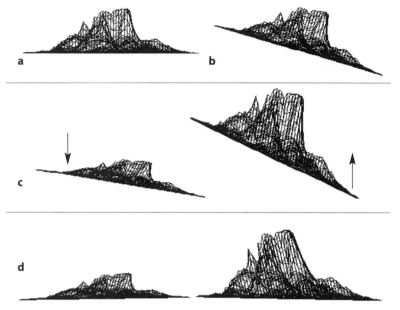

Figure 16.17 Creating an overhang: a) Beginning terrain; b) rotated; c) short-ened or heightened; d) rotated back to level.

3. Shorten or heighten the terrain along the *y* axis (see Figure 16.17c). Shortening and heightening cause the terrain to lean in opposite directions.

4. Rotate back on the *z* axis so that the bottom of the terrain is level again (see Figure 16.17d). Notice that the peaks of your mountain are all drooping toward one side. Instant overhang!

The more you rotate the terrain before changing it along the *y* axis, the more extreme the terrain's angle will be (see Figure 16.18). The parts of the figure are marked a, b, c, and d to match the steps from the previous recipe.

Look at angled terrains from another angle, all you Photoshop fans. Take a terrain map into Photoshop and apply the Wind filter. The resulting terrain map is lighter on one side than another (see Figure 16.19a). This creates a leaning geological for-mation of another sort (see Figure 16.19b). If you have the KPT 3 Lens f/x filter, try the Smudge with a Lighten Only or Screen apply mode to obtain a similar directional result.

For the terrain's surface appearance, give the 3D Solid Texture an angled setting. Rotate the noise in the Deep Texture Editor's Set Noise dialog box to shift the grain to an angle.

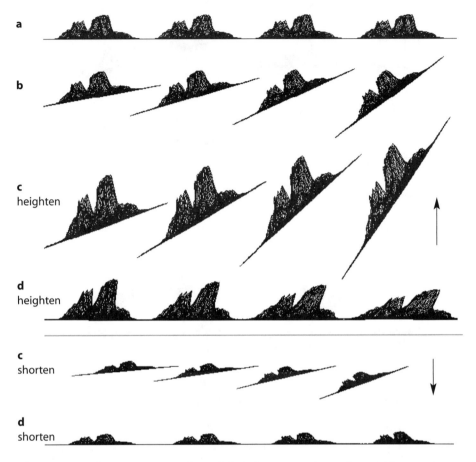

a

b

c
heighten

d
heighten

c
shorten

d
shorten

Figure 16.18 The more extreme the rotation, the more extreme the resulting overhang.

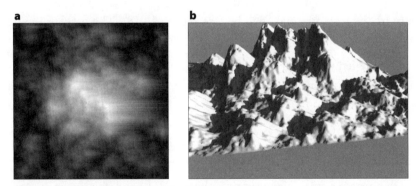

a   b

Figure 16.19 a) Photoshop's Wind filter applied to a terrain, resulting in b) an angled effect.

Finally, take any of these terrains and plop them under a regular terrain for those jutting rock protrusions (see Figure 16.20).

If you have Play's Amorphium, you can export your terrain from Bryce into Amorphium and distort its shape, then bring your distorted terrain back into Bryce again. Of course, once you export a terrain, it's no longer a terrain but a mesh, which you cannot edit further in the Terrain Editor.

Figure 16.20 Jutting rocks: an angled terrain placed below another terrain.

UNDERSEA WORLDS

One of the disadvantages of being creatures with lungs is that we don't have the same opportunities to observe undersea landscapes as we do mammal-inhabiting landscapes. But don't let this prevent the Jacques Cousteau fans among you from creating undersea scenes. There are a few things to bear in mind while you create exotic waterlogged vistas.

The undersea world has two limits: the sea floor below and the water's surface above. When creating undersea worlds with Bryce, use these two objects to provide the limits of your watery world: the ground primitive becomes the sea floor, and an infinite plane becomes the surface water above. Add terrains to taste. Terrains that go above the surface of the infinite plane are all the more convincing.

Use Sky & Fog settings to make your sea look as realistic as possible. Set them to make your undersea world cool and murky. Besides water, there are plankton, minerals, and nutrients suspended in this liquid soup! A crystal-clear "sky" won't create the right impression. A high Haze setting (70 or more) will give everything its proper briny appearance. Adjust Altitude (Cloud Height) and, in the Sky Lab, Haze's Base Height to fine-tune your haze. Even on a clear day, you can never see forever underwater. Haze Color is the main Sky & Fog setting that gives your sea its color. Keep your colors on the cool side: blues, greens, olives, drab browns, purples. Crank down the saturation so that they aren't so vivid, unless, of course, you're in a tropical undersea world. Experiment with color nuances by using Color Perspective with your haze.

Combine the haze with a complementary Fog Color. Fog will cling to the sea floor, creating a second localized murk color. Give fog a high amount and low height. You needn't keep the color aqua-cool. Sandy colors and drab olives as well as deep ultramarines will give you some intriguing sea effects.

Figure C16.21 in the color section shows the same sea scene using different colors. The haze and fog amounts are constant; only the colors change.

Creating Underwater Plant Life

To create underwater plant life for your scene, you will have to coax Bryce to grow seaweed. Use primitives and wrap plant forms around them, whether they are picture textures or textures generated within Bryce's Texture Generator.

Figure 16.22 shows a series of undersea plant studies. Inverted cones, spheres, symmetrical lattices, and rocks make different types of seaweed. For each of the rock objects in the figure, there are two stone objects of the same shape and nearly identical size. The inner stone object is your normal stone. Then it is duplicated and enlarged ever-so-slightly. The outer rock is given a seaweed mossy plant material, with alpha-driven transparency so that the rock underneath shows through.

Figure 16.22 Seaweed studies.

A RIVER RUNS THROUGH IT

To make a meandering river, create a fairly flat terrain, then use the Terrain Editor's brush tool to paint a rambling path through the terrain. Or copy your Terrain Canvas to the Clipboard and open it in Photoshop or some other image editor and paint your river there. Remember, water doesn't usually travel in a straight line, unless California Civil Engineers have built concrete channels to contain it. Left to its own, water usually meanders.

Figure 16.23a shows an image created from a Julia Set in the KPT Fractal Explorer. The wireframe and the Julia Set river source are shown in Figure 16.23b. A Julia Set has the right S-shapes for a river. After a bit of cleanup, it was made into a terrain, where a river ran through it!

a

b

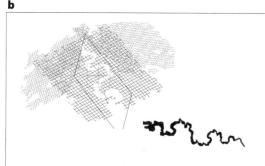

Figure 16.23 River created from Julia Set: a) Rendered image; b) top view wireframe and Julia set source.

For the riverbed terrain, the darker part is the river. Create a plane in the scene. Stretch it out to fill the same area as the riverbed. The plane becomes the river surface. Lower it into the river terrain.

If you've got a waterfall in your scene, then this method won't work. For a river that turns into a waterfall, you'll have to create the water surface from a terrain. A copy of the land terrain is a good place to start, as it will follow the contours of that particular area. Here's a very quick description of the waterfall terrain. A thorough recipe can be found in Chapter 8, "Terrains, Symmetrical Lattices, and the Terrain Editor."

Give your waterfall terrain two flat levels. The higher level is the water surface before the fall, and the lower level is the pool or river below. To fit the waterfall or a limited body of water snugly in your terrain, you'll need to clip off the unused portions of the terrain (see Figure C16.24 in the color section).

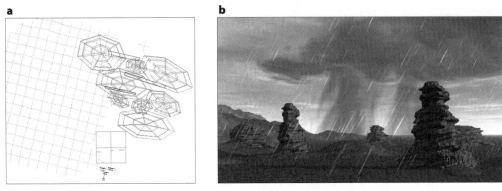

Figure 16.25 *Rainy Day*: a) Top view wireframe; b) rendered scene. *Art by Eric Wenger.*

RAINY WEATHER

How can it rain a world that lives inside your computer? It will be sufficient if you provide evidence that it's raining. Here are a few tips. (If you want a source of weather ideas, get *The Peterson Field Guide: Atmosphere: Clouds, Rain, Snow, Storms*, by Vincent J. Schaefer and John A. Day, published by Houghton Mifflin.) To create sheets of rain that fall from your clouds, create a plane (not an infinite plane or an airplane!). Give it a material setting with a 2D Picture texture; you'll find some on the CD-ROM. A nice, smudgy image makes a good picture texture for your sheets of rain. This scene by Eric Wenger (see Figure 16.25) uses grayscale PICT images to create rain smudges.

The 2D Picture texture is used again as its own Opacity Map. With alpha-driven Transparency to cut away the excess, you have a rain smudge. The top view of the image (Figure 16.25a) shows the placement of the weather-smudge rain sheets amidst the clouds.

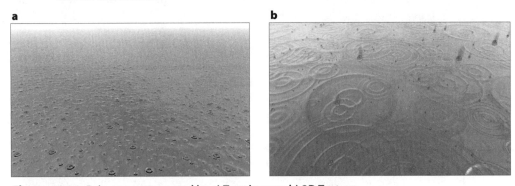

Figure 16.26 Rain on water created by a) Terrain map; b) 3D Texture.

If you want to create rain falling on a watery surface with puddle drops, then use the KPT Gradient designer to create concentric circles. Or if you're feeling really adventuresome, try creating the raindrop effect in the Deep Texture Editor. Figure 16.26 shows two different solutions using pictures and texture means to create droplets on the water's surface.

USGS MAPS G2H INFORMATION

If you want to create superlative nature imagery, how about recreating real places? Render real terrains from actual places on Earth! The USGS has created DEMs (Digital Elevation Models) for the United States, which can be converted to grayscale information in order to make terrains or imported directly into Bryce as mesh objects. See Chapter 8 for more information.

THE GREENING OF BRYCE

Why is it so hard to make a tree look natural in Bryce? You may have noticed by now that Bryce does not have an icon for a tree in the Create Palette. You have some precreated greenery in the Object libraries, and the ability to import 3D objects, and there are software applications that specialize in 3D foliage: TreePro, by Onyx, and Tree Druid (Win only), by Zenstar. They create all manner of foliage, however expensive in render time. To create trees that have as much depth and detail as the rest of the objects in Bryce you'd need to be able to model all of the different surfaces of foliage. For a tree with thousands of leaves, that is a lot of computation.

There are more options for creating foliage besides the render-intensive TreePro/Tree Druid method. The lack of tree tools within Bryce has spurred Brycers on to find new ways to introduce virtual chlorophyll for ray-tracing photosynthesis in Bryce. Here are a few methods:

- *Terrain Forest.* If you're looking at a faraway scene, you can create a terrain with many pointy spires to emulate a forest of trees. Use the Terrain Editor's Sharpen feature or the Spikes control. Have the spiky terrain poke out through the surface of another terrain for large patches of forest. The terrain map in Figure 16.27a resulted in the rendered forest shown in Figure 16.27b.

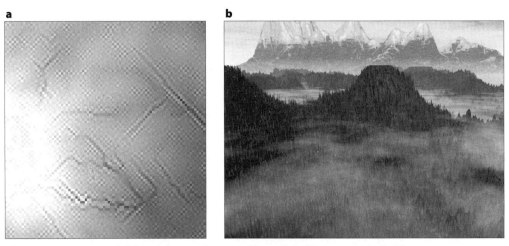

Figure 16.27 *Four Aest:* a) Terrain map for trees; b) rendered image. *Art by Kai Krause.*

- *Variation on a Terrain Forest.* Use a terrain or a symmetrical lattice to create tree shapes. In the scene *African After Dream*, Eric Wenger used both (see Figure 16.28a). A symmetrical lattice used for the trees in the fore- to mid-ground provides the full shape of the foliage crown. The no-texture render of this scene shows the shape of the objects more clearly than the final textured render (see Figure 16.28b). The symmetrical lattice and the other terrains (which are more or less the same shape and clipped at the bottom) all share a material created from a 3D texture, complete with transparency for the foliage appearance.

Figure 16.28 *African After Dream:* a) Rendered scene without textures; b) rendered with textures. *Scene by Eric Wenger.*

- *Picture-based Greenery.* In this technique, Sandy Birkholz brought specimens of an Oregon rainforest into Bryce for this scene called *Gorge Creek* (see Figures C16.29 and 16.30). She uses either a digital camera or a film camera to make her foliage shots. Ideal shooting conditions are on overcast days,

Figure 16.30 *Gorge Creek* foliage study: a) Rendered scene; b) wireframe view of scene; c) terrain map; d) image used in terrain and for terrain's texture; e) Picture library for scene; f) scene rendered without textures. *Art by Sandy Birkholz.*

which provide more uniform lighting. Shadows are soft. If an overcast day cannot be procured, then Sandy recommends shooting in the shade. She then uses her pictures twice in Bryce. First, the picture is the basis for a terrain. She generally avoids retouching the photo before importing as a terrain, using the picture-generated terrain as is. Second, the terrain's material is the same picture, mapped using Parametric mode. So the picture that creates the terrain's shape is then mapped onto that terrain. Sandy doesn't attempt to isolate one plant by extensive alpha-channel creation; instead, she just lets 'em all exist side by side. Her picture resolution is roughly 512 × 512. She avoids placing the picture-plant objects too near the camera in Bryce; they tend deteriorate into pixelated messes (perhaps exacerbated by the fact that the terrain is based on the picture, too). Scene files constructed using this method are rather large since they're chock-full of so many terrains and picture textures.

- *Picture Trees.* You can take a picture of a tree, cut out the nontree parts with an alpha-channel mask, and assign it to a plane in your scene. Of course, you will need to be facing in the direction of the tree. Setting the 2D object to track the camera will ensure that the tree picture does face the viewer. Or, take the same plane and create several copies that all rotate around the common center. Figure 16.31a is a set of wireframe planes, also shown in top view (Figure 16.31b). The Picture Library shows how the alpha mask cuts away the extraneous nontree area (see Figure 16.31c) to result in a final rendered tree image (see Figure 16.31d). Eric's *Abisko Pine Trees* uses this method. Some individual trees in *African After Dream* also use this method to create the trunk, with additional foliage pictures mapped to the top of spheres to create the branches and leaves of the tree.

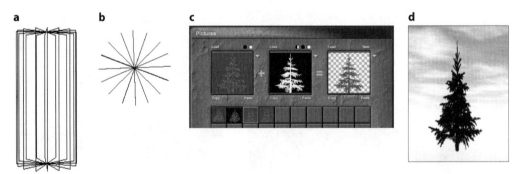

Figure 16.31 *Abisko Pine Trees*: a) Wireframe from main and b) top view; c) Picture Library with trees and their masks; d) rendered tree.

- *Terrain Trees.* This method, similar to the Picture Tree method just described, has been around since the early days of Bryce. Susan first saw the solution posed by Andrew Penick. A cone serves as the trunk, and small terrains make the branches on trees with picture images (see Figure 16.32). Penick has focused on smaller-scale horticulture in the scene, *Bushes*. Very low resolution terrains (set to 16)

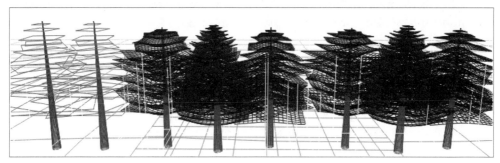

Figure 16.32 Andrew Penick's terrain tree collection.

provide the shape; the leaves are a picture texture. By the time all the terrains are assembled (see Figure 16.33), the number—and results—are quite staggering, as you can see in Figure C16.34.

- *Painting Trees.* Paint your own trees, whether as an after-the-render post-process, or as a before-the-render element for the scene. Dennis Berkla's *The Garden Hose* uses Corel Painter's Image Hose as a means to get foliage elements onto a digital canvas. It is a good resource for creating foliage elements.

a
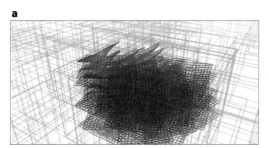

b
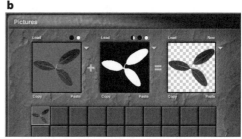

Figure 16.33 The making of *Bushes*, by Andrew Penick: a) A detail view of the wireframe; b) picture texture.

BRYCE STAR GALACTICA

Although Bryce's original purpose was to make outdoor scenery, with a click and a drag here and there on the Sky & Fog Palette, you can have instant outer-space Brycescapes.

Recipe for Space Scenes

This recipe walks you through the steps to create space scenes. You'll make a multi-sphere planet world and a planet with rings.

For space scenes to be convincing, your planets must live inside a hostile environment, maybe even one that's devoid of atmosphere. That's easy enough to arrange, as follows:

1. In the Sky & Fog Palette, under the Sky Mode pop-up menu, select the No Atmosphere option. Then use the color swatch to select the color for your Sky Backdrop. Black or extremely deep colors are good.

2. For Fog and Haze, you have a few options. Set them to zero for "deep space." Or use them judiciously to create some additional color. If you do include haze, you will need to position your objects and camera angle so that you miss the horizon. Aim the camera up somewhat. Then choose a nice dark, rich color for haze, just to add a sense of mystery. Likewise, with fog, take the *height* all the way to maximum and make the *amount* rather small. Choose a deep color for the fog and watch it mix with the haze.

Create your planets with sphere primitives. Your planet system can be as easy as one-two-three:

• *One* is a solitary sphere, the planet itself, devoid of atmosphere.

• *Two* is a planet with rings, where the second sphere is larger, yet squashed to be nearly flat.

• *Three* is a planet with atmospheric conditions—the planet sphere, the cloud layer sphere, and the diffuse atmosphere layer sphere.

Solitary Sphere

We'll focus first on the settings for the planets and then discuss the two- and three-sphere systems.

Start with the initial sphere, your planet. Now, "Make it so!" via the Materials Lab, as follows:

1. Set the Shading mode to either Normal Shading or Additive in the Material Options pop-up menu.

2. Establish settings in the Illumination (Value) channels. No Ambience. Lots of Diffusion and some Specularity. Your planet is not self-illuminating; it is lit by the major stellar light source. In some cases you may want to have lots of Specularity with brightly lit Specular Halo (see Step 5 for more about this).

3. For Optics, make sure Reflection and Transparency are off. (If your planet has water on it that is somewhat reflective and your Alpha is set for reflection, then set Reflection low for greater realism.)

4. By all means, put a bit of Bump Height in there! Keep it subtle, though, because by the time you get into outer space, the difference in elevation between Death Valley and Mount Everest appears negligible.

5. If your color is driven by a Texture Source, then let the texture drive both Diffuse and Specular color. Maximize the Specular Halo for high contrast between lit and shaded parts of the planet.

Two-Sphere Planet—Saturn Rings

Now that you have your first sphere—your planet, duplicate it (or create another sphere) to make your rings. Enlarge it proportionally so that it extends considerably beyond the planet itself. Reduce it along the *y* axis to flatten it, then rotate it to a jaunty angle. Next, you need to create some type of ring pattern on it. Some parts will be transparent and others will be "ring-y." You need an alpha channel arrangement of some sort in order to create transparency. There are two ways to use alpha-driven Transparency in the Materials Lab: with a 2D Picture and with a 3D Texture.

2D Picture Texture

To create an alpha channel, you need to make a mask for transparency. You can create a color layer to color the rings—or not—but you definitely need an alpha mask. Use the KPT Gradient Designer to make one.

It's possible to make a 2D Picture and mask; however, you'll find that it requires too much going back and forth—from the application you use to create the mask, to Bryce, to the object, back for more refinements of the image, and so on. You'll also need to set your image resolution high enough so that the rings aren't affected by antialiasing at the curved edges.

However, if you're adept at using the Deep Texture Editor (and since you've a guide in Chapter 10, you will be!) then use the following method, 3D Texture, because you can perfect your planet rings without ever leaving Bryce.

3D Texture

In the Materials Preset Library, find the preset Wild & Fun > Dali Bee Stripes—it has stripy yellow lines (see Figure 16.35a). Figure 16.35b shows an example of this preset.

a

This preset is a good starting place, because it already has stripes and Alpha Transparency to cut out the other half of the stripes. When applied to the flattened sphere, it makes a good start for rings. With a few adjustments and some noodling, you'll have your rings. The specifics of the noodling is presented as a tutorial, "Recipe for the Ringed Planet Material Adjustment," toward the end of Chapter 10, "Material World II: Picture Textures and the Deep Texture Editor."

b

Figure 16.35 Planet rings: a) Dali Bee Stripes preset; b) planet rings created from that preset.

Three-Sphere Planet—Planet, Clouds, and Atmosphere

This planet and atmosphere world comprises three spheres set inside each other: the planet proper, a cloud layer atop the planet, and a fuzzy atmospheric layer.

1. Start with your basic planet, select it, and duplicate twice. You now have three spheres (even though it appears that you have one).

2. Select only one sphere: Control/Ctrl-click the spheres to elicit a pop-up menu from which to choose one of the three. Make that sphere slightly smaller using the Proportional Resize tool on the Edit Palette. This will be the planet's surface. Name the sphere (planet sphere) and assign it its own family (wireframe color) so that you can tell easily which sphere is which.

3. Select another sphere and enlarge it using Proportional Resize. Name it (atmosphere) and assign it to a unique family. This sphere will be your atmosphere layer.

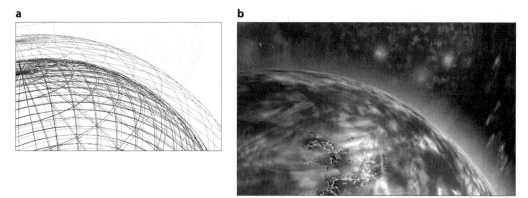

Figure 16.36 Three-sphere planet world: a) Wireframes for the planet, cloud layer, and atmosphere layer; b) rendered image.

Figure 16.36 shows (a) wireframes and (b) the resulting render of a three-sphere planet.

You now have three spheres. The one you didn't change is your cloud layer. Inside that is your actual planet. Outside both of those is your outer atmospheric sphere.

Now what about the Materials settings for each? All of your spheres have a planet Materials setting (assuming you created one following the previous steps). Now you need to change the settings for the outer two spheres to cloud and fuzzy atmosphere, respectively.

Clouds

The cloud layer sits just outside of the planet's edges. The 3D Texture called Atmosphere (in the pop-up menu from one of the four Texture Sources) is a good one for providing clouds, as are any of the other cloudy ones (Stratus, Cumulus, Low Smog, TurboCloud).

- *Shading Mode.* Normal.

- *Illumination (Value).* Lots of Diffusion, some Specularity, and no Ambience (well, maybe an eensy bit, but clouds don't show up when in shadow).

- *Optics.* You'll want to see the planet underneath the cloud layer, so there will be some Transparency. In this case, Transparency is driven by the texture. Thin out the cloud layer by adding more Transparency (using the slider) to taste.

- *Color.* Global uniform color using the swatches. For clouds, they should be white (or another color if you want your clouds to be a strange alien-world color).

Atmosphere

This is the little extra glowing part, where the atmosphere extends beyond the planet's surface.

- *Shading Mode*. Fuzzy Additive (the edge of the atmosphere is not crisply defined and the atmosphere glows).

- *Illumination*. High Diffusion, low Ambience, Specularity to taste. (All are global illumination settings.)

- *Optics and Bump*. Some Transparency, depending on how strong an atmosphere you want.

- *Color*. Choose a color for your atmosphere.

Add some space effects in one or more infinite planes for stars and intergalactic phenomena. Then render.

MOVING ON...

From scenic nature on Earth to nature outer space, you've been culling all your Bryce skills to make your own virtual nature scenery. This chapter only scratched the surface of what can be done. In the next chapter, be inspired by the work of other Brycers as we present Bryce Eye Candy.

CHAPTER SEVENTEEN

Bryce Eye Candy

IN THIS CHAPTER...

- Still Images by the Pros

- Animation Examples

For most of this book's discussion of Bryce, we've been focusing carefully on one aspect at a time, delving into all there is to know about camera, or editing, or terrains, or materials, or lights, and so forth. It's been necessary to look through a magnifying glass at each section individually in order to understand how the software works. In the previous chapter, we stopped for a bit, stepped back, and looked around at what goes into making good nature imagery. This final chapter continues the previous chapter's work of integrating all those pieces and parts into a cohesive whole. We offer for your delectation Bryce Eye Candy and present work done by Bryce artists, both still images and animation. In our discussion of each image, you'll recognize techniques described elsewhere in this book (and even some departures!). When working on a scene, the Bryce artist isn't thinking only about terrains or only about primitive object modeling, or only of skies or only lighting. Although it's true that in particular images, one or two features of Bryce may dominate, in the end, in complete works, all the different aspects of generating scenes work together to create the final image.

STILL IMAGE LANDSCAPES

We begin our tour of Bryce imagery with the kind of landscape images that Bryce is most noted for, offering some classic landscapes from space and from Earth.

David Palermo—*Alien Starburst*

http://www.davidpalermo.com/

Alien Starburst (see Figure C17.1 in the color section) is a dramatic other-worldly landscape, thanks to a combination of work in Bryce and in Photoshop. To create the leaning land formations, David rotated terrains and then resized them in World Space to give them that shear. The other object in the composition is a water plane in the foreground with aqua-colored Specularity. The most dramatic part of the scene, the sky changing from purple to green, is the result of both Bryce sky work and some Photoshop tweaking. David chose the Custom Sky Mode, with different hues for Sky Color and Sun Glow Color. The colors in the original Bryce render were more subtle than what you see here, ranging from an aqua blue to green. In addition, very low amplitude cumulus clouds contributed another color to the sky. When David brought the completed render into Photoshop, he used Levels to adjust the image, and the result after clicking the Auto button was so dramatic and pleasing that he accepted the unplanned result. The starburst patterns were applied using a Knoll Starburst filter in Photoshop.

Martin Murphy

http://www.netcom.ca/~m.murphy

If you have Bryce, you've seen Martin Murphy's work; the image on the product box is his creation. We show one of his works in color and one in black and white.

Old Shore

Martin created *Old Shore* (see Figure C17.2) entirely in Bryce 4 as an illustration for a magazine that was reviewing the software. In the foreground is a terrain and several rocks, plus some trees. The rocks came from object presets, the trees and grasses came from object presets or from the Content CD-ROM that ships with Bryce 4. After placing the foliage in the scene, Martin ungrouped and individually placed the plants and trees. He removed some of the branches that made the trees too bushy, moving leaves into the lower left corner of the scene. Martin spent a lot

Figure 17.3 *Ansel Tribute. Scene by Martin Murphy,* ©1999

of time working on the distant mountains, which are comprised of some six or
seven terrains. In order to get that sharp drop-off appearance, he chopped sides off
in the Terrain Editor using the circular brush and then painted the terrain with
low elevation. He duplicated the left terrain and placed it on the right. For the
atmosphere, Martin used Color Perspective to generate a blue haze in the background without sucking the life out of the foreground oranges and reds.

Ansel Tribute

The Ansel Tribute (see Figure 17.3) is a scene Martin created as an exploration of
volume clouds. His goal was to generate classic, romantic puffy clouds in Bryce.
He worked first with three very large spheres for volume clouds, with perhaps a

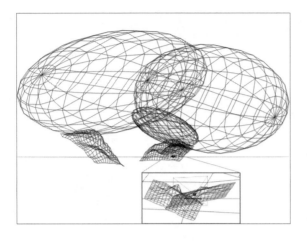

Figure 17.4 Side view of Ansel tribute scene with an inset showing the camera in more detail; note the size of the cloud spheres compared with the terrains and camera.

single gratuitous terrain in his scene. See the final scene file in top view wireframe in Figure 17.4. Getting the clouds to look just so took a lot of time; Martin worked on a laptop while watching TV, working over the course of a couple of days. He made an adjustment and let it render. "Nope, that's not it," he said and made another adjustment. "Nope. Hmm, try that." He made most of his adjustments to the Frequency in the Edit Texture controls in the Materials Lab and to the material's Base Density. Once the clouds were set, he worked on the terrains. There are four terrains, one of which was put through an application of the KPT Swirl filter. The terrains poke out from one another, and the snow material frequency is slightly different than that of the rocks.

The scene that Martin worked on all this time was a color scene, with soft golds and a very light blue sky. It was also a horizontal aspect ratio, as the wireframe window in Figure 17.4 shows; he compressed it all into a vertical format in order to get more dramatic puffiness out of the clouds. The final render contained one unfortunate seam from an application of the Sawtooth control in the Terrain Editor, which Martin sought to fix in Photoshop. As he looked at each of the RGB channels of the image, saw a gorgeous grayscale image reminiscent of Ansel Adams. And the rest, as they say, is history.

Chris Pappathan—*Alaskan Spring*

http://people.ne.mediaone.net/cpapp

Alaskan Spring (see Figure C17.5) was inspired by a commercial about a documentary on Alaska. The shape of the shoreline and the deep coastline inspired Chris to make the image in Bryce. He deliberately chose an image composition that had a foreground (the trees), midground (the smooth rolling snow-covered hills), and a background (the tall, snow-covered mountains). The foreground trees were Bryce preset trees. He spent the most time getting the distant mountains to work. The snow and terrain was not created by applying materials, but by working with two different terrains, one being the mountain and the second, the snow. The long stripes of snow and rock on the mountain peaks and valleys are the result of artfully combining the two terrains. In fact, there are three terrains in this scene—the third one had spikes applied, which became the pine trees in the midground. Figure 17.6 is a side view cutaway showing how the shapes of each of the three terrains interact with one another.

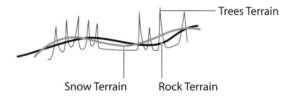

Figure 17.6 Side view cutaway representation of three terrains that make up the mountains in Chris Pappathan's *Alaskan Spring* scene: Rocky terrain, snow terrain and spiky tree terrain each poke above the surface in different ways to convey a snow-covered mountain.

WATER, WATER, EVERYWHERE

Moving from landscapes to seascapes, we explore the ways artists have portrayed water and the ever-moving boundary that lives between land and water.

Barb Ingersoll

http://members.aol.com/bjing/BJIDesigns.html

Brave Boat Harbor

This is an image (see Figure C17.7) inspired by a waterway accessed by a road of the same name. It's a shallow place; boats that venture in here are indeed brave. Barb's work on this and her other images are close-up studies of nature, and she seeks to put in as much detail as possible using leaves, rocks and mud—a pristine world is not a natural world. Bryce can create terrains with natural shapes; to get the rest of the natural phenomena, including dense foliage, the artist has to introduce detail and disorder into the environment. Barb has used various plant-based models that she disassembled after importing in order to get the right kind of plant forms. The arcing grass in the foreground of Figure C17.7, for instance, is the top of a stalk of wheat. The stalk was removed and the wheat head was positioned so that the curving spikes would become grass. Barb has gotten a lot of her plant models from the meshes available at http://www.baument.com/.

Shore

This scene (Figure C17.8) is another close-up view of a place where water meets land. Barb's work here includes lots of leaves and other things to imply debris. The group of pebbles in the center-right section of the image are, in fact, created from a 2D picture object of stones. What with the various plant models that she imports into her scenes, her Bryce file sizes grow to around 60 MB.

Water Under Water

The third of Barb Ingersoll's images (see Figure C17.9) began as a simple underwater scene. As happens so often in Bryce, during construction some part of the scene suggests something, and the artist, following that suggestion, gets taken into a flight of fancy, or whimsy as the case is here. The green "island" in the lower-center part of the image appeared, and she put trees on it. Then it simply had to have a domicile, so she added the little house. At that point, thinking from the perspective of what it would like to live there, she decided the inhabitants needed to have their own water, so she added the lake. The boat in the lake, the bridges from the green island and the nearer islands complete the view. Barb created the water's caustic appearance by putting a 2D pict object in front of the camera lens as a "filter" for us to look through onto the scene. The effect is that of watery, wavy lines. The wavy lines are white and an alpha channel makes the rest of the image transparent. An additional Global Transparency added to the picture object gives only a subtle hint of the undersea world.

Mark Longo—*Heavy Seas*

http://www.HighmarkDesign.com/

For the scene *Heavy Seas* (see Figure C17.10a), Mark Longo modeled a Tsunami buoy, set it atop a terrain, and worked with the sky and shadows to get a marvelously realistic scene. The first thing Mark said about how his image works is, "Hide the damn horizon!" though he said it with a smile in his tone. His having hidden the horizon places the viewer in the scene at the bottom trough of the wave, with no telltale horizon shouting "Hey! I was made in Bryce!" Mark comments that the composition is what makes the scene work. The composition is fairly simple: water, buoy, clouds, sky. The water is a terrain made with one of the Fractal presets. The buoy was modeled completely out of Bryce primitives, an exercise to figure out how Bryce's modeling capabilities worked. Figure C17.10 b shows a detailed view of the buoy from another scene, so you can see how it was modeled. The sky is a variation on the Afternoon Wedding Sky preset, with the cloud's Frequency and Amplitude adjusted, and with a change in sun position. Mark placed the sun at an angle to convey late afternoon sun. Notice the placement of the clouds in the sky and their reflection in the water. The one dark spot on the water might be a shadow; it's probably a reflection of a darker, clear spot in the sky. That unplanned but serendipitous patch of dark sky adds to the brooding, clouded appearance of the scene.

Mark Longo retouched the rendered image in Photoshop afterwards, taking a bit of excessive swirl out of the clouds and softening the shadow on the buoy. Take a second look at that buoy and shadow—by softening Bryce's hard-edged shadows, Longo made the dull overcast appearance convincing. Sometimes it's the very small details that make an image utterly realistic.

Ruth "Calyxa" Fry—*Rocks, Water, Sand*

http://www.chucko.com/calyxa/pearl/galleries.html

Rocks, Water, Sand (see Figure C17.11) is a straightforward seaside landscape showing a tidal area, in which the viewer's perspective is facing land from a little way out to sea, rather than looking to sea from the shore. There are five terrains and two infinite planes (ground plane, water plane). The water plane has a material whose bump is driven by an A-B-C texture. The alpha channel in C mixes a standard bump and Texture Source B's no bump, making the water flat in places. The material for the sand is also an A-B-C texture, varying between slight pink and tan-colored sand, and Texture Source D uses an altitude texture to drive Diffusion, so that the sand is darker at water's edge, appearing to be wet.

Sandy Birkholz

http://hometown.aol.com/sanbir/

Sandy Birkholz, who was trained in classical art forms, has learned from her work as a watercolorist to let the medium do the work for her. Her approach to work in Bryce is to start out in one direction and then explore from there. She's also very fond of using things—whether pictures, objects, materials or presets—in unexpected ways. In her experience, Bryce rewards that approach with contributions of its own.

Tides

The *Tides* image (see Figure C17.12) was made primarily in Bryce, with some post-work in Photoshop. The sea is a series of some eight or so terrains. Sandy first rendered the top view of a water material, and loaded that image into the Terrain Editor as the basis for a grayscale map, resulting in the waves out at sea. The sand in the foreground is a terrain with marks in it made by the bump map of a material. This scene started to take off for her when her camera was pointing at the terrain's edge with the patterns in the sand and the water nearby. She set a 2D plane with a Bubble material to make the very shallow water on the sand. There are many little details to make the seashore. The green-brown sludgy seaweed is a sphere with a volume material. The seafoam is made from both surface and volume cloud materials applied to flattened spheres. The rocks, unsurprisingly, are rock objects. The branching seaweed is a picture texture applied to a sphere; Sandy painted the seaweed in Photoshop. She absconded the seashells from the bra of a Poser Zygote mermaid figure, and gave them a Bryce procedural material. The tiny bubbles are small spheres with Bubble material applied.

Woodlights

Woodlights (see Figure C17.13) is a Bryce scene whose appearance is derived mostly from picture textures. (Sandy's technique was described in the previous chapter in the section, "The Greening of Bryce.") In addition, there are terrains, rocks and trees and bushes. The bush forms are imported into Bryce; they are L-systems plants made by Bryan Smith. The tree textures are pictures, as are the water and the ferny backdrop. The scene is lit by spotlights set to Volume Visible, creating shafts of light. Sandy says it took lots of playing around to get those lights looking right. Additionally, there are little dots of light from a spotlight. The uniform color is green, and the light uses a Pict Gel with a black field and white dots. The rocks in the foreground use a mossy picture texture, with a bump map generated from the identical picture information; the mapping at the rock edges is a kind of mistake, where the texture looks stretched, but because it resembles wet hanging moss, Sandy kept it.

FANTASTIC VISIONS

Departing from scenic landscapes, we turn our attention to other forms, whether still-life images, surrealistic constructions or abstract Brycework.

Martin Murphy—*Statue*

The Statue (see Figure C17.14) is a modeling and lighting exercise based on a large (5½-foot high) statue in Martin Murphy's home. He plunked his PowerBook down on a table facing the statue and went to work modeling each and every detail of that statue. Various portions were made in Bryce, in Poser and in Ray Dream Studio. The figure is from Poser, and the hair, hat, feathers and scarf were made in Ray Dream. The terrain at the base was made in Bryce, as were the grapes and leaves. The leaves are a sphere with a picture texture with transparency and another alpha channel for a bump map. Martin made the cougar in Poser from the body of a lion and a head of a cat. He removed the cat's ears and made new ones in Ray Dream Studio. The horse is from Poser, but the mesh was augmented in Ray Dream Studio. He removed the original jaw and modeled new mesh to make an open mouth with a lower jaw. He also tweaked the mesh to make the horse's legs bonier.

The assembled model has a single material applied, a very very very dark bronze. What gives the whole thing life and dimensionality is the lighting. There are tons of lights in this scene, mostly soft, small, round spotlights that focus on one or another part of the statue and bring out the detail. The scene is lit entirely by light objects; there is no sun. There is one radial light, set to not cast shadows, in order to fill in a little detail in shadowy portions of the scene. The background wall is a simple cube, with a radial spotlight with a Dirty Wall Gel casting its light in the background.

Finally, after the scene was rendered, Martin slightly softened the hard edges of the shadow that the statue cast onto the ground.

Chaz Fricke—*Coagulation*

http://acidsky.com/

Chaz Fricke's *Coagulation* (see Figure C17.15) is an image that belongs in the category affectionately known as a "bloop," (coined by someone on the Bryce email list), an abstract Bryce image made from a volume slab and a volume material.

Bloop refers to the appearance of the volume texture. For this, Chaz worked with a variation of the Alien texture and put a radial light in the scene. The name of the scene, *Coagulation*, came from an earlier version of the scene, in which the texture was red and looked like blood. Chaz moved away from those colors with a lime-green sun, a yellow-orange sky dome and pale orange haze. The radial light in the scene is white, and the color of the texture itself changed from red to the colors you now see. The result is a fascinating abstract. Of the texture itself, Chaz says, "The beauty of volumetric textures is that, much like fractals and clouds, the deeper you look into them the more things you can see."

Mike Pucciarelli's Altered States

http://www.alteredstate.net/digital.htm

Mike Pucciarelli, who takes lots of inspiration from the works of H. R. Giger, works with painting terrains and symmetrical lattices to realize his visions in Bryce.

Lotus

The centerpiece of the *Lotus* scene (see Figure C17.16a) was constructed from several sets of symmetrical lattices, which were then duplicated to form a circular lotus. For each piece of the construction, Mike painted the form freehand in the Terrain Editor using the Elevation Brush, working against one edge of the Terrain Canvas. Duplicating and flipping and fitting together the two lattices produced the symmetry down the center of the image. Of course, each arm of the lotus was duplicated and repositioned. He used the same mirroring effect for each symmetrical lattice. The supporting structures that lie in the water were also done this way, though it's just a single set of symmetrical lattices making up each metallic petal.

Organikscape

For this scene (see Figure C17.16b), Mike created a symmetrical lattice arch, generated freehand using the Terrain Editor's Brush tool. He duplicated it and flipped it to form both left and right sides of the arch. He grouped and duplicated those in order to construct a cave, complete with a solid ceiling to block out the outside sky. He lit the scene with a radial light at one end of the cave and placed the sun as light source at the other end, and a used high Haze setting to provide the misty sense of depth. When the render was complete, he airbrushed the root-like objects in Corel Photo-Paint. As a final touch, he took the top half of the image, duplicated it and flipped it in order to create a bottom half that perfectly mirrors the top.

Techscape

Techscape is another Giger-inspired scene. (see Figure C17.16c) It's constructed from a plethora of tori and cylinders and spheres, with a background made from a terrain. The background terrain was painted in Corel Photo-Paint as a grayscale image and brought into the Terrain Editor as a picture-based terrain. The bumpy concrete-like constructions were done in the Terrain Editor by freehand painting with the Elevation Brush. Most of the objects have the same material. There is a subtle color difference from one portion of the image to another, thanks to a mostly-transparent application of KPT Noize (from KPT 5).

Ernst

Mike's *Ernst* image (see Figure C17.16d) is inspired by a painting by Max Ernst titled *The Eye of Silence*, an image of surreal, organic-looking forms with figures and embedded gems. Mike took the green color, the towering constructions and organic shapes as his inspiration. The freestanding forms were constructed from painted symmetrical lattices (except for the two pillars, which were constructed from sphere primitives). There are a couple of Poser skeletons and a female figure (also from Poser) in the scene. He adapted a material preset (Flaky Paint) that he found on the Web, changing it from red to green. The faces were painted as grayscale maps in Photo-Paint. After rendering, Mike used some of Photo-Paint's brush tools to add the texture to rocks that support the entire set of objects.

What's in a Game?—*The Shahnra Project*

http://www.phase2.net/claygraphics/Intro.html

The *Shahnra Project* is Clay Hagebusch's conceptual exploration of environments for a game he's designing. We feature several different examples of his work.

Alien Borealis

In *Alien Borealis* (see Figure C17.17), Clay composed the image so that the sky dominates the scene, with the horizon line set very low in the image. His explorations of different-looking skies prove that you *can* wish upon a star in Bryce, even during the daytime. The dramatic sky juxtaposes sun and starfield. To get starfields to appear in the daytime sky, he set the Sky Mode to Custom Sky on the Sky & Fog Palette, and chose black (or very nearly black) for the color swatches. The most important of the three color swatches is the Sky Color (the center swatch), followed by the Sun Glow color, especially when the sun is visible in the scene. The Horizon Color can be a lighter color. When stars are activated and the sky is dark enough, the stars *will* appear. Though the starfield is Bryce-generated, the bright star in the upper left was augmented in Photoshop.

Clay worked on the cloud texture in the Sky Lab, editing the texture in the Deep Texture Editor. The swirly other-worldly appearance comes from the use of Auto-Phase mode in the DTE's Noise Editor.

She Plays With Magic

She Plays With Magic (see Figure C17.18) features a Poser figure imported into a Bryce scene. The rest of the image was constructed from Bryce primitives, except for the top part of the metal railing, which was modeled in Specular Infini-D, and the bird (Poser) and the book (Infini-D). Her dress also came from Poser, but the material was created in Bryce. The background sky was created using the same technique used in *Alien Borealis*. The star twinkles and the female's hair were added in Photoshop after the render was complete. The scene is lit by two light sources, the sun and a light that the female holds in her hand. You can see the light from her hand on her face and the one foot that is positioned slightly in front of her body. The clouds surrounding the female are three spheres with cloudy volume materials.

Galahfana's Amulet

This scene depicts a close-up of an artifact in The Shahnra Project game (see Figure C17.19). The object was constructed in Bryce, except for the chain, which was modeled in Infini-D. The main body of the amulet was made with a symmetrical lattice. The shape was designed in Adobe Illustrator (check out Symbol and Dingbat fonts for shape ideas!), and with the help of Photoshop and the Terrain Editor it grew to the shape you see here. If you were to look at the object from a side view, you'd see a hemisphere shape, thanks to a judicous application of the Gaussianize control in the Terrain Editor. The center glassy part is constructed from a sphere and a cylinder. The sphere—half a sphere, actually—is clear glass, set atop a cylinder backing. The cylinder's material is a gold picture image map. The green and rust-colored spheres in the center of the amulet are constructed of two spheres each. A sphere with a metallic material is enclosed in a sphere with a glass material to get additional shine and make the objects appear more jewel-like.

Tollerè Submersible

The *Tollerè Submersible* (see Figure C17.20) is an object made entirely from Bryce primitives except for the chain, created in Infini-D. The propeller and the hooks suspending the submersible were constructed from symmetrical lattices. In case you can't see the other primitives, the rivets are spheres and there are cylinders and tori to create fittings. In addition, the scene has lots of boolean constructions. The grid-like grating on all the glass sections is made from a material with alpha-driven transparency carving out the grid from the rest of the primitive object.

For the material, Clay created an aged rusty appearance in the Deep Texture Editor, and then applied a separate picture-driven Texture Source to apply as bump that gives the metal a subtly paneled look.

The background is pure white and the ground plane is reflective water.

Timerip

Timerip (Figure C17.21) is nearly pure sky work, using the techniques described for *Alien Borealis* and *Mikkahl Desert Region* (the following scene). The ground plane is a mirror, reflecting the sky. There is one small but significant addition to the scene that gives it that fantastic touch. Clay placed a sphere in the scene that enclosed the camera. He lengthened the sphere so that it extended far out in front, and then assigned it a volume material that's a variation on the Supernova volume presets. Figure 17.22 shows the wireframe of the scene in top and Camera views.

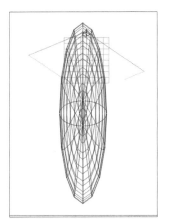
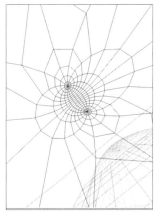

Figure 17.22 Timerip scene in wireframe view: a) Top view showing camera within elongated sphere; b) scene from camera's perspective.

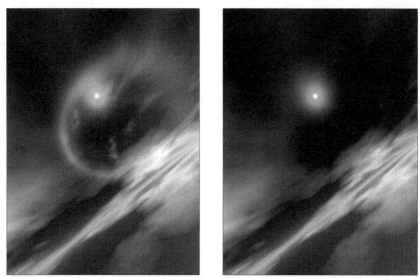

Figure 17.23 The Timerip scene: a) With and b) without the volume sphere.

Figure 17.23 compares the results when the sphere is present and when it's absent. The halo from the sphere wasn't planned, but was a happy accident.

Mikkahl Desert Region

The most notable thing about *Mikkahl Desert Region* (Figure C17.24) is the banking of the camera. There's a very wide encompassing zoom in the image composition. Clay prefers to set the scale of the 2D Projection plane to around 44 (the default is 100). Once he's zoomed out that far, he's careful of his object placement; objects positioned near the periphery of the scene will become distorted (spheres warp into oblong eggs).

Clay created the sky using the same techniques as in *Alien Borealis* and *She Plays With Magic*. In this scene you can see the result of another part of that technique, in which the stars have a hazy glow. To add the hazy glow to the stars, Clay activated Color Perspective in the Sky Lab. He set the Haze Color to match other atmospheric phenomena, and then tweaked the numbers for R, G and B to match. Equal numbers result in a gray tone and adjusting the numbers makes one or another color dominate. This technique will either call upon your mastery of RGB color theory or force you develop it.

The lens flares were added with KPT 6's Lens Flare.

Mystic's Rock

The landforms in *Mystic's Rock* (see Figure C17.25) are comprised of three terrains and one symmetrical lattice (for the arch). The landforms use the same rocky material as in *Mikkahl Desert Region*, with changes made to the texture's color. For the water (as for the water in many of Clay's scenes) he uses an infinite slab with the Caribbean Water materials preset (plus tweaks to Transparency, bump, and Specularity). Then he places an infinite cloud plane in the infinite slab, fairly close to the surface; it's the cloud plane that provides the aquatic highlights from under the water. The ground plane has the same material as the landforms.

Rocky Beach

This misty, watery scene (see Figure C17.26) is comprised primarily of terrains: a terrain for the sand, a terrain for the imposing cliff on the right, and three different terrains for the rocks piled on the beach. The sand's wet appearance is a trick done with a somewhat complex DTE texture in which the Altitude filter is output as alpha, which then drives the diffusion channel for the material. (Susan covered this technique in BryceTalk; the scene file is included on the CD-ROM, so you can figure it out for yourself.) The rocks' materials were generated in the DTE, with two noises output to color, alpha and bump. (To set the green seaweed on top of the rocks, Clay assigned the texture's lightest alpha value a green color, so that green corresponded with the highest parts of the bump map.)

Clay used haze with Color Perspective active to create a damp, drizzly mist. The Haze Color was white and the numbers for R, G, and B were identical to create a balanced white.

The fern is a 3D model that he found on the Web and assigned to it the Mediterranean Hills material preset.

PAINTERLY POST-PROCESSING

To those of you who consider yourselves to be part of the Pure Bryce school of thought, who believe that the ultimate be-all and end-all is to work in Bryce and only Bryce (well, okay, with a little 3D-modeling thrown into the Bryce scene), we cheerfully debunk that standard. Bryce is a tool. It's a powerful tool, and with it you may create amazing worlds and images, but we don't believe that you should unnecessarily restrict yourself to working solely in Bryce. Post-render touch-up is okay (Susan even did that for the book's cover image!). Using a Bryce render as the basis for a painting is okay. You have our full permission to let Bryce coexist with your other digital art tools and to make Bryce imagery that, in the end, may not look like Bryce imagery. As an example of painterly post-processing, we explore the work of Sylvia Lutnes.

Sylvia Lutnes

http://www.cricketcage.com/

Ned's Dock

In the series of four *Ned's Dock* images, Sylvia worked with a rather simple scene made up of water, a large cloud sphere, a model of a dock and boats and a boathouse. An original Bryce render of the scene is at the top left of the four images shown in Figure C17.27. Then she worked with the rendered image using Photo-Paint. She says that there's no way that she could describe the specific steps that led from a plain ol' Bryce render to her painterly results, since the process was filled with experimentation. The gist is that she took copies of the image and ran different paint-effect processes on them, and then composited a series of layers together. At any time, she may have had open several windows with various-looking treatments, combining them this way and that until she got a finished result. In addition to complex compositing of effects, she also applied hand-painting to the image, for instance, on the ropes that tie the boats to the dock. The seabirds were images added with Photo-Paint and hand-tweaked to match the rest of the scene and painting effects.

Rocky Shore

There was a minimal amount of post-processing in the *Rocky Shore* image (see C17.28). After rendering the image, Sylvia selected the sky—*sans* birds—and applied KPT Equalizer in order to enhance the contrast. Between the texture for the clouds and the contrast enhancement, it appears as though the sky might have been painted. Notice the dock and boats in this image and in the dock set of images. She imported the same 3D Studio MAX model into both scenes. Sylvia prefers simple models that she can use in different contexts, rather than a model so complex or distinctive that it draws excessive attention to itself and doesn't act as a supporting cast member to the whole environment.

Another technique that she likes to use is to render objects separately in Bryce and create additional mask renders, and then import the rendered result and mask as a 2D picture object. (Susan wholeheartedly concurs with this technique—the trees on the book's front cover were imported models from Onyx's Tree Professional, rendered in Bryce and imported into the scene as a 2D picture object.)

Eagle

The *Eagle* image shown in Figure C17.29 did not have any post-processing; Sylvia used Bryce's Sky Lab to get the appearance of the sky. She began with a scene with a wide field of view, then set the sky to Custom Color. The Sky Color is pale lavender, and black (yes!) is the Sun Glow color. The Horizon Color is a desaturated purple (rather like the dark purple of Mac OS icons). The Sun Color is orange, and the Ambient Color is a very dark gray. Haze is light blue. Those are all the color settings in the Sky & Fog Palette; but there are further interesting sky settings in Sky Lab, mostly in the Atmosphere tab. Haze Density is high—82—and Thickness is at 50. In addition, Color Perspective is active, with the default settings weighted toward blue. Finally, Blend With Sun is active (with both Color and Luminosity set to maximum), so that the blue tones of sky and haze are blended with the orange of the sun. Opposite the sun's position, the lack of sun's luminance in the haze dulls it to a dark gray. There is a stripe in between the sun-influenced haze and the dull gray haze, a vertical stripe of pure lavender—the color the sky would be all over if Blend With Sun were inactive. In the *Eagle* image, it happens to be positioned right behind the eagle. Color Perspective is what tints the mountains blue. For being a complete and utter Bryce sky, it certainly produces an amazingly painterly effect!

MARTIAN WATER IMAGES

In these images for *Scientific American*'s November 1996 issue discussing water on Mars (see Figure C17.30), Susan sought to re-create a portion of the Martian landscape, showing it at different epochs of the planet's history—at present, and in the past when Mars had plenty of water on its surface.

The scenes use actual Martian elevation data. To create the grayscale image data, Susan used the Digital Elevation Models (DEMs) that come on the CD-ROM for Vista Pro, a sister product to Bryce. (Although Vista Pro creates digital landscapes, it lacks the ray-tracing renderer, the complex sky model, and Procedural Texture Generator that give such photo-realism to Brycean rendered images, to say nothing of the interface and look and feel that give Bryce its soul.) Vista Pro was great for importing Martian DEMs and converting them to grayscale PICTs to use in Bryce. Susan imported sixteen Martian DEMs at a time, and generated a grayscale map from that information. After generating four quadrants for a large terrain map (from a total of 64 individual DEMs), she made alignment adjustments in Photoshop, and imported the resulting image to Bryce. The view is a site near the Olympus Mons (a very b-i-i-i-i-g mountain) on Mars.

Like the "One small step for man, one giant leap for mankind" statement, these images are more than dual pictures of an interesting landscape under differing climatic conditions, created with Brycean expertise. The snow-and-water image harkens back to the time when the surface of Mars was flowing with water—the dry, red planet is the planet of today. That is the small step. The giant leap is the ability to make visible what has heretofore been impossible to see. These images are a demonstration of the ability to take information gleaned from a place that no human has visited—information gathered by interplanetary explorer craft and beamed back to earth from millions of miles away. The information has made its way into a digital elevation format, which, after being converted to grayscale, becomes cloaked in a Brycean environment, where you can wander at will with the Brycean camera (or create QTVR movies to wander at will over rendered landscapes!). With Bryce as the culmination of various technologies, you are virtually taken onto the surface of our nearest neighbor planet, far, far away from our home world. The fine details of surface are left to your imagination, but you are transporting yourself to the Martian surface—or transporting the Martian surface to your computer! Beam me up!

ANIMATION

Bryce is not simply for still images, as is attested by the heft of 200 of this book's pages on animation. Following are a few examples of Bryce animation. See movies of the examples on the CD-ROM in this chapter's folder.

Infinity's Child

http://www.infinityschild.com/

First there was Third Planet Productions' *Planetary Traveler*, the first feature-length (40 minutes) animated movie created completely on desktop computers (Macs and Mac clones). It was made using several different development versions of Bryce between versions 1.0 and 2.0, and the experiences of the *Planetary Traveler* crew (of which Susan was a part) were taken into account for feature development of versions 2 and 3D of Bryce. For the sequel, *Infinity's Child*, a small portion of the original *Planetary Traveler* crew made for a more intimate production—Jan Nickman as director, Bill Ellsworth contributing and animating his Bryce worlds, animation and production by Rodney L'Ongnion, and music by Paul Haslinger. For a change, *Infinity's Child* was produced entirely on the commercially shipping version of Bryce 4 (though the original scene files date back as early as Bryce 1). Figure C17.31 shows a couple of still images from *Infinity's Child*.

Here are some technical notes on the production that are worth the attention of the ambitious Bryce animator:

- *Cross-platform work environment*. Scenes were created and animated on the Mac OS, then rendered on the Windows renderfarm. Gamma correction (Render options pop-up menu) was switched *off* during the creation and rendering of scenes.

- *Renderfarm*. There were a total of nine computers devoted to rendering scenes, 24 hours a day, seven days a week. (Multiple machines shared a common monitor, so that Rodney could switch back and forth to keep track of render progress.)

- *Render details*. In order to minimize temporal noise (an undesirable sparkly shimmer in the animation), Rodney and Bill both reduced the frequencies of noises in their materials, and, more importantly, rendered the final images at 1080×810, one-and-a-half times larger than the 720×540 resolution needed. Reducing the image size to the required resolution managed to hush much of the temporal noise.

- *Render tests*. Rodney and Bill conducted many render tests (at smaller sizes, and using the Fast Preview and Textures Off Render modes) in order to make sure that the animation was as desired. Better to have an abundance of render tests than copious piles of needless pixels on their cutting-room floor.

- *Rendered image sequences*. All movies—including render tests—were rendered as image sequences. If the electricity went out or if a render had to be stopped, the only thing lost was the current frame. (They kept their place with an interrupted render by saving the scene file with the Time Scrubber on the current frame; resuming render began at that spot.) In addition, if a sequence needed to be split up and rendered on two or more machines, rendering to image frames made that possible.

- *24 to 30 frames.* The scenes were rendered at 24 frames per second, identical to motion picture film speed. They were then converted to video using what's called a *3:2 pulldown.* There were three advantages to working this way: Fewer frames needed to be rendered, the human eye has been trained to see motion pictures in this manner, and the conversion process also aided in reducing temporal noise.

There is a movie trailer and a scene file from *Infinity's Child* on the CD-ROM in this chapter's folder. (The scene file on this book's CD-ROM came from the movie's DVD-ROM, which has several scene files that you can examine.)

Michael "renato!" Sigmon—*Rube Goldberg*

http://www.30fps.com/

Michael "renato!" Sigmon's *Rube Goldberg* movie was inspired by the board game Mousetrap, where the game-play involves constructing an elaborate mousetrap. A Rube Goldberg device works along the same lines, a convoluted series of events leading to a fairly simple end result. Michael generated all sorts of quirky workings that were put in place to accomplish a goal. A steel ball rolls along a set of double rails, tripping and triggering various other mechanical devices as it makes its way along the path. A still image of the scene is shown in Figure 17.32. He generated many motion tests of the proof-of-concept, including rolling the ball, tripping flag switches, triggering catapults, and more. (The purpose behind the *Rube*

Figure 17.32 A still image from the *Rube Goldberg* animated sequence shows the metal ball on a spiral track, while in the distance, more track and objects can be seen. ©2000 Michael "renato!" Sigmon, 30fps Video + Digital Design

Goldberg movie was to fully explore all the different concepts and workarounds for animation in Bryce.) As he continued working on his motion tests, the elaborate events leading to a simple conclusion suggested the proper ending for the movie. We won't give any spoilers here, just tell you that the proof-of-concept pushed the story to its logical conclusion. Get thee hence to the CD-ROM's folder for this chapter and see it for yourself!

The entire animation is 15 seconds in duration. All object animation took place in a master scene file. Getting all the objects animated first freed up Michael to experiment with camera shots. The advantage to this approach was that it made conditions similar to how it would be to shoot a film using a physical set. On a physical set with an actual Rube Goldberg device, once that ball is set in motion, it would follow the same path, no matter where the viewer is positioned.

Michael broke each shot into a separate scene file. Though each scene file's full duration was still 15 seconds long, he set the Working Range for each scene to include only the portion of time concerned with that shot. There were about a dozen shot variations. For any given shot, Michael sometimes finessed the object's animation to improve what was taking place during that shot.

Birth/Death Event

One technique that Michael used in this scene was not discussed in Chapters 14 and 15; it's in response to this situation: How do you deal with an object that needs to be independent in one section of the animation, and, in another section needs to be a part of a group or a linked hierarchy? Because they are states, you cannot switch groups or links off and on during the course of an animation.

The technique, a birth/death event, duplicates the object in question and pulls a switcheroo at a given frame. As with other sleights of hand, the viewer doesn't notice that the switch took place. The object that's going to die starts out in the scene, animating away until it reaches the switcheroo moment, when it's instantly whisked offstage. The object to be born waits offstage until the switcheroo moment, when it enters the scene and continues animating on its merry way. Nothing up my sleeves! From the viewer's perspective, it's all one single animated object. (This is the resurrection variety of birth/death events, since death comes before birth; you theologians talk about it among yourselves.)

Two keyframes need to be set, one for the frame immediately preceding the switcheroo, and the second for the switcheroo frame itself. Table 17.1 walks through the keyframes that need to be set in order to make a birth/death event transpire for an event that takes place at a mythical Frame 12 of an animated sequence. You can also check out the scene BOUNCE-DEATHBIRTH on the CD-ROM in this chapter's folder, in which the Bounce tutorial scene is altered to have a birth/death event.

		Object A Independent		Object B Child of a Parent Object
Frames 1–10		Animates toward position		Offstage
Frame 11		KEY in position		KEY offstage
Frame 12	Death:	KEY to offstage	Birth:	KEY to position
Frames 13–25		Offstage		Animates from position

Table 17.1 Setting keyframes for a birth/death event in order to switch two objects during an animated sequence.

Greg Moore—*Bryce Terrain Flyover*

Synergy543@aol.com

Greg Moore created four terrain flyover movies in Bryce 4 for Sony. Figure 17.33 shows small stills of each of the four animations that are on the CD-ROM. The spaceships were created by Greg's son, Aaron Moore, in Strata StudioPro, then they were imported into Bryce and had materials applied. The scene files for the series are huge, given the size of the imported DXF models and the abundance of terrains that the spaceships fly by—especially the ones in which the flyovers pass

Figure 17.33 Stills from *Bryce Terrain Flyover*. *Terrain modeling and animation by Gregory D. Moore; Models created by Aaron O. Moore.*

numerous terrains, most of which are at 1024 resolution. (The highest scene-file size was a whopping 230 megabytes!)

The animations range in length from seven to 15 seconds. About the process of animating, Greg says, "We used different methods for animating but mostly one shown to us by Rodney L'Ongnion (of *Planetary Traveler* and *Infinity's Child* fame) where we used an invisible track ball (the parent) to which all of the moving objects (the children) were linked." Although each child object follows the parent, there's also freedom for the child object to move independently. It took many low-resolution test renders to smooth out all the kinks in the motion trajectories. Another technique that Greg used was generating keyframes at fixed, regular intervals, which helped provide orientation for where things should be at a given point in time. Using many keyframes helped in the creation of trajectories in tight spots, as well as controlling speed. (This was animation using both trajectories and motion paths).

INDEX

2D graphics import formats, 338
2D pict object, 115
2D picture textures
   and opacity maps, 494–495
   and Picture Library, 485–494
   steps for creating, 484–485
   supported file formats, 484
2D Primitives, 115
2D Projection dialog box. *See* Camera & 2D
   Projection dialog box.
360 Panorama Render, 667–669
3D applications, 9, 22–23
3D "clip art," 154
3D graphics export formats, 398
3D modeling, 149, 154
3D objects. *See also* mesh.
   importing, 149–154
   sources of, on Web, 154–155
3D Preview area, AML, 786, 802–803
3D Primitives, 114–115
3D ray tracing. *See* ray tracing.
3D Studio MAX, 153, 934
3D Textures
   editing with Deep Texture Editor, 497–528
   mathematical basis for, 496
   miscellaneous advice on working with,
     529–532
   purpose of, 496
3D Transformations dialog box
   accessing via Three Rs controls, 204
   changing numbers in, 228–231
   contrasted with Object Attributes dialog
     box, 223–232
   and Space settings, 224–225
3DMF format, 153
3DS format, 153
48-bit Dithering, 654

A

A-B blend option, for textures, 454–456
A-B-C blend option, for textures, 456–461, 461
"A file error has occurred" alert message,
   783–784
A icon, 119
Abisko Pine Trees scene, 886, 888, 912
Absolute coordinates, 124
Absolute/Definition Coordinates pop-up
   menu, 124
Absolute filter, 519
academia, and computer graphics, 8–9
ACCEL ENGINE.TME file, 185
ACM, 9
active image area, 2D plane, 82
Acuris, 155
Adaptive Triangulation, 403
additive color theory, 426–427
Additive option, Materials Lab, 464–465, 477,
   611–612
Adobe After Effects, 823
Adobe Photoshop. *See* Photoshop.
Adobe Premiere, 823
Advanced Motion Lab, 786–818
   illustration of, 787
   keyboard shortcuts, 794, 798, 803
   main areas of, 786–787
     3D Preview, 786, 802–803
     Hierarchy List, 787, 788–794
     Sequencer, 787, 795–801
     Time Mapping Editor, 786, 787, 803–813
     Time/Playback controls, 786, 787, 797
   methods of accessing, 786
   and object hierarchies, 303–304
   purpose of, 29, 786
   removing keyframes in, 878, 879
   and .TME files, 185
   undoing actions in, 788

Advanced Motion Lab *(continued)*
  walkthroughs
    acceleration and other time mapping
      adjustments, 814–818
    displaying hierarchies, 790–791
aerial perspective, 597
Aerial Preview feature, 96–97
aesthetics, and lighting, 639–642
African After Dream scene, 910, 912
Alaskan Spring scene, 922–923
alert message, "A file error has occurred,"
    783–784
Alford, Janak, 647
algorist, 7
algorithms, mathematical, 7, 9
Alien Borealis scene, 929–930
Alien Starburst scene, 920
Align control, Edit Palette
  location of, 196, 248–249
  snappy options, 255–258
Align option, Object Attributes dialog box, 769
Align to Trajectory option, Object Attributes
    dialog box, 735–736
Align X commands, 249, 250
alignment
  Anchor-Based, 189, 250, 252
  bounding box, 250, 251
  on centers of objects, 253
  and earlier Bryce versions, 250
  edge, 253–254
  of object and path, 769
  "on" or "along" an axis, 249
  practice exercises, 254, 264–266
  with snappy options, 255–258
alpha channel
  applying filters to, 495
  creating optics and illumination with,
    494–495
  creating photographic two-dimensional
    image with, 484–485
Alpha output type, 521, 522, 528
Alpha Scaling, 444–447, 479
Alt key (Windows)
  and panning up and down, 79
  and resetting of Memory Dots, 106

Alt key (Windows) *(continued)*
  and resizing of objects, 213
  and rotation of objects, 222
  and swiveling of viewpoint, 100
Alt-nudge unit. *See* Option/Alt-nudge unit.
Alt+Clicking (Windows), 179
Alternate VCR Mode, 140, 142, 189
Altitude filter, 520
Altitude Minus Slope filter, 521
Altitude Render, 394–395, 675–678
Altitude scale, and Sun control, 563–564
Alton, John, 639
Ambience channel, Materials Lab, 45–46,
    415, 416
Ambient Color
  and Brycean skies, 587, 588, 593–594
  contrasted with Diffuse Color, 424
  and glowing objects, 610–612
AML. *See* Advanced Motion Lab.
AML Doorway tool, 708
AML Hierarchy List. *See* Hierarchy List.
amplitude, phase, 513
Anchor-Based Aligning, 189, 250, 252
AND boolean operation, 276
animatable objects, 709–712, 714–721
animation
  birth/death event, 939–940
  controls, 332, 693, 712–714 *(See also*
    Advanced Motion Lab; Time Palette.)
  copying and pasting, 880
  editing sequences together, 822–823
  examples
    Bouncing Ball, 686, 743, 814–818
    Bryce Terrain Flyover, 940–941
    Camera Crane, 305–308, 823–834
    Gears, 854
    Helix, 848–854
    Infinity's Child, 936–938
    Jet Race, 866–867
    Orbit, 842–848
    Pulsing Light, 840–842
    Rube Goldberg, 938–939
    Spiral Motion, 848–854
  of groups, 880
  how it works, 686

animation *(continued)*
  introduction of, in Bryce 3D, 15–16
  merging scenes, 880
  motion tricks, 835–862
  and object linking, 291, 823–835
  and object tracking, 91–93, 775–778, 823
  planning, 814–822
  post-production work, 822–823
  previewing, 49–50, 176, 687, 703–706, 780
  process for creating, 25, 687–688
  proof-of-concept, 821–822
  rendering, 50–52, 178, 778–784
  storyboarding, 687, 821
  of textures and materials, 870–879
  timing considerations, 688–690
  walkthrough, 46–52
Animation controls, 332, 693, 712–714. *See also* Advanced Motion Lab; Time Palette.
Animation Options pop-up menu, 702–703, 712
Animation Palette, 702
Animation Preview controls
  Advanced Motion Lab, 802–803
  Time Palette, 703–706
Animation settings, Preferences dialog box, 189
Animation Setup dialog box, 690–693
  illustrations of, 691
  methods of accessing, 691, 798
  purpose of, 690
  walkthrough, 692–693
  warning against increasing/decreasing time in, 797–798
Animation tab, Object Attributes dialog box, 127
Ansel Tribute scene, 921–922
antialiasing
  Fine Art setting, 652, 653
  and Mask Render, 681–684
  Normal Quality, 652
  practice exercise, 682–684
  Render options for, 652–654
  and Render Report, 658
  Sampling Blur as form of, 478
  Superfine, 652

Antiqued Column exercise, 329–330
Apply button, Filter control, 353, 355
array, light, 645–646
Arrow controls, 74, 139, 140–141, 209
artificial light, 642–643
ArtMatic, 10
ArtMixer, 9, 10
Association of Computing Machinery, 9
astronomy, Bryce, 559–568
atmosphere, 28, 588–589
Atmosphere Off setting, 602
atmospheric perspective, 597
augmenting light, 643
Auto-Key
  impact on file size, 189–190
  and keyframing, 721–731
  main trick to working with, 725
  purpose of, 161
  and scene file size, 725
  turning on/off, 189, 721–726, 728–729
  walkthroughs, 722, 724
Auto Update setting
  Nano Preview, 160–161
  Sky & Fog, 558
Autodesk, 152, 153
Avalon, 154
Average Blend option, Deep Texture Editor, 525
AVI file, 782
Axiom, 13–14
axis, aligning "on" or "along," 249
Azimuth scale, and Sun control, 563–564

B

B. *See* Bryce unit.
Background Pattern control, 170, 171
"bad media" error message, 783–784
Bailey, Robert, 15, 318
Banking control, 64, 80, 90
Base Density, 468, 479
Base Height setting
  for fog, 576, 577–581
  for haze, 582, 583

Basic Altitude 29 texture, 538–540
Basic Shading, 475
batch rendering, 178, 663
Bates, Josh, 16, 17
Berkla, Dennis, 913
Bernard, Gary, 640
bias, trajectory, 740, 741
binary numbering, Bryce's special, 124, 202
Birkholz, Sandy, 910, 925–926
Birn, Jeremy, 636
birth/death event, 939–940
Blend modes/options
    Deep Texture Editor, 523–527
    Terrain Editor, 360
    Volume Color, 466–467, 478–479
Blend Transparency shading mode, 462–463
blue pyramid, 40, 93
Blur effects, and Distance Render, 673–675
Blur More filter, 674
BMP file, 25, 26, 180, 484
Bogdan, Todd, 13, 14, 16
Boole, George, 276
boolean attributes, 122, 278–279
boolean logic, 276–277
boolean objects
    animating, 711
    editing, 280
    grouping, 267, 274, 286
    online primer for, 278
    sample images, 289–290
    setting up, 278–279
    special techniques for using, 281–289
    surfaces of, 280–281
    terrains as, 287–289
Boolean Objects section, Objects Preset
    Library, 186
boolean operations
    examples of, 277–278
    most commonly used, 276
    and renderer, 279–281
"Boolean Potato Skins" images, 624
BOUNCE-DEATHBIRTH scene file, 940
BOUNCE scene file, 686, 743
BOUNCEAMLSTART scene file, 814

Bouncing Ball animation, 686, 743, 814–818
bounding box alignment, 250, 251
BR4 file, 26, 180
Brave Boat Harbor scene, 923–924
BRC file, 180
Bretagnolle, Pierre, 10
BRT file, 185
Brush Behavior
    Erosion option, 352
    Minimum/Maximum options, 351–352
    Paint/Unpaint Effects, 350
    pop-up menu, 349, 350
    walkthrough, 350–352
Brush controls, Terrain Editor, 332, 333,
    348–350
brushes
    choosing color for, 349–350
    controlling behavior of, 348–349
    creating custom, 387
    determining size of, 348
Brushing Beauties practice exercise, 370
Bryce. *See also* specific versions.
    binary numbering, 124, 202
    contrasted with other 3D applications,
        9, 22–23
    controlling, 28
    and the creative process, 56–58
    as cross-platform product, 13–14
    derivation of name, 18
    emotional experience of working with,
        18–19
    file structure, 25–26
    hardware limitations, 22
    history of, 8–17
        and Eric Wenger, 9–10, 13, 14, 496
        and Kai Krause, 10, 11–12, 13
        and Ken Musgrave, 8–9, 17
    interface, 11–12, 13, 19, 23, 26–30
    launching, 23
    ownership of, 17
    performance considerations, 157–161
    purpose of, 22
    and river metaphor, 1–2, 4, 5–6, 7–8
    talking with other users of, 29

Bryce *(continued)*
    as three-dimensional world, 52–55
    time-saving strategies, 161–170
Bryce 1
    camera, 65
    hardware requirements, 157–158
    interface, 12
    ship date, 12
    and Unity command, 234–235
Bryce 2
    and behavior of lights, 609–610, 618
    camera, 65
    cycling through object types with, 141
    development team, 14
    interface, 12
    Macintosh version, 13
    new features included in, 13
    ship date, 13, 14
    and Unity command, 271
    Windows version, 13–15
Bryce 3D
    and Deep Texture Editor, 496
    development team, 15–16
    interface, 12
    new features included in, 15
    and object tracking, 91
    ship date, 16
    and Unity command, 234–235, 271
Bryce 4
    and behavior of lights, 609–610, 618
    development team, 17
    and image resolution, 493
    interface, 12
    and KPT filters, 386–387
    new features included in, 16–17
    and object tracking, 91
    and Photoshop filters, 384
    ship date, 17
    and Torus Editor, 237
    and Unity command, 234, 271
Bryce astronomy, 559–568
Bryce Big Rig images, 318
Bryce Canyon, 18
Bryce Classic fractal terrain, 340–341, 344

Bryce objects. *See* objects.
Bryce Spaces, 197. *See also* specific spaces.
Bryce Terrain Flyover animation, 940–941
Bryce unit
    and camera position, 88
    defined, 88
    and internal grid, 200
    and Torus Editor, 238
Brycean Units and Measurement Council, 200
Brycean Universe
    and Absolute coordinates, 124
    internal grid, 200–203
    underlying structure of, 197–203
    units of measure in, 200–203
BryceTalk, 29
BSK file, 185
Bubble Show, Lawrence Welk, 261–263,
    264–266
bump
    how it works, 412
    and render time, 167
    and Texture Sources, 432
Bump Height
    and Distance Blur option, 466
    and Materials Lab channels, 421–422
    texture-driven, 438–439
Bump output type, 521, 528
Bushes scene, 912–913

C

calibration, monitor, 655
California, University of, 6
camera
    animating, 711
    banking, 64, 80, 90
    compared with eye, 60–61
    and Field of View controls, 80–81
    holding slippery, 95
    lenses, 80, 85
    lowering to "eye level," 76
    modes of rotation for, 77–79
    moving, contrasted with scrolling 2D plane,
        82–83

Camera *(continued)*
  as object, 232
  point of origin of, 79, 89
  positioning
    with Cross controls, 72–73, 74, 86, 88,
        92–93, 95
    by manipulating directly, 93–95
    with numerical settings, 86
    with Position settings of Camera
        dialog box, 88
    practice exercises, 102–104
    with Trackball controls, 77–80, 86
    on Windows and Macintosh
        platforms, 79
  precise placement of, 95–96
  saving views, 105–106
  selecting, 118, 140
  tilting, 80
  tracking object with, 91–93, 103–104
  undoing manipulation of, 95
Camera & 2D Projection dialog box, 77, 79,
    87, 89, 92. *See also* Camera dialog box.
Camera controls
  illustration of, 64
  location of, 27
  pop-up menu options, 74–77
  purpose of, 64
Camera Crane animation, 305–308, 823–834
Camera Crosses pop-up menu, 86
Camera dialog box
  accessing from orthogonal views, 77
  illustration of, 87
  purpose of, 77, 86
  settings
    Field of View, 90
    Origin, 89
    Pan, 91
    Position, 88
    Rotate, 89–90
    Scale, 90
Camera Options pop-up menu, 40
Camera Space, 54–55
  repositioning objects in, 197, 206–207
  resizing objects in, 197, 218–220

Camera Space *(continued)*
  rotating objects in, 197, 222–223
  and *xyz* axes, 197–199
Camera to Director command, 76
Camera View
  contrasted with Director's View, 65–66
  defined, 40
  and point of origin, 79
  tip for navigating quickly to, 67
canyons
  Bryce, 18
  eroded, 896–900
  hard-rock, 898
  stair-step, 899–900
Casady, Chris, 318–319, 383, 384, 494
Cast Shadow option, 465, 478, 574–575,
    623–624
castle, boolean image of, 290
Castle Hall scene, 647
Cattrone, Paul, 14, 17
caustic light, 636–637, 643
center alignment, 253
Center commands, 74–76
center point, for scene, 75
Center Scene command, 74–75
Center Selection command, 74, 75–76
Center to Selection mode, 78
Centered Transform option, Picture
    Mapping, 450
Chandelier scene, 646
channels, Materials Lab, 412–414
chaos theory, 1–2, 6, 15
character, building, 756
child object, 291, 292, 294, 301–302
cinematography, 819
circle, multi-replicating into, 309–311,
    315–317
circle/disk, as 2D Primitive, 115
Clamp Minimum/Maximum options, Terrain
    Export Lab, 403
Clevenger, Phil, 11, 13, 387–388
cliffs, 898
clip art, 3D data, 154
Clip filter, 515–518

Clipping Bracket, 332, 360–363
close-ups, 84–85
Cloud Cover Panel, 39, 586
Cloud Height setting, 585
Cloud Motion setting, 575
clouds, 569–575
    adjusting shape of, 569–574
    alternative, 606–608
    animating, 575
    blocking sun with, 574–575
    creating layers of, 606–607
    limitations of Brycean, 606
    and nature imagery, 890–892
    practice exercise, 569–574
    types of, 569
CMY color picker, 423
Coagulation scene, 927–928
coastline, computer-generated, 6
coin flipping, and random walk, 4–5
color. *See also* Diffuse Color; Volume Color.
    Ambient, 414, 424, 588, 593–594
    blend modes/options, 466–467, 478–479,
        596–597
    and Brycean skies, 587–606
        controls for adjusting, 588–589
        practice exercises, 589–600
    choosing brush, 349–350
    and computer display problems, 654–655
    grouping objects by, 135–137
    light source, 619–623
    sun, 588, 591–593
    as surface property, 411
    texture-driven, 439–441
Color-Bump output type, 544, 545
Color channels, Materials Lab, 411, 413,
    414, 422–430
color correction, 654–655
Color Mapping control, Terrain Editor, 333
Color output type, 521, 528
color perspective
    controlling, 589, 597–599
    defined, 597
    and Renaissance paintings, 598

color perspective *(continued)*
    source of technical document
        regarding, 597
color pickers
    complaint regarding, 423
    descriptions of specific, 422–423
    tip for using, 588
Column exercise, 322–330
Combine Blend option, Deep Texture
    Editor, 525
comets, 28, 567
Command key (Macintosh), 100
Complexity button, 573–574
COMPOSITE OBJECT.MOV file, 856
compositing software, 823
composition
    recommended book on, 108
    tips for creating better, 106–109
Compression Settings dialog box, 862
computer graphics, and SIGGRAPH, 9
computers, and chaos theory, 6
Computing Machinery, Association of, 9
cone, as 3D Primitive, 115
Cone Campground Start scene, 267–270
Confetti variation, Lawrence Welk Bubble
    Show, 263–264
conglomerate objects
    adding terrains and symmetrical lattices to,
        318–319
    contrasted with group, 274
    managing elements of, 319–320
    merging scenes from, 320–321
    and Multi-Replicate command, 309
    shortcuts for building, 274–275
constrain keys
    for repositioning objects, 204–205
    for rotating by precise increments, 222
    using with Trackball for precise camera
        movement, 79
Constrain setting, Object Attributes dialog
    box, 768–769
container item, 874–875
continuity, trajectory, 740, 741

Control key (Macintosh), 74, 79, 144–145
Control Palette
    location of, 27
    and point of view, 26–27
    and Preferences dialog box, 188
    and Render controls, 651
Copy button, Picture Library, 489, 495
Copy Matrix command, 105, 127, 129
Corel, purchase of Bryce by, 17
Corel Painter, 384
Corel Photo-Paint. *See* Photo-Paint.
Corkscrew Spiral animation, 848–854
Coroniti, Sam, 17
Corrado, Fernando, 169
CPU, and render time, 157–158, 168–169
Crane animation, 305–308, 823–834
Create Palette
    illustration of, 112
    purpose of, 24, 27
    steps for placing rocks in scene with, 40–42
Create Path command, 762
Create Picture Object icon, 484
Create Stone icon, 40
Create Terrain icon, 24, 25
creative process, Bryce and, 56–58
Crop controls, Terrain Editor, 333, 365
Cross controls
    changing perspective with, 34–36
    keyboard navigation for, 74
    positioning camera with, 72–73, 74, 86,
        88, 92–93
Ctrl key (Windows), 74, 79, 100, 144–145
cube, as 3D Primitive, 114
cumulus cloud, 569, 588. *See also* clouds.
Cumulus Color, 594
Current Time Indicator, 694, 797
Custom Sky mode, 587, 589, 600–602
cylinder
    as 3D Primitive, 114
    practice exercises
        cylinder creation, 322–325
        flattened cylinder/cube, 326–327
        fluted cylinder, 323–325
cylindrical parallel light, 614

D

D, Texture Source, 461–462
D3, 9
Dark Sky mode, 587, 589, 604
Day, John A., 908
Day/Night toggle, 562, 565
Decal Colors, 451–452
Deep Texture Editor, 496–532
    blend modes, 524–527
    editing cloud textures with, 573
    editing noise in, 503–512 (*See also* Noise
        Editor.)
    evolution of, 496
    filtering noise in, 514–521
    housekeeping hints, 529–532
    illustrations of, 497, 499
    methods of accessing, 496, 531–532
    output types, 432, 521–528
    practice exercises
        selecting components, 499–500
        using existing preset to create another
            effect, 540–542
        working with bump and reflection,
            547–551
    process for creating texture with, 497–498
    undoing actions in, 534, 535
    user interface
        combination window, 501–502
        component windows, 499–501
        controls, 498–499
    working with phases in, 512–513
Deep Undulating Canyon scene, 681–682
DEF ACCEL ENGINE.TME file, 185
default, resetting, 179
DEFAULT.BR4 file, 191
Definition Coordinates
    pop-up menu, 124
    practice exercise, 226–228
    purpose of, 228
Delete All command, Picture Library, 491
Delete All Keyframes command, AML,
    793–794
DEMs, 395–397, 909, 935–936
density, 467, 468, 479

Density setting
  for fog, 576, 577–581
  for haze, 582, 583
  for volume materials, 468, 479
depth cueing, 93, 95, 134
Design Basics, 108
dialog boxes, 29, 194. *See also* specific dialog
  boxes.
Difference Blend option, Deep Texture
  Editor, 527
Diffuse Color
  contrasted with Ambient Color, 424
  image map, 405–406
  and Materials Lab, 414
  and Metallicity, 424–425
  modulation of, 428
  and Refract Index setting, 427–428
Diffusion channel, Materials Lab, 415
Digital Elevation Models. *See* DEMs.
Digital Exchange Format. *See* DXF format.
dimensions
  fractional, 5
  names of, in 3D world, 52
  noise, 505, 506, 508
Diorama control, 41
Direct3D, and Flat Shaded Preview, 176
Direct Imagination, 494, 495
direction, noise, 507–508
Director to Camera command, 76
Director's View
  contrasted with Camera View, 65–66
  defined, 40
  limitations of, 65–66
  manipulating camera from, 93
  setting Trackball in, 77–78
  tips for navigating quickly to, 66–67
dirty surface, 436
Disable Cast Shadows switch, 623–624
dispersion, and Randomize control, 259–261
Display controls
  descriptions of specific, 170–174
  location of, 170
  purpose of, 28
Display Palette, 170, 188

Display/Wireframe Palette, 28
Distance Blur option, Materials Lab, 466
DISTANCE OFFSET SIXSOME file, 298
Distance Render, 673–675
Distance setting, Object Attributes dialog box,
  294–300
Dithering, 48-bit, 654
Document Resolution settings, 162
Document Setup dialog box, 50, 82, 162
Dots. *See* Memory Dots.
DOUBLE-HIERARCHY scene file, 301, 790
DOUBLE-HIERARCHY.MOV file, 301
Doucet, Moe, 16
dragging
  camera, 93
  Elevation editors, 339–340
  repositioning objects via, 204–205, 207
  resizing objects via, 213–215
drawing, 56
Drawing on the Right Side of the Brain, 639
DTE. *See* Deep Texture Editor.
Duplicate command, 241–243
duplicating objects, 241–245
  contrasted with replicating, 245
  location of command for, 241
  practice exercise, 242–245
DXF format, 152–153, 167
Dynamic Light and Shade, 639

E

E icon, 331
Eagle scene, 935
earth, as two-dimensional surface, 5
earth formations, 893–900
Easter Egg
  for cycling through AML colors, 795
  for multi-replicating, 867–870
  for positioning sun in sky, 565
edge alignment, 253–254
Edge Softness, 469
Edit Current Camera command, 77, 86
Edit icon, 331

Edit Lights dialog box, 614–634
    color controls, 618–623
    illustration of, 614
    intensity control, 615–618
    methods of accessing, 614
    pop-up menu options, 623–628
    preview feature, 615, 623
    softness control, 618–619
Edit Lights pop-up menu
    Disable Cast Shadows option, 623–624
    Falloff options, 624–628
    Infinite Light option, 628
    Remove Gel option, 623
    Render Window Preview option, 623
Edit Materials control, 120, 196
Edit Mesh dialog box, 150–151
Edit Noise dialog box. *See also* Noise Editor.
    description of controls in, 504–512
    illustration of, 503
    positioning on screen, 504
Edit Object icon, 119, 120
Edit Palette
    enlarging terrain with, 33–34
    illustration of, 196
    list of controls on, 196
    organization of, 248
    purpose of, 27
    relationship to Object Attributes and 3D
        Transformations dialog boxes, 224
Edit Phase dialog box, 512–513
Edit Terrain/Object control
    location of, 196
    and torus, 236–241
Edit Texture Palette, 442–444
editing, 195–196. *See also* Deep Texture Editor;
    Edit Palette.
    boolean objects, 280
    cloud textures, 573
    noise, 503–512
    Path object, 764–767
    single *vs.* multiple objects, 203
    videos, 823
Edwards, Betty, 639
Elbow Crane animation, 305–308, 832–834

Elevation controls
    Brush Behavior, 349
    Terrain Editor, 332, 333, 336–348
Ellsworth, Bill, 175
empty world, 24
Energy Saver Control Panel, PowerBook,
    159–160
enlargements, proportional, 216
Enter key, and mouse movements, 101
environment controls, 28
Ernst scene, 929
Eroded control, Terrain Editor, 31, 336, 337
Erosion option, Brush Behavior, 350, 352
error message, "A file error has occurred,"
    783–784
Escher House image, 290
Eternal Lake scene, 457
exercises. *See* practice exercises.
Explorer icon, 25–26
exporting
    movies, 17
    presets, 183–184
    supported file formats, 398
    symmetrical lattices, 397
    terrains, 16, 29, 397–406 (*See also* Terrain
        Export Lab.)
eye, compared with camera, 60–61
Eye Candy, 919–941
    animation, 936–941
    Martian water images, 935–936
    seascapes, 923–926
    still-image landscapes, 920–923
    surrealistic/abstract, 927–933
Eye-Level Camera command, 76
eyedropper, 350

F

face, as 2D Primitive, 115
"face" orientation, and object tracking,
    776–777
fairy-tale castle, image of, 290
families. *See* Object Families.
Families icon, 119

Families pop-up menu, 135, 144
Family dialog box, 118
Fast Preview mode, 166, 169, 660–662
faults, geologic, 896
Fenimore, Michael, 835
Field of View
    and Camera dialog box, 90
    illustrations of different settings for, 81
    increasing/decreasing, 80
    and picture composition, 109
"file error has occurred" alert message,
        783–784
file formats/extensions
    2D graphics import, 338
    3D graphics export, 398
    3D graphics import, 151
    image document, 25–26
    scene document, 25–26
file naming, 178–180
film, setting size of, 82
*Film Directing Shot by Shot: Visualizing from
        Concept to Screen,* 819
Filter Palette, 498–499, 514
Filter Presets, 355–356
Filter ramp, 355, 356
Filtering controls, Terrain Editor, 352–358
    components of, 352–353
    contrasted with "action of filtering," 352
    and Filter Presets, 355–356
    Horizontal and Vertical options, 356–358
    purpose of, 352
    and symmetrical lattice, 383
Filtering index card, Terrain Editor, 352–353
filters
    and Deep Texture Editor, 514–521
    KPT, 386–387
    Photoshop, 384–386, 489–490
    purpose of, 352
    as "side view," 353–355
Final Cut Pro, 823
Finder icon, 25–26
Fine Art setting, Render pop-up menu,
        652–653
First Keyframe button, 51

Fit function, Terrain Editor, 365–366
Fjord Mud scenes, 884, 885, 888
flame light, 646
Flat Shaded Preview, 176–177
Flat Shading, 474–475
Flattened Cylinder/Cube practice exercise,
        326–327
Flemish painting, and color perspective, 598
Flip controls, 216–217
flipping coin, and random walk, 4–5
Flow control, for brushes, 349
Fluted Cylinder practice exercise, 323–325
Flyaround Center, 101
Flyaround Space, 96
Flyaround view
    and mouse movement, 98–100
    previewing scene in, 96–97
focal length, 80, 85
focal point, and lighting, 642
fog, 575–582. *See also* Sky & Fog Palette.
    adjusting color of, 588
    Base Height setting, 576, 577–581
    blending with sun, 589
    creating freestanding, 582
    Density setting, 576, 577–581
    parameters determining appearance of,
        575–576
    Thickness setting, 576, 577–581
    walkthrough, 587
Fog Color, 595–596
foliage imagery, 909–913
fps, 689
Fractal control, Terrain Editor, 337, 340–346
Fractal Design, 10
fractal geometry, 2–5
fractal mountain, 6
Fractal Noise map, 331
fractal patterns, 344
Fractal Stone noise, 505
fractal terrains. *See also* fractals.
    illustrations of, 341–344
    randomness settings for, 341, 344
    source of, 340
    tiling, 346–348, 366

fractal terrains *(continued)*
    trick to "shopping" for, 345–346
    and Zoom controls, 366–368
Fractal Terrains pop-up menu, 340
fractals. *See also* fractal terrains.
    and computer-generated landscapes, 6
    defined, 3
    fractional dimensions of, 5
    iterative process for generating, 4–5
    and random walk, 4–5
    self-similarity of, 4
fractional dimensions, 5
frames, counting, 688, 690
frames per second, 689
Free Camera mode, 77, 79
frequency, adjusting, 505–507, 530
Frequency slider, Texture Source, 442
Fricke, Chaz, 927–928
Fry, Ruth "Calyxa," 925
Full Shading, 475–476
Fuzzy Factor, 469–470
Fuzzy shading mode, 463–464, 610–611

G

G icon. *See* Group Objects icon.
G2H map, 332, 333, 353–354
Galahfana's Amulet scene, 930
Game Over practice exercise, 374
Gamma Correction, 654–655
Garden Hose, 913
Gaussian Blur filter, 674
Gaussian filter, 519
gears, creating/rotating, 316–317
Gears animation, 854
gel cookies, 644–645
gels, 620–623, 623, 631
General tab, Object Attributes dialog box, 121–125
geometry, 2–5, 22
geometry points, for Path object, 764–765
George Washington University, 8
GIF file, 484
glaciers, 895–896

Global Frequency control, Edit Texture, 506, 530
GlockenFondue images, 387–388
glowing objects, 610–613
Gorge Creek scene, 910–911
Gradient Designer, KPT, 393
"Grammer of Ornament" CD-ROM, 494, 495
Gray Galets 29 texture, 537–538
gray pyramid, 93
grayscale-to-height map, 318, 332. *See also* G2H map.
grid
    Bryce's internal, 200–203
    Materials Lab, 430, 453
Grid pop-up menu, 333, 334
Grid Triangulation, 402–403
Ground/Land Object icon, 120
group. *See also* grouping.
    animating, 880
    assigning boolean property to, 286
    contrasted with conglomerate, 274
    naming, 140
    selecting, 140
    as special-case object, 117
    and Unity command, 271
    ways of using, 267, 275–276
Group command, 135, 266
Group Objects icon, 119, 121, 266
grouping. *See also* group.
    advantages of, 275–276
    basic method for, 266
    consequences of, 267
    contrasted with object linking, 293–294
    by family/wireframe color, 135–137
    practice exercises, 136–137, 267–270

H

Hagebusch, Clay, 929–933
Hall of Kings scene, 647–648
halo, 28
Halo Rings, 566
Halo, Specular. *See* Specular Halo.
Hand tool, 82

hard-rock valleys, 898
Hardness control, for brushes, 349
hardware requirements, 157–158
haze
    adjusting color of, 588
    animating, 46–49
    Base Height setting, 582, 583
    blending with sun, 589
    controlling appearance of, 37–39, 582, 583
    Density setting, 582, 583
    Thickness setting, 582, 583
    walkthrough, 587
Haze Color, 594–595, 596, 889–890
Haze control, 37–39, 582, 583
Heavy Seas scene, 924–925
HELIX PATH.MOV file, 853
HELIX scene file, 848
HELIX.MOV file, 848
hidden object, 122
Hide/Show Underground Lines control,
    132–133
Hierarchy List, 788–794
    color-coding scheme, 788–789
    display options, 789–793
    how materials appear in, 870–872
    illustrations of, 304, 791, 871
    keyboard shortcuts, 794
    and keyframes, 793–794
    limitations of, 303–304
    pop-up menu options, 793–794
    walkthrough, 790–791
high-contrast detail, and render time, 167
Hills 29 texture, 535–537
history, Bryce, 8–17
Hogarth, Burne, 639
Holeček, Aleš, 14, 16, 17
hoodoos, 18, 357
Horizon Color, 600
Horizon Illusion slider, 565–566
horizon line, varying, 107
Horizontal options, Filtering control,
    356–358
horizontal panning, 91
hot spot, and Specular Halo, 425–426

HOW HELIX 1-2-3 scene file, 849
HSC Software, 10

I

IBM Research Lab, 6
icons
    Create Picture Object, 484
    Create Stone, 40
    Create Terrain, 24, 25
    Explorer, 25–26
    Finder, 25–26
    Object Control, 91–92, 119–121
    Object Selection, 139
    Padlock, 89
    Preview Animation, 49
    Select Stones, 43
IFF file, 484
illumination, 28, 410, 435–437
Illumination channels, Materials Lab, 413, 414,
    415–416
image
    changing magnification of, 84
    featuring dominant element of, 107–109
    file formats/extensions, 25–26, 338, 398
    rendering large, 664–666
    saving with scene file, 36
image document, 25–26
image editors, 333, 383–388. *See also* Terrain
    Editor.
Image Map controls, Terrain Export Lab, 399,
    404–406
image size, and resolution, 493–494
Image Thumbnail Area, Picture Library, 486
imagery. *See* nature imagery.
importing
    3D objects, 149–154
    meshes, 116–117
    presets, 183–184, 185–186
    supported file formats, 151, 338
    tips for, 154
Index card controls, Terrain Editor, 332
infinite cloud slab, 606–608
Infinite Light option, 628

infinite plane
adding depth to, 112–113
as cloud layer, 606–608
default appearance of, 113
types of, 112
infinite slab, 113
Infinity's Child animation, 936–938
Ingersoll, Barb, 923–924
inheritance of properties, parent-to-child, 294, 298–300
"injection mold" object, 383
intensity, light source, 615–618
interface
development of, 11–12, 13, 19
dialog boxes, 29
illustrations of, 12, 23
palettes, 26–30
Interface Max/Min control, 170
internal grid, Bryce's, 200–203
intersect object, 277
Intersection operation, 277, 285–286

J

Jet Race animation, 866–867
JET RACE HOW.MOV file, 867
JPG file, 484

K

Kai's Power Tools, 11, 606. *See also* KPT.
Katz, Steven D., 819
key event, 721. *See also* keyframe.
keyboard shortcuts
3D Preview, 803
for accessing Deep Texture Editor, 531–532
for accessing Object Attributes dialog box, 121
for accessing palettes, 192
for assigning boolean attributes, 279
Hierarchy List, 794
for navigating to specific views, 66–67
Playback controls, 696

keyboard shortcuts *(continued)*
for selecting objects, 138, 144
Sequencer, 798
Time Mapping Curve, 813
for zooming in/out, 84
keyframe
and animation scenarios, 726–729
and birth/death event, 939–940
defined, 721
and QTVR movies, 859–861
removing, 729–731, 793–794, 878, 879
strategies for generating, 721–724
Keyframe button, 51
Keyframe tools, 706–708, 713
keyframing
with Auto-Key Off, 722–724
with Auto-Key On, 721–722
pros and cons of each approach, 724–731
Kitchens, Susan, 387–388, 935–936
Kotay, Sree, 13, 16
KPT
filters, 386–387
Gradient Designer, 393
Krause, Kai, 10, 11–12, 13

L

labs, 29. *See also* specific labs.
Land Object icon, 119, 120
landscape software, 9–10
landscapes. *See also* nature imagery.
classic examples, 920–923
computer-generated, 6, 7, 56–57
lattice. *See* symmetrical lattice.
Lattice mode, displaying wireframe object in, 175
Lauer, David A., 108
Launch to Default State, 187
Launch to Previous State, 187, 190
Lawrence Welk Bubble Show, 261–263, 264–266
lenses, camera
and Field of View controls, 80
and focal length, 80, 85

Leonardo da Vinci, and color perspective, 598
Leonardo image, 490, 495
Leopard noise, 505, 506
light. *See also* light object; light source;
    lighting.
    artificial, 642–643
    augmenting, 643
    caustic, 636–637, 643
    example scenes using, 646–648
    negative-intensity, 634–635
    pseudo-, 609, 610–613, 646
    stealth, 643–644
    studio, 643
    tips for setting up, 644
    ways of using, 642–644
light array, 645–646
light object
    animating, 712
    secondary illumination of, 636
    and Solo mode, 639
    types of, 613–614
Light Sensitive Shading, 476–477
Light Shading mode, 464, 613
light source. *See also* lighting.
    adjusting with Edit Lights dialog box,
        614–628
    alternatives to sun and moon, 28, 116
    falloff options, 624–628
    intensity settings, 615–618
    previewing placement of, 615
    and radiosity, 636
    and render time, 167, 637–639
    Smoky Spotlight walkthrough, 632–634
    softness settings, 618–619
    types of, 613–614
    visible *vs.* invisible, 628–631
lighting. *See also* light source.
    aesthetic considerations, 639–642
    controlling with Sky & Fog Palette, 28
    and disabling of shadows, 624
    important functions of, 640–642
    real-world contrasted with ray-trace
        process, 636–637
    recommended books on, 639–640

lighting *(continued)*
    and render time, 167, 637–639
    and time of day, 109
    ways of using in Bryce, 639–646
        example scenes, 646–648
Linear Falloff, 624–625
Linear Interpolation, 522–523
linear perspective, 597
Link Clouds to View option, 575
Link Object icon, 119
Link Sun to View option, 96, 189, 560–561
Link Timeline Scale option, 796
linked links, 301
linking. *See* object linking.
Linking icon, 291
Linking Practice scene, 291
Linking section, Camera & 2D dialog box, 92
Linking tab, Object Attributes dialog box,
    126, 294
Load button, Picture Library, 487
Load Image pop-up menu, 359
locked object, 122–123
L'Ongnion, Rodney, 289, 941
Longo, Mark, 924–925
Lotus scene, 928
LST file, 491
Lutnes, Sylvia, 934–935

M

M icon, 119, 120
Macaulay, David, 854
Macintosh platform
    and behavior of lights, 609–610, 618
    and boolean operations, 278
    and Bryce 1, 12
    and Bryce 2, 13
    and color correction, 655
    color picker, 423
    Control key, 74, 79
    file formats, 25–26
    mouse movement, in Flyaround mode, 100
    Option key, 79, 100, 106, 213, 222
    performance considerations, 158–160

Macintosh platform *(continued)*
  and QuickTime VR, 862
  and render times, 169
  resetting defaults, 179
  resetting Memory Dots, 106
  and unity units, 201
  video-editing and compositing
    software, 823
  Zoom controls, 84
Magic Wand, Photoshop, 377
magnifier tools, 84. *See also* Zoom controls.
management, model, 319–321
Mandelbrot, Benoit B., 2–3, 4, 6–7
Mandelbrot set, 2–3, 4
Mann, Robert, 643, 645
mapping
  color, 333
  parametric, 434
  picture, 447–451
  texture, 433–435
  time, 185, 803–818 (*See also* Time Mapping
    Curve; Time Mapping Editor.)
maps, USGS, 909
Mask Render, 678–684
  and antialiasing, 681–684
  for finished rendering, 681
  how it works, 678–679
  practice exercise, 680–681
  and transparent objects, 680–681
  for work in progress, 679
MAT file, 185
Material Options pop-up menu, 462, 474
materials. *See also* Materials Lab.
  animating, 719–721, 870–879
  basic properties of, 410
  contrasted with texture, 409
  differentiating between container and
    animated items, 874–875
Materials Grid, 453
Materials Lab, 407–481
  adjusting sliders in, 414
  Animation controls, 712, 713
  channel categories, 412–414 (*See also*
    specific categories.)

Materials Lab *(continued)*
  color picker, 423
  icon for accessing, 119, 120
  illustrations of controls/user interface, 410,
    430, 453
  Material Options pop-up menu, 462
  purpose of, 29, 407–409
  steps for using, 44–46
  Texture Source box, 430–431
  tips for opening/exiting, 481
  and volume properties, 409, 467–468
Materials Preset Library, 32, 181, 185, 186
materials timeline, 719–720
mathematics
  and computer-generated art, 6–7
  and fractal geometry, 2
matrix
  commands, 105, 127, 129
  defined, 127
  practical uses for, 129
Maximum Blend option, Deep Texture
    Editor, 524
Maximum option, Brush Behavior, 351–352
measurement units
  for Bryce's internal grid, 200–202
  for rotation, 203
Memory Dots
  and Animation Palette, 702
  color-coding of, 105
  how they work, 105–106
  saving camera settings in, 105
  and Sky & Fog Palette, 558
Merge command, 320–321, 327
merging scenes
  advantages of, 880
  practice exercises, 322–330
  steps to follow for, 320–321
  theory behind, 320
mesh
  selecting, 140
  smoothing surface of, 150
  as special case object, 116–117
Mesh controls, Terrain Export Lab, 399–403
Mesh Editor, 150

Mesh Preview window, Terrain Export Lab, 400–401

MetaCreations, 10, 17

Metallicity
and Materials Lab channels, 410, 420–421, 424–425
texture-driven, 441

MetaSynth, 9–10

MetaTerrain Export, 398

MetaTools, 10, 11

Mid Winter preset, 542, 546

Mikkahl Desert Region scene, 932

Minimum Blend option, Deep Texture Editor, 524

Minimum option, Brush Behavior, 351–352

mix-and-match method, combining Texture Sources with, 453–454

model management, 319–321

modes. *See also* specific modes.
Bryce's basic, 25
camera rotation, 77–79
toggling between render and wireframe, 25

modifier keys
and mouse actions, 101
for nudging objects, 210

modulation, noise, 509–512

Mona Lisa, and color perspective, 598

monitor
and 3D images, 22
calibration of, 655

mood, lighting and, 640

moon
controlling phases of, 566
as light source, 28
location in Bryce sky dome, 562
setting diameter of, 565–566
surrounding with Halo Ring, 566

Moon Phase controls, 566

Moore, Aaron, 940

Moore, Carla, 646

Moore, Greg, 940–941

Motion Lab. *See* Advanced Motion Lab.

motion path, 731

Motion Picture and Television Engineers, Society of. *See* SMPTE.

Motion setting, Wireframe Resolution, 130–131

motion tricks, 835–862

Mountain Eroded scene, 163–165

mountains
how they're created, 893–895
and terrain objects, 113

mouse
movements, in Flyaround mode, 98–101
table of modifier keys, actions, and results, 101
and three-dimensional images, 22

MOV file, 782

MOVE AND CONSTRAIN scene file, 199, 222

MoviePlayer, QuickTime Pro, 823

Mud Cracks fractal style, 384

Multi-Replicate command
building spiral staircase using, 312–313
and conglomerate objects, 309
contrasted with Replicate command, 246
creating/rotating gears with, 316–317
practice exercise, 323
setting relationships by hand *vs.* calculation, 312
and torus, 314–315
using to rotate (without offset), 314

Multi-Replicate dialog box
adjusting numbers in, 230, 231, 246
contrasted with 3D Transformations dialog box, 246
determining numbers to be entered in, 309
purpose of, 246
and relative offset, 311
Scale Translation option, 247

multi-replication
along path, 863
Easter Egg, 867
practice exercise, 868–870

Multiply Blend option, Deep Texture Editor, 525–526

Murphy, Martin, 920–922, 927

Musgrave, Ken, 6–7, 8–9, 10, 17, 597
Mutation Marbles, 606
Mystic's Rock scene, 933

N

NAME.BRT file, 185
NAME.BSK file, 185
NAME.MAT file, 185
NAME.OBP file, 185
naming
    Family, 137
    group, 140
    images in Picture Library, 493
    object, 121
    scene files, 179–180
Nano Edit mode, 177
Nano Editor, 170, 171–172
Nano Preview
    Auto Update setting, 160–161
    choosing image quality with, 69
    compared with Sky Lab preview, 557–558
    defined, 27
    manual *vs.* automatic rendering with, 69
    purpose of, 68
    walkthrough, 70–71
Nano Preview options, Preferences dialog
    box, 188
NANO RENDER ME! scene file, 177
nature imagery
    Eric Wenger as master of, 884
    recommended books showing pictures of,
        896, 908
    specific types
        boulder-like stones, 901–902
        canyons, 896–900
        faults, 896
        glaciers, 895–896
        mountains, 893–895
        outer-space, 914–918
        rainy weather, 908–909
        rivers, 907
        trees and foliage, 909–913
        undersea worlds, 905–906

nature imagery, specific types *(continued)*
    valleys, 897–898
    vertical cliffs, 898
    volcanoes, 893–894, 900
    techniques/resources for creating realistic
        angled terrains, 902–905
        material frequency detail, 889
        multiple terrains, 901–905
        sky settings, 889–892
        terrain placement, 887–889
        USGS maps, 909
Necrofelinia images, 387–388
Ned's Dock scene, 934
negative-intensity light, 634–635
negative object, 122, 277, 282–284
neutral object, 122, 277, 281
New button, Picture Library, 487
New Image dialog box, Picture Library, 487
Night/Day toggle, 562, 565
Noise Editor, 503–512
    adjusting noise frequency with, 505–507
    changing Octave setting, 508–509
    changing orientation of noise with,
        507–508
    description of controls in, 504–512
    display bug, 505
    and noise modulation, 509–512
    positioning on screen, 504
    resetting noise to original state with, 512
    selecting noise type with, 505
    setting noise dimensions with, 505, 508
    working with phases in, 512–513
noise filtering, 514–521
noise modulation, 509–512
noise output types, 521–528
Noise Palette, Deep Texture Editor,
    498–499, 503
Normal shading mode, 462
NOT boolean operation, 276
nudge unit, 201
nudging
    moving objects via, 208–210
    practice exercises, 210–211, 215
    units of measure for, 201

numeric keypad, shifting between views with, 67

O

OBJ format, 153
Object Attributes dialog box
  Align option, 769
  Animation tab, 127, 734
  , changing numbers in, 228–231
  Constrain setting, 768–769
  contrasted with 3D Transformations dialog box, 223–232
  General tab, 121–125
  Linking tab, 126, 292, 294, 768
  methods of accessing, 119, 121
  purpose of, 119, 204
  setting up tracking relationship in, 775–777
  and Space settings, 224–225
Object Attributes icon, 119
Object Control icons
  descriptions of, 119–121
  illustrations of, 119
  and object linking, 291
  and object tracking, 91
Object Conversion control, 196, 235–236
Object Families, 118, 135–137
Object Hierarchy List. *See* Hierarchy List.
object linking, 291–308
  and animation, 291, 823–835
  contrasted with grouping, 293–294
  hierarchical implications of, 300–304
  keeping track of, 302–304
  and Object Attributes dialog box, 126, 292, 294
  practice exercise, 305–308
  and propagation of parent/child properties, 294–300
  purpose of, 291
  role of parent/child objects in, 291, 292, 294
object matrix. *See* matrix.
Object Parent Name pop-up menu, 292
object path, 731, 761. *See also* Path object.
Object Selection icons, 139

Object Space
  and Definition Coordinates, 124
  repositioning objects in, 206–207
  resizing objects in, 218–220
  rotating objects in, 222–223
  and texture mapping, 434
  and *xyz* axes, 54, 197, 198
object types
  changing from one to another, 235–236
  cycling through, 141
  selecting, 43
Object Worx, 862
objects
  aligning, 248–258
  animating, 709–712, 714–721
  building complex, 273–276
  controls associated with, 119–121
  cycling through, 140–141
  defining basic properties of, 121–125, 409
  descriptions of specific, 112–118
  duplicating, 241–245
  editing, 203–204, 223 (*See also* Edit Palette.)
  flipping, 216–217
  grouping (*See* grouping.)
  importing, 149–154
  linking, 126, 291–308 (*See also* object linking.)
  naming, 121
  nudging, 208–211
  numerical attributes for, 123–125
  organizing by family/wireframe color, 135–137
  palettes for working with, 27
  randomizing, 258–266
  replicating, 245–248, 309–317
  repositioning, 204–211
  resizing, 211–220 (*See also* Resize control.)
  rotating, 220–223 (*See also* Rotate control.)
  selecting, 41, 43, 138–145
  smoothing, 150–151
  special case, 116–118
  tracking, 91–93, 103–104, 126, 775–778
Objects Preset Library, 182, 185, 186
OBP file, 185

Octave setting, Noise Editor, 508–509
Offset
   and 3D Transformations dialog box,
      225–226
   defined, 124
   and Object Attributes dialog box, 225–226,
      294, 295, 298
   relationship to Reposition tool, 224
Offset X setting, 249
Old Shore scene, 920–921
Onyx, 909
OpenGL
   and camera placement, 95–96
   and Flat Shaded Preview, 176
optics, texture-driven, 437–438
Optics channels, Materials Lab, 411–412, 414,
   416–420
Option/Alt-nudge unit, 201–202, 210
Option-clicking (Macintosh), 179
Option key (Macintosh)
   and panning up and down, 79
   and resetting of Memory Dots, 106
   and resizing or objects, 213
   and rotation of objects, 222
   and swiveling of viewpoint, 100
Option-nudge. *See* Option/Alt-nudge unit.
OR boolean operation, 276
Orbit animation, 842–848
ORBIT-ORIGIN scene file, 842
Organikscape scene, 928
orientation, noise, 507–508
Orientation filter, 521
Origin Handle, 123
origin point, for camera, 79, 89
Origin setting, Camera dialog box, 89
orthogonal view
   accessing Camera dialog box from, 77
   and Center commands, 74
   contrasted with perspective view, 64
   defined, 67
   editing with Camera & 2D Projection
      dialog box, 91
   manipulating camera from, 93
   and zooming, 86

outdoor scenery. *See* nature imagery.
outer-space imagery, 914–918

P

Padlock icon, 89
Paint Effect setting, Brush Behavior, 350, 351
painting
   process of, contrasted with Bryce process,
      56–57
   using Bryce render as basis for, 934
Painting with Light, 639
Palermo, David, 669, 920
Palette Positions options, Preferences dialog
   box, 188
palettes. *See also* specific palettes.
   descriptions of, 26–28
   dual-monitor setups, 193
   keyboard shortcuts for accessing, 192
   repositioning, 191, 192–193
Pan control
   and active image area, 82
   altering 2D plane with, 81
   location of, 64
   resetting to default state, 83
Pan V/Pan H settings, Camera dialog box, 91
panning, 82–83, 91
panorama movie, 669
panorama rendering, 667–669
Pappathan, Chris, 922–923
Parallel Blend option, Deep Texture
   Editor, 525
parallel light, 614
parallel spotlight, 116
parametric mapping, 434
parent object, 291, 292, 294, 301–302
Paste button, Picture Library, 489, 495
Paste Matrix command, 105, 127, 129
Path object, 761–775, 862–867
   changing constraints for, 768–769
   contrasted with trajectory, 761–762
   creating, 762–763
   defined, 118
   editing, 764–767

Path object *(continued)*
    geometry points, 764–765
    linking object to, 768
    and multi-replication, 863
    selecting, 140
    storing, 763
    walkthrough, 771–775
    ways of working with, 863–867
    when not to use, 762
PCT file, 26, 179
PCX file, 484
pendulum
    animating single swing, 836–837
    components of, 836
    defined, 835
    practice exercise, 836–840
    repeating action over time, 839–840
    and Time Mapping Curve, 837–839
PENDULUM-NOANIM scene file, 836
PENDULUM scene file, 836
Penick, Andrew, 912–913
Pentak, Stephen, 108
Pentium processor, and render time, 169
Perlin, Ken, 9, 10
Perlin Hills terrain type, 9
perspective
    controlling, 34–36, 597–599
    types of, 597
Perspective Render, 672
perspective views, 64. *See also* Camera View;
    Director's View.
Peterson Field Guide: Atmosphere: Clouds, Rain,
    Snow, Storms, 908
Pfeiffer, Andreas, 10
phase amplitude, 513
Phase Palette, Deep Texture Editor,
    498–499, 512
Photo-Paint, 384, 928, 929, 934
photographer, thinking like, 106–109
photography
    and lighting conditions, 639
    process of, contrasted with Bryce process,
        56–57, 109

Photoshop
    as alternative to Terrain Editor, 377,
        383, 384
    creating custom brushes in, 387
    creating sloping letters in, 392
    filters, 384–386, 489–490
    and Picture Library, 489–490
PICT file, 25, 26, 179, 484
Pict Gel, 620–622, 644–645
Pict Interpolation option, 450–451, 493–494
pict object, 2D, 115
Picture Library, 485–495
    contents of, 483
    editing pictures in, 495
    filtering images in, 489–490
    generating new image within, 487–488
    global behaviors and commands, 490–492
    loading pictures into, 484–485, 487
    methods of accessing, 485
    naming images in, 493
    purpose of, 490
    sample work session in, 492–493
    saving contents to disk, 491
    undoing actions in, 490–491
    user interface, 485–490
Picture Mapping options, Texture Source,
    447–451
Pictures controls, Terrain Editor, 333, 337,
    358–360
Pictures index card, Terrain Editor, 359
Pixel 3D, 13
Plain Vanilla! scene, 559, 567–568, 570, 589,
    604–605
plane
    altering 2D, with Pan control, 81
    infinite, 112–113, 606–608
Planes and Terrains category, Materials
    Library, 32
Planetary Traveler animation, 289, 936–937
planets, 914–918
planning, animation, 814–822
Playback controls
    Advanced Motion Lab, 786, 797
    Time Palette, 695–697, 703, 707, 713

plop-render display, 194

Plop Render pop-up menu, 84, 85

plop-up dialog boxes, 194

Plop-Up Render control, 170, 173

plug-ins, import/export, 16

PNG file, 484

point of origin, for camera, 79, 89

point of view, 26–27, 59

Polygon-Memory ratio, and imported
    images, 154

Polygonal Mesh Preview window, Terrain
    Export Lab, 399

polyhedron, 116–117. *See also* mesh.

polymesh, 140. *See also* mesh.

Poser, 153, 929, 930

position, object
    compared with offset, 124
    default, 125
    units for measuring, 124

Position settings, Camera dialog box, 88

positioning of camera
    with Cross controls, 72–73, 74, 86, 88,
      92–93
    by manipulating directly, 93–95
    with numerical settings, 86
    with Position settings in Camera dialog
      box, 88
    practice exercises, 102–104
    with Trackball controls, 77–80
    on Windows and Macintosh platforms, 79

positive object, 122, 277, 282

post-processing, painterly, 933–935

post-production work, animation, 822–823

post-render processing, 933–935

Posterize control, 339

Power Tools. *See* Kai's Power Tools.

PowerBook, running Bryce on, 159–160

practice exercises. *See also* walkthroughs.
    adjusting cloud shape, 569–574
    aligning objects, 254, 264–266
    changing sky color and effects, 589–600,
      601–602, 604, 605
    creating and merging column and base,
      322–330

practice exercises *(continued)*
    creating photographic 2D image with alpha
      channel, 484–485
    creating QTVR movie, 670–672
    creating scene mixing antialiasing and non-
      antialiasing, 682–684
    creating terrain from text, 389–394
    creating terrain using Altitude Render, 395
    duplicating objects, 242–245
    entering Definition Coordinates, 226–228
    grouping objects, 136–137, 267–270
    linking objects, 305–308
    making a scene as efficient as possible, 177
    multi-replicating linked hierarchy, 868–870
    nudging objects, 210–211, 215
    positioning camera, 102–104
    positioning terrains, 287–288
    putting sun and moon in Brycean sky,
      567–568
    randomizing objects, 261–266
    rendering mask for transparent object,
      680–681
    replicating objects, 245, 322–323
    repositioning objects, 206–211
    resizing objects, 215, 218, 263–266
    rotating objects, 222–223, 263–266
    using Altitude Renders to work with
      terrains, 677–678
    using Deep Texture Editor, 499–500,
      540–542, 547–551
    using existing preset to create another
      effect, 540–542
    using Picture Library, 492–493
    using Sky & Fog Palette, 36–38, 589–600
    using Sun control, 567–568
    using Terrain Editor, 370–382
    working with bump and reflection,
      547–551

preferences
    default settings, 187–189
    global *vs.* local, 187
    Launch to Previous State *vs.* Launch to
      Default State, 187, 190

Preferences dialog box, 187–189
Preset Libraries
    accessing, 180
    adding/deleting preset, 182–183
    applying preset from, 181
    file types, 185
    importing/exporting presets, 183–184,
        185–186
    manipulating large volume of presets,
        184–185
    purpose of, 180
    viewing categories in, 180–181
Presets, Filter, 355–356
Preview Animation icon, 49
Preview area, AML, 786, 802–803
Preview controls
    Advanced Motion Lab, 802–803
    Terrain Editor, 332, 335–336, 364–365
    Time Palette, 703–706
Preview Gradient, Terrain Editor, 332
previewing
    animation, 49–50, 176, 687, 703–706, 780
    grayscale map in Terrain Editor, 335–336
    placement of light sources, 615
    render progress, 660–662
Primary Rays, 656, 658
primitives
    2D, 115
    3D, 114–115
    adding glow effects to, 610
    as building blocks for conglomerate
        object, 274
    default dimensions for squashed and
        stretched, 124
    types of light source, 613–614
Procedural Blend, 527
Procedural Texture, 496
processor speed, and render time, 157–158,
        168–169
proof-of-concept animation, 821–822
proportional enlargements/reductions, 216
PSD file, 484
pseudo-light, 609, 610–613, 646

publishing, computer graphics, 9
Pucciarelli, Mike, 928–929
Pulsing Light animation, 840–842
PULSINGLIGHT scene file, 841
PULSINGLIGHT.MOV file, 841
pyramid
    as 3D Primitive, 115
    blue, 40, 93
    gray, 93

Q

QTVR Edit Object, 862
QTVR Make Panorama 2 applet, 670–672
QTVR movie
    animating, 859–861
    calculating frame count for, 859
    creating, 669–670
        multi-row, 857–859
        single-row, 856–857
    defined, 855
    development of, 669
    ensuring smooth playback of, 857–858
    exporting, 17, 672
    practice exercise, 670–672
    recommended book on, 669, 855
    rendering, 667, 861–862
    software tools, 670, 862
    types of, 669
QTVR MULTIROW OBJECT MOVIE scene
        file, 859
Quality/Speed settings, and render time,
        470–474, 480–481
Quantize filter, 518, 545
QuickDraw, 153
QuickShow, 605
QuickTime movie, 781. *See also* QTVR movie.
QuickTime Player, 782
QuickTime Pro, 823
QuickTime Virtual Reality. *See* QTVR movie.
QuickTime VR Authoring Studio, 862
QuickTime VR Book, The, 669, 855
QuickTime Web site, 862

R

radial light, 116, 613

radiosity, 636, 637

rainbow, 28, 584–585

Rainy Day scene, 908

rainy weather, 908–909

Raise/Lower editor, 337, 339

Raise/Lower Terrain practice exercise, 371

RAM, and Flat Shaded Preview, 176

ramp. *See* Filter ramp.

Random Blend option, Deep Texture
Editor, 527

Random Continuous noise, 522

Random Lines noise, 544

Random Sky control, 606

random walk, 4–5, 6

Randomize Amount control, 258, 259

Randomize Combination button, Deep
Texture Editor, 502

Randomize control, Edit Palette
components of, 258–259
location of, 196
practice exercises, 261–266
working with, 259–261

Randomize Mode Selector, 258

Randomize Options menu, 258, 259

Randomize Rotation control, 260

Randomize Size control, 260

randomness settings, for fractal terrains,
341, 344

Ranged Falloff, 627–628

Ray Hit/Miss settings, 658

Ray Spray Render tool, 170, 174

Ray Spray tool, 659

ray tracing, 60–64, 650. *See also* rendering.

Realtime Linking option, 795

Receive Shadow option, Materials Lab,
465, 478

Recorded Area, 698

Recorded Range, 698–700

red object, 24

red padlock icon, 89

reductions, proportional, 216

reflection, and render time, 167

Reflection channel, Materials Lab, 413,
416–417, 419–420

Refract Index, Materials Lab, 418–419,
427–428

release dates. *See* ship dates.

Remove Gel option, 623

Remove Shear command, 219–220

Renaissance painting, and color
perspective, 598

Render Animation dialog box, 51, 781–784

Render button, 23–24, 662

Render controls
descriptions of specific
48-bit Dithering, 654
360 Panorama Render, 667–669
Altitude Render, 394–395, 675–678
Antialiasing, 652–654
color adjustments, 654–655
Mask Render, 678–684
Report Render Time, 655–658
Spatial Optimization, 651–652
illustration of, 651
location of, 27

Render mode
contrasted with Wireframe mode, 25
using Ray Spray tool in, 659
and Zoom to Selection option, 84–85

Render pop-up menu
advanced options, 664–684
360° rendering, 667–672
post-processing, 672–684
rendering large images, 664–666
descriptions of controls on, 651–658
illustration of, 651

Render Report, 655–658

Render Resolution settings, 50–51, 163

Render Scene button, 23–24, 662

render time
factors contributing to, 166–167, 194, 480,
636–637
report on, 655–658
strategies for reducing, 165, 166, 194
table comparing various processors, 169

Render Times Web page, 169

Render to Disk option, 665–666
rendered view, 23. *See also* Render mode.
rendering. *See also* Render controls.
    animations, 50–52, 178, 778–784
    basic steps for, 24–25
    and boolean operations, 279–281
    to disk, 665–666
    large images, 664–666
    and lighting effects, 167, 637–639
    post-processing of initial, 672–684
    and processor speed, 157–158, 168–169
    and Quality/Speed settings, 470–474,
        480–481
    and screen savers, 194
    in Solo mode, 148
    test, 779–781, 783
    touching up after, 933–934
    types of
        360° Panorama, 665–666
        Altitude Render, 394–395, 675–678
        batch, 178.663
        Distance Render, 673–675
        final, 662–663
        Mask Render, 678–684
        on-the-fly, 658–662
        Perspective Render, 672
        progressive, 63
    what happens during, 30
Repeat Tiling option, Picture Mapping, 449
Replicate command, 245–246. *See also*
    Multi-Replicate command.
Replicate dialog box. *See* Multi-Replicate
    dialog box.
replicating objects, 309–317
    building a spiral staircase by, 312–313
    into a circle, 309–311, 315–317
    contrasted with duplicating, 245
    practice exercise, 245.322–323
Replication folder, 248
Report Render Time, 655–658
Reposition control, 127, 196, 197, 204, 205
repositioning
    objects, 204–211 (*See also* Reposition
        control.)

repositioning *(continued)*
    palettes, 191, 192–193
Reset button, Filter control, 352–353, 355
reset command, 106
Reset Noise control, Noise Editor, 512
Reset Views option, 68
Resize control, 127, 196, 197, 211–213
resizing objects. *See also* Resize control.
    methods for, 211–215, 216, 218–220
    practice exercises, 215, 218, 263–266
resolution
    and image size, 493–494
    and imported images, 154
    terrain, 334–335, 368–370, 402
    wireframe, 130–132, 176
Resolution Grid, Terrain Editor, 332
Return key, and mouse movements, 101
Revert to Saved command, 187, 235
RGB color picker, 423
RGB color theory, 426–427
Rhodes, Hilary, 290
ribbon trajectory, 735
Rice Paddies practice exercise, 372
Riegel, Glenn, 647
Ringed Planet preset, 540–542
RINGS N THINGS scene file, 853
river imagery, 907
river metaphor, and Bryce, 1–2, 4, 5–6, 7–8
Rivers and Deltas practice exercise, 372–373
RLE file, 484
RND Continuous noise, 505, 510
RND Lines noise, 544
Rocks, Water, Sand scene, 925
Rocks & Stones category, Materials Library, 45
Rocky Beach scene, 933
Rocky Shore scene, 934–935
rooms, 29
Rotate control, Edit Palette
    how it works, 220–222
    illustration of, 196
    and object matrix, 127
    pop-up menu for, 197
    practice exercise, 222–223
    and *xyz* axes, 197

Rotate settings, Camera dialog box, 89–90

rotation

of camera, 77–79, 232

of objects, 220–223, 263–266

and Space settings, 222–223

units of measure for, 203

Rotation setting, Object Attributes dialog box, 294–295, 299–300

round parallel spotlight, 116

round spotlight, 116

Rube Goldberg animation, 820–821, 938–939

RUBE.MOV file, 820

S

Sampling Blur, 478

Santa Cruz, University of California at, 6

Save As dialog box, 186

Save List command, Picture Library, 491

saving

camera settings, 105

camera views, 105–106

rendered image with scene, 36

scene, 36, 180, 186–187

Sawtooth practice exercise, 371

SawWave filter, 518

Scale control, 795

Scale Pict Size option, Picture Mapping, 449–450

Scale setting, Camera dialog box, 90

Scale Timeline tool, 700–701

Scale Translation function, 247–248

scene document, 25–26

scene file

file extension for, 180

naming, 179–180

Scene Window, 23

scenery. *See* nature imagery.

scenes

adjusting view of, 34–36, 80–81

contrasted with sequences, 685

creating default, 191

determining center point of, 75

merging, 320–321

scenes *(continued)*

naming, 179–180

placing objects in, 163–164

previewing in Flyaround view, 96–97

saving, 36, 180, 186–187

setting up, 161–170

ways of looking at, 40

Schaefer, Vincent J., 908

Scientific American, 935

screen savers, using Bryce with, 194

Scrubber. *See* Time Scrubber.

"scuffed" surface, 436

SDTS file, 395–397

Seiwert, Harald, 290

Select All command, 140

Select by Family button, 139

Select Camera command, 140

Select Groups command, 140

Select Inverse command, 140, 147

Select Meshes command, 140

Select None command, 140

Select Options pop-up menu, 139, 140

Select Paths command, 140

Select Stones icon, 43

Select Web Links command, 140

Selected setting, Wireframe Resolution, 130–131

selecting

camera, 118

mesh, 140

noise type, 505

object, 41, 43, 138–145

ticker mark, 799

Selection Arrows, 139, 140–141, 142. *See also* Arrow controls.

Selection icons, and Shift key, 143–144

Selection Palette

controls on, 139–141

location of, 138

purpose of, 27

selecting objects by type with, 43

walkthrough, 141

Selection Palette Options pop-up menu, 95

Self Shadow option, Materials Lab, 465–466, 478

sequence, contrasted with scene, 685

Sequencer, 795–801
    color-coded "temperature bars," 795
    illustration of, 796
    and key event ticker marks, 799–801
    keyboard shortcuts, 798
    Time controls, 796

serif fonts, and text terrains, 393–394

Set as Unity command, 234, 271

shading
    and render time, 480
    for surface materials, 462–464
    for volume materials, 474–477, 480

Shading mode, and glowing primitives, 610–611

Shadow options, Materials Lab, 465–466, 477–488

Shadow Ray setting, 658

shadows
    combining with other Sky & Fog elements, 586
    controlling harshness of, 585, 645
    disabling, 623–624
    and light array, 645–646
    and render time, 480
    walkthrough, 587
    wireframe, 133
    working with, in Materials Lab, 465–466, 477–488, 585–586

Shahnra Project, 929–933

shapes, and fractal geometry, 2–5

Sharpen editor, 337, 339

She Plays With Magic scene, 930

shear, 219–220

Shift key
    and nudging of objects, 210
    and resizing of objects, 213–214
    and rotation of objects, 222
    and selection of objects, 142–144

ship dates
    Bryce 1, 12
    Bryce 2, 13

ship dates *(continued)*
    Bryce 3D, 16
    Bryce 4, 17

Shoji Lantern scene, 646–647

Shore scene, 924

shortcuts. *See* keyboard shortcuts.

shot
    alternatives to single, continuous, 820–821
    defined, 819

Show as Box option, 123, 175

Show/Hide Underground Lines control, 132–133

Sierpinski sieve, 2, 3

SIGGRAPH, 9

Sigmon, Michael "renato," 820, 938–940

Sine noise, 510, 522

Sine Wave filter, 518

size, units for measuring object, 124

Size setting, Object Attributes dialog box, 294, 299–300

sky. *See also* sky color; sky dome.
    animating, 715–719
    storing options for, 186
    strategies for rendering quickly, 166

Sky & Fog Palette
    and Auto Update, 558
    compared with Edit Palette, 555
    illustration of, 554
    and Memory Dots, 558
    practice exercises, 36–38, 589–600
    purpose of, 28, 553
    randomizing settings for, 606
    using controls on, 554–555

Sky & Fog Preset Library, 36–37, 182, 185, 186, 558

Sky Auto Update On/Off, 189

sky color, 587–606
    "normal" *vs.* custom, 587, 589
    practice exercises, 589–600
    and time of day, 590–591

sky dome
    adjusting illumination of, 589, 603–604
    location of sun and moon in, 562

Sky Dome Color, 603–604

Sky Lab
    altering sun and moon in, 562–567
    Animation controls, 712, 713
    development of, 16, 17
    editing cloud textures with, 573
    fine-tuning haze with, 37–38
    illustrations of, 556
    practice exercise, 587
    preview feature, 557–558
    purpose of, 29, 553
    user interface, 555–556
sky modes, 587, 589, 600–602, 604
slab
    infinite, 113
    infinite cloud, 606–608
Sleepware, 12
slide-show application, 605
sliders, adjusting, 414
Slope filter, 520
sloping-letters terrain, 392
Smoky Spotlight walkthrough, 632–634
Smooth button
    Edit Mesh dialog box, 150–151, 151
    Filter control, 353, 355
Smooth Clip filter, 518
Smooth editor, 337, 339
SMPTE, 688, 689–690
Snap to Frames option, 795
Snap to Grid command, 200, 255
Snap to Ground command, 255
Snap to Land command, 255–258
Snap to World Center command, 255
Snap Together command, 255
Snow Puddles filter, 521, 543
Snowed Under scene, 542
"snowy" surface, 437
Society of Motion Picture and Television
    Engineers. *See* SMPTE.
soft-rock valleys, 897
Soft Sky mode, 587, 589, 604
softness settings, light source, 618–619
Solo mode
    activating, 145
    contrasted with Normal mode, 146

Solo mode *(continued)*
    and groups, 146
    influence of lights in, 639
    purpose of, 145–146
    rendering in, 148
    ways of using, 146–148
Solo Mode button, 139
space bar, pausing aerial rotation with, 100
space scenes, recipe for, 914–918
Spaces, Bryce, 197. *See also* specific spaces.
Spatial Data Transfer Standard, 395–397
Spatial Optimization
    Off/Low/High settings, 651–652
    and render time, 169
Special Case objects, 116–118
Special Interest Group for Graphics, 9
Specular Color
    defined, 425
    interaction with Specular Halo, 426–427
    texture-driven, 440
Specular Halo
    and hot-spot size, 425–426
    interaction with Specular Color, 426–427
    and texture-driven color, 440
Specular Halo channel, Materials Lab, 414,
    415, 416
Specularity channel, Materials Lab, 414,
    415, 416
sphere, as 3D Primitive, 114
Spiral Motion animation, 848–854
spiral staircase, replicating objects to build,
    312–313
spline, removing from trajectory, 740
Spot noise, 505
spotlights
    illustrations of, 116
    types of, 116, 614
square, as 2D Primitive, 115
square spotlight, 116, 614
Squared Falloff, 624–627, 647
squashed-and-stretched primitive,
    measuring, 124
Sree3D
    creator of, 16

Sree3D *(continued)*
    and Flat Shaded Preview, 176
stars, 28, 567
states, animating, 710
states, object, 277
Static setting, Wireframe Resolution, 130–131
Statue scene, 927
Status Text area, Control Palette, 27
stealth light, 643–644
Step-by-Step folder, 368
stone object, 113–114
Storyboard Preview, 780
storyboarding, 687, 821
Strata StudioPro, 940
stratus cloud, 569. *See also* clouds.
studio light, 643
Subtraction operation, 277, 282–284
sun
    adjusting color of, 588, 591–593
    animating, 46–49, 715
    blending haze/fog with, 589
    default position of, 563
    impact on rainbows, 585
    location of, in Bryce sky dome, 562
    setting diameter of, 565–566
    surrounding with Halo Ring, 566
Sun Color, 591–593
Sun control
    altering numbers for, 562–565
    and Azimuth/Altitude scales, 563–564
    dragging, 562–563
    illustrations of, 37, 560
    and Link Sun to View option, 560–561
    practice exercise, 567–568
    purpose of, 559–560
    setting time of day with, 590–591
Sun Glow Color, 600
Superfine AntiAliasing, 652
surface properties
    of boolean objects, 280–281
    categories of, 410–412
    contrasted with volume properties, 409
    controlling with Materials Lab, 409
    isolating part of, 460

surface properties *(continued)*
    "material" contrasted with "texture," 409
    and Material Options pop-up menu, 462
    uniform *vs.* non-uniform, 430
surface visible light, 628–631
Surface/Volume toggle, 410, 412, 474
Symmetric Tiling option, Picture
    Mapping, 449
symmetrical lattice
    adding to conglomerate object, 318–319
    compared with terrain object, 113–114
    creating "injection mold" object with, 383
    exporting, 397
    and Filtering controls, 383
    minimizing seam in, 383

T

Tab key, and object selection, 142
Talk feature, 29
tangent, trajectory, 733
targa file, 484
Target icon. *See* Track Object icon.
Tchaitchian, Hessan, 14
Techscape scene, 929
telephoto lens, 80
tension, trajectory, 740, 741
terrain, 885–886
    adding to conglomerate object, 318–319
    adjusting with Terrain Editor, 30–31
    and Altitude Renders, 676–678
    animating, 714–715
    applying surface material to, 32
    as boolean object, 287–289
    clipping, 360–363
    controlling shape of, 332
    creating
        from existing land forms, 395–397
        from image source, 387
        from render of top-view object,
            394–395
        from text, 389–394
    cropping, 365
    enlarging, 33–34

terrain *(continued)*
    exporting, 16, 29, 397–406 (*See also* Terrain
        Export Lab.)
    fitting into smaller area, 365–366
    fractal, 340–346
    positioning, 34–36, 287–288
    practice exercises, 287–288, 370–382,
        389–394, 395
    previewing/changing color of, 364–365
    resolution of, 334–335, 368–370, 402
    tiling, 346–348, 366
Terrain Canvas
    and Brush controls, 348–350
    and G2H information, 333
    illustrations of, 332, 334
    purpose of, 30
Terrain Editor, 331–368
    accessing Deep Texture Editor from,
        531–532
    alternatives to, 383–387
    controls, 332–334, 712, 713
    illustration of, 332
    practice exercises, 370–382
    purpose of, 29
    steps for adjusting terrain with, 30–31
Terrain Export Lab, 399–406
    accessing, 398
    development of, 16, 17
    illustration of, 399
    Image Maps section of, 404–406
    Mesh controls, 399–403
    purpose of, 399
Terrain Flyover animation, 940–941
Terrain From DTE scene, 532
terrain object, 113–114
TERRAIN TILING CAMERA.MOV
    file, 835
Terrel, John, 14, 16
test render, 779–781, 783
text terrain, 389–394
Texture Gel, 622–623
Texture Library, 433, 529–530
Texture Mapping Mode pop-up menu,
    444, 447

Texture Source, 430–435
    accessing, 430
    and Alpha Scaling, 444–447
    Edit Texture Palette, 442–444
    Frequency slider, 442, 530
    illustration of controls for, 431
    Picture Mapping options, 447–451
    practical tips for using, 481
    purpose of, 431
    strategies for combining, 453–461
    and texture mapping, 433–435
    texture properties windows, 432
Texture Source D, 461–462, 481
texture timeline, 720–721
textured-sheen surface, 437
textures. *See also* 2D picture textures; 3D
    Textures.
    adjusting frequency, rotation, and position
        of, 442, 530
    analyzing, 533–535
    animating, 870–879
    combining, 527–528
    contrasted with material, 409
    copying, 529
    creating with Deep Texture Editor, 497
        (*See also* Deep Texture Editor.)
    saving, 527–528
    two main types of, 483
    uniform *vs.* non-uniform, 430
    using for illumination, 435–437
    in Whole Mountain preset, 535–540
Textures On/Off button, 165, 166,
    168–169, 660
Textures Preset Library, 185
TGA file, 484
The Way Things Work, 854
Thickness setting
    for fog, 576, 577–581
    for haze, 582, 583
Third Planet Productions, 936
three-dimensional images. *See also* 3D.
    computer-intensive nature of, 22–23
    hardware constraints when working
        with, 22

three-dimensional images *(continued)*
   taking two-dimensional snapshots of, 25
three-dimensional world, Bryce as, 52–55
Three Rs controls, 127. *See also* specific
      controls.
ticker marks
   choosing number of frames between, 703
   deleting, 800, 801
   duplicating, 800
   key commands for, 696
   moving, 799–800
   purpose of, 701
   scaling, 801
   selecting, 799
   and Sequencer, 799–801
   walkthrough, 701–702
Tides scene, 926
TIF file, 484
tiling options
   Picture Mapping, 449
   Terrain Editor, 346–348
tilt control, for camera, 80
time. *See also* render time.
   Bryce's method of measuring, 688
   mapping, 185, 803–818
   and SMPTE standards, 689–690
Time Mapping Curve, 805–813
   adding/removing points, 810–811
   illustrations of, 806, 811, 815, 816, 817, 840
   keyboard shortcuts, 813
   and pendulum movement, 837–839
   presets, 810
   sample files, 813
   significance of, 805
   straightening, 812
   and .TME file extension, 185
   zooming in/out on, 812–813
Time Mapping Editor, 803–818
   descriptions of component parts of,
      804–813
   illustration of, 804
   keyboard shortcuts, 813
   numerical readout, 808–809
   purpose of, 803

Time Mapping Editor *(continued)*
   walkthrough, 814–818
   zooming in/out with, 812–813
time of day, adjusting, 109, 590–591
Time Palette, 693–708
   descriptions of controls on
      AML Doorway tool, 708
      Animation Preview, 703–706
      Keyframe tools, 706–708
      time/playback tools, 694–703
   illustrations of, 47, 694
   purpose of, 28
   walkthroughs, 695–698, 700–703,
      705–707, 708
Time/Playback controls, AML, 786, 797
Time Ruler, 786, 795, 796, 797, 798
time-saving strategies, 161–170
Time Scrubber, 47, 694–697
Time/Selection Palette toggle, 139
time settings, for animation sequences,
      690–693
time tools, Time Palette, 694–703
timeline
   collapsing, 792
   expanding, 700–701, 792
   materials, 719–720
   purpose of, 694
   texture, 720–721
   and Time Mapping Editor, 804
Timeline Options pop-up menu, 47
Timerip scene, 931–932
Ting, Jackson, 15, 17, 318
TME file, 185
Tollerè Submersible scene, 931
topographical information, storing, 395
torus
   as 3D Primitive, 114
   adjusting size and shape of, 236
   characteristics of, 114
   and Edit Terrain/Object control, 236–241
   and Multi-Replicate command, 314–315
Torus Editor, 236–239
Tower architecture image, 318–319, 383, 494
Track Object icon, 91, 92, 119, 120

Track Object pop-up menu, 92
Trackball control
   and Center to Selection mode, 78
   changing camera position with, 77–80
   changing perspective with, 34–36
   and Free Camera mode, 78
   and Trackball mode, 77–78
   and Tripod mode, 78–79
Trackball mode, 77–78
Trackball pop-up menu, 77
tracking, 91–93, 103–104, 126, 775–778, 823
Tracking icon. *See* Track Object icon.
TRAJ-TO-PATH-BEFORE scene file, 771
trajectory, 731–761
   aligning objects to, 735–737
   components of, 733
   controlling appearance of, 734–735
   controlling behavior of, 737–738
   creating, 732–738
   creating Path object from, 763
   defined, 731
   moving, 739
   removing spline from, 740–742
   showing/hiding, 733–734
   straightening, 740–742
   walkthrough, 743–761
TRAJECTORY BEHAVIOR scene file, 737
trajectory handle
   illustration of, 733
   moving, 738–743
   purpose of, 731
   showing/hiding, 734
Transform options, Picture Mapping, 450
transformation, of parent and child objects, 301–302
Transformations dialog box. *See* 3D Transformations dialog box.
transparency
   and Mask Render, 680–681
   and render time, 167
Transparency channel, Materials Lab, 413, 417–418, 419–420

Transparent Color, 427–429
   adding to texture-driven color, 440–441
   effect of Volume Color on, 429–430
   and Materials Lab channels, 414
   modulation of, 428
Tree Druid, 909
tree tools, 909
TreePro, 909
trees, options for creating, 909–913
Triad: Live at the Hammersmith Odeon scene, 643
Triangulation, Adaptive/Grid, 402–403
Tripod mode, 77, 78–79, 79
Tucker, Scott, 109
turbulence, 512
Turbulence button, 573–574
twist
   and Path object, 766–767, 769–770
   and trajectory, 740
two-dimensional images, 22. *See also* 2D.

U

U icon. *See* Ungroup Objects icon.
U&I Software, 9–10
Underground Lines control, 132–133
undersea world, 905–906
underwater effects, and Volume slab, 430
Undo command, 232–233, 534, 535. *See also* Revert to Saved command.
Ungroup Objects icon, 119, 121, 266
Union operation, 277, 282
units of measurement
   for Bryce's internal grid, 200–202
   for rotation, 203
Unity command, 233–235, 271
unity unit, 200–201, 210
University of California, 6
UNIX, 8
Unpaint Effect setting, Brush Behavior, 350, 351
upwarping, 895
user interface. *See* interface.
USGS, 395, 909

V

valleys, formation of, 897–898
Value channels, Materials Lab, 410, 412,
    414–416, 420–422
VCR controls, 140
VCR mode, 140, 142
vertical cliffs, techniques for creating, 898
Vertical options, Filtering controls, 356–358
vertical panning, 91
video-editing software, 823
view
    orthogonal *vs.* perspective, 64
    rendered *vs.* wireframe, 23
    saving, 105–106
View control, 64, 66–67
View Diorama control, 41
View Options pop-up menu, 66, 68
Viewpoint Data Laboratories, 154–155
visible light, 628–634
Vista Pro, 935
volcanoes, 893–894, 900
volume clouds, and nature imagery, 890–892
Volume Color
    blend options, 466–467, 478–479
    effect of Transparent Color on, 429–430
    how it works, 429–430
    importance of, 429
    and Materials Lab, 414
    movie files, 467
    and underwater effects, 430
volume material
    Additive option, 477
    and Alpha Scaling, 479
    Blend options, 478–479
    changing a material to, 468
    and Sampling Blur, 478
    shading for, 474–477, 480
    Shadow options, 477–478
    tips for working with, 480–481
volume properties
    contrasted with surface properties, 409
    controlling with Materials Lab, 409,
        467–468
    defined, 412

volume properties *(continued)*
    descriptions of, 468–479
    and render time, 167, 480
volume shading styles, 474–477
volume visible light, 628–631, 632
Volumetric World, 167, 647–648
Voronoi noise, 505
Vortex Noise, 505
Voss, Richard, 6
VR Toolbox, 670, 862
VR Worx, 862

W

Wagner, Brian, 13, 14, 16, 17
walkthroughs. *See also* practice exercises.
    Advanced Motion Lab
        acceleration and other time mapping
            adjustments, 814–818
        displaying hierarchies, 790–791
    Animation Setup dialog box, 692–693
    Auto-Key On/Off, 722, 724
    Brush Behavior, 350–352
    Bryce basics, 23–26
    Bryce interface/controls, 30–52
        adjusting haze for sky and sun position,
            36–39
        adjusting rocks, 42–44
        adjusting terrain, 30–31
        adjusting view of scene, 34–36
        animating sun and haze, 46–49
        chancing stones' surface appearance,
            44–46
        enlarging terrain, 33–34
        placing rocks in scene, 40–42
        previewing animation, 49–50
        rendering animation, 50–52
        turning terrain into island, 32
    haze, fog, and shadow, 587
    Memory Dots, 702
    Nano Preview, 70–71
    paths, 771–775
    Selection Palette, 141
    Time Mapping Editor, 814–818

walkthroughs *(continued)*
Time Palette controls
AML Doorway tool, 708
Animation Preview, 705–706
Keyframe tools, 708
Playback/Navigation, 696–697
Scale Timeline, 700
ticker marks, 701–702
Time Scrubber, 695
Working Range, 697–698
trajectory, 743–761
volume visible lights, 632–634
Water Temple at Night scene, 646
Water Under Water scene, 924
Waterfall practice exercise, 374–382
Waterfall Start scene, 376
Waters & Liquids category, Materials
Library, 32
Wavefront OBJ format, 153
Waves noise, 505
Way Things Work, The, 854
weather imagery, 908
web links, 118, 126, 140
Wenger, Eric
Abisko Pine Trees scene, 884, 886, 890, 912
African After Dream scene, 910, 912
and Bryce development, 9–10, 13, 14
and Deep Texture Editor, 496
Eternal Lake scene, 457
Fjord Mud scene, 884, 885, 887
Mountain Eroded scene, 163–164
and nature imagery, 884–893
Rainy Day scene, 908
Valley scene, 884, 886, 888–889
"wet" terrain, 436
Whole Mountain preset, 457–460, 535–540
wide-angle lens, 80
Wilczak, John, 10
Windows Media Player, 782
Windows platform
Alt key, 79, 100, 106, 213, 222
and boolean operations, 278
and Bryce 1, 12
and Bryce 2, 13–15

Windows platform *(continued)*
and Bryce 3D, 15
and color correction, 655
color picker, 423
Ctrl key, 74, 79, 100
file formats, 25–26
mouse movement, in Flyaround mode, 100
performance considerations, 160
and QuickTime VR, 862
and render times, 169
and rendering procedure, 650
resetting defaults, 179
resetting Memory Dots, 106
and unity units, 201
video-editing and compositing
software, 823
Zoom controls, 84
Wine Cellar scene, 640, 643
wireframe color
default, 136
grouping objects by, 135–137
Wireframe controls, 28, 176
Wireframe mode. *See also* wireframe view.
contrasted with Render mode, 25
using Ray Spray tool in, 659
and Zoom to Selection option, 84–85
wireframe object
controlling appearance and behavior of,
28, 130–137
depth cueing in, 134
displaying as box, 123, 175
playing back, 176
previewing, 176
resolution settings, 130–132, 176
selecting, 138–142
showing/hiding underground lines in,
132–133
using shadows in, 133
Wireframe Preview, 176, 780
Wireframe Resolution pop-up menu, 130
wireframe shadow, 133
wireframe view. *See also* Wireframe mode.
contrasted with render view, 130
defined, 23

wireframe view *(continued)*
   illustration of, 23
   making adjustments in, 130–134
   performance considerations, 174–175, 176
Woodlights scene, 926
words, creating terrains from, 389–394
Working Range, 697–698
Working Window, 23
workspaces, 29
world
   adding objects to, 24
   Bryce as 3D, 52–55
   empty, 24
   rendering, 24–25
   Volumetric, 167, 647–648
World Center, 125
World Space
   and Absolute/Definition coordinates, 124
   orientation of arrow keys in, 209
   overview of, 52–53
   repositioning objects in, 206–207
   resizing objects in, 218–220
   rotating objects in, 222–223
   and texture mapping, 433–435
   and *xyz* axes, 197–198
World Space Top, mapping texture to, 434–435

X

x axis, 52–55, 197–198
X Power filter, 519–520

xyz space, 52, 54, 197–199
XZ Control, 35

Y

y axis, 52–55, 197–198
Yale University, 6–7

Z

z axis, 52–55, 197–198
Zenstar, 909
zero, and frame numbering, 688, 690
zigzag pattern, for tiling terrains, 348
Zoom Area, Terrain Editor, 365–368
Zoom controls
   camera
      altering 2D plane with, 81
      ambiguity of terms, 85
      and Camera dialog box, 90
      keyboard shortcuts, 84
      location of, 64
      magnifier tools, 84
      resetting default magnification, 84
   Terrain Editor, 332, 333, 365–368
Zoom In/Out tools, 84, 85, 90. *See also*
      Zoom controls.
Zoom to Selection option, 84–85
zooming, 84–86
Zygote, 155